Discuss 620-629

606-619

Native American Natural Resources Law

Native American Natural Resources Law

Cases and Materials

FOURTH EDITION

Judith V. Royster
Professor of Law
Co-Director, Native American Law Center
University of Tulsa College of Law

Michael C. Blumm
Jeffrey Bain Faculty Scholar & Professor of Law
Lewis & Clark Law School

Elizabeth Ann Kronk Warner
Professor of Law
Director, Tribal Law & Government Center
University of Kansas School of Law

Carolina Academic Press
Durham, North Carolina

Copyright © 2018
Carolina Academic Press, LLC
All Rights Reserved

ISBN 978-1-5310-0701-0
eISBN 978-1-53100-702-7
LCCN 2018944087

Carolina Academic Press
700 Kent Street
Durham, North Carolina 27701
Telephone (919) 489-7486
Fax (919) 493-5668
www.cap-press.com

Printed in the United States of America
2021 Printing

We dedicate this book to Indian Law students everywhere who are concerned about the wise use of the environment of Indian country.

Contents

Table of Cases	xv
Preface to the Fourth Edition	xxv
Introduction	xxvii
Themes of Native American Natural Resources Law	xxvii
Chapter 1 · Land, Religion, and Culture	**3**
A. Indians and the Land	3
Frank Pommersheim, *The Reservation as Place: A South Dakota Essay*	3
Michael C. Blumm, *Sacrificing the Salmon: A Legal and Policy History of the Decline of Columbia Basin Salmon*	6
Navajo Nation Code, Tit. I, § 205	8
Rebecca Tsosie, *Tribal Environmental Policy in an Era of Self-Determination: The Role of Ethics, Economics, and Traditional Ecological Knowledge*	8
Ezra Rosser, *Ahistorical Indians and Reservation Resources*	10
B. Legal Protection of Sacred and Cultural Sites	11
Lyng v. Northwest Indian Cemetery Protective Association	11
Notes	21
Navajo Nation v. United States Forest Service	22
Notes	34
Bear Lodge Multiple Use Association v. Babbitt [Bear Lodge II]	35
Executive Order 13007—Indian Sacred Sites	41
Notes	42
Note on Federal Protection of Cultural Property Under the Antiquities Act: Bears Ears National Monument	43
Note on Cultural Protection Under Other Statutes	44
USDA Forest Service Lake Tahoe Basin Management Unit Record of Decision for Cave Rock Management Direction Final Environmental Impact Statement	48
Notes	54
Note on the Native American Graves Protection and Repatriation Act	55
Bonnichsen v. United States	58
Notes	64

Chapter 2 · Some Basics of Federal Indian Law — 71
A. History of Federal Indian Policy — 71
B. The Cherokee Cases — 78
    Cherokee Nation v. Georgia — 80
    Worcester v. Georgia — 83
    Notes — 88
C. Tribal Sovereignty — 90
    Felix S. Cohen, *Handbook of Federal Indian Law* — 90
    Cohen's *Handbook of Federal Indian Law* § 4.01[1][a] — 91
    Notes — 92
D. The Federal Role in Indian Country — 94
    Lone Wolf v. Hitchcock — 95
    Notes — 99
    Note on Federal Power over Indians — 99
    Notes on the Trust Doctrine — 100
E. Indian Country — 103
    1. Scope and Extent of Indian Country — 103
        Note on Indian Country — 103
        Oklahoma Tax Comm'n v. Sac and Fox Nation — 104
        Note on the Definition of Reservation — 107
        Alaska v. Native Village of Venetie Tribal Government — 108
        Notes — 113
        Note on Alaskan Subsistence — 115
        Mustang Production Co. v. Harrison — 117
        Note on Tribal Courts and Tribal Court Exhaustion — 120
        Note on Indian Country in Oklahoma — 121
    2. Expanding Indian Country — 122
        Buzzard v. Oklahoma Tax Commission — 122
        Notes — 124
    3. Contracting Indian Country: Reservation Diminishment — 129
        Solem v. Bartlett — 130
        Note on the Canons of Construction — 138
        South Dakota v. Yankton Sioux Tribe — 138
        Notes — 146
        Nebraska v. Parker — 146
        Notes — 151

Chapter 3 · Land: The Fundamental Resource — 155
A. Aboriginal Title — 155
    Johnson and Graham's Lessee v. M'Intosh — 155
    Notes — 159
    City of Sherrill v. Oneida Indian Nation — 163
    Notes — 167
        United States ex rel. Hualpai Indians v. Santa Fe Pacific Railroad Co. — 170

Notes	175
Tee-Hit-Ton Indians v. United States	180
Notes	184
Note on the Federal Claims Process	186
B. Recognized Title	188
United States v. Shoshone Tribe of Indians	188
Notes	191
United States v. Sioux Nation of Indians	192
Notes	205
C. Executive Order Reservations	209
Sioux Tribe of Indians v. United States	209
Notes	213
D. Submerged Lands	215
Montana v. United States	215
Notes	219
United States v. Cherokee Nation of Oklahoma	223
Note on Cherokee Claims to the Arkansas River	226
E. Allotted Lands	229
Northern Cheyenne Tribe v. Hollowbreast	231
Note on Fractionation	235
Babbitt v. Youpee	237
Notes	242
Chapter 4 · Land Use and Environmental Protection	**247**
A. Authority to Control Land Use	247
Worcester v. Georgia	248
Notes	248
Montana v. United States	249
Notes	253
New Mexico v. Mescalero Apache Tribe	257
Notes	263
Brendale v. Confederated Tribes and Bands of the Yakima Indian Nation	264
Notes	272
South Dakota v. Bourland	273
Notes	274
Strate v. A-1 Contractors	275
Notes	276
Nevada v. Hicks	276
Notes	279
B. Environmental Protection	282
1. Environmental Authority in Indian Country	282
Phillips Petroleum Co. v. U.S. Environmental Protection Agency	282
Notes	283

EPA Policy for the Administration of Environmental Programs
   on Indian Reservations 284
Notes 285
*State of Washington, Department of Ecology v. United States
   Environmental Protection Agency* 286
Notes 291
City of Albuquerque v. Browner 295
Notes 300
Arizona Public Service Co. v. Environmental Protection Agency ... 304
Notes 311
Backcountry against Dumps v. Environmental Protection Agency ... 313
Notes 316
Note on Tribal Environmental Law 319
2. Application of Environmental Laws to Tribes 320
Notes 320
Blue Legs v. United States Bureau of Indian Affairs 322
Notes 325
3. Environmental Impacts of Development 327
Davis v. Morton 327
Notes 331
Sangre De Cristo Development Co., Inc. v. United States 332
Metcalf v. Daley 335
Notes 342
Note on Environmental Justice 344
An Environmental Justice Case Study: Dakota Access Pipeline 346

Chapter 5 · Natural Resource Development 349
A. The Federal-Tribal Relationship in Resource Management 349
1. The Role of the Department of the Interior 350
Reid Peyton Chambers & Monroe E. Price, *Regulating
   Sovereignty: Discretion and the Leasing of Indian Lands* 350
Mary Christina Wood, *Protecting the Attributes of Native
   Sovereignty: A New Trust Paradigm for Federal Actions
   Affecting Tribal Lands and Resources* 352
Notes 353
2. Tribal Resource Development Statutes 356
Note on Resource Development Statutes 356
Note on Renewable Energy Resources 362
3. Energy Rights-of-Way 363
Blackfeet Indian Tribe v. Montana Power Company 363
Notes 366
Nebraska Public Power Dist. v. 100.95 Acres of Land 367
Notes 369
Note on Tribal Regulatory Authority over Rights-of-Way 370

B. The Breach of Trust Action for Federal Resource Mismanagement	372
Nell Jessup Newton, *Enforcing the Federal-Indian Trust Relationship after* Mitchell	372
United States v. Navajo Nation	374
United States v. White Mountain Apache Tribe	386
Notes	392
Jicarilla Apache Tribe v. Supron Energy Corp.	396
Notes	397
C. The Tribal Role in Resource Management	401
Jicarilla Apache Tribe v. Andrus	401
Note on the Environmental Effects of Mining	406
United Nuclear Corp. v. United States	407
Notes	412
Quantum Exploration, Inc. v. Clark	414
Notes	418
Chapter 6 · Taxation of Natural Resources	**419**
A. Federal Taxation	419
Squire v. Capoeman	419
Notes	421
B. Tribal Taxation	424
Merrion v. Jicarilla Apache Tribe	425
Notes	432
Kerr-McGee Corp. v. Navajo Tribe of Indians	432
Notes	435
Atkinson Trading Co., Inc. v. Shirley	435
Notes	438
C. State Taxation	440
Note on State Taxation of Tribal Interests	440
County of Yakima v. Confederated Tribes and Bands of the Yakima Indian Nation	441
Cass County v. Leech Lake Band of Chippewa Indians	445
Notes	448
Montana v. Blackfeet Tribe of Indians	449
Notes	452
White Mountain Apache Tribe v. Bracker	453
Cotton Petroleum Corp. v. New Mexico	458
Notes	463
Chapter 7 · Water Rights	**471**
A. Introduction to Reserved Rights	471
United States v. Winans	471
Winters v. United States	474
Notes	477
Note on State Water Law Systems	479

B. Extending the *Winters* Doctrine	481
Arizona v. California	481
Notes	484
C. Scope and Extent of Water Rights	485
1. Reservation Purposes, Priority Dates, and Quantification	485
Note on Reservation Purposes	485
Note on Methods of Quantification	486
United States v. Adair [Adair I]	487
Notes	493
In re General Adjudication of All Rights to Use Water in the Big Horn River System [Big Horn I]	499
In re General Adjudication of All Rights to Use Water in the Gila River System and Source	504
Notes	511
2. Rights to Groundwater	513
In re General Adjudication of All Rights to Use Water in the Big Horn River System [Big Horn I]	513
Agua Caliente Band of Cahuilla Indians v. Coachella Valley Water Dist.	514
Notes	519
3. Use of Water Rights	521
In re General Adjudication of All Rights to Use Water in the Big Horn River System [Big Horn III]	521
Notes	528
Note on Water Marketing	529
4. Rights of Allottees and Subsequent Purchasers	530
Colville Confederated Tribes v. Walton	530
Notes	536
5. Right to Water Quality	538
United States v. Gila Valley Irrigation District	538
D. Determination of Water Rights	545
Notes	545
Pyramid Lake Paiute Tribe of Indians v. Morton	547
Nevada v. United States	551
Notes	561
Note on the McCarran Amendment and State Water Adjudications	566
Arizona v. San Carlos Apache Tribe of Arizona	567
Notes	576
Note on Water Settlements	577
Chapter 8 · Usufructuary Rights: Hunting, Fishing, and Gathering	**585**
A. Off-Reservation Rights	586
1. Modern Survival of the Rights	586

Minnesota v. Mille Lacs Band of Chippewa Indians	586
Notes	601
Note on the Non-Indian Backlash	603
Public Access Shoreline Hawaii (PASH) v. Hawai'i County Planning Commission	606
Notes	610
2. Defeasible Usufructuary Rights	612
State of Washington v. Buchanan	612
Notes	619
3. Regulation of Treaty Rights	620
Puyallup Tribe v. Department of Game of Washington [Puyallup I]	620
Notes	624
Department of Game of the State of Washington v. Puyallup Tribe [Puyallup II]	625
Note on Limiting Treaty Rights on Public Safety Grounds	626
Note on Tribal Hunting and Fishing Regulations	627
Note on On-Reservation versus Off-Reservation Rights	628
4. Scope and Extent of "the Right of Taking Fish"	629
United States v. Winans	629
Notes	630
Washington v. Washington State Commercial Passenger Fishing Vessel Association	633
Notes	642
Lac Courte Oreilles Band of Lake Superior Chippewa Indians v. Wisconsin [LCO-Timber]	647
5. Habitat Protection for the Treaty Fishing Right	649
Notes	650
United States v. Washington	654
Notes	656
United States v. Washington	657
Notes	661
B. Loss and Diminishment of the Rights	665
Menominee Tribe of Indians v. United States	665
Oregon Dept. of Fish and Wildlife v. Klamath Indian Tribe	670
Note on the Restoration of Menominee and Klamath Tribes	677
United States v. Dion	678
Notes	683
Anderson v. Evans	687
Note on Abrogation versus Regulation	693
Chapter 9 · International Approaches to Indigenous Lands and Resources	695
A. International Instruments for the Protection of Indigenous Rights	695
Note: U.N. Declaration on the Rights of Indigenous Peoples	695

U.N. Declaration on the Rights of Indigenous Peoples	696
Note: ILO Convention No. 169	700
The Convention Concerning Indigenous and Tribal Peoples in Independent Countries, 1989	700
Note: American Declaration on the Rights of Indigenous Peoples	702
American Declaration on the Rights of Indigenous Peoples	703
B. Indian Claims before International Forums	711
Inter-American Commission on Human Rights, Report No. 75/02, Case 11.140, Mary and Carrie Dann	712
Note: The Inter-American Human Rights System	717
Committee on the Elimination of Racial Discrimination: Early Warning and Urgent Action Procedure, Decision 1 (68): United States of America	718
Notes	719
Index	721

Table of Cases

The principal cases are in bold type. Cases cited in principal cases and within other quoted materials are not included.

Access Fund v. United States Department of Agriculture, 54
Agua Caliente Band of Cahuilla Indians v. Coachella Water Dist., 514
Alabama-Coushatta Tribe v. United States, 161
Alaska v. Babbitt, 116
Alaska v. Native Village of Venetie Tribal Gov't, 104, 108, 185
Alaska ex rel. Yukon Flats School District v. Native Village of Venetie Tribal Government, 115
Alaska Wilderness League v. Kempthorne, 343
Alcea Band of Tillamooks v. United States, 214
Amoco Production Co. v. Southern Ute Tribe, 191
Amoco Production Co. v. Village of Gambell, 117
Anderson v. Evans, 343, 687, 694
Arizona v. California, 214, 479, 481, 484–486, 492, 503, 512, 528, 562, 639, 640
Arizona v. California II, 528
Arizona v. California III, 562
Arizona v. California (Quechan Tribe), 484–485
Arizona v. San Carlos Apache Tribe, 567
Arizona Department of Revenue v. Blaze Construction Co., Inc., 469
Arizona Public Service Co. v. Environmental Protection Agency, 304
Arrow Midstream Holdings v. 3 Bears Construction, 371
Arviso v. Commissioner of Internal Revenue, 422
Ashley v. United States Department of the Interior, 394
Atiak Native Community v. Environmental Protection Agency, 117
Atkinson Trading Co. v. Shirley, 272, 279, 435, 438, 440
Atlantic States Legal Foundation v. Salt River Pima-Maricopa Indian Community, 326
Attorney General v. Ngati Apa, 179
Babbitt v. Youpee, 237, 244
Backcountry Against Dumps v. Environmental Protection Agency, 291, 313, 316, 319
Baley v. United States, 496
Bangor Hydro-Electric Co. v. United States Department of the Interior, 43
Bear Lodge Multiple Use Association v. Babbitt (Bear Lodge I), 40
Bear Lodge Multiple Use Association v. Babbitt (Bear Lodge II), 35, 42, 55
Big Eagle v. United States, 422
Big Horn County Electric Cooperative v. Adams, 276, 438

Black Hills Institute of Geological Research v. South Dakota School of Mines & Technology, 192
Blackfeet Indian Tribe v. Montana Power Company, 363
Blatchford v. Native Village of Noatak, 220
Blaze Construction Co. v. Taxation and Revenue Department, 466, 469
Blue Legs v. United States Bureau of Indian Affairs, 322, 325, 326
Boarhead Corp. v. Erickson, 47
Bobby v. Alaska, 116
Bonnichsen v. United States, 57, 58, 64
Brendale v. Confederated Tribes and Bands of the Yakima Indian Nation, 264, 306
Brewer-Elliott Oil & Gas Co. v. United States, 222
Burlington Northern Railroad Co. v. Blackfeet Tribe, 438–439
Burlington Northern Railroad Co. v. Red Wolf, 371
Burlington Northern Santa Fe Railroad Co. v. Assiniboine and Sioux Tribes of the Fort Peck Reservation, 439
Buzzard v. Oklahoma Tax Commission, 122
Cabazon Band of Mission Indians v. Wilson, 466
Calder v. Attorney General for British Columbia, 176
Cappaert v. United States, 519
Carcieri v. Norton, 126
Carcieri v. Salazar, 128
Cardin v. De La Cruz, 264
Cass County v. Leech Lake Band of Chippewa Indians, 445, 448, 449
Cayuga Indian Nation of New York v. Pataki, 168
Cayuga Indian Nation v. Seneca County, 169
Center for Biological Diversity v. Salazar, 332

Central New York Fair Business Ass'n v. Jewel, 127
Cherokee Nation v. Georgia, 73, 80, 101, 159, 255
Cherokee Nation v. State of Oklahoma, 227
Cherokee Nation of Oklahoma v. United States (Claims Court), 227, 228
Cherokee Nation of Oklahoma v. United States (Federal Circuit), 228
Cherokee Nation of Oklahoma v. United States (10th Circuit), 227
Cherokee Tobacco, The, 421, 422
Chevron, U.S.A. Inc. v. Natural Resources Defense Council, Inc., 291–293
Cheyenne-Arapaho Tribes of Oklahoma v. Oklahoma, 122
Chippewa Cree Tribe of the Rocky Boy's Reservation v. United States, 394
Choctaw Nation v Oklahoma, 219, 222, 223, 226
Cholla Ready Mix, Inc. v. Civish, 46
Churchill County v. Norton, 547, 564
Citizens for a Better Way v. U.S. Dept. of the Interior, 331
City of Albuquerque v. Browner, 295, 301
City of Boerne v. Flores, 686
City of Sherrill v. Oneida Indian Nation, 163, 167, 168
City of Roseville v. Norton, 128
Cobell v. Babbitt, 400
Cobell v. Kempthorne, 400
Cobell v. Norton, 400
Cobell v. Salazar, 400
Colorado River Water Conservation District v. United States, 566–567, 577
Colville Confederated Tribes v. Cavenham Forest Industries, 264
Colville Confederated Tribes v. Condon, 320

Colville Confederated Tribes v. Everybodytalksabout, 627
Colville Confederated Tribes v. Walton, 478, 494, 528, **530**, 536, 537, 651
Comanche Nation v. United States, 34
Confederated Salish and Kootenai Tribes v. Clinch, 512
Confederated Salish and Kootenai Tribes v. Namen, 264
Confederated Salish and Kootenai Tribes of the Flathead Reservation v. Stultz, 520
Confederated Tribes v. Bonneville Power Administration, 653
Confederated Tribes of Siletz Indians of Oregon v. United States, 129
Confederated Tribes of the Colville Reservation v. Anderson, 627
Confederated Tribes of the Colville Reservation v. Hoover, 280
Confederated Tribes of the Grand Ronde Community of Oregon v. Jewell, 129
Cotton Petroleum Corp. v. New Mexico, 382, **458**
Cougar Den, Inc. v. Washington State Department of Licensing, 468
County of Oneida v. Oneida Indian Nation, 163
County of Yakima v. Confederated Tribes and Bands of the Yakima Indian Nation, 441, 448, 452
Critzer v. United States, 422
Crow Creek Sioux Tribe v. Brownlee, 45
Crow Tribe of Indians v. Repsis, 620
Cutter v. Wilkerson, 34
Cypress v. United States, 424
Davila v. Enable Midstream Partners L.P., 370
Davis v. Morton, **327**, 332, 333, 404, 405
Delgamuukw v. British Columbia, 176
Department of Game of the State of Washington v. Puyallup Tribe (Puyallup II), **625**, 629, 631, 642, 643, 645
Department of the Interior v. Klamath Water Users Protective Association, 42, 565, 566
Department of the Interior v. South Dakota, 125
Dillon v. United States, 422
Dollar General v. Mississippi Band of Choctaw Indians, 280
Duro v. Reina, 255, 256
Earl v. Commissioner, 423
Ellis v. Page, 121
Ellis v. State, 121
Ex Parte Crow Dog, 74
Ex Parte Young, 220, 221
Flathead Joint Board of Control v. United States Department of the Interior, 565
Fort Mojave Indian Tribe v. United States, 562
Gila River Indian Community v. Waddell, 466
Gila River Pima-Maricopa Indian Community v. United States, 519
Gobin v. Snohomish County, 273
Governing Council of Pinoleville Indian Community v. Mendocino County, 264
Gros Ventre Tribe v. United States, 396
Guerin v. The Queen, 176
Hagen v. Utah, 141, 152, 165
Hodel v. Irving, 235, 237, 238, 241
Holt v. Commissioner, 422
Hoopa Valley Tribe v. Nevins, 465
Hopi Tribe v. United States, 393, 561
Hopi Tribe v. Trump, 44
Housing Authority v. Harjo, 121
Hydro Resources, Inc. v. United States Environmental Protection Agency, 113
Idaho v. Coeur d'Alene Tribe, 220
Idaho v. United States, 222, 498

In re General Adjudication of All Rights to Use Water in the Big Horn River System (Big Horn I), 486, **499**, 512, 513, 536

In re General Adjudication of All Rights to Use Water in the Big Horn River System (Big Horn III), 521

In re General Adjudication of All Rights to Use Water in the Big Horn River System (Big Horn IV), 537

In re General Adjudication of All Rights to Use Water in the Gila River System, 504, 519, 563

In re General Adjudication of All Rights to Use Water in the Gila River System (Gila River-Groundwater), 519

In re SRBA, 498

In the Matter of Water Use Permit Applications, 611

In the Matter of the Application of Beneficial Water Use Permit Nos. 66459-76L, Ciotti, 512

In re Ninety Mile Beach, 179

In re Yakima River Drainage Basin, 563

Iowa Mutual Insurance Co. v. LaPlante, 120, 321

Jackson v. United States, 399

Jamul Action Comm. v. Chaudhuri, 331

Jango v. Northern Territory, 178

Jicarilla Apache Tribe v. Andrus, 401

Jicarilla Apache Tribe v. Supron Energy Corp., 394, 396

Johnson and Graham's Lessee v. M'Intosh, 71, 72, 73, 79, **155**, 159–161, 169, 171, 176, 184–185

Joint Board of Control of the Flathead, Mission, and Jocko Irrigation Districts v. United States, 494, 565

Ka Pa'Akai O Ka'Aina v. Land Use Comm'n, 611

Kansas Indians, The, 440

Karuk Tribe of California v. Ammon, 214

Kenaitze Indian Tribe v. Alaska, 116

Kerr-McGee Corp. v. Navajo Tribe of Indians, 432

Keweenaw Bay Indian Community v. Naftaly, 448

King Mountain Tobacco Comp. Inc. v. McKenna, 467

Kiowa Tribe of Oklahoma v. Manufacturing Technologies, Inc., 321

Kittitas Reclamation District v. Sunnyside Valley Irrigation District, 494, 577, 652

Klamath Tribes v. United States Forest Service, 662

Knight v. Shoshone & Arapaho Indian Tribes, 264

Lac Courte Oreilles Band of Lake Superior Chippewa Indians v. Voigt, 603, 612

Lac Courte Oreilles Band of Lake Superior Chippewa Indians v. Wisconsin (LCO II), 620

Lac Courte Oreilles Band of Lake Superior Chippewa Indians v. Wisconsin (LCO III), 644

Lac Courte Oreilles Band of Lake Superior Chippewa Indians v. Wisconsin (LCO IV), 626, 628

Lac Courte Oreilles Band of Lake Superior Chippewa Indians v. Wisconsin (LCO-Timber), 647

Lac du Flambeau Band of Lake Superior Chippewa Indians v. Stop Treaty Abuse-Wisconsin, 605

Lone Wolf v. Hitchcock, 76, **95**, 99, 132, 198, 200, 204, 242, 669, 679

Lucas v. South Carolina Coastal Council, 611

Lummi Indian Tribe v. Hallauer, 264

Lyng v. Northwest Indian Cemetery Protective Ass'n, 11, 21–22, 42, 46

Mabo v. Queensland, 178

Mackinac Tribe v. Jewell, 94

Madison v. Alaska Department of Fish and Game, 116

Match-E-Be-Nash-She-Wish Band v. Patchak, 127
McClanahan v. State Tax Commission of Arizona, 106, 440
McDonald v. Means, 276
McDowell v. Alaska, 116
Menominee Tribe of Indians v. United States, 664, 665
Merrion v. Jicarilla Apache Tribe, 425, 432, , 439, 463
Mervyn v. Western Australia, 179
Mescalero Apache Tribe v. Jones, 103, 125, 468, 620
Metcalf v. Daley, 335, 694
Michigan v. Bay Mills Indian Community, 103, 321
Michigan v. Environmental Protection Agency, 311
Mid States Coalition for Progress v. Surface Transportation Board, 207
Milirrpum v. Nabalco, 178
Minnesota v. Mille Lacs Band of Chippewa Indians, 586, 602–603, 610, 612, 620, 684
Mitchel v. United States, 171, 616
Montana v. Blackfeet Tribe of Indians, 449, 452, 463
Montana v. Crow Tribe of Indians, 464
Montana v. United States, 215, 219, 247, **249,** 256, 424, 538, 628, 629
Montana v. United States Environmental Protection Agency, 308
Muckleshoot v. Hall, 652
Muckleshoot Indian Tribe v. Lummi Indian Nation, 646
Murphy v. Royal, 121
Murphy v. Sirmons, 121
Mustang Production Co. v. Harrison, 117, 435
Nance v. Environmental Protection Agency, 291, 315
Narragansett Indian Tribe v. Warwick Sewer Authority, 48
National Farmers Union Insurance Cos. v. Crow Tribe, 321
National Mining Association v. Slater, 48
Nat'l Wildlife Fed'n v. Nat'l Marine Fisheries Service, 653
Navajo Nation v. Peabody Holding Co., 394
Navajo Nation v. United States Forest Service, 22
Nebraska v. Parker, 146, 151
Nebraska Public Power Dist. v. 100.95 Acres of Land, 367
Nevada v. Hicks, 78, 276, 279, 321, 438, 439
Nevada v. United States, 551, 662
New Mexico v. Mescalero Apache Tribe, 257, 628, 629
New Mexico ex rel. Reynolds v. Aamodt, 519
New York Indians, The, 167, 440
Nez Perce Tribe v. Idaho Power Company, 662, 663
Ninilchik Traditional Council v. United States, 117
No Oilport! v. Carter, 652
Northern Cheyenne Tribe v. Hollowbreast, 231
Northern Cheyenne Tribe v. United States Bureau of Land Management, 48
Northwest Indian Cemetery Protective Association v. Peterson, 22
Northwest Sea Farms v. United States Army Corps of Engineers, 652
Oglala Sioux Tribe v. United States, 207
Oglala Sioux Tribe of Pine Ridge Indian Reservation v. United States Army Corps of Engineers, 46
Oklahoma v. Environmental Protection Agency, 311
Oklahoma Tax Commission v. Chickasaw Nation, 441

Oklahoma Tax Commission v. Citizen Band Potawatomi Indian Tribe of Oklahoma, 305
Oklahoma Tax Commission v. Sac and Fox Nation, 104, 113, 440–441
Oliphant v. Suquamish Indian Tribe, 78, 209, 255–256
Oneida Indian Nation v. County of Oneida, 162, 163
Oneida Indian Nation v. State of New York, 169
Oneida Nation v. Madison County, 168
Oregon Department of Fish and Wildlife v. Klamath Indian Tribe, 670
Osage Nation v. Irby, 121, 151
Osage Tribal Council v. Department of Labor, 326, 327
Osage Tribe of Indians of Oklahoma v. United States, 394
Otoe-Missouria Tribe of Indians v. United States, 399
Ottawa Tribe of Oklahoma v. Logan, 160, 602
Pakootas v. Teck Cominco Metals Ltd., 327
Parravano v. Babbitt, 214
Phillips Petroleum Co. v. United States Environmental Protection Agency, 282, 283
Pittsburg & Midway Coal Mining Co. v. Watchman, 435
Plains Commerce Bank v. Long Family Land and Cattle Co., 280
Public Access Shoreline Hawaii (PASH) v. Hawai'i County Planning Commission, 606, 612, 662
Public Service Co. v. Shoshone-Bannock Tribes, 327
Public Service Co. of New Mexico v. Approximately 15.49 Acres of Land, 369, 370
Public Service Co. of New Mexico v. Barboan, 370

Pueblo of Sandia v. United States, 43, 47
Puget Sound Gillnetters v. United States District Court, 632
Puget Sound Gillnetters Association v. Moos, 632
Purse Seine Vessel Owners Association v. Tollefson, 632
Puyallup Indian Tribe v. Port of Tacoma, 220
Puyallup Tribe v. Department of Game of Washington (Puyallup I), 620, 624, 629, 631, 642
Puyallup Tribe v. Department of Game of State of Washington (Puyallup III), 628, 629, 631
Pyramid Lake Paiute Tribe of Indians v. Morton, 547, 611, 662
Quantum Exploration, Inc. v. Clark, 414
Quapaw Tribe of Oklahoma v. Blue Tee Corp., 318
Quechan Tribe of the Fort Yuma Reservation v. United States Department of the Interior, 48
Quinault Indian Nation v. Grays Harbor County, 448
R. v. Marshall, 177
Red Lake Band of Chippewa Indians v. United States, 422
Reppun v. Board of Water Supply, 608, 611
Rice v. Rehner, 256
Robinson v. Jewell, 185
San Carlos Apache Tribe v. United States, 47
Sangre de Cristo Development Co., Inc. v. United States, 332
Santa Clara Pueblo v. Martinez, 321, 416
Santa Rosa Band of Indians v. Kings County, 124
Satiacum, 422, 639
Seminole Tribe of Florida v. Stranburg, 468

Seufert Bros. v. United States, 619, 630
Settler v. Lameer, 628
Shivwits Band of Paiute Indians v. Utah, 263
Shoshone Indian Tribe of the Wind River Reservation v. United States, 394
Simon v. The Queen, 176
Sioux Tribe of Indians v. United States, 209, 214
Skeem v. United States, 530
Skokomish Indian Tribe v. Mosbarger, 281
Skokomish Indian Tribe v. United States, 494, 664
Snoqualmie Indian Tribe v. Federal Energy Regulatory Commission, 48
Sohappy v. Smith, 632
Solem v. Bartlett, 121, 129, **130**, 138, 146, 151
South Dakota v. Bourland, 273, 274, 432, 628
South Dakota v. United States Department of the Interior, 124, 125, 128
South Dakota v. Yankton Sioux Tribe, 138, 146, 151, 152, 153, 602
Sparrow v. R., 176
Squire v. Capoeman, 419, 421, 422, 423
Standing Rock Sioux Tribe v. U.S. Army Corps of Eng'rs, 347, 348
State v. Elliott, 169
State v. Hanapi, 610
State v. Jim, 644
State v. Klindt, 122
State v. Littlechief, 122
State Department of Ecology v. Acquavella, 497
State Engineer v. South Fork Bank of the Te Moak Tribe, 577
State ex. rel Greely v. Confederated Salish & Kootenai Tribes, 536
State ex rel. Martinez v. Kerr-McGee, 497
State ex. rel Martinez v. Lewis, 486

State ex rel. May v. Seneca-Cayuga Tribe, 122
State of Washington v. Buchanan, 612, 619
Strate v. A-1 Contractors, 275, 276, 281, 321, 370–371, 438–439
Strom v. Commissioner of Internal Revenue, 423
Superintendent of Five Civilized Tribes v. Commissioner of Internal Revenue, 422
Tee-Hit-Ton Indians v. United States, 180, 185, 188
Temoak Band of Western Shoshone Indians v. United States, 711
Thompson v. County of Franklin, 448
Tooisgah v. United States, 121
Tsilhot'in Nation v. British Columbia, 177
Tulee v. Washington, 631, 642
Tweedy v. Texas Co., 519
Union Pacific Railroad Co. v. Runyon, 665
Union Pacific Railroad v. Wasco County, 665
United Nuclear Corp. v. United States, 407
United States v. 43 Gallons of Whiskey, 422
United States v. Abousleman, 478
United States v. Adair (Adair I), 486, 487, 494–495, 497, 529, 611
United States v. Adair (Adair II), 495, 496
United States v. Ahtanum Irrigation Dist., 563
United States v. Alaska, 222
United States v. Anderson (taxation), 423
United States v. Anderson (water rights–district court), 494, 651
United States v. Anderson (water rights–9th Cir.), 537, 538
United States v. Antoine, 687

United States v. Billie, 683
United States v. Braren, 496
United States v. Bresette, 684
United States v. Brown, 685
United States v. Cherokee Nation of Oklahoma, 223
United States v. Clapox, 74
United States v. Confederated Tribes of the Colville Indian Reservation, 646
United States v. Daney, 422
United States v. Dann, 170, 711
United States v. Dion, 103, 214, 497, 678, 683–684, 685, 693–694
United States v. District Court in and for Eagle County, 566
United States v. Friday, 686
United States v. Gerber, 46
United States v. Gila Valley Irrigation District, 538
United States v. Hardman, 686
United States v. Hicks, 618, 620
United States v. Holt State Bank, 216
United States v. Hugs, 686
United States v. Idaho, 222, 498
United States v. Jicarilla Apache Nation, 395
United States v. John, 108
United States v. Kagama, 74, 75, 101–102
United States v. Lara, 255
United States v. Lummi Nation, 647
United States v. Lummi Tribe, 646
United States v. Mazurie, 428
United States v. McBratney, 248
United States v. Midwest Oil Co., 211–213
United States v. Mitchell (Mitchell II), 394
United States v. Muckleshoot Tribe, 646
United States v. Navajo Nation, 374, 392
United States v. Navajo Nation (Navajo II), 392, 393
United States v. New Mexico, 485

United States v. Newmont USA Ltd., 326
United States v. Oklahoma Gas & Electric Co., 121
United States v. Oliver, 686
United States v. Oregon, 129, 576
United States v. Orr Water Ditch Company, 520, 529, 564, 565
United States v. Osage Wind, LLC, 362
United States v. Ramsey, 122
United States v. Roberts, 126
United States v. Sandoval, 109, 111–113
United States v. Shoshone Tribe of Indians, 188, 191, 192
United States v. Sioux Nation of Indians, 102, **192**, 207, 208–209, 214
United States v. Tawahongva, 686
United States v. Tohono O'Odham Nation, 398
United States v. Truckee-Carson Irrigation Dist., 565
United States v. Vasquez-Ramos, 687
United States v. Washington (Boldt Decision) (district court), 495, 632, 645, 646, 647
United States v. Washington (Boldt Decision) (9th Circuit), 632
United States v. Washington (Chehalis Tribe), 646
United States v. Washington (disestablishment of Puyallup reservation), 628
United States v. Washington (habitat protection cases), 643, 650–651, **654**, **657**, 661
United States v. Washington (hatchery fish), 642, 644, 645
United States v. Washington (Lummi water rights), 511, 520
United States v. Washington (shellfish), 664
United States v. Washington Department of Ecology, 286
United States v. Webb, 153

United States v. White Mountain Apache Tribe, **386**, 393, 394
United States v. Wilgus, 686
United States v. Winans, 76, 219, **471**, 477, 478, 494, 498, 612, 629, 630, 642, 643, 663
United States ex rel. Hualpai Indians v. Santa Fe Pacific Railroad Co., **170**, 175, 176, 602
Upper Skagit Indian Tribe v. Washington, 646
Ute Indian Tribe v. Utah, 152
Ute Mountain Ute Tribe v. Rodriguez, 464
Ute Tribe of the Uintah and Outray Reservation v. Myton, 152
Vieux Carre Prop. Owners, Residents & Assoc., Inc. v. Brown, 47
Wagnon v. Prairie Band of Potawatomi Nation, 467
Ward v. Race Horse, 601–602
Washington v. Confederated Tribes of the Colville Indian Reservation, 209, 263, 424
Washington v. Washington State Commercial Passenger Fishing Vessel Ass'n, 495, 626, **633**, 642, 643, 644, 647, 650–651
Washington Department of Ecology v. United States Environmental Protection Agency, **286**
Washington Department of Ecology v. Yakima Reservation Irrigation District, 497
Western Energy Alliance v. U.S. Dep't of the Interior, 372
Wheeler v. United States, 252, 255
White Mountain Apache Tribe v. Bracker, 256, **453**, 463, 466–467, 469
Wik Peoples v. Queensland, 178
Williams v. City of Chicago, 602
Williams v. Lee, 120, 248, 249, 255, 256
Winters v. United States, 76, 471, **474**, 477, 478, 479, 480, 485, 496, 546, 611
Wisconsin v. Environmental Protection Agency, 301
Wisconsin v. Yoder, 21
Worcester v. Georgia, 73, **83**, 88, 101, 138, 248, 255
Wyoming v. U.S. Dep't of the Interior, 354, 355
Wyoming v. U.S. Envtl. Protection Agency, 312
Wyoming v. United States, 486, 499, 511–513, 577
Wyoming v. Zinke, 354
Yankton Sioux Tribe v. Gaffey, 153
Yankton Sioux Tribe v. Podhradsky, 113, 124, 153
Youngbull v. United States, 188

Preface to the Fourth Edition

We have been quite pleased with the reception of the first three editions of Native American Natural Resources Law. It has been especially gratifying to see our efforts encourage the establishment of a new course in the law school curriculum, one which bridges Indian law and natural resources and environmental law. Some of our colleagues have been uncommonly enthusiastic about both the casebook and the subject matter. *See, e.g.,* Debra Donahue, *A Call for Native American Natural Resources in the Law School Curriculum,* 24 Journal of Land, Resources, and Environmental Law 211 (2004).

In the five years since the third edition, the field of Native American natural resources law has continued to expand, and this edition reflects those developments: in legislatures, in the courts, and in the legal commentary. Recent legislation has been particularly important in the energy field. On the federal judicial level, the tension between Congress and the Supreme Court continues: while the Supreme Court has continued its apparent hostility toward tribal sovereignty, tribal governments continue to gain important regulatory roles under federal statutes. And although some state courts have read tribal water rights extremely narrowly, for the most part, tribal property rights continue to gain judicial recognition and protection.

We continue to believe that this book is adaptable to either an advanced course in Indian law for students whose principal interest is Indian law, or an advanced natural resources law course for students whose principal interest is in natural resources law, or for students whose interest lies in the intersection between the two fields. We have tried to design this book so that students need not have taken either the basic Indian law course or the basic natural resources law course to take this course.

A word about editing in this edition: in order to increase the book's readability, we have generally eliminated ellipses in our edits of cases and commentary, retaining ellipses only to indicate material that has been edited out within a paragraph.

We look forward to continuing to follow developments in this dynamic field for years to come.

JRV
MCB
EKW

Introduction

Native American Natural Resources Law is a growing, dynamic, exciting area of the law, involving important environmental and economic resources. Yet it has deep historical roots which are inextricably linked to the nation's ethical and legal obligations to the continent's first peoples. The field includes transcendent issues, such as compensation for or restoration of lost resources, as well as pragmatic concerns, such as the ability to site or maintain major facilities, the allocation of water supplies, and pollution control. In a larger sense, the study of Native American Natural Resource Law is a worthy endeavor because, as Felix Cohen noted, it serves as a reflection of the dominant society's tolerance for diversity. Moreover, by providing new laboratories to test novel management approaches, the dominant society may learn valuable natural resources lessons for the future.

Themes of Native American Natural Resources Law

There are several enduring themes in this text. We believe the material is better understood if the following points are introduced at the outset:

1) Most of the core conflicts in this field are jurisdictional: conflicts over which government has sovereign control over which resources.

2) What you learned in high school civics class—that the United States has a federal system of government with dual sovereigns, the states and the federal government—is not true. Tribal governments are an important third source of sovereignty that play an increasingly important role in natural resources allocation.

3) A critical distinction, one not always recognized in the case law, concerns the difference between questions of sovereignty—which government has authority to control natural resource allocation—and questions of property, that is, ownership of resources.

4) Large variations in the history of Native American policy continue to influence natural resources allocation today. In particular, the legacy of the allotment era (1887–1934), when tribes lost more than sixty percent of their land base in a purported effort to "assimilate" the tribes into the mainstream of American life, looms large.

5) The historical record reveals that, although the federal Congress and Executive have trust responsibilities to protect tribal lands and resources, they have not always been able to fulfill those responsibilities without assistance from the federal courts.

6) Ironically, however, some of the most innovative aspects of Native American Natural Resources Law in recent years have come from the U.S. Environmental Protection Agency, when Congress has authorized treatment of tribes as states for pollution control purposes. These initiatives come at a time when the United States Supreme Court has frequently treated tribal claims of inherent sovereignty with hostility.

7) Perhaps the chief characteristic of this field of law is its relative lack of universal principles that apply to all situations. The great diversity in Indian Country in terms of distinct treaties, statutes, executive orders, and histories—what Charles Wilkinson has called the "scattering forces" in Indian Country—makes case-by-case adjudication the norm and generic statements hazardous.

Native American Natural Resources Law

Chapter 1

Land, Religion, and Culture

This chapter explores the relationship between Indian tribes and the land, the ways in which that relationship differs from Anglo-American concepts of lands and resources, and the response of the American legal system to those cultural distinctions.

The considerable differences between the Indian view of the relationship between humans and nature and the view of those who colonized North America are difficult to exaggerate. These differences produced profound changes in the ecology of the continent, led to startling declines in the populations of both Indians and the animals on which they depended for subsistence, and created significant wealth for the colonists and settlers who exploited the continent's natural resources.

A. Indians and the Land

Frank Pommersheim, The Reservation as Place: A South Dakota Essay
34 S.D. L. Rev. 246, 246–247, 250–251 (1989)*

Indian reservations are often described as islands of poverty and despair cast adrift from the mainstream of national progress. Less often, they are extolled as places luckily isolated from the corrosive predations of the twentieth century. Each of these descriptions invokes, in part, the complex field of Indian law as a touchstone of both the past and future, as either the driving wedge for Indian natural resources and land and cultural breakup or as a countervailing force of restraint and an element of cultural renewal. Hidden in this web of description and claims lies the important notion of the reservation as place: a physical, human, legal, and spiritual reality that embodies the history, the dreams, and the aspirations of Indian people, their communities, and their tribes. A place that marks not only the enduring survival of Indian communities from a marauding western society, but also a place that holds the promise of fulfillment. As Lakota people say: "hecel lena Oyate nipikte" ("that these people may live"). The reservation constitutes an abiding place full of quotidian vitality and pressing dilemmas that continue to define modern Indian life.

---

* Copyright 1989 South Dakota Law Review; reprinted with permission of the South Dakota Law Review.

Land is inherent to Indian people; they often cannot conceive of life without it. They are part of it and it is part of them; it is their Mother. Nor is this just a romantic commonplace. For most Indian groups, including the Lakota people, it is a cultural centerpiece with wide-ranging implications for any attempt to understand contemporary reservation life. The importance of the land is severalfold. Beyond its obvious historical provision of subsistence, it is the source of spiritual origins and sustaining myth which in turn provides a landscape of cultural and emotional meaning. The land often determines the values of the human landscape. The harsh lands of the prairie helped to make Lakota tribal communities austere and generous, places where giving and sharing were first principles. The people needed the land and each other too much to permit wanton accumulation and ecological impairment to the living source of nourishment. Much of this is, of course, antithetical to western history and culture. As suggested by one commentator, the western ethos reflects a commitment:

> To *take* possession without becoming possessed: to take secure hold on the lands beyond and yet hold them at a rigidly maintained spiritual distance. It was never to merge, to mingle, to marry. To do so was to become an apostate from Christian history and so be lost in an eternal wilderness.

Such differing conceptions between Indians and non-Indians about the nature of land only adds tinder to the likelihood of adversity and misunderstanding. And sure enough, one of the results of over three centuries of contact has been the severance of much of this central, cultural taproot connecting Lakota people to the land. Impaired but not eradicated, this root is, nevertheless, being rediscovered and tended with renewed vigor and stewardship. In fact, this is so prevalent that it has been noted as a recurrent theme in contemporary Indian literature. The theme involves the loss of the old guardian spirits of place and how they might be made to speak again — how the land may become numinous once more and nod toward its dwellers.

This then is one pull of the land, the source of vital myth and cultural well-being. But there is also the complementary notion of a homeland where generations and generations of relatives have lived out their lives and destiny — that it is, after all, my home, my community, my reservation in Indian country. Many reservations may seem rural and isolated and they are, but many like the Rosebud Reservation are quite beautiful, captivating in the way the subtle paintbrush of the prairie often is. The Rosebud Reservation and others like it do not possess (fortunately) the grandeur for tourists, but a long stay makes lasting impressions on one's psyche. This notion of homeland is not, of course, unique to Indians alone, and despite the obvious irony, it is valued by many non-Indians, including non-Indian residents of the reservation.

These attractions and connections do not prevent people from leaving the reservation, but they make it hard. People do leave, most often for greater economic opportunity, as well as sometimes to escape violence and perceptions about inferior schools. But most who leave also return.

The reservation is home. It is a place where the land lives and stalks people, where the land looks after people and makes them live right, a place where the earth's ways provide solace and nurture. Yet, paradoxically, it is also a place where the land has been wounded and the sacred hoop has been broken; a place where there is the stain of violence and suffering. And it is this painful dilemma that also stalks the people and their Mother.

One of the most fundamental differences between Indian and Anglo views is the relationship of the land and the natural resources to the economic life of the community. In his landmark study, Changes in the Land: Indians, Colonists, and the Ecology of New England (Hill and Wang 1983), Professor William Cronon described the changes that took place in the New England countryside between 1600 and 1800. At the beginning, the Indians harvested game on unfenced, common lands mainly for domestic needs. By 1800, most of southern New England was largely emptied of game animals, its forests clearcut, and its soils exhausted, contaminated with European pests and diseases. Game animals were replaced by livestock, which necessitated fence construction. Deforestation increased temperature variations, dried soils, changed drainage patterns, and depleted streams. Fences inhibited traditional native migrations in search of game.

> [W]hereas Indian villages moved from habitat to habitat to find maximum abundance through minimal work, and so reduce their impact on the land, the English believed in and required permanent settlements. . . . English fixity sought to replace Indian mobility; here was the central conflict in the ways Indians and colonists interacted with their environments.

Id. at 53. Although Cronon observed that these changes were most dramatic near populated areas, he noted that "they heralded the future." *Id.* at 160. Similar changes would be repeated many times in many locations throughout the 19th century.

Cronon attributed the reason for the dramatic landscape changes to a complex multiplicity of causes, including new production techniques and political organization. But fundamental was the replacement of the Indians' hunter-gatherer society, in which game was harvested for household consumption, with a society in which land was viewed as a means of generating wealth. For the Indians, status was not a function of economic wealth but instead of personal relationships and kinship networks. As Cronon explains: "A wide range of resources furnished economic subsistence, while a narrow range of resources conferred economic status." *Id.* at 166. For the colonists, however, the situation was reversed: "though colonists perceived fewer *resources* in New England ecosystems than did the Indians, they perceived many more *commodities*." *Id.* at 167 (emphasis in original). Cattle, corn, furs, timber, and so forth, were not merely for subsistence; they were export commodities. Distant markets in Europe established the demand for these resources and set their price. With land cheap and labor dear, land became a form of capital that could be transformed into profits and wealth. *Id.* at 169.

The commodification of land in the colonial perspective led to wasteful practices. Europeans considered New England to be a land of abundance, a "landscape of great natural wealth." *Id.* at 168. This view encouraged the colonists to engage in widespread overgrazing of livestock, overplanting of grains, and overharvesting of timber and game. When the land played out, the settlers simply moved on, usually further west, leaving ecological destruction in their wake. Their behavior was as often dictated by European prices as by local markets. Thus, Cronon concluded that "the abstract concept of commodity informed colonial decision-making about the New England environment." *Id.* This commodification of ecosystems as "natural resources" defined the colonists' approach to the environment.

In the Pacific Northwest, white settlement came later, in the wake of the Lewis and Clark expedition of 1804–05 and the Great Migration along the Oregon Trail beginning in 1843. But the conflicting native and settler views of the environment remained about the same. Consider the following analysis of the effects of white settlement on Columbia Basin salmon and the tribal communities that depended on the fisheries.

Michael C. Blumm, Sacrificing the Salmon: A Legal and Policy History of the Decline of Columbia Basin Salmon
65–67 (2002)*

The Gift Economy vs. the Market Economy

The economy of the pre-white settlement Northwest has been described by Jim Lichatowich as a "gift economy," which had evolved over 1,500 years. In this economy, one attained social position not by accumulation of wealth but through the size of one's gifts. Gifts were the basic source of exchange and commerce. Natural resources, like salmon harvests and fishing sites, were gifts from nature, not for individual ownership and exclusive possession, but to be shared with others and passed on to succeeding generations. Salmon, which had a conscious spirit, would remain abundant if treated with respect. The natural world was filled with such spirits, which humans needed to cultivate to ensure a continuous food supply and other necessities.

The new market economy introduced by white settlers was fundamentally different. Salmon and other natural resources were commodities to be captured and sold for profit. Unlike the gift economy, in which cultural and religious taboos supplied an inherent check on excessive harvests, the market economy contained no such checks. As white settlers began to arrive in numbers—the non-native population of the state of Oregon grew from just over 50,000 in 1860, to over 90,000 in 1870, to over 175,000 in 1880, to over 300,000 in 1890, to over 400,000 in 1900—they overwhelmed the natives and their gift economy. By the turn of the century 1.1 million people lived in the states of Oregon, Washington, and Idaho. Fewer than 20,000 were natives, who had experienced a 95 percent decline in their numbers since the onset of white settlement, mostly due to disease.

The market economy the white settlers established had no internal checks of legends and taboos to moderate resource use. Natural resources were not kindred

---

* Copyright 2002 by BookWorld Publications, Inc. Reprinted with permission of Vandeplas Publishing.

spirits but commodities essential to maximizing profits. Profits were often a function of the demands of distant markets, not local subsistence. Short-term wealth became more important than long-term sustainable use.

The new market economy did more than just displace tribal fishers: it had devastating effects on the salmon resource. There were two reasons for this result: changed fishing techniques and loss of salmon habitat. Even if the white-dominated fishery of the 19th century did not harvest more aggregate fish from the Columbia than the native harvests—and recent estimates place peak harvests of both just over 40 million pounds—the manner of harvest was materially different, concentrated in the lower river and compressed into a four-month season (the tribes generally fished nine months of the year), in order to concentrate efforts on the most prized salmon species. New harvest technologies, including fish wheels, captured higher percentages of particular runs. Waste at canneries was widespread, something not condoned in the pre-existing gift economy.

The second consequence of the introduction of the market economy was habitat loss. As beavers were trapped, streams mined, farms irrigated, livestock grazed, trees logged, mills operated, and cities settled, salmon habitat shrunk. Joseph Taylor concisely summarized the situation:

> Oregon country Indians had harvested massive quantities of salmon for many centuries before whites arrived, but their impact on the rest of the landscape was relatively benign. Salmon encountered a far different world in the second half of the nineteenth century. . . . Trappers, farmers, miners, irrigators, loggers, and boosters transformed nature in ways that made it less hospitable to aquatic life. The clear, cool, unimpeded streams of precontact times had become dirtier, warmer, and more often obstructed. By 1900, Euro-American settlement had already reduced significantly the spawning ranges of salmon in the Columbia and other basins. This was the ecological context of the industrial fishery during the late nineteenth century.

[Joseph E. Taylor III, Making Salmon: An Environmental History of the Northwest Fisheries Crisis 59 (U. Washington Press, 1999).]

The new economy thus not only preempted tribal harvests, it damaged the salmon runs themselves. Harvests declined 50 percent between 1884 and 1889, rebounded briefly as harvesters switched from chinook to coho and sockeye, then fell again. Thirty-nine canneries in 1887 became twenty-one by 1889. By the turn of the century, harvests in both Alaska and British Columbia exceeded Columbia River harvests. This "free-for-all" was over within just thirty years. Never again would Columbia Basin salmon be thought of as a limitless resource. Throughout the 20th century, there would always be more harvest capacity than available salmon; the chief issue would become not who possessed the better harvest technology but who had the better harvest rights. Allocating an increasingly scarce resource would become a vexing problem for scientists, regulators, and reviewing courts.

Underlying much of the difference in tribal and Anglo worldviews toward the land and its resources is a fundamentally different ethic and sense of obligation. Consider the following excerpt from the Navajo Nation Code, apparently codifying natural law, and the analysis offered by Professor Tsosie.

Navajo Nation Code, Tit. I, § 205

Nahasdzáán Dóó Yádiłhił Bits'ádéé Beehaz'áanii — Diné Natural Law

Diné Natural Law declares and teaches that:

A. The four sacred elements of life, air, light/fire, water and earth/pollen in all their forms must be respected, honored and protected for they sustain life; and

B. The six sacred mountains, Sisnaajini, Tsoodził, Dook'o'oosliid, Dibe Nitsaa, Dził Na'orrdiłii, Dził Ch'ool'í'í, and all the attendant mountains must be respected, honored, and protected for they, as leaders, are the foundation of the Navajo Nation; and

C. All creation, from Mother Earth and Father Sky to the animals, those who live in water, those who fly and plant life have their own laws and have rights and freedoms to exist; and

D. The Diné have the sacred obligation and duty to respect, preserve and protect all that was provided for we were designated as the steward for these relatives through our use of the sacred gifts of language and thinking; and

E. Mother Earth and Father Sky is part of us as the Diné and the Diné is part of Mother Earth and Father Sky; The Diné must treat this sacred bond with love and respect without exerting dominance for we do not own our mother or father; and

F. The rights and freedoms of the people to the use of the sacred elements of life as mentioned above and to the use of land, natural resources, sacred sites and other living beings must be accomplished through the proper protocol of respect and offering and these practices must be protected and preserved for they are the foundation of our spiritual ceremonies and the Diné life way; and

G. It is the duty and responsibility of the Diné to protect and preserve the beauty of the natural world for future generations.

Rebecca Tsosie, Tribal Environmental Policy in an Era of Self-Determination: The Role of Ethics, Economics, and Traditional Ecological Knowledge

21 Vermont L. Rev. 225, 268, 274, 276, 279, 281–282 (1996)*

The diversity among American Indian people makes defining an "indigenous land ethic" somewhat difficult. Nevertheless, the similarities among indigenous world

---

* Copyright 1996 Rebecca Tsosie, reprinted with permission of Rebecca Tsosie and the Vermont Law Review.

views regarding the environment cannot be discounted. These similarities are useful for a comparative discussion of Euro-American and indigenous land ethics, and they provide a means to understand the often different values that underlie contemporary tribal environment decision-making.

A central feature of many indigenous world views is found in the spiritual relationship that Native American peoples appear to have with the environment. Indeed, as Vine Deloria has observed, a central task of tribal religions is to "determine the proper relationship that the people of the tribe must have with other living things and to develop the self-discipline within the tribal community so that man acts harmoniously with other creatures."

A central belief among many Native American cultures is that Earth is a living, conscious being that must be treated with respect and care.

[T]he animate universe that predominates among indigenous world views gives rise to a relational, rather than hierarchical, land ethic. This relational ethic situates the human being in a kinship role with respect to other aspects of the natural universe.

The indigenous understanding of the relationships between man and the natural environment is radically different from the Western understanding of such relationships. Euro-American values stemming from Christianity, capitalism, and technology promote a view of nature as a commodity, "as wilderness to be tamed," and as a "nonliving collection of natural resources to be exploited." Although European traditions may speak of the need to maintain balance in nature, these traditions do not suggest that humans are in a kinship relation with animals, or that humans owe a duty to animals. A duty would imply some right on the part of animals, an idea which has never achieved widespread support from ethicists or from the public at large.

In comparison, [some scholars] find that indigenous people "base their relationship with the environment on concepts of respect and duty rather than rights and claims." * * * For Indian people, "[r]espect and duty are flexible principles that situate the 'right' in a context of a relationship or many relationships and cannot be abstracted from the nature of those relationships."

Despite the fact that many tribal societies possess a different worldview toward the land and its resources, Indian tribes may still decide to pursue forms of economic development that are environmentally destructive for a variety of reasons. In the following excerpt, focusing on tribal decisions to exploit natural resources, Professor Ezra Rosser explores the romanticized "stereotype of Indians as environmental stewards." This issue, and the conflicts that may arise between Indian tribes and those holding a romanticized view, are revisited in later chapters.

Ezra Rosser, Ahistorical Indians and Reservation Resources
40 Envtl. L. 437, 465–468 (2010)*

Natural resource exploitation on reservations is antithetical to the stereotype of Indians as environmental stewards. With the publication, in print and as a public service television commercial in 1971 to 1972 of a stoic Indian crying because of pollution, "Indian and environmental concern became synonymous, and public discussion turned to whether America might somehow tap native wisdom in solving the environmental problems facing Mother Earth." The notion that Indians are by definition also environmentalists pervades popular culture and is thought by many academics to have explanatory power when considering reservation development. This mental shortcut raises the challenge of any other stereotype—namely that although the romantic notion of tribes as environmental stewards does not hold for all tribes or for all points in time, the stereotype nevertheless is grounded on some element of truth.

What is the stereotype? Born out of the idea that Indians are somehow different and less civilized, the stereotype is at once a description of Indians and also, by contrast, of non-Indians. In the early 1970s, Indians were popularly thought of "as the continent's first conservationists." The romantic conception of Indians preceded the birth of the environmental movement; as early as the 1830s Indians were thought of romantically as "children of Nature," unburdened by the troubles of civilized society. In American Indians & National Parks, Robert H. Keller and Michael F. Turek provide a nice summary of the stereotype, namely that "Indians had always lived in harmony with nature, revered Mother Earth as sacred, and offered a special wisdom to non-Indians." More subtle versions of the stereotype assume, for example, that Indians will necessarily reach better decisions than non-Indians or always favor preserving the environment over economic development.

There is some truth to the stereotype. As Donald Fixico observes, "the 'Mother Earth' concept is one of the few universal concepts among American Indians." The "Indian 'heritage' of 'environmental sensitivity'" positively has facilitated tribal takeover of environmental protection responsibilities, while also legitimizing arguably racist U.S. environmental policies. Simply rejecting the stereotype risks ignoring the truths it contains. Professor Rebecca Tsosie argues that "[t]he cultural connections between Native peoples and the land" should not be dismissed "as a 'romanticized' notion that is of limited utility in a modern era." And studies confirming or making note of the central place of nature and land in Indian belief and value systems are ubiquitous. What is required is to reject the stereotypes and the "environmental myths" surrounding Indians without "suppressing their historical associations with the land."

---

* Ezra Rosser, *Ahistorical Indians and Reservation Resources*, 40 Envtl. L. 437 (2010). First published by *Environmental Law*, Volume 40, Issue 2. Reprinted with permission.

Given that the stereotype on its face seems a positive one, why must it be rejected? The answer is that the stereotype is too readily accepted as truth both when it is deployed to explain environmentally protective decisions and when it is used to block a tribe's decision to participate in or cause environmental harms. The stereotype confines Indians to an ahistorical moment and potentially deprives tribes of their sovereignty. It is ahistorical because, while it is surely true that some tribes balanced concerns for the environment with economic development differently than non-Indians, it is impossible to reduce the history of every, or even any, tribe so neatly in this way. It is also ahistorical because in order to accept the stereotype, the pretension that Indian societies are static and have not always changed with time must also be accepted. The stereotype is "dehumanizing" and "masks cultural diversity." It operates independent of reality, such that a "romantic conception of what 'Indians' should be is frequently inconsistent with what 'Indians' actually are today."

B. Legal Protection of Sacred and Cultural Sites

As discussed above, many individual Indians and Indian tribes have a unique relationship with the land and its resources. The following excerpts explore how the American legal system has responded to this unique relationship and the resulting cultural distinctions. The context for this exploration is sacred sites—places and areas of religious and cultural importance to tribes. The materials consider two aspects of the protection of sacred sites: the extent to which the government is bound to protect Indians' free exercise of religion, and the extent to which the government is constrained by the establishment clause if it tries to do so.

Lyng v. Northwest Indian Cemetery Protective Association
485 U.S. 439 (1988)

JUSTICE O'CONNOR delivered the opinion of the Court.

This case requires us to consider whether the First Amendment's Free Exercise Clause forbids the Government from permitting timber harvesting in, or constructing a road through, a portion of a National Forest that has traditionally been used for religious purposes by members of three American Indian tribes in northwestern California. We conclude that it does not.

I

As part of a project to create a paved 75-mile road linking two California towns, Gasquet and Orleans, the United States Forest Service has upgraded 49 miles of previously unpaved roads on federal land. In order to complete this project (the G-O road), the Forest Service must build a 6-mile paved segment through the Chimney Rock section of the Six Rivers National Forest. That section of the forest is situated between two other portions of the road that are already complete.

In 1977, the Forest Service issued a draft environmental impact statement that discussed proposals for upgrading an existing unpaved road that runs through the

Chimney Rock area. In response to comments on the draft statement, the Forest Service commissioned a study of American Indian cultural and religious sites in the area. The Hoopa Valley Indian reservation adjoins the Six Rivers National Forest, and the Chimney Rock area has historically been used for religious purposes by Yurok, Karok, and Tolowa Indians. The commissioned study, which was completed in 1979, found that the entire area "is significant as an integral and indispensable [sic] part of Indian religious conceptualization and practice." Specific sites are used for certain rituals, and "successful use of the [area] is dependent upon and facilitated by certain qualities of the physical environment, the most important of which are privacy, silence, and an undisturbed natural setting." The study concluded that constructing a road along any of the available routes "would cause serious and irreparable damage to the sacred areas which are an integral and necessary part of the belief systems and lifeway of Northwest California Indian peoples." Accordingly, the report recommended that the G-O road not be completed.

In 1982, the Forest Service decided not to adopt this recommendation, and it prepared a final environmental impact statement for construction of the road. The Regional Forester selected a route that avoided archeological sites and was removed as far as possible from the sites used by contemporary Indians for specific spiritual activities. Alternative routes that would have avoided the Chimney Rock area altogether were rejected because they would have required the acquisition of private land, had serious soil stability problems, and would in any event have traversed areas having ritualistic value to American Indians. At about the same time, the Forest Service adopted a management plan allowing for the harvesting of significant amounts of timber in this area of the forest. The management plan provided for one-half mile protective zones around all the religious sites identified in the report that had been commissioned in connection with the G-O road.

After exhausting their administrative remedies, respondents—an Indian organization, individual Indians, nature organizations and individual members of those organizations, and the State of California—challenged both the road-building and timber-harvesting decisions in the United States District Court for the Northern District of California. Respondents claimed that the Forest Service's decisions violated the Free Exercise Clause, the Federal Water Pollution Control Act (FWPCA) [Clean Water Act], the National Environment Policy Act of 1969 (NEPA), several other federal statutes, and governmental trust responsibilities to Indians living on the Hoopa Valley Reservation.

After a trial, the District Court issued a permanent injunction forbidding the Government from constructing the Chimney Rock section of the G-O road or putting the timber-harvesting management plan into effect. The court found that both actions would violate the Free Exercise Clause * * * [and] the FWPCA, and that the environmental impact statements for construction of the road were deficient under the National Environmental Policy Act. Finally, the court concluded that both projects would breach the Government's trust responsibilities to protect water and fishing rights reserved to the Hoopa Valley Indians.

A panel of the Ninth Circuit affirmed in part. The panel unanimously rejected the District Court's conclusion that the Government's proposed actions would breach its trust responsibilities to Indians on the Hoopa Valley Reservation. * * * The District Court's decision, to the extent that it rested on statutory grounds, was otherwise unanimously affirmed. [The panel also affirmed, by a divided decision, the District Court's constitutional ruling.]

II

* * * Neither the District Court nor the Court of Appeals explained or expressly articulated the necessity for their constitutional holdings. Were we persuaded that those holdings were unnecessary, we could simply vacate the relevant portions of the judgment below without discussing the merits of the constitutional issue. The structure and wording of the District Court's injunctive order, however, suggests that the statutory holdings would not have supported all the relief granted.

Because it appears reasonably likely that the First Amendment issue was necessary to the decisions below, we believe that it would be inadvisable to vacate and remand without addressing that issue on the merits. This conclusion is strengthened by considerations of judicial economy. The Government, which petitioned for certiorari on the constitutional issue alone, has informed us that it believes it can cure the statutory defects identified below, intends to do so, and will not challenge the adverse statutory rulings. In this circumstance, it is difficult to see what principle would be vindicated by sending this case on what would almost certainly be a brief round trip to the courts below.

III A

The Free Exercise Clause of the First Amendment provides that "Congress shall make no law . . . prohibiting the free exercise [of religion]." U.S. Const., Amdt. 1. It is undisputed that the Indian respondents' beliefs are sincere and that the Government's proposed actions will have severe adverse effects on the practice of their religion. Respondents contend that the burden on their religious practices is heavy enough to violate the Free Exercise Clause unless the Government can demonstrate a compelling need to complete the G-O road or to engage in timber harvesting in the Chimney Rock area. We disagree.

In *Bowen v. Roy*, 476 U.S. 693 (1986), we considered a challenge to a federal statute that required the States to use Social Security numbers in administering certain welfare programs. Two applicants for benefits under these programs contended that their religious beliefs prevented them from acceding to the use of a Social Security number for their two-year-old daughter because the use of a numerical identifier would "'rob the spirit' of [their] daughter and prevent her from attaining greater spiritual power." Similarly, in this case, it is said that disruption of the natural environment caused by the G-O road will diminish the sacredness of the area in question and create distractions that will interfere with "training and ongoing religious experience of individuals using [sites within] the area for personal medicine and growth . . . and as integrated parts of a system of religious belief and practice which correlates ascending degrees of personal power with a geographic hierarchy of power." The Court rejected this kind of challenge in *Roy*:

> "The Free Exercise Clause simply cannot be understood to require the Government to conduct its own internal affairs in ways that comport with the religious beliefs of particular citizens. Just as the Government may not insist that [the Roys] engage in any set form of religious observance, so [they] may not demand that the Government join in their chosen religious practices by refraining from using a number to identify their daughter. . . .
>
> ". . . The Free Exercise Clause affords an individual protection from certain forms of governmental compulsion; it does not afford an individual a right to dictate the conduct of the Government's internal procedures."

The building of a road or the harvesting of timber on publicly owned land cannot meaningfully be distinguished from the use of a Social Security number in *Roy*. In both cases, the challenged government action would interfere significantly with private persons' ability to pursue spiritual fulfillment according to their own religious beliefs. In neither case, however, would the affected individuals be coerced by the Government's action into violating their religious beliefs; nor would either governmental action penalize religious activity by denying any person an equal share of the rights, benefits, and privileges enjoyed by other citizens.

We are asked to distinguish this case from *Roy* on the ground that the infringement on religious liberty here is "significantly greater," or on the ground that the government practice in *Roy* was "purely mechanical" whereas this case involves "a case-by-case substantive determination as to how a particular unit of land will be managed." Similarly, we are told that this case can be distinguished from *Roy* because "the government action is not at some physically removed location where it places no restriction on what a practitioner may do." The State suggests that the Social Security number in *Roy* "could be characterized as interfering with Roy's religious tenets from a subjective point of view, where the government's conduct of its own internal affairs' was known to him only secondhand and did not interfere with his ability to practice his religion." In this case, however, it is said that the proposed road will "physically destroy the environmental conditions and the privacy without which the [religious] practices cannot be conducted."

These efforts to distinguish *Roy* are unavailing. This Court cannot determine the truth of the underlying beliefs that led to the religious objections here or in *Roy*, and accordingly cannot weigh the adverse effects on the Roys and compare them with the adverse effects on respondents. Without the ability to make such comparisons, we cannot say that the one form of incidental interference with an individual's spiritual activities should be subjected to a different constitutional analysis than the other.

Respondents insist, nonetheless, that the courts below properly relied on a factual inquiry into the degree to which the Indians' spiritual practices would become ineffectual if the G-O road were built. They rely on several cases in which this Court has sustained free exercise challenges to government programs that interfered with individuals' ability to practice their religion. *See Wisconsin v. Yoder*, 406 U. S. 205 (1972) (compulsory school-attendance law).

Even apart from the inconsistency between *Roy* and respondents' reading of these cases, their interpretation will not withstand analysis. It is true that this Court has repeatedly held that indirect coercion or penalties on the free exercise of religion, not just outright prohibitions, are subject to scrutiny under the First Amendment. * * * This does not and cannot imply that incidental effects of government programs, which may make it more difficult to practice certain religions but which have no tendency to coerce individuals into acting contrary to their religious beliefs, require government to bring forward a compelling justification for its otherwise lawful actions. The crucial word in the constitutional text is "prohibit": "For the Free Exercise Clause is written in terms of what the government cannot do to the individual, not in terms of what the individual can exact from the government."

Whatever may be the exact line between unconstitutional prohibitions on the free exercise of religion and the legitimate conduct by government of its own affairs, the location of the line cannot depend on measuring the effects of a governmental action on a religious objector's spiritual development. The Government does not dispute, and we have no reason to doubt, that the logging and road-building projects at issue in this case could have devastating effects on traditional Indian religious practices. Those practices are intimately and inextricably bound up with the unique features of the Chimney Rock area, which is known to the Indians as the "high country." Individual practitioners use this area for personal spiritual development; some of their activities are believed to be critically important in advancing the welfare of the tribe, and indeed, of mankind itself. The Indians use this area, as they have used it for a very long time, to conduct a wide variety of specific rituals that aim to accomplish their religious goals. According to their beliefs, the rituals would not be efficacious if conducted at other sites than the ones traditionally used, and too much disturbance of the area's natural state would clearly render any meaningful continuation of traditional practices impossible. To be sure, the Indians themselves were far from unanimous in opposing the G-O road, and it seems less than certain that construction of the road will be so disruptive that it will doom their religion. Nevertheless, we can assume that the threat to the efficacy of at least some religious practices is extremely grave.

Even if we assume that we should accept the Ninth Circuit's prediction, according to which the G-O road will "virtually destroy the Indians' ability to practice their religion," the Constitution simply does not provide a principle that could justify upholding respondents' legal claims. However much we might wish that it were otherwise, government simply could not operate if it were required to satisfy every citizen's religious needs and desires. A broad range of government activities—from social welfare programs to foreign aid to conservation projects—will always be considered essential to the spiritual well-being of some citizens, often on the basis of sincerely held religious beliefs. Others will find the very same activities deeply offensive, and perhaps incompatible with their own search for spiritual fulfillment and with the tenets of their religion. The First Amendment must apply to all citizens alike, and it can give to none of them a veto over public programs that do not prohibit the free exercise of religion. The Constitution does not, and courts cannot, offer to reconcile the various competing demands on government, many of them rooted in sincere religious belief, that inevitably arise in so diverse a society as ours. That task, to the extent that it is feasible, is for the legislatures and other institutions.

One need not look far beyond the present case to see why the analysis in *Roy* * * * offers a sound reading of the Constitution. Respondents attempt to stress the limits of the religious servitude that they are now seeking to impose on the Chimney Rock area of the Six Rivers National Forest. While defending an injunction against logging operations and the construction of a road, they apparently do not *at present* object to the area's being used by recreational visitors, other Indians, or forest rangers. Nothing in the principle for which they contend, however, would distinguish this case from another lawsuit in which they (or similarly situated religious objectors) might seek to exclude all human activity but their own from sacred areas of the public lands. The Indian respondents insist that "privacy during the power quests is required for the practitioners to maintain the purity needed for a successful journey." Similarly: "The practices conducted in the high country entail intense meditation and require the practitioner to achieve a profound awareness of the natural environment. Prayer seats are oriented so there is an unobstructed view, and the practitioner must be surrounded by undisturbed naturalness." No disrespect for these practices is implied when one notes that such beliefs could easily require de facto beneficial ownership of some rather spacious tracts of public property. Even without anticipating future cases, the diminution of the Government's property rights, and the concomitant subsidy of the Indian religion, would in this case be far from trivial: the District Court's order permanently forbade commercial timber harvesting, or the construction of a two-lane road, anywhere within an area covering a full 27 sections (i.e., more than 17,000 acres) of public land.

The Constitution does not permit government to discriminate against religions that treat particular physical sites as sacred, and a law forbidding the Indian respondents from visiting the Chimney Rock area would raise a different set of constitutional questions. Whatever rights the Indians may have to the use of the area, however, those rights do not divest the Government of its right to use what is, after all, *its* land.

B

Nothing in our opinion should be read to encourage governmental insensitivity to the religious needs of any citizen. The Government's rights to the use its own land, for example, need not and should not discourage it from accommodating religious practices like those engaged in by the Indian respondents. It is worth emphasizing, therefore, that the Government has taken numerous steps in this very case to minimize the impact that construction of the G-O road will have on the Indians' religious activities. First, the Forest Service commissioned a comprehensive study of the effects that the project would have on the cultural and religious value of the

Chimney Rock area. The resulting 423-page report was so sympathetic to the Indians' interests that it has constituted the principal piece of evidence relied on by respondents' throughout this litigation.

Although the Forest Service did not in the end adopt the report's recommendation that the project be abandoned, many other ameliorative measures were planned. No sites where specific rituals take place were to be disturbed. In fact, a major factor in choosing among alternative routes for the road was the relation of the various routes to religious sites: the route selected by the Regional Forester is, he noted, "the farthest removed from contemporary spiritual sites; thus, the adverse audible intrusions associated with the road would be less than all other alternatives." Nor were the Forest Service's concerns limited to "audible intrusions." As the dissenting judge below observed, ten specific steps were planned to reduce the visual impact of the road on the surrounding country.

Except for abandoning its project entirely, and thereby leaving the two existing segments of road to deadend in the middle of a National Forest, it is difficult to see how the Government could have been more solicitous. Such solicitude accords with "the policy of the United States to protect and preserve for American Indians their inherent right of freedom to believe, express, and exercise the traditional religions of the American Indian . . . including but not limited to access to sites, use and possession of sacred objects, and the freedom to worship through ceremonials and traditional rites." American Indian Religious Freedom Act (AIRFA), 42 U.S.C. § 1996.

Respondents, however, suggest that AIRFA goes further and in effect enacts their interpretation of the First Amendment into statutory law. * * * This argument is without merit. After reciting several legislative findings, AIRFA "resolves" upon the policy quoted above. A second section of the statute required an evaluation of federal policies and procedures, in consultation with native religious leaders, of changes necessary to protect and preserve the rights and practices in question. The required report dealing with this evaluation was completed and released in 1979. Nowhere in the law is there so much as a hint of any intent to create a cause of action or any judicially enforceable individual rights.

What is obvious from the face of the statute is confirmed by numerous indications in the legislative history. The sponsor of the bill that became AIRFA, Representative Udall, called it "a sense of Congress joint resolution," aimed at ensuring that "the basic right of the Indian people to exercise their traditional religious practices is not infringed without a clear decision on the part of the Congress or the administrators that such religious practices must yield to some higher consideration." Representative Udall emphasized that the bill would not "confer special religious rights on Indians," would "not change any existing State or Federal law," and in fact "has no teeth in it."

IV

The decision of the court below, according to which the First Amendment precludes the Government from completing the G-O road or from permitting timber harvesting in the Chimney Rock area, is reversed. In order that the District Court's injunction may be reconsidered in light of this holding, and in the light of any other relevant events that may have intervened since the injunction issued, the case is remanded for further proceedings consistent with this opinion.

JUSTICE BRENNAN, with whom JUSTICE MARSHALL and JUSTICE BLACKMUN join, dissenting.

"'The Free Exercise Clause,'" the Court explains today, "'is written in terms of what the government cannot do to the individual, not in terms of what the individual can exact from the government.'" Pledging fidelity to this unremarkable constitutional principle, the Court nevertheless concludes that even where the Government uses federal land in a manner that threatens the very existence of a Native American religion, the Government is simply not "doing" anything to the practitioners of that faith. Instead, the Court believes that Native Americans who request that the Government refrain from destroying their religion effectively seek to exact from the Government de facto beneficial ownership of federal property. These two astonishing conclusions follow naturally from the Court's determination that federal land-use decisions that render the practice of a given religion impossible do not burden that religion in a manner cognizable under the Free Exercise Clause, because such decisions neither coerce conduct inconsistent with religious belief nor penalize religious activity. The constitutional guarantee we interpret today, however, draws no such fine distinctions between types of restraints on religious exercise, but rather is directed against any form of governmental action that frustrates or inhibits religious practice. Because the Court today refuses even to acknowledge the constitutional injury respondents will suffer, and because this refusal essentially leaves Native Americans with absolutely no constitutional protection against perhaps the gravest threat to their religious practices, I dissent.

I

For at least 200 years and probably much longer, the Yurok, Karok, and Tolowa Indians have held sacred an approximately 25 square-mile area of land situated in what is today the Blue Creek Unit of Six Rivers National Forest in northwestern California. As the Government readily concedes, regular visits to this area, known to respondent Indians as the "high country," have played and continue to play a "critical" role in the religious practices and rituals of these tribes. Those beliefs, only briefly described in the Court's opinion, are crucial to a proper understanding of respondents' claims.

In marked contrast to traditional western religions, the belief systems of Native Americans do not rely on doctrines, creeds, or dogmas. * * * Where dogma lies at the heart of western religions, Native American faith is inextricably bound to the use of land. The site-specific nature of Indian religious practice derives from the Native American perception that land is itself a sacred, living being. Rituals are performed in prescribed locations not merely as a matter of traditional orthodoxy, but because land, like all other living things, is unique, and specific sites possess different spiritual properties and significance. Within this belief system, therefore, land is not fungible; indeed, at the time of the Spanish colonization of the American southwest, "all . . . Indians held in some form a belief in a sacred and indissoluble bond between themselves and the land in which their settlements were located."

For respondent Indians, the most sacred of lands is the high country where, they believe, pre-human spirits moved with the coming of humans to the earth. Because these spirits are seen as the source of religious power, or "medicine," many of the tribes' rituals and practices require frequent journeys to the area. Thus, for example, religious leaders preparing for the complex of ceremonies that underlie the tribes' World Renewal efforts must travel to specific sites in the high country in order to attain the medicine necessary for successful renewal. Similarly, individual tribe members may seek curative powers for the healing of the sick, or personal medicine for particular purposes such as good luck in singing, hunting, or love. A period of preparation generally precedes such visits, and individuals must select trails in the sacred area according to the medicine they seek and their abilities, gradually moving to increasingly more powerful sites, which are typically located at higher altitudes. Among the most powerful of sites are Chimney Rock, Doctor Rock, and Peak 8, all of which are elevated rock outcroppings.

According to the Theodoratus Report [commissioned by the Forest Service], the qualities "of silence, the aesthetic perspective, and the physical attributes, are an extension of the sacredness of [each] particular site." The act of medicine making is akin to meditation: the individual must integrate physical, mental and vocal actions in order to communicate with the pre-human spirits. As a result, "successful use of the high country is dependent upon and facilitated by certain qualities of the physical environment, the most important of which are privacy, silence, and an undisturbed natural setting." Although few tribe members actually make medicine at the most powerful sites, the entire tribe's welfare hinges on the success of the individual practitioners.

II

The Court does not for a moment suggest that the interests served by the G-O road are in any way compelling, or that they outweigh the destructive effect construction of the road will have on respondents' religious practices. Instead, the Court embraces the Government's contention that its prerogative as landowner should always take precedence over a claim that a particular use of federal property infringes religious practices. Attempting to justify this rule, the Court argues that the First Amendment bars only outright prohibitions, indirect coercion, and penalties on the free exercise of religion. All other "incidental effects of government programs," it concludes, even those "which may make it more difficult to practice certain religions but which have no tendency to coerce individuals into acting contrary to their religious beliefs," simply do not give rise to constitutional concerns. Since our recognition nearly half a century ago that restraints on religious conduct implicate the concerns of the Free Exercise Clause, we have never suggested that the protections of the guarantee are limited to so narrow a range of governmental burdens. The land-use decision challenged here will restrain respondents from practicing their religion as surely and as completely as any of the governmental actions we have struck down in the past, and the Court's efforts simply to define away respondents' injury as nonconstitutional is both unjustified and ultimately unpersuasive.

C

Prior to today's decision, several courts of appeals had attempted to fashion a test that accommodates the competing "demands" placed on federal property by the two cultures. Recognizing that the Government normally enjoys plenary authority over federal lands, the courts of appeals required Native Americans to demonstrate that any land-use decisions they challenged involved lands that were "central" or "indispensable" to their religious practices. Although this requirement limits the potential number of free exercise claims that might be brought to federal land management decisions, and thus forestalls the possibility that the Government will find itself ensnared in a host of lilliputian lawsuits, it has been criticized as inherently ethnocentric, for it incorrectly assumes that Native American belief systems ascribe religious significance to land in a traditionally western hierarchical manner. It is frequently the case in constitutional litigation, however, that courts are called upon to balance interests that are not readily translated into rough equivalents. At their most absolute, the competing claims that both the Government and Native Americans assert in federal land are fundamentally incompatible, and unless they are tempered by compromise, mutual accommodation will remain impossible.

I believe it appropriate, therefore, to require some showing of "centrality" before the Government can be required either to come forward with a compelling justification for its proposed use of federal land or to forego that use altogether. "Centrality," however, should not be equated with the survival or extinction of the religion itself. * * * Because of their perceptions of and relationship with the natural world, Native Americans consider all land sacred. Nevertheless, the Theodoratus Report reveals that respondents here deemed certain lands more powerful and more directly related to their religious practices than others. Thus, in my view, while Native Americans need not demonstrate, as respondents did here, that the Government's land-use decision will assuredly eradicate their faith, I do not think it is enough to allege simply that the land in question is held sacred. Rather, adherents challenging a proposed use of federal land should be required to show that the decision poses a substantial and realistic threat of frustrating their religious practices. Once such a showing is made, the burden should shift to the Government to come forward with a compelling state interest sufficient to justify the infringement of those practices.

III

Today, the Court holds that a federal land-use decision that promises to destroy an entire religion does not burden the practice of that faith in a manner recognized by the Free Exercise Clause. Having thus stripped respondents and all other Native Americans of any constitutional protection against perhaps the most serious threat to their age-old religious practices, and indeed to their entire way of life, the Court assures us that nothing in its decision "should be read to encourage governmental insensitivity to the religious needs of any citizen." I find it difficult, however, to imagine conduct more insensitive to religious needs than the Government's determination to build a marginally useful road in the face of uncontradicted evidence that the road will render the practice of respondents' religion impossible. Nor do I believe that respondents will derive any solace from the knowledge that although the practice of their religion will become "more difficult" as a result of the Government's actions, they remain free to maintain their religious beliefs. Given today's ruling, that freedom amounts to nothing more than the right to believe that their religion will be destroyed. The safeguarding of such a hollow freedom not only makes a mockery of the "'policy of the United States to protect and preserve for American Indians their inherent right of freedom to believe, express, and exercise their traditional religions,'" it fails utterly to accord with the dictates of the First Amendment.

Notes

1. **Native religion versus Catholic religion.** Justice O'Connor confidently stated that *Lyng* "cannot meaningfully be distinguished from the use of a Social Security number in *Roy [v. Bowen]*. . . . In neither case . . . would the affected individual be coerced by the government's action into violating their religious beliefs, nor would either governmental action penalize religious activity by denying any person an equal share of the rights, benefits, and privileges enjoyed by other citizens."

How sensitive was Justice O'Connor to Indian religion? She acknowledged that the timber harvesting and road building "could have devastating effects on traditional Indian religious practices. . . . We can assume the threat to religious practices is extremely grave." Nevertheless, she worried that giving the tribes a veto over the project would result in a "diminution of the Government's property rights, and concomitant subsidy of the Indian religion." Suppose a government action would not merely destroy a Catholic church, but also the place where an alleged religious miracle occurred? Would such an action penalize religion? (Justices Kennedy and Scalia, part of the six-member majority in *Lyng*, are Catholics.) Would the Court describe enjoining the project to protect the free exercise rights of Catholics as a subsidy to the religion?

2. **Justice O'Connor and *Wisconsin v. Yoder*.** Justice O'Connor made little attempt to explain why the government needed a compelling state interest to justify imposing a compulsory school requirement on Amish children in *Wisconsin v. Yoder*, 406 U.S. 205 (1972), but not for destroying sacred native religious sites through federal timber harvests and road building. According to Professor Getches, Justice O'Connor was "capable of employing foundation principles [of Indian jurisprudence] to justify an outcome that fits her views of what ought to be; however, she does not hesitate to invoke a subjectivist approach and disregard foundation principles if necessary to produce a desired result contradicting those principles." David H. Getches, *Conquering the Cultural Frontier: The New Subjectivism of the Supreme Court in Indian Law,* 84 Cal. L. Rev. 1573, 1642 (1996).

3. Property rights in sacred sites. Professor Kristen Carpenter critiqued the decision in *Lyng* as denying Indian free exercise rights on the basis of federal ownership of sacred sites. She argued that this "ownership model" of property law is neither accurate nor appropriate, and advanced property-based arguments for the rights of nonowners as a way of protecting tribal interests in sacred lands. Kristen A. Carpenter, *A Property Rights Approach to Sacred Sites Cases: Asserting a Place for Indians as Nonowners*, 52 UCLA L. Rev. 1061 (2005).

4. The aftermath of *Lyng*. The G-O Road at issue in the *Lyng* case was part of a larger Forest Service plan to harvest 733 million board feet of timber over an 80-year period from the Blue Creek Unit. That plan was aborted by the 1984 California Wilderness Act, which designated much of the area as wilderness. However, that statute also exempted from wilderness designation a 1200-foot wide strip, which apparently left the issue of whether to build the road to the Forest Service's discretion.

The Supreme Court decision on the First Amendment issue did not authorize construction of the road, since the Forest Service was still subject to the lower court's injunction for violating NEPA and the Clean Water Act, two issues on which the Supreme Court did not accept *certiorari*. *Northwest Indian Cemetery Protective Ass'n v. Peterson*, 795 F.2d 688, 695–97 (9th Cir. 1986). The Forest Service never remedied these statutory violations, and the road was never built. In 1990 Congress included the Blue Creek Unit in the Smith River National Recreation Area, 16 U.S.C. §§ 460bbb–460bbb-11.

Navajo Nation v. United States Forest Service
535 F.3d 1058 (9th Cir. 2008) (en banc)

BEA, Circuit Judge:

In this case, American Indians ask us to prohibit the federal government from allowing the use of artificial snow for skiing on a portion of a public mountain sacred in their religion. At the heart of their claim is the planned use of recycled wastewater, which contains 0.0001% human waste, to make artificial snow. The Plaintiffs claim the use of such snow on a sacred mountain desecrates the entire mountain, deprecates their religious ceremonies, and injures their religious sensibilities. We are called upon to decide whether this government-approved use of artificial snow on government-owned park land violates the Religious Freedom Restoration Act of 1993 ("RFRA") [and other statutes]. We hold that it does not, and affirm the district court's denial of relief on all grounds.

Plaintiff Indian tribes and their members consider the San Francisco Peaks in Northern Arizona to be sacred in their religion.[1] They contend that the use of recycled wastewater to make artificial snow for skiing on the Snowbowl, a ski area that

---

1. The Plaintiffs-Appellants in this case are the Navajo Nation, the Hopi Tribe, the Havasupai Tribe, the Hualapai Tribe, the Yavapai-Apache Nation, the White Mountain Apache Nation, Bill Bucky Preston (a member of the Hopi Tribe), Norris Nez (a member of the Navajo Nation), Rex

covers approximately one percent of the San Francisco Peaks, will spiritually contaminate the entire mountain and devalue their religious exercises. The district court found the Plaintiffs' beliefs to be sincere; there is no basis to challenge that finding. The district court also found, however, that there are no plants, springs, natural resources, shrines with religious significance, or religious ceremonies that would be physically affected by the use of such artificial snow. No plants would be destroyed or stunted; no springs polluted; no places of worship made inaccessible, or liturgy modified. The Plaintiffs continue to have virtually unlimited access to the mountain, including the ski area, for religious and cultural purposes. On the mountain, they continue to pray, conduct their religious ceremonies, and collect plants for religious use.

Thus, the sole effect of the artificial snow is on the Plaintiffs' subjective spiritual experience. That is, the presence of the artificial snow on the Peaks is offensive to the Plaintiffs' feelings about their religion and will decrease the spiritual fulfillment Plaintiffs get from practicing their religion on the mountain. Nevertheless, a government action that decreases the spirituality, the fervor, or the satisfaction with which a believer practices his religion is not what Congress has labeled a "substantial burden"—a term of art chosen by Congress to be defined by reference to Supreme Court precedent—on the free exercise of religion. Where, as here, there is no showing the government has coerced the Plaintiffs to act contrary to their religious beliefs under the threat of sanctions, or conditioned a governmental benefit upon conduct that would violate the Plaintiffs' religious beliefs, there is no "substantial burden" on the exercise of their religion.

Were it otherwise, any action the federal government were to take, including action on its own land, would be subject to the personalized oversight of millions of citizens. Each citizen would hold an individual veto to prohibit the government action solely because it offends his religious beliefs, sensibilities, or tastes, or fails to satisfy his religious desires. Further, giving one religious sect a veto over the use of public park land would deprive others of the right to use what is, by definition, land that belongs to everyone.

"[W]e are a cosmopolitan nation made up of people of almost every conceivable religious preference." Our nation recognizes and protects the expression of a great range of religious beliefs. Nevertheless, respecting religious credos is one thing; requiring the government to change its conduct to avoid any perceived slight to them is quite another. No matter how much we might wish the government to conform its conduct to our religious preferences, act in ways that do not offend our religious sensibilities, and take no action that decreases our spiritual fulfillment, no government—let alone a government that presides over a nation with as many religions as the

---

Tilousi (a member of the Havasupai Tribe), Dianna Uqualla (a member of the Havasupai Tribe), the Sierra Club, the Center for Biological Diversity, and the Flagstaff Activist Network.

United States of America—could function were it required to do so. *Lyng v. Nw. Indian Cemetery Protective Ass'n,* 485 U.S. 439, 452 (1988).

I. Factual and Procedural Background

The Snowbowl ski area ("the Snowbowl") is located on federally owned public land and operates under a special use permit issued by the United States Forest Service ("the Forest Service"). Specifically, the Snowbowl is situated on Humphrey's Peak, the highest of the San Francisco Peaks ("the Peaks"), located within the Coconino National Forest in Northern Arizona. The Peaks cover about 74,000 acres. The Snowbowl sits on 777 acres, or approximately one percent of the Peaks.

The Forest Service designated the Snowbowl as a public recreation facility after finding the Snowbowl "represented an opportunity for the general public to access and enjoy public lands in a manner that the Forest Service could not otherwise offer in the form of a major facility anywhere in Arizona." The Snowbowl has been in operation since the 1930s and is the only downhill ski area within the Coconino National Forest.

The Peaks have long-standing religious and cultural significance to Indian tribes. The tribes believe the Peaks are a living entity. They conduct religious ceremonies, such as the Navajo Blessingway Ceremony, on the Peaks. The tribes also collect plants, water, and other materials from the Peaks for medicinal bundles and tribal healing ceremonies. According to the tribes, the presence of the Snowbowl desecrates for them the spirituality of the Peaks. Certain Indian religious practitioners believe the desecration of the Peaks has caused many disasters, including the September 11, 2001 terrorist attacks, the Columbia Space Shuttle accident, and increases in natural disasters.

* * * In 2002, the Snowbowl submitted a proposal to the Forest Service to upgrade its operations. The proposal included a request for artificial snowmaking from recycled wastewater for use on the Snowbowl. The Snowbowl had suffered highly variable snowfall for several years; this resulted in operating losses that threatened its ski operation. Indeed, the district court found that artificial snowmaking is "needed to maintain the viability of the Snowbowl as a public recreational resource."

The recycled wastewater to be used for snowmaking is classified as "A+" by the Arizona Department of Environmental Quality ("ADEQ"). A+ recycled wastewater is the highest quality of recycled wastewater recognized by Arizona law and may be safely and beneficially used for many purposes, including irrigating school ground landscapes and food crops. Further, the ADEQ has specifically approved the use of recycled wastewater for snowmaking.

The Forest Service conducted an extensive review of the Snowbowl's proposal. As part of its review, the Forest Service made more than 500 contacts with Indian tribes, including between 40 and 50 meetings, to determine the potential impact of the proposal on the tribes. In a December 2004 Memorandum of Agreement, the Forest Service committed to, among other things: (1) continue to allow the tribes access to the Peaks, including the Snowbowl, for cultural and religious purposes; and (2) work with the tribes periodically to inspect the conditions of the religious and cultural sites on the Peaks and ensure the tribes' religious activities on the Peaks are uninterrupted.

Following the review process, the Forest Supervisor approved the Snowbowl's proposal, including the use of recycled wastewater to make artificial snow, and issued a Final Environmental Impact Statement and a Record of Decision in February 2005. [The Plaintiffs unsuccessfully pursued an administrative appeal. In their federal court action, the district court granted summary judgment on all claims to the Defendants. A panel of the Ninth Circuit reversed, holding that the use of recycled wastewater violated RFRA.] We took the case en banc to revisit the panel's decision and to clarify our circuit's interpretation of "substantial burden" under RFRA.

III. Religious Freedom Restoration Act of 1993

Plaintiffs contend the use of artificial snow, made from recycled wastewater, on the Snowbowl imposes a substantial burden on the free exercise of their religion, in violation of the Religious Freedom Restoration Act of 1993 ("RFRA"). We hold that the Plaintiffs have failed to establish a RFRA violation. The presence of recycled wastewater on the Peaks does not coerce the Plaintiffs to act contrary to their religious beliefs under the threat of sanctions, nor does it condition a governmental benefit upon conduct that would violate their religious beliefs, as required to establish a "substantial burden" on religious exercise under RFRA.

RFRA was enacted in response to the Supreme Court's decision in *Employment Division v. Smith,* 494 U.S. 872 (1990). In *Smith,* the Supreme Court held that the Free Exercise Clause does not bar the government from burdening the free exercise of religion with a "valid and neutral law of general applicability." Applying that standard, the *Smith* Court rejected the Free Exercise Clause claims of the plaintiffs, who were denied state unemployment compensation after being discharged from their jobs for ingesting peyote for religious purposes.

* * * With the enactment of RFRA, Congress created a cause of action for persons whose exercise of religion is substantially burdened by a government action, regardless of whether the burden results from a neutral law of general applicability.

To establish a prima facie RFRA claim, a plaintiff must present evidence sufficient to allow a trier of fact rationally to find the existence of two elements. First, the activities the plaintiff claims are burdened by the government action must be an "exercise of religion." Second, the government action must "substantially burden" the plaintiff's exercise of religion. If the plaintiff cannot prove either element, his RFRA claim fails. Conversely, should the plaintiff establish a substantial burden on his exercise of religion, the burden of persuasion shifts to the government to prove that the challenged government action is in furtherance of a "compelling governmental interest" and is implemented by "the least restrictive means." If the government cannot so prove, the court must find a RFRA violation.

We now turn to the application of these principles to the facts of this case. The first question is whether the activities Plaintiffs claim are burdened by the use of recycled wastewater on the Snowbowl constitute an "exercise of religion." RFRA defines "exercise of religion" as "any exercise of religion, whether or not compelled by, or central to, a system of religious belief." The Defendants do not contest the district court's holding that the Plaintiffs' religious beliefs are sincere and the Plaintiffs' religious activities on the Peaks constitute an "exercise of religion" within the meaning of RFRA.

The crux of this case, then, is whether the use of recycled wastewater on the Snowbowl imposes a "substantial burden" on the exercise of the Plaintiffs' religion. RFRA does not specifically define "substantial burden." Fortunately, we are not required to interpret the term by our own lights. Rather, we are guided by the express language of RFRA and decades of Supreme Court precedent.

A.

Our interpretation begins, as it must, with the statutory language. RFRA's stated purpose is to "restore the compelling interest test as set forth in *Sherbert v. Verner,* 374 U.S. 398 (1963) and *Wisconsin v. Yoder,* 406 U.S. 205 (1972) and to guarantee its application in all cases where free exercise of religion is substantially burdened." RFRA further states "the compelling interest test as set forth in ... Federal court rulings [prior to *Smith*] is a workable test for striking sensible balances between religious liberty and competing prior governmental interests."

Of course, the "compelling interest test" cited in the above-quoted RFRA provisions applies only if there is a substantial burden on the free exercise of religion. That is, the government is not required to prove a compelling interest for its action or that its action involves the least restrictive means to achieve its purpose, unless the plaintiff first proves the government action substantially burdens his exercise of religion. The same cases that set forth the compelling interest test also define what kind or level of burden on the exercise of religion is sufficient to invoke the compelling interest test. Therefore, the cases that RFRA expressly adopted and restored—*Sherbert, Yoder,* and federal court rulings prior to *Smith*—also control the "substantial burden" inquiry.

B.

In *Sherbert,* a Seventh-day Adventist was fired by her South Carolina employer because she refused to work on Saturdays, her faith's day of rest. Sherbert filed a claim for unemployment compensation benefits with the South Carolina Employment Security Commission, which denied her claim, finding she had failed to accept work without good cause. The Supreme Court held South Carolina could not, under the Free Exercise Clause, condition unemployment compensation so as to deny benefits to Sherbert because of the exercise of her faith. Such a condition unconstitutionally forced Sherbert "to choose between following the precepts of her religion and forfeiting benefits, on the one hand, and abandoning one of the precepts of her religion in order to accept work, on the other hand."

In *Yoder*, defendants, who were members of the Amish religion, were convicted of violating a Wisconsin law that required their children to attend school until the children reached the age of sixteen, under the threat of criminal sanctions for the parents. The defendants sincerely believed their children's attendance in high school was "contrary to the Amish religion and way of life." The Supreme Court reversed the defendants' convictions, holding the application of the compulsory school-attendance law to the defendants "unduly burden[ed]" the exercise of their religion, in violation of the Free Exercise Clause. According to the Court, the Wisconsin law "affirmatively compel[led the defendants], under threat of criminal sanction, to perform acts undeniably at odds with fundamental tenets of their religious beliefs."

The Supreme Court's decisions in *Sherbert* and *Yoder*, relied upon and incorporated by Congress into RFRA, lead to the following conclusion: Under RFRA, a "substantial burden" is imposed only when individuals are forced to choose between following the tenets of their religion and receiving a governmental benefit (*Sherbert*) or coerced to act contrary to their religious beliefs by the threat of civil or criminal sanctions (*Yoder*). Any burden imposed on the exercise of religion short of that described by *Sherbert* and *Yoder* is not a "substantial burden" within the meaning of RFRA, and does not require the application of the compelling interest test set forth in those two cases.

Applying *Sherbert* and *Yoder*, there is no "substantial burden" on the Plaintiffs' exercise of religion in this case. The use of recycled wastewater on a ski area that covers one percent of the Peaks does not force the Plaintiffs to choose between following the tenets of their religion and receiving a governmental benefit, as in *Sherbert*. The use of recycled wastewater to make artificial snow also does not coerce the Plaintiffs to act contrary to their religion under the threat of civil or criminal sanctions, as in *Yoder*. The Plaintiffs are not fined or penalized in any way for practicing their religion on the Peaks or on the Snowbowl. Quite the contrary: the Forest Service "has guaranteed that religious practitioners would still have access to the Snowbowl" and the rest of the Peaks for religious purposes.

The only effect of the proposed upgrades is on the Plaintiffs' subjective, emotional religious experience. That is, the presence of recycled wastewater on the Peaks is offensive to the Plaintiffs' religious sensibilities. To plaintiffs, it will spiritually desecrate a sacred mountain and will decrease the spiritual fulfillment they get from practicing their religion on the mountain. Nevertheless, under Supreme Court precedent, the diminishment of spiritual fulfillment—serious though it may be—is not a "substantial burden" on the free exercise of religion.[12]

---

12. [T]he sole question is whether a government action that affects only subjective spiritual fulfillment "substantially burdens" the exercise of religion. For all of the rich complexity that describes the profound integration of man and mountain into one, the burden of the recycled wastewater can only be expressed by the Plaintiffs as damaged spiritual feelings. Under Supreme Court precedent, government action that diminishes subjective spiritual fulfillment does not "substantially burden" religion.

The Supreme Court's decision in *Lyng v. Northwest Indian Cemetery Protective Ass'n* is on point. * * * The Supreme Court rejected the Indian tribes' Free Exercise Clause challenge.[13] * * * [T]here is nothing to distinguish the road-building project in *Lyng* from the use of recycled wastewater on the Peaks. We simply cannot uphold the Plaintiffs' claims of interference with their faith and, at the same time, remain faithful to *Lyng*'s dictates.

D.

In support of their RFRA claims, the Plaintiffs rely on two of our RLUIPA decisions. For two reasons, RLUIPA is inapplicable to this case. First, RLUIPA, by its terms, prohibits only state and local governments from applying regulations that govern land use or institutionalized persons to impose a "substantial burden" on the exercise of religion. RLUIPA does not apply to a federal government action, which is the only issue in this case. Second, even for state and local governments, RLUIPA applies only to government land-use regulations of private land-such as zoning laws-not to the government's management of its own land.

VI. Conclusion

We affirm the district court's entry of judgment in favor of the Defendants on the RFRA claim.

WILLIAM A. FLETCHER, Circuit Judge, dissenting, joined by Judge PREGERSON and Judge FISHER:

The en banc majority today holds that using treated sewage effluent to make artificial snow on the most sacred mountain of southwestern Indian tribes does not violate the Religious Freedom Restoration Act ("RFRA").

I. Religious Freedom Restoration Act A. Background

The Forest Service has acknowledged that the Peaks are sacred to at least thirteen formally recognized Indian tribes, and that this religious significance is of centuries' duration. There are differences among these tribes' religious beliefs and practices associated with the Peaks, but there are important commonalities. As the Service has noted, many of the tribes share beliefs that water, soil, plants, and animals from the Peaks have spiritual and medicinal properties; that the Peaks and everything on them form an indivisible living entity; that the Peaks are home to deities and other spirit beings; that tribal members can communicate with higher powers through prayers and songs focused on the Peaks; and that the tribes have a duty to protect the Peaks.

The Arizona Snowbowl is a ski area on Humphrey's Peak, the most sacred of the San Francisco Peaks.

Until now, the Snowbowl has always depended on natural snowfall. In dry years, the operating season is short, with few skiable days and few skiers. * * * ASR, the

---

13. That *Lyng* was a Free Exercise Clause, not RFRA, challenge is of no material consequence. Congress expressly instructed the courts to look to pre-*Smith* Free Exercise Clause cases, which include *Lyng*, to interpret RFRA.

current owner, purchased the Snowbowl in 1992 for $4 million, with full knowledge of weather conditions in northern Arizona.

Under the [approved snowmaking plan], the City of Flagstaff would provide the Snowbowl with up to 1.5 million gallons per day of its treated sewage effluent—euphemistically called "reclaimed water"—from November through February. A 14.8-mile pipeline would be built between Flagstaff and the Snowbowl to carry the treated effluent. The Snowbowl would be the first ski resort in the nation to make artificial snow entirely from undiluted treated sewage effluent.

The effluent that emerges after treatment by Flagstaff satisfies the requirements of Arizona law for "reclaimed water." However, as the FEIS explains, the treatment does not produce pure water. * * * Under Arizona law, the treated sewage effluent must be free of "detectable fecal coliform organisms" in only "four of the last seven daily reclaimed water samples." The FEIS acknowledges that the treated sewage effluent also contains "many unidentified and unregulated residual organic contaminants." Treated sewage effluent may be used for many things, including irrigation and flushing toilets, but the Arizona Department of Environmental Quality ("ADEQ") requires that precautions be taken to avoid ingestion by humans.

Under the [approved plan], treated sewage effluent would be sprayed on 205.3 acres of Humphrey's Peak during the ski season. In November and December, the Snowbowl would use the effluent to build a base layer of artificial snow. The Snowbowl would then make more snow from the effluent depending on the amount of natural snowfall. The Snowbowl would also construct a reservoir on the mountain with a surface area of 1.9 acres to hold treated sewage effluent. The stored effluent would allow snowmaking to continue after Flagstaff cuts off the supply at the end of February.

B. Religious Freedom Restoration Act

The majority contends that the phrase "substantial burden" refers only to burdens that are created by two mechanisms—the imposition of a penalty, or the denial of a government benefit. But the phrase "substantial burden" has a plain and ordinary meaning that does not depend on the presence of a penalty or deprivation of benefit. A "burden" is "[s]omething that hinders or oppresses." Black's Law Dictionary (8th ed. 2004). A burden is "substantial" if it is "[c]onsiderable in importance, value, degree, amount, or extent." American Heritage Dictionary (4th ed. 2000). In RFRA, the phrase "substantial burden" modifies the phrase "exercise of religion." Thus, RFRA prohibits government action that "hinders or oppresses" the exercise of religion "to a considerable degree."

The text of RFRA does not describe a particular *mechanism* by which religion cannot be burdened. Rather, RFRA prohibits government action with a particular *effect* on religious exercise.

* * * *Sherbert* and *Yoder* held that certain interferences with religious exercise trigger the compelling interest test. But neither case suggested that religious exercise

can be "burdened," or "substantially burdened," *only* by the two types of interference considered in those cases.

Lyng did not hold that the road at issue would cause no "substantial burden" on religious exercise. The Court in *Lyng* never used the phrase "substantial burden." Rather, *Lyng* held that government action that did not coerce religious practices or attach a penalty to religious belief was insufficient to trigger the compelling interest test *despite* the presence of a significant burden on religion. The Court explicitly recognized this in *Smith* when it wrote, "In [*Lyng*], we declined to apply *Sherbert* analysis to the Government's logging and road construction activities on lands used for religious purposes by several Native American Tribes, even though it was undisputed that the activities '*could have devastating effects on traditional Indian religious practices.*'"

The majority's attempt to read *Lyng* into RFRA is not just flawed. It is perverse. In refusing to apply the compelling interest test to the "severe adverse effects on the practice of [plaintiffs'] religion" in *Lyng,* the Court reasoned that the protections of the First Amendment "cannot depend on measuring the effects of a governmental action on a religious objector's spiritual development." The Court directly incorporated this reasoning into *Smith.* Congress then rejected this very reasoning when it restored the application of strict scrutiny "in all cases where free exercise of religion is substantially burdened."

The express purpose of RFRA was to reject the restrictive approach to the Free Exercise Clause that culminated in *Smith* and to restore the application of strict judicial scrutiny "in all cases where free exercise of religion is substantially burdened." The majority's approach is fundamentally at odds with this purpose.

As should be clear, RFRA creates a legally protected interest in *the exercise of religion.* The protected interest in *Sherbert* was the right to take religious rest on Saturday, not the right to receive unemployment insurance. The protected interest in *Yoder* was the right to avoid secular indoctrination, not, as the majority contends, the right to avoid criminal punishment.

Such interests in religious exercise can be severely burdened by government actions that do not deny a benefit or impose a penalty. For example, a court would surely hold that the government had imposed a "substantial burden" on the "exercise of religion" if it purchased by eminent domain every Catholic church in the country. Similarly, a court would surely hold that the Forest Service had imposed a "substantial burden" on the Indians' "exercise of religion" if it paved over the entirety of the San Francisco Peaks.

D. Misunderstanding of Religious Belief and Practice

In addition to misstating the law under RFRA, the majority misunderstands the nature of religious belief and practice. The majority concludes that spraying up to 1.5 million gallons of treated sewage effluent per day on Humphrey's Peak, the most sacred of the San Francisco Peaks, does not impose a "substantial burden" on the

Indians' "exercise of religion." In so concluding, the majority emphasizes the lack of physical harm. According to the majority, "[T]here are no plants, springs, natural resources, shrines with religious significance, nor any religious ceremonies that would be physically affected" by using treated sewage effluent to make artificial snow. In the majority's view, the "sole effect" of using treated sewage effluent on Humphrey's Peak is on the Indians' "subjective spiritual experience."

The majority's emphasis on physical harm ignores the nature of religious belief and exercise, as well as the nature of the inquiry mandated by RFRA. The majority characterizes the Indians' religious belief and exercise as merely a "subjective spiritual experience." Though I would not choose precisely those words, they come close to describing what the majority thinks it is *not* describing—a genuine religious belief and exercise. Contrary to what the majority writes, and appears to think, religious exercise invariably, and centrally, involves a "subjective spiritual experience."

Religious belief concerns the human spirit and religious faith, not physical harm and scientific fact. Religious exercise sometimes involves physical things, but the physical or scientific character of these things is secondary to their spiritual and religious meaning. The centerpiece of religious belief and exercise is the "subjective" and the "spiritual." As William James wrote, religion may be defined as "the feelings, acts, and experiences of individual men [and women] in their solitude, so far as they apprehend themselves to stand in relation to whatever they may consider the divine."

The majority's misunderstanding of the nature of religious belief and exercise as merely "subjective" is an excuse for refusing to accept the Indians' religion as worthy of protection under RFRA. According to undisputed evidence in the record, and the finding of the district court, the Indians in this case are sincere in their religious beliefs. The record makes clear that their religious beliefs and practice do not merely require the continued existence of certain plants and shrines. They require that these plants and shrines be spiritually pure, undesecrated by treated sewage effluent.

Perhaps the strength of the Indians' argument in this case could be seen more easily by the majority if another religion were at issue. For example, I do not think that the majority would accept that the burden on a Christian's exercise of religion would be insubstantial if the government permitted only treated sewage effluent for use as baptismal water, based on an argument that no physical harm would result and any adverse effect would merely be on the Christian's "subjective spiritual experience." Nor do I think the majority would accept such an argument for an orthodox Jew if the government permitted only non-Kosher food.

E. Proper Application of RFRA b. Substantial Burden on the Indians' Exercise of Religion

* * * Because the Indians' religious beliefs and practices are not uniform, the precise burdens on religious exercise vary among the Appellants. Nevertheless, the burdens fall roughly into two categories: (1) the inability to perform a particular religious ceremony, because the ceremony requires collecting natural resources from the Peaks that would be too contaminated—physically, spiritually, or both—for sacramental use; and (2) the inability to maintain daily and annual religious practices comprising an entire way of life, because the practices require belief in the mountain's purity or a spiritual connection to the mountain that would be undermined by the contamination.

The first burden—the inability to perform religious ceremonies because of contaminated resources—has been acknowledged and described at length by the Forest Service. The FEIS summarizes: "Snowmaking and expansion of facilities, especially the use of reclaimed water, would contaminate the natural resources needed to perform the required ceremonies that have been, and continue to be, the basis for the cultural identity for many of these tribes." Further, "the use of reclaimed water is believed by the tribes to be impure and would have an irretrievable impact on the use of the soil, plants, and animals for medicinal and ceremonial purposes throughout the entire Peaks, as the whole mountain is regarded as a single, living entity."

Three Navajo practitioners' testimony at trial echoed the Forest Service's assessment in describing how the proposed action would prevent them from performing various ceremonies. [The testimony emphasized the threat that using sewage effluent to produce snow posed to the tribes' religious ceremonies, medicine practices, and cultural ceremonies.] *** Larry Foster, a Navajo practitioner who is training to become a medicine man *** testified that if treated sewage effluent were used on the Peaks he would no longer be able to go on the pilgrimages to the Peaks that are necessary to rejuvenate the medicine bundles, which are, in turn, a part of every Navajo healing ceremony.

Appellant Navajo medicine man Norris Nez testified that the proposed action would prevent him from practicing as a medicine man. He told the district court that the presence of treated sewage effluent would "ruin" his medicine, which he makes from plants collected from the Peaks. He also testified that he would be unable to perform the fundamental Blessingway ceremony, because "all [medicine] bundles will be affected and we will have nothing to use eventually."

The second burden the proposed action would impose—undermining the Indians' religious faith, practices, and way of life by desecrating the Peaks' purity—is also shown in the record. The Hopi presented evidence that the presence of treated sewage effluent on the Peaks would fundamentally undermine all of their religious practices because their way of life, or "beliefway," is largely based on the idea that the Peaks are a pure source of their rains and the home of the Katsinam.

Antone Honanie, a Hopi practitioner, testified that he would have difficulty preparing for religious ceremonies, because treated sewage effluent is "something you can't get out of your mind when you're sitting there praying" to the mountain, "a place where everything is supposed to be pure." Emory Sekaquaptewa, a Hopi tribal member and research anthropologist, testified that the desecration of the mountain would cause Katsinam dance ceremonies to lose their religious value. They would "simply be a performance for performance['s] sake" rather than "a religious effort."

Summarizing the Hopi's testimony, the district court wrote:

> The individual Hopi's practice of the Hopi way permeates every part and every day of the individual's life from birth to death.... The Hopi Plaintiffs testified that the proposed upgrades to the Snowbowl have affected and will continue to negatively affect the way they think about the Peaks, the Kachina and themselves when preparing for any religious activity involving the Peaks and the Kachina—from daily morning prayers to the regular calendar of religious dances that occur throughout the year.... The Hopi Plaintiffs also testified that this negative effect on the practitioners' frames of mind due to the continued and increased desecration of the home of the Kachinas will undermine the Hopi faith and the Hopi way. According to the Hopi, the Snowbowl upgrades will undermine the Hopi faith in daily ceremonies and undermine the Hopi faith in their Kachina ceremonies as well as their faith in the blessings of life that they depend on the Kachina to bring.

The record supports the conclusion that the proposed use of treated sewage effluent on the San Francisco Peaks would impose a burden on the religious exercise of all four tribes discussed above—the Navajo, the Hopi, the Hualapai, and the Havasupai. However, on the record before us, that burden falls most heavily on the Navajo and the Hopi. The Forest Service itself wrote in the FEIS that the Peaks are the most sacred place of both the Navajo and the Hopi; that those tribes' religions have revolved around the Peaks for centuries; that their religious practices require pure natural resources from the Peaks; and that, because their religious beliefs dictate that the mountain be viewed as a whole living being, the treated sewage effluent would in their view contaminate the natural resources throughout the Peaks. Navajo Appellants presented evidence in the district court that, were the proposed action to go forward, contamination by the treated sewage effluent would prevent practitioners from making or rejuvenating medicine bundles, from making medicine, and from performing the Blessingway and healing ceremonies. Hopi Appellants presented evidence that, were the proposed action to go forward, contamination by the effluent would fundamentally undermine their entire system of belief and the associated practices of song, worship, and prayer, that depend on the purity of the Peaks, which is the source of rain and their livelihoods and the home of the *Katsinam* spirits.

In light of this showing, it is self-evident that the Snowbowl expansion prevents the Navajo and Hopi "from engaging in [religious] conduct or having a religious experience" and that this interference is "more than an inconvenience."

III. Conclusion

The San Francisco Peaks have been at the center of religious beliefs and practices of Indian tribes of the Southwest since time out of mind. Humphrey's Peak, the holiest of the San Francisco Peaks, will from this time forward be desecrated and spiritually impure. In part, the majority justifies its holding on the ground that what it calls "public park land" is land that "belongs to everyone." There is a tragic irony in this justification. The United States government took this land from the Indians by force. The majority now uses that forcible deprivation as a justification for spraying treated sewage effluent on the holiest of the Indians' holy mountains, and for refusing to recognize that this action constitutes a substantial burden on the Indians' exercise of their religion.

RFRA was passed to protect the exercise of all religions, including the religions of American Indians. If Indians' land-based exercise of religion is not protected by RFRA in this case, I cannot imagine a case in which it will be. I am truly sorry that the majority has effectively read American Indians out of RFRA.

Notes

1. Criticism of *Navajo Nation*. Professors Kristen A. Carpenter, Sonia K. Katyal, and Angela R. Riley, in *In Defense of Property*, 118 Yale L. J. 1022 (2009), criticized the en banc opinion for elevating the dominance of federal property rights over tribal religious and cultural interests. They proposed instead a "stewardship model" of property that can protect cultural property in the absence of title.

2. Medicine Bluffs case. In an unreported decision, one district court adopted the *Navajo Nation* dissent's view of "substantial burden" under RFRA. *Comanche Nation v. United States,* 2008 WL 4426621 (W.D. Okla. Sept. 23, 2008). The Army proposed to construct a 43,000 square foot warehouse at Fort Sill, Oklahoma, to carry out obligations imposed by the Base Realignment and Closure Commission. The warehouse would have blocked the last unobstructed view of the Medicine Bluffs, an area sacred to the Comanche people. Because of the spiritual importance of the unobstructed southern viewscape, the district court held that the warehouse would "substantially burden" native religious practices. The court further determined that the warehouse advanced a compelling government interest in training soldiers, but that the Army had not proved construction at that location was the least restrictive means. The court issued a preliminary injunction, and the commander at Fort Still subsequently cancelled the project.

3. The affirmation of the RLUIPA. The Religious Land Use and Institutionalized Persons Act (RLUIPA) of 2000, 42 U.S.C. § 2000cc *et seq.*, which was passed unanimously by Congress, aimed to correct the constitutional problems with the Religious Freedom Restoration Act by limiting its scope to incarcerated prisoners and land use ordinances restricting religious practices. The RLUIPA prohibits states and localities from imposing substantial burdens on religious practices absent the least restrictive means of furthering a compelling state interest. In *Cutter v. Wilkerson,* 544 U.S. 709 (2005), a unanimous Supreme Court upheld the RLUIPA as a permissible accommodation of religion in the context of incarcerated prisoners, expressly declining to reach the statute's constitutionality concerning land use ordinances.

The cases explored above addressed the question of what accommodation is required when Indians consider the land in question to be sacred. The case below addresses the opposite question: what accommodations are constitutionally permissible on public land owned by the federal government.

Bear Lodge Multiple Use Association v. Babbitt [*Bear Lodge II*]
2 F. Supp. 2d 1448 (D. Wyo. 1998), *aff'd* 175 F.3d 814 (10th Cir. 1999)

DOWNES, District Judge.

The United States Department of the Interior, National Park Service ("NPS") issued a Final Climbing Management Plan ("FCMP")/Finding of No Significant Impact for Devils Tower National Monument[1] in February of 1995. The FCMP "sets a new direction for managing climbing activity at the tower for the next three to five years", its stated purpose being, "to protect the natural and cultural resources of Devils Tower and to provide for visitor enjoyment and appreciation of this unique feature." To protect against any new physical impacts to the tower, the FCMP provides that no new bolts or fixed pitons will be permitted on the tower, and new face routes requiring new bolt installation will not be permitted. The FCMP does allow individuals to replace already existing bolts and fixed pitons. In addition, the plan calls for access trails to be rehabilitated and maintained, and requires camouflaged climbing equipment, and climbing routes to be closed seasonally to protect raptor nests. The FCMP further provides that "[i]n respect for the reverence many American Indians hold for Devils Tower as a sacred site, rock climbers will be asked to voluntarily refrain from climbing on Devils Tower during the culturally significant month of June." The FCMP does not identify any other reason for the June "voluntary closure."[2]

---

1. The Devils Tower National Monument is located in northeast Wyoming. The FCMP reports that the Tower is a "sacred site" to several American Indian peoples of the northern plains who are increasingly traveling to the monument to perform "traditional cultural activities." Devils Tower is also eligible for inclusion to the national Register of Historic Places as a traditional cultural property. The FCMP further reports:

   Recreational climbing at Devils Tower has increased dramatically from 312 climbers in 1973 to over 6,000 annually. New route development in the last ten years resulted [in] accelerated route development and bolt placement. Today the tower has about 220 named routes. Approximately 600 metal bolts are currently embedded in the rock along with several hundred metal pitons. Devils Tower is world famous for its crack climbing, which depends primarily on removable protection placed by climbers in cracks.

   Activities performed by the numerous climbers on the tower during the bear spring through fall climbing season have affected nesting raptors, soil, vegetation, the integrity of the rock, the area's natural quiet, and the rock's physical appearance. Some American Indians have complained that the presence of climbers on the sacred butte and the placement of bolts in the rock has adversely impacted their traditional activities and seriously impaired the spiritual quality of the site.

2. The Defendants attempt to characterize these measures as relating solely to American Indian culture and being wholly separate from any religious practices. The Court is not persuaded that a legitimate distinction can be drawn in this case between the "religious" and "cultural" practices of those American Indians who consider Devils Tower a sacred site.

The NPS represents that it will not enforce the voluntary closure, but will instead rely on climbers' self-regulation and a new "cross-cultural educational program" "to motivate climbers and other park visitors to comply." The NPS has also placed a sign at the base of the Tower in order to encourage visitors to stay on the trail surrounding the Tower. Despite the FCMP's reliance on self-regulation, it also provides that if the voluntary closure proves to be "unsuccessful," the NPS will consider taking several actions including: (a) revising the climbing management plan; (b) reconvening a climbing management plan work group; (c) instituting additional measures to further encourage compliance; (d) change the duration and nature of the voluntary closure; (e) converting the June closure to mandatory; and (f) writing a new definition of success for the voluntary closure. Factors indicating an unsuccessful voluntary closure include, little to no decrease in the number of climbers, an increase in the number of unregistered climbers and increased conflict between user groups in the park. The NPS, however, states that the voluntary closure will be "fully successful" only "when every climber personally chooses not to climb at Devils Tower during June out of respect for American Indian cultural values."

The NPS plans to fully comply with its own June closure by not allowing NPS staff to climb on the tower in June except to enforce laws and regulations or to perform emergency operations. Originally the plan also contained a provision stating that commercial use licenses for June climbing guide activities would not be issued by the NPS for the month of June. Plaintiffs filed a Motion for Preliminary Injunction seeking to enjoin Defendants from the commercial climbing ban during the month of June. This Court granted that motion in June of 1996. In December of that year, Defendant issued a decision revoking the commercial climbing ban.

The Plaintiffs challenge several practices adopted in the FCMP. While the FCMP no longer calls for a ban on commercial climbing in the month of June, Plaintiffs argue that the Defendant wrongfully contends that it has the power to impose such a rule. Other provisions objected to by the Plaintiffs remain a part of the plan. These include the "voluntary" ban on climbing in June; an interpretive education program which explains the religious and cultural significance that the Monument has among some Native Americans; and finally, the placement of signs which encourage people to remain on the trail surrounding the Tower.

STANDARD OF REVIEW

Judicial review of agency action is governed by § 706 of the Administrative Procedures Act ("APA"). The Plaintiffs in this case implicate the subsections of § 706 which require a reviewing court to hold unlawful and set aside agency action, findings, and conclusions found to be: arbitrary, capricious, an abuse of discretion, or otherwise not in accordance with law.

In this case Plaintiffs contend that * * * the NPS's plan wrongfully promotes religion in violation of the establishment clause of the first amendment.

Commercial Climbing Ban

The Defendants assert that any challenge to the ban on commercial climbing at the Monument has now been mooted. In November of 1996 the NPS found that "at the current time there is no necessity to restrict commercial guided climbing. . . ." As a result they did away with the mandatory commercial climbing ban that they had initially approved as part of the FCMP.

While the Court could permanently enjoin the NPS from instituting any commercial climbing ban, such an order would constitute relief to a hypothetical and non-existent injury. Consequently, any permanent injunction at this stage would be futile. Whatever the Government's motives, the ban against commercial climbing is no longer a live controversy. For this Court to treat it as such would serve only an advisory purpose. Therefore the commercial climbing ban issue is moot and will not be addressed by this Court. However, it is important to note that any subsequent effort to resuscitate this ill-conceived ban would only serve to impair the Defendants' credibility with this Court.

Standing

Defendants contest the Plaintiffs' standing to challenge the FCMP's provision providing for a cultural interpretive program and the NPS's decision to place signs at the base of the Tower. Plaintiffs allege that the interpretive program adopted by the NPS promotes the religion of American Indians in violation of the establishment clause of the First Amendment. In particular, the Plaintiffs allege that the program proselytizes school children who visit the Monument under the guise of educating children about the heritage surrounding the Memorial.

[The court held that the plaintiffs did not have standing because they alleged only a generalized grievance, and had not submitted affidavits showing injury in fact. Plaintiffs' affidavits established that public school children visited the Monument and were exposed to the interpretive program, but not that any of the parents of these children were members of the plaintiff association. Similarly, plaintiffs submitted affidavits which asserted that children were coerced by the signs into staying on the trails, and thus into complying with Indian religious beliefs, but none of the affidavits alleged that the parents were members of the plaintiff association.]

Voluntary Climbing Ban

The Establishment Clause of the First Amendment states that "Congress shall make no law respecting an establishment of religion. . . ." The Courts of this country have long struggled with the type and extent of limitations on government action which these ten words impose. At its most fundamental level, the United States Supreme Court has concluded that this provision prohibits laws "which aid one religion, aid all religions, or prefer one religion over another." *Everson v. Board of Ed. of Ewing*, 330 U.S. 1, 15 (1947). Defining this prohibition on a case by case basis has proven a difficult endeavor, but the Court has developed a number of useful frameworks for conducting the analysis. In *Lemon v. Kurtzman*, 403 U.S. 602 (1971), the

Court established a three part test for delineating between proper and improper government actions. According to this test a governmental action does not offend the Establishment Clause if it (1) has a secular purpose, (2) does not have the principal or primary effect of advancing or inhibiting religion, and (3) does not foster an excessive entanglement with religion. *Lemon*, 403 U.S. at 612–13. In a concurring opinion in the case of *Lynch v. Donnelly*, 465 U.S. 668 (1984), Justice O'Connor sought to clarify the *Lemon* analysis by focusing on whether the government action endorsed religion. "Applying Justice O'Connor's refined analysis, the government impermissibly endorses religion if its conduct has either (1) the purpose or (2) the effect of conveying a message that religion or a particular religious belief is favored or preferred." *Bauchman v. West High School*, 132 F.3d 542, 551 (10th Cir. 1997). Noting the current disarray surrounding the analysis of Establishment Clause challenges, the Tenth Circuit has adopted the approach that an action must satisfy both prongs of Justice O'Connor's "endorsement" and *Lemon*'s excessive entanglement test in order to be proper.

Balanced in the analysis of the permissibility or impermissibility of the Government's actions is the ability of government to accommodate religious practices. The Supreme Court "has long recognized that the government may (and sometimes must) accommodate religious practices and that it may do so without violating the Establishment Clause." *Hobbie v. Unemployment Appeals Comm'n of Florida*, 480 U.S. 136, 144 (1987). The Constitution actually "mandates accommodation, not merely tolerance, of all religions, and forbids hostility toward any." *Lynch v. Donnelly*, 465 U.S. 668, 673 (1984). The Defendants acknowledge that the voluntary climbing ban is intended to confer benefits on Native American worshipers, but they contend this is appropriate accommodation falling well within the confines of the Establishment Clause.

Purpose

The ability to accommodate religious practices is an important consideration in determining what constitutes a proper purpose under the *Lemon* test and Justice O'Connor's endorsement test. The Plaintiffs can succeed on this prong only if they show that the action has no clear secular purpose or that despite a secular purpose the actual purpose is to endorse religion. The Supreme Court has noted that requiring a government action to serve a secular legislative purpose, "does not mean that the [policy's] purpose must be unrelated to religion." *Corporation of the Presiding Bishop of the Church of Jesus Christ of Latter-day Saints v. Amos*, 483 U.S. 327, 335 (1987). In cases of accommodation the Court has stated that "it is a permissible ... purpose to alleviate significant governmental interference with the ability of religious organizations to define and carry out their religious missions." 483 U.S. at 336.

In this case the Defendants contend that the climbing plan was designed, in part, to eliminate barriers to American Indians' free practice of religion. They argue that this type of accommodation is particularly appropriate in situations like this where impediments to worship arise because a group's sacred place of worship is found on property of the United States. Defendants assert that their actions are also aimed at fostering the preservation of the historical, social and cultural practices of Native Americans which are necessarily intertwined with their religious practices. While the purposes behind the voluntary climbing ban are directly related to Native American religious practices, that is not the end of the analysis. The purposes underlying the ban are really to remove barriers to religious worship occasioned by public ownership of the Tower. This is in the nature of accommodation, not promotion, and consequently is a legitimate secular purpose.

Effect

Accommodation also plays a role in considering whether the principal effect of a policy is to advance religion. * * * "[O]n occasion some advancement of religion will result from governmental action." *Lynch*, 465 U.S. at 683. This is particularly true in cases of accommodation. Appropriate accommodation does not have a principal effect of advancing religion. Appropriate accommodation, however, is a matter of degree. Actions step beyond the bounds of reasonable accommodation when they force people to support a given religion.

In the context of the Free Exercise Clause, the Tenth Circuit drew a line demarcating impermissible accommodation in the area of public lands ruling that the "[e]xercise of First Amendment freedoms may not be asserted to deprive the public of its normal use of an area." *Badoni v. Higginson*, 638 F.2d 172, 179 (1980). The record clearly reveals that climbing at the Devils Tower National Monument is a "legitimate recreational and historic" use of Park Service lands. If the NPS is, in effect, depriving individuals of their legitimate use of the monument in order to enforce the tribes' rights to worship, it has stepped beyond permissible accommodation and into the realm of promoting religion. The gravamen of the issue then becomes whether climbers are allowed meaningful access to the monument. Stated another way, is the climbing ban voluntary or is it actually an improper exercise of government coercion?[6]

Plaintiffs argue that the "voluntary" ban is voluntary in name only. In support of their argument Plaintiffs note that the NPS has established a goal of having every climber personally choose not to climb at the Tower during June. Plaintiffs also cite to possible modifications to the FCMP if the NPS deems the voluntary ban unsuccessful. Specifically, they draw the Court's attention to the fact that if the plan does not result in a significant reduction of climbers on Devils Tower each June, then the NPS may convert the closure to a mandatory closure.

Neither of these factors is sufficient to transform the voluntary ban into a coerced ban. The Park Service's stated goals are not the measure of coercion, rather the implementation of those goals is. The goal of reducing the number of climbers to zero

---

6. Both Parties rely on the case of *Lyng v. Northwest Indian Cemetery Protective Assoc.*, 485 U.S. 439 (1988), in an effort to support their respective cases. The Court has concluded that the *Lyng* case is largely irrelevant to the issues at hand. That case addresses the other side of the issues presented here, namely what accommodation is constitutionally required when American Indians consider public land sacred. Here, the Court must determine what type of accommodation is constitutionally permissible on lands considered sacred by American Indians.

may or may not be a desirable one,[7] but coercion only manifests itself in the NPS's actions, not in its aspirations. The Park Service's stated goals would not be advanced at all by mandating that climbers not scale the Tower. Instead, it has stated that the "voluntary closure will be fully successful when every climber personally chooses not to climb at Devils Tower during June." Ordering climbers not to climb or deterring climbing through intimidation undermines this goal and robs individuals of the personal choice necessary to accomplish it. Yet, the Park Service's hopes that climbers will adhere to the voluntary climbing ban cannot be viewed as coercive.

The other purported indicia of coercion also fails to establish that the voluntary climbing ban is, in fact, mandatory. Although the NPS has stated that an unsuccessful voluntary ban may lead it to make the ban mandatory, that is far from an inevitable result. To the contrary, the conversion to a mandatory ban is only one of eight options which the NPS may consider in the event of a failed voluntary ban. While a more direct threat of a mandatory ban in the wake of a failed voluntary ban could evidence coercion, the remote and speculative possibility of a mandatory ban found in this case is insufficient to transform the Government's action into a coercive measure.

Excessive Entanglement

The Court concludes that the voluntary climbing ban also passes muster when measured against the excessive entanglement test. To determine whether a given policy constitutes an excessive entanglement the Court must look at "the character and purposes of the institutions that are benefitted, the nature of the aid that the State provides, and the resulting relationship between the government and religious authority." *Lemon*, 403 U.S. at 615. In making this analysis the Court must be mindful that "[e]ntanglement is a question of kind and degree." *Lynch*, 465 U.S. at 668. The organizations benefitted by the voluntary climbing ban, namely Native American tribes, are not solely religious organizations, but also represent a common heritage and culture. As a result, there is much less danger that the Government's actions will inordinately advance solely religious activities. The very limited nature of government involvement in this case also tends to undermine any argument of excessive entanglement. The government is merely enabling Native Americans to worship in a more peaceful setting. In doing so, the Park Service has no involvement in the manner of worship that takes place, but only provides an atmosphere more conducive to worship. This type of custodial function does not implicate the dangerously close relationship between state and religion which offends the excessive entanglement prong of the *Lemon* test.

---

7. In fact, a complete elimination of climbing from the Tower in the month of June would serve as powerful evidence of actual coercion. [Editor's note: In *Bear Lodge I*, the district court struck down a plan that included a mandatory closure during the month of June on the ground that it "require[d] climbers to conform their conduct" to tribal religious practices and thus "amounts to impermissible governmental entanglement with religion." *Bear Lodge Multiple Use Ass'n v. Babbitt*, No. 96-CV-063-D (D. Wyo. June 8, 1996).]

CONCLUSION

The Plaintiffs have challenged four aspects of the NPS's Final Climbing Management Plan. Three of these four challenges are not susceptible to judicial review. The fourth, the voluntary climbing ban, is a policy that has been carefully crafted to balance the competing needs of individuals using Devil's Tower National Monument while, at the same time, obeying the edicts of the Constitution. As such, the plan constitutes a legitimate exercise of the Secretary of the Interior's discretion in managing the Monument.

Executive Order 13007 — Indian Sacred Sites
61 Fed. Reg. 26,771 (1996)

By the authority vested in me as President by the Constitution and the laws of the United States, in furtherance of Federal treaties, and in order to protect and preserve Indian religious practices, it is hereby ordered:

Section 1. Accommodation of Sacred Sites. (a) In managing Federal lands, each executive branch agency with statutory or administrative responsibility for the management of Federal lands shall, to the extent practicable, permitted by law, and not clearly inconsistent with essential agency functions, (l) accommodate access to and ceremonial use of Indian sacred sites by Indian religious practitioners and (2) avoid adversely affecting the physical integrity of such sacred sites. Where appropriate, agencies shall maintain the confidentiality of sacred sites.

(b) For purposes of this order:

* * *

(iii) "Sacred site" means any specific, discrete, narrowly delineated location on Federal land that is identified by an Indian tribe, or Indian individual determined to be an appropriately authoritative representative of an Indian religion, as sacred by virtue of its established religious significance to, or ceremonial use by, an Indian religion; provided that the tribe or appropriately authoritative representative of an Indian religion has informed the agency of the existence of such a site.

Section 2. Procedures. (a) Each executive branch agency with statutory or administrative responsibility for the management of Federal lands shall, as appropriate, promptly implement procedures for the purposes of carrying out the provisions of section 1 of this order, including, where practicable and appropriate, procedures to ensure reasonable notice is provided of proposed actions or land management policies that may restrict future access to or ceremonial use of, or adversely affect the physical integrity of, sacred sites.

Section 3. Nothing in this order shall be construed to require a taking of vested property interests. Nor shall this order be construed to impair enforceable rights to use of Federal lands that have been granted to third parties through final agency action.

Section 4. This order is intended only to improve the internal management of the executive branch and is not intended to, nor does it, create any right, benefit, or trust responsibility, substantive or procedural, enforceable at law or equity by any party against the United States, its agencies, officers, or any person.

Notes

1. Sacred sites and raptor nests. Note that the FCMP for Devils Tower calls for the seasonal closure of trails to protect raptor nests. Why is it acceptable for the National Park Service to deny access to the Tower at certain seasons to protect raptor nests, but not to protect the practice of tribal religious rites and ceremonies? Is this a sensible distinction for the law to make?

2. Executive Order 13007 and the sacred sites cases. Executive Orders are typically not enforceable against federal agencies by private parties (see section 4 of EO 13007) However, if EO 13007 were in effect at the time of the events in *Lyng* and enforceable by private parties, would it have affected the outcome in that case? In its modified FCMP for Devils Tower in *Bear Lodge II*, the NPS stated its belief that the voluntary June closure met the directives of the executive order. Devils Tower National Monument: Reconsideration of Certain Climbing Limitations in the Final Climbing Management Plan 10 (Nov. 26, 1996). Do you agree?

3. Executive Order 13007 and FOIA. One major problem with the executive order is that tribes which take advantage of it may be subject to the Freedom of Information Act (FOIA), 5 U.S.C. § 552. FOIA requires all federal agencies to make available to the public upon request final opinions and orders in adjudications, "those statements of policy and interpretations which have been adopted by the agency and are not published in the Federal Register," and staff manuals and instructions that affect the public. There are nine exceptions: (1) national defense and foreign policy secrets; (2) internal personnel matters; (3) specifically exempt by statute; (4) "trade secrets and commercial or financial information obtained from a person and privileged or confidential;" (5) "inter-agency or intra-agency memorandums or letters which would not be available by law to a party other than an agency in litigation with the agency;" (6) personnel and medical files; (7) law enforcement information, under certain circumstances; (8) reports on financial institutions; and (9) geological and geophysical data.

Federal agencies can be compelled under FOIA to disclose information provided to them by Indian tribes that does not fall within one of the nine exemption categories. *See Dep't of the Interior v. Klamath Water Users Protective Ass'n*, 532 U.S. 1 (2001). In *Klamath Water Users*, the Klamath Indian Tribes submitted various documents to the Department of the Interior at the agency's request. The tribes submitted some of the documents, which included legal analyses and theories concerning the tribes' claims to water, in connection with a state court adjudication in which the federal government was representing the tribes' interests. Other documents were in connection with Interior's development of a plan to manage irrigation water in the Klamath River basin. The Court held that none of the documents was exempt under § 5 of FOIA, and thus that all documents had to be provided to the Water Users Association, whose interests were adverse to the tribes in both the irrigation project and the litigation. The Court expressly rejected the government's argument that its trust responsibilities to the tribes protected the documents from disclosure. *See also Bangor Hydro-Electric Co. v. U.S. Dep't of the Interior*, 903 F. Supp. 169 (D. Me. 1995) (holding that the Department of Interior had to disclose information provided to it by the Penobscot Nation in connection with the relicensing of Bangor's hydroelectric power project on the Penobscot River).

Many Indian tribes find it imperative to keep secret the locations of their sacred sites, whether for religious reasons or to prevent curiosity seekers. *See, e.g., Pueblo of Sandia v. United States*, 50 F.3d 856 (10th Cir. 1995) (describing traditional Pueblo secrecy). Can Indian tribes take advantage of EO 13007 without disclosing the location of sacred sites? Section 1(b)(iii) requires that tribes inform the appropriate agency "of the existence of such a site." Does this require the tribe to disclose the location? Even if it does not, won't the agency be required to locate the site in order to comply with EO 13007? And won't that information then be available under FOIA? Section 1(a) of EO 13007 provides that "[w]here appropriate, agencies shall maintain the confidentiality of sacred sites." Can that language be used to argue that the location of sacred sites falls under exception (4) of FOIA? If you represented a tribe to whom secrecy was crucial, would you advise the tribe to risk it? As a result of these issues, EO 13007 has proved ineffectual for those tribes unwilling to risk the public disclosure of their sacred sites.

More protection may be available if the sacred site is also an historic resource under the National Historic Preservation Act, discussed below at pages 46–48. The Act provides that federal agencies "shall withhold from disclosure to the public, information about the location, character, or ownership of a historic resource if the Secretary [of the Interior] and the agency determine that disclosure may—(1) cause a significant invasion of privacy; ... or (3) impede the use of a traditional religious site by practitioners." 16 U.S.C. § 470w-3(a).

For a discussion of sacred sites, FOIA, and disclosure under the National Environmental Policy Act, see Ethan Plaut, Comment, *Tribal-Agency Confidentiality: A Catch-22 for Sacred Site Management?*, 36 Ecol. L.Q. 137 (2009).

4. **The U.N. position on sacred sites.** On May 31, 2001, the United Nations General Assembly adopted Resolution 55/254: Protection of Religious Sites. The Resolution "[c]ondemns all acts or threats of violence, destruction, damage or endangerment" aimed at religious sites and "[c]alls upon all States to exert their utmost efforts to ensure that religious sites are fully respected and protected." In addition, the Resolution encourages "a culture of tolerance and respect for the diversity of religions and religious sites."

Note on Federal Protection of Cultural Property Under the Antiquities Act: Bears Ears National Monument

Under the Antiquities Act of 1906, 54 U.S.C. §§ 320301-03, the President may establish national monuments from federal lands to protect significant natural, cultural, or scientific features. In late 2016, President Obama proclaimed Bears Ears National Monument in southeastern Utah, a 1.35 million-acre area of deep sandstone canyons, desert mesas, and meadow mountaintops, constituting one of the most significant cultural landscapes in the United States. According to the proclamation, "abundant rock art, ancient cliff dwellings, ceremonial sites, and countless other artifacts provide an extraordinary archaeological and cultural record that is important to us all, but most notably the land is profoundly sacred to many Native American tribes, including the Ute Mountain Ute Tribe, Navajo Nation, Ute Indian Tribe of the Uintah Ouray, Hopi Nation, and Zuni Tribe." There is evidence of native habitation in the area as far back as 13,000 years ago.

In 2015, an intertribal coalition of nearby tribes petitioned the President to use his Antiquities Act authority to protect the area, and the 2016 proclamation established an unprecedented intertribal commission to advise the management agencies—the U.S. Forest Service and the Bureau of Land Management—on a plan to govern the monument. However, in 2017, under an executive order from President Trump, the Secretary of Interior reviewed some 27 large national monuments established during the previous two decades, including Bears Ears, that were "created or expanded without adequate public outreach and coordination with relevant stakeholders . . . that may create barriers to achieving energy independence, restrict public access to and use of Federal lands, burden State, tribal, and local governments, and otherwise curtail economic growth." Although none of these criteria are evident in the Antiquities Act, and the Secretary received over 585,000 public comments in favor of maintaining the 2016 monument, President Trump reduced the size of the monument by eighty-five percent and disbanded the intertribal commission. While there is no question that Congress may revoke or diminish monuments, the authority of the President to do so is subject to serious legal questions. *See* Mark Squillace, Eric Biber, Nicholas Bryner & Sean Hecht, *Presidents Lack Authority to Abolish or Diminish National Monuments*, 103 Va. L. Rev. Online 55 (2017) (construing § 204 of the Federal Land Policy and Management Act); Arnold & Porter's Kaye Scholer, *The President Has No Power Unilaterally to Abolish or Materially Change a National Monument Designation Under the Antiquities Act*, https://www.npca.org/resources/3197-legal-analysis-of-presidential-ability-to-revoke-national-monuments#sm.000015n94vl5ief2jukt3aeup6q5f. The tribes quickly filed suit, challenging the president's authority to diminish the monument. *Hopi Tribe et al. v. Trump*, Civ. No. 17-cv-02590 (D.D.C. Dec. 4, 2017) (suit by the Hopi Tribe, the Pueblo of Zuni, and the Ute Mountain Ute Tribe). Other suits were filed by the Navajo Nation and the Utah Ute Tribe. Updates from the Bears Ears Coalition are available at the coalition's website: http://bearsearscoalition.org.

Note on Cultural Protection Under Other Statutes

There are three other federal statutes that form the federal framework for the protection of places and objects of religious, cultural, or historical importance to Indian tribes: the Archaeological Resources Protection Act (ARPA), the National Historic Preservation Act (NHPA), and the Native American Graves Protection and Repatriation Act (NAGPRA). The first two of these are discussed in the notes below; NAGPRA is discussed later in this chapter. For a fuller exploration of these statutes and the tribal role in carrying out cultural property protection in Indian country, see Dean B. Suagee, *Tribal Voices in Historic Preservation: Sacred Landscapes, Cross-Cultural Bridges, and Common Ground*, 21 Vermont L. Rev. 145 (1996); Dean B. Suagee & Karen J. Funk, *Cultural Resources Conservation in Indian Country*, 7 Natural Res. & Env't 30 (Spring 1993).

These statutes can offer substantial protections for tribal interests. For example, in *Crow Creek Sioux Tribe v. Brownlee*, 331 F.3d 912 (D.C. Cir. 2003), the tribe challenged a transfer of land from the U.S. Army Corps of Engineers to the state of South Dakota under the Water Resources Development Act (WRDA) of 1999. The tribe sought to enjoin the transfer on the ground that it would "eviscerate the Secretary of the Army's ability to enforce federal cultural protection statutes on the transferred lands, thus injuring the Tribe's rights under these statutes." *Id.* at 913. The court ruled, however, that the tribe failed to show imminent injury necessary for standing because the WRDA expressly provided that the three federal laws—ARPA, the NHPA, and NAGPRA—would continue to apply to the land after the transfer of title to the state. Nonetheless, the court noted that if the harm the tribe worried about occurred, the tribe would then have standing to enforce those federal laws.

1. Archaeological Resources Protection Act of 1979, 16 U.S.C. §470aa *et seq.* This Act focuses on protecting archaeological resources and sites on federal public lands and Indian lands. Archaeological activities on such lands require a permit, and the Act provides criminal and civil penalties, including forfeiture, for violations of the Act. The Act also provides that no person may sell, purchase, transport, etc. any archaeological resource taken in violation of any state law.

In 1985, General Electric purchased agricultural land and began to excavate it for a highway. In the course of construction in 1988, workers unearthed odd-shaped rocks which one worker, a collector of Indian artifacts, recognized. The highway was running through a Hopewell burial mound which would prove to be one of the five largest ever discovered. Hopewell burial mounds are the product of a civilization more than 1500 years old, which built "large earthen mounds over prepared mound floors containing human remains plus numerous ceremonial artifacts and grave goods." The worker who recognized the artifacts contacted Gerber, "a well-known collector of Indian artifacts and promoter of annual Indian 'relic shows.'" Gerber paid $6000 for the location of the mound and over time excavated and removed "hundreds of additional artifacts including silver earspools, copper axeheads, pieces of worked leather, and rare silver musical instruments, some with the original reeds preserved." Gerber subsequently sold some of the artifacts at his annual "relic show."

Gerber acknowledged that he had committed criminal trespass and conversion in violation of Indiana law, but argued that ARPA was inapplicable to private lands. The Seventh Circuit concluded that Gerber's conduct was prohibited by the Act:

> it is almost inconceivable that Congress would have wanted to encourage amateur archaeologists to violate state laws in order to amass valuable collections of Indian artifacts * * *. It is also unlikely that a Congress sufficiently interested in archaeology to impose substantial criminal penalties for the violation of archaeological regulations would be so parochial as to confine its interests to archaeological sites and artifacts on federal and Indian lands merely because that is where most of them are.

United States v. Gerber, 999 F.2d 1112 (7th Cir. 1993).

2. National Historic Preservation Act, 16 U.S.C. § 470 *et seq.* Under the National Historic Preservation Act, the Secretary of the Interior, acting through the National Park Service, established the National Register of Historic Places.

a. Tribal cultural properties. The 1992 amendments to the NHPA provide that properties "of traditional religious and cultural importance" to a tribe may be eligible for inclusion on the National Register. However, neither a designation of eligibility for listing nor a listing on the National Register, in itself, necessarily protects an historic property. One demonstration of that is the fact that the government determined that the area at issue in *Lyng* was eligible for the National Register in 1981; that area has since been listed as an example of a "traditional cultural property." *See* National Park Service, National Register Bulletin 38: Guidelines for Evaluating and Documenting Traditional Cultural Properties (1998), available at www.nps.gov/history/nr/publications/bulletins/nrb38/.

Eligibility for listing on the National Register may, however, prompt government action with positive impacts on tribal cultural properties. An interesting establishment clause challenge was brought by a mining company that mines aggregate materials used for road construction from Woodruff Butte in Arizona. The Butte has religious, cultural, and historical importance to the Hopi, Zuni, and Navajo nations; all three enacted resolutions opposing the mining. In 1999, the state of Arizona adopted a policy against using materials from mines with potential adverse effects on places eligible for inclusion on the National Register of Historic Places. As a result, the plaintiff could not provide its aggregate materials for state highway construction projects, although it remained free to sell to the private market. The Ninth Circuit upheld the state's action, finding that: "the Establishment Clause does not bar the government from protecting an historically and culturally important site simply because the site's importance derives at least in part from its sacredness to certain groups." *Cholla Ready Mix, Inc. v. Civish*, 382 F.3d 969, 977 (9th Cir. 2004). Consider as well the Cave Rock decision following this note. *But see Oglala Sioux Tribe of Pine Ridge Indian Reservation v. U.S. Army Corps of Engineers*, 570 F.3d 327 (D.C. Cir. 2009) (the NHPA does not require the Army Corps of Engineers to evaluate Indian sites within a former reservation for inclusion on the National Register of Historic Places within a particular timeframe).

Identifying properties of traditional cultural significance may pose challenges. Thus, in *Pueblo of Sandia v. United States*, 50 F.3d 856 (10th Cir. 1995), the court held that the U.S. Forest Service violated the NHPA by failing to make a reasonable effort to identify historic properties. Given traditional Pueblo secrecy regarding religion, as well as the existence of federal regulations warning that tribes may be hesitant to disclose specifics, once the tribes had communicated to the Service that the area was of great religious and traditional importance, the Service was obligated to investigate, and it did not.

Under the NHPA, state historic preservation officers (SHPOs) are generally responsible for evaluating properties for historic significance and nominating properties for inclusion in the National Register. The NHPA amendments of 1992 directed the Secretary of the Interior to establish a program "to assist Indian tribes in preserving their particular historic properties." 16 U.S.C. § 470a(d). The program, to be initiated no later than October 1, 1994, is to be developed in cooperation with tribes, federal agencies, SHPOs, and other interested parties, and is "to ensure that tribal values are taken into account to the extent feasible."

The amendments provide that a tribe may assume the functions of a SHPO with respect to tribal lands upon the request of the tribe, if the tribe designates a preservation official and develops a preservation plan approved by the Secretary. A tribal plan must allow a nonmember who owns land in fee to request the SHPO to share preservation responsibilities with the tribal official for that land. Once a tribal preservation plan has federal approval, the tribe may also enter into contracts or cooperative agreements to assist the Secretary in such functions as identification, preservation, and maintenance of historic properties.

b. Tribal consultation. Section 106 of the NHPA requires a consultation process for any "undertakings" by a federal agency, or assisted or licensed by a federal agency, that may have an effect on "any district, site, building, structure, or object" that is on, or is eligible to be included in, the National Register. The consultation process is largely managed by state historic preservation officers (SHPOs).

The Ninth Circuit analogized this mandatory consultation process to that required under the National Environmental Policy Act (NEPA), 42 U.S.C. §§ 4321–4370, noting that "what § 106 of NHPA does for sites of historical import, NEPA does for our natural environment." *San Carlos Apache Tribe v. United States*, 417 F.3d 1091, 1097 (9th Cir. 2005). In that case, the tribe had brought a claim directly under the NHPA, seeking to enjoin the federal government from releasing water from the San Carlos Reservoir. However, the Ninth Circuit held that, like NEPA, the NHPA creates no private right of action against the federal government; thus, the tribe must proceed under the Administrative Procedure Act, 5 U.S.C. §§ 701 *et seq. Id.* at 1096. *But see Boarhead Corp. v. Erickson*, 923 F.2d 1011, 1017 (3rd Cir.1991); *Vieux Carre Prop. Owners, Residents & Assoc., Inc. v. Brown*, 875 F.2d 453, 458 (5th Cir.1989) (both holding that the NHPA impliedly creates a private right of action).

The implementing regulations for § 106 were challenged as violating the Establishment Clause because of the requirement that federal agencies "consult with any Indian Tribe or Native Hawaiian organization that attaches religious and cultural significance" to properties of religious or cultural importance. 36 C.F.R. §§ 800.2(c)(2)(ii)(D), 800.4(c)(1), 800.4(d)(1), 800.5(c)(2)(ii) (implementing 16 U.S.C. § 470a(d)(6)(B)). A federal district court held that the regulations were not unconstitutional, and noted that the same result would apply to the statute itself. *National Mining Ass'n v. Slater*, 167 F.Supp.2d 265, 295 & n.37 (D.D.C. 2001). The court noted that, unlike situations in which government action aids a religion, "this case is about government action that advances the purpose of historic preservation."

Tribes have had mixed success with claims that agencies have violated the consultation requirement. In an unpublished decision, one district court held that the Bureau of Land Management had violated the NHPA's consultation requirement, and further that the failure to comply "constituted a breach of the agency's trust obligations to the Tribe." *Northern Cheyenne Tribe v. U.S. Bureau of Land Management*, 32 Ind. L. Rptr. 3270, 3274 (D. Mont. 2005). Another district court faulted the Interior Department for failing to adequately consult with the Quechan Tribe concerning its decision to approve a solar energy project on federal public lands in the California Desert that the tribe believed would destroy hundreds of ancient cultural sites and the habitat of the flat-tailed horned lizard, a species of considerable cultural significance to the tribe; the court consequently enjoined the project. *Quechan Tribe of the Fort Yuma Reservation v. U.S. Dept of the Interior*, 755 F.Supp.2d 1104 (S.D. Cal. 2010). In contrast, the First Circuit rejected a tribe's claim of an NHPA violation in *Narragansett Indian Tribe v. Warwick Sewer Authority*, 334 F.3d 161 (1st Cir. 2003), agreeing with the district court that a local sewer authority adequately consulted with the tribe in determining that its project would have no effect on historic properties. The court noted that the sewer authority kept the tribe informed and took seriously the tribe's "belated objections," adjusting its plans in light of those objections. *Id.* at 169. The Ninth Circuit ruled that the Federal Energy Regulatory Commission was not obligated to consult with the Snoqualmie Tribe concerning a hydropower relicensing decision because that tribe was not a federally recognized tribe. *Snoqualmie Indian Tribe v. Federal Energy Regulatory Comm'n*, 545 F.3d 1207, 1216 (9th Cir. 2009).

c. **The ban on climbing at Cave Rock.** In 2003, the Forest Service banned climbing at Cave Rock, located on Lake Tahoe in Nevada. The Record of Decision of the Forest Supervisor is excerpted below. As you read it, consider the following questions. Why is it lawful for the Forest Service to ban all climbing at Cave Rock, but not lawful for the National Park Service to ban climbing one month a year at Devil's Tower? Is the distinction a sensible one for the law to make?

USDA Forest Service Lake Tahoe Basin Management Unit Record of Decision for Cave Rock Management Direction Final Environmental Impact Statement

August 5, 2003

It is my decision to implement Alternative 6 of the Cave Rock Management Direction: Final Environmental Impact Statement (EIS) as modified in this Record of

Decision (ROD). * * * Cave Rock is a site eligible for listing on the National Register of Historic Places (National Register) as a Traditional Cultural Property (TCP), historic transportation district, and archaeological site. This management direction's purpose is to:

> protect the Cave Rock heritage resource and regulate uses there in a manner that, consistent with mandates and restrictions of law and regulation, preserves the historic and cultural characteristics that make the property eligible for listing in the National Register. As caretaker of a property eligible for listing in the National Register, the Forest Service has a responsibility to assess and manage for the appropriateness of activities occurring at Cave Rock.

The management direction's need is to address the fact that:

> ongoing activities in the area have been identified as adversely affecting the integrity of the National Register-eligible properties. In addition, any long-term continuation of existing use restrictions requires a NEPA decision to implement.

The new management direction allows open access to the public and allows identified activities to occur while protecting and preserving the cultural and historical resource values at Cave Rock. The management policy provides the basis for prohibiting the recreational activity of rock climbing as well as any new, non-historic activities that might be proposed at the site. Consistent with the policy, this decision provides for the removal of all bolts and other climbing equipment that are technically feasible to remove. The decision also provides that modern graffiti and historic graffiti that do not contribute to historic districts will be removed when doing so will not physically damage Cave Rock. New graffiti will be removed if it occurs. The masonry flooring within the cave will be removed and disposed of. No motorized vehicles will be allowed outside of the highway corridor. Non-historic activities will not be permitted at Cave Rock; however other non-invasive recreation activities, consistent with the historic period will be allowed to continue.

I am making one clarification to the selected alternative (Alternative 6).[*] Examples of non-invasive activities that are consistent with the historic period (time

---

[*] [Editor's note: Alternative 6 is as follows:

This alternative provides maximum immediate protection of heritage resources by managing Cave Rock in a manner that minimizes the effects of modern activities and technology. All climbing, both sport and traditional climbing, would be prohibited immediately following adoption of the management direction. Alterative 6 would allow activities and protect, preserve, enhance, and interpret improvements that are consistent with the historic period at Cave Rock beginning with the arrival of the Washoe Tribe to Lake Tahoe through 1965, the year of Henry Rupert's death. (Henry Rupert was a Washoe spiritual practitioner whose association with Cave Rock contributed to its National Register eligibility). Activities and improvements that adversely affect the qualities for which the property was found eligible to the National Register would be restricted or removed. Thus, climbing would be prohibited as inconsistent with the setting, feel, and association

immemorial through 1965) that are allowed at Cave Rock are as follows: hiking, walking, picnicking, site seeing, fishing, and traditional Native American rituals and ceremonies. If monitoring indicates that these activities are occurring at or increase to levels significantly higher than the historic period, the need for further restrictions will be assessed. Specifically, rock climbing, motorized vehicle use, commercial activities, bungee jumping, and any activity that damages or defaces Cave Rock will be prohibited. If activities not listed above occur and it is not clear if they are allowed or not, I or the current Forest Supervisor will assess the activity and determine if it is consistent with the historic period.

The National Historic Preservation Act, 16 U.S.C. 470 et seq., authorizes the Secretary of the Interior to establish and to maintain a National Register of districts, sites, buildings, structures and objects significant in American history, architecture, archeology, engineering and culture. Pursuant to 36 C.F.R. 60.9, in September of 1998, the Forest Service submitted a request for determination of eligibility for Cave Rock to be included on the National Register. In October of 1998, the Keeper of the National Register notified the Forest Service that Cave Rock was eligible for inclusion on the National Register of Historic Places as a Traditional Cultural Property. It is significant as a place of accumulated spiritual power that has played a central role in Washoe Indian traditions, beliefs, and practices since time immemorial and it embodies significant aspect of the Washoe world view (Criterion A). Cave Rock is believed by traditional Washoe to be the location of important mythological events that are central to Washoe cosmology. It is also believed to be the location: where water babies (powerful dwarf-beings, common in Washoe cosmology) congregate, of a white sand path traveled by Washoe doctors, and where an enormous man-eating bird (Ang) would take its victims. Traditional Washoe continue to believe that the health and integrity of their society may be jeopardized if traditional practices are not observed there.

Cave Rock is also eligible to the National Register as a historic transportation district (Criterion A). Remnants of the trestle built around Cave Rock to carry the Lake Tahoe Wagon Trail, later designated as the Lincoln Highway, are extant. The south bound tunnel constructed on the west side of Cave Rock in 1931 when the road was designated Highway 50 and the north bound tunnel constructed in 1957 are still in use today. Together these features represent and characterize the evolution of the modern Highway 50 transportation corridor.

Additionally, Cave Rock is significant for its associations with important historical personalities in Washoe oral tradition. The development and practice of several influential historic Washoe spiritual leaders, the most notable being Weleiwkushkush and Henry Rupert was closely tied to Cave Rock (Criterion B). Welewkushkush was

---

of the historic property, while general public access would be allowed as it had occurred during the historic period. When conflicts between National Register properties arise, they will be managed in favor of the Cave Rock TCP.]

known to visit Cave Rock to acquire power. Henry "Moses" Rupert was the subject and informant of the only ethnographic study of Washoe spiritual practice and was known to have continued traditional use of Cave Rock throughout his lifetime.

Finally, Cave Rock is eligible to the National Register as an archaeological property. Excavations conducted in 1953 and 1957 at Cave Rock represent the first archaeological explorations in Douglas County as part of the earliest baseline investigations into Sierra Nevada prehistory by distinguished archaeologists Robert F. Heiser and Albert B. Elsasser. This is the only instance to date of the excavation of a shamanic archaeological deposit. Additionally, woodrat middens and dendrochronological specimens containing paleoenvironmental data have been located at Cave Rock as well as possible examples of prehistoric rock art. All these contribute to Cave Rock's National Register eligibility for its data potential (Criterion D).

Cave Rock is a significant Traditional Cultural Property, Historic Transportation District, and Archaeological site. As such, it is unique as the quintessential symbol of the Washoe people's culture. Its significance as a symbol of cultural identity is analogous to the Statue of Liberty for many U.S. citizens. Throughout the Washoe tenure at Lake Tahoe and in spite of their 20th century exclusion, Cave Rock has endured as an important symbol of Washoe traditional values and helped maintain the viability of Washoe culture.

The Washoe Tribe is a living community. As both a physical and symbolic feature, Cave Rock is historically rooted in the tribe's beliefs, customs, and practices. Cave Rock is fundamental to their traditions regarding the creation of a landscape central to their heritage and cultural identity. Traditional Washoe practitioners, who have been called by greater powers to seek power or knowledge at the rock, affect cures for the Washoe people. So powerful and important is Cave Rock that many Washoe continue to believe that the health and integrity of their society may be jeopardized if traditional practices are not observed there.

Historic and modern land development and recreational uses have introduced modern human presence and related activities into this traditionally sensitive setting. Recently, Cave Rock has gained an international reputation as an environmentally unique and extremely challenging sport-climbing venue. Local climbers, without Forest Service approval, established the first permanently bolted routes in 1987. Since then, the unapproved routes have expanded to include 46 routes ranging in difficulty from class 5.10c to 5.14a. Approximately 60% of the climbing routes are in the main cave and 40% are outside of the main cave area.

Rationale for the Decision

I became the Lake Tahoe Basin Management Unit's Forest Supervisor in 2000. At that time, the NEPA process for this EIS was well under way with a Draft EIS having been circulated and comments received. Reviewing the EIS myself, discussing it with my staff, reviewing the Forest Plan, and considering the comments that had been received, I became convinced that the preferred alternative in the Draft EIS (alternative 2)** did not adequately satisfy the Purpose and Need stated in the document. In fact, it did little to reverse the documented impacts to Cave Rock other than to remove a few rock climbing routes that were health and safety concerns. Significantly, alternative 2 also was not consistent with General Management direction in the Forest Plan (Chapter IV-18).

My staff, key regional subject specialists and I went back with fresh eyes and re-reviewed the Draft EIS. The pre-NEPA collaborative meetings documented that many Washoe view Cave Rock as a sacred or spiritual site and the Draft EIS documented that Washoe spiritual activity does take place there. It also documented an extensive array of historic, cultural, archaeological and traditional values that are historic rather than religious in nature. Key to clarifying this issue is direction found in the US Department of Interior, National Park Service, National Register Bulletin 38: Guidelines for Evaluation and Documenting Traditional Cultural Properties (USDI 1994). Generally, a religious property is excluded from eligibility to the National Register of Historic Places and thus from the protections afforded by the National Historic Preservation Act. However, the bulletin notes:

> Applying the "religious exclusion" without careful and sympathetic consideration to properties of significance to a traditional cultural group can result in discriminating against the group by effectively denying the legitimacy of its history and culture. The history of a Native American group, as conceived by its indigenous cultural authorities, is likely to reflect a kind of belief in supernatural beings and events that Euroamerican culture categorizes as religious, although the group involved, as is often the case with Native American groups, may not even have a word in its language for "religion". To exclude from the National Register a property of cultural and historical importance to such a group, because its significance tends to be expressed in terms that to the Euroamerican observer appear to be "religious" is ethnocentric in the extreme.

> In simplest terms, the fact that a property is used for religious purposes by a traditional group, such as seeking supernatural visions, collecting or preparing native medicines, or carrying out ceremonies, or is described by the group in terms that are classified by the outside observer as "religious" should

---

** [Editor's note: Alternative 2 was described as below:
This alternative would manage Cave Rock consistent with the activities occurring at the time Cave Rock was determined eligible as a TCP. Under this alternative sport climbing would be allowed; however routes above the highway and several other selected routes would be removed. The installation of new climbing routes and the use of artificial light for climbing would be prohibited. The Forest Service would work with the climbing community to camouflage existing bright-colored and shiny climbing equipment to blend with the natural colors of the rock. If non-camouflaged equipment remains after 6 months following adoption of the management direction, it will be an indicator that the routes are not being used and the routes will be removed. Maintenance of the existing routes would be conducted only with permission of the Forest Service.]

not by itself be taken to make the property ineligible, since these activities may be expressions of traditional cultural beliefs and may be intrinsic to the continuation of traditional cultural practices. Similarly, the fact that the group that owns a property—for example, an American Indian tribe—describes it in religious terms, or constitutes a group of traditional religious practitioners, should not automatically be taken to exclude the property from inclusion in the Register. Criteria Consideration A was included in the Criteria for Evaluation in order to avoid allowing historical significance to be determined on the basis of religious doctrine, not in order to exclude arbitrarily any property having religious associations. National Register guidelines stress the fact that properties can be listed in or determined eligible for the Register for their association with religious history, or with persons significant in religion, if such significance has "scholarly, secular recognition" (again, found in How to Complete the National Register Form). The integral relationship among traditional Native American culture, history, and religion is widely recognized in secular scholarship (for example see U.S. Commission on Civil Rights 1983; Michaelson 1986). Studies leading to the nomination of traditional cultural properties to the Register should have among their purposes the application of secular scholarship to the association of particular properties with broad patterns of traditional history and culture. The fact that traditional history and culture may be discussed in religious terms does not make it less historical or less significant to culture, nor does it make properties associated with traditional history and culture ineligible for inclusion in the National Register.

This is precisely the case with the Cave Rock Traditional Cultural Property. Although it is spoken of in religious terms and is associated with spiritual figures, it has significant cultural and historical significance that make it eligible to the National Register of Historic Places. Its significance is not based on "Washoe religious doctrine" but rather on the secularly-derived historic and ethnographic record. This significance has been recognized and documented by my staff and regional experts; it has been concurred with by experts at the Nevada State Historic Preservation Office, and has been determined eligible by the Keeper of the National Register of Historic Places. The planning record shows no dissension to the determination of eligibility either from the professional or lay community. Therefore, it is clear to me that Cave Rock is a significant property as defined by the National Historic Preservation Act and a resource whose cultural and historical values I should protect from activities that adversely impact it.

Having determined that Cave Rock was a valid historic and cultural resource for which I was responsible and should protect, I viewed this as a conflict between resource values and user impacts. This is the type of conflict that Forest Supervisors resolve by balancing the importance and value of the resource against the activity that is impacting it. I found that the Lake Tahoe Basin Management Unit's Land Management Plan gives direction for resource conflicts of this type. The plan directs:

In resolving conflicts, the following list of resources or uses are in order of priority and will normally apply:

c. Preservation of cultural resources determined or believed to be of significance;

g. Establishment of a variety of outdoor recreation facilities and uses at a level that assures a 'fair share' of the basin capacity;

This management direction prioritizes the protection of cultural resources over outdoor recreation. This direction was established in the Land Management Plan after careful thought, consideration and public input precisely so that in cases like this, general priorities would already be established without the need to rehash already decided issues.

* * * [T]he direction to establish a variety of outdoor recreation facilities and uses at a level that assures a 'fair share' of the basin capacity does not require the agency to allow every activity everywhere. Because of resource impacts, campfires are not allowed in Desolation Wilderness. Similarly, bicycles are not allowed on the Pacific Crest Trail. Restrictions are placed on activities when unacceptable impacts are recognized to important resources. In the case of rock climbing, 26 climbing locations are noted in Rock Climbing: Lake Tahoe (Carville, 1999). Most of these are located on federally managed land; and of these, only Cave Rock will have climbing restrictions, unless resource impacts are later identified at other sites. Allowing climbing at 95% of the identified climbing locations does more than assure a 'fair share' of the basin capacity. The Access Fund in communication with my staff and I, as well as on its web site, has voiced and demonstrated a sincere sensitivity to traditional and historical values that may be at risk, and a willingness to work with the Forest Service to craft solutions that will allow its members to continue climbing. It has also expressed a concern that this decision will set a precedent that will open the floodgates to closing climbing areas due to traditional cultural conflicts. I wish to assure the Access Fund that I have no intention to close climbing areas unless valid resource concerns exist. Cave Rock's significance is well documented and undisputed. Adverse effects to the site are also undisputed by experts in the field of cultural resource management. Consultation with the State Historic Preservation Officer and the Advisory Council on Historic Preservation to mitigate the adverse effects to the site and find an acceptable management direction for the property has been lengthy and extensive.

The decision to select Alternative 6 is consistent with the Forest Plan, as amended.

Notes

1. Judicial affirmation. Both the Nevada district court and the Ninth Circuit affirmed the Forest Service's Cave Rock decision. *See Access Fund v. U.S. Dept. of Agriculture*, 499 F.3d 1036 (9th Cir. 2007). The Ninth Circuit determined that the Forest Service's ban on climbing at Cave Rock had neither the purpose nor the effect of advancing or endorsing religion. With respect to the purpose of the government's action, the court ruled that "the Forest Service acted pursuant to a secular purpose—the preservation of a historic cultural area." With respect to the effect, the court noted:

> the climbing ban cannot be fairly perceived as an endorsement of Washoe religious practices. Indeed, during the public comment phase, the Washoe Tribe favored an alternative that would have precluded all activities inconsistent with traditional Washoe belief. This alternative would have denied non-Washoe access to the traditional cultural property and banned hiking and other recreational uses at the rock.
>
> The Forest Service's chosen alternative not only provides for general public use and access well beyond members of the Washoe Tribe, but also permits activities that are incompatible with Washoe beliefs. When a government action challenged under the Establishment Clause explicitly violates some of the core tenets of the religion it allegedly favors, such action will typically be considered permissible accommodation rather than impermissible endorsement.
>
> That a group of religious practitioners benefits in part from the government's policy does not establish endorsement. Significantly, the ban does not involve the Forest Service in any respect in Washoe religious practice. It does not require the Forest Service to monitor religious practice nor does it require the Forest Service to develop expertise on Washoe religious worship or evaluate the merits of different religious practices or beliefs.

The Ninth Circuit distinguished *Bear Lodge II*, excerpted at page 30:

> That case differs from this one in two significant respects—in *Bear Lodge*, the *only* reason for the closure was to facilitate current religious practice, and the Park Service specifically recognized that climbing was a "legitimate recreational and historic" use of the land. Here, the ban on climbing seeks to preserve the historic and cultural value of the site, and climbing has never been a legitimate historic use of the land. To the contrary, the Forest Service noted that the construction of the masonry floor and installation of climbing hardware were done without permission.

The court concluded that "the Establishment Clause does not bar the government from protecting an historically and culturally important site simply because the site's importance derives at least in part from its sacredness to certain groups."

2. The lesson. If you are a federal land manager wishing to protect an off-reservation sacred tribal site, what lesson do you derive from the Bear Lodge and Cave Rock decisions?

Note on the Native American Graves Protection and Repatriation Act

One of the sorriest parts of Native American history concerns the displaying of deceased native people in museums, universities, and tourist attractions. Estimates are that between 100,000 and 2 million people have been dug up and their remains placed on display. Virtually every tribe has been affected by grave looting. In 1868, a Surgeon General's order instituted a policy of army personnel procuring Indian crania and other body parts for the Army Medical Museum. Some 4,000 heads were collected under this order. In 1906, the Antiquities Act defined Indians dead on federal lands as "archeological resources" and authorized their collection under federal permits "for the[ir] permanent preservation in public museums." 16 U.S.C. § 432.

Under these initiatives an enormous amount of cultural property was transferred from tribes to public and private collections, mostly during the half-century following the Surgeon General's order. Many of these transfers were acquired illegally. NAGPRA, enacted in 1990, seeks to return this property to Indian owners. *See generally* Jack F. Trope & Walter R. Echohawk, *The Native American Graves Protection and Repatriation Act: Background and Legislative History,* 24 Ariz. St. L. J. 35 (1992).

a. NAGRPA, 25 U.S.C. § 3001 et seq. The Act provides for ownership and control of cultural items taken from or discovered on federal or tribal lands after the effective date of the Act. Human remains and associated funerary objects belong first to the lineal descendants. For other funerary, sacred, or cultural objects—and for those human remains and associated funerary objects where the lineal descendants cannot be identified—ownership and control vests in the tribe on whose land the objects were discovered or which has the closest cultural affiliation with the objects or which aboriginally occupied the land. Excavation and removal of cultural items from federal or tribal lands is prohibited unless the items are excavated and removed pursuant to a federal permit after proof of consultation with or consent of the tribe. 25 U.S.C. § 3002.

The Act further directs all federal agencies and museums to inventory Native American human remains and cultural items, and provide or make available to tribes the information assembled. 25 U.S.C. §§ 3003–3004. At the request of a lineal descendant or the tribe, human remains and cultural objects are to be "expeditiously returned" by the agency or museum. 25 U.S.C. § 3005.

One notable cultural item that became the subject of a NAGPRA suit was the Willamette Meteorite, a 15.5 ton meteorite which fell to earth some 10,000 years ago and is the largest meteorite ever discovered in the continental United States. The Confederated Tribes of the Grand Ronde claimed the meteorite under NAGPRA from the American Museum of Natural History, which has displayed the meteorite for nearly a century after purchasing it from the Oregon Iron and Steel Company for $20,600 in 1906. In June 2000, a settlement was reached, under which the meteorite will remain with the museum, which will keep it so long as it remains on display. If it does not, the meteorite will be returned to the tribes, which retain title. The agreement calls for the museum to expand its exhibit to include a description of the importance of the meteorite to the cultural and religious history of the tribes and to allow the tribes to schedule ceremonial visits. John Sullivan, *Pact Leaves Meteorite With Museum*, N.Y. Times, June 23, 2000, at B3.

In 2010, the Government Accountability Office concluded that several key federal agencies, including the Bureau of Indian Affairs, the U.S. Forest Service, and the

National Park Service, had yet to fully comply with NAGPRA, twenty years after enactment of the statute. Through fiscal year 2009, agencies had repatriated only 55% of human remains and 68% of associated funerary objects published in notices of inventory completion. U.S. Gov't Accountability Office, *Native American Grave Protection and Repatriation Act: After Almost Twenty Years, Key Federal Agencies Have Still Not Fully Complied with the Act,* GAO-10-768 (June 2010).

b. Kennewick Man. On July 28, 1996, college students discovered human remains on federal land managed by the Army Corps of Engineers on the Columbia River, near Kennewick, Washington. Initial studies suggested that the remains, dubbed "the Kennewick Man," were more than 9000 years old. Under NAGPRA, the Umatilla Tribe, located on the south side of the Columbia River, near Pendleton, Oregon, claimed cultural ties to the Kennewick Man and petitioned the Corps of Engineers to release the remains for burial under § 3001 of NAGPRA.

Because Kennewick Man was of great interest to archaeologists and the scientific community, there has been immense pressure to examine the remains. But that desire conflicts with the wishes of tribal leaders, who feel legally entitled and spiritually required to bury the Kennewick Man's remains. The result was a lawsuit by the scientific community to conduct DNA analysis and other testing on Kennewick Man. *Bonnichsen v. United States*, 969 F.Supp. 628 (D. Or. 1997) (rejecting a group of scientists' claim to study the remains and remanding the case to the Corps of Engineers to determine whether the tribes had a NAGPRA claim). *See* Renee M. Kosslak, *The Native American Graves Protection and Repatriation Act: The Death Knell for Scientific Study?*, 24 Am. Indian L. Rev. 129 (2000).

The legal controversy concerned the meaning of "Native American." NAGPRA requires a finding of indigenous and cultural ties by a tribe before repatriation occurs, but the statute does not define the term. A related problem is that it is quite difficult to establish cultural affiliation. It is nearly impossible, for example to demonstrate whether the Umatilla tribe was on the banks of the Columbia River thousands of years ago. The *Bonnichsen* court laid out procedures for determining cultural standing for the Bureau of Indian Affairs (BIA), retaining jurisdiction over the case. In a subsequent opinion the BIA stated that the Kennewick Man was 9300 years old, well before the arrival of the Europeans. Tribes argued this is evidence that Kennewick Man is "the Ancient One" and must be of Native American descent. However, a BIA study suggested that the remains were of Asian descent. *See* Mark Anthony Rolo, *Kennewick Man Still in Limbo; Tribes Want Burial, Scientists Want Access*, Indian Country Today (Nov. 1, 1999).

Under an agreement between the Department of the Army and the Department of the Interior, Interior agreed to determine the proper disposition of the Kennewick Man remains. In 2000, Interior Secretary Babbitt announced that the remains would be returned to the five tribes—Colville, Umatilla, Yakama, Nez Perce, and the non-federally recognized Wanapum Band—that have claimed Kennewick Man as an ancestor, on the grounds that the remains are "culturally affiliated" with those five tribes, and that the Umatilla and Nez Perce had aboriginal occupation of the area where the remains were found. Letter from Bruce Babbitt, Secretary of the Interior, to Louis Caldera, Secretary of the Army (Sept. 21, 2000) (available at http://www.cr.nps.gov/archeology/kennewick/babb_letter.htm).

Secretary Babbitt's decision was challenged by the scientists, who claimed he did not consider all available evidence and erroneously defined "Native American" to include anyone in the United States before Columbus' arrival in 1492. In 2002, the District Court of Oregon struck down the Secretary's decision, ruling that, under NAGPRA, the Secretary had failed to show that the 9,000-year-old remains of Kennewick Man had a cultural affiliation with the plaintiff tribes because the tribes were unable to establish an identifiable group of predecessors, and the record failed to support a conclusion that the remains were Native American for purposes of NAGPRA. *Bonnichsen v. United States,* 217 F. Supp. 2d 1116 (D. Or. 2002). The Secretary and others appealed, leading to the following decision.

Bonnichsen v. United States
367 F.3d 864 (9th Cir. 2004)

GOULD, Circuit Judge:

This is a case about the ancient human remains of a man who hunted and lived, or at least journeyed, in the Columbia Plateau an estimated 8340 to 9200 years ago, a time predating all recorded history from any place in the world, a time before the oldest cities of our world had been founded, a time so ancient that the pristine and untouched land and the primitive cultures that may have lived on it are not deeply understood by even the most well-informed men and women of our age. Seeking the opportunity of study, a group of scientists [including Smithsonian anthropologists and other experts] as Plaintiffs in this case brought an action against, inter alia, the United States Department of the Interior, challenging various Indian tribes' claim to one of the most important American anthropological and archaeological discoveries of the late twentieth century, and challenging the Interior Department's decision honoring the tribes' claim. The discovery that launched this contest was that of a human skeleton, estimated by carbon dating to be 8340 to 9200 years old, known popularly and commonly as "Kennewick Man," but known as "the Ancient One" to some American Indians who now inhabit regions in Washington, Idaho, and Oregon, roughly proximate to the site on the Columbia River at Kennewick, Washington, where the bones were found. From the perspective of the scientists Plaintiffs, this skeleton is an irreplaceable source of information about early New World populations that warrants careful scientific inquiry to advance knowledge of distant times. Yet, from the perspective of the intervenor-Indian tribes the skeleton is that of an ancestor who, according to the tribes' religious and social traditions, should be buried immediately without further testing.

Plaintiffs filed this lawsuit seeking to stop the transfer of the skeleton by the government to the tribes for burial, and the district court held in favor of the scientists-Plaintiffs. The Secretary of the Interior and the intervenor-Indian tribes appeal. We

*** affirm the judgment of the district court barring the transfer of the skeleton for immediate burial and instead permitting scientific study of the skeleton.

I

In July 1996, teenagers going to a boat race discovered a human skull and bones near the shore of the Columbia River just outside Kennewick, Washington. The remains were found on federal property under the management of the United States Army Corps of Engineers ("Corps") and, at the request of the county coroner, were removed for analysis by an anthropologist, Dr. James Chatters, pursuant to an Archaeological Resources Protection Act of 1979 ("ARPA") permit. *** A minute quantity of metacarpal bone was radiocarbon dated. The laboratory estimated the age of the bones to be between 8340 and 9200 years old.

The skeleton attracted attention because some of its physical features, such as the shape of the face and skull, differed from those of modern American Indians. Many scientists believed the discovery might shed light on the origins of humanity in the Americas. ***

Indian tribes from the area of the Columbia River opposed scientific study of the remains on religious and social grounds. Four Indian groups (the "Tribal Claimants") demanded that the remains be turned over to them for immediate burial. The Tribal Claimants based their demand on the Native American Graves Protection and Repatriation Act ("NAGPRA"), 25 U.S.C. § 3001 et seq. The Corps agreed with the Tribal Claimants and, citing NAGPRA, seized the remains on September 10, 1996, shortly before they could be transported to the Smithsonian. The Corps also ordered an immediate halt to DNA testing, which was being done using the remainder of the bone sample that had been submitted earlier for radiocarbon dating. After investigation, the Corps decided to give the remains to the Tribal Claimants for burial. ***

The scientists and others, including the Smithsonian Institution, objected to the Corps' decision, arguing that the remains were a rare discovery of national and international significance.

On March 24, 1998, the Corps and the Secretary of the Interior entered into an agreement that effectively assigned to the Secretary responsibility to decide whether the remains were "Native American" under NAGPRA, and to determine their proper disposition. The Department of the Interior then assumed the role of lead agency on this case.

* * *

The [DOI] experts compared the physical characteristics of the remains—e.g., measurements of the skull, teeth, and bones—with corresponding measurements from other skeletons. They concluded that Kennewick Man's remains were unlike those of any known present-day population, American Indian or otherwise.

The Secretary's experts cautioned, however, that an apparent lack of physical resemblance between the Kennewick Man's remains and present-day American Indians did not completely rule out the possibility that the remains might be biologically ancestral to modern American Indians. Moreover, although Kennewick Man's morphological traits did not closely resemble those of modern American Indian populations, the Secretary's experts noted that Kennewick Man's physical attributes are generally consistent with the very small number of human remains from this period that have been found in North America.

Relying solely on the age of the remains and the fact that the remains were found within the United States, on January 13, 2000, the Secretary pronounced Kennewick Man's remains "Native American" within NAGPRA's meaning. And on September 25, 2000, the Secretary determined that a preponderance of the evidence supported the conclusion that the Kennewick remains were culturally affiliated with present-day Indian tribes. For this reason, the Secretary announced his final decision to award Kennewick Man's remains to a coalition of the Tribal Claimants. The Corps and the Secretary also denied Plaintiffs' request to study the remains.

* * * As pertinent to this appeal, the district court vacated the Secretary's decisions as contrary to the Administrative Procedure Act ("APA") on the ground that the Secretary improperly concluded that NAGPRA applies. The district court also held that, because NAGPRA did not apply, Plaintiffs should have the opportunity to study Kennewick Man's remains under ARPA. Defendants and the Tribal Claimants appealed, and we stayed the district court's order granting Plaintiffs-scientists' study of the remains pending our decision herein.

III

NAGPRA vests "ownership or control" of newly discovered Native American human remains in the decedent's lineal descendants or, if lineal descendants cannot be ascertained, in a tribe "affiliated" with the remains. NAGPRA mandates a two-part analysis. The first inquiry is whether human remains are Native American within the statute's meaning. If the remains are not Native American, then NAGPRA does not apply. However, if the remains are Native American, then NAGPRA applies, triggering the second inquiry of determining which persons or tribes are most closely affiliated with the remains.

The parties dispute whether the remains of Kennewick Man constitute Native American remains within NAGPRA's meaning. NAGPRA defines human remains as "Native American" if the remains are "of, or relating to, a tribe, people, or culture that is indigenous to the United States." The text of the relevant statutory clause is written in the present tense ("of, or relating to, a tribe, people, or culture that is indigenous"). Thus the statute unambiguously requires that human remains bear some relationship to a presently existing tribe, people, or culture to be considered Native American.

It is axiomatic that, in construing a statute, courts generally give words not defined in a statute their "ordinary or natural meaning."

In the context of NAGPRA, we conclude that Congress's use of the present tense is significant. The present tense "in general represents present time." R. Pence and D. Emery, A Grammar of Present Day English 262 (2d ed.1963). Congress, by using the phrase "is indigenous" in the present tense, referred to presently existing tribes, peoples, or cultures. We must presume that Congress gave the phrase "is indigenous" its ordinary or natural meaning. We conclude that Congress was referring to presently existing Indian tribes when it referred to "a tribe, people, or culture that is indigenous to the United States."

NAGPRA also protects graves of persons not shown to be of current tribes in that it protects disjunctively remains "of, or relating to" current indigenous tribes. Thus, NAGPRA extends to all remains that relate to a tribe, people, or culture that is indigenous to the United States.

Our conclusion that NAGPRA's language requires that human remains, to be considered Native American, bear some relationship to a presently existing tribe, people, or culture accords with NAGPRA's purposes. As regards newly discovered human remains, NAGPRA was enacted with two main goals: to respect the burial traditions of modern-day American Indians and to protect the dignity of the human body after death. NAGPRA was intended to benefit modern American Indians by sparing them the indignity and resentment that would be aroused by the despoiling of their ancestors' graves and the study or the display of their ancestors' remains.

Congress's purposes would not be served by requiring the transfer to modern American Indians of human remains that bear no relationship to them. Yet, that would be the result under the Secretary's construction of the statute, which would give Native American status to any remains found within the United States regardless of age and regardless of lack of connection to existing indigenous tribes. The exhumation, study, and display of ancient human remains that are unrelated to modern American Indians was not a target of Congress's aim, nor was it precluded by NAGPRA.

NAGPRA was also intended to protect the dignity of the human body after death by ensuring that Native American graves and remains be treated with respect. Congress's purpose is served by requiring the return to modern-day American Indians of human remains that bear some significant relationship to them.

Despite the statute's language and legislative history, the Secretary argues that the district court's interpretation "improperly collapses" NAGPRA's first inquiry (asking whether human remains are Native American) into NAGPRA's second inquiry (asking which American Indians or Indian tribe bears the closest relationship to Native American remains). The Secretary is mistaken. Though NAGPRA's two inquiries have some commonality in that both focus on the relationship between human remains and present-day Indians, the two inquiries differ significantly. The first inquiry requires only a general finding that remains have a significant relationship to a presently existing "tribe, people, or culture," a relationship that goes beyond features common to all humanity. The second inquiry requires a more specific finding that remains are most closely affiliated to specific lineal descendants or to a specific Indian tribe. The district court's interpretation of NAGPRA preserves the statute's two distinct inquiries. Because the record shows no relationship of Kennewick Man to the Tribal Claimants, the district court was correct in holding that NAGPRA has no application.

* * * The Secretary by regulation has defined "Native American" to mean "of, or relating to, a tribe, people, or culture indigenous to the United States." 43 C.F.R. § 10.2(d). The Secretary's regulation, enacted through notice and comment rulemaking, defines Native American exactly as NAGPRA defines it, with one critical exception: the regulation omits the present-tense phrase "that is." * * * We hold that, notwithstanding 43 C.F.R. § 10.2(d), NAGPRA requires that human remains bear a significant relationship to a presently existing tribe, people, or culture to be considered Native American. The district court did not err in reaching that conclusion.

The requirement that we must give effect, if possible, to every word Congress used supports our holding that human remains must be related to a currently existing tribe to come within NAGPRA's protection. * * * By reading NAGPRA's definition of "Native American" literally, meaning is given to each of its terms. Some remains may be covered because they are remains of a tribe, people, or culture that is indigenous, while other remains may be covered because they are "related to" a currently existing indigenous tribe, people, or culture.

* * *

The "United States" is a political entity that dates back to 1789. This term supports that Congress's use of the present tense ("that is indigenous") referred to tribes, peoples, and cultures that exist in modern times, not to those that may have existed thousands of years ago but who do not exist now. By contrast, when Congress chose to harken back to earlier times, it described a geographic location ("the area that now constitutes the State of Hawaii") rather than a political entity ("the United States").

* * *

Although NAGPRA does not specify precisely what kind of a relationship or precisely how strong a relationship ancient human remains must bear to modern Indian groups to qualify as Native American, NAGPRA's legislative history provides some guidance on what type of relationship may suffice. The House Committee on Interior and Insular Affairs emphasized in its report on NAGPRA that the statute was being enacted with modern-day American Indians' identifiable ancestors in mind. Human remains that are 8340 to 9200 years old and that bear only incidental genetic resemblance to modern-day American Indians, along with incidental genetic resemblance to other peoples, cannot be said to be the Indians' "ancestors" within Congress's meaning. Congress enacted NAGPRA to give American Indians control over the remains of their genetic and cultural forbearers, not over the remains of people bearing no special and significant genetic or cultural relationship to some presently existing indigenous tribe, people, or culture.

The age of Kennewick Man's remains, given the limited studies to date, makes it almost impossible to establish any relationship between the remains and presently existing American Indians. At least no significant relationship has yet been shown. We cannot give credence to an interpretation of NAGPRA advanced by the government and the Tribal Claimants that would apply its provisions to remains that have at most a tenuous, unknown, and unproven connection, asserted solely because of the geographical location of the find.

IV

Finally, we address the Secretary's determination that Kennewick Man's remains are Native American, as defined by NAGPRA. We must set aside the Secretary's decision if it was "arbitrary" or "capricious" because the decision was based on inadequate factual support. * * *

The administrative record contains no evidence—let alone substantial evidence—that Kennewick Man's remains are connected by some special or significant genetic or cultural relationship to any presently existing indigenous tribe, people, or culture. An examination of the record demonstrates the absence of evidence that Kennewick Man and modern tribes share significant genetic or cultural features.

No cognizable link exists between Kennewick Man and modern Columbia Plateau Indians. When Kennewick Man's remains were discovered, local coroners initially believed the remains were those of a European, not a Native American, because of their appearance. Later testing by scientists demonstrated that the cranial measurements and features of Kennewick Man most closely resemble those of Polynesians and southern Asians, and that Kennewick Man's measurements and features differ significantly from those of any modern Indian group living in North America.

* * *

The Secretary's only evidence, perhaps, of a possible cultural relationship between Kennewick Man and modern-day American Indians comes in the form of oral histories. * * * But we conclude that these accounts are just not specific enough or reliable enough or relevant enough to show a significant relationship of the Tribal Claimants with Kennewick Man. Because oral accounts have been inevitably changed in context of transmission, because the traditions include myths that cannot be considered as if factual histories, because the value of such accounts is limited by concerns of authenticity, reliability, and accuracy, and because the record as a whole does not show where historical fact ends and mythic tale begins, we do not think that the oral traditions of interest to [DOI's expert] were adequate to show the required significant relationship of the Kennewick Man's remains to the Tribal Claimants. As the district court observed, 8340 to 9200 years between the life of Kennewick Man and the present is too long a time to bridge merely with evidence of oral traditions.

Considered as a whole, the administrative record might permit the Secretary to conclude reasonably that the Tribal Claimants' ancestors have lived in the region for a very long time. However, because Kennewick Man's remains are so old and the information about his era is so limited, the record does not permit the Secretary to conclude reasonably that Kennewick Man shares special and significant genetic or cultural features with presently existing indigenous tribes, people, or cultures. We thus hold that Kennewick Man's remains are not Native American human remains within the meaning of NAGPRA and that NAGPRA does not apply to them. Studies of the Kennewick Man's remains by Plaintiffs-scientists may proceed pursuant to ARPA.

Notes

1. **The court's reasoning.** According to the Ninth Circuit, NAGPRA requires a two-part finding to repatriate: 1) a general finding that remains have a significant relationship to a presently existing "tribe, people, or culture"; and 2) a more specific finding that remains are most closely affiliated to specific lineal descendants or to a specific Indian tribe. *Bonnichsen v. United States*, 367 F.3d 864, 876–77 (9th Cir. 2004). But NAGPRA requires a connection to a present-day tribe only to determine whether Native American remains should be returned to a particular tribe. The Ninth Circuit decided that there needed to be an additional connection as to whether the remains were "Native American" at all, a connection that the statute does not appear to require.

2. **The effect of DNA testing.** In 2015, a study by University of Copenhagen (Denmark) geneticists concluded that, based on DNA testing, Kennewick Man's closest contemporary relatives were Native Americans, not Asian Americans, as earlier studies based on craniometric studies that did not incorporate DNA analysis had suggested. But since the DNA study did not indicate to which current tribe the skeleton was most closely related, that information would not lead to repatriation of the remains under the court's ruling. *See* Carl Zimmer, *New DNA Results Show Kennewick Man Was Native American*, N.Y. Times, June 18, 2015, https://www.nytimes.com/2015/06/19/science/new-dna-results-show-kennewick-man-was-native-american.html.

3. **The ultimate disposition.** Scientists proceeded to study the remains and published their findings. Douglas W. Owsley & Richard L. Jantz (eds.), Kennewick Man, The Scientific Investigation of an Ancient American Skeleton (Texas A&M University Press, 2014). In 2016, Congress passed legislation to return the ancient bones to a coalition of Columbia Basin tribes for reburial according to their traditions. The coalition includes the Confederated Tribes of the Colville Reservation, the Confederated Tribes and Bands of the Yakama Nation, the Nez Perce Tribe, the Confederated Tribes of the Umatilla Reservation, and the Wanapum Band of Priest Rapids. The remains were buried in 2017, witnessed by 200 tribal members, at an undisclosed location in the area. *See Tribes Lay Remains of Kennewick Man to Rest*, Spokesman-Review, Feb. 20, 2017, http://www.spokesman.com/stories/2017/feb/20/tribes-lay-remains-of-kennewick-man-to-rest/.

4. **Another finding of ancient human remains.** In 2013, archaeologists in Alaska uncovered the remains of two infants in a burial pit below a hearth dating back 11,500 years. Genetic testing, reported in early 2018, revealed that the six-week-old child, named Xach'itee'aanenh T'eede Gaay (sunrise girl-child in Middle Tanana), was, like Kennewick Man, more closely related to modern Native Americans than to any other population. Carl Zimmer, *In the Bones of a Buried Child, Signs of a Massive Human Migration to the Americas*, N.Y. Times (Jan. 3, 2018). The DNA testing was

approved by the Healy Lake Village Council and the Tanana Chiefs Conference. A FAQ prepared by an archaeologist from the University of Alaska Fairbanks and a member of the Tanana Chiefs Conference explains:

> When we found the human remains, we followed the inadvertent discovery protocols agreed upon by the State of Alaska, National Science Foundation, the local Native Alaskan tribe and Tanana Chiefs Conference. We immediately stopped the excavation, reported the find to Native and State representatives, and consulted with everyone regarding the next step. It was agreed by all that the human remains should be protected by careful, meticulous excavation and recovery. This was also the first step to help understand the context of the finds.
>
> At the time of discovery, only a small portion of the find had been excavated. Once the scientists determined that the tiny bone fragments were human, they halted excavation, and immediately initiated consultation with the local Tribe. Through subsequent Tribal consultation, an understanding of the unique opportunity this discovery provided to further understand the deep human history of the region outweighed a more traditional approach of leaving the remains in the ground. It was also concluded that the rarity of this find make it vulnerable to vandalism and possible desecration based on previous experiences at local Indian cemeteries.
>
> The remains of these ancient children are being conserved in an environmentally controlled setting with physical security to protect against theft or vandalism. The location is being kept confidential to ensure the protection of the remains. The treatment and final disposition will be determined through further consultation between the lead federal agency, the State of Alaska, scientists, the local federally recognized Tribe and affiliated Tribal organizations.

https://www.tananachiefs.org/upward-sun-river-site-frequently-asked-questions/.

5. Why was NAGPRA necessary? Consider the following from Allison M. Dussias, *Kennewick Man, Kinship, and the "Dying Race": The Ninth Circuit's Assimilationist Assault on the Native American Graves Protection and Repatriation Act*, 84 Neb. L. Rev. 55, 61–72 (2005):*

> At the time that NAGPRA was enacted, all fifty states, as well as the District of Columbia, had statutes that regulated cemeteries and sought to protect graves from vandalism and desecration. Grave robbers and those who mutilated the dead could be subjected to criminal penalties. Most states guaranteed that all persons, including the indigent, prisoners, and unidentified persons, were entitled to a decent burial, and disinterment of the dead was permissible only in very limited circumstances. In short, existing state

---

* Copyright 2005; reprinted with permission of Allison M. Dussias.

law reflected a deep respect for the remains of deceased human beings, and a conviction that human remains should be properly buried and thereafter left undisturbed.

These legal protections had not, however, prevented the remains of many thousands of deceased Native Americans—perhaps as many as two million—from being wrenched from their resting places and taken away by government agencies, museums, educational institutions, and operators of tourist attractions. The remains were obtained by a wide variety of people—soldiers, other government employees, private collectors, museum collectors, and academics—acting from a variety of motivations, including profit-seeking, entertainment, and scientific curiosity. To these collectors, the remains of deceased Native Americans were not worthy of the respect given to the remains of deceased Euro-Americans. This attitude allowed the collectors to treat the remains in a way that undoubtedly would have appalled them if it had been applied to the remains of their own family and friends. This point is made forcefully at the beginning of Tony Hillerman's 1989 mystery novel Talking God, in which a Smithsonian Institution conservator receives a box filled with the recently unearthed bones of her grandparents, which had been sent to her to protest the museum's failure to repatriate Native American remains.

* * *

More extensive and systematic collection of Native American remains geared up in the nineteenth century, spurred by the popularization of craniology, the study of brain size and skull shape, by Samuel G. Morton. Morton, a physician who was a seminal figure in the development of American physical anthropology, collected large numbers of Native American skulls, to support his argument that measurements of the skulls of Native Americans proved that they were racially inferior. Morton believed that cranial measurements could be used for race classification and for measuring mental capability and a race's level of development. * * *

Morton was able to enlist the support of physicians in the western United States, both those in civilian and in military practice, by having them send to him Native American crania, and as a result of the enthusiastic support that he received Morton was able to build the largest collection of crania in the United States. Morton and his allies were aware of but indifferent to Native American opposition to the robbing of their graves, an attitude made abundantly clear in a letter from a field collector to Morton:

> It is rather a perilous business to procure Indians' skulls in this country—The natives are so jealous of you that they watch you very closely while you are wandering near their mausoleums & instant & sanguinary vengeance would fall upon the luckless—who would presume to interfere

with the sacred relics . . . . There is an epidemic raging among them which carries them off so fast that the cemeteries will soon lack watchers — I don't rejoice in the prospects of death of the poor creatures certainly, but then you know it will be very convenient for my purposes.

* * *

Morton's work was widely viewed as giving scientific validity to white claims of racial superiority, and government policymakers saw Morton's findings as supporting the relocation of the tribes and the taking of the land of this dying race. * * *

* * * [T]he federal government also sought to promote the work of Morton and his colleagues by making the collecting of Native American crania part of government policy. In 1868, the Surgeon General of the Army issued an order that directed army personnel, who had already been collecting skulls on a less formal basis for Morton and others since the early 1800's, to obtain Native American skulls and other body parts for the Army Medical Museum for the purpose of aiding "the progress of anthropological science by obtaining measurements of a large number of skulls of the aboriginal races of North America." The response to the order was so enthusiastic that over 4,000 heads were collected pursuant to the order in the following decades. These skulls eventually became part of the Smithsonian Institution's collection of about 18,500 bodies. While some skulls were taken from fresh graves, burial scaffolds, and burial grounds, in other cases, skulls were taken by decapitating Native Americans who had never been buried, such as those who were killed on battlefields or in massacres or who died in POW camps or army hospitals.

Anthropologists and ethnologists were not the only academics who were interested in collecting Native American crania; researchers from other fields also collected skulls as opportunities arose. For example, Edward Drinker Cope, a prominent nineteenth century American paleontologist, was not above desecrating Native American burials during his dinosaur fossil-hunting expeditions on tribal lands. His description of one incident provides insight into the attitudes of collectors like Cope toward the remains of Native Americans:

[A] day or so ago I gathered a number of skulls and skeletons of Sioux with a bag of tools buried with a chief, and brought them to the boat [on the Missouri River] and boxed them. The uproar it created among the poor white element that run the lesser offices scared the captain so that he ordered them all taken back to the place where I obtained them. He . . . said that I had "immolated the graves of the dead." . . . [T]he bones had to go. But I have a little bill of $120 for the bones . . . . It is not a nice job, taking dirty skulls from skeletons not carefully prepared, and it is done at some risk to life. So I am indignant . . . .

* * * [T]he collecting of Native American skulls in the name of science legitimized the desecration of tribal burial sites and the mutilation of Native American remains, and led [many Americans] to envision deceased Native Americans as objects of curiosity to be collected by those whose careers so required. This spawned a tradition of grave-looting and collecting of remains and burial offerings by amateurs, often referred to as "pothunters," which continues to this day. * * *

Systematic desecration of Native American graves by archaeologists, anthropologists, and others, oblivious to the objections of Native Americans, continued unabated into the twentieth century. Moreover, as was the case with Samuel Morton, recognized leaders in these fields were particularly active and unapologetic collectors. Franz Boas, considered to be the father of cultural anthropology, complained that stealing bones from graves is unpleasant work, but concluded that he had to be philosophical about it: "[W]hat is the use, someone has to do it." While visiting British Columbia in the 1880s, Boas professed friendship for the Native Canadians he met and an interest in their oral traditions, while secretly stealing corpses, which he hoped to sell for profit.

Some of the most chilling incidents involving the taking of Native American bodies from burial sites were generated by the activities of the Smithsonian Institution's own Ales Hrdlicka, as he was building his reputation as the "patriarch" of American physical anthropology. Hrdlicka spent forty years at the Smithsonian, during which time he served as Curator of the Division of Physical Anthropology, founded the American Journal of Physical Anthropology, and amassed the world's most complete collection of human bones. He collected Native Alaskans' remains during the 1920s and 1930s, in pursuit of evidence, which he believed could be derived from human crania's physical characteristics, to support his personal theory as to the arrival of humans in the Americas. He was almost exclusively interested in collecting crania, and was "generally unconcerned with the archaeological history of the places he excavated." Hrdlicka's determination to collect remains was so great that in one of his projects alone, the Larsen Bay project on Kodiak Island, he collected the remains of about 1,000 individuals.

Hrdlicka excavated not only old burial sites, but also carried off recently buried bodies, such as those of the victims of a 1918 influenza epidemic, without permission and despite community opposition. While plundering one grave, for example, he noticed "an old woman who appeared to be provoked at something and was talking rather loudly," and learned that "the old woman claimed the bones to be those of her long departed husband." This kind of encounter simply prompted Hrdlicka to better conceal his activities, as his description of a 1926 Yukon River excavation demonstrates: "Some of the burials are quite recent. Open three older ones. In two the remains are too fresh yet, but secure a good female skeleton, which I pack in a practically new heavy pail, thrown out probably on the occasion of the last funeral. Then back, farther out, to avoid notice, through swamps and over moss...."

* * *

His concealment efforts were not always successful, as he noted in recounting another 1926 excavation. He had tried to hide bones that he had just dug up in his boat and to "strike off as far as possible from the shore so none could see what is carried," but noticed that an "old Indian and his crone nevertheless stand on the bank and look at us. They know already."

Hrdlicka had no qualms about examining even the remains of individuals whom he had known in life. In 1897, he met and examined six Inuits whom Polar explorer and entrepreneur Robert Peary had just brought from Greenland to New York City, where they were initially housed in the American Museum of Natural History's basement. When four of them died within a two-month period in 1898, Hrdlicka was able to examine the corpse of one of them, a man named Qisuk, and to obtain the deceased man's brain for study. For men like Hrdlicka, "one brief but final breath separate[d] a human curiosity from a scientific specimen," and whether alive or dead the Inuits did not receive the degree of respect to which Euro-Americans were entitled. Despite a state statute requiring that all dead human bodies "be decently buried within a reasonable period of time after death," Qisuk's skeleton was exhibited in the museum, as his son Minik, who had accompanied Qisuk to New York City and had been eight years old when his father died, was horrified to learn ten years after his father's death. In short, museum officials refused to treat the body of Qisuk, or of any of the other deceased Inuits, as that of a human being, whose fundamental dignity in death would be protected by the statutory burial requirement. If prominent anthropologists treated recently deceased Native Americans with so little dignity, then it is small wonder that it became accepted practice within the profession to treat the skeletal remains of earlier Native Americans, including those dating to antiquity, with little respect.

This, then, is the backdrop against which the Native American Graves Protection and Repatriation Act, commonly referred to as NAGPRA, was proposed and became law....

Chapter 2

Some Basics of Federal Indian Law

The materials in this chapter are intended to introduce the basic concepts of the field of federal Indian law: that is, the relationships among the tribes, the federal government, and the states. The chapter begins with a brief history of the twists and turns of federal Indian policy. An understanding of the historical policies, their purposes and their problems, is crucial to an understanding of the law. The historical overview is followed by the *Cherokee Cases*: two early nineteenth century opinions written by Chief Justice John Marshall that form the foundations of modern Indian law.

The remaining sections of this chapter survey concepts introduced in the *Cherokee Cases* and explored in more detail throughout these materials. The central issues of tribal sovereignty, federal plenary power, and the federal trust doctrine are briefly addressed. The chapter closes with an examination of the concept of "Indian country," the geographical determinant of federal Indian law.

A. History of Federal Indian Policy

An understanding of the history of federal Indian policy is crucial to an understanding of the development of federal Indian law. Like a perpetual wave machine, federal policy has flowed between two poles: the protection of tribal autonomy on the one hand, and the incorporation and assimilation of Indians into the majority society on the other. The dichotomy in national approaches to the indigenous peoples is as old as European colonization and settlement, as reflected in Chief Justice John Marshall's articulation of the law of conquest in the 1824 case of *Johnson v. M'Intosh* (page 115).

Federal Indian policy has gone through a series of distinct periods, often entering a new era when one of the competing norms becomes dominant over the other. The following materials briefly describe the eras and the major legal developments associated with them, with an emphasis on federal policies affecting lands and natural resources. For fuller treatments of the history of federal Indian policy, see Cohen's Handbook of Federal Indian Law ch. 1 (Nell Jessup Newton, et al. eds. 2012); Francis Paul Prucha, The Great Father: The United States Government and the American Indians (1984); Angie Debo, A History of the Indians of the United States (1970).

COLONIAL PERIOD (UP TO 1789)

The colonizing powers of western Europe generally recognized the Law of Nations (international law) applicable to indigenous peoples. Molded by the writings of the Spaniard Franciscus de Victoria in 1532, the Law of Nations contained both a doctrine of discovery and a law of conquest, which vested sovereign rights in the colonizing nations but which also preserved some measure of rights in the native populations. These doctrines subsequently formed the basis of federal Indian law. *See Johnson v. M'Intosh*, page 115.

Great Britain, as the dominant European power in what is now the United States, dealt with the Indian tribes as separate sovereigns. Britain generally set Indian policy, but left the management and implementation of Indian affairs to the individual colonies. As the colonies moved toward independence, they agitated for a greater say in Indian affairs, and in particular for the right to control the acquisition and disposition of Indian lands. The British government responded with the Proclamation of 1763, which asserted Crown control over all Indian land cessions.

EARLY REPUBLIC (1789–1830)

Following the Revolutionary War, the tension over Indian affairs power between Britain and its colonies transferred to the United States and its states. Although the Articles of Confederation attempted to provide roles for both the federal and state governments in Indian affairs, the Constitution placed Indian affairs authority squarely with the federal government. Congress is empowered to "regulate Commerce... with the Indian tribes," Art. I, §8, cl. 3; the President is empowered to make treaties, with the consent of the Senate, Art. II, §2, cl. 2; and the Supremacy Clause guarantees that treaties, as well as the Constitution and federal statutes, are the supreme law of the land, Art. VI.

The first Congress enacted the first of a series of Trade and Intercourse Acts in 1790. 1 Stat. 137 (1790). The final version, enacted in 1834, 4 Stat. 729, remains in the United States Code today. The Acts set forth the boundaries of the Indian country, provided for federal regulation of Indian traders, and established a criminal and compensatory scheme for depredations committed by non-Indians against Indians and vice versa. Of most importance to the subject matter of this course is the provision sometimes called the Nonintercourse Act, which prohibited the alienation or lease of tribal rights in property without federal consent and provided penalties for non-Indians who attempted to purchase Indian lands. The 1834 version of the Nonintercourse Act, codified at 25 U.S.C. §177, is reprinted at page 120. The Trade and Intercourse Acts thus centralized Indian affairs power in the federal government and regulated the relations between tribes and the United States and its citizens. But nothing in the Acts purported to intervene in the internal affairs of the Indian tribes.

During this period, the young United States generally continued Great Britain's policy of dealing with the Indian tribes as separate sovereigns. Against the backdrop of the Nonintercourse Acts, the federal government entered into treaties to regulate relations with specific tribes.

REMOVAL ERA (1820–1860)

As the American population grew, demand for additional land became critical and the states agitated for access to Indian lands. The "removal" of Indians to federal territory west of the Mississippi River, a proposal raised by several presidents during the early nineteenth century, gradually became official policy. After the War of 1812, many treaties contained removal provisions. Andrew Jackson, a vigorous advocate of removal, was elected president in 1828, and in 1830 Congress enacted the Removal Act, 4 Stat. 411, authorizing the removal of the eastern tribes. Under its auspices, many of the eastern tribes were forcibly removed from their territories under conditions of extreme hardship. The Trail of Tears traveled by the Five "Civilized" Tribes of the southeast to the Indian Territory (now Oklahoma) is the best-known example.

During this period, the United States Supreme Court was formulating the nation's legal approach to the Indian tribes. In three cases decided between 1823 and 1832, Chief Justice John Marshall laid the foundations of federal Indian law. The first of the Marshall trilogy of cases was *Johnson v. M'Intosh*, excerpted at page 115. In *M'Intosh*, the Court ruled that Indian tribes had only a right of occupancy, now commonly known as Indian title or aboriginal title. In the second and third cases, known as the *Cherokee Cases*, the Court began to define the contours of the legal relationship among the tribes, the federal government, and the states. In *Cherokee Nation v. Georgia*, excerpted at page 58, the Court held that Indian tribes were not foreign states, but "domestic dependent nations" whose relationship to the United States "resembles that of a ward to his guardian." 30 U.S. (5 Pet.) 1, 17 (1831). The next year, in *Worcester v. Georgia*, excerpted at page 61, the Court clarified that Indian tribes were "distinct political communities, having territorial boundaries, within which their authority is exclusive." 31 U.S. (6 Pet.) 515, 557 (1832). Marshall concluded that the laws of the states "can have no force" within tribal territories.

At the close of the removal era, as a symbol of the changing view of Indian tribes — no longer independent sovereigns, but rather domestic dependent nations — the Indian Office (now Bureau of Indian Affairs) was moved in 1849 from the War Department to the Department of the Interior.

RESERVATION ERA (1850–1887)

As white settlement of the trans-Mississippi West boomed, the focus of federal Indian policy began to shift. Although a number of tribes were removed to the Indian Territory in the years following the Civil War, the federal goal of locating all Indians in a single separate territory began to appear increasingly unrealistic. Federal policy thus shifted to the creation of reservations, pockets of tribal territory usually carved out of vast tracts of aboriginal lands. The reservations were held "in trust" for the tribes, with the remainder of the tribal territory ceded to the United States.

The reservation policy that marked these decades represented a slow transition from one dominant approach to Indian affairs to the other. On the one hand, reservations, like removal, ensured the separatism of the tribes and recognized their autonomy within a defined territory. On the other, federal policymakers viewed reservations as living laboratories where Indians, under the leadership of the federal Indian agent, would learn the virtues of agriculture and Christianity.

In 1871, Congress ended the practice of treaty-making with the Indian tribes, 25 U.S.C. §71, largely because members of the House of Representatives objected to their exclusion from the treaty confirmation process. Existing treaties were not affected, and the government continued its practice of negotiating cession and reservation agreements with the Indian tribes. But reservations created after 1871 were set aside by federal statute or, until the practice was ended by Congress in 1919, by executive order.

The transition years between the reservation policy era and the allotment era to follow were marked by the first federal incursions into the internal affairs of Indian tribes. In 1883, the Interior Department, without statutory authorization, promulgated a federal Code of Indian Offenses and established Courts of Indian Offenses to enforce it. A federal court upheld the Department's power to create the Code and punish Indians for violating it, on the ground that the courts were "mere educational and disciplinary instrumentalities." *United States v. Clapox*, 35 Fed. 575, 577 (D. Or. 1888). Then in 1885, Congress enacted the first federal statute that regulated the relations among tribal Indians. In response to the decision in *Ex parte Crow Dog*, 109 U.S. 556 (1883), that the murder of one tribal member by another was within the exclusive jurisdiction of the tribe, Congress enacted the Major Crimes Act, creating federal criminal jurisdiction for certain crimes between Indians occurring in the Indian country. In *United States v. Kagama*, 118 U.S. 375 (1886), the Court upheld the validity of the statute.

ALLOTMENT AND ASSIMILATION ERA (1871–1934)

No other era of federal Indian policy is as important for the subject matter of this course as the allotment and assimilation era of the late nineteenth and early twentieth centuries. The effects of the allotment policy will be found in virtually every chapter of these materials.

The allotment policy was formally ushered in by the General Allotment Act (or Dawes Act) of 1887. 24 Stat. 388. Inspired by both land hunger and "friends of the Indians" who believed assimilation was the key to Indian prosperity, the Act was a massive experiment in social engineering. Its primary purpose was to promote the assimilation of individual Indians into the majority culture, economy, and religion; as assimilation progressed, the tribes, viewed as the major obstacle to Indian advancement, would wither and eventually disappear. The primary means of achieving these ends was the replacement of the existing communal tribal ownership of land with individual ownership of allotments to encourage productive agrarian pursuits.

The Act authorized the President to allot tribal lands to individual tribal members in 80–160 acre parcels, to be held in trust for the individual for a period of twenty five years. During that time, the allottee was expected to assimilate to citizenship, agriculture, and Christianity. At the end of the period, the allottee would receive a patent (federal deed) in fee simple absolute. The Act was amended in 1906 (the Burke

Act, 34 Stat. 182) to authorize the early issuance of fee patents to allottees deemed "competent" to manage their affairs.

The allotment of land was a disaster for Indian tribes. For the most part, allottees did not adapt to an individualized agrarian lifestyle, whether from lack of interest, lack of tools and implements, or lack of suitable land. Once allottees received their patents in fee, their land could be sold, encumbered, and often taxed. Unable to meet these financial obligations, vast numbers of allottees lost their lands to sales to non-Indians (voluntary or forced), fraud, and sheriffs' auctions for nonpayment of taxes. Lands were allotted on 118 reservations. By the end of allotment in 1934, two-thirds of the land allotted — 27 million acres — had passed into non-Indian hands.

Serious problems existed even where allotments remained in Indian ownership. The Act subjected allotments, whether in trust or fee, to the intestacy laws of the state. The result has been severe fractionation of ownership, a topic explored in Chapter III, Section E. In addition to heirship issues, widespread leasing of both allotted and tribal trust lands meant that most of the economic benefit of the lands was reaped by non-Indian lessees rather than the allottees or tribes. With the failure of the small-farmer model, Congress first authorized the leasing of some tribal and allotted lands in 1891. 25 U.S.C. § 397. That initial statute was followed in 1909 by general authorization for allottees to lease their lands for mining, 25 U.S.C. § 396, and a variety of statutes expanding mineral leasing of tribal lands, see 25 U.S.C. §§ 398, 398a–398e, and 399. Timber sales on Indian lands were first generally authorized in 1910. 25 U.S.C. §§ 406–407. Issues arising from the leasing of lands are the subject of Chapter VI.

In addition to the allotment of land to tribal members, the General Allotment Act also authorized the President to dispose of the "surplus" lands left over after allotments were made. Of the 118 reservations subject to allotment, 44 had their surplus lands opened to non-Indian settlement. Approximately 60 million acres of tribal trust lands were lost to the surplus lands program. The modern legacy of this program, the issue of reservation diminishment or disestablishment, is covered *infra* in Chapter II, Section E.2.

As a result of these land programs, Indian reservations subject to allotment became a "checkerboard" of land ownership. Depending upon the extent of allotment and whether the surplus lands had been opened to settlement, any particular reservation might contain land held in trust for the tribe, allotted land held in trust for individual tribal members, land owned in fee by individual Indians and perhaps by the tribe as well, and land owned in fee by non-Indian individuals and entities, including the state and the federal governments. The complexities of environmental and land use regulation resulting from this checkerboard are the focus of Chapter IV.

Coextensive with the allotment and assimilation era of congressional and executive policy was the plenary power era of Supreme Court jurisprudence. This era was marked by extreme judicial deference to Congress, even in the absence of a clear constitutional basis. In *United States v. Kagama*, 118 U.S. 375 (1886), for example, the

Court upheld the Major Crimes Act despite finding that it was not supported by the grant of power in the Indian Commerce Clause. Instead, the Court relied on general federal power over the "dependent" tribes:

> The power of the General Government over these remnants of a race once powerful, now weak and diminished in numbers, is necessary to their protection, as well as to the safety of those among whom they dwell. It must exist in that government, because it never has existed anywhere else, because the theatre of its exercise is within the geographical limits of the United States, because it has never been denied, and because it alone can enforce its laws on all the tribes.

118 U.S. at 385. Another of the central cases of the plenary power era, *Lone Wolf v. Hitchcock*, 187 U.S. 553 (1903), is excerpted at page 71.

At the same time, however, this period also saw the development of the reserved rights doctrine in the Supreme Court, recognizing that tribes retained important property rights to natural resources. In *United States v. Winans*, 198 U.S. 371 (1905), and *Winters v. United States*, 207 U.S. 564 (1908), both excerpted in Chapter VII, the Court articulated doctrines recognizing implied rights in the Indian tribes. *Winans* recognized implied rights necessary to fulfill express reservations of rights in treaties, and *Winters* recognized implied rights to water. These issues are explored in Chapters VII and VIII.

REORGANIZATION ERA (1928–1950)

In 1928, the Meriam Report—the outcome of a nongovernmental study undertaken at the request of the Secretary of the Interior—detailed the economic, social, and cultural devastation of the allotment policy. Then, in 1934, Congress formally ended the allotment of lands and officially repudiated the allotment policy. In the Indian Reorganization Act (IRA) of 1934, 25 U.S.C. § 5101 *et seq.* (formerly § 461), Congress declared a new federal Indian policy, based on the protection of Indian lands and the encouragement of tribal self-government.

The IRA prohibited any further allotment of Indian lands and provided that any allotments still held in trust for the Indian owners would continue in trust until Congress provided otherwise. 25 U.S.C. §§ 5101–5102 (formerly §§ 461–462). Section 5 of the IRA authorized the Secretary to take lands back into trust and add lands to existing reservations. 25 U.S.C. § 5108 (formerly § 465) (see page 95). The IRA also provided a mechanism for tribes to organize as constitutional governments and to obtain business charters. 25 U.S.C. §§ 5123–5124 (formerly §§ 476–477).

Under the influence of this new policy era, Congress instituted some reforms to the leasing statutes. Section 6 of the IRA required the Secretary of the Interior to promulgate regulations for the management of Indian timber resources on a sustained yield basis. 25 U.S.C. § 5109. In 1938, Congress enacted the Indian Mineral Leasing Act, 25 U.S.C. §§ 396a–396g, designed in part to further the IRA goal of revitalizing tribal government by placing leasing authority with tribal councils, subject to secretarial approval.

In essence, the IRA halted allotment where it stood in 1934, while also prompting some reforms in Indian resource use. But what the IRA did not do was restore surplus lands to tribal ownership, or attempt to return lost allotments to either the tribes or the allottees.

TERMINATION ERA (1945–1970)

The IRA's recognition of tribalism and autonomy, although somewhat limited, was subject to criticism almost immediately. With the rise of pro-assimilationist social forces after World War II, federal policy swung back to assimilation with a vengeance. In 1953, Congress announced a new policy of termination, intended "as rapidly as possible" to make Indians subject to "the same laws" as all other citizens and to end the federal trust relationship. H. Con. Res. 108, 83d Cong., 1st Sess., 67 Stat. B132 (1953). Two major congressional initiatives mark the termination era.

First were the termination acts. In a series of acts between 1954 and 1962, Congress terminated its federal-tribal relationship with approximately 109 bands and tribes. The termination acts were implemented through termination plans between 1955 and 1970.

The second major legislation of the era was Public Law 280, enacted in 1953. Pub. L. No. 83-280, 67 Stat. 588 (1953) (codified at 18 U.S.C. § 1162 and 28 U.S.C. § 1360). Public Law 280 subjected most tribes in a number of states to the full civil and criminal jurisdiction of the state, and authorized all other states to take steps to assume the same jurisdiction.

SELF-DETERMINATION ERA (1968–PRESENT)

Even as the final termination plans were being implemented, federal policy once again turned against the forcible assimilation of Indians. In 1968, President Johnson issued a statement on "The Forgotten American" and Congress enacted the Indian Civil Rights Act (ICRA), providing that states could not assume Public Law 280 jurisdiction without tribal consent. 25 U.S.C. § 1321 *et seq.*

In 1970, President Nixon issued the first formal modern presidential policy on Indian affairs. Nixon called for federal encouragement and promotion of tribal self-determination and management of reservation affairs. In response, Congress enacted in 1974 the first of a series of acts restoring many of the terminated tribes to federal recognition, as well as such major legislation as the Indian Financing Act of 1974, 25 U.S.C. § 1451 *et seq.*, and the Indian Self-Determination and Education Assistance Act of 1975, 25 U.S.C. § 450 *et seq.*

In 1983, President Reagan reaffirmed Nixon's policy, and added the concept of a "government-to-government" relationship between the tribes and the United States. Presidents George H.W. Bush, William Clinton, and George W. Bush reaffirmed this executive policy.

On December 19, 2009, President Barack Obama signed into law the Department of Defense Appropriations Act of 2009, which included an "Apology to Native Peoples of the United States." The apology recognized the "special legal and political relationship" between Indian tribes and the United States, expressed regret over its "official depredations, ill-conceived policies, and the breaking of covenants," and urged state governments to "work toward reconciling relationships with Indian tribes with their boundaries." The apology did not authorize any legal action against the United States, however. Public Law No. 111-118, § 8113, 123 Stat. 3409, 3453–54 (2009).

From the late 1970s through the 1990s, numerous statutes and administrative actions promoted the presidential policy of self-determination and government-to-government relations. For example, Congress has attempted to address the problem of fractionated allotment ownership in the Indian Land Consolidation Act, first enacted in 1983 and most recently amended in 2004; the Act is discussed at pages 179–187. The federal Environmental Protection Agency became the first federal agency to develop an Indian policy, issued in 1984, and pursued a largely successful campaign to amend the federal environmental statutes to treat Indian tribes on a par with states; these developments are the subject of Chapter IV, Section B. Congress enacted new schemes for increasing tribal control over the development of mineral resources, timber, and grazing and agricultural lands; these issues are explored in Chapter V. Other congressional actions, such as the American Indian Religious Freedom Act of 1978 and the Native American Graves Protection and Repatriation Act of 1990, were studied in Chapter I.

In the twenty-first century, Congress and the executive branch appear firmly committed to the policy of tribal self-determination. The Supreme Court, however, continues to pursue an apparently conflicting approach. In a series of cases beginning with *Oliphant v. Suquamish Indian Tribe*, 435 U.S. 191 (1978) (prohibiting tribal criminal jurisdiction over non-Indians), and continuing with *Nevada v. Hicks*, 533 U.S. 353 (2001), excerpted at page 214 (limiting tribal civil jurisdiction over state officials on trust lands), the Court has departed from the approach pursued by the other two branches. These cases and their impact on land use and environmental regulation are explored in Chapter IV.

Moreover, the Supreme Court's certiorari process has had a particularly acute effect in Indian law. As Professor Matthew Fletcher pointed out, "there is virtually zero chance the Supreme Court will grant a certiorari petition filed by tribal interests," while the Court grants more than a quarter of petitions filed by traditional opponents of tribal sovereignty. As a result, "the number of cases where a tribal party is the respondent—and at a clear disadvantage statistically—is overwhelming." Matthew L. M Fletcher, *Factbound and Splitless: The Certiorari Process as a Barrier to Justice for Indian Tribes*, 51 Ariz. L. Rev. 933 (2008). Fletcher's study included 162 petitions filed between 1986 and 1994.

B. The Cherokee Cases

The *Cherokee Cases* are the second and third cases of the Marshall trilogy: three decisions written by Chief Justice John Marshall between 1823 and 1832 that formed the foundations of federal Indian law. The first case in the Marshall trilogy—*Johnson v. M'Intosh*, 21 U.S. (8 Wheat.) 543 (1823)—is reprinted at page 115. As a brief introduction to the cases that follow, the Court held in *Johnson v. M'Intosh* that Indian tribes retain a legally protected right to their lands, although they do not possess fee title.

The political context of the *Cherokee Cases* is important to a full understanding of the decisions and their importance.

> In 1802 Georgia ceded its western lands to the United States in return for a promise that the federal government on behalf of the state would purchase all Indian lands within the state boundary as soon as possible and on reasonable terms. By the 1820s little progress had been made in extinguishing Indian titles. The Cherokees had taken up agriculture and refused to sell any more of their lands. In 1827 they adopted a constitution and declared themselves an independent state. In response Georgia enacted a series of laws seizing Cherokee territory, extending state law over this territory, and annulling all Indian customs and laws. These extreme actions encountered no opposition from the [President Andrew] Jackson administration, which lent a sympathetic ear to assertions of state sovereignty, particularly in regard to Indian affairs. In 1830 the administration secured passage of the Indian Removal Act, by which the Indians could choose to remove west of the Mississippi River or submit to state law. In these circumstances the Cherokees, supported by well- placed politicians and statesmen motivated both by genuine sympathy for the plight of the Indians and by desire to embarrass the administration, brought their cause to the Supreme Court.
>
> The state of Georgia refused to appear in court and made clear its intention to ignore any decree the Supreme Court might issue directing the state to rescind its Cherokee laws. An equally important consideration was whether the executive department would enforce such a decree. Jackson's political opponents eagerly spread rumors that the president would ignore the Court's mandate. While no direct evidence could be cited to substantiate this charge, the president and his party did denounce these judicial proceedings as being part of a broader political campaign designed to unseat them in the election of 1832. Shortly before the case was argued, Congress debated a resolution to repeal section 25 of the Judiciary Act, which would have abolished the Supreme Court's appellate review of state court decisions.

Charles F. Hobson, The Great Chief Justice: John Marshall and the Rule of Law 171, 174 (U. Press of Kan. 1996).*

---

* Copyright 1996 by the University Press of Kansas. All rights reserved. Reprinted with permission of the University Press of Kansas.

Cherokee Nation v. Georgia
30 U.S. (5 Pet.) 1 (1831)

Mr. Chief Justice MARSHALL delivered the opinion of the Court.

This bill is brought by the Cherokee nation, praying an injunction to restrain the state of Georgia from the execution of certain laws of that state, which, as is alleged, go directly to annihilate the Cherokees as a political society, and to seize, for the use of Georgia, the lands of the nation which have been assured to them by the United States in solemn treaties repeatedly made and still in force.

If courts were permitted to indulge their sympathies, a case better calculated to excite them can scarcely be imagined. A people once numerous, powerful, and truly independent, found by our ancestors in the quiet and uncontrolled possession of an ample domain, gradually sinking beneath our superior policy, our arts and our arms, have yielded their lands by successive treaties, each of which contains a solemn guarantee of the residue, until they retain no more of their formerly extensive territory than is deemed necessary to their comfortable subsistence. To preserve this remnant, the present application is made.

Before we can look into the merits of the case, a preliminary inquiry presents itself. Has this court jurisdiction of the cause?

The third article of the constitution describes the extent of the judicial power. The second section closes an enumeration of the cases to which it is extended, with "controversies" "between a state or the citizens thereof, and foreign states, citizens, or subjects." A subsequent clause of the same section gives the supreme court original jurisdiction in all cases in which a state shall be a party. The party defendant may then unquestionably be sued in this court. May the plaintiff sue in it? Is the Cherokee nation a foreign state in the sense in which that term is used in the constitution?

The counsel for the plaintiffs have maintained the affirmative of this proposition with great earnestness and ability. So much of the argument as was intended to prove the character of the Cherokees as a state, as a distinct political society, separated from others, capable of managing its own affairs and governing itself, has, in the opinion of a majority of the judges, been completely successful. They have been uniformly treated as a state from the settlement of our country. The numerous treaties made with them by the United States recognize them as a people capable of maintaining the relations of peace and war, of being responsible in their political character for any violation of their engagements, or for any aggression committed on the citizens of the United States by any individual of their community. Laws have been enacted in the spirit of these treaties. The acts of our government plainly recognize the Cherokee nation as a state, and the courts are bound by those acts.

A question of much more difficulty remains. Do the Cherokees constitute a foreign state in the sense of the constitution?

The counsel have shown conclusively that they are not a state of the union, and have insisted that individually they are aliens, not owing allegiance to the United

States. An aggregate of aliens composing a state must, they say, be a foreign state. Each individual being foreign, the whole must be foreign.

This argument is imposing, but we must examine it more closely before we yield to it. The condition of the Indians in relation to the United States is perhaps unlike that of any other two people in existence. In the general, nations not owing a common allegiance are foreign to each other. The term foreign nation is, with strict propriety, applicable by either to the other. But the relation of the Indians to the United States is marked by peculiar and cardinal distinctions which exist nowhere else.

The Indian territory is admitted to compose a part of the United States. In all our maps, geographical treatises, histories, and laws, it is so considered. In all our intercourse with foreign nations, in our commercial regulations, in any attempt at intercourse between Indians and foreign nations, they are considered as within the jurisdictional limits of the United States, subject to many of those restraints which are imposed upon our own citizens. They acknowledge themselves in their treaties to be under the protection of the United States; they admit that the United States shall have the sole and exclusive right of regulating the trade with them, and managing all their affairs as they think proper; and the Cherokees in particular were allowed by the treaty of Hopewell, which preceded the constitution, "to send a deputy of their choice, whenever they think fit, to congress." Treaties were made with some tribes by the state of New York, under a then unsettled construction of the confederation, by which they ceded all their lands to that state, taking back a limited grant to themselves, in which they admit their dependence.

Though the Indians are acknowledged to have an unquestionable, and, heretofore, unquestioned right to the lands they occupy, until that right shall be extinguished by a voluntary cession to our government; yet it may well be doubted whether those tribes which reside within the acknowledged boundaries of the United States can, with strict accuracy, be denominated foreign nations. They may, more correctly, perhaps, be denominated domestic dependent nations. They occupy a territory to which we assert a title independent of their will, which must take effect in point of possession when their right of possession ceases. Meanwhile they are in a state of pupilage. Their relation to the United States resembles that of a ward to his guardian.

They look to our government for protection; rely upon its kindness and its power; appeal to it for relief to their wants; and address the president as their great father. They and their country are considered by foreign nations, as well as by ourselves, as being so completely under the sovereignty and dominion of the United States, that any attempt to acquire their lands, or to form a political connection with them, would be considered by all as an invasion of our territory, and an act of hostility.

These considerations go far to support the opinion, that the framers of our constitution had not the Indian tribes in view, when they opened the courts of the union to controversies between a state or the citizens thereof, and foreign states.

In considering this subject, the habits and usages of the Indians, in their intercourse with their white neighbors, ought not to be entirely disregarded. At the time the constitution was framed, the idea of appealing to an American court of justice for an assertion of right or a redress of wrong, had perhaps never entered the mind of an Indian or of his tribe. Their appeal was to the tomahawk, or to the government. This was well understood by the statesmen who framed the constitution of the United States, and might furnish some reason for omitting to enumerate them among the parties who might sue in the courts of the union. Be this as it may, the peculiar relations between the United States and the Indians occupying our territory are such, that we should feel much difficulty in considering them as designated by the term foreign state, were there no other part of the constitution which might shed light on the meaning of these words. But we think that in construing them, considerable aid is furnished by that clause in the eighth section of the third article; which empowers congress to "regulate commerce with foreign nations, and among the several states, and with the Indian tribes."

In this clause they are as clearly contradistinguished by a name appropriate to themselves, from foreign nations, as from the several states composing the union. They are designated by a distinct appellation; and as this appellation can be applied to neither of the others, neither can the appellation distinguishing either of the others be in fair construction applied to them. The objects, to which the power of regulating commerce might be directed, are divided into three distinct classes—foreign nations, the several states, and Indian tribes. When forming this article, the convention considered them as entirely distinct. We cannot assume that the distinction was lost in framing a subsequent article, unless there be something in its language to authorize the assumption.

The counsel for the plaintiffs contend that the words "Indian tribes" were introduced into the article, empowering congress to regulate commerce, for the purpose of removing those doubts in which the management of Indian affairs was involved by the language of the ninth article of the confederation. Intending to give the whole power of managing those affairs to the government about to be instituted, the convention conferred it explicitly; and omitted those qualifications which embarrassed the exercise of it as granted in the confederation. This may be admitted without weakening the construction which has been intimated: Had the Indian tribes been foreign nations, in the view of the convention; this exclusive power of regulating intercourse with them might have been, and most probably would have been, specifically given, in language indicating that idea, not in language contradistinguishing them from foreign nations. Congress might have been empowered "to regulate commerce with foreign nations, including the Indian tribes, and among the several states." This language would have suggested itself to statesmen who considered the Indian tribes as foreign nations, and were yet desirous of mentioning them particularly.

If it be true that the Cherokee nation have rights, this is not the tribunal in which those rights are to be asserted. If it be true that wrongs have been inflicted, and that still greater are to be apprehended, this is not the tribunal which can redress the past or prevent the future.

The motion for an injunction is denied.

[Concurrences by Justices Johnson and Baldwin are omitted.]

Mr. Justice THOMPSON, dissenting.

It is a rule which has been repeatedly sanctioned by this court, that the judicial department is to consider as sovereign and independent states or nations those powers, that are recognized as such by the executive and legislative departments of the government; they being more particularly entrusted with our foreign relations.

If we look to the whole course of treatment by this country of the Indians, from the year 1775, to the present day, when dealing with them in their aggregate capacity as nations or tribes, and regarding the mode and manner in which all negotiations have been carried on and concluded with them; the conclusion appears to me irresistible, that they have been regarded, by the executive and legislative branches of the government, not only as sovereign and independent, but as foreign nations or tribes, not within the jurisdiction nor under the government of the states within which they were located.

Upon the whole, I am of opinion,

1. that the Cherokees compose a foreign state within the sense and meaning of the constitution, and constitute a competent party to maintain a suit against the state of Georgia.

2. That the bill presents a case for judicial consideration, arising under the laws of the United States, and treaties made under their authority with the Cherokee nation, and which laws and treaties have been, and are threatened to be still further violated by the laws of the state of Georgia referred to in this opinion.

3. That an injunction is a fit and proper writ to be issued, to prevent the further execution of such laws, and ought therefore to be awarded.

And I am authorized by my brother Story to say, that he concurs with me in this opinion.

Worcester v. Georgia
31 U.S. (6 Pet.) 515 (1832)

[In 1830, the State of Georgia enacted a law which required any person residing within the Cherokee Nation to have a state license or permit and to take an oath of loyalty. Other Georgia laws purported to annex the Cherokee Nation territory to the state, extend state law over the Cherokees, and disqualify Indians from testifying in state court. Samuel Worcester and other white missionaries living in the Cherokee territory were arrested for failing to have state permits. The missionaries were offered pardons on the condition that they swear an oath of loyalty and leave Cherokee territory. Worcester and one other refused, were convicted, and sentenced to four years in prison. They appealed their criminal convictions to the United States Supreme Court.]

Mr. Chief Justice MARSHALL delivered the opinion of the Court.

This cause, in every point of view in which it can be placed, is of the deepest interest. The defendant is a state, a member of the union, which has exercised the powers of government over a people who deny its jurisdiction, and are under the protection of the United States. The plaintiff is a citizen of the state of Vermont, condemned to hard labour for four years in the penitentiary of Georgia; under colour of an act which he alleges to be repugnant to the constitution, laws, and treaties of the United States. The legislative power of a state, the controlling power of the constitution and laws of the United States, the rights, if they have any, the political existence of a once numerous and powerful people, the personal liberty of a citizen, are all involved in the subject now to be considered.

It has been said at the bar, that the acts of the legislature of Georgia seize on the whole Cherokee country, parcel it out among the neighbouring counties of the state, extend her code over the whole country, abolish its institutions and its laws, and annihilate its political existence.

The extra-territorial power of every legislature being limited in its action, to its own citizens or subjects, the very passage of this act is an assertion of jurisdiction over the Cherokee nation, and of the rights and powers consequent on jurisdiction.

The first step, then, in the inquiry, which the constitution and laws impose on this court, is an examination of the rightfulness of this claim.

America, separated from Europe by a wide ocean, was inhabited by a distinct people, divided into separate nations, independent of each other and of the rest of the world, having institutions of their own, and governing themselves by their own laws. It is difficult to comprehend the proposition, that the inhabitants of either quarter of the globe could have rightful original claims of dominion over the inhabitants of the other, or over the lands they occupied; or that the discovery of either by the other should give the discoverer rights in the country discovered, which annulled the pre-existing rights of its ancient possessors.

But power, war, conquest, give rights, which, after possession, are conceded by the world; and which can never be controverted by those on whom they descend. We proceed, then, to the actual state of things, having glanced at their origin; because holding it in our recollection might shed some light on existing pretensions.

Soon after Great Britain determined on planting colonies in America, the king granted charters to companies of his subjects who associated for the purpose of carrying the views of the crown into effect, and of enriching themselves. The first of these charters was made before possession was taken of any part of the country. They purport, generally, to convey the soil, from the Atlantic to the South Sea. This soil was occupied by numerous and warlike nations, equally willing and able to defend their possessions. The extravagant and absurd idea, that the feeble settlements made on the seacoast, or the companies under whom they were made, acquired legitimate power by them to govern the people, or occupy the lands from sea to sea, did not enter the mind of any man. They were well understood to convey the title which, according to the common law of European sovereigns respecting America, they might rightfully convey, and no more. This was the exclusive right of purchasing such lands as the natives were willing to sell. The crown could not be understood to grant what the crown did not affect to claim; nor was it so understood.

Certain it is, that our history furnishes no example, from the first settlement of our country, of any attempt on the part of the crown to interfere with the internal affairs of the Indians, farther than to keep out the agents of foreign powers, who, as traders or otherwise, might seduce them into foreign alliances. The king purchased their lands when they were willing to sell, at a price they were willing to take; but never coerced a surrender of them. He also purchased their alliance and dependence by subsidies; but never intruded into the interior of their affairs, or interfered with their self-government, so far as respected themselves only.

Such was the policy of Great Britain towards the Indian nations inhabiting the territory from which she excluded all other Europeans; such her claims, and such her practical exposition of the charters she had granted: she considered them as nations capable of maintaining the relations of peace and war; of governing themselves, under her protection; and she made treaties with them, the obligation of which she acknowledged.

This was the settled state of things when the war of our revolution commenced. The influence of our enemy was established; her resources enabled her to keep up that influence; and the colonists had much cause for the apprehension that the Indian nations would, as the allies of Great Britain, add their arms to hers. This, as was to be expected, became an object of great solicitude to congress. Far from advancing a claim to their lands, or asserting any right of dominion over them, congress resolved "that the securing and preserving the friendship of the Indian nations appears to be a subject of the utmost moment to these colonies."

During the war of the revolution, the Cherokees took part with the British. After its termination, the United States [and the Cherokee Nation entered into a peace treaty, the Treaty of Hopewell.]

The third article [of the Treaty of Hopewell] acknowledges the Cherokees to be under the protection of the United States of America, and of no other power.

This stipulation is found in Indian treaties, generally. It was introduced into their treaties with Great Britain; and may probably be found in those with other European powers. Its origin may be traced to the nature of their connection with those powers; and its true meaning is discerned in their relative situation.

* * * The Indians perceived in this protection only what was beneficial to themselves—an engagement to punish aggressions on them. It involved, practically, no claim to their lands, no dominion over their persons. It merely bound the nation to the British crown, as a dependent ally, claiming the protection of a powerful friend and neighbour, and receiving the advantages of that protection, without involving a surrender of their national character. This is the true meaning of the stipulation, and is undoubtedly the sense in which it was made. Neither the British government, nor the Cherokees, ever understood it otherwise.

The same stipulation entered into with the United States, is undoubtedly to be construed in the same manner. They receive the Cherokee nation into their favour and protection. The Cherokees acknowledge themselves to be under the protection of the United States, and of no other power. Protection does not imply the destruction of the protected.

This relation [of the Cherokee Nation to the United States] was that of a nation claiming and receiving the protection of one more powerful: not that of individuals abandoning their national character, and submitting as subjects to the laws of a master.

This treaty, thus explicitly recognizing the national character of the Cherokees, and their right of self-government; thus guarantying their lands; assuming the duty of protection, and of course pledging the faith of the United States for that protection; has been frequently renewed, and is now in full force.

From the commencement of our government, congress has passed acts to regulate trade and intercourse with the Indians; which treat them as nations, respect their rights, and manifest a firm purpose to afford that protection which treaties stipulate. All these acts, and especially that of 1802, which is still in force, manifestly consider the several Indian nations as distinct political communities, having territorial boundaries, within which their authority is exclusive, and having a right to all the lands within those boundaries, which is not only acknowledged, but guaranteed by the United States.

The treaties and laws of the United States contemplate the Indian territory as completely separated from that of the states; and provide that all intercourse with them shall be carried on exclusively by the government of the union.

* * * [The United States Constitution] confers on congress the powers of war and peace; of making treaties, and of regulating commerce with foreign nations, and among the several states, and with the Indian tribes. These powers comprehend all that is required for the regulation of our intercourse with the Indians. They are not limited by any restrictions on their free actions. The shackles imposed on this power, in the confederation, are discarded.

The Indian nations had always been considered as distinct, independent political communities, retaining their original natural rights, as the undisputed possessors of the soil, from time immemorial, with the single exception of that imposed by irresistible power, which excluded them from intercourse with any other European potentate than the first discoverer of the coast of the particular region claimed: and this was a restriction which those European potentates imposed on themselves, as well as on the Indians. The very term "nation," so generally applied to them, means "a people distinct from others." The constitution, by declaring treaties already made, as well as those to be made, to be the supreme law of the land, has adopted and sanctioned the previous treaties with the Indian nations, and consequently admits their rank among those powers who are capable of making treaties. The words "treaty" and "nation" are words of our own language, selected in our diplomatic and legislative proceedings, by ourselves, having each a definite and well understood meaning. We have applied them to Indians, as we have applied them to the other nations of the earth. They are applied to all in the same sense.

The actual state of things at the time, and all history since, explain these charters; and the king of Great Britain, at the treaty of peace, could cede only what belonged to his crown. These newly asserted titles can derive no aid from the articles so often repeated in Indian treaties; extending to them, first, the protection of Great Britain, and afterwards that of the United States. These articles are associated with others, recognizing their title to self-government. The very fact of repeated treaties with them recognizes it; and the settled doctrine of the law of nations is, that a weaker power does not surrender its independence—its right to self-government, by associating with a stronger, and taking its protection. A weak state, in order to provide for its safety, may place itself under the protection of one more powerful, without stripping itself of the right of government, and ceasing to be a state. Examples of this kind are not wanting in Europe. "Tributary and feudatory states," says Vattel, "do not thereby cease to be sovereign and independent states, so long as self- government and sovereign and independent authority are left in the administration of the state." At the present day, more than one state may be considered as holding its right of self-government under the guarantee and protection of one or more allies.

The Cherokee nation, then, is a distinct community occupying its own territory, with boundaries accurately described, in which the laws of Georgia can have no force, and which the citizens of Georgia have no right to enter, but with the assent of the Cherokees themselves, or in conformity with treaties, and with the acts of congress. The whole intercourse between the United States and this nation, is, by our constitution and laws, vested in the government of the United States.

The act of the state of Georgia, under which the plaintiff in error was prosecuted, is consequently void, and the judgment a nullity.

Mr. Justice MCLEAN, concurring.

[I]s there no end to the exercise of this power over Indians within the limits of a state, by the general government? The answer is, that, in its nature, it must be limited by circumstances.

If a tribe of Indians shall become so degraded or reduced in numbers, as to lose the power of self-government, the protection of the local law, of necessity, must be extended over them. The point at which this exercise of power by a state would be proper, need not now be considered: if indeed it be a judicial question. Such a question does not seem to arise in this case. So long as treaties and laws remain in full force, and apply to Indian nations, exercising the right of self-government, within the limits of a state, the judicial power can exercise no discretion in refusing to give effect to those laws, when questions arise under them, unless they shall be deemed unconstitutional.

The exercise of the power of self-government by the Indians, within a state, is undoubtedly contemplated to be temporary.

At best they can enjoy a very limited independence within the boundaries of a state, and such a residence must always subject them to encroachments from the settlements around them; and their existence within a state, as a separate and independent community, may seriously embarrass or obstruct the operation of the state laws. If, therefore, it would be inconsistent with the political welfare of the states, and the social advance of their citizens, that an independent and permanent power should exist within their limits, this power must give way to the greater power which surrounds it, or seek its exercise beyond the sphere of state authority.

Notes

1. The "actual state of things." Chief Justice Marshall noted that "[i]t is difficult to comprehend the proposition [the European discovers] could have rightful original claims of the dominion over [Indian tribes]." But he acknowledged that "power, war, conquest" cannot be denied and courts must deal with "the actual state of things." Thus, he examined British-tribal relations in the years prior to the Revolution, which included "[t]he extravagant and absurd idea, that the feeble settlements made on the sea coast . . . acquired legitimate power by them to govern the [tribes]." Notice that his interpretation of the British claims in these cases was restricted to claims of sovereignty, the right to govern. Proprietary rights and titles were another matter: through discovery the crown obtained only "the exclusive right of purchasing such lands as the natives were willing to sell."

This "actual state of things" was altered only slightly by treaties with the United States, such as the Treaty of Hopewell. According to Marshall, what did the Cherokee Nation gain from this treaty? What did it lose? How does this interpretation affect the authority of the state of Georgia?

2. Justice McLean's concurrence. Unlike Chief Justice Marshall, who assumed that tribes were enduring political bodies with a geographical base, Justice McLean considered tribal self-government to be a temporary status, "always subject . . . to encroachments from the settlements around them." Where tribal self-government became "inconsistent with the political welfare of the states, and the social advance of its citizens," it would give way to state law. This competing vision of tribal sovereignty became dominant in the assimilationist era following the Civil War, producing what might be termed *de facto* (or judicial) terminations.

3. What Jackson allegedly said. The *Worcester* decision generated one of the more famous, although likely apocryphal, statements of President Andrew Jackson. The decision also had the potential to generate a constitutional crisis, which was avoided in part by Chief Justice Marshall's adjourning the Court immediately following the issuance of the *Worcester* opinion. Marshall's decision thus had substantial impacts on American politics and American law. What impact did it have for the Cherokee Nation? Consider the following:

> Of this case President Jackson was alleged to have said, "John Marshall has made his decision, now let him enforce it." There is no proof that Jackson

ever uttered this statement; indeed, there is no evidence that he ignored his constitutional duty to enforce the Court's judgment even though from the beginning he bitterly resented the judiciary's interference in the Cherokee business. The president was not legally required to do anything until the state of Georgia first refused to carry out the Court's mandate. The state, as expected, ignored the order, but a second mandate that might have obliged the executive to act was never issued. In response to the impending crisis posed by South Carolina's attempt to nullify federal tariff laws, the Jackson administration persuaded the Georgia governor to [release] Worcester, who in turn dropped further proceedings on behalf of the Cherokees. The upshot was that the Jackson administration had a stronger hand to deal with nullification, the state of Georgia did not yield its sovereign pretensions, the Supreme Court preserved its authority, and the Cherokees gave up further legal efforts to prevent their removal from ancient tribal lands.

Chief Justice Marshall stretched the limits of judicial power as far as he could in *Worcester* to give the Cherokee tribe's legal claims a full hearing at the bar of the Supreme Court. In this decision, perhaps more than in any other, the jurist went beyond strict legal necessity to make a pronouncement that trenched upon the political sphere. Although recognizing that the vindication of Cherokee legal rights would invite censure as trespassing upon the political realm, Marshall was genuinely moved by the Indians' plight and outraged by what he regarded as Georgia's unlawful conduct toward the tribe. Here law and morality were so clearly on the same side that a jurist might indulge his feelings to a greater extent than was possible in other cases * * *.

* * * Sympathetic as he was to the dire predicament of the Cherokees, Marshall had other reasons for seizing the opportunity to pronounce the law in their case. To have remained silent in the face of a state's manifest violation of the Constitution and laws of the United States would have seriously compromised the Supreme Court's claim to be the guardian and expositor of the nation's fundamental law, if not the keeper of the nation's moral conscience. To risk this consequence, the chief justice must have reckoned, was a less acceptable alternative than to incur the wrath of a defiant state or to provoke a confrontation with the federal executive. Even though a favorable decision was not likely to be of any practical benefit to the Indians, still it mattered greatly that the Court should be perceived as faithfully discharging its duty.

Charles F. Hobson, The Great Chief Justice: John Marshall and the Rule of Law 179–80 (U. Press of Kan. 1996).*

---

* Copyright 1996 by the University Press of Kansas. All rights reserved. Reprinted with permission of the University Press of Kansas.

4. The pardon. Over 160 years after jailing Samuel Worcester and his fellow missionary, Elizur Butler, the state of Georgia formally pardoned the two on November 25, 1992. The state's pardon called the incident "a stain on the history of criminal justice in Georgia," acknowledging that it usurped the tribe's sovereignty and ignored the Supreme Court. Worcester and Butler were sentenced to four years at hard labor and served sixteen months before being released in time to join the Cherokee on the Trail of Tears, the forced march of 17,000 to west of the Mississippi River. *See Georgia To Pardon Two in 1831 Case*, N.Y. Times, Nov. 23, 1992, at A7.

C. Tribal Sovereignty

The sovereign status of Indian tribes, and the inherent nature of that sovereignty, are the cornerstone concepts of federal Indian law. The following excerpts, from the original Handbook of Federal Indian Law by Felix S. Cohen in 1942, and the most recent edition of Cohen's Handbook of Federal Indian Law in 2012, explore the meaning of inherent tribal sovereignty for the development of federal Indian law.

Felix S. Cohen, Handbook of Federal Indian Law
122–23 (1942)

The Indian's right of self-government is a right which has been consistently protected by the courts, frequently recognized and intermittently ignored by treaty-makers and legislators, and very widely disregarded by administrative officials. That such rights have been disregarded is perhaps due more to lack of acquaintance with the law of the subject than to any drive for increased power on the part of administrative officials.

The most basic of all Indian rights, the right of self-government, is the Indian's last defense against administrative oppression, for in a realm where the states are powerless to govern and where Congress, occupied with more pressing national affairs, cannot govern wisely and well, there remains a large no-man's-land in which government can emanate only from officials of the Interior Department or from the Indians themselves. Self-government is thus the Indians' only alternative to rule by a government department.

Indian self-government, the decided cases hold, includes the power of an Indian tribe to adopt and operate under a form of government of the Indians' choosing, to define conditions of tribal membership, to regulate domestic relations of members, to prescribe rules of inheritance, to levy taxes, to regulate property within the jurisdiction of the tribe, to control the conduct of members by municipal legislation, and to administer justice.

Perhaps the most basic principle of all Indian law, supported by a host of decisions hereinafter analyzed, is the principle that *those powers which are lawfully vested in an Indian tribe are not, in general, delegated powers granted by express acts of*

Congress, but rather inherent powers of a limited sovereignty which has never been extinguished. Each Indian tribe begins its relationship with the Federal Government as a sovereign power, recognized as such in treaty and legislation. The powers of sovereignty have been limited from time to time by special treaties and laws designed to take from the Indian tribes control of matters which, in the judgment of Congress, these tribes could no longer be safely permitted to handle. The statutes of Congress, then, must be examined to determine the limitations of tribal sovereignty rather than to determine its sources or its positive content. What is not expressly limited remains within the domain of tribal sovereignty.

The acts of Congress which appear to limit the powers of an Indian tribe are not to be unduly extended by doubtful inference.

SECTION 2. THE DERIVATION OF TRIBAL POWERS

From the earliest years of the Republic the Indian tribes have been recognized as "distinct, independent, political communities," and, as such, qualified to exercise powers of self-government, not by virtue of any delegation of powers from the Federal Government, but rather by reason of their original tribal sovereignty. Thus treaties and statutes of Congress have been looked to by the courts as limitations upon original tribal powers, or, at most, evidences of recognition of such powers, rather than as the direct source of tribal powers. This is but an application of the general principle that "It is only by positive enactments, even in the case of conquered and subdued nations, that their laws are changed by the conqueror."

The whole course of judicial decision on the nature of Indian tribal powers is marked by adherence to three fundamental principles: (1) An Indian tribe possesses, in the first instance, all the powers of any sovereign state. (2) Conquest renders the tribe subject to the legislative power of the United States and, in substance, terminates the external powers of sovereignty of the tribe, *e.g.*, its power to enter into treaties with foreign nations, but does not by itself affect the internal sovereignty of the tribe, *i.e.*, its powers of local self-government. (3) These powers are subject to qualification by treaties and by express legislation by Congress, but, save as thus expressly qualified, full powers of internal sovereignty are vested in the Indian tribes and in their duly constituted organs of government.

Cohen's Handbook of Federal Indian Law § 4.01[1][a]*

Nell Jessup Newton et al. eds., LexisNexis 2012

The history of tribal self-government forms the basis for the exercise of modern powers. Indian tribes consistently have been recognized, first by the European nations, and later by the United States, as "distinct, independent political communities" qualified to exercise powers of self-government, not by virtue of any delegation of powers, but rather by reason of their original tribal sovereignty. The right of

---

* Copyright 2012. Reprinted with permission of the American Indian Law Center, Inc.

tribes to govern their members and territories flows from a preexisting sovereignty limited, but not abolished, by their inclusion within the territorial bounds of the United States. Tribal powers of self-government are recognized by the Constitution, legislation, treaties, judicial decisions, and administrative practice. Neither the passage of time nor the apparent assimilation of native peoples can be interpreted as diminishing or abandoning a tribe's status as a self-governing entity. Once recognized as a political body by the United States, a tribe retains its sovereignty until Congress acts to divest that sovereignty.

Perhaps the most basic principle of all Indian law, supported by a host of decisions, is that those powers lawfully vested in an Indian nation are not, in general, delegated powers granted by express acts of Congress, but rather "inherent powers of a limited sovereignty which has never been extinguished." The Supreme Court has observed that "Indian tribes still possess those aspects of sovereignty not withdrawn by treaty or statute, or by implication as a necessary result of their dependent status." This principle guides determinations of the scope of tribal authority. The tribes began their relationship with the federal government with the sovereign powers of independent nations. They came under the authority of the United States through treaties and agreements between tribes and the federal government and through the assertion of authority by the United States. Federal treaties and congressional enactments have imposed certain limitations on tribal governments, especially on their external political relations, and the Supreme Court has created common law that introduces further limitations. But from the beginning the United States permitted, then protected, continued internal tribal government * * *.

Notes

1. Contemporary tribal sovereignty. For a cogent justification of tribal sovereignty, see Joseph William Singer, *The Indian States of America: Parallel Universes & Overlapping Sovereignty*, 38 Am. Indian L. Rev. 1 (2014) (listing all (then) 566 recognized tribes in an appendix).

2. Felix S. Cohen. Felix Cohen, who had both a law degree and a Ph.D in philosophy, was a government attorney for fourteen years beginning in 1933, serving as an Associate Solicitor in the Interior Department and a Special Assistant to the Attorney General. He was a principal drafter of the Indian Reorganization Act of 1934, which brought to an end the allotment era. Although he wrote widely in both law and philosophy, his most enduring work was his Handbook of Federal Indian Law, which was based on a forty-six volume collection of federal laws and treaties compiled by Cohen and his colleague, Theodore H. Haas, who were directed by the Attorney General to produce an "Indian Law Survey." The result was the Handbook, published in 1942 under the auspices of the Department of the Interior.

According to the introduction of the 1982 edition of the Handbook:

> Cohen was the Blackstone of American Indian Law. He brought organization and conceptual clarity to the field. Although the 1942 work was

prefaced with the disclaimer that "this handbook does not purport to be a cyclopedia," it was in fact a thorough and comprehensive treatise that attended to virtually every nook and cranny of the field. The 1942 Handbook was also blessed with a philosophical breadth that only a scholar of Cohen's background and vision could provide.

The original Handbook was remarkable in another respect. Indian law is a field in which the extent of federal power over Indians is constantly being tested. Yet the official government treatise was of such scholarly integrity that it took the view that in many areas federal power was limited by Indian legal rights.

Felix S. Cohen's Handbook of Federal Indian Law viii–ix (Rennard Strickland, ed. 1982).

Cohen left government service in 1948. Upon his retirement he was awarded the Department of the Interior's highest honor, the Distinguished Service Award. He continued to practice, teach, and write about Indian law and other legal and philosophical matters until his premature death in 1953, at the age of forty-six.

3. Federal recognition of tribes. As the previous materials indicate, the federal government "recognizes" Indian tribes. Federal recognition is significant because it means that the United States has a political government-to-government relationship with the recognized tribes. With recognition, the federal government acknowledges both the tribe's inherent authority to exercise political powers and the federal trust responsibility to the tribe. In addition, recognized tribal governments have access to numerous federal programs that provide funding and support to the tribes and their members.

Congress and the Executive have broad power to recognize Indian tribes. Usually a tribe is considered federally recognized if Congress or the Executive has a continuing political relationship with the tribe. *See* Cohen's *Handbook of Federal Indian Law* § 3.02[3] (Nell Jessup Newton et al. eds. 2012). The Department of the Interior periodically publishes a list of federally-recognized tribes. For a recent list of the 567 "Indian Entities Recognized and Eligible to Receive Services from the Bureau of Indian Affairs," see 77 Fed. Reg. 47868 (Aug. 10, 2012).

Indian groups not presently recognized as tribes may petition the Bureau of Indian Affairs for acknowledgment under regulations codified at 25 C.F.R. § 83. The key provision is § 83.11 which, *inter alia*, requires petitioning tribes to show three basic elements:

(a) Facts demonstrating that the petitioner has been identified as an American Indian entity on a "substantially continuous" basis since 1900.

(b) Evidence that the petitioner comprises a distinct community and has existed as a community since 1900.

(c) Evidence that the petitioner has maintained political influence or authority over its members as an autonomous entity since 1900 until the present.

In 2015, the Secretary revised the Part 83 acknowledgement regulations, 25 C.F.R. § 83, 80 Fed. Reg. 37,862 (July 21, 2015). The revisions state that the BIA will not require conclusive proof of facts and only "substantially continuous" community or political influence from 1900 is required. Moreover, the government will consider "any and all evidence," including a petitioner's own contemporaneous records. But tribes must meet all seven criteria specified in § 83.11 of the regulations (identification, community, political influence, and so forth.). The bulk of the comments on the revisions concerned the 1900 date, as it is squarely within the allotment/assimilation era. However, the BIA decided that a uniform 1900 date in the case of the "identification" criterion had shown to be workable over two decades, records are generally available from that date, and the agency thought that a uniform date for all the criteria would ease the documentary burden on the petitioners. Nonetheless, a leading treatise has maintained that the federal recognition process is lengthy, expensive, lacking in clear standards and precedents, and "too political. In short, the process is designed to root our fraudulent tribes, but utilizes 18th century ethnocentric conceptions of what an Indian nation appears to be." Matthew L.M. Fletcher, Federal Indian Law 172 (West 2016).

In *Mackinac Tribe v. Jewell,* 829 F.3d 754 (D.C. Cir. 2016), the court affirmed a district court decision that ruled that the tribal petitioner must exhaust its administrative remedies under the BIA's regulations before filing suit claiming federal recognition was warranted. An aspect of federal recognition is the potential for intertribal conflict over scarce resources. In 1997, the Department proposed a finding against recognizing the Chinook Indian Tribe of Washington because it failed to show it functioned as a single social community after 1880 and because it failed to show political authority over its members continuously after 1856. 62 Fed. Reg. 44,714 (Aug. 22, 1997). But in early 2001, the Department reversed itself, primarily on the basis of the new documents and other documents that the tribe claimed the Department ignored in its initial decision. 66 Fed. Reg. 1690 (Jan. 9, 2001). The Department also acknowledged the Cowlitz Indian Tribe. 65 Fed. Reg. 8436 (Feb. 18, 2000). Both the Chinook and Cowlitz acknowledgments were challenged by the Quinault Tribe, which feared that federal recognition could lead to claims on its reservation. Although the Cowlitz Tribe survived this challenge and received recognition, *see* 67 Fed. Reg. 607 (Jan. 4, 2002), the Chinook Tribe did not. 67 Fed. Reg. 46,204 (July 12, 2002). Thus, despite Professor Stephen Dow Beckham's insistence that the Chinook are among the best-documented tribes in the Pacific Northwest, officially the tribe does not exist. Lewis Kamb, *Tribe that Aided Lewis and Clark Now Seeks Help: Lawmakers Try and Reverse Federal Ruling that Deemed Group Extinct*, Seattle Post-Intelligencer, June 2, 2003, WL 2967749l.

D. The Federal Role in Indian Country

The federal role in Indian country is broadly characterized by two main themes. The first is the exercise of federal power, both to regulate the country's relations with the Indian tribes and to exercise authority over Indians and Indian tribes themselves. The second is the federal trust relationship with the Indian tribes, incorporating the notion of federal fiduciary duties toward the tribes. The concepts of federal power and federal responsibilities are intertwined throughout the history of federal Indian law. To complicate matters further, neither the concept of federal power nor the concept of the federal trusteeship has remained constant over time. Both doctrines have shifted meaning, more than once and generally in a symbiotic fashion.

This section begins with the case of *Lone Wolf v. Hitchcock*, one of the foundation cases of the so-called plenary power era of judicial decisions, which roughly corresponded to the allotment era of federal Indian policy. During the plenary power era, the federal government's powers were viewed at their most expansive, and *Lone Wolf* is one of the prime examples of that view. As you read *Lone Wolf*, watch for the interplay of the doctrines of federal power and federal trusteeship.

Lone Wolf v. Hitchcock
187 U.S. 553 (1903)

The provisions in article 12 of the Medicine Lodge treaty of 1867 with the Kiowa and Comanche Indians [are] to the effect that no treaty for the cession of any part of the reservation therein described, which may be held in common, shall be of any force or validity as against the Indians unless executed and signed by at least three fourths of all the adult male Indians occupying the same * * *.

In 1867 a treaty was concluded with the Kiowa and Comanche tribes of Indians, and such other friendly tribes as might be united with them, setting apart a reservation for the use of such Indians. By a separate treaty the Apache tribe of Indians was incorporated with the two former-named, and became entitled to share in the benefits of the reservation. 15 Stat. 581, 589.

The first named treaty is usually called the Medicine Lodge treaty. By the sixth article thereof it was provided that heads of families might select a tract of land within the reservation, not exceeding 320 acres in extent, which should thereafter cease to be held in common, and should be for the exclusive possession of the Indian making the selection, so long as he or his family might continue to cultivate the land....

The three tribes settled under the treaties upon the described land. On October 6, 1892, 456 male adult members of the confederated tribes signed, with three commissioners representing the United States, an agreement concerning the reservation. The Indian agent, in a certificate appended to the agreement, represented that there were then 562 male adults in the three tribes. Four hundred and fifty-six male adults therefore constituted more than three fourths of the certified number of total male adults in the three tribes. In form the agreement was a proposed treaty, the terms of which, in substance, provided for a surrender to the United States of the rights of the tribes in the reservation, for allotments out of such lands to the Indians in severalty, the fee simple title to be conveyed to the allottees or their heirs after the expiration of twenty-five years; and the payment or setting apart for the benefit of the tribes of two million dollars as the consideration for the surplus of land over and above the allotments which might be made to the Indians. * * * Eliminating 350,000 acres of mountainous land, the quantity of surplus lands, suitable for farming and grazing purposes was estimated at 2,150,000 acres.

Soon after the signing of the foregoing agreement it was claimed by the Indians that their assent had been obtained by fraudulent misrepresentations of its terms by the interpreters, and it was asserted that the agreement should not be held binding upon the tribes because three fourths of the adult male members had not assented thereto, as was required by the twelfth article of the Medicine Lodge treaty.

* * * [V]arious bills were introduced in both Houses of Congress designed to give legal effect to the agreement made by the Indians in 1892. These bills were referred to the proper committees, and before such committees the Indians presented their objections to the propriety of giving effect to the agreement.

* * * [The Senate] on January 25, 1899, adopted a resolution calling upon the Secretary of the Interior for information as to whether the signatures attached to the agreement comprised three fourths of the male adults of the tribes. In response the Secretary of the Interior informed the Senate * * * [that] it appeared that there were 725 males over eighteen years of age, of whom 639 were twenty-one years and over." The Secretary further * * * observed:

> "If 18 years and over be held to be the legal age of those who were authorized to sign the agreement, the number of persons who actually signed was 87 less than three fourths of the adult male membership of the tribes; and if 21 years be held to be the minimum age, then 23 less than three fourths signed the agreement. In either event, less than three fourths of the male adults appear to have so signed."

[No bill passed that session.] In the meanwhile, about October, 1899, the Indians had, at a general council at which 571 male adults of the tribes purported to be present, protested against the execution of the provisions of the agreement of 1892, and adopted a memorial to Congress, praying that body should not give effect to the agreement. * * * [With that memorial before it, Congress enacted a statute in 1900 giving effect to the 1892 agreement, although the statute differed from the agreement in a number of respects.]

[Lone Wolf then filed a class action suit on behalf of himself and all other members of the Kiowa, Comanche, and Apache tribes residing in the Territory of Oklahoma, claiming that the statute was invalid because it violated article 12 of the Treaty and because it violated due process. Relief was denied in the courts below.]

MR. JUSTICE WHITE delivered the opinion of the court.

* * * The twelfth article [of the Treaty of Medicine Lodge of 1867, 15 Stat. 581] reads as follows:

> "Article 12. No treaty for the cession of any portion or part of the reservation herein described, which may be held in common, shall be of any

validity or force as against the said Indians, unless executed and signed by at least three fourths of all the adult male Indians occupying the same, and no cession by the tribe shall be understood or construed in such manner as to deprive, without his consent, any individual member of the tribe of his rights to any tract of land selected by him as provided in article III (VI) of this treaty."

The appellants base their right to relief on the proposition that by the effect of the article just quoted the confederated tribes of Kiowas, Comanches and Apaches were vested with an interest in the lands held in common within the reservation, which interest could not be divested by Congress in any other mode than that specified in the said twelfth article, and that as a result of the said stipulation the interest of the Indians in the common lands fell within the protection of the Fifth Amendment to the Constitution of the United States, and such interest—indirectly at least—came under the control of the judicial branch of the government. We are unable to yield our assent to this view.

The contention in effect ignores the status of the contracting Indians and the relation of dependency they bore and continue to bear towards the government of the United States. To uphold the claim would be to adjudge that the indirect operation of the treaty was to materially limit and qualify the controlling authority of Congress in respect to the care and protection of the Indians, and to deprive Congress, in a possible emergency, when the necessity might be urgent for a partition and disposal of the tribal lands, of the power to act, if the assent of the Indians could not be obtained.

Now, it is true that in decisions of this court, the Indian right of occupancy of tribal lands, whether declared in a treaty or otherwise created, has been stated to be sacred, or as sometimes expressed, as sacred as the fee of the United States in the same lands. But in none of these cases was there involved a controversy between Indians and the government respecting the power of Congress to administer the property of the Indians. The questions considered in the cases referred to, which either directly or indirectly had relation to the nature of the property rights of the Indians, concerned the character and extent of such rights as respected States or individuals. In one of the cited cases it was clearly pointed out that Congress possessed a paramount power over the property of the Indians, by reason of its exercise of guardianship over their interests, and that such authority might be implied, even though opposed to the strict letter of a treaty with the Indians.

Plenary authority over the tribal relations of the Indians has been exercised by Congress from the beginning, and the power has always been deemed a political one, not subject to be controlled by the judicial department of the government. Until the year 1871 the policy was pursued of dealing with the Indian tribes by means of treaties, and, of course, a moral obligation rested upon Congress to act in good faith in performing the stipulations entered into on its behalf. But, as with treaties made with foreign nations, the legislative power might pass laws in conflict with treaties made with the Indians.

The power exists to abrogate the provisions of an Indian treaty, though presumably such power will be exercised only when circumstances arise which will not only justify the government in disregarding the stipulations of the treaty, but may demand, in the interest of the country and the Indians themselves, that it should do so. When, therefore, treaties were entered into between the United States and a tribe of Indians it was never doubted that the power to abrogate existed in Congress, and that in a contingency such power might be availed of from considerations of governmental policy, particularly if consistent with perfect good faith towards the Indians. In *United States v. Kagama*, (1885) 118 U.S. 375, speaking of the Indians, the court said * * *:

> "It seems to us that this is within the competency of Congress. These Indian tribes are the wards of the nation. They are communities dependent on the United States. Dependent largely for their daily food. Dependent for their political rights. They owe no allegiance to the States, and receive from them no protection. Because of the local ill feeling, the people of the States where they are found are often their deadliest enemies. From their very weakness and helplessness, so largely due to the course of dealing of the Federal government with them and the treaties in which it has been promised, there arises the duty of protection, and with it the power. This has always been recognized by the Executive and by Congress, and by this court, whenever the question has arisen.
>
> "The power of the general government over these remnants of a race once powerful, now weak and diminished in numbers, is necessary to their protection, as well as to the safety of those among whom they dwell. It must exist in that government, because it never has existed anywhere else, because the theatre of its exercise is within the geographical limits of the United States, because it has never been denied, and because it alone can enforce its laws on all the tribes."

In view of the legislative power possessed by Congress over treaties with the Indians and Indian tribal property, we may not specially consider the contentions pressed upon our notice that the signing by the Indians of the agreement of October 6, 1892, was obtained by fraudulent misrepresentations and concealment, that the requisite three fourths of adult male Indians had not signed, as required by the twelfth article of the treaty of 1867, and that the treaty as signed had been amended by Congress without submitting such amendments to the action of the Indians, since all these matters, in any event, were solely within the domain of the legislative authority and its action is conclusive upon the courts.

The act of June 6, 1900, which is complained of in the bill, was enacted at a time when the tribal relations between the confederated tribes of Kiowas, Comanches and Apaches still existed, and that statute and the statutes supplementary thereto dealt with the disposition of tribal property and purported to give an adequate consideration for the surplus lands not allotted among the Indians or reserved for their benefit. Indeed, the controversy which this case presents is concluded by the decision in *Cherokee Nation v. Hitchcock*, 187 U.S. 294, decided at this term, where it was held that full administrative power was possessed by Congress over Indian tribal property. In effect, the action of Congress now complained of was but an exercise of such power, a mere change in the form of investment of Indian tribal property, the property of those who, as we have held, were in substantial effect the wards of the government. We must presume that Congress acted in perfect good faith in the dealings with the Indians of which complaint is made, and that the legislative branch of the government exercised its best judgment in the premises. In any event, as Congress possessed full power in the matter, the judiciary cannot question or inquire into the motives which prompted the enactment of this legislation. If injury was occasioned, which we do not wish to be understood as implying, by the use made by Congress of its power, relief must be sought by an appeal to that body for redress and not to the courts. The legislation in question was constitutional, and the demurrer to the bill was therefore rightly sustained.

[F]or the reasons previously given and the nature of the controversy, we think the decree below should be affirmed.

Notes

1. The effect of treaties. Why is it that treaties do not bind Congress? Why can't the Court consider whether an agreement to dispose of tribal lands was fraudulently obtained? What did the Court assume about the exercise of congressional power?

2. A mere change in investment? What did the Court mean when it said that Congress merely changed "the form of investment of Indian tribal property"? Are tribal lands investments in the same sense as, say, stock portfolios?

3. Critiques of the *Lone Wolf* decision. For critiques from a variety of perspectives, see *Symposium:* Lone Wolf v. Hitchcock: *One Hundred Years Later*, 38 Tulsa L. Rev. 1–157 (2002).

Note on Federal Power over Indians

The courts have consistently deferred to other branches of government concerning challenges to federal authority over Indian affairs. In part this is due to history. At the founding, Indian tribes were a threat to the national government and often sided with foreign powers. Thus, since Congress and the Executive dealt with the tribes as foreign nations, Indian affairs was a branch of foreign affairs. Consequently, the courts gave deference to the political branches under what is known as the "political question" doctrine. This deference allowed the courts to avoid challenges to federal policies regulating the amount of contact between the Indians and whites along the frontier and controlling the acquisition of Indian land, arguably reducing conflicts that could have produced more bloodshed than which occurred.

Even after the tribes were no longer a national security threat to the United States, the courts persisted in sustaining nearly every challenge to federal legislation regulating Indian tribes. Under what became known as the "plenary power" doctrine, the courts continued to defer to the political branches. As Professor (now Dean) Nell

Jessup Newton noted, the plenary power and political question doctrines were "not so much justifications for decisional outcomes as they are restatements of the Court's intent to defer to other branches of government and, concomitantly, to abdicate any role in defining the unique status of Indian tribes in our constitutional system or accommodating their legitimate claims of tribal sovereignty and preservation of property." Nell Jessup Newton, *Federal Power over Indians: Its Sources, Scope, and Limitations*, 132 U. Pa. L. Rev. 195, 196 (1984). The plenary power doctrine has been subjected to withering criticism by Professor Robert Clinton, who claimed it was a complete fabrication, untethered to any constitutional grant of authority. Robert N. Clinton, *There is No Federal Supremacy Over Indian Tribes*, 34 Ariz. St. L.J. 113 (2002) (asserting that the doctrine — which was invoked as a source of broad and unilateral federal authority over Indian affairs — is not only extra-constitutional, but was the product of deeply-rooted late-nineteenth century notions of racial superiority and racial hegemony).

Although the racist overtones of the plenary power doctrine have been expunged from recent judicial decisions, and the notion that Indian affairs is a political question beyond the judiciary's power to review has been repudiated, the courts have largely rejected tribal efforts to challenge federal authority or to suggest that the federal authority to control and manage tribal natural resources imposes fiduciary duties on the government. According to Professor Newton, "vestiges of the judicial attitude of nonintervention developed and nurture in the plenary power era remain, especially in the areas of tribal sovereignty and property rights," where the Supreme Court seems to recognize an almost unlimited inherent federal power over Indian affairs. The Court's deference to Congress on these matters, Professor Newton asserted, "appears in the modern cases not as a refusal to address the merits of a claim but in the refusal to find any merit in the claim addressed." Newton, 132 U. Pa. L. Rev. at 233 (explaining that the Court has indicated that tribal sovereignty exists only at the "sufferance" of Congress, and that the Court recognizes the "paramount power" of Congress over tribal property).

Given that the plenary power doctrine arose out of colonial attitude of racial and cultural superiority, that the colonial attitude has long since been repudiated, and that federal policy for the last forty years has been to promote tribal self-determination, why should the Supreme Court continue to adhere to this position of judicial deference? As Professor Newton noted, the dangers of extreme judicial deference are real. "[T]he Court's continued failure to attempt to define the extent of Congress's power over Indian affairs has encouraged further undue assertions of that power. If congressional policy were to shift again to one of forced assimilation, legislators might not be blamed for thinking the Court would place no limits on their actions." Newton, 132 U. Pa. L. Rev. at 236.

Notes on the Trust Doctrine

1. The federal trust responsibility to Indian tribes. The foremost treatise in Indian law explains that: "One of the basic principles in Indian law is that the federal government has a trust or special relationship with Indian tribes. Courts have invoked language of guardian and ward, or more recently trustee and beneficiary, to describe this relationship in a variety of legal settings." Cohen's Handbook of Federal Indian Law § 5.04[3][a] (Nell Jessup Newton et al. eds. 2012).

2. **The origins of the trust responsibility.** The origins of the federal trust relationship are most commonly traced to the *Cherokee Cases*, which are excerpted in Chapter II, Section B. In particular, in *Cherokee Nation v. Georgia* the Court coined the term "domestic dependent nations" to describe the status of Indian tribes, and stated that the relationship between the tribes and the federal government "resembles that of a ward to his guardian." 30 U.S. 1, 17 (1831). Early treaties too used language of federal protection, commonly providing that the tribe acknowledged itself to be under the protection of the United States "and of no other sovereign whosoever." Treaty with the Cherokee, 1875, art. III, 7 Stat.18.

3. **Evolution of the trust doctrine.** Professor Mary Wood has described the trusteeship of the early period of federal-Indian relations as a "sovereign trusteeship," aimed at protecting the separatism and sovereignty of the Indian tribes. Mary Christina Wood, *Indian Land and the Promise of Native Sovereignty: The Trust Doctrine Revisited*, 1994 Utah L. Rev. 1471, 1498. She posits that this concept of the trust relationship was "forcefully articulated" in *Worcester v. Georgia* in 1832. She then traces the fate of the trusteeship during the plenary power era:

> Just a half-century after *Worcester*, the Supreme Court defined a set of parameters to determine federal-tribal relations in a way that greatly obscured the native sovereignty basis for the trusteeship. In *United States v. Kagama* [118 U.S. 375 (1886)], the Court considered whether the federal government had authority to extend its criminal jurisdiction into Indian Country—a consequence which would unquestionably intrude into tribal sovereignty. Finding no such authority in the Constitution, the Court tapped the dependency relationship [that developed during the nineteenth century] and the duty of protection as an independent source of federal authority over the tribes:
>
>> These Indian tribes *are* the wards of the nation. They are communities *dependent* on the United States. . . . From their very weakness and helplessness, so largely due to the course of dealing of the Federal Government with them and the treaties in which it has been promised, there arises the duty of protection, and with it the power.
>
> *Kagama* brought forth what is now known as the "plenary power" doctrine to justify nearly total federal authority over tribal lands and internal tribal governance, even though such authority lacks any textual basis in the Constitution or treaties. The doctrine is essentially a judicial ratification of what, as a practical matter, amounted to considerable federal power over the tribes after decades of relentless subjugation. *Kagama*'s plenary power doctrine is perhaps best understood as a judicial approach which defines native rights

by their tragic violations. After *Kagama*, what was earlier conceived as a sovereign trusteeship giving rise to affirmative national obligations became obscured by new rhetoric that described federal plenary power resting on a guardian-ward relationship.

The *Kagama* and *Worcester* cases, then, suggest very distinct paradigms resting at opposite ends of the spectrum of federal-Indian relations. At one end is the sovereign trust model which presumes native sovereignty and very limited federal power, and obligates the federal government to protect the separatism of the native nations. At the other end of the spectrum is the *Kagama* "guardian-ward" model which draws on tribal dependency and the federal duty of protection to support nearly unchecked federal power over tribes, including power over their internal governments. The *Kagama* model is directed less at assuring viable separatism and more toward promoting assimilation.

* * * In evaluating contemporary use of the trust doctrine, it is important to note that, while many modern cases refer to the "guardian-ward" relationship in describing federal-Indian relations, the *Kagama* case did not wholly displace *Worcester*'s sovereign trust model. Rather, the *Worcester* and *Kagama* cases have left coexisting, if confused, legacies.

* * * [I]t is critical to delink the trust doctrine and the plenary power doctrine. Notions of federal responsibility existed long before *Kagama*, and a sovereign trust paradigm such as the one suggested in *Worcester* would support federal responsibility apart from unfettered federal dominion.

* * * [A]ny effort to "decolonize" federal Indian law by dismantling the notion of plenary power should not correspondingly destroy the notion of continuing federal obligations which benefit the tribes. * * * The trust responsibility should be recognized as a doctrine of federal restraint, not permission, and as an important source of protection for Indian rights.

Id. at 1502–05, 1507–08.

Professor Lincoln Davis has suggested that tribal sovereignty and the federal trust are not reconcilable, that the former is "morally, historically, and politically" superior, and that a better model to promote native sovereignty would be to allow tribes to be treated as states. Lincoln L. Davis, *Skull Valley Crossroads: Reconciling Native Sovereignty and the Federal Trust*, 68 Md. L. Rev. 290 (2009) (concerning a proposal to store high-level nuclear waste on tribal land).

4. The modern trust doctrine. Beginning in the mid-twentieth century, the concept of the trust doctrine began to shift away from that exemplified in *Lone Wolf*. The notion of Indian affairs as a political question, with unreviewable congressional authority, was modified. Congressional action today is subject to constitutional challenges, *see, e.g., United States v. Sioux Nation*, 448 U.S. 371 (1980) (5th amendment takings of land), excerpted at page 145, as well as interpretive rules designed to ensure that Congress intended to adversely impact tribal rights. *See, e.g., United States* *v. Dion*, 476 U.S. 734 (1986), excerpted at page 535. Perhaps the most significant change, however, was the development of the breach of trust action against federal administrative authority, turning the trust doctrine into a sword that tribes could, with varied success, wield against federal agencies. This aspect of the trust doctrine is explored in Chapter V.

5. The trust status of Indian lands. The trust doctrine has particular application to Indian lands and resources. Most tribal lands, and millions of acres of allotted lands, are held in trust for the Indian owners by the federal government. Title vests in the United States, with beneficial ownership in the tribe or the individual allottee. Trust lands may not be alienated, encumbered, or otherwise restricted without the express authorization of the federal government. *See generally* Cohen's Handbook of Federal Indian Law §§ 15.03, 15.06 (Nell Jessup Newton, et al. eds. LexisNexis 2012).

E. Indian Country

1. Scope and Extent of Indian Country

Note on Indian Country

For the most part, the doctrines of federal Indian law apply geographically: that is, within "Indian country." Outside Indian country, state law is generally applicable to Indians as to anyone else. "Absent express federal law to the contrary, Indians going beyond reservation boundaries have generally been held subject to nondiscriminatory state law otherwise applicable to all citizens of the State." *Mescalero Apache Tribe v. Jones*, 411 U.S. 145 (1973). Within the territory known as Indian country, however, the application of state law is limited. In Indian country, federal and tribal law generally prevail.

That statement, however, provides only a starting point for the analysis of jurisdiction involving Indians and Indian tribes. In some instances, federal laws applicable to Native Americans apply anywhere in the country. *See*, *e.g.*, the Indian Child Welfare Act of 1978, 25 U.S.C. § 1901 *et seq*. In rare instances, generally where tribes have expressly reserved rights in treaties and agreements, tribal authority extends outside Indian country. *See* Chapter VIII. In addition, tribal sovereign immunity from suit without congressional consent or tribal waiver runs to the tribe, not the tribe's Indian country, and thus applies to tribal actions taken outside Indian country as well as within tribal territories. *Kiowa Tribe v. Manufacturing Technologies, Inc.*, 523 U.S. 751 (1998); see also *Michigan v. Bay Mills Indian Community*, 134 S. Ct. 2024 (2014) (barring a state suit challenging a tribal casino on lands purchased by the tribe under a land trust on grounds of tribal sovereign immunity). And while state authority in Indian country has been historically limited, recent Supreme Court decisions have permitted increasing state jurisdiction within tribal territories. *See* Chapter IV, Section A.

"Indian country" is defined at 18 U.S.C. § 1151:

> [T]he term "Indian country" as used in this chapter means (a) all land within the limits of any Indian reservation under the jurisdiction of the United States Government, notwithstanding the issuance of any patent, and, including rights-of-way running through the reservation, (b) all dependent Indian communities within the borders of the United States whether within the original or subsequently acquired territory thereof, and whether within or without the limits of a state, and (c) all Indian allotments, the Indian titles to which have not been extinguished, including rights-of-way running through the same.

Although the definition is contained in the federal criminal code, the Supreme Court has stated that the definition "also generally applies to questions of civil jurisdiction." *Alaska v. Native Village of Venetie Tribal Government*, 522 U.S. 520, 527 (1998).

The following cases focus on the statutory definition of Indian country. The first case looks at § 1151(a): If Indian country includes all land within a reservation, what constitutes a "reservation"?

Oklahoma Tax Comm'n v. Sac and Fox Nation
508 U.S. 114 (1993)

JUSTICE O'CONNOR delivered the opinion of the Court.

In this case, we consider whether the State of Oklahoma may impose income taxes or motor vehicle taxes on the members of the Sac and Fox Nation.

I

The Sac and Fox Nation (Tribe) is a federally recognized Indian tribe located in the State of Oklahoma. Until the mid-eighteenth century, the Tribe lived in the Great Lakes region of the United States. In 1789, it entered into its first treaty with the United States and ceded much of its land. That was only the first of many agreements between the Government and the Tribe in which the Tribe surrendered its land and moved elsewhere. As part of its gradual, treaty-imposed migration, the Tribe stopped briefly along the Mississippi and Missouri Rivers in what are now the States of Illinois, Missouri, Iowa, and Nebraska. In the mid-nineteenth century, the Sac and Fox Nation ceded land in several States for two reservations in Kansas, but the Government eventually asked it to cede these as well. In 1867, the Sac and Fox Nation moved for the final time to the Sac and Fox Reservation in Indian Territory.

By the 1880s, however, white settlers increasingly clamored for the land the Sac and Fox and other tribes held in Indian Territory. In response, Congress passed two statutes that greatly affected the Tribe: the General Allotment Act (Dawes Act), which provided for allotting reservation land to individual tribal members and purchasing the surplus land for the use of white settlers; and the Oklahoma Territory Organic

Act, which established the Oklahoma Territory in what is now the western half of the State of Oklahoma. This new Oklahoma Territory included the Sac and Fox Nation's Reservation. In June 1890, the Government and the Tribe concluded their final treaty—a treaty designed to effectuate the provisions of the Dawes Act. Congress ratified the treaty in 1891 (hereinafter 1891 Treaty). Concerning the Tribe's cession of land, the 1891 Treaty states:

> "ARTICLE I. The said the Sac and Fox Nation hereby cedes, conveys, transfers, surrenders and forever relinquishes to the United States of America, all their title, claim or interest, of every kind or character, in and to the following described tract of land or country, in the Indian Territory, to-wit: [the Reservation land granted the Tribe in the Treaty of 1867].
>
> "Provided however the quarter section of land on which is now located the Sac and Fox Agency shall not pass to the United States by this cession, conveyance, transfer, surrender and relinquishment, but shall remain the property of said Sac and Fox Nation, to the full extent that it is now the property of said Nation—subject only to the rights of the United States therein, by reason of said Agency being located thereon, and subject to the rights, legal and equitable, of those persons that are now legally located thereon.... And the section of land now designated and set apart near the Sac and Fox Agency, for a school and farm, shall not be subject either to allotment to an Indian or to homestead entry under the laws of the United States—but shall remain as it now is and kept for school and farming purposes, so long as said Sac and Fox Nation shall so use the same...."

Under the 1891 Treaty, the Tribe retained the 800 acres discussed in the proviso. Each of the Tribe's members, adults and minors, had the right to choose an allotment of one quarter section (160 acres) within the boundaries of the ceded land.

Today, the Sac and Fox Nation has approximately 2,500 members. It has a fully functioning tribal government with its headquarters on the 800 acres reserved to it under the 1891 Treaty. The United States recognizes and encourages the Tribe's sovereign right to self-governance within "the family of governments in the federal constitutional system." Compact of Self-Governance Between the Sac and Fox Nation and the United States of America 2 (June 26, 1991), see 25 U.S.C. §5321 (formerly §450). To this end, the Tribe has a Constitution and a Code of Laws, as well as a court system in which to enforce them. It employs approximately 140 to 150 people, most of whom are tribal members.

[The State of Oklahoma sought to impose its income tax on employees of the Tribe, and to impose its motor vehicle taxes on tribal members who lived and garaged their cars within Sac and Fox territory. The tribe claimed immunity from the state taxes. The district court held for the tribe, and the Tenth Circuit affirmed, rejecting the state's argument that tribal immunity to state taxation applied only within the boundaries of established reservations, 967 F.2d 1425 (10th Cir. 1992).]

II A

In *McClanahan v. Arizona State Tax Comm'n*, 411 U.S. 164 (1973), we held that a State was without jurisdiction to subject a tribal member living on the reservation, and whose income derived from reservation sources, to a state income tax absent an express authorization from Congress. The Commission contends that the *McClanahan* presumption against jurisdiction comes into effect only when the income is earned from reservation sources by a tribal member residing on the reservation. Under the Commission's reading of *McClanahan*, the District Court erred in not determining whether the Sac and Fox Reservation has been disestablished or reduced because unless the members of the Sac and Fox Nation live on a reservation the State has jurisdiction to tax their earnings and their vehicles. The Commission is partially correct: The residence of a tribal member is a significant component of the *McClanahan* presumption against state tax jurisdiction. But our cases make clear that a tribal member need not live on a formal reservation to be outside the State's taxing jurisdiction; it is enough that the member live in "Indian country." Congress has defined Indian country broadly to include formal and informal reservations, dependent Indian communities, and Indian allotments, whether restricted or held in trust by the United States. *See* 18 U.S.C. § 1151.

Our decision in *McClanahan* relied heavily on the doctrine of tribal sovereignty. We found a "deeply rooted" policy in our Nation's history of "leaving Indians free from state jurisdiction and control." Indian nations, we noted, long have been "'distinct political communities, having territorial boundaries, within which their authority is exclusive.'" The Indian sovereignty doctrine, which historically gave state law "no role to play" within a tribe's territorial boundaries, did not provide "a definitive resolution of the issues," but it did "provide a backdrop against which the applicable treaties and federal statutes must be read." Although "exemptions from tax laws should, as a general rule, be clearly expressed," the tradition of Indian sovereignty requires that the rule be reversed when a State attempts to assert tax jurisdiction over an Indian tribe or tribal members living and working on land set aside for those members.

To determine whether a tribal member is exempt from state income taxes under *McClanahan*, a court first must determine the residence of that tribal member. To the extent that the Court of Appeals ruled without such a reference, it erred. The Commission, however, contends that the relevant boundary for taxing jurisdiction is the perimeter of a formal reservation, not merely land set aside for a tribe or its members. In the Commission's view, Indian sovereignty serves as a "backdrop" only for those tribal members who live on the reservation, and all others fall outside *McClanahan*'s presumption against taxation. It is true that we began our discussion in *McClanahan* by emphasizing that we were not "dealing with Indians who have left or never inhabited reservations set aside for their exclusive use or who do not possess the usual accouterments of tribal self-government." Here, in contrast, some of the Tribe's members may not live within a reservation; indeed, if the Commission's interpretation of the 1891 Treaty is correct and the Reservation was disestablished, none do.

Nonetheless, in *Oklahoma Tax Comm'n v. Citizen Band Potawatomi Indian Tribe of Okla.*, [498 U.S. 505 (1991)], we rejected precisely the same argument—and from precisely the same litigant. There the Commission contended that even if the State did not have jurisdiction to tax cigarette sales to tribal members on the reservation, it had jurisdiction to tax sales by a tribal convenience store located outside the reservation on land held in trust for the Potawatomi. We noted that we have never drawn the distinction Oklahoma urged. Instead, we ask only whether the land is Indian country.

On remand, it must be determined whether the relevant tribal members live in Indian country—whether the land is within reservation boundaries, on allotted lands, or in dependent communities. If the tribal members do live in Indian country, our cases require the court to analyze the relevant treaties and federal statutes against the backdrop of Indian sovereignty. Unless Congress expressly authorized tax jurisdiction in Indian country, the *McClanahan* presumption counsels against finding such jurisdiction. Because all of the tribal members earning income from the Tribe may live within Indian country, we need not determine whether the Tribe's right to self-governance could operate independently of its territorial jurisdiction to preempt the State's ability to tax income earned from work performed for the Tribe itself when the employee does not reside in Indian country.

B

The Commission also argues that the Court of Appeals erred in holding that the State could not impose state motor vehicle taxes on tribal members who live on tribal land, garage their cars principally on tribal land, and register their vehicles with the Tribe. * * * That argument fails for the same reasons it fails with regard to income taxes.

III

Absent explicit congressional direction to the contrary, we presume against a State's having the jurisdiction to tax within Indian country, whether the particular territory consists of a formal or informal reservation, allotted lands, or dependent Indian communities. Because the Court of Appeals did not determine whether the tribal members on whom Oklahoma attempts to impose its income and motor vehicle taxes live in Indian country, its judgment is vacated. We remand this case for further proceedings consistent with this opinion.

Note on the Definition of Reservation

If a reservation for purposes of § 1151(a) includes "informal" as well as "formal" reservations, what then is an informal reservation? In *Oklahoma Tax Comm'n v. Citizen Band Potawatomi Indian Tribe of Oklahoma*, 498 U.S. 505 (1991), relied on in *Sac and Fox*, the Court stated:

The State contends that the Potawatomis' cigarette sales do not, in fact, occur on a "reservation." Relying upon our decision in *Mescalero Apache Tribe v. Jones*, 411 U.S. 145 (1973), Oklahoma argues that the tribal convenience store should be held subject to State tax laws because it does not operate on a formally designated "reservation," but on land held in trust for the Potawatomis. Neither *Mescalero* nor any other precedent of this Court has ever drawn the distinction between tribal trust land and reservations that Oklahoma urges. In *United States v. John*, 437 U.S. 634 (1978), we stated that the test for determining whether land is Indian country does not turn upon whether that land is denominated "trust land" or "reservation." Rather, we ask whether the area has been "validly set apart for the use of the Indians as such, under the superintendence of the Government."

* * * As in *John*, we find that this trust land is "validly set apart" and thus qualifies as a reservation for tribal immunity purposes.

Does this mean that all land held in trust for an Indian tribe is Indian country?

Alaska v. Native Village of Venetie Tribal Government
522 U.S. 520 (1998)

Justice THOMAS delivered the opinion of the Court.

In this case, we must decide whether approximately 1.8 million acres of land in northern Alaska, owned in fee simple by the Native Village of Venetie Tribal Government pursuant to the Alaska Native Claims Settlement Act, 43 U.S.C. § 1601 *et seq.*, is "Indian country." We conclude that it is not, and we therefore reverse the judgment below.

I

The Village of Venetie, which is located in Alaska above the Arctic Circle, is home to the Neets'aii Gwich'in Indians. In 1943, the Secretary of the Interior created a reservation for the Neets'aii Gwich'in out of the land surrounding Venetie and another nearby tribal village, Arctic Village. This land, which is about the size of Delaware, remained a reservation until 1971, when Congress enacted the Alaska Native Claims Settlement Act (ANCSA), a comprehensive statute designed to settle all land claims by Alaska Natives.

In enacting ANCSA, Congress sought to end the sort of federal supervision over Indian affairs that had previously marked federal Indian policy. ANCSA's text states that the settlement of the land claims was to be accomplished

> "without litigation, with maximum participation by Natives in decisions affecting their rights and property, without establishing any permanent racially defined institutions, rights, privileges, or obligations, [and] without creating a reservation system or lengthy wardship or trusteeship."

To this end, ANCSA revoked "the various reserves set aside . . . for Native use" by legislative or executive action, except for the Annette Island Reserve inhabited by the

Metlakatla Indians, and completely extinguished all aboriginal claims to Alaska land. In return, Congress authorized the transfer of $962.5 million in federal funds and approximately 44 million acres of Alaska land to state-chartered private business corporations that were to be formed pursuant to the statute; all of the shareholders of these corporations were required to be Alaska Natives. The ANCSA corporations received title to the transferred land in fee simple, and no federal restrictions applied to subsequent land transfers by them.

Pursuant to ANCSA, two Native corporations were established for the Neets'aii Gwich'in, one in Venetie, and one in Arctic Village. In 1973, those corporations elected to make use of a provision in ANCSA allowing Native corporations to take title to former reservation lands set aside for Indians prior to 1971, in return for forgoing the statute's monetary payments and transfers of nonreservation land. The United States conveyed fee simple title to the land constituting the former Venetie Reservation to the two corporations as tenants in common; thereafter, the corporations transferred title to the land to the Native Village of Venetie Tribal Government (the Tribe).

[In 1986, the Tribe sought to collect its business activities tax from a private contractor which, pursuant to a joint venture with the State of Alaska, was constructing a public school in Venetie. The State filed suit in federal district court to enjoin collection of the tax. The district court concluded that ANCSA extinguished Indian Country, even though the village was a federally recognized tribe. The Ninth Circuit reversed, concluding that the village constituted a "dependent Indian community" within Indian Country, 101 F.3d 1286 (9th Cir. 1996).]

II A

"Indian country" is currently defined at 18 U.S.C. § 1151. * * * Because ANCSA revoked the Venetie Reservation, and because no Indian allotments are at issue, whether the Tribe's land is Indian country depends on whether it falls within the "dependent Indian communities" prong of the statute. Since 18 U.S.C. § 1151 was enacted in 1948, we have not had an occasion to interpret the term "dependent Indian communities." We now hold that it refers to a limited category of Indian lands that are neither reservations nor allotments, and that satisfy two requirements — first, they must have been set aside by the Federal Government for the use of the Indians as Indian land; second, they must be under federal superintendence. Our holding is based on our conclusion that in enacting § 1151, Congress codified these two requirements, which previously we had held necessary for a finding of "Indian country" generally.

Before § 1151 was enacted, we held in three cases that Indian lands that were not reservations could be Indian country and that the Federal Government could therefore exercise jurisdiction over them. *See United States v. Sandoval*, 231 U.S. 28 (1913); *United States v. Pelican*, 232 U.S. 442 (1914); *United States v. McGowan*, 302 U.S. 535 (1938). The first of these cases, *United States v. Sandoval*, posed the question whether the Federal Government could constitutionally proscribe the introduction of "intoxicating liquor" into the lands of the Pueblo Indians. We rejected the contention that federal power could not extend to the Pueblo lands because, unlike Indians living on reservations, the Pueblos owned their lands in fee simple. We indicated that the Pueblos' title was not fee simple title in the commonly understood sense of the term. Congress had recognized the Pueblos' title to their ancestral lands by statute, and Executive orders had reserved additional public lands "for the [Pueblos'] use and occupancy." In addition, Congress had enacted legislation with respect to the lands "in the exercise of the Government's guardianship over th[e] [Indian] tribes and their affairs," including federal restrictions on the lands' alienation. Congress therefore could exercise jurisdiction over the Pueblo lands, under its general power over "all dependent Indian communities within its borders, whether within its original territory or territory subsequently acquired, and whether within or without the limits of a State."

In *United States v. Pelican*, we held that Indian allotments—parcels of land created out of a diminished Indian reservation and held in trust by the Federal Government for the benefit of individual Indians—were Indian country. We stated that the original reservation was Indian country "simply because it had been validly set apart for the use of the Indians as such, under the superintendence of the Government." After the reservation's diminishment, the allotments continued to be Indian country, as "the lands remained Indian lands set apart for Indians under governmental care; ... we are unable to find ground for the conclusion that they became other than Indian country through the distribution into separate holdings, the Government retaining control."

In *United States v. McGowan*, we held that the Reno Indian Colony in Reno, Nevada was Indian country even though it was not a reservation. We reasoned that, like Indian reservations generally, the Colony had been "'validly set apart for the use of the Indians ... under the superintendence of the Government.'" We noted that the Federal Government had created the Colony by purchasing the land with "funds appropriated by Congress" and that the Federal Government held the Colony's land in trust for the benefit of the Indians residing there. We also emphasized that the Federal Government possessed the authority to enact "regulations and protective laws respecting th[e] [Colony's] territory," which it had exercised in retaining title to the land and permitting the Indians to live there. For these reasons, a federal statute requiring the forfeiture of automobiles carrying "intoxicants" into the Indian country applied to the Colony; we noted that the law was an example of the protections that Congress had extended to all "dependent Indian communities" within the territory of the United States.

In each of these cases, therefore, we relied upon a finding of both a federal set-aside and federal superintendence in concluding that the Indian lands in question constituted Indian country and that it was permissible for the Federal Government to exercise jurisdiction over them. Section 1151 does not purport to alter this definition of Indian country, but merely lists the three different categories of Indian country mentioned in our prior cases: Indian reservations, see *Donnelly v. United States*,

228 U.S. 243, 269 (1913); dependent Indian communities, see *United States v. McGowan, supra*, at 538–539; *United States v. Sandoval, supra*, at 46; and allotments, see *United States v. Pelican, supra*, at 449. The entire text of § 1151(b), and not just the term "dependent Indian communities," is taken virtually verbatim from *Sandoval*, which language we later quoted in *McGowan*. Moreover, the Historical and Revision Notes to the statute that enacted § 1151 state that § 1151's definition of Indian country is based "on [the] latest construction of the term by the United States Supreme Court in *U.S. v. McGowan* . . . following *U.S. v. Sandoval. (See also Donnelly v. U.S.)*. . . . Indian allotments were included in the definition on authority of the case of *U.S. v. Pelican*."

We therefore must conclude that in enacting § 1151(b), Congress indicated that a federal set-aside and a federal superintendence requirement must be satisfied for a finding of a "dependent Indian community"—just as those requirements had to be met for a finding of Indian country before 18 U.S.C. § 1151 was enacted.[5] These requirements are reflected in the text of § 1151(b): The federal set-aside requirement ensures that the land in question is occupied by an "Indian community";[6] the federal superintendence requirement guarantees that the Indian community is sufficiently "dependent" on the Federal Government that the Federal Government and the Indians involved, rather than the States, are to exercise primary jurisdiction over the land in question.

B

The Tribe's ANCSA lands do not satisfy either of these requirements. After the enactment of ANCSA, the Tribe's lands are neither "validly set apart for the use of the Indians as such," nor are they under the superintendence of the Federal Government.

With respect to the federal set-aside requirement, it is significant that ANCSA, far from designating Alaskan lands for Indian use, revoked the existing Venetie Reservation, and indeed revoked all existing reservations in Alaska "set aside by legislation or by Executive or Secretarial Order for Native use," save one. In no clearer

---

5. * * * [T]he Tribe asks us to adopt a different conception of the term "dependent Indian communities." Borrowing from Chief Justice Marshall's seminal opinions in *Cherokee Nation v. Georgia* and *Worcester v. Georgia*, the Tribe argues that the term refers to political dependence, and that Indian country exists wherever land is owned by a federally recognized tribe. Federally recognized tribes, the Tribe contends, are "dependent domestic nations," and thus ipso facto under the superintendence of the Federal Government.

This argument ignores our Indian country precedents, which indicate both that the Federal Government must take some action setting apart the land for the use of the Indians "as such," and that it is the land in question, and not merely the Indian tribe inhabiting it, that must be under the superintendence of the Federal Government.

6. The federal set-aside requirement also reflects the fact that because Congress has plenary power over Indian affairs, *see* U.S. Const., Art. I, § 8, cl. 3, some explicit action by Congress (or the Executive, acting under delegated authority) must be taken to create or to recognize Indian country.

fashion could Congress have departed from its traditional practice of setting aside Indian lands.

The Tribe argues—and the Court of Appeals majority agreed—that the ANCSA lands were set apart for the use of the Neets'aii Gwich'in, "as such," because the Neets'aii Gwich'in acquired the lands pursuant to an ANCSA provision allowing Natives to take title to former reservation lands in return for forgoing all other ANCSA transfers. The difficulty with this contention is that ANCSA transferred reservation lands to private, state-chartered Native corporations, without any restraints on alienation or significant use restrictions, and with the goal of avoiding "any permanent racially defined institutions, rights, privileges, or obligations." By ANCSA's very design, Native corporations can immediately convey former reservation lands to non-Natives, and such corporations are not restricted to using those lands for Indian purposes. Because Congress contemplated that non-Natives could own the former Venetie Reservation, and because the Tribe is free to use it for non-Indian purposes, we must conclude that the federal set-aside requirement is not met. *Cf. United States v. McGowan*, 302 U.S. at 538 (noting that the land constituting the Reno Indian Colony was held in trust by the Federal Government for the benefit of the Indians); *see also United States v. Pelican*, 232 U.S. at 447 (noting federal restraints on the alienation of the allotments in question).

Equally clearly, ANCSA ended federal superintendence over the Tribe's lands. As noted above, ANCSA revoked the Venetie Reservation along with every other reservation in Alaska but one, and Congress stated explicitly that ANCSA's settlement provisions were intended to avoid a "lengthy wardship or trusteeship." After ANCSA, federal protection of the Tribe's land is essentially limited to a statutory declaration that the land is exempt from adverse possession claims, real property taxes, and certain judgments as long as it has not been sold, leased, or developed. These protections, if they can be called that, simply do not approach the level of superintendence over the Indians' land that existed in our prior cases. In each of those cases, the Federal Government actively controlled the lands in question, effectively acting as a guardian for the Indians. *See United States v. McGowan, supra*, at 537–539 (emphasizing that the Federal Government had retained title to the land to protect the Indians living there); *United States v. Pelican, supra*, at 447 (stating that the allotments were "under the jurisdiction and control of Congress for all governmental purposes, relating to the guardianship and protection of the Indians"); *United States v. Sandoval*, 231 U.S. at 37, n.1 (citing federal statute placing the Pueblos' land under the "'absolute jurisdiction and control of the Congress of the United States'"). Finally, it is worth noting that Congress conveyed ANCSA lands to state-chartered and state-regulated private business corporations, hardly a choice that comports with a desire to retain federal superintendence over the land.

The Tribe contends that the requisite federal superintendence is present because the Federal Government provides "desperately needed health, social, welfare, and economic programs" to the Tribe. The Court of Appeals majority found this argument persuasive. Our Indian country precedents, however, do not suggest that the mere provision of "desperately needed" social programs can support a finding of Indian country. Such health, education, and welfare benefits are merely forms of general federal aid; considered either alone or in tandem with ANCSA's minimal land-related protections, they are not indicia of active federal control over the Tribe's land sufficient to support a finding of federal superintendence.

The Tribe's federal superintendence argument, moreover, is severely undercut by its view of ANCSA's primary purposes, namely, to effect Native self-determination and to end paternalism in federal Indian relations. The broad federal superintendence requirement for Indian country cuts against these objectives, but we are not free to ignore that requirement as codified in 18 U.S.C. § 1151. Whether the concept of Indian country should be modified is a question entirely for Congress.

Notes

1. **Defining "dependent Indian communities."** Under *Venetie*, except for the Pueblos and the Five "Civilized" Tribes of eastern Oklahoma, *see United States v. Sandoval*, 231 U.S. 28, 48 (1913), must land be held in trust for a tribe in order to be a dependent Indian community? If so, what is now the relationship between "informal reservations" and dependent Indian communities? If tribal trust lands qualify as informal reservations under *Sac and Fox*, does 18 U.S.C. § 1151(b) retain any meaning for tribes other than the Pueblos and the Five Tribes? The Eighth Circuit has held that it does. That court concluded that lands acquired under authority other than 25 U.S.C. § 5108 (the Indian Reorganization Act) (formerly § 465) did not qualify as "reservation" lands but instead were dependent Indian communities. *Yankton Sioux Tribe v. Podhradsky*, 606 F.3d 994 (8th Cir. 2010).

The difficulties involved in determining what constitutes a dependent Indian community are illustrated by *Hydro Resources, Inc. v. U.S. Environmental Protection Agency*, 608 F.3d 1131 (10th Cir. 2010). On rehearing en banc, a deeply divided Tenth Circuit reversed, 6–5, a 2009 panel decision concerning the Indian country status of a checkerboarded area near the Navajo Reservation. Hydro Resources proposed a uranium mining operation on fee lands within the checkerboarded area. EPA determined that the mine site was within a dependent Indian community, and thus subject to federal rather than state regulation. The panel agreed, concluding that the proper "community of reference," or the relevant geographical area, was the Church Rock Chapter of the Navajo Nation, where 78% of the chapter land was set aside for the use of Navajos, and where the federal government exercised superintendence over the land.

The en banc court reversed, rejecting the community of reference test. Relying on *Venetie*, the majority concluded that it must look only at the specific land in question, and that this land would be a dependent Indian community only if it had been explicitly set aside by Congress or the executive for the use of Indians. Because the mine site was on fee land, the court held that it could not be a dependent Indian community. The five dissenting judges argued that the community of reference test was not inconsistent with *Venetie*; instead, they maintained that community of reference test determined the "land in question" to which the *Venetie* test applied.

2. The Alaska Native Claims Settlement Act, Pub. L. No. 92-203, 85 Stat. 668, codified as amended at 43 U.S.C. § 1601 *et seq.* ANCSA extinguished all Native aboriginal title in Alaska, and re-conveyed to the Alaska Native people 44 million acres, more than 10% of the land in Alaska, plus $962 million. But ANCSA also imposed a corporate structure on Alaska Natives: it created over 200 village corporations and 12 regional corporations, all chartered under state corporations law. All assets under ANCSA—both land and money—were conveyed to these corporations. Native corporation land that remained undeveloped and unleased to third parties was immunized from state taxation for 20 years. Each Alaska Native born before the effective date of the Act (Dec. 18, 1971) was entitled to an equal number of shares in the corporations. Native corporate stock could not be alienated for 20 years. As of 1991, however, all shares and land would be freely alienable.

Compounding the problems posed by the corporate structure and alienability was the fact that a majority of the village corporations were insolvent, and would be forced to sell ANCSA lands to avoid bankruptcy. The regional corporations had better success, but they faced the possibility of hostile takeovers after their shares became alienable in 1991.

Consequently, in 1988, President Reagan signed the "1991 Amendments" to ANCSA. Pub. L. No. 100-241, 101 Stat. 1788. Among other provisions, the amendments established a general rule that corporation stock will be inalienable in perpetuity, unless the shareholders of a Native corporation amend its articles of incorporation to terminate the restriction. In addition, the 1991 Amendments authorized corporations to transfer certain ANCSA lands and other assets into settlement trusts. Placing land and assets in trust status removes the risk of involuntary loss of the Alaska Native land base. There is also an automatic extension of tax-exempt status (previously available only through a cumbersome process) to all undeveloped, unleased, and unmortgaged land. *See generally* David S. Case & David A. Voluck, Alaska Natives and American Laws (U. Alaska Press 3d ed. 2012); Thomas J. Berger, Village Journey (Hill and Wang 1985).

3. ANCSA and the federal-tribal trust relationship. In *Venetie*, the Court found a deep inconsistency between ANCSA's purpose of furthering Native self-determination and the federal set-aside requirement for Indian country. The Ninth Circuit, however, was able to reconcile ANCSA and Indian country:

> The answer is found in the unique relationship that Native Americans share with the federal government. On July 8, 1970, President Nixon enunciated a federal policy toward Indians that continues to this day: self-determination without termination of the trust relationship. The President "called for rejection of the extremes of termination and paternalism: termination because it ignored the moral and legal obligations involved in the special

relationship between tribes and the federal government, and paternalism because it resulted in 'the erosion of Indian initiative and morale.'" [Citing the 1982 Cohen treatise, at 186 (quoting Richard M. Nixon, Special Message to the Congress on Indian Affairs (July 8, 1970)]. The reconciliation of self-determination and superintendence is reflected in the Indian Self-Determination and Education Assistance Act of 1975, where Congress declared its commitment

> to the maintenance of the Federal Government's unique and continuing relationship with, and responsibility to, individual Indian tribes and to the Indian people as a whole through the establishment of a meaningful Indian self-determination policy which will permit an orderly transition from the Federal domination of programs for, and services to, Indians to effective and meaningful participation by the Indian people in the planning, conduct, and administration of those programs and services.

The federal government is fulfilling, not abandoning, its trust responsibilities when it facilitates Indian self-determination. Moreover, as expressed by the Self-Determination Act, Indian self-determination involves increased participation of Native Americans in the administration of federal programs, not the elimination of those programs nor the removal of federal officials from a supervisory role over those programs.

We believe that ANCSA also implemented the federal policy of self-determination without termination of the trust relationship. Accordingly, we find that Native self-determination and ongoing federal superintendence may coexist, and that this is precisely the federal-tribal relationship that was introduced by ANCSA.

Alaska ex rel. Yukon Flats School Dist. v. Native Village of Venetie Tribal Government, 101 F.3d 1286, 1299 (9th Cir. 1996), *rev'd*, 522 U.S. 520 (1998). Which court is correct? Is the federal trust responsibility fundamentally incompatible with federal promotion of tribal autonomy?

4. Property versus sovereignty. The Supreme Court's decision emphasized the fact that under ANCSA Alaska Natives received land in fee, without the trust limits the Court felt were essential to a finding of federal superintendence. Absent federal superintendence, the lands were not "set aside" for Alaska Natives, and therefore, the tribe lacked sovereign authority. Is that a sensible approach to determining whether sovereignty exists? Note that under *Venetie* the more control Alaska Natives have over their land, the less likely they are to have sovereign control. Whether proprietorship should influence sovereignty determinations is itself questionable, but the idea that the greater the property interest, the less likely there is to be sovereign control, seems counterintuitive.

Note on Alaskan Subsistence

One of the most controversial natural resource issues in Alaska concerns subsistence hunting and fishing, a way of life for most Alaskans not living in urban areas, nearly half of the state's population. There were no express provisions regarding subsistence uses in the 1971 Alaska Native Claims Settlement Act, but the legislative history indicated that Congress expected the Secretary of the Interior to protect subsistence uses. When the Secretary did not, Congress included several provisions concerning subsistence in the 1980 Alaskan National Interest Lands Conservation Act (ANILCA). The most significant of these promised a federal priority for subsistence harvesters in rural areas. 16 U.S.C. § 3114 (priority for "the taking on public lands of fish and wildlife for nonwasteful subsistence uses"). ANILCA did not include a preference for Native subsistence, substituting the rural subsistence provision after state officials claimed that a Native preference would conflict with the state's constitution. But Congress did note that an ANILCA purpose was to preserve a way of life "essential to Native physical, economic, traditional, and social existence."

ANILCA offered the state the opportunity to manage subsistence harvests on federal lands if the state afforded "long-term protection to the subsistence way of life" and recognized the rural priority in the federal statute. The state initially attempted to implement rural subsistence under pre-existing statutory authority, but the Alaska Supreme Court struck down the administrative regulations as being unauthorized by the statute. *Madison v. Alaska Dept. of Fish and Game*, 696 P.2d 168 (Alaska 1985). In order to avoid losing the ability to regulate subsistence on federal lands, the state legislature amended the statute to authorize a rural priority, but the Ninth Circuit ruled that the state's regulatory definition of "rural" was overly restrictive, excluding vast areas of the state. *Kenaitze Indian Tribe v. Alaska*, 860 F.2d 312 (9th Cir. 1988). Then, the federal district court struck down amended regulations because their limits on seasons and bag limits failed to accommodate traditional hunting practices. *Bobby v. Alaska*, 718 F. Supp. 764 (D. Alaska 1989).

Finally, the Alaska Supreme Court struck down the state statute establishing the rural subsistence priority on state constitutional grounds in *McDowell v. Alaska*, 785 P.2d 1 (Alaska 1989) (on the basis of provisions reserving fish and wildlife for "common use" and declaring that natural resources "shall apply equally to all persons similarly situated"). The effect of the decision was to make the state out of compliance with ANILCA's rural preference, and thus the state lost regulatory control over subsistence harvests on federal lands. The federal government therefore assumed control over federal land subsistence on July 1, 1990. 55 Fed. Reg. 27,114 (June 29, 1990). However, the federal government excluded navigable waters from the reach of the regulations, even though ANILCA defined "lands" subject to the rural subsistence to include "waters, and interests therein," title to which is in the United States. The Ninth Circuit subsequently ruled that under the statutory definition, federal subsistence regulations had to include waters in which the federal government has reserved water rights, and that it was up to the federal government to identify those waters. *Alaska v. Babbitt*, 72 F.3d 698 (9th Cir. 1995), *aff'd*, 297 F.3d 1032 (9th Cir. 2001) (en banc). The federal government amended its regulations accordingly. 64 Fed. Reg. 1276 (Jan. 8, 1999) (codified at 36 C.F.R. § 242, 50 C.F.R. § 100).

In *Ninilchik Traditional Council v. United States*, 227 F.3d 1186 (9th Cir. 2000), the court upheld antler-size restrictions imposed by the Federal Subsistence Board (established by ANILCA regulations) because the Board demonstrated that this subsistence restriction was necessary to "protect the continued viability" of the moose population, as required by section 3114 of ANILCA. However, the court struck down a two-day exclusive season for subsistence hunters in one "game management unit" because it did not provide subsistence hunters with a "meaningful preference" as required by section 3114. The court did uphold a ten-day exclusive season for another game management unit.

Title VIII of ANILCA also requires special consideration of public land management activities which affect subsistence and subsistence habitat. Federal agencies with control over such actions must specifically evaluate their effect on subsistence and consider alternatives which would reduce or eliminate the need to adversely affect subsistence. For activities which would significantly restrict subsistence, agencies must also: 1) give notice of the proposal; 2) hold a hearing in the vicinity of the involved area; and 3) determine that a significant restriction on subsistence is necessary, consistent with sound management, and will involve "the minimum of public lands necessary" to accomplish the purpose, and that reasonable steps will be taken to minimize adverse effects on subsistence. *See* Joris Naimen, *ANILCA Section 810: An Undervalued Protection for Alaskan Villagers' Subsistence*, 7 Fordham Envt'l L.J. 211 (1996).

In 1987, the Supreme Court ruled that outer continental shelf oil and gas leasing was not burdened by the subsistence habitat protection procedures described above, since the outer continental shelf was not within ANILCA's definition of "in Alaska." *Amoco Production Co. v. Village of Gambell*, 480 U.S. 531 (1987). This decision raises the question of whether the Alaska Native Claims Settlement Act's extinguishment of aboriginal title was effective on the outer continental shelf, because that statute contains the same geographical scope of applicability as ANILCA. *See* Marlyn J. Twitchell, Amoco Production Co. v. Village of Gambell: *Subsistence Protection Ends at Alaska's Border*, 18 Envtl. L. 635 (1988).

In 2010, the Ninth Circuit rejected a Native challenge to the Environmental Protection Agency's approval of Alaska's application to administer the National Pollutant Discharge Elimination System of the Clean Water Act. *Atiak Native Community v. Environmental Protection Agency*, 625 F.3d 1162 (9th Cir. 2010). The court concluded that the delegation of authority would not impair protection of subsistence resources protection under ANILCA.

Mustang Production Co. v. Harrison
94 F.3d 1382 (10th Cir. 1996)

Tacha, Circuit Judge.

The issue in this case is whether the Cheyenne-Arapaho Tribes of Oklahoma ("the Tribes") may impose a severance tax on oil and gas production on allotted lands held in trust for their members. The appellants are nineteen oil and gas companies and one individual (collectively referred to as "Mustang") who hold oil and gas leases on the allotted lands. The appellees are members of the Business Committee and the Tax Commission, the tribal government entities responsible for promulgating and enforcing the tax at issue. The Cheyenne-Arapaho District Court ("the Tribal Court"), the Tribal Supreme Court, and the federal district court all held that allotted lands are subject to taxation by the Tribes. Our jurisdiction arises under 28 U.S.C. § 1291, and we affirm.

BACKGROUND

In 1865, the United States signed a treaty creating a reservation for the Tribes in western Oklahoma. An 1869 Executive Order implemented the treaty and delineated the boundaries of the reservation ("the 1869 reservation"). In 1890, the United States and the Tribes signed an Allotment and Cession Agreement ("the Agreement"), the subject of which was the land within the 1869 reservation as well as other land which had been mistakenly reserved to the Tribe by a treaty signed in 1867. The Agreement took effect by an Act of Congress on March 3, 1891 ("the Act").

Article I of the Act provided that the Tribes would cede to the United States all land mistakenly reserved to the Tribes in the 1867 treaty. Article II stated that, subject to the allotment of land to individual members of the Tribes, the Tribes would cede all land within the boundaries of the 1869 reservation. Article III provided allotments of land to all members of the Tribe "out of the lands ceded, conveyed, transferred, relinquished, and surrendered by Article II." The allotted lands were to be held in trust by the federal government for individual members of the Tribe. All of the allotted lands involved in this case continue to be held in trust.

DISCUSSION

Mustang argues that the Tribes do not have authority over the allotted lands and thus cannot tax oil and gas production on those lands. Mustang contends that the Tribes lost jurisdiction over all of the lands in the 1869 reservation, including allotted lands, when the 1890 Agreement disestablished the reservation. According to Mustang, when the Agreement set aside allotted lands for individual tribal members, it also divested the Tribe of its jurisdiction over those lands.

As the district court correctly concluded, however, disestablishment of the reservation is not dispositive of the question of tribal jurisdiction. In order to determine whether the Tribes have jurisdiction we must instead look to whether the land in question is Indian country. Indian country encompasses those areas that have been "validly set apart for the use of the Indians as such, under the superintendence of the Government."

In *Oklahoma Tax Commission v. Sac and Fox Nation*, 508 U.S. 114 (1993), the Supreme Court specifically stated that "Indian allotments, whether restricted or held in trust by the United States," are Indian country. In that case, the state argued that members of the Sac and Fox Nation were subject to state taxation because an 1891 treaty disestablished their reservation. The Court rejected this argument and held that "a tribal member need not live on a formal reservation to be outside the State's taxing jurisdiction; it is enough that the member live in 'Indian country.'"

Mustang argues that *Sac and Fox Nation* does not apply because the issue in that case was a state's, rather than a tribe's, civil jurisdiction. We agree with the district court, however, that "the issue is analogous—whether one government can tax citizens of another government engaging in activities on allotted lands." "Indian tribes are 'domestic dependent nations' that exercise inherent sovereign authority over their members and territories." The sovereign authority of Indian tribes includes the inherent power to tax non-Indians who conduct business on tribal lands and who benefit from governmental services provided by the tribes. As discussed above, Indian tribes have jurisdiction over lands that are Indian country, and allotted lands constitute Indian country. Thus, we agree with the district court that the Tribes have "an inherent sovereign power to tax economic activities on their lands, and because the allotted lands are within their jurisdiction, the Tribes have the power to enact and enforce a severance tax on oil and gas production from allotted lands."

Mustang argues that the Tribes would have authority over allotted lands only if Congress passed an act specifically granting them jurisdiction, and that the Indian country statute, 18 U.S.C. § 1151 *et seq.*, grants criminal but not civil jurisdiction over allotted lands. The Indian country statute defines Indian country to include "all Indian allotments, the Indian titles to which have not been extinguished, including rights-of-way running through the same." Although the statute appears in Title 18, which deals primarily with crimes and criminal procedures, the Supreme Court has held that § 1151 applies to civil jurisdiction as well. *DeCoteau*, 420 U.S. at 427 n.2; *see also Pittsburg & Midway Coal Mining v. Watchman*, 52 F.3d 1531, n.10 (10th Cir. 1995) ("The principle that § 1151 defines Indian country for both civil and criminal jurisdiction purposes is firmly established. Any suggestion to the contrary... is simply erroneous."). Thus, Mustang's argument that § 1151 does not apply to civil jurisdiction is incorrect, and the statute supports our conclusion that the Tribes have jurisdiction over the allotted lands.

The language of the 1891 Act, which ratified verbatim the agreement between the Tribes and the United States, also supports our conclusion. Article II of the Act provides:

> Subject to the allotment of land in severalty to the individual members of the Cheyenne and Arapaho tribes of Indians, as hereinafter provided for and subject to the conditions hereinafter imposed, for the considerations hereinafter mentioned the said Cheyenne and Arapaho Indians hereby cede, convey, transfer, relinquish, and surrender forever and absolutely, without any reservation whatever, express or implied, all their claim, title and interest, of every kind and character, in and to the lands [in the 1869 reservation].

The "subject to the allotment of land" clause modifies the cession language and expressly conditions the cession of some lands on the allotment of other lands. In addition, the "subject to the allotment of lands" provision implicitly excludes the allotted lands from the ceded lands. Therefore, the comprehensive terms of the cession do not apply to the allotted lands.

Article III of the Act describes the details of the allotment procedure:

> Out of the lands ceded, conveyed, transferred, relinquished, and surrendered by Article II hereof, and in part consideration for the cession of lands named in the preceding article, it is agreed by the United States that each member of the said Cheyenne and Arapaho tribes of Indians over the age of eighteen years shall have the right to select for himself or herself one hundred and sixty acres of land, to be held and owned in severalty....

Mustang contends that because allotments were selected "out of the lands ceded," the allotted lands were ceded as well. This reading of the provision is incorrect. Article III merely describes who was entitled to allotments, identifies the land from which the allotments were to be selected, and describes the size of the allotments—it says nothing about which land is ceded, a subject covered in Articles I and II. Article I unconditionally cedes the land that was mistakenly reserved to the Tribes. Article II cedes the land in the 1869 reservation, but not unconditionally: the cession in Article II is subject to allotment. The plain language of the Act indicates that while the allotted lands were selected from the lands ceded, the allotted lands themselves were not ceded. Instead, the allotted lands were set aside for the use of the Indians, remaining part of Indian country even after the reservation was disestablished.

In conclusion, we hold that the allotted lands constitute Indian country over which the Tribes have civil jurisdiction. Thus, the Tribes have the power to enact and enforce a severance tax on oil and gas produced on allotted lands. Accordingly, the decision of the district court is affirmed.

Note on Tribal Courts and Tribal Court Exhaustion

The federal courts in *Mustang Production* implemented the tribal exhaustion doctrine under which courts decline to exercise jurisdiction over matters that fall within tribal jurisdiction until the appropriate tribal remedies have been exhausted. The doctrine grew out of the Supreme Court's decision in *Williams v. Lee*, 358 U.S. 217 (1958), where the Court reversed a state supreme court decision holding that state courts had jurisdiction over on-reservation transactions between a federal licensee and a tribal member because "to allow the exercise of state jurisdiction... would undermine the authority of the tribal courts over Reservation affairs and hence would infringe on the right of the Indians to govern themselves." *Id.* at 223. Tribal courts offer efficiencies by allowing federal courts to benefit from tribal court expertise, and the doctrine reaffirms the federal policy of tribal sovereignty. The Supreme Court has announced that tribal courts "play a vital role in tribal self-government... and the federal government has consistently encouraged their development." *Iowa Mutual Insurance Co. v. LaPlante*, 480 U.S. 9, 14-15 (1987); *see* Sandra Day O'Connor, *Lessons From the Third Sovereign*, 33 Tulsa L.J. 1 (1997). By the turn of the 21st century, over 175 tribes had tribal courts. Cohen's Handbook on Federal Indian Law § 4.04[3][C][iv][A], at 263-64 (Nell Jessup Newton, ed. 2012).

Note on Indian Country in Oklahoma

Virtually all of what is now Oklahoma was originally set aside as the Indian Territory. Around the turn of the twentieth century, however, with the allotment of tribal lands and the admission of Oklahoma as a state, legal questions were raised about the existence of Indian country in the state.

1. Oklahoma reservations. During the nineteenth century, several Indian reservations were established in what is now western Oklahoma. In 1904, Congress abolished the reservation boundaries of the Ponca, Otoe, and Missouria Reservations. Act of Apr. 21, 1904, 33 Stat. 189, 218. In a number of cases in the 1940s, 1950s and 1960s, state and federal courts held that certain reservations in Oklahoma no longer existed. *See United States v. Oklahoma Gas & Electric Co.*, 318 U.S. 206 (1943) (holding Kickapoo Reservation "obliterated"); *Tooisgah v. United States*, 186 F.2d 93 (10th Cir. 1950) (holding Kiowa, Comanche and Apache Reservation disestablished); *Ellis v. State*, 386 P.2d 326 (Okla. Crim. App. 1963) (holding Cheyenne-Arapaho Reservation disestablished); *Ellis v. Page*, 351 F. 2d 250 (10th Cir. 1965) (same). Together, those three ex-reservations comprised a large chunk of western Oklahoma. These cases led to a widespread presumption (still held today) that no reservations existed in Oklahoma.

The presumption against the survival of Oklahoma reservations had been applied in eastern Oklahoma as well. Relying in large part on that presumption, and citing statements from historians and a single statement in the legislative history of the Oklahoma Indian Welfare Act of 1936, federal courts initially concluded that both the Muscogee (Creek) Nation and the Osage Nation reservations were disestablished. *Murphy v. Sirmons*, 497 F. Supp. 2d 1257 (E.D. Okla. 2007) (Muscogee (Creek) Nation); *Osage Nation v. Irby*, 597 F.3d. 1117 (10th Cir. 2010). But in 2017, the Tenth Circuit ruled that the Muscogee (Creek) Nation reservation remains intact—neither diminished nor disestablished—relying primarily on the lack of a clearly expressed congressional intent in the statutes or treaties with the Muscogee Creeks and concluding that the Oklahoma Court of Criminal Appeals and the federal district court had erred in finding state jurisdiction over a murder case. *Murphy v. Royal*, 866 F.3d 1164 (10th Cir. 2017) (determining that Congress never disestablished or diminished the reservation, applying the Supreme Court's decision *Solem v. Bartlett*, page 130 below, in an exhaustive 126-page opinion), *cert. granted*, 2018 WL 747674 (May 21, 2018).

2. Dependent Indian communities. Oklahoma also contains Indian country in the form of dependent Indian communities. For example, in 1990, the Oklahoma Supreme Court held that non-restricted land owned and developed by the Seminole Housing Authority was a dependent Indian community. *Housing Authority v. Harjo*, 790 P.2d 1098 (Okla. 1990). The decision was, however, 5–4. The dissent argued that the fee title status of the Housing Authority land should be dispositive: that is, should lead to the automatic conclusion that the land was not Indian country. Is *Harjo* still good law after *Venetie*?

3. Indian allotments. Restricted Indian allotments are also Indian country in Oklahoma. As far back as 1926, the Supreme Court held that a restricted Osage allotment was Indian country. *United States v. Ramsey*, 271 U.S. 467 (1926). In the 1970s and 1980s, lower federal and state courts similarly held that trust allotments in western Oklahoma were Indian country. *See Cheyenne-Arapaho Tribes of Oklahoma v. Oklahoma*, 618 F.2d 665 (10th Cir. 1980); *State v. Littlechief*, 573 P.2d 263 (Okla. Crim. App. 1978) (Kiowa). Finally, in the 1980s, Oklahoma courts determined that trust and restricted allotments in eastern Oklahoma were also Indian country. *See State ex rel. May v. Seneca-Cayuga Tribe*, 711 P.2d 77 (Okla. 1985) (Quapaw and Seneca-Cayuga); *State v. Klindt*, 782 P.2d 401 (Okla. Crim. App. 1989) (Cherokee).

2. Expanding Indian Country

Buzzard v. Oklahoma Tax Commission
992 F.2d 1073 (10th Cir. 1993)

Godbold, Circuit Judge.

The United Keetoowah Band of Cherokee Indians in Oklahoma (UKB) purchased land subject to a restriction against alienation requiring the approval of the U.S. Secretary of the Interior. This case presents the issue whether the land can be considered Indian country and therefore exempt from state jurisdiction. The UKB, contending that land purchased by it subject to this restriction was Indian country, sought injunctive relief prohibiting Oklahoma from enforcing state tobacco taxing statutes against the UKB's smokeshops. The district court held that the restriction against alienation by itself was insufficient to make the UKB's land Indian country and granted summary judgment to Oklahoma. We agree and affirm the grant of summary judgment.

The UKB's tribal charter permits it to purchase land in fee simple but prohibits the UKB from disposing of land without the approval of the Secretary of the Interior. The UKB operates smokeshops on land purchased by it subject to this restriction. It contended in the district court that cigarette sales made in these smokeshops should not be subject to Oklahoma's state tobacco taxes[3] because the shops were located in Indian country.

For purposes of both civil and criminal jurisdiction, the primary definition of Indian country is 18 U.S.C. § 1151. Section 1151 defines Indian country to include: (1) land within the limits of any Indian reservation; (2) dependent Indian communities; and (3) Indian allotments, the Indian titles to which have not been

---

3. Even if land purchased by the UKB were Indian country, however, Oklahoma could require the UKB to collect taxes on cigarette sales to nontribal members. *Oklahoma Tax Comm'n v. Potawatomi Indian Tribe*, 498 U.S. 505 (1991).

extinguished. In addition the Supreme Court has held that Indian country includes land "'validly set apart for the use of the Indians as such, under the superintendency of the Government.'" Applying this test, the Court has concluded that Indian country includes land designated as an "Indian colony," and land held in trust by the United States for the use of an Indian tribe.

In *McGowan* the Supreme Court held that the Reno Indian Colony had been set apart by the government for the use of Indians because it had been purchased by the United States for the purpose of providing lands for needy Indians. Similarly, trust land is set apart for the use of Indians by the federal government because it can be obtained only by filing a request with the Secretary of the Interior, 25 C.F.R. § 151.9 (1992), who must consider, among other things, the Indian's need for the land, and the purposes for which the land will be used. If the request is approved, the United States holds the land as trustee. Thus, land is "validly set apart for the use of Indians as such" only if the federal government takes some action indicating that the land is designated for use by Indians.

Superintendency over the land requires the active involvement of the federal government. This involvement was shown in *McGowan* by the federal government's retention of title to the land and its regulation of activities in the Colony. The United States also holds title to trust land, although only as trustee. In addition, before agreeing to acquire trust land, the Secretary must consider several factors including the authority for the transactions, the impact on the state resulting from the removal of the land from the tax rolls, and jurisdictional problems that might arise. These requirements show that, when the federal government agrees to hold land in trust, it is prepared to exert jurisdiction over the land.

The UKB has not shown that its smokeshops are located on land validly set apart for the UKB's use by the federal government. Although it must obtain the Secretary of the Interior's approval before disposing of land, the UKB has the right to acquire land unilaterally. The smokeshops thus were located on land purchased by the UKB in the same manner as land purchased by any other property owner. In contrast to the Reno Indian Colony or trust land, title is held by the UKB in fee simple. No action has been taken by the federal government indicating that it set aside the land for use by the UKB. A restriction against alienation requiring government approval may show a desire to protect the UKB from unfair dispositions of its land, but does not of itself indicate that the federal government intended the land to be set aside for the UKB's use.

Nor has the UKB shown that its smokeshops are located on land superintended by the federal government. The federal government has not retained title to this land or indicated that it is prepared to exert jurisdiction over the land. At most it has agreed to approve transactions disposing the land. But the ability to veto a sale does not require the sort of active involvement that can be described as superintendence of the land. Because the UKB cannot show that its lands were validly set apart for its use under the superintendence of the government, we hold that the UKB's smokeshops are not located in Indian country.

Consideration of the consequences of determining that land is Indian country supports this conclusion. Within Indian country the federal and tribal governments have exclusive jurisdiction over the conduct of Indians and interests in Indian property. This limits a state's criminal jurisdiction over activities that occur in Indian country and involve Indians, and its authority to tax those activities. If the restriction against alienation were sufficient to make any land purchased by the UKB Indian country, the UKB could remove land from state jurisdiction and force the federal government to exert jurisdiction over that land without either sovereign having any voice in the matter. Nothing in *McGowan* or the cases concerning trust land indicates that the Supreme Court intended for Indian tribes to have such unilateral power to create Indian country.

Notes

1. Section 5108 (formerly § 465) lands and Indian country. Section 5 of the Indian Reorganization Act of 1934, 25 U.S.C. § 5108, is the primary statutory authority for the acquisition of lands in trust. Section 5108 (formerly § 465) provides:

> The Secretary of the Interior is hereby authorized, in his discretion, to acquire, through purchase, relinquishment, gift, exchange, or assignment, any interest in lands, water rights, or surface rights to lands, within or without existing reservations, including trust or otherwise restricted allotments, whether the allottee be living or deceased, for the purpose of providing land for Indians.

Lands taken into trust pursuant to 25 U.S.C. § 5108 are not necessarily formal reservations. Instead, § 5110 (formerly § 467) authorizes the Secretary of the Interior to "proclaim new Indian reservations" on lands acquired pursuant to § 5108 (formerly § 465) or to add those lands to existing reservations. Thus, the Eighth Circuit found it unnecessary to determine whether a district court was in error in ruling that a parcel of land contiguous to the Flandreau Santee Sioux Tribe's reservation that would be taken into trust would constitute Indian country. *South Dakota v. U.S. Dept. of the Interior*, 487 F.3d 548 (8th Cir. 2007). The appeals court noted that once the land was in trust, the tribe would petition to have the land proclaimed reservation land, "which should resolve the jurisdictional issues." Nonetheless, courts have not always required technical adherence to § 5110. *See Santa Rosa Band of Indians v. Kings County*, 532 F.2d 655, 666 (9th Cir. 1975): "We are confident that when Congress in 1934 authorized the Secretary to purchase and hold title to lands for the purpose of providing land for Indians, it understood and intended such lands to be held in the legal manner and condition in which trust lands were held under applicable court decisions—free of state regulation."

In 2010, the Eighth Circuit distinguished between lands added to existing reservations and lands comprising new reservations under § 5108 (formerly § 465). Although the latter require a proclamation under § 5110 (formerly § 467) that they are reservation lands, the former do not. *Yankton Sioux Tribe v. Podhradsky*, 606 F.3d 994 (8th Cir. 2010). The lands at issue in that case were within the borders of the Yankton Sioux's original 1858 reservation. Although the reservation has been diminished—see *South Dakota v. Yankton Sioux Tribe*, excerpted at page 107—it was never disestablished. The court decided that when the government took the lands back into trust, they automatically became reservation lands within the meaning of the Indian country statute. The court also ruled that lands acquired for the tribe in trust other than under § 5108 (formerly 465) constituted dependent Indian communities.

The United States Supreme Court interpreted § 5108 (formerly § 465) in *Mescalero Apache Tribe v. Jones*, 411 U.S. 145 (1973). The Mescalero Tribe leased land from the United States Forest Service on a long-term lease and constructed a ski resort. The land was located adjacent to the Mescalero Reservation, but was never taken into trust for the Tribe because, the United States Solicitor General explained, "it would have been meaningless for the United States, which already had title to the forest, to convey title to itself for the use of the Tribe." The State of New Mexico sought to impose its gross receipts tax and a use tax on personalty on the Mescalero ski resort operations.

The Court first found that the ski resort was an *off-reservation* enterprise, and stated the rule regarding state authority over Indians outside Indian country. "Absent express federal law to the contrary, Indians going beyond reservation boundaries have generally been held subject to nondiscriminatory state law otherwise applicable to all citizens of the State." The Court also found, however, that the peculiarities of the lease arrangement were sufficient to bring the Tribe's leasehold interest within § 5108 (formerly § 465). And § 5108 provides that any acquired trust lands or rights "shall be exempt from State and local taxation." Accordingly, the Court held that New Mexico could impose its gross receipts tax on business income, but could not impose its use tax on personalty. The former tax, the Court held, was unconnected to the land. By contrast, the latter tax was a tax on the use of permanent improvements upon the land and therefore functionally a tax on the property itself.

2. The constitutionality of section 5108 (formerly § 465). In 1995, the Eighth Circuit declared § 5108 (formerly § 465) unconstitutional. *South Dakota v. U.S. Department of the Interior*, 69 F.3d 878 (8th Cir. 1995). The court held that § 5108 contained no "intelligible principles" or "boundaries" limiting the Secretary's discretion. The U.S. Supreme Court granted certiorari, vacated the judgment, and remanded to the Eighth Circuit with instructions to vacate the judgment of the district court "and remand the matter to the Secretary of the Interior for reconsideration of his administrative decision." *Department of the Interior v. South Dakota*, 519 U.S. 919 (1996). The Court apparently expected the Secretary to reconsider the decision in light of regulations promulgated in 1995. The regulations governing the Secretary's decision to acquire lands in trust are reprinted below in note 3.

In 2005, the Eighth Circuit upheld the district court ruling on remand that § 5108 was a constitutional delegation of authority to the Secretary of the Interior. *South Dakota v. U.S. Dept. of the Interior*, 423 F.3d 790 (8th Cir. 2005). Relying on the language and legislative history of the statute, but *not* the revised regulations, the court held that Congress had set general policies and boundaries to the Secretary's discretion, satisfying the nondelegation doctrine. In so holding, the Eighth Circuit noted that it joined the First and Tenth Circuits in finding § 5108 constitutional. *See United States v. Roberts*, 185 F.3d 1125 (10th Cir. 1999); *Carcieri v. Norton*, 398 F.3d 22 (1st Cir. 2005).

3. The land into trust process. Federal regulations for taking land into trust vary somewhat depending upon whether the land is within or contiguous to, or outside, an existing reservation. For an analysis of the process, see Frank Pommersheim, *Land into Trust: An Inquiry into Law, Policy, and History*, 49 Idaho L. Rev. 519 (2013); Mary Jane Sheppard, *Taking Indian Land Into Trust*, 44 S.D. L. Rev. 681 (1998–1999); *see also U.S. Bureau of Indian Affairs, Fee-to-Trust Handbook: Version IV* (June 28, 2016), available at https://www.bia.gov/sites/bia.gov/files/assets/public/raca/handbook/pdf/idc1-024504.pdf.

In evaluating requests for the acquisition of land in trust when the land is located within or contiguous to an Indian reservation, the Secretary of the Interior is to consider the following factors:

(a) The existence of statutory authority for the acquisition and any limitations contained in such authority;

(b) The need of the individual Indian or the tribe for additional land;

(c) The purposes for which the land will be used;

(d) If the land is to be acquired for an individual Indian, the amount of trust or restricted land already owned by or for that individual and the degree to which he needs assistance in handling his affairs;

(e) If the land to be acquired is in unrestricted fee status, the impact on the State and its political subdivisions resulting from the removal of the land from tax rolls;

(f) Jurisdictional problems and potential conflicts of land use which may arise; and

(g) If the land to be acquired is in fee status, whether the Bureau of Indian Affairs is equipped to discharge the additional responsibilities resulting from the acquisition of the land in trust status.

(h) The extent to which the applicant has provided information that allows the Secretary to comply with [the National Environmental Policy Act and hazardous substances determinations].

25 C.F.R. § 151.10.

In considering the acquisition of lands in trust when the land is located outside and not contiguous to a reservation, the Secretary is to consider the factors from § 151.10, plus the following:

(b) The location of the land relative to state boundaries, and its distance from the boundaries of the tribe's reservation, shall be considered as follows: as the distance between the tribe's reservation and the land to be acquired increases, the Secretary shall give greater scrutiny to the tribe's justification of anticipated benefits from the acquisition. The Secretary shall give greater weight to the concerns raised pursuant to paragraph (d) of this section.

(c) Where land is being acquired for business purposes, the tribe shall provide a plan which specifies the anticipated economic benefits associated with the proposed use.

(d) Contact with state and local governments pursuant to 151.10(e) and (f) shall be completed as follows: upon receipt of a tribe's written request to have lands taken in trust, the Secretary shall notify the state and local governments having regulatory jurisdiction over the land to be acquired. The notice shall inform the state and local government that each will be given 30 days in which to provide written comment as to the acquisition's potential impact on regulatory jurisdiction, real property taxes and special assessments.

25 C.F.R. § 151.11.

4. Challenging land into trust status. The Secretary's decision to take land into trust may be challenged under the Administrative Procedure Act as arbitrary and capricious or beyond statutory authority. *Match-E-Be-Nash-She-Wish Band v. Patchak*, 567 U.S. 209 (2012) (neighboring landowners may challenge the taking of land into trust for gaming purposes). Justice Sotomayor, the lone dissenter in *Patchak*, complained that "[a]fter today, any person may sue under the Administrative Procedure Act (APA) to divest the Federal Government of title to and possession of land held in trust for Indian tribes—relief expressly forbidden by the QTA—so long as the complaint does not assert a personal interest in the land." One of the problems Justice Sotomayor noted was that challenges to land-into-trust decisions no longer needed to be brought within the 30-day period provided for by regulation, but could be brought at any time within the APA's six-year statute of limitations. An additional problem not noted by the Justice is that the majority's decision may allow serial challenges. In the case before the Court, for example, an anti-gaming organization had filed suit within the 30-day regulatory window, claiming a violation of the National Environmental Policy Act and that § 5108 (formerly § 465) was unconstitutional.

After the *Patchak* Court's decision, while the case was again under consideration by the district court, Congress enacted the Gun Lake Act in 2014, a statute directing that any case "relating to" the litigation "shall promptly be dismissed." But the statute did not amend and of the underlying law affecting the case. After the district court dismissed the case, and the D.C. Circuit affirmed, 820 F.3d 995 (D.C. Cir. 2016), the Supreme Court affirmed, a plurality of the Court concluding that the 2014 statute was a permissible exercise of Congress's power to strip the federal courts of jurisdiction. *Patchak v. Zinke*, 138 S. Ct. 897 (2018).

Other recent noteworthy land-into-trust cases include *Central New York Fair Business Ass'n v. Jewell*, 673 Fed. Appx. 63 (2d Cir. 2016) (affirming a district court decision upholding a government decision to take 13,000 acres of land into trust for the Oneida Nation); *Confederated Tribes of the Grand Ronde v. Jewell*, 830 F.3d 552 (D.C.

Cir. 2016) (affirming a district court decision upholding a decision to take into trust 152 acres of land for Cowlitz Indian Tribe for gaming, over the objections of a tribe with a rival casino); *South Dakota v. U.S. Dept. of the Interior*, 487 F.3d 548 (8th Cir. 2007) (affirming a district court decision upholding the taking of land into trust of 310 acres of land contiguous to reservation).

5. **Land into trust and federal recognition of tribes.** In 2009, the Supreme Court held that the Secretary of Interior may take lands into trust under §5108 (formerly §465) only for tribes that were federally recognized in 1934. *Carcieri v. Salazar*, 555 U.S. 379 (2009). The IRA defines Indians to "include all persons of Indian descent who are members of any recognized Indian tribe now under Federal jurisdiction." 25 U.S.C. §5129 (formerly §479). Overturning decades of prior practice, the Court focused on the word "now," concluding that the statute unambiguously referred only to those tribes under federal supervision on the date Congress enacted the IRA. As a result, the Secretary had no authority to take a 31-acre parcel into trust for the Narragansett Tribe of Rhode Island because, although the Narragansett Tribe was a state-recognized tribe in 1934, it was not federally-recognized until 1983.

6. **Lands acquired for gaming purposes.** Different regulations govern the acquisition of lands for purposes of gaming activities. The Indian Gaming Regulatory Act, 25 U.S.C. §2719, generally prohibits gaming on lands acquired after the effective date of the Act (October 17, 1988) unless the later-acquired lands are within or contiguous to existing reservations or, in the case of a tribe without a reservation, are within the tribe's last-recognized reservation or in Oklahoma and within the boundaries of the tribe's former reservation. There are two additional exceptions. One exempts lands taken into trust as part of a land settlement, as an initial reservation for a newly recognized tribe, or as land restoration for a tribe restored to federal recognition. The D.C. Circuit affirmed a district court ruling dismissing a challenge to a decision of the Secretary of Interior to accept land into trust for a terminated but later restored tribe. Even though the land was not within the tribe's former reservation, the court upheld the Secretary's action because the land was within the meaning of "restoration of lands" under the Indian Gaming Regulatory Act. *City of Roseville v. Norton*, 348 F.3d 1020 (D.C. Cir. 2003). The remaining exemption provides that:

> the Secretary, after consultation with the Indian tribe and appropriate State and local officials, including officials of other nearby Indian tribes, determines that a gaming establishment on newly acquired lands would be in the best interest of the Indian tribe and its members, and would not be detrimental to the surrounding community, but only if the Governor of the State in which the gaming activity is to be conducted concurs in the Secretary's determination.

25 U.S.C. §2719(b)(1)(A). Under this provision, the Siletz Tribe of Oregon proposed taking into trust a 16-acre tract in Salem, Oregon, located 50 miles from the Siletz Reservation, for the purpose of establishing a $7 million casino. Over the objections of the Governor of Oregon, the Department of the Interior concluded that the

proposal met the statutory criteria. The governor refused to concur, and DOI denied the tribe's application. The Tribe brought suit to reverse DOI's determination.

The district court held that §2719(b)(1)(A) was unconstitutional because it violated both the Appointments Clause and general principles of separation of powers by giving a state official veto power over a determination made by an Executive Branch agency. *Confederated Tribes of Siletz Indians of Oregon v. United States*, 841 F.Supp. 1479 (D. Or. 1994), *aff'd on other grounds*, 110 F.3d 688 (9th Cir. 1997). Because there was thus no constitutional mechanism for the tribe to acquire the land, the court denied the tribe's request to overturn DOI's decision. The Ninth Circuit reversed on the constitutional issues, finding no violation of either the Appointments Clause or separation of powers, but affirmed the denial of the tribe's claim on the ground that the Oregon governor had refused to concur.

In *Confederated Tribes of the Grand Ronde Community of Oregon v. Jewell*, 830 F.3d 552 (D.C. Cir. 2016), the court upheld a decision of the Secretary to take 152 acres into trust for the Cowlitz Tribe, which had achieved federal recognition only in 2002. Nonetheless, the court determined that the tribe satisfied the statutorily required language of "under Federal jurisdiction" in 1934 due to series of government actions with the tribe in the wake of failed 1855 treaty negotiations (which failed due to government plans to remove the tribe to the Pacific coast), including communication with tribal chiefs in the late 19th century, provision of government services in the 20th century, and supervision of a local tribal agency in the 1920s. The court concluded that the tribe satisfied the Secretary's two-part test of 1) establishing federal obligations, duties, and responsibility or authority over the tribe in 1934, and 2) continuing federal jurisdiction in the years following 1934.

3. Contracting Indian Country: Reservation Diminishment

The central question in the reservation diminishment cases is whether the opening of reservation land to homesteading during the allotment era effected either a diminishment or a complete disestablishment of the reservation, and consequently a loss of the opened lands as Indian country. Although the terms "diminishment" and "disestablishment" tend to be used interchangeably, there is a distinction. If a reservation is diminished, the reservation itself remains intact, but the homesteaded lands are no longer a part of it. If a reservation is disestablished, the reservation itself ceases to exist, although as we have seen, tribal trust lands and trust allotments within the former reservation boundaries would still remain Indian country.

The issue has received a great deal of attention from the Supreme Court. Between 1961 and 1998, the Court decided seven disestablishment cases. The first case below, *Solem v. Bartlett*, is the fifth of those cases and the one in which the Court attempted to bring order out of the chaos of the four preceding decisions. How successful is the Court in reconciling its prior case law and deciphering a "fairly clean analytical structure" for determining disestablishment?

Solem v. Bartlett
465 U.S. 463 (1984)

JUSTICE MARSHALL delivered the [unanimous] opinion of the Court.

On May 29, 1908, Congress authorized the Secretary of the Interior to open 1.6 million acres of the Cheyenne River Sioux Reservation for homesteading. Act of May 29, 1908, ch. 218, 35 Stat. 460 *et seq.* (Act or Cheyenne River Act). The question presented in this case is whether that Act of Congress diminished the boundaries of the Cheyenne River Sioux Reservation or simply permitted non-Indians to settle within existing reservation boundaries.

I

In 1979, the State of South Dakota charged respondent John Bartlett, an enrolled member of the Cheyenne River Sioux Tribe, with attempted rape. Respondent pleaded guilty to the charge, and was sentenced to a 10-year term in the state penitentiary at Sioux Falls. After exhausting state remedies, respondent filed a pro se petition for a writ of habeas corpus in the United States District Court for the District of South Dakota. Respondent contended that the crime for which he had been convicted occurred within the Cheyenne River Sioux Reservation, established by Congress in the Act of Mar. 2, 1889; that, although on May 29, 1908, Congress opened for settlement by non-Indians the portion of the reservation on which respondent committed his crime, the opened portion nonetheless remained Indian country; and that the State therefore lacked criminal jurisdiction over respondent.

Relying on previous decisions of the Eighth Circuit dealing with the Act of May 29, 1908, the District Court accepted respondent's claim that the Act had not diminished the original Cheyenne River Sioux Reservation, and issued a writ of habeas corpus. On appeal, the Eighth Circuit, sitting en banc, affirmed, two judges dissenting. Because the Supreme Court of South Dakota has issued a pair of opinions offering a conflicting interpretation of the Act of May 29, 1908, we granted certiorari. We now affirm.

II

In the latter half of the 19th century, large sections of the Western States and Territories were set aside for Indian reservations. Towards the end of the century, however, Congress increasingly adhered to the view that the Indian tribes should abandon their nomadic lives on the communal reservations and settle into an agrarian economy on privately owned parcels of land. This shift was fueled in part by the belief that individualized farming would speed the Indians' assimilation into American society and in part by the continuing demand for new lands for the waves of homesteaders moving west. As a result of these combined pressures, Congress passed a series of surplus land acts at the turn of the century to force Indians onto individual allotments carved out of reservations and to open up unallotted lands for non-Indian settlement. Initially, Congress legislated its Indian allotment program on a national scale, but by the time of the Act of May 29, 1908, Congress was dealing with the surplus land question on a reservation-by-reservation basis, with each surplus land act employing its own statutory language, the product of a unique set of tribal negotiation and legislative compromise.

The modern legacy of the surplus land Acts has been a spate of jurisdictional disputes between state and federal officials as to which sovereign has authority over lands that were opened by the Acts and have since passed out of Indian ownership.[8] As a doctrinal matter, the States have jurisdiction over unallotted opened lands if the applicable surplus land act freed that land of its reservation status and thereby diminished the reservation boundaries. On the other hand, federal, state, and tribal authorities share jurisdiction over these lands if the relevant surplus land act did not diminish the existing Indian reservation because the entire opened area is Indian country under 18 U.S.C. § 1151(a).

Unfortunately, the surplus land acts themselves seldom detail whether opened lands retained reservation status or were divested of all Indian interests. When the surplus land Acts were passed, the distinction seemed unimportant. The notion that reservation status of Indian lands might not be coextensive with tribal ownership was unfamiliar at the turn of the century. Indian lands were judicially defined to include only those lands in which the Indians held some form of property interest: trust lands, individual allotments, and, to a more limited degree, opened lands that had not yet been claimed by non-Indians. Only in 1948 did Congress uncouple reservation status from Indian ownership, and statutorily define Indian country to include lands held in fee by non-Indians within reservation boundaries.

Another reason why Congress did not concern itself with the effect of surplus land Acts on reservation boundaries was the turn-of-the-century assumption that Indian reservations were a thing of the past. Consistent with prevailing wisdom, members of Congress voting on the surplus land acts believed to a man that within a short time—within a generation at most—the Indian tribes would enter traditional American society and the reservation system would cease to exist. Given this expectation, Congress naturally failed to be meticulous in clarifying whether a particular piece of legislation formally sliced a certain parcel of land off one reservation.

Although the Congresses that passed the surplus land acts anticipated the imminent demise of the reservation and, in fact, passed the acts partially to facilitate the process, we have never been willing to extrapolate from this expectation a specific congressional purpose of diminishing reservations with the passage of every surplus land act. Rather, it is settled law that some surplus land acts diminished reservations,

---

8. Regardless of whether the original reservation was diminished, federal and tribal courts have exclusive jurisdiction over those portions of the opened lands that were and have remained Indian allotments. In addition, opened lands that have been restored to reservation status by subsequent Acts of Congress, *see, e.g.*, Indian Reorganization Act of 1934, ch. 576, 48 Stat. 984 (codified at 25 U.S.C. § 461 *et seq.* (1982 ed.) (authorizing the return of opened lands to the original reservations)), fall within the exclusive criminal jurisdiction of federal and tribal courts. [Ed. note: the IRA has been recodified at 25 U.S.C. §§ 5101-5144.]

see, e.g., Rosebud Sioux Tribe v. Kneip, 430 U.S. 584 (1977); *DeCoteau v. District County Court*, 420 U.S. 425 (1975), and other surplus land acts did not, *see, e.g., Mattz v. Arnett*, 412 U.S. 481 (1973); *Seymour v. Superintendent*, 368 U.S. 351 (1962). The effect of any given surplus land act depends on the language of the act and the circumstances underlying its passage.[10]

Our precedents in the area have established a fairly clean analytical structure for distinguishing those surplus land acts that diminished reservations from those acts that simply offered non-Indians the opportunity to purchase land within established reservation boundaries. The first and governing principle is that only Congress can divest a reservation of its land and diminish its boundaries. Once a block of land is set aside for an Indian reservation and no matter what happens to the title of individual plots within the area, the entire block retains its reservation status until Congress explicitly indicates otherwise.[11]

Diminishment, moreover, will not be lightly inferred. Our analysis of surplus land acts requires that Congress clearly evince an "intent . . . to change . . . boundaries" before diminishment will be found. *Rosebud Sioux Tribe v. Kneip, supra*, at 615. The most probative evidence of congressional intent is the statutory language used to open the Indian lands. Explicit reference to cession or other language evidencing the present and total surrender of all tribal interests strongly suggests that Congress meant

---

10. At one extreme, for example, the Act of Mar. 3, 1891, ch. 543, 26 Stat. 1035 *et seq.*, expressly stated that the Lake Traverse Indian Tribe agreed to "cede, sell, relinquish and convey" all interest in unallotted lands on the Lake Traverse Indian Reservation, and the Act further provided that the Tribe would receive full compensation in consideration for its loss. In *DeCoteau v. District County Court*, we found that the Lake Traverse Act, with its express language of cession, diminished the Lake Traverse Indian Reservation. At the other extreme, the Act of Mar. 22, 1906, ch. 1126, § 1, 34 Stat. 80, simply authorized the Secretary of the Interior "to sell or dispose of" unallotted lands on a portion of the Colville Indian Reservation; under the Act, the Colville Tribe received whatever proceeds these sales generated, rather than a sum certain. In *Seymour v. Superintendent*, we held that, because the Colville Act lacked an unconditional divestiture of Indian interest in the lands, the Act simply opened a portion of the Colville Reservation to non-Indian settlers and did not diminish the reservation. *See also Mattz v. Arnett*.

Between these extremes was the case of the Rosebud Sioux Reservation. In 1901, the Rosebud Sioux Tribe voted in favor of an agreement to cede a portion of their land in Gregory County to the United States in exchange for a sum certain. Three years later, Congress passed the Act of Apr. 23, 1904, ch. 1484, 33 Stat. 254–258, which incorporated the agreement's cession language, but replaced sum-certain payment with a provision guaranteeing the Tribe only the proceeds from the sale of the opened lands. Over the following years, Congress passed two more surplus land acts involving Rosebud Reservation land in other counties; each of the subsequent Acts authorized the sale and disposal of additional lands and promised the tribes the proceeds of the sales. Although none of the Rosebud Acts clearly severed the Tribe from its interest in the unallotted opened lands and even though the last two Acts were strikingly similar to the 1906 Act found not to have diminished the Colville Reservation in *Seymour v. Superintendent, supra*, this Court held that the circumstances surrounding the passage of the three Rosebud Acts unequivocally demonstrated that Congress meant for each Act to diminish the Rosebud Reservation. *Rosebud Sioux Tribe v. Kneip.*

11. At one time, it was thought that Indian consent was needed to diminish a reservation, but in *Lone Wolf v. Hitchcock*, 187 U.S. 553 (1903), this Court decided that Congress could diminish reservations unilaterally.

to divest from the reservation all unallotted opened lands. *DeCoteau v. District County Court, supra,* at 444–445; *Seymour v. Superintendent, supra,* at 355. When such language of cession is buttressed by an unconditional commitment from Congress to compensate the Indian tribe for its opened land, there is an almost insurmountable presumption that Congress meant for the tribe's reservation to be diminished.

As our opinion in *Rosebud Sioux Tribe* demonstrates, however, explicit language of cession and unconditional compensation are not prerequisites for a finding of diminishment. When events surrounding the passage of a surplus land act—particularly the manner in which the transaction was negotiated with the tribes involved and the tenor of legislative reports presented to Congress—unequivocally reveal a widely held, contemporaneous understanding that the affected reservation would shrink as a result of the proposed legislation, we have been willing to infer that Congress shared the understanding that its action would diminish the reservation, notwithstanding the presence of statutory language that would otherwise suggest reservation boundaries remained unchanged. To a lesser extent, we have also looked to events that occurred after the passage of a surplus land act to decipher Congress' intentions. Congress' own treatment of the affected areas, particularly in the years immediately following the opening, has some evidentiary value, as does the manner in which the Bureau of Indian Affairs and local judicial authorities dealt with unallotted open lands.

On a more pragmatic level, we have recognized that who actually moved onto opened reservation lands is also relevant to deciding whether a surplus land act diminished a reservation. Where non-Indian settlers flooded into the opened portion of a reservation and the area has long since lost its Indian character, we have acknowledged that de facto, if not de jure, diminishment may have occurred. *See Rosebud Sioux Tribe v. Kneip, supra,* at 588, n. 3, and 604–605; *DeCoteau v. District County Court, supra,* at 428. In addition to the obvious practical advantages of acquiescing to de facto diminishment,[12] we look to the subsequent demographic history of opened lands as one additional clue as to what Congress expected would happen once land on a particular reservation was opened to non-Indian settlers.[13]

There are, of course, limits to how far we will go to decipher Congress' intention in any particular surplus land act. When both an act and its legislative history fail to provide substantial and compelling evidence of a congressional intention to diminish Indian lands, we are bound by our traditional solicitude for the Indian tribes to rule that diminishment did not take place and that the old reservation boundaries

---

12. When an area is predominately populated by non-Indians with only a few surviving pockets of Indian allotments, finding that the land remains Indian country seriously burdens the administration of state and local governments. Conversely, problems of an imbalanced checkerboard jurisdiction arise if a largely Indian opened area is found to be outside Indian country.

13. Resort to subsequent demographic history is, of course, an unorthodox and potentially unreliable method of statutory interpretation. However, in the area of surplus land acts, where various factors kept Congress from focusing on the diminishment issue, the technique is a necessary expedient.

survived the opening. *Mattz v. Arnett*, 412 U.S., at 505; *Seymour v. Superintendent*, 368 U.S. 351 (1962).

III A

We now turn to apply these principles to the Act of May 29, 1908. We begin with the Act's operative language, which reads:

> "[The] Secretary of the Interior . . . is hereby . . . authorized and directed, as hereinafter provided, to sell and dispose of all that portion of the Cheyenne River and Standing Rock Indian reservations in the States of South Dakota and North Dakota lying and being within the following described boundaries. . . .
>
> "[From] the proceeds arising from the sale and disposition of the lands aforesaid, exclusive of the customary fees and commissions, there shall be deposited in the Treasury of the United States, to the credit of the Indians belonging and having tribal rights on the reservation aforesaid in the States of South Dakota and North Dakota the sums to which the respective tribes may be entitled. . . ."

These provisions stand in sharp contrast to the explicit language of cession employed in the Lake Traverse and 1904 Rosebud Acts discussed in our opinions in *DeCoteau* and *Rosebud Sioux Tribe*. See n.10, *supra*. Rather than reciting an Indian agreement to "cede, sell, relinquish and convey" the opened lands, the Cheyenne River Act simply authorizes the Secretary to "sell and dispose" of certain lands. This reference to the sale of Indian lands, coupled with the creation of Indian accounts for proceeds, suggests that the Secretary of the Interior was simply being authorized to act as the Tribe's sales agent. Indeed, when faced with precisely the same language in *Seymour v. Superintendent*, *supra*, at 356, we concluded that such provisions "did no more than to open the way for non-Indian settlers to own land on the reservation in a manner which the Federal Government, acting as guardian and trustee for the Indians, regarded as beneficial to the development of its wards."[15]

The balance of the Cheyenne River Act is largely consistent with the implication of the operative language that the Act opened but did not diminish the Cheyenne River Sioux Reservation. Nowhere else in the Act is there specific reference to the cession of Indian interests in the opened lands or any change in existing reservation boundaries. In fact, certain provisions of the Act strongly suggest that the unallotted opened lands would for the immediate future remain an integral part of the Cheyenne River Reservation. In § 1 of the Act, the Secretary was authorized to set aside

---

15. As petitioners stress, the operative language of the Cheyenne River Act is also similar to language in the 1907 and 1910 Rosebud Acts, which this Court held diminished the Rosebud Sioux Reservation. Our analysis of [the] Rosebud Acts, however, was strongly colored by the existence of a 1904 Rosebud Act containing cession language "precisely suited" to disestablishment, and the admission of the Indians that the second two Rosebud Acts must have diminished their reservation if the previous Act did. *Rosebud Sioux Tribe v. Kneip*, 430 U.S., at 597, 606, and n.29; *see* n.10, *supra*.

portions of the opened lands "for agency, school, and religious purposes, to remain reserved as long as needed, and as long as agency, school, or religious institutions are maintained thereon for the benefit of said Indians." It is difficult to imagine why Congress would have reserved lands for such purposes if it did not anticipate that the opened area would remain part of the reservation. This interpretation is supported by § 2 of the Act, under which Cheyenne River Indians were given permission to continue to obtain individual allotments on the affected portion of the reservation before the land was officially opened to non-Indian settlers. Also in § 2, Congress instructed the Geological Survey to examine the opened area for "lands bearing coal" and exempted those sections from allotment or disposal, the apparent purpose being to reserve those mineral resources for the whole tribe.

This case is made more difficult, however, by the presence of some language in the Cheyenne River Act that indirectly supports petitioners' view that the reservation was diminished. For instance, in a provision permitting Indians already holding an allotment on the opened lands to obtain new allotments in the unopened territories, the Act refers to the unopened territories as "within the respective reservations thus diminished." Elsewhere, the Act permits tribal members to harvest timber on certain parts of the opened lands, but conditions the grant for "only as long as the lands remain part of the public domain." On the assumption that Congress would refer to opened lands as being part of the public domain only if the lands had lost all vestiges of reservation status, petitioners and several amici point to the term "public domain" as well as the phrase "reservations thus diminished" as evidence that Congress understood the Cheyenne River Act to divest unallotted open lands of their reservation status.

Undisputedly, the references to the opened areas as being in "the public domain" and the unopened areas as constituting "the reservation thus diminished" support petitioners' view that the Cheyenne River Act diminished the reservation. These isolated phrases, however, are hardly dispositive.[17] And, when balanced against the Cheyenne River Act's stated and limited goal of opening up reservation lands for sale to non-Indian settlers, these two phrases cannot carry the burden of establishing an express congressional purpose to diminish. The Act of May 29, 1908, read as a whole, does not present an explicit expression of congressional intent to diminish the Cheyenne River Sioux Reservation.

B

The circumstances surrounding the passage of the Cheyenne River Act also fail to establish a clear congressional purpose to diminish the reservation. In contrast to

---

17. There is also considerable doubt as to what Congress meant in using these phrases. In 1908, "diminished" was not yet a term of art in Indian law. When Congress spoke of the "reservation thus diminished," it may well have been referring to diminishment in common lands and not diminishment of reservation boundaries. Similarly, even without diminishment, unallotted opened lands could be conceived of as being in the "public domain" inasmuch as they were available for settlement.

the Lake Traverse Act and 1904 Rosebud Act, the Cheyenne River Act did not begin with an agreement between the United States and the Indian Tribes, in which the Indians agreed to cede a portion of their territory to the Federal Government. The Cheyenne River Act had its origins in "[a] bill to authorize the sale and disposition of a portion of the surplus and unallotted lands in the Cheyenne River and Standing Rock Indian reservations," introduced by Senator Gamble of South Dakota on December 9, 1907. Once the bill was under consideration, the Secretary of the Interior dispatched an Inspector McLaughlin to the two affected reservations to consult with the Tribes about the bills.

During his meeting with members of the Cheyenne River Tribe, Inspector McLaughlin admittedly spoke in terms of cession and the relinquishment of Indian interests in the opened territories. However, it is impossible to say that the Tribe agreed to the terms that McLaughlin presented. Due to bad weather during McLaughlin's visit, only 63 members of the Tribe attended his meeting. At the close of McLaughlin's presentation, the president of the Cheyenne River Business Council said that he would have to discuss the matter with the entire Tribe before he could respond to the proposed bill. McLaughlin agreed to delay submission of his report to Congress until he had received word from the Tribe, but, when the Tribe's vote had not reached Washington 14 days later, McLaughlin sent his report to Congress with the conclusion: "The general sentiment of the Indians in council with me at the agency was in favor of the relinquishment [of the opened lands]." McLaughlin, however, also informed Congress of the low attendance at his meeting with the Cheyenne River Tribe and acknowledged that he had never received formal approval from the Tribe.

With a full report of Inspector McLaughlin's meeting with the Cheyenne River Tribe before it, Congress considered the Cheyenne River Act in April and May 1908. In neither floor debates nor legislative reports is there a clear statement that Congress interpreted Inspector McLaughlin's report to establish an agreement on the part of the Cheyenne River Indians to cede the opened areas.[21] Indeed, the most explicit statement of Congress' view of the Indians' position was: "The Indians upon both reservations are satisfied to have the surplus and unallotted lands disposed of under the provisions of the bill as amended." For the most part, the legislative debate of the Cheyenne River Act centered on how much money the Indians would be paid for certain sections of the opened area that the United States was going to buy for school lands, and no mention was made of the Act's effect on the reservation's boundaries or whether state or federal officials would have jurisdiction over the opened areas.

To be sure, there are a few phrases scattered through the legislative history of the Cheyenne River Act that support petitioners' position. Both the Senate and House Reports refer to the "reduced reservation" and state that "lands reserved for the use of

---

21. One reason why Congress may not have interpreted the McLaughlin report as evidence of tribal agreement to cede the land is that a delegation from the Tribe followed McLaughlin back to Washington to urge Congress not to pass the proposed legislation. The particulars of the delegation's trip are not known.

the Indians upon both reservations as diminished . . . are ample . . . for the present and future needs of the Indians of the respective tribes." However, it is unclear whether Congress was alluding to the reduction in Indian-owned lands that would occur once some of the opened lands were sold to settlers or to the reduction that a complete cession of tribal interests in the opened area would precipitate. Without evidence that Congress understood itself to be entering into an agreement under which the Tribe committed itself to cede and relinquish all interests in unallotted opened lands, and in the absence of some clear statement of congressional intent to alter reservation boundaries, it is impossible to infer from a few isolated and ambiguous phrases a congressional purpose to diminish the Cheyenne River Sioux Reservation.

C

The subsequent treatment of the Cheyenne River Sioux Reservation by Congress, courts, and the Executive is so rife with contradictions and inconsistencies as to be of no help to either side. For instance, two years after the Cheyenne River Act, Congress passed a bill to sell a portion of the opened lands and called the area "surplus and unallotted lands in the Cheyenne River Indian Reservation," suggesting that the opened area was still part of the reservation. But, 12 years after that, Congress passed another piece of legislation referring to the opened lands as "the former" Cheyenne River Sioux Reservation and suggesting that the reservation had been diminished. Ample additional examples pointing in both directions leave one with the distinct impression that subsequent Congresses had no clear view whether the opened territories were or were not still part of the Cheyenne River Reservation. A similar state of confusion characterizes the Executive's treatment of the Cheyenne River Sioux Reservation's opened lands. Moreover, both parties have been able to cite instances in which state and federal courts exerted criminal jurisdiction over the disputed area in the years following opening. Neither sovereign dominated the jurisdictional history of the opened lands in the decades immediately following 1908.

What is clear, however, is what happened to the Cheyenne River Sioux Tribe after the Act of May 29, 1908, was passed. Most of the members of the Tribe obtained individual allotments on the lands opened by the Act. Because most of the Tribe lived on the opened territories, tribal authorities and Bureau of Indian Affairs personnel took primary responsibility for policing and supplying social services to the opened lands during the years following 1908. The strong tribal presence in the opened area has continued until the present day. Now roughly two-thirds of the Tribe's enrolled members live in the opened area. The seat of tribal government is now located in a town in the opened area, where most important tribal activities take place.

Also clear is the historical fact that the opening of the Cheyenne River Sioux Reservation was a failure. Few homesteaders perfected claims on the lands, due perhaps in part to the price of the land but probably more importantly to the fact that the opened area was much less fertile than the lands in southern South Dakota opened by other surplus land acts. As a result of the small number of homesteaders who settled on the opened lands and the high percentage of tribal members who continue to live in the area, the population of the disputed area is now evenly divided between

Indian and non-Indian residents. Under these circumstances, it is impossible to say that the opened areas of the Cheyenne River Sioux Reservation have lost their Indian character.

IV

Neither the Act of May 29, 1908, the circumstances surrounding its passage, nor subsequent events clearly establish that the Act diminished the Cheyenne River Sioux Reservation. The presumption that Congress did not intend to diminish the reservation therefore stands, and the judgment of the Eighth Circuit is affirmed.

Note on the Canons of Construction

The Court's diminishment opinions refer to the manner in which courts interpret treaties and agreements with Indian tribes. Largely in recognition of the unequal bargaining power of the parties, the Supreme Court has developed a set of canons of treaty construction. In essence, these canons provide that:

(1) treaties are construed as the Indians understood them;

(2) treaties, statutes, and agreements are liberally construed in favor of the Indians;

(3) all ambiguities are resolved in favor of the Indians;

(4) tribal sovereignty and property rights are preserved unless Congress clearly and unambiguously provides otherwise.

See Cohen's Handbook of Federal Indian Law § 2.02[1] (Nell Jessup Newton et al., eds. (2012). The rudiments of these canons are traceable to Chief Justice Marshall's interpretation of the Treaty of Hopewell in *Worcester v. Georgia*, 31 U.S. 515 (1832), excerpted at page 61.

Did the *Solem* decision appropriately employ the canons? Does the *Yankton Sioux* Court in the following case? As you read the cases in the chapters that follow, pay attention to whether the courts refer to and/or apply the canons in interpreting statutes, treaties, and agreements with Indian tribes.

South Dakota v. Yankton Sioux Tribe
522 U.S. 329 (1998)

JUSTICE O'CONNOR delivered the [unanimous] opinion of the Court.

This case presents the question whether, in an 1894 statute that ratified an agreement for the sale of surplus tribal lands, Congress diminished the boundaries of the Yankton Sioux Reservation in South Dakota. The reservation was established pursuant to an 1858 treaty between the United States and the Yankton Sioux Tribe. Subsequently, under the General Allotment Act of 1887 (the Dawes Act), individual members of the Tribe received allotments of reservation land, and the Government then negotiated with the Tribe for the cession of the remaining, unallotted lands. The issue we confront illustrates the jurisdictional quandaries wrought by the allotment policy: We must decide whether a landfill constructed on non-Indian fee land that falls within the boundaries of the original Yankton Reservation remains subject to federal environmental regulations. If the divestiture of Indian property in 1894 effected a diminishment of Indian territory, then the ceded lands no longer constitute "Indian country" as defined by 18 U.S.C. § 1151(a), and the State now has primary jurisdiction over them. In light of the operative language of the 1894 Act, and the circumstances surrounding its passage, we hold that Congress intended to diminish the Yankton Reservation and consequently that the waste site is not in Indian country.

I A

At the outset of the 19th century, the Yankton Sioux Tribe held exclusive dominion over 13 million acres of land between the Des Moines and Missouri rivers, near the boundary that currently divides North and South Dakota. In 1858, the Yanktons entered into a treaty with the United States renouncing their claim to more than 11 million acres of their aboriginal lands in the north-central plains.

The retained portion of the Tribe's lands, located in what is now the southeastern part of Charles Mix County, South Dakota, was later surveyed and determined to encompass 430,405 acres. In consideration for the cession of lands and release of claims, the United States pledged to protect the Yankton Tribe in their "quiet and peaceable possession" of this reservation and agreed that "no white person," with narrow exceptions, would "be permitted to reside or make any settlement upon any part of the [reservation]." The Federal Government further promised to pay the Tribe, or expend for the benefit of members of the Tribe, $1.6 million over a 50-year period, and appropriated an additional $50,000 to aid the Tribe in its transition to the reservation through the purchase of livestock and agricultural implements, and the construction of houses, schools, and other buildings.

In accordance with the Dawes Act, each member of the Yankton Tribe received a 160-acre tract from the existing reservation, held in trust by the United States for 25 years. Members of the Tribe acquired parcels of land throughout the 1858 reservation, although many of the allotments were clustered in the southern part, near the Missouri River. By 1890, the allotting agent had apportioned 167,325 acres of reservation land, 95,000 additional acres were subsequently allotted under the Act of February 28, 1891, and a small amount of acreage was reserved for government and religious purposes. The surplus amounted to approximately 168,000 acres of unallotted lands.

In 1892, the Secretary of the Interior dispatched a three-member Yankton Indian Commission to Greenwood, South Dakota, to negotiate for the acquisition of these surplus lands. When the Commissioners arrived on the reservation in October 1892, they informed the Tribe that they had been sent by the "Great Father" to discuss the cession of "this land that [members of the Tribe] hold in common," and they abruptly encountered opposition to the sale from traditionalist tribal leaders. In the lengthy negotiations that followed, members of the Tribe raised concerns about the suggested price per acre, the preservation of their annuities under the 1858 Treaty, and other outstanding claims against the United States, but they did not discuss the future boundaries of the reservation. Once the Commissioners garnered a measure of support for the sale of the unallotted lands, they submitted a proposed agreement to the Tribe.

Article I of the agreement provided that the Tribe would "cede, sell, relinquish, and convey to the United States" all of the unallotted lands on the reservation. Pursuant to Article II, the United States agreed to compensate the Tribe in a single payment of $600,000, which amounted to $3.60 per acre.[2] Much of the agreement focused on the payment and disposition of that sum. * * * The saving clause in Article XVIII, the core of the current disagreement between the parties to this case, stated that nothing in the agreement's terms "shall be construed to abrogate the treaty [of 1858]" and that "all provisions of the said treaty . . . shall be in full force and effect, the same as though this agreement had not been made."[#]

By March 1893, the Commissioners had collected signatures from 255 of the 458 male members of the Tribe eligible to vote, and thus obtained the requisite majority endorsement. The Yankton Indian Commission filed its report in May 1893, but congressional consideration was delayed by an investigation into allegations of fraud in the procurement of signatures. On August 15, 1894, Congress finally ratified the 1892 agreement, together with similar surplus land sale agreements between the United States and the Siletz and Nez Perce Tribes. Act of Aug. 15, 1894, 28 Stat. 286. The 1894 Act incorporated the 1892 agreement in its entirety and appropriated the necessary funds to compensate the Tribe for the ceded lands * * *.

President Cleveland issued a proclamation opening the ceded lands to settlement as of May 21, 1895, and non-Indians rapidly acquired them. By the turn of the century, 90 percent of the unallotted tracts had been settled. A majority of the individual allotments granted to members of the Tribe also were subsequently conveyed in fee by the members to non-Indians. Today, the total Indian holdings in the region consist of approximately 30,000 acres of allotted land and 6,000 acres of tribal land.

[In 1992, a group of South Dakota counties formed a waste management district, and acquired a landfill site within the boundaries of the 1858 Yankton Sioux Reservation. The site was acquired in fee from a non-Indian, and the Court determined

---

2. In 1980, the Court of Claims concluded that the land ceded by the Tribe had a fair market value of $6.65 per acre, or $1,337,381.50, that the $600,000 paid pursuant to the 1892 agreement was "unconscionable and grossly inadequate," and that the Tribe was entitled to recover the difference. *Yankton Sioux Tribe v. United States*, 224 Ct. Cl. 62, 623 F.2d 159, 178.

* [Editor's note. Article XVIII provided in its entirety:
  Nothing in this agreement shall be construed to abrogate the treaty of April 19th, 1858, between the Yankton tribe of Sioux Indians and the United States. And after the signing of this agreement, and its ratification by Congress, all provisions of the said treaty of April 19th, 1858, shall be in full force and effect, the same as though this agreement had not been made, and the said Yankton Indians shall continue to receive their annuities under the said treaty of April 19th, 1858.]

that it was located on land ceded in the 1894 Act. The state issued a landfill permit to the waste district over the environmental objections of the Tribe, and the Tribe filed suit in federal district court to enjoin construction of the landfill. The district court held that the 1894 Act did not diminish the reservation, and thus that the landfill site was within the Yankton Sioux Reservation. The Eighth Circuit affirmed.]

* * * We now reverse the Eighth Circuit's decision and hold that the unallotted lands ceded as a result of the 1894 Act did not retain reservation status.

II

States acquired primary jurisdiction over unallotted opened lands where "the applicable surplus land Act freed that land of its reservation status and thereby diminished the reservation boundaries." *Solem*, 465 U.S. at 467. In contrast, if a surplus land Act "simply offered non-Indians the opportunity to purchase land within established reservation boundaries," *id.*, at 470, then the entire opened area remained Indian country. Our touchstone to determine whether a given statute diminished or retained reservation boundaries is congressional purpose. Congress possesses plenary power over Indian affairs, including the power to modify or eliminate tribal rights. Accordingly, only Congress can alter the terms of an Indian treaty by diminishing a reservation, and its intent to do so must be "clear and plain."

Here, we must determine whether Congress intended by the 1894 Act to modify the reservation set aside for the Yankton Tribe in the 1858 Treaty. Our inquiry is informed by the understanding that, at the turn of this century, Congress did not view the distinction between acquiring Indian property and assuming jurisdiction over Indian territory as a critical one, in part because "the notion that reservation status of Indian lands might not be coextensive with tribal ownership was unfamiliar," *Solem*, 465 U.S. at 468, and in part because Congress then assumed that the reservation system would fade over time. "Given this expectation, Congress naturally failed to be meticulous in clarifying whether a particular piece of legislation formally sliced a certain parcel of land off one reservation." *Ibid.*; *see also Hagen [v. Utah]*, 510 U.S. [399] at 426 [1994] (Blackmun, J., dissenting). Thus, although "the most probative evidence of diminishment is, of course, the statutory language used to open the Indian lands," we have held that we will also consider "the historical context surrounding the passage of the surplus land Acts," and, to a lesser extent, the subsequent treatment of the area in question and the pattern of settlement there. Throughout this inquiry, "we resolve any ambiguities in favor of the Indians, and we will not lightly find diminishment."

A

Article I of the 1894 Act provides that the Tribe will "cede, sell, relinquish, and convey to the United States all their claim, right, title, and interest in and to all the unallotted lands within the limits of the reservation"; pursuant to Article II, the United States pledges a fixed payment of $600,000 in return. This "cession" and "sum certain" language is "precisely suited" to terminating reservation status. *See DeCoteau*, 420 U.S. at 445. Indeed, we have held that when a surplus land Act contains both explicit language of cession, evidencing "the present and total surrender of all tribal interests," and a provision for a fixed-sum payment, representing "an unconditional commitment from Congress to compensate the Indian tribe for its opened land," a "nearly conclusive," or "almost insurmountable," presumption of diminishment arises. *Solem, supra*, at 470; *see also Hagen, supra*, at 411.

The terms of the 1894 Act parallel the language that this Court found terminated the Lake Traverse Indian Reservation in *DeCoteau*, and, as in *DeCoteau*, the 1894 Act ratified a negotiated agreement supported by a majority of the Tribe. Moreover, the Act we construe here more clearly indicates diminishment than did the surplus land Act at issue in *Hagen*, which we concluded diminished reservation lands even though it provided only that "all the unallotted lands within said reservation shall be restored to the public domain."

The 1894 Act is also readily distinguishable from surplus land Acts that the Court has interpreted as maintaining reservation boundaries. In both *Seymour v. Superintendent of Wash. State Penitentiary*, 368 U.S. 351, 355 (1962), and *Mattz v. Arnett*, 412 U.S. 481, 501–502 (1973), we held that Acts declaring surplus land "subject to settlement, entry, and purchase," without more, did not evince congressional intent to diminish the reservations. Likewise, in *Solem*, we did not read a phrase authorizing the Secretary of the Interior to "sell and dispose" of surplus lands belonging to the Cheyenne River Sioux as language of cession. In contrast, the 1894 Act at issue here— a negotiated agreement providing for the total surrender of tribal claims in exchange for a fixed payment—bears the hallmarks of congressional intent to diminish a reservation.

B

The Yankton Tribe and the United States, appearing as amicus for the Tribe, rest their argument against diminishment primarily on the saving clause in Article XVIII of the 1894 Act. The Tribe asserts that because that clause purported to conserve the provisions of the 1858 Treaty, the existing reservation boundaries were maintained. The United States urges a similarly "holistic" construction of the agreement, which would presume that the parties intended to modify the 1858 Treaty only insofar as necessary to open the surplus lands for settlement, without fundamentally altering the Treaty's terms.

Such a literal construction of the saving clause, as the South Dakota Supreme Court noted in *State v. Greger*, 1997 S.D. 14, 559 N.W.2d 854, 863 (S.D. 1997), would "impugn the entire sale." The unconditional relinquishment of the Tribe's territory for settlement by non-Indian homesteaders can by no means be reconciled with the central provisions of the 1858 Treaty, which recognized the reservation as the Tribe's "permanent" home and prohibited white settlement there. Moreover, the Government's contention that the Tribe intended to cede some property but maintain the entire reservation as its territory contradicts the common understanding of the time: that tribal ownership was a critical component of reservation status. We "cannot ignore plain language that, viewed in historical context and given a fair appraisal, clearly runs counter to a tribe's late claims."

Rather than read the saving clause in a manner that eviscerates the agreement in which it appears, we give it a "sensible construction" that avoids this "absurd conclusion." The most plausible interpretation of Article XVIII revolves around the annuities in the form of cash, guns, ammunition, food, and clothing that the Tribe was to receive in exchange for its aboriginal claims for 50 years after the 1858 Treaty. Along with the proposed sale price, these annuities and other unrealized Yankton claims dominated the 1892 negotiations between the Commissioners and the Tribe. The tribal historian testified, before the District Court, that the loss of their rations would have been "disastrous" to the Tribe, and members of the Tribe clearly perceived a threat to the annuities. At a particularly tense point in the negotiations, when the tide seemed to turn in favor of forces opposing the sale, Commissioner John J. Cole warned:

> "I want you to understand that you are absolutely dependent upon the Great Father to-day for a living. Let the Government send out instructions to your agent to cease to issue these rations, let the Government instruct your agent to cease to issue your clothes. . . . Let the Government instruct him to cease to issue your supplies, let him take away the money to run your schools with, and I want to know what you would do. Everything you are wearing and eating is gratuity. Take all this away and throw this people wholly upon their own responsibility to take care of themselves, and what would be the result! Not one-fourth of your people could live through the winter, and when the grass grows again it would be nourished by the dust of all the balance of your noble tribe." Council of the Yankton Indians (Dec. 10, 1892), transcribed in S. Exec. Doc. No. 27, at 74.

Given the Tribe's evident concern with reaffirmance of the Government's obligations under the 1858 Treaty, and the Commissioners' tendency to wield the payments as an inducement to sign the agreement, we conclude that the saving clause pertains to the continuance of annuities, not the 1858 borders.

The language in Article XVIII specifically ensuring that the "Yankton Indians shall continue to receive their annuities under the [1858 Treaty]" underscores the limited purpose and scope of the saving clause. It is true that the Court avoids interpreting statutes in a way that "renders some words altogether redundant." But in light of the fact that the record of the negotiations between the Commissioners and the Yankton Tribe contains no discussion of the preservation of the 1858 boundaries but many references to the Government's failure to fulfill earlier promises, it seems most likely that the parties inserted and understood Article XVIII, including both the general statement regarding the force of the 1858 Treaty and the particular provision that payments would continue as specified therein, to assuage the Tribes' concerns about their past claims and future entitlements.

Indeed, apart from the pledge to pay annuities, it is hard to identify any provision in the 1858 Treaty that the Tribe might have sought to preserve, other than those plainly inconsistent with or expressly included in the 1894 Act. * * * [The Tribe] contends that because Article XVIII affirms that the 1858 Treaty will govern "the same as though [the 1892 agreement] had not been made," without reference to consistency between those agreements, it has more force than the standard saving clause. While the language of the saving clause is indeed unusual, we do not think it is meaningfully distinct from the saving clauses that have failed to move this Court to find that pre-existing treaties remain in effect under comparable circumstances. Furthermore, "it is a commonplace of statutory construction that the specific" cession and sum certain language in Articles I and II "governs the general" terms of the saving clause. *See Morales v. Trans World Airlines, Inc.*, 504 U.S. 374, 384 (1992).

Finally, the Tribe argues that, at a minimum, the saving clause renders the statute equivocal, and that confronted with that ambiguity we must adopt the reading that favors the Tribe. The principle according to which ambiguities are resolved to the benefit of Indian tribes is not, however, "a license to disregard clear expressions of tribal and congressional intent." *DeCoteau*, 420 U.S. at 447. In previous decisions, this Court has recognized that the precise cession and sum certain language contained in the 1894 Act plainly indicates diminishment, and a reasonable interpretation of the saving clause does not conflict with a like conclusion in this case.

III

Although we perceive congressional intent to diminish the reservation in the plain statutory language, we also take note of the contemporary historical context, subsequent congressional and administrative references to the reservation, and demographic trends. Even in the absence of a clear expression of congressional purpose in the text of a surplus land Act, unequivocal evidence derived from the surrounding circumstances may support the conclusion that a reservation has been diminished. *See Solem*, 465 U.S. at 471. In this case, although the context of the Act is not so compelling that, standing alone, it would indicate diminishment, neither does it rebut the "almost insurmountable presumption" that arises from the statute's plain terms.

[The Court found that the contemporary historical context revealed an "understanding that the proposed legislation modified the reservation," but that subsequent governmental references were so contradictory and inconsistent as to have little force "in light of the strong textual and contemporaneous evidence of diminishment." The Court then turned to the demographics of the Yankton Sioux Reservation.]

"Where non-Indian settlers flooded into the opened portion of a reservation and the area has long since lost its Indian character, we have acknowledged that de facto, if not de jure, diminishment may have occurred." *Id.* at 471. This final consideration is the least compelling for a simple reason: Every surplus land Act necessarily resulted in a surge of non-Indian settlement and degraded the "Indian character" of the reservation, yet we have repeatedly stated that not every surplus land Act diminished the affected reservation. The fact that the Yankton population in the region promptly and drastically declined after the 1894 Act does, however, provide "one additional clue as to what Congress expected," *id.* at 472. Today, fewer than ten percent of the 1858 reservation lands are in Indian hands, non-Indians constitute over two-thirds of the population within the 1858 boundaries, and several municipalities inside those boundaries have been incorporated under South Dakota law. The opening of the tribal casino in 1991 apparently reversed the population trend; the tribal presence in the area has steadily increased in recent years, and the advent of gaming has stimulated the local economy. In addition, some acreage within the 1858 boundaries has reverted to tribal or trust land. Nonetheless, the area remains "predominantly populated by non-Indians with only a few surviving pockets of Indian allotments," and those demographics signify a diminished reservation. *Solem, supra*, at 471, n.12.

The State's assumption of jurisdiction over the territory, almost immediately after the 1894 Act and continuing virtually unchallenged to the present day, further reinforces our holding. As the Court of Appeals acknowledged, South Dakota "has quite consistently exercised various forms of governmental authority over the opened lands," and the "tribe presented no evidence that it has attempted until recently to exercise civil, regulatory, or criminal jurisdiction over nontrust lands." Finally, the Yankton Constitution, drafted in 1932 and amended in 1962, defines the Tribe's territory to include only those tribal lands within the 1858 boundaries "now owned" by the Tribe.

IV

The allotment era has long since ended, and its guiding philosophy has been repudiated. Tribal communities struggled but endured, preserved their cultural roots, and remained, for the most part, near their historic lands. But despite the present-day understanding of a "government-to-government relationship between the United States and each Indian tribe," *see, e.g.,* 25 U.S.C. §3601, we must give effect to Congress' intent in passing the 1894 Act. Here, as in *DeCoteau*, we believe that Congress spoke clearly, and although "some might wish [it] had spoken differently . . . we cannot remake history."

The 1894 Act contains the most certain statutory language, evincing Congress' intent to diminish the Yankton Sioux Reservation by providing for total cession and fixed compensation. Contemporaneous historical evidence supports that conclusion, and nothing in the ambiguous subsequent treatment of the region substantially controverts our reasoning. The conflicting understandings about the status of the reservation, together with the fact that the Tribe continues to own land in common, caution us, however, to limit our holding to the narrow question presented: whether unallotted, ceded lands were severed from the reservation. We need not determine whether Congress disestablished the reservation altogether in order to resolve this case, and accordingly decline to do so. Our holding in *Hagen* was similarly limited, as was the State Supreme Court's description of the Yankton reservation in *Greger*.

In sum, we hold that Congress diminished the Yankton Sioux Reservation in the 1894 Act, that the unallotted tracts no longer constitute Indian country, and thus that the State has primary jurisdiction over the waste site and other lands ceded under the Act. * * *

Notes

1. **Reconciling *Yankton Sioux* and *Solem*?** Can you reconcile the apparently contradictory results in *Solem* and in *Yankton Sioux*? Note that both decisions were unanimous, albeit fourteen years apart.

2. **The "actual state of things."** How much are the divergent results in the two cases due to what Chief Justice John Marshall referred to as the "actual state of things?" In other words, how much is the legal reasoning influenced by current settlement patterns in the disputed areas? If current settlement patterns influence the legal results, doesn't that guarantee that tribes will retain sovereign authority only over lands that were not highly prized by white settlers? In short, land with valuable resources would have been homesteaded in proportions great enough to make the current character of the land look non-Indian. Land without valuable resources would not likely have been sought by white settlers, leaving the Indian character of the lands intact and making a judicial finding of tribal sovereignty more likely. Moreover, doesn't this approach depend upon a "snapshot" of the reservation demographics at the time of the case? In *Yankton Sioux*, for example, the tribe was reestablishing its population and economic base. If it continues on that path, is there a point at which the reservation becomes de facto "re-established"?

Nebraska v. Parker
136 S. Ct. 1072 (2016)

Justice THOMAS delivered the opinion of the Court.

The village of Pender, Nebraska sits a few miles west of an abandoned right-of-way once used by the Sioux City and Nebraska Railroad Company. We must decide whether Pender and surrounding Thurston County, Nebraska, are within the boundaries of the Omaha Indian Reservation or whether the passage of an 1882 Act empowering the United States Secretary of the Interior to sell the Tribe's land west of the right-of-way "diminished" the reservation's boundaries, thereby "free[ing]" the disputed land of "its reservation status." We hold that Congress did not diminish the reservation in 1882 and that the disputed land is within the reservation's boundaries.

I. A.

Centuries ago, the Omaha Tribe settled in present-day eastern Nebraska. By the mid–19th century, the Tribe was destitute and, in exchange for much-needed revenue, agreed to sell a large swath of its land to the United States. [The Court explained a series of treaties and ensuing land sales between 1859 and 1872.]

Then came the 1882 Act, central to the dispute between petitioners and respondents. In that Act, Congress again empowered the Secretary of the Interior "to cause to be surveyed, if necessary, and sold" more than 50,000 acres lying west of a right-of-way granted by the Tribe and approved by the Secretary of the Interior in 1880 for use by the Sioux City and Nebraska Railroad Company. Act of Aug. 7, 1882 (1882 Act), 22 Stat. 341. The land for sale under the terms of the 1882 Act overlapped substantially with the land Congress tried, but failed, to sell in 1872. Once the land was appraised "in tracts of forty acres each," the Secretary was "to issue [a] proclamation" that the "lands are open for settlement under such rules and regulations as he may prescribe." §§ 1, 2, *id.*, at 341. Within one year of that proclamation, a nonmember could purchase up to 160 acres of land (for no less than $2.50 per acre) in cash paid to the United States, so long as the settler "occup[ied]" it, made "valuable improvements thereon," and was "a citizen of the United States, or . . . declared his intention to become such." § 2, *id.*, at 341. The proceeds from any land sales, "after paying all expenses incident to and necessary for carrying out the provisions of th[e] act," were to "be placed to the credit of said Indians in the Treasury of the United States." § 3, *id.*, at 341. Interest earned on the proceeds was to be "annually expended for the benefit of said Indians, under the direction of the Secretary of the Interior." *Ibid*.

The 1882 Act also included a provision, common in the late 19th century, that enabled members of the Tribe to select individual allotments as a means of encouraging them to depart from the communal lifestyle of the reservation. The 1882 Act provided that the United States would convey the land to a member or his heirs in fee simple after holding it in trust on behalf of the member and his heirs for 25 years. Members could select allotments on any part of the reservation, either east or west of the right-of-way.

After the members selected their allotments—only 10 to 15 of which were located west of the right-of-way—the Secretary proclaimed that the remaining 50,157 acres west of the right-of-way were open for settlement by nonmembers in April 1884. One of those settlers was W.E. Peebles, who "purchased a tract of 160 acres, on which he platted the townsite for Pender."

B.

The village of Pender today numbers 1,300 residents. Most are not associated with the Omaha Tribe. Less than 2% of Omaha tribal members have lived west of the right-of-way since the early 20th century.

Despite its longstanding absence, the Tribe sought to assert jurisdiction over Pender in 2006 by subjecting Pender retailers to its newly amended Beverage Control Ordinance. The ordinance requires those retailers to obtain a liquor license (costing $500, $1,000, or $1,500 depending upon the class of license) and imposes a 10% sales tax on liquor sales. Nonmembers who violate the ordinance are subject to a $10,000 fine.

The village of Pender and Pender retailers, including bars, a bowling alley, and social clubs, brought a federal suit against members of the Omaha Tribal Council in their official capacities to challenge the Tribe's power to impose the requirements of the Beverage Control Ordinance on nonmembers. Federal law permits the Tribe to regulate liquor sales on its reservation and in "Indian country" so long as the Tribe's regulations are (as they were here) "certified by the Secretary of the Interior, and published in the Federal Register." 18 U.S.C. §1161. The challengers alleged that they were neither within the boundaries of the Omaha Indian Reservation nor in Indian country and, consequently, were not bound by the ordinance.

The State of Nebraska intervened on behalf of the plaintiffs, and the United States intervened on behalf of the Omaha Tribal Council members. The State's intervention was prompted, in part, by the Omaha Tribe's demand that Nebraska share with the Tribe revenue that the State received from fuel taxes imposed west of the right-of-way. In addition to the relief sought by Pender and the Pender retailers, Nebraska sought a permanent injunction prohibiting the Tribe from asserting tribal jurisdiction over the 50,157 acres west of the abandoned right-of-way.

After examining the text of the 1882 Act, as well as the contemporaneous and subsequent understanding of the 1882 Act's effect on the reservation boundaries, the District Court concluded that Congress did not diminish the Omaha Reservation in 1882. Accordingly, the District Court denied the plaintiffs' request for injunctive and declaratory relief barring the Tribe's enforcement of the Beverage Control Ordinance. The Eighth Circuit affirmed. We granted certiorari to resolve whether the 1882 Act diminished the Omaha Reservation.

II.

We must determine whether Congress "diminished" the Omaha Indian Reservation in 1882. If it did so, the State now has jurisdiction over the disputed land. If Congress, on the other hand, did not diminish the reservation and instead only enabled nonmembers to purchase land within the reservation, then federal, state, and tribal authorities share jurisdiction over these "opened" but undiminished reservation lands.

The framework we employ to determine whether an Indian reservation has been diminished is well settled. [The Court explained the three-part test established in *Solem*.]

A.

As with any other question of statutory interpretation, we begin with the text of the 1882 Act, the most "probative evidence" of diminishment. . . .

The 1882 Act bore none of these hallmarks of diminishment. The 1882 Act empowered the Secretary to survey and appraise the disputed land, which then could be purchased in 160–acre tracts by nonmembers. 22 Stat. 341. The 1882 Act states that the disputed lands would be "open for settlement under such rules and regulations as [the Secretary of the Interior] may prescribe." Ibid. And the parcels would be sold piecemeal in 160-acre tracts. *Ibid*. So rather than the Tribe's receiving a fixed sum for all of the disputed lands, the Tribe's profits were entirely dependent upon how many nonmembers purchased the appraised tracts of land.

From this text, it is clear that the 1882 Act falls into another category of surplus land Acts: those that "merely opened reservation land to settlement and provided that the uncertain future proceeds of settler purchases should be applied to the Indians' benefit." ***

Our conclusion that Congress did not intend to diminish the reservation in 1882 is confirmed by the text of earlier treaties between the United States and the Tribe. In drafting the 1882 Act, Congress legislated against the backdrop of the 1854 and 1865 Treaties—both of which terminated the Tribe's jurisdiction over their land "in unequivocal terms." *Ibid.* Those treaties "ced[ed]" the lands and "relinquish[ed]" any claims to them in exchange for a fixed sum. 10 Stat. 1043–1044; see also 14 Stat. 667 ("The Omaha tribe of Indians do hereby *cede, sell, and convey* to the United States a tract of land from the north side of their present reservation . . ." (emphasis added)). The 1882 Act speaks in much different terms, both in describing the way the individual parcels were to be sold to nonmembers and the way in which the Tribe would profit from those sales. That 1882 Act also closely tracks the 1872 Act, which petitioners do not contend diminished the reservation. The change in language in the 1882 Act undermines petitioners' claim that Congress intended to do the same with the reservation's boundaries in 1882 as it did in 1854 and 1865. Petitioners have failed at the first and most important step. They cannot establish that the text of the 1882 Act evinced an intent to diminish the reservation.

B

We now turn to the history surrounding the passage of the 1882 Act. The mixed historical evidence relied upon by the parties cannot overcome the lack of clear textual signal that Congress intended to diminish the reservation. That historical evidence in no way "*unequivocally* reveal[s] a widely held, contemporaneous understanding that the affected reservation would shrink as a result of the proposed legislation."

Petitioners rely largely on isolated statements that some legislators made about the 1882 Act. Senator Henry Dawes of Massachusetts, for example, noted that he had been "assured that [the 1882 Act] would *leave an ample reservation*" for the Tribe. 13 Cong. Rec. 3032 (1882) (emphasis added). And Senator John Ingalls of Kansas observed "that this bill practically breaks up that portion at least of the reservation which is to be sold, and provides that it shall be disposed of to private purchasers." *Id.*, at 3028. Whatever value these contemporaneous floor statements might have, other such statements support the opposite conclusion—that Congress never intended to diminish the reservation. Senator Charles Jones of Florida, for example, spoke of "white men purchas[ing] titles to land *within* this reservation and settl[ing] down with the Indians on it." *Id.*, at 3078 (emphasis added). Such dueling remarks by individual legislators are far from the "clear and plain" evidence of diminishment required under this Court's precedent. *Yankton Sioux*, 522 U.S., at 343 (internal quotation marks omitted); see also *Solem*, 465 U.S., at 478 (noting that it was unclear whether statements referring to a "'reduced reservation'" alluded to the "reduction in Indian-owned lands that would occur once some of the opened lands were sold to settlers or to the reduction that a complete cession of tribal interests in the opened area would precipitate").

More illuminating than cherry-picked statements by individual legislators would be historical evidence of "the manner in which the transaction was negotiated" with the Omaha Tribe. *Id.*, at 471, In *Yankton Sioux*, for example, recorded negotiations between the Commissioner of Indian Affairs and leaders of the Yankton Sioux Tribe unambiguously "signaled [the Tribe's] understanding that the cession of the surplus lands dissolved tribal governance of the 1858 reservation." No such unambiguous evidence exists in the record of these negotiations. In particular, petitioners' reliance on the remarks of Representative Edward Valentine of Nebraska, who stated, "You cannot find one of those Indians that does not want the western portion sold," and that the Tribe wished to sell the land to those who would "'reside upon it and cultivate it'" so that the Tribe members could "benefit of these improvements," 13 Cong. Rec. 6541, falls short. Nothing about this statement or other similar statements unequivocally supports a finding that the existing boundaries of the reservation would be diminished.

C

Finally, we consider both the subsequent demographic history of opened lands, which serves as "one additional clue as to what Congress expected would happen once land on a particular reservation was opened to non-Indian settlers," as well as the United States' "treatment of the affected areas, particularly in the years immediately following the opening," which has "some evidentiary value." Our cases suggest that such evidence might "reinforc[e]" a finding of diminishment or nondiminishment based on the text. *Mattz*, 412 U.S., at 505; see also, e.g., *Rosebud Sioux Tribe v. Kneip*, 430 U.S. 584, 604–605 (1977) (invoking subsequent history to reject a petitioner's "strained" textual reading of a congressional Act). But this Court has never relied solely on this third consideration to find diminishment.

As petitioners have discussed at length, the Tribe was almost entirely absent from the disputed territory for more than 120 years. Brief for Petitioners 24–30. The Omaha Tribe does not enforce any of its regulations—including those governing businesses, fire protection, animal control, fireworks, and wildlife and parks—in Pender or in other locales west of the right-of-way. 996 F.Supp.2d, at 832. Nor does it maintain an office, provide social services, or host tribal celebrations or ceremonies west of the right-of-way.

This subsequent demographic history cannot overcome our conclusion that Congress did not intend to diminish the reservation in 1882. And it is not our role to "rewrite" the 1882 Act in light of this subsequent demographic history. After all, evidence of the changing demographics of disputed land is "the least compelling" evidence in our diminishment analysis, for "[e]very surplus land Act necessarily resulted in a surge of non-Indian settlement and degraded the 'Indian character' of the reservation, yet we have repeatedly stated that not every surplus land Act diminished the affected reservation."

Evidence of the subsequent treatment of the disputed land by Government officials likewise has "limited interpretive value." Petitioners highlight that, for more than a century and with few exceptions, reports from the Office of Indian Affairs and in opinion letters from Government officials treated the disputed land as Nebraska's. It was not until this litigation commenced that the Department of the Interior definitively changed its position, concluding that the reservation boundaries were in fact not diminished in 1882. For their part, respondents discuss late-19th century statutes referring to the disputed land as part of the reservation, as well as inconsistencies in maps and statements by Government officials. This "mixed record" of subsequent treatment of the disputed land cannot overcome the statutory text, which is devoid of any language indicative of Congress' intent to diminish.

Petitioners' concerns about upsetting the "justifiable expectations" of the almost exclusively non-Indian settlers who live on the land are compelling, but these expectations alone, resulting from the Tribe's failure to assert jurisdiction, cannot diminish reservation boundaries. Only Congress has the power to diminish a reservation. And though petitioners wish that Congress would have "spoken differently" in 1882, "we cannot remake history." * * *

In light of the statutory text, we hold that the 1882 Act did not diminish the Omaha Indian Reservation. Because petitioners have raised only the single question of diminishment, we express no view about whether equitable considerations of laches and acquiescence may curtail the Tribe's power to tax the retailers of Pender in light of the Tribe's century-long absence from the disputed lands. Cf. *City of Sherrill v. Oneida Indian Nation of N.Y.*, 544 U.S. 197, 217–221, (2005).

The judgment of the Court of Appeals for the Eighth Circuit is affirmed.

Notes

1. The importance of subsequent demographic history. The state of Nebraska sought Supreme Court review to challenge the Eighth Circuit's alleged discounting of the third *Solem* factor, claiming that it overlooked 130 years of non-Indian settlement and reasonable reliance on state jurisdiction. After *Parker*, what is the role in diminishment cases of an area's subsequent demographic history?

2. Disestablishing the Osage Reservation. Based on its interpretation of *Solem*, the Tenth Circuit concluded that Congress disestablished the Osage Reservation. *Osage Nation v. Irby*, 597 F.3d 1117 (10th Cir. 2010). The court read *Solem* to create a three-part test for determining whether a reservation was disestablished or diminished: 1) express statutory language; 2) contemporaneous circumstances surrounding the opening of the reservation; and 3) subsequent events like congressional actions or the demographic history of the lands. Although there was no explicit congressional termination, the court decided that Congress disestablished the reservation under the second and third factors, relying on events surrounding the enactment of the Osage Allotment Act and ensuing demographics (non-tribal members accounting for over 90% of the population during the last century). *Irby* represents the first disestablishment case decided without a surplus lands act. Unlike the reservations in *Solem*, *Yankton Sioux*, and the other Supreme Court cases, the entire Osage Reservation had been allotted to tribal members.

3. Diminishment of the Wind River Reservation. In 2017, the Tenth Circuit ruled in a split decision in *Wyoming v. U.S. Environmental Protection Agency*, 875 F.3d 505 (10th Cir. 2017), that a 1905 statute diminished the Wind River Reservation in west-central Wyoming that is shared by the Eastern Shoshone and Northern Arapahoe Tribes. The court reversed a 2011 determination by the U.S. Environmental Protection Agency approving the tribes as qualified to administer certain provisions of the Clean Air Act on the reservation. EPA had agreed with the tribes that they had jurisdiction over most of the lands within the boundaries established by their 1868 treaty. Wyoming and the Wyoming Farm Bureau appealed, and the Tenth Circuit reversed on the basis that the language of the 1905 law, its surrounding circumstance, and the subsequent treatment of the area indicated that Congress intended to diminish the reservation. The majority emphasized that the statutory language, in which the tribes "for the consideration hereinafter named, do hereby cede, grant, and relinquish to the United States, all right, title, and interest" to the lands at issue, was similar to language in cases like *Yankton Sioux* in which the Supreme Court has concluded that Congress intended diminishment. The majority gave little or no deference to a legal opinion by the Interior Solicitor that concluded that the 1905 statute did not diminish the reservation. The dissent thought that the 1905 statute did not diminish the reservation, since it lacked clear language concerning diminishment and contained no "sum certain" payment to the tribes. The tribes filed a petition for certiorari in February 2018.

4. Non-diminishment of the Ute Reservation. A long-running saga concerning the Ute tribe's Unitah and Ouray Reservation may have finally played itself out. The Tenth Circuit in an opinion by Judge (now Justice) Gorsuch ruled that the state lacked jurisdiction of the criminal prosecution of a tribal member on land within the town of Myton, Utah, because the alleged crime took place in Indian Country, a matter decided in earlier litigation. The court also decided that laches did not bar the tribe's suit challenging the state's prosecution, and that checkerboard jurisdiction could not be remedied by equitable principles. *Ute Tribe of the Uintah and Outray Reservation v. Myton*, 832 F.2d 1220 (10th Cir. 2016) (land within the town of Myton that was returned to the tribe under the Indian Reorganization Act in 1945 was part of tribe's reservation and subject to the jurisdiction of the tribe; also reassigning further proceedings to a different district judge). In 1985, an en banc Tenth Circuit ruled that all lands within the original reservation's boundaries, including those that passed into non-Indian hands during allotment, remained Indian Country, *Ute Indian Tribe v. Utah*, 773 F.2d 1087 (10th Cir. 1985), cert. denied, 479 U.S. 994 (1986). But the Supreme Court later agreed with the Utah Supreme Court that lands owned by nonmembers were not Indian Country in *Hagen v. Utah*, 510 U.S. 399 (1994). Although Myton sought certiorari of Judge Gorsuch's decision, after he joined the Court it withdrew its petition and agreed to negotiate an intergovernmental jurisdiction arrangement. *See* UBMedia.biz, *Ute Tribe secures victory in dismissal of Myton Supreme*

Court Case (July 11, 2017), http://www.ubmedia.biz/news/article_4dde0590-61ad-11e7-b855-df11e5680eff.html.

5. Diminishment of former allotments. The Court in *Yankton Sioux* expressly limited its holding to the "unallotted, ceded lands" of the reservation. On remand, the South Dakota district court ruled that only the surplus lands were diminished from the reservation; the reservation was otherwise intact. *Yankton Sioux Tribe v. Gaffey*, 14 F. Supp. 2d 1135 (D.S.D. 1998). The Eighth Circuit affirmed in part, agreeing that the reservation had never been disestablished, but reversed on the issue of former allotments. *Yankton Sioux Tribe v. Gaffey*, 188 F.3d 1010 (8th Cir. 1999). The court held that when the 1894 Act was "viewed in its full historical context . . . it is clear that the parties did not intend for the tribe to retain control over allotted lands which passed out of trust status and into non-Indian hands." Former allotments now owned by non-Indians were therefore no longer Indian country.

On remand, the district court ruled that lands taken into trust under the Indian Reorganization Act were part of the Yankton Sioux Reservation, and that other trust lands within the original reservation boundaries were dependent Indian communities, and the Eighth Circuit affirmed. However, the appellate court reversed the district court's decision that former allotments continuously held in fee by Indian owners were reservation lands, concluding that the lack of a fully developed record on those parcels made the issue not yet ripe. *Yankton Sioux Tribe v. Podhradsky*, 606 F.3d 994 (8th Cir. 2010).

In *United States v. Webb*, 219 F.3d 1127 (9th Cir. 2000), the Ninth Circuit arrived at a different conclusion. The court construed an agreement with "cede, sell, relinquish, and convey" language similar to that construed by the Supreme Court in *Yankton Sioux*, but concluded that this language did not diminish the boundaries of the Nez Perce reservation. The Ninth Circuit distinguished *Yankton Sioux* on its facts, finding a "critical distinction" between the fact that *Yankton Sioux* involved unallotted, surplus lands that were ceded back to the federal government, while the lands at issue in *Webb* were allotted to the Nez Perce. The court concluded that allotments which had passed into fee status remained Indian country.

6. The legacy of allotment. Although Congress repudiated the policy of allotment more than seventy years ago, in the 1934 Indian Reorganization Act, the case law makes clear that the Supreme Court remains heavily influenced by that era's effects on the tribal land base. *See generally* Judith V. Royster, *The Legacy of Allotment*, 27 Ariz. St. L.J. 1 (1995).

Chapter 3

Land: The Fundamental Resource

Of all the natural resources available to tribes, land is the most pervasive and important. The following sections explore the various types of title in land owned by tribes, starting with aboriginal title.

A. Aboriginal Title

Johnson and Graham's Lessee v. M'Intosh

21 U.S. 543 (1823)

Mr. Chief Justice MARSHALL delivered the opinion of the Court.

The plaintiffs in this cause claim the land, in their declaration mentioned, under two grants, purporting to be made, the first in 1773, and the last in 1775, by the chiefs of certain Indian tribes, constituting the Illinois and the Piankeshaw nations; and the question is, whether this title can be recognized in the Courts of the United States?

The facts, as stated in the case agreed, show the authority of the chiefs who executed this conveyance, so far as it could be given by their own people; and likewise show, that the particular tribes for whom these chiefs acted were in rightful possession of the land they sold. [In 1795 the tribes ceded the land in question to the United States by treaty. In 1818, the defendant, William M'Intosh, received a grant of the land, located in what is now Illinois, from the United States.] The inquiry, therefore, is, in a great measure, confined to the power of Indians to give, and of private individuals to receive, a title which can be sustained in the Courts of this country.

On the discovery of this immense continent, the great nations of Europe were eager to appropriate to themselves so much of it as they could respectively acquire. Its vast extent offered an ample field to the ambition and enterprise of all; and the character and religion of its inhabitants afforded an apology for considering them as a people over whom the superior genius of Europe might claim an ascendancy. The potentates of the old world found no difficulty in convincing themselves that they made ample compensation to the inhabitants of the new, by bestowing on them civilization and Christianity, in exchange for unlimited independence. But, as they were all in pursuit of nearly the same object, it was necessary, in order to avoid conflicting settlements, and consequent war with each other, to establish a principle, which all should acknowledge as the law by which the right of acquisition, which they all asserted, should be regulated as between themselves. This principle was, that discovery gave title to the government by whose subjects, or by whose authority, it was made, against all other European governments, which title might be consummated by possession.

The exclusion of all other Europeans, necessarily gave to the nation making the discovery the sole right of acquiring the soil from the natives, and establishing settlements upon it. It was a right with which no Europeans could interfere. It was a right which all asserted for themselves, and to the assertion of which, by others, all assented.

Those relations which were to exist between the discoverer and the natives, were to be regulated by themselves. The rights thus acquired being exclusive, no other power could interpose between them.

In the establishment of these relations, the rights of the original inhabitants were, in no instance, entirely disregarded; but were necessarily, to a considerable extent, impaired. They were admitted to be the rightful occupants of the soil, with a legal as well as just claim to retain possession of it, and to use it according to their own discretion; but their rights to complete sovereignty, as independent nations, were necessarily diminished, and their power to dispose of the soil at their own will, to whomsoever they pleased, was denied by the original fundamental principle, that discovery gave exclusive title to those who made it.

While the different nations of Europe respected the right of the natives, as occupants, they asserted the ultimate dominion to be in themselves; and claimed and exercised, as a consequence of this ultimate dominion, a power to grant the soil, while yet in possession of the natives. These grants have been understood by all, to convey a title to the grantees, subject only to the Indian right of occupancy.

No one of the powers of Europe gave its full assent to this principle, more unequivocally than England. The documents upon this subject are ample and complete. So early as the year 1496, her monarch granted a commission to the Cabots, to discover countries then unknown to Christian people, and to take possession of them in the name of the king of England. Two years afterwards, Cabot proceeded on this voyage, and discovered the continent of North America, along which he sailed as far south as Virginia. To this discovery the English trace their title.

In this first effort made by the English government to acquire territory on this continent, we perceive a complete recognition of the principle which has been mentioned. The right of discovery given by this commission, is confined to countries 'then unknown to all Christian people;' and of these countries Cabot was empowered to take possession in the name of the king of England. Thus asserting a right to take possession, notwithstanding the occupancy of the natives, who were heathens, and, at the same time, admitting the prior title of any Christian people who may have made a previous discovery.

Thus has our whole country been granted by the crown while in the occupation of the Indians. These grants purport to convey the soil as well as the right of dominion to the grantees.

Further proofs of the extent to which this principle has been recognized, will be found in the history of the wars, negotiations, and treaties, which the different nations, claiming territory in America, have carried on, and held with each other.

Between France and Great Britain, whose discoveries as well as settlements were nearly contemporaneous, contests for the country, actually covered by the Indians, began as soon as their settlements approached each other, and were continued until finally settled in the year 1763, by the treaty of Paris.

This treaty expressly cedes, and has always been understood to cede, the whole country, on the English side of the dividing line, between the two nations, although a great and valuable part of it was occupied by the Indians. Great Britain, on her part, surrendered to France all her pretensions to the country west of the Mississippi. It has never been supposed that she surrendered nothing, although she was not in actual possession of a foot of land. She surrendered all right to acquire the country; and any after attempt to purchase it from the Indians, would have been considered and treated as an invasion of the territories of France.

Thus, all the nations of Europe, who have acquired territory on this continent, have asserted in themselves, and have recognized in others, the exclusive right of the discoverer to appropriate the lands occupied by the Indians. Have the American States rejected or adopted this principle?

By the treaty which concluded the war of our revolution, Great Britain relinquished all claim, not only to the government, but to the 'propriety and territorial rights of the United States,' whose boundaries were fixed in the second article. By this treaty, the powers of government, and the right to soil, which had previously been in Great Britain, passed definitively to these States. We had before taken possession of them, by declaring independence; but neither the declaration of independence, nor the treaty confirming it, could give us more than that which we before possessed, or to which Great Britain was before entitled. It has never been doubted, that either the United States, or the several States, had a clear title to all the lands within the boundary lines described in the treaty, subject only to the Indian right of occupancy, and that the exclusive power to extinguish that right, was vested in that government which might constitutionally exercise it.

The United States, then, have unequivocally acceded to that great and broad rule by which its civilized inhabitants now hold this country. They hold, and assert in themselves, the title by which it was acquired. They maintain, as all others have maintained, that discovery gave an exclusive right to extinguish the Indian title of occupancy, either by purchase or by conquest; and gave also a right to such a degree of sovereignty, as the circumstances of the people would allow them to exercise.

We will not enter into the controversy, whether agriculturists, merchants, and manufacturers, have a right, on abstract principles, to expel hunters from the territory they possess, or to contract their limits. Conquest gives a title which the Courts of the conqueror cannot deny, whatever the private and speculative opinions of individuals may be, respecting the original justice of the claim which has been successfully asserted. The British government, which was then our government, and whose rights have passed to the United States, asserted title to all the lands occupied by Indians, within the chartered limits of the British colonies. It asserted also a limited sovereignty over them, and the exclusive right of extinguishing the title which occupancy gave to them. These claims have been maintained and established as far west as the river Mississippi, by the sword. The title to a vast portion of the lands we now hold, originates in them. It is not for the Courts of this country to question the validity of this title, or to sustain one which is incompatible with it.

Although we do not mean to engage in the defence of those principles which Europeans have applied to Indian title, they may, we think, find some excuse, if not justification, in the character and habits of the people whose rights have been wrested from them.

The title by conquest is acquired and maintained by force. The conqueror prescribes its limits. Humanity, however, acting on public opinion, has established, as a general rule, that the conquered shall not be wantonly oppressed, and that their condition shall remain as eligible as is compatible with the objects of the conquest. Most usually, they are incorporated with the victorious nation, and become subjects or citizens of the government with which they are connected. The new and old members of the society mingle with each other; the distinction between them is gradually lost, and they make one people. Where this incorporation is practicable, humanity demands, and a wise policy requires, that the rights of the conquered to property should remain unimpaired; that the new subjects should be governed as equitably as the old, and that confidence in their security should gradually banish the painful sense of being separated from their ancient connexions, and united by force to strangers.

When the conquest is complete, and the conquered inhabitants can be blended with the conquerors, or safely governed as a distinct people, public opinion, which not even the conqueror can disregard, imposes these restraints upon him; and he cannot neglect them without injury to his fame, and hazard to his power. But the tribes of Indians inhabiting this country were fierce savages, whose occupation was war, and whose subsistence was drawn chiefly from the forest. To leave them in possession of their country, was to leave the country a wilderness; to govern them as a distinct people, was impossible, because they were as brave and as high spirited as they were fierce, and were ready to repel by arms every attempt on their independence.

Frequent and bloody wars, in which the whites were not always the aggressors, unavoidably ensued. European policy, numbers, and skill, prevailed. As the white population advanced, that of the Indians necessarily receded. The country in the immediate neighborhood of agriculturists became unfit for them. The game fled into thicker and more unbroken forests, and the Indians followed. The soil, to which the crown originally claimed title, being no longer occupied by its ancient inhabitants, was parcelled out according to the will of the sovereign power, and taken possession of by persons who claimed immediately from the crown, or mediately, through its grantees or deputies.

That law which regulates, and ought to regulate in general, the relations between the conqueror and conquered, was incapable of application to a people under such circumstances. The resort to some new and different rule, better adapted to the actual state of things, was unavoidable. Every rule which can be suggested will be found to be attended with great difficulty.

However extravagant the pretension of converting the discovery of an inhabited country into conquest may appear; if the principle has been asserted in the first instance, and afterwards sustained; if a country has been acquired and held under it; if the property of the great mass of the community originates in it, it becomes the law of the land, and cannot be questioned. So, too, with respect to the concomitant principle, that the Indian inhabitants are to be considered merely as occupants, to be protected, indeed, while in peace, in the possession of their lands, but to be deemed incapable of transferring the absolute title to others. However this restriction may be opposed to natural right, and to the usages of civilized nations, yet, if it be indispensable to that system under which the country has been settled, and be adapted to the actual condition of the two people, it may, perhaps, be supported by reason, and certainly cannot be rejected by Courts of justice.

[The Court affirmed the judgment of the District Court of Illinois in favor of defendant M'Intosh.]

Notes

1. Sovereignty and property. *M'Intosh* is the first of the Marshall trilogy of cases that set the foundations of federal Indian law. The other two cases in the trilogy—the *Cherokee Cases*—are excerpted at pages 80 and 83. *M'Intosh* is in some ways a harbinger of the holding in *Cherokee Nation v. Georgia* that Indian tribes are "domestic dependent nations." Under the doctrine of discovery that Marshall employed in *M'Intosh*, the tribes' "rights to complete sovereignty, as independent nations, were necessarily diminished."

But the doctrine of discovery is also a property rule. What happened to the indigenous populations' property rights under that doctrine? What sticks in the bundle of property rights did the tribes retain after *M'Intosh*? What sticks did they lose to the discovering nations? What kind of "title" to Indian lands did the United States, as the successor to Great Britain, hold? What restrictions, if any, did *M'Intosh* place on the "rights" of non-Indian citizens to acquire and hold property? To what extent were these property rules driven by "the actual state of things"—settled expectations—rather than legal doctrine? For a reconsideration of *Johnson v. M'Intosh*, see Michael C. Blumm, *Retracing the Discovery Doctrine: Aboriginal Title, Tribal Sovereignty, and Their Significance to the Treaty-Making Process and Modern Natural Resource Policy in Indian Country*, 28 Vermont L. Rev. 713 (2004) (suggesting that the result in *M'Intosh* should have been interpreted to leave the tribes with fee title subject to a partial restraint on alienation and to the federal government's right of preemptive purchase).

Scholars frequently note Marshall's tone of apology and embarrassment in the *M'Intosh* opinion. And yet Marshall purported to find "some excuse, if not justification" for the rules he announces "in the character and habits" of the Indians. In particular, he noted that: "To leave them in possession of their country, was to leave the country a wilderness." What is wrong with leaving the country a wilderness? Refer back to the materials at pages 3–9.

Can we view the rule laid down in *M'Intosh* as protective of the Indians? The tribes lost the right to convey title to anyone not the U.S. government (a partial restraint on alienation). But however poorly the tribes fared in dealings with the federal sovereign, were they likely to have done any better in dealings with the states or the locals on the frontier? If *M'Intosh* served the tribes badly, what outcome would have served them better?

The doctrine of discovery and the *M'Intosh* case have been the subjects of considerable recent scholarship. In addition to Professor Blumm's article, cited above, see Lindsay G. Robertson, Conquest by Law: How the Discovery of America Dispossessed Indigenous Peoples of Their Lands (Oxford U. Press 2005); Michael C. Blumm, *Why Aboriginal Title Is a Fee Simple Absolute,* 15 Lewis & Clark L. Rev. 975 (2011); Blake A. Watson, *John Marshall and Indian Land Rights: A Historical Rejoinder to the Claim of "Universal Recognition" of the Doctrine of Discovery*, 36 Seton Hall L. Rev. 481 (2006); Robert J. Miller, *The Doctrine of Discovery in American Indian Law*, 42 Idaho L. Rev. 1 (2005).

For a case using the temporary nature of "the right of occupancy" to deny tribal fishing rights in Lake Erie, see *Ottawa Tribe of Oklahoma v. Logan,* 577 F.3d 634 (6th Cir. 2009) (discussed on page 602).

2. *M'Intosh* **as law and economics.** Professor Eric Kades applied a law and economics approach to Chief Justice Marshall's ruling. Eric Kades, *The Dark Side of Efficiency:* Johnson v. M'Intosh *and the Expropriation of American Indian Lands*, 148 U. Pa. L. Rev. 1065 (2000). He argued that *M'Intosh* can best be understood not in normative terms, but as the centerpiece of a system for the efficient expropriation of Indian lands.

> This Article . . . explains the process of expropriating Indian lands in terms of minimizing the costs, broadly defined (for example, value of lives, risks borne, and time spent on unproductive warfare), to the European colonizers. Simply put, customs and legal rules promulgated by colonial and later American courts and legislatures promoted not simply expropriation (right or wrong), but *efficient* expropriation. The thesis of this Article is that colonists established rules to minimize the costs associated with dispossessing the natives. If it had been cheaper to be more brutal, then Europeans would have been more brutal. Such brutality, however, was not cheap at all.
>
> Likewise, if it had been cheaper to show more humanity, the Europeans would have exhibited more, such as extending Indians full rights to sell (or

keep) their land. Such a legal rule, however, would have been far from cheap. *Johnson v. M'Intosh* was an essential part of the regime of efficient expropriation because it ensured that Europeans did not bid against each other to acquire Indian lands, thus keeping prices low.

Id. at 1071–72. From whose point of view was the *M'Intosh* rule "efficient"? Is Professor Kades correct that the values espoused in the *M'Intosh* rule were only those of economic efficiency? For a critique of Professor Kades' thesis that the Marshall Court was consciously pursuing an agenda of least-cost appropriation of Indian lands, *see* Blumm, *supra* note 1, 28 Vt. L. Rev. at 746–47 n. 216.

3. The Nonintercourse Act. A significant part of the holding in *M'Intosh* had already found legislative expression. In 1790, the first Congress enacted the Nonintercourse Act, 1 Stat. 137, asserting the paramount and exclusive right of the federal government to acquire Indian lands. The Act was subsequently amended and re-enacted. The current version, enacted in 1834, provides:

> No purchase, grant, lease, or other conveyance of lands, or of any title or claim thereto, from any Indian nation or tribe of Indians, shall be of any validity in law or equity, unless the same be made by treaty or convention entered into pursuant to the Constitution. Every person who, not being employed under the authority of the United States, attempts to negotiate such treaty or convention, directly or indirectly, or to treat with any such nation or tribe of Indians for the title or purchase of any lands by them held or claimed, is liable to a penalty of $1,000. The agent of any State who may be present at any treaty held with Indians under the authority of the United States, in the presence and with the approbation of the commissioner of the United States appointed to hold the same, may, however, propose to, and adjust with, the Indians the compensation to be made for their claim to lands within such State, which shall be extinguished by treaty.

25 U.S.C. § 177.

Notice that had the Nonintercourse Act applied to the conveyances at issue in *M'Intosh,* the result would have been precisely the same as Justice Marshall achieved via the common law. In other words, his interpretation of the common law was previously codified by congressional statute.

4. *Alabama-Coushatta Tribe v. United States.* A case reflecting the principles laid down in *Johnson v. M'Intosh* and the Nonintercourse Act is *Alabama-Coushatta Tribe v. United States*, 2000 WL 1013532 (Ct. Fed. Cl., June 19, 2000) (unpub. op.). The Court of Federal Claims ruled that the tribe established aboriginal title to some 5.5 million acres of land in East Texas by 1830, and that subsequent land grants and settlement did not extinguish the tribe's aboriginal title. Moreover, the panel ruled that neither Spain, Mexico, nor the Republic of Texas extinguished aboriginal title prior to the admission of Texas to the Union in 1845. Nor did statehood or subsequent federal statutes extinguish the tribe's aboriginal title. Absent effective extinguishment, land grants could convey only fees subject to the Indians' continued right of occupancy. As a result, the involuntary and forceful dispossession of the tribe from its lands was unlawful.

The tribe also alleged, and the Court of Federal Claims agreed, that the federal government's failure to protect the tribe's lands against encroachment by non-Indian settlers after statehood was a violation of its statutory duty under the Nonintercourse Act for which the federal government was liable for trespass damages. However, the federal government was not liable for pre-statehood dispossession because it did not assume a duty to protect the tribe's lands until statehood. And the federal government terminated its trust responsibility to the tribe in 1954, transferring it to the state. But between statehood in 1845 and 1954—a 109-year period—the federal government owed the tribe a fiduciary duty to protect its lands. Thus, it was liable to the tribe for some 2.85 million of 5.5 million acres that were lost, although all 5.5 million acres remain subject to the tribe's aboriginal title.

5. Eastern land claims. One of the primary modern uses of the Nonintercourse Act was a series of land claims cases brought by eastern tribes. The classic eastern land claim is that of the Oneida Nation.

In 1970, the Oneida Nation filed suit against two New York counties. The Nation claimed that a 1795 agreement which conveyed 100,000 acres to the State of New York was void on the ground that it violated the Nonintercourse Act of 1793. As damages, the Nation sought fair rental value for the previous two years of that portion of the 100,000 acres presently owned and occupied by the counties.

The Oneida Nation held aboriginal title to approximately six million acres in what is now central New York State. Under pressure to make the Oneida lands available for settlement, the state entered into a "treaty" with the tribe in 1788. The state purchased the vast majority of the tribe's land, and the Oneidas retained a reservation of about 300,000 acres. In 1795, the state entered into negotiations to purchase the remaining Oneida lands. Although Secretary of War Pickering warned the governor of New York that the Nonintercourse Act required the appointment of federal commissioners to supervise the land transaction, the state ignored the warnings and concluded the agreement to purchase nearly all the remaining Oneida lands.

The district court determined that a prima facie case of a violation of the Nonintercourse Act required the Oneida Nation to establish four elements: (1) it was an Indian tribe; (2) the lands at issue were covered by the Act "as tribal land"; (3) the United States never consented to the alienation of the tribal land; and (4) the trust relationship with the tribe had never been terminated or abandoned. The court found that all four requirements were satisfied. *Oneida Indian Nation v. County of Oneida*, 434 F. Supp. 527 (N.D.N.Y. 1977).

On appeal, the New York defendants did not contest the district court's holding that the land transactions violated the Nonintercourse Act. Instead, they argued that (1) the Act preempted any common law cause of action; (2) the Oneida Nation did not have a private right of action under the Act; (3) any cause of action was time-barred by a statute of limitations or the common law doctrine of laches; (4) any cause of action was a nonjusticiable political question; and (5) the United States had ratified the agreement by subsequent federally-approved treaties. The court of appeals rejected all the defendants' arguments and found them liable to the Nation for rent. The Supreme Court affirmed. *County of Oneida v. Oneida Indian Nation*, 470 U.S. 226 (1985). Compare the foregoing with the Supreme Court's decision in the case below:

City of Sherrill v. Oneida Indian Nation
544 U.S. 197 (2005)

Justice GINSBURG delivered the opinion of the Court.

This case concerns properties in the city of Sherrill, New York, purchased by the Oneida Indian Nation of New York (OIN or Tribe) in 1997 and 1998. The separate parcels of land in question, once contained within the Oneidas' 300,000-acre reservation, were last possessed by the Oneidas as a tribal entity in 1805. For two centuries, governance of the area in which the properties are located has been provided by the State of New York and its county and municipal units. In *County of Oneida v. Oneida Indian Nation of N.Y.*, 470 U.S. 226 (1985) (*Oneida II*), this Court held that the Oneidas stated a triable claim for damages against the County of Oneida for wrongful possession of lands they conveyed to New York State in 1795 in violation of federal law. In the instant action, OIN resists the payment of property taxes to Sherrill on the ground that OIN's acquisition of fee title to discrete parcels of historic reservation land revived the Oneidas' ancient sovereignty piecemeal over each parcel. Consequently, the Tribe maintains, regulatory authority over OIN's newly purchased properties no longer resides in Sherrill.

Our 1985 decision recognized that the Oneidas could maintain a federal common-law claim for damages for ancient wrongdoing in which both national and state governments were complicit. Today, we decline to project redress for the Tribe into the present and future, thereby disrupting the governance of central New York's counties and towns. Generations have passed during which non-Indians have owned and developed the area that once composed the Tribe's historic reservation. And at least since the middle years of the 19th century, most of the Oneidas have resided elsewhere. Given the longstanding, distinctly non-Indian character of the area and its inhabitants, the regulatory authority constantly exercised by New York State and its counties and towns, and the Oneidas' long delay in seeking judicial relief against parties other than the United States, we hold that the Tribe cannot unilaterally revive its ancient sovereignty, in whole or in part, over the parcels at issue. The Oneidas long ago relinquished the reins of government and cannot regain them through open-market purchases from current titleholders.

This brings us to the present case, which concerns parcels of land in the city of Sherrill, located in Oneida County, New York. According to the 2000 census, over 99% of the population in the area is non-Indian: American Indians represent less than 1% of the city of Sherrill's population and less than 0.5% of Oneida County's population. OIN owns approximately 17,000 acres of land scattered throughout the

Counties of Oneida and Madison, representing less than 1.5% of the counties' total area. OIN's predecessor, the Oneida Nation, had transferred the parcels at issue to one of its members in 1805, who sold the land to a non-Indian in 1807. The properties thereafter remained in non-Indian hands until OIN's acquisitions in 1997 and 1998 in open-market transactions. OIN now operates commercial enterprises on these parcels: a gasoline station, a convenience store, and a textile facility.

Because the parcels lie within the boundaries of the reservation originally occupied by the Oneidas, OIN maintained that the properties are exempt from taxation, and accordingly refused to pay the assessed property taxes. The city of Sherrill initiated eviction proceedings in state court, and OIN sued Sherrill in federal court. In contrast to *Oneida I* and *II*, which involved demands for monetary compensation, OIN sought equitable relief prohibiting, currently and in the future, the imposition of property taxes. OIN also sued Madison County, seeking a declaration that the Tribe's properties in Madison are tax exempt. The litigation involved a welter of claims and counterclaims. Relevant here, the District Court concluded that parcels of land owned by the Tribe in Sherrill and Madison are not taxable.

A divided panel of the Second Circuit affirmed.

We granted the city of Sherrill's petition for a writ of certiorari, and now reverse the judgment of the Court of Appeals.

II

OIN and the United States argue that because the Court in *Oneida II* recognized the Oneidas' aboriginal title to their ancient reservation land and because the Tribe has now acquired the specific parcels involved in this suit in the open market, it has unified fee and aboriginal title and may now assert sovereign dominion over the parcels. When the Oneidas came before this Court 20 years ago in *Oneida II*, they sought money damages only. The Court reserved for another day the question whether "equitable considerations" should limit the relief available to the present-day Oneidas.

"The substantive questions whether the plaintiff has any right or the defendant has any duty, and if so what it is, are very different questions from the remedial questions whether this remedy or that is preferred, and what the measure of the remedy is." "[S]tandards of federal Indian law and federal equity practice" led the District Court, in the litigation revived after *Oneida II*, to reject OIN's plea for ejectment of 20,000 private landowners. In this action, OIN seeks declaratory and injunctive relief recognizing its present and future sovereign immunity from local taxation on parcels of land the Tribe purchased in the open market, properties that had been subject to state and local taxation for generations. We now reject the unification theory of OIN and the United States and hold that "standards of federal Indian law and federal equity practice" preclude the Tribe from rekindling embers of sovereignty that long ago grew cold.

The appropriateness of the relief OIN here seeks must be evaluated in light of the long history of state sovereign control over the territory. From the early 1800s into the 1970s, the United States largely accepted, or was indifferent to, New York's governance of the land in question and the validity *vel non* of the Oneidas' sales to the State. In fact, the United States' policy and practice through much of the early 19th century was designed to dislodge east coast lands from Indian possession. Moreover, the properties here involved have greatly increased in value since the Oneidas sold them 200 years ago. Notably, it was not until lately that the Oneidas sought to regain ancient sovereignty over land converted from wilderness to become part of cities like Sherrill.

This Court has observed in the different, but related, context of the diminishment of an Indian reservation that "[t]he longstanding assumption of jurisdiction by the State over an area that is over 90% non-Indian, both in population and in land use," may create "justifiable expectations." *Rosebud Sioux Tribe v. Kneip,* 430 U.S. 584, 604–605 (1977); accord *Hagen v. Utah,* 510 U.S. 399, 421 (1994) ("jurisdictional history" and "the current population situation . . . demonstrat[e] a practical acknowledgment" of reservation diminishment; "a contrary conclusion would seriously disrupt the justifiable expectations of the people living in the area" (internal quotation marks omitted)). Similar justifiable expectations, grounded in two centuries of New York's exercise of regulatory jurisdiction, until recently uncontested by OIN, merit heavy weight here.

The wrongs of which OIN complains in this action occurred during the early years of the Republic. For the past two centuries, New York and its county and municipal units have continuously governed the territory. The Oneidas did not seek to regain possession of their aboriginal lands by court decree until the 1970s. And not until the 1990s did OIN acquire the properties in question and assert its unification theory to ground its demand for exemption of the parcels from local taxation. This long lapse of time, during which the Oneidas did not seek to revive their sovereign control through equitable relief in court, and the attendant dramatic changes in the character of the properties, preclude OIN from gaining the disruptive remedy it now seeks.

The principle that the passage of time can preclude relief has deep roots in our law, and this Court has recognized this prescription in various guises. It is well established that laches, a doctrine focused on one side's inaction and the other's legitimate reliance, may bar long-dormant claims for equitable relief.

* * * When a party belatedly asserts a right to present and future sovereign control over territory, longstanding observances and settled expectations are prime considerations. There is no dispute that it has been two centuries since the Oneidas last exercised regulatory control over the properties here or held them free from local taxation. Parcel-by-parcel revival of their sovereign status, given the extraordinary passage of time, would dishonor "the historic wisdom in the value of repose."

Finally, this Court has recognized the impracticability of returning to Indian control land that generations earlier passed into numerous private hands. The District Court, in the litigation dormant during the pendency of *Oneida II,* rightly found these pragmatic concerns about restoring Indian sovereign control over land "magnified exponentially here, where development of every type imaginable has been ongoing for more than two centuries."

In this case, the Court of Appeals concluded that the "impossibility" doctrine had no application because OIN acquired the land in the open market and does not seek to uproot current property owners. But the unilateral reestablishment of present and future Indian sovereign control, even over land purchased at the market price, would have disruptive practical consequences similar to those that led this Court in *Yankton Sioux* to initiate the impossibility doctrine. The city of Sherrill and Oneida County are today overwhelmingly populated by non-Indians. A checkerboard of alternating state and tribal jurisdiction in New York State—created unilaterally at OIN's behest—would "seriously burde[n] the administration of state and local governments" and would adversely affect landowners neighboring the tribal patches. If OIN may unilaterally reassert sovereign control and remove these parcels from the local tax rolls, little would prevent the Tribe from initiating a new generation of litigation to free the parcels from local zoning or other regulatory controls that protect all landowners in the area

Recognizing these practical concerns, Congress has provided a mechanism for the acquisition of lands for tribal communities that takes account of the interests of others with stakes in the area's governance and well being. Title 25 U.S.C. § 465[*] authorizes the Secretary of the Interior to acquire land in trust for Indians and provides that the land "shall be exempt from State and local taxation." The regulations implementing § 465 are sensitive to the complex interjurisdictional concerns that arise when a tribe seeks to regain sovereign control over territory. Before approving an acquisition, the Secretary must consider, among other things, the tribe's need for additional land; "[t]he purposes for which the land will be used"; "the impact on the State and its political subdivisions resulting from the removal of the land from the tax rolls"; and "[j]urisdictional problems and potential conflicts of land use which may arise." Section 465 provides the proper avenue for OIN to reestablish sovereign authority over territory last held by the Oneidas 200 years ago.

In sum, the question of damages for the Tribe's ancient dispossession is not at issue in this case, and we therefore do not disturb our holding in *Oneida II*. However, the distance from 1805 to the present day, the Oneidas' long delay in seeking equitable relief against New York or its local units, and developments in the city of Sherrill spanning several generations, evoke the doctrines of laches, acquiescence, and impossibility, and render inequitable the piecemeal shift in governance this suit seeks unilaterally to initiate.

[Justice SOUTER's concurring opinion is omitted.]

Justice STEVENS, dissenting.

* * * [I]t is abundantly clear that all of the land owned by the Tribe within the boundaries of its reservation qualifies as Indian country. Without questioning the

---

[*] Ed. note: Section 465 has been recodified at 25 U.S.C. § 5108.

accuracy of that conclusion, the Court today nevertheless decides that the fact that most of the reservation has been occupied and governed by non-Indians for a long period of time precludes the Tribe "from rekindling embers of sovereignty that long ago grew cold." * * * In the present case, the Tribe is not attempting to collect damages or eject landowners as a remedy for a wrong that occurred centuries ago; rather, it is invoking an ancient immunity against a city's present-day attempts to tax its reservation lands.

Without the benefit of relevant briefing from the parties, the Court has ventured into legal territory that belongs to Congress. Its decision today is at war with at least two bedrock principles of Indian law. First, only Congress has the power to diminish or disestablish a tribe's reservation. Second, as a core incident of tribal sovereignty, a tribe enjoys immunity from state and local taxation of its reservation lands, until that immunity is explicitly revoked by Congress. Far from revoking this immunity, Congress has specifically reconfirmed it with respect to the reservation lands of the New York Indians. Ignoring these principles, the Court has done what only Congress may do—it has effectively proclaimed a diminishment of the Tribe's reservation and an abrogation of its elemental right to tax immunity. Under our precedents, whether it is wise policy to honor the Tribe's tax immunity is a question for Congress, not this Court, to decide.

In any event, as a matter of equity I believe that the "principle that the passage of time can preclude relief," should be applied sensibly and with an even hand. It seems perverse to hold that the reliance interests of non-Indian New Yorkers that are predicated on almost two centuries of inaction by the Tribe do not foreclose the Tribe's enforcement of judicially created damages remedies for ancient wrongs, but do somehow mandate a forfeiture of a tribal immunity that has been consistently and uniformly protected throughout our history. In this case, the Tribe reacquired reservation land in a peaceful and lawful manner that fully respected the interests of innocent landowners—it purchased the land on the open market. To now deny the Tribe its right to tax immunity—at once the most fundamental of tribal rights and the least disruptive to other sovereigns—is not only inequitable, but also irreconcilable with the principle that only Congress may abrogate or extinguish tribal sovereignty. I would not decide this case on the basis of speculation about what may happen in future litigation over other regulatory issues. For the answer to the question whether the City may require the Tribe to pay taxes on its own property within its own reservation is pellucidly clear. Under settled law, it may not.

Notes

1. **Responses to *City of Sherrill*.** For sharp critiques of the *City of Sherrill* decision, see Joseph William Singer, *Nine-Tenths of the Law: Title, Possession & Sacred Obligations*, 38 Conn. L. Rev. 605 (2006) (delineating nine separate barriers preventing the Oneida Nation from seeking relief in court earlier than it did); Sarah Krakoff, City of Sherrill v. Oneida Indian Nation of New York: *A Regretful Postscript to the Taxation Chapter in Cohen's Handbook of Federal Indian Law*, 41 Tulsa L. Rev. 5 (2005).

The Second Circuit invoked the Supreme Court's *Sherrill* decision in deciding that a land claim by the Cayuga Indian Nation of New York and the Seneca-Cayuga Tribe of Oklahoma was barred by laches. *Cayuga Indian Nation of New York v. Pataki*, 413 F.3d 266 (2d Cir. 2005). The district court had held that the tribes were dispossessed of their lands in the eighteenth century in violation of the Nonintercourse Act, awarding some $248 million in damages and prejudgment interest. The Second Circuit reversed, noting that: "We understand *Sherrill* to hold that equitable doctrines, such as laches, acquiescence, and impossibility can, in appropriate circumstances, be applied to Indian land claims, even when such a claim is legally viable and within the statute of limitations." In response to the argument by the tribes and the United States that *City of Sherrill* should not affect monetary damages, the court stated that the Cayuga claim "is and has always been one sounding in ejectment." It therefore found *Sherrill* applicable, and laches appropriate.

In a subsequent case, the Oneida Nation filed a federal common law claim for damages in connection with the disposition of its lands. The tribe alleged that the state purchased about 250,000 acres of its lands at an unconscionably low price: about one-seventh of what the state charged white homesteaders upon resale. Although the district court ruled that the tribe's claim could proceed, the Second Circuit again reversed. Applying *Sherrill* and *Cayuga*, the court concluded that equitable defenses such as laches also barred this claim, as did the state's sovereign immunity and the Nonintercourse Act. *Oneida Indian Nation of New York v. County of Oneida*, 617 Fed. 114 (2d. Cir. 2010).

In 2007, in a case involving the same lands at issue in *Sherrill*, a district court enjoined two counties from foreclosing against Oneida Nation properties for failure to pay local taxes on grounds of sovereign immunity, the Nonintercourse Act, constitutional due process, and exemptions under state law. *Oneida Nation v. Madison County*, 432 F.Supp.2d 285 (N.D. N.Y. 2006). The Second Circuit affirmed on sovereign immunity grounds. 605 F.3d 149 (2d Cir. 2010). After the U.S. Supreme Court accepted certiorari in the case, the tribe passed an ordinance waiving its sovereign immunity, and the Court consequently vacated and remanded the case to the Second Circuit. The Second Circuit proceeded to rule for the counties on all counts. Case No. 06-5168 (Oct. 20, 2011).

In 2013, the Oneida Nation and the State of New York entered into a settlement agreement that covered a variety of taxation, gaming, and land issues. Then-existing litigation was dismissed, and the state agreed not to challenge a 2008 decision by the Secretary of the Interior to take some 13,000 acres of land into trust for the Oneida Nation. The state also agreed not to oppose the Oneida's application to take any subsequently-acquired land into trust, and the tribe agreed not to designate more than 25,370 acres of reacquired land as "Nation Land" not taxable by the state or county. *See* http://theoneidanation.com/publicaffairs/wp-content/uploads/NYS-Nation-Counties-Settlement-Agreement.pdf.

In a case involving the Cayuga Indian Nation, the Second Circuit reaffirmed its ruling in *Madison County* that an Indian tribe has sovereign immunity from suit by a county to foreclose on tribally-owned fee land for nonpayment of ad valorem property taxes. *Cayuga Indian Nation v. Seneca County*, 761 F.3d 218 (2d Cir. 2014). The court declined to "attempt to discern the implied message" in the Court's vacatur of *Madison County* in light of subsequent Supreme Court opinions upholding tribal sovereign immunity and stated that "we read no implied abrogation of tribal sovereign immunity from suit" into *Sherrill*.

2. The wilderness theme. Note the following statement from the Court's decision: "it was not until lately that the Oneidas sought to regain ancient sovereignty over land converted from wilderness to become part of cities like Sherrill." Recall Chief Justice Marshall's statement in *Johnson v. M'Intosh* that to leave the Indians in possession was to "leave the country a wilderness." Why, in the 21st century, is the idea of an Indian wilderness still invoked?

3. Pre-constitutional claims. In a previous claim to land acquired by the State of New York in 1785 and 1788, prior to passage of the Nonintercourse Act, the Oneida Nation did not fare well, either. The Oneida Nation alleged that the land transactions were invalid under the Articles of Confederation for lack of consent by the Congress. The Articles of Confederation provided, in relevant part, that:

> The United States in Congress assembled shall also have the sole and exclusive right and power of . . . regulating the trade and managing all affairs with the Indians, not members of any of the States, provided that the legislative right of any State within its own limits be not infringed or violated. . . .

Article IX, cl. 4. On appeal, the Second Circuit concluded that this Article gave "the states the power to purchase Indian land within their borders and extinguish Indian title to such land so long as such activity did not interfere with Congress's paramount powers over war and peace with the Indians." *Oneida Indian Nation v. State of New York*, 860 F.2d 1145, 1154 (2d Cir. 1988). The court ruled that congressional consent was not required for the land purchases, and thus the 1780s transactions were valid. How consistent is this result with the common law ruling of Chief Justice Marshall in *M'Intosh*?

4. Aboriginal title. "Indian title" is now commonly referred to as aboriginal title. One state court decision has explained the concept as follows:

> "Aboriginal title" gives members of a viable Native American tribe a right of occupancy to lands that is protected against claims by anyone else unless the tribe abandons the lands or the sovereign extinguishes the right. The right arises from a tribe's occupation of a definable, ancestral homeland before the onset of European colonization. The occupation must have been exclusive of the occupation by other tribes. The validity of aboriginal title is not dependent on treaty, statute, or other formal governmental recognition, but a group making a claim under the doctrine must present sufficient proof that they have constituted a tribe throughout relevant history and have never voluntarily abandoned their tribal status.

State v. Elliott, 616 A.2d 210 (Vt. 1992).

Although most aboriginal title is tribal, the United States Supreme Court has recognized that individual aboriginal title may exist as well. *See United States v. Dann*, 470 U.S. 39 (1985). The story of the Dann sisters, Western Shoshone ranchers who claim aboriginal title to their grazing lands, is the most well-known example. *See* Allison M. Dussias, *Squaw Drudges, Farm Wives, and the Dann Sisters' Last Stand: American Indian Women's Resistance to Domestication and the Denial of Their Property Rights*, 77 N.C. L. Rev. 637, 707–726 (1999). The Dann sisters' pursuit of their claim in international forums is discussed at pages 711–720.

The following case further illustrates some of the implications of the concept of aboriginal title.

United States ex rel. Hualpai Indians v. Santa Fe Pacific Railroad Co.

314 U.S. 339 (1941)

MR. JUSTICE DOUGLAS delivered the opinion of the Court

This is a suit brought by the United States, in its own right and as guardian of the Indians of the Walapai (Hualpai) Tribe in Arizona to enjoin respondent from interfering with the possession and occupancy by the Indians of certain land in northwestern Arizona. Respondent claims full title to the lands in question under the grant to its predecessor, the Atlantic and Pacific Railroad Co., provided for in the Act of July 27, 1866, 14 Stat. 292. The bill sought to establish that respondent's rights under the grant of 1866 are subject to the Indians' right of occupancy both inside and outside their present reservation which was established by the Executive Order of President Arthur, January 4, 1883. The bill consists of two causes of action — the first relating to lands inside, and the second, to lands outside, that reservation. The bill prayed, inter alia, that title be quieted and that respondent "account for all rents, issues and profits derived from the leasing, renting or use of the lands subject to said right of occupancy" by the Indians. Respondent moved to dismiss on the ground that the facts alleged were "insufficient to constitute a valid cause of action in equity." The District Court granted that motion. The Circuit Court of Appeals affirmed. We granted the petition for certiorari because of the importance of the problems raised in the administration of the Indian laws and the land grants.

Sec. 2 of the Act of July 27, 1866, the Act under which respondent's title to the lands in question derived, provided: "The United States shall extinguish, as rapidly as may be consistent with public policy and the welfare of the Indians, and only by their voluntary cession, the Indian title to all lands falling under the operation of this act and acquired in the donation to the road named in the act."

Basic to the present causes of action is the theory that the lands in question were the ancestral home of the Walapais, that such occupancy constituted "Indian title" within the meaning of § 2 of the 1866 Act, which the United States agreed to extinguish, and that in absence of such extinguishment the grant to the railroad "conveyed the fee subject to this right of occupancy." The Circuit Court of Appeals concluded that the United States had never recognized such possessory rights of Indians within the Mexican Cession and that in absence of such recognition the Walapais had no such right good against grantees of the United States.

Occupancy necessary to establish aboriginal possession is a question of fact to be determined as any other question of fact. If it were established as a fact that the lands in question were, or were included in, the ancestral home of the Walapais in the sense that they constituted definable territory occupied exclusively by the Walapais (as distinguished from lands wandered over by many tribes), then the Walapais had "Indian title" which, unless extinguished, survived the railroad grant of 1866.

"Unquestionably it has been the policy of the Federal Government from the beginning to respect the Indian right of occupancy, which could only be interfered with or determined by the United States." *Cramer v. United States*, 261 U.S. 219, 227. This policy was first recognized in *Johnson v. M'Intosh*, and has been repeatedly reaffirmed. As stated in *Mitchel v. United States*, [9 Pet. 711], 746, Indian "right of occupancy is considered as sacred as the fee simple of the whites." Whatever may have been the rights of the Walapais under Spanish law, the *Cramer* case assumed that lands within the Mexican Cession were not excepted from the policy to respect Indian right of occupancy. Though the *Cramer* case involved the problem of individual Indian occupancy, this Court stated that such occupancy was not to be treated differently from "the original nomadic tribal occupancy." Perhaps the assumption that aboriginal possession would be respected in the Mexican Cession was, like the generalizations in *Johnson v. M'Intosh*, not necessary for the narrow holding of the case. But such generalizations have been so often and so long repeated as respects land under the prior sovereignty of the various European nations, including Spain, that, like other rules governing titles to property they should now be considered no longer open. Furthermore, treaties negotiated with Indian tribes, wholly or partially within the Mexican Cession, for delimitation of their occupancy rights or for the settlement and adjustment of their boundaries, constitute clear recognition that no different policy as respects aboriginal possession obtained in this area than in other areas. Certainly it would take plain and unambiguous action to deprive the Walapais of the benefits of that policy. For it was founded on the desire to maintain just and peaceable relations with Indians. The reasons for its application to other tribes are no less apparent in case of the Walapais, a savage tribe which in early days caused the military no end of trouble.

Nor is it true, as respondent urges, that a tribal claim to any particular lands must be based upon a treaty, statute, or other formal government action. As stated in the *Cramer* case, "The fact that such right of occupancy finds no recognition in any statute or other formal governmental action is not conclusive."

Extinguishment of Indian title based on aboriginal possession is of course a different matter. The power of Congress in that regard is supreme. The manner, method and time of such extinguishment raise political, not justiciable, issues. As stated by Chief Justice Marshall in *Johnson v. M'Intosh*, "the exclusive right of the United States to extinguish" Indian title has never been doubted. And whether it be done by treaty, by the sword, by purchase, by the exercise of complete dominion adverse to the right of occupancy, or otherwise, its justness is not open to inquiry in the courts.

If the right of occupancy of the Walapais was not extinguished prior to the date of definite location of the railroad in 1872, then the respondent's predecessor took the fee subject to the encumbrance of Indian title. For on that date the title of respondent's predecessor attached as of July 27, 1866.

Certainly, prior to 1865 any right of occupancy of the Walapais to the lands in question was not extinguished; nor was the policy of respecting such Indian title changed. The Indian Trade and Intercourse Act of June 30, 1834 was extended over "the Indian tribes in the Territories of New Mexico and Utah" by §7 of the Act of February 27, 1851. * * * The Act of 1851 obviously did not create any Indian right of occupancy which did not previously exist. But it plainly indicates that in 1851 Congress desired to continue in these territories the unquestioned general policy of the Federal Government to recognize such right of occupancy. As stated by Chief Justice Marshall in *Worcester v. Georgia*, the Indian trade and intercourse acts "manifestly consider the several Indian nations as distinct political communities, having territorial boundaries, within which their authority is exclusive, and having a right to all the lands within those boundaries, which is not only acknowledged, but guaranteed by the United States."

This brings us to the Act of March 3, 1865, which provided: "All that part of the public domain in the Territory of Arizona, lying west of a direct line from Half-Way Bend to Corner Rock on the Colorado River, containing about seventy-five thousand acres of land, shall be set apart for an Indian reservation for the Indians of said river and its tributaries." It is plain that the Indians referred to included the Walapais. The suggestion for removing various Indian tribes in this area to a reservation apparently originated with a former Indian agent, Superintendent Poston, who was a Territorial Representative in Congress in 1865. His explanation on the floor of the House of the bill, which resulted in the creation of the 1865 reservation, indicates that he had called a council of the confederated tribes of the Colorado, including the Walapais, and had told them that "they should abandon" their lands and confine themselves to the place on the Colorado river which was later proposed for a reservation. He entered into no agreement with them nor did he propose a treaty. He merely stated that if elected to Congress he would try to get Congress to provide for them. As stated by the Commissioner of Indian Affairs in 1864, "Assuming that the Indians have a right of some kind to the soil, Mr. Poston's arrangement proposes a compromise with these Indians, by which on their confining themselves to their reservation, and yielding all claims to lands beyond it, they shall, in lieu of an annuity in money or supplies, be furnished by government with an irrigating canal, at a cost estimated at something near $100,000, which, by insuring them their annual crops, will enable them to support themselves, independently of other aid by the government."

We search the public records in vain for any clear and plain indication that Congress in creating the Colorado River reservation was doing more than making an offer to the Indians, including the Walapais, which it was hoped would be accepted as a compromise of a troublesome question. We find no indication that Congress by creating that reservation intended to extinguish all of the rights which the Walapais had in their ancestral home. That Congress could have effected such an extinguishment is not doubted. But an extinguishment cannot be lightly implied in view of the avowed solicitude of the Federal Government for the welfare of its Indian wards. As stated in *Choate v. Trapp*, 224 U.S. 665, 675, the rule of construction recognized without exception for over a century has been that "doubtful expressions, instead of being resolved in favor of the United States, are to be resolved in favor of a weak and defenseless people, who are wards of the nation, and dependent wholly upon its protection and good faith." Nor was there any plain intent or agreement on the part of the Walapais to abandon their ancestral lands if Congress would create a reservation. Furthermore, the Walapais did not accept the offer which Congress had tendered. In 1874 they were, however, forcibly removed to the Colorado River reservation on order from the Indian Department. But they left it in a body the next year. And it was decided "to allow them to remain in their old range during good behavior." They did thereafter remain in their old country and engaged in no hostilities against the whites. No further attempt was made to force them onto the Colorado River reservation, even though Congress had made various appropriations to defray the costs of locating the Arizona Indians in permanent abodes, including the Colorado River reservation. On these facts we conclude that the creation of the Colorado River reservation was, so far as the Walapais were concerned, nothing more than an abortive attempt to solve a perplexing problem. Their forcible removal in 1874 was not pursuant to any mandate of Congress. It was a high-handed endeavor to wrest from these Indians lands which Congress had never declared forfeited. No forfeiture can be predicated on an unauthorized attempt to effect a forcible settlement on the reservation, unless we are to be insensitive to the high standards for fair dealing in light of which laws dealing with Indian rights have long been read. Certainly, a forced abandonment of their ancestral home was not a "voluntary cession" within the meaning of § 2 of the Act of July 27, 1866.

The situation was, however, quite different in 1881. Between 1875 and that date there were rather continuous suggestions for settling the Walapais on some reservation. In 1881 the matter came to a head. A majority of the tribe, "in council assembled," asked an officer of the United States Army in that region "to aid them and represent to the proper authorities" the following proposal:

> "They say that in the country, over which they used to roam so free, the white men have appropriated all the water; that large numbers of cattle have been introduced and have rapidly increased during the past year or two; that in many places the water is fenced in and locked up; and they are driven from all waters. They say that the Railroad is now coming, which will require more water, and will bring more men who will take up all the small springs remaining. They urge that the following reservation be set aside for them while there is still time; that the land can never be of any great use to the Whites; that there are no mineral deposits upon it, as it has been thoroughly

prospected; that there is little or no arable land; that the water is in such small quantities, and the country is so rocky and void of grass, that it would not be available for stock raising. I am credibly informed, and from my observations believe, the above facts to be true. I, therefore, earnestly recommend that the hereafter described Reservation be, at as early a date as practicable, set aside for them."

Pursuant to that recommendation, the military reservation was constituted on July 8, 1881, subject to the approval of the President. The Executive Order creating the Walapai Indian Reservation was signed by President Arthur on January 4, 1883. There was an indication that the Indians were satisfied with the proposed reservation. A few of them thereafter lived on the reservation; many of them did not. While suggestions recurred for the creation of a new and different reservation, this one was not abandoned. For a long time it remained unsurveyed. Cattlemen used it for grazing, and for some years the Walapais received little benefit from it. But in view of all of the circumstances, we conclude that its creation at the request of the Walapais and its acceptance by them amounted to a relinquishment of any tribal claims to lands which they might have had outside that reservation and that that relinquishment was tantamount to an extinguishment by "voluntary cession" within the meaning of § 2 of the Act of July 27, 1866. The lands were fast being populated. The Walapais saw their old domain being preempted. They wanted a reservation while there was still time to get one. That solution had long seemed desirable in view of recurring tensions between the settlers and the Walapais. In view of the long standing attempt to settle the Walapais' problem by placing them on a reservation, their acceptance of this reservation must be regarded in law as the equivalent of a release of any tribal rights which they may have had in lands outside the reservation. They were in substance acquiescing in the penetration of white settlers on condition that permanent provision was made for them too. In view of this historical setting, it cannot now be fairly implied that tribal rights of the Walapais in lands outside the reservation were preserved. That would make the creation of the 1883 reservation, as an attempted solution of the violent problems created when two civilizations met in this area, illusory indeed. We must give it the definitiveness which the exigencies of that situation seem to demand. Hence, acquiescence in that arrangement must be deemed to have been a relinquishment of tribal rights in lands outside the reservation and notoriously claimed by others.

On January 23, 1941, the date of the filing of this petition for certiorari, respondent quitclaimed to the United States all lands claimed by it under the Act of July 27, 1866, within the Walapai Indian Reservation. Since the decree below must stand as to the second cause of action and since by virtue of the quitclaim deeds the United States has received all the lands to which the first cause of action relates, the decree will not be reversed. It is apparent, however, that it must be modified so as to permit the accounting as respects lands in the first cause of action. It does not appear whether those lands were included in the ancestral home of the Walapais in the sense that they were in whole or in part occupied exclusively by them or whether they were lands wandered over by many tribes. As we have said, occupancy necessary to establish aboriginal possession is a question of fact. The United States is entitled to an accounting as respects any or all of the lands in the first cause of action which the Walapais did in fact occupy exclusively from time immemorial.[24]

Such statements by the Secretary of the Interior as that "title to the odd-numbered sections" was in the respondent do not estop the United States from maintaining this suit. For they could not deprive the Indians of their rights any more than could the unauthorized leases in *Cramer v. United States*.

Hence, an accounting as respects such lands in the reservation which can be proved to have been occupied by the Walapais from time immemorial can be had. To the extent that the decree below precludes such proof and accounting, it will be modified. And as so modified, it is affirmed.

Notes

1. Extinguishing aboriginal title. Notice that the Supreme Court ruled that neither the 1865 statute establishing a reservation for the Colorado River tribes, nor the railroad grant act of 1866, nor the location of the railroad right-of-way in 1872 extinguished the Hualapai's (the Court spelled the tribe's name phonetically as Walapai) aboriginal title. Why not? How then did the Hualapai Reservation established in the early 1880s work an extinguishment?

2. Railroad land grants. The *Hualpai Tribe* case involved ownership of lands along railroad rights-of-way running through Indian reservations. The decision cited a statement by the Secretary of the Interior that the railroad held title to the odd-numbered sections. This is a reference to the congressional practice of land grants to the railroads. In particular, the federal government awarded vast amounts of land to the transcontinental railroads:

> The Union Pacific and Central Pacific—the two companies that shared the first transcontinental route—received 20 odd-numbered sections of land [a section is one square mile] for each mile of track they constructed. * * * The largest grant, however, went to the Northern Pacific Railroad. In 1864 the Northern Pacific received 20 sections per mile when building through states and 40 sections per mile when building through the territories. The grant to the Northern Pacific gave that railroad about 40 million acres, or an area roughly the size of New England.

Richard White, "It's Your Misfortune and None of My Own": A History of the American West 145–47 (U. Okla. Press 1991). Professor White noted that by the time Congress ended land grants to the railroads in 1871, some seven to 10 percent of all

---

24. In case of any lands in the reservation which were not part of the ancestral home of the Walapais and which had passed to the railroad under the 1866 Act, the railroad's title would antedate the creation of the reservation in 1883 and hence not be subject to the incumbrance of Indian title.

the land in the United States had been granted to them. The lands were granted to the railroads on both sides of their rights-of-way in "patterns resembling section-by-section checkerboards," creating access problems and frustrating attempts of federal land managers to engage in the coordinated planning and management called for by modern public land statutes. *See* George C. Coggins & Robert L. Glicksman, Public Natural Resources Law § 2.02[3][c] (2007).

3. The background of the *Hualpai* case. Christian McMillen's book, Making Indian Law: The Hualapai Land Case and the Birth of Ethnohistory (Yale 2007), explains the near dispossession of the tribe at the hands of the government and the railroad during the late nineteenth and early twentieth centuries, the government lawyers' erroneous claim that the Hualapai had abandoned the reservation, and the influence of Fred Mahone, a Hualapai historian, on John Collier, Commissioner of Indian Affairs, in getting the government to oppose diminishing the reservation in favor of the railroad. Collier's legal team, which included Felix Cohen, unsuccessfully argued in the lower courts that the railroad's occupation of the reservation was illegal. But they convinced the Supreme Court to reverse, based largely on Cohen's brief that, under *Johnson v. M'Intosh*, the tribe retained an inherent property right to the land, even without an affirmative grant from the government. *See* Mathew L.M. Fletcher, *Book Review*, 31 Am. Indian Culture & Research J. 225 (2007).

4. Application abroad. The rule that generic statutory land grants do not extinguish aboriginal title would have important ramifications if adopted by other English-speaking countries. In both British Columbia and Australia, for example, the argument against the existence of aboriginal title is based on generic land grants from the Crown, not on treaties or statutes expressly terminating aboriginal title.

a. Canada. In Canada, after a long period of judicial hostility, described in Douglas Sanders, *Aboriginal Rights in Canada: An Overview*, 2 L. & Anthro. 177 (1987), the Canadian Supreme Court split on the issue of whether general land ordinances could extinguish aboriginal rights. *Calder v. Attorney General for British Columbia*, [1973] S.C.R. 313. But in 1982 the Canadian Constitution Act entrenched the Canadian Charter of Rights and Freedoms. Included among the rights and freedoms was section 35(1), stating: "The existing aboriginal and treaty rights of the aboriginal peoples of Canada are hereby recognized and affirmed." Two years later, in *Guerin v. The Queen* [1984], S.C.R. 335, the Supreme Court ruled that the Crown had a fiduciary obligation to protect native lands "surrendered" to the Crown for management. Then, in *Simon v. The Queen*, [1985], 2 S.C.R. 387, the Court ruled that extinguishment of a treaty right "cannot be lightly implied," and that "strict proof" would be required to prove an intent to extinguish Indian rights. And in *Sparrow v. R.*, [1990] 1 S.C.R. 1075, the Court held that the federal Fisheries Act and its regulations failed to demonstrate "clear and plain" intent to extinguish aboriginal fishing rights, and that while regulation in the interest of conservation was permissible, native fishing rights—entrenched by the Constitution Act—had to be accorded "top priority" in allocating harvests. In *Delgamuukw v. British Columbia*, [1997] 3 S.C.R. 1010, the

Supreme Court overruled a lower decision and allowed oral testimony to establish the existence of aboriginal title.

In *R. v. Marshall*, [1999] 3 S.C. R. 456, the Canadian Supreme Court concluded that the Mi'kmaq Treaty of 1760–61 could serve as a defense to a charge of fishing without a federal license. The Court interpreted the treaty to enable Mi'kmaq to provide for their own sustenance by obtaining "necessaries" ("food, clothing, and housing supplemented by a few amenities"). Permissible harvest restrictions were limited to those which satisfied the *Sparrow* decision's priority, and which allowed the tribe to procure a moderate living under present-day standards. Just two months after this decision, the Court clarified, in *R. v. Marshall II*, [1999] 3 S.C.R. 533, that the government could restrict native harvests on conservation grounds "or other grounds of public importance," such as economic or regional fairness and historic reliance on a fishery by non-native groups. Gathering rights, the Court made clear, extended only to resources gathered in 1760, not to commercial logging or mineral development.

In 2014, *Tsilhot'in Nation v. British Columbia*, 2014 S.C.C. 44, the Supreme of Canada handed down a highly significant aboriginal rights decision concerning the claims of a seminomadic grouping of six bands sharing common culture and history, which lived in a remote valley bounded by rivers and mountains in central British Columbia. The bands are among hundreds of indigenous groups in British Columbia with unresolved land claims. In 1983, B.C. granted commercial logging licenses on land considered by the Tsilhqot'in to be part of their traditional territory. The bands objected and sought a declaration prohibiting commercial logging on the land. After negotiations failed, the bands filed suit. Their aboriginal rights claim was opposed by both the federal and provincial governments. A trial court upheld the claim, but the British Columbia Court of Appeal largely reversed, indicating that aboriginal title was limited to small intensively-used tracts.

The Canadian Supreme Court disagreed, ruling that aboriginal title requires only evidence of regular and exclusive use and occupation of land. The use and occupation must be sufficient, continuous, and exclusive. In determining what constitutes sufficient occupation, which was the heart of the Tsilhot'in appeal, the Court determined that aboriginal title is not confined to specific sites of settlement but instead extends to tracts of land regularly used for hunting, fishing, or otherwise exploiting resources and over which the group exercised effective control at the time of assertion of European sovereignty. The court consequently upheld the trial judge's determination: even though the Tsilhot'in population was small, there was sufficient evidence that the parts of the land were regularly used by the Tsilhqot'in. The evidence also showed that historically the Tsilhqot'in repelled other peoples from their land and demanded permission from outsiders who wished to pass over it.

The Court stated that the nature of aboriginal title is that it confers on the group that holds it the exclusive right to decide how the land is used and the right to benefit from those uses, subject to the restriction that the uses must be consistent with the group nature of the interest and the enjoyment of the land by future generations.

Moreover, prior to establishment of title, the Crown must consult in good faith with any aboriginal groups asserting title to the land about proposed uses of the land and, if appropriate, accommodate the interests of such groups. The level of consultation and accommodation required varies with the strength of the aboriginal group's claim to the land and the seriousness of the potentially adverse effect upon the interest claimed.

Where aboriginal title has been established, the Crown must not only comply with its procedural duties, but must also justify any incursions on aboriginal title lands by ensuring that the proposed government action is substantively consistent with the requirements of section 35 of the Canadian Constitution Act of 1982, which requires a demonstration of both a compelling and substantial governmental objective, and that the government action is consistent with the fiduciary duty owed by the Crown to the aboriginal group. According to the Court, the government must act in a way that respects the fact that aboriginal title is a group interest that inheres in present and future generations. Fulfilling that duty requires consultation with and consent by the group. The Court concluded that the province breached its duty by issuing the 1983 licenses, since the honor of the Crown required consultation with the Tsilhqot'in and accommodation of their interests.

b. Australia. In Australia, aboriginal rights were denied for most of the country's history. For example, in *Milirrpum v. Nabalco*, [1973] 17 F.L.R 141 (N.T. Sup. Ct.), a lower court denied the existence of aboriginal rights, employing the legal fiction that Australia was a "settled country," uninhabited before colonization. *See* Garth Nettheim, *Australian Aborigines and the Law*, 2 L. & Anthro. 371 (1987). In 1988, in *Mabo v. Queensland*, [1988] 83 A.L.R 14, the Australia High Court invalidated a law passed by the state of Queensland that declared the state owned all the land claimed by aboriginal peoples; the Court ruled that the state law conflicted with the federal Racial Discrimination Act. Four years later, reaching the merits of the aboriginal peoples' claim, the Court for the first time recognized the existence of aboriginal title. However, the Court also determined, 4–3, that extinguishment of aboriginal title does not require compensation. *Mabo v. Queensland*, [1992] 107 A.L.R 1. And in *Wik Peoples v. Queensland*, [1996] 121 A.L.R 129, the High Court ruled that aboriginal title and Crown pastoral leases for livestock grazing and other purposes can coexist; in other words, grazing leases do not extinguish native title because they are not necessarily inconsistent with the native titleholder's rights. *See* In the Wake of Wik: Old Dilemmas; New Directions in Native Title Law (Nat'l Native Title Tribunal, Gary D. Meyers, ed. 1999); Gary D. Meyers & Sally Raine, *Australian Aboriginal Land Rights in Transition (Part II): The Legislative Response to the High Court's Decisions in Mabo v. Queensland and Wik v. Queensland*, 9 Tulsa J. Comp. & Int'l L. 95 (2001); *see also* Dr. Lisa Strelein, *From Mabo to Yorta Yorta: Native Title Law in Australia*, 19 Wash. U. J.L. & Pol'y 225 (2005).

After a 25-year fight, the Ngaanyatjarra won the biggest indigenous land claim in Australian history in 2006. *Jango v. Northern Territory*, BC200601675 (Fed. Ct. Australia, 2006). The claim encompassed over 73,000 square miles in the Australian

Outback. In 2005, the Ngaanyatjarra settled the biggest indigenous land claim in Australian history. *Mervyn (on behalf of the peoples of the Ngaanyatjarra Lands) v. Western Australia,* BC200504470 (Fed. Ct. Australia, 2005). The claim encompassed over 72,000 square miles of Crown and reserve lands on Western Australia's eastern border. A summary of current Australian native title applications and determinations including relevant maps and case-links can be found at the Australian National Native Title Tribunal's website: http://www.nntt.gov.au/.

c. New Zealand. New Zealand's courts have been even slower than Australia and Canada to recognize the concept of aboriginal title, not doing so until 2003. In *Attorney-General v. Ngati Apa,* [2003] 3 N.Z.L.R. 643, a case involving a dispute between the government and the Maori over the title to certain stretches of country's foreshore and seabed, the New Zealand Court of Appeal (the highest court in New Zealand) finally recognized that aboriginal title, which the court referred to as "customary title," may exist in certain parts of the country's foreshore and seabed. In so holding, it overruled a 1963 case, *In re Ninety Mile Beach,* [1963] N.Z.L.R. 461, that rested on the nineteenth century assumption that the Maori lacked the social sophistication to possess customary property rights, stating:

> Maori custom and usage recognising property in foreshore and seabed lands displaces any English Crown Prerogative and is effective as a matter of New Zealand law, unless such property interests have been lawfully extinguished. The existence and extent of any such customary property interest is determined in application of tikanga. That is a matter for the Maori Land Court to consider on application to it or on reference by the High Court. Whether any such interests have been extinguished is a matter of law. Extinguishment depends on the effect of the legislation and actions relied upon as having that effect.

"Tikanga" are the Maori customs and traditions that have been handed down through time. In response to the Court of Appeal's decision, the New Zealand government exercised its "absolute Parliamentary supremacy" and passed the Foreshore and Seabed Act of 2004. The Act vests full legal and beneficial title of the public foreshore and seabed in the government, thus precluding any Maori claims of common law customary title in those lands. For a discussion of the Maori's struggle for aboriginal title in the country's foreshore and seabed, see F.M. (Jock) Brookfield, *Maori Claims and the "Special" Juridical Nature of Foreshore and Seabed,* 2 N.Z. L. Rev. 179 (2005). For a comparative property rights approach to native fishing rights in Canada, New Zealand, and the United States, see Michael C. Blumm, *Native Fishing Rights and Environmental Protection in North America and New Zealand: A Comparative Analysis of Profits A Prendre and Habitat Servitudes,* 18 Wis. Intl. L.J. 1 (1989).

The following case explores the ramifications of aboriginal title in the context of Alaska. There is little or no disagreement that the Tee-Hit-Ton Indians held aboriginal title to the territory in question. The issue before the Court was whether the federal government would be required to compensate the tribe for the confiscation of its timber.

Tee-Hit-Ton Indians v. United States
348 U.S. 272 (1955)

MR. JUSTICE REED delivered the opinion of the Court

This case rests upon a claim under the Fifth Amendment by petitioner, an identifiable group of American Indians of between 60 and 70 individuals residing in Alaska, for compensation for a taking by the United States of certain timber from Alaskan lands allegedly belonging to the group. The area claimed is said to contain over 350,000 acres of land and 150 square miles of water. The Tee-Hit-Tons, a clan of the Tlingit Tribe, brought this suit in the Court of Claims under 28 U.S.C. § 1505. The compensation claimed does not arise from any statutory direction to pay. Payment, if it can be compelled, must be based upon a constitutional right of the Indians to recover. This is not a case that is connected with any phase of the policy of the Congress, continued throughout our history, to extinguish Indian title through negotiation rather than by force, and to grant payments from the public purse to needy descendants of exploited Indians. The legislation in support of that policy has received consistent interpretation from this Court in sympathy with its compassionate purpose.

[The Court of Claims] held that petitioner was an identifiable group of American Indians residing in Alaska; that its interest in the lands prior to purchase of Alaska by the United States in 1867 was "original Indian title" or "Indian right of occupancy." It was further held that if such original Indian title survived the Treaty of 1867, 15 Stat. 539, by which Russia conveyed Alaska to the United States, such title was not sufficient basis to maintain this suit as there had been no recognition by Congress of any legal rights in petitioner to the land in question. The court said that no rights inured to plaintiff by virtue of legislation by Congress.

The Alaskan area in which petitioner claims a compensable interest is located near and within the exterior lines of the Tongass National Forest. By Joint Resolution of August 8, 1947, 61 Stat. 920, the Secretary of Agriculture was authorized to contract for the sale of national forest timber located within this National Forest "notwithstanding any claim of possessory rights." The Resolution defines "possessory rights"[7] and provides for all receipts from the sale of timber to be maintained in a special account in the Treasury until the timber and land rights are finally determined. Section 3 (b) of the Resolution provides:

---

7. "That 'possessory rights' as used in this resolution shall mean all rights, if any should exist, which are based upon aboriginal occupancy or title * * * whether claimed by native tribes, native villages, native individuals, or other persons, and which have not been confirmed by patent or court decision or included within any reservation."

"Nothing in this resolution shall be construed as recognizing or denying the validity of any claims of possessory rights to lands or timber within the exterior boundaries of the Tongass National Forest."

The Secretary of Agriculture, on August 20, 1951, pursuant to this authority contracted for sale to a private company of all merchantable timber in the area claimed by petitioner. This is the sale of timber which petitioner alleges constitutes a compensable taking by the United States of a portion of its proprietary interest in the land.

The problem presented is the nature of the petitioner's interest in the land, if any. Petitioner claims a "full proprietary ownership" of the land; or, in the alternative, at least a "recognized" right to unrestricted possession, occupation and use. Either ownership or recognized possession, petitioner asserts, is compensable. If it has a fee simple interest in the entire tract, it has an interest in the timber and its sale is a partial taking of its right to "possess, use and dispose of it." It is petitioner's contention that its tribal predecessors have continually claimed, occupied and used the land from time immemorial; that when Russia took Alaska, the Tlingits had a well-developed social order which included a concept of property ownership; that Russia while it possessed Alaska in no manner interfered with their claim to the land; that Congress has by subsequent acts confirmed and recognized petitioner's right to occupy the land permanently and therefore the sale of the timber off such lands constitutes a taking pro tanto of its asserted rights in the area.

The Government denies that petitioner has any compensable interest. It asserts that the Tee-Hit-Tons' property interest, if any, is merely that of the right to the use of the land at the Government's will; that Congress has never recognized any legal interest of petitioner in the land and therefore without such recognition no compensation is due the petitioner for any taking by the United States.

I. Recognition.—The question of recognition may be disposed of shortly. Where the Congress by treaty or other agreement has declared that thereafter Indians were to hold the lands permanently, compensation must be paid for subsequent taking. The petitioner contends that Congress has sufficiently "recognized" its possessory rights in the land in question so as to make its interest compensable. Petitioner points specifically to two statutes to sustain this contention. The first is § 8 of the Organic Act for Alaska of May 17, 1884, 23 Stat. 24. The second is § 27 of the Act of June 6, 1900, which was to provide for a civil government for Alaska, 31 Stat. 321, 330.

We have carefully examined these statutes and the pertinent legislative history and find nothing to indicate any intention by Congress to grant to the Indians any permanent rights in the lands of Alaska occupied by them by permission of Congress. Rather, it clearly appears that what was intended was merely to retain the status quo until further congressional or judicial action was taken. There is no particular form for congressional recognition of Indian right of permanent occupancy. It may be established in a variety of ways but there must be the definite intention by congressional action or authority to accord legal rights, not merely permissive occupation.

This policy of Congress toward the Alaskan Indian lands was maintained and reflected by its expression in the Joint Resolution of 1947 under which the timber contracts were made.

II. Indian Title.—(a) The nature of aboriginal Indian interest in land and the various rights as between the Indians and the United States dependent on such interest are far from novel as concerns our Indian inhabitants. It is well settled that in all the States of the Union the tribes who inhabited the lands of the States held claim to such lands after the coming of the white man, under what is sometimes termed original Indian title or permission from the whites to occupy. That description means mere possession not specifically recognized as ownership by Congress. After conquest they were permitted to occupy portions of territory over which they had previously exercised "sovereignty," as we use that term. This is not a property right but amounts to a right of occupancy which the sovereign grants and protects against intrusion by third parties but which right of occupancy may be terminated and such lands fully disposed of by the sovereign itself without any legally enforceable obligation to compensate the Indians.

This position of the Indian has long been rationalized by the legal theory that discovery and conquest gave the conquerors sovereignty over and ownership of the lands thus obtained. The great case of *Johnson v. M'Intosh* denied the power of an Indian tribe to pass their right of occupancy to another. It confirmed the practice of two hundred years of American history "that discovery gave an exclusive right to extinguish the Indian title of occupancy, either by purchase or by conquest."

In *Beecher v. Wetherby*, 95 U.S. 517, a tract of land which Indians were then expressly permitted by the United States to occupy was granted to Wisconsin. In a controversy over timber, this Court held the Wisconsin title good.

> "The grantee, it is true, would take only the naked fee, and could not disturb the occupancy of the Indians: that occupancy could only be interfered with or determined by the United States. It is to be presumed that in this matter the United States would be governed by such considerations of justice as would control a Christian people in their treatment of an ignorant and dependent race. Be that as it may, the propriety or justice of their action towards the Indians with respect to their lands is a question of governmental policy, and is not a matter open to discussion in a controversy between third parties, neither of whom derives title from the Indians. The right of the United States to dispose of the fee of lands occupied by them has always been recognized by this court from the foundation of the government."

No case in this Court has ever held that taking of Indian title or use by Congress required compensation. The American people have compassion for the descendants of those Indians who were deprived of their homes and hunting grounds by the drive of civilization. They seek to have the Indians share the benefits of our society as citizens of this Nation. Generous provision has been willingly made to allow tribes to recover for wrongs, as a matter of grace, not because of legal liability.

(b) There is one opinion in a case decided by this Court that contains language indicating that unrecognized Indian title might be compensable under the Constitution when taken by the United States. *United States v. Tillamooks*, 329 U.S. 40 [1946].

Recovery was allowed under a jurisdictional Act of 1935 that permitted payments to a few specific Indian tribes for "legal and equitable claims arising under or growing out of the original Indian title" to land, because of some unratified treaties negotiated with them and other tribes. The other tribes had already been compensated. Five years later this Court unanimously held that none of the former opinions in Vol. 329 of the United States Reports expressed the view that recovery was grounded on a taking under the Fifth Amendment. *United States v. Tillamooks*, 341 U.S. 48 [1951]. Interest, payable on recovery for a taking under the Fifth Amendment, was denied. * * * [In a later case, *Hynes v. Grimes Packing Co.*, 337 U.S. 86, 106 n.28, we] commented as to the first *Tillamook* case: "That opinion does not hold the Indian right of occupancy compensable without specific legislative direction to make payment."

[T]his Court in the second *Tillamook* case held that the first case was not "grounded on a taking under the Fifth Amendment." Therefore no interest was due.

We think it must be concluded that the recovery in the *Tillamook* case was based upon statutory direction to pay for the aboriginal title in the special jurisdictional act to equalize the Tillamooks with the neighboring tribes, rather than upon a holding that there had been a compensable taking under the Fifth Amendment. This leaves unimpaired the rule derived from *Johnson v. M'Intosh* that the taking by the United States of unrecognized Indian title is not compensable under the Fifth Amendment.

This is true, not because an Indian or an Indian tribe has no standing to sue or because the United States has not consented to be sued for the taking of original Indian title, but because Indian occupation of land without government recognition of ownership creates no rights against taking or extinction by the United States protected by the Fifth Amendment or any other principle of law.

(c) What has been heretofore set out deals largely with the Indians of the Plains and east of the Mississippi. The Tee-Hit-Tons urge, however, that their stage of civilization and their concept of ownership of property takes them out of the rule applicable to the Indians of the States. They assert that Russia never took their lands in the sense that European nations seized the rest of America. The Court of Claims, however, saw no distinction between their use of the land and that of the Indians of the Eastern United States. That court had no evidence that the Russian handling of the Indian land problem differed from ours. The natives were left the use of the great part of their vast hunting and fishing territory but what Russia wanted for its use and that of its licensees, it took. The court's conclusion on this issue was based on strong evidence.

In considering the character of the Tee-Hit-Tons' use of the land, the Court of Claims had before it the testimony of a single witness who was offered by plaintiff. He stated that he was the chief of the Tee-Hit-Ton tribe. He qualified as an expert on the Tlingits, a group composed of numerous interconnected tribes including the Tee-Hit-Tons. His testimony showed that the Tee-Hit-Tons had become greatly reduced in numbers. Membership descends only through the female line. At the present time there are only a few women of childbearing age and a total membership of some 65.

The witness pointed out that their claim of ownership was based on possession and use. The use that was made of the controverted area was for the location in winter of villages in sheltered spots and in summer along fishing streams and/or bays. The ownership was not individual but tribal. As the witness stated, "Any member of the tribe may use any portion of the land that he wishes, and as long as he uses it that is his for his own enjoyment, and is not to be trespassed upon by anybody else, but the minute he stops using it then any other member of the tribe can come in and use that area."

* * * From all that was presented, the Court of Claims concluded, and we agree, that the Tee-Hit-Tons were in a hunting and fishing stage of civilization, with shelters fitted to their environment, and claims to rights to use identified territory for these activities as well as the gathering of wild products of the earth. We think this evidence introduced by both sides confirms the Court of Claims' conclusion that the petitioner's use of its lands was like the use of the nomadic tribes of the States Indians.

The line of cases adjudicating Indian rights on American soil leads to the conclusion that Indian occupancy, not specifically recognized as ownership by action authorized by Congress, may be extinguished by the Government without compensation. Every American schoolboy knows that the savage tribes of this continent were deprived of their ancestral ranges by force and that, even when the Indians ceded millions of acres by treaty in return for blankets, food and trinkets, it was not a sale but the conquerors' will that deprived them of their land.

In the light of the history of Indian relations in this Nation, no other course would meet the problem of the growth of the United States except to make congressional contributions for Indian lands rather than to subject the Government to an obligation to pay the value when taken with interest to the date of payment. Our conclusion does not uphold harshness as against tenderness toward the Indians, but it leaves with Congress, where it belongs, the policy of Indian gratuities for the termination of Indian occupancy of Government-owned land rather than making compensation for its value a rigid constitutional principle.

The judgment of the Court of Claims is Affirmed.

Notes

1. **Property and sovereignty (again).** At the outset of this book, we emphasized the importance of distinguishing between sovereignty and proprietary issues. How well does Justice Reed do in this regard? He noted that in *Johnson v. M'Intosh*, Chief Justice Marshall stated that "discovery gave an exclusive right to extinguish the Indian title of occupancy, whether by purchase or conquest." In *M'Intosh*, the government

purchased the lands; in Alaska, there was no purchase. Was there conquest? Justice Reed also asserted that aboriginal title is not a property right, apparently on the basis of *M'Intosh*. Review the holding of that case again. What stick(s) in the bundle of property rights did Chief Justice Marshall rule that the tribes did not possess? Does this mean that they had no property rights? How would you classify Indian title in traditional property law terms?

2. **Use rights.** Justice Reed seemed to suggest that the Tlingit tradition of tribal use rights cannot be considered property rights. Aren't usufructuary rights recognized as property under Anglo-American law? For example, easements are property rights, are they not?

3. **What "every American schoolboy knows."** Why does what schoolboys "knew" in the 1950s matter to the Supreme Court? The historical record, as demonstrated by Felix Cohen, would seem to be more relevant. Cohen showed that, despite the myth that native lands were taken by force, "the historic fact is that all of the real estate acquired by the United States since 1776 was purchased not from Napoleon or any other emperor or czar but from its original Indian owners. What we acquired from Napoleon in the Louisiana Purchase was not real estate . . . but simply the power to govern and to tax." Felix S. Cohen, *Original Indian Title*, in Readings in American Indian Law: Recalling the Rhythm of Survival 65 (Jo Carrillo ed., 1998).

4. ***Tee-Hit-Ton* in context.** Professor Newton posited that fiscal and political considerations were at the heart of the decision in *Tee-Hit-Ton*. Oil was discovered on the Arctic Slope in the 1940s and 1950s, and the resources wealth of Alaska was becoming known by the time the Court decided *Tee-Hit-Ton* in 1955. Under the rule of the case, the Court left Congress free to extinguish aboriginal title to all of Alaska, in preparation for statehood in 1959, without incurring the cost of compensating the Native people for their lands. Moreover, *Tee-Hit-Ton* was decided in the middle of the Termination Era of federal Indian policy, one year after Congress passed House Concurrent Resolution 108, calling for termination of the federal trust responsibility. *See* Nell Jessup Newton, *At the Whim of the Sovereign: Aboriginal Title Reconsidered*, 31 Hastings L.J. 1215, 1248–53 (1980).

5. **The Alaska Native Claims Settlement Act.** The outcome of the *Tee-Hit-Ton* case led to agitation in Congress and eventual passage of the Alaska Native Claims Settlement Act (ANCSA) of 1971. Pub. L. No. 92-203, codified as amended at 43 U.S.C. § 1601 *et seq*. ANCSA is described and interpreted in *Alaska v. Native Village of Venetie Tribal Government* and the accompanying notes, at page 114.

6. **The Tejon Ranch claim.** In 2015, the Ninth Circuit affirmed a district court's rejection of the non-recognized Kawaiisu Tribe's aboriginal claim to Tejon Ranch, some 270,000 acres of private lands in southern California, because of the tribe's failure to present the claim to a board of commissioners established by the California Land Claims Act of 1851. The court also ruled that a subsequent treaty did not recognize the tribe's aboriginal claim, nor did an unratified treaty. *Robinson v. Jewell*, 790 F.3d 910 (9th Cir. 2015).

Note on the Federal Claims Process

Tee-Hit-Ton was an appeal from the Court of Claims. The claims process has been, and continues to be, of enormous importance in Indian law. Tribal access to the claims process, however, has a tortuous history. *See generally* Nell Jessup Newton, *Indian Claims in the Courts of the Conqueror*, 41 Am. U.L. Rev. 753 (1992).

1. Indian claims before 1946. In 1855, Congress created the federal Court of Claims. Act of Feb. 24, 1855, 10 Stat. 612. A few tribes filed suit, but no cases had been adjudicated before Congress, in 1863, expressly barred claims based on treaties with the Indian tribes. Act of Mar. 3, 1863, §9, 12 Stat. 765, 767. Despite the apparently limited nature of the exception, it was held to bar all tribal claims unless authorized by specific acts of Congress. *See* Newton, *supra*, at 770.

Not until 1881 did the first tribe win congressional authorization to bring suit in the Court of Claims. In the next 42 years (until Indians were awarded citizenship in 1924), Congress permitted only 39 cases to reach the Court of Claims; just 17 resulted in awards to the Indian plaintiffs. Between 1923 and 1927, as many claims were filed as in the previous 42 years. By 1946, some 200 claims had been approved for adjudication.

But the process was slow. In one four-year period in the 1930s, 96 bills were introduced in Congress to allow tribes to litigate claims, but only one was enacted. Of the 200 claims that had reached the court by 1946, only 29 had produced awards for the tribes. Most of the remainder had been dismissed, not on the merits, but because of flaws in the jurisdictional acts.

As a result, when the Indian Claims Commission Act was proposed in 1946, it had the backing of two camps: first, those who believed that long-overdue justice was due the Indians for the loss of their lands; and second, those who favored termination and assimilation. The termination era was just around the corner, and its proponents believed that settling Indian claims, with the resulting cash awards, would help free the government of dependent tribes.

2. Indian Claims Commission. The Indian Claims Commission (ICC) was created to hear "ancient claims": those claims by tribes against the United States that accrued prior to August 13, 1946. Indian Claims Commission Act of 1946, Pub. L. No. 726, ch. 959, 60 Stat. 1049. All such claims had to be filed within five years; 375 were. These claims were subsequently divided up into over 600 "dockets."

Adjudication before the ICC took on a pattern. First, establish the claim to the land. Second, determine the fair market value of the land as of the time of the cession. And third, compare this price with the amount actually paid by the government, including any offsets. Offsets included any government expenditures to the tribes that were not required by treaty, such as rations, tools, education, and medical care.

Remedies were limited to money damages for the loss of the land. For the tribes, this was the worst part of the ICC Act. With the exception of the Taos Pueblo, which recovered the sacred Blue Lake through congressional action, no tribe received its land back.

Once an award was determined by the ICC, money had to be appropriated by Congress. In no instance did Congress refuse to do so, but the appropriations bill could take more than one session of Congress to be enacted. Even then, the money would not be released to the tribe until it had prepared a plan, acceptable to Congress, for spending the money. Under the trust doctrine, the Bureau of Indian Affairs required plans to include provisions for at least some of the money to be used for education, economic development, or other purposes that the BIA deemed worthwhile. Most tribes would have preferred a straight per capita distribution of the entire award.

Congress originally intended the ICC to function for 10 years, but extended the Commission until 1978. By that time, the ICC had adjudicated more than 500 claims, mostly relating to land. About 60 percent of the claims resulted in awards to the tribes, totaling about $800 million. Nonetheless, 102 dockets remained, and were transferred to the Court of Claims. In 1990, there were still 12 of these original ICC claims remaining in the Claims Court.

3. Claims accruing after August 1946. Any claim of any tribe against the federal government, arising under federal law (including treaties), that accrued after August 13, 1946, had to be brought in the Court of Claims. 28 U.S.C. § 1505. Note that the Tee-Hit-Ton Indians, whose claim arose after 1946, filed suit directly in the Court of Claims, seeking compensation for the taking of their timber.

The jurisdiction of the Court of Federal Claims* is determined by the Tucker Act and the Indian Tucker Act. The Indian Tucker Act, 28 U.S.C. § 1505, provides:

> The United States Claims Court shall have jurisdiction of any claim against the United States accruing after August 13, 1946, in favor of any tribe, band, or other identifiable group of American Indians residing within the territorial limits of the United States or Alaska whenever such claim is one arising under the Constitution, laws or treaties of the United States, or Executive orders of the President, or is one which otherwise would be cognizable in the Claims Court if the claimant were not an Indian tribe, band or group.

The last basis for jurisdiction is a reference to the Tucker Act, 28 U.S.C. § 1491(a)(1), which provides:

> The United States Claims Court shall have jurisdiction to render judgment upon any claim against the United States founded either upon the Constitution, or any Act of Congress or any regulation of an executive department, or upon any express or implied contract with the United States, or for liquidated or unliquidated damages in cases not sounding in tort.

---

*The name of the claims court has undergone a number of changes over the years. The Court of Claims was replaced in 1982 by the Claims Court, which was in turn replaced in 1993 by the Court of Federal Claims.

The Court of Federal Claims has offered the following explanation of its jurisdiction:

> For the Claims Court to adjudicate claims — even actions stemming from the Constitution, a federal statute, or an executive regulation — the claimant must seek money damages. Moreover the claimant must find an entitlement to money damages in a source of federal law other than the Tucker Act. Neither the Tucker Act nor its counterpart for claims brought by Indian tribes supply [sic] an independent basis for monetary relief in the Claims Court. The Tucker Act merely confers jurisdiction upon the Claims Court to enforce independent rights to monetary relief.
>
> Thus, plaintiffs must show both that their claim springs from violation of a duty embodied in federal law independent of the Tucker Act and that the independent law "can be fairly interpreted as mandating compensation by the Federal Government for the damage sustained." In sum, plaintiffs must show a right to monetary relief for violation of a federal law outside the Tucker Act.

Youngbull v. United States, No. 31-88 L, 1990 U.S. Cl. Ct. LEXIS 3, *9–10 (Cl. Ct. Jan. 4, 1990).

The U.S. Court of Appeals for the Federal Circuit hears appeals from the Court of Federal Claims.

B. Recognized Title

As noted in *Tee-Hit-Ton*, Congress can "recognize" Indian title to the land by treaty, agreement, or statute. The following cases explore the ramifications of recognized title. The first case establishes the modern understanding of what recognized title encompasses. The second case addresses the issue of compensability for the confiscation of recognized-title land.

United States v. Shoshone Tribe of Indians
304 U.S. 111 (1938)

MR. JUSTICE BUTLER delivered the opinion of the Court.

The Shoshone Tribe brought this suit to recover the value of part of its reservation taken by the United States by putting upon it, without the tribe's consent, a band of Arapahoe Indians.

The sole question for decision is whether, as the United States contends, the Court of Claims erred in holding that the right of the tribe included the timber and mineral resources within the reservation.

The findings show: The United States, by the treaty of July 2, 1863, set apart for the Shoshone Tribe a reservation of 44,672,000 acres located in Colorado, Utah, Idaho and Wyoming. By the treaty of July 3, 1868, the tribe ceded that reservation to the United States. And by it the United States agreed that the "district of country" 3,054,182 acres definitely described "shall be and the same is set apart for the absolute and undisturbed use and occupation of the Shoshone Indians . . . , and the United States now solemnly agrees that no persons," with exceptions not important here, "shall ever be permitted to pass over, settle upon, or reside in" that territory. The Indians agreed that they would make the reservation their permanent home.

[The United States] stipulated that no treaty for the cession of any portion of the reservation held in common should be valid as against the Indians, unless signed by at least a majority of all interested male adults; and that no cession by the tribe should be construed to deprive any member of his right to any tract of land selected by him.

When the treaty of 1868 was made, the tribe consisted of full blood blanket Indians, unable to read, write, or speak English. Upon consummation of the treaty, the tribe went, and has since remained, upon the reservation. It was known to contain valuable mineral deposits—gold, oil, coal and gypsum. It included more than 400,000 acres of timber, extensive well-grassed bench lands and fertile river valleys conveniently irrigable. It was well protected by mountain ranges and a divide, and was the choicest and best-watered portion of Wyoming.

In 1904 the Shoshones and Arapahoes ceded to the United States 1,480,000 acres to be held by it in trust for the sale of such timber lands, timber and other products, and for the making of leases for various purposes. The net proceeds were to be credited to the Indians. From 1907 to 1919 there were allotted to members of the tribes 245,058 acres.

The court's finding of the ultimate fact is: "The fair and reasonable value of a one-half undivided interest of the Shoshone or Wind River Reservation of a total of 2,343,540 acres, which was taken by the United States on March 19, 1878, from the Shoshone Tribe of Indians for the Northern Arapahoe Tribe, was, on March 19, 1878, $1,581,889.50." That is $1.35 per acre for 1,171,770 acres, one-half of the reservation in 1878, at the time of taking. The United States does not challenge the principle or basis upon which the court determined the amount to be added to constitute just compensation. >$33,297,865 in 2023

The substance of the Government's point is that in fixing the value of the tribe's right, the lower court included as belonging to the tribe substantial elements of value, ascribable to mineral and timber resources, which in fact belonged to the United States.

It contends that the Shoshones' right to use and occupy the lands of the reservation did not include the ownership of the timber and minerals and that the opinion of the court below departs from the general principles of law regarding Indian land tenure and the uniform policy of the Government in dealing with Indian tribes. It asks for reversal with "directions to determine the value of the Indians' right of use and occupancy but to exclude therefrom 'the net value of the lands' and 'the net value of any timber or minerals.'"

In [an earlier opinion in] this case we have held that the tribe had the right of occupancy with all its beneficial incidents; that, the right of occupancy being the primary one and as sacred as the fee, division by the United States of the Shoshones' right with the Arapahoes was an appropriation of the land pro tanto; that although the United States always had legal title to the land and power to control and manage the affairs of the Indians, it did not have power to give to others or to appropriate to its own use any part of the land without rendering, or assuming the obligation to pay, just compensation to the tribe, for that would be, not the exercise of guardianship or management, but confiscation.

It was not then necessary to consider, but we are now called upon to decide, whether, by the treaty, the tribe acquired beneficial ownership of the minerals and timber on the reservation. The phrase "absolute and undisturbed use and occupation" is to be read, with other parts of the document, having regard to the purpose of the arrangement made, the relation between the parties, and the settled policy of the United States fairly to deal with Indian tribes. In treaties made with them the United States seeks no advantage for itself; friendly and dependent Indians are likely to accept without discriminating scrutiny the terms proposed. They are not to be interpreted narrowly, as sometimes may be writings expressed in words of art employed by conveyancers, but are to be construed in the sense in which naturally the Indians would understand them.

The principal purpose of the treaty was that the Shoshones should have, and permanently dwell in, the defined district of country. To that end the United States granted and assured to the tribe peaceable and unqualified possession of the land in perpetuity. Minerals and standing timber are constituent elements of the land itself. For all practical purposes, the tribe owned the land. Grants of land subject to the Indian title by the United States, which had only the naked fee, would transfer no beneficial interest. The right of perpetual and exclusive occupancy of the land is not less valuable than full title in fee.

The treaty, though made with knowledge that there were mineral deposits and standing timber in the reservation, contains nothing to suggest that the United States intended to retain for itself any beneficial interest in them. The words of the grant, coupled with the Government's agreement to exclude strangers, negative the idea that the United States retained beneficial ownership. The grant of right to members of the tribe severally to select and hold tracts on which to establish homes for themselves and families, and the restraint upon cession of land held in common or individually, suggest beneficial ownership in the tribe. As transactions between a guardian and his wards are to be construed favorably to the latter, doubts, if there were any, as to ownership of lands, minerals or timber would be resolved in favor of the tribe. The cession in 1904 by the tribe to the United States in trust reflects a construction by the parties that supports the tribe's claim, for if it did not own, creation of a trust to sell or lease for its benefit would have been unnecessary and inconsistent with the rights of the parties.

Although the United States retained the fee, and the tribe's right of occupancy was incapable of alienation or of being held otherwise than in common, that right is as sacred and as securely safeguarded as is fee simple absolute title. Subject to the conditions imposed by the treaty, the Shoshone Tribe had the right that has always been understood to belong to Indians, undisturbed possessors of the soil from time immemorial. Provisions in aid of teaching children and of adult education in farming, and to secure for the tribe medical and mechanical service, to safeguard tribal and individual titles, when taken with other parts of the treaty, plainly evidence purpose on the part of the United States to help to create an independent permanent farming community upon the reservation. Ownership of the land would further that purpose. In the absence of definite expression of intention so to do, the United States will not be held to have kept it from them.

The lower court did not err in holding that the right of the Shoshone Tribe included the timber and minerals within the reservation.

Notes

1. **A split estate.** According to the *Shoshone Tribe* Court, the federal title in Indian lands is "only the naked fee;" the tribes retain all beneficial interest. As the Court stated: "For all practical purposes, the tribe owned the land." This concept of a split property estate, arising out of the federal trust obligation, is a central feature of most Indian land title. The split estate concept is conceptually important as well, because it separates the title questions from usufructuary rights. Use rights were always central to native life, as the notes and excerpts which began this text illustrated. They remain a critical part of Native American natural resources law, as ensuing chapters will demonstrate.

2. **"Constituent elements of the land."** Because of the tribe's full beneficial ownership, the government owed the Shoshone Tribe compensation for the loss of "constituent elements of the land," like minerals and timber. Is there any reason to think that if minerals and timber are constituent elements of the land, subsurface water (groundwater) is not? Water rights are explored in Chapter VII.

3. **Coalbed methane gas.** As *Shoshone Tribe* holds, tribal trust ownership of land generally extends to the mineral resources under the land unless Congress has provided otherwise. Nonetheless, surface and subsurface estates may be split, with ownership divided among the tribes, allottees, fee owners, the state, or the federal government. In one instance, the mineral estate itself was divided between the tribe and the non-Indian fee owners of the surface lands. *See Amoco Production Co. v. Southern Ute Tribe*, 526 U.S. 865 (1999).

Once considered a nuisance or a hazardous waste product associated with mining coal, coalbed methane gas (CMG) is now a valuable resource, comprising an estimated 15 percent of the nation's potential gas reserves. Whether CMG is a constituent element of the coal or a separate mineral estate has been the subject of dispute for over two decades. Most courts considering the question held that CMG was a component of the coal, but a 1981 opinion of the Interior Solicitor disagreed, suggesting that the gas was a separate estate from the coal. The issue was of particular importance to the Southern Ute Tribe, whose reservation today contains lands that had been ceded to the federal government and subsequently patented to homesteaders under the 1909 and 1910 Coal Lands Acts, which reserved to the federal government "all coal" and the rights to mine it. In 1938, the government restored the lands it retained to the tribe, along with the coal, subject to the homestead patents. Relying on the 1981 Solicitor's opinion, non-Indian surface owners began to sell their CMG rights to energy companies such as Amoco, and the tribe sued Amoco for back royalties of approximately $1 billion. In *Amoco Production*, however, the Supreme Court held that the tribe did not own the CMG. The Court ruled that in light of contemporary dictionary definitions and industry practices, the 1909 Congress intended the term "coal" to include only the solid rock mineral, and not the associated gas.

4. A dinosaur named Sue. An unusual application of the *Shoshone Tribe* rule occurred in 1990, when employees of the private Black Hills Institute of Geological Research discovered a Tyrannosaurus Rex skeleton approximately 65 million years old. The skeleton, named "Sue" after the discoverer, is one of only eleven complete T. Rex skeletons in existence. The land on which the fossil was discovered was a trust allotment located within the boundaries of the Cheyenne River Sioux Reservation. The Institute paid the allottee $5000 "for title to the fossil and the right to excavate the fossil from his land." It then excavated the skeleton and removed it to the Institute headquarters outside the reservation, where the fossil was subsequently seized by federal marshals.

In a suit to quiet title to the fossil, the federal court held that the T. Rex skeleton "was a component part of [the allotted] land, just like the soil, the rocks, and whatever other naturally-occurring materials make up the earth of the ranch." *Black Hills Institute of Geological Research v. South Dakota School of Mines & Technology*, 12 F.3d 737 (8th Cir. 1993). As an interest in land, the fossil could be conveyed only upon the approval of the Secretary of the Interior. Because no approval had been obtained, the severance and sale of the fossil were unlawful, and the Institute acquired no ownership or possessory rights in the skeleton.

The result was that the allottee owned the T. Rex skeleton in trust. The Bureau of Indian Affairs, as trustee, authorized the allottee to sell the fossil and keep the proceeds. In 1997, Sue was auctioned by Sotheby's in Manhattan, and acquired by The Field Museum of Natural History in Chicago for $8.36 million. Malcolm W. Browne, *Tyrannosaur Skeleton Is Sold to a Museum for $8.36 Million*, N.Y. Times, Oct. 5, 1997, at Sec. 1, p. 37.

United States v. Sioux Nation of Indians
448 U.S. 371 (1980)

Mr. Justice BLACKMUN delivered the opinion of the Court.

This case concerns the Black Hills of South Dakota, the Great Sioux Reservation, and a colorful, and in many respects tragic, chapter in the history of the Nation's West. Although the litigation comes down to a claim of interest since 1877 on an award of over $17 million, it is necessary, in order to understand the controversy, to review at some length the chronology of the case and its factual setting.

I

For over a century now the Sioux Nation has claimed that the United States unlawfully abrogated the Fort Laramie Treaty of April 29, 1868, in Art. II of which the United States pledged that the Great Sioux Reservation, including the Black Hills, would be "set apart for the absolute and undisturbed use and occupation of the Indians herein named." The Fort Laramie Treaty was concluded at the culmination of the Powder River War of 1866–1867, a series of military engagements in which the Sioux tribes, led by their great chief, Red Cloud, fought to protect the integrity of earlier-recognized treaty lands from the incursion of white settlers.[1]

The Fort Laramie Treaty included several agreements central to the issues presented in this case. First, it established the Great Sioux Reservation, a tract of land bounded on the east by the Missouri River, on the south by the northern border of the State of Nebraska, on the north by the forty-sixth parallel of north latitude, and on the west by the one hundred and fourth meridian of west longitude,[2] in addition to certain reservations already existing east of the Missouri. The United States "solemnly agree[d]" that no unauthorized persons "shall ever be permitted to pass over, settle upon, or reside in [this] territory."

Second, the United States permitted members of the Sioux tribes to select lands within the reservation for cultivation. In order to assist the Sioux in becoming civilized farmers, the Government promised to provide them with the necessary services and materials, and with subsistence rations for four years.[3]

Third, in exchange for the benefits conferred by the treaty, the Sioux agreed to relinquish their rights under the Treaty of September 17, 1851, to occupy territories outside the reservation, while reserving their "right to hunt on any lands north of North Platte, and on the Republican Fork of the Smoky Hill river, so long as the

---

1. The Sioux territory recognized under the Treaty of September 17, 1851, included all of the present State of South Dakota, and parts of what is now Nebraska, Wyoming, North Dakota, and Montana.

2. The boundaries of the reservation included approximately half the area of what is now the State of South Dakota, including all of that State west of the Missouri River save for a narrow strip in the far western portion. The reservation also included a narrow strip of land west of the Missouri and north of the border between North and South Dakota.

3. The treaty called for the construction of schools and the provision of teachers for the education of Indian children, the provision of seeds and agricultural instruments to be used in the first four years of planting, and the provision of blacksmiths, carpenters, millers, and engineers to perform work on the reservation. In addition, the United States agreed to deliver certain articles of clothing to each Indian residing on the reservation, "on or before the first day of August of each year, for thirty years." An annual stipend of $10 per person was to be appropriated for all those members of the Sioux Nation who continued to engage in hunting; those who settled on the reservation to engage in farming would receive $20. Subsistence rations of meat and flour (one pound of each per day) were to be provided for a period of four years to those Indians upon the reservation who could not provide for their own needs.

buffalo may range thereon in such numbers as to justify the chase." The Indians also expressly agreed to withdraw all opposition to the building of railroads that did not pass over their reservation lands, not to engage in attacks on settlers, and to withdraw their opposition to the military posts and roads that had been established south of the North Platte River.

Fourth, Art. XII of the treaty provided:

> "No treaty for the cession of any portion or part of the reservation herein described which may be held in common shall be of any validity or force as against the said Indians, unless executed and signed by at least three fourths of all the adult male Indians, occupying or interested in the same."[4]

The years following the treaty brought relative peace to the Dakotas, an era of tranquility that was disturbed, however, by renewed speculation that the Black Hills, which were included in the Great Sioux Reservation, contained vast quantities of gold and silver. In 1874 the Army planned and undertook an exploratory expedition into the Hills, both for the purpose of establishing a military outpost from which to control those Sioux who had not accepted the terms of the Fort Laramie Treaty, and for the purpose of investigating "the country about which dreamy stories have been told." Lieutenant Colonel George Armstrong Custer led the expedition of close to 1,000 soldiers and teamsters, and a substantial number of military and civilian aides. Custer's journey began at Fort Abraham Lincoln on the Missouri River on July 2, 1874. By the end of that month they had reached the Black Hills, and by mid-August had confirmed the presence of gold fields in that region. The discovery of gold was widely reported in newspapers across the country. Custer's florid descriptions of the mineral and timber resources of the Black Hills, and the land's suitability for grazing and cultivation, also received wide circulation, and had the effect of creating an intense popular demand for the "opening" of the Hills for settlement.[7] The only obstacle to "progress" was the Fort Laramie Treaty that reserved occupancy of the Hills to the Sioux.

Having promised the Sioux that the Black Hills were reserved to them, the United States Army was placed in the position of having to threaten military force, and occasionally to use it, to prevent prospectors and settlers from trespassing on lands reserved to the Indians. For example, in September 1874, General Sheridan sent instructions to Brigadier General Alfred H. Terry, Commander of the Department of Dakota, at Saint Paul, directing him to use force to prevent companies of prospectors from trespassing on the Sioux Reservation. At the same time, Sheridan let it

---

4. The Fort Laramie Treaty was considered by some commentators to have been a complete victory for Red Cloud and the Sioux. In 1904 it was described as "the only instance in the history of the United States where the government has gone to war and afterwards negotiated a peace conceding everything demanded by the enemy and exacting nothing in return."

7. * * * The Sioux regarded Custer's expedition in itself to be a violation of the Fort Laramie Treaty. In later negotiations for cession of the Black Hills, Custer's trail through the Hills was referred to by a chief known as Fast Bear as "that thieves' road."

be known that he would "give a cordial support to the settlement of the Black Hills," should Congress decide to "open up the country for settlement, by extinguishing the treaty rights of the Indians." Sheridan's instructions were published in local newspapers.[8]

Eventually, however, the Executive Branch of the Government decided to abandon the Nation's treaty obligation to preserve the integrity of the Sioux territory. In a letter dated November 9, 1875, to Terry, Sheridan reported that he had met with President Grant, the Secretary of the Interior, and the Secretary of War, and that the President had decided that the military should make no further resistance to the occupation of the Black Hills by miners, "it being his belief that such resistance only increased their desire and complicated the troubles." These orders were to be enforced "quietly," and the President's decision was to remain "confidential." (letter from Sheridan to Sherman).

With the Army's withdrawal from its role as enforcer of the Fort Laramie Treaty, the influx of settlers into the Black Hills increased. The Government concluded that the only practical course was to secure to the citizens of the United States the right to mine the Black Hills for gold. Toward that end, the Secretary of the Interior, in the spring of 1875, appointed a commission to negotiate with the Sioux. The commission was headed by William B. Allison. The tribal leaders of the Sioux were aware of the mineral value of the Black Hills and refused to sell the land for a price less than $70 million. The commission offered the Indians an annual rental of $400,000, or payment of $6 million for absolute relinquishment of the Black Hills. The negotiations broke down.

In the winter of 1875–1876, many of the Sioux were hunting in the unceded territory north of the North Platte River, reserved to them for that purpose in the Fort Laramie Treaty. On December 6, 1875, for reasons that are not entirely clear, the Commissioner of Indian Affairs sent instructions to the Indian agents on the reservation to notify those hunters that if they did not return to the reservation agencies by January 31, 1876, they would be treated as "hostiles." Given the severity of the winter, compliance with these instructions was impossible. On February 1, the Secretary of the Interior nonetheless relinquished jurisdiction over all hostile Sioux, including those Indians exercising their treaty-protected hunting rights, to the War Department. The Army's campaign against the "hostiles" led to Sitting Bull's notable victory over

---

8. General William Tecumseh Sherman, Commanding General of the Army, as quoted in the Saint Louis Globe in 1875, described the military's task in keeping prospectors out of the Black Hills as "the same old story, the story of Adam and Eve and the forbidden fruit." In an interview with a correspondent from the Bismarck Tribune, published September 2, 1874, Custer recognized the military's obligation to keep all trespassers off the reservation lands, but stated that he would recommend to Congress "the extinguishment of the Indian title at the earliest moment practicable for military reasons." Given the ambivalence of feeling among the commanding officers of the Army about the practicality and desirability of its treaty obligations, it is perhaps not surprising that one chronicler of Sioux history would describe the Government's efforts to dislodge invading settlers from the Black Hills as "feeble."

Custer's forces at the battle of the Little Big Horn on June 25. That victory, of course, was short-lived, and those Indians who surrendered to the Army were returned to the reservation, and deprived of their weapons and horses, leaving them completely dependent for survival on rations provided them by the Government.

In the meantime, Congress was becoming increasingly dissatisfied with the failure of the Sioux living on the reservation to become self-sufficient.[11] The Sioux' entitlement to subsistence rations under the terms of the Fort Laramie Treaty had expired in 1872. Nonetheless, in each of the two following years, over $1 million was appropriated for feeding the Sioux. In August 1876, Congress enacted an appropriations bill providing that "hereafter there shall be no appropriation made for the subsistence" of the Sioux, unless they first relinquished their rights to the hunting grounds outside the reservation, ceded the Black Hills to the United States, and reached some accommodation with the Government that would be calculated to enable them to become self-supporting. Act of Aug. 15, 1876.[12] Toward this end, Congress requested the President to appoint another commission to negotiate with the Sioux for the cessation of the Black Hills.

---

11. In Dakota Twilight (1976), a history of the Standing Rock Sioux, Edward A. Milligan states: "Nearly seven years had elapsed since the signing of the Fort Laramie Treaty and still the Sioux were no closer to a condition of self-support than when the treaty was signed. In the meantime the government had expended nearly thirteen million dollars for their support. The future treatment of the Sioux became a matter of serious moment, even if viewed from no higher standard than that of economics." *Id.* at 52.

One historian has described the ration provisions of the Fort Laramie Treaty as part of a broader reservation system designed by Congress to convert nomadic tribesmen into farmers. Hagan, The Reservation Policy: Too Little and Too Late, *in* Indian-White Relations: A Persistent Paradox 157–169 (J. Smith & R. Kvasnicka, eds., 1976). In words applicable to conditions on the Sioux Reservation during the years in question, Professor Hagan stated:

"The idea had been to supplement the food the Indians obtained by hunting until they could subsist completely by farming. Clauses in the treaties permitted hunting outside the strict boundaries of the reservations, but the inevitable clashes between off-reservation hunting parties and whites led this privilege to be first restricted and then eliminated. The Indians became dependent upon government rations more quickly than had been anticipated, while their conversion to agriculture lagged behind schedule.

"The quantity of food supplied by the government was never sufficient for a full ration, and the quality was frequently poor. But in view of the fact that most treaties carried no provision for rations at all, and for others they were limited to four years, the members of Congress tended to look upon rations as a gratuity that should be terminated as quickly as possible. The Indian Service and military personnel generally agreed that it was better to feed than to fight, but to the typical late nineteenth-century member of Congress, not yet exposed to doctrines of social welfare, there was something obscene about grown men and women drawing free rations. Appropriations for subsistence consequently fell below the levels requested by the secretary of the interior.

"That starvation and near-starvation conditions were present on some of the sixty-odd reservations every year for the quarter century after the Civil War is manifest." *Id.* at 161.

12. The chronology of the enactment of this bill does not necessarily support the view that it was passed in reaction to Custer's defeat at the Battle of the Little Big Horn on June 25, 1876, although some historians have taken a contrary view.

This commission, headed by George Manypenny, arrived in the Sioux country in early September and commenced meetings with the head men of the various tribes. The members of the commission impressed upon the Indians that the United States no longer had any obligation to provide them with subsistence rations. The commissioners brought with them the text of a treaty that had been prepared in advance. The principal provisions of this treaty were that the Sioux would relinquish their rights to the Black Hills and other lands west of the one hundred and third meridian, and their rights to hunt in the unceded territories to the north, in exchange for subsistence rations for as long as they would be needed to ensure the Sioux' survival. In setting out to obtain the tribes' agreement to this treaty, the commission ignored the stipulation of the Fort Laramie Treaty that any cession of the lands contained within the Great Sioux Reservation would have to be joined in by three-fourths of the adult males. Instead, the treaty was presented just to Sioux chiefs and their leading men. It was signed by only 10% of the adult male Sioux population.[13]

Congress resolved the impasse by enacting the 1876 "agreement" into law as the Act of Feb. 28, 1877 (1877 Act). The Act had the effect of abrogating the earlier Fort

---

13. The commission's negotiations with the chiefs and head men is described by Robinson, *supra* n.1. [D. Robinson, A History of the Dakota or Sioux Indians 356–381 (1904), *reprinted in* 2 South Dakota Historical Collections (1904).] He states:

"As will be readily understood, the making of a treaty was a forced put, so far as the Indians were concerned. Defeated, disarmed, dismounted, they were at the mercy of a superior power and there was no alternative but to accept the conditions imposed upon them. This they did with as good grace as possible under all of the conditions existing."

Another early chronicler of the Black Hills region wrote of the treaty's provisions in the following chauvinistic terms:

"It will be seen by studying the provisions of this treaty, that by its terms the Indians from a material standpoint lost much, and gained but little. By the first article they lose all rights to the unceded Indian territory in Wyoming from which white settlers had then before been altogether excluded; by the second they relinquish all right to the Black Hills, and the fertile valley of the Belle Fourche in Dakota, without additional material compensation; by the third conceding the right of way over the unceded portions of their reservation; by the fourth they receive such supplies only, as were provided by the treaty of 1868, restricted as to the points for receiving them. The only real gain to the Indians seems to be embodied in the fifth article of the treaty [Government's obligation to provide subsistence rations]. The Indians, doubtless, realized that the Black Hills was destined soon to slip out of their grasp, regardless of their claims, and therefore thought it best to yield to the inevitable, and accept whatever was offered them.

"They were assured of a continuance of their regular daily rations, and certain annuities in clothing each year, guaranteed by the treaty of 1868, and what more could they ask or desire, than that a living be provided for themselves, their wives, their children, and all their relations, including squaw men, indirectly, thus leaving them free to live their wild, careless, unrestrained life, exempt from all the burdens and responsibilities of civilized existence? In view of the fact that there are thousands who are obliged to earn their bread and butter by the sweat of their brows, and that have hard work to keep the wolf from the door, they should be satisfied."

Laramie Treaty, and of implementing the terms of the Manypenny Commission's "agreement" with the Sioux leaders.[14]

The passage of the 1877 Act legitimized the settlers' invasion of the Black Hills, but throughout the years it has been regarded by the Sioux as a breach of this Nation's solemn obligation to reserve the Hills in perpetuity for occupation by the Indians. One historian of the Sioux Nation commented on Indian reaction to the Act in the following words:

> "The Sioux thus affected have not gotten over talking about that treaty yet, and during the last few years they have maintained an organization called the Black Hills Treaty Association, which holds meetings each year at the various agencies for the purpose of studying the treaty with the intention of presenting a claim against the government for additional reimbursements for the territory ceded under it. Some think that Uncle Sam owes them about $9,000,000 on the deal, but it will probably be a hard matter to prove it." F. Fiske, The Taming of the Sioux 132 (1917).

Fiske's words were to prove prophetic.

IV. A.

In reaching its conclusion that the 1877 Act effected a taking of the Black Hills for which just compensation was due the Sioux under the Fifth Amendment, the Court of Claims relied upon the "good faith effort" test developed in its earlier decision in *Three Tribes of Fort Berthold Reservation v. United States*, 390 F.2d 686 ([Cl. Ct.] 1968). The *Fort Berthold* test had been designed to reconcile two lines of cases decided by this Court that seemingly were in conflict. The first line, exemplified by *Lone Wolf v. Hitchcock*, 187 U.S. 553 (1903), recognizes "that Congress possesse[s] a paramount power over the property of the Indians, by reason of its exercise of guardianship over

---

14. The 1877 Act "ratified and confirmed" the agreement reached by the Manypenny Commission with the Sioux tribes. It altered the boundaries of the Great Sioux Reservation by adding some 900,000 acres of land to the north, while carving out virtually all that portion of the reservation between the one hundred and third and one hundred and fourth meridians, including the Black Hills, an area of well over 7 million acres. The Indians also relinquished their rights to hunt in the unceded lands recognized by the Fort Laramie Treaty, and agreed that three wagon roads could be cut through their reservation.

In exchange, the Government reaffirmed its obligation to provide all annuities called for by the Fort Laramie Treaty, and "to provide all necessary aid to assist the said Indians in the work of civilization; to furnish to them schools and instruction in mechanical and agricultural arts, as provided for by the treaty of 1868." In addition, every individual was to receive fixed quantities of beef or bacon and flour, and other foodstuffs, in the discretion of the Commissioner of Indian Affairs, which "shall be continued until the Indians are able to support themselves." The provision of rations was to be conditioned, however, on the attendance at school by Indian children, and on the labor of those who resided on lands suitable for farming. The Government also promised to assist the Sioux in finding markets for their crops and in obtaining employment in the performance of Government work on the reservation.

Later congressional actions having the effect of further reducing the domain of the Great Sioux Reservation are described in *Rosebud Sioux Tribe v. Kneip*, 430 U.S. 584, 589 (1977).

their interests, and that such authority might be implied, even though opposed to the strict letter of a treaty with the Indians." The second line, exemplified by the more recent decision in *Shoshone Tribe v. United States*, 299 U.S. 476 (1937), concedes Congress' paramount power over Indian property, but holds, nonetheless, that "[t]he power does not extend so far as to enable the Government 'to give the tribal lands to others, or to appropriate them to its own purposes, without rendering, or assuming an obligation to render, just compensation.'" In *Shoshone Tribe*, Mr. Justice Cardozo, in speaking for the Court, expressed the distinction between the conflicting principles in a characteristically pithy phrase: "Spoliation is not management."

The *Fort Berthold* test distinguishes between cases in which one or the other principle is applicable:

> "It is obvious that Congress cannot simultaneously (1) act as trustee for the benefit of the Indians, exercising its plenary powers over the Indians and their property, as it thinks is in their best interests, and (2) exercise its sovereign power of eminent domain, taking the Indians' property within the meaning of the Fifth Amendment to the Constitution. In any given situation in which Congress has acted with regard to Indian people, it must have acted either in one capacity or the other. Congress can own two hats, but it cannot wear them both at the same time.
>
> "Some guideline must be established so that a court can identify in which capacity Congress is acting. The following guideline would best give recognition to the basic distinction between the two types of congressional action: Where Congress makes a good faith effort to give the Indians the full value of the land and thus merely transmutes the property from land to money, there is no taking. This is a mere substitution of assets or change of form and is a traditional function of a trustee."

Applying the *Fort Berthold* test to the facts of this case, the Court of Claims concluded that, in passing the 1877 Act, Congress had not made a good-faith effort to give the Sioux the full value of the Black Hills. The principal issue presented by this case is whether the legal standard applied by the Court of Claims was erroneous.[26]

---

26. It should be recognized at the outset that the inquiry presented by this case is different from that confronted in the more typical of our recent "taking" decisions. *E.g., Kaiser Aetna v. United States*, 444 U.S. 164 (1979); *Penn Central Transp. Co. v. New York City*, 438 U.S. 104 (1978). In those cases the Court has sought to "determin[e] when 'justice and fairness' require that economic injuries caused by public action be compensated by the Government, rather than remain disproportionately concentrated on a few persons." Here, there is no doubt that the Black Hills were "taken" from the Sioux in a way that wholly deprived them of their property rights to that land. The question presented is whether Congress was acting under circumstances in which that "taking" implied an obligation to pay just compensation, or whether it was acting pursuant to its unique powers to manage and control tribal property as the guardian of Indian welfare, in which event the Just Compensation Clause would not apply.

B.

The Government contends that the Court of Claims erred insofar as its holding that the 1877 Act effected a taking of the Black Hills was based on Congress' failure to indicate affirmatively that the consideration given the Sioux was of equivalent value to the property rights ceded to the Government. It argues that "the true rule is that Congress must be assumed to be acting within its plenary power to manage tribal assets if it reasonably can be concluded that the legislation was intended to promote the welfare of the tribe." The Government derives support for this rule principally from this Court's decision in *Lone Wolf v. Hitchcock*.

The foregoing considerations support our conclusion that the passage from *Lone Wolf* here relied upon by the Government has limited relevance to this case. More significantly, *Lone Wolf*'s presumption of congressional good faith has little to commend it as an enduring principle for deciding questions of the kind presented here. In every case where a taking of treaty-protected property is alleged,[29] a reviewing court must recognize that tribal lands are subject to Congress' power to control and manage the tribe's affairs. But the court must also be cognizant that "this power to control and manage [is] not absolute. While extending to all appropriate measures for protecting and advancing the tribe, it [is] subject to limitations inhering in . . . a guardianship and to pertinent constitutional restrictions."

As the Court of Claims recognized in its decision below, the question whether a particular measure was appropriate for protecting and advancing the tribe's interests, and therefore not subject to the constitutional command of the Just Compensation Clause, is factual in nature. The answer must be based on a consideration of all the evidence presented. We do not mean to imply that a reviewing court is to second-guess, from the perspective of hindsight, a legislative judgment that a particular measure would serve the best interests of the tribe. We do mean to require courts, in considering whether a particular congressional action was taken in pursuance of Congress' power to manage and control tribal lands for the Indians' welfare, to engage in a thoroughgoing and impartial examination of the historical record. A presumption of congressional good faith cannot serve to advance such an inquiry.

C.

We turn to the question whether the Court of Claims' inquiry in this case was guided by an appropriate legal standard. We conclude that it was. In fact, we approve that court's formulation of the inquiry as setting a standard that ought to be emulated by courts faced with resolving future cases presenting the question at issue here:

---

29. Of course, it has long been held that the taking by the United States of "unrecognized" or "aboriginal" Indian title is not compensable under the Fifth Amendment. *Tee-Hit-Ton Indians v. United States*, 348 U.S. 272 (1955). The principles we set forth today are applicable only to instances in which "Congress by treaty or other agreement has declared that thereafter Indians were to hold the lands permanently." In such instances, "compensation must be paid for subsequent taking."

"In determining whether Congress has made a good faith effort to give the Indians the full value of their lands when the government acquired [them], we therefore look to the objective facts as revealed by Acts of Congress, congressional committee reports, statements submitted to Congress by government officials, reports of special commissions appointed by Congress to treat with the Indians, and similar evidence relating to the acquisition. . . .

"The 'good faith effort' and 'transmutation of property' concepts referred to in *Fort Berthold* are opposite sides of the same coin. They reflect the traditional rule that a trustee may change the form of trust assets as long as he fairly (or in good faith) attempts to provide his ward with property of equivalent value. If he does that, he cannot be faulted if hindsight should demonstrate a lack of precise equivalence. On the other hand, if a trustee (or the government in its dealings with the Indians) does not attempt to give the ward the fair equivalent of what he acquires from him, the trustee to that extent has taken rather than transmuted the property of the ward. In other words, an essential element of the inquiry under the *Fort Berthold* guideline is determining the adequacy of the consideration the government gave for the Indian lands it acquired. That inquiry cannot be avoided by the government's simple assertion that it acted in good faith in its dealings with the Indians."[30]

D.

We next examine the factual findings made by the Court of Claims, which led it to the conclusion that the 1877 Act effected a taking. First, the court found that "[t]he only item of 'consideration' that possibly could be viewed as showing an attempt by Congress to give the Sioux the 'full value' of the land the government took from them was the requirement to furnish them with rations until they became self-sufficient." This finding is fully supported by the record, and the Government does not seriously contend otherwise.[31]

---

30. An examination of this standard reveals that, contrary to the Government's assertion, the Court of Claims in this case did not base its finding of a taking solely on Congress' failure in 1877 to state affirmatively that the "assets" given the Sioux in exchange for the Black Hills were equivalent in value to the land surrendered. Rather, the court left open the possibility that, in an appropriate case, a mere assertion of congressional good faith in setting the terms of a forced surrender of treaty-protected lands could be overcome by objective indicia to the contrary. And, in like fashion, there may be instances in which the consideration provided the Indians for surrendered treaty lands was so patently adequate and fair that Congress' failure to state the obvious would not result in the finding of a compensable taking.

31. The 1877 Act, purported to provide the Sioux with "all necessary aid to assist the said Indians in the work of civilization," and "to furnish to them schools and instruction in mechanical and agricultural arts, as provided for by the treaty of 1868." The Court of Claims correctly concluded that the first item "was so vague that it cannot be considered as constituting a meaningful or significant element of payment by the United States." As for the second, it "gave the Sioux nothing to which they were not already entitled [under the 1868 treaty]."

Second, the court found, after engaging in an exhaustive review of the historical record, that neither the Manypenny Commission, nor the congressional Committees that approved the 1877 Act, nor the individual legislators who spoke on its behalf on the floor of Congress, ever indicated a belief that the Government's obligation to provide the Sioux with rations constituted a fair equivalent for the value of the Black Hills and the additional property rights the Indians were forced to surrender. This finding is unchallenged by the Government.

A third finding lending some weight to the court's legal conclusion was that the conditions placed by the Government on the Sioux' entitlement to rations, "further show that the government's undertaking to furnish rations to the Indians until they could support themselves did not reflect a congressional decision that the value of the rations was the equivalent of the land the Indians were giving up, but instead was an attempt to coerce the Sioux into capitulating to congressional demands."

Finally, the Court of Claims rejected the Government's contention that the fact that it subsequently had spent at least $43 million on rations for the Sioux (over the course of three-quarters of a century) established that the 1877 Act was an act of guardianship taken in the Sioux' best interest. The court concluded: "The critical inquiry is what Congress did—and how it viewed the obligation it was assuming—at the time it acquired the land, and not how much it ultimately cost the United States to fulfill the obligation." It found no basis for believing that Congress, in 1877, anticipated that it would take the Sioux such a lengthy period of time to become self-sufficient, or that the fulfillment of the Government's obligation to feed the Sioux would entail the large expenditures ultimately made on their behalf. We find no basis on which to question the legal standard applied by the Court of Claims, or the findings it reached, concerning Congress' decision to provide the Sioux with rations.

The Government has placed some reliance in this Court on the fact that the 1877 Act extended the northern boundaries of the reservation by adding some 900,000 acres of grazing lands. In the Court of Claims, however, the Government did "not contend . . . that the transfer of this additional land was a significant element of the consideration the United States gave for the Black Hills." And Congress obviously did not intend the extension of the reservation's northern border to constitute consideration for the property rights surrendered by the Sioux. The extension was effected in that article of the Act redefining the reservation's borders; it was not mentioned in the article which stated the consideration given for the Sioux' "cession of territory and rights." Moreover, our characterizing the 900,000 acres as assets given the Sioux in consideration for the property rights they ceded would not lead us to conclude that the terms of the exchange were "so patently adequate and fair" that a compensable taking should not have been found.

Finally, we note that the Government does not claim that the Indian Claims Commission and the Court of Claims incorrectly valued the property rights taken by the 1877 Act by failing to consider the extension of the northern border. Rather, the Government argues only that the 900,000 acres should be considered, along with the obligation to provide rations, in determining whether the Act, viewed in its entirety, constituted a good-faith effort on the part of Congress to promote the Sioux' welfare.

E.

The aforementioned findings fully support the Court of Claims' conclusion that the 1877 Act appropriated the Black Hills "in circumstances which involved an implied undertaking by [the United States] to make just compensation to the tribe."[32] We make only two additional observations about this case. First, dating at least from the decision in *Cherokee Nation v. Southern Kansas R. Co.*, 135 U.S. 641 (1890), this Court has recognized that Indian lands, to which a tribe holds recognized title, "are held subject to the authority of the general government to take them for such objects as are germane to the execution of the powers granted to it; provided only, that they are not taken without just compensation being made to the owner." In the same decision the Court emphasized that the owner of such lands "is entitled to reasonable, certain and adequate provision for obtaining compensation before his occupancy is disturbed." The Court of Claims gave effect to this principle when it held that the Government's uncertain and indefinite obligation to provide the Sioux with rations until they became self-sufficient did not constitute adequate consideration for the Black Hills.

Second, it seems readily apparent to us that the obligation to provide rations to the Sioux was undertaken in order to ensure them a means of surviving their transition from the nomadic life of the hunt to the agrarian lifestyle Congress had chosen for them. Those who have studied the Government's reservation policy during this period of our Nation's history agree. It is important to recognize that the 1877 Act, in addition to removing the Black Hills from the Great Sioux Reservation, also ceded the Sioux' hunting rights in a vast tract of land extending beyond the boundaries of that reservation. Under such circumstances, it is reasonable to conclude that

---

32. The dissenting opinion suggests that the factual findings of the Indian Claims Commission, the Court of Claims, and now this Court, are based upon a "revisionist" view of history. The dissent fails to identify which materials quoted herein or relied upon by the Commission and the Court of Claims fit that description. The dissent's allusion to historians "writing for the purpose of having their conclusions or observations inserted in the reports of congressional committees," is also puzzling because, with respect to this case, we are unaware that any such historian exists.

The primary sources for the story told in this opinion are the factual findings of the Indian Claims Commission and the Court of Claims. A reviewing court generally will not discard such findings because they raise the specter of creeping revisionism, as the dissent would have it, but will do so only when they are clearly erroneous and unsupported by the record. No one, including the Government, has ever suggested that the factual findings of the Indian Claims Commission and the Court of Claims fail to meet that standard of review.

A further word seems to be in order. The dissenting opinion does not identify a single author, nonrevisionist, neorevisionist, or otherwise, who takes the view of the history of the cession of the Black Hills that the dissent prefers to adopt, largely, one assumes, as an article of faith. Rather, the dissent relies on the historical findings contained in the decision rendered by the Court of Claims in 1942. That decision, and those findings, are not before this Court today. Moreover, the holding of the Court of Claims in 1942, to the extent the decision can be read as reaching the merits of the Sioux' taking claim, was based largely on the conclusive presumption of good faith toward the Indians which that court afforded to Congress' actions of 1877. The divergence of results between that decision and the judgment of the Court of Claims affirmed today, which the dissent would attribute to historical revisionism, is more logically explained by the fact that the former decision was based on an erroneous legal interpretation of this Court's opinion in *Lone Wolf*.

Congress' undertaking of an obligation to provide rations for the Sioux was a quid pro quo for depriving them of their chosen way of life, and was not intended to compensate them for the taking of the Black Hills.[33]

V.

In sum, we conclude that the legal analysis and factual findings of the Court of Claims fully support its conclusion that the terms of the 1877 Act did not effect "a mere change in the form of investment of Indian tribal property." *Lone Wolf v. Hitchcock*, 187 U.S., at 568. Rather, the 1877 Act effected a taking of tribal property, property which had been set aside for the exclusive occupation of the Sioux by the Fort Laramie Treaty of 1868. That taking implied an obligation on the part of the Government to make just compensation to the Sioux Nation, and that obligation, including an award of interest, must now, at last, be paid.

The judgment of the Court of Claims is affirmed.

Mr. Justice REHNQUIST, dissenting.

In 1942, the Sioux Tribe filed a petition for certiorari requesting this Court to review the Court of Claims' ruling that Congress had not unconstitutionally taken the Black Hills in 1877, but had merely exchanged the Black Hills for rations and grazing lands—an exchange Congress believed to be in the best interests of the Sioux and the Nation. This Court declined to review that judgment. Yet today the Court permits Congress to reopen that judgment which this Court rendered final upon denying certiorari in 1943, and proceeds to reject the 1942 Court of Claims' factual interpretation of the events in 1877. I am convinced that Congress may not constitutionally require the Court of Claims to reopen this proceeding, that there is no judicial principle justifying the decision to afford the respondents an additional opportunity to litigate the same claim, and that the Court of Claims' first interpretation of the events in 1877 was by all accounts the more realistic one. I therefore dissent.

Although the Court refrains from so boldly characterizing its action, it is obvious from [the facts of the jurisdictional history of the case] that Congress has reviewed

---

33. We find further support for this conclusion in Congress' 1974 amendment to §2 of the Indian Claims Commission Act, 25 U.S.C. §70a. That amendment provided that in determining offsets, "expenditures for food, rations, or provisions shall not be deemed payments on the claim." The Report of the Senate Committee on Interior and Insular Affairs, which accompanied this amendment, made two points that are pertinent here. First, it noted that "[a]lthough couched in general terms, this amendment is directed to one basic objective—expediting the Indian Claims Commission's disposition of the famous Black Hills case." Second, the Committee observed:

> "The facts are, as the Commission found, that the United States disarmed the Sioux and denied them their traditional hunting areas in an effort to force the sale of the Black Hills. Having violated the 1868 Treaty and having reduced the Indians to starvation, the United States should not now be in the position of saying that the rations it furnished constituted payment for the land which it took. In short, the Government committed two wrongs: first, it deprived the Sioux of their livelihood; secondly, it deprived the Sioux of their land. What the United States gave back in rations should not be stretched to cover both wrongs."

the decisions of the Court of Claims, set aside the judgment that no taking of the Black Hills occurred, set aside the judgment that there is no cognizable reason for relitigating the claim, and ordered a new trial. I am convinced that this is nothing other than an exercise of judicial power reserved to Art. III courts that may not be performed by the Legislative Branch under its Art. I authority.

Article III vests "the judicial Power . . . of the United States" in federal courts. Congress is vested by Art. I with *legislative* powers, and may not itself exercise an appellate-type review of judicial judgments in order to alter their terms, or to order new trials of cases already decided.

Even if I could countenance the Court's decision to reach the merits of this case, I also think it has erred in rejecting the 1942 court's interpretation of the facts. That court rendered a very persuasive account of the congressional enactment. As the dissenting judges in the Court of Claims opinion under review pointedly stated: "The majority's view that the rations were not consideration for the Black Hills is untenable. What else was the money for?"

I think the Court today rejects that conclusion largely on the basis of a view of the settlement of the American West which is not universally shared. There were undoubtedly greed, cupidity, and other less-than-admirable tactics employed by the Government during the Black Hills episode in the settlement of the West, but the Indians did not lack their share of villainy either. It seems to me quite unfair to judge by the light of "revisionist" historians or the mores of another era actions that were taken under pressure of time more than a century ago.

Different historians, not writing for the purpose of having their conclusions or observations inserted in the reports of congressional committees, have taken different positions than those expressed in some of the materials referred to in the Court's opinion. This is not unnatural, since history, no more than law, is not an exact (or for that matter an inexact) science.

But the inferences which the Court itself draws * * * leave a stereotyped and one-sided impression both of the settlement regarding the Black Hills portion of the Great Sioux Reservation and of the gradual expansion of the National Government from the Proclamation Line of King George III in 1763 to the Pacific Ocean.

That there was tragedy, deception, barbarity, and virtually every other vice known to man in the 300-year history of the expansion of the original 13 Colonies into a Nation which now embraces more than three million square miles and 50 States cannot be denied. But in a court opinion, as a historical and not a legal matter, both settler and Indian are entitled to the benefit of the Biblical adjuration: "Judge not, that ye be not judged."

Notes

1. The meaning of the Black Hills. Lakota medicine man Pete Catches was quoted in Indian Country Today on the significance of the Black Hills:

> To the Indian spiritual way of life, the Black Hills is the center of the Lakota people. There, ages ago, before Columbus came over the sea, seven spirits came to the Black Hills. They selected that area, the beginning of sacredness to the Lakota people.
>
> The two are tied together. Our people that have passed on, their spirits are contained in the Black Hills. This is why it is the center of the universe, and this is why it is sacred to the Oglala Sioux. In this life and the life hereafter, the two are together.
>
> I'd like a life to look forward to after this life. Generations and generations ago, our people have looked upon the Black Hills as the center of the world, and it's a circle. We began from there and we make a complete circle of life, and we go there after our demise from this world. That is why it is sacred to us.

Mario Gonzalez, *The Black Hills: Why the Black Hills Are Sacred to Lakota*, Indian Country Today, Feb. 29–Mar. 4, 1996, at A6.

2. The history of the Black Hills claim. The Sioux Nation never recognized the taking of its land, and in particular the 1877 taking of the Black Hills. The Nation's struggle to get its claim heard, and its continuing fight for the return of the land, are summarized by Professor Newton:

> The Sioux people * * * continuously made demands for the return of this land, or at least the portion of the Great Sioux Reservation containing the Black Hills. In 1920, the tribe obtained a special jurisdictional statute permitting suit against the Government. In 1942, the Court of Claims dismissed the claim in an opinion remarkable for its lack of clarity on the basis of the dismissal. In 1950, the Sioux again filed a claim for their land invoking the more liberal bases in the Indian Claims Commission Act. The Commission held there had not been a taking, in part because their attorney working with very limited resources had not made proper offers of proof that the Sioux land had, in fact, been confiscated. New attorneys for the Sioux convinced the Court of Claims to reopen the case, on the grounds that the tribe's former attorney had developed a serious drinking problem and was incompetent. Finally in 1975, the court again dismissed the Sioux Nation's case for failure to state a claim. After an intense lobbying effort by the new tribal attorneys in 1978, Congress revived the claim.
>
> By the time of the claim's revival, many members of the Sioux Tribe decided that the claim was misguided. In 1977, the Oglala Sioux Tribe, one of the signatories of the Treaty of Fort Laramie, refused to renew its attorney's contract and passed a tribal resolution advising Congress of their desire to seek return of the Black Hills. Because taking money for the land created the impression that the tribe had no right to the land, the Oglala Sioux Tribe decided it did not want the money.

Although this decision may have been ill-considered in light of the chances of getting any land back, courts usually do not interfere when litigants dismiss their attorneys. The Court of Claims would not let the attorneys withdraw from the case, however, and judgment was eventually entered in favor the tribe. The Supreme Court affirmed in a case briefed and argued by the attorneys who had been dismissed by the Oglala Sioux Tribe. [*United States v. Sioux Nation of Indians*, at page 148.] Although the Court affirmed an award of $122 million to the Sioux Nation, each of the tribes refused to accept it. The account has now grown to over $300 million.

Nell Jessup Newton, *Indian Claims in the Courts of the Conqueror*, 41 Am. U.L. Rev. 753, 764–65 (1992).*

Subsequent attempts to invalidate the confiscation of Sioux land failed. The Eighth Circuit dismissed the Oglala Sioux Tribe's quiet title claim to the Black Hills on the ground that, because the claim arose prior to 1946, it was within the exclusive jurisdiction of the Indian Claims Commission. *Oglala Sioux Tribe v. United States*, 650 F.2d 140, 143–44 (8th Cir. 1981). Subsequently, the same court rejected an argument by Sioux tribes that the 1889 statute which broke up the Great Sioux Reservation was invalid for failing to comply with the tribal consent provisions of the 1868 Fort Laramie Treaty. *Mid States Coalition for Progress v. Surface Transportation Board*, 345 F.3d 520, 555–56 (8th Cir. 2003). The court also rejected a claim that a railroad project required tribal consent, because the route was located outside the boundaries of any current reservation.

3. The land and the money. The Court confirmed an award of more than $17 million, plus interest from the date of the takings, for Docket 74-B (takings of the Black Hills). With interest, the amount in the Treasury grew rapidly: from $380 million in 1996, to $570 million in 2011, to $757 million in 2007. By 2011, Docket 74-B funds had grown to around $1 billion. Maria Streshinsky, *Saying No to $1 Billion*, The Atlantic (March 2011), http://www.theatlantic.com/magazine/archive/2011/02/saying-no-to-1-billion/8380.

In addition, in 1970 the Indian Claims Commission, in Docket 74-A, awarded the tribes $40 million concerning a claim for 14 million acres of aboriginal title land and 34 million acres of recognized title land east of the Black Hills. Avis Little Eagle, *Black Hills Land Claim*, Indian Country Today, May 21–28, 1996, at A1. By 2007, those funds were nearly $106 million. Tim Giago, *The Black Hills: A Case of Dishonest Dealings*, The Huffington Post (posted June 3, 2007), www.huffingtonpost.com/tim-giago/.

In the late 1990s, both the Santee Sioux and the Fort Peck Assiniboine Sioux expressed interest in receiving their shares of the Docket 74-A funds. *See* Little Eagle, *supra*, at A1-A2; K. Marie Porterfield, *Fort Peck Sioux Vote to Accept Black Hills Money*, Indian Country Today, Dec. 1–8, 1997, at A1. The chairman of the Santee Sioux stated:

---

* Copyright 1992, Nell Jessup Newton. Reprinted with permission of Nell Jessup Newton.

"We are being realistic. We know we will never get those lands back. We could use that money to buy land here." Little Eagle, *supra*, at A1–A2. In both cases, other Sioux leaders and tribes questioned the right of the Santee and Fort Peck Assiniboine to a share of the funds. *See* Avis Little Eagle, *Sioux Tribes Try to Block Santee*, Indian Country Today, Aug. 12–19, 1996, at A1; Porterfield, *supra*, at A1–A2. No distribution appears to have taken place, however, and a 2007 report stated that the Sioux continued to refuse to accept the money; "the poorest people in all of America refuse to accept one single penny of the award." Giago, *supra*.

The Conservation Alliance of The Great Plains proposed establishing a "Greater Black Hills Wildlife Protected Area" to restore the grasslands of the Northern Great Plains through a public-private partnership that would manage perhaps a million acres or more, centered around the Black Hills, according to principles of conservation biology. For an argument that this proposal should be amended to include restoration of the Black Hills to the Sioux peoples and management of adjacent lands according to conservation values and subject to significant tribal control, see John P. LaVelle. *Rescuing Paha Sapa: Achieving Environmental Justice by Restoring the Great Grasslands and Returning the Sacred Black Hills to the Great Sioux Nation*, 5 Great Plains Nat. Resources J. 40 (2001).

4. Taos Blue Lake. The only successful fight to reclaim sacred land was that of the Taos Pueblo for Blue Lake, which the federal government put into the Carson National Forest in 1906. In 1933, the Senate Indian Affairs Committee recommended that Blue Lake be restored to the Pueblo; the result was a statute providing permits for Pueblo use of the area, although no permit was issued until 1940. In 1951, the Pueblo filed suit in the Indian Claims Commission, and, in 1965, the ICC held that Blue Lake and the surrounding area were taken unjustly. After failed attempts at legislation to return the area in 1966 and 1968, H.R. 471 was introduced in 1969. Opponents of H.R. 471 included the National Wildlife Federation, which believed that the Forest Service would better protect and conserve the area, local landowners who were concerned about water supplies, and a New Mexico senator who voiced concern on the Senate floor that restoring Blue Lake would open an Indian run on public domain lands. Nonetheless, H.R. 471 was signed into law in December 1970 by President Nixon. Public Law 91-550 granted the Taos Pueblo title in trust to some 48,000 acres, including Blue Lake. *See generally* R.C. Gordon-McCutchan, The Taos Indians and the Battle for Blue Lake (Red Crane Books 1995).

5. The Rehnquist dissent and the use of history. Justice Rehnquist's dissent in *Sioux Nation*, in which he argued against a "revisionist" interpretation of history, is worth noting. Between his appointment to the Court in 1972 and 1996, Rehnquist wrote ten majority opinions in Indian cases, profoundly affecting the concept of tribal sovereignty. The late Professor Ralph Johnson, a respected Indian law scholar, considered his opinions to be "advocating and implementing a judicial termination policy." Ralph W. Johnson & Berrie Martinis, *Chief Justice Rehnquist and the Indian Cases*, 16 Pub. Land L. Rev 1, 24 (1995).

Two years before his dissent in *Sioux Nation*, Rehnquist's majority opinion in *Oliphant v. Suquamish Indian Tribe*, 435 U.S. 191 (1978), held that it would be "inconsistent with their status for tribes to exercise criminal jurisdiction over non-Indians." *Id.* at 208. He thus created a third category of inherent limits on tribal sovereignty, adding to the restrictions on foreign affairs and land title alienability recognized by Chief Justice Marshall in the early 19th century as a result of the doctrine of discovery. In *Oliphant*, and in his 1980 partial concurrence in *Washington v. Confederated Tribes of the Colville Indian Reservation*, 447 U.S. 134, 176 (1980) (Rehnquist, J. concurring in part and dissenting in part), in which the Court allowed state taxation of cigarette sales on the reservation to nonmembers, Rehnquist relied on historical notions of tribal authority to resolve contemporary questions of sovereignty. According to the late Dean David Getches, this historical approach obviated the need to ascertain a specific act of Congress limiting tribal sovereignty, completely inverting the usual analysis:

> [Rehnquist] urged that early notions of tribal powers and immunities as reflected in historical records, generally supporting the perceptions of non-Indians, should determine the outcome. Thus, unless a review of historical information showed actual tribal exercise of the specific type of jurisdiction, Rehnquist would require an Act of Congress to preempt state law.... [B]oth opinions [in *Oliphant* and *Colville*] indulged in a search for historical indicators as to how Indian sovereignty should be treated rather than a search for congressional limitations.

David H. Getches, *Conquering the Cultural Frontier: The New Subjectivism of the Supreme Court in Indian Law*, 84 Cal. L. Rev. 1573, 1633–34 (1996).

C. Executive Order Reservations

If confiscation of aboriginal territory is not compensable, but confiscation of recognized title land is compensable, what about federal confiscation of lands set aside by executive order?

Sioux Tribe of Indians v. United States
316 U.S. 317 (1942)

MR. JUSTICE BYRNES delivered the opinion of the Court.

This is an action to recover compensation for some 52 million acres of land allegedly taken from the petitioner tribe in 1879 and 1884. * * * The Court of Claims denied recovery, and we brought the case here on certiorari.

The facts as found by the Court of Claims are as follows:

In 1868 the United States and the Sioux Tribe entered into the Fort Laramie Treaty. By Article II of this treaty, a certain described territory, known as the Great Sioux

Reservation and located in what is now South Dakota and Nebraska, was "set apart for the absolute and undisturbed use and occupation" of the Tribe.

The eastern boundary of the Great Sioux Reservation, as constituted by the Ft. Laramie Treaty, was the low water mark on the east bank of the Missouri River. The large tract bordering upon and extending eastward from the east bank of the river remained a part of the public domain open to settlement and afforded easy access to the Reservation. As a result, great numbers of white men "infested" the region for the purpose of engaging in the liquor traffic. Anxiety over this development led the Commissioner of Indian Affairs, on January 8, 1875, to suggest to the Secretary of the Interior that he request the President to issue an executive order withdrawing from sale and setting apart for Indian purposes a certain large tract of the land along the eastern bank of the Missouri River. In the Commissioner's letter to the Secretary of the Interior, and in the latter's letter of January 9th to the President, the reason advanced for the proposed executive order was that it was "deemed necessary for the suppression of the liquor traffic with the Indians upon the Missouri River." On January 11, 1875, the President signed the suggested order. It described the territory affected and provided that it "be, and the same hereby is, withdrawn from sale and set apart for the use of the several tribes of Sioux Indians as an addition to their present reservation." On two occasions thereafter, once in February and again in May, white persons who had settled on the land in question prior to the issuance of the executive order and who feared that its effect was to deprive them of their holdings, were informed by the Commissioner of Indian Affairs that the object of the executive order was "to enable the suppression of the liquor traffic with the Indians on the Missouri River," that it did not affect the existing rights of any persons in the area, that it was not "supposed that the withdrawal will be made permanent," and that no interference with the peaceful occupancy of the territory had been intended.

[In 1875 and 1876, three more tracts of land were set aside by executive orders for the same reasons.]

About two and a half years after the last of these four executive orders withdrawing lands from sale and setting them apart for the use of the Sioux, the Commissioner of Indian Affairs submitted to the Secretary of the Interior a report upon a suggestion that the orders be modified so as to permit the return of the lands to the public domain. The report, dated June 6, 1879, reviewed the problems arising from the liquor trade during the years following the Fort Laramie treaty, recalled that the purpose of the four executive orders of 1875 and 1876 had been to eliminate this traffic, observed that they had "to a great extent accomplished the object desired, viz: the prevention of the sale of whiskey to the Indians," and concluded that any change in the boundaries established by the executive orders would "give renewed life to this unlawful traffic, and be detrimental to the best interests of the Indians."

Three weeks later, however, upon reconsideration, the Commissioner informed the Secretary that, in his opinion, the lands included in the executive orders of 1875 and 1876 might be "restored to the public domain, and the interests of the Indians still be protected."

* * * On August 9, 1879, an executive order [restoring the land to the public domain] was promulgated * * *. [In 1884, three small parcels excepted from the 1879 order were also restored by executive order to the public domain.]

One additional event remains to be noted. In the Indian Appropriation Act for 1877, approved August 15, 1876, Congress provided:

"... hereafter there shall be no appropriation made for the subsistence of said Indians [i.e., the Sioux], unless they shall first agree to relinquish all right and claim to any country outside the boundaries of the permanent reservation established by the treaty of eighteen hundred and sixty-eight [the Fort Laramie treaty] for said Indians; and also so much of their said permanent reservation as lies west of the one hundred and third meridian of longitude [the western boundary set by the Fort Laramie treaty had been the 104th meridian], and shall also grant right of way over said reservation to the country thus ceded for wagon or other roads, from convenient and accessible points on the Missouri River..."

On September 26, 1876—a date subsequent to the first three of the four executive orders setting apart additional lands for the use of the Sioux, but about two months prior to the last of those orders—the Sioux Tribe signed an agreement conforming to the conditions imposed by Congress in the Indian Appropriation Act and promised to "relinquish and cede to the United States all the territory lying outside the said reservation, as herein modified and described..."

Petitioner's position is that the executive orders of 1875 and 1876 were effective to convey to the Tribe the same kind of interest in the lands affected as it had acquired in the lands covered by the Fort Laramie Treaty, that the executive orders of 1879 and 1884 restoring the lands to the public domain deprived petitioner of this interest, and that it is entitled to be compensated for the fair value of the lands as of 1879 and 1884.

Section 3 of Article IV of the Constitution confers upon Congress exclusively "the power to dispose of and make all needful rules and regulations respecting the territory or other property belonging to the United States." Nevertheless, "from an early period in the history of the government it has been the practice of the President to order, from time to time, as the exigencies of the public service required, parcels of land belonging to the United States to be reserved from sale and set apart for public uses." As long ago as 1830, Congress revealed its awareness of this practice and acquiesced in it. By 1855 the President had begun to withdraw public lands from sale by executive order for the specific purpose of establishing Indian reservations. From that date until 1919, hundreds of reservations for Indian occupancy and for other purposes were created by executive order. Although the validity of these orders was occasionally questioned, doubts were quieted in *United States v. Midwest Oil Co., supra*. In that case, it was squarely held that, even in the absence of express statutory authorization, it lay within the power of the President to withdraw lands from the public domain.

The Government therefore does not deny that the executive orders of 1875 and 1876 involved here were effective to withdraw the lands in question from the public domain. It contends, however, that this is not the issue presented by this case. It urges that, instead, we are called upon to determine whether the President had the power to bestow upon the Sioux Tribe an interest in these lands of such a character as to require compensation when the interest was extinguished by the executive orders of 1879 and 1884. Concededly, where lands have been reserved for the use and occupation of an Indian Tribe by the terms of a treaty or statute, the tribe must be compensated if the lands are subsequently taken from them. [*e.g., United States v. Shoshone Tribe*, 304 U.S. 111.] Since the Constitution places the authority to dispose of public lands exclusively in Congress, the executive's power to convey any interest in these lands must be traced to Congressional delegation of its authority. The basis of decision in *United States v. Midwest Oil Co.* was that, so far as the power to withdraw public lands from sale is concerned, such a delegation could be spelled out from long continued Congressional acquiescence in the executive practice. The answer to whether a similar delegation occurred with respect to the power to convey a compensable interest in these lands to the Indians must be found in the available evidence of what consequences were thought by the executive and Congress to flow from the establishment of executive order reservations.

It is significant that the executive department consistently indicated its understanding that the rights and interests which the Indians enjoyed in executive order reservations were different from and less than their rights and interests in treaty or statute reservations. The annual reports of the Commissioner of Indian Affairs during the years when reservations were frequently being established by executive order contain statements that the Indians had "no assurance for their occupation of these lands beyond the pleasure of the Executive," that they "are mere tenants at will, and possess no permanent rights to the lands upon which they are temporarily permitted to remain," and that those occupying land in executive order reservations "do not hold it by the same tenure with which Indians in other parts of the Indian Territory possess their reserves."

Although there are abundant signs that Congress was aware of the practice of establishing Indian reservations by executive order, there is little to indicate what it understood to be the kind of interest that the Indians obtained in these lands. However, in its report in 1892 upon a bill to restore to the public domain a portion of the Colville executive order reservation, the Senate Committee on Indian Affairs expressed the opinion that under the executive order "the Indians were given a license to occupy the lands described in it so long as it was the pleasure of the Government they should do so, and no right, title, or claim to such lands has vested in the Indians by virtue of this occupancy."

Perhaps the most striking proof of the belief shared by Congress and the Executive that the Indians were not entitled to compensation upon the abolition of an executive order reservation is the very absence of compensatory payments in such situations. It was a common practice, during the period in which reservations were created by executive order, for the President simply to terminate the existence of a reservation by cancelling or revoking the order establishing it. That is to say, the procedure followed in the case before us was typical. No compensation was made, and neither the Government nor the Indians suggested that it was due.

We conclude therefore that there was no express constitutional or statutory authorization for the conveyance of a compensable interest to petitioner by the four executive orders of 1875 and 1876, and that no implied Congressional delegation of the power to do so can be spelled out from the evidence of Congressional and executive understanding. The orders were effective to withdraw from sale the lands affected and to grant the use of the lands to the petitioner. But the interest which the Indians received was subject to termination at the will of either the executive or Congress and without obligation to the United States. The executive orders of 1879 and 1884 were simply an exercise of this power of termination, and the payment of compensation was not required.

Affirmed.

Notes

1. **Executive order reservations.** The process of establishing Indian reservations by executive order dates to 1855, but became particularly important after Congress, in 1871, prohibited further treaty-making with tribes. 25 U.S.C. § 71. After 1871, tribal land cessions and the setting aside of reservations continued unabated. In many instances, land dealings were accomplished through negotiated agreements ratified by Congress through enactment of a statute. Lands set aside for tribes by that process carry recognized title. But millions of acres of land were also set aside by executive order.

There was initially some doubt about the authority of the President to create Indian reservations by executive order, but the Supreme Court held in 1915 that the executive had authority, even absent a statutory basis, to withdraw lands from the public domain. *United States v. Midwest Oil Co.*, 236 U.S. 459 (1915). That authority stems primarily from Congress' long-standing acquiescence in the practice.

In 1919, however, Congress put an end to the creation of reservations by executive order. The Act of June 30, 1919, provided that: "No public lands of the United States shall be withdrawn by Executive Order, proclamation, or otherwise, for or as an Indian reservation except by act of Congress." 43 U.S.C. § 150. Nonetheless, between 1855 and 1919, some 23 million acres of land were set aside as reservation lands by executive orders.

In 1927, Congress similarly terminated any right of the President to alter the boundaries of executive order lands: "Changes in the boundaries of reservations created by Executive order, proclamation, or otherwise for the use and occupation of Indians shall not be made except by Act of Congress." 25 U.S.C. § 398d.

2. **Tribal rights in executive order reservations.** Tribes generally have the same rights in executive order reservations as they do in reservations set aside by treaty or

statute. As the Supreme Court has noted: "Indian reservations created by statute, agreement, or executive order normally carry with them the same implicit hunting rights as those created by treaty." *United States v. Dion*, 476 U.S. 734, 745 n.8 (1986). *See also Parravano v. Babbitt*, 70 F.3d 539, 547 (9th Cir. 1995) ("we emphasize that Indian [fishing] rights arising from executive orders are entitled to the same protection against non-federal interests as Indian rights arising from treaties."). Similarly, executive order reservations include federally-reserved rights to water. *Arizona v. California*, 373 U.S. 546, 598 (1963) ("these reservations, like those created directly by Congress, were not limited to land, but included waters as well.").

3. Takings of executive order reservations. The Indian Claims Commission Act of 1946 provided that takings of executive order lands prior to 1946 would be compensable. 25 U.S.C. § 70a. Takings of executive order lands after 1946 are also apparently compensable in the Court of Federal Claims. *See* 28 U.S.C. § 1505. All takings of executive order lands, however, are considered takings of "non-recognized" title. As such, they are subject to the no-interest rule. *Alcea Band of Tillamooks v. United States*, 341 U.S. 48 (1951). That is, awards of compensation are valued as of the date of the taking, and no interest is paid. Tribes thus could be awarded judgments of a few dollars per acre (the value of the land in the nineteenth century, when the takings occurred) for land that today is worth several hundred times that much. For example, if the no-interest rule had applied to the Black Hills, the Sioux Nation's compensation award would have been $17 million, rather than $122 million at the time of the *Sioux Nation* decision or close to $1 billion in 2011.

4. Reconsidering *Sioux Tribe*. How clear is it that the *Sioux Tribe* Court stands for the proposition that no takings of executive order reservations are protected by the Fifth Amendment? What was the purpose of the reservations in this case? Did revocation of the reservation status of the lands lead to dispossession of the tribes? Perhaps if an executive order reservation was established to provide a homeland rather than a buffer zone, a court might confine *Sioux Tribe* to its facts and the revocation would entitle the tribe to just compensation.

For a contrary view, however, see *Karuk Tribe of California v. Ammon*, 209 F.3d 1366 (Fed. Cir. 2000). The Hoopa Valley Reservation was set aside in 1876 by executive order; a second executive order added an addition in 1891. In 1994, Congress enacted a settlement act that severed the two parts of the reservation, making the 1891 addition a reservation for the Yurok Tribe. The plaintiff Yurok and Karuk Tribes claimed a taking of their property rights in the 1876 area, which remained a reservation for the Hoopa Valley Tribe. The Federal Circuit ruled that the plaintiffs had no compensable property right in the 1876 reservation, because "Indian occupancy may be extinguished by the government without compensation, unless an Act of Congress has specifically recognized the Indians' ownership rights." *Id.* at 1380. The dissent was vigorous: "It is not tenable, at this late date in the life of the Republic, to rule that Native Americans living on a Reservation are not entitled to the constitutional protections of the Fifth Amendment." *Id.* (Newman, J., dissenting).

D. Submerged Lands

The following materials address a particular subset of lands: land submerged below rivers and lakes. As the cases below illustrate, tribal ownership of these submerged lands can be crucial from both a sovereignty and a proprietary perspective. In *Montana v. United States*, below, the Crow Tribe was primarily interested in asserting regulatory jurisdiction over non-Indian hunting and fishing on the Big Horn River within the Crow Reservation. As we will see in Chapter IV, Section A, tribes generally have authority to regulate non-Indian conduct on tribal lands. Accordingly, if the Crow Tribe could establish that it owned the riverbed, its ability to regulate hunting and fishing on the river was virtually assured. In the Arkansas River cases following *Montana*, below, the tribal concern appears to be more proprietary. The disputed Arkansas River bedlands contain extremely valuable sand, gravel, and oil and gas deposits. If the Cherokee and Choctaw Tribes could establish that they owned the riverbed, then they also owned those mineral deposits. As a result of these and similar concerns, tribal ownership of submerged lands has taken on greater significance than the amount of land involved might seem to indicate.

Montana v. United States
450 U.S. 544 (1981)

JUSTICE STEWART delivered the opinion of the Court.

This case concerns the sources and scope of the power of an Indian tribe to regulate hunting and fishing by non-Indians on lands within its reservation owned in fee simple by non-Indians. Relying on its purported ownership of the bed of the Big Horn River, on the treaties which created its reservation, and on its inherent power as a sovereign, the Crow Tribe of Montana claims the authority to prohibit all hunting and fishing by nonmembers of the Tribe on non-Indian property within reservation boundaries. We granted certiorari to review a decision of the United States Court of Appeals for the Ninth Circuit that substantially upheld this claim.

I

The Crow Indians originated in Canada, but some three centuries ago they migrated to what is now southern Montana. In the 19th century, warfare between the Crows and several other tribes led the tribes and the United States to sign the First Treaty of Fort Laramie of 1851, in which the signatory tribes acknowledged various designated lands as their respective territories. The treaty identified approximately 38.5 million acres as Crow territory and, in Article 5, specified that, by making the treaty, the tribes did not "surrender the privilege of hunting, fishing, or passing over" any of the lands in dispute. In 1868, the Second Treaty of Fort Laramie established a Crow Reservation of roughly 8 million acres, including land through which the Big Horn River flows. By Article II of the treaty, the United States agreed that the reservation "shall be . . . set apart for the absolute and undisturbed use and occupation" of the Crow Tribe, and that no non-Indians except agents of the Government "shall ever be permitted to pass over, settle upon, or reside in" the reservation.

Several subsequent Acts of Congress reduced the reservation to slightly fewer than 2.3 million acres.

[The United States, in its own right and on behalf of the Crow Tribe, brought suit for, among other relief, a declaratory judgment quieting title to the bed of the Big Horn River in the United States as trustee for the Tribe.]

II

The respondents seek to establish a substantial part of their claim of power to control hunting and fishing on the reservation by asking us to recognize their title to the bed of the Big Horn River. The question is whether the United States conveyed beneficial ownership of the riverbed to the Crow Tribe by the treaties of 1851 or 1868, and therefore continues to hold the land in trust for the use and benefit of the Tribe, or whether the United States retained ownership of the riverbed as public land which then passed to the State of Montana upon its admission to the Union. *Choctaw Nation v. Oklahoma*, 397 U.S. 620, 627–628 [1970].

Though the owners of land riparian to nonnavigable streams may own the adjacent riverbed, conveyance by the United States of land riparian to a navigable river carries no interest in the riverbed. Rather, the ownership of land under navigable waters is an incident of sovereignty. As a general principle, the Federal Government holds such lands in trust for future States, to be granted to such States when they enter the Union and assume sovereignty on an "equal footing" with the established States. After a State enters the Union, title to the land is governed by state law. The State's power over the beds of navigable waters remains subject to only one limitation: the paramount power of the United States to ensure that such waters remain free to interstate and foreign commerce. It is now established, however, that Congress may sometimes convey lands below the high-water mark of a navigable water,

> "[and so defeat the title of a new State,] in order to perform international obligations, or to effect the improvement of such lands for the promotion and convenience of commerce with foreign nations and among the several States, or to carry out other public purposes appropriate to the objects for which the United States hold the Territory." *Shively v. Bowlby*, 152 U.S. 1, 48.

But because control over the property underlying navigable waters is so strongly identified with the sovereign power of government, it will not be held that the United States has conveyed such land except because of "some international duty or public exigency." A court deciding a question of title to the bed of a navigable water must, therefore, begin with a strong presumption against conveyance by the United States, and must not infer such a conveyance "unless the intention was definitely declared or otherwise made plain," or was rendered "in clear and especial words," or "unless the claim confirmed in terms embraces the land under the waters of the stream."

In *United States v. Holt State Bank*, this Court applied these principles to reject an Indian Tribe's claim of title to the bed of a navigable lake. The lake lay wholly within the boundaries of the Red Lake Indian Reservation, which had been created by treaties entered into before Minnesota joined the Union. In these treaties the United States promised to "set apart and withhold from sale, for the use of" the Chippewas, a large tract of land, and to convey "a sufficient quantity of land for the permanent homes" of the Indians. The Court concluded that there was nothing in the treaties "which even approaches a grant of rights in lands underlying navigable waters; nor anything evincing a purpose to depart from the established policy . . . of treating such lands as held for the benefit of the future State." Rather, "[the] effect of what was done was to reserve in a general way for the continued occupation of the Indians what remained of their aboriginal territory."

The Crow treaties in this case, like the Chippewa treaties in *Holt State Bank*, fail to overcome the established presumption that the beds of navigable waters remain in trust for future States and pass to the new States when they assume sovereignty. The 1851 treaty did not by its terms formally convey any land to the Indians at all, but instead chiefly represented a covenant among several tribes which recognized specific boundaries for their respective territories. Treaty of Fort Laramie, 1851, Art. 5. It referred to hunting and fishing only insofar as it said that the Crow Indians "do not surrender the privilege of hunting, fishing, or passing over any of the tracts of country heretofore described," a statement that had no bearing on ownership of the riverbed. By contrast, the 1868 treaty did expressly convey land to the Crow Tribe. Article II of the treaty described the reservation land in detail and stated that such land would be "set apart for the absolute and undisturbed use and occupation of the Indians herein named. . . ." Second Treaty of Fort Laramie, May 7, 1868, Art. II. The treaty then stated:

> "[The] United States now solemnly agrees that no persons, except those herein designated and authorized to do so, and except such officers, agents, and employees of the Government as may be authorized to enter upon Indian reservations in discharge of duties enjoined by law, shall ever be permitted to pass over, settle upon, or reside in the territory described in this article for the use of said Indians. . . ."

Whatever property rights the language of the 1868 treaty created, however, its language is not strong enough to overcome the presumption against the sovereign's conveyance of the riverbed. The treaty in no way expressly referred to the riverbed, nor was an intention to convey the riverbed expressed in "clear and especial words," or "definitely declared or otherwise made very plain." Rather, as in *Holt*, "[the] effect of what was done was to reserve in a general way for the continued occupation of the Indians what remained of their aboriginal territory."

Though Article 2 gave the Crow Indians the sole right to use and occupy the reserved land, and, implicitly, the power to exclude others from it, the respondents' reliance on that provision simply begs the question of the precise extent of the conveyed lands to which this exclusivity attaches. The mere fact that the bed of a navigable water lies within the boundaries described in the treaty does not make the riverbed part of the conveyed land, especially when there is no express reference to the riverbed that might overcome the presumption against its conveyance. In the Court of Appeals' *Finch* decision, on which recognition of the Crow Tribe's title to the riverbed rested in this case, that court construed the language of exclusivity in the 1868 treaty as granting to the Indians all the lands, including the riverbed, within the described boundaries. Such a construction, however, cannot survive examination. As the Court of Appeals recognized, and as the respondents concede, the United States retains a navigational easement in the navigable waters lying within the described boundaries for the benefit of the public, regardless of who owns the riverbed. Therefore, such phrases in the 1868 treaty as "absolute and undisturbed use and occupation" and "no persons, except those herein designated . . . shall ever be permitted," whatever they seem to mean literally, do not give the Indians the exclusive right to occupy all the territory within the described boundaries. Thus, even if exclusivity were the same as ownership, the treaty language establishing this "right of exclusivity" could not have the meaning that the Court of Appeals ascribed to it.[5]

Moreover, even though the establishment of an Indian reservation can be an "appropriate public purpose" within the meaning of *Shively v. Bowlby*, 152 U.S., at

---

5. In one recent case, *Choctaw Nation v. Oklahoma*, [397 U.S. 620 (1970)], this Court did construe a reservation grant as including the bed of a navigable water, and the respondents argue that this case resembles *Choctaw Nation* more than it resembles the established line of cases to which *Choctaw Nation* is a singular exception. But the finding of a conveyance of the riverbed in *Choctaw Nation* was based on very peculiar circumstances not present in this case.

Those circumstances arose from the unusual history of the treaties there at issue, a history which formed an important basis of the decision. Immediately after the Revolutionary War, the United States had signed treaties of peace and protection with the Cherokee and Choctaw Tribes, reserving them lands in Georgia and Mississippi. In succeeding years, the United States bought large areas of land from the Indians to make room for white settlers who were encroaching on tribal lands, but the Government signed new treaties guaranteeing that the Indians could live in peace on those lands not ceded. The United States soon betrayed that promise. It proposed that the Tribes be relocated in a newly acquired part of the Arkansas Territory, but the new territory was soon overrun by white settlers, and through a series of new cession agreements the Indians were forced to relocate farther and farther west. Ultimately, most of the Tribes' members refused to leave their eastern lands, but Georgia and Mississippi, anxious for the relocation westward so they could assert jurisdiction over the Indian lands, purported to abolish the Tribes and distribute the tribal lands. The Choctaws and Cherokees finally signed new treaties with the United States aimed at rectifying their past suffering at the hands of the Federal Government and the states.

Under the Choctaw treaty, the United States promised to convey new lands west of the Arkansas Territory in fee simple, and also pledged that "no Territory or State shall ever have a right to pass laws for the government of the Choctaw Nation . . . and that no part of the land granted to them shall ever be embraced in any Territory or State." Treaty of Dancing Rabbit Creek, Sept. 27, 1830, 7 Stat. 333–334. In 1835, the Cherokees signed a treaty containing similar provisions granting reservation lands in fee simple and promising that the tribal lands would not become part of any State or Territory. In concluding that the United States had intended to convey the riverbed to the Tribes before the admission of Oklahoma to the Union, the *Choctaw* Court relied on these circumstances surrounding the treaties and placed special emphasis on the Government's promise that the reserved lands would never become part of any State. Neither the special historical origins of the Choctaw and Cherokee treaties nor the crucial provisions granting Indian lands in fee simple and promising freedom from state jurisdiction in those treaties have any counterparts in the terms and circumstances of the Crow treaties of 1851 and 1868.

48, justifying a congressional conveyance of a riverbed, the situation of the Crow Indians at the time of the treaties presented no "public exigency" which would have required Congress to depart from its policy of reserving ownership of beds under navigable waters for the future States. As the record in this case shows, at the time of the treaty the Crows were a nomadic tribe dependent chiefly on buffalo, and fishing was not important to their diet or way of life.

For these reasons, we conclude that title to the bed of the Big Horn River passed to the State of Montana upon its admission into the Union, and that the Court of Appeals was in error in holding otherwise.

[The concurring opinion of Justice Stevens is omitted.]

JUSTICE BLACKMUN, with whom JUSTICE BRENNAN and JUSTICE MARSHALL join, dissenting in part.

Only two years ago, this Court reaffirmed that the terms of a treaty between the United States and an Indian tribe must be construed "'in the sense in which they would naturally be understood by the Indians.'" In holding today that the bed of the Big Horn River passed to the State of Montana upon its admission to the Union, the Court disregards this settled rule of statutory construction. Because I believe that the United States intended, and the Crow Nation understood, that the bed of the Big Horn was to belong to the Crow Indians, I dissent from so much of the Court's opinion as holds otherwise.

Notes

1. *Choctaw Nation.* Only eleven years before *Montana v. United States,* in *Choctaw Nation v. Oklahoma,* 397 U.S. 620 (1970), the Court ruled that the Choctaw Nation owned the bed of the Arkansas River. *See* footnote 5 in *Montana,* at page 218. Why wasn't that decision controlling in the case of the Crow Reservation?

2. *Bedlands and the canons of construction.* Justice Blackmun's dissent charged the majority with disregarding the canons of construction. In addition to the canons described at page 138, the Court declared in *United States v. Winans,* 198 U.S. 371 (1905), that a "treaty was not a grant of rights to the Indians, but a grant of rights from them—a reservation of those not granted." (*Winans* is excerpted at page 471.) Yet in *Montana* the Court stated that: "The question is whether the United States *conveyed* beneficial ownership of the riverbed in the treaties." Why aren't reserved rights principles controlling in the case of bedlands?

3. *Holt State Bank.* Note that in the *Holt State Bank* case, on which the *Montana* Court relied, the Chippewa treaty made no mention of the lakebed, merely reserving lands for continued tribal occupation. But one of the purposes of the treaty was to allow the tribes to continue to hunt and fish. Presumably the fishing purpose required the lake.

4. *Post-Montana claims to bedlands.* Of seven bedlands ownership claims brought by tribes or the United States on behalf of tribes in the ten years following *Montana,*

the tribal claim prevailed in five. Thomas H. Pacheco, *Indian Bedlands Claims: A Need to Clear the Waters*, 15 Harv. Envt'l L. Rev. 1, 26 (1991). Mr. Pacheco summarized the results as follows: "In the decisions in which the tribal claim prevailed, the courts relied primarily on the Indians' dependence on resources found within the areas at issue, as well as on the canon of interpretation focusing on the perceptions of the tribal members at the time of the grant." *Id.* In particular, the tribes' dependence upon lake or river fisheries seemed a crucial factor in the courts' decisions. For example, in *Puyallup Indian Tribe v. Port of Tacoma,* 717 F.2d 1251, 1258 (9th Cir. 1983), the court ruled:

> [W]here a grant of real property to an Indian tribe includes within its boundaries a navigable water and the grant is made to a tribe dependent on the fishery resource in that water for survival, the grant must be construed to include the submerged lands if the Government was plainly aware of the vital importance of the submerged lands and the water resource to the tribe at the time of the grant.

The issue of tribal claims to bedlands returned to the Supreme Court in a pair of cases involving Lake Coeur d'Alene in Idaho.

a. The Lake Coeur d'Alene claim and state sovereign immunity. In *Idaho v. Coeur d'Alene Tribe*, 521 U.S. 261 (1997), the Supreme Court held that the Eleventh Amendment barred the tribe's suit for a declaratory judgment that it owned the submerged lands of Lake Coeur d'Alene and various related navigable streams within the boundaries of the original Coeur d'Alene Reservation. Under the Eleventh Amendment, states enjoy sovereign immunity from suits brought by Indian tribes. *See Blatchford v. Native Village of Noatak*, 501 U.S. 775 (1991). Despite the Eleventh Amendment, however, the Court has allowed certain suits without state consent: those seeking declaratory and injunctive relief against state officers in their individual capacities for violations of federal law. *See Ex parte Young*, 209 U.S. 123 (1908).

In *Coeur d'Alene*, the Supreme Court held that the Tribe could not take advantage of the *Ex parte Young* exception to the Eleventh Amendment. The Court agreed that the tribe's

> allegation of an on-going violation of federal law where the requested relief is prospective is ordinarily sufficient to invoke the *Young* fiction. However, this case is unusual in that the Tribe's suit is the functional equivalent of a quiet title action which implicates sovereignty interests.
>
> [T]he declaratory and injunctive relief the Tribe seeks is close to the functional equivalent of quiet title in that substantially all benefits of ownership and control would shift from the State to the Tribe. This is especially troubling when coupled with the far-reaching and invasive relief the Tribe seeks, relief with consequences going well beyond the typical stakes in a real property quiet title action. The suit seeks, in effect, a determination that the lands in question are not even within the regulatory jurisdiction of the State. The requested injunctive relief would bar the State's principal officers from

exercising their governmental powers and authority over the disputed lands and waters. The suit would diminish, even extinguish, the State's control over a vast reach of lands and waters long deemed by the State to be an integral part of its territory. To pass this off as a judgment causing little or no offense to Idaho's sovereign authority and its standing in the Union would be to ignore the realities of the relief the Tribe demands.

* * * [The relief requested] would divest the State of its sovereign control over submerged lands, lands with a unique status in the law and infused with a public trust the State itself is bound to respect. As we stressed in *Utah Div. of State Lands v. United States*, 482 U.S. 193, 195–98 (1987), lands underlying navigable waters have historically been considered "sovereign lands." State ownership of them has been "considered an essential attribute of sovereignty." *Id.* at 195.

Under these particular and special circumstances, we find the *Young* exception inapplicable. The dignity and status of its statehood allows Idaho to rely on its Eleventh Amendment immunity and to insist upon responding to these claims in its own courts, which are open to hear and determine the case.

521 U.S. at 281–88.

Justice Souter, joined by Justices Stevens, Ginsburg, and Breyer, dissented on the *Ex parte Young* issue:

Congress has implemented the Constitution's grant of federal-question jurisdiction by authorizing federal courts to enforce rights arising under the Constitution and federal law. The federal courts have an obligation to exercise that jurisdiction, and in doing so have applied the doctrine of *Ex parte Young*, that in the absence of some congressional limitation a federal court may entertain an individual's suit to enjoin a state officer from official action that violates federal law. * * * The Tribe's suit falls squarely within the *Young* doctrine and the District Court had an obligation to hear it.

Id. at 297–98. For a thorough discussion of the case and its implications, see John P. LaVelle, *Sanctioning a Tyranny: The Diminishment of Ex Parte Young, Expansion of Hans Immunity, and Denial of Indian Rights in Coeur d'Alene Tribe*, 31 Ariz. St. L.J. 787 (1999).

Is it sufficient that the Idaho state courts "are open" to the tribe's bedlands claim? If tribes seek to vindicate rights under federal law and treaties, shouldn't they be able to do so in federal court? Are there special reasons why Indian tribes, as opposed to private plaintiffs, should have access to a federal forum to seek redress of those rights?

b. The Lake Coeur d'Alene claim on the merits. The Eleventh Amendment does not bar the United States from bringing suit against states. (Note that in *Montana*, the United States filed suit against the state.) Following the Court's decision in *Coeur d'Alene Tribe*, when the state began to authorize developments in the lake, the federal government sued to quiet title to the bedlands as trustee for the tribe. Both the federal district court of Idaho and the Ninth Circuit ruled that Congress intended to reserve the lakebed for the tribe prior to statehood. The Supreme Court, in a 5–4 decision, affirmed. *Idaho v. United States*, 533 U.S. 262 (2001).

In the Supreme Court, Idaho conceded that the 1873 executive order creating the Coeur d'Alene Reservation included submerged lands. The Court then decided that Congress was on notice prior to Idaho statehood in 1890 that the reservation included submerged lands. Thus, the Court concluded that the two-step test for defeating state "equal footing" title to submerged lands established in *United States v. Alaska*, 521 U.S. 1, 41–46, 55–61 (1997)—(1) an executive reservation clearly including submerged lands, and (2) congressional recognition of the reservation in a way that demonstrates an intent to defeat state title—was satisfied. Chief Justice Rehnquist, for the four-member dissent, complained that the evidence of congressional intent, on which the majority relied, was insufficient to meet the high standard required to defeat state title to submerged navigable waters. He maintained that the 1891 congressional action which confirmed negotiations recognizing the tribe's ownership of the submerged lands was too late to annul the effect of the 1890 statehood act.

5. Nonnavigable waters. In *Choctaw Nation v. Oklahoma*, 397 U.S. 620 (1970), discussed in footnote 5 of the *Montana* decision, at page 218, the Supreme Court addressed ownership of the Arkansas River in Cherokee and Choctaw territory, below the junction of the Arkansas and the Grand Rivers. The Court noted that there was "no question" but that the Arkansas River below the junction is a navigable river.

Where a river is nonnavigable, however, different rules apply. In *Choctaw Nation*, for example, the Court distinguished its holding half a century earlier in *Brewer-Elliott Oil & Gas Co. v. United States*, 260 U.S. 77 (1922):

> The facts involved in *Brewer-Elliott* were essentially similar to those of the present cases. There the United States had established a reservation for the Osage Indians which was bounded on one side by "the main channel of the Arkansas river." The United States brought suit to establish the Indians' right to the river bed and the oil reserves beneath it, and the State of Oklahoma intervened to claim that the river bed had passed to it at statehood. * * * This Court held that in the region in question the Arkansas River was nonnavigable and that "the title of the Osages as granted certainly included the bed of the river as far as the main channel, because the words of the grant expressly carry the title to that line." The question whether it would have been beyond the power of the United States to make the grant had the river been navigable was reserved for future decision.

6. The navigation servitude. In *Montana*, Justice Stewart used the navigation servitude (referred to as a navigation "easement"), a sovereignty concept, to resolve the tribe's claims to property. The navigation servitude, discussed further in the following case, allows the federal government to interfere with the flow of navigable waters or to affect the bed and banks of navigable waters up to the high water mark without payment of compensation. *See* 2 Waters and Water Rights § 35.02 (3d ed., Amy K. Kelley, ed., 2014). According to Justice Stewart, the retention of this federal servitude meant that treaty phrases such as the tribe's right to "absolute and undisturbed use and occupation" could not have been meant literally. Thus, a sovereignty concept was employed to deny the tribe's property ownership. And as we will see in a further excerpt from the case at page 249, the denial of the tribe's property claim then became the basis for denying the tribe's regulatory authority to control access to fishing on the river. So a sovereignty concept was used to deny proprietary claims which in turn were used to deny the tribe's sovereign authority. Would it have made any difference in terms of federal authority under the navigation servitude if the tribe owned the riverbed instead of the state?

As noted in *Montana*'s footnote 5, at page 218, the Cherokee and Choctaw Tribes prevailed in their claim to ownership of the bed and banks of the Arkansas River. *Choctaw Nation v. Oklahoma*, 397 U.S. 620 (1970). The following case addresses the Cherokee Nation's attempt to recover from the United States for damage to the riverbed resulting from the McClellan-Kerr Project, which channelized the Arkansas River from Catoosa, Oklahoma to the Mississippi River. If the Cherokee Nation owns the riverbed in its territory, why is it barred from recovering compensation for damages caused by the United States?

United States v. Cherokee Nation of Oklahoma

480 U.S. 700 (1987)

CHIEF JUSTICE REHNQUIST delivered the opinion of the Court.

In *Choctaw Nation v. Oklahoma*, 397 U.S. 620 (1970), the Court determined that certain treaties between the Cherokee, Chickasaw, and Choctaw Tribes and the United States granted to the Tribes fee simple title to the riverbed underlying specified portions of the Arkansas River in Oklahoma. The Court found the circumstances sufficient to overcome the "strong presumption against conveyance by the United States" of title to the bed of a navigable water. *Montana v. United States*, 450 U.S. 544, 552 (1981). The question presented in this case is whether the United States must pay the Cherokee Nation compensation for damage to these riverbed interests caused by navigational improvements which it has made on the Arkansas River. The damage to sand and gravel deposits resulted from the McClellan-Kerr Project, approved by Congress in 1946, and designed to improve navigation by construction of a channel in the Arkansas River from its mouth at the Mississippi to Catoosa, Oklahoma. The project was completed in 1971.

After our decision in *Choctaw Nation*, the Cherokee Nation sought compensation from the Government. Congress refused to fund the claim after the Department of the Interior and the Army Corps of Engineers concluded that the United States' navigational servitude rendered it meritless. Congress did, however, provide respondent with the opportunity to seek judicial relief, conferring jurisdiction on the United States District Court for the Eastern District of Oklahoma to determine "any claim which the Cherokee Nation of Oklahoma may have against the United States for any and all damages to Cherokee tribal assets related to and arising from the construction of the [McClellan-Kerr Project]."

The Cherokee Nation filed a complaint contending that the construction of the McClellan-Kerr Project resulted in a taking under the Fifth Amendment of the Tribe's riverbed interests without just compensation. * * * The District Court granted the Tribe's motion for summary judgment.

A divided panel of the Court of Appeals for the Tenth Circuit affirmed, adopting a different analysis. The court rejected the District Court's conclusion that the United States' failure to reserve its navigational servitude defeated that interest. It found it "certain [that] the United States retained a navigational servitude in the Arkansas River." Nevertheless, the court held that the servitude was insufficient to protect the United States from liability. Finding that "the assertion of a navigational servitude on particular waters acknowledges only that the property owner's right to use these waters is shared with the public at large," the court believed that the effect of the navigational servitude varied with the owner's intended use: "When the exercise of that public power affects private ownership rights not connected to a navigational use, the court must balance the public and private interests to decide whether just compensation is due." Applying this test, the court concluded that though the Cherokee Nation could not interfere with the United States' exercise of the navigational servitude, it had a right to compensation for any consequent loss of property or diminution in value.

We think the Court of Appeals erred in formulating a balancing test to evaluate this assertion of the navigational servitude. No such "balancing" is required where, as here, the interference with in-stream interests results from an exercise of the Government's power to regulate navigational uses of "the deep streams which penetrate our country in every direction." Though "this Court has never held that the navigational servitude creates a blanket exception to the Takings Clause whenever Congress exercises its Commerce Clause authority to promote navigation," there can be no doubt that "[the] Commerce Clause confers a unique position upon the Government in connection with navigable waters." It gives to the Federal Government "a 'dominant servitude,' which extends to the entire stream and the stream bed below ordinary high-water mark. The proper exercise of this power is not an invasion of any private property rights in the stream or the lands underlying it, for the damage sustained does not result from taking property from riparian owners within the meaning of the Fifth Amendment but from the lawful exercise of a power to which the interests of riparian owners have always been subject."

These well-established principles concerning the exercise of the United States' dominant servitude would, in the usual case, dictate that we reject respondent's "takings" claim. We do not understand respondent to argue otherwise. Instead, the Cherokee Nation asserts that its title to the Arkansas River bed is unique in scope and that interference with that interest requires just compensation. Respondent does not rely explicitly on any language of the relevant treaties, but rather on its reading of *Choctaw Nation v. Oklahoma*, 397 U.S. 620 (1970). We have noted that *Choctaw Nation* involved "very peculiar circumstances," *Montana v. United States*, 450 U.S., at 555, n.5, in that "the Indians were promised virtually complete sovereignty over their new lands." These circumstances allowed the claimants to overcome the strong presumption against conveyance of riverbed interests by the United States, designed to protect the interests of the States under the equal-footing doctrine. Respondent urges that these circumstances further indicate that the United States abandoned its navigational servitude in the area. Thus, in respondent's view, the treaties by which it gained fee simple title to the bed of the Arkansas River were such as to make the Arkansas River a "private stream," "not intended as a public highway or artery of commerce."

We think that the decision in *Choctaw Nation* was quite generous to respondent, and we refuse to give a still more expansive and novel reading of respondent's property interests. There is certainly nothing in *Choctaw Nation* itself that suggests such a broad reading of the conveyance. To the contrary, the Court expressly noted that the United States had no interest in retaining title to the submerged lands because "all it was concerned with in its navigational easement via the constitutional power over commerce." The parties, including respondent here, clearly understood that the navigational servitude was dominant no matter how the question of riverbed ownership was resolved. *See*, *e.g.*, Brief for Petitioner in Cherokee Nation v. Oklahoma, O.T. 1969, No. 59, p. 19 ("[There] is nothing in the conveyance of title to the land beneath the navigable waters which conflicts with the power of the Government to hold such lands for navigation").

Any other conclusion would be wholly extraordinary, for we have repeatedly held that the navigational servitude applies to all holders of riparian and riverbed interests. Indeed, even when the sovereign States gain "the absolute right to all their navigable waters and the soils under them for their own common use" by operation of the equal-footing doctrine, this "absolute right" is unquestionably subject to "the paramount power of the United States to ensure that such waters remain free to interstate and foreign commerce." If the States themselves are subject to this servitude, we cannot conclude that respondent—though granted a degree of sovereignty over tribal lands—gained an exemption from the servitude simply because it received title to the riverbed interests. Such a waiver of sovereign authority will not be implied, but instead must be "'surrendered in unmistakable terms.'" Respondent can point to no such terms.

We also reject respondent's suggestion that the fiduciary obligations of the United States elevate the Government's actions into a taking. It is, of course, well established that the Government in its dealings with Indian tribal property acts in a fiduciary capacity. When it holds lands in trust on behalf of the tribes, the United States may not "give the tribal lands to others, or . . . appropriate them to its own purposes, without rendering, or assuming an obligation to render, just compensation for them." These principles, however, do little to aid respondent's cause, for they do not create property rights where none would otherwise exist but rather presuppose that the United States has interfered with existing tribal property interests. As we have explained, the tribal interests at issue here simply do not include the right to be free from the navigational servitude, for exercise of the servitude is "not an invasion of any private property rights in the stream or the lands underlying it. . . ."

The judgment of the Court of Appeals is reversed, and the case is remanded for further proceedings consistent with this opinion.

Note on Cherokee Claims to the Arkansas River

As noted, the Supreme Court ruled in 1970 that the Choctaw and Cherokee Tribes owned the bed of the Arkansas River where it formed the boundary between the two nations. *Choctaw Nation v. Oklahoma*, 397 U.S. 620 (1970). The materials in this note follow the saga of the Cherokee Nation's attempts to put the holding of *Choctaw Nation* into practice.

1. Relief against the State of Oklahoma. The State of Oklahoma had asserted ownership of the Arkansas River bed since statehood. On remand from *Choctaw Nation v. Oklahoma*, 397 U.S. 620 (1970), the district court canceled all state-issued leases given to the riverbed; ordered an accounting of all bonuses, rents, and royalties paid to the state; and determined the disposition of the moneys. On appeal, the Tenth Circuit noted that the district court had

> three alternatives, (1) to permit Oklahoma to retain the lease considerations, (2) to require Oklahoma to return those considerations to the lessees, or (3) to award the lease considerations to the Indians as the true owners of the leased land. The first merits little consideration. Oklahoma received money for leasing land which it did not own. To permit it to retain such money would approve unjust enrichment contrary to well recognized principles of equity. The suggestions of Oklahoma that laches of the Indians precludes their recovery does not impress us. The unexplained delay in title determination was mutual. The record contains nothing to show that any action, or nonaction, of the Indians disadvantaged Oklahoma. Oklahoma has suffered, and will suffer, no detriment other than payment to the rightful owners of the money which it wrongfully received as lessor.

> In our opinion Oklahoma has no right to retain the lease considerations. The right thereto lies between the lessees and the Indians. The lessees and Oklahoma made a mutual mistake of law. The documents determinative of title were all a matter of public record. We find nothing to suggest that Oklahoma engaged in conduct which misled or prejudiced the lessees. The trial court found, and we perceive nothing in the record to dispute the finding, that the lessees "got what they bargained for." The court decree protects the lessees against accountability to the Indians for actions taken under the leases. This includes damages for trespass. The lessees are not entitled to this protection plus return of the money which they paid for the leases.

> Whatever might be the situation if we were concerned only with the respective rights of Oklahoma and its lessees, we are confronted with the fact that the lessees have had the use of the land and have paid Oklahoma, not the rightful owner, therefor. If the lessees were awarded the return of the lease considerations which they have paid to Oklahoma, they would have received the use of the land for nothing and by the decree would be protected against trespass claims by the real owners. Equity will not condone such a result. The lessees are not entitled to return of the lease considerations.
>
> This leaves us with the third alternative, accounting to the Indians for the lease considerations. No party questions the amounts of bonuses, rentals, and royalties. There is no claim that they were either exorbitant or inadequate. For all that the record shows, they were at the going rates for such leases. We perceive no reason why the Indians should not be entitled thereto.

Cherokee Nation v. State of Oklahoma, 461 F.2d 674 (10th Cir. 1972). The court concluded: "We believe that [the district court] properly and satisfactorily disposes of a troublesome problem."

2. **The Senate report.** Seventeen years after the Tenth Circuit's opinion, little had changed. The Final Report and Legislative Recommendations of the Senate Select Committee on Indian Affairs Special Committee on Investigations, S. Rep. 216, 101st Cong. 129–32 (1989) found that:

> In 1970 the U.S. Supreme Court held that the Cherokee, Choctaw and Chickasaw Nations, three of the four largest Indian tribe in Oklahoma, owned title to ninety-six miles of Arkansas Riverbed lands in eastern Oklahoma. Unfortunately, at the time of the decision, the Riverbed lands were already occupied by hundreds of private landowners who were, in effect, trespassers. The tribes themselves were then, and are now, powerless to evict the trespassers because by statute all eviction actions on Indian lands must be substantiated by surveys conducted and certified by the Bureau of Land Management. Without the BLM surveys, the tribes are barred from court. BLM, however, will only survey the Riverbed land if it receives a request from BIA. The ultimate responsibility for initiating surveys of the Riverbed thus resides with BIA.
>
> Even though BIA has been charged with this specific responsibility since 1970, in 19 years it has obtained surveys of only 789 of the 22,000 Riverbed acres. The BIA's minimal efforts to initiate surveys and reclaim the Arkansas Riverbed have cost the Cherokee, Choctaw and Chickasaw Nations more than $5 million a year.

The report noted that the tribes were losing significant oil and gas royalties, revenues from sand and gravel sales, and agricultural lease and crop revenues. It estimated the total market value of the oil and gas reserves under the riverbed at $40 million, and the total market value of the sand and gravel on the riverbed at $32 million.

3. **The breach of trust claim.** In *Cherokee Nation of Oklahoma v. United States*, 21 Cl. Ct. 565 (1990), the tribe sought damages for the government's breach of fiduciary

duties regarding the submerged lands of the Arkansas River. The court ruled that the tribe could prosecute its claims regarding lands outside the geographic area where the United States exercises its navigation servitude. The Claims Court then held, however, that the government had no duty to survey the bedlands, and no duty to evict casual trespassers from those lands; both were discretionary actions. Nonetheless, the court noted that the government did have a trust responsibility to administer the tribe's mineral estate and collect royalties. In order to carry out that duty, the court held, "the government must remove trespassers who take oil or gas illegally." The court thus left intact the claims alleging failure to remove trespassers from, and issue leases on, the tribe's mineral lands; claims for unauthorized use of tribal lands; and claims for unauthorized use of land for rights-of-way.

The United States subsequently filed a motion for a more definite statement. The Claims Court granted the motion and ordered the Cherokee Nation to specify exactly which lands were involved in its claim, specify who the alleged trespassers were for each parcel; identify with specificity the leases at issue; and identify with particularity when the claims first accrued. The Cherokee Nation argued that it could not provide the specifics because of the absence of U.S. Bureau of Land Management (BLM) surveys. The Claims Court reiterated its holding that the BLM was under no fiduciary obligation to conduct surveys, and struck the portions of the complaint where the Cherokee Nation "has failed to provide the requisite degree of specificity." *Cherokee Nation of Oklahoma v. United States*, 23 Cl. Ct. 117 (1991).

4. Further proceedings in the Court of Federal Claims. In 1994, the claims court denied the federal government's motion for summary judgment, but issued an indefinite stay of the Cherokee, Choctaw, and Chickasaw Tribes' claims pending the outcome of suits to quiet title to the disputed lands. On appeal, the Federal Circuit vacated the stay on the ground that it was unfair to the tribes. The court noted:

> [T]he trial court's stay seriously impairs the Tribes' access to court. For almost 100 years, the United States has been trustee for the Tribes, but the United States has yet to take any legal action to preserve the Tribes' lands. Since 1970, the United States allegedly has been in various stages of preparing to file quiet title suits on behalf of the Tribes. Yet, it has filed none. Even now, eight years after the Tribes filed this suit, the United States has yet to take such action on behalf of its beneficiary.
>
> The stay also has the cruel effect of placing the Tribes at the mercy of the party against whom they seek redress. Under the trial court's stay, the Tribes cannot pursue their claims against the Government until the Government files and prosecutes the quiet title actions. The potential conflict of interest is manifest. As litigation adversaries go, the United States may be a relatively trustworthy sentry, but this court is confident the Tribes would prefer to have a neutral party guard the "hen house."

Cherokee Nation of Oklahoma v. United States, 124 F.3d 1413, 1418 (Fed. Cir. 1997).

5. The BLM survey. The Bureau of Land Management survey of the Arkansas riverbed was finally completed in 1994. The 28 miles of the riverbed just west of the Arkansas border—owned jointly by the Cherokee and the Choctaw and Chickasaw tribes—are the most usable lands for the tribes. For that section, the survey identified approximately 3000 trespassers, many of whom are tribal members.

6. The settlement act. In 2002, Congress enacted the Cherokee, Choctaw, and Chickasaw Nations Claims Settlement Act, 25 U.S.C. § 1779 *et seq.* The Act extinguished the three tribes' claims to certain lands lying above the ordinary high water mark (known as the "disclaimed drybed lands"), but did not extinguish the tribes' claims to other drybed lands or to lands below the current ordinary high water mark. The Act authorized Congress to appropriate a total of $40 million over four years ($10 million per year), allocated 50 percent to the Cherokee Nation, 37.5 percent to the Choctaw Nation, and 12.5 percent to the Chickasaw Nation. These funds could not be distributed per capita but could be used for a wide variety of governmental purposes—health care facilities, law enforcement, cultural and educational activities, economic development, social services, and land acquisition—in the discretion of the tribe. The lands acquired could be taken into trust for the appropriate tribe under Department of Interior regulations.

E. Allotted Lands

Recall that the General Allotment Act of 1887 authorized the allotment of reservation lands in severalty. 24 Stat. 388 (1887) (codified in part at 25 U.S.C. §§ 331–381). Under the Act, individual Indians received a certain number of acres of reservation land, generally between 80 and 160, to be held in trust for the allottee for a period of 25 years. At the expiration of the trust period, when the allottee was supposed to have sufficiently assimilated to agriculture, Christianity, and citizenship, the individual would receive a patent in fee (fee title) to the land, free of encumbrance and fully alienable. The account below explains some of efforts to shorten this trust period and the disastrous resulting effects.

> The twenty-five year trust period came under attack, however, by those who viewed the continued federal guardianship as an obstacle to the goal of assimilation. As a result, Congress amended the General Allotment Act in 1906 to authorize the early issuance of fee patents. The Burke Act authorized the Secretary of the Interior to issue a fee patent to an allottee at any time, upon a determination that the individual was "competent and capable of managing his or her affairs." Upon the issuance of one of these premature patents, the land was expressly subject to alienation, encumbrance, and taxation.
>
> The effect of the Burke Act was immediate and substantial. In the three years following the passage of the 1906 act, patents were issued upon the recommendation of the Indian superintendent. Of the 2744 applications made

during those years, all but 68 were granted. Surveys in 1908 showed that more than 60 percent of the premature patentees lost their lands. In 1909, an alarmed Commissioner of Indian Affairs began requiring a more detailed showing that the allottee was competent, and the approval rate dropped to approximately seventy percent of all applicants.

That relief was short-lived. In 1913, a new Commissioner of Indian Affairs not only reinstated the liberalized policy, but expanded upon it. Initially, the Indian superintendents were ordered to submit the names of competent Indians, but that procedure was soon replaced by "competency commissions," charged with roaming the reservations in search of allottees who could be issued premature patents. Under pressure to liberate the Indians from federal guardianship, the Indian Office issued patents to unqualified allottees and, in many cases, to allottees who neither applied for nor wanted to accept them. Despite reports showing that in many cases 90 percent or more of premature and forced-fee allottees lost their lands, the liberalized policy was formalized and further expanded in 1917.

In that year, Indian Commissioner Sells announced that fee patents would simply be issued to all allottees of less than one-half Indian ancestry, while competency determinations would still be required for those of one-half or more Indian blood. The effects were again devastating. In the eighteen months following Sells' policy announcement, the Indian Office issued premature patents for approximately one million acres, more than had been patented in the previous ten years. Similarly, between 1917 and 1920, more than 17,000 patents were issued, twice as many as were issued in the previous ten years. The havoc caused by Sells' policy resulted in a loss of support for liberalized patenting, and in 1920 a new Commissioner abolished the competency commissions and declared that no fee patents would issue without a determination of competency regardless of blood quantum.

Between the two methods—expiration of the trust period and premature patents—thousands of patents in fee were issued, often amounting to several thousand in a single year. Once a patent in fee was issued, the land could be alienated, encumbered, and at least as to Burke Act patents, taxed. Thousands of Indian owners disposed of their lands by voluntary or fraudulent sales; many others lost their lands at sheriffs' sales for nonpayment of taxes or other liens. By the end of the allotment era, two-thirds of all the land allotted—approximately 27 million acres—had passed into non-Indian ownership.

* * * In 1921, the liberal policy of granting forced-fee and other premature patents was officially abandoned, and the number of premature patents steadily declined throughout the 1920s. By the early 1930s, the Indian Office rejected more than 50 percent of patent applications, and issued fewer than 300 patents in a two-year period. Nonetheless, patentees continued to lose their lands in "staggering" numbers. As a result, the Indian Office began to

urge legislation that would permit the cancellation of forced-fee patents, a proposal that received considerable impetus from a Ninth Circuit decision holding that fee title did not pass to the allottee under a forced-fee patent. Congress responded in 1927, authorizing the Secretary of the Interior to cancel forced-fee patents. The effect of the legislation was limited, however; patents could be canceled only if the patent was issued without the application or consent of the allottee and if the owner had not sold or mortgaged the land. Because of those limitations, the Interior Department ultimately canceled only some 470 forced-fee patents out of approximately 10,000 that were issued.

Judith V. Royster, *The Legacy of Allotment*, 27 Ariz. St. L.J. 1, 10–12, 15–16 (1995).*

Between 1887 and 1934, the federal government implemented the allotment policy on 118 reservations through individual allotment acts.

In 1934, the Indian Reorganization Act ended the allotment policy. Act of June 18, 1934, 48 Stat. 984 (codified as amended at 25 U.S.C. §§ 5101–5143 (formerly §§ 461–495)). The IRA prohibited further allotment of tribal land and provided that any allotments then held in trust status would continue in trust until Congress provided otherwise. It did not, however, restore any allotted land to tribal ownership. Nonetheless, many reservations today contain substantial amounts of land held in trust by allottees and their heirs and devisees.

The following materials explore some of the tensions between tribal interests in reservation land and the interests of the individual allottees.

Northern Cheyenne Tribe v. Hollowbreast
425 U.S. 649 (1976)

JUSTICE BRENNAN delivered the opinion of the Court.

The question to be decided is whether the Northern Cheyenne Allotment Act, Act of June 3, 1926, gave the allottees of surface lands vested rights in the mineral deposits underlying those lands. The District Court for the District of Montana held that the Act did not grant the allottees vested rights in the mineral deposits. The Court of Appeals for the Ninth Circuit reversed. We granted certiorari. We agree with the District Court and reverse.

I

The 1926 Act statutorily established the Northern Cheyenne Reservation pursuant to the federal policy expressed in the General Allotment Act of 1887,[1] and

---

* Copyright 1995 by Judith V. Royster. Reprinted with permission of Judith V. Royster.

1. The objects of this policy were to end tribal land ownership and to substitute private ownership, on the view that private ownership by individual Indians would better advance their assimilation as self-supporting members of our society and relieve the Federal Government of the need to continue supervision of Indian affairs.

provided for the allotment of tracts of land to individual tribal members. Section 1 of the Act declared the lands constituting the reservation "to be the property of [the Northern Cheyenne] Indians, subject to such control and management of said property as the Congress of the United States may direct." Section 2 set up a procedure for allotment of agricultural and grazing lands. Section 3, upon which the question for decision in this case turns, reads as follows:

> "That the timber, coal or other minerals, including oil, gas, and other natural deposits, on said reservation are hereby reserved for the benefit of the tribe and may be leased with the consent of the Indian council under such rules and regulations as the Secretary of the Interior may prescribe: Provided, That at the expiration of fifty years from the date of the approval of this Act the coal or other minerals, including oil, gas, and other natural deposits, of said allotments shall become the property of the respective allottees or their heirs: Provided further, That the unallotted lands of said tribe of Indians shall be held in common, subject to the control and management thereof as Congress may deem expedient for the benefit of said Indians."

On its face, § 3 provides that title to the mineral deposits would pass to the allottees, or their heirs, 50 years after approval of the Act, or in 1976. But the phrasing might also be read to imply a reserved power in Congress to terminate the allottees' interest before that date. Thus, the critical question is whether Congress could, as it purports to have done in 1968, terminate the grant without rendering the United States constitutionally liable to pay the allottees just compensation.

A supervening event of particular significance was the considerable increase in value of coal reserves under the allotted lands that occurred in the 1960s due to increasing energy demand and the concomitant need for new sources of energy.[3] Until this occurred, the reservation of the deposits until 1976 for the benefit of the Tribe had not significantly benefited it, because mining of most of the coal was not economically feasible. There was also substantial concern that, because one-third of the allottees did not live on the reservation, if control of strip mining passed in 1976 to the individual allottees, serious adverse consequences might be suffered by the Indians living on the reservation. In addition, Congress believed that injustice might result if the benefits to be realized by individual Indians depended upon whether coal was found under particular allotted lands. These considerations led Congress in 1968 to terminate the grant to allottees and to reserve the mineral rights "in perpetuity for the benefit of the Tribe." The termination was, however, expressly conditioned upon a prior judicial determination that the allottees had not been granted vested rights to the mineral deposits by the 1926 Act. Congress so conditioned the termination to avoid the possibility of a successful claim for damages against the United States by the allottees under the Just Compensation Clause of the Fifth Amendment.

---

3. Petitioner informs us that its "conservative" estimate of the value of the coal reserves is $2 billion, based on a recent offer for coal under the Crow Reservation, which adjoins the Northern Cheyenne Reservation.

The 1968 amendment authorized the Tribe to commence an action against the allottees in the District Court for Montana "to determine whether under [the 1926 Act] the allottees, their heirs or devisees, have received a vested property right in the minerals which is protected by the fifth amendment," and provided that the reservation of the minerals in perpetuity for the benefit of the Tribe "shall cease to have any force or effect" if the court determines that "the allottees, their heirs or devisees, have a vested interest in the minerals which is protected by the fifth amendment."

II

Both the Tribe and the allottees argue that the plain meaning of § 3 of the 1926 Act, providing that the mineral deposits "shall become the property of the respective allottees" 50 years after the effective date of the Act, compels a declaratory judgment in their favor. The Tribe argues that this provision can only be read to grant an expectancy, while the allottees maintain that it unequivocally grants a vested future interest. Both interpretations are consistent with the wording of the Act, and we therefore must determine the intent of Congress by looking to the legislative history against the background of principles governing congressional power to alter allotment plans.

* * * The Court has consistently recognized the wide-ranging congressional power to alter allotment plans until those plans are executed. This principle has specifically been applied to uphold congressional imposition on allottees of restraints against alienation of their interests or expansion of the class of beneficiaries under an allotment Act. The extensiveness of this congressional authority, as well as "Congress' unique obligation toward the Indians," underlies the judicially fashioned canon of construction that these statutes are to be read to reserve Congress' powers in the absence of a clear expression by Congress to the contrary.

Read in this light, the statutory history of the Northern Cheyenne Reservation allotment supports the District Court's reading of the Act. Although prior to 1925 allotment Acts had been enacted for nearly all Indian reservations, none yet applied to the Northern Cheyenne Reservation. The Tribe in 1925 petitioned Senator Walsh of Montana to have the reservation allotted. The petition read in pertinent part:

> "We, the undersigned members of the Northern Cheyenne Indian Tribe, of the State of Montana, do hereby humbly beseech you to do all in your power to have a Bill introduced and passed in Congress, to have an allotment of not less than 320 acres of tillable farm land made to each and every member of the Northern Cheyenne Indians.
>
> "To reserve all mineral, timber, and coal lands for the benefit of the Northern Cheyenne Indian Tribe, said tribe to have absolute control of same."

Thus, the Tribe from the outset sought allotment provisions that would retain, for the benefit of the entire Tribe, the rights to the coal and other minerals underlying the reservation.

The proposed bill (H.R. 9558) introduced in the House [provided that:] * * * "if any of the land shall be found to contain coal or other minerals, only the surface thereof may be allotted, and all minerals on said lands are hereby reserved for the benefit of the tribe."

This language is clear evidence of an intent to sever the surface estate from the interest in the minerals, at least wherever minerals are found to exist. But nothing appears in the legislative history explaining the object of the proviso:

> "Provided, That at the expiration of fifty years from the date of the approval of this Act, the coal or other mineral deposits of said allotments shall become the property of the respective allottees or their heirs or assigns."

We are persuaded for several reasons that it was not intended to grant the allottees a vested future interest in the mineral deposits and thereby relinquish congressional "control and management thereof as Congress may deem expedient for the benefit of said Indians."

The proposed bill plainly reveals a purpose to sever the mineral rights from the surface estate; "only the surface . . . may be allotted" under the bill. In fact, the limited object of the bill, as stated in its title, was "to provide for allotting in severalty agricultural lands" within the reservation.

* * * Only the surface lands were to be subject to allotment.

The Senate Committee reported out the House bill with several amendments * * * [and] substituted the following as § 3 of its bill:

> "That the timber, coal or other minerals, including oil, gas, and other natural deposits on said reservation, are hereby reserved for the benefit of the tribe: Provided, That at the expiration of fifty years from the date of the approval of this act the coal or other minerals, including oil, gas, and other natural deposits of said allotments shall become the property of the respective allottees or their heirs: Provided further, That the unallotted lands of said tribe of Indians shall be held in common, subject to the control and management thereof as Congress may deem expedient for the benefit of said Indians."

The changes from the House bill indicate no difference in purpose. The coal and other mineral rights were still "reserved for the benefit of the tribe," with no suggestion from the Senate Committee that it attached any more import to the 50-year provision than had the House. Most significantly, and a critical fact supporting the District Court's construction of § 3, the Committee added an express reservation of congressional authority over "unallotted lands." Since the House bill clearly allotted only the surface lands, we are compelled to conclude that when both Houses adopted the bill as amended by the Senate, "unallotted lands" in § 3 included the mineral deposits.[11]

---

11. A reasonable explanation for the provision that the mineral rights would become the property of the allottees after 50 years is that it may have been thought to further the policy of assimilation underlying the allotment policy; the provision is consistent with a desire to give the mineral

The conclusion we reach is also supported by the wording of the allotment trust patents. The patents "reserved for the benefit of the Northern Cheyenne Indians, all the coal or other minerals, including oil, gas, and all natural deposits in said land," without any reference to the allottees' future interest. Thus, the agency charged with executing the Act construed it as not granting the allottees any vested rights. "While not conclusive, this construction given to the [allotment] act in the course of its actual execution is entitled to great respect."

Reversed.

Note on Fractionation

Perhaps the most serious problem today with respect to allotted lands is that of fractionation: the continually increasing fragmentation of ownership over the generations. Congress attempted to address the problem in the Indian Lands Consolidation Act (ILCA), 25 U.S.C. § 2206, originally enacted in 1983 and amended in 1984, in 2000, and most recently in 2004 as the American Indian Probate Reform Act. The Supreme Court considered the escheat provisions of both the original and the first amended version of ILCA, and found them both unconstitutional. The original 1983 version was struck down in *Hodel v. Irving*, 481 U.S. 704 (1987), which provides the best explanation of the problem and its origins.

> Towards the end of the 19th century, Congress enacted a series of land Acts which divided the communal reservations of Indian tribes into individual allotments for Indians and unallotted lands for non-Indian settlement. This legislation seems to have been in part animated by a desire to force Indians to abandon their nomadic ways in order to "speed the Indians' assimilation into American society," and in part a result of pressure to free new lands for further white settlement. Two years after the enactment of the General Allotment Act of 1887, Congress adopted a specific statute authorizing the division of the Great Reservation of the Sioux Nation into separate reservations and the allotment of specific tracts of reservation land to individual Indians, conditioned on the consent of three-fourths of the adult male Sioux. Under the Act, each male Sioux head of household took 320 acres of land and most other individuals 160 acres. In order to protect the allottees from the improvident disposition of their lands to white settlers, the Sioux allotment statute provided that the allotted lands were to be held in trust by the United States. Until 1910, the lands of deceased allottees passed to their heirs "according to the laws of the State or Territory" where the land was located, and after 1910, allottees were permitted to dispose of their interests by will in accordance with regulations promulgated by the

---

rights to the allottees after they became assimilated. On the other hand, the vesting of an irrevocable future interest in 1926 would not be wholly consistent with that policy, particularly since the policy was already losing its appeal by 1926, and Congress might more logically be expected to have been reluctant to surrender its power to modify the Act.

Secretary of the Interior. Those regulations generally served to protect Indian ownership of the allotted lands.

The policy of allotment of Indian lands quickly proved disastrous for the Indians. Cash generated by land sales to whites was quickly dissipated, and the Indians, rather than farming the land themselves, evolved into petty landlords, leasing their allotted lands to white ranchers and farmers and living off the meager rentals. The failure of the allotment program became even clearer as successive generations came to hold the allotted lands. Thus 40-, 80-, and 160-acre parcels became splintered into multiple undivided interests in land, with some parcels having hundreds, and many parcels having dozens, of owners. Because the land was held in trust and often could not be alienated or partitioned, the fractionation problem grew and grew over time.

A 1928 report commissioned by the Congress found the situation administratively unworkable and economically wasteful. L. Meriam, Institute for Government Research, *The Problem of Indian Administration* 40–41. Good, potentially productive, land was allowed to lie fallow, amidst great poverty, because of the difficulties of managing property held in this manner. In discussing the Indian Reorganization Act of 1934, Representative Howard said:

> "It is in the case of the inherited allotments, however, that the administrative costs become incredible.... On allotted reservations, numerous cases exist where the shares of each individual heir from lease money may be 1 cent a month. Or one heir may own minute fractional shares in 30 or 40 different allotments. The cost of leasing, bookkeeping, and distributing the proceeds in many cases far exceeds the total income. The Indians and the Indian Service personnel are thus trapped in a meaningless system of minute partition in which all thought of the possible use of land to satisfy human needs is lost in a mathematical haze of bookkeeping."

In 1934, in response to arguments such as these, the Congress acknowledged the failure of its policy and ended further allotment of Indian lands. Indian Reorganization Act of 1934, 25 U.S.C. §461 *et seq.*

But the end of future allotment by itself could not prevent the further compounding of the existing problem caused by the passage of time. Ownership continued to fragment as succeeding generations came to hold the property, since, in the order of things, each property owner was apt to have more than one heir. In 1960, both the House and the Senate undertook comprehensive studies of the problem. These studies indicated that one-half of the approximately 12 million acres of allotted trust lands were held in fractionated ownership, with over 3 million acres held by more than six heirs to a parcel. Further hearings were held in 1966, but not until the Indian Land Consolidation Act of 1983 did the Congress take action to ameliorate the problem of fractionated ownership of Indian lands.

The fractionation problem on Indian reservations is extraordinary and may call for dramatic action to encourage consolidation. The Sisseton-Wahpeton Sioux Tribe, appearing as amicus curiae in support of the Secretary of the Interior, is a quintessential victim of fractionation. Forty-acre tracts on the Sisseton-Wahpeton Lake Traverse Reservation, leasing for about $1,000 annually, are commonly subdivided into hundreds of undivided interests, many of which generate only pennies a year in rent. The average tract has 196 owners and the average owner undivided interests in 14 tracts. The administrative headache this represents can be fathomed by examining Tract 1305, dubbed "one of the most fractionated parcels of land in the world." Tract 1305 is 40 acres and produces $1,080 in income annually. It is valued at $8,000. It has 439 owners, one-third of whom receive less than $.05 in annual rent and two-thirds of whom receive less than $1. The largest interest holder receives $82.85 annually. The common denominator used to compute fractional interests in the property is 3,394,923,840,000. The smallest heir receives $.01 every 177 years. If the tract were sold (assuming the 439 owners could agree) for its estimated $8,000 value, he would be entitled to $.000418. The administrative costs of handling this tract are estimated by the Bureau of Indian Affairs at $17,560 annually.

Hodel, 481 U.S. at 706–09, 712–13.

Fractionation continues to be a problem of enormous importance in Indian country. According to the Department of the Interior, there are approximately 150 locations with 97,970 fractionated tracts in trust or restricted fee, comprising about 10.8 million acres. More than 34,000 of these tracts have 20 or more owners, and the average per tract is 30 owners. At one location, each fractionated tract has an average of 149 owners. In addition, each owner of a fractionated interest has, on average, an interest in 10 different tracts of land. Some 63 percent of the fractionated tracts generated no income in fiscal year 2016. U.S. Dep't of the Interior, Land Buy-Back Program for Tribal Nations: 2016 Status Report 10 (Nov. 7, 2016), https://www.doi.gov/sites/doi.gov/files/uploads/2016_buy-back_program_final_0.pdf.

Congress has attempted to address the problem of fractionation through the Indian Land Consolidation Act (and its 2004 amendment, the American Indian Probate Reform Act) and the establishment in 2010 of a Trust Land Consolidation Fund. The following case explains the reasoning in *Hodel v. Irving* and addresses the 1984 amendments to ILCA. The notes after the case discuss the 2004 and 2010 statutes.

Babbitt v. Youpee

519 U.S. 234 (1997)

JUSTICE GINSBURG delivered the opinion of the Court.

In this case, we consider for a second time the constitutionality of an escheat-to-tribe provision of the Indian Land Consolidation Act (ILCA). Specifically, we address § 207 of the ILCA, as amended in 1984. Congress enacted the original provision in

1983 to ameliorate the extreme fractionation problem attending a century-old allotment policy that yielded multiple ownership of single parcels of Indian land. Amended § 207 provides that certain small interests in Indian lands will transfer—or "escheat"—to the tribe upon the death of the owner of the interest. In *Hodel v. Irving*, 481 U.S. 704 (1987), this Court held that the original version of § 207 of the ILCA effected a taking of private property without just compensation, in violation of the Fifth Amendment to the United States Constitution. We now hold that amended § 207 does not cure the constitutional deficiency this Court identified in the original version of § 207.

I

In 1983, Congress adopted the ILCA in part to reduce fractionated ownership of allotted lands. Section 207 of the Act—the "escheat" provision—prohibited the descent or devise of small fractional interests in allotments.[1] Instead of passing to heirs, such fractional interests would escheat to the tribe, thereby consolidating the ownership of Indian lands. Congress defined the targeted fractional interest as one that both constituted 2 percent or less of the total acreage in an allotted tract and had earned less than $100 in the preceding year. Section 207 made no provision for the payment of compensation to those who held such interests.

In *Hodel v. Irving*, this Court invalidated § 207 on the ground that it effected a taking of property without just compensation, in violation of the Fifth Amendment. The appellees in *Irving* were, or represented, heirs or devisees of members of the Oglala Sioux Tribe. But for § 207, the appellees would have received 41 fractional interests in allotments; under § 207, those interests would escheat to the Tribe. This Court tested the legitimacy of § 207 by considering its economic impact, its effect on investment-backed expectations, and the essential character of the measure. Turning first to the economic impact of § 207, the Court in *Irving* observed that the provision's income-generation test might fail to capture the actual economic value of the land. The Court next indicated that § 207 likely did not interfere with investment-backed expectations. Key to the decision in *Irving*, however, was the "extraordinary" character of the Government regulation. As this Court noted, § 207 amounted to the "virtual abrogation of the right to pass on a certain type of property." Such a complete abrogation of the rights of descent and devise could not be upheld.

II

In 1984, while *Irving* was still pending in the Court of Appeals for the Eighth Circuit, Congress amended § 207.[2] Amended § 207 differs from the original escheat

---

1. As originally enacted, § 207 provided:
"No undivided fractional interest in any tract of trust or restricted land within a tribe's reservation or otherwise subjected to a tribe's jurisdiction shall descedent [sic] by intestacy or devise but shall escheat to that tribe if such interest represents 2 per centum or less of the total acreage in such tract and has earned to its owner less than $100 in the preceding year before it is due to escheat."

2. * * * Amended § 207 provides:
"(a) Escheat to tribe; rebuttable presumption

provision in three relevant respects. First, an interest is considered fractional if it both constitutes 2 percent or less of the total acreage of the parcel and "is incapable of earning $100 in any one of the five years [following the] decedent's death"—as opposed to one year before the decedent's death in the original § 207. If the interest earned less than $100 in any one of five years prior to the decedent's death, "there shall be a rebuttable presumption that such interest is incapable of earning $100 in any one of the five years following the death of the decedent." Second, in lieu of a total ban on devise and descent of fractional interests, amended § 207 permits devise of an otherwise escheatable interest to "any other owner of an undivided fractional interest in such parcel or tract" of land. Finally, tribes are authorized to override the provisions of amended § 207 through the adoption of their own codes governing the disposition of fractional interests; these codes are subject to the approval of the Secretary of the Interior. In *Irving*, "we expressed no opinion on the constitutionality of § 207 as amended."

Under amended § 207, the interests in this case would escheat to tribal governments. The initiating plaintiffs, respondents here, are the children and potential heirs of William Youpee. An enrolled member of the Sioux and Assiniboine Tribes of the Fort Peck Reservation in Montana, William Youpee died testate in October 1990. His will devised to respondents, all of them enrolled tribal members, his several undivided interests in allotted trust lands on various reservations in Montana and North Dakota. These interests, as the Ninth Circuit reported, were valued together at $1,239. Each interest was devised to a single descendant. Youpee's will thus perpetuated existing fractionation, but it did not splinter ownership further by bequeathing any single fractional interest to multiple devisees.

"No undivided interest held by a member or nonmember Indian in any tract of trust land or restricted land within a tribe's reservation or outside of a reservation and subject to such tribe's jurisdiction shall descend by intestacy or devise but shall escheat to the reservation's recognized tribal government, or if outside of a reservation, to the recognized tribal government possessing jurisdiction over the land if such interest represents 2 per centum or less of the total acreage in such tract and is incapable of earning $100 in any one of the five years from the date of the decedent's death. Where the fractional interest has earned to its owner less than $100 in any one of the five years before the decedent's death, there shall be a rebuttable presumption that such interest is incapable of earning $100 in any one of the five years following the death of the decedent.

"(b) Escheatable fractional interest

"Nothing in this section shall prohibit the devise of such an escheatable fractional interest to any other owner of an undivided fractional interest in such parcel or tract of trust or restricted land.

"(c) Adoption of Indian tribal code

"Notwithstanding the provisions of subsection (a) of this section, any Indian tribe may, subject to the approval of the Secretary, adopt its own code of laws to govern the disposition of interests that are escheatable under this section, and such codes or laws shall take precedence over the escheat provisions of subsection (a) of this section, provided, the Secretary shall not approve any code or law that fails to accomplish the purpose of preventing further descent or fractionation of such escheatable interests."

III

In determining whether the 1984 amendments to § 207 render the provision constitutional, we are guided by *Irving*. The United States maintains that the amendments, though enacted three years prior to the *Irving* decision, effectively anticipated the concerns expressed in the Court's opinion. As already noted, amended § 207 differs from the original in three relevant respects: it looks back five years instead of one to determine the income produced from a small interest, and creates a rebuttable presumption that this income stream will continue; it permits devise of otherwise escheatable interests to persons who already own an interest in the same parcel; and it authorizes tribes to develop their own codes governing the disposition of fractional interests. These modifications, according to the United States, rescue amended § 207 from the fate of its predecessor. The Government maintains that the revisions moderate the economic impact of the provision and temper the character of the Government's regulation; the latter factor weighed most heavily against the constitutionality of the original version of § 207.

The narrow revisions Congress made to § 207, without benefit of our ruling in *Irving*, do not warrant a disposition different than the one this Court announced and explained in *Irving*. Amended § 207 permits a five-year window rather than a one-year window to assess the income-generating capacity of the interest. As the Ninth Circuit observed, however, argument that this change substantially mitigates the economic impact of § 207 "misses the point." Amended § 207 still trains on income generated from the land, not on the value of the parcel. The Court observed in *Irving* that "even if . . . the income generated by such parcels may be properly thought of as de minimis," the value of the land may not fit that description. The parcels at issue in *Irving* were valued by the Bureau of Indian Affairs at $2,700 and $1,816, amounts we found "not trivial." The value of the disputed parcels in this case is not of a different order; as the Ninth Circuit reported, the value of decedent Youpee's fractional interests was $1,239. In short, the economic impact of amended § 207 might still be palpable.

Even if the economic impact of amended § 207 is not significantly less than the impact of the original provision, the United States correctly comprehends that *Irving* rested primarily on the "extraordinary" character of the governmental regulation. *Irving* stressed that the original § 207 "amounted to virtually the abrogation of the right to pass on a certain type of property—the small undivided interest—to one's heirs." The *Irving* Court further noted that the original § 207 "effectively abolished both descent and devise [of fractional interests] even when the passing of the property to the heir might result in consolidation of property." As the United States construes *Irving*, Congress cured the fatal infirmity in § 207 when it revised the section to allow transmission of fractional interests to successors who already own an interest in the allotment.

Congress' creation of an ever-so-slight class of individuals equipped to receive fractional interests by devise does not suffice, under a fair reading of *Irving*, to rehabilitate the measure. Amended § 207 severely restricts the right of an individual to direct the descent of his property. Allowing a decedent to leave an interest only to a current owner in the same parcel shrinks drastically the universe of possible successors. And, as the Ninth Circuit observed, the "very limited group [of permissible devisees] is unlikely to contain any lineal descendants." Moreover, amended § 207 continues to restrict devise "even in circumstances when the governmental purpose sought to be advanced, consolidation of ownership of Indian lands, does not conflict with the further descent of the property." William Youpee's will, the United States acknowledges, bequeathed each fractional interest to one heir. Giving effect to Youpee's directive, therefore, would not further fractionate Indian land holdings.

The United States also contends that amended § 207 satisfies the Constitution's demand because it does not diminish the owner's right to use or enjoy property during his lifetime, and does not affect the right to transfer property at death through non-probate means. These arguments did not persuade us in *Irving* and they are no more persuasive today.

The third alteration made in amended § 207 also fails to bring the provision outside the reach of this Court's holding in *Irving*. Amended § 207 permits tribes to establish their own codes to govern the disposition of fractional interests; if approved by the Secretary of the Interior, these codes would govern in lieu of amended § 207. The United States does not rely on this new provision to defend the statute. Nor does it appear that the United States could do so at this time: Tribal codes governing disposition of escheatable interests have apparently not been developed.

For the reasons stated, the judgment of the Court of Appeals for the Ninth Circuit is Affirmed.

JUSTICE STEVENS, dissenting.

Section 207 of the Indian Land Consolidation Act, did not, in my view, effect an unconstitutional taking of William Youpee's right to make a testamentary disposition of his property. As I explained in *Hodel v. Irving*, the Federal Government, like a State, has a valid interest in removing legal impediments to the productive development of real estate. For this reason, the Court has repeatedly "upheld the power of the State to condition the retention of a property right upon the performance of an act within a limited period of time." I remain convinced that "Congress has ample power to require the owners of fractional interests in allotted lands to consolidate their holdings during their lifetimes or to face the risk that their interests will be deemed to be abandoned." The federal interest in minimizing the fractionated ownership of Indian lands—and thereby paving the way to the productive development of their property—is strong enough to justify the legislative remedy created by § 207, provided, of course, that affected owners have adequate notice of the requirements of the law and an adequate opportunity to adjust their affairs to protect against loss.

In my opinion, William Youpee did have such notice and opportunity. With regard to notice, the requirements of § 207 are set forth in the United States Code. "Generally, a legislature need do nothing more than enact and publish the law, and afford the citizenry a reasonable opportunity to familiarize itself with its terms and to comply.... It is well established that persons owning property within a [jurisdiction] are charged with knowledge of relevant statutory provisions affecting the control or disposition of such property." Unlike the landowners in *Hodel*, Mr. Youpee also had adequate opportunity to comply. More than six years passed from the time § 207 was amended until Mr. Youpee died on October 19, 1990 (this period spans more than seven years if we count from the date § 207 was originally enacted). During this time, Mr. Youpee could have realized the value of his fractional interests (approximately $1,239) in a variety of ways, including selling the property, giving it to his children as a gift, or putting it in trust for them. I assume that he failed to do so because he was not aware of the requirements of § 207. This loss is unfortunate. But I believe Mr. Youpee's failure to pass on his property is the product of inadequate legal advice rather than an unconstitutional defect in the statute.

Accordingly, I respectfully dissent.

Notes

1. ILCA and *Lone Wolf*. Recall the decision in *Lone Wolf v. Hitchcock*, 187 U.S. 553 (1903), excerpted at page 95. In that case, the Court rejected Lone Wolf's claim that implementation of the allotment policy to allot tribal lands to individuals and sell the surplus was a taking under the Fifth Amendment of the U.S. Constitution. In light of *Lone Wolf*, consider the following commentary on ILCA:

> Irony is not new to federal Indian law, but seldom is it as striking as the present scenario. Congressional authority was upheld when Congress took millions of acres held by tribal governments and allotted those lands to individuals, yet the tribal governments were never compensated. However, Congress now lacks the authority to mandate an escheat from a tribal member back to the tribal government even of extremely small, economically worthless ownership interests. Congressional plenary power has often been upheld when it diminishes tribal land base, but seldom to restore it.

Stacy L. Leeds, *The Burning of Blackacre: A Step Toward Reclaiming Tribal Property Law*, 10 Kan. J.L. & Pub. Pol'y 491, 492 (Spring 2001). Why is the taking of an interest in an allotment and restoring it to tribal ownership a constitutional taking, while the taking of tribal land for allotments was not?

2. American Indian Probate Reform Act of 2004. Congress amended the Indian Land Consolidation Act (ILCA) for the second time in 2000, Pub. L. No. 106-462. But even before the 2000 amendments became effective, Congress enacted amendments in 2004, known as the American Indian Probate Reform Act (AIPRA) of 2004, Pub. L. 108-374, codified as amended at 25 U.S.C. §§ 2201–2221. The 2004 Act addressed devise and escheat, tribal probate codes, and tribal land consolidation and purchase.

a. Devise and escheat. The 2004 Act institutes a new descent and distribution scheme (25 U.S.C. § 2206), providing that in the absence of a will, trust property will descend according to an approved tribal probate code, if one exists. If there is no tribal probate code, the surviving spouse receives a life estate in trust lands of the decedent. If there is no surviving spouse, trust land descends to an "eligible heir" in the following order: children and grandchildren, great grandchildren, parents, and siblings. The statute defines an eligible heir as a relative who is Indian or a lineal descendant "within 2 degrees of consanguinity of an Indian" or owns a trust or restricted interest in the decedent's parcel of land. If there is no eligible heir, the property passes to the tribe, although a co-owner of the parcel may instead acquire the decedent's interest by paying fair market value to the estate. The 2004 Act restricts devises of trust or other restricted interests to a lineal descendant, any person who owns a pre-existing trust interest in the parcel, the Indian tribe, or any Indian. Otherwise, the owner may devise a life estate to any person, with the remainder to an eligible heir, or a fee interest to any other person, if the lands are not Indian Reorganization Act Lands.

Under *Hodel* and *Youpee*, is this version constitutional?

b. Tribal probate codes. The American Indian Probate Reform Act of 2004 (formerly ILCA) stipulates that:

> (a)(1) Notwithstanding any other provision of law, any Indian tribe may adopt a tribal probate code to govern descent and distribution of trust or restricted lands that are —
>
> (A) located within that Indian tribe's reservation, or
>
> (B) otherwise subject to the jurisdiction of that Indian tribe.

25 U.S.C. § 2205. Tribal probate codes, which may include rules of intestate succession, must be approved by the Secretary of the Interior. The Secretary may not approve a code unless it "promotes the policies" of ILCA, or if it "prohibits the devise of an interest in trust or restricted land to — an Indian lineal descendant of the original allottee."

In addition, this section provides that a tribe may acquire, by paying fair market value, any interest in trust or restricted property that has been devised to a non-Indian pursuant to § 207, although that provision does not apply if the non-Indian devisee renounces the interest in favor of an Indian person while the estate is pending before the Secretary. The Act also allows a non-Indian devisee to retain a life estate in the property, with the amount of the tribe's payment for the property reduced to reflect the value of the life estate.

c. Tribal land consolidation and purchase. An important provision of ILCA enables any tribe to adopt, with the approval of the Secretary of the Interior, a land consolidation plan. 25 U.S.C. § 2203(a). The plan's purpose is to eliminate fractionated interests and consolidate tribal land holdings. The act authorizes tribes to purchase interests in allotments, at fair market value, from any consenting owner. *Id.* § 2204(a). The tribe may also purchase all of the interests in an allotment with the consent of a majority of the owners, provided that the tribe obtains secretarial approval, except that any allottee of the tract in actual use or possession for at least three years may purchase the entire tract by matching the tribe's offer. *Id.* §2204(a)-(b). *See generally* Douglas R. Nash & Cecelia E. Burke, *The Changing Landscape of Indian Estate Planning and Probate: The American Indian Probate Reform Act,* 5 Seattle J. for Soc. Just. 121 (2006).

The act also created a pilot program under which the Secretary may acquire, at fair market value, fractional interests in trust or restricted lands and hold those interests in trust for the Indian tribe. *Id.* §2212. The program authorizes the Secretary of the Interior to "give priority to the acquisition of fractional interests representing two percent or less of a parcel of trust or restricted land, especially those interests that would have escheated to a tribe but for the Supreme Court's decision in *Babbitt v. Youpee.*" An alternative proposal is for tribes to create tribal land corporations, which would acquire fractionated interests in land in exchange for shares in the corporation. *See* Brian Sawers, *Tribal Land Corporations: Using Incorporation to Combat Fractionation,* 88 Neb. L. Rev. 385 (2009).

3. Land Buy-Back Program. The Claims Resolution Act of 2010 that ended the *Cobell* trust litigation—see note 4, pages 399–401—included a $2 billion Trust Land Consolidation Fund. Over $1.5 billion of that was set aside for the purchase of fractionated interests in allotments. By statute, the funds must be expended by late November 2022.

The Land Buy-Back Program for Tribal Nations allows individuals to voluntarily sell their interests in fractionated tracts, with the land placed immediately in trust for the tribe with jurisdiction. The initial implementation plan in 2012 reported over 10 and a half million fractionated acres, with close to 3 million fractionated interests in them, and over 90,000 tracts that are fractionated.

The program concentrates on the 40 reservations that the government believes will experience the most benefit from the consolidation of land administration. The first reservation on which allotment owners received offers to sell was the Pine Ridge Reservation in South Dakota, considered the most fractionated of all reservations. Pine Ridge had over 6000 fractionated tracts with close to 196,000 interests eligible for purchase. *See* https://www.doi.gov/news/pressreleases/interior-announces-first-purchase-offers-to-facilitate-cobell-land-consolidation-efforts.

At the end of fiscal year 2016, the Department of the Interior reported that:

> The Program began land consolidation purchases in December 2013 and thus far has made more than $2 billion in offers to nearly 102,600 unique individuals for interests at 30 locations [in 13 states]. In Fiscal Year (FY) 2016 alone, the Program paid more than $207 million to landowners who accepted offers. The Program has paid landowners approximately $900 million since its inception, and it has created or increased tribal ownership in more than 30,000 tracts of allotted land—with nearly 1,200 of those tracts reaching 100 percent tribal trust ownership. The Program has restored the equivalent of nearly 1.7 million acres of land to tribal trust ownership.

U.S. Dep't of the Interior, Land Buy-Back Program for Tribal Nations: 2016 Status Report 1-2 (Nov. 7, 2016), https://www.doi.gov/sites/doi.gov/files/uploads/2016_buy-back_program_final_0.pdf. The report notes that 45,600 individuals accepted buy-back offers. *Id.* at 2. In addition, 485,253 fractional interests had been returned to Indian tribes, and 10,891 tracts had reached greater than 50 percent tribal ownership. *Id.* at unnumbered page.

Chapter 4

Land Use and Environmental Protection

This chapter focuses on regulatory authority: primarily the issues surrounding state-tribal conflicts over who regulates. Part A of the chapter considers these issues in the common law context of land use, and Part B considers them in the context of the federal environmental statutes.

A. Authority to Control Land Use

The next set of cases focuses on the issue of which government—the tribe or the state—has the authority to regulate the use of land and other resources within Indian country. In determining regulatory authority, the Supreme Court has focused on the interplay of two factors. The first factor is the citizenship of the person subject to the regulation. As seen below (*e.g., Montana v. United States*, at page 249), the Court drew a distinction between Indians and non-Indians. In the later cases, the distinction has shifted to that between members of the tribe asserting governmental authority and nonmembers, including both non-Indians and Indians who are members of other tribes.

The second factor is the status of the land on which the regulated conduct occurs. Here, the Court has tended to distinguish two broad categories of lands within Indian country. One category is "Indian lands," which includes land owned by the tribe, land held in trust for the tribe, and land held in trust for members of the tribe (trust allotments). This category also likely includes land owned in fee by members of the tribe. The other category is "fee lands," which includes land owned by nonmember individuals as well as lands owned by the federal government, the states, and their political subdivisions.

Based on these two factors, the issues generally fall into three categories:

- Who regulates the conduct of tribal members?
- Who regulates the conduct of nonmembers on Indian lands?
- Who regulates the conduct of nonmembers on fee land?

As you read the cases in this section, note which factors the Court considers important in each of these situations. If the Court treats the situations differently, what is the difference and why does the Court draw a distinction? Has the Court's approach changed over time? If so, how?

Worcester v. Georgia
31 U.S. 515 (1832)

Worcester v. Georgia is excerpted at page 83. Recall the ultimate holding of the case:

> The Cherokee nation, then, is a distinct community occupying its own territory, with boundaries accurately described, in which the laws of Georgia can have no force, and which the citizens of Georgia have no right to enter, but with the assent of the Cherokees themselves, or in conformity with treaties, and with the acts of congress. The whole intercourse between the United States and this nation, is, by our constitution and laws, vested in the government of the United States.

Notes

1. Nineteenth century developments. Recall that *Worcester* involved an attempt by the State of Georgia to regulate the conduct of Samuel Worcester, a non-Indian, within Indian territory by requiring him to obtain a state license to enter Cherokee lands. The Court's decision in *Worcester* is phrased in absolutist terms: absent some treaty provision, or the consent of Congress, or the consent of the tribes, the states have no authority within Indian country.

Nonetheless, some cracks in this absolute approach began to appear in the late nineteenth century. In particular, the Supreme Court held that crimes occurring in Indian country that involved only non-Indians were within the jurisdiction of the state. *See, e.g., United States v. McBratney*, 104 U.S. 621 (1881). The underlying rationale of the *McBratney* line of cases appears to be that crimes not involving Indians as either victims or perpetrators do not affect Indian interests. Accordingly, the reasoning ran, state jurisdiction over those matters would not interfere with tribal self-government.

2. State laws protecting health and education. Occasionally, Congress has authorized state regulatory jurisdiction within Indian country. For example, in 1929, Congress passed a law, now codified at 25 U.S.C. §231, which authorizes the Secretary of the Interior to prescribe rules allowing state officials to enter "Indian tribal lands, reservations, or allotments therein" to inspect health and education conditions and enforce sanitation and quarantine regulations. *See* 25 C.F.R. §31.4 (compulsory school attendance).

3. *Williams v. Lee*. The late nineteenth-century rationale for state jurisdiction found expression in the termination-era case of *Williams v. Lee*, 358 U.S. 217 (1959). In that case, a non-Indian who owned a store on the Navajo reservation sued a Navajo couple in state court for nonpayment of goods sold on credit. The Navajo defendants moved to dismiss the state court action on the ground that the proper forum was tribal court. Rather than adopt the *Worcester* approach that state jurisdiction could not reach within Indian country, the Supreme Court articulated a standard for determining when state jurisdiction over on-reservation affairs would be allowed:

> Essentially, absent governing Acts of Congress, the question has always been whether the state action infringed on the right of reservation Indians to make their own laws and be ruled by them.

Id. at 220. Based on that standard, the Court found that state court jurisdiction over a civil dispute involving an Indian defendant, where the cause of action arose on the reservation, would infringe on Navajo self-government.

Is the *Williams v. Lee* analysis applied in *Montana v. United States*, below? Why or why not?

4. Authority to control the use of land. The Supreme Court's first modern pronouncement on the question of state versus tribal authority over the use of land was *Montana v. United States* in 1981, in which the Crow Tribe claimed the authority to regulate (in fact, to prohibit) non-Indian hunting and fishing everywhere within the boundaries of its reservation. The tribe first claimed that right based on its ownership of the Big Horn riverbed. As we saw in the earlier excerpt from *Montana* at page 215, however, the Court held that title to the riverbed vested in the state. The Crow Tribe then argued that it was nonetheless entitled to regulate the non-Indian conduct, even though that conduct occurred on non-Indian land.

Note that the Court addressed two separate grounds for tribal authority to regulate non-Indians on fee lands. The first source of authority is based on treaty rights, and the second on inherent rights of sovereignty aside and apart from the treaties. What is the relationship between these two kinds of tribal rights? How did the Court deal with each of these arguments?

Montana v. United States
450 U.S. 544 (1981)

Justice STEWART delivered the opinion of the Court.

This case concerns the sources and scope of the power of an Indian tribe to regulate hunting and fishing by non-Indians on lands within its reservation owned in fee simple by non-Indians. Relying on its purported ownership of the bed of the Big Horn River, on the treaties which created its reservation and on its inherent power as a sovereign, the Crow Tribe of Montana claims the authority to prohibit all hunting and fishing by nonmembers of the Tribe on non-Indian property within reservation boundaries. We granted certiorari to review a decision of the United States Court of Appeals for the Ninth Circuit that substantially upheld this claim.

I

The Crow Indians originated in Canada, but some three centuries ago they migrated to what is now southern Montana. In the 19th century, warfare between the Crows and several other tribes led the tribes and the United States to sign the First Treaty of Fort Laramie of 1851, in which the signatory tribes acknowledged various designated lands as their respective territories. The treaty identified approximately 38.5 million acres as Crow territory and, in Article 5, specified that, by making the treaty, the tribes did not "surrender the privilege of hunting, fishing, or passing over" any of the lands in dispute. In 1868, the Second Treaty of Fort Laramie established a Crow Reservation of roughly 8 million acres, including land through which the Big Horn River flows. By Article II of the treaty, the United States agreed that the reservation "shall be . . . set apart for the absolute and undisturbed use and occupation" of the Crow Tribe, and that no non-Indians except agents of the Government "shall ever be permitted to pass over, settle upon, or reside in" the reservation.

Several subsequent Acts of Congress reduced the reservation to slightly fewer than 2.3 million acres. In addition, the General Allotment Act of 1887, and the Crow Allotment Act of 1920, authorized the issuance of patents in fee to individual Indian allottees within the reservation. Under these Acts, an allottee could alienate his land to a non-Indian after holding it for 25 years. Today, roughly 52 percent of the reservation is allotted to members of the Tribe and held by the United States in trust for them, 17 percent is held in trust for the Tribe itself, and approximately 28 percent is held in fee by non-Indians. The State of Montana owns in fee simple 2 percent of the reservation, the United States less than 1 percent.

Since the 1920s, the State of Montana has stocked the waters of the reservation with fish, and the construction of a dam by the United States made trout fishing in the Big Horn River possible. The reservation also contains game, some of it stocked by the State. Since the 1950s, the Crow Tribal Council has passed several resolutions respecting hunting and fishing on the reservation, including Resolution No. 74-05, the occasion for this lawsuit. That resolution prohibits hunting and fishing within the reservation by anyone who is not a member of the Tribe. The State of Montana, however, has continued to assert its authority to regulate hunting and fishing by non-Indians within the reservation.

[The Court concluded that the State of Montana, not the Crow Tribe, held title to the bed of the Big Horn River. This portion of the case is excerpted at page 215.]

III — Control

Though the parties in this case have raised broad questions about the power of the Tribe to regulate hunting and fishing by non-Indians on the reservation, the regulatory issue before us is a narrow one. The Court of Appeals held that the Tribe may prohibit nonmembers from hunting or fishing on land belonging to the Tribe or held by the United States in trust for the Tribe, and with this holding we can readily agree. We also agree with the Court of Appeals that if the Tribe permits nonmembers to fish or hunt on such lands, it may condition their entry by charging a fee or establishing bag and creel limits. What remains is the question of the power of the Tribe to regulate non-Indian fishing and hunting on reservation land owned in fee by nonmembers of the Tribe. The Court of Appeals held that, with respect to fee-patented lands, the Tribe may regulate, but may not prohibit, hunting and fishing by non-member resident owners or by those, such as tenants or employees, whose occupancy is authorized by the owners. The court further held that the Tribe may totally prohibit hunting and fishing on lands within the reservation owned by non-Indians who do not occupy that land.

The Court of Appeals found two sources for this tribal regulatory power: the Crow treaties, "augmented" by 18 U.S.C. § 1165, and "inherent" Indian sovereignty. We believe that neither source supports the court's conclusion.

A.

The purposes of the 1851 treaty were to assure safe passage for settlers across the lands of various Indian Tribes; to compensate the Tribes for the loss of buffalo, other game animals, timber, and forage; to delineate tribal boundaries; to promote intertribal peace; and to establish a way of identifying Indians who committed depredations against non-Indians. As noted earlier, the treaty did not even create a reservation, although it did designate tribal lands. Only Article 5 of that Treaty referred to hunting and fishing, and it merely provided that the eight signatory tribes "do not surrender the privilege of hunting, fishing, or passing over any of the tracts of country heretofore described." The treaty nowhere suggested that Congress intended to grant authority to the Crow Tribe to regulate hunting and fishing by nonmembers on nonmember lands. Indeed, the Court of Appeals acknowledged that after the treaty was signed non-Indians, as well as members of other Indian tribes, undoubtedly hunted and fished within the treaty-designated territory of the Crows.

The 1868 Fort Laramie Treaty reduced the size of the Crow territory designated by the 1851 treaty. Article II of the treaty established a reservation for the Crow Tribe, and provided that it be "set apart for the *absolute and undisturbed use and occupation* of the Indians herein named, and for such other friendly tribes or individual Indians as from time to time they may be willing, with the consent of the United States, to admit amongst them . . . ," (emphasis added) and that "the United States now solemnly agrees that no persons, except those herein designated and authorized so to do . . . shall ever be permitted to pass over, settle upon, or reside in the territory described in this article for the use of said Indians. . . ." The treaty, therefore, obligated the United States to prohibit most non-Indians from residing on or passing through reservation lands used and occupied by the Tribe, and, thereby, arguably conferred upon the Tribe the authority to control fishing and hunting on those lands. But that authority could only extend to land on which the Tribe exercises "absolute and undisturbed use and occupation." And it is clear that the quantity of such land was substantially reduced by the allotment and alienation of tribal lands as a result of the passage of the General Allotment Act of 1887, and the Crow Allotment Act of 1920. If the 1868 treaty created tribal power to restrict or prohibit non-Indian hunting and fishing on the reservation, that power cannot apply to lands held in fee by non-Indians.

In *Puyallup Tribe v. Washington Game Dept.*, 433 U.S. 165 (*Puyallup III*), the relevant treaty included language virtually identical to that in the 1868 Treaty of Fort Laramie. The Puyallup Reservation was to be "set apart, and, so far as necessary, surveyed and marked out for their exclusive use . . . [and no] white man [was to] be permitted to reside upon the same without permission of the tribe. . . ." The Puyallup Tribe argued that those words amounted to a grant of authority to fish free of state interference. But this Court rejected that argument, finding, in part, that it "clashe[d] with the subsequent history of the reservation . . . ," notably two Acts of Congress under which the Puyallups alienated, in fee simple, the great majority of the lands in the reservation, including all the land abutting the Puyallup River. Thus, "[n]either the Tribe nor its members continue to hold Puyallup River fishing grounds for their 'exclusive use.'" *Puyallup III* indicates, therefore, that treaty rights with respect to reservation lands must be read in light of the subsequent alienation of those lands. Accordingly, the language of the 1868 treaty provides no support for tribal authority to regulate hunting and fishing on land owned by non-Indians.

B. Inherent sovereignty

Beyond relying on the Crow treaties and 18 U.S.C. § 1165 as source for the Tribe's power to regulate non-Indian hunting and fishing on non-Indian lands within the reservation, the Court of Appeals also identified that power as an incident of the inherent sovereignty of the Tribe over the entire Crow Reservation. But "inherent sovereignty" is not so broad as to support the application of Resolution No. 74-05 to non-Indian lands. This Court most recently reviewed the principles of inherent sovereignty in *United States v. Wheeler*, 435 U.S. 313. In that case, noting that Indian tribes are "unique aggregations possessing attributes of sovereignty over both their members and their territory," the Court upheld the power of a tribe to punish tribal members who violate tribal criminal laws. But the Court was careful to note that, through their original incorporation into the United States as well as through specific treaties and statutes, the Indian tribes have lost many of the attributes of sovereignty. The Court distinguished between those inherent powers retained by the tribes and those divested:

> "The areas in which such implicit divestiture of sovereignty has been held to have occurred are those involving *the relations between an Indian tribe and nonmembers of the tribe.* . . .
>
> "These limitations rest on the fact that the dependent status of Indian tribes within our territorial jurisdiction is necessarily inconsistent with their freedom independently *to determine their external relations.* But the powers of self-government, including the power to prescribe and enforce internal criminal laws, are of a different type. They involve *only the relations among members of a tribe.* Thus, they are not such powers as would necessarily be lost by virtue of a tribe's dependent status." (Emphasis added.)

Thus, in addition to the power to punish tribal offenders, the Indian tribes retain their inherent power to determine tribal membership, to regulate domestic relations among members, and to prescribe rules of inheritance for members. But exercise of tribal power beyond what is necessary to protect tribal self-government or to control internal relations is inconsistent with the dependent status of the tribes, and so cannot survive without express congressional delegation. Since regulation of hunting and fishing by nonmembers of a tribe on lands no longer owned by the tribe bears no clear relationship to tribal self-government or internal relations, the general principles of retained inherent sovereignty did not authorize the Crow Tribe to adopt Resolution No. 74-05.

The Court recently applied these general principles in *Oliphant v. Suquamish Indian Tribe*, 435 U.S. 191 [1978], rejecting a tribal claim of inherent sovereign authority to exercise criminal jurisdiction over non-Indians. Stressing that Indian tribes cannot exercise power inconsistent with their diminished status as sovereigns, the Court quoted Justice Johnson's words in his concurrence in *Fletcher v. Peck*, 6 Cranch 87—the first Indian case to reach this Court—that the Indian tribes have lost any "right of governing every person within their limits except themselves." Though *Oliphant* only determined inherent tribal authority in criminal matters, the principles on which it relied support the general proposition that the inherent sovereign powers of an Indian tribe do not extend to the activities of nonmembers of the tribe. To be sure, Indian tribes retain inherent sovereign power to exercise some forms of civil jurisdiction over non-Indians on their reservations, even on non-Indian fee lands. A tribe may regulate, through taxation, licensing, or other means, the activities of nonmembers who enter consensual relationships with the tribe or its members, through commercial dealing, contracts, leases, or other arrangements. A tribe may also retain inherent power to exercise civil authority over the conduct of non-Indians on fee lands within its reservation when that conduct threatens or has some direct effect on the political integrity, the economic security, or the health or welfare of the tribe.

No such circumstances, however, are involved in this case. Non-Indian hunters and fishermen on non-Indian fee land do not enter any agreements or dealings with the Crow Tribe so as to subject themselves to tribal civil jurisdiction. And nothing in this case suggests that such non-Indian hunting and fishing so threaten the Tribe's political or economic security as to justify tribal regulation. The complaint in the District Court did not allege that non-Indian hunting and fishing on fee lands imperil the subsistence or welfare of the Tribe. Furthermore, the District Court made express findings, left unaltered by the Court of Appeals, that the Crow Tribe has traditionally accommodated itself to the State's "near exclusive" regulation of hunting and fishing on fee lands within the reservation. And the District Court found that Montana's statutory and regulatory scheme does not prevent the Crow Tribe from limiting or forbidding non-Indian hunting and fishing on lands still owned by or held in trust for the Tribe or its members.

IV

For the reasons stated in this opinion, the judgment of the Court of Appeals is reversed, and the case is remanded to that court for further proceedings.

Notes

1. Treaty interpretation and abrogation. Is the Court's interpretation of the Crow treaties consistent with the canons of construction for Indian treaties? Is it consistent with the congressional definition of Indian country? Does the Court's interpretation abrogate the treaties, if only in part? If so, is the Crow Tribe entitled to compensation under the Fifth Amendment for a taking of its property rights? Consider the following:

> When tribes would benefit from being classified as property holders, the courts often classify them as sovereigns. Thus, when the courts cut back on the property rights of American Indian nations, they claim they are simply limiting the sovereign power of those nations. Given the history of the plenary power doctrine, the Supreme Court has come more and more to assume that tribal sovereignty concerns personal power over tribal members rather than geographic power over land bases on the reservations. By classifying the tribes as public entities, rather than as private property owners, the Court can cut back on tribal control over tribal land without appearing to violate the takings clause. According to the Supreme Court, when Congress took from the [tribe] the right to exclude nonmembers from its territory, it was not taking a property right but simply cutting back on tribal sovereignty. The [tribe] was not a property owner for purposes of obtaining protection from loss of its property to the state.
>
> On the other hand, when tribes would benefit from being classified as sovereigns, the courts often treat them as private associations. Thus, when the Court analyzes the extent of the sovereign power of Indian nations, it assumes that it is inappropriate for those nations to exercise sovereignty over nonmembers. The Court does this despite the fact that all states in the nation have the power to exercise sovereign authority over outsiders that come into those states. * * * Yet, according to the Supreme Court, nonmembers who own property inside the [tribe's] reservation have the right not to be regulated in most instances by the tribal government of the [Indian nation]. The [tribe] is not treated as a sovereign for the purpose of exercising power in a way that affects nonmembers.
>
> The Supreme Court has therefore given Indian nations the worst of both worlds. They are often not treated as property owners for the purpose of protection from confiscation of their property by the state, and they are often not treated as sovereigns for the purpose of governing the conduct of nonmembers inside their territory.

Joseph William Singer, *Sovereignty and Property*, 86 Nw. U. L. Rev. 1, 55–56 (1991).*

For an argument that the treaty right to undisturbed use and occupation recognizes and preserves tribes' full authority over nonmembers on trust lands, see Judith V. Royster, *Revisiting Montana: Indian Treaty Rights and Tribal Authority over Nonmembers on Trust Lands*, 57 Ariz. L. Rev. 889 (2015).

---

* Copyright 1991, Joseph William Singer. Reprinted with permission of Joseph William Singer.

2. The doctrine of implicit divestiture. The *Montana* Court relied heavily on the doctrine of implicit divestiture: that tribes are, by implication, divested of those sovereign powers not necessary to protect internal self-government. As the Court stated in *Montana*: "exercise of tribal power beyond what is necessary to protect tribal self-government or to control internal relations is inconsistent with the dependent status of the tribes, and so cannot survive without express congressional delegation."

This doctrine is traceable back to the Marshall cases. In *Cherokee Nation v. Georgia*, excerpted at page 80, Chief Justice Marshall held that the domestic dependent status of the tribes divested them of certain sovereign powers: "They and their country are considered by foreign nations, as well as by ourselves, as being so completely under the sovereignty and dominion of the United States, that any attempt to acquire their lands, or to form a political connexion with them, would be considered by all as an invasion of our territory, and an act of hostility." By implication, then, the tribes were divested of the powers to freely alienate their lands and to enter into foreign relations. Note that these are powers of dealings with the world outside the tribe's territory, not powers of regulating affairs that take place within tribal territories.

Marshall's notion that tribes lost certain sovereign powers by virtue of their dependent status remained dormant for 150 years. The doctrine was revived by Chief Justice Rehnquist in 1978, in *Oliphant v. Suquamish Indian Tribe*, 435 U.S. 191, 208 (1978), in which the Court held that tribal criminal jurisdiction over non-Indians was a power "inconsistent with their status" and therefore barred to the tribes. Two weeks later, the Court dubbed this doctrine "implicit divestiture." *See Wheeler v. United States*, 435 U.S. 313, 326 (1978). For a detailed critique of the doctrine, see John P. LaVelle, *Implicit Divestiture Reconsidered: Outtakes from the Cohen's Handbook Cutting-Room Floor*, 38 Conn. L. Rev. 731 (2006).

How has the doctrine of implicit divestiture been used or expanded in *Montana*? Is the decision in *Montana* consistent with the holding of *Worcester v. Georgia*? Which branch of government is doing the implicit divesting? Is that consistent with the Court's approach in *Williams v. Lee*?

3. Congressional override of implicit divestiture. As noted above, the Court ruled in 1978 in *Oliphant* that tribes possessed no inherent criminal jurisdiction over non-Indians. The Court subsequently decided, in *Duro v. Reina*, 495 U.S. 676 (1990), that tribes also possessed no criminal jurisdiction over Indians who were not members of the governing tribe. Congress immediately responded with an amendment to the Indian Civil Rights Act that included within the definition of powers of self-government the following language: "the inherent power of Indian tribes, hereby recognized and affirmed, to exercise criminal jurisdiction over all Indians." 25 U.S.C. § 1301(2).

In *United States v. Lara*, 541 U.S. 193 (2004), the Supreme Court upheld that statute. Billy Jo Lara, a member of the Turtle Mountain Chippewa, was prosecuted first by the federal government and then by the Spirit Lake Sioux Tribe for the same conduct. He claimed the second prosecution was barred by the double jeopardy clause of the U.S. Constitution because the tribe was exercising federally-delegated powers under § 1301(2). The Supreme Court held, however, that the federal statute was a valid recognition of inherent tribal power, noting that the political branches of the federal government may impose restrictions on tribal sovereign powers. The Court's decisions in cases such as *Oliphant* and *Duro*, and by implication *Montana* and its progeny as well, were judicial interpretations of the limits imposed by Congress and treaties. But if Congress can impose restrictions on tribes, the Court ruled, Congress may also "relax the restrictions imposed by the political branches" on inherent tribal powers. 541 U.S. at 205. Nothing in the Constitution prevents Congress from altering "judicially-made federal Indian law." *Id.* at 206. The Court's Indian law decisions, the Court determined, are common law rather than constitutional law.

4. **The infringement/preemption test.** The "infringement" test of *Williams v. Lee* did not survive intact for long. By the time of *Montana v. United States* in 1981, the Supreme Court had already articulated a different approach. In 1980, the Court declared that there were:

> two independent but related barriers to the assertion of state regulatory authority over tribal reservations and members. First, the exercise of such authority may be pre-empted by federal law. Second, it may unlawfully infringe "on the right of reservation Indians to make their own laws and be ruled by them."

White Mountain Apache Tribe v. Bracker, 448 U.S. 136, 142 (1980). Even this formulation, however, was short-lived. Within a few years, the Court had decided that there was a "trend" away from reliance on tribal sovereignty to bar state jurisdiction, and toward virtually total reliance on the notion of federal preemption. *See Rice v. Rehner*, 463 U.S. 713, 718 (1983).

5. **Indian law preemption.** After *White Mountain Apache Tribe v. Bracker*, preemption became the dominant analysis. But Indian law preemption differs in material ways from the standard preemption analysis under the Supremacy Clause of the Constitution. In *Bracker*, the Court described the Indian law preemption analysis as follows:

> When on-reservation conduct involving only Indians is at issue, state law is generally inapplicable, for the State's regulatory interest is likely to be minimal and the federal interest in encouraging tribal self-government is at its strongest. More difficult questions arise where, as here, a State asserts authority over the conduct of non-Indians engaging in activity on the reservation. In such cases we have examined the language of the relevant federal treaties and statutes in terms of both the broad policies that underlie them and the notions of sovereignty that have developed from historical traditions of tribal independence. This inquiry is not dependent on mechanical or absolute conceptions of State or tribal sovereignty, but has called for a particularized inquiry into the nature of the State, Federal, and tribal interests at stake, an inquiry designed to determine whether, in the specific context, the exercise of state authority would violate federal law.

448 U.S. at 143.

Notice that "the particularized inquiry" that the Court called for invites considerable balancing of equities. How consistent is this balancing with the foundation principle that only Congress may terminate tribal rights?

The next case, *New Mexico v. Mescalero Apache Tribe*, involves superficially similar facts to the situation in *Montana*. Once again, the tribe claimed the right to regulate non-Indian hunting and fishing on the tribe's reservation. Does the Court employ the same analysis as in *Montana*? Given the outcome in that earlier case, why does the Court find in favor of the tribe in *Mescalero Apache*?

New Mexico v. Mescalero Apache Tribe
462 U.S. 324 (1983)

Justice MARSHALL delivered the [unanimous] opinion of the Court.

We are called upon to decide in this case whether a State may restrict an Indian Tribe's regulation of hunting and fishing on its reservation. With extensive federal assistance and supervision, the Mescalero Apache Tribe has established a comprehensive scheme for managing the reservation's fish and wildlife resources. Federally approved Tribal ordinances regulate in detail the conditions under which both members of the Tribe and nonmembers may hunt and fish. New Mexico seeks to apply its own laws to hunting and fishing by nonmembers on the reservation. We hold that this application of New Mexico's hunting and fishing laws is preempted by the operation of federal law.

I

The Mescalero Apache Tribe (Tribe) resides on a reservation located within Otero County in south central New Mexico. The reservation, which represents only a small portion of the aboriginal Mescalero domain, was created by a succession of Executive Orders promulgated in the 1870s and 1880s. The present reservation comprises more than 460,000 acres, of which the Tribe owns all but 193.85 acres. Approximately 2,000 members of the Tribe reside on the reservation, along with 179 non-Indians, including resident federal employees of the Bureau of Indian Affairs and the Indian Health Service.

The Tribe is organized under the Indian Reorganization Act of 1934, which authorizes any tribe residing on a reservation to adopt a constitution and bylaws, subject to the approval of the Secretary of the Interior (Secretary). The Tribe's Constitution, which was approved by the Secretary on January 12, 1965, requires the Tribal Council

> "[t]o protect and preserve the property, wildlife and natural resources of the tribe, and to regulate the conduct of trade and the use and disposition of tribal property upon the reservation, providing that any ordinance directly

affecting non-members of the tribe shall be subject to review by the Secretary of Interior."

The Constitution further provides that the Council shall

"adopt and approve plans of operation to govern the conduct of any business or industry that will further the economic well-being of the members of the tribe, and to undertake any activity not inconsistent with Federal law or with this constitution, designed for the social or economic improvement of the Mescalero Apache people, . . . subject to review by the Secretary of the Interior."

Anticipating a decline in the sale of lumber which has been the largest income-producing activity within the reservation, the Tribe has recently committed substantial time and resources to the development of other sources of income. The Tribe has constructed a resort complex financed principally by federal funds, and has undertaken a substantial development of the reservation's hunting and fishing resources. These efforts provide employment opportunities for members of the Tribe, and the sale of hunting and fishing licenses and related services generates income which is used to maintain the Tribal government and provide services to Tribe members.

Development of the reservation's fish and wildlife resources has involved a sustained, cooperative effort by the Tribe and the Federal Government. Indeed, the reservation's fishing resources are wholly attributable to these recent efforts. Using federal funds, the Tribe has established eight artificial lakes which, together with the reservation's streams, are stocked by the Bureau of Sport Fisheries and Wildlife of the U.S. Fish and Wildlife Service, Department of the Interior, which operates a federal hatchery located on the reservation. None of the waters are stocked by the State. The United States has also contributed substantially to the creation of the reservation's game resources. Prior to 1966 there were only 13 elk in the vicinity of the reservation. In 1966 and 1967 the National Park Service donated a herd of 162 elk which was released on the reservation. Through its management and range development the Tribe has dramatically increased the elk population, which by 1977 numbered approximately 1,200. New Mexico has not contributed significantly to the development of the elk herd or the other game on the reservation, which includes antelope, bear and deer.

The Tribe and the Federal Government jointly conduct a comprehensive fish and game management program. Pursuant to its Constitution and to an agreement with the Bureau of Sport Fisheries and Wildlife, the Tribal Council adopts hunting and fishing ordinances each year. The tribal ordinances, which establish bag limits and seasons and provide for licensing of hunting and fishing, are subject to approval by the Secretary under the Tribal Constitution and have been so approved. The Tribal Council adopts the game ordinances on the basis of recommendations submitted by a Bureau of Indian Affairs range conservationist who is assisted by full-time conservation officers employed by the Tribe. The recommendations are made in light of the conservation needs of the reservation, which are determined on the basis of annual game counts and surveys. Through the Bureau of Fish and Wildlife, the Secretary also determines the stocking of the reservation's waters based upon periodic surveys of the reservation.

Numerous conflicts exist between State and tribal hunting regulations. For instance, tribal seasons and bag limits for both hunting and fishing often do not coincide with those imposed by the State. The Tribe permits a hunter to kill both a buck and a doe; the State permits only buck to be killed. Unlike the State, the Tribe permits a person to purchase an elk license in two consecutive years. Moreover, since 1977, the Tribe's ordinances have specified that State hunting and fishing licenses are not required for Indians or non-Indians who hunt or fish on the reservation. The New Mexico Department of Game and Fish has enforced the State's regulations by arresting non-Indian hunters for illegal possession of game killed on the reservation in accordance with tribal ordinances but not in accordance with State hunting regulations.

In 1977 the Tribe filed suit against the State and the Director of its Fish and Game Department in the United States District Court for the District of New Mexico, seeking to prevent the State from regulating on-reservation hunting or fishing by members or nonmembers. On August 2, 1978, the District Court ruled in favor of the Tribe and granted declaratory and injunctive relief against the enforcement of the State's hunting and fishing laws against any person for hunting and fishing activities conducted on the reservation. The United States Court of Appeals for the Tenth Circuit affirmed. Following New Mexico's petition for a writ of certiorari, this Court vacated the Tenth Circuit's judgment, and remanded the case for reconsideration in light of *Montana v. United States*, 450 U.S. 544 (1981). On remand, the Court of Appeals adhered to its earlier decision. We granted certiorari, and we now affirm.

II

New Mexico concedes that on the reservation the Tribe exercises exclusive jurisdiction over hunting and fishing by members of the Tribe and may also regulate the hunting and fishing by nonmembers. New Mexico contends, however, that it may exercise concurrent jurisdiction over nonmembers and that therefore its regulations governing hunting and fishing throughout the State should also apply to hunting and fishing by nonmembers on the reservation. Although New Mexico does not claim that it can require the Tribe to permit nonmembers to hunt and fish on the reservation, it claims that, once the Tribe chooses to permit hunting and fishing by nonmembers, such hunting and fishing is subject to any State-imposed conditions. Under this view the State would be free to impose conditions more restrictive than the Tribe's own regulations, including an outright prohibition. The question in this case is whether the State may so restrict the Tribe's exercise of its authority.

Our decision in *Montana v. United States*, does not resolve this question. Unlike this case, *Montana* concerned lands located within the reservation but not owned by the Tribe or its members. We held that the Crow Tribe could not as a general matter regulate hunting and fishing on those lands. But as to "lands belonging to the Tribe or held by the United States in trust for the Tribe," we "readily agree[d]" that a Tribe may "prohibit nonmembers from hunting or fishing . . . [or] condition their entry by charging a fee or establish bag and creel limits." We had no occasion to decide whether a Tribe may only exercise this authority in a manner permitted by a State.

A.

It is beyond doubt that the Mescalero Apache Tribe lawfully exercises substantial control over the lands and resources of its reservation, including its wildlife. As noted above, and as conceded by New Mexico, the sovereignty retained by the Tribe under the Treaty of 1852 includes its right to regulate the use of its resources by members as well as non-members. In *Montana v. United States*, we specifically recognized that tribes in general retain this authority.

Moreover, this aspect of tribal sovereignty has been expressly confirmed by numerous federal statutes. Pub. L. 280 specifically confirms the power of tribes to regulate on-reservation hunting and fishing. This authority is afforded the protection of the federal criminal law by 18 U.S.C. § 1165, which makes it a violation of federal law to enter Indian land to hunt, trap or fish without the consent of the tribe. The 1981 amendments to the Lacey Act, further accord tribal hunting and fishing regulations the force of federal law by making it a federal offense "to import, export, transport, sell, receive, acquire, or purchase any fish or wildlife . . . taken or possessed in violation of any . . . Indian tribal law."

B.

Several considerations strongly support the Court of Appeals' conclusion that the Tribe's authority to regulate hunting and fishing preempts State jurisdiction. It is important to emphasize that concurrent jurisdiction would effectively nullify the Tribe's authority to control hunting and fishing on the reservation. Concurrent jurisdiction would empower New Mexico wholly to supplant tribal regulations. The State would be able to dictate the terms on which nonmembers are permitted to utilize the reservation's resources. The Tribe would thus exercise its authority over the reservation only at the sufferance of the State. The tribal authority to regulate hunting and fishing by nonmembers, which has been repeatedly confirmed by federal treaties and laws and which we explicitly recognized in *Montana v. United States*, would have a rather hollow ring if tribal authority amounted to no more than this. Furthermore, the exercise of concurrent State jurisdiction in this case would completely "disturb and disarrange", *Warren Trading Post Co. v. Arizona Tax Comm'n*, 380 U.S. 685, 691 (1965), the comprehensive scheme of federal and tribal management established pursuant to federal law. As described above, federal law requires the Secretary to review each of the Tribe's hunting and fishing ordinances. Those ordinances are based on the recommendations made by a federal range conservationist employed by the Bureau of Indian Affairs. Moreover, the Bureau of Sport Fisheries and Wildlife stocks the reservation's waters based on its own determinations concerning the availability of fish, biological requirements, and the fishing pressure created by on-reservation fishing.

Concurrent State jurisdiction would supplant this regulatory scheme with an inconsistent dual system: members would be governed by Tribal ordinances, while nonmembers would be regulated by general State hunting and fishing laws. This could severely hinder the ability of the Tribe to conduct a sound management program. Tribal ordinances reflect the specific needs of the reservation by establishing the optimal level of hunting and fishing that should occur, not simply a maximum level that should not be exceeded. State laws in contrast are based on considerations not necessarily relevant to, and possibly hostile to, the needs of the reservation. For instance, the ordinance permitting a hunter to kill a buck and a doe was designed to curb excessive growth of the deer population on the reservation. Enforcement of the State regulation permitting only buck to be killed would frustrate that objective. Similarly, by determining the Tribal hunting seasons, bag limits, and permit availability, the Tribe regulates the duration and intensity of hunting. These determinations take into account numerous factors, including the game capacity of the terrain, the range utilization of the game animals, and the availability of tribal personnel to monitor the hunts. Permitting the State to enforce different restrictions simply because they have been determined to be appropriate for the State as a whole would impose on the Tribe the possibly insurmountable task of ensuring that the patchwork application of State and Tribal regulations remains consistent with sound management of the reservation's resources.

Federal law commits to the Secretary and the Tribal Council the responsibility to manage the reservation's resources. It is most unlikely that Congress would have authorized, and the Secretary would have established, financed, and participated in Tribal management if it were thought that New Mexico was free to nullify the entire arrangement. Requiring Tribal ordinances to yield whenever State law is more restrictive would seriously "undermine the Secretary's [and the Tribe's] ability to make the wide range of determinations committed to [their] authority."

The assertion of concurrent jurisdiction by New Mexico not only would threaten to disrupt the federal and tribal regulatory scheme, but would also threaten Congress' overriding objective of encouraging tribal self-government and economic development. The Tribe has engaged in a concerted and sustained undertaking to develop and manage the reservation's wildlife and land resources specifically for the benefit of its members. The project generates funds for essential tribal services and provides employment for members who reside on the reservation. This case is thus far removed from those situations, such as on-reservation sales outlets which market to nonmembers goods not manufactured by the tribe or its members, in which the tribal contribution to an enterprise is de minimis. The Tribal enterprise in this case clearly involves "value generated on the reservation by activities involving the Trib[e]." The disruptive effect that would result from the assertion of concurrent jurisdiction by New Mexico would plainly "stan[d] as an obstacle to the accomplishment of the full purposes and objectives of Congress".

C.

The State has failed to "identify any regulatory function or service . . . that would justify" the assertion of concurrent regulatory authority. The hunting and fishing permitted by the Tribe occur entirely on the reservation. The fish and wildlife resources are either native to the reservation or were created by the joint efforts of the Tribe and the Federal Government. New Mexico does not contribute in any significant respect to the maintenance of these resources, and can point to no other "governmental functions it provides" in connection with hunting and fishing on the reservation by nonmembers that would justify the assertion of its authority.

The State also cannot point to any off-reservation effects that warrant State intervention. Some species of game never leave tribal lands, and the State points to no specific interest concerning those that occasionally do. Unlike *Puyallup Tribe v. Washington Game Dept.*, this is not a case in which a Treaty expressly subjects a tribe's hunting and fishing rights to the common rights of nonmembers and in which a State's interest in conserving a scarce, common supply justifies State intervention. The State concedes that the Tribe's management has not had an adverse impact on fish and wildlife outside the reservation.

We recognize that New Mexico may be deprived of the sale of state licenses to nonmembers who hunt and fish on the reservation, as well as some federal matching funds calculated in part on the basis of the number of State licenses sold. However, any financial interest the State might have in this case is simply insufficient to justify the assertion of concurrent jurisdiction. The loss of revenues to the State is likely to be insubstantial given the small numbers of persons who purchase tribal hunting licenses. Moreover, unlike *Confederated Tribes* [*Washington v. Confederated Tribes of the Colville Indian Reservation*, 447 U.S. 134 (1980)], and *Moe* [*v. Salish & Kootenai Tribes*, 425 U.S. 463 (1976)] [cases involving taxation of on-reservation cigarette sales, in which the Court upheld the right of the states to tax sales to nonmembers because the cigarettes were not value generated on the reservation], the activity involved here concerns value generated on the reservation by the tribe. Finally, as already noted, the State has pointed to no services it has performed in connection with hunting and fishing by nonmembers which justify imposing a tax in the form of a hunting and fishing license, and its general desire to obtain revenues is simply inadequate to justify the assertion of concurrent jurisdiction in this case.

IV.

In this case the governing body of an Indian Tribe, working closely with the Federal Government and under the authority of federal law, has exercised its lawful authority to develop and manage the reservation's resources for the benefit of its members. The exercise of concurrent jurisdiction by the State would effectively nullify the Tribe's unquestioned authority to regulate the use of its resources by members and nonmembers, interfere with the comprehensive tribal regulatory scheme, and threaten Congress' firm commitment to the encouragement of tribal self-sufficiency and economic development. Given the strong interests favoring exclusive tribal jurisdiction and the absence of State interests which justify the assertion of concurrent authority, we conclude that the application of the State's hunting and fishing laws to the reservation is preempted.

Accordingly, the judgment of the Court of Appeals is AFFIRMED.

Notes

1. *Mescalero Apache* versus *Montana*. Contrast the facts of *Mescalero Apache* and *Montana*. Consider the demographics of the two reservations, the efforts of the tribes versus the efforts of the states with respect to managing wildlife habitat, and the aim of the tribal regulations in terms of excluding non-members.

Note that in *Mescalero Apache*, Justice Marshall emphasized that "[t]he Tribal enterprise in this case clearly involves 'value generated on the reservation by activities involving the Trib[e].'" What did he mean? See *Washington v. Confederated Tribes of the Colville Indian Reservation*, 447 U.S. 134 (1980), where the Court discussed the "value generated" concept in the context of smokeshop sales of tobacco products to non-Indians:

> While the Tribes do have an interest in raising revenues for essential governmental programs, that interest is strongest when the revenues are derived from value generated on the reservation by activities involving the Tribes and when the taxpayer is the recipient of tribal services. The State also has a legitimate governmental interest in raising revenues, and that interest is likewise strongest when the tax is directed at off-reservation value and when the taxpayer is the recipient of state services.

With respect to cigarette sales to non-Indians, the Court concluded: "It is painfully apparent that the value marketed by the smokeshops to persons coming from outside is not generated on the reservation by activities in which the Tribes have a significant interest."

2. Preemption of state regulation. Justice Marshall concluded that the state regulations are preempted. What laws or actions preempted the state?

For an example of the preemption analysis in the lower courts, see *Shivwits Band of Paiute Indians v. Utah*, 428 F.3d 966 (10th Cir. 2005). In that case, Utah claimed the right to regulate billboards erected by a non-Indian company on leased parcels of trust land along a highway. The state asserted the right under both the federal Highway Beautification Act (HBA) and its own police power. The court concluded that even if the HBA applied to trust lands, it was unenforceable by the state against trust property. In addition, the court held that Utah's police power was preempted. The court found strong federal and tribal interests, as shown by the trust status of the land, the lack of any significant environmental impact from the billboards, a federal regulation providing that state land use laws are not applicable to trust lands (*see* 25 C.F.R. § 1.4), and the economic importance of the billboard lease to the tribe. By contrast, the court determined that the state's interests in regulating were not substantial: there was no indication that the state would face federal penalties under the HBA; the "visual pollution" argument was undercut by significant development of the area in question; and the tribe was not merely marketing an exemption from state law.

3. Cooperative management agreements. One alternative to conflicts over regulations of resources is the use of cooperative management agreements between tribes and states, tribes and the federal government, or all three sovereigns. *See, e.g.,*

Intergovernmental Accord Between the Federally Recognized Indian Tribes in Michigan and the Governor of the State of Michigan Concerning Protection of Shared Water Resources (May 12, 2004) (www.michigan.go/documents/Accord_91058_7.pdf). Increasingly tribes are using cooperative agreements to gain some measure of regulatory authority over lands they ceded long ago to the federal government which are still in federal hands. For examples, there are cooperative agreements between the federal government and Northern California tribes concerning sacred sites on public lands; the Nez Perce Tribe and the federal government concerning wolf reintroduction in Idaho; and the Klamath Tribes and the federal government giving the tribes a voice in the management of 1.2 million acres of national forest lands on what was the former Klamath Reservation in south-central Oregon. For a survey of some agreements, see Debra L. Donahue, *Education and Cooperative Management of Tribal Natural Resources*, 42 Tulsa L. Rev. 5 (2006).

4. *Montana* **in the tribal and federal courts.** Post-*Montana* cases on the tribal right to regulate non-Indian conduct in Indian country concentrated on the second exception: the "direct effects" test. Tribes were, virtually without exception, able to convince lower federal courts and tribal courts that a range of non-Indian conduct on fee lands would have sufficient direct effects on tribal sovereignty to justify tribal regulation. *See Cardin v. De La Cruz*, 671 F.2d 363 (9th Cir. 1982) (tribal building, health and safety codes); *Confederated Salish and Kootenai Tribes v. Namen*, 665 F.2d 951 (9th Cir. 1982) (tribal regulation of rights to use riparian land); *Lummi Indian Tribe v. Hallauer*, 9 Indian L. Rep. 3025 (W.D. Wash. 1982) (tribal sewer hook-up requirements). In particular, courts were amenable to claims that zoning of fee lands was within inherent tribal sovereign authority. *See Knight v. Shoshone & Arapaho Indian Tribes*, 670 F.2d 900 (10th Cir. 1982); *Governing Council of Pinoleville Indian Community v. Mendocino County*, 684 F. Supp. 1042 (N.D. Cal. 1988); *Colville Confederated Tribes v. Cavenham Forest Industries*, 14 Indian L. Rep. 6043 (Colv. Tr. Ct. 1987). The direct effects exception seemed to swallow the "general proposition" that tribes were divested of sovereign authority over non-Indian fee lands.

5. **The *Brendale* decision(s).** Despite the expansive reading given the *Montana* exceptions by tribal and lower federal courts, the Supreme Court was not willing to follow their lead. When the issue of regulatory authority over the use of land within Indian country returned to the Supreme Court in *Brendale* in 1989, excerpted below, the Court was not able to produce a majority opinion. Instead, the Court split 4–2–3, with the two-justice opinion providing the swing votes in the split decision. Each of the three opinions takes a different approach to the *Montana* "direct effects" test. Note what those differences are, and how they lead the justices to differing conclusions.

Brendale v. Confederated Tribes and Bands of the Yakima Indian Nation
492 U.S. 408 (1989)

[Justice White delivered the judgment of the Court concerning Wilkinson's property in the "open" area and dissented concerning Brendale's property in the "closed" area; he was joined by the Chief Justice and Justices Scalia and Kennedy. Justice Stevens delivered the judgment of the Court concerning Brendale's property and concurred as to Wilkinson's property; he was joined by Justice O'Connor. Justice Blackmun concurred in the judgment of the Court as to Brendale's property and dissented as to Wilkinson's property; he was joined by Justices Brennan and Marshall.]

[Justice White's opinion follows:]

The issue presented by these three consolidated cases is whether the Yakima Indian Nation or the County of Yakima, a governmental unit of the State of Washington, has the authority to zone fee lands owned by nonmembers of the Tribe located within the boundaries of the Yakima Reservation.

I. A.

The Reservation is located in the southeastern part of the State of Washington. Approximately 1.3 million acres of land are located within its boundaries. Of that land, roughly 80% is held in trust by the United States for the benefit of the Yakima Nation or individual members of the Tribe. The remaining 20% of the land is owned in fee by Indian or non-Indian owners. Most of the fee land is found in Toppenish, Wapato, and Harrah, the three incorporated towns located in the northeastern part of the Reservation. The remaining fee land is scattered throughout the Reservation in a "checkerboard" pattern.

The parties to this litigation, as well as the District Court and the Court of Appeals, have treated the Yakima Reservation as divided into two parts: a "closed area" and an "open area." The closed area consists of the western two-thirds of the Reservation and is predominantly forest land. Of the approximately 807,000 acres of land in the closed area, 740,000 acres are located in Yakima County. Twenty-five thousand acres of the seven hundred and forty thousand acres are fee land. The closed area is so-named because it has been closed to the general public at least since 1972 when the Bureau of Indian Affairs restricted the use of federally maintained roads in the area to members of the Yakima Nation and to its permittees, who must be record land owners or associated with the Tribe. Access to the open area, as its name suggests, is not likewise restricted to the general public. The open area is primarily rangeland, agricultural land, and land used for residential and commercial development. Almost half of the land in the open area is fee land.

B.

The Yakima Nation adopted its first zoning ordinance in 1970. The ordinance was amended to its present form in 1972. By its terms, the Yakima Nation ordinance applies to all lands within the Reservation boundaries, including fee lands owned by Indians or non-Indians. Yakima County adopted its present comprehensive zoning ordinance in 1972, although the county had regulated land use as early as 1946. The county ordinance applies to all real property within county boundaries, except for Indian trust lands. The ordinance establishes a number of use districts, which generally govern agricultural, residential, commercial, industrial, and forest-watershed uses. The particular zoning designations at issue are "forest watershed" and "general rural."

The fee lands located in the closed area are zoned by the county ordinance as forest watershed. That designation permits development of single family dwellings, commercial camp grounds, small overnight lodging facilities, restaurants, bars, general stores and souvenir shops, service stations, marinas, and saw mills. The minimum lot size is one-half acre. None of these uses would be permitted by the zoning designation "reservation restricted area," which applies to the closed area under the Yakima Nation zoning ordinance.

The general rural zoning designation, applicable to land in the open area, is one of three use districts governing agricultural properties. The minimum lot size for land zoned general rural is smaller than that specified for agricultural land in the Yakima Nation ordinance, although the other county use districts for agricultural properties have larger minimum lot sizes than the Yakima Nation ordinance.

C.

Petitioner Philip Brendale, who is part-Indian but not a member of the Yakima Nation, owns [in fee] a 160-acre tract of land near the center of the forested portion of the closed area. * * * The land is zoned as reservation restricted area by the Yakima Nation. It is zoned forest watershed by Yakima County. [Brendale proposed to develop a 20-acre parcel into ten 2-acre lots for summer cabins.] The proposed development would not have been permissible under the Yakima Nation ordinance.

Petitioner Stanley Wilkinson, a non-Indian and a nonmember of the Yakima Nation, owns [in fee] a 40-acre tract of land in the open area of the Reservation. * * * It is zoned agricultural by the Yakima Nation and general rural by Yakima County. [Wilkinson sought to subdivide 32 acres of his land into 20 lots, ranging in size from 1.1 acres to 4.5 acres, each to be used for single family homes.] The proposed development would not have been permissible under the Yakima Nation ordinance.

[In both cases, the planning department approved the developments and the Yakima Nation appealed to the County Board of Commissioners on the ground that the county lacked authority to zone the lands. In both cases, the Board concluded that the appeal was properly before it. In the Brendale case, the Board determined that an environmental impact statement was necessary.]

II

The present actions were brought by the Yakima Nation to require development occurring on property within the boundaries of its Reservation to proceed in accordance with the Yakima Nation zoning ordinance. The Tribe is necessarily contending that it has the exclusive authority to zone all of the property within the Reservation, including the projects at issue here. We therefore examine whether the Yakima Nation has the authority, derived either from its treaty with the United States or from its status as an independent sovereign, to zone the fee lands owned by Brendale and Wilkinson.

A.

[The Yakima Nation argued that its treaty right to the "exclusive use and benefit" of the reservation encompassed the right to exclude and therefore the authority over the lands at issue. Justice White, however, applied the reasoning of *Montana* that allotment had stripped the tribe of the exclusive use and benefit of lands now alienated to non-Indians. "We would follow *Montana* and conclude that, for the reasons stated there, any regulatory power the Tribe might have under the treaty "cannot apply to lands held in fee by non-Indians."]

B.

An Indian tribe's treaty power to exclude nonmembers of the tribe from its lands is not the only source of Indian regulatory authority. In *Merrion v. Jicarilla Apache Tribe*, 455 U.S. 130, 141 (1982), the Court held that tribes have inherent sovereignty independent of that authority arising from their power to exclude. * * * Thus, an Indian tribe generally retains sovereignty by way of tribal self-government and control over other aspects of its internal affairs.

A tribe's inherent sovereignty, however, is divested to the extent it is inconsistent with the tribe's dependent status, that is, to the extent it involves a tribe's "external relations." Those cases in which the Court has found a tribe's sovereignty divested generally are those "involving the relations between an Indian tribe and nonmembers of the tribe." For example, Indian tribes cannot freely alienate their lands to non-Indians, cannot enter directly into commercial or governmental relations with foreign nations, and cannot exercise criminal jurisdiction over non-Indians in tribal courts.

Therefore under the general principle enunciated in *Montana*, the Yakima Nation has no authority to impose its zoning ordinance on the fee owned lands by petitioners Brendale and Wilkinson.

C.

Our inquiry does not end here because the opinion in *Montana* noted two "exceptions" to its general principle. First, "[a] tribe may regulate, through taxation, licensing, or other means, the activities of nonmembers who enter consensual relationships with the tribe or its members, through commercial dealing, contracts, leases, or other arrangements." Second, "[a] tribe may also retain inherent power to exercise civil authority over the conduct of non-Indians on fee lands within its reservation when that conduct threatens or has some direct effect on the political integrity, the economic security, or the health or welfare of the tribe."

The parties agree that the first *Montana* exception does not apply in this case. Brendale and Wilkinson do not have a "consensual relationship" with the Yakima Nation simply by virtue of their status as landowners within reservation boundaries, as *Montana* itself necessarily decided. The Yakima Nation instead contends that the Tribe has authority to zone under the second *Montana* exception. We disagree.

* * * The governing principle is that the tribe has no authority itself, by way of tribal ordinance or actions in the tribal courts, to regulate the use of fee land. The

inquiry thus becomes whether and to what extent the tribe has a protectable interest in what activities are taking place on fee land within the reservation and, if it has such an interest, how it may be protected. * * * *Montana* suggests that in the special circumstances of checkerboard ownership of lands within a reservation, the tribe has an interest under federal law, defined in terms of the impact of the challenged uses on the political integrity, economic security, or the health or welfare of the tribe. But, as we have indicated above, that interest does not entitle the tribe to complain or obtain relief against every use of fee land that has some adverse effect on the tribe. The impact must be demonstrably serious and must imperil the political integrity, economic security or the health and welfare of the tribe. This standard will sufficiently protect Indian tribes while at the same time avoiding undue interference with state sovereignty and providing the certainty needed by property owners.

* * * The Tribe in this case, as it should have, first appeared in the county zoning proceedings, but its submission should have been, not that the county was without zoning authority over fee land within the Reservation, but that its tribal interests were imperiled.

[Justice Stevens' opinion follows:]

The United States has granted to many Indian tribes, including the Yakima Nation—"a power unknown to any other sovereignty in this Nation: a power to exclude nonmembers entirely from territory reserved for the tribe." *Merrion v. Jicarilla Apache Tribe*, 455 U.S. 130, 160 (1982) (STEVENS, J., dissenting). That power necessarily must include the lesser power to regulate land use in the interest of protecting the tribal community. Thus, the proper resolution of these cases depends on the extent to which the Tribe's virtually absolute power to exclude has been either diminished by federal statute or voluntarily surrendered by the Tribe itself.

I

Zoning is the process whereby a community defines its essential character. Whether driven by a concern for health and safety, esthetics, or other public values, zoning provides the mechanism by which the polity ensures that neighboring uses of land are not mutually—or more often unilaterally—destructive.

An Indian tribe's power to exclude nonmembers from a defined geographical area obviously includes the lesser power to define the character of that area. * * * It is difficult to imagine a power that follows more forcefully from the power to exclude than the power to require that nonmembers, as a condition of entry, not disturb the traditional character of the reserved area.

At one time, the Yakima Nation's power to exclude nonmembers from its reservation was near-absolute. This power derived from two sources: The Tribe's aboriginal sovereignty over vast reaches of land in the Pacific Northwest and the express provisions of its 1855 treaty with the United States. Even in the absence of a treaty provision expressly granting such authority, Indian tribes maintain the sovereign power of exclusion unless otherwise curtailed.

The Dawes Act did not itself transfer any regulatory power from the Tribe to any state or local governmental authority. Nonetheless, by providing for the allotment and ultimate alienation of reservation land, the Act in some respect diminished tribal authority.

* * * [A]s early as 1954 the Tribe had divided its Reservation into two parts, which the parties and the District Court consistently described as the "closed area" and the "open area," and that it continues to maintain the closed area as a separate community. That division, which was made many years before either petitioner Brendale or petitioner Wilkinson acquired title to reservation land, is of critical importance and requires a different disposition of their respective cases.

II

Petitioner Brendale's property is located in the heart of this closed portion of the Reservation.

Although the logging operations, the construction of BIA roads, and the transfer of ownership of a relatively insignificant amount of land in the closed area unquestionably has diminished the Tribe's power to exclude non-Indians from that portion of its reservation, this does not justify the conclusion that the Tribe has surrendered its historic right to regulate land use in the restricted portion of the Reservation. By maintaining the power to exclude nonmembers from entering all but a small portion of the closed area, the Tribe has preserved the power to define the essential character of that area. In fact, the Tribe has exercised this power, taking care that the closed area remains an undeveloped refuge of cultural and religious significance, a place where tribal members "may camp, hunt, fish, and gather roots and berries in the tradition of their culture."

The question is then whether the Tribe has authority to prevent the few individuals who own portions of the closed area in fee from undermining its general plan to preserve the character of this unique resource by developing their isolated parcels without regard to an otherwise common scheme. More simply, the question is whether the owners of the small amount of fee land may bring a pig into the parlor. In my opinion, just as Congress could not possibly have intended in enacting the Dawes Act [i.e., General Allotment Act] that tribes would maintain the power to exclude bona fide purchasers of reservation land from that property, it could not have intended that tribes would lose control over the character of their reservations upon the sale of a few, relatively small parcels of land.

I therefore agree with Justice Blackmun that the Tribe may zone the Brendale property.

III

The authority of the Tribe to enact and enforce zoning ordinances applicable in the open area—where petitioner Wilkinson's property is located—requires a different analysis. Although the Tribe originally had the power to exclude non-Indians from the entire Reservation, the "subsequent alienation" of about half of the property in the open area has produced an integrated community that is not economically or culturally delimited by reservation boundaries. Because the Tribe no longer has the power to exclude nonmembers from a large portion of this area, it also lacks the power to define the essential character of the territory. As a result, the Tribe's interest in preventing inconsistent uses is dramatically curtailed. For this reason, I agree with Justice White that the Tribe lacks authority to regulate the use of Wilkinson's property. So long as the land is not used in a manner that is pre-empted by federal law, the Tribe has no special claim to relief. It, of course, retains authority to regulate the use of trust land, and the county does not contend otherwise.

Unlike the closed area, the Tribe makes no attempt to control access to the open area. [The county maintains roads in the open area. Yakima members comprise less than 20 percent of the population, and the open area is not of particular religious or spiritual significance to the Yakima Nation. Almost half the land in the open area is owned in fee. The majority of fee land is located in the three towns. The remainder is about 143,000 acres of farmland. Of this, 63,179 acres are owned by non-members; 67,466 acres are owned by the Yakima Nation or its members, but leased to non-Indians; and only 12,355 acres are farmed by tribal members.]

Given that a large percentage of the land in the open area is owned in fee by nonmembers—and that an additional portion is leased to nonmembers—even if the Tribe had exercised its power to exclude nonmembers from trust land, it would have been unable thereby to establish the essential character of the region. In such circumstances, allowing a nonmember to use his or her land in a manner that might not be approved by the Tribal Council does not upset an otherwise coherent scheme of land use. * * * Moreover, it is unlikely that Congress intended to give the Tribe the power to determine the character of an area that is predominantly owned and populated by nonmembers, who represent 80 percent of the population yet lack a voice in tribal governance. I therefore agree with Justice White's conclusion that the Tribe lacks authority to zone the Wilkinson property.

[Justice Blackmun's opinion follows:]

The Court's combined judgment in these consolidated cases—splitting tribal zoning authority over non-Indian fee lands between the so-called "open" and "closed" areas of the Yakima Indian Reservation—is Solomonic in appearance only. This compromise result arises from two distinct approaches to tribal sovereignty, each of which is inconsistent with this Court's past decisions and undermines the Federal Government's longstanding commitment to the promotion of tribal autonomy. Because the Court's judgment that the tribe does not have zoning authority over non-Indian fee lands in the "open" area of its reservation is wrong, in my view, as a matter of law and fashions a patently unworkable legal rule, I dissent in [Wilkinson's case]. Because Justice Stevens' opinion reaches the right result for the wrong reason with respect to the Tribe's authority to zone non-Indian fee lands in the closed portion of the Reservation, I concur in the judgment in [Brendale's case].

I. A.

It would be difficult to conceive of a power more central to "the economic security, or the health or welfare of the tribe," than the power to zone. * * * This fundamental sovereign power of local governments to control land use is especially vital to Indians, who enjoy a unique historical and cultural connection to the land. * * * I am hard pressed to find any reason why zoning authority, a critical aspect of self-government and the ultimate instrument of "territorial management," should not be deemed to lie within the inherent sovereignty of the tribes as well. Thus, if *Montana* is to fit at all within this Court's Indian sovereignty jurisprudence, zoning authority—even over fee lands—must fall within the scope of tribal jurisdiction under *Montana*.

* * * *Montana*'s literal language does not require, as [Justice White] claims, a parcel-by-parcel, use-by-use determination whether a proposed use of fee land will threaten the political integrity, economic security, or health or welfare of the tribe. The threat to the tribe does not derive solely from the proposed uses of specific parcels of fee lands (which admittedly would vary over time and place). The threat stems from the loss of the general and longer-term advantages of comprehensive land management.

What the majority offers the tribes falls far short of meeting their legitimate needs. * * * [T]he opportunity to engage in protracted litigation over every proposed land use that conflicts with tribal interests does nothing to recognize the tribe's legitimate sovereign right to regulate the lands within its reservation, with the view to the long-term, active management of land use that is the very difference between zoning and case-by-case nuisance litigation.

B

While Justice White's opinion misreads the Court's decisions defining the limits of inherent tribal sovereignty, Justice Stevens' opinion disregards those decisions altogether.

On a practical level, Justice Stevens' approach to zoning authority poses even greater difficulties than Justice White's approach. Justice Stevens' opinion not only would establish a self-defeating regime of "checkerboard" zoning authority in "open" areas of every reservation, but it would require an intrinsically standardless threshold determination as to when a section of a reservation contains sufficient non-Indian land holdings to warrant an "open" classification. Justice Stevens' opinion suggests no benchmark for making this determination, and I can imagine none.

Moreover, to the extent that Justice Stevens' opinion discusses the characteristics of a reservation area where the Tribe possesses authority to zone because it has preserved the "essential character of the reservation," these characteristics betray a stereotyped and almost patronizing view of Indians and reservation life. * * * In my view, even under Justice Stevens' analysis, it must not be the case that tribes can retain the "essential character" of their reservations (necessary to the exercise of zoning authority), only if they forgo economic development and maintain those reservations according to a single, perhaps quaint, view of what is characteristically "Indian" today.

Notes

1. **The fractured Supreme Court.** The badly fractured *Brendale* Court consisted of a plurality opinion in which four justices suggested that tribal zoning authority was a function of tribal or member land ownership, a three-justice dissent which clung to the view that tribal zoning authority generally extended throughout the reservation, regardless of land ownership, and Justice Stevens' opinion which decided the outcome for both the Brendale and Wilkinson tracts. Justice Stevens' "factual approach" calls for case by case decision making by courts in order to account for, in Chief Justice John Marshall's words, "the actual state of things." This balancing enabled Justice Stevens to conceptually split the Yakima (now Yakama) Reservation into open and closed sections. Is this judicial line-drawing the rough equivalent of saying that part of the Yakama Reservation resembles the Crow Reservation in the *Montana* case, and part resembles the Mescalero Apache Reservation in the case of the same name?

2. **The open-versus-closed distinction.** In its more recent cases, the Court appears to have repudiated, or at least severely limited, the open/closed distinction that controlled the outcome in *Brendale*. In *Atkinson Trading Co., Inc. v. Shirley*, 532 U.S. 645 (2001), excerpted at page 435, the Court stated:

> Respondents extrapolate from [*Brendale*'s] holding that Indian tribes enjoy broad authority over nonmembers wherever the acreage of non-Indian fee land is minuscule in relation to the surrounding tribal land. But we think it plain that the judgment in *Brendale* turned on both the closed nature of the non-Indian fee land and the fact that its development would place the entire area "in jeopardy." Irrespective of the percentage of non-Indian fee land within a reservation, *Montana*'s second exception grants Indian tribes nothing "'beyond what is necessary to protect tribal self-government or to control internal relations.'"

3. **Justice Stevens' subjectivism.** According to the late Professor Getches, "[m]ore than any other member of the Court, Stevens employed a subjectivist approach to tribal jurisdiction questions ... He has no allegiance to the foundational principles ... [but instead employs] an *ad hoc* judicial weighing of demographic facts to design an Indian policy." David H. Getches, *Conquering the Cultural Frontier: The New Subjectivism of the Supreme Court in Indian Law*, 84 Cal. L. Rev. 1573, 1635–36 (1996). Under the new subjectivism, the Court sees tribal sovereignty as a product of an equitable balancing of changing social, political, and economic conditions and of non-Indian expectations.

4. **On-reservation fee lands owned by tribal members.** The Ninth Circuit limited *Brendale* by ruling that a county does not have land use authority over land owed in

fee by tribal members within reservation boundaries. *Gobin v. Snohomish County*, 304 F.3d 909 (9th Cir. 2002). The court held that federal statutes removing restrictions on alienation of lands allotted to tribal members did not amount to an "unmistakably clear" reflection of congressional intent to authorize county land use regulations. The court also ruled that allowing concurrent county regulation would interfere with tribal self-determination.

3. The Court's subsequent *Montana*-test decisions. In the years following *Brendale*, the Court has heard a number of cases in which it has applied the *Montana* direct effects test. As in *Brendale* and *Montana*, these decisions focus on two factors: the status of the land on which the non-member conduct occurs, and the type of non-member conduct that might rise to the level of sufficient effects to justify tribal regulation. Pay careful attention to how the Court addresses these two factors in each of the cases that follow.

South Dakota v. Bourland
508 U.S. 679 (1993)

[Four years after *Brendale*, the Court considered whether the Cheyenne River Sioux Tribe could regulate non-Indian hunting and fishing on lands within the reservation that had been purchased by the United States for the Oahe Dam and Reservoir project pursuant to the Flood Control Act of 1944 and the Cheyenne River Act of 1954. The Fort Laramie Treaty of 1868 had guaranteed the Sioux Nation the "absolute and undisturbed use and occupation" of the reservation lands, but the Court, in an opinion by Justice Thomas, held as follows:]

Montana and *Brendale* establish that when an Indian tribe conveys ownership of its tribal lands to non-Indians, it loses any former right of absolute and exclusive use and occupation of the conveyed lands. The abrogation of this greater right, at least in the context of the type of area at issue in this case, implies the loss of regulatory jurisdiction over the use of the land by others. In taking tribal trust lands and other reservation lands for the Oahe Dam and Reservoir Project, and broadly opening up those lands for public use, Congress, through the Flood Control and Cheyenne River Acts eliminated the Tribe's power to exclude non-Indians from these lands, and with that the incidental regulatory jurisdiction formerly enjoyed by the Tribe.

The Court of Appeals found *Montana* inapposite with respect to the 104,420 acres of former trust lands because "the purpose of the [Cheyenne River] Act, unlike that of the Allotment Act at issue in Montana, was not the destruction of tribal self-government, but was only to acquire the property rights necessary to construct and operate the Oahe Dam and Reservoir." To focus on purpose is to misread *Montana*. In *Montana* the Court did refer to the purpose of the Allotment Acts and discussed the legislative debates surrounding the allotment policy, as well as Congress' eventual repudiation of the policy in 1934 by the Indian Reorganization Act. However, at the end of this discussion the Court unequivocally stated that "what is relevant . . .

is the *effect of the land alienation occasioned by that policy on Indian treaty rights tied to Indian use and occupation of reservation land.*" (emphasis added) Thus, regardless of whether land is conveyed pursuant to an Act of Congress for homesteading or for flood control purposes, when Congress has broadly opened up such land to non-Indians, the effect of the transfer is the destruction of pre-existing Indian rights to regulatory control. Although *Montana* involved lands conveyed in fee to non-Indians within the Crow Reservation, *Montana*'s framework for examining the "effect of the land alienation" is applicable to the federal takings in this case.

Notes

1. The congressional purpose. Justice Blackmun, joined by Justice Souter, dissented in *Bourland*, arguing that the purpose for which the lands were purchased was crucial. The dissenters noted that Congress's purpose in acquiring the Cheyenne River Sioux lands was "simply to build a dam," and asserted that continued tribal authority over non-Indian hunting and fishing on the lands was fully consistent with that congressional purpose. Why isn't congressional purpose relevant, according to Justice Thomas? What is determinative?

2. Non-Indian equities. Arguably, in *Montana*, the Supreme Court was upholding the authority of the state to continue to regulate fish and game harvests, as it had been doing for some time. In *Brendale*, arguably the Court was protecting the expectations of non-Indian landowners on reservations. What interest was the Court vindicating in *Bourland*? Federal recreational licensees? Should their interest outweigh those to whom the federal government owes a trust obligation?

3. The Eighth Circuit decision on remand. The *Bourland* Court expressly left for remand the issue whether the Tribe retained its inherent powers to regulate on the taken area under the *Montana* exceptions. On remand, the Eighth Circuit found that non-Indian hunting did not amount to a direct effect on tribal interests. *South Dakota v. Bourland*, 39 F.3d 868 (8th Cir. 1994).

> The Tribe contends that the record supports a finding that the Tribe is directly affected or threatened by the conduct of non-Indian hunters and fishermen. It is true that the court found that non-Indians "may have harassed cattle grazing on the taken area or on tribal lands, failed to close pasture gates, or let down wires on fences." The court also found that non-Indian deer hunting "on the taken area and the nonmember fee lands does reduce the amount of deer available to tribal members," but "does not decrease subsistence hunting by members as few deer are harvested by members for subsistence purposes." These incidents undeniably are vexatious to the individual Indians affected, but we think it is plain that they do not amount to a direct effect on the political integrity, the economic security, or the health or welfare of the Tribe as a whole, and we are satisfied the District Court did not err in finding that they do not threaten these tribal concerns such that tribal regulatory authority over non-Indians attaches under the second *Montana* exception.

The court noted that if non-Indian conduct in the future "escalate[s] in severity" to the point where it has a direct effect on tribal interests, the Tribe may seek relief in district court.

After this decision, what might be sufficient for a direct effect on the tribal interests listed in *Montana*? Does the next case shed any light on that issue?

Strate v. A-1 Contractors
520 U.S. 438 (1997)

[This case involved a tort action arising out of an accident on a state highway running through a reservation. Both the plaintiff and the defendants were nonmembers. The plaintiff brought suit in tribal court, and the defendants contested the court's subject matter jurisdiction. The Supreme Court first held that an Indian tribe's judicial jurisdiction (its subject matter jurisdiction to hear a lawsuit) "does not exceed" its regulatory or legislative jurisdiction. 520 U.S. at 453. Consequently, tribal court jurisdiction over nonmember defendants would be judged by the same standards as tribal regulatory jurisdiction.]

We consider next the argument that *Montana* does not govern this case because the land underlying the scene of the accident is held in trust for the Three Affiliated Tribes and their members. Petitioners and the United States point out that in *Montana*, as in later cases following *Montana*'s instruction[,] the challenged tribal authority related to nonmember activity on alienated, non-Indian reservation land. We "can readily agree," in accord with *Montana*, that tribes retain considerable control over nonmember conduct on tribal land. On the particular matter before us, however, we agree with respondents: The right-of-way North Dakota acquired for the State's highway renders the 6.59-mile stretch equivalent, for nonmember governance purposes, to alienated, non-Indian land.

Forming part of the State's highway, the right-of-way is open to the public, and traffic on it is subject to the State's control. The Tribes have consented to, and received payment for, the State's use of the 6.59-mile stretch for a public highway. They have retained no gatekeeping right. So long as the stretch is maintained as part of the State's highway, the Tribes cannot assert a landowner's right to occupy and exclude. We therefore align the right-of-way, for the purpose at hand, with land alienated to non-Indians. Our decision in *Montana*, accordingly, governs this case.

The second exception to *Montana*'s general rule concerns conduct that "threatens or has some direct effect on the political integrity, the economic security, or the health or welfare of the tribe." Undoubtedly, those who drive carelessly on a public highway running through a reservation endanger all in the vicinity, and surely jeopardize the safety of tribal members. But if *Montana*'s second exception requires no more, the exception would severely shrink the rule.

Read in isolation, the *Montana* rule's second exception can be misperceived. Key to its proper application, however, is the Court's preface: "Indian tribes retain their inherent power [to punish tribal offenders,] to determine tribal membership, to regulate domestic relations among members, and to prescribe rules of inheritance for members. . . . But [a tribe's inherent power does not reach] beyond what is necessary to protect tribal self-government or to control internal relations." Neither regulatory nor adjudicatory authority over the state highway accident at issue is needed to preserve "the right of reservation Indians to make their own laws and be ruled by them." [citing *Williams v. Lee*, 358 U.S. 217, 220 (1959).] The *Montana* rule, therefore, and not its exceptions, applies to this case.

[The plaintiff] may pursue her case against [the defendants] in the state forum open to all who sustain injuries on North Dakota's highway. Opening the Tribal Court for her optional use is not necessary to protect tribal self-government; and requiring [the defendants] to defend against this commonplace state highway accident claim in an unfamiliar court is not crucial to "the political integrity, the economic security, or the health or welfare of the [tribe]."

Notes

1. **Lower court interpretations of *Montana* after *Strate*.** In contrast to the early post-*Montana* cases noted at page 264, the post-*Strate* cases in the lower federal courts tend to employ a far more restrictive vision of what constitutes a direct effect on core tribal governmental interests such as health and welfare. *See, e.g., Big Horn County Electric Coop. v. Adams*, 219 F.3d 944 (9th Cir. 2000), noted at page 438–439.

2. **Status of tribal and BIA roads.** The Ninth Circuit ruled that a Bureau of Indian Affairs (BIA) road is a tribal road for purposes of tribal court jurisdiction. *McDonald v. Means*, 300 F.3d 1037 (9th Cir. 2002). A minor member of the Northern Cheyenne Tribe was injured in a collision with a horse owned by a member of a different tribe who owned fee lands on the Northern Cheyenne Reservation. The court reversed a lower court decision which held that the BIA road was, like the state highway in *Strate*, the functional equivalent of fee land for jurisdictional purposes. The Ninth Circuit distinguished the BIA road from a state highway, based on the federal trust obligation the agency owes the tribe and BIA regulations which give tribal governments gate-keeping authority over BIA roads.

3. **Highways as rights-of-way.** Highways and other state roads through reservations are governed by federal statutes for rights-of-way. Rights-of-way in the context of energy development are discussed in Chapter 5, section A.3.

Nevada v. Hicks
533 U.S. 353 (2001)

[This case, the Court's most recent word on the *Montana* analysis, concerned tribal court jurisdiction over a damages action against state officials who allegedly damaged a tribal member's property while conducting searches authorized by warrants issued by a state court and approved by the tribal court. The searches were conducted on trust land within the Fallon Paiute-Shoshone Reservation. Hicks, claiming the officials damaged the property that was seized and subsequently returned to him, filed suit in Fallon Tribal Court. The state of Nevada challenged the tribal court's jurisdiction in federal court. The federal district court upheld the tribal court's jurisdiction and the Ninth Circuit affirmed in a 2–1 decision. The Supreme Court, in an opinion by Justice Scalia, reversed without dissent.]

Both *Montana* and *Strate* rejected tribal authority to regulate nonmembers' activities on land over which the tribe could not "assert a landowner's right to occupy and exclude." Respondents and the United States argue that since Hicks's home and yard *are* on tribe-owned land within the reservation, the Tribe may make its exercise of regulatory authority over nonmembers a condition of nonmembers' entry. Not necessarily. While it is certainly true that the non-Indian ownership status of the land was central to the analysis in both *Montana* and *Strate*, the reason that was so was *not* that Indian ownership suspends the "general proposition" derived from *Oliphant [v. Suquamish Tribe]* that "the inherent sovereign powers of an Indian tribe do not extend to the activities of nonmembers of the tribe" except to the extent "necessary to protect tribal self-government or to control internal relations." *Oliphant* itself drew no distinctions based on the status of land. And *Montana*, after announcing the general rule of no jurisdiction over nonmembers, cautioned that "[t]o be sure, Indian tribes retain inherent sovereign power to exercise some forms of civil jurisdiction over non-Indians on their reservations, even on non-Indian fee lands"—clearly implying that the general rule of *Montana* applies to both Indian and non-Indian land. The ownership status of land, in other words, is only one factor to consider in determining whether regulation of the activities of nonmembers is "necessary to protect tribal self-government or to control internal relations." It may sometimes be a dispositive factor. Hitherto, the absence of tribal ownership has been virtually conclusive of the absence of tribal civil jurisdiction; with one minor exception, we have never upheld under *Montana* the extension of tribal civil authority over nonmembers on non-Indian land. But the existence of tribal ownership is not alone enough to support regulatory jurisdiction over nonmembers.

Our cases make clear that the Indians' right to make their own laws and be governed by them does not exclude all state regulatory authority on the reservation. State sovereignty does not end at a reservation's border. Though tribes are often referred to as "sovereign" entities, it was "long ago" that "the Court departed from Chief Justice Marshall's view that 'the laws of [a State] can have no force' within reservation boundaries."

That is not to say that States may exert the same degree of regulatory authority within a reservation as they do without. To the contrary, the principle that Indians have the right to make their own laws and be governed by them requires "an accommodation between the interests of the Tribes and the Federal Government, on the one hand, and those of the State, on the other." *Washington v. Confederated Tribes of Colville Reservation,* 447 U.S. 134, 156 (1980). "When on-reservation conduct involving only Indians is at issue, state law is generally inapplicable, for the State's regulatory interest is likely to be minimal and the federal interest in encouraging tribal self-government is at its strongest." When, however, state interests outside the reservation are implicated, States may regulate the activities even of tribe members on tribal land, as exemplified by our decision [holding that tribes could be required to collect state tobacco taxes from nonmember customers].

We conclude today, in accordance with these prior statements, that tribal authority to regulate state officers in executing process related to the violation, off reservation, of state laws is not essential to tribal self-government or internal relations—to "the right to make laws and be ruled by them." [Citing *Williams v. Lee*.] The State's interest in execution of process is considerable, and even when it relates to Indian-fee lands it no more impairs the tribe's self-government than federal enforcement of federal law impairs state government.

[There were four concurring opinions, two of which are excerpted below. Both concurrences disputed Justice Scalia's expansion of the *Montana* tests: one thought he did not go far enough and the other thought he went too far. Justice Souter, joined by Justices Kennedy and Thomas, wrote:]

* * * I would go right to *Montana*'s rule that a tribe's civil jurisdiction generally stops short of nonmember defendants, subject only to two exceptions, one turning on "consensual relationships," the other on respect for "the political integrity, the economic security, or the health or welfare of the tribe."

Montana applied this presumption against tribal jurisdiction to nonmember conduct on fee land within a reservation; I would also apply it where, as here, a nonmember acts on tribal or trust land, and I would thus make it explicit that land status within a reservation is not a primary jurisdictional fact, but is relevant only insofar as it bears on the application of one of *Montana*'s exceptions to a particular case. Insofar as I rest my conclusion on the general jurisdictional presumption, it follows for me that, although the holding in this case is "limited to the question of tribal-court jurisdiction over state officers enforcing state law," one rule independently supporting that holding (that as a general matter "the inherent sovereign powers of an Indian tribe do not extend to the activities of nonmembers of the tribe") is not so confined.

[On the other hand, Justice O'Connor, joined by Justices Stevens and Breyer, accused the Court of issuing a decision that "is unmoored from our precedents." In an opinion that concurred in part and concurred in the judgment, but often sounded like a dissent, Justice O'Connor wrote:]

* * * The Court's reasoning suffers from two serious flaws: It gives only passing consideration to the fact that the state officials' activities in this case occurred on land owned and controlled by the Tribes, and it treats as dispositive the fact that the nonmembers in this case are state officials.

The majority's rule undermining tribal interests is all the more perplexing because the conduct in this case occurred on land owned and controlled by the Tribes. Although the majority gives a passing nod to land status at the outset of its opinion, that factor is not prominent in the Court's analysis. This oversight is significant.

Montana recognizes that tribes may retain inherent power to exercise civil jurisdiction when the nonmember conduct "threatens or has some direct effect on the political integrity, the economic security, or the health or welfare of the tribe." These interests are far more likely to be implicated where, as here, the nonmember activity takes place on land owned and controlled by the tribe. If *Montana* is to bring coherence to our case law, we must apply it with due consideration to land status, which has always figured prominently in our analysis of tribal jurisdiction.

This case involves state officials acting on tribal land. The Tribes' sovereign interests with respect to nonmember activities on its land are not extinguished simply because the nonmembers in this case are state officials enforcing state law. Our cases concerning tribal power often involve the competing interests of state, federal, and tribal governments. The actions of state officials on tribal land in some instances may affect tribal sovereign interests to a greater, not lesser, degree than the actions of private parties. In this case for example, it is alleged that state officers, who gained access to Hicks' property by virtue of their authority as state actors, exceeded the scope of the search warrants and damaged Hicks' personal property.

The Court's reasoning does not reflect a faithful application of *Montana* and its progeny. Our case law does not support a broad *per se* rule prohibiting tribal jurisdiction over nonmembers on tribal land whenever the nonmembers are state officials. If the Court were to remain true to the principles that have governed in prior cases, the Court would reverse and remand the case to the Court of Appeals for a proper application of *Montana* to determine whether there is tribal jurisdiction.

Notes

1. *Hicks'* **effect on the** *Montana* **analysis.** What exactly is the majority's holding in *Hicks*? Does the "main rule" of *Montana*—that tribes are divested of jurisdiction over nonmembers on fee lands absent one of the two exceptions—now apply to all nonmember conduct on trust lands as well? Or does it apply only if the nonmember in question is a state official? Or only if the nonmember is a state official serving process in connection with an off-reservation violation of state law? Justice Ginsburg found it necessary to write separately to make the point that, in her estimation, the Court had not announced a general rule concerning tribal court authority over nonmembers on tribal lands. "As the Court plainly states, and as Justice Souter recognizes, the 'holding in this case is limited to the question of tribal-court jurisdiction over state officers enforcing state law.'" 533 U.S. at 386 (Ginsburg, J., concurring).

2. *Hicks* **and trust land status.** How many of the justices in *Hicks* thought that the trust status of Hicks' property should be dispositive? Justice Souter was the most dismissive of the importance of trust status. His concurrence in *Hicks*, as well as his concurrence in *Atkinson Trading Company Inc. v. Shirley*, 532 U.S. 645 (2001) (noted at page 435), expressed the view that the status of reservation land as fee or trust is merely one factor to consider in tribal civil jurisdiction over nonmembers. For a critique of this approach, see Judith V. Royster, Montana *at the Crossroads*, 38 Conn. L.

Rev. 631 (2006). Professor Royster argues that Justice Souter conflated the two lines of reasoning in *Montana*—treaty rights and inherent sovereignty—ignoring the Court's analysis that treaty rights to absolute and undisturbed use and occupation of trust lands recognize tribal authority over activities on those lands, including the activities of nonmembers.

3. **Narrowing *Montana*'s consensual relations exception.** The Court has been no more expansive in its approach to the consensual relations exception from *Montana* than it has to the direct effects exception. In *Plains Commerce Bank v. Long Family Land and Cattle Co.*, 554 U.S. 316 (2008), a 5–4 Supreme Court refused to apply the first *Montana* exception, concerning consensual relations, to an anti-discrimination claim brought in tribal court against a bank that had extensive on-reservation dealings with tribal members. The majority characterized the *Montana* rule as prohibiting the exercise of tribal jurisdiction over nonmembers, and the consensual relation exception as extending only to activities on-reservation. However, the majority explained that a land sale of a mortgage in default was not related to the bank's commercial dealings with the tribe, and therefore the tribal court lacked jurisdiction to either grant a tribal family an option to repurchase or award damages. The four-member dissent (per Justice Ginsberg) would have found tribal court jurisdiction to award damages for discrimination, rejecting the majority's distinction between on-reservation land sales and activities on the land.

In *Dollar General v. Mississippi Band of Choctaw Indians*, 136 S. Ct. 2159 (2016), an equally divided Supreme Court affirmed the Fifth Circuit's decision in the case without opinion. The Fifth Circuit, 732 F.3d 409 (5th Cir. 2013), invoked the *Montana* consensual relations exception (the first circuit court to do so) to find tribal court jurisdiction over a tort claim against a nonmember whose action took place on trust land.

4. ***Montana* in the tribal courts.** In contrast to the Supreme Court, tribal courts often employ a more expansive view of tribal health and welfare needs. Consider, for example, the thorough analysis of the *Montana* factors in *Confederated Tribes of the Colville Reservation v. Hoover*, 28 Indian L. Rptr. 6103 (Colv. Tr. Ct. 1998). In 1977, the Colville Tribes designated a 100,400-acre corner of their reservation as the Hellsgate Game Reserve. Land ownership in the reserve area is approximately 87% tribal trust; 11% fee, and 1% federal. In 1987, Hoover, a non-Indian, purchased a parcel of fee land in the reserve adjoining the shorelands of Lake Roosevelt. Hoover submitted a plat to the county to subdivide his property into several lots, and indicated that he did not intend to apply for tribal permits. The Colville Tribal Court held that the tribes had jurisdiction to regulate land use on fee lands within the reserve area.

> Although only a small minority of the Hellsgate Reserve land base is in fee status, high density development in these areas will seriously impact wildlife populations that are sensitive to human presence and development. Single unregulated developments, such as that proposed by defendant, can have negative impacts on water resources, riparian areas and sensitive wildlife species. The impacts escalate with cumulative, uncontrolled growth.

Much of the fee land in the Reserve is concentrated at low elevations along waterways which are a critical component of the Reserve ecosystem and an important wintering habitat for large game species.

The plants and animals placed at risk by unregulated fee land development in the Reserve are integral to Colville people's culture, religion, and way of life. Hunting of animals and gathering of traditional foods and medicines have defined the Colville culture for generations. Hunting camps, vision quests and other traditional and religious practices carried out in the Reserve are often not compatible with increased development and housing density. The animals and plants of the Reserve are an important source of food, medicine, and culture of the Colville people. Without land use controls designating certain contiguous areas of the Reservation such as Hellsgate for greater protection and conservation, fundamental aspects of tribal culture will be placed in serious jeopardy.

Consistent with the unique cultures and traditions of the Bands of the Colville Tribes, protection of subsistence and ceremonial game is necessary for the health and welfare of the Tribes and tribal members.

Development in the Reserve without strict tribal environmental review and in violation of the Tribes' land use plan seriously threatens the political integrity of the Colville Tribes by placing in jeopardy tribal medicines, tribal foods, tribal cultural practices, tribal religious practices and tribal food sources that provide the base for sustaining the people and their economy.

Exempting fee lands in the Reserve also will have negative impacts on the economic security of the Colville Tribes and its members.

The subsistence food sources are an important part of the economy of the Reservation. With median income of $7,561 and unemployment at approximately 48%, many tribal members depend on deer meat and native plants for food.

Would these legal conclusions be sufficient to convince the U.S. Supreme Court today?

In another tribal court decision, *Skokomish Indian Tribe v. Mosbarger*, Case No. I 12774 (VII NW Intertribal Ct. App. Ops 90, 2006), the Skokomish Court of Appeals upheld the speeding conviction of a non-member within a school zone on a highway within the exterior boundaries of the tribe's reservation. The court concluded that the speeding threatened or had a direct effect on the tribe's health and welfare, thus satisfying the *Montana* test. The court distinguished *Strate* by emphasizing that the Skokomish Tribe was a party to this litigation which, according to the court, was evidence that the case concerned internal issues, tribal citizens, and tribal self-government—unlike *Strate*, which the U.S. Supreme Court limited to the external relations and powers of tribes. Thus, the tribal court ruled that violating the tribe's speed limit in a school zone met the second *Montana* exception, giving the tribe jurisdiction over the dispute.

B. Environmental Protection

1. Environmental Authority in Indian Country

This section explores the interplay of federal, tribal, and state authority for environmental protection in Indian country. In particular, these materials focus on which of the governments is authorized to carry out the federal environmental programs in Indian country. An initial question, however, is why the federal environmental statutes apply in Indian country. Today, virtually all the major federal laws have been amended to expressly apply to Indian tribes, but did those amendments confer jurisdiction on the U.S. Environmental Protection Agency (EPA) that did not otherwise exist?

Phillips Petroleum Co. v. U.S. Environmental Protection Agency
803 F.2d 545 (10th Cir. 1986)

[In 1983, EPA promulgated rules for underground injection control programs on Indian lands under the Safe Drinking Water Act (SDWA), § 1401, 42 U.S.C. §§ 300f–300j10. The following year, EPA adopted an underground injection control program for the Osage Reserve in Oklahoma. Phillips Petroleum challenged the program on the ground that the EPA had no jurisdiction over Indian lands. (The SDWA was not amended to apply specifically to tribes until 1986). In *Phillips Petroleum*, the court held that EPA was empowered under the SDWA to promulgate the program for the Osage Reserve.]

The nub of Phillips' jurisdiction argument is that the EPA can only regulate under Part C of the SDWA where state governments can, but fail to do so. All parties agree that the Oklahoma state government has no power to prescribe an underground injection control program regulating the Osage Indian Reserve. Therefore, Phillips argues, the EPA has no power either. The matter is supposedly left by Congress to the Bureau of Indian Affairs.

We are not persuaded by Phillips. Its view of the statute is too narrow. Considering the amount of oil and gas exploration and production on Indian lands from 1974 to 1986, the SDWA would be eviscerated in large part by Phillips' interpretation. * * * It is readily apparent from the legislative history that the underground drinking water provisions of the SDWA apply throughout the country, border to border, ocean to ocean. It is triggered by area (state) designations by the Administrator, but its reach covers the country. * * * Phillips interprets the statute by emphasizing borders (state political entity versus Indian land). Congress emphasizes a national policy of clean water. So, therefore, must we in interpreting the statute.

We conclude, therefore, that there is no sound policy reason to exclude Indian lands from the SDWA's application, and every reason to include them. As indicated above, the SDWA clearly establishes national policy with respect to clean water, including sources of underground water. To hold, as Phillips suggests, that the EPA did not have authority to promulgate underground injection control programs for Indian lands would contradict the clear meaning and purpose of the SDWA by creating, prior to 1986, a vacuum of authority over underground injections on Indian lands, leaving vast areas of the nation devoid of protection from groundwater contamination.

The conclusion that the SDWA empowered the EPA to prescribe regulations for Indian lands is also consistent with the presumption that Congress intends a general statute applying to all persons to include Indians and their property interests. *See Federal Power Commission v. Tuscarora Indian Nation*, 362 U.S. 99, 116–18 (1960). Although this rule of construction can be rescinded where a tribe raises a specific right under a treaty or statute which is in conflict with the general law to be applied, no such right under statute or treaty has been demonstrated. To the contrary, the Osage Indian Tribe supports the EPA's adoption of the injection program on the reserve.

Notes

1. State authority. Why do "[a]ll parties agree that the Oklahoma state government has no power to prescribe an underground injection control program regulating the Osage Indian Reserve"?

2. Environmental federalism. Most of the federal environmental laws are premised on a federal-state partnership idea. Broadly speaking, the federal government will establish the programs and standards, and the states will implement them. *See generally* Robert V. Percival, *Environmental Federalism: Historical Roots and Contemporary Models*, 54 Md. L. Rev. 1141 (1995); Judith V. Royster & Rory SnowArrow Fausett, *Control of the Reservation Environment: Tribal Primacy, Federal Delegation, and the Limits of State Intrusion*, 64 Wash. L. Rev. 581, 614–19 (1989).

Under statutes such as the SDWA, the Clean Water Act, and the Clean Air Act, the federal government establishes programs and sets uniform minimum standards applicable nationwide, and the states may seek "primacy" from the EPA to implement and administer the federal programs within their borders. The general purpose of state primacy is to combine national uniformity of minimum pollution control standards with local program implementation. To that end, the pollution control laws expressly preserve the right of the states, when they assume primacy, to set more stringent standards than those established under the federal laws. In the absence of an approved state program, the EPA will administer the federal program within the state to ensure implementation of the national standards.

3. EPA's Indian law policy. As *Phillips Petroleum* indicates, prior to 1986 the federal environmental statutes did not generally address the role of Indian tribes. EPA, however, had already developed an agency Indian policy. In 1983, President Reagan issued an Indian policy, reaffirming the existing federal policy of tribal control and economic self-sufficiency, and calling for a "government-to-government" relationship between the tribal and federal governments. *Statement on Indian Policy*, 1 Pub. Papers 96 (1983). Building on Reagan's statement, EPA became the first federal agency to issue an Indian policy of its own.

EPA Policy for the Administration of Environmental Programs on Indian Reservations
(1984)

1. *The Agency stands ready to work directly with Indian Tribal Governments on a one-to-one basis (the "government-to-government" relationship), rather than as subdivisions of other governments.* EPA recognizes Tribal Governments as sovereign entities with primary authority and responsibility for the reservation populace. Accordingly, EPA will work directly with Tribal Governments as the independent authority for reservation affairs, and not as political subdivisions of States or other governmental units.

2. *The Agency will recognize Tribal Governments as the primary parties for setting standards, making environmental policy decisions and managing programs for reservations, consistent with agency standards and regulations.* In keeping with the principle of Indian self-government, the Agency will view Tribal Governments as the appropriate non-Federal parties for making decisions and carrying out program responsibilities affecting Indian reservations, their environments, and the health and welfare of the reservation populace. Just as EPA's deliberations and activities have traditionally involved the interests and/or participation of State Governments, EPA will look directly to Tribal Governments to play this lead role for matters affecting reservation environments.

3. *The Agency will take affirmative steps to encourage and assist Tribes in assuming regulatory and program management responsibilities for reservation lands.* The Agency will assist interested Tribal Governments in developing programs and in preparing to assume regulatory and program management responsibilities for reservation lands. Within the constraints of EPA's authority and resources, this aid will include providing grants and other assistance to Tribes similar to that we provide State Governments. The Agency will encourage Tribes to assume delegable responsibilities, (i.e. responsibilities which the Agency has traditionally delegated to State Governments for non-reservation lands) under terms similar to those governing delegations to States.

Until Tribal Governments are willing and able to assume full responsibility for delegable programs, the Agency will retain responsibility for managing programs for reservations (unless the State has an express grant of jurisdiction from Congress sufficient to support delegation to the State Government). Where EPA retains such responsibility, the Agency will encourage the Tribe to participate in policy-making and to assume appropriate lesser or partial roles in the management of reservation programs.

4. *The Agency will take appropriate steps to remove existing legal and procedural impediments to working directly and effectively with Tribal Governments on reservation programs.*

5. *The Agency, in keeping with the federal trust responsibility, will assure that Tribal concerns and interests are considered whenever EPA's actions and/or decisions may affect reservation environments.*

6. *The Agency will strive to assure compliance with environmental statutes and regulations on Indian reservations.*

Notes

1. EPA's Indian program. EPA has consistently reaffirmed its commitment to the 1984 government-to-government policy. *See* U.S. Envt'l Protection Agency, *Federal, Tribal and State Roles in the Protection and Regulation of Reservation Environments: A Concept Paper* (1991); Memorandum from EPA Administrator Christine Todd Whitman, July 11, 2001; Memorandum from Michael O. Leavitt, Sept. 17, 2004; Memorandum from Stephen L. Johnson, Sept. 26, 2005. Barack Obama's EPA Administrator, Lisa Jackson, reaffirmed the 1984 policy on July 22, 2009.[1] In March 2010, Jackson created the Office of International and Tribal Affairs (OITA). The American Indian Environmental Office, formerly located within the Office of Water, is now part of the combined OITA. *See* U.S. Environmental Protection Agency, *EPA Policy on Consultation and Coordination with Indian Tribes* (May 4, 2011). For a detailed history of EPA-tribal relations, see James M. Grijalva, *The Origins of EPA's Indian Program*, 15. Kan. J. L. & Pub. Poly 191 (2006); *see also* James M. Grijalva, *EPA's Indian Policy at Twenty-Five*, 25 Nat. Res. & Envt. 12 (Summer 2010).

On January 9, 2014, EPA Administrator Gina McCarthy reaffirmed the EPA's Indian Policy first adopted in 1984. In her statement, Administrator McCarthy stated:

> the EPA reiterates its recognition that the United States has a unique legal relationship with tribal governments based on the Constitution, treaties, statutes, executive orders and court decisions. The EPA recognizes the right of the tribes as sovereign governments to self-determination and acknowledges the federal government's trust responsibility to tribes. The EPA works with tribes on a government-to-government basis to protect the land, air and water in Indian Country.

Memorandum from Gina McCarthy, EPA Administrator, to All EPA Employees (January 9, 2014).

2. The role of the states. Under the concept of environmental federalism, as noted above, the states are the primary agents for carrying out the programs of the federal environmental statutes. In its 1984 policy, what role does the EPA envision for the states? Is EPA's approach consistent with the concept of environmental federalism?

---

1. [Editors' Note: The reaffirmation cited in the 3rd edition of this casebook does not appear on the EPA website at the time of writing.]

In the following case, the State of Washington sought primacy from EPA to apply its hazardous waste program everywhere within the state, including on "Indian lands." EPA denied interim authorization as to Indian lands, and the Ninth Circuit affirmed. How does the court reconcile EPA's approach with the federal statutory scheme of environmental federalism?

State of Washington, Department of Ecology v. United States Environmental Protection Agency

752 F.2d 1465 (9th Cir. 1985)

CANBY, Circuit Judge.

The Resource Conservation and Recovery Act (RCRA), 42 U.S.C. §6901 *et seq.*, creates a comprehensive federal program of hazardous waste management administered by the Environmental Protection Agency (EPA). RCRA also authorizes the states to develop and implement their own hazardous waste management programs "in lieu of" the federal program. This case presents the question whether EPA violated the requirements of RCRA when it refused to permit the State of Washington to apply its state hazardous waste regulations to the activities of all persons, Indians and non-Indians, on "Indian lands." We conclude that EPA has adopted a reasonable interpretation of RCRA and we therefore affirm the agency's decision.

I

RCRA requires EPA to promulgate regulations governing the generation, transportation, storage, and disposal of hazardous wastes. EPA also must establish a permit system covering all hazardous waste facilities, to enforce the regulations. The RCRA requirements apply to all persons. The statute defines "person" to include, inter alia, Indian tribes.

Like several other federal environmental statutes, RCRA provides a mechanism by which the states can administer their own hazardous waste programs "in lieu of the Federal program." The state must apply to the EPA Administrator for authorization to implement its own program. The Administrator is required to authorize a state program on an interim basis if the state demonstrates that the program is "substantially equivalent" to the federal program. The Administrator authorizes a permanent state program when he determines that the program is "equivalent" to the federal program, consistent with the federal program and other state programs, and adequately enforceable. If a state chooses not to set up its own program, or if the Administrator decides that the state does not qualify for authorization, EPA continues to administer the federal program in that state. Where a state program is in effect, EPA retains certain oversight and enforcement powers, including the power to withdraw authorization if the state program fails to comply with the federal requirements.

On May 3, 1982, the Governor of the State of Washington submitted an application for interim authorization pursuant to Section 3006(c). The complete application included an analysis by the Washington Attorney General of the state's authority over activities on Indian lands, as required by 40 C.F.R. § 123.125(c) (recodified at 40 C.F.R. § 271.125(c) (1984)). The Attorney General's analysis asserted that RCRA authorizes the State of Washington to regulate the hazardous waste-related activities of Indians on reservation lands. After the requisite review and public comment, EPA approved Washington's application for interim authorization "except as to Indian lands." With respect to Indian lands, EPA concluded that the state had not adequately demonstrated its legal authority to exercise jurisdiction. EPA found that RCRA does not give the state jurisdiction over Indian lands, and that states could possess such jurisdiction only through an express act of Congress or by treaty. Since Washington had cited no independent authority for its jurisdictional claim, EPA retained jurisdiction to operate the federal hazardous waste management program "on Indian lands in the State of Washington."[1]

It is important at the outset to define the issue raised by the State of Washington's petition. Washington sought EPA authorization to apply its hazardous waste program to both Indian and non-Indian residents of Indian reservations. In the Attorney General's analysis of state jurisdiction and again before this court, Washington contended that RCRA confers on the state the right to regulate all hazardous waste activities within the state, with no exceptions for Indian tribes or Indian lands. We hold today that the EPA Regional Administrator properly refused to approve the proposed state program because RCRA does not authorize the states to regulate Indians on Indian lands. We do not decide the question whether Washington is empowered to create a program reaching into Indian country when that reach is limited to non-Indians. Contrary to the assumption of amicus State of California, Washington has made clear that it did not present such a program to EPA. Since our function is to review EPA's administrative decision, we will consider only the program that Washington did present. We do not address the legality of other programs that the state might have proposed.

III

RCRA does not directly address the problem of how to implement a hazardous waste management program on Indian reservations.[3] The statutory language on which Washington relies sets forth the state's general regulatory powers, but does not

---

1. Washington expresses some confusion over the precise meaning of the term "Indian lands." The term appears several times in the RCRA regulations, but the regulations do not define it. In the course of this litigation, EPA has regarded it as synonymous with "Indian country", which is defined at 18 U.S.C. § 1151 to include all lands (including fee lands) within Indian reservations, dependent Indian communities, and Indian allotments to which Indians hold title. We accept this definition as a reasonable marker of the geographic boundary between state authority and federal authority.

3. As the current controversy illustrates, the problem is not merely academic. The parties and the amici Tribes agree that industrial activities on Indian lands within Washington create a potentially significant hazardous waste problem. Conversely, Indian reservations may be considered as potential locations for hazardous waste disposal sites, in Washington and elsewhere, because they often are remote from heavily populated areas.

specify its authority over Indian tribes or lands. The only mention of Indians in the statute is in Section 1004(13), 42 U.S.C. § 6903(13), which defines "municipality" to include "an Indian tribe or authorized tribal organization." This reference indicates only that tribes are regulated entities under RCRA, since "municipality" is included in the statutory definition of "person", and the enforcement provisions of the statute apply to "any person". The statute does not say whether the states have authority to enforce state hazardous waste regulations against tribes or individual Indians on Indian lands. The legislative history of RCRA is totally silent on the issue of state regulatory jurisdiction on the reservations. Congress apparently did not consider whether state programs authorized "in lieu of" the federal program would apply in Indian country.

When a statute is silent or unclear with respect to a particular issue, we must defer to the reasonable interpretation of the agency responsible for administering the statute. By leaving a gap in the statute, Congress implicitly has delegated policy-making authority to the agency. *Chevron, U.S.A. Inc. v. Natural Resources Defense Council*, 104 S. Ct. 1778, 2782 (1984). In such a case, we may not substitute our judgment for that of the agency as long as the agency has adopted a reasonable construction of the statute. We must defer to the agency's interpretation even if the agency could also have reached another reasonable interpretation, or even if we would have reached a different result had we construed the statute initially. The agency's interpretation is especially weighty where statutory construction involves "reconciling conflicting policies, and a full understanding of the force of the statutory policy in the given situation (depends) upon more than ordinary knowledge respecting the matters subjected to agency regulations." *Chevron, U.S.A.*, 104 S. Ct. at 2783, *quoting United States v. Shimer*, 367 U.S. 374, 382 (1961).

Applying this deferential standard of review, we hold that EPA reasonably has interpreted RCRA not to grant state jurisdiction over the activities of Indians in Indian country. The statutory language cited by Washington does not express Congressional intent to extend state jurisdiction with sufficient clarity for us to conclude that the agency's interpretation is wrong. Implementation of hazardous waste management programs on Indian lands raises questions of Indian policy as well as environmental policy. It is appropriate for us to defer to EPA's expertise and experience in reconciling these policies, gained through administration of similar environmental statutes on Indian lands.

Our conclusion that the EPA construction is a reasonable one is buttressed by well-settled principles of federal Indian law. States are generally precluded from exercising jurisdiction over Indians in Indian country unless Congress has clearly expressed an intention to permit it. This rule derives in part from respect for the plenary authority of Congress in the area of Indian affairs. Accompanying the broad congressional power is the concomitant federal trust responsibility toward the Indian tribes. That responsibility arose largely from the federal role as a guarantor of Indian rights against state encroachment. We must presume that Congress intended to exercise its power in a manner consistent with the federal trust obligation.

The Washington tribes that appeared as amici in this case fear that their reservations will become "dumping grounds" for off-reservation hazardous wastes if the state is permitted to control the hazardous waste program on the reservations. Whether or not that fear is well-founded, the United States in its role as primary guarantor of Indian interests legitimately may decide that such tribal concerns can best be addressed by maintaining federal control over Indian lands. EPA's interpretation of RCRA permits this option. Respect for the long tradition of tribal sovereignty and self-government also underlies the rule that state jurisdiction over Indians in Indian country will not be easily implied. Vague or ambiguous federal statutes must be measured against the "backdrop" of tribal sovereignty, especially when the statute affects an area in which the tribes historically have exercised their sovereign authority or contemporary federal policy encourages tribal self-government.

In this case, of course, the state is being required to yield to an exercise of jurisdiction by the federal government, not by a tribe. The sovereign role of the tribes, however, does not disappear when the federal government takes responsibility for the management of a federal program on tribal lands. The federal government has a policy of encouraging tribal self-government in environmental matters.[5] That policy has been reflected in several environmental statutes that give Indian tribes a measure of control over policymaking or program administration or both. These statutes include the Federal Insecticide, Fungicide, and Rodenticide Act (FIFRA), 7 U.S.C. § 136(u), which permits the EPA Administrator to delegate authority for operating pesticide applicator certification programs to tribes, and the Clean Air Act, 42 U.S.C. § 7474(c), which allows tribes to control air quality on their reservations under the "Prevention of Significant Deterioration" program.[6]

---

5. The current Administration has reaffirmed the national commitment "to strengthen tribal governments and lessen federal control over tribal government affairs. . . . Our policy is to reaffirm dealing with Indian tribes on a government-to-government basis and to pursue the policy of self-government for Indian tribes without threatening termination." Statement by the President: Indian Policy, January 24, 1983, at 2. Likewise, Congress, in the Indian Self-Determination Act of 1975, declared its "commitment to the maintenance of the Federal Government's unique and continuing relationship with and responsibility to the Indian people through the establishment of a meaningful Indian self-determination policy which will permit an orderly transition from Federal domination of programs for and services to Indians to effective and meaningful participation by the Indian people in the planning, conduct, and administration of those programs and services."

6. Certain environmental statutes provide that they are not meant to change the jurisdictional status of Indian lands. Safe Drinking Water Amendments of 1977, 42 U.S.C. § 300j–6(c)(1); Surface Mining and Reclamation Act of 1977, 30 U.S.C. § 1300(h). Washington argues that the absence of a similar provision in RCRA demonstrates Congress' intent to sweep away tribal powers of self-government in the area of hazardous waste regulation. This contention, if accepted, would reverse the fundamental principle that the established jurisdictional relationships between Indian tribes and the states remain intact unless Congress clearly expresses its desire to change them. We cannot assume that Congress intended in RCRA to substitute state authority for tribal authority on Indian lands, where the statute is unclear and other expressions of federal Indian policy are inconsistent with that result.

The policies and practices of EPA also reflect the federal commitment to tribal self-regulation in environmental matters. In a 1980 statement approved by the Deputy Administrator, EPA announced that its policy is to "promote an enhanced role for tribal government in relevant decisionmaking and implementation of Federal environmental programs on Indian reservations." EPA Policy for Program Implementation on Indian Lands, December 19, 1980 at 5.[7] EPA has carried out the policy of self-determination in administering the various environmental statutes. For example, EPA promulgated regulations under FIFRA authorizing tribes to develop their own programs for certification of pesticide applicators, at a time when the statute provided only that "states" could submit certification plans. Similarly, EPA delegated to Indian tribes the authority to classify their reservations under the "Prevention of Significant Deterioration" (PSD) standards of the Clean Air Act, even though the Act did not specifically authorize such delegation. As noted above, Congress subsequently amended both statutes expressly to permit tribal participation as set forth in the regulations. We cannot foreclose the possibility of similar developments under RCRA.

This court has endorsed the EPA effort to promote tribal self-government in environmental matters. In *Nance v. EPA*, 645 F.2d 701 (9th Cir. 1981), we upheld the delegation of authority to Indian governments under the PSD regulations, against the contention that the Clean Air Act permitted delegation only to the states. The Clean Air Act specifies that "[e]ach State shall have the primary responsibility for assuring air quality within the entire geographic region comprising such state." Despite that language, we held that the statute permitted EPA to allow tribes to set their own air quality goals on their reservations. Citing the inherent sovereignty of Indian tribes and the principle of deference to an agency's interpretation of a statute, we concluded that "within the . . . context of reciprocal impact of air quality standards on land use, the states and Indian tribes occupying federal reservations stand on substantially equal footing." We accordingly declined to subordinate the tribes to state authority.

In the case at bar, as in *Nance*, the tribal interest in managing the reservation environment and the federal policy of encouraging tribes to assume or at least share in management responsibility are controlling. We cannot say that RCRA clearly evinces a Congressional purpose to revise federal Indian policy or to diminish the independence of Indian tribes. Section 3006 of RCRA is far less explicit than the Clean Air Act provision at issue in *Nance*, which gave the states primary responsibility for the "entire geographic region" within the state. RCRA merely authorizes state hazardous

---

7. A more recent "discussion paper" prepared by the EPA Office of Federal Activities similarly recommended that the agency "endeavor where appropriate to give tribal governments the primary role in environmental program management and decisionmaking relative to Indian lands." Administration of Environmental Programs on Indian Lands, at 35. The paper noted that this approach advances the President's stated policy of tribal self-determination.

waste programs "in lieu of" the federal program. Since EPA could exclude state authority from Indian lands in *Nance*, it can certainly do so here.

EPA, having retained regulatory authority over Indian lands in Washington under the interpretation of RCRA that we approve today, can promote the ability of the tribes to govern themselves by allowing them to participate in hazardous waste management. To do so, it need not delegate its full authority to the tribes. We therefore need not decide, and do not decide, the extent to which program authority under Section 3006 of RCRA is delegable to Indian governments. It is enough that EPA remains free to carry out its policy of encouraging tribal self-government by consulting with the tribes over matters of hazardous waste management policy, such as the siting of waste disposal facilities. Other avenues of accommodating tribal sovereignty will doubtless become clear in the concrete administration of the federal program. The "backdrop" of tribal sovereignty, in light of federal policies encouraging Indian self-government, consequently supports EPA's interpretation of RCRA.

We therefore conclude that EPA correctly interpreted RCRA in rejecting Washington's application to regulate all hazardous waste-related activities on Indian lands. We recognize the vital interest of the State of Washington in effective hazardous waste management throughout the state, including on Indian lands. The absence of state enforcement power over reservation Indians, however, does not leave a vacuum in which hazardous wastes go unregulated. EPA remains responsible for ensuring that the federal standards are met on the reservations. Those standards are designed to protect human health and the environment. The state and its citizens will not be without protection.

The decision of the EPA Regional Administrator is AFFIRMED.

Notes

1. *Nance v. EPA.* The *Washington DOE* court referred to *Nance v. EPA*, 645 F.2d 701 (9th Cir. 1981), decided fully nine years before Congress amended the Clean Air Act to expressly authorize EPA to approve tribal programs for treatment as states. In *Nance*, the Ninth Circuit upheld EPA's interpretation of the Act allowing the agency to approve the Northern Cheyenne Tribe's prevention of significant deterioration program. Contrast *Nance* and *Backcountry Against Dumps v. EPA,* excerpted at page 313.

2. **The *Chevron* doctrine.** All of the decisions in this section arise from challenges to agency action. As administrative law decisions, they are governed by the standards of review of agency action set forth in the key case of *Chevron U.S.A. Inc. v. Natural Resources Defense Council, Inc.*, 467 U.S. 837 (1984). Note the two-step approach to judicial review of agency rules that the *Chevron* Court articulated:

> When a court reviews an agency's construction of the statute which it administers, it is confronted with two questions. First, always, is the question whether Congress has directly spoken to the precise question at issue. If the intent of Congress is clear, that is the end of the matter; for the court,

as well as the agency, must give effect to the unambiguously expressed intent of Congress.[9] If, however, the court determines Congress has not directly addressed the precise question at issue, the court does not simply impose its own construction on the statute, as would be necessary in the absence of an administrative interpretation. Rather, if the statute is silent or ambiguous with respect to the specific issue, the question for the court is whether the agency's answer is based on a permissible construction of the statute.[11]

"The power of an administrative agency to administer a congressionally created . . . program necessarily requires the formulation of policy and the making of rules to fill any gap left, implicitly or explicitly, by Congress." *Morton v. Ruiz*, 415 U.S. 199, 231 (1974). If Congress has explicitly left a gap for the agency to fill, there is an express delegation of authority to the agency to elucidate a specific provision of the statute by regulation. Such legislative regulations are given controlling weight unless they are arbitrary, capricious, or manifestly contrary to the statute. Sometimes the legislative delegation to an agency on a particular question is implicit rather than explicit. In such a case, a court may not substitute its own construction of a statutory provision for a reasonable interpretation made by the administrator of an agency.

We have long recognized that considerable weight should be accorded to an executive department's construction of a statutory scheme it is entrusted to administer, and the principle of deference to administrative interpretations:

> "has been consistently followed by this Court whenever decision as to the meaning or reach of a statute has involved reconciling conflicting policies, and a full understanding of the force of the statutory policy in the given situation has depended upon more than ordinary knowledge respecting the matters subjected to agency regulations.
>
> ". . . If this choice represents a reasonable accommodation of conflicting policies that were committed to the agency's care by the statute, we should not disturb it unless it appears from the statute or its legislative history that the accommodation is not one that Congress would have sanctioned." *United States v. Shimer*, 367 U.S. 374, 382, 383 (1961).

Chevron, 467 U.S. at 842–45. The *Chevron* doctrine thus recognizes two steps. At step one, the reviewing court determines "whether Congress has directly spoken to the

---

9. The judiciary is the final authority on issues of statutory construction and must reject administrative constructions which are contrary to clear congressional intent. If a court, employing traditional tools of statutory construction, ascertains that Congress had an intention on the precise question at issue, that intention is the law and must be given effect.

11. The court need not conclude that the agency construction was the only one it permissibly could have adopted to uphold the construction, or even the reading the court would have reached if the question initially had arisen in a judicial proceeding.

precise question at issue." If it has not, the court moves on to step two: whether the agency's approach is reasonable.

In the cases in this section, note which step of the *Chevron* analysis is at issue. Are the courts according proper deference, too much deference, or not enough deference to EPA's interpretations of the law?

3. The role of the tribes under the federal environmental laws: tribes as states. To carry out the promises of its 1984 Indian policy, excerpted at page 284, EPA embarked on a legislative agenda of amending federal environmental laws as they came up for reauthorization. Beginning with the round of reauthorizations in 1986, Congress amended the federal statutes administered by EPA to include provisions treating tribes as states for all or most of the programs authorized by the statutes. New environmental laws, moreover, generally provided equivalent treatment to tribal and state governments.

Between 1986 and 1990, three of the major federal environmental statutes were amended to include a tribes-as-states (TAS) provision. The primary programs of the Clean Water Act and the Safe Drinking Water Act are described below. The Clean Air Act programs are described in the notes following the next two cases. (Note that the federal laws considered in this chapter represent the major federal environmental laws, but by no means the only environmental statutes that apply to tribes in Indian country. For a comprehensive treatment of environmental laws in Indian country, see Cohen's Handbook of Federal Indian Law, ch.10 (Nell Jessup Newton et al., eds. 2012)).

a. Clean Water Act (CWA), 33 U.S.C. § 1251 *et seq*. The CWA establishes two primary permit programs. One is the National Pollutant Discharge Elimination System (NPDES) program, under which a permit must be obtained before any "point source" may discharge pollutants into navigable waters. A "point source" is defined as "any discernible, confined and discrete conveyance," such as a pipe, ditch, conduit, well, container, or vessel "from which pollutants are or may be discharged." The second program is the permit program for the discharge into navigable waters of dredged or fill material, known as the § 404 permit program after the section of the statute that created it. In addition, the CWA authorizes states to set water quality standards, subject to federal review and oversight, and encourages states to establish management programs for "nonpoint" sources of water pollution.

The Clean Water Act Amendments of 1987 required EPA to treat tribes as states for most purposes and programs of the Act. 33 U.S.C. § 1377. Tribes can be treated as states for purposes of certain grant programs as well as for setting water quality standards (WQS) for waters within reservations, administering the NPDES permit program, assuming permitting authority for the § 404 program, granting or denying certification for federally permitted activities that may result in discharges of pollutants into the waters, and developing management programs for nonpoint source pollution.

A tribal government that assumes responsibility for programs under the CWA may exercise its authority over water resources held by the tribe, by the United States in trust for the tribe or a member, or "otherwise within the borders of an Indian reservation." 33 U.S.C. §1377(e)(2). The EPA has stated that it considers "trust lands formally set apart for the use of Indians" to be reservation lands, citing *Oklahoma Tax Comm'n v. Citizen Band Potawatomi Indian Tribe of Oklahoma*, 498 U.S. 505, 511 (1991). 56 Fed. Reg. 64876, 64881 (Dec. 12, 1991).

The CWA also contains a provision for federal settlement of disputes between states and tribes sharing common bodies of water. The EPA must "provide a mechanism for the resolution of any unreasonable consequences that may arise as a result of differing water quality standards that may be set by States and Indian tribes located on common bodies of water." 33 U.S.C. §1377.

b. Safe Drinking Water Act (SDWA), 42 U.S.C. §300f *et seq*. The SDWA establishes three major programs. The first is the public water systems program, which sets drinking water quality standards. The second program is the underground injection control (UIC) program, which regulates the injection of fluids into the ground because injection may cause contamination of underground waters that supply public water systems. The third program is for the protection of wellhead areas, defined as the surface and subsurface area surrounding a water well or wellfield that supplies a public water system.

The SDWA amendments of 1986 authorized EPA "to treat Indian Tribes as States," and specifically provided that tribes may assume primary enforcement responsibility for both public water systems and UIC programs. 42 U.S.C. §300j-11(a). Tribal primacy under the UIC program also is addressed at §300h-1(e), which exempts tribes from certain time limits placed upon states, and promises that EPA will prescribe a UIC program where one does not exist for a tribe.

Where treatment of a tribe as a state is considered "inappropriate, administratively infeasible or otherwise inconsistent with the purposes" of the SDWA, however, EPA may promulgate "other means for administering such provision in a manner that will achieve the purpose of the provision." 42 U.S.C. §300j-11(b). The SDWA also defines "municipality" to include Indian tribes, and "person" to include municipalities. 42 U.S.C. §§300f(10) and (12). The EPA has stated that tribes which do not meet the tribes-as-states criteria of SDWA will be treated as municipalities. 53 Fed. Reg. 37,396, 37,397 (Sept. 26, 1988).

4. Implementing TAS. In order to be treated as states under the CWA and the SDWA, Indian tribes must meet three statutory and regulatory criteria. The first and third requirements of the two statutes are virtually identical. First, the tribe must show that it is a federally-recognized tribe with a governing body carrying out substantial governmental duties and powers. The third criterion requires the tribe to show that it is reasonably capable of carrying out the functions to be exercised in a manner consistent with the terms and purposes of the statute.

The middle requirement for TAS serves a similar purpose in the two statutes, but varies in its coverage. For the Clean Water Act, a tribe must show that the functions to be exercised by the Indian tribe pertain to the management and protection of water resources which are held by an Indian tribe, held by the United States in trust for Indians, held by a member of an Indian tribe if such property interest is subject to a trust restriction on alienation, or otherwise within the borders of an Indian reservation. 33 U.S.C. § 1377(e). For the SDWA, a tribe must show that the functions to be exercised by the Indian tribe are within the area of the tribal government's jurisdiction. 42 U.S.C. § 300j-11(b)(1). Based on the difference in language, the EPA has determined that a tribe may seek TAS under the CWA for the surface waters within its reservation only, 56 Fed. Reg. 64,876, 64,881 (Dec. 12, 1991), whereas under the SDWA a tribe may apply for TAS for "any lands over which it believes it has jurisdiction." 53 Fed. Reg. 37,396, 37,400 (Sept. 26, 1988).

A tribe must qualify as a state under each act or even under each program within an act. Qualification under one act or program does not constitute qualification as a state under all, because each act or program may require specialized authorities or capabilities. *See, e.g.,* 56 Fed. Reg. 64,876, 64,883 (Dec. 12, 1991). However, EPA has interpreted the CWA to require tribes to submit the basic application only once, with subsequent additional information as needed. EPA expects "that once a Tribe has qualified for one program, the key step toward assumption of other programs, in most cases, will be demonstrating appropriate capability." *Id.* at 64885. Moreover, in a memorandum dated November 10, 1992, EPA observed that if a tribe satisfies the federal recognition and governmental duties and powers requirements under one act, that showing will be satisfactory for all acts with TAS provisions.

If a tribe's application for TAS is not acceptable, EPA will generally not deny the tribe's request, but will work with the tribe to resolve deficiencies in the application or the tribal program so that TAS may be authorized. 56 Fed. Reg. 64,876, 64,885 (Dec. 12, 1991).

5. **TAS in Oklahoma.** In 2005, as a last-minute amendment to a massive transportation bill, Congress limited the ability of Indian tribes in Oklahoma to acquire TAS and expanded the authority of the state. The statute provides that if EPA approves the state of Oklahoma to administer any environmental statute in the state for areas that are not Indian country, then on request of the state, EPA must approve state program authority in Oklahoma Indian country as well. In addition, any tribe qualifying for TAS under any federal environmental law within EPA's jurisdiction may receive that authority only if the state of Oklahoma agrees and the tribe and state enter into a cooperative agreement. Pub. L. No. 109-59, § 10211, 119 Stat. 1144 (2005).

City of Albuquerque v. Browner
97 F.3d 415 (10th Cir. 1996)

McKAY, Circuit Judge.

The City of Albuquerque [Albuquerque] filed a complaint challenging the U.S. Environmental Protection Agency's [EPA] approval of the Pueblo of Isleta's [Isleta Pueblo] water quality standards on numerous grounds. After denying Albuquerque a temporary restraining order and a preliminary injunction, the district court denied its motion for summary judgment while granting the Defendant EPA's motion for summary judgment. Albuquerque now appeals the district court's judgment.

I. Background

In 1987, Congress amended the Clean Water Act to authorize the Defendant EPA to treat Indian tribes as states under certain circumstances for purposes of the Clean Water Act. Through the amendment Congress merged two of the four critical elements necessary for tribal sovereignty—water rights and government jurisdiction[2]—by granting tribes jurisdiction to regulate their water resources in the same manner as states. Congress's authorization for the EPA to treat Indian tribes as states preserves the right of tribes to govern their water resources within the comprehensive statutory framework of the Clean Water Act. This case involves the first challenge to water quality standards adopted by an Indian tribe under the Clean Water Act amendment.[4]

The Rio Grande River flows south through New Mexico before turning southeast to form the border between Texas and Mexico. Plaintiff City of Albuquerque operates a waste treatment facility which dumps into the river approximately five miles north of the Isleta Pueblo Indian Reservation. The EPA recognized Isleta Pueblo as a state for purposes of the Clean Water Act on October 12, 1992. The Isleta Pueblo adopted water quality standards for Rio Grande water flowing through the tribal reservation, which were approved by the EPA on December 24, 1992.[5] The Isleta

---

2. The other two critical elements to tribal sovereignty are land and mineral rights.

4. The Clean Water Act provides two measures of water quality. One measure is an "effluent limitations guideline." Effluent limitations guidelines are uniform, technology-based standards promulgated by the EPA, which restrict the quantities, rates and concentrations of specified substances discharged from point sources. The other measure of water quality is a "water quality standard." Unlike the technology-based effluent limitations guidelines, water quality standards are not based on pollution control technologies, but express the desired condition or use of a particular waterway. Water quality standards supplement technology-based effluent limitations guidelines "so that numerous point sources, despite individual compliance with effluent limitations, may be further regulated to prevent water quality from falling below acceptable levels." In this case, the water quality standards of the Isleta Pueblo are at issue.

There are three elements of water quality standards under the Clean Water Act: (1) one or more designated "uses" of each waterway (e.g., public water supply, recreation, or agriculture) consistent with the goals of the Act as articulated in 33 U.S.C. § 1251; (2) "criteria" expressed in numerical concentration levels or narrative statements specifying the amount of various pollutants that may be present in the water and still protect the designate uses; and (3) an anti-degradation provision.

5. The EPA provides states with substantial guidance in drafting water quality standards. States must adopt criteria that protect the designated uses. The Clean Water Act requires the EPA to develop criteria for water quality that reflect the latest scientific knowledge, and to provide those criteria to the states as guidance. States can draw upon the EPA's recommended water quality criteria or use other criteria for which they have sound scientific support.

Prior to adopting or revising any water quality standard, the state must provide notice and an opportunity for a public hearing. The criteria may be based on EPA guidance, EPA guidance modified to reflect conditions at the site, or on other scientifically defensible methods. After adoption, the states must submit the water quality standards to the EPA for review and approval. The

Pueblo's water quality standards are more stringent than the State of New Mexico's standards.

The Albuquerque waste treatment facility discharges into the Rio Grande under a National Pollution Discharge Elimination System [NPDES] permit issued by the EPA. The EPA sets permit discharge limits for waste treatment facilities so they meet state water quality standards. Albuquerque filed this action as the EPA was in the process of revising Albuquerque's NPDES permit to meet the Isleta Pueblo's water quality standards.

In its complaint, Albuquerque challenged the EPA's approval of Isleta Pueblo's water quality standards on numerous grounds. The district court denied Albuquerque's request for a temporary restraining order and a preliminary injunction. Then, the district court denied Plaintiff's motion for summary judgment while granting the Defendant EPA's motion for summary judgment.

Albuquerque now appeals the district court's judgment. On April 15, 1994, Albuquerque, the EPA, the State of New Mexico, and Isleta Pueblo agreed to a new four-year NPDES permit for Albuquerque pursuant to a stipulation and agreement. The stipulation and agreement does not mention the claims in this suit, and the EPA's regulations and the Isleta Pueblo's revised water quality standards are in effect. During the briefing stage of this appeal, Albuquerque filed a motion requesting an order vacating the district court's judgment due to mootness and remand with instructions to dismiss its complaint without prejudice.

Albuquerque has raised seven issues on appeal: (1) whether the district court's opinion and order should be vacated because the case is mooted by an agreement negotiated by the parties; (2) whether the EPA reasonably interpreted § 1377 of the Clean Water Act as providing the Isleta Pueblo's authority to adopt water quality standards that are more stringent than required by the statute, and whether the Isleta Pueblo standards can be applied by the EPA to upstream permit users; (3) whether the EPA complied with the Administrative Procedure Act's notice and comment requirements in approving the Isleta Pueblo's standards under the Clean Water Act; (4) whether the EPA's approval of the Isleta Pueblo's standards was supported by a rational basis; (5) whether the EPA's adoption of regulations providing for mediation or arbitration to resolve disputes over unreasonable consequences of a tribe's water quality standards is a reasonable interpretation of § 1377(e) of the Clean Water Act; (6) whether the EPA's approval of the Isleta Pueblo's ceremonial use designation offends the Establishment Clause of the First Amendment; and (7) whether the Isleta Pueblo's standards approved by the EPA are so vague as to deprive Albuquerque of due process.

[All seven issues were resolved against the City of Albuquerque. The court affirmed the district court's grant of summary judgment to the EPA and denial of summary

---

EPA reviews the state's water quality standards to ensure that they are consistent with the Act's requirements.

judgment to the City in all aspects. Only the court's decision on the second issue is excerpted here.]

III. Tribal Sovereignty Under the Clean Water Act

Albuquerque acknowledges that the 1987 amendment to the Clean Water Act authorizes the EPA to treat tribes as states. Albuquerque contends, however, that 33 U.S.C. §1377 does not allow tribes to establish water quality standards more stringent than federal standards and does not permit tribal standards to be enforced beyond tribal reservation boundaries.

In *Chevron, USA, Inc. v. Natural Resources Defense Council*, 467 U.S. 837, 842–43 (1984), the Supreme Court established a two-step approach to judicial review of agency interpretations of acts of Congress. First, the reviewing court must determine whether there is a clear and unambiguous congressional intent concerning the precise question at issue. If congressional intent is clear and unambiguous, then that intent is the law and must be given effect. A reviewing court proceeds to the second step "if the statute is silent or ambiguous with respect to the specific issue." Then, "the question for the court is whether the agency's answer is based on a permissible construction of the statute." The EPA, however, is entitled to considerable deference in its interpretation of the Clean Water Act because it is charged with administering the Act.

In regard to the first question at issue, we reach the second step of *Chevron* because congressional intent is unclear and ambiguous. Under Albuquerque's interpretation of §1377, tribes could devise water quality standards which are neither more nor less stringent than federal standards. Albuquerque's statutory construction is based on a negative implication inferred from Congress's failure to incorporate all provisions of the Clean Water Act in §1377(e). We find that Congress's intent is unclear and ambiguous in regard to §1377(e) but that the EPA's construction of the 1987 amendment to the Clean Water Act is reasonable and permissible.

Congress's objective in the Clean Water Act is to "restore and maintain the chemical, physical, and biological integrity of the Nation's waters" through the elimination of pollutant discharge into those waters. Through the Act, Congress designed a comprehensive regulatory scheme that recognized and preserved a primary role for the states in eliminating pollution from our waterways. The power of states under the Act is underlined by their ability to force the development of technology by setting stringent water quality standards that the EPA can enforce against upstream polluters. In the Clean Water Act, Congress provided the EPA "substantial statutory discretion." Pursuant to the 1987 amendment of the Clean Water Act, the EPA can treat Indian tribes as states under the Act, provided that the tribes meet certain criteria listed in 33 U.S.C. §1377(e) and 40 C.F.R. §131.8(a). The 1987 amendment further provides:

(a) Policy

Nothing in this section shall be construed to affect the application of section 1251(g) of this title, and all of the provisions of this section shall be carried out in accordance with the provisions of such section 1251(g) of this title. Indian tribes shall be treated as States for purposes of such section 1251(g) of this title.

. . . .

(e) Treatment as States

The Administrator is authorized to treat an Indian tribe as a State for purposes of subchapter II of this chapter and sections 1254, 1256, 1313, 1315, 1318, 1319, 1324, 1329, 1341, 1342, and 1344 of this title to the degree necessary to carry out the objectives of this section, ...[9]

In its letter approving the Isleta Pueblo's standards, the EPA cites 33 U.S.C. § 1370 as the basis for Isleta Pueblo's authority to set water quality standards that are more stringent than those recommended by the EPA under the Clean Water Act. Albuquerque argues that tribes cannot adopt discharge limits more stringent than those of the EPA because § 1377 does not make reference to § 1370. Section 1370 prohibits states from imposing standards which are less stringent than those imposed by the federal government, while acknowledging states' inherent right to impose standards or limits that are more stringent than those imposed by the federal government.[11] Congress's intent in excluding § 1370 from § 1377(e) is unclear and ambiguous. We decline to read § 1377 as incorporating § 1370 because it was not explicitly included in § 1377(e), as other sections are.

The EPA, however, also construes § 1370 as a savings clause that merely recognizes powers already held by the states. Thus, Congress's failure to incorporate § 1370 into § 1377 does not prevent Indian tribes from exercising their inherent sovereign power to impose standards or limits that are more stringent than those imposed by the federal government. Indian tribes have residual sovereign powers that already guarantee the powers enumerated in § 1370, absent an express statutory elimination of

---

9. Section 1251(g) generally preserves the authority of states to regulate water within their jurisdiction. Together, §§ 1377 and 1251(g) preserve the authority of Indian tribes—acting as states—to regulate water within their jurisdiction.

11. Section 1370 provides:

Except as expressly provided in this chapter, nothing in this chapter shall (1) preclude or deny the right of any State or political subdivision thereof or interstate agency to adopt or enforce (A) any standard or limitation respecting discharges of pollutants, or (B) any requirement respecting control or abatement of pollution; except that if an effluent limitation, or other limitation, effluent standard, prohibition, pretreatment standard, or standard of performance is in effect under this chapter, such State or political subdivision or interstate agency may not adopt or enforce any effluent limitation, or other limitation, effluent standard, prohibition, pretreatment standard, or standard of performance which is less stringent than the effluent limitation, or other limitation, effluent standard, prohibition, pretreatment standard, or standard of performance under this chapter; or (2) be construed as impairing or in any manner affecting any right or jurisdiction of the States with respect to the waters (including boundary waters) of such States.

those powers. In *Arkansas* [Arkansas v. Oklahoma, 503 U.S. 91 (1992)], the Court explained that § 1370 "only concerns *state* authority and does not constrain the *EPA's* authority," (emphasis in original); likewise, we do not view § 1370 as implicitly constraining tribes' sovereign authority. We conclude that the EPA's construction of the 1987 amendment to the Clean Water Act—that tribes may establish water quality standards that are more stringent than those imposed by the federal government—is permissible because it is in accord with powers inherent in Indian tribal sovereignty.

In the second question at issue, Albuquerque argues that § 1377 does not expressly permit Indian tribes to enforce effluent limitations or standards under § 1311 to upstream point source dischargers outside of tribal boundaries. Albuquerque misconstrues the Clean Water Act by selectively reading isolated sections; the Clean Water Act is a comprehensive regulatory scheme, and it must be read as such. The express incorporation in § 1377(e) of §§ 1341 and 1342 gives the EPA the authority to issue NPDES permits in compliance with a tribe's water quality standards.[13] Section 1341 authorizes states to establish NPDES programs with the EPA, and § 1342 authorizes the EPA to issue NPDES permits in compliance with downstream state's water quality standards. Under the statutory and regulatory scheme, tribes are not applying or enforcing their water quality standards beyond reservation boundaries.[14] Instead, it is the EPA which is exercising its own authority in issuing NPDES permits in compliance with downstream state and tribal water quality standards. In regard to this question, therefore, the 1987 amendment to the Clean Water Act clearly and unambiguously provides tribes the authority to establish NPDES programs in conjunction with the EPA. Under §§ 1311, 1341, 1342 and 1377, the EPA has the authority to require upstream NPDES dischargers, such as Albuquerque, to comply with downstream tribal standards.

Notes

1. Tribal water quality standards. As of early 2018, 54 tribes are eligible to administer WQS, and 44 now have EPA-approved WQS. In addition, EPA has promulgated federal WQS for one tribe (Colville Reservation). *See* https://www.epa.gov/wqs-tech/epa-approvals-tribal-water-quality-standards-and-contacts. For a discussion of tribal WQS, see generally Marren Sanders, *Clean Water in Indian Country: The Risks (and Rewards) of Being Treated in the Same Manner as a State*, 36 W. Mitchell L. Rev. 533 (2010).

---

13. While § 1377 incorporates § 1342, § 1342 incorporates § 1311 and thereby provides the EPA the authority to issue NPDES permits to upstream point source dischargers which are in compliance with downstream state's and tribe's water quality standards.

14. Although, Indian tribes could have inherent jurisdiction over non-Indian conduct or non-Indian resources if there is "some direct effect on the political integrity, the economic security, or the health or welfare of the tribe." *Montana v. United States*, 450 U.S. 544, 566 (1981).

2. Protection of traditional water uses. In upholding the Isleta Pueblo's ability to enact water quality standards (WQS) that are stricter than its neighboring state's, the court in *City of Albuquerque* also affirmed the tribe's ability to designate unique tribal water uses upon which those WQS are based. A number of tribes with TAS status have taken advantage of this aspect of the CWA, designating unique cultural water uses and enacting WQS that are stricter than their neighboring states. *See generally* Case Studies in Tribal Water Quality Standards Programs, https://www.epa.gov/wqs-tech/case-studies-video-and-publications-tribal-water-quality-standards.

One example among many is the Sokaogon Chippewa Community of Wisconsin's WQS. In 2005, the Sokaogon Chippewa designated uses that include the "[u]se of all Tribal Waters for cultural, subsistence, spiritual, medicinal, ceremonial, and aesthetic purposes that include any element of the environment that is ecologically associated with Tribal Waters." Sokaogon Chippewa Community Water Quality Standards, § II.A., p. 4 (2005). In order to protect these and other tribal uses, the tribe took the unique step of classifying all of its water bodies as "Outstanding National Resource Waters" (ONRW). EPA regulations state that there can be no new or increased discharges to ONRWs or to tributaries of ONRWs that would lower the overall water quality of the ONRWs. 40 C.F.R. § 131.12. In addition to the ONRW designation, the tribe established both numeric and narrative water quality criteria designed to protect its uses.

The Hoopa Valley Tribe in Northern California provides another example. The tribe's WQS establish 16 different designated uses for their water bodies including ceremonial and cultural water use, fish spawning, and water contact recreation. One such ceremonial use is the tribe's annual boat dance, which takes place on the Trinity River. The 10-day boat dance usually occurs in late August when the river is low. Thus, each year, a few days prior to the ceremony, the tribe contacts the U.S. Bureau of Reclamation to release water from an upstream reservoir.

3. TAS for state-owned submerged lands. As discussed at pages 219–225, states generally assert title to the submerged lands under navigable waters located within Indian country, under the equal footing doctrine. The State of Wisconsin challenged EPA's grant of TAS status to the Sokaogon Chippewa Community (Mole Lake Band of Lake Superior Chippewa Indians) for the purpose of setting water quality standards. Although the Sokaogon Reservation is held entirely in trust for the tribe, Wisconsin claimed that because it owned the bedlands of Rice Lake, the tribe could not exercise regulatory authority over those lands. In *Wisconsin v. Environmental Protection Agency*, 266 F.3d 741 (7th Cir. 2001), the court held that, even assuming the state did have title to the lake bed, state ownership would not affect TAS authority. "Because the state does not contend that its ownership of the beds would preclude the federal government from regulating the waters within the reservation, it cannot now complain about the federal government allowing tribes to do so." *Id.* at 747.

4. Regulation of nonmembers. The *City of Albuquerque* case broadly affirmed TAS status for tribes under the water quality standards program of the CWA. As noted, the EPA approved the Isleta Pueblo's water quality standards for the section of the Rio Grande that runs through the Pueblo.

What happens when a tribe seeks TAS for the purpose of establishing water quality standards for water bodies that are surrounded by a mix of Indian and fee lands? The EPA takes the position that environmental authority in Indian country should not be checkerboarded, that sound environmental management requires that only one government have regulatory authority over the whole of Indian country. Thus, the EPA's position is that it will grant primacy in Indian country only to that government—state or tribe—that can demonstrate its authority to regulate pollution sources throughout the tribal territory. U.S. Envt'l Protection Agency, *Federal, Tribal and State Roles in the Protection and Regulation of Reservation Environments* 3 (1991).

Initially, the EPA took the position that the TAS provision of the Clean Water Act recognized inherent tribal authority. As a result, the EPA required tribes, in order to take authority over nonmember activities on fee lands, to show that the regulated activities met the second *Montana* exception, as interpreted by *Brendale*: serious and substantial effects on "the political integrity, the economic security, or the health or welfare of the tribe." 56 Fed. Reg. 64,876 (1991). Because of the demonstrated health and welfare effects of water pollutants, the EPA believed that tribes could usually meet the *Montana* test by making a factual showing of the impact on waters within their reservations. The EPA's interpretation of the CWA was upheld in *Montana v. U.S. Envtl. Protection Agency*, 137 F.3d 1135 (9th Cir. 1998).

In 2016, EPA published its revised interpretation of the CWA's TAS provision to help streamline how tribes apply for TAS status under the CWA. EPA concluded "definitively that section 518 [the TAS provision] includes an express delegation of authority by Congress to eligible Indian tribes to administer regulatory programs over their entire reservations." 81 Fed. Reg. 30,183 (May 16, 2016). This reinterpretation makes EPA's interpretation of the CWA consistent with the agency's interpretation of the Clean Air Act, discussed below. The reinterpretation is also consistent with the EPA's interpretation of tribal regulation under the CAA, and eliminates the need for tribes to demonstrate inherent authority to regulate. *Id.*

5. The Clean Air Act: structure. The CAA requires the EPA to promulgate national ambient air quality standards for "each air pollutant for which air quality criteria have been issued," and establishes programs to address each of two types of air quality areas. In nonattainment areas, those for which the air quality is in violation of the national standards for any of the regulated pollutants, the Act calls for the "expeditious attainment" of the national air quality standards through measures such as emission limitations and permits for the construction and operation of new sources of air pollutants. For "clean," or attainment areas, the CAA establishes a program for the prevention of significant deterioration (PSD) of air quality. Attainment areas are divided into three classes: Class I for the protection of pristine air quality, Class II permitting some air quality deterioration, and Class III tolerating even greater deterioration, although in no case may air quality fall below the national standards.

The CAA gives the tribes exclusive authority to redesignate air quality for attainment-area reservations. The Act provides that "[l]ands within the exterior boundaries of reservations of federally recognized Indian tribes may be redesignated only by the appropriate Indian governing body." 42 U.S.C. § 7474(c). The Seventh Circuit held that Michigan lacked standing to challenge a reclassification of the Forest County Potawatomi Community's lands from Class II to Class I. The court ruled that the state lacked constitutional injury-in-fact; instead, the potentially injured parties were emitting sources within the state. *Michigan v. U.S. Environmental Protection Agency*, 581 F.3d 524 (7th Cir. 2009).

The 1990 CAA amendments included a TAS provision, under which the EPA must promulgate rules "specifying those provisions of this Act for which it is appropriate to treat Indian tribes as states . . . [for] the management and protection of air resources within the exterior boundaries of the reservation or other areas within the tribes jurisdiction." 42 U.S.C. § 7601(d)(2). The EPA rules treat tribes as states for virtually all purposes of the statute, with limited exceptions such as deadlines for submittal of various plans and criminal enforcement. *See* 40 C.F.R. pt. 49.

The CAA also expressly permits tribes to develop tribal implementation plans (TIPs, equivalent to state implementation plans) for the implementation, maintenance, and enforcement of reservation air quality standards. 42 U.S.C. § 7601(d)(3). Tribal authority under a TIP extends to all lands within the reservation, notwithstanding the issuance of fee patents. *Id.* § 7410(o). In 2007, the Saint Regis Mohawk Tribe and the Mohegan Tribe of Connecticut became the first tribes to receive EPA approval of their TIPs. In approving the Saint Regis Mohawk TIP, however, the EPA approved only those portions that did not conflict with or supplement federal standards, and rejected proposed tribal standards that were more stringent than federal standards. *See* 72 Fed. Reg. 45397 (Aug. 14, 2007).

In the absence of a tribal TIP, EPA's regulations call for a federal plan to fill the regulatory gap. The EPA adopted a federal plan for the Four Corners Power Plant on the Navajo Reservation that essentially replicated New Mexico state standards, which the plant had historically complied with. In *Arizona Public Serv. Co. v. EPA*, 562 F.2d 1116, 1124–26 (10th Cir. 2009), the Tenth Circuit rejected claims by environmental organizations that EPA was required to adopt more stringent federal standards, noting that the CAA requires only that standards maintain, not improve, air quality.

In addition, the CAA provides for federal resolution of disputes between tribal governments and states where either government objects to redesignation by the other or to a permit for a new emission source that would cause or contribute to air pollution in excess of that allowed by the tribal or state government. Either government may request the EPA to enter into negotiations with the governments involved, and to make recommendations to resolve the dispute. If the parties do not reach agreement, however, the EPA "shall resolve the dispute," and the federal determination then becomes part of the government's air quality plans. *Id.* § 7474(e).

Arizona Public Service Co. v. Environmental Protection Agency
211 F.3d 1280 (D.C. Cir. 2000)

HARRY T. EDWARDS, Chief Judge.

In 1990, Congress passed a compendium of amendments to the Clean Air Act ("CAA" or "the Act"). This case concerns those amendments that specifically address the power of Native American nations (or "tribes") to implement air quality regulations under the Act. Petitioners challenge the Environmental Protection Agency's ("EPA" or "the Agency") regulations, promulgated in 1998, implementing the 1990 Amendments. *See* Indian Tribes: Air Quality Planning and Management, 63 Fed. Reg. 7254 (1998) (to be codified at 40 C.F.R. pts. 9, 35, 49, 50, and 81) ("Tribal Authority Rule"). Petitioners' principal contention is that EPA has granted too much authority to tribes.

Petitioners' primary challenges focus on two issues. The first is whether Congress expressly delegated to Native American nations authority to regulate air quality on all land within reservations, including fee land held by private landowners who are not tribe members. The second is whether EPA has properly construed "reservation" to include trust lands and Pueblos. * * * [Petitioners also argue] that EPA violated the Act in authorizing tribes to administer programs affecting nonreservation "allotted lands" and "dependent Indian communities".

We find petitioners' challenges to be mostly meritless. We hold that the Agency did not err in finding delegated authority to Native American nations to regulate all land within reservations, including fee land owned by nonmembers. We also uphold EPA's construction of "reservation" to include trust lands and Pueblos.

I. BACKGROUND

A. Statutory Background

The Act establishes a framework for a federal-state partnership to regulate air quality. The provisions of the 1990 Amendments under review, fairly read, constitute an attempt by Congress to increase the role of Native American nations in this partnership.

Importantly, the 1990 Amendments added language to the Act granting EPA the "author[ity] to treat Indian tribes as States under this chapter," provided tribes meet the following requirements:

(c) the Indian tribe is reasonably expected to be capable, in the judgment of the Administrator, of carrying out the functions to be exercised in a manner consistent with the terms and purposes of this chapter and all applicable regulations.

The 1990 Amendments also directed EPA to promulgate regulations "specifying those provisions of this chapter for which it is appropriate to treat Indian tribes as States." If the Agency "determines that the treatment of Indian tribes as identical to States is inappropriate or administratively infeasible," EPA may announce other ways for the Agency to administer the program "so as to achieve the appropriate purpose."

B. The Challenged Rule

* * * On February 12, 1998, after receiving and responding to public comments, EPA issued the final Tribal Authority Rule. The Agency first found that the 1990 Amendments constitute a delegation of federal authority to regulate air quality to Native American nations within the boundaries of reservations, regardless of whether the land is owned by the tribes. The Agency read the statute to support this "territorial view of tribal jurisdiction," authorizing a "tribal role for all air resources within the exterior boundaries of Indian reservations without distinguishing among various categories of on-reservation land." EPA believed that this "territorial approach . . . best advances rational, sound, air quality management." Thus, the Agency determined that Congress delegated to tribes the authority to regulate air quality in areas within the exterior boundaries of a reservation.

The Act does not define "reservation" for the purposes of tribal regulation. EPA interpreted "reservation" to include "trust lands that have been validly set apart for the use of a tribe even though the land has not been formally designated as a reservation." The Agency explained that this interpretation was consistent with the Supreme Court's definition of "reservation" in *Oklahoma Tax Commission v. Citizen Band Potawatomi Indian Tribe of Oklahoma*, 498 U.S. 505 (1991). EPA held that it would decide on a case-by-case basis whether other types of land may be considered "reservations" under the Act.

For areas not within a "reservation," the Agency determined that a tribe would be allowed to regulate such areas if the tribe could demonstrate inherent jurisdiction over the particular non-reservation area under general principles of federal Indian law. This means that tribes may propose air quality regulations in "allotted land" and "dependent Indian communities" provided they can otherwise demonstrate inherent jurisdiction over these areas.

II. ANALYSIS

We analyze EPA's interpretation of the Act under familiar principles. "Where congressional intent is ambiguous, . . . an agency's interpretation of a statute entrusted to its administration is entitled to deference, so long as it is reasonable." Our primary concern under *Chevron* is to ensure that an agency acts within the bounds of congressional delegation. "[A]s long as the agency stays within [Congress'] delegation, it is free to make policy choices in interpreting the statute, and such interpretations are entitled to deference." *Arent v. Shalala*, 70 F.3d 610, 615 (D.C. Cir. 1995).

In evaluating the extent of congressional delegation, a reviewing court first exhausts the traditional tools of statutory construction to determine whether a congressional act admits of plain meaning. If, in light of its text, legislative history, structure, and purpose, a statute is found to be plain in its meaning, "then Congress has expressed its intention as to the question, and deference is not appropriate." If congressional intent is ambiguous, then we move to the second step of the *Chevron* analysis, and uphold an agency's interpretation if it is reasonable. The reasonableness prong includes an inquiry into whether the agency reasonably filled a gap in the statute left by Congress.

A. Express Delegation of Authority to Native American Nations

It is undisputed that Native American nations retain significant sovereign power. Native American nations have inherent power to determine forms of tribal government, to determine tribal membership, to make substantive criminal and civil laws governing internal matters, to administer tribal judicial systems, to exclude others from tribal lands, and, to some extent, to exercise civil jurisdiction over nonmembers, including non-Indians. *See* Cohen, Handbook of Federal Indian Law, at 247–53; *Montana v. United States*, 450 U.S. 544, 564 (1981). It is this last category of power that is at issue in the instant case, because petitioners claim that the 1990 Amendments to the Act do not authorize tribes to administer the Act over fee land within a reservation that is owned by nonmembers. As the Supreme Court has held,

> exercise of tribal power beyond what is necessary to protect tribal self-government or to control internal relations is inconsistent with the dependent status of the tribes, and so cannot survive without express congressional delegation.

Montana, 450 U.S. at 564.

There is no doubt that tribes hold "inherent sovereign power to exercise some forms of civil jurisdiction over non-Indians on their reservations, even on non-Indian fee lands." *Id.* at 565. For instance, if the behavior of non-Indians on fee lands within the reservation "threatens or has some direct effect on the political integrity, the economic security, or the health or welfare of the tribe," the tribe may regulate that activity. To satisfy this standard, however, a tribe must show, on a case-by-case basis, that the disputed activity constitutes a "demonstrably serious" impact that "imperil[s] the political integrity, the economic security, or the health and welfare of the tribe." *Brendale v. Confederated Tribes and Bands of the Yakima Indian Nation*, 492 U.S. 408, 431 (1989) (plurality opinion). EPA suggests, not implausibly, that "inherent sovereign power" may apply to tribal regulation under the Act of fee lands within a reservation, but the Agency does not press this argument on appeal. Rather, EPA contends that the 1990 Amendments constitute an express congressional delegation to the tribes of the authority to regulate air quality on fee lands located within the exterior boundaries of a reservation.

"There are few examples of congressional delegation of authority to tribes." Cohen, Handbook of Federal Indian Law, at 253. However, as is the case in any situation in which we are called upon to find congressional intent in construing a contested statute, we start with traditional sources of statutory interpretation, including the statute's text, structure, purpose, and legislative history. Our review of the CAA indicates that EPA's interpretation comports with congressional intent.

Section 7601(d), in pertinent part, authorizes EPA to treat otherwise eligible tribes as states if "the functions to be exercised by the Indian tribe pertain to the management and protection of air resources within the exterior boundaries of the reservation or other areas within the tribe's jurisdiction." The statute's clear distinction between areas "within the exterior boundaries of the reservation" and "other areas within the tribe's jurisdiction" carries with it the implication that Congress considered the areas within the exterior boundaries of a tribe's reservation to be per se within the tribe's jurisdiction. Thus, EPA correctly interpreted § 7601(d) to express congressional intent to grant tribal jurisdiction over nonmember owned fee land within a reservation without the need to determine, on a case-specific basis, whether a tribe possesses "inherent sovereign power" under *Montana*.

Petitioners do not dispute that an important purpose of the Act is to ensure effective enforcement of clean air standards. Obviously, this is best done by allowing states and tribes to establish uniform standards within their boundaries.

Accepting petitioners' interpretation of the 1990 Amendments would result in a "checkerboard" pattern of regulation within a reservation's boundaries that would be inconsistent with the purpose and provisions of the Act. Indeed, the Supreme Court has condemned such an approach. *See Moe v. Confederated Salish and Kootenai Tribes of Flathead Reservation*, 425 U.S. §§ 463, 479 (1976) (rejecting checkerboard approach in interpreting § 6 of the General Allotment Act, 25 U.S.C. § 349); *Seymour v. Superintendent of Washington State Penitentiary*, 368 U.S. 351, 358 (1962) (terming "impractical" a pattern of checkerboard jurisdiction under 18 U.S.C. § 1151).

Finally, we note that the legislative history of the 1990 Amendments supports EPA's interpretation. As originally introduced, 42 U.S.C. § 7601(d) differed in significant respect from the final adopted version. The original § 7601(d)(2)(B) provided that treatment of tribes as states was authorized if "the functions to be exercised by the Indian tribe are *within the area of the tribal government's jurisdiction*." S. 1630, 101st Cong. § 113(a) (1990), *reprinted in* Senate Comm. On Env't and Pub. Works, 103d Cong., Legislative History of the Clean Air Act Amendments of 1990, at 4283 (1993) (emphasis added); see also H.R. 2323, 101st Cong. § 604 (1989), reprinted in Legislative History of the Clean Air Act Amendments of 1990, at 4101. The statute as finally enacted, however, treats tribes and states as equivalent if the tribe is to exercise functions "within the exterior boundaries of the reservation or other areas within the tribe's jurisdiction."

Thus, Congress moved from authorizing tribal regulation over the areas "within the tribal government's jurisdiction" (an admittedly general category) to a bifurcated classification of all areas within "the exterior boundaries of the reservation" and "other areas within the tribe's jurisdiction." This change strongly suggests that Congress viewed all areas within "the exterior boundaries of the reservation" to be "within the area of the tribal government's jurisdiction." The change also indicates that Congress knew how to draft the 1990 Amendments to support petitioners' interpretation. The fact that Congress specifically rejected language favorable to petitioners' position and enacted instead language that is consistent with EPA's interpretation only strengthens our conclusion that the Agency has correctly ascertained Congress' intent in passing the 1990 Amendments.

Finally, petitioners note that the Agency declined to find an express delegation of power to regulate fee lands under §§ 518(e) and (h) of the Clean Water Act; this is noteworthy to petitioners, because they can glean no difference between the cited provisions under the Clean Water Act and the disputed provisions in this case under the Clean Air Act. We find no merit in this argument. The Clean Water Act states that "[t]he Administrator is authorized to treat an Indian tribe as a State . . . if . . . the functions to be exercised by the Indian tribe pertain to the management and protection of water resources which are held by an Indian tribe . . . within the borders of an Indian reservation." 33 U.S.C. § 1377(e)(2) (1994). "Reservation" is defined as "all land within the limits of any Indian reservation under the jurisdiction of the United States Government, notwithstanding the issuance of any patent, and including rights-of-way running through the reservation." *Id.* § 1377(h)(1). In construing these provisions, EPA concluded that because the legislative history was "ambiguous and inconclusive," it would not find that the Clean Water Act expanded or limited the scope of tribal authority beyond that inherent in the tribe. *Amendments to the Water Quality Standards Regulation That Pertain to Standards on Indian Reservations*, 56 Fed. Reg. 64,876, 64,880 (1991) (codified at 40 C.F.R. pt. 131).

The situation here is quite different from what EPA found with respect to the Clean Water Act. Although the disputed language in the Clean Air Act and the Clean Water Act is somewhat similar, it is far from identical. As noted above, EPA correctly relied on the CAA's clear distinction between areas "within the exterior boundaries of the reservation" and "other areas within the tribe's jurisdiction" to find a congressional intention to define the areas within the exterior boundaries of a tribe's reservation to be per se within the tribe's jurisdiction. Furthermore, as we have already indicated, the legislative history of the 1990 Amendments plainly supports EPA's interpretation. Thus, the legislative history underlying the Clean Air Act is not "ambiguous and inconclusive," as was found to be the case with respect to the Clean Water Act.

It is also of some significance that EPA's interpretation of the Clean Water Act never has been subject to judicial review on the question of the presence or absence of an express delegation to tribes to regulate fee lands within the bounds of reservations. One federal court has observed, in dicta, that "the statutory language [in the Clean Water Act] seems to indicate plainly that Congress did intend to delegate . . . authority to tribes." *State of Montana v. EPA*, 941 F.Supp. 945, 951 (D. Mont. 1996). The court noted, however, that in construing the provisions of the Clean Water Act, "EPA determined that it would take the more cautious view, that Congress did not expressly delegate jurisdiction to tribes over non-Indians and that tribes would have to prove on a case-by-case basis that they possess such jurisdiction." There was no reason for EPA to take a similarly "cautious view" with respect to the Clean Air Act, because the language and legislative history of the 1990 Amendments differ from that of the Clean Water Act.

B. EPA's Interpretation of "Reservation"

Given that EPA correctly interpreted § 7601(d) to expressly delegate jurisdiction to otherwise eligible tribes over all land within the exterior boundaries of reservations, including fee land, the next question is what areas are covered by a "reservation." EPA interprets "reservation" as used in three different statutory provisions

(42 U.S.C. §§ 7410(o), 7474(c), 7601(d)(2)(B)) to mean formally designated reservations as well as "trust lands that have been validly set apart for the use of a tribe even though the land has not been formally designated as a reservation." This includes what EPA terms "Pueblos" and tribal trust land. * * * Petitioners ignore the status of Pueblos and concentrate their attack on EPA's interpretation of "reservation" to include tribal trust land.

The Secretary of the Interior is authorized to acquire land in trust for a tribe under 25 U.S.C. § 5108 (formerly § 465), and such land can only formally be designated a reservation via the process provided by 25 U.S.C. § 467 (1994). Petitioners claim that EPA's interpretation contravenes the Act's plain language and renders 25 U.S.C. § 467 superfluous by ignoring the distinction between "trust lands" and "reservations." EPA counters that the statute is ambiguous, and that its reasonable interpretation is entitled to *Chevron* deference. [The court concluded that the meaning of "reservation" was ambiguous.]

Accordingly, we turn to step two of the *Chevron* inquiry. That is, did the Agency reasonably interpret the term "reservation" to include formal reservations, Pueblos, and trust lands? EPA supported its interpretation of "reservation" by looking to relevant case law, in particular Supreme Court precedent holding that there is no relevant distinction between tribal trust land and reservations for the purpose of tribal sovereign immunity. *See Oklahoma Tax Comm'n*, 498 U.S. at 511. This view is consonant with other federal court holdings that an Indian reservation includes trust lands.

* * * In light of the ample precedent treating trust land as reservation land in other contexts, and the canon of statutory interpretation calling for statutes to be interpreted favorably towards Native American nations, we cannot condemn as unreasonable EPA's interpretation of "reservations" to include Pueblos and tribal trust land.

C. Areas over which Tribes May Exercise Jurisdiction to Propose TIPs and Redesignations

The next issue that arises in this case is whether EPA defensibly interprets the extent of Native American authority to redesignate geographic areas and propose TIPs [Tribal Implementation Plans] under the Act. Native American nations are authorized to redesignate "[l]ands within the exterior boundaries of reservations of federally recognized Indian tribes." 42 U.S.C. § 7474(c). Similarly, Indian tribes may submit TIPs "applicable to all areas . . . located within the exterior boundaries of the reservation, notwithstanding the issuance of any patent and including rights-of-way running through the reservation." 42 U.S.C. § 7410(o).

EPA interpreted both of these provisions to authorize tribal redesignation and implementation of TIPs not just within the limits of reservations (including trust lands and Pueblos), but also within allotted lands and dependent Indian communities. No one argues that allotted lands and dependent Indian communities are within the compass of a "reservation." Instead, EPA contends that so long as a tribe demonstrates inherent jurisdiction over non-reservation areas, it may issue redesignations and TIPs for those lands. In other words, although tribes do not have express delegated authority to issue redesignations and TIPs for nonreservation areas, neither does the Act bar tribes from acting on a case-by-case basis pursuant to demonstrated inherent sovereign power.

Petitioners contend that both § 7474(c) and 7410(o) operate as geographical limitations on the power of tribes to redesignate areas and issue TIPs. Petitioners' argument with respect to § 7474(c) falls flat. This provision says that "[l]ands within the exterior boundaries of reservations of federally recognized Indian tribes may be redesignated only by the appropriate Indian governing body." Petitioners seek to twist this language into the following: "Indian tribes may only redesignate lands within the exterior boundaries of reservations." All § 7474(c) establishes, however, is the exclusive power of Indian tribes to redesignate land within a reservation; it does not address the inherent power of tribes to redesignate land in nonreservation areas.

Nor do petitioners fare better with respect to § 7410(o), which states that EPA-approved TIPs "shall become applicable to all areas (except as expressly provided otherwise in the plan) located within the exterior boundaries of the reservation, notwithstanding the issuance of any patent and including rights-of-way running through the reservation." Petitioners read this to mean that EPA may only approve a TIP if it applies within reservation areas. As EPA points out, petitioners' interpretation cannot stand for several reasons. First, § 7410(o) cross-references § 7601(d), which allows for tribes to exercise jurisdiction over reservation areas or "other areas within the tribe's jurisdiction." Most importantly, § 7410(o) provides that TIPs apply to all areas within the borders of a reservation once the plan "becomes effective in accordance with the regulations promulgated under section 7601(d) of this title." Therefore, it is permissible for EPA to give § 7410(o) the reading it proffers: a reinforcement of tribes' jurisdiction to implement TIPs in reservation land. Petitioners would instead read the statute as an express limitation of tribal jurisdiction. Under step one of *Chevron*, we cannot say that congressional intent is free of ambiguity on this question.

Accordingly, we turn to whether EPA's interpretation is reasonable. We believe that it is undoubtedly so. To read the statute otherwise would result in several anomalies. First, EPA notes without dispute that petitioners' interpretation would allow a state's implementation plan to apply to non-reservation areas, even where a tribe has demonstrated inherent jurisdiction over those areas. Second, petitioners' reading would disable a tribe from comprehensively administering the Act. A tribe could implement, in non-reservation areas, new source performance standards under the Act, but not administer a TIP, even though the regulated activity "threatens or has some direct effect on the . . . health or welfare of the tribe." *Montana*, 450 U.S. at 566. EPA's reading of the statute to allow such regulation is a reasonable interpretation of §§ 7410(o) and 7601(d).

DOUGLAS GINSBURG, Circuit Judge, dissenting in part:

With certain exceptions, of which more later, an Indian tribe lacks inherent authority to regulate the conduct of a nonmember on land he owns within the boundaries of the tribe's reservation. Lacking inherent authority, a tribe may exercise regulatory authority over such non-Indian lands only by express congressional delegation. The court today determines that § 301(d)(2)(B) of the Clean Air Act, 42 U.S.C. § 7601(d)(2)(B), expressly delegates to tribes—contingent upon approval by the EPA Administrator—authority to enforce the Clean Air Act on nonmembers' lands within a reservation. Finding no such express delegation in § 301(d)(2)(B), I dissent from Part II.A of the opinion for the court.

* * * [I]t seems to me clear that the 1990 Amendments do contain an express delegation of authority over fee lands and rights of way—but not in § 301(d), which governs tribal enforcement of all Clean Air Act programs specified by the Administrator. Rather, the delegation is in § 110(o), which governs only tribal implementation plans (TIPs).

Notes

1. Indian country "in question." The District of Columbia Circuit struck down a portion of EPA's CAA rules in *Michigan v. Environmental Protection Agency*, 268 F.3d 1075 (D.C. Cir. 2001). EPA stated that it would administer and enforce a federal permit program for those lands whose Indian country status was "in question" until and unless the status of the lands was resolved. *See* 40 C.F.R. § 71.4(b). The federal court ruled, however, that EPA had exceeded its statutory authority because the CAA authorized it to implement a federal program in Indian country, not in areas where the Indian country status was in question. Thus, EPA was required to determine the Indian country status of the lands prior to instituting a federal program. The court further determined that EPA, in making a determination of Indian country status, was required to use notice and comment rulemaking.

The District of Columbia Circuit struck down a similar argument in *Oklahoma v. Environmental Protection Agency*, 740 F.3d 185 (D.C. Cir. 2014). EPA attempted to establish a federal rule for attainment of national ambient air quality standards in Indian County not located within reservations. 76 Fed. Reg. 38,748 (July 1, 2011). According to the CAA, tribes may manage and protect resources within "the exterior boundaries of the reservation or other areas within the tribe's jurisdiction." 42 U.S.C. § 7601(d)(2)(B). Under the EPA's tribal authority rule (TAR), upheld in *Arizona Public Service Co. v. EPA*, a tribe may implement the CAA within its reservation without proving jurisdiction, but must demonstrate jurisdiction over non-reservation areas. Under the TAR, a federal implementation plan applied to all of Indian country nationwide except where EPA had already approved a tribal program. Oklahoma challenged the rule, alleging that a state's plan applied to pollution sources outside reservations until EPA demonstrates the existence of tribal regulatory authority. The court agreed with the state, finding that the newly promulgated rule was arbitrary and capricious under the Administrative Procedure Act for two reasons. First, no regulatory gap (a justification for the new rule) existed because the State Implementation Plan applied unless a tribe demonstrated regulatory authority. Second, EPA cannot institute a Federal Implementation Plan until it has determined that the jurisdiction's plan is inadequate. The court did not reach the second issue, as it found in Oklahoma's favor on the first issue. Until a tribe demonstrates jurisdiction over non-reservation Indian country, the court found that jurisdiction resides in the state. Accordingly, the court determined that EPA's interpretation under the newly promulgated rule was not entitled deference because its interpretation violates the CAA and was therefore arbitrary and capricious.

Further, in December 2008, the Eastern Shoshone and Northern Arapaho Tribes of the Wind River Reservation applied to the EPA for treatment as a state under the CAA. The Tribes asserted jurisdiction over Riverton, Wyoming in their application. In 2013, EPA approved the Tribes' application, including jurisdiction over Riverton. On appeal to the Tenth Circuit, however, the court held that a 1905 statute diminished the Wind River Reservation, vacated the EPA's TAS order, and remanded for further proceedings. *Wyoming v. U.S. Envtl. Protection Agency*, 875 F.3d 505 (10th Cir. 2017). For a discussion of reservation diminishment, see Chapter 2, pages 129–153.

2. No tribes-as-states provision: the Resource Conservation and Recovery Act. Congress enacted RCRA, 42 U.S.C. § 6901 *et seq.*, to reduce or eliminate the generation of hazardous waste, and to treat and store existing hazardous waste in a manner that will minimize the threat to human health and the environment. RCRA's ambitious purpose is to regulate and manage hazardous waste from generation through final disposal, popularly referred to as "cradle to grave" management, through measures such as identification of hazardous wastes and waste sites; standards for generators, transporters, and owners and operators of treatment, storage, and disposal facilities; and permits for the treatment, storage, and disposal of hazardous waste. The hazardous waste program of RCRA was at issue in *Washington DOE*, page 286.

RCRA also regulates non-hazardous wastes, although less stringently. Under Subtitle D of RCRA, EPA promulgated regulations establishing minimum national criteria for all municipal solid waste landfills. 40 CFR pt. 258. The regulations, enforced through state permit programs, apply to owners and operators of all new and existing municipal solid waste landfills and to other solid waste disposal facilities not regulated under the hazardous waste regulations of Subtitle C. The regulations cover location restrictions, operating and design criteria, groundwater monitoring and corrective action, closure and post-closure requirements, and financial assurance criteria. Any municipal landfill failing to meet the federal criteria is considered an open dump, and open dumps are prohibited under RCRA.

RCRA is the only major federal environmental law which does not treat tribes as states. Legislation to reauthorize RCRA was introduced in the 102nd Congress, but did not come to a vote before the session adjourned. The proposed Senate amendments to RCRA contained a provision authorizing EPA to treat tribes as states, and it is anticipated that any final reauthorization of RCRA which is eventually enacted will contain a TAS provision.

When Congress failed to act, EPA proposed rules for tribes to take primacy for the RCRA Subtitle D municipal solid waste landfill permit program, 61 Fed. Reg. 2584 (Jan. 26, 1996), and the Subtitle C hazardous waste management program, 61 Fed. Reg. 30472 (June 14, 1996). The following case addresses the fate of those regulations and of EPA's approval of tribal permit programs under RCRA.

Backcountry against Dumps v. Environmental Protection Agency

100 F.3d 147 (D.C. Cir. 1996)

TATEL, Circuit Judge.

The Campo Band of Mission Indians, a small tribe in San Diego County, California, applied to the Environmental Protection Agency for approval of its solid waste permitting plan pursuant to the Resource Conservation and Recovery Act. That Act requires states to submit solid waste permitting plans to the agency for approval. The Act defines Indian tribes as municipalities, not states, and says nothing about municipalities submitting permitting plans for the agency's review. The EPA nonetheless determined that it had authority to approve the tribe's permitting program. Because we find that the Act does not give the EPA such authority, we grant the petition for review and vacate the agency's decision.

I.

The Resource Conservation and Recovery Act (RCRA), 42 U.S.C. §6901 *et seq.* (1994), establishes a "comprehensive federal program to regulate the handling of solid wastes." Subtitle C addresses the treatment, storage, and disposal of hazardous waste. Subtitle D governs the disposal of nonhazardous solid waste and of small-quantity hazardous solid waste not regulated under Subtitle C.

[Pursuant to the Subtitle D requirements, the EPA established minimum federal standards for municipal solid waste landfills. Section 6945(c) of RCRA requires states to implement permit programs to ensure that landfills comply with those standards. A state with an EPA-approved permit program must meet the federal operating standards, but is allowed flexibility in its choice of design standards.]

The focus of this case is the statute's definition of "state." Section 6903(31) defines a "state" as "any of the several States, the District of Columbia, the Commonwealth of Puerto Rico, the Virgin Islands, Guam, American Samoa, and the Commonwealth of the Northern Mariana Islands." Indian tribes are listed in the statute's definition of "municipality:"

> The term "municipality" (A) means a city, town, borough, county, parish, district, or other public body created by or pursuant to State law, with responsibility for the planning or administration of solid waste management, or an Indian tribe or authorized tribal organization or Alaska Native village or organization, and (B) includes any rural community or unincorporated

town or village or any other public entity for which an application for assistance is made by a State or political subdivision thereof.

As "municipalities," Indian tribes are eligible for federal funding to develop solid waste management and resource recovery programs, and are also subject to citizen suits to enforce the revised criteria.

The Campo Band of Mission Indians occupies an approximately 23-square-mile reservation just north of the Mexican border in San Diego County, California. About 200 of its members live on the reservation. The tribe is governed by a General Council composed of all of its adult members.

In 1990, Mid-American Waste Systems, Inc. proposed developing a 600-acre landfill in the southeast corner of the Campo reservation. The landfill site is bordered on the east, south, and southwest by non-Indian farms and residences, including the residence of petitioner Donna Tisdale. As proposed by Mid-American, the landfill would have a 28-million-ton capacity, to be used over approximately 30 years. According to Tisdale and the other petitioner, Backcountry Against Dumps, the landfill would be the nation's largest solid-waste facility on an Indian reservation. The Bureau of Indian Affairs estimated the Band's share of facility revenues would be about $1.6 million a year.

Also in 1990, the tribe's General Council adopted the Tribal Environmental Policy Act of 1990 and a Solid Waste Management Code governing the construction and operation of solid-waste facilities on the reservation. These in turn established the Campo Environmental Protection Agency. With authority over all solid-waste operations on reservation land, this agency has primary responsibility for the enforcement of federal environmental laws on the reservation. The Tribe also established the Campo Band Environmental Appeals Court to hear appeals from final actions of the Campo Environmental Protection Agency, prohibited open dumping of solid waste within the reservation, and established a detailed system for managing solid waste.

[The Campo Band sought approval of its solid waste program under RCRA §6945(c). In granting approval, the EPA admitted that RCRA did not expressly treat tribes as states, but stated its belief that "adequate authority existed under RCRA" for tribal programs.]

II.

Petitioners argue that the EPA lacks authority to approve the Campo Band's solid waste permitting process, pointing out that the tribe is not a state under RCRA, but a municipality. According to the EPA, since RCRA does not indicate whether entities other than states may submit solid waste permitting plans for the agency's approval, we must defer to the agency's reasonable interpretation of the statute.

To resolve this dispute, we look to the familiar standards set forth in *Chevron U.S.A. Inc. v. Natural Resources Defense Council, Inc.*, 467 U.S. 837 (1984). Using "traditional tools of statutory construction," we first examine whether the statute "directly [speaks] to the precise question at issue"—here, whether the statute authorizes the

EPA to approve solid waste permitting plans submitted by Indian tribes. If so, we follow the statute's instructions. If Congress has not addressed the issue, we defer to the agency's interpretation if it is reasonable.

We begin and end our analysis at *Chevron*'s first step. Section 6945(c) is clear on its face: "States" are required to submit solid waste management plans to the EPA for review and approval. Indian tribes are defined as municipalities, not states. Section 6945(c) says nothing about municipalities submitting their own solid waste permitting plans to the EPA. In approving the Campo Band's plan, the EPA essentially removed Indian tribes from their statutory status as "municipalities," creating a new, intermediate status for Indian tribes in section 6945(c), a status equivalent to that of a state. Not only does the agency's interpretation of section 6945(c) conflict with the plain language of RCRA's definitional provisions, but it also rewrites section 6945(c) itself. According to the agency, the formerly clear permitting provision now reads: "States must, and Indian tribes may, but other local governments may not" adopt permit programs and submit them to the agency for review and approval. This is not what the statute says.

We think it significant that when Congress wants to treat Indian tribes as states, it does so in clear and precise language. For example, a provision of the Clean Air Act authorizes the EPA Administrator to "treat Indian tribes as States" and requires the Administrator to promulgate regulations specifying the provisions of the Act under which it is appropriate to treat tribes as states. Likewise, the Safe Drinking Water Act authorizes the EPA Administrator to "treat Indian Tribes as States" and to delegate primary enforcement responsibility to tribes. A provision of the Clean Water Act provides that "Indian tribes shall be treated as States" for purposes of that Act. These clear statements of Congressional intent to treat Indian tribes as states stand in marked contrast to RCRA's equally clear requirement that "states"—not municipalities, and therefore not Indian tribes—must submit permitting plans for EPA's review.

Attempting to move past *Chevron* step one, the EPA argues that, since section 6945(c) is silent as to its application to Indian tribes, the statute is "ambiguous." Therefore, it argues, we must defer to its reasonable interpretation of the statute.

[T]he statute here is neither silent nor ambiguous. It is quite clear. "States" must submit solid waste management plans to the EPA. Indian tribes are not states under the statute; they are municipalities. The EPA would have a stronger case if Indian tribes were not defined anywhere in the statute. *See, e.g., Nance v. EPA*, 645 F.2d 701, 713–14 (9th Cir. 1981) (where Indian tribes not treated as "states" or "municipalities" prior to the amendment of the Clean Air Act, EPA filled gap in statute and allowed tribe to designate air quality standards on its land). Were that the case, we would move to *Chevron*'s second step. But because Indian tribes are explicitly defined as municipalities, and because only states may submit solid waste management plans for EPA approval, the agency's position that it may approve plans submitted by Indian tribes is inconsistent with the statute's plain language.

Our determination that EPA lacks authority to approve the Campo Band's solid waste management plan does not, as both the agency and the Campo Band argue, strip the tribe of its sovereign authority to govern its own affairs. With its comprehensive environmental codes and an agency and court devoted solely to enforcing tribal and federal environmental regulations, the tribe has as much authority to create and enforce its own solid waste management plan as it ever did. The only difference between the Campo Band and states with approved plans is that a landfill operating on the reservation must comply with the part 258 design standards in addition to the operating standards. Referring back to our earlier example, a landfill operating on the reservation must use the "six-inches-of-earthen-cover" design rather than any equally effective alternative. In other words, what the tribe loses is the ability to take advantage of the leeway built into the regulations, including the ability to take site-specific factors into account.

According to the EPA, if it cannot review and approve tribal solid waste management plans, a "regulatory gap" will exist on reservation land, conjuring up the specter of Indian reservations as safe havens for all manner of illegal dumping activity. But this argument ignores the fact that even in the absence of an EPA-approved solid waste management plan, the revised criteria automatically apply to owners and operators of solid-waste facilities. Individuals aggrieved by a facility's failure to comply with federal regulations may institute citizen suits against the offending facility owner, and Indian tribes are not exempted from citizen suits. The EPA, of course, may also initiate emergency abatement actions if it has evidence that an "imminent and substantial endangerment to health or the environment" exists. What the EPA complains of is not a "regulatory gap" at all, but the statute's different treatment of states and Indian tribes. Although treating tribes differently from states may be unfair as a policy matter, and may be the result of Congressional inadvertence, the remedy lies with Congress, not with the EPA or the courts.

The Campo Band and the EPA, however, need not wait for Congress to act to give the tribe the flexibility it seeks. At oral argument, all parties agreed that the Campo Band could seek EPA approval for a site-specific regulation, which would satisfy both RCRA and the tribe's desire for flexibility in designing and monitoring a landfill on its reservation. In fact, Campo Band's counsel told us at oral argument that, because the reservation is located in a seismic zone, the tribe may have to seek such a site-specific ruling in order to maintain a landfill facility.

We grant the petition for review and vacate the EPA's Notice of Final Determination.

Notes

1. ***Backcountry Against Dumps* versus *Washington DOE*.** Is the D.C. Circuit's decision in *Backcountry Against Dumps* inconsistent with the Ninth Circuit's decision in *Washington DOE*, page 286? After the D.C. Circuit's decision, who regulates landfill siting on the Campo Reservation? After the Ninth Circuit's decision, who regulates hazardous waste on reservations in Washington?

2. Environmental remediation statutes. RCRA addresses the regulation of hazardous waste and, to a lesser extent, other solid wastes, in part to reduce any possibility of a release into the environment. Once environmental contamination occurs, whether from a hazardous waste or other hazardous substance, other federal programs address issues of environmental remediation.

a. Comprehensive Environmental Response, Compensation, and Liability Act (CERCLA, also known as Superfund), 42 U.S.C. §9601 *et seq*. CERCLA is aimed primarily at cleaning up hazardous waste sites and spills. To that end, CERCLA provides for notification procedures and federal remedial action in case of the release of a hazardous substance; a "Superfund" to pay the costs of responding to a release; and standards for clean up of hazardous materials releases. The Act also establishes a national priorities list of sites most in need of remedial action.

The Superfund Amendments and Reauthorization Act of 1986 (SARA) provides that a tribal government "shall be afforded substantially the same treatment as a State" with respect to a number of the provisions of CERCLA, including notification of releases, consultation on remedial actions, access to information, roles and responsibilities under the national contingency plan, and submittal of priorities for remedial action. 42 U.S.C. §9626. The statute authorizes tribes to enter into contracts or cooperative agreements with the federal government to carry out removal or other remedial actions in case of releases of hazardous substances, 42 U.S.C. §9604(d), and to assert claims against the Superfund for damages to tribal natural resources and for the costs of restoring or replacing damaged resources. 42 U.S.C. §9611(b)(1).

Some express exceptions to the general TAS provision exist. Each state is entitled to have one facility on the national list of priorities for remedial action. The treatment of tribes as states, however, specifically excludes the entitlement for one facility on the national list. Tribes also are exempt from certain assurances of future maintenance and cost-sharing required of states in the case of federal remedial actions, and from certain time limitations placed on state governments.

b. Oil Pollution Act of 1990 (OPA), 33 U.S.C. §2701 *et seq*. The OPA provides, among other things, for the recovery of damages for injury to or destruction of natural resources caused by oil spills. 33 U.S.C. §2702. Liability for damages to natural resources shall be to the government which owns, manages, or controls the resources. The provision for tribes parallels those for the federal and state governments: "[L]iability shall be . . . to any Indian tribe for natural resources belonging to, managed by, controlled by, or appertaining to such Indian tribe". Tribes, like states, are authorized to designate a trustee for natural resources to assess natural resources damages and develop and implement a plan for restoration, rehabilitation, and replacement of the resources. 33 U.S.C. §2706. Tribes may recover costs incurred in carrying out the trustee functions from the Oil Spill Liability Trust Fund. 33 U.S.C. §2712.

3. Natural resource damages (NRD) actions. Under both CERCLA and the OPA, when a release of hazardous substances or oil damages affect an Indian tribe's natural resources, Indian tribal trustees may act on behalf of the tribe to recover compensatory damages. Typically, Indian tribal trustees are the head of the tribe's governing body or a tribal official designated by the tribal governing body. 40 C.F.R. § 300.610. The Bureau of Indian Affairs also may act as a trustee "for those natural resources for which the Indian tribe would otherwise act as trustee in those cases where the United States acts on behalf of the Indian tribe." *Id.*§ 300.600.

Under both statutes, "natural resources" include "land, fish, wildlife, biota, air, water, ground water, drinking water supplies, and other such resources belonging to managed by, held in trust by, appertaining to, or otherwise controlled by . . . any Indian tribe." 42 U.S.C. § 9601(16) (CERCLA); 33 U.S.C. § 2701(20) (OPA). This definition embraces more than those resources that are "owned" by a tribe or the federal government in trust, including inherently migratory resources like wildlife and waters that are "managed by, controlled by, or appertaining to" the tribe. Thus, the release of a hazardous substance need not occur within the boundaries of a reservation in order for a tribal natural resource to be adversely affected. The only requirement is that the damaged resource be a resource that the tribe holds in trust for its members. Thus, when a release is discovered, the initial question is which trustees' resources have been adversely affected. The answer to this question is not always easy.

Once damage to natural resources has occurred, and the interested trustees have been identified and notified, the trustees must determine the extent of the harm and the most appropriate compensatory measures. This is typically accomplished via a natural resource damage assessment (NRDA).

The Superfund site known as Commencement Bay in Washington provides an example of how the NRDA settlement process works. The Commencement Bay case originally involved over 150 potentially responsible parties (PRPs). The PRPs included landowners conducting industrial and commercial activities on or adjacent to waterways that feed into the Bay. These activities resulted in the contamination of the Bay, which in turn affected Bay resources like salmon, which use the Bay as a migratory pathway. In 1991, trustees, including the BIA, the Puyallup Tribe of Indians, and the Muckleshoot Indian Tribe, formally began to assess damages. Since that time, numerous settlement agreements have been reached by responsible parties and trustees. These agreements all provide funds for restoration projects and typically designate a resource trustee to oversee the restoration project. The settlements also typically provide for damage payments to be made directly to the trustees. Examples of settlement agreements from the NRDA process at Commencement Bay and the resulting projects can be found at: https://darrp.noaa.gov/hazardous-waste/commencement-bay.

Responsible parties are not liable for damages that occurred prior to CERCLA's enactment, although some damages can be the result of non-human activities that occurred post-enactment like passive water migration. Pre-CERCLA natural resource damages may be reached through a common law NRD action. *See Quapaw Tribe of Oklahoma v. Blue Tee Corp.*, 653 F. Supp. 2d 1166 (N.D. Okla. 2009) (holding that the tribe had *parens patriae* standing to protect its quasi-sovereign interests in natural resources "within the Tribe's authority," specifically including resources on tribal lands, that were damaged by early 20th century lead and zinc mining).

Note on Tribal Environmental Law

The materials on environmental authority thus far have focused on the application of federal environmental laws to Indian country. But in addition to federal law, tribes are free to enact their own tribal environmental laws. As the D.C. Circuit explained in *Backcountry against Dumps*, the tribe's inability to be treated as a state under RCRA "does not, as both the agency and the Campo Band argue, strip the tribe of its sovereign authority to govern its own affairs. With its comprehensive environmental codes and an agency and court devoted solely to enforcing tribal and federal environmental regulations, the tribe has as much authority to create and enforce its own solid waste management plan as it ever did." Tribal environmental laws therefore can play an important role in regulating the environment in Indian country.

For many tribes, environmental protection begins with a traditional "environmental ethic." *See* Rebecca Tsosie, *Tribal Environmental Policy in an Era of Self-Determination: The Role of Ethics, Economics and Traditional Ecological Knowledge*, 21 Vt. L. Rev. 225 (1996) (excerpted at page 8). Traditional environmental norms, however, are seldom put into written law. This can present a problem for tribes trying to enforce their tribal environmental customs, especially if enforcement is sought against a non-member.

> The continuation of indigenous environmental management systems, therefore, may depend on a coherent understanding and acceptance of the group's traditional norms and values, rather than norms inculcated by market forces or individual liberalism. Indigenous environmental management systems also depend on the group's ability to enforce its rules through traditional institutions which have authority that is recognized as legitimate by tribal members. To the extent that cultural attrition and the presence of non-members on the reservation undermine the social cohesiveness of earlier, unwritten systems of tribal common law, it is possible that the effectiveness of traditional norms will ultimately depend on some formalization as tribal law, rather than as mere "custom."

Id. at 294.

The development of tribal environmental laws can sometimes prove complicated as tribes work to harmonize traditional customs and beliefs with the legal expectations associated with the American legal system. As Professor Tsosie notes, "traditional indigenous institutions must be reconciled with those organized by tribes under centralized governmental structures, based largely on norms and values imposed by federal legislation." *Id.* at 293. For example, the Confederated Salish and Kootenai Natural Resources Department codified its environmental scheme in a wilderness management plan, which details how the Tribes will manage their natural resources. A central purpose of the Tribes' Plan is to preserve the Tribes' designated wilderness under the tribal environmental code for future generations. *See* Confederated Salish & Kootenai Tribes Wildland Recreation Department, Mission Mountains Tribal Wilderness Management Plan 3 (June, 1982).

For an example of a tribe that has codified its environmental law related to waste disposal, see *Colville Confederated Tribes v. Condon*, No. FW-2003–03063 (Confederated Tribes of the Colville Res. Tr. Ct., May 12, 2008). In *Condon*, the tribal court held that the tribal member defendant had failed to come into compliance with the Tribes' applicable waste disposal provisions and was therefore subject to a civil fine.

In addition to assisting tribes in addressing environmental challenges within their territories, tribal environmental laws are also an expression of tribal self-determination and sovereignty. For discussions of how the enactment of tribal environmental laws promotes tribal sovereignty, see Dean B. Suagee, *Tribal Environmental Policy Acts and the Landscape of Environmental Law*, 23 Nat. Resources & Env't 12 (Spr. 2009); Jill Elise Grant, *The Navajo Nation EPA's Experience with "Treatment as a State" and Primacy*, 21 Nat. Resources & Env't 9 (Wtr. 2007).

In light of the foregoing, what issues should you consider if called upon to draft a tribe's environmental code? Is it more important that tribal environmental laws conform to the environmental ethics of the tribal community or to the expectations of the legal non-tribal community?

A recent study looked at the tribal environmental codes of 74 federally recognized tribes located within Arizona, Montana, New York and Oklahoma. The study determined that approximately half of the tribal codes reviewed, or the tribal codes of 36 tribes, included code provisions related to air pollution, water pollution, solid waste disposal or environmental quality generally. Elizabeth Ann Kronk Warner, *Examining Tribal Environmental Law*, 39 Colum. J. Envt'l L. 42 (2014). Examining the environmental tribal laws of the same 74 federally recognized tribes, a second article considered how tribes have adopted and adapted federal environmental laws within the tribal context. Elizabeth Ann Kronk Warner, *Tribes as Innovative Environmental "Laboratories,"* 86 U. Colo. L. Rev. 789 (2015). The third article in the series considers sources of law, other than tribal codes, adopted by tribes under their inherent sovereignty to regulate their environments. The article also argues that tribes are truly innovating in the area of environmental regulation, and are therefore valuable regulatory laboratories that other sovereigns can look to for guidance as to effective environmental regulation. Elizabeth Ann Kronk Warner, *Justice Brandeis and Indian Country: Lessons from the Tribal Environmental Laboratory*, 47 Ariz. St. L.J. 857 (2015).

2. Application of Environmental Laws to Tribes

Notes

The materials thus far have focused on who regulates under the federal environmental laws. But tribes may also be subject to regulation under those statutes. The cases that follow raise issues of tribal sovereign immunity and tribal-versus-federal court jurisdiction. The notes following offer some background on those issues.

1. Tribal sovereign immunity. Like any sovereign, tribal governments enjoy sovereign immunity from suit without the consent of the sovereign. *See Michigan v. Bay Mills Indian Community*, 134 S. Ct. 2024 (2014); *Kiowa Tribe of Oklahoma v. Manufacturing Technologies, Inc.*, 523 U.S. 751 (1998). Tribal sovereign immunity may be waived by the tribe or abrogated by Congress. *Kiowa Tribe*, 523 U.S. at 754. Congressional consent to lawsuits against tribes should not be implied, but rather should be "unequivocally expressed." *See Santa Clara Pueblo v. Martinez*, 436 U.S. 49, 58 (1977). Did the Eighth Circuit, in the case that follows, properly apply this principle?

2. Exhaustion of tribal remedies. In two cases in the mid-1980s, the Supreme Court ruled that defendants in actions in tribal courts are generally required to exhaust their tribal court remedies before proceeding in federal court, even if the federal court properly had jurisdiction over the lawsuit. *National Farmers Union Insurance Cos. v. Crow Tribe*, 471 U.S. 845 (1985) (federal court proceeding predicated on federal question jurisdiction); *Iowa Mutual Insurance Co. v. LaPlante*, 480 U.S. 9 (1987) (federal court proceeding predicated on diversity jurisdiction). Subsequently, lower federal courts generally have applied the exhaustion doctrine even if there is no pending tribal court action. The exhaustion doctrine, designed to further tribal self-government by litigating cases within tribal jurisdiction in tribal courts, encourages federal courts to stay proceedings or dismiss lawsuits pending exhaustion of tribal remedies. Once tribal remedies are exhausted, the defendant may seek federal court review on the issue of whether the tribal court jurisdiction was proper as a matter of federal law.

The Supreme Court addressed tribal court jurisdiction in *Strate v. A-1 Contractors*, 520 U.S. 438 (1997), excerpted at page 275. At the end of the excerpted material, the Court attached a footnote:

> When, as in this case, it is plain that no federal grant provides for tribal governance of nonmembers' conduct on [fee land or its jurisdictional equivalent], it will be equally evident that tribal courts lack adjudicatory authority over disputes arising from such conduct. * * * Therefore, when tribal-court jurisdiction over an action such as this one is challenged in federal court, the otherwise applicable exhaustion requirement must give way, for it would serve no purpose other than delay.

Id. at 459 n.14. More recently, in *Nevada v. Hicks*, 533 U.S. 353 (2001), excerpted at page 277, the Court quoted the footnote from *Strate*, admitted that the exception was "technically inapplicable" because in *Hicks* the search in question took place on trust lands, but claimed the reasoning behind the exception applied "[s]ince it is clear ... that tribal courts lack jurisdiction over state officials for causes of action relating to the performance of official duties." Thus, the Court concluded that "the tribal exhaustion requirement in such cases would serve no purpose other than delay, and is therefore unnecessary." *Id.* at 369.

The following case rejects the exhaustion doctrine. For what reasons? How, if at all, might the reasoning in *Strate* or *Hicks* affect the Eight Circuit's decision?

Blue Legs v. United States Bureau of Indian Affairs
867 F.2d 1094 (8th Cir. 1989)

HEANEY, Circuit Judge.

Taylor Wallace Blue Legs and Margaret Jenkins are members of the Oglala Sioux Tribe (Tribe) of Indians and reside on the Pine Ridge Indian Reservation (Reservation). They brought suit against the Environmental Protection Agency (EPA), the EPA's Administrator, the Bureau of Indian Affairs (BIA), the Indian Health Service (IHS) and subsequently joined the Tribe, complaining that garbage dumps located on the Reservation were maintained in violation of federal law. The United States District Court for the District of South Dakota dismissed the EPA and its Administrator. It ordered the Tribe, the BIA and IHS to submit a plan within 120 days to bring the dump sites into compliance (stayed pending our review).

On appeal, the Tribe argues that it is immune from suit, that resort must first be made to tribal courts, and that in any event, BIA and IHS are solely responsible for compliance. BIA and IHS argue that they have no legal duty to clean up the dumps; rather, the Tribe is responsible. We affirm the district court and hold that the Tribe, BIA and IHS share the responsibility of bringing the garbage dumps into compliance.

BACKGROUND

The district court's order covered fourteen dump sites located on the Reservation. "Most of the sites are in the vicinity of or near one or more of the following: houses, schools, and streams or springs." The court found that twelve sites are unfenced. Six sites lack sanitary trenches. No site has a dirt covering. No site is supervised. All locations have had fires at the sites. Laboratory analysis of water samples from the sites showed "significant contamination," including organisms capable of "caus[ing] disease in wildlife and frequently in humans *** urinary tract infections and infections of the respiratory system *** neonatal infections, involving the central nervous system and other organs." Children, pets and others can easily come in contact with the sites given the present condition of the dumps. Moreover, the sites represent a danger even to those who do not wander near them.

BIA and IHS operate schools, a hospital, a health station, and own over 47 homes and other residences on the Reservation. BIA and IHS dispose of their trash through the Pine Ridge Village Garbage Service (Service), an adjunct of the Tribe. At some locations BIA personnel transport the waste directly to disposal facilities; at other locations the Service collects the waste. Immediately, infectious waste is incinerated at the IHS health stations. IHS provides technical assistance to the Tribe in the form of information and research about solid waste disposal, and has in the past provided some money to help purchase relevant equipment. Neither agency supervises the Tribe's waste disposal but both are aware of the conditions on the Reservation and continue to contract with the Service for disposal in violation of law.

There is little disagreement between the parties about these facts. This dispute concerns who is to pay for the initial clean-up and subsequent maintenance.

I. THE TRIBE

The Tribe argues that it is immune from this suit, that the plaintiffs must exhaust tribal remedies before proceeding in federal court and that the federal defendants are solely responsible for cleaning up the sites. The district court rejected the Tribe's first two contentions, as do we.

A. Sovereign Immunity

Over the course of the last two centuries Indian tribes have evolved into dependent associations with limited powers of self-government. Where Congress clearly indicates that Indian tribes are subject to a given law, no tribal sovereignty exists to bar the reach or enforcement of that law. We turn to the question of whether Congress has abrogated the tribe's immunity in this matter.

Congress passed the Resource Conservation and Recovery Act of 1976 (RCRA) to remedy national problems caused by hazardous waste and solid waste disposal. Congress was concerned that a failure to address all sources of pollution would render efforts aimed at other sources ineffectual.

Congress also decided to regulate the disposal of discarded materials on reservations. Under the RCRA, citizens are permitted to bring compliance suits "against any person (including (a) the United States, and (b) any other governmental instrumentality or agency * * *) who is alleged to be in violation * * *." "Person" is subsequently defined to include municipalities. Municipalities include "an Indian tribe or authorized tribal organization * * *." It thus seems clear that the text and history of the RCRA clearly indicates congressional intent to abrogate the Tribe's sovereign immunity with respect to violations of the RCRA.

B. Exhaustion

The Tribe makes a related claim that even if it is not immune from suit, respect for tribal self-government requires that the plaintiffs initially bring suit in tribal courts. The government defendants endorsed this claim but clearly indicated under questioning that they would not submit to the jurisdiction of a tribal court.

The judicial preference for tribal court exhaustion is an adjunct to Congress' general preference for tribal self-government. We agree that tribal courts are presumed to have civil jurisdiction over the actions of non-Indians on reservation lands absent the affirmative limitations of federal treaties and statutes. Determining the "extent of a tribal court's jurisdiction * * * require[s] a careful examination of tribal sovereignty, the extent to which the sovereignty has been altered, divested, or diminished, as well as a detailed study of relevant statutes, Executive Branch policy as embodied in treaties and elsewhere, and administrative or judicial decisions." Our examination of the RCRA leads us to conclude that exhaustion of tribal remedies is not required in this case.

The RCRA places exclusive jurisdiction in federal courts for suits brought pursuant to section 6972(a)(1) of the Resource Conservation and Recovery Act.

Any action under paragraph (a)(1) of this subsection [as this case is] shall be brought in the district court for the district in which the alleged violation occurred.

Moreover, Congress has expressed a preference for prompt federal adjudication of citizen suits to enforce the RCRA.

C. The Tribe's Responsibilities

Finally, the Tribe argues that the federal defendants are responsible for cleaning up the dump sites pursuant to the RCRA and other laws. We agree. We do not accept, however, the Tribe's contention that the Tribe possesses no responsibility to help.

The district court found that the Tribe established and operated the dumps through the Service. The Tribe also generated waste dumped at these sites. We agree with the district court that the Tribe must share responsibility with BIA and IHS for bringing the dumps into compliance. In determining the Tribe's share, the district court must consider the Tribe's ability to pay a portion of the costs and still provide essential services to its people.

II. THE FEDERAL DEFENDANTS

BIA and IHS argue that the RCRA does not obligate them to participate in compliance efforts. We disagree.

The RCRA obligates the BIA and IHS to insure compliance with Environmental Protection Agency regulations. BIA and IHS are admittedly engaged in some activities in violation of the RCRA's open dumping provisions.[3] These activities trigger corresponding obligations in two ways.

First, the RCRA prohibits "any solid waste management practice or disposal of solid waste or hazardous waste which constitutes the open dumping of solid waste."

The district court found that BIA and IHS contributed to open dumping on the Reservation by generating solid waste, contracting for its disposal and, in some instances, transporting solid waste to dumps operated in violation of federal law. They were therefore "engaged in activity resulting in the disposal of solid waste" within the meaning of the statute. Thus, the district court has the power to order BIA and IHS to undertake whatever compliance efforts are necessary.

---

3. Both federal agencies operate facilities on the Reservation which generate waste. Most of the waste generated at these facilities is transported to tribal dumps by a tribal agency, the Pine Ridge Village Garbage Service. In this case, the two agencies violate the requirements of Section 4005 of RCRA, in two respects only: one is where employees of the Bureau of Indian Affairs transport solid waste directly to three tribal dumps, and the other is where the IHS at two sites burns waste in open drums. The agencies recognize that these direct violations of RCRA must cease.

The IHS contracts with the Pine Ridge Village Garbage Service and has informal arrangements with BIA contractors to remove the solid waste generated at its facilities on the Reservation. These haulers transport the trash to open dumps operated by the Tribe.

Second, the district court held that BIA and IHS were engaged in solid waste management activities in violation of 42 U.S.C. §6964. We agree.

* * * Throughout the RCRA, "the term 'solid waste management' means the systematic administration of activities which provide for the collection, source separation, storage, transportation, transfer, processing, treatment, and disposal of solid waste." BIA and IHS together collect, separate, transport and dispose of hazardous and non-hazardous waste at their facilities on the Reservation. Therefore, they do have "jurisdiction" over facilities, "the operation or administration of which involves such agency" in the generation and disposal of solid waste. They administer facilities, the administration of which engages them in regulated activities.

For these reasons, we agree with the district court's conclusion that, under the RCRA, BIA and IHS must share the blame and responsibility for the conditions of these sites.

CONCLUSION

Our holding that BIA and IHS have a duty to clean up the dumps is buttressed by the existence of the general trust relationship between these agencies and the Tribe. The existence of a trust duty between the United States and an Indian or Indian tribe can be inferred from the provisions of a statute, treaty or other agreement, "reinforced by the undisputed existence of a general trust relationship between the United States and the Indian people."

The provisions of the RCRA require that executive agencies refrain from activities resulting in violations. Congress intended the obligations of BIA and IHS under the RCRA to be exercised consistent with their trust obligation. Accord *State of Washington Dep't. of Ecology*, 752 F.2d at 1470 (9th Cir. 1985). BIA and IHS have not merely violated the RCRA, but, in so doing, they have violated their fiduciary obligation toward the plaintiffs and the Tribe. They are required to insure that the dumps are cleaned up, even if others contributed to the problem and even if the RCRA does not clearly set forth what role BIA and IHS are to play under the statute.

Thus, we reject the government's contention that BIA and IHS owe no obligation to the plaintiffs because they merely contracted with the Service for garbage disposal.

Accordingly, we affirm the district court.

Notes

1. United States' liability. Why is the United States held liable in *Blue Legs*? Under RCRA, citizen suits may be brought against past or present owners, operators, generators, and transporters. 42 U.S.C. §6972(a)(1)(B). Which was the United States? How does the federal trust responsibility toward the tribes affect federal liability in this case? The trust doctrine is explored in Chapter V.

The Comprehensive Environmental Response, Compensation, and Liability Act (CERCLA) (see note 2.a, at page 317) similarly places liability on past and present owners, operators, arrangers, and transporters of hazardous substances. In *United States v. Newmont USA Ltd.*, 504 F. Supp. 2d 1050 (E.D. Wash. 2007), the court held that the United States was the "owner" of a uranium mining site on the Spokane Reservation for purposes of liability under CERCLA. The Midnight Mine Superfund Site was located on lands held in trust for the Spokane Tribe and on a trust allotment. The court determined that the United States was not only the holder of legal title to the lands, but also exercised sufficient "indicia of ownership" through its trust responsibilities for the lands and minerals, and its exercise of various authority under the uranium mining leases.

2. The Indian Lands Open Dump Clean-Up Act. In response to the open dump problem in Indian country, Congress enacted the Indian Lands Open Dump Cleanup Act of 1994, 25 U.S.C. §§ 3901–3908. The Act called for an Indian Health Service (IHS) survey and inventory of open dumps on Indian lands and a ten-year plan to address solid waste disposal needs in Indian country. Any tribe may request an inventory of its open dumps, after which IHS shall provide financial and technical assistance to the tribe to close the dumps and provide postclosure maintenance. IHS is directed to carry out its duties by contracting with tribes "to the maximum extent feasible."

3. Citizen suits. Relying on *Blue Legs*, a federal district court held that environmental organizations could maintain a citizen suit against the Salt River Pima-Maricopa Indian Community under both RCRA and the Clean Water Act. *Atlantic States Legal Foundation v. Salt River Pima-Maricopa Indian Community*, 827 F. Supp. 608 (D. Ariz. 1993). The court noted that the CWA, like RCRA, permitted a citizen suit against any "person" alleged to be in violation of the act; that person was defined to include municipalities; and that municipality was defined to include Indian tribes. *Id.* at 609. On the other hand, EPA regulations specifically exclude tribal governments from citizen suits under the Clean Air Act. 43 C.F.R. § 49.4(o). For an argument that subjecting tribes to citizen suits is contrary to the doctrine requiring Congress to clearly state its intent to abrogate tribal sovereign immunity and will interfere with EPA's policy of government-to-government relations with tribes, see James M. Grijalva, *Environmental Citizen Suits in Indian Country*, *in* 8th Annual Conf. on Env't & Dev. in Indian Country (ABA SONREEL 1996). *See also* Michael P. O'Connell, *Citizen Suits Against Tribal Governments and Tribal Officials Under Federal Environmental Statutes*, 36 Tulsa L.J. 335 (2000).

Citizen suits may, on the other hand, prove useful to Indian tribes as a means of addressing particular violations "without presenting the legal risks tribes face when they attempt direct regulation of non-Indians." James M. Grijalva, *The Tribal Sovereign as Citizen: Protecting Indian Country Health and Welfare Through Federal Environmental Citizen Suits*, 12 Mich. J. Race & L. 33, 34 (2006).

4. Other waivers of tribal sovereign immunity. Courts have concluded that other provisions of various environmental statutes also abrogate tribal sovereign immunity. The Tenth Circuit ruled that the whistleblower provisions of the SDWA constituted an express waiver of tribal immunity from suit. *Osage Tribal Council v. Dep't of Labor*, 187 F.3d 1174 (10th Cir. 1999). The court cited *Blue Legs* for the proposition that a statute abrogates tribal sovereign immunity if it authorizes action against any person, defines person as including municipality, and municipality as including Indian tribe. *Osage Tribal Council*, 187 F.3d at 1182. Similarly, the Ninth Circuit concluded that the Hazardous Materials Transportation Act (HMTA) contained an express waiver of tribal immunity from suit. The court therefore determined that the utility's claim—that tribal regulation of shipments of spent nuclear fuel across the reservation was preempted by the HMTA—could proceed. *Public Serv. Co. v. Shoshone-Bannock Tribes*, 30 F.3d 1203 (9th Cir. 1994).

In contrast, one district court held that Indian tribes are not subject to counterclaims for contribution under CERCLA because tribes are not included within the meaning of "person" under that statute. *Pakootas v. Teck Cominco Metals, Ltd.*, 632 F. Supp.2d 1029 (E.D. Wash. 2009). The court held that "CERCLA's definition of 'person' is plain. It does not include 'Indian tribes.' . . . Whereas CERCLA specifically provides for liability *to* an Indian tribe, it contains no specific provision for the liability *of* an Indian tribe. Further, sovereigns will not be read into the term 'person' unless there is affirmative evidence that Congress intended to include sovereigns." The court noted that although CERCLA defines "person" to include "municipality," it does not define municipality. Thus, unlike RCRA, the CWA, and the SDWA, there is no definitional chain connecting Indian tribes to CERCLA's definition of "persons."

3. Environmental Impacts of Development

Davis v. Morton
469 F.2d 593 (10th Cir. 1972)

HILL, Circuit Judge.

This is an appeal from the United States District Court for the District of New Mexico for dismissing appellants' action against the United States government. Appellants allege the government failed to follow the provisions of the National Environmental Policy Act (NEPA), 42 U.S.C. § 4321 *et seq.*, and of 25 U.S.C. § 415 before approving a 99-year lease on the Tesuque Indian Reservation in Santa Fe County, New Mexico.

The facts are simple and uncontroverted. On April 17, 1970, a 99-year lease of restricted Indian lands was executed by the Pueblo of Tesuque (Pueblo), as lessor, and Sangre de Cristo Development Company, Inc. (Sangre), a New Mexico corporation, as lessee. The agreement granted Sangre a lease on a 1300-acre tract of land called "Tract 1" and granted lease options on four other tracts, thereby subjecting approximately 5400 acres to the lease. The purpose of the lease is to develop the property for residential, recreational and commercial purposes. Ultimately a small city is planned with a population of approximately 15,000 inhabitants.

On May 24, 1970, appellee Walter O. Olson, Area Supervisor for the New Mexico District of the Bureau of Indian Affairs of the Department of the Interior, approved the lease agreement pursuant to 25 U.S.C. § 415. Olson's authority was granted to him by appellee Lewis R. Bruce, Commissioner of Indian Affairs in the Department of the Interior, and by appellee Rogers C. B. Morton, Secretary of the Interior of the United States. Subsequent to this initial lease approval, appellees have approved a master plan for the development of the total acreage, a plat plan for the first phase of development, deed restrictions, the make-up of an architectural and engineering review board, and the plan for the development of a condominium apartment complex on Tract 1 of the leased premises. Appellants, two of whom are landowners living near the leased Indian property and two of whom are non-profit corporations concerned with protection of the environment, filed the complaint on October 22, 1971, asking for a preliminary injunction enjoining future work by Sangre on the leased premises. Appellants charged that appellees were without authority to grant the lease since no environmental impact study was conducted prior to approval of the lease as required by NEPA.[1]

They further asserted that appellees violated 25 U.S.C. §415(a)[3] by approving the lease on Indian lands without first being assured that certain statutory mandates had been met.

Two issues are presented on appeal. First, does the Secretary's authority to ratify or reject leases relating to Indian lands constitute major federal action? Second, does 25 U.S.C. §415, as amended, have any effect on a lease signed before the amendment's enactment date? As we answer the first issue in the affirmative, it will be unnecessary to discuss the retroactive effect of §415.

Appellees' primary thesis is that although the contractual relationship between Sangre and the Pueblo is a lease, it is not a federal lease and therefore does not constitute major federal action. The United States did not initiate the lease, was not a

---

1. [NEPA provides that:]
The Congress authorizes and directs that, to the fullest extent possible: ... (2) all agencies of the Federal Government shall— ... (C) include in every recommendation or report on proposals for legislation and other major Federal actions significantly affecting the quality of the human environment, a detailed statement by the responsible official on—(I) the environmental impact of the proposed action, (ii) any adverse environmental effects which cannot be avoided should the proposal be implemented, (iii) alternatives to the proposed action, (iv) the relationship between local short-term uses of man's environment and the maintenance and enhancement of long-term productivity, and (v) any irreversible and irretrievable commitments of resources which would be involved in the proposed action should it be implemented. ...

3. 25 U.S.C. §415, as amended:
(a) Any restricted Indian lands, whether tribally, or individually owned, may be leased by the Indian owners, with the approval of the Secretary of the Interior, for public, religious, educational, recreational, residential, or business purposes.... Prior to approval of any lease or extension of an existing lease pursuant to this section, the Secretary of the Interior shall first satisfy himself that adequate consideration has been given to the relationship between the use of the leased lands and the use of neighboring lands; the height, quality, and safety of any structures or other facilities to be constructed on such lands; the availability of police and fire protection and other services; the availability of judicial forums for all criminal and civil causes arising on the leased lands; and the *effect on the environment* of the uses to which the leased lands will be subject. (Emphasis added.)

party, possessed no interest in either the lease or the development, did not participate financially or benefit from the lease in any way. Before federal action will constitute major federal action under the mandates of NEPA, the government must initiate, participate in or benefit from the project.

We feel the government's interpretation of NEPA is too constrained for our court to adopt. Title 42 U.S.C. § 4331(b) states:

> [I]t is the continuing responsibility of the Federal Government to use all practicable means, consistent with other essential considerations of national policy, to . . . (2) assure for all Americans safe, healthful, productive, and esthetically and culturally pleasing surroundings; (3) attain the widest range of beneficial uses of the environment without degradation, risk to health or safety, or other undesirable and unintended consequences; (4) preserve important historic, cultural, and natural aspects of our national heritage, and maintain, wherever possible, an environment which supports diversity and variety of individual choice;. . . .

These general mandates reflect Congress' attitude toward preserving our environment. To ensure the implementation of these substantive requirements, Congress established procedural guidelines. One in particular applies to the instant case, 42 U.S.C. § 4332(2)(C). This section directs all agencies to present a detailed statement on the environmental impact of the proposed action. This impact statement will aid the agency in determining what proper course of action should be taken in each situation as it arises.

It is clear Congress passed this legislation out of concern for our natural environment. NEPA requires all federal agencies to consider values of environmental preservation in their spheres of activity. As the court stated in *Calvert Cliffs' Coord. Comm. v. United States Atomic Energy Comm'n*, 449 F.2d 1109 (1971):

> NEPA, first of all, makes environmental protection a part of the mandate of every federal agency and department. The Atomic Energy Commission, for example, had continually asserted, prior to NEPA, that it had no statutory authority to concern itself with the adverse environmental effects of its actions. Now, however, its hands are no longer tied. It is not only permitted, but compelled, to take environmental values into account. Perhaps the greatest importance of NEPA is to require the Atomic Energy Commission and other agencies to consider environmental issues just as they consider other matters within their mandates.

Senator Jackson, NEPA's principal sponsor, said on the floor just before final Senate approval that the Act "directs all agencies to assure consideration of the environmental impact of their actions in decision-making." Reading the Act and its legislative history together, there is little doubt that Congress intended all agencies under their authority to follow the substantive and procedural mandates of NEPA.

The problem boils down to whether granting leases on Indian lands constitutes major federal action as required in NEPA. Upon review of the lease and relevant case law, we feel the lower court erred in holding the lease did not constitute major federal action. The lease refers to the United States government countless times. All notices and approvals must be made by the Pueblo and the United States. The Secretary is required to give written approval before encumbrances can be made on the leased land. The lease protects the United States government against damage or injury to people or property on the leased premises. Certainly the fact the United States government might be held liable for injury or damages incurred on the Indian land unless the lease provides otherwise makes the government more than an impartial, disinterested party to the contract between Pueblo and Sangre.

It is interesting to note that appellees proffer no case law to support their arguments. The fact Indian lands are held in trust does not take it out of NEPA's jurisdiction. All public lands of the United States are held by it in trust for the people of the United States. To accept appellees' contention would preclude all federal lands from NEPA jurisdiction, something clearly not intended by Congress in passing the Act.

Appellees' second contention that Congress did not intend to enmesh the discretionary execution of these fiduciary duties in the procedural and bureaucratic web imposed by NEPA § 102(2)(C) also falls on deaf ears. In *Calvert Cliffs' Coord. Comm. v. United States A.E. Comm'n, supra,* the court answered this problem by stating that "Section 102 duties are not inherently flexible . . . Considerations of administrative difficulty, delay or economic cost will not suffice to strip the section of its fundamental importance."

We conclude approving leases on federal lands constitutes major federal action and thus must be approved according to NEPA mandates. As our court had occasion to consider once before, this Act was intended to include all federal agencies, including the Bureau of Indian Affairs.

The lower court felt NEPA did not apply to Indian lands or otherwise the amendment to 25 U.S.C. § 415 would not have addressed the problem of environmental concerns. We do not draw that conclusion. NEPA is a very broad statute covering both substantive and procedural problems relating to the environment. The amendment to 25 U.S.C. § 415 deals primarily with the addition of Indian tribes to the group having long-term lease authority. Only briefly is the environmental problem discussed. The amendment only requires the Secretary to satisfy himself on the environmental issue; nowhere are any specific procedural guidelines set out as in NEPA. In *Calvert Cliffs' Coord. Comm. v. United States A.E. Comm'n*, a similar problem arose. The court correctly determined that unless the obligations of another statute are clearly mutually exclusive with the mandates of NEPA, the specific requirements of NEPA will remain in force. The reasoning is applicable in the instant case. The general statement in § 415 in no way implies leases on Indian lands were not covered by NEPA. The amendment merely reaffirms congressional intent that environmental considerations are to play a factor in any Bureau of Indian Affairs decisions.

For the reasons stated above, we feel the lower court erred in dismissing appellants' request for a temporary and permanent injunction enjoining appellees from approving or acting on any submissions or approvals under the lease until the environmental impact of the project is studied and evaluated.

The judgment appealed from is reversed, and the case is remanded to the trial court with directions to grant the relief prayed for.

Notes

1. NEPA. The National Environmental Policy Act, 42 U.S.C. § 4321 *et seq.*, was enacted in 1969 as the nation's basic environmental charter. *See* Michael C. Blumm, *The National Environmental Policy Act at Twenty: A Preface*, 20 Envt'l. L. 447 (1990); *see generally NEPA at Twenty: The Past, Present and Future of the National Environmental Policy Act*, 20 Envt'l. L. 447–810 (1990).

NEPA requires any federal agency which proposes legislation or major federal action "significantly affecting the quality of the human environment" to prepare an Environmental Impact Statement (EIS) and take public comment on the proposed action. The EIS must include evaluations of adverse environmental impacts of the proposed action, and a discussion of possible alternatives. The EIS requirement is intended to prohibit uninformed actions, but it does not prohibit actions which may adversely affect the environment. NEPA is a procedural statute, and though an agency may find adverse consequences, NEPA does not mandate any substantive result. The details of NEPA compliance are set forth in regulations promulgated by the Council on Environmental Quality, 40 C.F.R. § 1500 *et seq.*

An EIS need not be prepared for all federal actions. By rulemaking, federal agencies designate certain types of actions, such as personnel actions, as "categorical exclusions" from the EIS process. In addition, the agencies may designate certain types of actions as major actions significantly affecting the environment, and therefore automatically requiring the preparation of an EIS. All other actions require the agency to prepare an environmental assessment (EA) to determine whether an EIS is necessary. The EA will result either in a determination that the action is a major one significantly affecting the environment and thus requiring that an EIS be prepared, or in a Finding of No Significant Impact (FONSI), in which case the agency's obligations under NEPA have been met.

2. NEPA and Indian country development. NEPA can apply to actions of the Bureau of Indian Affairs related to Indian county. *See, e.g., Citizens for a Better Way v. U.S. Dept. of the Interior*, 2015 WL 5648925 (E.D. Cal., Sept. 24, 2015) (NEPA applied to a fee-to-trust acquisition project related to a proposed casino, although the court found that the BIA had not violated NEPA).

In *Jamul Action Comm. v. Chaudhuri*, 2016 WL 3910597 (9th Cir. Aug. 19, 2016), however, the court found that NEPA did not apply, as the application of NEPA would create an irreconcilable statutory conflict with the Indian Gaming Regulatory Act. In that case, plaintiffs argued that the National Indian Gaming Commission acted in an arbitrary and capricious manner when it failed to comply with NEPA prior to approving the Jamul Indian Village's gaming ordinance for a casino. In reaching its decision for the Commission, the court explained that one exception to the application of NEPA occurs when an irreconcilable statutory conflict exists. Given that the Indian Gaming Regulatory Act requires the Commission to act within 90 days of a tribal gaming ordinance or resolution being submitted, and it typically takes at least 360 days to prepare an environmental impact statement under the EIS, the court found that it was impossible to reconcile the requirements of NEPA with this specific requirement of the Indian Gaming Regulatory Act.

On NEPA in Indian country, see William H. Rodgers, Jr., Environmental Law in Indian Country §§ 1:14–1:26 (Thompson/West 2005); Dean B. Suagee, *The Application of the National Environmental Policy Act to "Development" in Indian Country*, 16 Am. Indian L. Rev. 377 (1991).

3. Benefits and disadvantages of NEPA in Indian country. NEPA may act as both "shield and sword" for Indian tribes. Cohen's Handbook of Federal Indian Law § 10.08 (Nell Jessup Newton et al., eds. 2012). As a shield, "tribes can use the NEPA process to reach better decisions, at least in the environmental sense. Tribes can also use the NEPA process to make the BIA do likewise." Suagee, *supra*, at 427. But NEPA, which requires the agency to look at the environment of the affected area, "may also introduce nontribal considerations into the Secretary of the Interior's approval process for projects on tribal lands" because nontribal entities may submit comments through the NEPA process related to tribal projects and development. Cohen's Handbook at § 10.08. Nonetheless, as Cohen's Handbook notes, the Secretary's primary obligation in project approval is to act in the best interests of the tribe.

On remand, the *Davis v. Morton* case raised the specter of a further disadvantage to the NEPA process in Indian country. That follow-up case appears below.

As an example of how tribes attempted to use NEPA as a "shield," see *Center for Biological Diversity v. Salazar*, 706 F.3d 1065 (9th Cir. 2013). Environmental organizations, the Kaibab Band of Paiute Indians, and the Havasupai Tribe alleged that the Secretary of the Interior and Bureau of Land Management (BLM) violated NEPA, in addition to the Federal Land Policy and Management Act and BLM regulations, when the agencies permitted a mining company to restart uranium mining after a 17-year hiatus without a new mine plan or a new environmental impact statement. The 9th Circuit upheld the district court's decision to allow the restart because the court deferred both to BLM's interpretation of its mine plan regulations and its interpretation of its NEPA responsibilities, including its determination that a required gravel permit qualified for a categorical exclusion.

Sangre De Cristo Development Co., Inc. v. United States
932 F.2d 891 (10th Cir. 1991)

EBEL, Circuit Judge.

Appellants seek damages against the United States for harm suffered when the Department of the Interior allegedly canceled a lease agreement reached between the appellants and the Tesuque Indian Pueblo. The appellants claim that the alleged lease cancellation by the Department of the Interior deprived them of a vested property interest and as a result entitles them to recover just compensation under the takings clause of the Fifth Amendment.

The United States District Court for the District of New Mexico found for the United States on all the appellants' claims. The district court held that because the Department of the Interior's actions did not deprive the appellants of a vested property interest, the appellants' Fifth Amendment just compensation claim was without merit. * * * We affirm.

FACTS

[Following the decision in *Davis v. Morton*, the court remanded the case] to the district court with instructions that it grant the relief requested by the neighboring landowners and environmental groups and enjoin the United States "from approving, allowing or acting in any way on submissions or approvals required or permitted under the lease agreement until the environmental impact of the project had been studied and evaluated." The injunction issued on January 31, 1973.

Over the course of the next four and one-half years, a number of entities, including the Bureau of Indian Affairs ("BIA"), the Council on Environmental Quality ("CEQ"), the Assistant Solicitor for Environmental Law, and Sangre, worked to prepare the environmental impact statement ("EIS"). In early 1976, the Pueblo, under new tribal leadership, began to express reservations regarding the lease. By April of 1976, the Pueblo formally requested that the Department void the lease. On August 25, 1977, the Department announced that it would rescind its prior approval of the lease based upon environmental considerations as well as the Pueblo's opposition to the lease. On October 26, 1977, Sangre was subjected to involuntary bankruptcy proceedings. The trustee of Sangre's estate has brought this civil action on behalf of the estate.

DISCUSSION

Sangre argues that when the Department "rescinded" its approval of the lease on August 25, 1977, that this action constituted a taking under the Fifth Amendment, thereby entitling Sangre to recover "just compensation." As Sangre admits in its brief, for it to be successful on this argument, it must prevail on two separate points: (1) that at the time the alleged taking occurred, Sangre had a vested interest protectable under the Fifth Amendment; and (2) that the Department's action constituted a taking under the Fifth Amendment. Because we hold that Sangre did not possess a vested interest in the lease at the time the Department rescinded its approval, we need not address the issue of whether the Department's action constituted a taking.

In *Davis v. Morton* we instructed the district court to grant the relief requested by the environmental groups and the neighboring landowners: "the case is remanded to the trial court with directions to grant the relief prayed for." The relief requested by the environmental groups and the neighboring landowners was

> to issue a preliminary and permanent injunction enjoining [the United States] from approving, allowing or acting in any way on submissions or approvals required or permitted under the lease agreement until the environmental impact of the project had been studied and evaluated. [The environmental groups and the neighboring landowners] further requested the court issue a Writ of Mandamus requiring [the United States] to follow mandates of NEPA before taking any future action on the Pueblo lease.

Sangre contends that this language indicates that we did not invalidate the lease, but that we simply enjoined the project from continuing until the NEPA requirements were fulfilled. We disagree. We held that the initial approval of the lease by the Department was invalid because it was not preceded by the requisite environmental study. That the requested relief only sought an injunction against future action did not narrow the holding that the lease itself had never been validly approved.

In order for the lease to have been valid, the Department's approval was required:

> Any restricted Indian lands, whether tribally or individually owned, may be leased by the Indian owners, with the approval of the Secretary of the Interior, for public, religious, educational, recreational, residential or business purposes.... All leases so granted shall be for a term of not to exceed twenty-five years, except leases of land on the ... pueblo of Tesuque ... which may be for a term of not to exceed ninety-nine years....

25 U.S.C. §415(a) (1970). Further, not just any Departmental approval would suffice—the approval must have been a valid approval. *See Gray v. Johnson*, 395 F.2d 533, 537 (10th Cir.), *cert. denied*, 392 U.S. 906 (1968), where we held that when the BIA approved a lease that was contrary to regulations and not in the best interest of the Indian lessors, the lessee never acquired a vested interest in the lease. In *Gray* we said, "actions by the local agency contrary to the regulations and contrary to the best interest of the Indian do not create a vested interest in the lease. Agents of the government must act within the bounds of their authority; and one who deals with them assumes the risk that they are so acting." In *Davis* we agreed with the environmental groups and the neighboring landowners that the Department was "without authority to grant the lease since no environmental impact study was conducted prior to approval of the lease as required by NEPA...." Because we read 25 U.S.C. §415(a) as requiring a valid approval from the Department in order for the lease contract to have legal effect, the invalid lease contract between Sangre and the Pueblo vested no property interest in Sangre.

The Department's August 25, 1977 action, regardless of whether it is referred to as a recision or merely a failure to approve, did not divest Sangre of a leasehold interest because Sangre's interest never vested in the first place. Therefore, we affirm the district court's dismissal of Sangre's Fifth Amendment takings claim.

Metcalf v. Daley
214 F.3d 1135 (9th Cir. 2000)

TROTT, Circuit Judge.

I. FACTUAL BACKGROUND

The Makah, who reside in Washington state on the northwestern Olympic Peninsula, have a 1500 year tradition of hunting whales. In particular, the Makah target the California gray whale ("gray whale"), which annually migrates between the North Pacific and the coast of Mexico. During their yearly journey, the migratory gray whale population travels through the Olympic Coast National Marine Sanctuary ("Sanctuary"), which Congress established in 1993 in order to protect the marine environment in a pristine ocean and coastal area. A small sub-population of gray whales, commonly referred to as "summer residents," live in the Sanctuary throughout the entire year.

In 1855, the United States and the Makah entered into the Treaty of Neah Bay, whereby the Makah ceded most of their land on the Olympic Peninsula to the United States in exchange for "[t]he right of taking fish and of whaling or sealing at usual and accustomed grounds and stations. . . ." Treaty of Neah Bay, 12 Stat. 939, 940 (1855). Despite their long history of whaling and the Treaty of Neah Bay, however, the Makah ceased whaling in the 1920s because widespread commercial whaling had devastated the population of gray whales almost to extinction. Thus, the Tribe suspended whale hunting for seventy years, notwithstanding the important cultural role this practice played in their community.

Because the gray whale had become virtually extinct, the United States signed in 1946 the International Convention for the Regulation of Whaling in order "to provide for the proper conservation of whale stocks and thus make possible the orderly development of the whaling industry. . . ." International Convention for the Regulation of Whaling, 62 Stat. 1716, 1717 (1946). The International Convention for the Regulation of Whaling enacted a schedule of whaling regulations ("Schedule") and established the International Whaling Commission ("IWC") [to regulate whaling, including establishing harvest quotas].

Subsequently, in 1949, Congress passed the Whaling Convention Act to implement domestically the International Convention for the Regulation of Whaling. *See* 16 U.S.C.A. § 916 *et seq.* (1985). The * * * Act prohibits whaling in violation of the International Convention [and directs] the National Oceanic and Atmospheric Administration ("NOAA") and the National Marine Fisheries Service ("NMFS") [to promulgate implementing regulations].

When the IWC was established on December 2, 1946, it took immediate action to protect the beleaguered mammal. Specifically, the IWC amended the Schedule to impose a complete ban on the taking or killing of gray whales. However, the IWC included an exception to the ban "when the meat and products of such whales are to be used exclusively for local consumption by the aborigines." This qualification is referred to as the "aboriginal subsistence exception."

In addition to being shielded from commercial whaling under international law, the gray whale received increased protection in 1970 when the United States designated the species as endangered under the Endangered Species Conservation Act of 1969, the predecessor to the Endangered Species Act of 1973 ("ESA"). In 1993, however, NMFS determined that the eastern North Pacific stock of gray whales had recovered to near its estimated original population size and was no longer in danger of extinction. As such, this stock of gray whales was removed from the endangered species list in 1994. At that point, and as required by the ESA, NMFS began a five-year monitoring program to document and to evaluate the viability of the stock subsequent to delisting.

After these gray whales were removed from the endangered species list, the Makah decided to resume the hunting of whales who migrated through the Sanctuary. To execute this plan, the Makah turned to the United States government — the Department of Commerce, NOAA, and NMFS — for assistance. The Tribe asked representatives from the Department of Commerce to represent it in seeking approval from the IWC for an annual quota of up to five gray whales [and the government agreed to help the Makah obtain an aboriginal subsistence quota from the IWC].

In January 1996, Will Martin, an NOAA representative, sent an e-mail message to his colleagues informing them that "we now have interagency agreement to support the Makah's application in IWC for a whaling quota of 5 grey whales." Shortly thereafter, on March 22, 1996, NOAA entered into a formal written Agreement with the Tribe, which provided that "[a]fter an adequate statement of need is prepared [by the Makah], NOAA, through the U.S. Commissioner to the IWC, will make a formal proposal to the IWC for a quota of gray whales for subsistence and ceremonial use by the Makah Tribe." Furthermore, the Agreement provided for cooperation between NOAA and the Makah Tribal Council ("Council") in managing the harvest of gray whales.

Pursuant to the Agreement, the Makah prepared an adequate statement of need, and the United States presented a formal proposal to the IWC for a quota of gray whales for the Tribe at the IWC annual meeting in June 1996. Several member nations supported the Makah whaling proposal, while others expressed concerns and indicated that they would vote against it. In short order, the proposal turned controversial. As the annual meeting was in progress, the United States House of Representatives Committee on Resources unanimously passed a resolution, introduced by Representatives Jack Metcalf (R-Washington) and George Miller (D-California), opposing the proposal. Ultimately, the United States realized that it did not have the three-quarters majority required to approve it. Thus, after consulting with the Makah, the United States withdrew the proposal in order to give the Tribe an opportunity to address the delegates' concerns.

In June 1997, an attorney representing the organizations Australians for Animals and BEACH Marine Protection wrote a letter to NOAA and NMFS alleging that the United States Government had violated NEPA by authorizing and promoting the

Makah whaling proposal without preparing an EA or an EIS. In response, the Administrator for NOAA wrote to Australians for Animals and BEACH Marine Protection on July 25, 1997, informing them *that an EA would be prepared*. Twenty-eight days later, on August 22, 1997, a draft EA was distributed for public comment. [NOAA issued a final EA and Finding of No Significant Impact ("FONSI") on October 17, 1997 indicating that whaling would be limited to taking four whales and attempting to avoid taking of summer residents.]

The 1997 IWC annual meeting was held on October 18, 1997, one day after the final EA had been issued. Before this meeting, however, the United States (representing the Makah) and the Russian Federation (representing a Siberian aboriginal group called the Chukotka) had met to discuss the possibility of submitting a joint proposal for a gray whale quota, as the IWC previously had granted a gray whale quota for the benefit of the Chukotka. After conferring, the United States and the Russian Federation decided to submit a joint proposal for a five-year block quota of 620 whales. The total quota of 620 assumed an average annual harvest of 120 whales by the Chukotka and an average annual harvest of four whales by the Makah. We note in passing that because "not every gray whale struck will be landed," the EA eventually concluded that the cumulative impact of the removal of injured gray whales by the Makah would total not just twenty whales over a five-year period, but forty-one. The EA makes no explicit mention of the decision to submit this joint proposal to the IWC, which would include a block quota of 620 whales for the Chukotka.

Shortly thereafter, the quota was approved by consensus with no objections.

On April 6, 1998, NOAA issued a Federal Register Notice setting the domestic subsistence whaling quotas for 1998. The Notice stated that the Makah's subsistence and cultural needs had been recognized by both the United States and the IWC. Accordingly, the Notice allowed the Makah to engage in whaling pursuant to the IWC-approved quota and Whaling Convention Act regulations.

II. PROCEDURAL BACKGROUND

On October 17, 1997, the same day as the release of the FONSI, appellants, including, inter alia, Congressman Metcalf, Australians for Animals, and BEACH Marine Protection, filed a complaint against the Federal Defendants in the United States District Court for the District of Columbia. Appellants alleged that the Federal Defendants had violated NEPA, the Whaling Convention Act, and the Administrative Procedure Act in connection with their support of the Makah whaling proposal. After granting the Makah's motion to intervene, the district court transferred the case to the Western District of Washington.

Ultimately, the parties filed cross-motions for summary judgment on the merits, which were briefed and argued during the spring and summer of 1998. On September 21, 1998, the district court denied appellants' motion for summary judgment and granted the Federal Defendants' and the Makah's motions for summary judgment. Appellants now appeal.

IV: NEPA CLAIM

A.

* * * We have characterized [NEPA] as "primarily procedural," and held that "agency action taken without observance of the procedure required by law will be set aside." *Save the Yaak*, 840 F.2d at 717. In this respect, we have observed in connection with the preparation of an EA that "[p]roper timing is one of NEPA's central themes. An assessment must be 'prepared early enough so that it can serve practically as an important contribution to the decisionmaking process and will not be used to rationalize or justify decisions already made.'"

In summary, the comprehensive "hard look" mandated by Congress and required by the statute must be timely, and it must be taken objectively and in good faith, not as an exercise in form over substance, and not as a subterfuge designed to rationalize a decision already made.

In this case, the Federal Defendants did (1) prepare an EA, (2) decide that the Makah whaling proposal would not significantly affect the environment, and (3) issue a FONSI, but they did so after already having signed two agreements binding them to support the Tribe's proposal. Appellants assert that, in so doing, the Federal Defendants violated NEPA in several ways. Appellants argue that, although NOAA/NMFS ultimately prepared an EA, they violated NEPA because they prepared the EA too late in the process. According to appellants, "by making a commitment to authorize and fund the Makah whaling plan, and then drafting a NEPA document which simply rubber-stamped the decision . . . , defendants eliminated the opportunity to choose among alternatives, . . . and seriously imped[ed] the degree to which their planning and decisions could reflect environmental values." Additionally, appellants contend that the Federal Defendants violated NEPA by preparing an inadequate EA, and by issuing a FONSI instead of preparing an EIS.

B.

We begin by considering appellants' argument that the Federal Defendants failed timely and in the proper sequence to comply with NEPA. As provided in the regulations promulgated to implement NEPA, "[a]gencies shall integrate the NEPA process with other planning at the earliest possible time to insure that planning and decisions reflect environmental values, to avoid delays later in the process, and to head off potential conflicts." Furthermore, this court has interpreted these regulations as requiring agencies to prepare NEPA documents, such as an EA or an EIS, "before any irreversible and irretrievable commitment of resources." *Conner v. Burford*, 848 F.2d 1441, 1446 (9th Cir.1988). Thus, the issue we must decide here is whether the Federal Defendants prepared the EA too late in the decision-making process, *i.e.*, after making an irreversible and irretrievable commitment of resources. We conclude that they did.

The purpose of an EA is to provide the agency with sufficient evidence and analysis for determining whether to prepare an EIS or to issue a FONSI. Because the very important decision whether to prepare an EIS is based solely on the EA, the EA is fundamental to the decision-making process. In terms of timing and importance to the goals of NEPA, we see no difference between an EA and an EIS in connection with when an EA must be integrated into the calculus. In the case at bar, the Makah first asked the Federal Defendants to help them secure IWC approval for a gray whale quota in 1995; however, NOAA/NMFS did not prepare an EA until 1997. During these two years, the United States and the Makah worked together toward obtaining a gray whale quota from the IWC. In January 1996, an NOAA representative informed his colleagues that "we now have interagency agreement to support the Makah's application in IWC for a whaling quota of 5 grey whales." More importantly, in March 1996, more than a year before the EA was prepared, NOAA entered into a contract with the Makah pursuant to which it committed to (1) making a formal proposal to the IWC for a quota of gray whales for subsistence and ceremonial use by the Makah and (2) participating in the management of the harvest. To demonstrate the firmness of this commitment, we need only to look at the EA, which says, "In early 1996, [NOAA and the Makah Tribal Council] signed an agreement in which the United States committed to make a formal request to the IWC...."

The Federal Defendants did not engage the NEPA process "at the earliest possible time." Instead, the record makes clear that the Federal Defendants did not even consider the potential environmental effects of the proposed action until long after they had already committed in writing to support the Makah whaling proposal. The "point of commitment" in this case came when NOAA signed the contract with the Makah in March 1996 and then worked to effectuate the agreement. It was at this juncture that it made an "irreversible and irretrievable commitment of resources." As in *Save the Yaak*, the "contracts were awarded prior to the preparation of the EAs.... These events demonstrate that the agency did not comply with NEPA's requirements concerning the timing of their environmental analysis, thereby seriously impeding the degree to which their planning and decisions could reflect environmental values." Although it could have, NOAA did not make its promise to seek a quota from the IWC and to participate in the harvest conditional upon a NEPA determination that the Makah whaling proposal would not significantly affect the environment.

Had NOAA/NMFS found after signing the Agreement that allowing the Makah to resume whaling would have a significant effect on the environment, the Federal Defendants would have been required to prepare an EIS, and they may not have been able to fulfill their written commitment to the Tribe. As such, NOAA would have been in breach of contract.

It is highly likely that because of the Federal Defendants' prior written commitment to the Makah and concrete efforts on their behalf, the EA was slanted in favor of finding that the Makah whaling proposal would not significantly affect the environment. As the court below noted, "the longer the defendants worked with the Tribe toward the end of whaling, the greater the pressure to achieve this end.... [A]n EA prepared under such circumstances might be subject to at least a subtle pro-whaling bias." The EA itself somewhat disingenuously claims in 1997 that the "decision to be made" is "whether to support the Makah Tribe in its effort to continue its whaling tradition," when in point of fact that decision had already been made in contract form. To quote the 1996 Agreement, "after an adequate statement of need is prepared, NOAA ... will make a formal proposal to the IWC for a quota of gray whales...." The Makah satisfied its part of the bargain in 1996, binding the Federal Defendants to deliver on theirs, as they did at the IWC meeting in June 1996. Also, NOAA/NMFS's statement in the EA that "[a]ny perception that the U.S. Government is trying to withdraw its support for Makah whaling would likely plunge the Tribe into a difficult controversy with the United States" strongly suggests that the Federal Defendants were predisposed to issue a FONSI.

NEPA's effectiveness depends entirely on involving environmental considerations in the initial decisionmaking process. Moreover, the Supreme Court has clearly held that treaty rights such as those at stake in this case "may be regulated ... in the interest of conservation ..., provided the regulation ... does not discriminate against the Indians." *Puyallup Tribe v. Department of Game of Wash.*, 391 U.S. 392, 398 (1968). Here, before preparing an EA, the Federal Defendants signed a contract which obligated them both to make a proposal to the IWC for a gray whale quota and to participate in the harvest of those whales. We hold that by making such a firm commitment before preparing an EA, the Federal Defendants failed to take a "hard look" at the environmental consequences of their actions and, therefore, violated NEPA.

We want to make clear, however, that this case does not stand for the general proposition that an agency cannot begin preliminary consideration of an action without first preparing an EA, or that an agency must always prepare an EA before it can lend support to any proposal. * * * Rather, our holding here is limited to the unusual facts and circumstances of this case where the defendants already had made an "irreversible and irretrievable commitment of resources"—*i.e.*, by entering into a contract with the Makah before they considered its environmental consequences and prepared the EA.

V. REMEDY

Appellees argue that, even if the Federal Defendants did violate NEPA by preparing the EA after deciding to support Makah whaling, the issue is moot because the only relief that the court could order is the preparation of an adequate EA, which, appellees contend, already has been done. In making this argument, appellees rely on *Realty Income Trust v. Eckerd*, 564 F.2d 447 (D.C. Cir. 1977), in which the court refused to remand to the district court because an adequate EIS had been prepared before any action was taken that might harm the environment. The *Eckerd* court explained:

> The problem here, to repeat, was simply one of timing, that is, that there was not a timely filing of an EIS with Congress. No complaint remains on appeal that the statements in substance were inadequate in any way.

We conclude that the case at bar is distinguishable from *Eckerd* and, therefore, appellees' reliance on that case is misplaced. Unlike in *Eckerd*, appellants do not concede that the EA that ultimately was prepared is adequate. To the contrary, appellants contend that the EA is demonstrably suspect because the process under which the EA was prepared was fatally defective —*i.e.*, the Federal Defendants were predisposed to finding that the Makah whaling proposal would not significantly affect the environment. We agree. Moreover, appellants vigorously maintain that the EA is deficient with respect to its content and conclusions.

Our conclusions about the EA in this case raise an obvious question: Having already committed in writing to support the Makah's whaling proposal, can the Federal Defendants now be trusted to take the clear-eyed hard look at the whaling proposal's consequences required by the law, or will a new EA be a classic Wonderland case of first-the-verdict, then-the-trial? In order to avoid this problem and to ensure that the law is respected, must we — and can we — set aside the FONSI and require the Federal Defendants to proceed directly to the preparation of an Environmental Impact Statement? On reflection, and in consideration of our limited role in this process, we have decided that it is appropriate only to require a new EA, but to require that it be done under circumstances that ensure an objective evaluation free of the previous taint. Unlike many of the disputes we are called on to resolve, time here is not of the essence. Although the doctrine of laches cannot defeat Indian rights recognized in a treaty, see *United States v. Washington*, 157 F.3d 630, 649 (9th Cir.1998), the Makah's seventy year hiatus in connection with whale hunting suggests that a modest delay occasioned by the need to respect NEPA's commands will cause no harm.

The manner of ensuring that the process for which we remand this case is accomplished objectively and in good faith shall be left to the relevant agencies. Should a new EA come back to the courts for additional scrutiny, however, the burden shall be on the Federal Defendants to demonstrate to the district court that they have complied with this requirement.

Accordingly, we REVERSE and REMAND to the district court. The district court is directed to order the Federal Defendants to set aside the FONSI, suspend implementation of the Agreement with the Tribe, begin the NEPA process afresh, and prepare a new EA. Costs are awarded to Appellants Metcalf et al.

KLEINFELD, Circuit Judge, dissenting.

I respectfully dissent.

The federal government reconciled two policies, one favoring aboriginal Indian interests and another favoring preservation of sea mammals, by choosing to advance the Indian whale-hunting interests. But before allowing the Indians to hunt whales, the government took the "hard look" at environmental consequences that was required by law. Nothing more was required.

It is impractical to suppose that executive agencies will be uncommitted to policies when they prepare environmental assessments and environmental impact statements. It is precisely their determinations to move ahead with one proposal or another that occasions the assessments and impact statements. So long as the agency prepares an objective statement giving the initiative the required "hard look," prior to going ahead with it, it has done its duty, and even if it prepares the statement too late, it is pointless to require another one unless there is something wrong with the one the agency submitted. Environmental assessments and environmental impact statements are unlikely to persuade agency personnel, who initiated a project, to change their minds. Few things in government are as hard to shake as a bureaucratic policy choice.

The value of the environmental assessments and impact statements comes mostly after the agency has settled on a policy choice. The process of preparing them mobilizes groups that may generate political pressure sufficient to defeat the executive initiative. Exploration of the alternatives, and the facts brought out in preparation, may educate the agency, so that the initiative is modified in a useful way. The process may educate the agency about interests and concerns of which it was not aware, so that implementation will be more sensitive. The quality of the statement may persuade Congress or others who must pass on the agency proposal that the agency was wrong in its policy choice. The statement also stands as an archive with which the public may evaluate the correctness of the agency's policy choices after implementation, to decide whether the agency has done what it promised during implementation, and whether to repose more or less confidence in the agency's policy choices in the future. Preparation and publication of the statements eliminate the agency's monopoly of information, thus enabling other participants in the political process to use the information to overcome the agency's policy choice. None of these values were subverted in this case by the agency's commitment to the Makah Tribe. And nothing has been shown to be wrong with the environmental assessment. There is a legitimate clash of values between those who care more about whale hunting from the point of view of the hunter, and those who care more from the viewpoint of the whale. The political organs of government have the authority to choose. We have no warrant in this case to interfere.

Notes

1. NEPA compliance. What should NOAA have done to comply with NEPA in this case? When should it have done it? Why is this required? NOAA released a draft EIS on the proposed whaling in 2008, terminated the draft EIS in 2012 and issued a new draft EIS in March 2015. http://www.westcoast.fisheries.noaa.gov/protected _species/marine_mammals/cetaceans/chronology.html; 80 Fed. Reg. 14912 (March 20, 2015). No further action appears to have been taken on the draft EIS.

2. Whaling pending NEPA compliance? What must NOAA do now to comply with the court's order? Does the case mean that the IWC quota was unlawful? Does the NEPA apply to IWC actions? May the Makah exercise their whaling rights in the meantime? For a discussion of the Makah Tribe's successful national and international effort to restore its 1500-year old cultural and religious whaling traditions, see Robert J. Miller, *Exercising Cultural Self-Determination: The Makah Indian Tribe Goes Whaling*, 25 Am. Indian L. Rev. 165 (2001).

3. The effect of NEPA and the Marine Mammal Protection Act on Makah whaling rights. In 2002, the Ninth Circuit ruled that the Department of Commerce had to prepare an EIS prior to establishing a quota for the Makah Tribe for the taking of Pacific gray whales, reversing the district court, because of the scientific uncertainty concerning the effect of the harvest on a portion of the California gray whale population that summers in the local offshore Washington area. The court also ruled that the exercise of the Makah's treaty fishing rights was subject to the permit requirements of the Marine Mammal Protection Act. *Anderson v. Evans,* 314 F.3d 1006 (9th Cir. 2002). The court subsequently amended its earlier decision and, among other revisions, stated:

> [I]n holding that the MMPA [Marine Mammal Protection Act] applies to the Tribe, we need not and do not decide whether the Tribe's whaling rights have been abrogated by the MMPA. We simply hold that the Tribe, to pursue any treaty rights for whaling, must comply with the process prescribed in the MMPA for authorizing a "take" because it is the procedure that ensures the Tribe's whaling will not frustrate the conservation goals of the MMPA.

Anderson v. Evans, 350 F.3d 815, 822 (9th Cir. 2003).

4. Illegal whale kill. On September 8, 2007, some five-and-a-half years after the Makah's only federally authorized whale kill, and in apparent frustration at what they viewed as bureaucratic impediments imposed on their treaty right, five rogue members of the Makah Tribe illegally killed a gray whale. The whale kill was in violation of both tribal and federal law, and the tribe promised a vigorous prosecution. *See* Mike Lewis & Paul Shukovsky, *Tribe vows prosecution of killing of whale: Many fear effort to legalize new hunt will be derailed,* Seattle Post-Intelligencer, Sept. 10, 2007, http://seattlepi.nwsource.com/local/331060_whale10.html. The harvesters were ultimately convicted in federal court.

5. NEPA, offshore oil, and subsistence whaling in Alaska. In *Alaska Wilderness League v. Kempthorne,* 548 F.3d 815 (9th Cir. 2008), a divided Ninth Circuit agreed with a coalition of native and environmental groups and rejected an environmental assessment (EA) on a federal exploration plan in the Beaufort Sea by an outer continental shelf lessee. The court concluded that the EA failed to take the requisite "hard look" demanded by NEPA, faulting the EA for its lack of specificity concerning drilling sites and the potential effect of drilling on bowhead whales and native subsistence practices. The majority refused to accept the government's claim that a proposed post-leasing "conflict resolution" process that could be invoked by affected Inupiat communities would reduce the significance of the environmental impacts of the drilling, viewing the controversy surrounding the project as a reason to require an EIS. The dissent complained that the majority was engaging in "fine-grained judgments" on the evidence that the agency assembled and should defer to the agency absent systematic failures in its analysis.

6. Presidential Memorandum on mitigating environmental impacts. Beyond NEPA, the federal government has taken other steps to mitigate environmental damage. On November 3, 2015, the White House released a Presidential Memorandum titled "Mitigating Impacts on Natural Resources from Development and Encouraging Related Private Investment." Office of the Press Secretary, White House, *Mitigating Impacts on Natural Resources from Development and Encouraging Related Private Investment*, (Nov. 3, 2015), available at: https://www.whitehouse.gov/the-press-office/2015/11/03/mitigating-impacts-natural-resources-development-and-encouraging-related. The Memorandum states that "[i]t shall be the policy of the Departments of Defense, the Interior, and Agriculture; the Environmental Protection Agency; and the National Oceanic and Atmospheric Administration; and all bureaus or agencies within them . . . to avoid and then minimize harmful effects to land, water, wildlife, and other ecological resources (natural resources) caused by land- or water-disturbing activities, and to ensure that any remaining harmful effects are effectively addressed, consistent with existing mission and legal authorities. Agencies shall adopt a clear and consistent approach for avoidance and minimization of, and compensatory mitigation for, the impacts of their activities and projects they approve." The Memorandum encourages federal agencies to take advantage of existing plans, such as tribal plans, in their planning. The Memorandum, however, is intended for internal guidance for federal agencies, and is not legally enforceable by third parties.

Note on Environmental Justice

Environmental justice is a field related to environmental law, although it also has its roots in the civil rights movement, labor movement, and other social reform movements of the second half of the 20th century. Environmental justice typically applies to racial and lower socio-economic communities that are disproportionately affected by negative environmental consequences. The origins of the environmental justice movement are often connected to the United Church of Christ's release in 1987 of its groundbreaking report, *Toxic Wastes and Race*, http://www.ucc.org/about-us/archives/pdfs/toxwrace87.pdf; s*ee also Toxic Wastes and Race at Twenty 1987–2007*, http://www.ucc.org/environmental-ministries_toxic-waste-20.

Indian communities are often environmental justice communities, although the environmental justice concerns in Indian country may be different in kind than those in other affected communities.

> The Environmental Justice Movement ("EJM") emerged during the 1980s as a "grassroots response to evidence that environmental hazards disproportionately affect the health and well-being of low-income communities and communities of color." Although this work initially focused on the inequities suffered by poor African-American and Latino communities, the analysis was quickly extended to Native American communities, in large part because of the harmful legacy of mineral exploitation in Indian Country. Studies documented that uranium mining on Indian reservations throughout the United States resulted in severe, widespread contamination of land and water resources. Coal power plants located on or near reservations have

caused disproportionate levels of pollution and affect the health of tribal members. The American Academy of Sciences referred to Navajo lands in the Four Corners region as a "national sacrifice area" in reference to the permanent damage and pollution caused by coal strip-mining. In the 1990s, EJM activists focused on the efforts of solid and hazardous waste companies to site facilities on tribal lands, as well as in minority and low-income communities, and deemed this to constitute a civil rights issue. Indian nations resisted this attempt to be identified as "victims" of environmental "injustice." Tribal leaders and their legal advocates claimed that this was a "sovereignty" issue because tribes are governments capable of deciding whether and if such a facility can lease reservation lands. The only "injustice" to Indian nations was caused by the federal government's failure to acknowledge tribal sovereignty and the BIA's decisions to allow reservation resources to be exploited without adequate compensation or mitigation.

The lesson that emerged from the first generation of environmental justice claims for Native peoples was that equality of status as governments was the key to "justice," rather than the "equality of citizenship" that is the focus of environmental justice claims on behalf of poor and minority communities. The "justice" inquiry focuses on the ability of the tribal government to choose the appropriate type of economic development for the reservation, as well as determine the relevant balance between securing the economic benefit of resources and protecting the integrity of the reservation environment and the health of tribal members.

Rebecca Tsosie, *Climate Change, Sustainability and Globalization: Charting the Future of Indigenous Environmental Self-Determination*, 4 Envt'l & Energy L. & Pol'y J. 188, 210–211 (2009). For a discussion of the role of environmental justice in Indian country, see James Grijalva, Closing the Circle: Environmental Justice in Indian Country (Carolina Academic Press, 2008).

In 1994, President Clinton issued Executive Order 12898, directing executive agencies to take environmental justice into consideration before rendering decisions. Section 6-606 of the executive order provides: "Each Federal agency responsibility set forth under this order shall apply equally to Native American programs. In addition, the Department of the Interior, in coordination with the [Interagency] Working Group [on Environmental Justice], and, after consultation with tribal leaders, shall coordinate steps to be taken pursuant to this order that address Federally-recognized Indian Tribes."

Environmental justice advocates have used Title VI of the Civil Rights Act to challenge actions that may have environmental justice consequences. Title VI states that "[n]o person in the United States shall, on the ground of race, color, or national origin, be excluded from participation in, be denied the benefits of, or be subjected to discrimination under any program or activity receiving Federal financial assistance." 42 U.S.C. § 2000d. The federal government is therefore precluded from financially supporting a program operated in a racially discriminatory manner. Environmental justice advocates can thus use Title VI to combat the disproportionate impacts of pollution by arguing that federal funding should not be given (or should be rescinded) where there is evidence that environmental justice communities are unfairly bearing the burden of increased pollution. For a discussion of the use of Title VI in Indian country, see Elizabeth Ann Kronk, *Application of Title VI in Indian Country: The Key is Tribal Sovereignty*, 6 Fla. A&M U.L. Rev. 215 (2011). For more information on environmental justice generally, see Luke Cole and Sheila Foster, From the Ground Up: Environmental Racism and the Rise of the Environmental Justice Movement (NYU Press 2001).

On July 24, 2014, the EPA released the *EPA Policy on Environmental Justice for Working with Federally Recognized Tribes and Indigenous Peoples*, available at https://archive.epa.gov/partners/web/pdf/ej-indigenous-policy.pdf. The EPA defines "environmental justice" as the "fair and meaningful involvement of all people regardless of race, color, national origin, or income with respect to the development, implementation, and enforcement of environmental laws, regulations, and policies." The policy is designed to integrate environmental justice principles into the agency's work with federally recognized tribes and indigenous peoples. The policy is based on three key documents: 1) Executive Order 12898 (page 345); 2) the *EPA Policy for the Administration of Environmental Programs on Indian Reservations* (page 284); and 3) Plan EJ 2014, which is the EPA's overarching strategy for advancing environmental justice, available at https://www.epa.gov/environmentaljustice/plan-ej-2014. The policy divides 17 principles into four categories: 1) promoting environmental justice principles in EPA direct implementation of programs, policies, and activities; 2) promoting environmental justice principles in tribal environmental protection programs; 3) promoting environmental justice principles in EPA's engagement with indigenous peoples; and 4) promoting environmental justice principles in intergovernmental coordination and collaboration.

An Environmental Justice Case Study: Dakota Access Pipeline

The Dakota Access Pipeline transports crude oil from North Dakota across four states to facilities in Illinois, a roughly 1200 mile route that traverses mostly private lands but also covers 1851 treaty lands and traditional territories of the tribes in the region. The pipeline also runs near the Missouri River, upstream of the water supply of tribes, and crosses under the river at Lake Oahe, which is approximately a half mile north of the Standing Rock Sioux Tribe's reservation. The pipeline transports approximately 470,000 barrels per day with a capacity as high as 570,000 barrels per day. For more information on the pipeline, see http://landowners.daplpipelinefacts.com/.

In 2016, indigenous peoples and their supporters gathered in historic proportions near the Standing Rock Sioux Reservation in North Dakota. Beginning late in the summer, people gathered near the Reservation to protest the construction of the Dakota Access Pipeline. These "water protectors" challenged the construction of the pipeline and related pollution that will occur when it leaks. They argued that the Standing Rock Sioux Tribe was not adequately included in consultations leading to the pipeline approval (along with other potential legal arguments). Although the proposed pipeline did not cross existing reservation boundaries, it comes within a half a mile of the reservation and would threaten Lake Oahe, and potentially the Missouri River, which are sources of water vital to the Tribe's survival. Further, significant sites of tribal cultural, religious, and spiritual importance were located along the proposed route.

Many tribal water protectors were troubled that the federal government considered and rejected a proposed route for the pipeline that would have crossed the Missouri River ten miles north of Bismarck, North Dakota. This Bismarck route was rejected, in part, because of concerns about protecting municipal water supply wells from potential pipeline spills. It may be argued that this decision—to move the pipeline away from non-Native communities and towards a Native community—is evidence of the federal government's discriminatory intent against indigenous people. From an environmental justice perspective, such decisions disproportionately impact people of color.

The legal controversy initially focused on the Tribe's efforts to secure an emergency injunction to halt construction of the pipeline around the Lake Oahe area. The Tribe argued that an injunction was appropriate, because the federal government failed to participate in adequate tribal consultations under the National Historic Preservation Act (NHPA) prior to approval of the pipeline near tribal lands. (NHPA is described at note 2, page 46.) The U.S. District Court for the District of Columbia denied the Tribe's motion for preliminary injunction, finding that the Corps complied with NHPA and the Tribe failed to demonstrate irreparable harm. *Standing Rock Sioux Tribe v. U.S. Army Corps of Eng'rs*, 205 F. Supp. 3d 4 (D.D.C. 2016).

The Departments of Justice, the Army, and the Interior released a joint statement regarding the case on the same day the district court released its opinion. While these departments acknowledged and appreciated the district court's decision, they also recognized that important issues raised by the Tribe remained, despite the issues adjudicated by the court. The departments announced that "[t]he Army will not authorize constructing the Dakota Access pipeline on Corps land bordering or under Lake Oahe until it can determine whether it will need to reconsider any of its previous decisions regarding the Lake Oahe site under the National Environmental Policy Act (NEPA) or other federal laws." Press Release, Off. of Pub. Aff., Dept. of Just., Joint Statement from the Dep't of Justice, the Dep't of the Army, and the Dep't of the Interior Regarding Standing Rock Sioux Tribe v. U.S. Army Corps of Eng'rs (Sept. 9, 2016), https://www.justice.gov/opa/pr/joint-statement-department-justice-department-army-and-department-interior-regarding-standing.

On October 9, 2016, the U.S. Court of Appeals for the District of Columbia Circuit denied an emergency injunction request, finding, as the district court had, that the Tribe failed to meet its burden demonstrating that such an extraordinary remedy was appropriate. Court Order, *Standing Rock Sioux Tribe v. U.S. Army Corps of Eng'rs* (2016) (No. 16-5259). On December 4, 2016, the Army Corps of Engineers announced that it would not grant the easement for the Dakota Access Pipeline to cross Lake Oahe. On January 24, 2017, however, President Trump issued a presidential memorandum on the pipeline directing the Secretary of the Army to direct the appropriate assistant secretary to "review and approve in an expedited manner, to the extent permitted by law and as warranted, and with such conditions as are necessary or appropriate, requests for approvals to construct and operate the DAPL." Presidential Memorandum Regarding Construction of the Dakota Access Pipeline, Office of the Press Sec'y, The White House, to the Sec'y of the Army (Jan. 24, 2017), 82 Fed. Reg. 11129 (Feb. 17, 2017). On February 7, 2017, the Army Corps of Engineers announced its intention to approve the easement for the Dakota Access Pipeline under Lake Oahe. The camps were ultimately cleared and closed on February 23, 2017.

The federal litigation involving the controversial Dakota Access Pipeline took another turn when the United States District Court for the District of Columbia granted partial summary judgment finding that the U.S. Army Corps of Engineers' review of DAPL under the NEPA was inadequate. *Standing Rock Sioux Tribe v. U.S. Army Corps of Eng'rs*, 255 F. Supp. 3d 101 (D.D.C. June 14, 2017). Accordingly, the legal controversy surrounding the Pipeline continues at the time of writing.

Although the issues raised by the Standing Rock Sioux Tribe and others in response to the Dakota Access Pipeline are not yet resolved by early 2018, the case study presents numerous environmental justice issues, especially in the development of extractive industries. These issues concern the siting of such extractive infrastructure and the consultation methods used to engage indigenous peoples. Concerns exist regarding the revision of the pipeline pathway in such a way as to have greater potential impacts on indigenous peoples than majority populations. As mentioned above, Dakota Access, the company constructing the pipeline, originally considered a pathway that would have crossed the Missouri River ten miles north of Bismarck, North Dakota. Due in large part to factors related to the size of Bismarck and the location of that community's water resources, the pipeline's route was moved from close proximity to the non-diverse Bismarck community—where 90 percent of the population is white—to almost adjacent to the Standing Rock Sioux Reservation, where only 13.9 percent of the population is white. Even presuming that there is no overt racial discrimination in the siting of the pipeline, the result, at the very least, is a strong perception by many in the Standing Rock Sioux community that indigenous communities are being called upon to disproportionately bear the risk of environmental pollution.

For a full discussion of the environmental justice concerns related to the Dakota Access Pipeline, see Elizabeth Kronk Warner, *Environmental Justice: A Necessary Lens to Effectively View Environmental Threats to Indigenous Survival*, 26 Transnational Law & Contemporary Problems 343 (Summer 2017).

Chapter 5

Natural Resource Development

The resource base in Indian country is extensive. There are approximately 56.2 million acres of trust lands, including more than 10 million acres held in trust for individual tribal members.

Of these lands, more than 43 million acres—about three-fourths of Indian lands outside Alaska—are classified as grassland. In 2005, the federal government had approved grazing leases on more than three-quarters of eligible lands. Forest lands accounted for 16 million acres on 214 reservations in 23 states. More than 7 million of the forested acres were classified as timberland with species suitable for commercial logging, with over 5 million acres in use as commercial forest.

Mineral and energy resources are similarly abundant. Indian tribes are the third-largest owners of mineral resources in the country, behind only the federal government and the railroads. Indian lands contain approximately 3–4% of known oil and gas reserves, about a third of the coal west of the Mississippi, and a third or more of the nation's uranium supply. More than 10% of federal on-shore energy production occurs on Indian lands, representing more than 5% of domestic oil production, 8% of gas production, and 2% of coal production. In 2011, the Department of the Interior administered more than 4800 producing mineral leases on 2.7 million acres of Indian lands, resulting in revenues of over $545 million. The Department of the Interior estimates that some 15 million acres of energy resources remain undeveloped.

In addition to traditional mineral resources and fossil fuels, Indian lands contain an abundance of renewable energy resources. The Department of the Interior has identified 23 million acres on 77 reservations with significant wind power potential, and 118 reservations with a high potential for biomass production. The Department of Energy has identified 57 reservations with some potential for geothermal electrical production, and 83 reservations with the two highest levels of solar radiation energy potential.

A. The Federal-Tribal Relationship in Resource Management

Indian tribes have three basic options for natural resources development. First, tribes may choose to develop their resources directly. Some tribes engage in tribal agricultural, grazing, and even mining operations. Second, tribes may use the "638" program of the Indian Self-Determination and Education Assistance Act of 1974, Public Law 93-638, 88 Stat. 2203 (codified as amended in scattered sections of 25 U.S.C.), to enter into contracts and self-governance compacts to assume administration of federal Indian programs. For example, a study in the 1980s showed that 49 of 75 forestry tribes used the 638 program to take some degree of management control of their timber operations. The study concluded that "tribal control of forestry under PL 638 results in significantly better timber management," including increased output and higher timber prices. Matthew B. Krepps, *Can Tribes Manage Their Own Resources? The 638 Program and American Indian Forestry, in* What Can Tribes Do? Strategies and Institutions in American Indian Economic Development (Stephen Cornell & Joseph P. Kalt eds., 1992). The third option, however—entering into leases or other types of arrangements with non-Indian resource companies—remains the most common approach to resource development in Indian country.

1. The Role of the Department of the Interior

The federal government, through the Secretary of the Department of the Interior, has two primary roles in resource development in Indian country when non-Indian companies are involved in the development process. The first of these is the decision whether to approve a proposed non-Indian use of trust lands. Although tribes initially make the decision whether to permit development of tribal resources, federal approval is generally required for leases or other arrangements with non-Indians. This requirement of federal approval of non-Indian uses of trust lands derives from the Nonintercourse Act, reprinted at page 161, which prohibits the "purchase, grant, lease, or other conveyance" of Indian lands without federal approval. This section explores some of the issues involved in federal approval of non-Indian development of reservation resources and outlines the major resource statutes.

The second primary role of the federal government—its responsibilities to tribes and trust allottees once non-Indian development has been approved—is examined in Section B.

Reid Peyton Chambers & Monroe E. Price, Regulating Sovereignty: Discretion and the Leasing of Indian Lands*

26 Stan. L. Rev. 1061, 1063–68 (1974)

* * * The issues that come before the Secretary in the context of approval of long-term business leases are of enormous significance in terms of the lawmaking power of the tribe and its cultural and political future. Some leases may bring large

---

* Copyright 1974, Stanford Law Review. Used with permission of the Stanford Law Review, from Reid Peyton Chambers & Monroe E. Price, *Regulating Sovereignty: Discretion and the Leasing of Indian Lands*, 26 Stan. L. Rev. 1061 (1974); permission conveyed through Copyright Clearance Center, Inc.

numbers of non-Indians onto the reservation or may entice states to attempt to exercise regulatory and taxing powers over reservations. More than the landscape may be changed: an influx of non-Indians or state authority may interfere with tribal control over the reservation and continuation of tribal culture.

The Secretary has largely ignored these broader consequences of leasing. His principal view of Indian trust land is as a resource to be used singularly for the production of income in the form of lease revenues; that conception is embodied in the Secretary's regulations governing leases. A different approach to leasing and land management would be to emphasize the overall economic and social impact upon the tribe.

The two approaches are not necessarily antithetical, for an emphasis on jobs does not entirely deprecate the receipt of lease income, and the converse is also true. But a distinction can be made in the basic purposes and consequences of these two approaches. If reservation land is simply a source for income production, then it should be devoted to its "highest and best use" in order to maximize lease revenues. That is a conventional goal of trust management. If, on the other hand, reservation land has multiple purposes and should be utilized as a part of an overall resource development plan that has as its goal the economic and cultural viability of an Indian tribe, there would be trade-offs of various kinds which should be considered by the Secretary in exercising his approval power: between income and jobs, income and services, income and economic growth, income and conservation of an Indian culture on the land.

[I]t has become increasingly important to develop a coherent theory of the Secretary's trust duties and the purposes of his trusteeship. A virtually unconfined discretion now has potentially hazardous implications. Tribal self-government is endangered by the likelihood that the Secretary may have the authority and duty to disapprove leases desired by the tribe or its members. Unbounded discretion also creates the possibility of arbitrariness and uncertainty, two conditions that discourage development on reservation lands.

In order to determine the appropriate standards for exercise of the Secretary's approval power, a judgment must be made as to which policy goals are to be furthered by his leasing supervision. If the goal of leasing is merely the production of income, the Secretary's function could be limited to ensuring that the tribe or individual beneficiary receives fair financial value for the lease. If other policies are of equal or greater importance, however, more could be required: for example, the Secretary could be viewed as having some trust responsibility to preserve a reservation land base, to protect the tribe's continued political existence and governmental self-sufficiency, to preserve the environment of the reservation, to encourage development of a viable economic and social structure on the reservation to ensure equitable participation in the enterprise by the lessor, or to determine what law (state, tribal, or federal) should apply to disputes that arise from the lease enterprise. Perhaps the Secretary's trusteeship could even include an obligation to ensure that the lease is consistent with a broad, coherent rehabilitative strategy of the federal government.

These are not always exclusive or necessary considerations in the exercise of the approval power with regard to any particular lease. But there has been virtually no analysis of how the Secretary should resolve these often competing considerations.

Mary Christina Wood, Protecting the Attributes of Native Sovereignty: A New Trust Paradigm for Federal Actions Affecting Tribal Lands and Resources*
1995 Utah L. Rev. 109, 143–148

The requisite of federal approval as a condition of reservation development creates a difficult role for the federal government in light of the often intense conflicts within tribes over use of tribal lands. The federal action of approving a lease may be open to judicial challenge by dissenting members of the tribe. Like all federal actions affecting the interests of tribes, the approval action is appropriately measured according to trust standards. Often, however, the federal government simply defers to the decision of the tribal council and approves any development initially approved in the tribal forum.

While this approach seems on its face to promote the overriding policy of tribal self-determination where significant, long-term tribal land interests are at stake, there are compelling legal and policy arguments for measuring the federal approval decision against the trust obligation independent of the tribe's decision. Otherwise, the federal trust obligation essentially collapses into a rule of absolute deference to a tribal council's decision—an approach which excludes from the analysis other beneficiary tribal interests to which the trust obligation extends, including the interests of dissenting members of the tribe as well as the inchoate interests of future tribal generations.

In any given case, a court must evaluate the long-term interests of a tribe against the magnitude and permanence of the proposed development. And, as in all cases of judicial line-drawing, it is inherently difficult to determine at what point land development in response to perceived present economic needs impermissibly intrudes upon the interests of future tribal generations or the interests of present tribal members whose views are at odds with their tribal leaders. A prudent judicial approach to such conflicts might be to reserve decisions that depart from tribal council prerogatives for those cases presenting extreme circumstances; this approach is preferable to painting the trust obligation with the shades of gray that inevitably arise in close cases.

In searching out the extreme circumstances that may justify judicial relief, courts should be cognizant of some practical factors which frame reservation land use issues. [Professor Wood suggests three such factors: 1) whether the proposed use irrevocably or permanently converts Indian land to non-Indian use; 2) whether the proposed

---

* Copyright 1995, Mary Christina Wood. Reprinted with permission of Mary Christina Wood.

use involves a "critical mass" of the reservation territory; and 3) whether the proposed use will result in substantial environmental damage.]

Notes

1. Standards for secretarial approval of resource development. Chambers and Price, writing in 1974, noted the lack of clear standards for secretarial approval of tribal development decisions. Had those standards improved, or become clearer, by the time Professor Wood wrote more than twenty years later? What standards should the Secretary apply to the decision whether to approve non-Indian development? How much weight should the Secretary accord to a tribe's decision? What problems do the authors identify if the Secretary accords too much weight, or too little?

2. Interior deference to tribal decisions. Regulations for surface leases provide that the Department of the Interior will defer, "to the maximum extent possible," to the landowner's determination that a lease is in their best interest. 25 C.F.R. § 162.107(a) (agricultural and other surface leases); *id.* § 162.441(b) (business leases, including biomass); *id.* § 162.566(b) (wind and solar resource leases). Does this clarify the matters discussed by Chambers & Price and Wood?

3. The Executive Order on Consultation and Coordination with Tribal Governments. On November 6, 2000, President Clinton signed Executive Order No. 13175, which aimed to establish regular and meaningful consultation and collaboration with tribal officials, strengthen federal-tribal government-to-government relations, and reduce the imposition of unfunded mandates on Indian tribes. In the order, the government reaffirmed its commitment to tribal self-government and self-determination (§ 2(c)), promised to give tribal governments the maximum administrative discretion in implementing federal statutes and regulations (§ 3(b)), and, to the extent practicable and permitted by law, vowed to impose no new unfunded mandates on tribal government (§ 5(b)). The order stipulated that its purpose was "to improve the internal management of the executive branch, and is not intended to create any right, benefit, or trust responsibility, substantive or procedural, enforceable at law by a party against the United States, its agencies, or any person" (§ 10). Executive Order No. 13175, 36 Weekly Comp. Pres. Doc. 2806 (2000). In November 2009, President Obama directed the head of every federal agency to submit, after consultations with tribes and tribal officials, "a detailed plan of actions the agency will take to implement the policies and directives of Executive Order 13175." Progress and implementation reports are also required. *See* 74 Fed. Reg. 57881 (Nov. 5, 2009). On the issue of tribal consultation, see Gabriel S. Galanda, *The Federal Indian Consultation Right: A Frontline Defense Against Tribal Sovereignty Incursion*, Federal Indian Law (Fed. Bar Ass'n Indian Law Sect., Fall 2010) (arguing that tribes should assume a "preemptive" approach to consultation, in which tribes force federal agencies to consult prior to tribal disclosure of information or access to tribal facilities).

4. DOI's duty to consult. In 2011, the Secretary of the Department of the Interior issued Order No. 3317, setting forth the Department of the Interior Policy on

Consultation with Indian Tribes, designed to carry out Executive Order 13175: Consultation and Coordination with Indian Tribal Governments. Section 4 provides:

> a. Government-to-government consultation between appropriate Tribal officials and the Department requires Departmental officials to demonstrate a meaningful commitment to consultation by identifying and involving Tribal representatives in a meaningful way early in the planning process.
>
> b. Consultation is a process that aims to create effective collaboration with Indian tribes and to inform Federal decision-makers. Consultation is built upon government-to-government exchange of information and promotes enhanced communication that emphasizes trust, respect, and shared responsibility. Communication will be open and transparent without compromising the rights of Indian tribes or the government-to-government consultation process.
>
> c. Bureaus and offices will seek to promote cooperation, participation, and efficiencies between agencies with overlapping jurisdictions, special expertise, or related responsibilities when a Departmental action with Tribal implications arises. Efficiencies derived from the inclusion of Indian tribes in all stages of the tribal consultation will help ensure that future Federal action is achievable, comprehensive, long-lasting, and reflective of tribal input.

In 2016, the federal district court in Wyoming struck down a final rule by the Bureau of Land Management (BLM) regulating hydraulic fracturing (fracking) on federal and Indian lands. *Wyoming v. U.S. Dept. of the Interior*, 2016 WL 3509415 (D. Wyo. June 21, 2016) (unreported). The court determined that BLM had exceeded its delegated authority when it attempted to regulate fracking not involving the use of diesel fuels. The Tenth Circuit vacated the district court's decision and remanded with instructions to dismiss the case, on the basis that BLM was in the process of rescinding the fracking regulations. *Wyoming v. Zinke*, 871 F.3d 1133 (10th Cir. 2017). The BLM's final rule rescinding the fracking rule became effective December 29, 2017. 82 Fed. Reg. 61924 (2017).

The district court, in issuing its injunction against the fracking rule, did not address the intervenor Ute Tribe's claim that the rule was contrary to the federal trust obligation to tribes. On appeal to the Tenth Circuit, one judge dissented from the dismissal of the tribal claim. Judge Hartz would have affirmed the permanent injunction as to the tribe, because the tribe "adequately raised the issues specific to it" and the "other parties have failed to challenge the Tribe's reasoning." *Wyoming v. Zinke*, 871 F.3d at 1147 (Hartz, J., concurring and dissenting).

In an earlier opinion granting a preliminary injunction against implementation of the fracking rule, however, the district court did address BLM's responsibility to consult with Indian tribes:

> The Court also finds merit in the Ute Indian Tribe's argument that the BLM failed to consult with the Tribe on a government-to-government basis in accordance with its own policies and procedures.

Effective December 2, 2014, still prior to publication of the Fracking Rule, the DOI converted the provisions of Order No. 3317 to the DOI Departmental Manual. *See* Departmental Manual, Part 512, Chapters 4 and 5. * * * The DOI's policies and procedures reflect the unique relationship between Indian tribes and the federal government and recognize Indian tribes' right to self-governance and tribal sovereignty.

The BLM contends it engaged in extensive tribal consultation when promulgating the Fracking Rule by holding four regional tribal consultation meetings ("information sessions") and distributing copies of a draft rule to affected tribes for comment in January 2012, and offering to meet individually with tribes after those regional meetings. In June 2012, after publication of the proposed rule on May 11, 2012, and again after publication of the supplemental proposed rule in May of 2013, the BLM held additional regional consultation meetings and individual consultations with tribal representatives. In March 2014, the BLM invited tribes to another meeting in Lakewood, Colorado and offered to meet with individual tribes thereafter.

The BLM's efforts, however, reflect little more than that offered to the public in general. The DOI policies and procedures require extra, *meaningful* efforts to involve tribes in the decision-making process. The record reflects the BLM spent more than a year developing the proposed rule before initiating any consultation with Indian tribes. The BLM had already drafted a proposed rule by the time the agency initiated consultation with Indian tribes in January of 2012. Although the BLM asserts comments from affected tribes were considered in developing the final rule, the preamble cites only two changes resulting from tribal consultations: a clarification that tribal and state variances are separate from variances for a specific operator, and a requirement that operators certify to the BLM that operations on Indian lands comply with applicable tribal laws. Several tribal organizations attempted to assert their sovereignty by encouraging an "opt out" provision for Indian tribes or allowing the tribes to exercise regulatory authority over hydraulic fracturing. However, despite acknowledging "the importance of tribal sovereignty and self-determination," the BLM summarily dismissed these legitimate tribal concerns, simply citing its consistency in applying uniform regulations governing mineral resource development on Indian and federal lands and disavowing any authority to delegate regulatory responsibilities to the tribes. This failure to comply with departmental policies and procedures is arbitrary and capricious action.

Wyoming v. United States Dep't of the Interior, 136 F. Supp. 3d 1317, 1344–46 (D. Wyo. 2015), vacated and remanded, 2016 WL 3853806 (10th Cir. July 13, 2016) (unreported). For an argument that the final rule promulgated by the BLM (now rescinded) violated its responsibility to consult with tribes, relied on an improper interpretation of federal statutes to extend the rule to Indian lands, and was contrary to the federal trust responsibility to tribes, see Monte Mills, *What Should Tribes*

Expect from Federal Regulations? The Bureau of Land Management's Fracking Rule and the Problems with Treating Indian and Federal Lands Identically, 37 Pub. Land & Resources L. Rev. 1 (2016).

2. Tribal Resource Development Statutes*

The three major natural resources traditionally subject to leasing are agricultural and grazing lands, forests, and minerals. Each has been subject to federal statutes that follow a similar arc—comprehensive federal control and exploitation during the allotment period; a slight loosening of federal control, a requirement of tribal consent, and concern with tribal revenue streams in the reorganization period; and new approaches focusing more on tribal participation, partnerships, and increased control during the modern era of self-determination.

Note on Resource Development Statutes

1. Resource development in the allotment era. Leasing of all three types of natural resources began in the allotment era, under the federal idea that Indian lands should be made "productive." The allotment years were a period during which the federal government first authorized and then expanded the availability of Indian resources for development by non-Indians. After a cautious beginning in 1891, statute after statute opened more lands and more resources. Tribal consent was generally required for timber sales as well as for agricultural, grazing, oil and gas, and some other mineral leases, but not for mineral leases other than oil and gas in nine western states. Agricultural and grazing leases were set for fairly short terms, as were non-oil and gas leases outside the nine western states. The federal government was entirely in charge during this period—of what resources could be developed, for what length of time, and under what circumstances. In most cases, tribes could consent to non-Indian development, but had little control otherwise over the management and development of their natural resources.

2. Resource development in the reorganization era. Although the statutes of this era attempted to correct prior abuses and provide a measure of control to Indian tribes, federal management and control remained the norm for resource development.

a. Indian Reorganization Act. The Indian Reorganization Act (IRA) of 1934 authorized Indian tribes to form IRA constitutional governments and receive federal charters of incorporation. 25 U.S.C. §§ 5123–5124 (formerly §§ 476–477). For those tribes subject to them, IRA constitutions included a provision requiring tribal

---

* [Editor's note: parts of this section are adapted from Judith V. Royster, *Practical Sovereignty, Political Sovereignty, and the Indian Tribal Energy Development and Self-Determination Act*, 12 Lewis & Clark L. Rev. 1065, 1071–81 (2008). Copyright 2008, Judith V. Royster. *See also* Monte Mills, *Beyond a Zero-Sum Federal Trust Responsibility: Lessons from Federal Indian Energy Policy*, 6 Am. Indian L.J. 35 (2017).]

consent for leases or other encumbrances of tribal lands. Tribal business councils operating under IRA charters of incorporation were authorized to manage tribal property, including the authority to enter into leases of up to ten years without secretarial approval (extended to 25 years in 1990).

b. Indian Mineral Leasing Act. In 1938 Congress enacted the Indian Mineral Leasing Act (IMLA), 25 U.S.C. §§ 396a–396g, intended in part to help achieve the IRA goal of revitalizing tribal governments. The IMLA substituted a single set of mineral leasing procedures for the allotment-era jumble of mining laws, and required both tribal consent and secretarial approval. All leases were issued for a term not to exceed ten years and "as long thereafter as minerals are produced in paying quantities," often resulting in a de facto perpetual lease. The IMLA and its implementing regulations established a system of bonuses, rents, and royalties, and also eliminated the authorization in prior mining laws for states to tax Indian royalties.

c. Indian Long-Term Leasing Act. In 1955, during the termination era of federal Indian policy, Congress passed the Indian Long-Term Leasing Act, 25 U.S.C. § 415. Section 415 authorized 25-year leases of surface lands for a wide variety of purposes, including "[for] business purposes, including the development or utilization of natural resources in connection with operations under such lease, for grazing purposes, and for those farming purposes which require the making of a substantial investment in the improvement of land the for the production of specialized crops as determined by said Secretary." ILTLA leases of tribal lands required the consent of the tribe and the approval of the Secretary of the Interior.

d. Advantages and drawbacks. The reorganization era and subsequent decades were thus a time of consolidating and streamlining federal leasing statutes. In keeping with the federal policy focus on revitalizing tribal governments, tribal consent was uniformly required for resource development. Nonetheless, tribes had more authority over resource development on paper than in practice. IRA corporations could enter freely into leases, but the ten-year maximum lease term curtailed much real utility for resource development. Leasing was the sole route of development by non-Indians, and the Bureau of Indian Affairs set standard lease terms and lease forms. Mineral leases were essentially perpetual once minerals were produced in paying quantities, preventing tribes from renegotiating more favorable terms as conditions changed. Royalty rates were low, and industry often nominated tracts for sale, reducing the tribal role to simple consent. And because there were few federal surveys of Indian lands, tribes had little real information about their natural resources before entering into leases. In the reorganization era, therefore, the federal government retained most of the practical decision-making about Indian natural resources development and use.

3. Resource development in the self-determination era. In the modern era, Congress enacted new measures for each type of resource, providing for greater tribal participation in resource use and development. The legislative push under the self-determination policy began in earnest in the mid-1970s. Viewed through this new lens of tribal self-determination and management of resources, the resource statutes of the reorganization years were woefully out of sync.

Agitation for change started in the mining arena.* Western energy tribes, tired of their passive role and ever-smaller financial returns, took steps to assert more control. One was a moratorium on mineral development by several tribes while they engaged in careful planning for development. A second was the negotiation of mineral development agreements with energy companies. Relying on statutory authority to enter into service contracts "relative to their lands," 25 U.S.C. §81 (now amended), several tribes bypassed the restrictive provisions of the IMLA and entered into negotiated agreements that provided more tribal decision-making authority and greater tribal profits. The Secretary of the Interior initially approved several of these agreements, but determined in 1980 that the department did not have the authority to approve an oil and gas agreement. The result was to call into question the legitimacy of the existing approved agreements. But energy tribes had begun to exercise sovereignty over their mineral resources, and there was no going back.

a. Indian Mineral Development Act. Congress responded with the Indian Mineral Development Act (IMDA) of 1982, 25 U.S.C. §§ 2101–2108. Under the IMDA, any tribe was authorized to enter into a minerals agreement of any kind, including "any joint venture, operating, production sharing, service, managerial, lease or other agreement." Subject to the approval of the Secretary of the Interior, a tribe could choose the degree of control it wished to exercise, and the degree of risk it was willing to assume, by the method of structuring an agreement. The IMDA was a significant leap: not only were tribes authorized for the first time to directly negotiate the terms of their mineral development, but they could also enter into any type of arrangement they found beneficial.

b. Agriculture and forestry. Congress did not address increased tribal authority over farming, range, and forest resources until 1990. When it did, Congress took a different approach than it had to mineral resources, focusing on tribal resource and management plans and the development of tribal law, as well as federally-approved sales and leases. In 1990, Congress enacted both the American Indian Agricultural Resource Management Act (AIARMA), 25 U.S.C. §§ 3701–3745, and the National Indian Forest Resources Management Act (NIFRMA), 25 U.S.C. §§ 3101–3120. Both statutes call for increased tribal participation in managing the resources; state that the Secretary's participation in management should be consistent not only with federal trust responsibilities, but also with tribal objectives; and provide training and education opportunities for tribal members.

Both statutes require development of tribal resource plans. Tribes (or the Secretary if the tribe does not) are to develop agricultural resource plans for farm and range lands. Once approved, these plans govern management of agricultural lands by both the tribe and the federal government. As of 2007, approximately a quarter of tribal agricultural and grazing lands were subject to completed resource management plans.

---

* For a detailed look at the history and evolution of the major mineral statutes, see Judith V. Royster, *Mineral Development in Indian Country: The Evolution of Tribal Control Over Mineral Resources*, 29 Tulsa L.J. 541 (1994).

Forest management plans (FMPs), developed by the Secretary with "full and active consultation and participation" of the tribes, govern harvests of timber and other forest products, and incorporate critical tribal values for forests. By 2005, FMPs governed approximately 86 percent of Indian forest lands.

Tribes may choose to assume a significantly larger role in management of their agricultural and forest resources. AIARMA authorizes the use of "638 contracts" or self-governance compacts for tribes to develop agricultural resource management plans. (See Public Law 93–638 Contracting and Compacting, https://www.doi.gov/ost/tribal_beneficiaries/contracting, for an explanation of 638 contracts.) In addition, AIARMA regulations provide that tribes may develop tribal leasing laws that supersede federal regulations. NIFRMA similarly authorizes the Secretary to undertake forest management activities through contracts, grants, or cooperative agreements under the 638 program. The regulations provide that tribal forest enterprises, defined as Indian enterprises that are "initiated and organized" by the tribe, may contract with tribes for the use of tribal forest products and other purposes, subject to the approval of the Secretary.

c. Advantages. These self-determination era statutes represent a substantial increase in tribal sovereignty over resource development. Congress opened up options for tribes that wished to take advantage of them. Tribes may use 638 contracts to develop agricultural resource management plans and undertake forest management activities; enact tribal laws to govern the management of agricultural and forest lands; and structure negotiated minerals agreements. Congress also took important steps toward the Secretary's transition from decision-maker to advisor: providing education and training programs for agricultural and forestry management; giving financial support for tribal forestry programs; and supplying advice and assistance during the negotiations of minerals agreements.

Many Indian tribes have taken advantage of the new statutory opportunities. Tribes have widely adopted the IMDA alternative of negotiated minerals agreements, tribal forest management plans now cover the vast majority of tribal forest lands, and many tribes have adopted resource management plans for agricultural and grazing lands.

4. The "next generation" of statutes. Since 1934, Congress has occasionally granted exceptions to the Nonintercourse Act's requirement of federal approval for all encumbrances of Indian lands. Tribal corporations chartered under section 17 of the Indian Reorganization Act may "manage, operate, and dispose of property," although their leasing authority is time-limited. 25 U.S.C. § 5124 (formerly § 477). Originally, IRA corporations were authorized to issue leases for up to ten year terms, but in 1990 Congress extended that authority to 25 years. Similarly, in 2000 Congress amended the 1871 general statute addressing contracts and agreements with Indian tribes (25 U.S.C. § 81) to provide that agreements and contracts encumbering Indian lands for less than seven years do not require secretarial approval.

For the most part, this short-term leasing authority has not proved overly useful for the economic development of tribal natural resources. First, it appears that less than a third of federally-recognized tribes has a federal corporate charter. Most tribes, therefore, are unable to take advantage of the IRA provision for leasing without secretarial approval. Moreover, non-Indian companies entering into natural resource development leases or agreements may not be willing to accept terms that extend for seven to ten years. The 1990 extension of IRA corporate leasing to 25-year terms may result in greater use of IRA leases, perhaps particularly for agricultural purposes. But by the time Congress enacted that extension, many tribes with mineral resources had moved away from leases to the more flexible arrangements authorized by the 1982 IMDA.

Early in the self-determination era, Congress began to experiment cautiously with a new approach, one that eliminated secretarial approval of specific leases if the leases were issued in accordance with department-approved tribal regulations. In 1970, Congress amended the general surface leasing statute to authorize the Tulalip Tribes to issue surface leases that do not involve "the exploitation of any natural resource" for up to 15 years, or for longer periods if the lease is executed under tribal regulations approved by the Secretary. 25 U.S.C. §415(b). Specific leases that comply with these requirements do not require secretarial approval.

Thirty years later, in 2000, Congress again amended the general surface leasing statute to provide a broader authorization to the Navajo Nation to issue business and agricultural leases for up to 25 years and other surface leases for up to 75 years, if the lease is executed under tribal regulations approved by the Secretary. 25 U.S.C. §415(e). Congress specified, however, that the authorization did not extend to any lease for "the exploration, development, or extraction of any mineral resources." The Secretary is directed to approve tribal regulations if the regulations are consistent with Interior regulations for surface leasing and "provide for an environmental review process." As with the Tulalip provision, specific leases that comply with the special statutory requirements do not require secretarial approval. In enacting the statute, Congress expressly stated that one purpose was to "revitalize" the Navajo Nation "by promoting political self-determination, and encouraging economic self-sufficiency."

Congress first extended this approach beyond specific tribal authorizations in the 2004 American Indian Probate Reform Act, creating a category of "owner-managed interests" in individual trust and restricted lands. 25 U.S.C. §2220. The statute authorizes the owners of such lands to apply to the Secretary for the ability to lease the lands without secretarial approval. Once the Secretary has approved applications for all the owners of a parcel, the owners may lease the land for agricultural purposes for up to ten years without secretarial approval of the individual leases.

a. **Tribal Energy Resource Agreements.** In 2005, Congress expanded the new approach dramatically, reaching well beyond specific tribes or individual interests in agricultural land. As part of the massive Energy Policy Act, Congress enacted the Indian Tribal Energy Development and Self-Determination Act (ITEDSA), 25 U.S.C. §§ 3501–3506. ITEDSA has the potential to fundamentally change the way that tribal resource development occurs. ITEDSA authorizes Indian tribes, at their option, to enter into tribal energy resource agreements (TERAs) with the Department of the

Interior. 25 U.S.C. § 3504. The Secretary is mandated to approve a TERA if the proposed agreement complies with a slew of statutory requirements, foremost among which are that the tribe demonstrate "sufficient capacity to regulate the development" of the tribal resources and provide an environmental review process that closely mirrors that of the National Environmental Policy Act.

Once a tribe has an approved TERA, it is authorized to enter into leases and business agreements (of all kinds) for energy resource development, and to grant rights of way for pipelines and electric transmission and distribution lines, without the approval of the Secretary. With the exception of oil and gas leases, which may be made for the standard term of ten years and as long thereafter as the oil or gas is produced in paying quantities, leases, business agreements, and rights of way may be made for terms not to exceed 30 years. Thus, unlike the IMDA and its predecessor mineral leasing statutes, all of which require secretarial approval for each lease or minerals agreement that a tribe enters into, ITEDSA abolishes the need for secretarial approval of every specific instrument of development.

ITEDSA, designed to allow tribes more freedom of energy development, has so far proved to be "the solution that isn't." Judith V. Royster, *Tribal Energy Development: Renewables and the Problem of the Current Statutory Structures*, 31 Stan. Envt'l L.J. 91, 117 (2012). As of early 2018, no tribe had submitted a TERA application. "The front-end costs of time, money, and staffing to develop a TERA and shepherd it through the approval process are substantial, if not prohibitive. The back-end costs of providing an environmental review process and addressing public input into tribal decisions and compliance are similarly substantial. These costs mean that ITEDSA may ultimately be useful to only a small cadre of tribes with considerable energy resources to develop." *Id*. at 119–20. As Professor Kronk has noted, "tribes have failed to take advantage of the existing TERA provisions because they represent a mixture of federal paternalism, oversight, and limited liability that is not attractive to tribes." Elizabeth Ann Kronk, *Tribal Energy Resource Agreements: The Unintended 'Great Mischief for Indian Energy Development' and the Resulting Need for Reform*, 29 Pace Envt'l L. Rev. 811, 820 (2012).

Energy state senators have introduced legislation to streamline the TERA process to make it easier for tribes to enter into TERAs. S. 209 (primary sponsor: Sen. John Barrasso, R-WY) was introduced in January 2015, passed the Senate by unanimous consent, and was referred to various House committees in December 2015. But nothing happened in the House. S. 245 (primary sponsor: Sen. John Hoeven, R-ND) was introduced in January 2017, passed the Senate by unanimous consent, and was referred to various House committees in December 2017.

b. HEARTH Act. The most recent of the "next generation" statutes is the Helping Expedite and Advance Responsible Tribal Ownership (HEARTH) Act of 2012, 25 U.S.C. § 415(h) (note 2c above), which offers an alternative land leasing process for all tribes. Modeled on the TERA provision of ITEDSA, the HEARTH Act gives tribes that develop land leasing regulations approved by the Secretary of the Interior authority to negotiate and enter into surface leases of tribal trust lands for primary terms of 25 years and up to two renewals of 25 additional years (or a primary term of 75 years for residential, recreational, religious, or educational purposes). These leases would not require secretarial approval, but the Act requires public notice and environmental review, although the tribe could choose to maintain federal environmental review. Mineral leases, however, are not covered by the HEARTH Act.

The HEARTH Act has proved far more popular with tribes than the TERA provision of ITEDSA on which it was modeled. By late 2017, at least 27 tribes had received approval of their HEARTH Act regulations. Each received approval for residential and/or business leases, but a few are also authorized to enter into resource leases: Ho-Chunk Nation (agricultural), Makah Tribe (wind and solar leases), and Gila River Indian Community (solar). *See* https://www.bia.gov/bia/ots/hearth.

Note on Renewable Energy Resources

The traditional minerals statutes described above are designed for the development of traditional energy resources such as coal, oil, and natural gas. The IMDA includes "other energy" mineral resources in its definition, although Professor Royster has argued that its application to renewable energy resources is uncertain because those sources are not "minerals." See Judith V. Royster, *Tribal Energy Development: Renewables and the Problem of the Current Statutory Structures*, 31 Stan. Envt'l L.J. 91 (2012).

Alternative sources of energy, such as solar, wind, biomass, and geothermal, may be developed using TERAs, which expressly applies to "both renewable and nonrenewable energy sources." In the dozen years since TERAs have been available, however, no tribe has pursued this option.

Alternative energy resources that involve surface use only—such as wind or solar—might be developed using the surface leasing authority of 25 U.S.C. §415, and biomass resources might be developed using the agricultural or forestry statutes. If tribes may use only these latter statutes, and not the IMDA, they are limited to the role of lessor or seller rather than development partner available under the IMDA and with TERAs. *See* Royster, *supra*, at 112–17.

Surface development for wind or solar may still require a mineral lease or agreement, however, if the development includes "action upon the minerals in order to exploit the minerals themselves." *United States v. Osage Wind, LLC*, 871 F.3d 1078, 1089 (10th Cir. 2017). A private wind energy company leased surface rights to 8400 acres of private fee land in Osage County, Oklahoma. The mineral estate of the lands, once the Osage Reservation, is reserved to the tribe in trust. In order to install the 84 wind turbines, the company excavated holes to accommodate cement foundations ten feet deep and 60 feet in diameter. The process included extracting soil, sand, and rock of common mineral varieties; sorting the rock into pieces smaller or larger than three feet; crushing the smaller-sized rocks; and, after the foundations were poured and set, compacting the crushed rock into the holes to aid in structural support for the turbines. The company did not obtain a mineral lease, arguing that it was not "mining" if it did not sell the extracted minerals. The Tenth Circuit, however, determined that because the wind energy company had "acted upon the minerals by altering their natural size and shape in order to take advantage of them for a structural purpose," the company had engaged in mineral development without a federally-approved lease. *Id.* at 1091–92.

For a review of alternative energy projects and obstacles, see Elizabeth Ann Kronk, *Alternative Energy Development in Indian Country: Lighting the Way for the Seventh Generation*, 46 Idaho L. Rev. 449 (2010).

3. Energy Rights-of-Way

Recall that Indian country, as defined by federal statute:

> means (a) all land within the limits of any Indian reservation under the jurisdiction of the United States Government, notwithstanding the issuance of any patent, and, *including rights-of-way* running through the reservation, . . . and (c) all Indian allotments, the Indian titles to which have not been extinguished, *including rights-of-way* running through the same.

18 U.S.C. § 1151 (emphasis added). Rights-of-way across Indian lands include oil and gas pipelines and electric transmission and distribution lines, as well as roads and highways, railroads, telephone lines, and the like. Most rights-of-way are granted pursuant to the 1948 Indian Right-of-Way Act that authorized them for all purposes (25 U.S.C. §§ 323–328), but oil and gas pipelines are also authorized by a 1904 statute (25 U.S.C. § 321).

Blackfeet Indian Tribe v. Montana Power Company
838 F.2d 1055 (9th Cir. 1988)

The Blackfeet Indian Tribe seeks to have rights-of-way granted over tribal lands invalidated. The appeal presents the question of whether the Secretary of the Interior exceeded his authority by allowing a fifty-year term for natural gas pipeline rights-of-way across Blackfeet *tribal primacy* lands. We hold he did not.

I.

Between 1961 and 1969, the Secretary of the Interior ("Secretary") granted The Montana Power Company ("MPC") five rights-of-way for natural gas transmission pipelines across Blackfeet Indian Tribe ("Tribe") lands on the Blackfeet Indian Reservation *in taxation* Montana. Each right-of-way was granted by the Secretary pursuant to his approval power, and each was for a fifty-year term. At the time of approval, the Tribe also consented to each right-of-way.

In 1981, the Tribe objected to the fifty-year term and notified MPC of its objection. The Tribe contended the terms were limited to twenty rather than fifty years. * * * [T]he Tribe alleged the right-of-way had expired and MPC was therefore occupying the land as a trespasser.

II.

In 1904, Congress enacted a statute authorizing the Secretary to grant rights-of-way as easements for oil and gas pipelines through any Indian reservation for a period no longer than twenty years. The statute reads as follows:

> The Secretary of the Interior is authorized and empowered to grant a right of way in the nature of an easement for the construction, operation, and maintenance of pipe lines for the conveyance of oil and gas through any Indian reservation . . . *Provided,* That the rights herein granted shall not extend beyond a period of twenty years: *Provided further,* That the Secretary of the Interior, at the expiration of said twenty years, may extend the right to maintain any pipe line constructed under this section for another period not to exceed twenty years from the expiration of the first right, upon such terms and conditions as he may deem proper. The right to alter, amend, or repeal this section is expressly reserved.

25 U.S.C. § 321.

With the 1904 Act still in effect, in 1948 Congress passed the Indian Right-of-Way Act. The 1948 Act empowered the Secretary to grant rights-of-way across Indian lands for all purposes. The statute provides:

> The Secretary of the Interior be, and he is empowered to grant rights-of-way for all purposes, subject to such conditions as he may prescribe, over and across any lands now or hereafter held in trust by the United States for individual Indians or Indian tribes, communities, bands, or nations, or any lands now or hereafter owned, subject to restrictions against alienation, by individual Indians or Indian tribes, communities, bands, or nations, including the lands belonging to the Pueblo Indians in New Mexico, and any other lands heretofore or hereafter acquired or set aside for the use and benefit of the Indians.

25 U.S.C. § 323. The 1948 Act included a second statute which required tribal consent for rights-of-way, stating, in relevant part: "No grant of a right-of-way over and across any lands belonging to a tribe . . . shall be made without the consent of the proper tribal officials." 25 U.S.C. § 324. Additionally, the 1948 Act provided that:

> Sections 323 and 328 of this title shall not in any manner amend or repeal the provisions of the Federal Water Power Act, . . . nor shall any existing statutory authority empowering the Secretary of the Interior to grant rights-of-way over Indian lands be repealed.

25 U.S.C. § 326.

Pursuant to the authority granted by the 1948 Act, empowering the Secretary to grant rights-of-way "subject to such conditions as he may prescribe," the Secretary promulgated a regulation in 1960 which allowed rights-of-way for oil and gas pipelines for a period not to exceed fifty years. * * * In 1968, the regulation was amended to allow the Secretary to grant rights-of-way for *all* easements, *including* oil and gas pipelines, for an unlimited term of years.

However, the regulation promulgated pursuant to the 1904 Act limited oil and gas pipeline rights-of-way to not more than 20 years * * *. Thus the rights-of-way acquired by MPC could be subject to [the regulation] covering all rights-of-way and allowing unlimited terms; or subject to [the regulation] covering only oil and gas pipeline rights-of-way and limiting the term of years to not more than twenty; or subject to the original regulation providing for not more than a fifty-year term for all rights-of-way.

Because the rights-of-way at issue here were limited to fifty years, we need not consider the validity of the 1968 amendment insofar as it allowed terms in excess of fifty years. * * * As a result, the essential question is whether the 1904 Act, the 1948 Act, or both, control the five rights-of-way the Secretary granted MPC.

IV.

The starting point for an issue involving statutory construction is the language in the statute itself. Where two statutes are involved, legislative intent to repeal an earlier statute must be clear and manifest. In the absence of such intent, apparently conflicting statutes must be read to give effect to each if such can be done by preserving their sense and purpose. This is because statutory repeals by implication from a later enacted statute are disfavored. Also, where possible, we resolve legal ambiguities in favor of Indians, but we cannot ignore the plain intent of Congress.

Here, the language in neither Act speaks to the relationship of the Acts *inter se*. We therefore look to congressional intent with an eye toward upholding both statutes. The 1904 Act is specific. It authorizes the Secretary to grant rights-of-way for oil and gas pipelines for up to a twenty-year period. The later enacted Act of 1948 is more general; it grants the Secretary the power to grant "rights-of-way for *all* purposes" subject to the conditions he prescribed. Additionally, the 1948 Act stated that it was not to "in any manner amend or repeal . . . any existing statutory authority empowering the Secretary of the Interior to grant rights-of-way over Indian lands. . . ."

There is no express congressional intent to repeal § 321, even with the law's unaffected language contained in § 326. In 1904, the Secretary was given the authority to grant easements for oil and gas pipelines. Later, in an attempt to broaden the Secretary's powers in granting rights-of-way for access to Indian lands for other purposes, the 1948 Act was passed. It was meant to "satisfy the need for simplification and uniformity in the administration of Indian law." To avoid confusion, the existing special purpose statutes (such as section 321) were preserved in anticipation of implementation of the general purpose statute of § 323.

The Act of 1904 and the Act of 1948 can be read as coexisting. The former allows a term of 20 years, the later a term of 50 years. No matter which term the Secretary permits the consent of the Tribe is still required. Presumably, if the Tribe did not approve a 50-year term, approval of a 20-year term would be much more likely. In either case, the Tribe has preserved its election and its ability to protect Tribal interests. Thus the two Acts are not in direct conflict, and effect can be given to each while still preserving their sense and purpose.

Since effect can be given to both the 1904 and the 1948 Acts, both should be applied. This gave the Tribe a choice between either the 20-year term under the earlier statute or up to a 50-year term under the latter statute. The Tribe consented to a 50-year term. The term of years was controlled by both Acts and the Secretary did not exceed his authority in providing regulations allowing 50-year terms.

V.

We hold the term of years for the rights-of-way can be either 20 or 50 years. Since the Tribe consented to the 50-year term, the Secretary's regulations with respect to term of years are valid.

Notes

1. Indian Land Right-of-Way Study. In the Energy Policy Act of 2005, Congress directed the Departments of Energy and Interior to conduct a study of energy rights-of-way on tribal lands. *See* Energy Policy Act of 2005, Section 1813 Indian Land Rights-of-Way Study: Report to Congress (May 2007), https://energy.gov/sites/prod/files/oeprod/DocumentsandMedia/EPAct_1813_Final.pdf

One of the issues addressed by the study was complaints by energy companies that obtaining tribal consent to rights-of-way was a lengthy and occasionally contentious process, too often resulting in high costs and relatively short duration of the rights-of-way. The study concluded, however, that the problem was greatly exaggerated, that costs had not increased as a result of negotiations with tribes, and that any diminishment of tribal consent authority would undermine tribal sovereignty. Nonetheless, to help streamline the process, the study recommended a comprehensive right-of-way inventory to ensure that all parties were negotiating from a base of full information; the development of model or standard business practices (but not through legislation or federal regulation); and broadening the scope of energy right-of-way negotiations. It also recommended that if a failure of negotiations significantly affected regional or national supply, price, or reliability of energy resources, Congress should resolve the matter with legislation specific to the particular case, not with broad legislation that would adversely affect tribal sovereignty.

2. Rights-of-way under a tribal energy resource agreement. Under the Indian Tribal Energy Development and Self-Determination Act of 2005, tribes are authorized to enter into tribal energy resource agreements (TERAs) with the Department of the Interior. See note 4, at page 360. A tribe with an approved TERA may then enter into certain energy transactions without specific secretarial approval, including rights-of-way for pipelines and energy transmission and distribution lines. By early 2018, however, no tribe had applied for a TERA.

Nebraska Public Power Dist. v. 100.95 Acres of Land
719 F.2d 956 (8th Cir. 1983)

This case concerns the authority of a public utility to condemn tracts of land held in trust by the United States for individual Indians and for Indian tribes. We hold that pursuant to 25 U.S.C. § 357 the utility has the authority to condemn land allotted in severalty to Indians but not land in which the Indian tribe holds an interest.

This litigation arose from a plan of Nebraska Public Power District (NPPD) to construct an electric transmission line across the Winnebago Indian Reservation. The Winnebago Tribe has opposed construction of the proposed power line. NPPD brought this action in federal district court to condemn a right-of-way across twenty-nine tracts of land within the reservation. The tracts sought to be condemned by NPPD were allotted by the United States to individual Indians pursuant to either the Indian General Allotment Act or the treaty between the United States and the Winnebago Tribe.

I. ALLOTTED LAND

25 U.S.C. § 357, enacted by Congress in 1901, provides as follows:

> Lands allotted in severalty to Indians may be condemned for any public purpose under the laws of the State or Territory where located in the same manner as land owned in fee may be condemned, and the money awarded as damages shall be paid to the allottee.

Section 357 clearly authorizes the judicial condemnation of a right-of-way across allotted Indian land for the construction of an electric transmission line. The question on appeal is whether, as the district court held, section 357 has been impliedly repealed in part by the more recently enacted Indian Right-of-Way Act of 1948, which conditions condemnation of a right-of-way across allotted Indian land upon consent of the Secretary of Interior, and in certain cases, upon consent of the individual allottee.

To determine whether an earlier statute has been impliedly repealed by a later one, we are guided by familiar principles. The intent of Congress must be "clear and manifest" to support an implied repeal. The cardinal rule is that repeals by implication are not favored. Absent affirmative evidence of congressional intent to repeal the earlier statute "the only permissible justification for a repeal by implication is when the earlier and later statutes are irreconcilable." "[W]hen two statutes are capable of coexistence, it is the duty of the courts, absent a clearly expressed congressional intention to the contrary, to regard each as effective."

In this case, we find no clearly expressed congressional intent impliedly to repeal section 357. Prior to 1948, access across Indian lands was governed by an amalgam of special purpose access statutes dating back as far as 1875. This statutory scheme limited the nature of rights-of-way to be obtained, and in certain cases, created an unnecessarily complicated method for obtaining rights-of-way. Each application for a right-of-way across Indian land had to be examined painstakingly to assure that it fit into one of the narrow categories of rights-of-way authorized by statute. When a right-of-way was not authorized under one of the existing statutes, which often was the case, it became necessary to obtain easement deeds, approved by the Secretary of the Interior, from each of the Indian owners. Frequently, many individual Indians, often widely scattered, owned undivided interests in a single tract of land. Obtaining the signatures of all the owners was time-consuming and burdensome process, both for the party seeking the right-of-way and for the Interior Department.

The purpose of the 1948 Act was to simplify and facilitate this process of granting rights-of-way across Indian lands. * * * The 1948 Act does not, by its express terms, amend or repeal any existing legislation concerning rights-of-way across Indian lands. On the contrary, the statute provides that "any existing statutory authority empowering the Secretary of the Interior to grant rights-of-way over Indian lands" is not repealed. The legislative history explains that this provision "to preserve the existing statutory authority relating to rights-of-way over Indian lands" was included "to avoid any possible confusion which may arise, particularly in the period of transition from the old system to the new." This provision was aimed at the special purpose access statutes which authorized rights-of-way upon secretarial consent and does not expressly address section 357. Nevertheless, the explanation of this provision does suggest a general intent in the 1948 Act of adding to, rather than replacing, existing legislation concerning rights-of-way across Indian lands.

In sum, it is apparent from the legislative history that the 1948 Act was not enacted as a restrictive measure in response to problems engendered by section 357, which authorized condemnation pursuant to state law without secretarial consent. Rather, the 1948 Act was a response to quite the opposite problems; the limited nature of rights-of-way authorized by statute, and the difficulty of obtaining easement deeds from all the various owners. Conditioning rights-of-way in certain cases upon consent of only the Secretary was intended to make the law more lenient in situations where consent of all the owners previously had to be obtained. Thus, it is not consistent with the legislative history of the 1948 Act expansively to interpret the secretarial consent provision as an intended restriction upon obtaining all rights-of-way across Indian lands.

Finding no clearly expressed congressional intent to repeal section 357, we consider whether section 357 is in irreconcilable conflict with the 1948 Act.

The specific conflict presented in this case—the alleged inconsistency between section 357 and the 1948 Act— has been addressed in three courts of appeals decisions. In *Nicodemus v. Washington Water Power Co.,* 264 F.2d 614 (9th Cir.1959), the Ninth Circuit held that the 1948 Act and section 357 offered "two methods for the acquisition of an easement across allotted Indian land for the construction of an electric transmission line." In *Southern California Edison Co. v. Rice,* 685 F.2d [354 (9th Cir. 1982)], the Indian allottees contended that the 1948 Act was the exclusive means by which the company could obtain a right-of-way across the allotted Indian lands. The Ninth Circuit reaffirmed its holding in *Nicodemus* that section 357 "is an *alternative* method for the acquisition of an easement across allotted Indian land to which the United States has consented." Similarly, in *Yellowfish v. City of Stillwater*, 691 F.2d 926 (10th Cir. 1982), an Indian allottee contended that section 357 was impliedly repealed in part by the 1948 Act. The Tenth Circuit concluded that in spite of the 1948 Act, "federal courts have jurisdiction under section 357 to condemn rights-of-way over allotted Indian land without secretarial or Indian consent." The court found no irreconcilable conflict between section 357 and the 1948 Act. Indeed, it concluded that the two provisions could be harmonized: "The two statutes provide alternative methods for a state-authorized condemnor to obtain a right-of-way over *allotted* lands."

We agree with the other circuits that have considered the issue that section 357 and the 1948 Act can be reconciled. The statutes serve similar but not identical purposes: Section 357 authorizes the condemnation of land while the 1948 Act provides for the granting of consent for rights-of-way. Thus, based on the disfavor of an implied repeal of a statute, the absence of any clearly expressed congressional intent to repeal section 357, and finally, the compatibility of section 357 and the 1948 Act based on the case law of this and other circuits, we hold that the district court committed error in its conclusion that the 1948 Act impliedly repealed the authorization for obtaining rights-of-way by condemnation proceedings in section 357.

Notes

1. Consent of allottees. Why must tribes consent to rights-of-way, but allottees may be subject to rights-of-way by condemnation? Under current regulations, all individual landowners must be notified, but consent is required from only the owners of the majority interest in the allotment. 25 C.F.R. § 169.107(b). No owner needs to consent if there are 50 or more co-owners (and it is thus impracticable to obtain individual consent) and the BIA determines that the right-of-way will "cause no substantial injury" and that the landowners will be adequately compensated. Given those regulations, should consent (whether from allottees or the BIA) always be required for a right-of-way across allotted land?

2. Parcels co-owned by allottees and tribes. What if a parcel of land is held in trust for co-owners that include both individual tribal members and tribes? A public utility sought to condemn a right-of-way for an electric transmission line across five allotments. The Navajo Nation held an undivided beneficial interest in two of those allotments: a 13.6% interest in one and a 0.14% interest in the other. In *Public Service Co. of New Mexico v. Approximately 15.49 Acres of Land*, 167 F. Supp. 3d 1248 (D.N.M. 2016), the court held that condemnation was authorized only for individual lands, not tribal. If the tribe holds an interest in a tract, it is considered tribal land, and tribal consent is required for a right-of-way. A petition for a writ of certiorari in the case was denied in 2018. Note the potential effect of the Land Buy-Back Program described at note 3, page 244. Through fiscal year 2016, the program "has created or increased tribal ownership in more than 30,000 tracts of land."

Efforts by easement holders to condemn rights-of-way across tracts in which tribes hold an undivided interest have also faltered on civil procedure grounds. The tribe, as the holder of an interest, is a required party that cannot be joined without its consent because of tribal sovereign immunity. Courts routinely find that it is not feasible to proceed with the action in the absence of the tribal party. *See, e.g., Davilla v. Enable Midstream Partners, L.P.*, 2016 WL 4402064 (W.D. Okla. Aug. 18, 2016) (unreported); *Public Service Co. of New Mexico v. Approximately 15.49 Acres of Land*, 155 F. Supp. 3d 1151 (D.N.M. 2015). The Tenth Circuit affirmed the New Mexico decision on other grounds, but noted that "the district court's orders provide thorough and well-reasoned bases to affirm" on each question raised by the utility. *Public Service Co. of New Mexico v. Barboan*, 857 F.3d 1101, 1108 n.2 (10th Cir. 2017).

3. Trespass liability absent consent. A company that operates on a right-of-way without the required consent may be liable for trespass damages and/or required to move the utility. In *Davilla v. Enable Midstream Partners, L.P.*, 247 F. Supp. 3d 1233 (W.D. Okla. 2017) (appeal docketed Apr. 25, 2017), the BIA approved a 20-year easement for a natural gas transmission pipeline across a Kiowa trust allotment. The right-of-way expired in 2010, although the company had continued to operate the pipeline. In 2002, the pipeline company sought a new 20-year easement, and obtained the written consent of five of the co-owners, who collectively owned less than a 10% interest. At the time, 38 Indians and the Kiowa Tribe owned undivided interests in the tract. The tribe's interest, obtained sometime after 2008 under operation of the American Indian Probate Reform Act, is approximately 1.1%.

In 2015, plaintiffs (co-owners of the tract who had not consented) sued the company for trespass. The district court determined that state trespass law could provide the rule for decision if it was not inconsistent with federal law or policy. Oklahoma law provides that consent is a complete defense to trespass, and the company argued that the five written consents it obtained absolved it of any liability. The federal court, however, held that application of Oklahoma law would be clearly inconsistent with the federal requirement that the owners of a majority of the interests consent. The court consequently granted summary judgment to the plaintiffs on their trespass claim and permanently enjoined the use of the defendant's pipeline. The company was ordered to move the pipeline within six months.

Note on Tribal Regulatory Authority over Rights-of-Way

In 1997, the Supreme Court held that a highway right-of-way across reservation land was the "equivalent, for nonmember governance purposes, to alienated, non-Indian land." *Strate v. A1 Contractors*, 520 U.S. 438 (1997), excerpted at page 275. The Court relied on the concept that the tribe had retained no "gatekeeping" interests in the right-of-way:

> Forming part of the State's highway, the right-of-way is open to the public, and traffic on it is subject to the State's control. The Tribes have consented to, and received payment for, the State's use of the 6.59-mile stretch for a public highway. They have retained no gatekeeping right. So long as the stretch is maintained as part of the State's highway, the Tribes cannot assert a landowner's right to occupy and exclude. We therefore align the right-of-way, for

the purpose at hand, with land alienated to non-Indians. Our decision in *Montana,* accordingly, governs this case.

Applying the *Montana* framework [see page 249], the Court held that the tribal court lacked jurisdiction over a vehicle accident between two nonmembers on the highway right-of-way, finding no consensual relationship and no adverse effects on tribal self-government.

Lower federal and state courts subsequently expanded the idea of rights-of-way as fee-land equivalents to situations where the rights-of-way at issue were not broadly open to the public. *See Burlington Northern R.R. Co. v. Red Wolf,* 196 F.3d 1059 (9th Cir. 1999) (accident on railroad right-of-way that resulted in death of two tribal members); *Big Horn Electric Coop., Inc. v. Adams,* 219 F.3d 944 (9th Cir. 2000) (tribal property tax on utility property on right-of-way) [discussed at note 3, page 438]; *Arrow Midstream Holdings v. 3 Bears Construction,* 873 N.W.3d 16 (N.D. 2015) (lien against holder of pipeline right-of-way for oil, gas, and water lines). In each case, the courts applied the *Montana* framework and held against tribal jurisdiction over the nonmember holder of the right-of-way.

In 2016, the Department of the Interior issued amended right-of-way regulations. Among the provisions is 25 C.F.R. § 169.10, intended to address the problem created by *Strate* and its progeny:

> A right-of-way is a non-possessory interest in land, and title does not pass to the grantee. The Secretary's grant of a right-of-way will clarify that it does not diminish to any extent:
>
> (a) The Indian tribe's jurisdiction over the land subject to, and any person or activity within, the right-of-way;
>
> (b) The power of the Indian tribe to tax the land, any improvements on the land, or any person or activity within, the right-of-way;
>
> (c) The Indian tribe's authority to enforce tribal law of general or particular application on the land subject to and within the right-of-way, as if there were no grant of right-of-way;
>
> (d) The Indian tribe's inherent sovereign power to exercise civil jurisdiction over nonmembers on Indian land; or
>
> (e) The character of the land subject to the right-of-way as Indian country under 18 U.S.C. 1151.

Similarly, § 169.125(c)(1) provides that a grant of a right-of-way "will state that: The tribe maintains its existing jurisdiction over the land, activities, and persons within the right-of-way under § 169.10 and reserves the right of the tribe to reasonable access to the lands subject to the grant to determine grantee's compliance with consent conditions or to protect public health and safety."

The Part 169 regulations apply only to rights-of-way granted under the 1948 Indian Right-of-Way Act, 25 U.S.C. §§ 323-328. They do not apply to rights-of-way acquired on allotments by condemnation. *See* 25 C.F.R. § 169.1(a); *Public Service Co. of New*

Mexico v. Approximately 15.49 Acres of Land, 167 F. Supp. 3d 1248, 1261 (D.N.M. 2016) ("The new regulations and the comments reaffirm that the Amended Part 169 regulations do not govern condemnation actions under § 357.").

In March 2016, the Western Energy Alliance filed suit against the Department of the Interior, alleging that the ROW rule exceeded the Secretary's authority under the 1948 Act, was contrary to existing federal law regarding Indian rights-of-way, and was arbitrary and capricious. The federal district court denied the plaintiff's motion for a preliminary injunction. *Western Energy Alliance v. U.S. Dep't of the Interior*, No. 1:16-cv-050 (D.N.D. Apr. 19, 2016). The court found that the Secretary had "clear" authority to issue regulations under the 1948 Act, and that the plaintiff had not demonstrated a likelihood of success on the merits. Despite the ruling, the court opined that: "the need for this new Final Rule is unclear at best, particularly when the long-established process for obtaining BIA grants of rights-of-way across tribal lands seems to have worked relatively well for more than 60 years." Is the court correct that the previous process worked well? If so, for whom? Is the court exceeding its role in judicial review by opining on the necessity of the rule?

How should courts treat tribal jurisdiction over rights-of-way created by condemnation after April 2016 (when the amended regulations took effect)? If you represented a public utility seeking a new right-of-way across allotted land for an electric transmission line, would you prefer to seek the allottees' consent or to proceed by condemnation?

B. The Breach of Trust Action for Federal Resource Mismanagement

The federal government's fiduciary obligations with respect to trust lands and resources do not end with the Secretary's decision to approve or disapprove non-Indian development. The materials in this section explore the circumstances under which the federal government has a trust responsibility to the tribes concerning the way in which non-Indians carry out development activities, and the scope of that federal trust obligation to the tribes and allottees. These materials focus on the judicial development of the action for breach of trust.

Nell Jessup Newton, Enforcing the Federal-Indian Trust Relationship after *Mitchell*
31 Cath. U.L. Rev. 635, 635–39, 643–44 (1982)*

The legislative, judicial, and executive branches of the government have acknowledged Indian tribes' special relationship to the federal government. Borrowing concepts from trust law, courts have described this relationship most eloquently: the

---

* Copyright 1982. Reprinted with permission of Nell Jessup Newton and the Catholic University Law Review.

relationship is like "that of a ward to his guardian," imposing "moral obligations of the highest responsibility and trust," that should "be judged by the most exacting fiduciary standards." For six decades courts invoked this relationship, primarily, however, as the source of federal "plenary" power to regulate exclusively a wide spectrum of Indian affairs—from the management of Indian land and resources, to the application of federal criminal laws to tribal members on reservations, and even to the dissolution of Indian tribes' governing structures.

During the last twenty years, Indian tribes have sought to establish that this right of exclusive federal regulatory power gives rise to concomitant fiduciary duties. In response to the essential fairness of this claim, courts awarded equitable relief, and even money damages, to tribes suing the federal government for breach of trust in a handful of cases before 1980. Nevertheless, the exact source of this special relationship remains uncertain. Ownership of Indian land, the helplessness of Indian tribes in the face of a superior culture, higher law, the entire course of dealings between the government and Indian tribes, treaties, and "hundreds of cases and . . . a bulging volume of the U.S. Code" have all been cited as the source.

Pressed by the necessity of determining whether a breach of trust has in fact occurred, courts have defined somewhat more specifically the scope of the federal government's fiduciary duties by looking to treaties, statutes, the federal common law of trusts (heavily influenced by the Restatement of Trusts) and a combination of these sources for guidance. Furthermore, when relying on statutes and treaties as the source of enforceable fiduciary duties, courts have read them broadly, often applying rules of construction favoring Indian tribes. In the 1970s particularly, the courts handed down many favorable decisions. For example, courts have held the government liable for mismanagement of property, ordered the government to manage trust funds prudently, and imposed duties on the government to preserve water for a tribal lake. Nevertheless, before 1980 the scope of the government's fiduciary duties remained uncertain as the trust relationship doctrine continued its maturation. In 1980 that process took a decisive turn in *United States v. Mitchell*. To understand this new direction, the prerequisites for suing to enforce the trust relationship must be understood.

To sue the government for breach of trust, a tribe must satisfy three major threshold requirements: bring its claim in a competent court, one statutorily vested with subject matter jurisdiction; escape the doctrine of sovereign immunity by establishing the government's consent to be sued; and, finally, assert a claim, a federally recognized right entitling it to the relief requested.

The first requirement, subject matter jurisdiction, has been easily satisfied. Tribes seeking money damages for breach of trust have invoked the Tucker Act, empowering the Court of Claims (and the district courts in cases involving less than $10,000) to hear a variety of claims against the government, including claims "founded . . . upon . . . any Act of Congress." Since many statutes refer directly or indirectly to a trust relationship, the Court of Claims generally has invoked this provision as the basis for its jurisdiction. In the federal district courts, tribes usually have invoked general federal question jurisdiction or the Administrative Procedure Act (APA) as the jurisdictional bases of claims for declaratory and injunctive relief against agencies of the federal government. Except when tribes have attempted to avoid the Court of Claims by masking a money claim as one for equitable relief, federal district courts have accepted jurisdiction willingly over breach of trust claims.

The second requirement, a statutory consent to be sued, has posed no real problem, especially after Congress amended the Administrative Procedure Act in 1976, explicitly waiving sovereign immunity for claims based on the APA. Even before the amendment, however, many district courts had readily found consent to be sued in the APA and various other statutes, when they considered the question at all. The Court of Claims also found consent to be sued by viewing the same Tucker Act provision granting jurisdiction for claims based on statutes to be a waiver of immunity for such claims.

The final requirement, a claim upon which relief can be granted, has also been easily met, but based on uncertain analysis. In recent breach of trust claims, courts have turned most often to statutes and regulations, but sometimes to treaties and even the federal common law, as a basis for tribal claims for equitable remedies and money damages.

United States v. Navajo Nation
537 U.S. 488 (2003)

GINSBURG, J., delivered the opinion of the Court, in which REHNQUIST, C. J., and SCALIA, KENNEDY, THOMAS, and BREYER, JJ., joined. SOUTER, J., filed a dissenting opinion, in which STEVENS and O'CONNOR, JJ., joined.

JUSTICE GINSBURG delivered the opinion of the Court.

This case concerns the Indian Mineral Leasing Act of 1938 (IMLA), and the role it assigns to the Secretary of the Interior (Secretary) with respect to coal leases executed by an Indian Tribe and a private lessee. The controversy centers on 1987 amendments to a 1964 coal lease entered into by the predecessor of Peabody Coal Company (Peabody) and the Navajo Nation (Tribe), a federally recognized Indian Tribe. The Tribe seeks to recover money damages from the United States for an alleged breach of trust in connection with the Secretary's approval of coal lease amendments negotiated by the Tribe and Peabody. This Court's decisions in *United States v. Mitchell*, 445 U. S. 535 (1980) (*Mitchell I*), and *United States v. Mitchell*, 463 U. S. 206 (1983) (*Mitchell II*), control this case. Concluding that the controversy here falls within *Mitchell I*'s domain, we hold that the Tribe's claim for compensation from the Federal Government fails, for it does not derive from any liability-imposing provision of the IMLA or its implementing regulations.

I. A.

The IMLA, which governs aspects of mineral leasing on Indian tribal lands, states that "unallotted lands within any Indian reservation," or otherwise under federal jurisdiction, "may, with the approval of the Secretary . . . , be leased for mining purposes, by authority of the tribal council or other authorized spokesmen for such Indians, for terms not to exceed ten years and as long thereafter as minerals are produced in paying quantities." In addition "to provid[ing] Indian tribes with a profitable source of revenue," the IMLA aimed to foster tribal self-determination by "giv[ing] Indians a greater say in the use and disposition of the resources found on Indian lands."

Prior to enactment of the IMLA, decisions whether to grant mineral leases on Indian land generally rested with the Government. Indian consent was not required, and leases were sometimes granted over tribal objections. The IMLA, designed to advance tribal independence, empowers Tribes to negotiate mining leases themselves, and, as to coal leasing, assigns primarily an approval role to the Secretary.

Although the IMLA covers mineral leasing generally, in a number of discrete provisions it deals particularly with oil and gas leases. The IMLA contains no similarly specific prescriptions for coal leases; it simply remits coal leases, in common with all mineral leases, to the governance of rules and regulations promulgated by the Secretary.

During all times relevant here, the IMLA regulations provided that "Indian tribes ... may, with the approval of the Secretary ... or his authorized representative, lease their land for mining purposes." In line with the IMLA itself, the regulations treated oil and gas leases in more detail than coal leases. The regulations regarding royalties, for example, specified procedures applicable to oil and gas leases, including criteria for the Secretary to employ in setting royalty rates. As to coal royalties, in contrast, the regulations required only that the rate be "not less than 10 cents per ton." No other limitation was placed on the Tribe's negotiating capacity or the Secretary's approval authority.[1]

B

The Tribe involved in this case occupies the largest Indian reservation in the United States. Over the past century, large deposits of coal have been discovered on the Tribe's reservation lands, which are held for it in trust by the United States. Each year, the Tribe receives millions of dollars in royalty payments pursuant to mineral leases with private companies.

Peabody mines coal on the Tribe's lands pursuant to leases covered by the IMLA. This case principally concerns Lease 8580 (Lease or Lease 8580), which took effect upon approval by the Secretary in 1964. The Lease established a maximum royalty rate of 37.5 cents per ton of coal, but made that figure "subject to reasonable adjustment by the Secretary of the Interior or his authorized representative" on the 20-year anniversary of the Lease and every ten years thereafter.

---

1. In 1996, well after the events at issue here, the minimum rate on new coal leases was increased to "12-1/2 percent of the value of production produced and sold from the lease." The amended regulations further state, however, that "[a] lower royalty rate shall be allowed if it is determined to be in the best interest of the Indian mineral owner."

As the 20-year anniversary of Lease 8580 approached, its royalty rate of 37.5 cents per ton yielded for the Tribe only "about 2% of gross proceeds." This return was higher than the ten cents per ton minimum established by the then-applicable IMLA regulations. It was substantially lower, however, than the 12-1/2 percent of gross proceeds rate Congress established in 1977 as the minimum permissible royalty for coal mined on federal lands under the Mineral Leasing Act. For some years starting in the 1970s, to gain a more favorable return, the Tribe endeavored to renegotiate existing mineral leases with private lessees, including Peabody.

In March 1984, the Chairman of the Navajo Tribal Council wrote to the Secretary asking him to exercise his contractually conferred authority to adjust the royalty rate under Lease 8580. On June 18, 1984, the Director of the Bureau of Indian Affairs for the Navajo Area, acting pursuant to authority delegated by the Secretary, sent Peabody an opinion letter raising the rate to 20 percent of gross proceeds.

Contesting the Area Director's rate determination, Peabody filed an administrative appeal in July 1984, pursuant to 25 CFR § 2.3(a) (1985). The appeal was referred to the Deputy Assistant Secretary for Indian Affairs, John Fritz, then acting as both Commissioner of Indian Affairs and Assistant Secretary of Indian Affairs. In March 1985, Fritz permitted Peabody to supplement its brief and requested additional cost, revenue, and investment data. He thereafter appeared ready to reject Peabody's appeal. By June 1985, both Peabody and the Tribe anticipated that an announcement favorable to the Tribe was imminent.

On July 5, 1985, a Peabody Vice President wrote to Interior Secretary Donald Hodel, asking him either to postpone decision on Peabody's appeal so the parties could seek a negotiated settlement, or to rule in Peabody's favor. A copy of Peabody's letter was sent to the Tribe, which then submitted its own letter urging the Secretary to reject Peabody's request and to secure the Department's prompt release of a decision in the Tribe's favor. Peabody representatives met privately with Secretary Hodel in July 1985; no representative of the Tribe was present at, or received notice of, that meeting.

On July 17, 1985, Secretary Hodel sent a memorandum to Deputy Assistant Secretary Fritz. The memorandum "suggest[ed]" that Fritz "inform the involved parties that a decision on th[e] appeal is not imminent and urge them to continue with efforts to resolve this matter in a mutually agreeable fashion." "Any royalty adjustment which is imposed on those parties without their concurrence," the memorandum stated, "will almost certainly be the subject of protracted and costly appeals," and "could well impair the future of the contractual relationship" between the parties. Secretary Hodel added, however, that the memorandum was "not intended as a determination of the merits of the arguments of the parties with respect to the issues which are subject to the appeal."

The Tribe was not told of the Secretary's memorandum to Fritz, but learned that "'someone from Washington' had urged a return to the bargaining table." Facing "severe economic pressure," the Tribe resumed negotiations with Peabody in August 1985.

On September 23, 1985, the parties reached a tentative agreement on a package of amendments to Lease 8580. They agreed to raise the royalty rate to 12-1/2 percent of monthly gross proceeds, and to make the new rate retroactive to February 1, 1984. The 12-1/2 percent rate was at the time customary for leases to mine coal on federal lands and on Indian lands. The amendments acknowledged the legitimacy of tribal taxation of coal production, but stipulated that the tax rate would be capped at eight percent. In addition, Peabody agreed to pay the Tribe $1.5 million when the amendments became effective, and $7.5 million more when Peabody began mining additional coal, as authorized by the Lease amendments. The agreement "also addressed ancillary matters such as provisions for future royalty adjustments, arbitration procedures, rights of way, the establishment of a tribal scholarship fund, and the payment by Peabody of back royalties, bonuses, and water payments." "In consideration of the benefits associated with these lease amendments," the parties agreed to move jointly to vacate the Area Director's June 1984 decision, which had raised the royalty to 20 percent.

In August 1987, the Navajo Tribal Council approved the amendments. The parties signed a final agreement in November 1987, and Secretary Hodel approved it on December 14, 1987. Shortly thereafter, pursuant to the parties' stipulation, the Area Director's decision was vacated.

In 1993, the Tribe brought suit against the United States in the Court of Federal Claims, alleging, inter alia, that the Secretary's approval of the amendments to the Lease constituted a breach of trust. The Tribe sought $600 million in damages.

The Court of Federal Claims granted summary judgment for the United States. In no uncertain terms, that court found that the Government owed general fiduciary duties to the Tribe, which, in its view, the Secretary had flagrantly dishonored by acting in the best interests of Peabody rather than the Tribe. Nevertheless, the court concluded that the Tribe had entirely failed to link that breach of duty to any statutory or regulatory obligation which could "be fairly interpreted as mandating compensation for the government's fiduciary wrongs." Accordingly, the court held that the United States was entitled to judgment as a matter of law.

The Court of Appeals for the Federal Circuit reversed. The Government's liability to the Tribe, it said, turned on whether "the United States controls the Indian resources." Relying on 25 U.S.C. § 399 and regulations promulgated thereunder, the Court of Appeals determined that the measure of control the Secretary exercised over the leasing of Indian lands for mineral development sufficed to warrant a money judgment against the United States for breaches of fiduciary duties connected to coal leasing. The appeals court agreed with the Federal Claims Court that the Secretary's actions regarding Peabody's administrative appeal violated the Government's fiduciary obligations to the Tribe, in that those actions "suppress[ed] and conceal[ed]" the decision of the Deputy Assistant Secretary, and "thereby favor[ed] Peabody interests to the detriment of Navajo interests." Based on these determinations, the Court of Appeals remanded for further proceedings, including a determination of damages.

Judge Schall concurred in part and dissented in part. It was not enough, he maintained, for the Tribe to show a violation of a general fiduciary relationship stemming from federal involvement in a particular area of Indian affairs. Rather, a Tribe "must show the breach of a specific fiduciary obligation that falls within the contours of the statutes and regulations that create the general fiduciary relationship at issue." In his view, "the only government action in this case that implicated a specific fiduciary responsibility" was the Secretary's 1987 approval of the Lease amendments. The Secretary had been deficient, Judge Schall concluded, in approving the amendments without first conducting an independent economic analysis of the amended agreement.

The Court of Appeals denied rehearing. We granted certiorari, and now reverse.

II. A.

"It is axiomatic that the United States may not be sued without its consent and that the existence of consent is a prerequisite for jurisdiction." *Mitchell II*, 463 U. S., at 212. The Tribe asserts federal subject-matter jurisdiction under 28 U.S.C. § 1505, known as the Indian Tucker Act. That Act provides:

> "The United States Court of Federal Claims shall have jurisdiction of any claim against the United States accruing after August 13, 1946, in favor of any tribe . . . whenever such claim is one arising under the Constitution, laws or treaties of the United States, or Executive orders of the President, or is one which otherwise would be cognizable in the Court of Federal Claims if the claimant were not an Indian tribe, band, or group."

> "If a claim falls within the terms of the [Indian] Tucker Act, the United States has presumptively consented to suit."

Mitchell II, 463 U. S., at 216.

Although the Indian Tucker Act confers jurisdiction upon the Court of Federal Claims, it is not itself a source of substantive rights. To state a litigable claim, a tribal plaintiff must invoke a rights-creating source of substantive law that "can fairly be interpreted as mandating compensation by the Federal Government for the damages sustained." *Mitchell II*, 463 U. S., at 218. Because "[t]he [Indian] Tucker Act itself provides the necessary consent" to suit, however, the rights-creating statute or regulation need not contain "a second waiver of sovereign immunity."

B

Mitchell I and *Mitchell II* are the pathmarking precedents on the question whether a statute or regulation (or combination thereof) "can fairly be interpreted as mandating compensation by the Federal Government."

In *Mitchell I*, we considered whether the Indian General Allotment Act of 1887 (GAA) authorized an award of money damages against the United States for alleged mismanagement of forests located on lands allotted to tribal members. The GAA authorized the President of the United States to allot agricultural or grazing land to individual tribal members residing on a reservation, and provided that "the United

States does and will hold the land thus allotted . . . in trust for the sole use and benefit of the Indian to whom such allotment shall have been made."

We held that the GAA did not create private rights enforceable in a suit for money damages under the Indian Tucker Act. After examining the GAA's language, history, and purpose, we concluded that it "created only a limited trust relationship between the United States and the allottee that does not impose any duty upon the Government to manage timber resources." In particular, we stressed that sections 1 and 2 of the GAA removed a standard element of a trust relationship by making "the Indian allottee, and not a representative of the United States, . . . responsible for using the land for agricultural or grazing purposes." We also determined that Congress decided to have "the United States 'hold the land . . . in trust' not because it wished the Government to control use of the land . . . , but simply because it wished to prevent alienation of the land and to ensure that allottees would be immune from state taxation." Because "the Act [did] not . . . authoriz[e], much less requir[e], the Government to manage timber resources for the benefit of Indian allottees," we held that the GAA established no right to recover money damages for mismanagement of such resources. We left open, however, the possibility that other sources of law might support the plaintiffs' claims for damages.

In *Mitchell II*, we held that a network of other statutes and regulations did impose judicially enforceable fiduciary duties upon the United States in its management of forested allotted lands. "In contrast to the bare trust created by the [GAA]," we observed, "the statutes and regulations now before us clearly give the Federal Government full responsibility to manage Indian resources and land for the benefit of the Indians."

As to managing the forests and selling timber, we noted, Congress instructed the Secretary to be mindful of "the needs and best interests of the Indian owner and his heirs," and specifically to take into account:

> "(1) the state of growth of the timber and the need for maintaining the productive capacity of the land for the benefit of the owner and his heirs, (2) the highest and best use of the land, including the advisability and practicality of devoting it to other uses for the benefit of the owner and his heirs, and (3) the present and future financial needs of the owner and his heirs."

Proceeds from timber sales were to be paid to land owners "or disposed of for their benefit." Congress' prescriptions, Interior Department regulations, and "daily supervision over the harvesting and management of tribal timber" by the Department's Bureau of Indian Affairs, we emphasized, combined to place under federal control "[v]irtually every stage of the process."

Having determined that the statutes and regulations "establish[ed] fiduciary obligations of the Government in the management and operation of Indian lands and resources," we concluded that the relevant legislative and executive prescriptions could "fairly be interpreted as mandating compensation by the Federal Government for damages sustained." A damages remedy, we explained, would "furthe[r] the purposes of the statutes and regulations, which clearly require that the Secretary manage Indian resources so as to generate proceeds for the Indians."

To state a claim cognizable under the Indian Tucker Act, *Mitchell I* and *Mitchell II* thus instruct, a Tribe must identify a substantive source of law that establishes specific fiduciary or other duties, and allege that the Government has failed faithfully to perform those duties. If that threshold is passed, the court must then determine whether the relevant source of substantive law "can fairly be interpreted as mandating compensation for damages sustained as a result of a breach of the duties [the governing law] impose[s]." Although "the undisputed existence of a general trust relationship between the United States and the Indian people" can "reinforc[e]"the conclusion that the relevant statute or regulation imposes fiduciary duties, that relationship alone is insufficient to support jurisdiction under the Indian Tucker Act. Instead, the analysis must train on specific rights-creating or duty-imposing statutory or regulatory prescriptions. Those prescriptions need not, however, expressly provide for money damages; the availability of such damages may be inferred.

C

We now consider whether the IMLA and its implementing regulations can fairly be interpreted as mandating compensation for the Government's alleged breach of trust in this case. We conclude that they cannot.

1

The Tribe's principal contention is that the IMLA's statutory and regulatory scheme, viewed in its entirety, attaches fiduciary duties to each Government function under that scheme, and that the Secretary acted in contravention of those duties by approving the 12-1/2 percent royalty contained in the amended Lease. We read the IMLA differently. As we see it, the statute and regulations at issue do not provide the requisite "substantive law" that "mandat[es] compensation by the Federal Government."

The IMLA and its implementing regulations impose no obligations resembling the detailed fiduciary responsibilities that *Mitchell II* found adequate to support a claim for money damages.[11] The IMLA simply requires Secretarial approval before coal mining leases negotiated between Tribes and third parties become effective, and authorizes the Secretary generally to promulgate regulations governing mining operations. Yet the dissent concludes that the IMLA imposes "one or more specific statutory obligations, as in *Mitchell II*, at the level of fiduciary duty whose breach is compensable in damages." The endeavor to align this case with *Mitchell II* rather than *Mitchell I*, however valiant, falls short of the mark. Unlike the "elaborate" provisions

---

11. We rule only on the Government's role in the coal leasing process under the IMLA. As earlier recounted, both the IMLA and its implementing regulations address oil and gas leases in considerably more detail than coal leases. Whether the Secretary has fiduciary or other obligations, enforceable in an action for money damages, with respect to oil and gas leases is not before us.

before the Court in *Mitchell II*, the IMLA and its regulations do not "give the Federal Government full responsibility to manage Indian resources . . . for the benefit of the Indians." The Secretary is neither assigned a comprehensive managerial role nor, at the time relevant here, expressly invested with responsibility to secure "the needs and best interests of the Indian owner and his heirs."[12]

Instead, the Secretary's involvement in coal leasing under the IMLA more closely resembles the role provided for the Government by the GAA regarding allotted forest lands. Although the GAA required the Government to hold allotted land "in trust for the sole use and benefit of the Indian to whom such allotment shall have been made," that Act did not "authoriz[e], much less requir[e], the Government to manage timber resources for the benefit of Indian allottees." Similarly here, the IMLA and its regulations do not assign to the Secretary managerial control over coal leasing. Nor do they even establish the "limited trust relationship," existing under the GAA; no provision of the IMLA or its regulations contains any trust language with respect to coal leasing.

Moreover, as in *Mitchell I*, imposing fiduciary duties on the Government here would be out of line with one of the statute's principal purposes. The GAA was designed so that "the allottee, and not the United States, . . . [would] manage the land." Imposing upon the Government a fiduciary duty to oversee the management of allotted lands would not have served that purpose. So too here. The IMLA aims to enhance tribal self-determination by giving Tribes, not the Government, the lead role in negotiating mining leases with third parties. As the Court of Federal Claims recognized, "[t]he ideal of Indian self-determination is directly at odds with Secretarial control over leasing."

2

The Tribe nevertheless argues that the actions of the Secretary targeted in this case violated discrete statutory and regulatory provisions whose breach is redressable in an action for damages.

Citing 25 U.S.C. § 396a, the IMLA's general prescription, the Tribe next asserts that the Secretary violated his "duty to review and approve any proposed coal lease with care to promote IMLA's basic purpose and the [Tribe's] best interests." To support that assertion, the Tribe points to various Government reports identifying 20 percent as the appropriate royalty, and to the Secretary's decision, made after receiving ex parte communications from Peabody, to withhold departmental action.

In the circumstances presented, the Tribe maintains, the Secretary's eventual approval of the 12-1/2 percent royalty violated his duties under § 396a in two ways. First, the Secretary's approval was "improvident," because it allowed the Tribe's coal

---

12. Both the Tribe and the dissent refer to portions of 25 CFR pt. 211 that require administrative decisions affecting tribal mineral interests to be made in the best interests of the tribal mineral owner. We note, however, that the referenced regulatory provisions were adopted more than a decade after the events at issue in this case.

"to be conveyed for what [the Secretary] knew to be about half of its value." Second, Secretary Hodel's intervention into the Lease adjustment process "skewed the bargaining" by depriving the Tribe of the 20 percent rate, rendering the Secretary's subsequent approval of the 12-1/2 percent rate "unfair."

* * * [T]he § 396a arguments fail, for they assume substantive prescriptions not found in that provision. As to the "improviden[ce]" of the Secretary's approval, the Tribe can point to no guides or standards circumscribing the Secretary's affirmation of coal mining leases negotiated between a Tribe and a private lessee. Regulations under the IMLA in effect in 1987 established a minimum royalty of ten cents per ton. But the royalty contained in Lease 8580 well exceeded that regulatory floor.[14] At the time the Secretary approved the amended Lease, it bears repetition, 12-1/2 percent was the rate the United States itself customarily received from leases to mine coal on federal lands. Similarly, the customary rate for coal leases on Indian lands issued or readjusted after 1976 did not exceed 12-1/2 percent.

In sum, neither the IMLA nor any of its regulations establishes anything more than a bare minimum royalty. Hence, there is no textual basis for concluding that the Secretary's approval function includes a duty, enforceable in an action for money damages, to ensure a higher rate of return for the Tribe concerned. Similarly, no pertinent statutory or regulatory provision requires the Secretary, on pain of damages, to conduct an independent "economic analysis" of the reasonableness of the royalty to which a Tribe and third party have agreed.[16]

The Tribe's second argument under § 396a concentrates on the "skew[ing]" effect of Secretary Hodel's 1985 intervention, i.e., his direction to Deputy Assistant Secretary Fritz to withhold action on Peabody's appeal from the Area Director's decision setting a royalty rate of 20 percent. The Secretary's actions, both in intervening in the administrative appeal process, and in approving the amended Lease, the Tribe urges, were not based upon an assessment of the merits of the royalty issue; instead,

---

14. Because the Tribe does not contend that the amended Lease failed to meet the minimum royalty under the regulations then in effect, we need not decide whether the Secretary's approval of such a lease would trigger money damages.

16. Citing language from the legislative history, the dissent stresses that the IMLA aimed in part to "give the Indians the greatest return from their property," and suggests that the Secretary's approval role encompasses an enforceable duty to further that objective. We have cautioned against according "talismanic effect" to the Senate Report's "reference to 'the greatest return from [Indian] property,'" and have observed that it "overstates" Congress' aim to attribute to the Legislature a purpose "to guarantee Indian tribes the maximum profit available." *Cotton Petroleum Corp. v. New Mexico*, 490 U. S. 163, 179 (1989). Beyond doubt, the IMLA was designed "to provide Indian tribes with a profitable source of revenue." But Congress had as a concrete objective in that regard the removal of certain impediments that had applied particularly to mineral leases on Indian land. That impediment-removing objective is discrete from the Secretary's lease approval role under the IMLA. Again, we find no solid basis in the IMLA, its regulations, or lofty statements in legislative history for a legally enforceable command that the Secretary disapprove Indian coal leases unless they survive "an independent market study," or satisfy some other extratextual criterion of tribal profitability.

the Tribe maintains, they were attributable entirely to the undue influence Peabody exerted through ex parte communications with the Secretary. Underscoring that the Tribe had no knowledge of those communications or of Secretary Hodel's direction to Fritz, the Tribe asserts that its bargaining position was seriously compromised when it resumed negotiations with Peabody in 1985. The Secretary's ultimate approval of the 12-1/2 percent royalty, the Tribe concludes, was thus an outcome fundamentally unfair to the Tribe.

Here again, as the Court of Federal Claims ultimately determined, the Tribe's assertions are not grounded in a specific statutory or regulatory provision that can fairly be interpreted as mandating money damages. Nothing in § 396a, the IMLA's basic provision, or in the IMLA's implementing regulations proscribed the ex parte communications in this case, which occurred during an administrative appeal process largely unconstrained by formal requirements. Either party could have effected a transfer of Peabody's appeal to the Board of Indian Appeals.

Exercise of that option would have triggered review of a more formal character, in which ex parte communications would have been prohibited. But the Tribe did not elect to transfer the matter to the Board, and the regulatory proscription on ex parte contacts applicable in Board proceedings thus did not govern.

We note, moreover, that even if Deputy Assistant Secretary Fritz had rendered an opinion affirming the 20 percent royalty approved by the Area Director, it would have been open to the Secretary to set aside or modify his subordinate's decision. As head of the Department of the Interior, the Secretary had "authority to review any decision of any employee or employees of the Department." Accordingly, rejection of Peabody's appeal by the Deputy Assistant Secretary would not necessarily have yielded a higher royalty for the Tribe.

However one might appraise the Secretary's intervention in this case, we have no warrant from any relevant statute or regulation to conclude that his conduct implicated a duty enforceable in an action for damages under the Indian Tucker Act. The judgment of the United States Court of Appeals for the Federal Circuit is accordingly reversed, and the case is remanded for further proceedings consistent with this opinion.

JUSTICE SOUTER, with whom JUSTICE STEVENS and JUSTICE O'CONNOR join, dissenting.

The issue in this case is whether the Indian Mineral Leasing Act and its regulations imply a specific duty on the Secretary of the Interior's part, with a cause of action for damages in case of breach. The Court and I recognize that if IMLA indicates that a fiduciary duty was intended, it need not provide a damages remedy explicitly; once a statutory or regulatory provision is found to create a specific fiduciary obligation, the right to damages can be inferred from general trust principles, and amenability to suit under the Indian Tucker Act. I part from the majority because I take the Secretary's obligation to approve mineral leases under 25 U.S.C. § 396a as raising a substantial fiduciary obligation to the Navajo Nation (Tribe), which has pleaded and shown enough to survive the Government's motion for summary judgment. I would affirm the judgment of the Federal Circuit.

IMLA requires the Secretary's approval for the effectiveness of any lease negotiated by the Tribe with a third party. The Court accepts the Government's position that the IMLA approval responsibility places no substantive obligation on the Secretary, save for a minimal duty to withhold assent from leases calling for less than the minimum royalty rate set by IMLA regulations, whatever that may be. Since that rate is merely a general standard, which may be a bargain rate when applied to extractable material of high quality, the obligation to demand it may not amount to much. The legislative history and purposes of IMLA, however, illuminated by the Secretary's historical role in reviewing conveyances of Indian lands, point to a fiduciary responsibility to make a more ambitious assessment of the best interest of the Tribe before signing off.

The protective purpose of the Secretary's approval power has appeared in our discussions of other statutes governing Indian lands over the years. * * * The Secretary's approval power was understood to be a significant component of the Government's general trust responsibility. See Clinton, Isolated in Their Own Country: A Defense of Protection of Indian Autonomy and Self-Government, 33 Stan. L. Rev. 979, 1002–1003 (1981); Chambers & Price, Regulating Sovereignty: Secretarial Discretion and the Leasing of Indian Lands, 26 Stan. L. Rev. 1061, 1061–1068 (1974).

Congress's decision in IMLA to give the Secretary an approval authority is well understood in terms of this background, for in the enactment of IMLA, Congress devised a scheme of divided responsibility reminiscent of the old allotment legislation. While it changed the prior law by transferring negotiating authority from the Government to the tribes, it hedged that augmentation of tribal authority in leaving the Secretary with certain powers of oversight including the authority to approve or reject leases once the tribes negotiated them. The Secretary's signature was the final step in a scheme of "uniform leasing procedures designed to protect the Indians," *Montana v. Blackfeet Tribe*, 471 U. S. 759, 764 (1985), and imposed out of a concern that existing laws were not "adequate to give the Indians the greatest return from their property." The "basic purpose" of the Secretary's powers under IMLA is thus to "maximize tribal revenues from reservation lands." *Kerr-McGee Corp. v. Navajo Tribe*, 471 U. S. 195, 200 (1985). Consistent with this aim, the Secretary's own IMLA regulations (now in effect) provide that administrative actions, including lease approvals, are to be taken "[i]n the best interest of the Indian mineral owner."[1] Thus, viewed in light of IMLA's legislative history and the general trust relationship between the United States and the Indians, § 396a supports the existence of a fiduciary responsibility to review mineral leases for substance to safeguard the Indians' interest.

---

1. In addition, the Interior Department at all times relevant to this case had in place an internal policy providing that mineral leases would be approved only if "the terms and conditions of the lease are in the best interest of the Indian landowner."

I do not mean to suggest that devising a specific standard of responsibility is any simple matter, for we cannot ignore the tension between IMLA's two objectives. If we thought solely in terms of the aim to ensure that negotiated leases "maximize tribal revenues," we would ignore the object of IMLA to provide greater tribal responsibility, against which the Secretary's oversight is acting as a hedge. See Royster, Mineral Development in Indian Country: The Evolution of Tribal Control Over Mineral Resources, 29 Tulsa L. Rev. 541, 558–580 (1994) (noting the twin aims of IMLA). The more stringent the substantive obligation of the Secretary, the less the scope of tribal responsibility. The Court, however, errs in the opposite direction, giving overriding weight to the interest of tribal autonomy to the point of concluding that the Secretary's approval obligation cannot be an onerous one, thus losing sight of the mixture of congressional objectives. The standard of responsibility simply cannot give the whole hog to the one congressional policy or the other.

While this is not the case to essay any ultimate formulation of a balanced standard, even a reticent formulation of the fiduciary obligation would require the Secretary to withhold approval if he had good reason to doubt that the negotiated rate was within the range of reasonable market rates for the coal in question, or if he had reason to know that the Tribe had been placed under an unfair disadvantage at the negotiating table by his very own acts. See Restatement (Second) of Trusts §§ 170, 173, 174, 176 (1957). And those modest standards are enough to keep the present suit in court, for the Tribe has pleaded a breach of trust in each respect and has submitted evidence to get past summary judgment on either alternative.

The record discloses serious indications that the 12-1/2 percent royalty rate in the lease amendments was substantially less than fair market value for the Tribe's high quality coal. In the course of deciding that 20 percent would be a reasonable adjustment under the terms of the lease, the Area Director of the Board of Indian Affairs (BIA) considered several independent economic studies, each one of them recommending rates around 20 percent, and one specifically rejecting 121/2 percent as "inadequate." These conclusions were confirmed by the expert from the BIA's Energy and Mineral Division, in a supplemental report submitted after Peabody appealed the Area Director's decision. That report not only endorsed the 20 percent rate, but expressly found that the royalty rate "should be much higher than the 12.5% that the Federal Government receives for surface-mined coal" because the Navajo coal is "extremely valuable." No federal study ever recommended a royalty rate under 20 percent, and yet the Secretary approved a rate little more than half that. When this case was before the Federal Circuit, Judge Schall took the sensible position that the Secretary was obligated to obtain an independent market study to assess the rate in these circumstances, and the record as it stands shows the Secretary to be clearly open to the claim of fiduciary breach for approving the rate on the information he is said to have had. Of course I recognize that the Secretary's obligation is to approve leases, not royalty rates in isolation, but an allegation that he approved an otherwise unjustified rate apparently well below market for the particular resource deposit certainly raises a claim of breach.

What is more, the Tribe has made a powerful showing that the Secretary knew perfectly well how his own intervention on behalf of Peabody had derailed the lease adjustment proceeding that would in all probability have yielded the 20 percent rate. After his ex parte meeting with Peabody's representatives, the Secretary put his name on the memorandum, drafted by Peabody, directing Deputy Assistant Secretary Fritz to withhold his decision affirming the 20 percent rate; directing him to mislead the Tribe by telling it that no decision on the merits of the adjustment was imminent, when in fact the affirmance had been prepared for Fritz's signature; and directing him to encourage the Tribe to shift its attention from the Area Director's appealed award of 20 percent and return to the negotiating table, where 20 percent was never even a possibility. The purpose and predictable effect of these actions was to induce the Tribe to take a deep discount in the royalty rate in the face of what the Tribe feared would otherwise be prolonged revenue loss and uncertainty. The point of this evidence is not that the Secretary violated some rule of procedure for administrative appeals, or some statutory duty regarding royalty adjustments under the terms of the earlier lease. What these facts support is the Tribe's claim that the Secretary defaulted on his fiduciary responsibility to withhold approval of an inadequate lease accepted by the Tribe while under a disadvantage the Secretary himself had intentionally imposed.

All of this is not to say that the Tribe would end up with a recovery at the end of the day.

But the only issue here is whether the Tribe's claims address one or more specific statutory obligations, as in *Mitchell II*, at the level of fiduciary duty whose breach is compensable in damages. The Tribe has pleaded such duty, the record shows that the Tribe has a case to try, and I respectfully dissent.

United States v. White Mountain Apache Tribe
537 U.S. 465 (2003)

SOUTER, J., delivered the opinion of the Court, in which STEVENS, O'CONNOR, GINSBURG, and BREYER, JJ., joined. GINSBURG, J., filed a concurring opinion, in which BREYER, J., joined. THOMAS, J., filed a dissenting opinion, in which REHNQUIST, C.J., and SCALIA and KENNEDY, JJ., joined.

JUSTICE SOUTER delivered the opinion of the Court.

The question in this case arises under the Indian Tucker Act: does the Court of Federal Claims have jurisdiction over the White Mountain Apache Tribe's suit against the United States for breach of fiduciary duty to manage land and improvements held in trust for the Tribe but occupied by the Government. We hold that it does.

I

The former military post of Fort Apache dates back to 1870 when the United States established the fort within territory that became the Tribe's reservation in 1877. In 1922, Congress transferred control of the fort to the Secretary of the Interior

(Secretary) and, in 1923, set aside about 400 acres, out of some 7,000, for use as the Theodore Roosevelt Indian School. Congress attended to the fort again in 1960, when it provided by statute that "former Fort Apache Military Reservation" would be "held by the United States in trust for the White Mountain Apache Tribe, subject to the right of the Secretary of the Interior to use any part of the land and improvements for administrative or school purposes for as long as they are needed for the purpose." The Secretary exercised that right, and although the record does not catalog the uses made by the Department of the Interior, they extended to about 30 of the post's buildings and appurtenances, a few of which had been built when the Government first occupied the land. Although the National Park Service listed the fort as a national historical site in 1976, the recognition was no augury of fortune, for just over 20 years later the World Monuments Watch placed the fort on its 1998 List of 100 Most Endangered Monuments.

In 1993, the Tribe commissioned an engineering assessment of the property, resulting in a finding that as of 1998 it would cost about $14 million to rehabilitate the property occupied by the Government in accordance with standards for historic preservation. This is the amount the Tribe sought in 1999, when it sued the United States in the Court of Federal Claims, citing the terms of the 1960 Act, among others, and alleging breach of fiduciary duty to "maintain, protect, repair and preserve" the trust property.

[The Court of Federal Claims dismissed the action for lack of jurisdiction, holding that the 1960 Act created only a "bare trust" not enforceable in an action for money damages. The Court of Appeals for the Federal Circuit reversed, finding that federal use of the property triggered an obligation to preserve it and that the obligation to preserve was redressable by money damages.]

We granted certiorari to decide whether the 1960 Act gives rise to jurisdiction over suits for money damages against the United States, and now affirm.

II. A.

Jurisdiction over any suit against the Government requires a clear statement from the United States waiving sovereign immunity, together with a claim falling within the terms of the waiver. The terms of consent to be sued may not be inferred, but must be "unequivocally expressed," in order to "define [a] court's jurisdiction." The Tucker Act contains such a waiver, giving the Court of Federal Claims jurisdiction to award damages upon proof of "any claim against the United States founded either upon the Constitution, or any Act of Congress," and its companion statute, the Indian Tucker Act, confers a like waiver for Indian tribal claims that "otherwise would be cognizable in the Court of Federal Claims if the claimant were not an Indian tribe."

Neither Act, however, creates a substantive right enforceable against the Government by a claim for money damages. As we said in *Mitchell II*, a statute creates a right capable of grounding a claim within the waiver of sovereign immunity if, but only if, it "can fairly be interpreted as mandating compensation by the Federal Government for the damage sustained."

This "fair interpretation" rule demands a showing demonstrably lower than the standard for the initial waiver of sovereign immunity. "Because the Tucker Act supplies a waiver of immunity for claims of this nature, the separate statutes and regulations need not provide a second waiver of sovereign immunity, nor need they be construed in the manner appropriate to waivers of sovereign immunity." It is enough, then, that a statute creating a Tucker Act right be reasonably amenable to the reading that it mandates a right of recovery in damages. While the premise to a Tucker Act claim will not be "lightly inferred," a fair inference will do.

III. A.

The 1960 Act goes beyond a bare trust and permits a fair inference that the Government is subject to duties as a trustee and liable in damages for breach. The statutory language, of course, expressly defines a fiduciary relationship in the provision that Fort Apache be "held by the United States in trust for the White Mountain Apache Tribe." Unlike the Allotment Act, however, the statute proceeds to invest the United States with discretionary authority to make direct use of portions of the trust corpus. The trust property is "subject to the right of the Secretary of the Interior to use any part of the land and improvements for administrative or school purposes for as long as they are needed for the purpose," and it is undisputed that the Government has to this day availed itself of its option. As to the property subject to the Government's actual use, then, the United States has not merely exercised daily supervision but has enjoyed daily occupation, and so has obtained control at least as plenary as its authority over the timber in *Mitchell II*. While it is true that the 1960 Act does not, like the statutes cited in that case, expressly subject the Government to duties of management and conservation, the fact that the property occupied by the United States is expressly subject to a trust supports a fair inference that an obligation to preserve the property improvements was incumbent on the United States as trustee. This is so because elementary trust law, after all, confirms the commonsense assumption that a fiduciary actually administering trust property may not allow it to fall into ruin on his watch. "One of the fundamental common-law duties of a trustee is to preserve and maintain trust assets." Given this duty on the part of the trustee to preserve corpus, "it naturally follows that the Government should be liable in damages for the breach of its fiduciary duties."

B

The United States raises three defenses against this conclusion, the first being that the property occupied by the Government is not trust corpus at all. It asserts that in the 1960 Act Congress specifically "carve[d] out of the trust" the right of the Federal Government to use the property for the Government's own purposes. According to the United States, this carve-out means that the 1960 Act created even less than the "bare trust" in *Mitchell I*. But this position is at odds with a natural reading of the 1960 Act. It provided that "Fort Apache" was subject to the trust; it did not read that the trust consisted of only the property not used by the Secretary. Nor is there any apparent reason to strain to avoid the straightforward reading; it makes sense to treat even the property used by the Government as trust property, since any use the Secretary would make of it would presumably be intended to redound to the benefit of the Tribe in some way.

Next, the Government contends that no intent to provide a damages remedy is fairly inferable, for the reason that "[t]here is not a word in the 1960 Act — the only substantive source of law on which the Tribe relies — that suggests the existence of such a mandate." The argument rests, however, on a failure to appreciate [] the role of trust law in drawing a fair inference.

To the extent that the Government would demand an explicit provision for money damages to support every claim that might be brought under the Tucker Act, it would substitute a plain and explicit statement standard for the less demanding requirement of fair inference that the law was meant to provide a damage remedy for breach of a duty. To begin with, this would leave *Mitchell II* a wrongly decided case, for one would look in vain for a statute explicitly providing that inadequate timber management would be compensated through a suit for damages. But the more fundamental objection to the Government's position is that, if carried to its conclusion, it would read the trust relation out of Indian Tucker Act analysis; if a specific provision for damages is needed, a trust obligation and trust law are not. And this likewise would ignore *Mitchell I*, where the trust relationship was considered when inferring that the trust obligation was enforceable by damages. To be sure, the fact of the trust alone in *Mitchell I* did not imply a remedy in damages or even the duty claimed, since the Allotment Act failed to place the United States in a position to discharge the management responsibility asserted. To find a specific duty, a further source of law was needed to provide focus for the trust relationship. But once that focus was provided, general trust law was considered in drawing the inference that Congress intended damages to remedy a breach of obligation.

Finally, the Government argues that the inference of a damages remedy is unsound simply because damages are inappropriate as a remedy for failures of maintenance, prospective injunctive relief being the sole relief tailored to the situation. We think this is clearly wrong. If the Government is suggesting that the recompense for run-down buildings should be an affirmative order to repair them, it is merely proposing the economic (but perhaps cumbersome) equivalent of damages. But if it is suggesting that relief must be limited to an injunction to toe the fiduciary mark in the future, it would bar the courts from making the Tribe whole for deterioration already suffered, and shield the Government against the remedy whose very availability would deter it from wasting trust property in the period before a Tribe has gone to court for injunctive relief.

IV

The judgment of the Court of Appeals for the Federal Circuit is affirmed, and the case is remanded to the Court of Federal Claims for further proceedings consistent with this opinion.

JUSTICE GINSBURG, with whom JUSTICE BREYER joins, concurring.

I join the Court's opinion, satisfied that it is not inconsistent with the opinion I wrote for the Court in *United States v. Navajo Nation*.

Both *Navajo* and the instant case are guided by *United States v. Mitchell*, 445 U.S. 535 (1980) (*Mitchell I*), and *United States v. Mitchell*, 463 U.S. 206 (1983) (*Mitchell II*). While *Navajo* is properly aligned with *Mitchell I*, this case is properly ranked with *Mitchell II*.

In this case, the threshold set by the *Mitchell* cases is met. The 1960 Act, provides that Fort Apache shall be "held by the United States in trust for the White Mountain Apache Tribe" and, at the same time, authorizes the Government to use and occupy the fort. Thus, as the Court here observes, the Act expressly and without qualification employs a term of art ("trust") commonly understood to entail certain fiduciary obligations, and "invest[s] the United States with discretionary authority to make direct use of portions of the trust corpus." Further, as the Court describes, the Tribe tenably maintains that the Government has "availed itself of its option" to "exercis[e] daily supervision . . . [and] enjo[y] daily occupation" of the trust corpus, but has done so in a manner irreconcilable with its caretaker obligations. The dispositive question, accordingly, is whether the 1960 measure, in placing property in trust and simultaneously providing for the Government-trustee's use and occupancy, is fairly interpreted to mandate compensation for the harm caused by maladministration of the property.

Navajo, in contrast, turns on the threshold question whether the Indian Mineral Leasing Act (IMLA) and its regulations impose any concrete substantive obligations, fiduciary or otherwise, on the Government. *Navajo* answers that question in the negative. The "controversy . . . falls within *Mitchell I*'s domain," *Navajo* concludes, for "the Tribe's claim for compensation . . . does not derive from any liability-imposing provision of the IMLA or its implementing regulations." The coal-leasing provisions of the IMLA and its allied regulations, *Navajo* explains, lacked the characteristics that typify a genuine trust relationship: Those provisions assigned the Secretary of the Interior no managerial role over coal leasing; they did not even establish the "limited trust relationship" that existed under the law at issue in *Mitchell I*.

In the instant case, as the Court's opinion develops, the 1960 Act in fact created a trust not fairly characterized as "bare," given the trustee's authorized use and management. The plenary control the United States exercises under the Act as sole manager and trustee, I agree, places this case within *Mitchell II*'s governance. To the extent that the Government allowed trust property "to fall into ruin," I further agree, a damages remedy is fairly indexable.

JUSTICE THOMAS, with whom THE CHIEF JUSTICE, JUSTICE SCALIA and JUSTICE KENNEDY join, dissenting.

The majority's conclusion that the Court of Federal Claims has jurisdiction over this matter finds support in neither the text of the 1960 Act, nor our case law. As the Court has repeatedly held, the test to determine if Congress has conferred a substantive right enforceable against the Government in a suit for money damages is whether an Act "can fairly be interpreted as mandating compensation by the Federal Government for the damage sustained." Instead of faithfully applying this test, however, the Court engages in a new inquiry, asking whether common-law trust principles permit a "fair inference" that money damages are available, that finds no support in existing law. But even under the majority's newly devised approach, there is no basis for finding that Congress intended to create anything other than a "bare trust," which we have found insufficient to confer jurisdiction on the Court of Federal Claims in *Mitchell I*. Because the 1960 Act "can[not] fairly be interpreted as mandating compensation by the Federal Government for damage sustained" by the White Mountain Apache Tribe (Tribe), I respectfully dissent.

I

[T]he Court made clear in *Mitchell I* that the existence of a trust relationship does not itself create a claim for money damages.

The statute under review here provides no more evidence of congressional intent to authorize a suit for money damages than the General Allotment Act did in *Mitchell I*. The Tribe itself acknowledges that the 1960 Act is "silen[t]" not only with respect to money damages, but also with regard to any underlying "maintenance and protection duties" that can fairly be construed as creating a fiduciary relationship. Indeed, unlike the statutes and regulations at issue in *Mitchell II*, the 1960 Act does not "establish . . . 'comprehensive' responsibilities of the Federal Government in managing the" Fort Apache property. Because there is nothing in the statute that "clearly establish[es] fiduciary obligations of the Government in the management and operation of Indian lands," the 1960 Act creates only a "bare trust."

In addition, unlike the statutes and regulations at issue in *Mitchell I* and *Mitchell II*, "[n]othing in the 1960 Act imposes a fiduciary responsibility to manage the fort for the benefit of the Tribe and, in fact, it specifically carves the government's right to unrestricted use for the specified purposes out of the trust." The 1960 Act authorizes the "Secretary of the Interior to use any part of the land and improvements for administrative or school purposes for as long as they are needed for that purpose." The Government's use of the land does not have to inure to the benefit of the Indians. Nor is there any requirement that the United States cede control over the property now or in the future. Thus, if anything, there is less evidence of a fiduciary relationship in the 1960 Act than there was in the General Allotment Act at issue in *Mitchell I*.

If Congress intended to create a compensable trust relationship between the United States and the Tribe with respect to the Fort Apache property, it provided no indication to this effect in the text of the 1960 Act. Accordingly, I would hold that the 1960 Act created only a "bare trust" between the United States and the Tribe.

II

[T]his case does not involve the level of "*elaborate* control over" the Tribe's property that the Court found sufficient to create a compensable trust duty in *Mitchell II*. *Mitchell II* involved a "comprehensive" regulatory scheme that "addressed virtually every aspect of forest management," and under which the United States assumed "*full* responsibility to manage Indian resources and land for the benefit of the Indians." (emphasis added). Here, by contrast, there are no management duties set forth in any "fundamental document," and thus the United States has the barest degree of control over the Tribe's property. And, unlike *Mitchell II*, the bare control that is exercised by the United States over the property does not inure to the benefit of the Indians. In my view, this is more than sufficient to distinguish this case from *Mitchell II*.

Moreover, even assuming that *Mitchell II* can be read to support the proposition that mere factual control over property is sufficient to create compensable trust duties (which it cannot), the Court has never provided any guidance on the nature and scope of such duties. And, in any event, the Court has never before held that "control" alone can give rise to, as the majority puts it, the specific duty to "preserve the property." Indeed, had Congress wished to create such a duty, it could have done so expressly in the 1960 Act. Its failure to follow that course strongly suggests that Congress did not intend to create a compensable trust relationship between the United States and the Tribe.

In addition, the Court's focus on control has now rendered the inquiry open-ended, with questions of jurisdiction determined by murky principles of the common law of trusts, and a parcel-by-parcel determination whether "portions of the property were under United States control." Such an approach provides little certainty to guide Congress in fashioning legislation that insulates the United States from damages for breach of trust. Instead, to the ultimate detriment of the Tribe, Congress might refrain from creating trust relationships out of apprehension that the use of the word "trust" will subject the United States to liability for money damages.

The Court today fashions a new test to determine whether Congress has conferred a substantive right enforceable against the United States in a suit for money damages. In doing so, the Court radically alters the relevant inquiry from one focused on the actual fiduciary duties created by statute or regulation to one divining fiduciary duties out of the use of the word "trust" and notions of factual control. Because I find no basis for this approach in our case law or in the language of the Indian Tucker Act, I respectfully dissent.

Notes

1. Subsequent developments. On remand from the Supreme Court's decision, the Court of Federal Claims found no trust duties in other sources of law asserted by the Navajo Nation. The Federal Circuit reversed, finding that a "network of statutes and regulations" established trust duties, and that "the government exercised blanket control over the Nation's coal resources." In *United States v. Navajo Nation*, 556 U.S. 287 (2009) (*Navajo II*), the Supreme Court reversed. The Court concentrated its opinion on three statutory provisions, finding that two provisions of the Navajo-Hopi Rehabilitation Act did not impose money-mandating duties on the government, and that provisions of the Surface Mining Control and Reclamation Act (SMCRA) were inapplicable to the Navajo Nation's lease, which was issued years before SMCRA became law.

With respect to the suggestion of the Federal Circuit that the government's comprehensive control over the Navajo Nation's coal resources could give rise to trust duties, the Court stated:

> The Federal Government's liability cannot be premised on control alone. The text of the Indian Tucker Act makes clear that only claims arising under "the Constitution, laws or treaties of the United States, or Executive orders of the President" are cognizable (unless the claim could be brought by a non-Indian plaintiff under the ordinary Tucker Act). In *Navajo I* we reiterated that the analysis must begin with "specific rights-creating or duty-imposing statutory or regulatory prescriptions." *If* a plaintiff identifies such a prescription, and *if* that prescription bears the hallmarks of a "conventional fiduciary relationship," *White Mountain,* 537 U.S., at 473, *then* trust principles (including any such principles premised on "control") could play a role in "inferring that the trust obligation [is] enforceable by damages," *id.,* at 477. But that must be the second step of the analysis, not (as the Federal Circuit made it) the starting point.

556 U.S. at 301.

Can this statement be reconciled with *White Mountain Apache*? What "specific rights-creating or duty-imposing" provision was there in the 1960 statute that put the former Fort Apache into trust for the tribe?

The Supreme Court's direction in *Navajo II* that "liability cannot be premised on control alone" led the Court of Federal Claims to dismiss an action brought by the Hopi Tribe concerning its water resources, on the ground that the claims court lacked subject matter jurisdiction. In *Hopi Tribe v. United States,* 113 Fed. Cl. 43 (2013), the tribe sought damages for breach of trust for the federal government's failure to ensure that reservation drinking water contained safe levels of arsenic. Public water systems on the eastern part of the reservation contained arsenic at levels exceeding EPA standards. The tribe argued that the executive order and statute establishing the reservation, along with a slew of statutes relating to tribal and Hopi water supplies, gave the federal government sufficient control over the water supply to give rise to fiduciary obligations.

The court found no specific duties with respect to Hopi water supplies. It distinguished *White Mountain Apache* because "the specific statutory provision at issue simultaneously used the word 'trust' in connection with imparting to the federal government a right to 'use' the land," whereas the statute for the Hopi Reservation "does not confer on the federal government comparable authority or, indeed, any kind of authority to use or manage the land." Has the Court of Federal Claims effectively limited *White Mountain Apache* to situations where the federal government is in actual physical control of trust property?

2. Related proceeding. In a related action, the D.C. District Court held that the Supreme Court's decision did not collaterally estop the Navajo Nation from pursuing a Racketeer Influenced and Corrupt Organizations Act (RICO) claim against Peabody. *Navajo Nation v. Peabody Holding Co., Inc.*, 314 F. Supp. 2d 23 (D.D.C. 2004). The court observed that the issue of whether a private company "violated RICO and committed various common law torts when it hired a lobbyist to procure favorable government action at the expense of the Tribe" was a different action than whether the federal government was liable for breach of trust. *Id.* at 25–26.

3. Test(s) for enforceable fiduciary duties. The *Mitchell* cases in 1980 and 1983, discussed in both *Navajo Nation* and *White Mountain*, established the framework for determining whether the federal government owed enforceable fiduciary duties to the tribes or allottees. What test did the Supreme Court use in *Navajo Nation* to make this determination? Did the Court employ a different test in *White Mountain*? Does either test differ in any important way from the litmus test that the Court used in either of the *Mitchell* cases (as the dissent contended in *White Mountain*)? Are you convinced by Justice Ginsburg's opinion in *White Mountain* that the two decisions can be reconciled?

As a practical matter, neither *Navajo Nation* nor *White Mountain* seems to have substantially changed the lower courts' analyses. *See, e.g., Ashley v. U.S. Dept. of Interior*, 408 F.3d 997 (8th Cir. 2005) (Crow Creek Sioux Tribe Infrastructure Development Trust Fund Act of 1996 did not authorize the federal government to manage tribe's expenditures of trust payments, and thus did not impose a fiduciary duty on the government to ensure that the money was spent properly); *Osage Tribe of Indians of Oklahoma v. United States*, 68 Fed. Cl. 322, 333 (2005) (statute requiring the federal government to hold in trust moneys due the tribe created specific fiduciary duties mandating compensation for damages sustained from violations of those duties); *Chippewa Cree Tribe of the Rocky Boy's Reservation v. United States*, 69 Fed. Cl. 639 (2006) (provisions of statutes that distributed funds awarded by the Indian Claims Commission to compensate tribes for ceded lands indicated that the money was to be held in trust for the tribes; under investment statutes, the government had a fiduciary duty to invest the funds productively).

4. Coal versus oil and gas. In *Navajo Nation*, the Supreme Court suggested in footnote 11 that oil and gas leases might be treated differently than coal leases, noting that oil and gas leases were addressed "in considerably more detail" in the 1938 Indian Mineral Leasing Act (IMLA). In 1986, in a case involving oil and gas leases, the Tenth Circuit held that the federal government had a "pervasive" and "comprehensive" role; that the IMLA required the federal government to ensure the greatest return for the tribes; and that the government was required to act in the interests of the tribes. Consequently, the court determined that the IMLA created the same type of fiduciary duties as the timber management statutes and regulations at issue in *Mitchell II*. *Jicarilla Apache Tribe v. Supron Energy Corp.*, 782 F.2d 855 (10th Cir. 1986), excerpted at page 396.

Is *Supron* still good law after *Navajo Nation*? The Court of Federal Claims appears to think it is. In *Shoshone Indian Tribe of the Wind River Reservation v. United States*,

56 Fed. Cl. 639, 646 (2003), the court held that the "more elaborate statutory and regulatory framework" in the IMLA for oil and gas leases created enforceable fiduciary duties. The Navajo Nation conceded, however, that under the Supreme Court's ruling, it could not maintain a claim that the United States had failed to maximize its oil and gas lease revenues. *Id.* at 644.

5. The trust doctrine and the recent mineral development statutes. *Navajo Nation* dealt with federal trust responsibilities under the 1938 Indian Mineral Leasing Act. Subsequent mineral and energy statutes—the Indian Mineral Development Act (IMDA) of 1982 and the Indian Tribal Energy Development and Self-Determination Act (ITEDSA) of 2005—expressly address the trust doctrine. (The statutory provisions are outlined at pages 358 and 360.)

The IMDA expressly extends the trust doctrine to "the rights of a tribe or individual Indian . . . in the event of a violation of the terms of any Minerals Agreement by any other party to such agreement." Nonetheless, despite this clear recognition of the trust responsibility, the IMDA also provides that "the United States shall not be liable for losses sustained by a tribe or individual Indian" under a minerals agreement. The intent is that if tribes wish to become partners in development, tribes must take the risk of losses.

Like the IMDA, ITEDSA requires the Secretary to "act in accordance with the trust responsibility . . . [and] in good faith and in the best interests of the Indian tribes." Other than the provisions waiving secretarial approval of specific instruments authorized by tribal energy resource agreements, nothing in ITEDSA relieves the federal government of any trust obligations under treaties or other federal laws. Like the IMDA, ITEDSA obligates the Secretary to ensure protection of tribal rights and interests in cases where any other party to a lease, agreement, or right-of-way violates the terms of the instrument or any applicable federal law. Nonetheless, also like the IMDA, ITEDSA asserts that the federal government "shall not be liable" for any loss resulting from a lease or agreement entered into pursuant to a tribal energy resource agreement.

In the wake of *Navajo Nation*, what, if any, enforceable fiduciary duties exist under these statutes? What effect might the increased role of tribes under these statutes have on breach of trust claims?

6. Government disclosure of trust management communications to tribes. The Jicarilla Apache Nation, in a case alleging federal mismanagement of the tribe's trust accounts between 1972 and 1992, sought some 155 documents from the government. The Court of Federal Claims granted the request in part, concluding that the communication fell within "the fiduciary exception" to attorney-client privilege, and the Federal Circuit affirmed. 590 F.3d 1305 (Fed. Cir. 2009). But in *United States v. Jicarilla Apache Nation*, 564 U.S. 162 (2011), the Supreme Court reversed, explaining that the common-law fiduciary exception to the attorney-client privilege did not apply in this case because the federal government resembles a private trustee in only limited instances. The Court explained that two features must exist in order for the common-law fiduciary exception to apply: 1) a "real client" and 2) a duty to disclose information regarding the trust. The Court concluded that the *Jicarilla* case lacked both factors. First, the Court determined that the tribe was not a real client of the federal government's attorneys, since the tribe did not pay the attorneys. Additionally, the federal government sought advice from its attorneys in its role as a sovereign, not as a fiduciary. Moreover, the Court determined that the federal government had an interest in its capacity as a sovereign in the administration of the Indian trust accounts that was separate from the interests of the beneficiaries.

The Court also rejected the tribe's argument that the federal government had a statutory duty to disclose the documents, stating that "[w]hatever Congress intended, we cannot read the clause [providing that the government's trust responsibilities 'are not limited to' those set out in the statute] to include a general common-law duty to disclose all information related to the administration of Indian trusts. . . . Reading the statute to incorporate the full duties of a private, common-law fiduciary would vitiate Congress' specification of narrowly defined disclosure obligations."

7. Breach of trust for off-reservation actions. The tribes of the Fort Belknap Reservation brought a common law breach of trust action, alleging that the federal government failed to protect tribal resources. The government authorized two cyanide heap-leach gold mines upstream from the reservation, and the tribes claimed that the cyanide processing would cause downstream damage to reservation resources, in particular the waters. In *Gros Ventre Tribe v. United States*, 469 F.3d 801 (9th Cir. 2006), the court rejected the trust claim:

> But none of the treaties cited by the Tribes impose a specific duty on the United States to regulate parties or non-tribal resources for the benefit of the Tribes. Because the government's general trust obligations must be analyzed within the confines of generally applicable statutes and regulations, we reject the suggestion to create by judicial fiat a right of action Congress has not recognized by treaty or statute.

Jicarilla Apache Tribe v. Supron Energy Corp.
782 F.2d 855 (10th Cir. 1986)

[On rehearing en banc, the majority of the court adopted Judge Seymour's dissenting opinion from the panel decision, 728 F.2d 1555 (10th Cir. 1984). Judge Seymour determined that the federal government owed fiduciary duties to the tribe with respect to its oil and gas leases. In addition, she argued, and the en banc Tenth Circuit held, as follows:]

If the Secretary is obligated to act as a fiduciary to the Tribe in his administration of the Tribe's oil and gas reserves, and in his determination of what royalties the Tribe is due, then his actions must not merely meet the minimal requirements of administrative law, but must also pass scrutiny under the more stringent standards demanded of a fiduciary.

The trial court in this case concluded that Interior had breached its fiduciary duty in several respects: by failing to interpret correctly the royalty terms in the lease and regulations, by failing to insure that lessees comply with lease terms requiring diligent development, and by failing to insure the protection of leased lands from drainage. The trial court entered a declaratory judgment against the Secretary.[3] The majority opinion reverses the trial court's construction of the lease and the regulations, and finds it unnecessary to reach the other breach of trust issues. I disagree, and would affirm the trial court on each of these matters.

The Supreme Court has implicitly recognized that stricter standards apply to federal agencies when administering Indian programs. When the Secretary is acting in his fiduciary role rather than solely as a regulator and is faced with a decision for which there is more than one "reasonable" choice as that term is used in administrative law, he must choose the alternative that is in the best interests of the Indian tribe. In short, he cannot escape his role as trustee by donning the mantle of administrator.

Thus, the true issue in this case is not whether the Secretary's earlier application of the royalty terms was reasonable; rather, it is whether the alternative interpretation requiring dual accounting is also reasonable and better promotes the Tribe's interest. If so, dual accounting should have been required from the beginning.[4]

* * * As I have noted, our initial determination is whether the trial court's and the Secretary's construction of the royalty regulations is reasonable. I believe that it is. Given two reasonable interpretations, Interior's trust responsibilities require it to apply whichever accounting method (BTU or net realization) yields the Tribe the greatest royalties. I would affirm the trial court on this point.

Notes

1. The effect of the trust on administrative decision making. The Tenth Circuit suggested that normal administrative law principles—judicial deference to

---

3. The Tribe has, of course, another remedy for the Government's breach of its fiduciary obligations. "If in carrying out [its] role as representative [of the Tribe], the Government violated its obligations to the Tribe, then the Tribe's remedy is against the Government. . . ." That action lies in the Court of Claims. The Tribe has instituted a suit against the Government in the Court of Claims, which has been stayed pending this appeal.

4. [This footnote appears later in the opinion, but has been placed here for clarification.—eds.] * * * This case involves two methods of royalty calculation. The "BTU Method" calculates the value of gas produced by measuring the volume and BTU content of the wet gas at the wellhead, from which the "value" of the gas is derived. The second method, called the "net realization" or "aggregate value" method, is calculated by determining the values of the component gases after they have been extracted through processing. The ""value" of the gas is the aggregate value of the constituent gases, less a cost of processing allowance.

"Dual accounting," requiring the computation of the value of wet gas by both methods and the subsequent payment of royalties on the basis of whichever methods yields the higher value, allows a lessee to market gas by whichever methods it chooses and ensures that the lessor royalty holder receives the maximum return on its gas.

"reasonable" agency actions under the *Chevron* doctrine, see page 291—should give way to stricter standards when federal agencies administer Indian programs because of the federal trust responsibility. Consequently, the trust narrows the range of reasonable alternatives for federal administrators to "the alternative that is in the best interests of the Indian tribe." In other words, the only reasonable alternative for federal trustees is the alternative which is in the best interest of the tribe. For elaboration of the way in which the trust responsibility ought to affect environmental decision making, see Mary Christina Wood, *Fulfilling the Executive's Trust Responsibility Toward Native Nations on Environmental Issues: A Partial Critique of the Clinton Administration's Promises and Performance*, 25 Envtl. L. 733 (1995).

2. Breach of trust actions for declaratory and injunctive relief. Footnote 3 in *Supron* noted that the federal district courts and the federal claims court, now called the Court of Federal Claims, both have jurisdiction over breach of trust actions. The jurisdiction of the claims court is discussed at pages 187–188. As noted there, the Court of Federal Claims has jurisdiction only if the plaintiff seeks monetary damages. Plaintiffs seeking declaratory or injunctive relief for breach of trust must bring those claims in the federal district court, as the tribe did in *Supron*. For a discussion of injunctive relief cases, see Mary Christina Wood, *The Indian Trust Responsibility: Protecting Tribal Lands and Resources Through Claims of Injunctive Relief Against Federal Agencies*, 39 Tulsa L. Rev. 355 (2003).

3. Overlapping claims. Because of the concurrent jurisdiction noted above, tribes may not be able to pursue complete relief in either the federal district court or the Court of Federal Claims. Consequently, some tribes, as indicated in *Supron*, filed concurrent actions seeking declaratory and injunctive relief in district court and monetary damages in the claims court. In 2011, the Supreme Court limited this approach.

A federal statute enacted at the end of the Civil War prohibits the Court of Federal Claims (CFC) from exercising jurisdiction over "any claim for or in respect to which the plaintiff" then has pending before any other court. 28 U.S.C. § 1500. In *United States v. Tohono O'Odham Nation*, 563 U.S. 307 (2011), the Court ruled that the CFC had no jurisdiction over the Tohono O'Odham Nation's claim for money damages for breach of trust that it filed in the CFC one day after filing suit on the same facts for equitable relief, including an accounting, in federal district court. The Court determined that the "[t]wo suits are for or in respect to the same claim, precluding jurisdiction in the CFC, if they are based on substantially the same operative facts, regardless of the relief sought in each suit." *Id.* at 317. The Court explained that the statutory language "for or in respect to" referred to similar facts, so that different requested relief did not remove a claim from the preclusive effect of the statute.

Moreover, the Court explained that this result would not work a hardship on tribes because they could either file in the CFC alone for monetary damages, or "[i]t also seems likely that Indian tribes in the Nation's position could go to the district court first without losing the chance to later file in the CFC, for Congress has provided in every appropriations Act for the Department of Interior since 1990 that the statute of limitations on Indian trust mismanagement claims shall not run until the affected tribe has been given an appropriate accounting." *Id.* at 316–317. Finally, from a policy perspective, the Court pointed out that the Nation did not have a right to monetary relief, as damages were available only by the "grace" of Congress. Therefore, should a tribe disagree with the Court's decision, the proper remedy would be to bring a complaint to Congress.

Is the lesson that tribes must file suit first in the Court of Federal Claims or lose their money damages claims? In *Otoe-Missouria Tribe of Indians v. United States*, 105 Fed. Cl. 136 (2012), the court held that the order of filing was crucial. The tribe had filed in the morning in the Court of Federal Claims, and that same afternoon in federal district court. The claims court held that "pending" in the statute "refers to cases that are filed." At the time the tribe filed in the claims court, no other lawsuit had been filed. "It is from the moment of the filing, not necessarily the date of filing," that the court determines which lawsuit was filed first. Because no case was therefore pending when the tribe filed in the claims court, that court had proper subject matter jurisdiction.

The Court of Federal Claims ruled that it lacked jurisdiction, however, in a case filed in federal district court and transferred in part to the claims court. *Jackson v. United States*, 107 Fed. Cl. 495 (2012). Individual members of the Shoshone-Bannock Tribe filed claims for negligence and breach of fiduciary duty in federal district court. The court granted summary judgment against the tribal members on the negligence claims and transferred the breach of trust claims to the claims court. Under the transfer statute, 28 U.S.C. § 1631, the transferred claim is treated as if it were filed in the claims court on the date it was actually filed in district court. As a result, the claims in the district court and in the claims court were considered to be filed simultaneously. Under a 1999 case not involving Indian claims, the claims court had held that in that situation, the district court claims are "pending" for purposes of § 1500. The Court of Federal Claims appeared sympathetic to the Indian plaintiffs, but held itself bound by precedent to dismiss the case.

4. Management of Indian trust funds. Recall our study of the management problems associated with allotments in Chapter III, Section E. As we saw, the General Allotment Act of 1887 authorized the allotment of reservations into individually-owned parcels of land. Allottees, however, generally were poorly equipped to enter the market economy. As a result, Congress enacted a series of statutes authorizing allottees, with approval of the federal trustee, to lease their allotments to non-Indians, who grazed, irrigated, logged, or mined the land. The trustee, through the Bureau of Indian Affairs, was supposed to account to the lessors for the rents and royalties earned, but it proved incapable of doing so.

The BIA's record-keeping system was inept. Many documents were lost, destroyed, or never cataloged. Over time it became impossible to determine who owed what. As the D.C. Circuit observed:

> The federal government does not know the precise number of IIM [individual Indian money] trust accounts that it is to administer and protect. At

present, the Interior Department's system contains over 300,000 accounts covering an estimated 11 million acres, but the Department is unsure whether this is the proper number of accounts. Plaintiffs claim that the actual number of accounts is far higher, exceeding 500,000 trust accounts. Not only does the Interior Department not know the proper number of accounts, it does not know the proper balances for each IIM account, nor does Interior have sufficient records to determine the value of IIM accounts. As the district court found, "[a]lthough the United States freely gives out 'balances' to plaintiffs, it admits that currently these balances cannot be supported by adequate transactional documentation." Current account reconciliation procedures are insufficient to ensure that existing account records, reported account balances, or payments to IIM beneficiaries are accurate. As the Interior Secretary testified at trial, the Department is presently unable to render an accounting for a majority of the IIM trust beneficiaries. As a result, the government regularly issues payments to trust beneficiaries "in erroneous amounts — from unreconciled accounts — some of which are known to have incorrect balances." Thus, the district court concluded, and the government does not deny, that "[i]t is entirely possible that tens of thousands of IIM trust beneficiaries should be receiving different amounts of money — their own money — than they do today. Perhaps not. But no one can say. . . ."

Cobell v. Norton, 240 F.3d 1081, 1089 (D.C. Cir. 2001).

The system was, in short, in complete disarray.

In June 1996, a massive class action suit was filed in the District of Columbia District Court. *Cobell v. Babbitt*, 37 F. Supp. 2d 6 (D.D.C. 1999). The plaintiffs claimed that the federal government breached its trust obligation by failing to pay up to $10 billion due on trust accounts. They sought not only an accounting and payment of what was owed, but court appointment of a special master to overhaul the system.

The litigation was protracted and convoluted. It included contempt citations against the Secretary of the Interior and the Assistant Secretary for Indian Affairs (later vacated), and removal of the presiding judge. After a bench trial, the new presiding judge concluded that "it is now clear that completion of the required accounting is an impossible task." *Cobell v. Kempthorne*, 532 F. Supp. 2d 37, 39 (D.D.C. 2008). On appeal, however, the Federal Circuit held that the beneficiaries were statutorily entitled to an accounting. *Cobell v. Salazar*, 573 F.3d 808 (Fed. Cir. 2009).

In December 2009, the parties reached a settlement agreement. Congress ratified the agreement in 2010, creating a $1.4 billion Trust Accounting and Administration Fund and a $2 billion Trust Land Consolidation Fund with two groups of IIM account holders eligible to receive settlement payments. Claims Resolution Act of 2010, Pub. L. No. 111-291. The D.C. District Court approved the settlement in 2011, and in May 2012 the D.C. Circuit denied two appeals by class members and affirmed the district court's judgment.

All of the documents, opinions, and orders in the *Cobell* litigation and settlement can be found on the *Cobell* website: http://www.cobellsettlement.com.

C. The Tribal Role in Resource Management

The cases that follow involve Indian tribes' attempts to exert greater control over resource development within their Indian country. In each case, the tribe is seeking to terminate or avoid a mineral lease or other mineral agreement that the tribe no longer perceives as being in its best interests. To what extent are the tribes successful, and why?

Jicarilla Apache Tribe v. Andrus
687 F.2d 1324 (10th Cir. 1982)

HALLOWAY, Circuit Judge.

In 1976 the Jicarilla Apache Tribe (the Tribe) filed this action against the Secretary of the Interior and certain oil and gas lessees (lessee defendants or the companies), claiming that the Secretary failed to comply with his regulation, 25 CFR § 171.3, when advertising four sales of oil and gas leases on the Jicarilla Apache Indian Reservation. * * * The Tribe sought a declaration that the nonproducing leases were invalid and an order directing the Secretary to cancel them. In addition the Tribe sought an order that the Secretary prepare an environmental impact statement for producing leases and that he recommend changes in the lease terms based thereon.

The four lease sales were conducted by the Bureau of Indian Affairs (BIA) on April 22, 1970, July 14, 1971, November 17, 1971, and September 6, 1972, by sealed-bid auction pursuant to 25 U.S.C. § 396b. Of a total 415,885.90 acres offered, 276,117.61 acres were actually leased. At trial the companies essentially sought to demonstrate lack of violation of the regulations on notice procedures, lack of harm to the Tribe's interests, * * * and laches and unclean hands.

We turn first to the basic issue whether the Secretary's regulations were violated in giving notice of the lease sales.

I

The notice procedures which the Government must follow when offering oil and gas leases for sale on behalf of Indian tribes are set forth in 25 CFR § 171.3, promulgated pursuant to 25 U.S.C. § 396b.

The provision that publication may be at such times and in such manner as the Superintendent deems appropriate does not dispense with the clear mandate to "publish notices" and its close connection to their specified contents. In view of these mandatory provisions and their purpose, we are convinced that there had to be publication carrying the essentials of the notice—that oil and gas leases on specified tracts would be offered, that the offer was based on stipulated rentals and royalties, and that there was a reservation that the Secretary might reject bids not deemed in the interest of the Indians. In the context of this kind of notice, the ordinary meanings of publish "to make generally known . . . to make public announcement . . . to place before the public: Disseminate," Webster's New Collegiate Dictionary at 933 (1975), clearly point to general publication by a regular medium of publication. As the trial judge concluded: "The procedures employed, viewed as a whole, did not reach the Section 171.3 mark."

It is argued that an administrative interpretation of the regulation has been made by the Indian Affairs Manual and by the procedures used, to which deference should be given, particularly because of past reliance on them. We are convinced, however, that the plain, mandatory terms of the regulations do not leave room for deference to this interpretation, which does not serve the interest of the Indians. If there is any doubt, the interpretation should be made liberally in favor of the Indians for whose protection these provisions were promulgated. This rule of construction pertaining to statutes and treaties should also govern the interpretation of the regulations. Regulations are generally subject to the same rules of construction as statutes.

In sum we conclude, as did the trial court, that the publication procedures used failed to comply with the regulation.

II

Having found a technical violation of the regulation on notice procedures, the district judge declined to order outright cancellation and instead provided in his decree that cancellation of any of the leases could be avoided by payment of adjusted bonuses to the Tribe. The adjusted bonus payments were to be equal to the difference between the bonuses actually paid and 60% of the bonus payments which Mr. Reese, a geologist who testified as an expert for the Tribe, testified he would have recommended to a bidder. The trial judge stated that on the whole he found Reese's testimony competent and credible on the basis of Reese's long and extensive familiarity with the geology of the area, with specific reference to oil and gas development in the San Juan Basin. The judge stated that he had discounted Mr. Reese's estimate as to the amount of bonus payments which the leases should have generated to the extent the court felt that Reese had been impeached.

For reversal and a decree of cancellation, the Tribe argues that in light of the violations of the notice requirements of 25 CFR § 171.3, the leases were void ab initio and must be canceled, citing *Gray v. Johnson*, 395 F.2d 533 (10th Cir.), *cert. denied*, 392 U.S. 906 inter alia. That case, however, concerned court review of the Secretary's administrative decision to cancel a 10-year lease of an Indian's land which had earlier been approved, but which the Secretary found on administrative appeal to be void for violation of regulations limiting the length of leases on dry farming land to five years. We held that "the execution of the lease was an administrative error which the Secretary can correct by cancellation of the lease." We thus upheld the administrative determination there to cancel, but the case does not compel an equity court to order cancellation of all leases on Indian land for every procedural error in the leasing procedure. We feel the *Gray* case is distinguishable.

The equitable nature of this suit is of paramount importance. "When Congress leaves to the federal courts the formulation of remedial details, it can hardly expect them to break with historic principles of equity in the enforcement of federally-created equitable rights." If Congress had intended to make a drastic departure from the traditions of equity practice, an unequivocal statement of that purpose would have been made. An appeal to the equity jurisdiction of the federal district courts is an appeal to the sound discretion which guides the determinations of courts of equity. We should not "lightly assume that Congress has intended to depart from established (equitable) principles."

The equitable remedy of cancellation will be granted in the discretion of the chancellor. Cancellation is "an exertion of the most extraordinary power of a court of equity. The power ought not to be exercised except in a clear case . . ." It is not to be granted unless it appears no injustice will be done by placing the parties in the positions they occupied before the contract or conveyance was made. If the parties cannot be put back in status quo, cancellation will be ordered "only where the clearest and strongest equity imperatively demands it." Thus, a person coming into a court of equity cannot demand cancellation as a matter of right, and granting such relief is within the sound discretion of the court even if the ground on which the plaintiff seeks cancellation has been clearly established.

In light of the virtual impossibility of putting these parties back in status quo after years of exploration and development,[6] we do not think the district court abused its equitable discretion in refusing to grant outright cancellation.

We are persuaded that the trial judge had the power to exercise his discretion to provide for the payment of the adjusted bonuses as he did in this equitable action.

IV

As noted, the trial court held that the Tribe's claim of a NEPA violation was barred by laches and the doctrine of unclean hands. The Tribe had prayed for cancellation of the nonproducing leases, and an order directing the Secretary to prepare an environmental impact statement (EIS) for producing leases and to recommend changes in the lease terms based thereon. Due to its laches and unclean hands ruling the court did not reach the questions of whether the oil and gas leasing activity constituted major federal action significantly affecting the quality of the human environment and whether an EIS was required.

---

6. For example, Southland Royalty drilled eight wells at a cost of $556,149.75 and made $53,979 in geological expenditures before being served in this suit. Union Oil drilled two exploratory wells before the suit. Dugan Production drilled two wells before suit. Merrion and Bayless Drilling drilled four wells before the suit was commenced. Also before the suit, Amoco Production, Mesa Petroleum, and Huber Corp. participated together in one well on Lease 485, spending $287,000 for drilling and geological studies. Gulf Oil also conducted "some seismic operations."

The defense of laches is available in environmental litigation but is disfavored because of the interests of the public in environmental quality and because the agency would escape compliance with NEPA if laches were generally applied, thus defeating Congress' environmental policy. The question whether laches bars an action depends on the facts and circumstances of each case. The issue is primarily left to the discretion of the trial court, but that discretion is, of course, confined by recognized standards. The trial court must find (a) unreasonable delay in bringing suit by the party against whom the defense is asserted and (b) prejudice to the party asserting the defense as a result of this delay.

We are uncertain as to the appropriateness of this policy consideration, as Congress has mandated the completion of an EIS when major federal action significantly affecting the quality of the human environment is involved. Congress has chosen the procedural protections of NEPA to serve the public's interest in protecting the environment. This choice as the mandate of Congress could be undercut if other studies are accepted or if we make a substitute judgment on the public interest. We need not reach this issue, however, as we uphold the laches ruling due to the delay and prejudice factors.

Mere lapse of time does not amount to laches. When Government action is involved, members of the public are entitled to assume public officials will act in accordance with law. Laches may be found, however, where a party, having knowledge of the relevant facts, acquiesces for an unreasonable length of time in the assertion of a right adverse to his own. A party must exercise reasonable diligence in protecting his rights.

The record supports the finding of unreasonable delay by the Tribe in asserting its NEPA claim as a ground for attacking the leases. The Tribe commenced the action in April 1976. The four lease sales were held beginning in April 1970 and concluding in September 1972. During the period of lease sales, the law was unclear as to applicability of NEPA to the approval of lease sales by the BIA. In November 1972, however, this court held that NEPA was applicable to Government approval of a 99-year lease of Indian lands in New Mexico. *Davis v. Morton*, 469 F.2d 593, 597–98 (10th Cir.). It was more than three years after that decision when the Tribe brought this action.

The Tribe asserts that there was evidence showing that the Tribe first acquired knowledge of its NEPA claims in October 1975 and that the defendants offered no evidence to the contrary. Harold Tecube, an agency realty specialist for the BIA who had responsibility for oil and gas activity and its environmental consequences during the relevant time periods herein, did testify that the Tribe first became aware of the ramifications of NEPA with regard to these leases in October 1975 at a meeting of the Tribal Council. Tecube also testified that in the years from 1970 to 1974 the Tribe was dependent on the Bureau to answer questions relating to oil and gas development. The latter testimony was corroborated by Thomas Olson, the Tribe's general counsel from 1965 to 1973, who stated that he did not represent the Tribe on oil and gas or NEPA matters, and that during his representation the Tribe relied heavily on the BIA and United States Geological Survey and had no independent oil and gas consultants. The Tribe thus argues that its ignorance of the NEPA violation was attributable to its reliance on the BIA. The Tribe points to the fiduciary duty owed by the United States to protect Indian land and concludes that the suit was timely filed.

We disagree. The Tribe cannot rely on its lack of knowledge of the applicability of NEPA to the approval of lease sales. Laches does not depend on the subjective awareness of the legal basis on which a claim can be made. The Tribe clearly had knowledge of the Secretary's approval of the lease sales at the time of the sales, and the NEPA ruling in *Davis v. Morton* was made in November 1972. While the Tribe may not have known of the BIA's failure to comply with NEPA until October 1975, the Tribe would have acquired this knowledge had it exercised the proper diligence.

The trial court also found that the delay in bringing suit resulted in prejudice to the lessee defendants, stating:

> [T]he delay resulted in prejudice to the lessee defendants. Because they had no notice that anything was amiss with their Jicarilla leases until the institution of this suit, they have invested well over $12 million in the leases in the form of bonus payments, rentals, administrative overhead costs, plus exploration, drilling and production costs. Were they to lose their leases, much of that investment would be lost, not to mention the loss of future profits based on investments already made.

The Tribe does not dispute the finding that the lessee defendants made some expenditures prior to the bringing of this suit.

The Tribe says that the greater part of the monies spent by the lessee defendants has been for bonuses and delay rentals, that these contractual liabilities were incurred by defendants at the time of the lease sales and are not dependent on the Tribe's inaction in bringing suit, and that these expenditures could not have been made in reliance on the Tribe's inaction. We agree that the lease bonuses should not be controlling. These monies were paid before there was any reliance by the lessee defendants on the inaction of the Tribe. The same can be said as to those rentals paid before an unreasonable delay in the assertion of the Tribe's claim occurred. We feel it is clear, however, that the same result would have been reached by the court based on other expenditures and the loss of future profits, if cancellation on NEPA grounds occurred. The record amply supports the laches ruling.

Likewise, the trial court did not err in its application of the unclean hands doctrine. At approximately the same time the Tribe filed this suit, it entered into three joint venture agreements for oil and gas development on the reservation. The largest of these developments was for 5000–5500 acres; the smallest was for 640 acres. The economic benefits of these agreements are more attractive to the Tribe than the lease terms at issue. The Tribe, however, did not seek to enforce NEPA compliance with respect to the joint ventures. Environmental "reports" were prepared on the joint ventures for the benefit of the Tribe. They were not prepared by BIA personnel, but by private environmental experts approved by the oil companies and the Tribe. The Tribe, however, did not ask the BIA to prepare an EIS with respect to the joint ventures, nor did it file suit against the companies which are parties to the joint venture agreements to secure compliance with NEPA as it did against the lessee defendants here.

We feel the trial judge could reasonably find, as he did, that the Tribe was not motivated by good faith concerns for the environmental impact of oil and gas development, that it was motivated by its desire to obtain the maximum possible compensation for the development, and that it was unjust and inequitable to allow the Tribe to use NEPA as a device solely for economic gain.

In sum, we conclude that the district judge did not err in holding that the Tribe's NEPA claim was barred by the laches and unclean hands doctrines.

Note on the Environmental Effects of Mining

The tribe in *Andrus* tried unsuccessfully to raise environmental concerns by claiming a violation of the National Environmental Policy Act. NEPA and its application in Indian country are explored at pages 327–343.

Indian tribes whose lands are subject to coal development have available a special environmental statute: the Surface Mining Control and Reclamation Act of 1977 (SMCRA), 30 U.S.C. §§ 1201–1328. Although tribes may enter into leases under the 1938 Indian Mineral Leasing Act, or other mineral agreements under the 1982 Indian Mineral Development Act, for the mining of tribal coal resources, SMCRA regulates the environmental consequences of surface exploration, mining, and reclamation of Indian coal. Accordingly, Interior Department regulations require all coal leases for Indian lands to include a provision that the lessee must comply with the applicable provisions of SMCRA.

SMCRA established two major programs affecting surface mining: an abandoned mine reclamation program for mines abandoned prior to August 3, 1977 and a program to control the environmental effects of surface mining through the issuance of permits for the exploration and development of mines, including environmental protection performance standards and reclamation plans. The Act applies to "Indian lands," defined in SMCRA as all lands, regardless of ownership, within the exterior boundaries of an Indian reservation, plus any off-reservation lands in which the tribe owns either the mineral estate or the surface estate.

Under SMCRA, states may, with federal approval, take regulatory control over the issuance of permits for surface coal mining operations on state lands. If a state has an approved permit program, it may also seek approval for a state abandoned mine reclamation program. Although Indian tribes are defined as "states" for purposes of the abandoned mine reclamation program, tribes have been delegated no authority to assume general surface mining regulatory programs. Accordingly, tribes have been unable to take the regulatory authority over abandoned mines.

In the SMCRA regulations, the Interior Department's Office of Surface Mining (OSM) declared that it will "[b]e the regulatory authority on Indian lands." 30 C.F.R. § 750.6(a)(1). Although OSM is therefore the permitting agency for surface mining operations on Indian lands, OSM does not consult directly with the affected Indian tribes. Instead, the regulations make the Bureau of Indian Affairs responsible for tribal consultations; the BIA then makes recommendations to OSM concerning permits, and OSM determines whether to approve or disapprove the surface mining permits for Indian coal.

Congress has delegated statutory abandoned mine reclamation authority to selected tribes. In 1988, Congress authorized the Crow, Hopi, and Navajo Tribes to develop tribal programs for reclamation of mines abandoned prior to August 3, 1977, subject to approval by the Secretary of the Interior, notwithstanding the absence of a tribal permit program as required by SMCRA. 30 U.S.C. § 1235(k). All three tribes submitted plans, which were approved, and they now operate tribal abandoned mine reclamation programs. In 1992, Congress made those three tribes, plus the Northern Cheyenne, eligible for grants to develop tribal offices of surface mining regulation.

United Nuclear Corp. v. United States
912 F.2d 1432 (Fed. Cir. 1990)

FRIEDMAN, Circuit Judge.

The appellant, United Nuclear Corporation (United), entered into two leases with the Navajo Tribal Council (Tribal Council), which authorized United to conduct uranium mining on land in the Navajo Reservation. The leases were awarded to United through competitive bidding, and the Secretary of the Interior approved the leases, as well as United's exploration plans for the leased land. United's explorations, for which United spent more than $5 million, uncovered valuable uranium deposits. United then prepared a mining plan, which it submitted to the Secretary for approval, such approval being necessary before United could begin mining.

Although United's mining plan satisfied all of the requirements of the Secretary's regulations, the Secretary refused to approve it without tribal approval. During the next three years United unsuccessfully attempted to obtain tribal approval or to persuade the Secretary to approve the mining plan without tribal approval. The result was that United's leases terminated because United failed to begin mining within the period the lease specified. United then filed the present suit in the United States Claims Court alleging that the Secretary's refusal to approve the mining plan constituted a taking of its leases, for which it was entitled to just compensation.

The Claims Court dismissed the suit, holding that United had no "legally protected property right to approval of its mine plan" that was "the subject of a Fifth Amendment taking." We hold, however, that there has been a taking of United's property interest in the leases, and remand the case to the Claims Court to determine the amount of just compensation to which United is entitled.

I.

The basic facts, as found by the Claims Court and as shown by the record, are as follows:

The Navajo Reservation is located in the Grants Mineral Belt, "the premier uranium-producing area" in the United States. Three hundred and thirty million pounds of uranium (approximately 55 percent of all uranium produced in the United States) has come from this area. The potential for uranium mining in this area has been generally recognized since at least the late 1960s, when the Kerr-McGee Corporation had obtained uranium leases from the Tribal Council and conducted substantial exploration. These and other exploratory efforts "strongly suggested that there was a significant potential for uranium to be discovered on areas of the Navajo reservation not covered by the Kerr-McGee leases."

The Tribal Council in 1970 unanimously authorized the Secretary of the Interior to conduct public bidding for uranium mining of this area. In sealed bidding, United, a large domestic producer of uranium with extensive mining experience, was the successful bidder for the mining rights on two tracts of the reservation.

On June 29, 1971, United entered into two ten-year leases with the Navajo Tribe (Tribe). The leases were for "a term of 10 years from the date of . . . approval and as long thereafter as the minerals specified are produced in paying quantities." The leases provided for annual rent, a minimum annual royalty and additional royalties based upon the amount of minerals mined. United paid the Tribe a bonus of $79,000 upon signing the leases, and also paid total rent and royalties of more than $220,000. The Tribe has retained all this money.

On July 7, 1971, the Secretary approved the leases. Such approval was necessary for them to become effective.

The Secretary subsequently approved United's exploration plan, which approval was necessary before United could begin exploration. United spent $5,366,835 for exploration and related activities. Through this exploration, United discovered more than 20 million pounds of uranium on explored portions of the leased land, and believed there was a potential for 20 million additional pounds on unexplored portions.

Prior to commencing mining operations on the leased lands, United was required to obtain the Secretary's approval of its mining plan. On February 4, 1977, United submitted its mining plan to the United States Geological Survey (the "Survey"), a Bureau of the Department of the Interior. The Claims Court found that "[t]he mining plan satisfied each of the requirements set forth in the mining plan regulations," and the government concedes that United's "plan satisfied the technical requirements of the Department's regulations." The Regional Mining Supervisor, an Interior Department official who had served in that position since 1960, testified that he had never disapproved any of the hundreds of exploration or mining plans submitted for his approval.

The Claims Court found that although United's mining plan met all the regulatory requirements, the Department "withheld approval of the mining plan for a period of more than 4 years, deferring to the Navajo Tribe approval of the plan." In April 1978, at a meeting between United and Departmental officials, the latter informed United that the Department "was giving the Navajo Tribe a veto power over the mining plan and that the Department and the [Survey] were refusing to take any action on the mining plan until the Tribe approved it."

Tribal approval of mining plans never had been required previously. Only a few months earlier, when Kerr-McGee had sought the Secretary's approval for a mining plan on tribal land that it had leased, the Acting Director of the Survey wrote the Tribal Council that if the Survey did not receive tribal comments regarding Kerr-McGee's plan by a stated date, the Survey would "assume that the [Tribe] concurs with the plan as submitted and [the Survey] will proceed with administrative processing of the mine plan."

In a meeting on October 13, 1978, among tribal representatives, Department officials, and United, the General Counsel of the Tribe indicated that a "$10,000,000 adder might be needed" and a member of the Tribe indicated that "it was not enough." It was stated that the Tribe was "[c]oncerned about the depletion of Tribal water resources." The Claims Court found, however, that United "had met necessary environmental impact requirements."

The government itself recognized that the Tribe was using its veto power either to require United to pay more money or to cause the leases to lapse. The Chief of the Survey's Branch of Mining Operations wrote in the fall of 1978:

> The tribe is withholding comments and concurrence on approval of [United's mining] plan[ ] in hopes of forcing the lessees to take the tribe on as a partner in the operations. This is real leverage since the tribal leases will expire on July 7, 1981, unless production has commenced in paying quantities.

Moreover, there is testimony indicating that the Bureau of Indian Affairs also was aware that the Tribe was withholding approval because "the tribe wanted more bucks, more money." From the time of the April 1978 meeting, when United first was informed of the tribal approval requirement, United "made repeated and continuous efforts to gain such tribal approval . . . [and] sought to convince the Secretary to withdraw the requirement of tribal approval of the mining plan." Neither endeavor succeeded.

Following an unsuccessful judicial attempt by United to compel the Secretary (1) to approve or act upon the mining plan, or (2) to extend the leases, the leases expired as of July 7, 1981, because of United's failure to begin mining.

On May 4, 1984, United filed a complaint in the United States Claims Court alleging that the Secretary's failure to approve the mining plan constituted a taking of United's property without just compensation, in violation of the fifth amendment, and seeking damages.

II

The determination whether government action constitutes a taking of property under the fifth amendment rather than a mere exercise of the government's regulatory authority frequently is a close, difficult, and complex process. In *Connolly v. Pension Benefit Guaranty Corp.*, 475 U.S. 211 (1986), the Supreme Court noted that while its cases "have eschewed the development of any set formula for identifying a 'taking' forbidden by the Fifth Amendment, and have relied instead on ad hoc, factual inquiries into the circumstances of each particular case," there are "three factors which have 'particular significance'" "[t]o aid in this determination": (1) "the economic impact of the regulation on the claimant"; (2) "the extent to which the regulation has interfered with distinct investment-backed expectations"; and (3) "the character of the governmental action."

1. The Economic Impact of the Regulation on the Claimant. As the Claims Court found, the economic impact of the regulation (giving the Tribe a veto power over the mining plan) upon United "has been severe." United has paid the Tribe approximately $300,000 as a bonus for the leases and as rent and minimum royalties. It also expended more than $5 million in exploration and related activity. It is unlikely that United will be able to recover any of this money.

Equally or perhaps more significant, United's exploration indicated that a substantial amount of uranium existed on the leased land. The extraction and sale of this uranium by United presumably would have produced significant profits for the company. The Secretary prevented United from commencing mining operations by refusing to approve United's mining plan, thus causing the leases to expire. As a result, United lost whatever profits it would have made had it been permitted to mine the leased land.

2. The Extent to Which the Regulation Has Interfered With Distinct Investment-Backed Expectations. United invested more than $5 million in the project and presumably expected to derive substantial profits from the venture. Prior to the April 1978 meeting with Departmental officials, United had no indication or even suggestion that tribal approval of the mining plan would be required before the Secretary would approve it. Indeed, previously tribal approval of mining plans had not been required. United's mining plan concededly satisfied the requirements of the applicable regulations. Prior to the meeting, United justifiably believed and expected that if its mining plan met the requirements, the Secretary would approve it—as he had done for United's exploration plan.

The Secretary's new requirement of tribal approval of the mining plan was not adopted or included in any regulation of the Secretary. If the Secretary had proposed such a regulation, United would have had the opportunity to oppose it.

The fact that United agreed that the leases would be subject to future regulations does not indicate that United fairly can be said to have anticipated that the Secretary would apply a new policy requiring tribal approval of mining plans to leases entered into almost six years earlier, in reliance on which United had expended some $5 million.

*** [T]he property interest that is the subject of the taking claim is United's leasehold interest in the minerals, which the government took by preventing United from mining under the leases, and not the mere expectation that United would be permitted to engage in mining. Contrary to the ruling of the Claims Court, we hold that the Secretary's refusal to approve the mining plan seriously interfered with United's investment-backed expectations by destroying them.

3. The Character of the Governmental Action. When the Interior Department officials first informed United that tribal approval was required for the mining plan, they gave no reason for or explanation of that decision. The Claims Court specified two factors that it believed explained the Secretary's decision: "[T]ribal concerns about potential reduction of scarce drinking water supplies in an arid region and the addition of another major uranium mining operation to an already large number of such mines operating in an area which could not handle the burgeoning population and increased traffic that would impact the area." The court also noted that United "had met necessary environmental impact requirements,"—a finding that seemingly undercuts and perhaps vitiates the court's speculation regarding the reasons for the Secretary's decision.

The record leaves no doubt that the real reason for the Tribe's refusal to approve United's mining plan was an attempt to obtain substantial additional money from United. The general counsel of the Tribe indicated at a meeting that an additional $10 million would be necessary. Interior Department officials were aware that the Tribe's true motive for refusing to approve the mining plan was that the Tribe "wanted . . . more money." This fact, which the Claims Court did not mention, is inconsistent with that court's view that the reason the Tribal Council would not approve the mining plan was "tribal concerns regarding potential loss of the Tribe's drinking water supplies and the cumulative effects of the proliferation of uranium mines in the area," since these concerns apparently would have disappeared if United had paid the Tribe substantial additional money.

In its brief before us, the government asserts that the Secretary's requirement of tribal approval of the mining plan was intended to promote the Indians' right to and development of self-determination. It is difficult to understand, however, how encouraging the Indians not to live up to their contractual obligations, which they entered into freely and with the Secretary's approval, could be said to encourage self-determination. To the contrary, one would think that the best way to make the Indians more responsible citizens would be to require them to live up to their contractual commitments.

The present case is very different from *Allied-General*. In that case a company had constructed a plant for reprocessing used nuclear fuel. While the Nuclear Regulatory Commission was considering the company's application for an operating permit for the plant, the President barred the operation of any reprocessing plants because of concern that permitting the plant to operate could lead to a proliferation of nuclear weapons that could threaten the safety of the United States.

The Claims Court dismissed a suit for just compensation based on the government's alleged taking of the plant. This court affirmed, holding that "the claimant had no legally protected property right to operate the plant, which could have been the subject of a fifth amendment taking, as against the fear it would injure the national security." This court applied "the basic rule . . . that as against reasonable state regulation, no one has a legally protected right to use property in a manner that is injurious to the safety of the general public."

The Secretary's requirement of tribal consent in the present case is a far cry from the kind of Presidential power invoked in *Allied-General*. The Secretary's action reflects not concern over national safety, but an attempt to enable the Tribe to exact additional money from a company with whom it had a valid contract, which the government euphemistically describes as an attempt to encourage and promote Indian self-determination. The considerations upon which the court based its decision in *Allied-General* are inapplicable here.

CONCLUSION

We hold that there was a taking, and accordingly reverse the judgment of the Claims Court dismissing the complaint. The case is remanded to that court to determine the just compensation to which United Nuclear Corporation is entitled. In so remanding, we indicate no views concerning the basis upon which just compensation is to be determined or the amount to be awarded.

Notes

1. Distinguishing *Allied-General*. Why is it that barring the operation of a constructed nuclear fuel reprocessing plant is not a taking but requiring tribal approval of a uranium mining plan is?

2. Uranium mining on the Navajo Reservation. Was the Navajo Tribe concerned only with money? Consider the following: Uranium mining on the Navajo Reservation resulted from discovery of the mineral carnotite, which contains both uranium and vanadium. Vanadium is important in the production of steel, and in the early twentieth century, uranium was found to be the source of the medicinal element radium. Later in the century, national defense needs for the minerals accelerated mining in Navajo country.

Most of the mining took place in the Monument Valley, with typical operations consisting of both the mine and a processing mill. Although the federal government had been aware of the health problems associated with radium and radiation since the 1920s, and set exposure standards for workers in the 1940s, uranium mines and mills were exempt from those standards. In 1949, the U.S. Public Health Service, at the request of the Office of Indian Affairs, conducted a survey of mining on the Navajo Reservation. The survey results showed that miners were exposed to from twice to almost ten times modern allowable radiation levels. In some cases, miners exceeded annual allowable levels in a week's time. Concentrated uranium oxide dust, or yellowcake, was everywhere in the mines, coating the mouths and clothes of the workers. No uncontaminated drinking water was available, so miners drank the water that trickled down the mine walls. Nearby residents used discarded waste rock from the mining process to build their homes. Living in those homes was equivalent to living in a uranium mine.

Today, the Navajo Nation is attempting to reclaim the 1200 uranium mines in its Indian country. Despite some progress, numerous problems remain. Many of the open mine pits, filled with rainwater, have become a source of contaminated drinking water for wildlife and livestock. Wastewater seepage has contaminated the groundwater. Respiratory disease and cancer, likely the result of long-term radiation exposure, are appearing in Navajo families. *See generally* Peter H. Eichstaedt, If You Poison Us: Uranium and Native Americans (Red Crane Books 1994).

3. The Church Rock spill. Most people have heard of Three Mile Island, the most serious nuclear power plant accident in this country's history. But Three Mile Island was not the most serious radioactive spill in this country's history. That record belongs to Church Rock.

> An ominous illustration of the hazards of mill tailings disposal occurred on July 16, 1979, at the United Nuclear Corporation processing facility at Church Rock, New Mexico. On that day, a massive crack cleaved an earthen dam, spilling more than 93 million gallons of contaminated liquids and 1,100 tons of radioactive solid wastes from the corporation's tailings pond into a dry arroyo that empties into the Rio Puerco. The Rio Puerco, a stream used by Navajo herdsmen as a watering hole for their livestock, carried the residues more than 100 miles.
>
> Ironically, this dam had been a new, improved design, using earth instead of tailings themselves to dam the tailings pond, recommended by the NRC [Nuclear Regulatory Commission] itself. Special design criteria had been devised by the NRC prior to licensing of the dam. However, the corporation did not follow these criteria. Nor did it undertake regular inspections of the completed dam, although independent consultants hired by the firm had strongly recommended that it do so. Even after a consulting firm had observed and notified the corporation of a dangerously high settlement rate and the beginnings of small cracks in the dam as of 1977, it still took little or no preventive action. At leas[t] three federal and state regulatory agencies overseeing the licensing and construction of the dam could have predicted that the dam would break, but failed to do so.
>
> The spill immediately contaminated the waters of the Rio Puerco and Little Colorado rivers, rendering them unfit for consumption by humans or livestock. Navajo residents were instructed not to use the water or to eat livestock that had drunk the contaminated water, but many Navajos could neither read the newspaper reports of the spill nor the signs posted by government officials in the affected areas.

Lise Young, *What Price Progress? Uranium Production on Indian Lands in the San Juan Basin*, 9 Am. Indian L. Rev. 1, 21–22 (1981).* *See also Mill Tailings Dam Break at Church Rock, New Mexico: Oversight Hearing Before the Subcomm. on Energy and the Environment of the House Comm. on Interior and Insular Affairs*, 96th Cong., 1st Sess. (1980).

4. The Navajo uranium ban. In 2005, the Navajo Nation Council enacted the following law: "No person shall engage in uranium mining and uranium processing on any sites within Navajo Indian Country." 18 Nav. Nat. Code § 1303. The Council made extensive findings about the cultural, social, environmental, health, and economic impacts of uranium mining. Among other findings, the Council noted:

> the Dine medicine peoples' . . . recitation of the ceremonies and stories that have been passed down from generation to generation warn that certain substances in the Earth (*doo nal yee dah*) that are harmful to the people and should not be disturbed, and that the people now know that uranium is one such substance, and therefore, that its extraction should be avoided as traditional practice and prohibited by Navajo law.

Id. § 1301(D). *See generally* Bradford D. Cooley, Note, *The Navajo Uranium Ban: Tribal Sovereignty v. National Energy Demands*, 26 J. Land Resources & Envtl. L. 393 (2006).

5. Litigation under the Indian Mineral Development Act of 1982. Most of the federal case law addressing the tribal role in mineral development has focused on the Indian Mineral Leasing Act of 1938. The following case appears to be the only reported decision under the IMDA of 1982.

Quantum Exploration, Inc. v. Clark
780 F.2d 1457 (9th Cir. 1986)

BRUNETTI, Circuit Judge.

Quantum Exploration, Inc., ("Quantum") appeals the district court's order dismissing its complaint for lack of standing. Quantum sought a decision that would bind the Blackfeet Indian Tribe to a mineral development agreement between Quantum and the Tribe. Additionally, Quantum requested a writ of mandamus pursuant to the Indian Mineral Development Act to compel the Secretary of the Interior ("Secretary") to approve or disapprove the agreement and to promulgate rules and regulations establishing a deadline before which the Secretary must begin compliance with the National Environmental Policy Act ("NEPA"). We affirm, albeit for reasons other than those set forth by the district court. The court may affirm on any ground finding support in the record.

---

* Copyright 1981. Reprinted with permission of the American Indian Law Review.

FACTUAL AND PROCEDURAL BACKGROUND

In 1982, Congress passed the Indian Mineral Development Act of 1982 (IMDA). 25 U.S.C. §§ 2101–2108. IMDA was enacted to provide Indian tribes with flexibility in the development and sale of mineral resources. Foremost among the beneficial effects of IMDA was the opportunity for Indian tribes to enter into joint venture agreements with mineral developers. The contractual relationships permitted by IMDA were designed to meet two objectives: "first, to further the policy of self-determination and second, to maximize the financial return tribes can expect for their valuable mineral resources."

On July 12, 1983, the Blackfeet Tribal Business Council approved a proposed joint venture agreement with Quantum subject to approval by the Secretary. The agreement was submitted to the Secretary after it was amended and approved by the tribe in March of 1984. The agreement allowed Quantum to select a specific amount of acreage of tribal and allotted lands on the Blackfeet Reservation for oil and gas exploration and development.

On August 8, 1984, prior to a decision by the Secretary, the Tribal Business Council issued a resolution rescinding the agreement. The Council found the agreement was not in the best interests of the Blackfeet Tribe. This result was reached after the Council conferred with the Bureau of Indian Affairs ("BIA") concerning contract problems envisioned by that agency.

On November 20, 1984, Quantum initiated the instant action alleging that the Secretary's failure to approve or disapprove the agreement violated IMDA § 2103(a). Quantum also alleged that the involvement of the BIA constituted a violation of IMDA and interfered with Quantum's contractual relations. Quantum sought an injunction barring the Secretary from considering lease proposals of competitors, and a writ of mandamus to compel the Secretary to approve or disapprove the agreement and to comply with NEPA. On November 29, 1984, the district court issued a temporary restraining order against the Secretary.

On December 7, 1984, the district court sua sponte dismissed Quantum's complaint, finding that the Secretary was in compliance with IMDA and that Quantum lacked standing to compel the Secretary to promulgate a regulation limiting the ability of the Secretary to delay compliance with NEPA.

We address two issues on appeal:

I. May the Blackfeet Indian Tribe unilaterally rescind a proposed joint venture agreement entered into with a mineral developer before the agreement has been approved or disapproved by the Secretary of the Interior pursuant to IMDA?

II. Did the BIA's consultations with the tribe after the proposed agreement was submitted to the Secretary violate IMDA?

STANDARD OF REVIEW

* * * [T]he district court's interpretation of IMDA is a question of law subject to de novo review. In construing IMDA, we defer to interpretations by the

Secretary that are consistent with congressional intent and supported by substantial evidence.

DISCUSSION

I. Tribal Rescission Prior to the Secretary's Decision.

IMDA requires the Secretary to approve or disapprove all submitted mineral agreements. No agreement stands submitted to the Secretary awaiting his review if the Tribe has effectively rescinded the agreement in question.

It is Quantum's position that a valid agreement remains before the Secretary abiding its fate. Quantum argues that an effective, binding agreement was formed between itself and the Tribe on March 8, 1984. According to Quantum, the Tribe's August 8, 1984, rescission of the agreement violates the terms of IMDA and existing case law and contravenes general principles of contract law.[4] Contrary to Quantum's assertions, IMDA's provisions and legislative history reveal a congressional intent to accord tribes the right to disentangle themselves from the negotiations and agreements entered into prior to the Secretary's final decision.

The enforceability of IMDA agreements between tribes and mineral developers is entirely dependent on the approval of the Secretary. IMDA states that "[a]ny Indian tribe, *subject to the approval of the Secretary* . . . may enter into any joint venture" for the development of mineral resources in which the tribe owns a beneficial or restricted interest. 25 U.S.C. § 2102(a) (emphasis added). Typically, language requiring governmental approval of Indian agreements under other statutes has been interpreted to mean that the agreements simply are invalid absent the requisite approval.

That secretarial approval is similarly prerequisite under § 2102(a) is evidenced by the statute's legislative history. Perhaps the clearest expression of congressional intent appears in the legislative history analyzing § 2103(c). Under that section, the Secretary must prepare written findings forming the basis of his intent to approve or disapprove a minerals agreement and provide them to the tribe at least thirty days prior to formal approval or disapproval. In its report on the then-pending version of IMDA, the Senate Select Committee on Indian Affairs noted that the purpose for having the Secretary report to the tribe was to ensure "that tribes are fully apprised of the potential risks, as well as potential benefits. Having the opportunity to review the Secretary's findings in advance of a decision, *tribes will have time to reassess and perhaps reconsider before final approval or disapproval.*" Quantum argues that the legislative history merely recognizes a right for the Indians to "consult" with the Secretary with no possibility to withdraw from the agreement. The plain language of the report, however, shows the converse to be true. The right to "reconsider" clearly indicates that the tribe has the right to rescind the agreement.

---

4. The Blackfeet Indian Tribe is a federally recognized tribe possessing "the common-law immunity from suit traditionally enjoyed by sovereign powers." *Santa Clara Pueblo v. Martinez*, 436 U.S. 49 (1978). Consequently, no action for breach of contract may be initiated against the tribe.

This conclusion is buttressed by the fact that congressional reports preceding the enactment of IMDA often classified tribal arrangements with developers merely as "proposed agreements" prior to secretarial approval.

Quantum argues that the Tribe is unable to rescind without the Secretary's approval. Quantum relies heavily on our decision in *Yavapai-Prescott Indian Tribe v. Watt*, 707 F.2d 1072 (9th Cir.), *cert. denied*, 464 U.S. 1017 (1983). The holding of *Yavapai-Prescott* is inapposite. The tribe as lessor in *Yavapai-Prescott* sought unilaterally to terminate a lease alleging that the agreement had been breached. Unlike the instant case, the original lease agreement had received the formal approval of the Secretary and was thus binding.

Of importance to this court in *Yavapai-Prescott* was the consideration that, were the tribe allowed to rescind approved leases without secretarial involvement, lessees would have no available remedy; the tribe is immune from suit and the Secretary's inability to prohibit the termination deprives the lessee of any administrative remedy. Quantum claims it is in the same position as the lessee referred to in *Yavapai-Prescott* because it would have no remedy if the Tribe is allowed to rescind prior to secretarial approval. As noted above, Congress intended to make tribal agreements with developers binding only after official secretarial approval. This being so, until the Secretary approves the agreement Quantum has no remediable claims.

II. BIA Advice to the Tribe.

It is evident in the Tribe's August 8, 1984, resolution rescinding the Quantum agreement, that the BIA had been actively advising the Tribe. The Tribe placed great weight on the Bureau's assessment that the agreement was rife with problems. Quantum argues that the BIA's involvement was not allowed under IMDA and openly violated the Act's provisions vesting the power of official approval or disapproval in the Secretary or his authorized delegate, the Assistant Secretary of the Interior for Indian Affairs.

Under § 2106, upon the request of the Tribe, the Secretary is required to provide assistance "during the negotiation" of mineral agreements. This assistance may be rendered by federal officials or independent consultants. Quantum contends that the phrase "during the negotiation" implies that BIA involvement is allowed only prior to the time the tribe and developer sign an agreement. Under Quantum's proposed construction of the term, the Tribe would be barred from consulting with the BIA or other agents of the Secretary from the time the proposed agreement is signed until the Secretary provided the Tribe with his pre-decision findings. Such a narrow interpretation is not required by the language of the provision and is incompatible with the Act's goal of providing the tribes with greater flexibility in entering into joint venture agreements.

The term "negotiation" encompasses the period starting at the time the developer first contacts tribal representatives and continuing until the Secretary renders an official decision. This interpretation is consistent with the Tribe's right to rescind prior to the Secretary's final determination, and favors the tribe by providing additional flexibility.

IMDA's legislative history suggests that the federal government's trust obligations concerning tribal mineral reserves continue under IMDA. This duty to provide advice and assistance runs for the life of the agreement without interruption: "the Secretary of the Interior has an obligation to assist tribes from the very inception of agreements and his responsibility to protect their interests will continue for the duration of the agreement."

The advice offered by the BIA after the proposed agreement was submitted to the Secretary was consistent with the Secretary's duty to assist the Tribe in all stages of the transaction. Authorization for the BIA's consultations operates independent of the Secretary's duty to formally approve or disapprove.

CONCLUSION

Under IMDA, the proposed joint venture agreement was unenforceable and, consequently, rescindable by the tribe prior to official approval by the Secretary. Accordingly, the tribe's August 8, 1984, rescission of the Quantum agreement did not violate IMDA.

Notes

1. Secretarial approval and self-determination. Are the requirements of secretarial consultation and approval consistent with the IMDA's goal of promoting tribal self-determination?

2. Doing business in Indian country. What lesson does the *Quantum* case teach to those who want to conduct business in Indian country? Is a development agreement with a tribe without Secretarial approval enforceable?

Chapter 6

Taxation of Natural Resources

This chapter takes up issues of taxation of lands and natural resource development in Indian country. There are three taxing governments:

- the federal government,
- the tribal government, and
- the state government.

And there are two primary classifications of taxpayers:

- Indian tribes and tribal members, and
- nonmembers, including non-Indians and Indians who are not members of the governing tribe.

The following materials explore which government(s) — federal, tribal, or state — have authority to tax which classes of potential taxpayers, and under what circumstances.

A. Federal Taxation

Squire v. Capoeman
351 U.S. 1 (1956)

MR. CHIEF JUSTICE WARREN delivered the opinion of the Court.

The question presented is whether the proceeds of the sale by the United States Government of standing timber on allotted lands on the Quinaielt Indian Reservation may be made subject to capital-gains tax, consistently with applicable treaty and statutory provisions and the Government's role as respondents' trustee and guardian.

Respondents, husband and wife, were born on the reservation, and are described by the Government as full-blood, noncompetent* Quinaielt Indians. They have lived

---

* [Editor's note: Under the Burke Act of 1906, discussed in the case, patents in fee could be issued prior to the expiration of the 25-year trust period if the allottee was deemed "competent and capable of managing his or her affairs." Accordingly, a "noncompetent" Indian referred to an allottee who was not awarded a forced-fee patent. The terminology is no longer used by the courts.]

on the reservation all their lives with the exception of the time served by respondent husband in the Armed Forces of the United States during World War II.

Pursuant to the treaty and under the General Allotment Act of 1887, respondent husband was allotted from the treaty-guaranteed reservation 93.25 acres and received a trust patent therefor dated October 1, 1907. During the tax year here in question, the fee title to this land was still held by the United States in trust for him, and was not subject to alienation or encumbrance by him, except with the consent of the United States Government, which consent had never been given.

The Government urges us to view this case as an ordinary tax case without regard to the treaty, relevant statutes, congressional policy concerning Indians, or the guardian-ward relationship between the United States and these particular Indians.

We agree with the Government that Indians are citizens and that in ordinary affairs of life, not governed by treaties or remedial legislation, they are subject to the payment of income taxes as are other citizens. We also agree that, to be valid, exemptions to tax laws should be clearly expressed. But we cannot agree that taxability of respondents in these circumstances is unaffected by the treaty, the trust patent or the Allotment Act.

The courts below held that imposition of the tax here in question is inconsistent with the Government's promise to transfer the fee "free of all charge or incumbrance whatsoever." Although this statutory provision is not expressly couched in terms of nontaxability, this Court has said that

> Doubtful expressions are to be resolved in favor of the weak and defenseless people who are the wards of the nation, dependent upon its protection and good faith.

* * * But Congress, in an amendment to the General Allotment Act, gave additional force to respondents' position. Section 6 of that Act was amended to include a proviso—

> "That the Secretary of the Interior may, in his discretion, and he is authorized, whenever he shall be satisfied that any Indian allottee is competent and capable of managing his or her affairs at any time to cause to be issued to such allottee a patent in fee simple, and thereafter all restrictions as to sale, incumbrance, or taxation of said land shall be removed and said land shall not be liable to the satisfaction of any debt contracted prior to the issuing of such patent . . ."

* * * The literal language of the proviso evinces a congressional intent to subject an Indian allotment to all taxes only after a patent in fee is issued to the allottee. This, in turn, implies that, until such time as the patent is issued, the allotment shall be free from all taxes, both those in being and those which might in the future be enacted.

[In 1925, the] Attorney General advised that he was—

"[U]nable, by implication, to impute to Congress under the broad language of our Internal Revenue Acts an intent to impose a tax for the benefit of the Federal Government on income derived from the restricted property of these wards of the nation; property the management and control of which rests largely in the hands of officers of the Government charged by law with the responsibility and duty of protecting the interests and welfare of these dependent people. In other words, it is not lightly to be assumed that Congress intended to tax the ward for the benefit of the guardian."

On the basis of these opinions and decisions, and a series of district and circuit court decisions, it was said by Felix S. Cohen, an acknowledged expert in Indian law, that "It is clear that the exemption accorded tribal and restricted Indian lands extends to the income derived directly therefrom."

The wisdom of the congressional exemption from tax embodied in Section 6 of the General Allotment Act is manifested by the facts of the instant case. Respondent's timber constitutes the major value of his allotted land. The Government determines the conditions under which the cutting is made. Once logged off, the land is of little value. The land no longer serves the purpose for which it was by treaty set aside to his ancestors, and for which it was allotted to him. It can no longer be adequate to his needs and serve the purpose of bringing him finally to a state of competency and independence. Unless the proceeds of the timber sale are preserved for respondent, he cannot go forward when declared competent with the necessary chance of economic survival in competition with others. This chance is guaranteed by the tax exemption afforded by the General Allotment Act, and the solemn undertaking in the patent. It is unreasonable to infer that, in enacting the income tax law, Congress intended to limit or undermine the Government's undertaking. To tax respondent under these circumstances would, in the words of the court below, be "at the least, a sorry breach of faith with these Indians."

Notes

1. **Applicability of federal tax laws.** A long-standing rule of construction of tax laws provides that "to be valid, exemptions to tax laws should be clearly expressed." *Squire*, 351 U.S. at 6. In some cases, Indian interests have been expressly exempted from general tax laws. *See, e.g.*, statutes cited in notes 4 and 5 below. In other cases, as in *Squire*, the courts have been willing to find congressional intent to exempt Indian interests from taxation where the exemption is not express.

What if a tax law conflicts with a treaty provision? In *The Cherokee Tobacco*, 78 U.S. 616 (1871), the Supreme Court first addressed this issue. An 1866 treaty with the Cherokee had guaranteed the tribe the right to sell natural and manufactured products without "paying any tax thereon which is now or may be levied by the United States." Two years later, in 1868, the federal government imposed an excise tax on liquor and tobacco "produced anywhere within the exterior boundaries of the United States." The Court held that, notwithstanding the treaty provision, the Cherokees were subject to the excise tax on their tobacco. The Court noted that an act of Congress may supersede a prior treaty, and stated that the excise tax act "embraces indisputably the Indian territories. Congress not having thought proper to exclude them, it is not for this court to make the exception. If the exemption had been intended it would doubtless have been expressed." A dozen years later, however, the Court refused to follow *The Cherokee Tobacco*, and held that federal laws must "be construed so as to conform to the provisions of a treaty, if it be possible to do so without violence to their language." *United States v. 43 Gallons of Whiskey*, 108 U.S. 491 (1883).

2. The "derived directly" test. Under the test articulated in *Squire*, income which is derived directly from allotments held in trust is not subject to federal taxation. Some courts have attempted to articulate a standard for determining which income is "derived directly" from allotted land. "Income is derived directly if is generated principally from the use of reservation land and resources. It is not derived directly if was earned primarily through a combination of taxpayer labor, the sale of goods produced off the reservation, and improvements constructed on the trust land." *Dillon v. United States*, 792 F.2d 849 (9th Cir. 1986). Income is not directly derived if it is attributable primarily to use of the capital improvements constructed on the land and the individual's management of those assets or business activities related to those assets. *Critzer v. United States*, 597 F.2d 708 (Ct. Cl. 1979).

Using these or similar formulations of the "derived directly" prong, courts have held that income which allottees earned from bonuses and royalties on minerals, from the rental or sale of crops, or from the sale or exchange of livestock, is tax exempt. *Big Eagle v. United States*, 300 F.2d 765 (Ct. Cl. 1962); *United States v. Daney*, 370 F.2d 791 (10th Cir. 1966); Rev. Rul. 62-16, 1962-1 C.B. 7. Conversely, reinvestment income or income derived from operation of a business is not derived directly from the land. *Superintendent of Five Civilized Tribes v. Commissioner of Internal Revenue*, 295 U.S. 418 (1935); *Critzer*, 597 F.2d 708; *Dillon*, 792 F.2d 849; *Satiacum*, T.C.M. (P-H) 1601 (1986).

The derived directly standard is fairly strictly construed. For example, the Tax Court considered the case of a Navajo woman who raised and trained quarterhorses on her allotment and derived income from the sale of the horses. She purchased the horses off the reservation. Water for the horses was piped in. And because she did not have grazing rights on the reservation, all feed for the horses was purchased off the reservation. The court concluded that her income from the sale of horses was taxable because it was not derived directly from the land. "She conducted her activities on the land but in no way exploited it so as to reduce its value, nor has she taken anything away from her land or relied on any resources peculiar to that land." *Arviso v. Commissioner of Internal Revenue*, T.C. Memo 1992-685, 20 Indian L. Rep. 7001 (1993).

3. Income derived from tribal trust lands. Under *Squire*, an individual's income is only tax exempt if it is derived directly from allotted lands held in trust for that individual. Courts have consistently refused to extend the reasoning of *Squire* to individual income derived from tribal trust lands. *See Holt v. Commissioner*, 364 F.2d 38 (8th Cir. 1966) (tribal member's income derived from grazing cattle on tribal trust lands). *See also Red Lake Band of Chippewa Indians v. United States*, 861 F.Supp. 841

(D. Minn. 1994) (refusing to find a treaty-based exemption for income of tribal members derived from logging activities on tribal trust lands).

4. Taxation of Indian treaty fishing rights. All tribes retain rights to hunt and fish within their reservations. *See* Chapter VIII. Moreover, many tribes—particularly in the Pacific Northwest and the western Great Lakes—reserved off-reservation hunting and fishing rights in their treaties. Given that these rights are guaranteed by treaty, can income from the exercise of these rights be taxed by the federal government? Can income from the off-reservation rights be taxed by the states?

Historically, the federal government did tax Indian commercial fishing income. First, federal courts found the *Squire* analysis inapplicable, analogizing the communal fishing right to communal tribal property. Accordingly, the courts found that fishing income derived from common, unallotted tribal property and was therefore taxable. The courts also rejected the argument that imposition of federal income taxes interfered with the right to fish guaranteed by treaty:

> We do not agree with the argument that the imposition of the tax upon income earned by these petitioners in carrying on a commercial fishing business on the Quinaielt River is a restriction upon the *right* to fish guaranteed by treaty.... The disputed income tax is not a burden upon the *right to fish*, but upon the income earned through the exercise of that right.

Strom v. Commissioner of Internal Revenue, 6 T.C. 621 (1946), *aff'd per curiam*, 158 F.2d 520 (9th Cir. 1947) (emphasis in original); *see also Earl v. Commissioner*, 78 T.C. 1014 (1982).

As for state taxation, a state generally cannot tax the income of tribal members who live and work within reservation boundaries. (*See infra* section C.) By definition, however, much of Indian commercial fishing income is earned through the exercise of off-reservation treaty rights. So, historically, that income was taxable as well by the states.

In 1988, however, Congress amended the Internal Revenue Code and Title 25 of the U.S. Code to prohibit both federal and state taxation of income from the exercise of treaty fishing rights. Note, however, that these laws technically apply to fishing rights only, and not to income earned through the exercise of hunting or other usufructuary rights reserved by treaty. *See* 26 U.S.C. § 7873 (federal tax) and 25 U.S.C. § 71 (state tax).

5. Federal taxation of tribes. Absent some express provision in a statute or a treaty, Indians and Indian tribes are generally subject to federal taxation as any other person or entity. *United States v. Anderson*, 625 F.2d 910 (9th Cir. 1980). Some federal statutes expressly exempt Indian tribes from certain taxes. For example, the Indian Tribal Intergovernmental Tax Status Act of 1982, 26 U.S.C. § 7871(a)(2), exempts tribes from a number of federal taxes such as the manufacturer's excise tax. In addition, the Internal Revenue Service has determined that an Indian tribe is not a taxable entity under the federal income tax statutes. *See* Rev. Ruling 67-284, 1967-2 C.B. 55. The federal income tax applies to every individual, estate and trust, and corporation; the IRS concluded that because an Indian tribe is none of these, it is not taxable on its income.

The federal courts, however, have allowed for the application of federal taxes on individual members of tribes, even when the income being taxed derives directly from a tribe's trust account. In *Cypress v. United States*, 646 Fed. Appx. 748 (11th Cir. 2016), sixteen members of the Miccosukee Tribe of Florida brought a claim against the United States and its representatives seeking declaratory relief in order to avoid federal income tax on distributions, including gaming proceeds, paid to them directly from the Tribe's trust account. The Eleventh Circuit affirmed the lower court's decision that the federal courts lacked subject matter jurisdiction over the claim, as the United States had not waived its sovereign immunity as to the members' claim.

6. Tribal access to tax-exempt bonds. Access to tax-exempt bonds is a key component for successful economic development within Indian country. For a discussion of tribes' ability to utilize tax-exempt bonds, see Gavin Clarkson, *Tribal Bonds: Statutory Shackles and Regulatory Restraints on Tribal Economic Development*, 85 N.C. L. Rev. 1009 (2007). Dr. Clarkson has also written extensively on other financial tools important for tribal economic development. *See* Gavin Clarkson, *Accredited Indians: Increasing the Flow of Private Equity into Indian Country as a Domestic Emerging Market*, 80 U. Colo. L. Rev. 285 (2009); Gavin Clarkson, *Wall Street Indians: Information Asymmetry and Barriers to Tribal Capital Market Access*, 12 Lewis & Clark L. Rev. 943 (2008).

B. Tribal Taxation

In the same way that tribes retain authority to regulate the conduct of their members inside Indian country and to regulate Indian lands within Indian country, see Chapter IV, tribes also retain the power to tax their members.

The issue of tribal taxation has generally arisen in the context of tribal attempts to tax non-Indians, particularly non-Indian mineral lessees. By the time that issue was squarely before the Supreme Court, however, the Court had already addressed tribal taxing authority twice. In *Washington v. Confederated Tribes of the Colville Indian Reservation*, 447 U.S. 134 (1980), the Court upheld tribal cigarette taxes on non-Indian purchasers at tribal stores:

> The power to tax transactions occurring on trust lands and significantly involving a tribe or its members is a fundamental attribute of sovereignty which the tribes retain unless divested of it by federal law or necessary implication of their dependent status. * * * The widely held understanding within the Federal Government has always been that federal law to date has not worked a divestiture of Indian taxing power.

The next year, in *Montana v. United States*, 450 U.S. 544 (1981) (excerpted at page 249), the Court recognized two circumstances under which tribes could retain regulatory authority over non-Indians in Indian country without congressional delegation or recognition: consensual relationships and direct effects on tribal governmental interests. The consensual relationship test provided that:

> A tribe may regulate, through *taxation*, licensing, or other means, the activities of nonmembers who enter into consensual relationships with the tribe or its members, through commercial dealing, contracts, *leases*, or other arrangements.

Id. at 565 (emphasis added). Nonetheless, the issue of the tribal power to tax lessees was not squarely before the Court until the *Merrion* case in 1982.

Merrion v. Jicarilla Apache Tribe
455 U.S. 130 (1982)

JUSTICE MARSHALL delivered the opinion of the Court.

Pursuant to long-term leases with the Jicarilla Apache Tribe, petitioners, 21 lessees, extract and produce oil and gas from the Tribe's reservation lands. In these two consolidated cases, petitioners challenge an ordinance enacted by the Tribe imposing a severance tax on "any oil and natural gas severed, saved and removed from Tribal lands." We granted certiorari to determine whether the Tribe has the authority to impose this tax.

I

The Jicarilla Apache Tribe resides on a reservation in northwestern New Mexico. Established by Executive Order in 1887,[1] the reservation contains 742,315 acres, all of which are held as tribal trust property. The 1887 Executive Order set aside public lands in the Territory of New Mexico for the use and occupation of the Jicarilla Apache Indians, and contained no special restrictions except for a provision protecting pre-existing rights of bona fide settlers. Approximately 2,100 individuals live on the reservation, with the majority residing in the town of Dulce, N. M., near the Colorado border.

The Tribe is organized under the Indian Reorganization Act of 1934, 25 U.S.C. § 461 *et seq.*, which authorizes any tribe residing on a reservation to adopt a constitution and bylaws, subject to the approval of the Secretary of the Interior (Secretary). The Tribe's first Constitution, approved by the Secretary on August 4, 1937, preserved all powers conferred by § 16 of the Indian Reorganization Act of 1934. In 1968, the Tribe revised its Constitution to specify:

> "The inherent powers of the Jicarilla Apache Tribe, including those conferred by Section 16 of the Act of June 18, 1934, shall vest in the tribal council and shall be exercised thereby subject only to limitations imposed by the Constitution of the United States, applicable Federal statutes and regulations of

---

1. * * * The fact that the Jicarilla Apache Reservation was established by Executive Order rather than by treaty or statute does not affect our analysis; the Tribe's sovereign power is not affected by the manner in which its reservation was created.

the Department of the Interior, and the restrictions established by this revised constitution."

The Revised Constitution provides that "[the] tribal council may enact ordinances to govern the development of tribal lands and other resources." It further provides that "[the] tribal council may levy and collect taxes and fees on tribal members, and may enact ordinances, subject to approval by the Secretary of the Interior, to impose taxes and fees on non-members of the tribe doing business on the reservation." The Revised Constitution was approved by the Secretary on February 13, 1969.

To develop tribal lands, the Tribe has executed mineral leases encompassing some 69% of the reservation land. Beginning in 1953, the petitioners entered into leases with the Tribe. The Commissioner of Indian Affairs, on behalf of the Secretary, approved these leases, as required by the Act of May 11, 1938, 25 U.S.C. §§ 396a–396g (1938 Act). In exchange for a cash bonus, royalties, and rents, the typical lease grants the lessee "the exclusive right and privilege to drill for, mine, extract, remove, and dispose of all the oil and natural gas deposits in or under" the leased land for as long as the minerals are produced in paying quantities. Petitioners may use oil and gas in developing the lease without incurring the royalty. In addition, the Tribe reserves the rights to use gas without charge for any of its buildings on the leased land, and to take its royalties in kind. Petitioners' activities on the leased land have been subject to taxes imposed by the State of New Mexico on oil and gas severance and on oil and gas production equipment. *See* Act of Mar. 3, 1927, 25 U.S.C. § 398c (permitting state taxation of mineral production on Indian reservations) (1927 Act).

Pursuant to its Revised Constitution, the Tribal Council adopted an ordinance imposing a severance tax on oil and gas production on tribal land. The ordinance was approved by the Secretary, through the Acting Director of the Bureau of Indian Affairs, on December 23, 1976. The tax applies to "any oil and natural gas severed, saved and removed from Tribal lands. . . ." The tax is assessed at the wellhead at $0.05 per million Btu's of gas produced and $0.29 per barrel of crude oil or condensate produced on the reservation, and it is due at the time of severance. Oil and gas consumed by the lessees to develop their leases or received by the Tribe as in-kind royalty payments are exempted from the tax.

In two separate actions, petitioners sought to enjoin enforcement of the tax by either the tribal authorities or the Secretary. The United States District Court for the District of New Mexico consolidated the cases, granted other lessees leave to intervene, and permanently enjoined enforcement of the tax. * * * The United States Court of Appeals for the Tenth Circuit, sitting en banc, reversed. * * * We granted certiorari, and we now affirm the decision of the Court of Appeals.

II

Petitioners argue, and the dissent agrees, that an Indian tribe's authority to tax non-Indians who do business on the reservation stems exclusively from its power to exclude such persons from tribal lands. Because the Tribe did not initially condition the leases upon the payment of a severance tax, petitioners assert that the Tribe is without authority to impose such a tax at a later time. We disagree with the premise that the power to tax derives only from the power to exclude. Even if that premise is accepted, however, we disagree with the conclusion that the Tribe lacks the power to impose the severance tax.

A.

In *Washington v. Confederated Tribes of Colville Indian Reservation*, 447 U.S. 134 (1980) (*Colville*), we addressed the Indian tribes' authority to impose taxes on non-Indians doing business on the reservation. We held that "[the] power to tax transactions occurring on trust lands and significantly involving a tribe or its members is a fundamental attribute of sovereignty which the tribes retain unless divested of it by federal law or necessary implication of their dependent status." The power to tax is an essential attribute of Indian sovereignty because it is a necessary instrument of self-government and territorial management. This power enables a tribal government to raise revenues for its essential services. The power does not derive solely from the Indian tribe's power to exclude non-Indians from tribal lands. Instead, it derives from the tribe's general authority, as sovereign, to control economic activity within its jurisdiction, and to defray the cost of providing governmental services by requiring contributions from persons or enterprises engaged in economic activities within that jurisdiction.

The petitioners avail themselves of the "substantial privilege of carrying on business" on the reservation. They benefit from the provision of police protection and other governmental services, as well as from "'the advantages of a civilized society'" that are assured by the existence of tribal government. Numerous other governmental entities levy a general revenue tax similar to that imposed by the Jicarilla Tribe when they provide comparable services. Under these circumstances, there is nothing exceptional in requiring petitioners to contribute through taxes to the general cost of tribal government.

As we observed in *Colville*, the tribe's interest in levying taxes on nonmembers to raise "revenues for essential governmental programs ... is strongest when the revenues are derived from value generated on the reservation by activities involving the Tribes and when the taxpayer is the recipient of tribal services." This surely is the case here. The mere fact that the government imposing the tax also enjoys rents and royalties as the lessor of the mineral lands does not undermine the government's authority to impose the tax. The royalty payments from the mineral leases are paid to the Tribe in its role as partner in petitioners' commercial venture. The severance tax, in contrast, is petitioners' contribution "to the general cost of providing governmental services." State governments commonly receive both royalty payments and severance taxes from lessees of mineral lands within their borders.

Viewing the taxing power of Indian tribes as an essential instrument of self-government and territorial management has been a shared assumption of all three branches of the Federal Government.

Thus, the views of the three federal branches of government, as well as general principles of taxation, confirm that Indian tribes enjoy authority to finance their governmental services through taxation of non-Indians who benefit from those services. Indeed, the conception of Indian sovereignty that this Court has consistently reaffirmed permits no other conclusion. As we observed in *United States v. Mazurie*, 419 U.S. 544, 557 (1975), "Indian tribes within 'Indian country' are a good deal more than 'private, voluntary organizations.'" They "are unique aggregations possessing attributes of sovereignty over both their members and their territory." Adhering to this understanding, we conclude that the Tribe's authority to tax non-Indians who conduct business on the reservation does not simply derive from the Tribe's power to exclude such persons, but is an inherent power necessary to tribal self-government and territorial management.

Of course, the Tribe's authority to tax nonmembers is subject to constraints not imposed on other governmental entities: the Federal Government can take away this power, and the Tribe must obtain the approval of the Secretary before any tax on nonmembers can take effect. These additional constraints minimize potential concern that Indian tribes will exercise the power to tax in an unfair or unprincipled manner, and ensure that any exercise of the tribal power to tax will be consistent with national policies.

We are not persuaded by the dissent's attempt to limit an Indian tribe's authority to tax non-Indians by asserting that its only source is the tribe's power to exclude such persons from tribal lands. Limiting the tribes' authority to tax in this manner contradicts the conception that Indian tribes are domestic, dependent nations, as well as the common understanding that the sovereign taxing power is a tool for raising revenue necessary to cover the costs of government.

* * * Instead, based on the views of each of the federal branches, general principles of taxation, and the conception of Indian tribes as domestic, dependent nations, we conclude that the Tribe has the authority to impose a severance tax on the mining activities of petitioners as part of its power to govern and to pay for the costs of self-government.

B.

Alternatively, if we accept the argument, advanced by petitioners and the dissent, that the Tribe's authority to tax derives solely from its power to exclude non-Indians from the reservation, we conclude that the Tribe has the authority to impose the severance tax challenged here. Nonmembers who lawfully enter tribal lands remain subject to the tribe's power to exclude them. This power necessarily includes the lesser power to place conditions on entry, on continued presence, or on reservation conduct, such as a tax on business activities conducted on the reservation. When a tribe grants a non-Indian the right to be on Indian land, the tribe agrees not to exercise its ultimate power to oust the non-Indian as long as the non-Indian complies with the initial conditions of entry. However, it does not follow that the lawful property right to be on Indian land also immunizes the non-Indian from the tribe's exercise of its lesser-included power to tax or to place other conditions on the non-Indian's conduct or continued presence on the reservation. A nonmember who enters the jurisdiction of the tribe remains subject to the risk that the tribe will later exercise its sovereign power. The fact that the tribe chooses not to exercise its power to tax when it initially grants a non-Indian entry onto the reservation does not permanently divest the tribe of its authority to impose such a tax.

Petitioners argue that their leaseholds entitle them to enter the reservation and exempt them from further exercises of the Tribe's sovereign authority. Similarly, the dissent asserts that the Tribe has lost the power to tax petitioners' mining activities because it has leased to them the use of the mineral lands and such rights of access to the reservation as might be necessary to enjoy the leases. However, this conclusion is not compelled by linking the taxing power to the power to exclude. Instead, it is based on additional assumptions and confusions about the consequences of the commercial arrangement between petitioners and the Tribe.

Most important, petitioners and the dissent confuse the Tribe's role as commercial partner with its role as sovereign. This confusion relegates the powers of sovereignty to the bargaining process undertaken in each of the sovereign's commercial agreements. It is one thing to find that the Tribe has agreed to sell the right to use the land and take from it valuable minerals; it is quite another to find that the Tribe has abandoned its sovereign powers simply because it has not expressly reserved them through a contract.

Confusing these two results denigrates Indian sovereignty. Indeed, the dissent apparently views the tribal power to exclude, as well as the derivative authority to tax, as merely the power possessed by any individual landowner or any social group to attach conditions, including a "tax" or fee, to the entry by a stranger onto private land or into the social group, and not as a sovereign power. * * * [I]n arguing that the Tribe somehow "lost" its power to tax petitioners by not including a taxing provision in the original leases or otherwise notifying petitioners that the Tribe retained and might later exercise its sovereign right to tax them, the dissent attaches little significance to the sovereign nature of the tribal authority to tax, and it obviously views tribal authority as little more than a landowner's contractual right.

Moreover, the dissent implies that the power to tax depends on the consent of the taxed as well as on the Tribe's power to exclude non-Indians. Whatever place consent may have in contractual matters and in the creation of democratic governments, it has little if any role in measuring the validity of an exercise of legitimate sovereign authority. Requiring the consent of the entrant deposits in the hands of the excludable non-Indian the source of the tribe's power, when the power instead derives from sovereignty itself. Only the Federal Government may limit a tribe's exercise of its sovereign authority. Indian sovereignty is not conditioned on the assent of a nonmember; to the contrary, the nonmember's presence and conduct on Indian lands are conditioned by the limitations the tribe may choose to impose.

Viewed in this light, the absence of a reference to the tax in the leases themselves hardly impairs the Tribe's authority to impose the tax. Contractual arrangements remain subject to subsequent legislation by the presiding sovereign. Even where the contract at issue requires payment of a royalty for a license or franchise issued by the governmental entity, the government's power to tax remains unless it "has been specifically surrendered in terms which admit of no other reasonable interpretation."

To state that Indian sovereignty is different than that of Federal, State or local Governments, does not justify ignoring the principles announced by this Court for determining whether a sovereign has waived its taxing authority in cases involving city, state, and federal taxes imposed under similar circumstances. Each of these governments has different attributes of sovereignty, which also may derive from different sources. These differences, however, do not alter the principles for determining whether any of these governments has waived a sovereign power through contract, and we perceive no principled reason for holding that the different attributes of Indian sovereignty require different treatment in this regard. Without regard to its source, sovereign power, even when unexercised, is an enduring presence that governs all contracts subject to the sovereign's jurisdiction, and will remain intact unless surrendered in unmistakable terms.

No claim is asserted in this litigation, nor could one be, that petitioners' leases contain the clear and unmistakable surrender of taxing power required for its extinction. We could find a waiver of the Tribe's taxing power only if we inferred it from silence in the leases. To presume that a sovereign forever waives the right to exercise one of its sovereign powers unless it expressly reserves the right to exercise that power in a commercial agreement turns the concept of sovereignty on its head, and we do not adopt this analysis.[14]

IV.

In *Worcester v. Georgia*, 6 Pet., at 559, Chief Justice Marshall observed that Indian tribes had "always been considered as distinct, independent political communities, retaining their original natural rights." Although the tribes are subject to the authority of the Federal Government, the "weaker power does not surrender its independence—its right to self-government, by associating with a stronger, and taking its protection." Adhering to this understanding, we conclude that the Tribe did not surrender its authority to tax the mining activities of petitioners, whether this authority is deemed to arise from the Tribe's inherent power of self-government or from its inherent power to exclude nonmembers. Therefore, the Tribe may enforce its severance

---

14. Petitioners and the dissent also argue that we should infer a waiver of the taxing power from silence in the Tribe's original Constitution. Although it is true that the Constitution in force when petitioners signed their leases did not include a provision specifically authorizing a severance tax, neither the Tribe's Constitution nor the Federal Constitution is the font of any sovereign power of the Indian tribes. Because the Tribe retains all inherent attributes of sovereignty that have not been divested by the Federal Government, the proper inference from silence on this point is that the sovereign power to tax remains intact. The Tribe's Constitution was amended to authorize the tax before the tax was imposed, and this is the critical event necessary to effectuate the tax.

tax unless and until Congress divests this power, an action that Congress has not taken to date.

JUSTICE STEVENS, with whom THE CHIEF JUSTICE and Justice REHNQUIST join, dissenting.

* * * In becoming part of the United States, however, the tribes yielded their status as independent nations; Indians and non-Indians alike answered to the authority of a new Nation, organized under a new Constitution based on democratic principles of representative government. In that new system of government, Indian tribes were afforded no general powers over citizens of the United States. Many tribes, however, were granted a power unknown to any other sovereignty in this Nation: a power to exclude nonmembers entirely from territory reserved for the tribe. Incident to this basic power to exclude, the tribes exercise limited powers of governance over nonmembers, though those nonmembers have no voice in tribal government. Since a tribe may exclude nonmembers entirely from tribal territory, the tribe necessarily may impose conditions on a right of entry granted to a nonmember to do business on the reservation.

The question presented in these cases is whether, after a tribe has granted nonmembers access to its reservation on specified terms and conditions to engage in an economic venture of mutual benefit, the tribe may impose a tax on the nonmembers' share of benefits derived from the venture. The Court today holds that it may do so. In my opinion this holding distorts the very concept of tribal sovereignty. Because I am convinced that the Court's treatment of these important cases gives inadequate attention to the critical difference between a tribe's powers over its own members and its powers over nonmembers, I set forth my views at greater length than is normally appropriate in a dissenting opinion.

* * * Tribal powers over nonmembers are appropriately limited because nonmembers are foreclosed from participation in tribal government. If the power to tax is limited to situations in which the tribe has the power to exclude, then the nonmember is subjected to the tribe's jurisdiction only if he accepts the conditions of entry imposed by the tribe. The limited source of the power to tax nonmembers—the power to exclude intruders—is thus consistent with this Court's recognition of the limited character of the power of Indian tribes over nonmembers in general. The proper source of the taxing authority asserted by the Jicarilla Apache Tribe in these cases, therefore, is not the Tribe's inherent power of self-government, but rather its power over the territory that has been set apart for its use and occupation.

The power to exclude petitioners would have supported the imposition of a discriminatory tribal tax on petitioners when they sought to enter the Jicarilla Apache Reservation to explore for minerals. Moreover, even if no tax had been imposed at the time of initial entry, a discriminatory severance tax could have been imposed as a condition attached to the grant of the privilege of extracting minerals from the earth. But the Tribe did not impose any tax prior to petitioners' entry or as a condition attached to the privileges granted by the leases in 1953. As a result, the tax imposed in 1976 is not valid unless the Tribe retained its power either to exclude petitioners from the reservation or to prohibit them from continuing to extract oil and gas from reservation lands.

Notes

1. Landowner or sovereign. The decision in *Merrion* reiterates a major theme in these materials as well as in Indian law generally: the dichotomy of proprietary rights versus sovereign powers. The Court gave two alternative reasons for upholding the Jicarilla Apache Tribe's power to tax: 1) the taxation power is inherent in the tribe until extinguished by Congress, and 2) the tribe retained the right to tax its mineral lessee because the lease did not clearly waive the tribe's sovereign powers. If the Court had agreed with the lessees, would the tribe have any authority beyond that of an ordinary landowner? Is the Court's approach here materially different from Justice Stevens' approach to regulatory authority in *Brendale,* at page 264, or Justice Thomas' majority opinion in *Bourland*, at page 273? If so, does it make sense for proprietary status to be more determinative of regulatory jurisdiction than tax jurisdiction?

2. Insight into the *Merrion* case. As part of the New Mexico Oral History Project of the University of New Mexico School of Law, Robert Nordhaus, the lead attorney for the Jicarilla Apache Tribe, recalled the case after twenty years. His account, based on the transcripts, is published as Robert J. Nordhaus, G. Emlen Hall & Anne Alise Rudio, *Revisiting* Merrion v. Jicarilla Apache Tribe: *Robert Nordhaus and Sovereign Indian Control over Natural Resources on Reservations*, 43 Nat. Resources J. 223 (2003).

3. Secretarial approval. In *Merrion*, the Court noted that the Jicarilla Apache Tribe must obtain the approval of the Secretary of the Interior before any tribal tax on nonmembers can take effect. The Court used that fact to help ease the fears of nonmember companies that tribes might "exercise the power to tax in an unfair or unprincipled manner." If secretarial approval was so apparently important to the outcome in *Merrion*, what explains the Court's decision in *Kerr-McGee* below? Why is neither federal approval of the Navajo Nation's constitution nor federal approval of the tax required before the Navajo Nation can tax a nonmember business on its reservation?

Kerr-McGee Corp. v. Navajo Tribe of Indians
471 U.S. 195 (1985)

BURGER, C. J., delivered the opinion of the Court, in which all Members joined, except POWELL, J., who took no part in the consideration or decision of the case.

We granted certiorari to decide whether the Navajo Tribe of Indians may tax business activities conducted on its land without first obtaining the approval of the Secretary of the Interior.

I

In 1978, the Navajo Tribal Council, the governing body of the Navajo Tribe of Indians, enacted two ordinances imposing taxes known as the Possessory Interest Tax and the Business Activity Tax. The Possessory Interest Tax is measured by the value of leasehold interests in tribal lands; the tax rate is 3% of the value of those interests. The Business Activity Tax is assessed on receipts from the sale of property produced or extracted within the Navajo Nation, and from the sale of services within the nation; a tax rate of 5% is applied after subtracting a standard deduction and specified expenses. The tax laws apply to both Navajo and non-Indian businesses, with dissatisfied taxpayers enjoying the right of appeal to the Navajo Tax Commission and the Navajo Court of Appeals.

The Navajo Tribe, uncertain whether federal approval was required, submitted the two tax laws to the Bureau of Indian Affairs of the Department of the Interior. The Bureau informed the Tribe that no federal statute or regulation required the Department of the Interior to approve or disapprove the taxes.

Before any taxes were collected, petitioner, a substantial mineral lessee on the Navajo Reservation, brought this action seeking to invalidate the taxes. Petitioner claimed in the United States District Court for the District of Arizona that the Navajo taxes were invalid without approval of the Secretary of the Interior. The District Court agreed and permanently enjoined the Tribe from enforcing its tax laws against petitioner.

The United States Court of Appeals for the Ninth Circuit reversed. * * * We granted certiorari. We affirm.

II

In *Merrion v. Jicarilla Apache Tribe*, 455 U.S. 130 (1982), we held that the "power to tax is an essential attribute of Indian sovereignty because it is a necessary instrument of self-government and territorial management." Congress, of course, may erect "checkpoints that must be cleared before a tribal tax can take effect." The issue in this case is whether Congress has enacted legislation requiring Secretarial approval of Navajo tax laws.

Petitioner suggests that the Indian Reorganization Act of 1934 (IRA or Act) is such a law. Section 16 of the IRA authorizes any tribe on a reservation to adopt a constitution and bylaws, subject to the approval of the Secretary of the Interior. The Act, however, does not provide that a tribal constitution must condition the power to tax on Secretarial approval. Indeed, the terms of the IRA do not govern tribes, like the Navajo, which declined to accept its provisions.

Many tribal constitutions written under the IRA in the 1930s called for Secretarial approval of tax laws affecting non-Indians. But there were exceptions to this practice. For example, the 1937 Constitution and By-laws of the Saginaw Chippewa Indian Tribe of Michigan authorized the Tribal Council, without Secretarial approval, to "create and maintain a tribal council fund by . . . levying taxes or assessments against members or nonmembers." Thus the most that can be said about this period of constitution writing is that the Bureau of Indian Affairs, in assisting the drafting of tribal constitutions, had a policy of including provisions for Secretarial approval; but that policy was not mandated by Congress.

Nor do we agree that Congress intended to recognize as legitimate only those tribal taxes authorized by constitutions written under the IRA. Long before the IRA was enacted, the Senate Judiciary Committee acknowledged the validity of a tax imposed by the Chickasaw Nation on non-Indians. And in 1934, the Solicitor of the Department of the Interior published a formal opinion stating that a tribe possesses "the power of taxation [which] may be exercised over members of the tribe and over nonmembers." The 73d Congress, in passing the IRA to advance tribal self-government, did nothing to limit the established, pre-existing power of the Navajos to levy taxes.

Some tribes that adopted constitutions in the early years of the IRA may be dependent on the Government in a way that the Navajos are not. However, such tribes are free, with the backing of the Interior Department, to amend their constitutions to remove the requirement of Secretarial approval.

Petitioner also argues that the Indian Mineral Leasing Act of 1938 requires Secretarial approval of Navajo tax laws. Sections 1 through 3 of the 1938 Act establish procedures for leasing oil and gas interests on tribal lands. And § 4 provides that "[all] operations under any oil, gas, or other mineral lease issued pursuant to the [Act] shall be subject to the rules and regulations promulgated by the Secretary of the Interior." Under this grant of authority, the Secretary has issued comprehensive regulations governing the operation of oil and gas leases. The Secretary, however, does not demand that tribal laws taxing mineral production be submitted for his approval.

Petitioner contends that the Secretary's decision not to review such tax laws is inconsistent with the statute. In *Merrion*, we emphasized the difference between a tribe's "role as commercial partner," and its "role as sovereign." The tribe acts as a commercial partner when it agrees to sell the right to the use of its land for mineral production, but the tribe acts as a sovereign when it imposes a tax on economic activities within its jurisdiction. Plainly Congress, in passing § 4 of the 1938 Act, could make this same distinction.

Even assuming that the Secretary could review tribal laws taxing mineral production, it does not follow that he must do so. We are not inclined to impose upon the Secretary a duty that he has determined is not needed to satisfy the 1938 Act's basic purpose—to maximize tribal revenues from reservation lands. Thus, in light of our obligation to "tread lightly in the absence of clear indications of legislative intent," we will not interpret a grant of authority to regulate leasing operations as a command to the Secretary to review every tribal tax relating to mineral production.

Finally, we do not believe that statutes requiring Secretarial supervision in other contexts, reveal that Congress has limited the Navajo Tribal Council's authority to tax non-Indians. As we noted in *New Mexico v. Mescalero Apache Tribe*, 462 U.S. 324 (1983), the Federal Government is "firmly committed to the goal of promoting tribal self-government." The power to tax members and non-Indians alike is surely an essential attribute of such self-government; the Navajos can gain independence from the Federal Government only by financing their own police force, schools, and social programs.

III

The Navajo Government has been called "probably the most elaborate" among tribes. The legitimacy of the Navajo Tribal Council, the freely elected governing body of the Navajos, is beyond question. We agree with the Court of Appeals that neither Congress nor the Navajos have found it necessary to subject the Tribal Council's tax laws to review by the Secretary of the Interior; accordingly, the judgment is affirmed.

Notes

1. Taxation of trust allotments. In *Mustang Production Co. v. Harrison*, 94 F.3d 1382 (10th Cir. 1996), excerpted at page 117, the court held that the Cheyenne-Arapaho Tribes retained the civil jurisdiction to tax oil and gas production on trust allotments located within the original boundaries of the Tribes' reservation, on the ground that the off-reservation allotments were Cheyenne-Arapaho Indian country. *See also Pittsburg & Midway Coal Mining Co. v. Watchman*, 52 F.3d 1531, 1542 n.11 (10th Cir. 1995) (noting that "we believe that the Navajo Nation has the authority to apply its Business Activities Tax to the source gains from the 47% portion of the South McKinley Mine that lies within individual Navajo trust allotments.").

2. Taxation of fee lands. If tribes retain the inherent sovereign authority to tax trust allotments because they are Indian country (see 18 U.S.C. § 1151(c)), do they also retain that authority as to fee lands, because fee lands within reservation borders are also Indian country under § 1151(a)? Or was the *Mustang Production* court, writing in 1996, really basing its conclusion on the trust status of the allotted land? In other words, is the jurisdiction to tax based on sovereignty or on property — on the power to exclude? See the unanimous decision of the Supreme Court in the following case.

Atkinson Trading Co., Inc. v. Shirley
532 U.S. 645 (2001)

[In 1992, the Navajo Nation enacted a hotel occupancy tax, imposing an eight percent tax on any hotel room located within the exterior boundaries of the Navajo Nation Reservation. The legal incidence of the tax is on the hotel guests, but the owner of the hotel must collect and remit the tax to the Navajo Tax Commission. Nonmember guests at the Cameron Trading Post paid approximately $84,000 in annual taxes. The owner of the Cameron Trading Post, Atkinson Trading Company, whose land was purchased by its predecessor from the federal government before Congress expanded the Navajo Reservation in 1934 to include its hotel, challenged the occupancy tax.]

[The challenge was rejected by both the Navajo Tax Commission and the Navajo Supreme Court. The U.S. District Court for New Mexico also upheld the tax. A divided panel of the Court of Appeals for the Tenth Circuit affirmed, finding that "a consensual relationship exists in that the nonmember guests could refrain from the privilege of lodging within the confines of the Navajo Reservation and therefore remain free from liability for the [tax]."]

Chief Justice REHNQUIST delivered the opinion of the Court.

In *Montana v. United States,* we held that, with limited exceptions, Indian tribes lack civil authority over the conduct of nonmembers on non-Indian fee land within a reservation. The question with which we are presented is whether this general rule applies to tribal attempts to tax nonmember activity occurring on non-Indian fee land. We hold that it does and that neither of *Montana's* exceptions obtains here.

Tribal jurisdiction is limited: For powers not expressly conferred upon them by federal statute or treaty, Indian tribes must rely upon their retained or inherent sovereignty. In *Montana,* the most exhaustively reasoned of our modern cases addressing this latter authority, we observed that Indian tribe power over nonmembers on non-Indian fee land is sharply circumscribed.

Citing our decision in *Merrion,* respondents submit that *Montana* and *Strate* do not restrict an Indian tribe's power to impose revenue-raising taxes. In *Merrion,* just one year after our decision in *Montana,* we upheld a severance tax imposed by the Jicarilla Apache Tribe upon non-Indian lessees authorized to extract oil and gas from tribal land.

Merrion, however, was careful to note that an Indian tribe's inherent power to tax only extended to "'transactions occurring on *trust lands* and significantly involving a tribe or its members.'" There are undoubtedly parts of the *Merrion* opinion that suggest a broader scope for tribal taxing authority than the quoted language above. But *Merrion* involved a tax that only applied to activity occurring on the reservation, and its holding is therefore easily reconcilable with the *Montana-Strate* line of authority, which we deem to be controlling. See *Merrion, supra,* at 142 ("[A] tribe has no authority over a nonmember until the nonmember enters tribal lands or conducts business with the tribe"). An Indian tribe's sovereign power to tax—whatever its derivation—reaches no further than tribal land.[5]

We therefore do not read *Merrion* to exempt taxation from *Montana's* general rule that Indian tribes lack civil authority over nonmembers on non-Indian fee land. Accordingly, as in *Strate,* we apply *Montana* straight up. [The Court thus applied the *Montana* tests:]

The consensual relationship must stem from "commercial dealing, contracts, leases, or other arrangements," and a nonmember's actual or potential receipt of tribal police, fire, and medical services does not create the requisite connection. If it did, the exception would swallow the rule: All non-Indian fee lands within a reservation

---

5. *** Our reference in *Merrion* to a State's ability to tax activities with which it has a substantial nexus was made in the context of describing an Indian tribe's authority over *tribal land*. Only full territorial sovereigns enjoy the "power to enforce laws against all who come within the sovereign's territory, whether citizens or aliens," and Indian tribes "can no longer be described as sovereigns in this sense." *Duro v. Reina,* 495 U.S. 676, 685 (1990).

benefit, to some extent, from the "advantages of a civilized society" offered by the Indian tribe. * * * We therefore reject respondents' broad reading of *Montana's* first exception, which ignores the dependent status of Indian tribes and subverts the territorial restriction upon tribal power.

Although the Court of Appeals did not reach *Montana's* second exception, both respondents and the United States argue that the hotel occupancy tax is warranted in light of the direct effects the Cameron Trading Post has upon the Navajo Nation. Again noting the Navajo Nation's provision of tribal services and petitioner's status as an "Indian trader," respondents emphasize that petitioner employs almost 100 Navajo Indians; that the Cameron Trading Post derives business from tourists visiting the reservation; and that large amounts of tribal land surround petitioner's isolated property. Although we have no cause to doubt respondents' assertion that the Cameron Chapter of the Navajo Nation possesses an "overwhelming Indian character," we fail to see how petitioner's operation of a hotel on non-Indian fee land "threatens or has some direct effect on the political integrity, the economic security, or the health or welfare of the tribe."[12]

We find unpersuasive respondents' attempt to augment this claim by reference to *Brendale v. Confederated Tribes and Bands of Yakima Nation*, 492 U.S. 408, 440 (1989) (opinion of STEVENS, J.). In this portion of *Brendale,* per the reasoning of two Justices, we held that the Yakima Nation had the authority to zone a small, non-Indian parcel located "in the heart" of over 800,000 acres of closed and largely uninhabited tribal land. Respondents extrapolate from this holding that Indian tribes enjoy broad authority over nonmembers wherever the acreage of non-Indian fee land is minuscule in relation to the surrounding tribal land. But we think it plain that the judgment in *Brendale* turned on both the closed nature of the non-Indian fee land[13] and the fact that its development would place the entire area "in jeopardy." Irrespective of the percentage of non-Indian fee land within a reservation, *Montana's* second exception grants Indian tribes nothing "'beyond what is necessary to protect tribal self-government or to control internal relations.'" Whatever effect petitioner's operation of the Cameron Trading Post might have upon surrounding Navajo land, it does not endanger the Navajo Nation's political integrity.

---

12. * * * The exception is only triggered by *nonmember conduct* that threatens the Indian tribe, [sic] it does not broadly permit the exercise of civil authority wherever it might be considered "necessary" to self-government. Thus, unless the drain of the nonmember's conduct upon tribal services and resources is so severe that it actually "imperil[s]" the political integrity of the Indian tribe, there can be no assertion of civil authority beyond tribal lands. Petitioner's hotel has no such adverse effect upon the Navajo Nation.

13. JUSTICE STEVENS' opinion in *Brendale* sets out in some detail the restrictive nature of "closed area" surrounding the non-Indian fee land. Pursuant to the powers reserved it in an 1855 treaty with the United States, the Yakima Nation closed this forested area to the public and severely limited the activities of those who entered the land through a "courtesy permit system." The record here establishes that, save a few natural areas and parks not at issue, the Navajo reservation is open to the general public.

Justice SOUTER, with whom Justice KENNEDY and Justice THOMAS join, concurring.

If we are to see coherence in the various manifestations of the general law of tribal jurisdiction over non-Indians, the source of doctrine must be *Montana v. United States,* and it is in light of that case that I join the Court's opinion. Under *Montana,* the status of territory within a reservation's boundaries as tribal or fee land may have much to do (as it does here) with the likelihood (or not) that facts will exist that are relevant under the exceptions to Montana's "general proposition" that "the inherent sovereign powers of an Indian tribe do not extend to the activities of nonmembers of the tribe." That general proposition is, however, the first principle, regardless of whether the land at issue is fee land or land owned by or held in trust for an Indian tribe.

Notes

1. Zoning versus taxing. In *Atkinson Trading Co.,* all nine justices ruled against the tribe's power to tax even though the land was on-reservation, and even though with less than four percent nonmember fee land, the land had hardly lost its Indian character. Does the power to zone nonmember fee land, which survived on the closed portion of the Yakama Reservation in *Brendale,* excerpted at page 264, survive *Atkinson Trading Company*? If it does, why is the power to zone "'vital to the maintenance of tribal integrity and self-determination,'" *Atkinson,* 532 U.S. at 658 n.14, while the power to tax is not?

2. Justice Souter's position on land status and the *Montana* tests. Note Justice Souter's concurrence in *Atkinson,* reprinted above in its entirety. His concurrence here foreshadows his concurrence on the same issue one month later in *Nevada v. Hicks,* excerpted at page 276.

3. Taxation of rights-of-way. Rights-of-way through reservations, such as railroads and state highways, are trust land. (Rights-of-way are discussed at pages 363–72.) Consequently, the Ninth Circuit upheld a tribe's right to impose a tax on a railroad's possessory interests within the reservation. *Burlington Northern Railroad Co. v. Blackfeet Tribe,* 924 F.2d 899, 904 (9th Cir. 1991). Six years later, however, the Supreme Court held that, for purposes of tribal jurisdiction over state highways, rights-of-way were the equivalent of fee land:

> Forming part of the State's highway, the right-of-way is open to the public, and traffic on it is subject to the State's control. The Tribes have consented to, and received payment for, the State's use of the 6.59-mile stretch for a public highway. They have retained no gatekeeping right. So long as the stretch is maintained as part of the State's highway, the Tribes cannot assert a landowner's right to occupy and exclude. We therefore align the right-of-way, for the purpose at hand, with land alienated to non-Indians.

Strate v. A-1 Contractors, 520 U.S. 438, 459 (1997) (excerpted at page 275).

Based on *Strate,* the Ninth Circuit expressly overruled *Burlington Northern. Big Horn County Electric Coop. v. Adams,* 219 F.3d 944 (9th Cir. 2000). The Crow Tribe enacted a Railroad and Utility Tax Code, assessing a three percent tax on the full fair market value of utility property located on tribal or trust lands within the Crow Reservation. The utility objected, claiming that the tribe had no authority to tax its property because the property was located on a congressionally granted right-of-way, the equivalent under *Strate* of fee land. The Ninth Circuit agreed that *Strate* governed, even though the tribe argued that the utility's rights-of-way were neither open to the public nor under the control of the state.

Applying the *Montana* tests for tribal authority over nonmembers on fee lands, the court held that neither exception permitted a tribal tax on utility property located on tribal trust lands. The court dismissed the first exception, even though the utility had a consensual relationship with the tribe. Under that exception, the court determined that a tribe could tax the *activities* of nonmembers, but not the value of property owned by nonmembers. In addition, the court determined that the second "direct effects" exception from *Montana* did not apply because the tax was not necessary to protect tribal self-government or control internal relations.

How are rights-of-way different from mineral leases? In *Burlington Northern*, the Ninth Circuit held that: "The Tribes' power to tax nonmembers derives from the Tribes' continuing property interest. Like the continuing property interest in the leases at issue in *Merrion* [citation omitted], this interest was not extinguished by the right-of-way grant." Is a right-of-way, a type of easement, less of a property right than a mineral lease? Does granting a right-of-way mean the land is no longer in trust? After *Nevada v. Hicks*, excerpted at page 276, how relevant is the distinction between trust lands and other lands in any case?

4. Taxation of property versus taxation of activities. As noted above, in *Big Horn Electric*, the Ninth Circuit held that under *Montana*'s consensual relations exception, tribes might be able to tax nonmember activities, but not nonmember property interests. In 2003, the same court affirmed in most respects a district court ruling that Burlington Northern Railroad was not generally subject to a tribal *ad valorem* tax on its right-of-way, but remanded to the district court to determine whether the railroad's activities were sufficient to bring it within the second *Montana* exception. *Burlington Northern Santa Fe Railroad Co. v. Assiniboine and Sioux Tribes of the Fort Peck Reservation*, 323 F.3d 767 (9th Cir. 2003). A concurrence stated that "if trains crossing a tribe's reservation carry toxic or dangerous chemicals, nuclear waste, biological dangers, or other threats to the reservation, then the tribe has a right to know . . . and . . . to assess whether any taxing strategy could fairly cover the tribe's protective costs." *Id.* at 776 (Gould, J., concurring).

Was the Ninth Circuit correct in distinguishing between the activities of nonmembers and the property of nonmembers for purposes of tribal taxation? Are the acquisition, ownership, and development of property not "activities"? If the Crow Tribe now enacted a tax on Big Horn Electric Coop's *use* of its right-of-way, rather than its property interest, would the Ninth Circuit find that tax to be within the consensual relations exception?

5. Continuing relevance of the "reservation" as a basis for jurisdiction. Recall that the Indian country statute defines a reservation as "all land within the limits of any Indian reservation under the jurisdiction of the United States Government, notwithstanding the issuance of any patent, and including rights-of-way running through the reservation." 18 U.S.C. § 1151(a). In *Atkinson Trading Company*, the Court found the Ninth Circuit's reliance on that statute "misplaced," noting that § 1151 is "a statute conferring upon Indian tribes jurisdiction over certain criminal acts." The Court explained:

> Although § 1151 has been relied upon to demarcate state, federal, and tribal jurisdiction over criminal and civil matters, we do not here deal with a claim of statutorily conferred power. Section 1151 simply does not address an Indian tribe's inherent or retained sovereignty over nonmembers on non-Indian fee land.

Is the Court saying that a "reservation" is relevant for jurisdictional purposes only if jurisdiction is delegated by the federal government? If so, what effect might this have on the environmental jurisdiction cases in Chapter IV, Section B.1?

Are the diminishment cases, see Chapter 2, section E.3, still relevant to the issue of tribal civil jurisdiction? The existence of a reservation within the meaning of § 1151(a) remains relevant to such issues as federal criminal jurisdiction, state taxing authority over tribal members, and the provision of federal services to Indians. But what relevance remains for the assertion of inherent tribal regulatory authority?

C. State Taxation

Note on State Taxation of Tribal Interests

As a general principle dating back at least to the mid-nineteenth century, states have no authority—absent congressional consent—to tax Indian tribes, their members, or Indian interests in Indian country. *See, e.g., The Kansas Indians*, 72 U.S. 667 (1867); *The New York Indians*, 72 U.S. 708 (1867). The modern articulation of the principle came in the case of *McClanahan v. State Tax Comm'n of Arizona*, 411 U.S. 164 (1973). In *McClanahan*, the Supreme Court held that state taxation of "a reservation Indian for income earned exclusively on the reservation" was preempted by federal law. *Id.* at 167, 180.

The Court expanded the *McClanahan* doctrine in *Oklahoma Tax Comm'n v. Sac and Fox Nation*, 508 U.S. 114 (1993), excerpted at page 104. In *Sac and Fox*, the Court made clear that the *McClanahan* doctrine extends throughout Indian country, not just on reservations. The *Sac and Fox* Court stated: "Absent explicit congressional direction to the contrary, we presume against a State's having the jurisdiction to tax within Indian country, whether the particular territory consists of a formal or informal reservation, allotted lands, or dependent Indian communities." *Id.* at 128.

More recently, the Court expressly rejected the use of a balancing test to determine whether states could impose taxes on Indians in Indian country. In *Oklahoma Tax Comm'n v. Chickasaw Nation*, 515 U.S. 450 (1995), the Court held unanimously:

> [Because] Congress has not expressly authorized the imposition of Oklahoma's fuels tax on fuel sold by the Tribe, we must decide if the State's exaction is nonetheless permitted. Oklahoma asks us to make the determination by weighing the relevant state and tribal interests, and urges that the balance tilts in its favor. Oklahoma emphasizes that the fuel sold is used "almost exclusively on state roads," imposing "very substantial costs on the State—but no burden at all on the Tribe." The State also stresses that "the levy does not reach any value generated by the Tribe on Indian land," i.e., the fuel is not produced or refined in Indian country, and is often sold to outsiders.
>
> We have balanced federal, state, and tribal interests in diverse contexts, notably, in assessing state regulation that does not involve taxation, and state attempts to compel Indians to collect and remit taxes actually imposed on non-Indians.
>
> But when a State attempts to levy a tax directly on an Indian tribe or its members inside Indian country, rather than on non-Indians, we have employed, instead of a balancing inquiry, "a more categorical approach: 'Absent cession of jurisdiction or other federal statutes permitting it,' we have held, a State is without power to tax reservation lands and reservation Indians." *County of Yakima v. Confederated Tribes and Bands of Yakima Nation*, 502 U.S. 251, 258 (1992). Taking this categorical approach, we have held unenforceable a number of state taxes whose legal incidence rested on a tribe or on tribal members inside Indian country.
>
> The initial and frequently dispositive question in Indian tax cases, therefore, is who bears the legal incidence of a tax. If the legal incidence of an excise tax rests on a tribe or on tribal members for sales made inside Indian country, the tax cannot be enforced absent clear congressional authorization.

Id. at 457–59.

The next three principal cases address the question of congressional consent to state taxation of tribal interests. The *Sac and Fox* Court said congressional authorization must be "explicit;" the *Chickasaw Nation* Court said it must be "clear." In the cases that follow, how clearly must congressional consent be expressed?

County of Yakima v. Confederated Tribes and Bands of the Yakima Indian Nation
502 U.S. 251 (1992)

Justice SCALIA delivered the opinion of the Court.

The question presented by these consolidated cases is whether the County of Yakima may impose an ad valorem tax on so-called "fee-patented" land located within the Yakima Indian Reservation, and an excise tax on sales of such land.

I.A

In the late 19th century, the prevailing national policy of segregating lands for the exclusive use and control of the Indian tribes gave way to a policy of allotting those lands to tribe members individually. The objectives of allotment were simple and clear cut: to extinguish tribal sovereignty, erase reservation boundaries, and force the assimilation of Indians into the society at large.

[The primary means of allotment was] the Indian General Allotment Act of 1887, also known as the Dawes Act, which empowered the President to allot most tribal lands nationwide without the consent of the Indian nations involved. The Dawes Act restricted immediate alienation or encumbrance by providing that each allotted parcel would be held by the United States in trust for a period of 25 years or longer; only then would a fee patent issue to the Indian allottee.

The policy of allotment came to an abrupt end in 1934 with passage of the Indian Reorganization Act. Returning to the principles of tribal self-determination and self-governance which had characterized the pre-Dawes Act era, Congress halted further allotments and extended indefinitely the existing periods of trust applicable to already allotted (but not yet fee-patented) Indian lands. In addition, the Act provided for restoring unallotted surplus Indian lands to tribal ownership, and for acquiring, on behalf of the tribes, lands "within or without existing reservations." Except by authorizing reacquisition of allotted lands in trust, however, Congress made no attempt to undo the dramatic effects of the allotment years on the ownership of former Indian lands. It neither imposed restraints on the ability of Indian allottees to alienate or encumber their fee-patented lands nor impaired the rights of those non-Indians who had acquired title to over two-thirds of the Indian lands allotted under the Dawes Act.

B

The Yakima Indian Reservation, which was established by treaty in 1855, covers approximately 1.3 million acres in southeastern Washington State. Eighty percent of the reservation's land is held by the United States in trust for the benefit of the Tribe or its individual members; 20 percent is owned in fee by Indians and non-Indians as a result of patents distributed during the allotment era. Some of this fee land is owned by the Yakima Indian Nation itself.

The reservation is located almost entirely within the confines of petitioner/cross-respondent Yakima County. Pursuant to Washington law, Yakima County imposes an ad valorem levy on taxable real property within its jurisdiction and an excise tax on sales of such land. According to the county, these taxes have been levied on the Yakima Reservation's fee lands and collected without incident for some time. In 1987, however, as Yakima County proceeded to foreclose on properties throughout the county for which ad valorem and excise taxes were past due, including a number of reservation parcels in which the Tribe or its members had an interest, respondent/cross-petitioner Yakima Nation commenced this action for declaratory and injunctive relief, contending that federal law prohibited these taxes on fee-patented lands held by the Tribe or its members.

II

* * * "[A]bsent cession of jurisdiction or other federal statutes permitting it," we have held, a State is without power to tax reservation lands and reservation Indians. *Mescalero Apache Tribe v. Jones,* 411 U.S. 145, 148 (1973). And our cases reveal a consistent practice of declining to find that Congress has authorized state taxation unless it has "made its intention to do so unmistakably clear." *Montana v. Blackfeet Tribe,* 471 U.S. 759, 765 (1985).

Yakima County persuaded the Court of Appeals, and urges upon us, that express authority for taxation of fee-patented land is found in § 6 of the General Allotment Act, as amended.[1] We have little doubt about the accuracy of that threshold assessment. Our decision in *Goudy v. Meath,* 203 U.S. 146, 149 (1906), without even mentioning the Burke Act proviso, held that state tax laws were "[a]mong the laws to which [Indian allottees] became subject" under § 6 upon the expiration of the Dawes Act trust period. And we agree with the Court of Appeals that by specifically mentioning immunity from land taxation "as one of the restrictions that would be removed upon conveyance in fee," Congress in the Burke Act proviso "manifest[ed] a clear intention to permit the state to tax" such Indian lands.

* * * But (and now we come to the misperception concerning the *structure* of the General Allotment Act) *Goudy* did not rest exclusively, or even primarily, on the § 6 grant of personal jurisdiction over allottees to sustain the land taxes at issue. Instead, it was the *alienability of the allotted lands*—a consequence produced in these cases not by § 6 of the General Allotment Act, but by § 5[3]—that the Court found of central significance. As the first basis of its decision, before reaching the "further" point of

---

1. Section 6 provides in pertinent part:
   "At the expiration of the trust period and when the lands have been conveyed to the Indians by patent in fee, . . . then each and every allottee shall have the benefit of *and be subject to* the laws, both civil and criminal, of the State or Territory in which they may reside. . . . *Provided,* That the Secretary of the Interior may, in his discretion, and he is authorized, whenever he shall be satisfied that any Indian allottee is competent and capable of managing his or her affairs at any time to cause to be issued to such allottee a patent in fee simple, *and thereafter all restrictions as to sale, incumbrance, or taxation of said land shall be removed.*" 25 U.S.C. § 349 (emphasis added).

3. Section 5 of the General Allotment Act provides in part:
   "[A]t the expiration of said [trust] period the United States will convey [the allotted lands] by patent to said Indian . . . in fee, discharged of said trust and free of all charge or incumbrance whatsoever. . . . And if any conveyance shall be made of the lands set apart and allotted as herein provided, or any contract made touching the same, before the expiration of the time above mentioned, such conveyance or contract shall be absolutely null and void. . . ." 25 U.S.C. § 348.

The negative implication of the last quoted sentence, of course, is that a conveyance of allotted land is permitted once the patent issues.

personal jurisdiction under §6, the *Goudy* Court said that, although it was certainly possible for Congress to "grant the power of voluntary sale, while withholding the land from taxation or forced alienation," such an intent would not be presumed unless it was "clearly manifested." For "it would seem strange to withdraw [the] protection [of the restriction on alienation] and permit the Indian to dispose of his lands as he pleases, while at the same time releasing it *[sic]* from taxation." Thus, when §5 rendered the allotted lands alienable and encumberable, it also rendered them subject to assessment and forced sale for taxes.

The Burke Act proviso, enacted in 1906, made this implication of §5 explicit, and its nature more clear. As we have explained, the purpose of the Burke Act was to change the outcome of our decision in *In re Heff,* 197 U.S. 488 (1905), so that §6's general grant of civil and criminal jurisdiction over Indian allottees would not be effective until the 25-year trust period expired and patents were issued in fee. The proviso, however, enabled the Secretary of the Interior to issue fee patents to certain allottees *before* expiration of the trust period. Although such a fee patent would not subject its Indian owner to *plenary* state jurisdiction, fee ownership would free the *land* of "all restrictions as to sale, incumbrance, or taxation." In other words, the proviso reaffirmed for such "prematurely" patented land what §5 of the General Allotment Act implied with respect to patented land generally: subjection to state real estate taxes.[4] And when Congress, in 1934, while putting an end to further allotment of reservation land, chose *not* to return allotted land to pre-General Allotment Act status, leaving it fully alienable by the allottees, their heirs, and assigns, it chose not to terminate state taxation upon those lands as well.

[The Court then held that Yakima County's "ad valorem tax constitutes 'taxation of . . . land' within the meaning of the General Allotment Act and is therefore prima facie valid." The excise tax, however, "is another matter." Noting that the Burke Act authorized "taxation of . . . land," the Court held:]

It does not exceed the bounds of permissible construction to interpret "taxation of land" as including taxation of the proceeds from sale of land; and it is even true that such a construction would be fully in accord with *Goudy*'s emphasis upon the consequences of alienability, which underlay the Burke Act proviso. That is surely not, however, the phrase's unambiguous meaning — as is shown by the Washington Supreme Court's own observation that "a tax upon the sale of property is not a tax upon the subject matter of that sale." It is quite reasonable to say, in other words, that though the object of the *sale* here is land, that does not make land the object of the *tax*, and hence does not invoke the Burke Act proviso. When we are faced with these two possible constructions, our choice between them must be dictated by a

---

4. Since the proviso is nothing more than an acknowledgment (and clarification) of the operation of §5 with respect to *all* fee-patented land, it is inconsequential that the trial record does not reflect "which (if any) of the parcels owned in fee by the Yakima Nation or individual members originally passed into fee status pursuant to the proviso, rather than at the expiration of the trust period. . . ." Brief for United States as *Amicus Curiae* 13, n. 10.

principle deeply rooted in this Court's Indian jurisprudence: "[S]tatutes are to be construed liberally in favor of the Indians, with ambiguous provisions interpreted to their benefit." *Montana v. Blackfeet Tribe,* 471 U.S., at 766.

The short of the matter is that the General Allotment Act explicitly authorizes only "taxation of . . . land," not "taxation with respect to land," "taxation of transactions involving land," or "taxation based on the value of land." Because it is eminently reasonable to interpret that language as not including a tax upon the sale of real estate, our cases require us to apply that interpretation for the benefit of the Tribe. Accordingly, Yakima County's excise tax on sales of land cannot be sustained.

[Opinion of Justice Blackmun, concurring in part and dissenting in part, is omitted.]

Cass County v. Leech Lake Band of Chippewa Indians
524 U.S. 103 (1998)

Justice THOMAS delivered the opinion of the Court.

We granted certiorari in this case to resolve whether state and local governments may tax reservation land that was made alienable by Congress and sold to non-Indians by the Federal Government, but was later repurchased by a tribe. We hold that ad valorem taxes may be imposed upon such land because, under the test established by our precedents, Congress has made "unmistakably clear" its intent to allow such taxation.

I

The Leech Lake Band of Chippewa Indians is a federally recognized Indian tribe. The Leech Lake Reservation, which today encompasses 588,684 acres within the northern Minnesota counties of Cass, Itasca, and Beltrami, was established by federal treaty in 1855 and was augmented by subsequent treaties and executive orders.

Most of the allotments made by the Federal Government were implemented pursuant to the General Allotment Act of 1887 (GAA).

For the Leech Lake Band and other Chippewa tribes in Minnesota, the allotment policy was implemented through the Nelson Act of 1889. The Nelson Act provided for the "complete cession and relinquishment" of tribal title to all reservation land in the state of Minnesota, except for parts of two reservations, to the United States. After such "complete cession and relinquishment," which "operate[d] as a complete extinguishment of Indian title," the lands were to be disposed of in one of three ways: under § 3, the United States would allot parcels to individual tribe members as provided in the GAA; under §§ 4 and 5, so-called "pine lands" (surveyed 40-acre lots with standing or growing pine timber) were to be sold by the United States at public auction to the highest bidder; and under § 6, the remainder of the reservation land (called "agricultural lands") was to be sold by the United States to non-Indian settlers under the provisions of the Homestead Act of 1862.

In 1977, the Leech Lake Band and individual Band members owned only about 27,000 acres—less than five percent—of Leech Lake Reservation land. Since then, the Leech Lake Band has sought to re-establish its land base by purchasing back parcels of reservation land that were allotted to individual Indians or sold to non-Indians during the allotment period.

In 1993, Cass County began assessing ad valorem taxes on 21 parcels of reservation land that had been alienated from tribal control under the various provisions of the Nelson Act and later reacquired by the Leech Lake Band. Thirteen of the parcels had been allotted to individual Indians under §3; seven had been sold to non-Indians as pine lands under §§4 and 5 for commercial timber harvest; and one parcel had been distributed to a non-Indian under §6 as a homestead plot. Under protest and to avoid foreclosure, the Leech Lake Band paid more than $64,000 in taxes, interest, and penalties.

In 1995, the Band filed suit in federal court seeking a declaratory judgment that Cass County could not tax the 21 parcels. [The District Court granted summary judgment to the county, on the ground that "alienability equals taxability" under *Yakima*. The Eighth Circuit reversed in part. It interpreted *Yakima* to authorize ad valorem taxation under the General Allotment Act. Accordingly, it held that the 13 parcels allotted under §3 of the Nelson Act were taxable if they had been patented after the Burke Act proviso, but that the remaining eight parcels sold as pine or homestead lands were not.]

We granted certiorari to decide whether Cass County may impose its ad valorem property tax on the seven parcels sold as pine lands and the one sold as a homestead to non-Indians.

II

In *Yakima*, we considered whether the GAA manifested an unmistakably clear intent to allow state and local taxation of reservation lands allotted under the GAA and owned in fee by either the Yakima Indian Nation or individual Indians. In holding that the lands could be taxed, we noted that the Burke Act proviso clearly manifested such an intent by expressly addressing the taxability of fee-patented land. We also indicated that the alienability of allotted lands itself, as provided by §5 of the GAA, similarly manifested an unmistakably clear intent to allow taxation. We reasoned that *Goudy [v. Meath*, 203 U.S. 146 (1906)], "without even mentioning the Burke Act proviso," had held that state tax laws applied to the Indian allottee at the expiration of the trust period: "[I]t was the alienability of the allotted lands . . . that the [*Goudy*] Court found of central significance." And we reiterated *Goudy*'s point that, although it is possible for Congress to render reservation land alienable and still forbid states from taxing it, this unlikely arrangement would not be presumed unless Congress "clearly manifested" such an intent.

The Court of Appeals thus erred in concluding that our holding in *Yakima* turned on the Burke Act proviso's express reference to taxability. *Yakima*, like *Goudy*, stands for the proposition that when Congress makes reservation lands freely alienable, it is "unmistakably clear" that Congress intends that land to be taxable by state and local governments, unless a contrary intent is "clearly manifested."

The foregoing principle controls the disposition of this case. In §§ 5 and 6 of the Nelson Act, Congress provided for the public sale of pine lands and agricultural "homestead" lands by the Federal Government to non-Indians. Congress thereby removed that reservation land from federal protection and made it fully alienable. Under *Goudy* and *Yakima*, therefore, it is taxable. Indeed, this conclusion flows a fortiori from *Goudy* and *Yakima*: those cases establish that Congress clearly intended reservation lands conveyed in fee to Indians to be subject to taxation; hence Congress surely intended reservation lands conveyed in fee to non-Indians also to be taxable. The Court of Appeals' contrary holding attributes to Congress the odd intent that parcels conveyed to Indians are to assume taxable status, while parcels sold to the general public are to remain tax-exempt.

The Band essentially argues that, although its tax immunity lay dormant during the period when the eight parcels were held by non-Indians, its reacquisition of the lands in fee rendered them non-taxable once again. We reject this contention. As explained, once Congress has demonstrated (as it has here) a clear intent to subject the land to taxation by making it alienable, Congress must make an unmistakably clear statement in order to render it non-taxable. The subsequent repurchase of reservation land by a tribe does not manifest any congressional intent to reassume federal protection of that land and to oust state taxing authority—particularly when Congress explicitly relinquished such protection many years before.

Further, if we were to accept the Leech Lake Band's argument, it would render partially superfluous § 465 of the Indian Reorganization Act. That section grants the Secretary of the Interior authority to place land in trust, to be held by the federal government for the benefit of the Indians and to be exempt from state and local taxation after assuming such status:

> "The Secretary of the Interior is authorized, in his discretion, to acquire, through purchase, relinquishment, gift, exchange, or assignment, and interest in lands ... within or without existing reservations ... for the purpose of providing land for Indians....
>
> "Title to any lands ... shall be taken in the name of the United States in trust for the Indian tribe or individual Indian for which the land is acquired, and such lands ... shall be exempt from State and local taxation."

In § 465, therefore, Congress has explicitly set forth a procedure by which lands held by Indian tribes may become tax-exempt. It would render this procedure unnecessary, as far as exemption from taxation is concerned, if we held that tax-exempt status automatically attaches when a tribe acquires reservation land. The Leech Lake Band apparently realizes this, because in 1995 it successfully applied to the Secretary of the Interior under § 465 to restore federal trust status to seven of the eight parcels at issue here.

When Congress makes Indian reservation land freely alienable, it manifests an unmistakably clear intent to render such land subject to state and local taxation. The repurchase of such land by an Indian tribe does not cause the land to reassume tax-exempt status. The eight parcels at issue here were therefore taxable unless and until they were restored to federal trust protection under §465. The judgment of the Court of Appeals with respect to those lands is reversed.

Notes

1. Land alienability. In *Leech Lake*, the Court made land alienability determinative of the county's taxing jurisdiction. Is the Court correct that such a result was foreordained by *County of Yakima*? Is all land within Indian country that is owned in fee by tribes and their members taxable? Consider the following cases.

In 2002, a divided Second Circuit ruled that land owned by a tribal member but not subject to federal restraints on alienation was subject to county property taxes. *Thompson v. County of Franklin*, 314 F.3d 79 (2d Cir. 2002). The judges in the majority disagreed about the need to decide whether the land was still within the St. Regis Mohawk Reservation, one judge determining that even on-reservation land which is alienable is subject to the county tax. *Id.* at 84 (Winter, J., concurring). The dissent maintained that the land was on-reservation, and that Congress had never made it "unmistakably clear" that it intended to diminish the reservation or to subject land owned by individual tribal members to the county property tax. *Id.* at 88 (Sack, J., dissenting).

In *Keweenaw Bay Indian Community v. Naftaly*, 452 F.3d 514 (6th Cir. 2006), the court held that lands within the reservation owned in fee by the tribe and its members as a result of the Treaty of 1854 were not taxable by the state. The court ruled that Article 11 of the treaty, which stated that "the Indians shall not be required to remove from the homes hereby set apart for them," was ambiguous as to whether it precluded all forms of involuntary alienation, including sale for unpaid taxes. Applying the Indian law canons of construction, the court interpreted the treaty in favor of the Indians, although it also noted that it found the tribe's approach "much more persuasive" in any case. In addition, the court distinguished *Leech Lake* and *County of Yakima*, because in both of those cases Congress had made the land in question freely alienable. In *Keweenaw Bay*, by contrast, the lands were alienable because of the treaty, not because of any statute or other action by Congress. Noting that Congress could make the lands alienable and therefore taxable, the court concluded that because Congress had not done so, the lands were not taxable.

2. The canons of construction. In both *Leech Lake* and *County of Yakima*, the Court agreed that Congress must be "unmistakably clear" in authorizing state and local taxes on Indian interests within reservation boundaries. How was Congress "unmistakably clear" in these cases?

In addition to the "unmistakably clear" rule, the canons of construction in Indian law provide that ambiguous statutes should be resolved in favor of Indian interests. At what point in its analysis does the Court employ this canon in *County of Yakima*? Does the Court invoke the Indian law canons in *Leech Lake*?

In *Quinault Indian Nation v. Grays Harbor County*, 310 F.3d 645 (9th Cir. 2002), the Ninth Circuit struck down the county's "compensating tax" on the transfer of land title from the tribe to the federal government in trust for the tribe. The land at issue was a 4500-acre on-reservation tract of forest land that had fallen out of trust status under the General Allotment Act. The court thought the county tax was closer to an impermissible excise tax than a permissible ad valorem tax.

3. The role of section 5108 (formerly 465). Note the advice that Justice Thomas gave in the last paragraph of the *Leech Lake* opinion. The current § 5108 standards for taking land into trust are excerpted at pages 124. Is Justice Thomas's advice an adequate response to the alienability-equals-taxation approach?

Montana v. Blackfeet Tribe of Indians
471 U.S. 759 (1985)

JUSTICE POWELL delivered the opinion of the Court.

This case presents the question whether the State of Montana may tax the Blackfeet Tribe's royalty interests under oil and gas leases issued to non-Indian lessees pursuant to the Indian Mineral Leasing Act of 1938, 25 U.S.C. § 396a *et seq.* (1938 Act).

I

Respondent Blackfeet Tribe filed this suit in the United States District Court for the District of Montana challenging the application of several Montana taxes[4] to the Tribe's royalty interests in oil and gas produced under leases issued by the Tribe. The leases involved unallotted lands on the Tribe's reservation and were granted to non-Indian lessees in accordance with the 1938 Act. The taxes at issue were paid to the State by the lessees and then deducted by the lessees from the royalty payments made to the Tribe. The Blackfeet sought declaratory and injunctive relief against enforcement of the state tax statutes.[5] * * * The District Court * * * granted the State's motion for summary judgment.

A panel of the United States Court of Appeals for the Ninth Circuit affirmed the District Court's decision. On rehearing en banc, the Court of Appeals reversed in part and remanded the case for further proceedings. * * * We granted the State's petition for certiorari to resolve whether Montana may tax Indian royalty interests arising out of leases executed after the adoption of the 1938 Act. We affirm the decision of the en banc Court of Appeals that it may not.

---

4. At issue are the taxes adopted in the following statutes: the Oil and Gas Severance Tax, Oil and Gas Net Proceeds, Oil and Gas Conservation, and the Resource Indemnity Trust Tax.

5. The Blackfeet properly invoked the jurisdiction of the District Court pursuant to 28 U.S.C. § 1362, which provides:

> "The district courts shall have original jurisdiction of all civil actions, brought by any Indian tribe or band with a governing body duly recognized by the Secretary of the Interior, wherein the matter in controversy arises under the Constitution, laws, or treaties of the United States."

* * * [A] suit by an Indian tribe to enjoin the enforcement of state tax laws is cognizable in the district court under § 1362 despite the general ban in 28 U.S.C. § 1341 against seeking federal injunctions of such laws.

II

Congress first authorized mineral leasing of Indian lands in the Act of Feb. 28, 1891, 25 U.S.C. §397 (1891 Act). The Act authorized leases for terms not to exceed 10 years on lands "bought and paid for" by the Indians. The 1891 Act was amended by the 1924 Act. The amendment provided in pertinent part:

> "Unallotted land . . . subject to lease for mining purposes for a period of ten years under section 397 . . . may be leased . . . by the Secretary of the Interior, with the consent of the [Indian] council . . . , for oil and gas mining purposes for a period of not to exceed ten years, and as much longer as oil or gas shall be found in paying quantities, and the terms of any existing oil and gas mining lease may in like manner be amended by extending the term thereof for as long as oil or gas shall be found in paying quantities: *Provided*, That the production of oil and gas and other minerals on such lands may be taxed by the State in which said lands are located in all respects the same as production on unrestricted lands, and the Secretary of the Interior is authorized and directed to cause to be paid the tax so assessed against the royalty interests on said lands: *Provided*, however, That such tax shall not become a lien or charge of any kind or character against the land or the property of the Indian owner." Act of May 29, 1924, 25 U.S.C. §398.

Montana relies on the first proviso in the 1924 Act in claiming the authority to tax the Blackfeet's royalty payments.

In 1938, Congress adopted comprehensive legislation in an effort to "obtain uniformity so far as practicable of the law relating to the leasing of tribal lands for mining purposes." Like the 1924 Act, the 1938 Act permitted, subject to the approval of the Secretary of the Interior, mineral leasing of unallotted lands for a period not to exceed 10 years and as long thereafter as minerals in paying quantities were produced. The Act also detailed uniform leasing procedures designed to protect the Indians. The 1938 Act did not contain a provision authorizing state taxation; nor did it repeal specifically the authorization in the 1924 Act. A general repealer clause was provided in §7 of the Act: "All Act [sic] or parts of Acts inconsistent herewith are hereby repealed." The question presented by this case is whether the 1924 Act's proviso that authorizes state taxation was repealed by the 1938 Act, or if left intact, applies to leases executed under the 1938 Act.

III

The Constitution vests the Federal Government with exclusive authority over relations with Indian tribes. Art. I, §8, cl. 3. As a corollary of this authority, and in recognition of the sovereignty retained by Indian tribes even after formation of the United States, Indian tribes and individuals generally are exempt from state taxation within their own territory.

In keeping with its plenary authority over Indian affairs, Congress can authorize the imposition of state taxes on Indian tribes and individual Indians. It has not done so often, and the Court consistently has held that it will find the Indians' exemption from state taxes lifted only when Congress has made its intention to do so unmistakably clear. The 1924 Act contains such an explicit authorization. As a result, in *British-American Oil Producing Co. v. Board of Equalization of Montana*, 299 U.S. 159 (1936), the Court held that the State of Montana could tax oil and gas produced under leases executed under the 1924 Act.

The State urges us that the taxing authorization provided in the 1924 Act applies to leases executed under the 1938 Act as well. It argues that nothing in the 1938 Act is inconsistent with the 1924 taxing provision and thus that the provision was not repealed by the 1938 Act. It cites decisions of this Court that a clause repealing only inconsistent Acts "implies very strongly that there may be acts on the same subject which are not thereby repealed," and that such a clause indicates Congress' intent "to leave in force some portions of former acts relative to the same subject-matter." The State also notes that there is a strong presumption against repeals by implication, especially an implied repeal of a specific statute by a general one. Thus, in the State's view, sound principles of statutory construction lead to the conclusion that its taxing authority under the 1924 Act remains intact.

The State fails to appreciate, however, that the standard principles of statutory construction do not have their usual force in cases involving Indian law. As we said earlier this Term, "[the] canons of construction applicable in Indian law are rooted in the unique trust relationship between the United States and the Indians." Two such canons are directly applicable in this case: first, the States may tax Indians only when Congress has manifested clearly its consent to such taxation; second, statutes are to be construed liberally in favor of the Indians, with ambiguous provisions interpreted to their benefit. When the 1924 and 1938 Acts are considered in light of these principles, it is clear that the 1924 Act does not authorize Montana to enforce its tax statutes with respect to leases issued under the 1938 Act.

IV

Nothing in either the text or legislative history of the 1938 Act suggests that Congress intended to permit States to tax tribal royalty income generated by leases issued pursuant to that Act. The statute contains no explicit consent to state taxation. Nor is there any indication that Congress intended to incorporate implicitly in the 1938 Act the taxing authority of the 1924 Act. Contrary to the State's suggestion, under the applicable principles of statutory construction, the general repealer clause of the 1938 Act cannot be taken to incorporate consistent provisions of earlier laws. The clause surely does not satisfy the requirement that Congress clearly consent to state taxation. Nor would the State's interpretation satisfy the rule requiring that statutes be construed liberally in favor of the Indians.

Moreover, the language of the taxing provision of the 1924 Act belies any suggestion that it carries over to the 1938 Act. The tax proviso in the 1924 Act states that "the production of oil and gas and other minerals on such lands may be taxed by the State in which said lands are located. . . ." Even applying ordinary principles of statutory construction, "such lands" refers to "[unallotted] land . . . subject to lease for mining purposes . . . under section 397 [the 1891 Act]." When the statute is "liberally construed . . . in favor of the Indians," it is clear that if the tax proviso survives at all, it reaches only those leases executed under the 1891 Act and its 1924 amendment.

V

In the absence of clear congressional consent to taxation, we hold that the State may not tax Indian royalty income from leases issued pursuant to the 1938 Act. Accordingly, the judgment of the Court of Appeals is affirmed.

Justice WHITE, with whom Justice REHNQUIST and Justice STEVENS join, dissenting.

* * * In my view, the proviso constitutes a sufficiently explicit expression of congressional intent to permit such taxation.

The majority apparently does not rest its contrary holding on the conclusion that the 1938 Act *repealed* the taxing authority contained in the 1924 Act. Although the majority does not appear to come to rest on the question whether the taxing proviso has been repealed, it is clear to me (as it was to both the majority and the dissent in the Court of Appeals) that the 1938 Act did not repeal the proviso. The 1938 Act repealed only Acts inconsistent with its terms, and there is no suggestion that taxation of mineral leases is actually inconsistent with any of the provisions of the 1938 Act. Indeed, given that the 1938 Act and its legislative history are completely silent on the question of taxation, it cannot seriously be suggested that the 1938 Act specifically repealed any taxing authority that might otherwise exist under the 1924 Act.

In so concluding, I am mindful of the general rule that statutes are to be liberally construed in favor of Indian tribes. But more to the point, to my way of thinking, is the proposition that this rule is no more than a canon of construction, and "[a] canon of construction is not a license to disregard clear expressions of . . . congressional intent." The proviso to the 1924 Act is a clear expression of congressional intent to allow the States to tax mineral production under leases of lands described in the Act; the proviso has never been repealed; and the lands that the Blackfeet have leased under the 1938 Act fall within the proviso's description of lands on which mineral production is subject to taxation.

Notes

1. Canons of construction. Because *Blackfeet Tribe* involved a state tax paid by the non-Indian mineral lessees and then deducted from royalty payments to the tribe, the Court treated the issue as one of state taxation of Indians. Compare the Court's analysis in *Blackfeet Tribe* with that in *County of Yakima* and *Leech Lake*. Which rules of statutory construction are used in *Blackfeet Tribe*? Are they same rules the Court used in the two property tax cases? What about the Court's analysis of congressional consent to state taxation? Did that analysis change between the 1985 decision in *Blackfeet Tribe* and the later decisions in *County of Yakima* and *Leech Lake*? If not, what explains the difference in outcome?

2. State taxation of non-Indians. Unlike the *Blackfeet* case, the following cases raise issues of state taxation of non-Indian companies engaged in resource extraction and development in Indian country. The basic analytical framework for determining the validity of state taxation of non-Indian parties was established by the Court in 1980 in the following case. To what extent are these non-Indians subject to state taxation? What factors does the Court consider controlling, and why?

White Mountain Apache Tribe v. Bracker
448 U.S. 136 (1980)

[Under a contract with the Fort Apache Timber Co. (FATCO), a White Mountain Apache tribal business created to manage, harvest, process, and sell timber, Pinetop Logging Co. (Pinetop), a non-Indian enterprise authorized to do business in Arizona, cut tribal timber on the Fort Apache Reservation and transported it to the tribal organization's sawmill. Pinetop's activities were performed solely on the reservation. The state sought to impose on Pinetop Arizona's motor carrier license tax, which is assessed on the basis of the carrier's gross receipts, and its use fuel tax, which is assessed on the basis of diesel fuel used to propel a motor vehicle on any highway within the State. Pinetop paid the taxes under protest and then brought suit in state court, asserting that under federal law the taxes could not lawfully be imposed on logging activities conducted exclusively within the reservation or on hauling activities on Bureau of Indian Affairs (BIA) and tribal roads. The trial court awarded summary judgment to the state, and the Arizona Court of Appeals affirmed in pertinent part, rejecting petitioners' pre-emption claim.]

Justice MARSHALL delivered the opinion of the Court.

II

Although "[generalizations] on this subject have become . . . treacherous," our decisions establish several basic principles with respect to the boundaries between state regulatory authority and tribal self-government. Long ago the Court departed from Mr. Chief Justice Marshall's view that "the laws of [a State] can have no force" within reservation boundaries, *Worcester v. Georgia*, 6 Pet. 515, 561 (1832). At the same time we have recognized that the Indian tribes retain "attributes of sovereignty over both their members and their territory." As a result, there is no rigid rule by which to resolve the question whether a particular state law may be applied to an Indian reservation or to tribal members. The status of the tribes has been described as "'an anomalous one and of complex character,'" for despite their partial assimilation into American culture, the tribes have retained "'a semi-independent position . . . not as States, not as nations, not as possessed of the full attributes of sovereignty, but as a separate people, with the power of regulating their internal and social relations, and thus far not brought under the laws of the Union or of the State within whose limits they resided.'"

Congress has broad power to regulate tribal affairs under the Indian Commerce Clause, Art. 1, § 8, cl. 3. This congressional authority and the "semi-independent position" of Indian tribes have given rise to two independent but related barriers to the assertion of state regulatory authority over tribal reservations and members. First, the exercise of such authority may be pre-empted by federal law. Second, it may unlawfully infringe "on the right of reservation Indians to make their own laws and be ruled by them." The two barriers are independent because either, standing alone, can be a sufficient basis for holding state law inapplicable to activity undertaken on the reservation or by tribal members. They are related, however, in two important ways. The right of tribal self-government is ultimately dependent on and subject to the broad power of Congress. Even so, traditional notions of Indian self-government are so deeply engrained in our jurisprudence that they have provided an important "backdrop," against which vague or ambiguous federal enactments must always be measured.

The unique historical origins of tribal sovereignty make it generally unhelpful to apply to federal enactments regulating Indian tribes those standards of pre-emption that have emerged in other areas of the law. Tribal reservations are not States, and the differences in the form and nature of their sovereignty make it treacherous to import to one notions of pre-emption that are properly applied to the other. The tradition of Indian sovereignty over the reservation and tribal members must inform the determination whether the exercise of state authority has been pre-empted by operation of federal law. As we have repeatedly recognized, this tradition is reflected and encouraged in a number of congressional enactments demonstrating a firm federal policy of promoting tribal self-sufficiency and economic development. Ambiguities in federal law have been construed generously in order to comport with these traditional notions of sovereignty and with the federal policy of encouraging tribal independence. We have thus rejected the proposition that in order to find a particular state law to have been pre-empted by operation of federal law, an express congressional statement to that effect is required. At the same time any applicable regulatory interest of the State must be given weight, and "automatic exemptions 'as a matter of constitutional law'" are unusual.

When on-reservation conduct involving only Indians is at issue, state law is generally inapplicable, for the State's regulatory interest is likely to be minimal and the federal interest in encouraging tribal self-government is at its strongest. More difficult questions arise where, as here, a State asserts authority over the conduct of non-Indians engaging in activity on the reservation. In such cases we have examined the language of the relevant federal treaties and statutes in terms of both the broad policies that underlie them and the notions of sovereignty that have developed from historical traditions of tribal independence. This inquiry is not dependent on mechanical or absolute conceptions of state or tribal sovereignty, but has called for a particularized inquiry into the nature of the state, federal, and tribal interests at stake, an inquiry designed to determine whether, in the specific context, the exercise of state authority would violate federal law.

III

With these principles in mind, we turn to the respondents' claim that they may, consistent with federal law, impose the contested motor vehicle license and use fuel taxes on the logging and hauling operations of petitioner Pinetop. At the outset we observe that the Federal Government's regulation of the harvesting of Indian timber is comprehensive. That regulation takes the form of Acts of Congress, detailed regulations promulgated by the Secretary of the Interior, and day-to-day supervision by the Bureau of Indian Affairs. Under 25 U.S.C. §§ 405–407, the Secretary of the Interior is granted broad authority over the sale of timber on the reservation. Timber on Indian land may be sold only with the consent of the Secretary, and the proceeds from any such sales, less administrative expenses incurred by the Federal Government, are to be used for the benefit of the Indians or transferred to the Indian owner. Sales of timber must "be based upon a consideration of the needs and best interests of the Indian owner and his heirs." The statute specifies the factors which the Secretary must consider in making that determination. In order to assure the continued productivity of timber-producing land on tribal reservations, timber on unallotted lands "may be sold in accordance with the principles of sustained yield." The Secretary is granted power to determine the disposition of the proceeds from timber sales. He is authorized to promulgate regulations for the operation and management of Indian forestry units.

Acting pursuant to this authority, the Secretary has promulgated a detailed set of regulations to govern the harvesting and sale of tribal timber. Among the stated objectives of the regulations is the "development of Indian forests by the Indian people for the purpose of promoting self-sustaining communities, to the end that the Indians may receive from their own property not only the stumpage value, but also the benefit of whatever profit it is capable of yielding and whatever labor the Indians are qualified to perform." The regulations cover a wide variety of matters: for example, they restrict clear-cutting, establish comprehensive guidelines for the sale of timber, regulate the advertising of timber sales, specify the manner in which bids may be accepted and rejected, describe the circumstances in which contracts may be entered into, require the approval of all contracts by the Secretary, call for timber-cutting permits to be approved by the Secretary, specify fire protective measures, and provide a board of administrative appeals. Tribes are expressly authorized to establish commercial enterprises for the harvesting and logging of tribal timber.

Under these regulations, the Bureau of Indian Affairs exercises literally daily supervision over the harvesting and management of tribal timber. In the present case, contracts between FATCO and Pinetop must be approved by the Bureau; indeed, the record shows that some of those contracts were drafted by employees of the Federal Government. Bureau employees regulate the cutting, hauling, and marking of timber by FATCO and Pinetop. The Bureau decides such matters as how much timber will be cut, which trees will be felled, which roads are to be used, which hauling equipment Pinetop should employ, the speeds at which logging equipment may travel, and the width, length, height, and weight of loads.

The Secretary has also promulgated detailed regulations governing the roads developed by the Bureau of Indian Affairs. Bureau roads are open to "[free] public use." Their administration and maintenance are funded by the Federal Government, with contributions from the Indian tribes. On the Fort Apache Reservation the Forestry Department of the Bureau has required FATCO and its contractors, including Pinetop, to repair and maintain existing Bureau and tribal roads and in some cases to construct new logging roads. Substantial sums have been spent for these purposes. In its federally approved contract with FATCO, Pinetop has agreed to construct new roads and to repair existing ones. A high percentage of Pinetop's receipts are expended for those purposes, and it has maintained separate personnel and equipment to carry out a variety of tasks relating to road maintenance.

In these circumstances we agree with petitioners that the federal regulatory scheme is so pervasive as to preclude the additional burdens sought to be imposed in this case. Respondents seek to apply their motor vehicle license and use fuel taxes on Pinetop for operations that are conducted solely on Bureau and tribal roads within the reservation. There is no room for these taxes in the comprehensive federal regulatory scheme. In a variety of ways, the assessment of state taxes would obstruct federal policies. And equally important, respondents have been unable to identify any regulatory function or service performed by the State that would justify the assessment of taxes for activities on Bureau and tribal roads within the reservation.

At the most general level, the taxes would threaten the overriding federal objective of guaranteeing Indians that they will "receive . . . the benefit of whatever profit [the forest] is capable of yielding. . . ." Underlying the federal regulatory program rests a policy of assuring that the profits derived from timber sales will inure to the benefit of the Tribe, subject only to administrative expenses incurred by the Federal Government. That objective is part of the general federal policy of encouraging tribes "to revitalize their self-government" and to assume control over their "business and economic affairs." The imposition of the taxes at issue would undermine that policy in a context in which the Federal Government has undertaken to regulate the most minute details of timber production and expressed a firm desire that the Tribe should retain the benefits derived from the harvesting and sale of reservation timber.

In addition, the taxes would undermine the Secretary's ability to make the wide range of determinations committed to his authority concerning the setting of fees and rates with respect to the harvesting and sale of tribal timber. The Secretary reviews and approves the terms of the Tribe's agreements with its contractors, sets fees for services rendered to the Tribe by the Federal Government, and determines stumpage rates for timber to be paid to the Tribe. Most notably in reviewing or writing the terms of the contracts between FATCO and its contractors, federal agents must predict the amount and determine the proper allocation of all business expenses, including fuel costs. The assessment of state taxes would throw additional factors into the federal calculus, reducing tribal revenues and diminishing the profitability of the enterprise for potential contractors.

Finally, the imposition of state taxes would adversely affect the Tribe's ability to comply with the sustained-yield management policies imposed by federal law. Substantial expenditures are paid out by the Federal Government, the Tribe, and its contractors in order to undertake a wide variety of measures to ensure the continued productivity of the forest. These measures include reforestation, fire control, wildlife promotion, road improvement, safety inspections, and general policing of the forest. The expenditures are largely paid for out of tribal revenues, which are in turn derived almost exclusively from the sale of timber. The imposition of state taxes on FATCO's contractors would effectively diminish the amount of those revenues and thus leave the Tribe and its contractors with reduced sums with which to pay out federally required expenses.

As noted above, this is not a case in which the State seeks to assess taxes in return for governmental functions it performs for those on whom the taxes fall. Nor have respondents been able to identify a legitimate regulatory interest served by the taxes they seek to impose. They refer to a general desire to raise revenue, but we are unable to discern a responsibility or service that justifies the assertion of taxes imposed for on-reservation operations conducted solely on tribal and Bureau of Indian Affairs roads. Pinetop's business in Arizona is conducted solely on the Fort Apache Reservation. Though at least the use fuel tax purports to "[compensate] the state for the use of its highways," Ariz. Rev. Stat. Ann. § 28-1552 (Supp. 1979), no such compensatory purpose is present here. The roads at issue have been built, maintained, and policed exclusively by the Federal Government, the Tribe, and its contractors. We do not believe that respondents' generalized interest in raising revenue is in this context sufficient to permit its proposed intrusion into the federal regulatory scheme with respect to the harvesting and sale of tribal timber.

Respondents' argument is reduced to a claim that they may assess taxes on non-Indians engaged in commerce on the reservation whenever there is no express congressional statement to the contrary. That is simply not the law. In a number of cases we have held that state authority over non-Indians acting on tribal reservations is pre-empted even though Congress has offered no explicit statement on the subject. The Court has repeatedly emphasized that there is a significant geographical component to tribal sovereignty, a component which remains highly relevant to the pre-emption inquiry; though the reservation boundary is not absolute, it remains an important factor to weigh in determining whether state authority has exceeded the permissible limits. "'The cases in this Court have consistently guarded the authority of Indian governments over their reservations.'" Moreover, it is undisputed that the economic burden of the asserted taxes will ultimately fall on the Tribe.[15] Where, as here, the Federal Government has undertaken comprehensive regulation of the harvesting and sale of tribal timber, where a number of the policies underlying the federal regulatory scheme are threatened by the taxes respondents seek to impose, and where respondents are unable to justify the taxes except in terms of a

---

15. Of course, the fact that the economic burden of the tax falls on the Tribe does not by itself mean that the tax is pre-empted. Our decision today is based on the pre-emptive effect of the comprehensive federal regulatory scheme, which * * * leaves no room for the additional burdens sought to be imposed by state law.

generalized interest in raising revenue, we believe that the proposed exercise of state authority is impermissible.

The decision of the Arizona Court of Appeals is *Reversed*.

[The dissenting opinion of Justice STEVENS joined by Justices STEWART and REHNQUIST, and the concurring opinion of Justice POWELL are omitted.]

Cotton Petroleum Corp. v. New Mexico
490 U.S. 163 (1989)

JUSTICE STEVENS delivered the opinion of the Court.

This case is a sequel to *Merrion v. Jicarilla Apache Tribe*, 455 U.S. 130 (1982), in which we held that the Jicarilla Apache Tribe (Tribe) has the power to impose a severance tax on the production of oil and gas by non-Indian lessees of wells located on the Tribe's reservation. We must now decide whether the State of New Mexico can continue to impose its severance taxes on the same production of oil and gas.

I

All 742,135 acres of the Jicarilla Apache Reservation are located in northwestern New Mexico. In 1887, President Cleveland issued an Executive Order setting aside this tract of public land "as a reservation for the use and occupation of the Jicarilla Apache Indians." The only qualification contained in the order was a proviso protecting bona fide settlers from defeasance of previously acquired federal rights. The land is still owned by the United States and is held in trust for the Tribe.

The Tribe, which consists of approximately 2,500 enrolled members, is organized under the Indian Reorganization Act. The Indian Mineral Leasing Act of 1938 (1938 Act) grants the Tribe authority, subject to the approval of the Secretary of the Interior (Secretary), to execute mineral leases. Since at least as early as 1953, the Tribe has been leasing reservation lands to nonmembers for the production of oil and gas. Mineral leases now encompass a substantial portion of the reservation and constitute the primary source of the Tribe's general operating revenues. In 1969, the Secretary approved an amendment to the Tribe's Constitution authorizing it to enact ordinances, subject to his approval, imposing taxes on nonmembers doing business in the reservation. The Tribe enacted such an ordinance in 1976, imposing a severance tax on "any oil and natural gas severed, saved and removed from Tribal lands." The Secretary approved the ordinance later that year, and in 1982 this Court upheld the Tribe's power to impose a severance tax on pre-existing as well as future leases. Subsequently, the Tribe enacted a privilege tax, which the Secretary also approved.

In 1976, Cotton Petroleum Corporation (Cotton), a non-Indian company in the business of extracting and marketing oil and gas, acquired five leases covering approximately 15,000 acres of the reservation. There were then 15 operating wells on the leased acreage and Cotton has since drilled another 50 wells. The leases were issued by the Tribe and the United States under the authority of the 1938 Act. Pursuant to the terms of the leases, Cotton pays the Tribe a rent of $125 per acre, plus a royalty of 12 1/2 percent of the value of its production. In addition, Cotton pays the Tribe's oil and gas severance and privilege taxes, which amount to approximately 6 percent of the value of its production. Thus, Cotton's aggregate payment to the Tribe includes an acreage rent in excess of $1 million, plus royalties and taxes amounting to about 18 1/2 percent of its production.

Prior to 1982, Cotton paid, without objection, five different oil and gas production taxes to the State of New Mexico.[4] The state taxes amount to about 8 percent of the value of Cotton's production. The same 8 percent is collected from producers throughout the State. Thus, on wells outside the reservation, the total tax burden is only 8 percent, while Cotton's reservation wells are taxed at a total rate of 14 percent (8 percent by the State and 6 percent by the Tribe). No state tax is imposed on the royalties received by the Tribe.

In 1982, Cotton paid its state taxes under protest and then brought an action in the District Court for Santa Fe County * * *. [After trial, the Jicarilla Apache Tribe sought and was granted leave to file an amicus curiae brief. After the tribe filed its brief, the New Mexico district court issued a decision upholding the state taxes. The New Mexico Court of Appeals affirmed.] * * * We now affirm the judgment of the New Mexico Court of Appeals.

II

[I]t is well settled that, absent express congressional authorization, a State cannot tax the United States directly. It is also clear that the tax immunity of the United States is shared by the Indian tribes for whose benefit the United States holds reservation lands in trust. *See Montana v. Blackfeet Tribe of Indians*, 471 U.S. 759, 764 (1985). Under current doctrine, however, a State can impose a nondiscriminatory tax on private parties with whom the United States or an Indian tribe does business, even though the financial burden of the tax may fall on the United States or tribe. Although a lessee's oil production on Indian lands is therefore not "automatically exempt from state taxation," Congress does, of course, retain the power to grant such immunity.

The question for us to decide is whether Congress has acted to grant the Tribe such immunity, either expressly or by plain implication. In addition, we must consider Cotton's argument that the "multiple burden" imposed by the state and tribal taxes is unconstitutional.

III

Although determining whether federal legislation has preempted state taxation of lessees of Indian land is primarily an exercise in examining congressional intent, the history of tribal sovereignty serves as a necessary "backdrop" to that process. As

---

4. The five taxes are the Oil and Gas Severance Tax, the Oil and Gas Conservation Tax, the Oil and Gas Emergency School Tax, the Oil and Gas Ad Valorem Production Tax, and the Production Equipment Ad Valorem Tax.

a result, questions of pre-emption in this area are not resolved by reference to standards of pre-emption that have developed in other areas of the law, and are not controlled by "mechanical or absolute conceptions of state or tribal sovereignty." Instead, we have applied a flexible pre-emption analysis sensitive to the particular facts and legislation involved. Each case "requires a particularized examination of the relevant state, federal, and tribal interests."

Against this background, Cotton argues that the New Mexico taxes are pre-empted by the "federal laws and policies which protect tribal self-government and strengthen impoverished reservation economies." Most significantly, Cotton contends that the 1938 Act exhibits a strong federal interest in guaranteeing Indian tribes the maximum return on their oil and gas leases. Moreover, Cotton maintains that the Federal and Tribal Governments, acting pursuant to the 1938 Act, its accompanying regulations, and the Jicarilla Apache Tribal Code, exercise comprehensive regulatory control over Cotton's on-reservation activity. Cotton describes New Mexico's responsibilities, in contrast, as "significantly limited." Thus, weighing the respective state, federal, and tribal interests, Cotton concludes that the New Mexico taxes unduly interfere with the federal interest in promoting tribal economic self-sufficiency and are not justified by an adequate state interest. We disagree.

The 1938 Act neither expressly permits state taxation nor expressly precludes it, but rather simply provides that "unallotted lands within any Indian reservation or lands owned by any tribe . . . may, with the approval of the Secretary of the Interior, be leased for mining purposes, by authority of the tribal council . . . , for terms not to exceed ten years and as long thereafter as minerals are produced in paying quantities." The Senate and House Reports that accompanied the Act, moreover — even when considered in their broadest possible terms — shed little light on congressional intent concerning state taxation of oil and gas produced on leased lands.

* * * Cotton argues that the 1938 Act embodies a broad congressional policy of maximizing revenues for Indian tribes. Cotton finds support for this proposition in *Montana v. Blackfeet Tribe*, 471 U.S. 759 (1985). That case raised the question whether the 1938 Act authorizes state taxation of a tribe's royalty interests under oil and gas leases issued to nonmembers. Applying the settled rule that a tribe may only be directly taxed by a State if "Congress has made its intention to [lift the tribe's exemption] unmistakably clear," we concluded that "the State may not tax Indian royalty income from leases issued pursuant to the 1938 Act." In a footnote we added the observation that direct state taxation of Indian revenues would frustrate the 1938 Act's purpose of "ensuring that Indians receive 'the greatest return from their property.'"

We thus agree that a purpose of the 1938 Act is to provide Indian tribes with badly needed revenue, but find no evidence for the further supposition that Congress intended to remove all barriers to profit maximization.

Our review of the legislation that preceded the 1938 Act provides no additional support for Cotton's expansive view of the Act's purpose. This history is relevant in that it supplies both the legislative background against which Congress enacted the 1938 Act and the relevant "backdrop" of tribal independence. * * * [W]hen Congress first authorized oil and gas leasing on Executive Order reservations in the 1927 Act, it expressly waived immunity from state taxation of oil and gas lessees operating in those reservations. Thus, at least as to Executive Order reservations, state taxation of nonmember oil and gas lessees was the norm from the very start. There is, accordingly, simply no history of tribal independence from state taxation of these lessees to form a "backdrop" against which the 1938 Act must be read.

We are also unconvinced that the contrast between the 1927 Act's express waiver of immunity and the 1938 Act's silence on the subject suggests that Congress intended to repeal the waiver in the 1938 Act and thus to diametrically change course by implicitly barring state taxation. The general repealer clause contained in the 1938 Act provides that "all Act[s] or parts of Acts inconsistent herewith are hereby repealed." Although one might infer from this clause that all preceding, nonconflicting legislation in the area, like the 1927 Act's waiver provision, is implicitly incorporated, we need not go so far to simply conclude that the 1938 Act's omission demonstrates no congressional purpose to close the door to state taxation.[14]

Cotton nonetheless maintains that our decisions in *White Mountain Apache Tribe v. Bracker*, 448 U.S. 136 (1980), and *Ramah Navajo School Bd., Inc. v. Bureau of Revenue of New Mexico*, 458 U.S. 832 (1982),* compel the conclusion that the New

---

14. Our decision in *Montana v. Blackfeet Tribe*, 471 U.S. 759 (1985), is not to the contrary. In that case we considered the distinct question whether the 1938 Act, through incorporation of the 1927 Act, expressly authorized direct taxation of Indian royalties. In concluding that it did not, we made clear that our holding turned on the rule that Indian tribes, like the Federal Government itself, are exempt from direct state taxation and that this exemption is "lifted only when Congress has made its intention to do so unmistakably clear." We stressed that the 1938 Act "contains no explicit consent to state taxation," and that the reverse implication of the general repealer clause that the 1927 waiver might be incorporated "does not satisfy the requirement that Congress clearly consent to state taxation." Our conclusion that the 1938 Act does not expressly authorize direct taxation of Indian tribes does not entail the further step that the Act impliedly prohibits taxation of nonmembers doing business on a reservation.

* [Editor's note: In *Ramah*, the Court held that New Mexico was preempted from imposing its gross receipts tax on a non-Indian construction company for payments received from the tribal school board for the on-reservation construction of a school for Indian children. The Court determined that the case "is indistinguishable in all relevant respects" from *Bracker*. First, the construction and financing of the school were governed by "detailed and comprehensive" federal regulations. Second, the state tax "necessarily impedes the clearly expressed federal interest in promoting the 'quality and quantity' of educational opportunities for Indians by depleting the funds available for the construction of Indian schools." And third, "the State does not seek to assess its tax in return for the governmental functions it provides to those who must bear the burden of paying this tax. . . . [n]or has the State asserted any specific, legitimate regulatory interest to justify the imposition of its gross receipts tax." The Court noted that the state's "only arguably specific interest" was the fact that it provided off-reservation services to the construction company. The Court rejected that interest because the "ultimate burden" of the tax fell on the tribe. "[W]e fail to see how these benefits can justify a tax imposed on the construction of school facilities *on tribal lands* pursuant to a contract between the tribal organization and the non-Indian contracting firm."]

Mexico taxes are pre-empted by federal law. In pressing this argument, Cotton ignores the admonition included in both of those decisions that the relevant pre-emption test is a flexible one sensitive to the particular state, federal, and tribal interests involved.

The factual findings of the New Mexico District Court clearly distinguish this case from both *Bracker* and *Ramah Navajo School Bd.* After conducting a trial, that court found that "New Mexico provides substantial services to both the Jicarilla Tribe and Cotton," costing the State approximately $3 million per year. Indeed, Cotton concedes that from 1981 through 1985 New Mexico provided its operations with services costing $89,384, but argues that the cost of these services is disproportionate to the $2,293,953 in taxes the State collected from Cotton. Neither *Bracker* nor *Ramah Navajo School Bd.*, however, imposes such a proportionality requirement on the States. Rather, both cases involved complete abdication or noninvolvement of the State in the on-reservation activity. The present case is also unlike *Bracker* and *Ramah Navajo School Bd.*, in that the District Court found that "no economic burden falls on the tribe by virtue of the state taxes," and that the Tribe could, in fact, increase its taxes without adversely affecting on-reservation oil and gas development. Finally, the District Court found that the State regulates the spacing and mechanical integrity of wells located on the reservation. Thus, although the federal and tribal regulations in this case are extensive, they are not exclusive, as were the regulations in *Bracker* and *Ramah Navajo School Bd.*

We thus conclude that federal law, even when given the most generous construction, does not pre-empt New Mexico's oil and gas severance taxes. This is not a case in which the State has had nothing to do with the on-reservation activity, save tax it. Nor is this a case in which an unusually large state tax has imposed a substantial burden on the Tribe.[17] It is, of course, reasonable to infer that the New Mexico taxes have at least a marginal effect on the demand for on-reservation leases, the value to the Tribe of those leases, and the ability of the Tribe to increase its tax rate. Any impairment to the federal policy favoring the exploitation of on-reservation oil and gas resources by Indian tribes that might be caused by these effects, however, is simply too indirect and too insubstantial to support Cotton's claim of pre-emption.

The judgment of the New Mexico Court of Appeals is affirmed.

JUSTICE BLACKMUN, with whom JUSTICE BRENNAN and JUSTICE MARSHALL join, dissenting.

---

17. We therefore have no occasion to reexamine our summary affirmance of the Court of Appeals for the Ninth Circuit's conclusion that Montana's unique severance and gross proceeds taxes may not be imposed on coal mined on Crow tribal property. *See Montana v. Crow Tribe*, 484 U.S. 997 (1988), *summarily aff'g* 819 F.2d 895 (1987). In that case, as the Ninth Circuit noted, the state taxes had a negative effect on the marketability of coal produced in Montana. Moreover, as the Solicitor General stated in urging that we affirm the judgment of the Court of Appeals, the Montana taxes at issue were "extraordinarily high." According to the Crow Tribe's expert, the combined effective rate of the Montana taxes was 32.9 percent, "more than twice that of any other state's coal taxes."

Although the Jicarilla Apache Tribe is not a party to the appeal, this case centrally concerns "the boundaries between state regulatory authority and [the Tribe's] self-government." The basic principles that define those boundaries are well established. The Court today, while faithfully reciting these principles, is less faithful in their application.

Pre-emption is essentially a matter of congressional intent. In this case, our goal should be to determine whether the State's taxation of Cotton Petroleum's reservation oil production is consistent with federal Indian policy as expressed in relevant statutes and regulations. First and foremost, we must look to the statutory scheme Congress has established to govern the activity the State seeks to tax in order to see whether the statute itself expresses Congress' views on the question of state taxation. * * * [T]he statute most relevant to this case [the Indian Mineral Leasing Act of 1938] makes clear that Congress intended to foreclose the kind of tax New Mexico has imposed. Second, we must consider other indications of whether federal policy permits the tax in question. * * * [U]nder established principles, state taxation is pre-empted by federal and tribal interests in this case. Because the record is more than adequate to demonstrate the pre-emptive force of federal and tribal interests, I dissent.

Notes

1. The role of state courts. Notice that both *Bracker* and *Cotton Petroleum* originated in state courts, which means that state courts were the fact finders in both cases. Did this have any effect on the outcome of the cases? Note also that the tribe in *Cotton Petroleum* was not a party to the lawsuit. Were there any facts the state court found which the tribe might have wanted to challenge?

2. Dual taxation. Prior to the 1982 decision in *Merrion*, page 425, non-Indian mining companies generally paid no tribal or state taxes out of pocket. The companies paid state taxes without protest because, using provisions of federal statutes from the 1920s, the companies deducted the state taxes from the royalty payments to the tribes. Then in 1985, the Court held in *Blackfeet Tribe*, page 449, that that practice was invalid under the 1938 Indian Mineral Leasing Act. Within a few years, then, non-Indian mining companies with IMLA leases went from paying no tax to paying both tribal and state taxes. That sudden dual tax burden, in turn, led to the lawsuit filed by Cotton Petroleum Corporation. The net effect of the *Cotton Petroleum* decision, however, is that the nonmember company is in fact subject to both state and tribal taxation. Why should the tribe care about double taxation of a nonmember company?

For a discussion of how state and tribal taxation (or dual taxation) impacts Indian country, see Kelly S. Croman & Jonathan B. Taylor, *Why beggar thy Indian neighbor? The case for tribal primacy in taxation in Indian country*, Joint Occasional Papers on Native Affairs, JOPNA 2016-1 (May 4, 2016), available at http://nni.arizona.edu/application/files/8914/6254/9090/2016_Croman_why_beggar_thy_Indian_neighbor.pdf

3. **Mineral taxation after *Cotton Petroleum*.** The Court's decision in *Cotton Petroleum* relies on the particular facts of that case: not only the economic situation, but also the fact that New Mexico regulated aspects of oil and gas production on the Jicarilla Reservation. In a subsequent case, however, the Court appeared to create a bright-line rule that in mineral cases, "neither the State nor the Tribe enjoys authority to tax to the total exclusion of the other." *Montana v. Crow Tribe of Indians*, 523 U.S. 696, 698 (1998). Although the federal scheme governing coal mining on the Crow lands at issue was exclusive, and Montana therefore regulated no aspect of the coal mining, the Court focused on the economic impact of the state taxes on the tribe. The Court determined that the state taxes did not deprive the tribe of its fair share of the value of the coal because the tribe could have taxed production as well, and because there was no evidence that the mining company would have paid a higher royalty to the tribe in the absence of state taxes.

The Ute Mountain Ute Tribe unsuccessfully alleged that the same five state taxes at issue in *Cotton Petroleum* were preempted as applied to oil and gas companies with Indian Mineral Leasing Act leases and Indian Mineral Development Act agreements on the New Mexico portion of the Ute Mountain Ute reservation. *Ute Mountain Ute Tribe v. Rodriguez*, 660 F.3d 1177 (10th Cir. 2011). The tribe claimed that the application of the taxes on its reservation was distinguishable from *Cotton Petroleum* because the state provided no on-reservation support services to either the tribe or the oil and gas companies to justify its taxes. Over a dissent, the Tenth Circuit disagreed, ruling that 1) the federal scheme regulating reservation oil and gas was not "exclusive" because the state regulated certain aspects of reservation leasing; 2) the tribe suffered only "indirect" economic harm by not being able to raise its own taxes without discouraging new companies faced with double-taxation; and 3) the state's interest was more than minimal, particularly concerning the off-reservation infrastructure that allowed the transportation of oil and gas to market. The dissent thought that the state was justified in taxing only the off-reservation activities of the oil and gas companies because the state's on-reservation presence was minimal.

4. **State taxation under the Indian Mineral Development Act.** *Cotton Petroleum* determined in part that state taxes on non-Indian mineral lessees were not preempted by the Indian Mineral Leasing Act of 1938. Review the materials on the IMLA and the Indian Mineral Development Act of 1982, at pages 357–358. Might state taxes be preempted by the IMDA? Note that in the *Ute Mountain Ute* case above, the Tenth Circuit determined that, like the IMLA, the IMDA neither clearly authorized nor prohibited state taxation of nonmembers. Might there be ways to structure minerals agreements under the 1982 Act to take advantage of tribal exemptions from state mineral taxes?

5. **State taxation under the HEARTH Act.** The HEARTH Act authorizes tribes, upon federal approval of tribal leasing regulations, to enter into surface and business leases of tribal lands without federal approval. *See* pages 361–362. In its notice

approving HEARTH Act regulations of the Seminole Tribe of Florida, the Department of Interior explained that tribal leasing regulations adopted under the HEARTH Act will preempt state and local taxation. 80 Fed. Reg. 47949 (Aug. 10, 2015). Specifically, "[t]he strong Federal and tribal interests against State and local taxation of improvements, leaseholds, and activities on land leased under the Department's leasing regulations apply equally to improvements, leaseholds, and activities on land leased pursuant to tribal leasing regulations approved under the HEARTH Act." *Id.*

6. Effect of *Cotton Petroleum* on other state taxes. What effect has the Court's decision in *Cotton Petroleum* had on subsequent state taxation cases? Did the Court alter the analysis for determining whether states may tax nonmembers? A number of subsequent federal court decisions have held that it did not. Typical of these is *Hoopa Valley Tribe v. Nevins*, 881 F.2d 657 (9th Cir. 1989), which held that California could not impose its timber yield tax on the harvest by non-Indian purchasers of timber owned by the tribe. With respect to *Cotton Petroleum*, the court found as follows:

> In *Cotton Petroleum* the Court reaffirmed the basic principles of *White Mountain* and *Ramah* while holding that New Mexico could impose its oil and gas severance tax on the production of oil and gas by non-Indians from tribal lands. The Court distinguished *White Mountain* and *Ramah* by recognizing that New Mexico regulated the oil and gas activities affected by the tax. Additionally, the Court noted that the New Mexico tax primarily burdened non-Indian taxpayers. "This is not a case in which the State has had nothing to do with the on-reservation activity, save tax it. Nor is this a case in which an unusually large state tax has imposed a substantial burden on the tribe." The Court also noted that it had no reason to reexamine its summary affirmance of our decision in *Crow Tribe*, because the Montana tax "had a negative effect on the marketability of coal produced in Montana." In contrast to New Mexico's regulation of oil and gas in *Cotton*, California plays no role in the Hoopa Valley Tribe's timber activities. Also unlike *Cotton*, the burden of the tax concededly falls on the tribe.
>
> The state argues that the district court erred because its interest in imposing the tax is much stronger than Arizona's interest in *White Mountain*. The state points out that in *White Mountain*, Arizona imposed motor vehicle taxes on entities that used reservation roads maintained by the BIA and not the state. Here, California notes that the timber tax helps fund various services used by tribal members, and that the services provided by the state to tribal members far exceed the income from the timber tax.
>
> The district court correctly determined that the state's interest was not strong enough to outweigh the substantial federal and tribal interests in timber harvesting on the reservation. The Supreme Court rejected a parallel argument in *Ramah*: "We are similarly unpersuaded by the State's argument

that the significant services it provides to the Ramah Navajo Indians justify the imposition of this tax. The State does not suggest these benefits are in any way related to the construction of schools on Indian land." Although California points to a variety of services that it provides to residents of the reservation and the surrounding area, none of those services is connected with the timber activities directly affected by the tax. To be valid, the California tax must bear some relationship to the activity being taxed. Showing that the tax serves legitimate state interests, such as raising revenues for services used by tribal residents and others, is not enough.

The state's general interest in revenue collection is insufficient to outweigh the specific federal and tribal interests with which the timber yield tax interferes. The services provided by the state and county are provided to all residents. The road, law enforcement, welfare, and health care services provided by the state and county benefit both tribal and non-tribal members. California admits that there is no direct connection between revenues from the timber yield tax and the provision of services to tribal members or area residents generally.

Because the timber yield tax does not fund services that directly relate to the harvesting of tribal timber and is otherwise unconnected with tribal timber activities, the timber yield tax should be preempted.

881 F.2d at 660–61.

Other post-*Cotton Petroleum* cases in the lower federal courts have similarly found state taxes on non-Indians doing business within Indian country preempted where there is a comprehensive federal scheme that leaves no room for state regulation or services. *See Gila River Indian Community v. Waddell*, 967 F.2d 1404 (9th Cir. 1992) (reversing trial court's dismissal of tribe's suit to enjoin state transaction privilege tax on ticket revenues); *Cabazon Band of Mission Indians v. Wilson*, 37 F.3d 430 (9th Cir. 1994) (state tax on off-track betting activities on tribal lands preempted by the Indian Gaming Regulatory Act). Although these lower court cases have adhered to the traditional preemption analysis, none of them has involved state taxation of mineral lessees.

Not all courts, however, agree that *Cotton Petroleum* simply "reaffirmed the basic principles" of existing law. The New Mexico Supreme Court, in *Blaze Construction Co. v. Taxation and Revenue Dep't*, 884 P.2d 803 (N.M. 1994), stated its understanding that *Cotton Petroleum* had changed the Indian law preemption test by providing that a state interest in raising revenue, rather than a direct link between state taxes and a state interest in the taxed activity, could justify a state tax.

7. **The "who" and the "where" of state taxes.** The threshold issues for application of the *Bracker* analysis for state taxation are first, where the legal incidence of the tax falls (on the tribe or its members, or on nonmembers); and second, where the activity or property being taxed is located.

For example, the U.S. Supreme Court upheld Kansas' imposition of a motor fuel excise tax on an off-reservation, non-Indian distributor for fuel supplied to a gas station that was operated by the tribe on the reservation. *Wagnon v. Prairie Band of Potawatomi Nation* 546 U.S. 95 (2005). At the appellate level, the Tenth Circuit held that, while the legal incidence of the tax rested on non-Indians, under *Bracker* the strong tribal and federal interest weighed against the imposition of the tax. In an opinion by Justice Thomas, the Supreme Court reversed, noting that "under our Indian tax immunity cases, the 'who' and the 'where' of the challenged tax have significant consequences." While the court agreed that the Tenth Circuit had gotten the "who" in this case correct, it disagreed as to "where" the tax was being imposed:

> The Nation maintains that we must apply the *Bracker* interest-balancing test, irrespective of the identity of the taxpayer (*i.e.*, the party bearing the legal incidence), because the Kansas fuel tax arises as a result of the *on-reservation* sale and delivery of the motor fuel. Notably, however, the Nation presented a starkly different interpretation of the statute in the proceedings before the Court of Appeals, arguing that "[t]he balancing test is appropriate even though the legal incidence of the tax is imposed on the Nation's non-Indian distributor and is triggered by the distributor's receipt of fuel *outside the reservation*." A "fair interpretation of the taxing statute as written and applied," confirms that the Nation's interpretation of the statute before the Court of Appeals was correct.

> Although Kansas' fuel tax is imposed on non-Indian distributors based upon those distributors' off-reservation receipt of motor fuel, the Tenth Circuit concluded that the tax was nevertheless still subject to the interest-balancing test this Court set forth in *Bracker*. As *Bracker* itself explained, however, we formulated the balancing test to address the "difficult questio[n]" that arises when "a State asserts authority over the conduct of non-Indians engaging in activity *on the reservation*." (emphasis added). The *Bracker* interest-balancing test has never been applied where, as here, the State asserts its taxing authority over non-Indians off the reservation. And although we have never addressed this precise issue, our Indian tax immunity cases counsel against such an application.

The Court held that the tax was a "nondiscriminatory tax imposed on an off-reservation transaction between non-Indians. Accordingly, the tax is valid and poses no affront to the Nation's sovereignty." Two Justices (Ginsberg and Kennedy) dissented.

The United States Court of Appeals for the Ninth Circuit decided that a treaty provision did not exempt a business owned by a tribal member and partially located within the tribe's reservation from a state escrow tax. *King Mountain Tobacco Comp. Inc. v. McKenna*, 768 F.3d 989 (9th Cir. 2014). The court upheld Washington's application of its escrow tax on the King Mountain Tobacco Company Inc., which is owned by a citizen of the Yakama Nation and which grows and processes some of its tobacco within the Nation's reservation. The escrow tax requires that money be put into an escrow account to reimburse Washington for health care costs related to the use of tobacco products. The company argued that a provision of the Nation's 1855 treaty precluded application of the tax. However, the court disagreed, explaining that because the escrow statute is a nondiscriminatory law and the company's activities and sales occurred largely off of the reservation, the escrow tax applied. Further, the court held that the plain text of the Nation's treaty did not create a federal exemption from the escrow statute.

In *Cougar Den, Inc. v. Washington State Department of Licensing*, 392 P.3d 1014 (Wash. 2017), the Supreme Court of Washington considered the same treaty provision, the right to travel provision, of the Treaty with the Yakamas, 12 Stat. 951, 952–53 (1855). In relevant part, the right to travel provision provides the Yakamas "the right, in common with citizens of the United States, to travel upon all public highways." Under this treaty provision, Cougar Den, which is a corporation of the Yakama Nation, had been transporting fuel to the Nation's reservation without possessing an importer's license or paying state fuel taxes. When the State of Washington sought to recover $3.6 million from the corporation in unpaid taxes, penalties, and licensing fees, the Nation appealed the fine. In reaching its decision that the fine should not apply, the court explained that there was no question that, absent the treaty provision, Cougar Den would be subject to taxation for its activities outside of the reservation. The court also explained, however, that the Indian canons of construction applied and the court should interpret the treaty as the Nation would have understood it at the time it entered into the treaty. In reviewing the historical record, the court concluded that the right to travel for commercial purposes was very important to the Nation at the time of the treaty, and that all parties understood the treaty to protect the Nation's right to travel for commercial purposes. Further, the court explained that the treaty provision was meant to apply to future commercial endeavors. The court also stated that, if the state had concerns about this treaty provision, Congress was the appropriate actor to make any revisions to the treaty. Therefore, the court concluded that the right of Cougar Den to transport the fuel on Washington highways without paying otherwise applicable taxes was protected under the treaty provision. On June 14, 2017, the State of Washington filed a petition with the U.S. Supreme Court seeking review of the decision. In October 2017, the U.S. Solicitor General was invited to submit a brief to the U.S. Supreme Court expressing the views of the federal government.

The Eleventh Circuit split its decision on two state taxes, finding one preempted and one not. *Seminole Tribe of Florida v. Stranburg*, 799 F.3d 1324 (11th Cir. 2015). In *Stranburg*, the Seminole Tribe opposed the application of a rental tax and a utility tax to two non-Indian corporations with twenty-five year leases to conduct food-court operations for the Tribe's casinos. The court determined that the state rental tax was not applicable for two reasons; first, it would be inconsistent with the U.S. Supreme Court's decision in *Mescalero Apache Tribe v. Jones*, 411 U.S. 145 (1973), prohibiting state taxation on the privileges of tribal ownership; and second, it was preempted under the *Bracker* analysis. The court, however, upheld the state utility tax. It found that the legal incidence of the tax fell on the utility company rather than the Tribe, and that the Tribe failed to show that the utility tax was preempted under the *Bracker* analysis.

8. State taxes on federal contractors working on-reservation. In 1999, a unanimous Supreme Court upheld the state of Arizona's right to impose a gross receipts tax on Blaze Construction, a company owned by the Blackfeet Tribe of Montana and engaged in road construction work on several Arizona reservations. *Arizona Dep't of Revenue v. Blaze Construction Co, Inc.*, 526 U.S. 32 (1999). The Arizona Court of Appeals held that the on-reservation tax was preempted by federal law, but the Supreme Court reversed in an opinion by Justice Thomas. The Court first ruled that Blaze Construction, although tribally-owned, was the equivalent of a non-Indian company because it was a nonmember corporation. The Court then determined that the *Bracker/Cotton Petroleum* test for preemption of state taxes placed on nonmembers doing business in Indian country was inapplicable because Blaze Construction was not a nonmember company doing business with the tribe or its members, but a nonmember company under contract with the federal government. Because the incidence of the tax fell on Blaze, not the tribe, the Court concluded that congressional immunity or a congressional exemption was necessary to shield Blaze from the state tax.

Chapter 7

Water Rights

A. Introduction to Reserved Rights

The next two chapters consider tribal reserved rights to resources: that is, rights reserved by or for tribes in the treaties, agreements, and other instruments that ceded aboriginal lands and/or created reservations. The two cases that follow are the foundation cases of the reserved rights doctrine. What are the differences between the reserved fishing rights recognized in *Winans* and the reserved water rights recognized in *Winters*?

United States v. Winans
198 U.S. 371 (1905)

MR. JUSTICE McKENNA delivered the opinion of the Court.

This suit was brought to enjoin the respondents from obstructing certain Indians of the Yakima Nation in the State of Washington from exercising fishing rights and privileges on the Columbia River in that State, claimed under the provisions of the treaty between the United States and the Indians, made in 1859.

The treaty is as follows:

> "Article III. * * * The exclusive right of taking fish in all the streams where running through or bordering said reservation, is further secured to said confederated tribes and bands of Indians, as also the right of taking fish at all usual and accustomed places, in common with citizens of the Territory, and of erecting temporary buildings for curing them; together with the privilege of hunting, gathering roots and berries, and pasturing their horses and cattle upon open and unclaimed land. . . ."

The respondents or their predecessors in title claim under patents of the United States the lands bordering on the Columbia River and under grants from the State of Washington to the shore land which, it is alleged, fronts on the patented land. They also introduced in evidence licenses from the State to maintain devices for taking fish, called fish wheels.

At the time the treaty was made the fishing places were part of the Indian country, subject to the occupancy of the Indians, with all the rights such occupancy gave.

The object of the treaty was to limit the occupancy to certain lands and to define rights outside of them.

The pivot of the controversy is the construction of the second paragraph [of Article III]. Respondents contend that the words "the right of taking fish at all usual and accustomed places in common with the citizens of the Territory" confer only such rights as a white man would have under the conditions of ownership of the lands bordering on the river, and under the laws of the State, and, such being the rights conferred, the respondents further contend that they have the power to exclude the Indians from the river by reason of such ownership. Before filing their answer respondents demurred to the bill. The court overruled the demurrer, holding that the bill stated facts sufficient to show that the Indians were excluded from the exercise of the rights given them by the treaty. The court further found, however, that it would "not be justified in issuing process to compel the defendants to permit the Indians to make a camping ground of their property while engaged in fishing." [An injunction was issued, but it was limited to unfenced areas and allowed the Winans brothers to exclude Indian fishers by erecting new fences.]

* * * [The court below stated:] "I find from the evidence that the defendants have excluded the Indians from their own lands, to which a perfect absolute title has been acquired from the United States Government by patents, and they have more than once instituted legal proceedings against the Indians for trespassing, and the defendants have placed in the river in front of their lands fishing wheels for which licenses were granted to them by the State of Washington, and they claim the right to operate these fishing wheels, which necessitates the exclusive possession of the space occupied by the wheels. Otherwise the defendants have not molested the Indians nor threatened to do so. The Indians are at the present time on an equal footing with the citizens of the United States who have not acquired exclusive proprietary rights, and this it seems to me is all that they can legally demand with respect to fishing privileges in waters outside the limits of Indian reservations under the terms of their treaty with the United States."

The remarks of the court clearly stated the issue and the grounds of decision. The contention of the respondents was sustained. In other words, it was decided that the Indians acquired no rights but what any inhabitant of the Territory or State would have. Indeed, acquired no rights but such as they would have without the treaty. This is certainly an impotent outcome to negotiations and a convention, which seemed to promise more and give the word of the Nation for more. And we have said we will construe a treaty with the Indians as "that unlettered people" understood it, and "as justice and reason demand in all cases where power is exerted by the strong over those to whom they owe care and protection," and counterpoise the inequality "by the superior justice which looks only to the substance of the right without regard to technical rules." How the treaty in question was understood may be gathered from the circumstances.

The right to resort to the fishing places in controversy was a part of larger rights possessed by the Indians, upon the exercise of which there was not a shadow of impediment, and which were not much less necessary to the existence of the Indians than the atmosphere they breathed. New conditions came into existence, to which those rights had to be accommodated. Only a limitation of them, however, was necessary and intended, not a taking away. In other words, the treaty was not a grant of rights to the Indians, but a grant of rights from them—a reservation of those not granted. And the form of the instrument and its language was adapted to that purpose. Reservations were not of particular parcels of land, and could not be expressed in deeds as dealings between private individuals. The reservations were in large areas of territory and the negotiations were with the tribe. They reserved rights, however, to every individual Indian, as though named therein. They imposed a servitude upon every piece of land as though described therein. There was an exclusive right of fishing reserved within certain boundaries. There was a right outside of those boundaries reserved "in common with citizens of the Territory." As a mere right, it was not exclusive in the Indians. Citizens might share it, but the Indians were secured in its enjoyment by a special provision of means for its exercise. They were given "the right of taking fish at all usual and accustomed places," and the right "of erecting temporary buildings for curing them." The contingency of the future ownership of the lands, therefore, was foreseen and provided for—in other words, the Indians were given a right in the land—the right of crossing it to the river—the right to occupy it to the extent and for the purpose mentioned. No other conclusion would give effect to the treaty. And the right was intended to be continuing against the United States and its grantees as well as against the State and its grantees.

It is further contended that the rights conferred upon the Indians are subordinate to the powers acquired by the state upon its admission into the Union. In other words, it is contended that the state acquired by its admission into the Union "upon an equal footing with the original states," the power to grant rights in or to dispose of the shore lands upon navigable streams, and such power is subject only to the paramount authority of Congress with regard to public navigation and commerce. The United States, therefore, it is contended, could neither grant nor retain rights in the shore or to the lands under water.

The elements of this contention and the answer to it are expressed in Shively v. Bowlby, 152 U.S. 1 [1894]. It is unnecessary, and it would be difficult, to add anything to the reasoning of that case. The power and rights of the states in and over shore lands were carefully defined, but the power of the United States, while it held the country as a territory, to create rights which would be binding on the states, was also announced * * *.

> "We cannot doubt, therefore, that Congress has the power to make grants of lands below high-water mark of navigable waters in any territory of the United States, whenever it becomes necessary to do so in order to perform international obligations, or to effect the improvement of such lands for the promotion and convenience of commerce with foreign nations and among the several states, or to carry out other public purposes appropriate to the objects for which the United States hold the territory."

The extinguishment of the Indian title, opening the land for settlement, and preparing the way for future states, were appropriate to the objects for which the United States held the territory. And surely it was within the competency of the nation to secure to the Indians such a remnant of the great rights they possessed as "taking fish at all usual and accustomed places." Nor does it restrain the state unreasonably, if at all, in the regulation of the right. It only fixes in the land such easements as enable the right to be exercised.

Decree reversed and the case remanded for further proceedings in accordance with this opinion.

Winters v. United States
207 U.S. 564 (1908)

This suit was brought by the United States to restrain appellants and others from constructing or maintaining dams or reservoirs on the Milk River in the State of Montana, or in any manner preventing the water of the river or its tributaries from flowing to the Fort Belknap Indian Reservation.

An interlocutory order was granted, enjoining the defendants in the suit from interfering in any manner with the use by the reservation of 5,000 inches of the water of the river. The order was affirmed by the Circuit Court of Appeals. Upon the return of the case to the Circuit Court, an order was taken pro confesso [defendant admits or fails to answer the charge] against five of the defendants. The appellants filed a joint and several answer, upon which and the bill a decree was entered making the preliminary injunction permanent. The decree was affirmed by the Circuit Court of Appeals.

The allegations of the bill, so far as necessary to state them, are as follows: On the first day of May, 1888, a tract of land, the property of the United States, was reserved and set apart "as an Indian reservation as and for a permanent home and abiding place of the Gros Ventre and Assiniboine bands or tribes of Indians in the State (then Territory) of Montana, designated and known as the Fort Belknap Indian Reservation." The tract has ever since been used as an Indian reservation and as the home and abiding place of the Indians. Its boundaries were fixed and defined as follows:

> "Beginning at a point in the middle of the main channel of Milk River, opposite the mouth of Snake Creek; thence due south to a point due west of the western extremity of the Little Rocky Mountains; thence due east to the crest of said mountains at their western extremity, and thence following the southern crest of said mountains to the eastern extremity thereof; thence in a northerly direction in a direct line to a point in the middle of the main channel of Milk River opposite the mouth of People's Creek; thence up Milk River, in the middle of the main channel thereof, to the place of beginning."

Milk River, designated as the northern boundary of the reservation, is a non-navigable stream. Large portions of the lands embraced within the reservation are well fitted and adapted for pasturage and the feeding and grazing of stock, and since the establishment of the reservation the United States and the Indians have had and have large herds of cattle and large numbers of horses grazing upon the land within the reservation, "being and situate along and bordering upon said Milk River." Other portions of the reservation are "adapted for and susceptible of farming and cultivation and the pursuit of agriculture, and productive in the raising thereon of grass, grain and vegetables," but such portions are of dry and arid character, and in order to make them productive require large quantities of water for the purpose of irrigating them. In 1889 the United States constructed houses and buildings upon the reservation for the occupancy and residence of the officers in charge of it, and such officers depend entirely for their domestic, culinary and irrigation purposes upon the water of the river. In the year 1889, and long prior to the acts of the defendants complained of, the United States, through its officers and agents at the reservation, appropriated and took from the river a flow of 1,000 miners' inches, and conducted it to the buildings and premises, used the same for domestic purposes and also for the irrigation of land adjacent to the buildings and premises, and by the use thereof raised crops of grain, grass and vegetables. Afterwards, but long prior to the acts of the defendants complained of, to wit, on the fifth of July, 1898, the Indians residing on the reservation diverted from the river for the purpose of irrigation a flow of 10,000 miners' inches of water to and upon divers and extensive tracts of land, aggregating in amount about 30,000 acres, and raised upon said lands crops of grain, grass and vegetables. And ever since 1889 and July, 1898, the United States and the Indians have diverted and used the waters of the river in the manner and for the purposes mentioned, and the United States "has been enabled by means thereof to train, encourage and accustom large numbers of Indians residing upon the said reservation to habits of industry and to promote their civilization and improvement." It is alleged with detail that all of the waters of the river are necessary for all those purposes and the purposes for which the reservation was created, and that in furthering and advancing the civilization and improvement of the Indians, and to encourage habits of industry and thrift among them, it is essential and necessary that all of the waters of the river flow down the channel uninterruptedly and undiminished in quantity and undeteriorated in quality.

It is alleged that "notwithstanding the riparian and other rights" of the United States and the Indians to the uninterrupted flow of the waters of the river the defendants, in the year 1900, wrongfully entered upon the river and its tributaries above the points of the diversion of the waters of the river by the United States and the Indians, built large and substantial dams and reservoirs, and by means of canals and ditches and waterways have diverted the waters of the river from its channel, and have deprived the United States and the Indians of the use thereof. And this diversion of the water, it is alleged, has continued until the present time, to the irreparable injury of the United States, for which there is no adequate remedy at law.

MR. JUSTICE MCKENNA, after making the foregoing statement, delivered the opinion of the court.

The case, as we view it, turns on the agreement of May, 1888, resulting in the creation of Fort Belknap Reservation. In the construction of this agreement there are certain elements to be considered that are prominent and significant. The reservation was a part of a very much larger tract which the Indians had the right to occupy and use and which was adequate for the habits and wants of a nomadic and uncivilized people. It was the policy of the Government, it was the desire of the Indians, to change those habits and to become a pastoral and civilized people. If they should become such the original tract was too extensive, but a smaller tract would be inadequate without a change of conditions. The lands were arid and, without irrigation, were practically valueless. And yet, it is contended, the means of irrigation were deliberately given up by the Indians and deliberately accepted by the Government. The lands ceded were, it is true, also arid; and some argument may be urged, and is urged, that with their cession there was the cession of the waters, without which they would be valueless, and "civilized communities could not be established thereon." And this, it is further contended, the Indians knew, and yet made no reservation of the waters. We realize that there is a conflict of implications, but that which makes for the retention of the waters is of greater force than that which makes for their cession. The Indians had command of the lands and the waters—command of all their beneficial use, whether kept for hunting, "and grazing roving herds of stock," or turned to agriculture and the arts of civilization. Did they give up all this? Did they reduce the area of their occupation and give up the waters which made it valuable or adequate? And, even regarding the allegation of the answer as true, that there are springs and streams on the reservation flowing about 2,900 inches of water, the inquiries are pertinent. If it were possible to believe affirmative answers, we might also believe that the Indians were awed by the power of the Government or deceived by its negotiators. Neither view is possible. The Government is asserting the rights of the Indians. But extremes need not be taken into account. By a rule of interpretation of agreements and treaties with the Indians, ambiguities occurring will be resolved from the standpoint of the Indians. And the rule should certainly be applied to determine between two inferences, one of which would support the purpose of the agreement and the other impair or defeat it. On account of their relations to the Government, it cannot be supposed that the Indians were alert to exclude by formal words every inference which might militate against or defeat the declared purpose of themselves and the Government, even if it could be supposed that they had the intelligence to foresee the "double sense" which might sometime be urged against them.

Another contention of appellants is that if it be conceded that there was a reservation of the waters of Milk River by the agreement of 1888, yet the reservation was repealed by the admission of Montana into the Union, February 22, 1889, "upon an equal footing with the original States." The language of counsel is that "any reservation in the agreement with the Indians, expressed or implied, whereby the waters of Milk River were not to be subject of appropriation by the citizens and inhabitants of said State, was repealed by the act of admission." But to establish the repeal counsel rely substantially upon the same argument that they advance against the intention of the agreement to reserve the waters. The power of the Government to reserve the waters and exempt them from appropriation under the state laws is not denied, and could not be. *United States v. Winans*, 198 U.S. 371. That the Government did reserve them we have decided, and for a use which would be necessarily continued through years. This was done May 1, 1888, and it would be extreme to believe that within a year Congress destroyed the reservation and took from the Indians the consideration of their grant, leaving them a barren waste—took from them the means of continuing their old habits, yet did not leave them the power to change to new ones.

Appellants' argument upon the incidental repeal of the agreement by the admission of Montana into the Union and the power over the waters of Milk River which the State thereby acquired to dispose of them under its laws, is elaborate and able, but our construction of the agreement and its effect make it unnecessary to answer the argument in detail. For the same reason we have not discussed the doctrine of riparian rights urged by the Government.

Decree affirmed.

Notes

1. Creation of reserved water rights. Compare the rights reserved in each of the foregoing cases. Who reserved the rights? Was the reservation for a new or an existing use? Was the reservation express or implied? Was the reservation for an on-reservation or an off-reservation use? Did the affected non-Indians have any effective notice of the rights prior to the Court's decisions?

2. The equal footing doctrine. In both cases, the non-Indian parties raised the equal footing doctrine as a defense against tribal rights. Is the Court consistent in its approach to this doctrine in the two cases?

3. The continuing importance of the *Winans* and *Winters* decisions. Together, *Winans* and *Winters* are the core cases of the reserved rights doctrine, centrally important to treaty interpretation and tribal sovereignty. Both cases have been the subject of significant recent scholarship. For a centennial look at the central importance of *Winans*, see Michael C. Blumm & James Brumberg, *"Not Much Less Necessary Than the Atmosphere They Breathed:" Salmon, Indian Treaties, and the Supreme Court—A Centennial Remembrance of* United States v. Winans *and Its Enduring Significance*, 46 Natural Res. J. 489 (2006). For a centennial look at *Winters*, see The Future of Indian and Federal Reserved Water Rights: The *Winters* Centennial (Barbara Cosens & Judith V. Royster, eds., Univ. New Mexico Press 2012). For historical treatments of *Winters*, see John Shurts, The *Winters* Doctrine: Origin and Development of the Indian Reserved Water Rights Doctrine in its Social and Legal Context, 1880s–1930s (U. Okla. Press 2000); Judith V. Royster, *Water, Legal Rights, and Actual Consequences: The Story of* Winters v. United States, *in* Indian Law Stories (Carole Goldberg, Kevin K. Washburn & Philip P. Frickey, eds., Found. Press 2011). *See also* A. Dan Tarlock, *Tribal Justice and Property Rights: The Evolution of* Winters v. United States, 50 Nat. Res. J. 471 (2010) (comparing *Winters* rights and Australian aboriginal rights).

4. Comparing *Winans* rights and *Winters* rights. Most tribal reserved rights to water arise under the *Winters* doctrine established in the 1908 case. That is, those rights are generally implied from the creation of a reservation, and encompass sufficient water to carry out the purposes for which the land was set aside. But the water rights of some tribes may perhaps be more appropriately traced to *Winans*. *See generally* 2 Waters and Water Rights §§ 37.01(b)(1), 37.02(a)(2) (Amy K. Kelley, ed., 3d ed. LexisNexis/Matthew Bender 2016).

In the Waters and Water Rights treatise, Professor Blumm suggested that *Winans* is the lodestar case where a tribe was using water in its aboriginal territory prior to the creation of the reservation, and a treaty or other instrument creating the reservation confirmed those uses of water. These aboriginal uses of water may include irrigation (Pima Indians of the Gila River Reservation) or fisheries (Pacific Northwest tribes). In those cases, "[t]he rights were not created by the [treaty], rather, the treaty confirmed the continued existence of these rights." *United States v. Adair*, 723 F.2d 1394, 1414 (9th Cir. 1983). Where water is reserved to a tribe under this approach, the tribe's priority date is "time immemorial," making the tribe the senior water user. *Id.*

On the other hand, Professor Royster has observed that federal courts have generally not made a distinction between *Winters* and *Winans* rights to water. *See* Judith V. Royster, *A Primer on Indian Water Rights*, 30 Tulsa L.J. 61 (1994). Although there are significant differences between water rights reserved to carry out new purposes (such as agriculture) and those reserved to continue aboriginal uses (such as fishing), the federal courts have tended to use *Winters* to determine whether water has been impliedly reserved to carry out the purposes of the reservation. The courts have generally viewed an express reservation of the right to fish, for example, as evidence that one purpose of the reservation was to allow the tribe to continue its aboriginal fishing way of life, and used *Winters* to find implied rights to water for that purpose. *See, e.g., United States v. Adair*, 723 F.2d 1394 (9th Cir. 1983); *Colville Confederated Tribes v. Walton*, 647 F.2d 42 (9th Cir. 1981), excerpted at pages 487 and 530.

Professor Blumm's approach has been adopted by at least one court. In the Jemez River adjudication in New Mexico, the federal district court rejected the applicability of *Winters* rights for Pueblo grant lands on the ground that the government did not impliedly reserve water for new uses on those lands. However, it refused to grant the state's motion for a ruling that *Winans* rights also did not apply to Pueblo grant lands. Noting that *Winans* rights are recognized aboriginal rights, the court ruled that whether the Pueblos have *Winans* rights depends upon whether the government recognized their aboriginal rights in the Treaty of Guadalupe Hildalgo. *United States v. Abousleman*, Civ. No. 83cv01041 MV-ACE, at 21–28 (D. N.M. Oct. 4, 2004).

5. The half-century after *Winters*. Following the Court's decision in *Winters*, there was no rush to implement the water rights recognized for Indian tribes. As explained by the National Water Commission:

> During most of this 50-year period, the United States was pursuing a policy of encouraging the settlement of the West and the creation of family-sized farms on its arid lands. In retrospect, it can be seen that this policy was pursued with little or no regard for Indian water rights and the *Winters* doctrine. With the encouragement, or at least the cooperation, of the Secretary of the Interior — the very office entrusted with protection of all Indian rights — many large irrigation projects were constructed on streams that flowed through or bordered Indian Reservations, sometimes above and more often below the Reservations. With few exceptions the projects were planned and built by the Federal Government without any attempt to define, let alone protect, prior rights that Indian tribes might have had in the waters used for the projects.... In the history of the United States Government's treatment of Indian tribes, its failure to protect Indian water rights for use on the Reservations it set aside for them is one of the sorrier chapters.

National Water Commission, Water Policies for the Future — Final Report to the President and to the Congress of the United States 474–75 (1973).

Nonetheless, the reserved water rights doctrine did not lay dormant between *Winters* and the *Arizona v. California* decision in 1963, excerpted at page 481. In fact, in states such as Montana and Utah, federal officials claimed, and federal courts accepted, reserved rights for a number of reservations. For elaboration, see John Shurts, The *Winters* Doctrine: Origin and Development of the Indian Reserved Water Rights Doctrine in its Social and Legal Context, 1880s–1930s (U. Okla. Press 2000).

Note on State Water Law Systems

With the exception of federal reserved rights, water rights are almost entirely creatures of state law. The eastern and western United States developed very different water law systems to accommodate very different climates. The main aspects of each system are described below.

1. Western water law. The main water law system in the western half of the United States is called prior appropriation. The appropriation system is predicated on the concept that in the West there is not enough water to go around, and so some means of allocating the scarce resource must be determined. Its main features are:

a. First in time, first in right. Water is allocated by priority date: that is, the first date that the water is put to beneficial use. In times of shortage, those appropriators with earlier priority dates (senior appropriators) get all their water before junior appropriators get any.

b. Prior appropriation rights are based not on ownership of land, but on putting the water to a "beneficial" use as defined by state law. Historically, a beneficial use is one which removes water from the stream and applies it elsewhere. For example, taking water out of the stream by way of a canal or ditch and using it to irrigate croplands is a traditional beneficial use.

Consequently, the water is often used at a location remote from the source of the water.

c. Use it or lose it. The appropriator retains rights to the water only so long as the water is actually put to a beneficial use, and retains rights to only so much of the water as is actually used. Non-use for a specified period of time, which may vary from state to state, constitutes forfeiture of the right.

If Indian tribes were required to conform to the states' prior appropriation systems, tribal rights to water would often be subordinate to the rights of non-Indians. Non-Indians tended to appropriate the water—that is, put it to diversionary, beneficial uses—earlier than did the tribes.

The doctrine of federal reserved water rights first articulated in *Winters*, and subsequently applied to other types of federally-reserved land such as national forests and national parks, mitigated much of the harshness that would have resulted from application of prior appropriation principles to Indian tribes. Under the reserved rights doctrine, reserved rights are appurtenant to the land; tribal beneficial ownership of the land is the basis for the assertion of reserved rights to water, although the water need not be used on the appurtenant land. The priority date for reserved rights is the date of the reservation, rather than the date when the water is put to use. Moreover, reserved rights are not lost through non-use, but may be asserted at any time.

2. Eastern water law. The main water law system in the eastern United States, by contrast, is that of riparian rights. Riparian rights, inherited from England, spring from land ownership, not from water diversion and use for a beneficial purpose. Riparian rights are not lost through non-use, and they generally cannot be separated from the lands to which they are appurtenant. Riparian owners are entitled to a correlative "reasonable use" of the stream, and in some jurisdictions that can mean a continuation of the flow of the stream. Shortages in the riparian world are shared. *See* 1 Waters and Water Rights §§ 6.01, 7.02(d) (Amy K. Kelley, eds., LexisNexis/Matthew Bender 3d ed. 2016).

No tribe in a riparian state has yet litigated its reserved water rights, although the Seminole Tribe of Florida entered into a negotiated water rights settlement. *See* Florida Indian (Seminole) Land Claims Settlement Act of 1987, 25 U.S.C. § 1772(e) (incorporating the Seminole Water Rights Compact, which is reprinted in *Seminole Indian Land Claims Settlement Act of 1987: Hearing on S. 1684 Before the Senate Select Comm. on Indian Affairs*, 100th Cong., 83–122 (1987)). Because tribal rights have generally been determined only in the context of appropriation states, integrating reserved rights with state-law riparian systems will pose special problems. *See generally* Judith V. Royster, Winters *in the East: Tribal Reserved Rights to Water in Riparian States*, 25 Wm & Mary Envtl. L. & Pol'y Rev. 169 (2000).

3. Reserved water rights as a hybrid? One of the reasons reserved water rights are so controversial is that, as federal rights, they follow neither prior appropriation nor riparian principles. Instead, they seem to combine elements of both. What elements of prior appropriation and riparianism are implicit in reserved water rights?

B. Extending the *Winters* Doctrine
Arizona v. California
373 U.S. 546 (1963)

MR. JUSTICE BLACK delivered the opinion of the Court.

In 1952 the State of Arizona invoked the original jurisdiction of this Court by filing a complaint against the State of California and seven of its public agencies. Later, Nevada, New Mexico, Utah, and the United States were added as parties either voluntarily or on motion. The basic controversy in the case is over how much water each State has a legal right to use out of the waters of the Colorado River and its tributaries. After preliminary pleadings, we referred the case to * * * [a] Special Master to take evidence, find facts, state conclusions of law, and recommend a decree, all "subject to consideration, revision, or approval by the Court." The Master conducted a trial lasting from June 14, 1956, to August 28, 1958, during which 340 witnesses were heard orally or by deposition, thousands of exhibits were received, and 25,000 pages of transcript were filled. Following many motions, arguments, and briefs, the Master in a 433-page volume reported his findings, conclusions, and recommended decree, received by the Court on January 16, 1961. The case has been extensively briefed here and orally argued twice, the first time about 16 hours, the second, over six.

The Colorado River itself rises in the mountains of Colorado and flows generally in a southwesterly direction for about 1,300 miles through Colorado, Utah, and Arizona and along the Arizona-Nevada and Arizona-California boundaries, after which it passes into Mexico and empties into the Mexican waters of the Gulf of California. On its way to the sea it receives tributary waters from Wyoming, Colorado, Utah, Nevada, New Mexico, and Arizona. The river and its tributaries flow in a natural basin almost surrounded by large mountain ranges and drain 242,000 square miles, an area about 900 miles long from north to south and 300 to 500 miles wide from east to west—practically one-twelfth the area of the continental United States excluding Alaska. Much of this large basin is so arid that it is, as it always has been, largely dependent upon managed use of the waters of the Colorado River System to make it productive and inhabitable. The Master refers to archaeological evidence that as long as 2,000 years ago the ancient Hohokam tribe built and maintained irrigation canals near what is now Phoenix, Arizona, and that American Indians were practicing irrigation in that region at the time white men first explored it.

V. CLAIMS OF THE UNITED STATES.

In these proceedings, the United States has asserted claims to waters in the main river and in some of the tributaries for use on Indian Reservations, National Forests, Recreational and Wildlife Areas and other government lands and works. While the Master passed upon some of these claims, he declined to reach others, particularly those relating to tributaries. We approve his decision as to which claims required adjudication, and likewise we approve the decree he recommended for the government claims he did decide. We shall discuss only the claims of the United States on behalf of the Indian Reservations.

The Government, on behalf of five Indian Reservations in Arizona, California, and Nevada,[97] asserted rights to water in the mainstream of the Colorado River. The Colorado River Reservation, located partly in Arizona and partly in California, is the largest. It was originally created by an Act of Congress in 1865, but its area was later increased by Executive Order. Other reservations were created by Executive Orders and amendments to them, ranging in dates from 1870 to 1907. The Master found both as a matter of fact and law that when the United States created these reservations or added to them, it reserved not only land but also the use of enough water from the Colorado to irrigate the irrigable portions of the reserved lands. The aggregate quantity of water which the Master held was reserved for all the reservations is about 1,000,000 acre-feet, to be used on around 135,000 irrigable acres of land. Here, as before the Master, Arizona argues that the United States had no power to make a reservation of navigable waters after Arizona became a State; that navigable waters could not be reserved by Executive Orders; that the United States did not intend to reserve water for the Indian Reservations; that the amount of water reserved should be measured by the reasonably foreseeable needs of the Indians living on the reservation rather than by the number of irrigable acres; and, finally, that the judicial doctrine of equitable apportionment should be used to divide the water between the Indians and the other people in the State of Arizona.

The last argument is easily answered. The doctrine of equitable apportionment is a method of resolving water disputes between States. It was created by this Court in the exercise of its original jurisdiction over controversies in which States are parties. An Indian Reservation is not a State. And while Congress has sometimes left Indian Reservations considerable power to manage their own affairs, we are not convinced by Arizona's argument that each reservation is so much like a State that its rights to water should be determined by the doctrine of equitable apportionment. Moreover, even were we to treat an Indian Reservation like a State, equitable apportionment would still not control since, under our view, the Indian claims here are governed by the statutes and Executive Orders creating the reservations.

Arizona's contention that the Federal Government had no power, after Arizona became a State, to reserve waters for the use and benefit of federally reserved lands rests largely upon statements in *Pollard's Lessee v. Hagan*, 3 How. 212 (1845), and *Shively v. Bowlby*, 152 U.S. 1 (1894). Those cases and others that followed them gave rise to the doctrine that lands underlying navigable waters within territory acquired by the Government are held in trust for future States and that title to such lands is automatically vested in the States upon admission to the Union. But those cases involved only the shores of and lands beneath navigable waters. They do not determine the problem before us and cannot be accepted as limiting the broad powers of

---

97. The Reservations were Chemehuevi, Cocopah, Yuma, Colorado River and Fort Mohave.

the United States to regulate navigable waters under the Commerce Clause and to regulate government lands under Art. IV, § 3, of the Constitution. We have no doubt about the power of the United States under these clauses to reserve water rights for its reservations and its property.

Arizona also argues that, in any event, water rights cannot be reserved by Executive Order. Some of the reservations of Indian lands here involved were made almost 100 years ago, and all of them were made over 45 years ago. In our view, these reservations, like those created directly by Congress, were not limited to land, but included waters as well. Congress and the Executive have ever since recognized these as Indian Reservations. Numerous appropriations, including appropriations for irrigation projects, have been made by Congress. They have been uniformly and universally treated as reservations by map makers, surveyors, and the public. We can give but short shrift at this late date to the argument that the reservations either of land or water are invalid because they were originally set apart by the Executive.

Arizona also challenges the Master's holding as to the Indian Reservations on two other grounds: first, that there is a lack of evidence showing that the United States in establishing the reservations intended to reserve water for them; second, that even if water was meant to be reserved the Master has awarded too much water. We reject both of these contentions. Most of the land in these reservations is and always has been arid. If the water necessary to sustain life is to be had, it must come from the Colorado River or its tributaries. It can be said without overstatement that when the Indians were put on these reservations they were not considered to be located in the most desirable area of the Nation. It is impossible to believe that when Congress created the great Colorado River Indian Reservation and when the Executive Department of this Nation created the other reservations they were unaware that most of the lands were of the desert kind—hot, scorching sands—and that water from the river would be essential to the life of the Indian people and to the animals they hunted and the crops they raised. In the debate leading to approval of the first congressional appropriation for irrigation of the Colorado River Indian Reservation, the delegate from the Territory of Arizona made this statement:

> "Irrigating canals are essential to the prosperity of these Indians. Without water there can be no production, no life; and all they ask of you is to give them a few agricultural implements to enable them to dig an irrigating canal by which their lands may be watered and their fields irrigated, so that they may enjoy the means of existence. You must provide these Indians with the means of subsistence or they will take by robbery from those who have. During the last year I have seen a number of these Indians starved to death for want of food."

The question of the Government's implied reservation of water rights upon the creation of an Indian Reservation was before this Court in *Winters v. United States*, decided in 1908. Much the same argument made to us was made in *Winters* to persuade the Court to hold that Congress had created an Indian Reservation without intending to reserve waters necessary to make the reservation livable. The Court rejected all of the arguments. * * * The Court in *Winters* concluded that the Government, when it created that Indian Reservation, intended to deal fairly with the Indians by reserving for them the waters without which their lands would have been useless. *Winters* has been followed by this Court as recently as 1939 in *United States v. Powers*, 305 U.S. 527. We follow it now and agree that the United States did reserve the water rights for the Indians effective as of the time the Indian Reservations were created. This means, as the Master held, that these water rights, having vested before the Act became effective on June 25, 1929, are "present perfected rights" and as such are entitled to priority under the Act.

We also agree with the Master's conclusion as to the quantity of water intended to be reserved. He found that the water was intended to satisfy the future as well as the present needs of the Indian Reservations and ruled that enough water was reserved to irrigate all the practicably irrigable acreage on the reservations. Arizona, on the other hand, contends that the quantity of water reserved should be measured by the Indians' "reasonably foreseeable needs," which, in fact, means by the number of Indians. How many Indians there will be and what their future needs will be can only be guessed. We have concluded, as did the Master, that the only feasible and fair way by which reserved water for the reservations can be measured is irrigable acreage. The various acreages of irrigable land which the Master found to be on the different reservations we find to be reasonable.

Finally, we note our agreement with the Master that all uses of mainstream water within a State are to be charged against that State's apportionment, which of course includes uses by the United States.

Notes

1. **Creating reserved water rights.** Who created the reserved water rights in this case? How?

2. **Quantification of water rights.** *Arizona v. California* addressed the issue of how to determine the amount of water Indian tribes are entitled to under the *Winters* doctrine. The practicably irrigable acreage (PIA) standard articulated in this case has proved to be the primary measure of tribal water rights, although its usefulness is increasingly being questioned. We explore these issues in the next section.

3. **Subsequent developments in the *Arizona v. California* litigation.** In 2000, the Supreme Court ruled that the Quechan Tribe could pursue its claim to water from the Colorado River to irrigate 25,000 acres of the Fort Yuma reservation along the Arizona-California border. The states claimed that the tribe was compensated for its reserved water rights in a $15 million land claim settlement in 1983. But the Court held, 6–3, in an opinion by Justice Ginsburg, that the tribe should be allowed to prove that the settlement was only for the wrongful use of its lands since the late 19th century, not for the lands themselves. The Court therefore remanded the case to a special master to determine whether the tribe still owns the lands and therefore still possesses reserved water rights. *Arizona v. California*, 530 U.S. 392 (2000). In 2006, under

settlement agreements between the Quechan Tribe, the United States, Arizona, and California, the Supreme Court entered a consolidated decree recognizing an additional 26,350 acre-feet for the tribe. *See Arizona v. California,* 547 U.S. 150 (2006). The Quechan Tribe now holds a reserved right to 77,966 acre-feet of water with a priority date of January 9, 1884.

C. Scope and Extent of Water Rights

The *Winters* case in 1908 established the existence and much of the measure of tribal reserved rights to water, and *Arizona v. California* in 1963 gave content to that right by creating the PIA standard for measuring the quantity of the tribal right to water based on agriculture. The cases in this section look at a variety of issues that have arisen in the decades since *Arizona v. California*, concerning the scope and extent of tribal reserved rights to water.

1. Reservation Purposes, Priority Dates, and Quantification

Under the *Winters* doctrine of water rights, water is impliedly reserved to fulfill the purposes for which a reservation was created. In order to ensure that the reserved water will fulfill those purposes, the water right (at least in western states) is assigned a "priority date" and quantified. The purposes for which a reservation was set aside, and the measure or quantification of the tribe's right to water, are closely linked. The priority date allows tribal reserved rights to function in an integrated system with western appropriation first-in-time, first-in-right state-law water rights. The cases and notes in this section explore these interrelated concepts.

Note on Reservation Purposes

As you read the cases in this section, note what the courts identify as the purpose or purposes of the Indian reservations. Do the courts identify a single purpose or multiple purposes? Do the courts identify specific purposes such as agriculture or fishing, or do they recognize a broader purpose of establishing a homeland for the tribe?

Also note the courts' discussions of *United States v. New Mexico*, 438 U.S. 696 (1978), in which the U.S. Supreme Court determined non-Indian federal reserved rights to water for the Gila National Forest. In that decision, the Court distinguished between the primary and secondary purposes for which the land was set aside, looking to "the specific purposes for which the land was reserved" and concluding that a federal reservation was entitled to reserved water rights for those primary purposes only. In the case of the Gila National Forest, this meant water to preserve timber and secure favorable water flows. It did not mean water for such "secondary uses" as recreation or fish and wildlife. Water rights for such secondary purposes must be obtained under state law.

The Supreme Court has not issued an Indian water rights opinion since *New Mexico*, and consequently it is an open question whether the *New Mexico* primary-versus-secondary purposes analysis will apply to *Winters* rights for Indian reservations. The various state and lower federal courts have not agreed on the question. Contrast the broad approach of the Ninth Circuit in *Adair I*, at page 487, with the strict interpretation of the Wyoming Supreme Court in *Big Horn I*, at page 499. Contrast both with the Arizona Supreme Court's rejection of the *New Mexico* test in *Gila River*, at page 504.

Note on Methods of Quantification

Once the purposes of a reservation have been determined, the court must quantify the tribe's right to water to fulfill those purposes. As you read the cases in this section, note how the courts quantify the tribal water right, and how that method of quantification correlates to the purposes that the courts found for the particular reservation. This note briefly describes the primary methods of quantification that courts have used.

a. Practicably irrigable acreage. Thus far, agriculture has been found to be either one of the purposes, or the sole purpose, of every reservation for which reserved rights have been litigated. As a result, the primary measure of tribal water rights is an agricultural measure: the practicably irrigable acreage (PIA) standard articulated in *Arizona v. California*, at page 481.

Determining PIA involves "[a]t least four disciplines... soil science, hydrology, engineering and economics." David H. Getches, Charles F. Wilkinson & Robert A. Williams, Jr., Federal Indian Law: Cases and Materials 833 (West 4th ed. 1998). The parties in the *Big Horn* litigation in Wyoming agreed on the following definition of PIA, which was adopted by the court:

> "those acres susceptible to sustained irrigation at reasonable costs." The determination of practicably irrigable acreage involves a two-part analysis, i.e., the PIA must be susceptible of sustained irrigation (not only proof of the arability but also of the engineering feasibility of irrigating the land) and irrigable "at reasonable cost."

In re General Adjudication of all Rights to Use Water in the Big Horn River System (Big Horn I), 753 P.2d 76, 101 (Wyo. 1988), *aff'd sub nom. by an equally divided Court, Wyoming v. United States*, 492 U.S. 406 (1989); *see also State ex rel. Martinez v. Lewis*, 861 P.2d 235, 247 (N.M. Ct. App. 1993) (adopting the same definitional language).

b. Instream flow right. If the purposes of reservations extend beyond agricultural purposes, courts will use other measures of water quantification. Thus, for example, if a continuation of aboriginal fishing practices is a purpose of a reservation, courts will award an "instream flow right" as the measure of the tribal water right.

Historically, an appropriator in a western state could receive a vested property right to the amount of water diverted and applied to a beneficial use. A diversion required that the water be physically removed from the source and applied elsewhere for uses such as irrigation, stock watering, mining, and manufacturing. However well that doctrine may have worked during the nineteenth and early twentieth centuries, it failed to take into account other values that are important in the twenty-first century. A century after the establishment of the prior appropriation system, the use of water for such "instream" purposes as fish and wildlife habitat, water quality maintenance, and recreation became as important as the traditional consumptive uses of water recognized by western states' water law.

Water required to be left in place is generally referred to as an instream flow right. An instream flow is any use of water that does not require a diversion or withdrawal of the water from the stream. It is the right to maintain a specified quantity of water in the stream for specified purposes. Those purposes may include those listed above, as well as navigation and hydropower generation. Most western states have now recognized instream flow rights through one mechanism or another. But observe that this late recognition of instream rights in a prior appropriation system, which gives priority to rights first in time, disadvantages latecomers, like instream rights, perpetually. On the issue of instream flow rights generally, see Michael C. Blumm, *Unconventional Waters: The Quiet Revolution in Federal and Tribal Minimum Streamflows*, 19 Ecol. L.Q. 445 (1992).

Note how an instream flow right is described in *Adair I*, below. An instream flow right is actually the right to prevent others from drawing down the water below a certain level. It is thus a right to prevent others from injuring a resource, rather than an affirmative right to take a resource. But although the tribes' water right might be in the nature of a negative right, the water right supports affirmative game and fish harvesting rights.

United States v. Adair [*Adair I*]

723 F.2d 1394 (9th Cir. 1983)

FLETCHER, Circuit Judge.

I BACKGROUND

A. History of the Litigation Area.

The Klamath Indians have hunted, fished, and foraged in the area of the Klamath Marsh and upper Williamson River for over a thousand years. In 1864 the Klamath Tribe entered into a treaty with the United States whereby it relinquished its aboriginal claim to some 12 million acres of land in return for a reservation of approximately 800,000 acres in south-central Oregon. This reservation included all of the Klamath Marsh as well as large forested tracts of the Williamson River watershed. Treaty between the United States of America and the Klamath and Moadoc Tribes and Yahooskin Band of Snake Indians, Oct. 14, 1864, 16 Stat. 707. Article I of the treaty gave the Klamath the exclusive right to hunt, fish, and gather on their reservation. Article II provided funds to help the Klamath adopt an agricultural way of life.

For 20 years, until 1887, the Klamath lived on their reservation under the terms of the 1864 treaty. In 1887 Congress passed the General Allotment Act, which fundamentally changed the nature of land ownership on the Klamath Reservation. Prior to the Act, the tribe held the reservation land in communal ownership. Pursuant to the terms of the Allotment Act, however, parcels of tribal land were granted to individual Indians in fee. Under the allotment system, approximately 25% of the original Klamath Reservation passed from tribal to individual Indian ownership. Over time, many of these individual allotments passed into non-Indian ownership.

The next major change in the pattern of land ownership on the Klamath Reservation occurred in 1954 when Congress approved the Klamath Termination Act. Act of Aug. 13, 1954, c. 732, § 1, 68 Stat. 718 (codified at 25 U.S.C. §§ 564–564w (1976)). Under this Act, tribe members could give up their interest in tribal property for cash. A large majority of the tribe chose to do this. In order to meet the cash obligation, in 1961, the United States purchased much of the former Klamath Reservation. The balance of the reservation was placed in a private trust for the remaining tribe members. In 1973, to complete implementation of the Klamath Termination Act, the United States condemned most of the tribal land held in trust. Payments from the condemnation proceeding and sale of the remaining trust land went to Indians still enrolled in the tribe. This final distribution of assets essentially extinguished the original Klamath Reservation as a source of tribal property.

Even though the Klamath Tribe no longer holds any of its former reservation, the United States still holds title to much of the former reservation lands. In 1958 the Government purchased approximately 15,000 acres of the Klamath Marsh, the heart of the former reservation, to establish a migratory bird refuge under the jurisdiction of the United States Fish and Wildlife Service. In 1961 and again in 1973, the Government purchased large forested portions of the former Klamath Reservation. This forest land became part of the Winema National Forest under the jurisdiction of the United States Forest Service. By these two purchases, the Government became the owner of approximately 70% of the former reservation lands. The balance of the reservation is in private, Indian and non-Indian, ownership either through allotment or sale of reservation lands at the time of termination.

III WATER RIGHTS

The district court declared reserved water rights within the litigation area to the Klamath Tribe, the Government, individual Indians, and non-Indian successors to Indian land owners.

A. A Reservation of Water to Accompany the Tribe's Treaty Right to Hunt, Fish, and Gather.

Article I of the 1864 treaty with the Klamath Tribe reserved to the Tribe the exclusive right to hunt, fish, and gather on its reservation. This right survived the Klamath Termination Act. *See Kimball v. Callahan*, 590 F.2d 768, 775 (9th Cir.), *cert. denied*, 444 U.S. 826 (1979) (*Kimball II*); [*Kimball v. Callahan*, 493 F.2d 564, 569 (9th Cir.), *cert. denied*, 419 U.S. 1019 (1974) (*Kimball I*)]. The issue presented for decision in this case is whether, as the district court held, these hunting and fishing rights carry with them an implied reservation of water rights.

1. Reservation of Water in the 1864 Treaty.

* * * In *New Mexico* [*United States v. New Mexico*, 438 U.S. 696 (1978)], the Supreme Court clarified the scope of the reserved water rights doctrine in the course of determining whether the United States had reserved water for use on the Gila National Forest in New Mexico. The Court indicated that water may be reserved under the *Winters* doctrine only for the primary purposes of a federal reservation. Hence, even though the Supreme Court agreed that hunting, fishing, and recreation are among the purposes for which the National Forest System is maintained, it determined that these purposes are secondary to the purposes of "securing favorable conditions of water flows," and furnishing "a continuous supply of timber." 16 U.S.C. § 475 (1976), quoted in *United States v. New Mexico*. Accordingly, only the latter purposes carried with them an implied reservation of water rights. *New Mexico* and *Cappaert* [*v. United States*, 426 U.S. 128 (1976)], while not directly applicable to *Winters* doctrine rights on Indian reservations, see F. Cohen, *Handbook of Federal Indian Law* 581–85 (1982 ed.), establish several useful guidelines. First, water rights may be implied only "where water is necessary to fulfill the very purposes for which a federal reservation was created," and not where it is merely "valuable for a secondary use of the reservation." *New Mexico*, 438 U.S. at 702. Second, the scope of the implied right is circumscribed by the necessity that calls for its creation. The doctrine "reserves only that amount of water necessary to fulfill the purpose of the reservation, no more." *Cappaert*, 426 U.S. at 141.

Article I of the Klamath Treaty expressly provides that the Tribe will have exclusive on-reservation fishing and gathering rights. * * * In view of the historical importance of hunting and fishing, and the language of Article I of the 1864 Treaty, we find that one of the "very purposes" of establishing the Klamath Reservation was to secure to the Tribe a continuation of its traditional hunting and fishing lifestyle. This was at the forefront of the Tribe's concerns in negotiating the treaty and was recognized as important by the United States as well.

At the same time, as the State and individual defendants argue, Articles II through V of the 1864 Treaty evince a purpose to convert the Klamath Tribe to an agricultural way of life. Article II provides that monies paid to the Tribe in consideration for the land ceded by the treaty "shall be expended . . . to promote the well-being of the Indians, advance them in civilization, *and especially agriculture*, and to secure their moral improvement and education." (emphasis added). A similar focus on agriculture is reflected in the language of Articles III, IV and V. It is apparent that a second essential purpose in setting aside the Klamath Reservation, recognized by both the Tribe and the Government, was to encourage the Indians to take up farming.

Neither *Cappaert* nor *New Mexico* requires us to choose between these activities or to identify a single essential purpose which the parties to the 1864 Treaty intended the Klamath Reservation to serve. In fact, in *Colville Confederated Tribes v. Walton*,

647 F.2d 42 (9th Cir.), *cert. denied*, 454 U.S. 1092 (1981) [excerpted at page 413], this court found that provision of a "homeland for the Indians to maintain their agrarian society," as well as "preservation of the tribe's access to fishing grounds," were dual purposes behind establishment of the Colville Reservation. Consequently the court found an implied reservation of water to support both of these activities. * * * We therefore have no difficulty in upholding the district court's finding that at the time the Klamath Reservation was established, the Government and the Tribe intended to reserve a quantity of the water flowing through the reservation not only for the purpose of supporting Klamath agriculture, but also for the purpose of maintaining the Tribe's treaty right to hunt and fish on reservation lands.

A water right to support game and fish adequate to the needs of Indian hunters and fishers is not a right recognized as a part of the common law doctrine of prior appropriation followed in Oregon. Indeed, one of the standard requirements of the prior appropriation doctrine is that some diversion of the natural flow of a stream is necessary to effect a valid appropriation. But diversion of water is not required to support the fish and game that the Klamath Tribe take in exercise of their treaty rights. Thus the right to water reserved to further the Tribe's hunting and fishing purposes is unusual in that it is basically non-consumptive. The holder of such a right is not entitled to withdraw water from the stream for agricultural, industrial, or other consumptive uses (absent independent consumptive rights). Rather, the entitlement consists of the right to prevent other appropriators from depleting the streams waters below a protected level in any area where the non-consumptive right applies. In this respect, the water right reserved for the Tribe to hunt and fish has no corollary in the common law of prior appropriations.[19]

2. Effect of the Klamath Termination Act on the Tribe's Hunting and Fishing Water Rights.

In 1954, Congress terminated federal supervision of the Klamath Tribe. The state and individual appellants now argue that the Termination Act also abrogated any water rights reserved by the 1864 Treaty to accompany the Tribe's right to hunt and fish. Appellants contend that when federal supervision was terminated, former reservation lands were sold at full market value without limitations on use. They conclude that recognition of a reserved water right to sustain the Tribe's hunting and fishing rights would impose a servitude or limitation on the use of former reservation lands in contravention of the Termination Act policy of unencumbered sale.

Appellants' argument, however, overlooks the substantive language of the Termination Act, the canons of construction for legislation affecting Indian Tribes, and the implications of our decision in *Kimball I*. Section 564m(a) of the Termination Act provides, "nothing in sections 564–564w of this title shall abrogate any water

---

19. The fact that water rights of the type reserved for the Klamath Tribe are not generally recognized under state prior appropriations law is not controlling as federal law provides an unequivocal source of such rights.

rights of the tribe and its members." This provision admits no exception, nor can it be read to exclude reserved water rights. * * * Because Congress in section 564m of the Termination Act explicitly protected tribal water rights and nowhere in the Act explicitly denied them, we can only conclude that such rights survived termination.

3. Priority of the Water Right Reserved to Accompany the Tribe's Treaty Right to Hunt and Fish.

The district court found that the Tribe's water right accompanying its right to hunt and fish carried a priority date for appropriation of time immemorial. The State and individual appellants argue that an implied reservation of water cannot have a priority date earlier than establishment of the reservation. The Government and the Tribe argue that a pre-reservation priority date is appropriate for tribal water uses that pre-date establishment of the reservation.

Foremost among [the relevant principles] is the principle that "the treaty is not a grant of rights to the Indians, but a grant of rights from them—a reservation of those not granted." *United States v. Winans*, 198 U.S. 371, 381 (1905). Further, Indian treaties should be construed as the tribes would have understood them. And any ambiguity in a treaty must be resolved in favor of the Indians. A corollary of these principles, also recognized by the Supreme Court, is that when a tribe and the Government negotiate a treaty, the tribe retains all rights not expressly ceded to the Government in the treaty so long as the rights retained are consistent with the tribe's sovereign dependent status.

In 1864, at the time the Klamath entered into a treaty with the United States, the Tribe had lived in Central Oregon and Northern California for more than a thousand years. This ancestral homeland encompassed some 12 million acres. Within its domain, the Tribe used the waters that flowed over its land for domestic purposes and to support its hunting, fishing, and gathering lifestyle. This uninterrupted use and occupation of land and water created in the Tribe aboriginal or "Indian title" to all of its vast holdings. * * * The Tribe's title also included aboriginal hunting and fishing rights, and by the same reasoning, an aboriginal right to the water used by the Tribe as it flowed through its homeland.

With this background in mind, we examine the priority date attaching to the Klamath Tribe's reservation of water to support its hunting and fishing rights. In Article I of the 1864 Treaty the Tribe expressly ceded "all [its] right, title and claim" to most of its ancestral domain. In the same article, however, the Tribe reserved for its exclusive use and occupancy the lands that became the Klamath Reservation, the same lands that are the subject of the instant suit. There is no indication in the treaty, express or implied, that the Tribe intended to cede any of its interest in those lands it reserved for itself. Nor is it possible that the Tribe would have understood such a reservation of land to include a relinquishment of its right to use the water as it had always used it on the land it had reserved as a permanent home. Further, we find no language in the treaty to indicate that the United States intended or understood the agreement to diminish the Tribe's rights in that part of its aboriginal holding reserved for its permanent occupancy and use. Accordingly, we agree with the district court that within the 1864 Treaty is a recognition of the Tribe's aboriginal water rights and a confirmation to the Tribe of a continued water right to support its hunting and fishing lifestyle on the Klamath Reservation.

Such water rights necessarily carry a priority date of time immemorial. The rights were not created by the 1864 Treaty, rather, the treaty confirmed the continued existence of these rights. To assign the Tribe's hunting and fishing water rights the later, 1864, priority date argued for by the State and individual appellants would ignore one of the fundamental principles of prior appropriations law—that priority for a particular water right dates from the time of first use. Furthermore, an 1864 priority date might limit the scope of the Tribe's hunting and fishing water rights by reduction for any pre-1864 appropriations of water. This could extinguish rights the Tribe held before 1864 and intended to reserve to itself thereafter. Thus, we are compelled to conclude that where, as here, a tribe shows its aboriginal use of water to support a hunting and fishing lifestyle, and then enters into a treaty with the United States that reserves this aboriginal water use, the water right thereby established retains a priority date of first or immemorial use.

This does not mean, however, as the individual appellants argue, that the former Klamath Reservation will be subject to a "wilderness servitude" in favor of the Tribe. Apparently, appellants read the water rights decreed to the Tribe to require restoration of an 1864 level of water flow on former reservation lands now used by the Tribe to maintain traditional hunting and fishing lifestyles. We do not interpret the district court's decision so expansively.

In its opinion discussing the Tribe's hunting and fishing water rights, the district court stated "the Indians are still entitled to as much water on the Reservation lands as they need to protect their hunting and fishing rights." We interpret this statement to confirm to the Tribe the amount of water necessary to support its hunting and fishing rights as currently exercised to maintain the livelihood of Tribe members, not as these rights once were exercised by the Tribe in 1864.

We find authority for such a construction of the Indians' rights in the Supreme Court's decision in *Washington v. Fishing Vessel Ass'n*, 443 U.S. 658 (1979). There, citing *Arizona v. California*, 373 U.S. 546 (1963), a reserved water rights case, the court stated "that Indian treaty rights to a natural resource that once was thoroughly and exclusively exploited by the Indians secures so much as, but not more than, is necessary to provide the Indians with a livelihood—that is to say, a moderate living." Implicit in this "moderate living" standard is the conclusion that Indian tribes are not generally entitled to the same level of exclusive use and exploitation of a natural resource that they enjoyed at the time they entered into the treaty reserving their interest in the resource, unless, of course, no lesser level will supply them with a moderate living. *See Washington v. Fishing Vessel Ass'n*, 443 U.S. at 686. As limited by the "moderate living" standard enunciated in *Fishing Vessel*, we affirm the district court's decision that the Klamath Tribe is entitled to a reservation of water with a priority date of immemorial use, sufficient to support exercise of treaty hunting and fishing rights.[24]

C. The United States' Water Rights in Former Klamath Reservation Lands.

The most significant water rights still held by the Klamath Tribe on former reservation lands are those that accompany their treaty hunting and fishing rights. These rights are essentially nonconsumptive in nature. Thus, to the extent that the United States now owns former reservation lands which may be benefitted by a compatible nonconsumptive use of water, the Government may participate in the enjoyment of the Klamath's hunting and fishing water rights.

We must point out, however, that the Government has no ownership interest in, or right to control the use of, the Klamath Tribe's hunting and fishing water rights. The hunting and fishing rights from which these water rights arise by necessary implication were reserved by the Tribe in the 1864 treaty with the United States. The hunting and fishing rights themselves belong to the Tribe and may not be transferred to a third party. Because the Klamath Tribe's treaty right to hunt and fish is not transferable, it follows that no subsequent transferee may acquire that right of use or the reserved water necessary to fulfill that use.[31]

Notes

1. Priority dates. Note that the reserved rights for water for the tribe's hunting and fishing are "time immemorial" rights, but the reserved rights for irrigation have a reservation date priority. Why are these priority dates different for the different

---

24. Appellants argue vigorously that the Tribe can no longer hold a water right to support its treaty hunting and fishing rights because the Tribe no longer owns land to which this water right is appurtenant. Their argument, however, misperceives the history and nature of the Klamath's reserved water rights.

In 1864, when the Klamath Reservation was created and water was impliedly reserved for the benefit of the Tribe, the Indians owned appurtenant land. The issue is whether these water rights, once reserved, are terminated by a transfer of the appurtenant land. We have already held in *Kimball I* that the Tribe's hunting and fishing rights guaranteed by the treaty survived despite the land transfer. To find that the water rights necessary to give meaning to these hunting and fishing rights have been lost because the Tribe has disposed of the appurtenant land would effectively overrule the *Kimball* decisions. We refuse to do so.

31. A forceful argument can be made that the Klamath's hunting and fishing water rights should not be treated differently from other reserved water rights, such as those for irrigation. Under this view, the Tribe's hunting and fishing water rights would be transferable to the United States. *Cf. Colville Confederated Tribe v. Walton*, 647 F.2d at 50–51 (transfer of reserved irrigation water rights). We decline to adopt this analogy, however, because even when the Tribe transfers the land to which the hunting and fishing water rights might be said to be appurtenant, it is the Tribe and its members, not some third party, that retains the right to hunt and fish and needs water to support that right. Where the Tribe transfers land without reserving the right to hunt and fish on it, there is no longer any basis for a hunting and fishing water right. For this reason, we find the Klamath Tribe's hunting and fishing water rights virtually unique and not subject to the ordinary rules of transfer and change of use.

water rights? Compare the earlier discussion of *Winans* versus *Winters* rights at page 478. Is the Klamath Tribe's water for hunting and fishing a *Winans* right, while the reservation irrigation rights are *Winters* rights? If the former is a *Winans* rights, is it because the Klamath Tribe's fishing right is an aboriginal practice, or because the fishing right is not appurtenant to reservation lands?

2. **Primary versus secondary purposes in the Ninth Circuit.** Although the Ninth Circuit in *Adair I* found the distinction between primary and secondary purposes to provide only "useful guidelines," that court has more recently indicated that it may adopt the distinction as law. In *Skokomish Indian Tribe v. United States*, 401 F.3d 979 (9th Cir. 2005), an en banc Ninth Circuit appeared to adopt that distinction without analysis, suggesting that fishing was not a primary purpose of the Skokomish Reservation, even though it was "important" to the tribe and clearly intended by Congress to continue. The en banc Ninth Circuit later amended its *Skokomish* decision to delete that portion of the original opinion addressing reserved water rights of the Skokomish Tribe. *Skokomish Indian Tribe v. United States*, 410 F.3d 506 (9th Cir. 2005). In a subsequent decision relying on the original *Skokomish* opinion, the Western District of Washington stated that: "*Skokomish* emphasized the narrow grant of *Winters* rights, and the applicability of *New Mexico* to Indian reserved water rights." *United States v. Washington Dep't of Ecology*, 2005 WL 1244797 (W.D. Wash. May 20, 2005). On reconsideration after *Skokomish* was amended, the district court removed all references to the *Skokomish* decision, but retained its ultimate conclusion that the primary purposes of the Lummi Reservation were only agricultural and domestic. *United States v. Washington Dep't of Ecology*, 375 F. Supp. 2d 1050 (W.D. Wash. 2005). The Lummi case, however, concerned only rights to groundwater, and the court consequently did not address reserved rights to water for fisheries purposes.

3. **Recognition of tribal instream flow rights.** A number of cases have recognized tribal non-consumptive water rights for hunting and fishing purposes. *See, e.g., Colville Confederated Tribes v. Walton*, 647 F.2d 42 (9th Cir. 1981), excerpted at page 530; *Joint Board of Control of the Flathead, Mission, and Jocko Irrigation Dists. v. United States*, 832 F.2d 1127 (9th Cir. 1987); *Kittitas Reclamation Dist. v. Sunnyside Valley Irrig. Dist.*, 763 F.2d 1032 (9th Cir. 1985). *See* Michael C. Blumm & Brett M. Swift, *The Indian Treaty Piscary Profit and Habitat Protection in the Pacific Northwest: A Property Rights Approach*, 69 U. Colo. L. Rev. 407, 471–75 (1998).

4. **Measure of instream flow rights.** When tribes are entitled to an instream flow right to protect and preserve hunting, fishing, and gathering rights, how much water is that? Exact quantification of the right may prove difficult. In one case, for example, a court held that the Spokane Tribe had the right to a sufficient quantity of water to keep the water temperature at 68° F or less because a higher temperature would endanger the native fish population. *United States v. Anderson*, 6 Indian L. Rep. F-129 (E.D. Wash. 1979).

The question of quantifying instream flow rights is closely linked to the federal courts' interpretation of the reserved rights to hunt, fish, and gather. Although we do not explore reserved rights to harvest food sources until the next chapter, this note considers the interrelationship of reserved fishing rights and reserved water rights.

For example, in *Adair I*, the Ninth Circuit was careful to indicate that whatever the scope of the tribes' hunting and fishing rights, it did not entitle the tribes to restoration of wilderness conditions — a "wilderness servitude," in the words of the court. However, the court did not foreclose restoration of river flows, stating that the tribes' reserved right entitled them to "the amount of water necessary to support its [sic] hunting and fishing rights as currently exercised to maintain the livelihood of the Tribe members, not as these rights once were exercised by the Tribe in 1864 . . . *unless of course no lesser level will supply them with a moderate living*" (emphasis added). The "moderate living" phrase was drawn from *Washington v. Washington State Commercial Passenger Fishing Vessel Association*, 443 U.S. 658, 686 (1979), excerpted at page 633, in which the Supreme Court affirmed the "Boldt Decision" that tribes were entitled to enough of the treaty-reserved resources to provide them with a moderate living, up to a maximum of fifty percent of the available resources. The Ninth Circuit's language in *Adair I* thus suggested that water flows necessary to restore increased tribal hunting and fishing harvests are within the tribes' reserved rights if they are necessary to supply the tribes with a moderate living.

In *Adair II*, the district court addressed the relationship between the "moderate living" standard and the quantification of tribal water rights. *United States v. Adair*, 187 F. Supp. 2d 1273 (D. Or. 2002). The court outlined a two-step process for determining the effect of the "moderate living" standard on the quantity of the tribes' reserved water. First, under *Adair I*, the tribes were entitled to ""whatever water is necessary to achieve the result of supporting productive habitat." The court rejected the notion that the tribes were entitled only to some "minimum amount" of water. Second, the court determined that the "moderate living" standard applied, in the words of the Supreme Court, only "if tribal needs may be satisfied by a lesser amount" than fifty percent, citing *Fishing Vessel Association*.

> However, this case is unlike *Fishing Vessel* where the reserved right could be reduced without completely frustrating the purpose of the reservation. For example, if the tribes' 50% allocation of the harvestable fish run at issue in *Fishing Vessel* would have been reduced to a 35% allocation, the reserved right would still survive after the reduction. In contrast, the Klamath Tribes' reserved water right does not readily lend itself to such a reduction. Ultimately, the water level cannot be reduced to a level below that which is required to support productive habitat, and the Tribes are entitled to "whatever water is necessary to achieve" the result of supporting productive habitat.

Any reduction below that level would, according to the district court, be an abrogation of the treaty that would require an act of Congress.

In addition, the court construed the "as currently exercised" phrase in the Ninth Circuit's *Adair I* decision as "refer[ring] only to the moderate living standard which recognizes that changing circumstances can affect the measure of a reserved right." Consequently, the court declined to adopt the state's suggestion that the Ninth Circuit intended to fix the scope of the tribes' water rights to the amount the tribes used in 1979 (the date of the district court decision in *Adair I*) or 1983 (the date of the Ninth Circuit's decision). The court concluded that "[f]ixing the tribal water rights to a specific date is not related to the fulfillment of purposes of the Klamath Indian Reservation, which is the paramount consideration mandated by *United States v. Winters*, 207 U.S. 564 (1908).''

The Ninth Circuit vacated the district court decision in *Adair II* as not ripe for federal court review. *United States v. Braren*, 338 F.3d 971 (9th Cir. 2003). The appellate court concluded that the state's narrow interpretation of the scope of the tribes' hunting and fishing rights and its denial of water rights for gathering were not final decisions, since they were reviewable both administratively and in state courts. The effect of this decision may be to limit federal court review of these issues to the U.S. Supreme Court's review of the state court's final decision. For a critique of the Ninth Circuit's decision, see Ryan Sudbury, Note, *When Good Streams Go Dry:* United States v. Adair *and the Unprincipled Elimination of a Federal Forum for Treaty Reserved Rights*, 25 Pub. Land & Resources L. Rev. 147 (2004); *see also* Michael C. Blumm, David H. Becker & Joshua D. Smith, *The Mirage of Indian Reserved Water Rights and Western Streamflow Protection: A Promise Unfulfilled*, 36 Envtl. L. 1157, 1168–69 (2006).

More recently, the Court of Federal Claims ruled that unquantified instream flow rights entitled the tribes "to prevent the diversion of at least as much water . . . as was necessary to fulfill the Bureau of Reclamation's Endangered Species Act obligations." *Baley v. United States*, 134 Fed. Cl. 619, 673 (2017), appeal filed (Dec. 21, 2017). The Bureau of Reclamation had temporarily halted delivery of water to farmers in the Klamath River Basin in southern Oregon and northern California, in order to fulfill its obligations under the ESA and the trust responsibility to the Klamath, Yurok, and Hoopa Valley tribes. The farmers sued, claiming a Fifth Amendment taking. The court held that the tribes held senior water rights and, although the water right was unquantified, it entitled the tribes to prevent withdrawals that would cause the endangerment or extinction of the fish. *Id*. at 672. The court concluded that all available water was necessary to satisfy ESA requirements and that the tribes, as senior rights holders, were entitled to have their rights satisfied before the junior appropriator farmers.

5. **"Diminished" instream flow rights.** In a long-running comprehensive adjudication of all water rights in the Yakima River Basin, a Washington trial court ruled in 1990 that the Yakama Tribe (which changed its spelling in 1994 to reflect historic spelling) had a treaty right to water for fish propagation, but held that the scope of the water right reserved for fish had been substantially diminished, despite their "time immemorial" priority date, as a result of government actions during most of the twentieth century. The trial court did rule, however, that the tribe was entitled to a minimum instream flow necessary to maintain salmon according to annual prevailing conditions. In 1993, the Washington Supreme Court affirmed, sanctioning a

new category of "diminished" water rights. *Washington Dept. of Ecology v. Yakima Reservation Irrig. Dist.*, 850 P.2d 1306 (Wash. 1993).

The court recognized the rules of treaty construction and purported to liberally construe the treaty language and interpret treaty language in the tribes' favor (the court even applied these rules to administrative agencies), concluding that the Yakama Reservation had both agricultural and fishing purposes. However, the court managed to avoid the prospect of having to restore river flows to treaty-time conditions. Instead, the court affirmed that an unspecified series of "congressional, executive, administrative, and judicial acts" between 1905 and 1968—while not abrogating the tribes' water rights for fisheries—diminished them because "there was encroachment upon and significant damage to the Indians' treaty fishing rights during this period." Thus, the court apparently concluded that an inconsistent series of actions could substantially diminish treaty water rights, despite a lack of clear intent to abrogate those rights, a result that appears inconsistent with the Supreme Court's standards for abrogation laid down in *United States v. Dion,* 476 U.S. 734 (1986), excerpted at page 678.

There is no precedent for the Washington court's concept of "diminished" water rights. The court relied on a 1968 settlement in an Indian Claims Commission case as evidence that the tribes' treaty rights to fish had been diminished. *Yakima Reservation Irrig. Dist.*, 850 P.2d at 1323–25. But the Claims Commission had no authority to extinguish—or even diminish—treaty rights. The New Mexico Court of Appeals subsequently considered the Washington Supreme Court's interpretation of the Claims Commission proceeding, and concluded that the Washington court "failed to analyze the effect of the [Commission's] limited jurisdiction." *State ex rel. Martinez v. Kerr-McGee*, 898 P.2d 1256, 1260 (N.M. Ct. App. 1995).

The Washington Supreme Court opinion seemed to send a crushing blow to the Yakama Nation's efforts to restore salmon runs in the Yakima Basin. In 1995, however, the trial court in the comprehensive adjudication (known as the *Aquavella* case) interpreted the Washington Supreme Court's recognition of a limited right of habitat protection "to maintain fish life" as requiring fish flows in Yakima Basin tributaries and flushing flows in the mainstem Yakima River to facilitate downstream salmon migration in the spring. *See State Dept. of Ecology v. Acquavella*, No. 77-2-OA84-5 Water Order Re Treaty Reserved Rights at Usual and Accustomed Fishing Places (Wash. Sup. Ct. Mar. 1, 1995); Order Re "Flushing Flows" (Wash. Sup. Ct. Apr. 13, 1995). The latter decision required the Bureau of Reclamation to release some 600 acre-feet of storage water for fish migration. *See* Michael C. Blumm, David H. Becker & Joshua D. Smith, *The Mirage of Indian Reserved Water Rights and Western Streamflow Protection in the McCarran Amendment Era: A Promise Unfulfilled*, 36 Envtl. L. 1157, 1180–82 (2006).

6. Off-reservation instream flow rights. In *Adair I*, the Ninth Circuit recognized tribal water rights for fisheries purposes even though the protected fishing places were located outside Indian country. One court, however, has expressly rejected off-reservation water rights. The Snake River Basin Adjudication Court (a special state water court) in Idaho concluded that the Nez Perce Tribe had no water rights appurtenant to its off-reservation fishing rights because reserved water rights were limited to reservation lands. *In re SRBA*, No. 39576, Subcase No. 03-10022 (Idaho Dist. Ct. Nov. 10, 1999). The SRBA judge held that the Nez Perce Treaty's express reservation of fishing rights off-reservation did not evince sufficient intent to reserve water. Such a specific intent was not required by the Supreme Court in *Winters*, however, where the Court found an implied water right in a treaty purpose to promote agriculture, or in *Winans*, where the Court found an implied servitude from a treaty fishing promise. *See* Michael C. Blumm, Dale D. Goble, Judith V. Royster & Mary C. Wood, *Judicial Termination of Treaty Water Rights: The Snake River Case*, 36 Idaho L. Rev. 449, 452, 470–71 (2000) (arguing that the SRBA court misunderstood the purpose of the treaty, misconstrued or ignored relevant Supreme Court cases, and "erroneously concluded that the tribe's reserved water rights were limited to" reservation lands).

In 2002, the Idaho Supreme Court dismissed as moot a motion brought by the Nez Perce Tribe to disqualify the former presiding judge in the SRBA adjudication. The tribe claimed he should have recused himself from the litigation because he and his family had undisclosed water rights at stake in the case that conflicted with the tribe's claims. But the state supreme court held that because he was no longer the presiding judge (having been removed by the supreme court after his brother-in-law was elected to the supreme court), the issue was moot. The judge also refused to rescind his rulings, due to the delay and financial hardship involved, as well as the fact that those rulings were subject to review by the supreme court. *United States v. Idaho*, 51 P.3d 1110 (Idaho 2002).

Rather than appeal the SRBA court's denial of reserved water rights to sustain off-reservation fishing rights, the Nez Perce Tribe entered into prolonged mediation in an attempt to settle out of court. In March 2005, the parties reached a settlement in which the state recognized tribal on-reservation water rights, but the tribe waived its claims to off-reservation water. As part of the settlement the state agreed to establish instream flows at nearly 200 locations, and protect nearly 600 streams. The instream flows, however, were subordinated to all existing water rights at the date of the settlement and also to future domestic, commercial, industrial and municipal water rights. *See* Alexander Hays, *The Nez Perce Water Rights Settlement and the Revolution in Indian Country*, 36 Envtl. L. 869 (2006); *Symposium on the Nez Perce Water Rights Settlement*, 42 Idaho L. Rev. 547 (2006); Michael C. Blumm, David H. Becker & Joshua D. Smith, *The Mirage of Indian Reserved Water Rights and Western Streamflow Restoration in the McCarran Amendment Era: A Promise Unfulfilled*, 36 Envtl. L. 1157, 1194–1201 (2006).

Idaho courts have also proved very reluctant to recognize federal reserved rights for non-Indian reservations like wilderness areas or wildlife refuges. *See* Michael C. Blumm, *Federal Reserved Water Rights as a Rule of Law*, 52 Idaho L. Rev. 369 (2015) (criticizing the Idaho decisions and arguing against the notion that there are no post-1955 reserved rights on grounds of a lack of congressional intent).

In re General Adjudication of All Rights to Use Water in the Big Horn River System [*Big Horn I*]

753 P.2d 76 (Wyo. 1988) *aff'd by an equally divided Court, Wyoming v. United States*, 492 U.S. 406 (1989)

This appeal is from the district court's order adjudicating rights to use water in the Big Horn River System and all other sources within the State's Water Division No. 3. [Water Division No. 3 includes the Wind River Indian Reservation.] The district court modified the special master's recommended decree. All parties have appealed from the district court's amended judgment and decree. We affirm in part and reverse in part.

[I]n 1865, the United States, hoping to preserve the peace and stability, reached an agreement delineating the area within which the Eastern Shoshone roamed, a 44,672,000 acre region comprising parts of Wyoming, Colorado and Utah. Following the Civil War, as the westward movement gained momentum, the United States government realized the size of the region set aside for Indians only was unrealistic, and on July 3, 1868, executed the Second Treaty of Fort Bridger with the Shoshone and Bannock Indians, establishing the Wind River Indian Reservation.

During their first years on the reservation, the Shoshone Indians were still dependent on the buffalo as the mainstay of their life, but as the supply rapidly decreased, they began to rely upon an agricultural economy. During the 1870s the Shoshone Indians increased their efforts in both farming and ranching. The Shoshone ceded lands beyond the Popo Agie back to the United States in the 1872 Brunot Agreement. The Arapahoe moved to the reservation in 1878. By the 1880s it was evident that the agricultural economy of the Indians was failing, and by 1895, the Indians on the Wind River Indian Reservation were totally dependent on the government for food, clothing and shelter. These economic misfortunes compelled them to sell more of their land to the United States. The First McLaughlin Agreement, or Thermopolis Purchase, was concluded in 1897; the Big Horn Hot Springs was the main feature of the lands ceded to the United States for cash payment. An additional 1,480,000 acres of reservation land were ceded to the Government in the Second McLaughlin Agreement in 1904–1905. The revenue derived helped to develop the remaining reservation lands (which came to be known as the "diminished reservation"). The United States Government offered the ceded lands for sale to others, under the provisions of the homestead, townsite, coal and mineral land laws, and reimbursed the Tribes or expended for the benefit of the Tribes the money raised by the sales.

The earliest non-Indian settlements in northwestern and north central Wyoming were near the gold and silver fields in the South Pass area of the Wind River Range. These mining camps soon expanded into permanent farming and ranching communities which relied primarily on cattle ranching and dryland or easily-irrigated farming for sustenance. By the mid-1800s, many small communities had been established by settlers who had obtained their land under the Congressional land disposal acts. By the early 1900s most of the best land in the region was occupied by ranches or irrigated farms. Yet the settlers continued to arrive, forcing gradual expansion onto the dry basin floors and prompting the development of many irrigation projects, often sponsored jointly by private citizens and the United States. The arrival of the homesteaders in the Wind River Basin significantly altered the Indians' economic base. As the number of settlers and their farms increased, the number of Indians working their own farms and ranches decreased, and they began to rent and eventually to sell their land while hiring themselves out as laborers.

In 1934, all remaining lands which had been ceded to the United States by the 1904 agreement were reserved from non-Indian settlement. In 1940, the Secretary of Interior began a series of restorations of certain undisposed lands to tribal ownership. These lands again became part of the existing Wind River Reservation. In addition, the United States later reacquired, in trust for the Tribes, additional ceded land and certain lands within the diminished reservation which previously had passed into private ownership. Since 1953, the size of the reservation has remained fairly stable.

[The court appointed a special master, who entered a 451-page "Report Concerning Reserved Water Right Claims by and on Behalf of the Tribes in the Wind River Reservation" on December 15, 1982.]

The report recognized a reserved water right for the Wind River Indian Reservation and determined that the purpose for which the reservation had been established was a permanent homeland for the Indians. A reserved water right for irrigation, stock watering, fisheries, wildlife and aesthetics, mineral and industrial, and domestic, commercial, and municipal uses was quantified and awarded.

The State of Wyoming, the United States, the Shoshone and Arapahoe Tribes, and numerous private parties presented objections to the master's report, and on May 10, 1983, Judge Joffe entered his Findings of Fact, Conclusions of Law and Judgment approving that portion of the master's report awarding reserved water rights for practicably irrigable acreage within the Wind River Indian Reservation and refusing to accept that portion of the master's report recommending an award of reserved water rights for other than agricultural purposes.

On May 13, 1983, the case was assigned to State District Judge Alan B. Johnson. The United States, the State of Wyoming and the Tribes then moved to alter or amend Judge Joffe's decree. On May 24, 1985, pursuant to Rule 54(b) W.R.C.P., the Amended Judgment and Decree from which this appeal is taken was entered.

The treaty establishing the Wind River Indian Reservation, signed on July 3, 1868, ratified on February 16, 1869, and proclaimed on February 24, 1869, Treaty of Ft. Bridger, is silent on the subject of water for the reservation. Yet both the district court and the special master found an intent to reserve water. We affirm.

IV. PURPOSES OF THE WIND RIVER INDIAN RESERVATION

The government may reserve water from appropriation under state law for use on the lands set aside for an Indian reservation. *Winters v. United States*, 207 U.S. 564. A reserved water right is implied for an Indian reservation where water is necessary to fulfill the purposes of reservation. The quantity of water reserved is the amount of water sufficient to fulfill the purpose of the lands set aside for the reservation. * * * We have already decided that Congress intended to reserve water for the Wind River Indian Reservation when it was created in 1868, and we accept the proposition that the amount of water impliedly reserved is determined by the purposes for which the reservation was created.

* * * The district court ascertained the purpose of the reservation from the treaty itself, stating: "On the very face of the Treaty, it is clear that its purpose was purely agricultural." This legal determination is fully reviewable by this court.

A. The Treaty

[The court quoted extensively from the 1868 Treaty with the Shoshones and Bannacks. The provisions on which the court relied are summarized by it below. In addition to the provisions relied upon by the court, article II of the treaty provided that the reservation was "set apart for the absolute and undisturbed use and occupation of" the Indians. In article IV the Indians agreed that "they will make said reservations their permanent home. . . ."]

The court in *Colville Confederated Tribes v. Walton*, 647 F.2d 42, did not mandate that a single purpose for the reservation be found. Rather, the court applied the specific purpose test outlined in *United States v. New Mexico*, 438 U.S. at 702, in an Indian reserved water case and found two primary purposes: "to provide a homeland for the Indians to maintain their agrarian society," for which practicably irrigable acreage was the measure, and to preserve the "tribes' access to fishing grounds." The validity of the Ninth Circuit's application of the *New Mexico* test has been drawn into question because the standards governing non-Indian federal reserved water rights differ from those governing Indian reserved water rights. In *United States v. Adair*, 723 F.2d at 1408, the Ninth Circuit agreed that non-Indian federal reservation reserved water rights cases only provide useful guidelines to Indian reserved water rights.

[W]e have no difficulty affirming the finding that it was the intent at the time to create a reservation with a sole agricultural purpose. Indian treaties should be interpreted generously, and liberally in favor of the Indians, and should not be given a crabbed or restrictive meaning. Nor should treaties be improperly construed in favor of Indians, for "'[W]e cannot remake history,'" and courts should not distort the words of a treaty to find rights inconsistent with its language. *Ward v. Race Horse*, 163 U.S. 504 (1896).

Article 7 of the treaty refers to "said agricultural reservations." Article 6 authorizes allotments for farming purposes; Article 8 provides seeds and implements for farmers; in Article 9 "the United States agreed to pay each Indian farming a $20 annual stipend, but only $10 to 'roaming' Indians"; and Article 12 establishes a $50 prize to the ten best Indian farmers. The treaty does not encourage any other occupation or pursuit. The district court correctly found that the reference in Article 4 to "permanent homeland" does nothing more than permanently set aside lands for the Indians; it does not define the purpose of the reservation. Rather, the purpose of the permanent-home reservation is found in Articles 6, 8, 9, and 12 of the treaty.

Although the treaty did not force the Indians to become farmers and although it clearly contemplates that other activities would be permitted (hunting is mentioned in Article 4, lumbering and milling in Article 3, roaming in Article 9), the treaty encouraged only agriculture, and that was its primary purpose. The Court in *United States v. Shoshone Tribe of Indians*, 304 U.S. 111, discussing the purpose of this treaty, stated:

> "Provisions in aid of teaching children and of adult education in farming, and to secure for the tribe medical and mechanical service, to safeguard tribal and individual titles, when taken with other parts of the treaty, plainly evidence purpose on the part of the United States to help to create an independent permanent farming community upon the reservation."

The Court, while recognizing that the Tribes were the beneficial owners of the reservation's timber and mineral resources, and that it was known to all before the treaty was signed that the Wind River Indian Reservation contained valuable minerals, nonetheless concluded that the purpose of the reservation was agricultural. The fact that the Indians fully intended to continue to hunt and fish does not alter that conclusion.

Agreements subsequent to the treaty acknowledge the continuance of non-agricultural activities on the reservation. The reports of the Indian agents are replete with descriptions of and plans for other activities. Yet not one of the cited reports neglects to report also on the progress of the farming and ranching operations. The primary purpose was clearly agricultural.

B. Fisheries

Reserved water rights for fisheries have been recognized where a treaty provision explicitly recognized an exclusive right to take fish on the reservation or the right to take fish at traditional off-reservation fishing grounds, in common with others.

Instream fishery flows have also been recognized where the Indians were heavily, if not totally, dependent on fish for their livelihood. In the case at bar, the Tribes introduced evidence showing that fish had always been part of the Indians' diet. The master, erroneously concluding that a reserved right for fisheries should be implied when the tribe is "at least partially dependent upon fishing," awarded an instream flow right for fisheries. The district court, however, finding neither a dependency upon fishing for a livelihood nor a traditional lifestyle involving fishing, deleted the [special master's] award [of water for fisheries]. The district court did not err. The evidence is not sufficient to imply a fishery flow right absent a treaty provision.

C. Mineral and Industrial

The Tribes were denied a reserved water right for mineral and industrial development. All parties to the treaty were well aware before it was signed of the valuable mineral estate underlying the Wind River Indian Reservation. The question of whether, because the Indians own the minerals, the intent was that they should have the water necessary to develop them must be determined, of course, by the intent in 1868. Neither the Tribes nor the United States has cited this court to any provision of the treaty or other evidence indicating that the parties contemplated in 1868 that a purpose of the reservation would be for the Indians to develop the minerals. The fact that the Tribes have since used water for mineral and industrial purposes does not establish that water was impliedly reserved in 1868 for such uses. The district court did not err in denying a reserved water right for mineral and industrial uses.

[The court upheld the trial court's rulings 1) allowing a reserved right for municipal, domestic, and commercial uses within the agricultural reserved right. 2) subsuming water for livestock with the agricultural right, and 3) and rejecting a reserved right for wildlife and aesthetics due to a lack of evidence of a tradition of wildlife and aesthetic preservation.]

The district court did not err in finding a sole agricultural purpose in the creation of the Wind River Indian Reservation. The Treaty itself evidences no other purpose, and none of the extraneous evidence cited is sufficient to attribute a broader purpose.

VI. QUANTIFICATION

A. The Measure

The measure of the Tribes' reserved water right is the water necessary to irrigate the practicably irrigable acreage on the reservation. In *Arizona v. California, supra* 373 U.S. at 600–601, a needs test was rejected as too uncertain, the Court opting instead for practicably irrigable acreage as the measure of a tribal agricultural reserved water right. * * * [T]he Court declined the invitation to re-examine the PIA standard in *Arizona v. California, supra* 460 U.S. at 625–626, and reaffirmed the value of the certainty inherent in the practicably irrigable acreage standard. The district court was correct in quantifying the Tribes' reserved water right by the amount of water necessary to irrigate all of the reservation's practicably irrigable acreage.

B. Future Lands

The Tribes and the United States claimed a reserved water right for lands on the reservation not yet developed for irrigation, but which were in their view, practicably irrigable acreage.

The master determined that the arable land base was 76,027 acres. [The court affirmed this finding.]

The master's determination that the Wind River Indian Reservation embraces practicably irrigable acreage is proper. We therefore affirm the district court's award of a reserved water right for future projects covering practicably irrigable acreage.

VII. PRIORITY DATES

A. Diminished Reservation

We recognized earlier in this opinion that there was indeed a federal water right impliedly reserved for the Indians when the Wind River Indian Reservation was created by the 1868 Treaty. Therefore, we affirm the rulings below that the tribal diminished-reservation lands have a water right with a priority date of 1868.

THOMAS, Justice, dissenting with whom HANSCUM, District Judge, joins.

I differ from the majority with respect to three propositions and must dissent from the disposition made in the majority opinion. Except for my three points of difference, I am in accord with the resolution of this case as set forth in that opinion. My three points of difference are: first, I do not agree that reserved water rights, to the extent that they properly are recognized under the reserved rights doctrine, should be limited in the manner suggested by the majority opinion; second, I believe that there should be a pragmatic limitation on the standard for quantification, the practicably irrigable acreage, which would eliminate those lands from the quantification formula which only could be irrigated by the construction of some future water project; and third, but most important, I do not believe that the reserved rights doctrine is applicable to that portion of the lands lying north of the "Big Wind River," i.e., the ceded portion of the Wind River Indian Reservation.

The purpose of establishing an Indian reservation, such as the Wind River Indian Reservation, is to provide a homeland for Indian peoples. If one is to assume that, pursuant to the reserved rights doctrine relating to water, there is an implied reservation of those waters essential to accomplish the purpose of the reservation of land, then I cannot agree that the implied reservation of water with respect to the Wind River Indian reservation should be limited, as the majority has held in approving the judgment of the district court. The fault that I find with such a limitation is that it assumes that the Indian peoples will not enjoy the same style of evolution as other people, nor are they to have the benefits of modern civilization. I would understand that the homeland concept assumes that the homeland will not be a static place frozen in an instant of time but that the homeland will evolve and will be used in different ways as the Indian society develops. For that reason, I would hold that the implied reservation of water rights attaching to an Indian reservation assumes any use that is appropriate to the Indian homeland as it progresses and develops.

In re General Adjudication of All Rights to Use Water in the Gila River System and Source
35 P.3d 68 (Ariz. 2001)

ZLAKET, Chief Justice.

We are presented with another issue in the Gila River general stream adjudication. * * * Today the court addresses issue 3: "What is the appropriate standard to be applied in determining the amount of water reserved for federal lands?"

> In its September 1988 decision, the trial court stated that each Indian reservation was entitled to such water as is necessary to effectuate the purpose of that reservation. While as to other types of federal lands courts have allowed controversy about what the purpose of the land is and how much water will

satisfy that purpose, as to Indian reservations the courts have drawn a clear and distinct line. It is that the amount is measured by the amount of water necessary to irrigate all of the *practicably irrigable acreage* (PIA) on that reservation.

(emphasis in original). We review this determination utilizing a de novo standard.

DISCUSSION

B. Purpose

Generally, the "purpose of a federal reservation of land defines the scope and nature of impliedly reserved water rights." However, when applying the *Winters* doctrine, it is necessary to distinguish between Indian and non-Indian reservations.

The government may exercise total dominion over water rights on federal non-Indian lands. But unlike those attached to Indian lands, which have reserved water rights for "future needs and changes in use," non-Indian reserved rights are narrowly quantified to meet the original, primary purpose of the reservation; water for secondary purposes must be acquired under state law. Thus, the primary purpose for which the federal government reserves non-Indian land is strictly construed after careful examination.

Indian reservations, however, are different. In its role as trustee of such lands, the government must act for the Indians' benefit. This fiduciary relationship is referred to as "one of the primary cornerstones of Indian law." Thus, treaties, statutes, and executive orders are construed liberally in the Indians' favor. Such an approach is equally applicable to the federal government's actions with regard to water for Indian reservations. "The purposes of Indian reserved rights . . . are given broader interpretation in order to further the federal goal of Indian self sufficiency."

The parties dispute the purposes of the several Indian reservations involved in this case. The United States and the tribal litigants argue that federal case law has pre-emptively determined that every Indian reservation was established as a permanent tribal homeland. The state litigants disagree, contending instead that the trial court must analyze each tribe's treaty or enabling documentation to determine that reservation's individual purpose. We need not decide whether federal case law has pre-emptively determined the issue. We agree with the Supreme Court that the essential purpose of Indian reservations is to provide Native American people with a "permanent home and abiding place," *Winters,* 207 U.S. at 565, that is, a "livable" environment. *Arizona I,* 373 U.S. at 599.

While courts may choose to examine historical documents in determining the purpose and reason for creating a federal reservation on non-Indian lands, the utility of such an exercise with respect to Indian reservations is highly questionable. This is so for a variety of reasons.

First, as pointed out by the state litigants, many Indian reservations were pieced together over time. For example, the boundaries of the Gila River Indian Community changed ten times from its creation in 1859 until 1915, resulting in overall growth from 64,000 to 371,422 acres. But some of the changes along the way actually decreased the size of the reservation or limited the scope of previous additions. If these alterations had different purposes, as the state litigants suggest, it might be argued that water reserved to a specific parcel could not be utilized elsewhere on the same reservation, or that water once available could no longer be accessed. Such an arbitrary patchwork of water rights would be unworkable and inconsistent with the concept of a permanent, unified homeland.

A second problem lies in the fact that congressional intent to reserve water for tribal land is not express, but implied. As [one commentator] points out, "because the intent is merely imputed — that is, its historical reality is irrelevant for purposes of establishing reserved rights — it seems strained to impute an historical definition to that imputed intent for the purpose of quantifying an extremely valuable right to a scarce resource."

Courts construe Indian treaties according to the way in which the Indians themselves would have understood them. *Minnesota v. Mille Lacs Band of Chippewa Indians,* 526 U.S. 172, 196 (1999). But the historical search for a reservation's purpose tends to focus only on the motives of Congress — tribal intent is easily and often left out of the equation. It is doubtful that any tribe would have agreed to surrender its freedom and be confined on a reservation without some assurance that sufficient water would be provided for its well-being.

The most recognizable difficulty with the historical approach is that many documents do not accurately represent the true reasons for which Indian reservations were created. It is well known that in the nineteenth century, the federal government made conflicting promises. On one hand, it offered white settlers free land, an abundance of resources, and safety if they would travel to and inhabit the West. The government also assured Indians that they would be able to live on their lands in peace. The promises to the tribes were not kept. As recognized in 1863 by the Superintendent of Indian Affairs, M. Steck, the invasion of white settlement caused the Apache Indian people to be

> divested... of all their peculiar and former means of subsistence, in contending with a race who, under the circumstances, can feel no sympathy with them, [such that] the Indian must soon be swept from the face of the earth. If every red man were a Spartan, they would find it impossible to withstand this overpowering influx of immigration. Humanity and religion, therefore, demand of us that we interpose a barrier for their safety....

Even after this humanitarian "barrier" was imposed, however, General William T. Sherman made clear that "if [the Indians] wander outside they at once become objects of suspicion, liable to be attacked by the troops as hostile." In a November 9, 1871 letter to the Secretary of War, Sherman closed by stating that General Crook, head of the Army in Arizona, "may feel assured that whatever measures of severity he may adopt to reduce these Apaches to a peaceful and subordinate condition will be approved by the War Department and the President."

Despite what may be set forth in official documents, the fact is that Indians were forced onto reservations so that white settlement of the West could occur unimpeded. As recognized by former Arizona Congressman Morris K. Udall, the federal government "can be kindly described as having been less than diligent in its efforts to secure sufficient water supplies for the [Indian] community to develop its arable lands and achieve meaningful economic self-sufficiency and self-determination."

The trial court here failed to recognize any particular purpose for these Indian reservations, only finding that the PIA standard should be applied when quantifying tribes' water rights. It is apparent that the judge was leery of being "drawn into a potential racial controversy" based on historical documentation. But it seems clear to us that each of the Indian reservations in question was created as a "permanent home and abiding place" for the Indian people, as explained in *Winters*. This conclusion comports with the belief that "[t]he general purpose, to provide a home for the Indians, is a broad one and must be liberally construed." *Colville Confederated Tribes v. Walton,* 647 F.2d 42, 47 (9th Cir.1981). Such a construction is necessary for tribes to achieve the twin goals of Indian self-determination and economic self-sufficiency.

> Limiting an Indian reservation's purpose to agriculture, as the PIA standard implicitly does, assumes that the Indian peoples will not enjoy the same style of evolution as other people, nor are they to have the benefits of modern civilization. I would understand that the homeland concept assumes that the homeland will not be a static place frozen in an instant of time but that the homeland will evolve and will be used in different ways as the Indian society develops.

In re General Adjudication of All Rights to Use Water in the Big Horn River System, 753 P.2d 76, 119 (Wyo.1988) (Thomas, J., dissenting) [*Big Horn I*].

Other right holders are not constrained in this, the twenty-first century, to use water in the same manner as their ancestors in the 1800s. Although over 40% of the nation's population lived and worked on farms in 1880, less than 5% do today. Likewise, agriculture has steadily decreased as a percentage of our gross domestic product. Just as the nation's economy has evolved, nothing should prevent tribes from diversifying their economies if they so choose and are reasonably able to do so. The permanent homeland concept allows for this flexibility and practicality. We therefore hold that the purpose of a federal Indian reservation is to serve as a "permanent home and abiding place" to the Native American people living there.

C. Primary-Secondary Purpose Test

Next arises the question of whether the primary-secondary purpose test applies to Indian reservations. In *New Mexico*, a case dealing with a national forest, the Supreme Court reaffirmed that "[w]here water is necessary to fulfill the very purposes for which a federal reservation was created," it is implied that the United States reserved water for it. However, where the "water is only valuable for a secondary use of the reservation," any right must be acquired according to state law. All parties agree that this distinction applies to non-Indian federal reservations. The trial court here rejected the primary-secondary test, finding that the "rule is a little different for entrusted lands, Indian reservations." We agree.

It is true that some courts have utilized the primary-secondary purpose test or looked to it for guidance when dealing with Indian lands. *See Adair* (stating that *New Mexico* is not directly applicable, but establishes "several useful guidelines"); *Walton* (applying the test); *In re the General Adjudication of all Rights to Use Water in the Big Horn River System*, 835 P.2d 273, 278–79 (Wyo.1992) [*Big Horn II*] (following the test). Nevertheless, we believe the significant differences between Indian and non-Indian reservations preclude application of the test to the former. As Judge Canby has noted, "[w]hile the purpose for which the federal government reserves other types of lands may be strictly construed, the purposes of Indian reservations are necessarily entitled to broader interpretation if the goal of Indian self-sufficiency is to be attained." W. Canby, *American Indian Law* 245–46 (1981) (citation omitted). Parenthetically, even if the *New Mexico* test were to apply, tribes would be entitled to the full measure of their reserved rights because water use necessary to the establishment of a permanent homeland is a primary, not secondary, purpose.

D. Quantifying Winters Rights

The *Winters* doctrine retains the concept of "minimal need" by reserving "only that amount of water necessary to fulfill the purpose of the reservation, no more." The method utilized in arriving at such an amount, however, must satisfy both present and future needs of the reservation as a livable homeland.

E. The PIA Standard

The United States and tribal litigants argue that federal case law has preemptively established PIA as the standard by which to quantify reserved water rights on Indian reservations. We disagree. As observed by Special Master Tuttle in his *Arizona II* report, "the Court did not necessarily adopt this standard as the universal measure of Indian reserved water rights...." Indeed, nothing in *Arizona I* or *II* suggests otherwise.

On its face, PIA appears to be an objective method of determining water rights. But while there may be some "value of the certainty inherent in the practicably irrigable acreage standard," *Big Horn I,* its flaws become apparent on closer examination.

The first objection to an across-the-board application of PIA lies in its potential for inequitable treatment of tribes based solely on geographical location. Arizona's topography is such that some tribes inhabit flat alluvial plains while others dwell in steep, mountainous areas. This diversity creates a dilemma that PIA cannot solve. As stated by two commentators:

> There can be little doubt that the PIA standard works to the advantage of tribes inhabiting alluvial plains or other relatively flat lands adjacent

to stream courses. In contrast, tribes inhabiting mountainous or other agriculturally marginal terrains are at a severe disadvantage when it comes to demonstrating that their lands are practicably irrigable.

Tribes who fail to show either the engineering or economic feasibility of proposed irrigation projects run the risk of not receiving any reserved water under PIA. This inequity is unacceptable and inconsistent with the idea of a permanent homeland.

Another concern with PIA is that it forces tribes to pretend to be farmers in an era when "large agricultural projects . . . are risky, marginal enterprises. This is demonstrated by the fact that no federal project planned in accordance with the Principles and Guidelines [adopted by the Water Resources Council of the Federal Government] has been able to show a positive benefit/cost ratio in the last decade [1981 to 1991]." A permanent homeland requires water for multiple uses, which may or may not include agriculture. The PIA standard, however, forces "tribes to prove economic feasibility for a kind of enterprise that, judging from the evidence of both federal and private willingness to invest money, is simply no longer economically feasible in the West."

Limiting the applicable inquiry to a PIA analysis not only creates a temptation for tribes to concoct inflated, unrealistic irrigation projects, but deters consideration of actual water needs based on realistic economic choices. We again agree with the analysis of Justice Richard V. Thomas in *Big Horn I*:

> I would be appalled . . . if the Congress . . . began expending money to develop water projects for irrigating these Wyoming lands when far more fertile lands in the midwestern states now are being removed from production due to poor market conditions. I am convinced that . . . those lands which were included as practicably irrigable acreage, based upon the assumption of the construction of a future irrigation project, should not be included for the purpose of quantification of the Indian peoples' water rights. They may be irrigable academically, but not as a matter of practicality. . . .

The PIA standard also potentially frustrates the requirement that federally reserved water rights be tailored to minimal need. Rather than focusing on what is necessary to fulfill a reservation's overall design, PIA awards what may be an overabundance of water by including every irrigable acre of land in the equation.

For the foregoing reasons, we decline to approve the use of PIA as the exclusive quantification measure for determining water rights on Indian lands.

F. Proper Factors for Consideration

Recognizing that the most likely reason for PIA's endurance is that "no satisfactory substitute has emerged," we now enter essentially uncharted territory. In *Gila III*, this court stated that determining the amount of water necessary to accomplish a reservation's purpose is a "fact-intensive inquir[y] that must be made on a reservation-by-reservation basis." We still adhere to the belief that this is the only way federally reserved rights can be tailored to meet each reservation's minimal need.

When *Big Horn I* went before the Supreme Court, one of the present state litigants, in an amicus brief, argued that there should be a "balancing of a myriad of factors" in quantifying reserved water rights. During oral argument in the present case, counsel for the Apache tribes made a similar argument. Considering the objective that tribal reservations be allocated water necessary to achieve their purpose as permanent homelands, such a multi-faceted approach appears best-suited to produce a proper outcome.

Tribes have already used this methodology in settling water rights claims with the federal government. One feature of such settlements has been the development of master land use plans specifying the quantity of water necessary for different purposes on the reservation.

While we commend the creation of master land use plans as an effective means of demonstrating water requirements, tribes may choose to present evidence to the trial court in a different manner. The important thing is that the lower court should have before it actual and proposed uses, accompanied by the parties' recommendations regarding feasibility and the amount of water necessary to accomplish the homeland purpose. In viewing this evidence, the lower court should consider the following factors, which are not intended to be exclusive.

[The court listed the following factors: a tribe's history; tribal culture; the tribal land's geography, topography, and natural resources, including groundwater; a tribe's economic base; past water use; and present and projected future population.]

The state litigants argue that courts should act with sensitivity toward existing state water users when quantifying tribal water rights. *See New Mexico,* 438 U.S. at 718 (Powell, J., dissenting in part) (concurring that the *Winters* doctrine "should be applied with sensitivity to its impact upon those who have obtained water rights under state law"). They claim that this is necessary because when a water source is fully appropriated, there will be a gallon-for-gallon decrease in state users' water rights due to the tribes' federally reserved rights. When an Indian reservation is created, the government impliedly reserves water to carry out its purpose as a permanent homeland. The court's function is to determine the amount of water necessary to effectuate this purpose, tailored to the reservation's minimal need. We believe that such a minimalist approach demonstrates appropriate sensitivity and consideration of existing users' water rights, and at the same time provides a realistic basis for measuring tribal entitlements.

Again, the foregoing list of factors is not exclusive. The lower court must be given the latitude to consider other information it deems relevant to determining tribal water rights. We require only that proposed uses be reasonably feasible. As with PIA, this entails a two-part analysis. First, development projects need to be achievable from a practical standpoint—they must not be pie-in-the-sky ideas that will likely never reach fruition. Second, projects must be economically sound. When water, a scarce resource, is put to efficient uses on the reservation, tribal economies and members are the beneficiaries.

CONCLUSION

We wish it were possible to dispose of this matter by establishing a bright line standard, easily applied, in order to relieve the lower court and the parties of having to engage in the difficult, time-consuming process that certainly lies ahead. Unfortunately, we cannot.

In a quote attributed to Mark Twain, it is said that "in the west, whiskey is for drinkin' and water is for fightin'." While this remains true in parts of Arizona, it is our hope that interested parties will work together in a spirit of cooperation, not antagonism. "Water is far too ecologically valuable to be used as a political pawn in the effort to resolve the centuries-old conflict between Native Americans and those who followed them in settling the West." This is especially so now, when the welfare and progress of our indigenous population is inextricably tied to and inseparable from the welfare and progress of the entire state.

Notes

1. Homeland purpose. A federal district court, in a case that addressed tribal rights to groundwater only, rejected the *Gila River* approach, and refused to find a homeland purpose for the Lummi Reservation. *United States v. Washington*, 375 F. Supp. 2d 1050 (D. Wash. 2005). The court, noting that the resulting water right would be "for a broad and almost unlimited range of activities," found the concept inconsistent with the "primary purpose" doctrine under federal law. Instead, the court limited the reservation's purpose—and therefore the quantification of the tribe's water right—to agriculture and domestic use. The court said that PIA was the proper method for determining the tribe's agricultural award, but found that the domestic award required independent consideration by the trial court.

2. "Sensitivity" to non-Indian water rights. Although the Gila River court rejected a "sensitivity" analysis, former Justice Sandra Day O'Connor argued in favor of just such an approach. In 1988, the Supreme Court took certiorari on the issue of whether PIA was the proper measurement of the Wind River tribes' water right. *See Wyoming v. United States*, 488 U.S. 1040 (1989). The entire Court heard oral argument, and Justice O'Connor drafted an opinion that would have dramatically altered the PIA analysis.

Although Justice O'Connor would have retained the fundamental PIA standard, she would have required that PIA be determined with "sensitivity" to the effect on non-Indian appropriators, including a reasonable likelihood that future irrigation projects would actually be constructed and that additional cultivation was necessary to meet the needs of the tribes. Justice O'Connor's opinion is analyzed in Andrew C. Mergen & Sylvia F. Liu, *A Misplaced Sensitivity: The Draft Opinions in* Wyoming v. United States, 68 U. Colo. L. Rev. 683 (1997); the draft opinions are appended to the article.

Subsequent to the drafting of the opinion, however, Justice O'Connor recused herself from taking part in the decision because her family's ranching corporation was a party to the Gila River adjudication in Arizona. The remaining justices split evenly, so an equally divided court affirmed the Wyoming Supreme Court's decision awarding water rights based on PIA. *Wyoming v. United States*, 492 U.S. 406 (1989), *aff'g by an equally divided court*, In re General Adjudication of All Rights to Use Water in the Big Horn River System (Big Horn I), 753 P.2d 76 (Wyo. 1988). The *Big Horn I* decision is excerpted at page 499.

If Justice O'Connor would wish for "sensitivity" to non-Indian appropriation rights, the Montana Supreme Court took a nearly opposite approach. In 2002, the Montana court held for the third time in seven years that the State of Montana could not issue permits for new appropriations within the Flathead Reservation until the tribal reserved rights were determined and quantified, because the state-law requirement of showing "legally available" water could not be met. *Confederated Salish and Kootenai Tribes of the Flathead Reservation v. Stults*, 59 P.3d 1093 (Mont. 2002); *see also Confederated Salish and Kootenai Tribes v. Clinch*, 992 P.2d 244, 250 (Mont. 1999); *In the Matter of the Application of Beneficial Water Use Permit Nos. 66459-76L, Ciotti*, 923 P.2d 1073 (Mont. 1996). In 2007, however, the court ruled, 5–2, that an appropriator's application for a change of use might be permissible. *Confederated Salish & Kootenai Tribes v. Clinch*, 158 P.3d 377, 388 (Mont. 2007). The court held that the state district court must first determine whether the state agency has the sovereign authority to process the application and, if it does, whether the appropriator can prove that granting the change of use will not adversely affect the tribes' reserved rights.

3. The future of PIA. Consider the following assessment of PIA and its future:

> The PIA standard may be criticized, as the Arizona Supreme Court did, for basing water awards on irrigated agriculture, a water use that in the late twentieth century is unlikely to provide an economic basis for tribal self-determination. And because irrigated agriculture is a highly consumptive use, the amount of the Indian water claims is large. One estimate suggests that the application of the PIA standard to all reservations in Arizona would require eleven times the state's total dependable surface water supply. Further, because the PIA standard is based on the flawed premise that water is free, it frequently identifies economically unrealistic water uses. Moreover, because the standard is one based on territory instead of people, it can, as noted by the Arizona Supreme Court, produce inequities among tribes.
>
> Yet the demise of the PIA standard is not inevitable. Its establishment in *Arizona v. California* was a consequence of the Court's unwillingness to tolerate the uncertainties inherent in a "reasonably foreseeable needs" standard, and the Court has reaffirmed, repeatedly, the need for certainty in water rights adjudications. Further, the Court also has affirmed *Arizona* more than once. And the standard is not so inflexible as it might first appear; there is a good deal of pliability in variables such as the cost of capital needed to develop

an irrigation system and the efficiency of water use. There is, moreover, no indication that the PIA standard is making Indians rich.

Perhaps the greatest virtue of the PIA standard is the incentive it supplies to parties to negotiate settlements, and it is through settlements that tribes may be able to secure the funding they need to make water useful to reservation lands and improve the quality of reservation life. Ironically, the uncertainty over the future of the PIA standard may undermine the predictability that is a necessary prerequisite to successful settlements.

2 Waters and Water Rights, § 37.02(c)(2) (Amy K. Kelley, ed., 3d ed. LexisNexis/Matthew Bender 2016).*

2. Rights to Groundwater

The question of whether groundwater is included within tribal reserved water rights has only recently reached the courts. Consider the following approaches.

In re General Adjudication of All Rights to Use Water in the Big Horn River System [*Big Horn I*]

753 P.2d 76 (Wyo. 1988) *aff'd by an equally divided Court, Wyoming v. United States*, 492 U.S. 406 (1989)

The logic which supports a reservation of surface water to fulfill the purpose of the reservation also supports reservation of groundwater. Certainly the two sources are often interconnected.

Acknowledging the above, we note that, nonetheless, not a single case applying the reserved water doctrine to groundwater is cited to us. The Ninth Circuit indicated that groundwater was reserved in *United States v. Cappaert* [a non-Indian case]. The United States Supreme Court, however, found the water in the pool reserved for preservation of the pupfish was not groundwater but surface water, protected from subsequent diversions from either surface or groundwater supplies. Nor have the other cases cited to us granted a reserved right in underground water. In *Colville Confederated Tribes v. Walton*, there is slight mention of the underground aquifer and of pumping wells, but the opinion does not indicate that "their wells" are a source of reserved water or even discuss a groundwater right.

The district court did not err in deciding there was no reserved groundwater right. * * * The State has not appealed the decision that the Tribe may continue to satisfy their domestic and livestock needs (part of the agricultural award) from existing wells at current withdrawal rates; therefore, we do not address that question.

---

* Reprinted from Waters and Water Rights with permission. Copyright 2011 Matthew Bender & Company, Inc., a part of LexisNexis. All rights reserved.

Agua Caliente Band of Cahuilla Indians v. Coachella Valley Water Dist.

849 F.3d 1262 (9th Cir. 2017)

TALLMAN, Circuit Judge:

> "When the well's dry, we know the worth of water."
> Benjamin Franklin (1706–1790), Poor Richard's Almanac.

The Coachella Valley Water District ("CVWD") and the Desert Water Agency ("DWA") (collectively, the "water agencies") bring an interlocutory appeal of the district court's grant of partial summary judgment in favor of the Agua Caliente Band of Cahuilla Indians (the "Tribe") and the United States. The judgment declares that the United States impliedly reserved appurtenant water sources, including groundwater, when it created the Tribe's reservation in California's arid Coachella Valley. We agree. In affirming, we recognize that there is no controlling federal appellate authority addressing whether the reserved rights doctrine applies to groundwater. However, because we conclude that it does, we hold that the Tribe has a reserved right to groundwater underlying its reservation as a result of the purpose for which the reservation was established.

I.A

The Agua Caliente Band of Cahuilla Indians has lived in the Coachella Valley since before California entered statehood in 1850. The bulk of the Agua Caliente Reservation was formally established by two Presidential Executive Orders issued in 1876 and 1877, and the United States, pursuant to statute, now holds the remaining lands of the reservation in trust for the Tribe. The reservation consists of approximately 31,396 acres interspersed in a checkerboard pattern amidst several cities within Riverside County, including Palm Springs, Cathedral City, and Rancho Mirage.

The Executive Orders establishing the reservation are short in length, but broad in purpose. In 1876, President Ulysses S. Grant ordered certain lands "withdrawn from sale and set apart as reservations for the permanent use and occupancy of the Mission Indians in southern California." Similarly, President Rutherford B. Hayes's 1877 Order set aside additional lands for "Indian purposes." These orders followed on the heels of detailed government reports from Indian agents, which identified the urgent need to reserve land for Indian use in an attempt to encourage tribal members to "build comfortable houses, improve their acres, and surround themselves with home comforts." In short, the United States sought to protect the Tribe and "secure the Mission Indians permanent homes, with land and water enough."

Establishing a sustainable home in the Coachella Valley is no easy feat, however, as water in this arid southwestern desert is scarce. Rainfall totals average three to six inches per year, and the Whitewater River System—the valley's only real source of surface water—produces an average annual supply of water that fluctuates between

4,000 and 9,000 acre-feet, most of which occurs in the winter months.[1] In other words, surface water is virtually nonexistent in the valley for the majority of the year. Therefore, almost all of the water consumed in the region comes from the aquifer underlying the valley—the Coachella Valley Groundwater Basin.

The Coachella Valley Groundwater Basin supports 9 cities, 400,000 people, and 66,000 acres of farmland. Given the demands on the basin's supply, it is not surprising that water levels in the aquifer have been declining at a steady rate. Since the 1980s, the aquifer has been in a state of overdraft,[3] which exists despite major efforts to recharge the basin with water delivered from the California Water Project and the Colorado River. In total, groundwater pumping has resulted in an average annual recharge deficit of 239,000 acre-feet, with cumulative overdraft estimated at 5.5 million acre-feet as of 2010.

The Tribe does not currently pump groundwater on its reservation. Rather, it purchases groundwater from Appellant water agencies. The Tribe also receives surface water from the Whitewater River System, particularly the Andreas and Tahquitz Creeks that sometimes flow nearby. The surface water received from this system is consistent with a 1938 California Superior Court adjudication—the Whitewater River Decree—which attempted to address state-law water rights for users of the river system. Because the United States held the lands in trust, it participated in the adjudication via a "Suggestion" on behalf of the Tribe and the resulting state court order included a water allotment for the Tribe's benefit.[4] The amount of water reserved for the Tribe from this adjudication, however, is minimal, providing enough water to irrigate approximately 360 acres. Further, most of this allotment is filled outside of the growing season because the river system's flow peaks between December and March. Thus, groundwater supplied by the water agencies remains the main source of water for all types of consumption on the reservation throughout the year.

III

Due to the unusual trifurcation of this litigation, we are concerned on appeal only with Phase I—whether the Tribe has a federal reserved right to the groundwater

---

1. An acre-foot is the volume of water sufficient to cover one acre in area at a depth of one foot. It is equivalent to 325,851 gallons. It takes about four acre-feet of water to irrigate one acre of land for a year in the Coachella Valley. Therefore, at 9,000 acre-feet per year, the river system provides enough water to irrigate around 2,250 acres. At 4,000 acre-feet per year, the system can only irrigate about 1,000 acres. Considering that the Tribe is not the only user of the Whitewater River System, and that its reservation alone accounts for 31,396 acres, even in a peak year the river system provides very little water for irrigation or for human consumption.

3. Overdraft occurs when the amount of water extracted from the underground basin exceeds its recharge rate.

4. In providing this "Suggestion," the government maintained that it was not "submitting the rights of the United States . . . to the jurisdiction of the Department of Public Works of the State of California" and that the court lacked "jurisdiction [to adjudicate] the water rights of the United States." The federal government continues to maintain this position before us.

underlying its reservation. This question, however, is best analyzed in three steps: whether the United States intended to reserve water when it created the Tribe's reservation; whether the reserved rights doctrine encompasses groundwater; and, finally, whether the Tribe's correlative rights under state law or the historic lack of drilling for groundwater on the reservation, or the water the Tribe receives pursuant to the Whitewater River Decree, impacts our answers to these questions. We address each in turn.

A

Despite the longstanding recognition that Indian reservations, as well as other reserved lands, require access to water, the *Winters* doctrine only applies in certain situations: it only reserves water to the extent it is necessary to accomplish the purpose of the reservation, and it only reserves water if it is appurtenant to the withdrawn land. Once established, however, *Winters* rights "vest[ ] on the date of the reservation and [are] superior to the rights of future appropriators."

B. 1

Given the limitations in the *Winters* doctrine, we must first decide whether the United States, in establishing the Agua Caliente Reservation, impliedly reserved water. *See United States v. New Mexico*, 438 U.S. 696, 701 (1978). We conclude that it did. * * *

* * * [T]he water agencies argue that *New Mexico* stands for the proposition that water is impliedly reserved only if other sources of water then available cannot meet the reservation's water demands. According to the water agencies, if other sources of water exist—and the lack of a federal right would not entirely defeat the purpose of the reservation—then Congress intended to defer to state water law and require the United States to obtain water rights like any other private user.

New Mexico, however, is not so narrow. Congress does not defer to state water law with respect to reserved rights. Instead, Congress retains "its authority to reserve unappropriated water . . . for use on appurtenant lands withdrawn from the public domain for specific federal purposes."

The federal purpose for which land was reserved is the driving force behind the reserved rights doctrine. "Each time [the] Court has applied the 'implied-reservation-of-water-doctrine,' it has carefully examined both the asserted water right and the specific purposes for which the land was reserved, and concluded that without the water the purposes of the reservation would be entirely defeated." But the question is not whether water stemming from a federal right is necessary at some selected point in time to maintain the reservation; the question is whether the purpose underlying the reservation envisions water use.

2

Because *New Mexico* holds that water is reserved if the primary purpose of the reservation envisions water use, we now determine the primary purpose of the Tribe's reservation and whether that purpose contemplates water use. To do so, we consider "the document and circumstances surrounding [the reservation's] creation, and the history of the Indians for whom it was created."

The Executive Orders establishing the Tribe's reservation declared that the land was to be set aside for "the permanent use and occupancy of the Mission Indians" or, more generally, for "Indian purposes." While imprecise, such a purpose is not indecipherable. Our precedent recognizes that "[t]he specific purposes of an Indian reservation . . . [are] often unarticulated. The general purpose, *to provide a home for the Indians*, is a broad one and must be liberally construed." Moreover, "[m]ost of the land in these reservations is and always has been arid," and it is impossible to believe that the United States was unaware "that water . . . would be essential to the life of the Indian people."

The situation facing the Agua Caliente Tribe is no different. Water is inherently tied to the Tribe's ability to live permanently on the reservation. Without water, the underlying purpose—to establish a home and support an agrarian society—would be entirely defeated. Put differently, the primary purpose underlying the establishment of the reservation was to create a home for the Tribe, and water was necessarily implicated in that purpose. Thus, we hold that the United States implicitly reserved a right to water when it created the Agua Caliente Reservation.

C

While we conclude that the federal government envisioned water use when it established the Tribe's reservation, that does not end our inquiry. We must now determine whether the *Winters* doctrine, and the Tribe's reserved water right, extends to the groundwater underlying the reservation. And while we are unable to find controlling federal appellate authority explicitly holding that the *Winters* doctrine applies to groundwater, we now expressly hold that it does.

Apart from the requirement that the primary purpose of the reservation must intend water use, the other main limitation of the reserved rights doctrine is that the unappropriated water must be "appurtenant" to the reservation. Appurtenance, however, simply limits the reserved right to those waters which are attached to the reservation. It does not limit the right to surface water only. *Cappaert* [*v. United States*, 426 U.S. 128 (1976),] itself hinted that impliedly reserved waters may include appurtenant groundwater when it held that "the United States can protect its water from subsequent diversion, whether the diversion is of surface or groundwater." If the United States can protect against groundwater diversions, it follows that the government can protect the groundwater itself.

Further, many locations throughout the western United States rely on groundwater as their only viable water source. More importantly, such reliance exists here, as surface water in the Coachella Valley is minimal or entirely lacking for most of the year. Thus, survival is conditioned on access to water—and a reservation without an adequate source of surface water must be able to access groundwater.

The *Winters* doctrine was developed in part to provide sustainable land for Indian tribes whose reservations were established in the arid parts of the country. And in many cases, those reservations lacked access to, or were unable to effectively capture, a regular supply of surface water. Given these realities, we can discern no reason to cabin the *Winters* doctrine to appurtenant surface water. As such, we hold that the *Winters* doctrine encompasses both surface water and groundwater appurtenant to reserved land.[10] The creation of the Agua Caliente Reservation therefore carried with it an implied right to use water from the Coachella Valley aquifer.

D

The final issue we must address is the contours of the Tribe's reserved right, including its relation to state water law and the Tribe's existing water rights.

A "reserved right in unappropriated water . . . vests on the date of the reservation and is superior to the rights of future appropriators." Further, reserved rights are not analyzed "in terms of a balancing test." Rather, they are federal water rights that preempt conflicting state law. Finally, the rights are not lost through non-use. Instead, they are flexible and can change over time.

Despite the federal primacy of reserved water rights, the water agencies argue that because (1) the Tribe has a correlative right to groundwater under California law and (2) the Tribe has not drilled for groundwater on its reservation, and (3) because the Tribe is entitled to surface water from the Whitewater River Decree, the Tribe does not need a federal reserved right to prevent the purpose of the reservation from being entirely defeated. Put differently, the water agencies argue that, because the Tribe is already receiving water pursuant to California's correlative rights doctrine and the Whitewater River Decree, a federal reserved right is unnecessary.

However, the water agencies' arguments fail for three reasons. First, state water rights are preempted by federal reserved rights. Second, the fact that the Tribe did not historically access groundwater does not destroy its right to groundwater now. And third, the *New Mexico* inquiry does not ask if water is currently needed to sustain the reservation; it asks whether water was envisioned as necessary for the reservation's purpose at the time the reservation was created. Thus, state water entitlements do not affect our analysis with respect to the creation of the Tribe's federally reserved water right.

IV

In sum, the *Winters* doctrine does not distinguish between surface water and groundwater. Rather, its limits derive only from the government's intent in withdrawing land for a public purpose and the location of the water in relation to the reservation created. As such, because the United States intended to reserve water when it established a home for the Agua Caliente Band of Cahuilla Indians, we hold that the district court did not err in determining that the government reserved appurtenant

---

10. The parties do not dispute appurtenance, nor could they. The Coachella Valley Groundwater Basin clearly underlies the Tribe's reservation.

water sources—including groundwater—when it created the Tribe's reservation in the Coachella Valley.

Finally, we recognize that the district court's failure to conduct a thorough *New Mexico* analysis with respect to whether the Tribe needs access to groundwater was largely a function of the parties' decision to trifurcate this case. We also understand that a full analysis specifying the scope of the water reserved under *New Mexico* will be considered in the subsequent phases of this litigation.

Presumably, however, the water agencies will continue to argue in these later phases that the *Winters* doctrine is dependent upon the Tribe's demonstrated need—that is, need above and beyond what the Tribe is already receiving under state-law entitlements or could receive through a paramount surface water right. And while we express no opinion on how much water falls within the scope of the Tribe's federal groundwater right, there can be no question that water in some amount was necessarily reserved to support the reservation created. Thus, to guide the district court in its later analysis, we hold that the creation of the Agua Caliente Reservation carried with it an implied right to use water from the Coachella Valley aquifer.

Notes

1. **Pre-*Big Horn I* groundwater cases.** The *Big Horn I* court was the first to rule expressly on the groundwater issue. Although it was technically correct that no cases had applied the *Winters* doctrine to groundwater, rights to groundwater had nonetheless been addressed in a number of cases prior to *Big Horn I*. Relying on the Supreme Court's decision in *Cappaert v. United States*, 426 U.S. 128 (1976), that off-reservation groundwater pumping could be restricted to protect the water level in a pool at a national monument, a federal district court held that Pueblo water rights extended to "the surface waters of the stream systems and the ground water physically interrelated to the surface water as an integral part of the hydrologic cycle." *New Mexico ex rel. Reynolds v. Aamodt*, 618 F. Supp. 993, 1010 (D.N.M. 1985). The Federal Circuit similarly noted that one source of irrigation water reserved for the Gila River Reservation was groundwater. *Gila River Pima-Maricopa Indian Community v. United States*, 695 F.2d 559, 561 (Fed. Cir. 1982). Another federal district court observed in dictum that the *Winters* right should extend to groundwater as well as surface water. *Tweedy v. Texas Co.*, 286 F. Supp. 383 (D. Mont. 1968).

2. **The *Gila River* groundwater decision.** The first court to disagree with *Big Horn I* was the Arizona Supreme Court in the comprehensive Gila River adjudication. "We can appreciate the hesitation of the *Big Horn* court to break new ground, but we do not find its reasoning persuasive. That no previous court has come to grips with an issue does not relieve a present court, fairly confronted with the issue, of the obligation to do so." *In re the General Adjudication of All Rights to Use Water in the Gila River System and Source*, 989 P.2d 739, 745 (Ariz. 1999). Relying on the cases discussed above in note 1, the court concluded:

> [I]f the United States implicitly intended, when it established reservations, to reserve sufficient unappropriated water to meet the reservations' needs,

it must have intended that reservation of water to come from whatever particular sources each reservation had at hand. The significant question for the purpose of the reserved rights doctrine is not whether the water runs above or below the ground but whether it is necessary to accomplish the purpose of the reservation.

Id. at 747. Nonetheless, the court imposed potential limitations on the groundwater right: "We do not, however, decide that any particular federal reservation, Indian or otherwise, has a reserved right to groundwater. A reserved right to groundwater *may only be found where other waters are inadequate to accomplish the purpose of a reservation.*" *Id.* at 748 (emphasis added).

3. The influence of the *Gila River* decision. The Arizona Supreme Court's decision was influential in other jurisdictions. Both the Montana Supreme Court and the Western District of Washington cited *Gila River* in deciding that the reserved rights doctrine extends to groundwater as well as surface water. *Confederated Salish and Kootenai Tribes of the Flathead Reservation v. Stultz*, 59 P.3d 1093 (Mont. 2002); *United States v. State of Washington Dep't of Ecology*, No. C01-0047Z (W.D. Wash. Feb. 24, 2003). In a subsequent decision, the Washington district court extended the Arizona approach, rejecting the notion that groundwater should be generally restricted to situations where surface waters are inadequate. "Evidence of other surface and groundwater sources available to the Lummi will not be considered as part of these proceedings [to determine rights to groundwater of the Lummi Peninsula], except as those sources relate to the calculation of the Lummi's PIA reserved water right." *United States v. Washington Dep't of Ecology*, 375 F. Supp. 2d 1050, 1068, 1070 (W.D. Wash. 2005).

For examination of groundwater issues, see Stephen V. Quesenberry, Timothy C. Seward & Adam P. Bailey, *Tribal Strategies for Protecting and Preserving Groundwater*, 41 Wm. Mitchell L. Rev. 431 (2015); Judith V. Royster, *Indian Tribal Rights to Groundwater*, 15 Kan. J. L. & Pub. Pol'y 489 (2006); Debbie Shosteck, *Beyond Reserved Rights: Tribal Control over Groundwater Resources in a Cold Winters Climate*, 28 Colum. J. Envt.l L. 325 (2003).

4. Groundwater and Indian water settlement acts. Congress has expressly recognized a right to groundwater in a number of Indian water rights settlements. "Of the twenty or so water settlement acts since 1978, more than half contain some provisions concerning tribal rights to groundwater. In general, groundwater is addressed as a primary source in settlements for tribes in the southern United States, while northern tribes' settlements tend to focus on surface water supplies." Judith V. Royster, *Indian Tribal Rights to Groundwater*, 15 Kan. J. L. & Pub. Pol'y 489, 501 (2006). Professor Royster observed that "[t]here is little uniformity or consistency in the groundwater provisions of water rights settlements."

5. Right to non-interference from groundwater use. In *United States v. Orr Water Ditch Co.*, 600 F.3d 1152 (9th Cir. 2010), the Pyramid Lake Paiute Tribe challenged a groundwater allocation by the Nevada State Engineer on the ground that it would adversely affect the tribe's senior rights in the Truckee River under the federal Orr Ditch decree. The Ninth Circuit acknowledged that the decree did not explicitly protect the tribe's water rights from groundwater diminution, but held that allowing such diminution would be inconsistent with the intent of the decree to assure "a reasonable amount of water" for the tribe. Moreover, the court cited *Winters* for the proposition that ambiguities should be resolved in favor of the tribes.

3. Use of Water Rights

In *Big Horn I*, excerpted at page 499, the Wind River Tribes were awarded more than 400,000 acre-feet of water—most of the Big Horn River's annual flow. The tribes' preferred use of the water, however—to restore reservation fisheries—was denied. Consequently, the tribes adopted a water code under which they attempted to dedicate some of the "future project" irrigation water to instream flows for fisheries. The following litigation ensued.

In re General Adjudication of All Rights to Use Water in the Big Horn River System [*Big Horn III*]
835 P.2d 273 (Wyo. 1992)

MACY, J., delivered the opinion of the Court, joined by Justice Thomas and Justice Cardine on the first issue and joined by Justice Thomas and Justice Brown (Retired) on the second issue; THOMAS, J., filed a specially concurring opinion; CARDINE, J., filed an opinion concurring on the first issue and dissenting on the second issue; BROWN, J. (RET.), filed an opinion dissenting on the first issue and concurring on the second issue, with Justice Golden joining in the part dissenting on the first issue; and GOLDEN, J., filed a dissenting opinion, with Justice Brown (Retired) joining in the part dissenting on the first issue.

The State of Wyoming and non-Indian water users appeal from a judgment entered by the district court which (1) decreed that the Shoshone and Northern Arapaho Tribes on the Wind River Indian Reservation may change the use of their reserved water right as they deem advisable without regard to Wyoming water law; and (2) substituted the tribal water agency for the state engineer as the administrator of both reserved and state-permitted water rights within the Wind River Indian Reservation.

We reverse.

The core issues stated in various ways by the several appellants are:

1. Whether the Tribes may change their right to divert future project water for agricultural purposes to a right to maintain an instream flow for fishery purposes without regard to Wyoming water law; and

2. Whether the Tribes have the right to administer all the water rights within the reservation to the exclusion of the Wyoming state engineer.

This is another appeal of an ongoing general adjudication of all water rights in the Big Horn River System, involving over 20,000 claimants. Because of its size and complexity, the adjudication is being conducted in phases. The dispute presently before this court relates to the interpretation of the amended judgment and decree entered on May 24, 1985, by Judge Alan B. Johnson (the 1985 decree) involving Phase I, wherein the Tribes were granted the right to divert water for agricultural purposes on reservation land historically irrigated, as well as on reservation land included within certain future projects. In *Big Horn I*, this court affirmed the 1985 decree, granting the Tribes the right to divert water from the Big Horn River System for agricultural purposes and subsuming livestock, municipal, domestic, and commerce uses within those purposes. This court also affirmed the district court's finding that an instream flow right for fisheries was not a subsuming use. The United States Supreme Court affirmed the *Big Horn I* decision in 1989. After the United States Supreme Court affirmed the Wyoming Supreme Court's decision, the Tribes announced their intent to dedicate a portion of their reserved water right, which had been awarded for future projects, to instream flow for fisheries and other nonsubsumed uses in the Wind River. To that end, the Tribes adopted a Wind River Interim Water Code, created the Wind River Water Resources Control Board, and, on April 12, 1990, granted themselves Instream Flow Permit No. 90-001, which authorized the dedication for the 1990 irrigation season of up to 252 cfs of water in the Wind River for "fisheries restoration and enhancement, recreational uses, ground water recharge downstream benefits to irrigators and other water users."

Shortly after the issuance of Permit No. 90-001, the Tribes complained to the state engineer that the diversion of water by holders of state-awarded water rights caused the Wind River flows to be less than that amount authorized by the permit. The state engineer informed the Tribes that their permit was unenforceable because the Tribes had been awarded only the right to divert water and that any change in the use of future project water covered by their reserved water right must be made following a diversion. The Tribes nevertheless thereafter requested that the state-awarded water rights of Midvale Irrigation District be curtailed so that the instream flows could be maintained. The state engineer refused to honor this request, which he viewed as being an unlawful selective call.

On July 30, 1990, the Tribes filed a motion in the district court for an order to show cause why the state engineer should not be held in contempt, why he should not be relieved of his duties, and why a special master should not be appointed to enforce the Tribes' reserved water right. The State filed its own motion for a determination of certain administrative matters. The district court referred the motions to a special master for a report. The special master agreed to hear all the issues raised except for the contempt issue involving the state engineer.

After hearing oral arguments on exceptions to the special master's report, the district court entered its judgment and decree on March 11, 1991, declaring that the Tribes were entitled to use their reserved water right on the reservation as they deemed advisable, including instream flow use, without regard to Wyoming water law. The district court did not distinguish that portion of the Tribes reserved water right quantified on the basis of historical use from that portion quantified on the basis of future practically irrigable acres when it issued its judgment and decree. The only issue properly before the district court was whether the Tribes could dedicate their future project water to instream flow for the purposes of maintaining fisheries, et cetera, without regard to Wyoming water law. We limit the scope of review on appeal accordingly. The court also ordered the substitution of the Tribes for the state engineer as the administrator of Indian and non-Indian water rights within the Wind River Indian Reservation. On May 3, 1991, this court stayed the judgment and decree from which this appeal is taken.

* * * The issue of whether or not the Tribes have unlimited discretionary use of their quantified reserved water right was decided in *Big Horn I*. We qualified the Tribes' use of their water right by stating:

> The government may reserve water from appropriation *under state law for use on the lands set aside* for an Indian reservation. . . .
>
> . . . .
>
> . . . Considering the well-established principles of treaty interpretation, the treaty itself, the ample evidence and testimony addressed, and the findings of the district court, we have no difficulty affirming the finding that it was the intent at the time to create a reservation with a sole agricultural purpose. . . .
>
> . . . .
>
> . . . The evidence is not sufficient to imply a fishery flow right absent a treaty provision.

Our opinion clearly and unequivocally stated that the Tribes had the right to use a quantified amount of water on their reservation solely for agricultural and subsumed purposes and not for instream purposes. If we had intended to specify what the water could be used for merely as a methodology to determine the amount of water the Tribes could use for any purpose, we would have said so. The contrary is unmistakable. *See* the dissenting opinions of Justice Thomas and Judge Hanscum in *Big Horn I*, wherein they stated that they would have allowed the Tribes to use the water for any purpose appropriate to the progress and development of the reservation rather than limiting the uses to those mentioned in the majority opinion. It is not necessary for us to discuss the Tribes' alternative contention that principles of federal law do not limit the uses to which they may put their water or the State's contention that the 1983 decision and the 1985 decree are not final orders. *Big Horn I*, having been affirmed by the United States Supreme Court, is final and controlling. The Tribes do not have the unfettered right to use their quantified amount of future project water for any purpose they desire.

We must now consider whether the district court erred when it decreed that the Tribes may change the use of their reserved future project water right from agriculture to any other purpose, including instream flows, without regard to Wyoming water law.

* * * We are persuaded by *United States v. New Mexico*, 438 U.S. 696 (1978), wherein the United States Supreme Court held that water is impliedly reserved only to the extent necessary to meet the primary purposes for which a reservation is made and that, where water is valuable for a secondary purpose, the inference arises that Congress intended for water to be acquired in the same manner as is employed by any other private or public appropriator. In *United States v. Adair*, 723 F.2d 1394 (9th Cir. 1983), *cert. denied*, 467 U.S. 1252 (1984), the United States attempted to convert Indian reserved water rights to forest and wildlife programs.

The Ninth Circuit Court of Appeals rejected the attempt and stated:

> The purpose of a federal reservation of land defines the scope and nature of impliedly reserved water rights. Because the reserved rights doctrine is an exception to Congress's explicit deference to state water law in other areas, the Supreme Court has emphasized the importance of the limitation of such rights to only so much water as is essential to accomplish the purpose for which the land was reserved. We conclude that it would be inconsistent with the principles expressed in *United States v. New Mexico* to hold that the Government may "tack" a currently claimed Winters right to a prior one by asserting that it has merely changed the purpose of its previously reserved water right.

We see no reason why this rationale should not apply to a change of use of the future project water acquired by the Tribes solely for agricultural purposes. We hold that the Tribes, like any other appropriator, must comply with Wyoming water law to change the use of their reserved future project water from agricultural purposes to any other beneficial use. We leave for another day the question of whether the Tribes may dedicate their historically used water to instream flow, as that issue is not directly presented for our review by the facts of this case.

Although our statutory scheme regulating the appropriation of water has contemplated an actual physical diversion of water, we have never said that a requirement to do so existed. This is understandable if we give consideration to the fact that, until passage of our instream flows act, it was necessary to actually divert water to put it to a beneficial use permitted by law in Wyoming. "Beneficial use" is, however, an evolving concept and can be expanded to reflect changes in society's recognition of the value of new uses of our resources. Actual diversion is neither constitutionally required nor an essential element of our appropriation doctrine. Beneficial use is the key element. Wyo. Stat. §41-3-101 (Supp. 1991) provides in relevant part: "Beneficial use shall be the basis, the measure and limit of the right to use water." We join the Idaho Supreme Court and hold that an actual diversion of water is not necessary to appropriate water for a beneficial use. This holding, however, is of no comfort to the Tribes or to the national and Wyoming wildlife federations which have filed an amicus curiae brief, as the appropriation of water for instream flow is not a beneficial use which is presently available to the Tribes. Wyo. Stat. §41-3-1002(e) (Supp. 1991) clearly provides: "No person other than the state of Wyoming shall own any instream flow water right."

The Wyoming legislature has for good reason precluded water right holders from unilaterally dedicating water to maintain instream flows. Water is the lifeblood of Wyoming. It is a scarce resource which must be effectively managed and efficiently used to meet the various demands of society. Wyoming's founding fathers also recognized the necessity of having state control over this vital resource. * * * Our decision today recognizes only that which has been the traditional wisdom relating to Wyoming water: Water is simply too precious to the well being of society to permit water right holders unfettered control over its use.[7]

We turn now to the State's contentions regarding that portion of the district court's March 11, 1991, judgment and decree which provided:

> The Tribal agency which regulates reserved water matters shall have the authority to administer all water rights within the stipulated boundaries of the reservation. Non-Indian rights will be administered according to state water law by the Tribal agency, with appropriate judicial review in state district court pursuant to Title 41 of the Wyoming statutes.

The State argues, among other things, that the district court violated the Wyoming Constitution by removing the state engineer from being the administrator of state water within the reservation.

Neither the constitution nor the statutes contemplate that a district court should have the authority to remove or replace the state engineer as the administrator of Wyoming water. The state engineer is an executive officer appointed by and subject to removal by only the governor of Wyoming. The district court's primary role in the instant case was to adjudicate the nature, extent, and relative priority of competing water interests in the Big Horn River System. We hold that the district court had no "inherent equitable enforcement authority," as argued by the Tribes, to effectuate a de facto removal and replacement of the state engineer as the administrator of state water within the reservation. A contrary position would result in a most unbalanced and unworkable form of government. The district court's action violated not only the separation of powers doctrine embodied in the Wyoming Constitution, but also the constitutional charge that the state engineer shall have "general supervision of the waters of the state."

As to the Tribes' concern that the separation of powers doctrine should not be applied in such a manner as to make the state engineer immune from judicial enforcement of the 1985 decree, we agree. The state engineer is obligated by the Wyoming

---

7. Even if the Tribes were to petition to change the use of their reserved water right from agricultural purposes to another beneficial use permitted by law, they would have to overcome the difficulty of complying with Wyo. Stat. § 41-3-104 (1977). Section 41-3-104 provides that changes in the use or place of use of water may be allowed if the water transferred does not (1) exceed the amount of water historically diverted under an existing use; (2) exceed the historic rate of diversion under a existing use; (3) increase the historic amount consumptively used under a existing use; (4) decrease the historic amount of return flow under an existing use; or (5) injure in any manner other lawful appropriators.

Constitution to "equally guard all the various interests" in the water of the State of Wyoming. Of the various interests to be protected is the Tribes' reserved water right. If the district court were to find in a future proceeding that the state engineer had shunned this constitutional mandate, then appropriate enforcement action should be undertaken. Our objection to the district court's action in the instant case goes only to the method employed, not to the underlying principle that the court should have authority to compel compliance with its lawful judgments and decrees.

This court addressed the role of the state engineer as the administrator of the Tribes' reserved water right in *Big Horn I*. We limited the state engineer's authority as the administrator in two respects. We initially acknowledged that the Indian reserved water right existed independent of state law and procedure regarding the perfection of usufructuary rights to Wyoming water. We then determined that the state engineer, as the monitor of the Indian reserved water right, could not shut down tribal headgates once he believed that the Tribes had exceeded either the nature or the extent of their decreed right. We explained that, assuming cooperative efforts were of no avail, the state engineer would have to seek judicial enforcement of the decree against the United States and the Tribes.

Our present decision is consistent with the duties and limitations imposed upon the state engineer in *Big Horn I*. The state engineer remains responsible to distribute the water within the Big Horn River System according to the nature, extent, and priority of right. When the nature, extent, and priority of the Indian reserved water right are clear and not respected by state appropriators, the state engineer must exercise his authority over the state appropriators to see that the tribal right is observed. When, on the other hand, it is impossible to determine if the tribal right is being violated because the right itself is in some respect ill-defined, the state engineer should promptly seek clarification from the district court so that appropriate remedial action, if needed, may be undertaken. Should the state engineer determine that the Tribes violated the decree, he should execute an enforcement action as outlined in *Big Horn I* and summarized in the preceding paragraph.

Reversed.

[The court issued several other opinions. Justice Cardine concurred in part and dissented in part. He agreed that "a paper water right, one that has never been applied to practicably irrigable acreage or subsumed uses, may not be transferred to instream flow." Instead, he believed that the tribes' water right "must first be put to use for agricultural purposes. . . . [O]nce a paper right has been converted to beneficial use by actually being applied to the practicably irrigable acreage, I would allow the Tribes to apply to change their use of the water." He disagreed with the majority that Wyoming law prevented a tribal instream flow right.]

[Justice Brown also concurred in part and dissented in part. He reminded the court "that the Tribes' water rights flow from the Treaty of 1868 and not from an appropriation under Wyoming law. The majority opinion treats the Tribes' reserved water right substantially the same as an appropriation under Wyoming statutes. The effect of the majority determination is to make marginal farmers out of the tribes forever. This defeats the purposes for which the Reservation was created." In particular, he noted that *Big Horn I* did not discuss or decide the issue of change of use of the tribe's agricultural water rights. "The majority pumps air into its *Big Horn I* decision, then cites the enhanced opinion for its determination that the Tribes cannot divert water for agricultural purposes to instream flows." He concluded there was no authority for the majority's conclusion that the tribe's water could not be used for fishery purposes, but he agreed with the majority that the state engineer should manage the water.]

[Justice Golden dissented. He agreed with Justice Brown that "the Tribes may use their water, whether it falls into the category of historic water or future water, for any purpose they deem to be to their benefit," including an instream flow. He also believed that the district court was well within its discretion in removing the state engineer from administering the contested water rights. He then supplied the following guide to the confusion caused by the numerous opinions the case generated:]

A GUIDE TO THE COURT'S PRESENT OPINION

If one looks closely at the fragmented opinions of my four brethren, it is not unlikely that bewilderment will ensue. It is unfortunate that clarity of vision and voice have eluded the court in this most important opinion. The Tribes' application of future waters to instream flow is denied, though no clear majority opinion exists to determine why. Justices Macy and Thomas conclude that state law precludes this dedication, and Justice Cardine views the Treaty as preventing it, though also concluding that state law does not govern its use.

At least three Justices (Macy, Thomas and Brown) conclude that the state engineer should regulate the water on the entire reservation, but the law that should be applied is federal, not state law, according to Justices Cardine, Golden, and Brown.

The result of the court is fragmented, providing no clear guidance to the parties. Pragmatically, it is difficult to imagine how this opinion can be implemented. The court has stated that two different types of law apply to two inter-related issues. A coherent opinion would have at least determined a consistent answer to the question of what law applies to Indian water rights on the reservation. All that is really clear from this narrow opinion is that the parties will continue to litigate their conflicts.

CONCLUSION

If one may mark the turn of the 20th century by the massive expropriation of Indian lands, then the turn of the 21st century is the era when the Indian tribes risk the same fate for their water resources.

[Joseph R. Membrino, *Indian Reserved Water Rights, Federalism and the Trust Responsibility*, 27 Land & Water L. Rev. 1, 14 (1992).]

Today some members of the court sound a warning to the Tribes that they are determined to complete the agenda initiated over one hundred years ago and are willing to pervert prior decisions to advance that aim. I cannot be a party to deliberate and transparent efforts to eliminate the political and economic base of the Indian peoples under the distorted guise of state water law superiority.

Notes

1. Use of water rights. In *Arizona v. California II*, in accordance with a stipulation of the parties, the Supreme Court declared that PIA was "the means of determining quantity of adjudicated water rights but shall not constitute a restriction of the usage of them to irrigation or other agricultural application." 439 U.S. 419, 422 (1979). Similarly, the Special Master in the *Arizona* litigation, after determining that PIA was the measure of the tribes' water rights, explained:

> This does not necessarily mean, however, that water reserved for Indian Reservations may not be used for purposes other than agriculture and related uses. . . . The measurement used in defining the magnitude of the water rights is the amount of water necessary for agriculture and related purposes because this was the initial purpose of the reservation, but the decree establishes a property right which the United States may utilize or dispose of for the benefit of the Indians as the relevant law may allow.

Report from Simon H. Rifkind, Special Master to the Supreme Court in Arizona v. California [373 U.S. 546 (1963)] 265–66 (Dec. 5, 1960) (received by the Court Jan. 16, 1961, 364 U.S. 940 (1961)).

Relying in part on the Special Master's report, the Ninth Circuit held that: "When the Tribe has a vested property right in reserved water, it may use it in any lawful manner. . . . [P]ermitting the Indians to determine how to use reserved water is consistent with the general purpose for the creation of an Indian reservation—providing a homeland for the survival and growth of the Indians and their way of life." *Colville Confederated Tribes v. Walton*, 647 F.2d 42, 48–49 (9th Cir. 1981) (see page 530). The Western District of Washington adopted the Ninth Circuit's approach, finding that once the Lummi Tribe's reserved right to groundwater for agricultural and domestic purposes was quantified, the tribe was free to use the water for "any purpose." *United States v. Washington Dept. of Ecology*, 375 F. Supp. 2d 1050, 1070 (W.D. Wash. 2005).

What weight should be given to the statements from the *Arizona* litigation? How much weight did the Ninth Circuit give them? How much weight did the Wyoming Supreme Court give them? Which court was correct?

2. Clean Water Act option. Does the decision in *Big Horn III* mean the tribes cannot restore water flows in the Big Horn River? Suppose the tribes sought to use their sovereign rather than their proprietary authority to establish instream flows, and obtained TAS (treatment as a state) status for water quality standards from the EPA. See pages 295–300. Suppose further that the tribes set flow parameters as part of their water quality standards and required all non-point sources of pollution, such as irrigation diversions, to certify that they were meeting water quality standards? Would EPA approve such a program?

3. Instream flow rights and change of use. In *Adair I* (see page 487), the Ninth Circuit held that if a tribe is awarded an instream flow right for the purpose of continuing an aboriginal right such as fisheries, the tribe may not change the use of the water:

> [T]he right to water reserved to further the Tribe's hunting and fishing purposes is unusual in that it is basically non-consumptive. The holder of such a right is not entitled to withdraw water from the stream for agricultural, industrial, or other consumptive uses (absent independent consumptive rights). Rather, the entitlement consists of the right to prevent other appropriators from depleting the streams waters below a protected level in any area where the non-consumptive right applies.

Should the same rule apply to *Winters* rights reserved for new and/or consumptive uses? For example, if the Wind River Tribes in the *Big Horn* cases put part of their existing water right to an instream use, could they later change the use back to a consumptive one? The "no injury" rule of state appropriation law permits a state appropriator to change the nature or place of use only if that change will not cause injury to a downstream junior appropriator. If the Wind River Tribes changed a non-consumptive instream flow to a consumptive use, there would be less water available downstream and injury to junior users would likely result. What effect, if any, should that state law doctrine have on Indian tribes' ability to change the use of their federal reserved rights?

A federal district court in Nevada ruled that in assessing potential injury to junior appropriators, the proper test was to compare "the impact of the Tribe's proposed change against those physical conditions that would exist *if* the Tribe used its entire water rights as decreed." *United States v. Orr Water Ditch Co.*, 309 F. Supp. 2d 1245, 1253 (D. Nev. 2004) (emphasis in original). The court reasoned that because the tribe's water right was judicially recognized and established, as a matter of law, the tribe would not injure others' water rights when it expanded its use within the boundaries of the decree.

Note on Water Marketing

Water marketing is the sale or lease of water or water rights, independent of the appurtenant land. In *Big Horn I* (see page 499), the Wyoming court addressed the issue of "exportation" of water, distinguishing between on-reservation and off-reservation sales or leases of water:

> The district court held that "[t]he Tribes can sell or lease any part of the water covered by their reserved water rights but the said sale or lease cannot be for exportation off of the Reservation." The Tribes did not seek permission to export reserved water, and the United States concedes that no federal law permits the sale of reserved water to non-Indians off the reservation.

The Nonintercourse Act, which prohibits any "purchase, grant, lease, or other conveyance of lands, or of any title or claim thereto" without federal consent, 25 U.S.C.

§ 177, probably applies to the marketing of water rights. Congress has authorized the inclusion of appurtenant water rights in surface leases of Indian lands. 25 U.S.C. § 415(a); *see also Skeem v. United States*, 273 F. 93 (9th Cir. 1921) (Indian reserved water rights may be exercised by lessees of Indian lands). However, no federal statute authorizes the sale or lease of Indian water rights separate and apart from the land. There is, therefore, presently no general congressional authorization for the off-reservation marketing of Indian water.

Most of the Indian water rights settlement acts include provisions authorizing water leasing or water marketing, although those acts benefit only the tribes that are parties to the settlements. *See* Judith V. Royster, *Indian Water and the Federal Trust: Some Proposals for Federal Action*, 46 Nat. Resources J. 375, 395 (2006). Professor Royster noted that the tribe-by-tribe

> legislative approach has benefitted only the few tribes with settlement agreements; the vast majority of tribes are unable to exercise the same authority. Nonetheless, the water rights of many of those tribes are presently in use by non-Indians. Under the prior appropriation regimes of the western states, any unused tribal water is available for use by junior non-Indian appropriators until it is claimed by the tribes. The result is that Indian water is in fact used by non-Indians—for free. Water marketing would permit tribes to capture the economic benefit of that non-Indian use.

4. Rights of Allottees and Subsequent Purchasers

Colville Confederated Tribes v. Walton

647 F.2d 42 (9th Cir. 1981)

WRIGHT, Circuit Judge.

The Colville Confederated Tribes initiated this case a decade ago. They sought to enjoin Walton, non-Indian owner of allotted lands, from using surface and ground waters in the No Name Creek basin. The State of Washington intervened, asserting its authority to grant water permits on reservation lands, and the case was consolidated with a separate suit brought by the United States against Walton.

I. BACKGROUND

A.

In 1871 the predecessors of the Colville Confederated Tribes had no treaty with the United States and no reservation. These Indians were contemporaneously described as "good farmers, [who] raise extensive crops, make good improvements, and own stocks of cattle and horses." [1871] *Report of the Commissioner of Indian Affairs*, 277.

After the Civil War, settlers had begun to encroach on Indian lands. The Farmer in charge at Fort Colville reported that violence was likely unless a reservation was established to protect Indian interests. In response to a request from the

Commissioner of Indian Affairs, President Grant created the Colville Reservation. Executive Order of July 2, 1872. Twenty years later, the northern half of the reservation was taken from the Indians and opened for entry and settlement.

In 1906, Congress ratified an agreement with the Colvilles that provided for distribution of reservation lands to the Indians pursuant to the General Allotment Act of 1887, and for disposition of the remainder by entry and settlement. The agreement was effectuated by Presidential proclamation in 1916.

In 1917, a row of seven allotments was created in the No Name Creek watershed. Walton, a non-Indian, now owns the middle three, numbers 525, 2371 and 894. He bought them in 1948 from an Indian, not a member of the Tribe, who had begun to irrigate the land by diverting water for 32 acres from No Name Creek. Walton immediately procured a permit from the state to irrigate 65 acres by diverting up to 1 cubic foot per second "subject to existing rights." He now irrigates 104 acres and uses additional water for domestic and stock water purposes.

The United States holds the remaining allotments in trust for the Colville Indians. Allotments 526 and 892 are north of Walton's property and allotments 901 and 903 are south. Allotments 892, 901 and 903 are held for heirs of the original allottees, but the Tribe has a long-term lease. Allotment 526 is beneficially owned by the Tribe.[5]

B.

The No Name Creek is a spring-fed creek flowing south into Omak Lake, which has no outlet and is saline. The No Name hydrological system, consisting of an underground aquifer and the creek, is located entirely on the Colville Reservation.

The aquifer lies under the Indians' northern allotments and the northern tip of Walton's allotment, number 525. No Name Creek originates on the southern tip of the Indians' allotment number 802 [sic; apparently should be 892] and flows through Walton's allotments and the Indians' southern allotments.

C.

Salmon and trout were traditional foods for the Colville Indians, but the salmon runs have been destroyed by dams on the Columbia River. In 1968, the Tribe, with the help of the Department of the Interior, introduced Lahonton cutthroat trout into Omak Lake. The species thrives in the lake's saline water, but needs fresh water to spawn. The Indians cultivated No Name Creek's lower reach to establish spawning grounds but irrigation use depleted the water flow during spawning season. The federal government has given the Indians fingerlings to maintain the stock of trout.

II. THE CASE BELOW

The trial court found that 1,000 acre feet per year of water were available in No Name Creek Basin in an average year. It calculated the quantity of the Colvilles' reserved water rights on the basis of irrigable acreage. The court excluded the

---

5. We assume that none of the Colvilles' allotments ever passed from Indian ownership.

northern-most allotment, number 526, because the evidence showed that it was formerly irrigated with the surface waters of Omak Creek, and the Tribe had not demonstrated that water to irrigate it was required from the No Name system.

The trial court determined the Indians had a reserved right to 666.4 acre feet per year of water from the No Name Creek Basin. It held that Walton was not entitled to share in the Colvilles' reserved water rights. The trial court found, however, that the Colvilles were irrigating only a portion of the irrigable acres included in its calculation.

Under the district court's findings, in an average year there are 333.6 acre feet per year of water not subject to the Indians' reserved right. There are an additional 237.6 acre feet per year of water to which the Indians have a reserved right, but which they are not currently using. This water is available for appropriation by non-Indians, subject to the Indians' superior right. The court held that Walton had a right to irrigate the 32 acres under irrigation at the time he acquired his land, with a priority date of the actual appropriation of water for that use.

The court also held that the Indians were potentially entitled to use water to propagate trout, but refused to award water for that purpose. It concluded that spawning was unnecessary because fingerlings were provided free by the federal government.

By post-trial motion, the Indians sought permission to use some of their irrigation water for trout spawning. The motion was granted and the Tribe has since pumped aquifer water from their wells into No Name Creek during spawning season.

Finally, the court decided that the state could regulate No Name water not reserved for Indian use.

Walton, the Tribe and the State appeal parts of the decision.

III. THE TRIBE'S WATER RIGHTS

[The court held that the Colville Reservation was set aside to serve dual purposes. The first was "to provide a homeland for the Indians to maintain their agrarian society," for which water would be awarded under the practicably irrigable acreage standard. The second purpose was "preservation of the tribe's access to fishing grounds." To fulfill that purpose, "we find an implied reservation of water from No Name Creek for the development and maintenance of replacement fishing grounds." The court thus affirmed "the district court's holding that the Colvilles have a reserved right to the quantity of water necessary to maintain the Omak Lake Fishery."]

IV. THE GENERAL ALLOTMENT ACT OF 1887

We next consider Walton's rights as the fee owner of allotted land, and reverse the district court's judgment that he has no right to reserved water.

A.

The General Allotment Act provided that land on reservations could be allotted for the exclusive use of individual Indians. Remaining land was to be made available for homesteading by non-Indians. After holding allotted lands in trust for individual Indians for a 25-year period, the federal government could convey the land to the allottee in fee, "discharged of said trust and free of all charge or incumbrance whatsoever."

Because the use of reserved water is not limited to fulfilling the original purposes of the reservation, Congress had the power to allot reserved water rights to individual Indians, and to allow for the transfer of such rights to non-Indians. Whether it did so is a question of congressional intent.

The only reference to water rights in the Act is found in section 7:

> In cases where the use of water for irrigation is necessary to render the lands within any Indian reservation available for agricultural purposes, the Secretary of the Interior is authorized to prescribe such rules and regulations as he may deem necessary to secure a just and equal distribution thereof among the Indians residing upon any such reservation; and no other appropriation or grant of water by an riparian proprietor shall be authorized or permitted to the damage of any other riparian proprietor.

The Act was passed over 20 years before the Supreme Court announced the implied-reservation doctrine in *Winters*. There is nothing to suggest Congress gave any consideration to the transferability of reserved water rights. To resolve this issue, we must determine what Congress would have intended had it considered it.

B.

It is settled that Indian allottees have a right to use reserved water. *United States v. Powers*, 305 U.S. 527 (1939). "[W]hen allotments were made for exclusive use and thereafter conveyed in fee, the right to use some portion of tribal waters essential for cultivation passed to the owners." We must determine whether non-Indian purchasers of allotted lands also obtain a right to some portion of reserved waters.

(1)

The general rule is that termination or diminution of Indian rights requires express legislation or a clear inference of Congressional intent gleaned from the surrounding circumstances and legislative history. Upon careful consideration, we conclude this principle supports the proposition that an Indian allottee may sell his right to reserved water.

The district court's holding that an Indian allottee may convey only a right to the water he or she has actually appropriated with a priority date of actual appropriation reduces the value of the allottee's right to reserved water. We think this type of restriction on transferability is a "diminution of Indian rights" that must be supported by a clear inference of Congressional intent.

By placing allotted lands in trust for 25 years, Congress evinced an intent to protect Indians by preventing transfer of those lands. But there is no basis for an inference that some restrictions survived beyond the trust period. Congress provided for extensions of the trust period, but directed that fee title be conveyed to the allottee when the period expired. We think the fee included the appurtenant right to share in reserved waters, and see no basis for limiting the transferability of that right.

(2)

In determining the nature of the right acquired by non-Indian purchasers, we consider three aspects of an allottee's right to use reserved waters.

First, the extent of an Indian allottee's right is based on the number of irrigable acres he owns. If the allottee owns 10% of the irrigable acreage in the watershed, he is entitled to 10% of the water reserved for irrigation (i.e., a "ratable share"). This follows from the provision for an equal and just distribution of water needed for irrigation.

A non-Indian purchaser cannot acquire more extensive rights to reserved water than were held by the Indian seller. Thus, the purchaser's right is similarly limited by the number of irrigable acres he owns.

Second, the Indian allottee's right has a priority as of the date the reservation was created. This is the principal aspect of the right that renders it more valuable than the rights of competing water users, and therefore applies to the right acquired by a non-Indian purchaser. In the event there is insufficient water to satisfy all valid claims to reserved water, the amount available to each claimant should be reduced proportionately.

Third, the Indian allottee does not lose by non-use the right to a share of reserved water. This characteristic is not applicable to the right acquired by a non-Indian purchaser. The non-Indian successor acquires a right to water being appropriated by the Indian allottee at the time title passes. The non-Indian also acquires a right, with a date-of-reservation priority date, to water that he or she appropriates with reasonable diligence after the passage of title. If the full measure of the Indian's reserved water right is not acquired by this means and maintained by continued use, it is lost to the non-Indian successor.

The full quantity of water available to the Indian allottee thus may be conveyed to the non-Indian purchaser. There is no diminution in the right the Indian may convey. We think Congress would have intended, however, that the non-Indian purchaser, under no competitive disability vis-a-vis other water users, may not retain the right to that quantity of water despite non-use.

C.

The district court's holding that Walton has no right to share in water reserved when the Colville reservation was created is reversed. On remand, it will need to determine the number of irrigable acres Walton owns, and the amount of water he appropriated with reasonable diligence in order to determine the extent of his right to share in reserved water.

V. STATE PERMITS

Finally, we consider Walton's claim to water rights based on state water permits. We hold that the state has no power to regulate water in the No Name system, and the permits are of no force and effect.

A.

State regulatory authority over a tribal reservation may be barred either because it is pre-empted by federal law, or because it unlawfully infringes on the right of reservation Indians to self-government. Although these barriers are independent, they are related by the concept of tribal sovereignty. "The tradition of Indian sovereignty over the reservation and tribal members must inform the determination whether the exercise of state authority has been pre-empted by operation of federal law."

A tribe's inherent power to regulate generally the conduct of non-members on land no longer owned by, or held in trust for the tribe was impliedly withdrawn as a necessary result of its dependent status. *Montana v. United States*, [450 U.S. 544] (1981). Exceptions to this implied withdrawal exist. A tribe retains the inherent power to exercise civil authority over the conduct of non-Indians on fee lands within its reservation when that conduct threatens or has some direct effect on the health and welfare of the tribe. This includes conduct that involves the tribe's water rights.

A water system is a unitary resource. The actions of one user have an immediate and direct effect on other users. The Colvilles' complaint in the district court alleged that the Waltons' appropriations from No Name Creek imperiled the agricultural use of downstream tribal lands and the trout fishery, among other things. *Cf. Montana* (complaint did not allege peril to subsistence or welfare of tribe from non-Indian hunting and fishing on fee lands).

Regulation of water on a reservation is critical to the lifestyle of its residents and the development of its resources. Especially in arid and semi-arid regions of the West, water is the lifeblood of the community. Its regulation is an important sovereign power.

B.

We hold that state regulation of water in the No Name system was preempted by the creation of the Colville Reservation. The geographic facts of this case make resolution of this issue somewhat easier than it otherwise might be. The No-Name water system is non-navigable and is entirely within the boundaries of the reservation. Although some of the water passes through lands now in non-Indian ownership, all of those lands are also entirely within the reservation boundaries.

The Supreme Court has held that water use on a federal reservation is not subject to state regulation absent explicit federal recognition of state authority. *Federal Power Commission v. Oregon*, 349 U.S. 435 (1955). Thus, in creating the Colville Reservation, the federal government preempted state control of the No Name system.

In *United States v. McIntire*, 101 F.2d 650, 654 (9th Cir. 1934), we held that state water laws are not controlling on an Indian reservation:

> [T]he Montana statutes regarding water rights are not applicable, because Congress at no time has made such statutes controlling in the reservation. In fact, the Montana enabling act specifically provided that Indian lands within the limits of the state, 'shall remain under the absolute jurisdiction and control of the Congress of the United States.'

Identical language appears in the Washington Enabling Act.

We adhere to this holding because we find no indication Congress intended the state to have this power. In a series of Acts culminating in the Desert Lands Act of 1877, Congress gave the states plenary control of water on the public domain. Based on this and other legislation, the Supreme Court concluded that Congress almost invariably defers to state water law when it expressly considers water rights.

This deference is not applicable to water use on a federal reservation, at least where such use has no impact off the reservation. The usual policy stems in part from the need to permit western states to fashion water rights regimes that are responsive to local needs, and in part from the "legal confusion that would arise if federal water law and state water law reigned side by side in the same locality."

Neither rationale is applicable here. Where land is set aside for an Indian reservation, Congress has reserved it for federal, as opposed to state needs. Because the No Name system is located entirely within the reservation, state regulation of some portion of its waters would create the jurisdictional confusion Congress has sought to avoid.

Finally, we note that the state's interest in extending its water law to the reservation is limited in this case. Tribal or federal control of No Name waters will have no impact on state water rights off the reservation.

Thus, we conclude that Walton's state permits are of no force and effect.

VI. CONCLUSION

On remand, the district court will calculate the respective rights of the parties. To the extent Walton's use of water exceeds his rights and interferes with the rights of the tribe, it will be enjoined.

Notes

1. **Water rights of allottees.** The *Walton* decision describes the basic features of the water rights obtained by Indians when reservations were allotted. This approach has been universally adopted. *See, e.g., In re General Adjudication of All Rights to Use Water in the Big Horn River System (Big Horn I)*, 753 P.2d 76, 112 (Wyo. 1988), *aff'd by an equally divided Court*, 492 U.S. 406 (1989) (page 499); *State ex rel. Greely v. Confederated Salish & Kootenai Tribes*, 712 P.2d 754, 764 (Mont. 1985).

In addition, the Wyoming Supreme Court in *Big Horn I* ruled that the same water rights are held by Indian fee owners of former allotments:

> The special master held that land within the reservation held in fee by individual Indians which never left Indian ownership held a priority date of 1868. In *United States v. Powers*, 305 U.S. at 533, the Court said it found nothing to show that Congress intended allottees be denied participation in the use of reserved water rights. We affirm.

2. *Walton* **rights of subsequent purchasers.** Boyd Walton, of course, was a non-Indian who purchased a former allotment in fee. Are his water rights prior

appropriation rights? Reserved rights? Are they federal rights, state rights, or tribal rights?

In 2002, the Wyoming Supreme Court issued another decision in the long-running *Big Horn* adjudication, ruling that non-Indian successors' *Walton* rights to federal reserved water were not lost, even though the water projects necessary to exercise those rights were not completed until some ten to thirty years after the Indian allottees transferred the land to the non-Indian claimants. The court noted that the claimants had a reasonable amount of time to put the water to beneficial use; in the court's judgment, that meant they had a reasonable time after the projects made the water available to them. *In re General Adjudication of All Rights to Use Water in the Big Horn River System*, 48 P.3d 1040 (Wyo. 2002).

3. Water rights for reacquired lands. Whether lands reacquired by an Indian tribe include reserved water rights depends upon how the lands were originally lost to tribal ownership. If a tribe reacquires former allotments, it acquires the water rights of its predecessor in interest—either allotment water rights if the fee owner was a tribal member, or *Walton* rights if the fee owner was a non-Indian. *United States v. Anderson*, 736 F.2d 1358, 1362 (9th Cir. 1984); *Big Horn I*, 753 P.2d at 112–113. However, reserved water rights did not survive on tribal lands sold to homesteaders. When these non-allotment lands are reacquired by a tribe, there are no *Winters* or *Walton* rights attached. The tribe will succeed only to the state-law water rights of its predecessor in interest, including the state-law priority date. *Anderson*, 736 F.2d at 1363; *In re Adjudication of All Rights to Use Water in the Big Horn River System (Big Horn IV)*, 899 P.2d 848, 855 (Wyo. 1995). If the predecessor in interest had no perfected water rights under state law, the tribe will acquire *Winters* rights on the land, but with a priority date of the reacquisition of the land. *Anderson*, 736 F.2d at 1363. *See generally* Nicole C. Salamander, *A Half Full Circle: The Reserved Rights Doctrine and Tribal Reacquired Lands*, 12 U. Denver Water L. Rev. 333 (2009).

4. Water rights on after-acquired lands. Section 5 of the Indian Reorganization Act (IRA), discussed at pages 124–126, authorizes the Secretary of the Interior to acquire in trust "any interest in lands, water rights, or surface rights to lands, within or without existing reservations... for the purpose of providing land for Indians." 25 U.S.C. § 5108 (formerly § 465). If lands taken into trust were originally tribal lands, then *Winters* rights to water would attach under the principles set forth in note 3 *above*. Lands outside existing reservations have been referred to after-acquired lands; as "new" Indian country, these lands should include *Winters* rights to water with a priority date of the acquisition. Tribal water rights settlement acts, however, may provide otherwise. *See* Arizona Water Settlements Act of 2004, Pub. L. No. 108-451, § 210(b), 118 Stat. 3478, 3523 (specifying that "[a]fter-acquired trust land shall not include federally reserved rights to surface water or groundwater.").

5. Regulatory control over reservation water rights. In *Walton*, the Ninth Circuit ruled that the Colville tribes were the water managers of all water rights on No Name Creek because these water rights had no off-reservation effects. The court noted that water is a "unitary resource" and the "actions of one user have an immediate and direct effect on other users." Compare the conclusions of EPA in its Clean Water Act regulations treating tribes as states, discussed at pages 293–294. *See also* U.S. Interior Solicitor, Entitlement to Water under the Southern Arizona Water Rights Settlement Act (Op. No. M-36982, March 30, 1995) (opining that tribes possess broad authority over reservation water resources, including allotment water rights).

Three years after *Walton*, however, the Ninth Circuit ruled that the decision was an exception to the "usual policy of deference" to state water law. *United States v. Anderson*, 736 F.2d 1358, 1365 (9th Cir. 1984). In *Anderson*, the Spokane Tribe sought regulatory control over non-Indian use of excess water from Chamokane Creek on its reservation. The court upheld state regulation of the water, explaining that "[t]he *Walton* decision was compelled by the geography and hydrology of the No Name Basin and its relationship to the Colville Reservation," and that, unlike *Walton*, where the creek was small, non-navigable, and located entirely within the reservation, Chamokane Creek begins and ends off-reservation, forming the eastern boundary of the reservation. *See also Big Horn III* (page 521) (rejecting tribal authority to administer non-Indian water rights on the Wind River Reservation).

Would a tribe have regulatory authority over all water rights if it owned the submerged lands of the water source? See Chapter III, Section D. Under *Montana v. United States*, 450 U.S. 544 (1981) (see page 249) and cited by the court in *Walton*, tribes retain regulatory authority on tribal lands. Note, however, that more recent U.S. Supreme Court cases may have cast some doubt on this absolute rule. See note 2, page 279.

5. Right to Water Quality

Most uses of water rights — including fisheries, irrigation, and domestic use — require water of an adequate quality to meet those intended uses. There is virtually no reserved rights case law, however, on the right to water quality.

The following case is the first, and still the only, one to directly address the interrelated issues of water quantity and water quality for Indian tribes. To what extent, however, is the court's decision based on the language of the Globe Equity Decree that the tribe was entitled to a water right from "the natural flow" of the river? Is the court's analysis applicable to common-law *Winters* rights? On the issue of water quality, see generally Margaret S. Treuer, *An Indian Right to Water Undiminished in Quality*, 7 Hamline L. Rev. 347 (1984).

United States v. Gila Valley Irrigation District
920 F. Supp. 1444 (D. Ariz. 1996), *aff'd*, 117 F.3d 425 (9th Cir. 1997)

This is the fourth phase of the most recent round of litigation concerning the enforcement of the Globe Equity Consent Decree of June 29, 1935 (hereafter "Decree") for the benefit of the Gila River Indian Community (hereafter "GRIC") and the San Carlos Apache Tribe (hereafter "Apache Tribe" or "Apaches"). [The Decree provided that the United States, on behalf of the San Carlos Apache Tribe, owned the right to divert 6000 acre feet of the Gila River during the irrigation season "from the natural flow in said river."]

The Apache Tribe argues that the waters of the Gila River are contaminated by farming practices in the upper valleys and that the Tribe is therefore deprived of its right under the Decree to the "natural flow" of the stream. UVDs [Upper Valley Defendants] argue that the water quality deteriorates as the river passes through the upper valleys due to natural causes, some of them unknown. For the reasons expressed below, the Court finds (1) that the water reaching the San Carlos Reservation is of significantly lower quality than the water in the upper valleys, (2) that UVDs are responsible to a significant degree for the degradation of the water reaching the reservation boundary, and (3) that equity requires that certain measures be adopted to protect the Tribe's water right.

The courts of the western states generally agree that a prior appropriator of water is entitled to protection, including injunctive relief, against material degradation of the quality of the water by junior appropriators upstream. Further, the Supreme Court has held:

> What diminution of quantity, or deterioration of quality, will constitute an invasion of the rights of the first appropriator will depend on the special circumstances of each case, considered with reference to the uses to which the water is applied. A slight deterioration in quality might render the water unfit for drink or domestic purposes, whilst it would not sensibly impair its value for mining or irrigation. In all controversies, therefore, between him and parties subsequently claiming the water, the question for determination is necessarily whether his use and enjoyment of the water to the extent of his original appropriation have been impaired by the acts of the defendant. *Atchison v. Peterson*, 87 U.S. 507, 514–15 (1974) . . .

There is no substantial dispute that the United States and the Apache Tribe bear the burden of proof on this issue.

A. Overview

The Gila River once supported irrigation from its surface flow in regions extending from above the New Mexico border to the confluence of the Gila and the Salt River. The river is now overdeveloped and overallocated. In the upper valleys, surface flow is heavily augmented with water pumped from wells. Further, the growers in the upper valleys on occasion divert the entire flow of the stream into irrigation canals to serve the acreage they farm. The return flows from diversions are often recycled, diverted again and applied to other fields. The effects of these and other practices contribute to a dramatic increase in both the salt load and the salinity of the Gila River. The salt load is increased, in part, by pumping groundwater that is higher in salt content than the surface flow and mixing it with the stream. Salinity increases as the river flows through the Safford Valley due to the diversion of the entire stream and the consumptive use of the water, but not the salt, by irrigated crops and other plants. By the time the flow, if any remains, reaches the San Carlos Reservation boundary, the water is degraded to such a degree that the Apache Tribe may be unable to grow the types of vegetable and grain crops that were once raised there.

B. Water Quality of the Gila River

There are two interrelated aspects to the water quality issue in this case: flow rate and contamination. The contaminant is salt, which prevents the successful cultivation of a variety of crops. The issue of flow rate is, in this case, inseparable from the issue of salt, given the general agreement among the testifying experts that flow rate is a primary factor affecting water quality: at a high level of generalization, the lower the flow rate, the poorer the quality of the water.

To see the difference in the quality of the water available to the UVDs and that available to the Apache Tribe, one need only compare salinity in the upper valleys and salinity at the reservation boundary. Plaintiffs' expert witnesses conducted extensive field studies in 1993 and 1994, sampling water and measuring flow rates at various sites in the upper valleys and on the reservation. [The tests showed salinity at the reservation border approximately three times greater than in the upper valley.] * * * The evidence at trial also demonstrated unequivocally that flow rate is inversely related to salinity.

C. Causes of Degradation of Water Quality

Plaintiffs, the government and the Apache Tribe, argue that the degradation of the Gila River water quality is the direct result of various farming practices in the upper valleys. UVDs dispute this. They argue that the degradation, if there is any, is the result of purely natural causes and that the water would be similarly degraded if cultivation in the upper valleys ceased and the lands were taken over by wild vegetation.

The Court finds abundant evidence supporting plaintiffs' view. There are two primary causes of the increased salinity and salt load in the river: pumping from the groundwater and diverting the entire natural flow of the stream.

Pumping from groundwater: The effect of pumping on the salt load and salinity is difficult to overstate. The amount of water pumped prior to the entry of the Decree was apparently quite small. By 1938, there were about 30 wells in the upper valleys. * * * The number of wells and the amount of water pumped steadily increased. Gookin Engineers estimates that there were 900 wells in the Safford Valley by 1958. * * * In general, UVDs pump greater amounts of water in dry years, when the surface flow is low, and lesser amounts in wet years, when there is more surface flow to meet their irrigation needs.

The expert witnesses disagreed about the extent to which groundwater pumping affects the water quality. The greater weight of the evidence and the more plausible analysis support plaintiffs' argument that the effects are significant. First, some of the wells in the Safford Valley tap into very high salinity water sources. The evidence was uncontroverted that there are natural high-salinity artesian seeps flowing into the Gila, but the flow from these seeps is very low, so their effect on overall salinity is minimal. Certain "hot" wells, however, are responsible for localized TDS [total dissolved solids] elevations of several hundred percent.

Second, all of the evidence indicates that the groundwater is higher in salts than undiverted surface flows. Pumping from the groundwater adds salt to the surface flow of the Gila River. The increased salt load in pumped water contributes directly to the increase in salinity as the river flows through the Safford Valley. Moreover, pumping during the dry summer months places the lower quality water in the stream at the time when natural flows are at their lowest and demand on the stream is at its highest.

Third, groundwater pumping contributes to a decline in the water table, leading to a "losing stream" phenomenon, in which the river loses water to the groundwater. Surface flow may be seriously depleted or eliminated due to nearby pumping. Also, a losing stream condition can exacerbate the salinity problem to the extent that surface flows of higher quality, such as from precipitation and sudden freshets, go to recharging the alluvial aquifer, rather than remaining on the surface.

Fourth, excessive pumping alters the relationship between the alluvial aquifer, immediately underlying the riverbed, and the basin-fill aquifer, which is an older geologic formation up to a hundred feet below the surface. Water in the basin-fill aquifer is at a higher pressure than that in the alluvial aquifer. When large amounts of water are pumped from the alluvium, the piezometric relationship between these two aquifers is altered and the water from the basin-fill aquifer seeps upward into the alluvial aquifer. Because the basin-fill aquifer is much higher in salts than the alluvial aquifer, this seepage increases salts in the alluvium and in the river.

Diversion of the entire flow of the stream: The evidence demonstrates that UVDs on occasion divert the entire flow of the stream at various canal headings. The water arriving back at the river consists largely of irrigation return flows that have absorbed salts from the soils to which the water was applied. This cycle is repeated when the entire flow is diverted at canal headings downstream. Thus, the river becomes an "agricultural drain" carrying salts from the soils of the cultivated acreage. Also, diversion of the entire flow of the river exacerbates the deleterious conditions created by pumping, including the losing stream phenomenon and the upward seepage from the basin-fill aquifer into the alluvial aquifer.

These practices contribute to salt load and salinity in a fairly straightforward manner: As water is diverted and used for irrigation, the ratio of salt to water increases, because the plants consume only the water, leaving the salt behind. Additions of salt to the system, from both natural and artificial sources, add to the burden of salt in the stream.

UVDs acknowledge that the quality of the Gila River deteriorates as it proceeds through the Safford Valley toward the San Carlos Reservation and that this deterioration is attributable to increased concentrations of salts. Further, UVDs concede that the greatest contributor of salt in the Safford Valley is the basin-fill aquifer. UVDs argue, however, that the influx of salt in the Safford Valley is from a natural cause. They further argue that the water is not significantly worse than it was in the early

1940s and that the Apaches would receive equally salty water if irrigated agriculture in the Safford Valley ceased.

The Court cannot agree that the influx of salt in the Safford Valley is primarily natural. * * * [T]he more carefully documented conclusion of other expert witnesses [demonstrates] that, absent pumping from the groundwater, the natural migration of water from the basin-fill aquifer has a relatively small effect. Pumping, however, causes immediate and significant increases in upward flow from the basin fill, in addition to directly affecting salinity by bringing the saline groundwater to the surface.

UVDs also argue that the Apache Tribe would receive equally degraded water if no irrigation at all occurred in the upper valleys, because UVDs' lands would be taken over by phreatophytes.[14] UVDs argue that their crops consume only about 2.5 acre feet per acre (AFA) per year and that if phreatophytes invaded their lands, the consumptive use would rocket to 5 AFA per year, leaving the river as salty, if not saltier, than it is now. UVDs assume, first, that half of their lands will give over to phreatophitic growth if crop irrigation ceased. There is no evidence to support this assumption. The argument also assumes, without supporting evidence, that wild phreatophytes will draw on the river in the same manner as a crop being irrigated during a growing season with diverted and pumped water. The evidence at trial indicates that this is an unreasonable assumption, both because wild phreatophytes do not receive water in the same way as irrigated crops and because UVDs would not, in any case, pump groundwater and divert the river to serve wild phreatophytes on their lands, some of which are several miles downstream of the canal headings.

Based on the evidence discussed here and the totality of the evidence presented at trial, the Court finds that the farming practices of UVDs, particularly pumping and diverting the entire stream flow, are significant causes of the degradation of the quality of the Gila River.

D. Extent of Water Quality Degradation

Plaintiffs' experts, compiling data from several sources, estimate that man-made contributions to salt load account for almost half of the increase in salt in the Safford Valley.

The Court cannot conclude that artificial contributions of salt account for a full half of the salt load leaving the Safford Valley. It is sufficient to conclude, for purposes of the issue before the Court, that UVDs' contributions to the salt load are significant enough to warrant injunctive relief, as described further below.

E. Effects of Water Quality Degradation

The Apaches argue that the degradation of the water reaching the San Carlos Reservation impedes their efforts to cultivate the types of salt-sensitive crops they once

---

14. A phreatophyte is a plant that depends on ground water within the reach of its roots for water. Although the consumptive use varies greatly among species of phreatophytes, in general, they consume more water than other plants in the same environment.

grew. UVDs argue that the effects are overstated and that recent experience justifies the conclusion that the Tribe can raise a variety of crops commercially.

The irrigated agriculture of the Apache Tribe prior to the entry of the Decree included a variety of crops, several of which are salt-sensitive and moderately salt-sensitive. Prior to the turn of the century, the Tribe cultivated and harvested wheat, barley, corn, and beans. Testimony at trial established that ancestors of Apaches on the reservation today grew sugar cane, corn, melon, cantaloupes, peppers, Apache squash, and a native sweet corn, in addition to oats, wheat, hay, and alfalfa and various garden vegetables. The Tribe states that it can no longer grow such moderately salt-sensitive crops as alfalfa, but must cultivate, if anything, salt-tolerant crops such as barley, wheat, and cotton.

UVDs argue that there is a lack of evidence that the Tribe grew salt-sensitive crops commercially. First, UVDs point out that there is little evidence that Apaches grew pinto beans, a particularly salt-sensitive crop. The Court agrees that, although the record demonstrates that Apaches grew beans, it is difficult to conclude that there were large harvests specifically of pinto beans. Upper Valleys farmers testify that pinto beans cannot be grown with Gila River water at all, due to a variety of rust whose spores are present in the stream flow. The Court agrees generally with the Tribe, however, that the historical record amply demonstrates harvests of a variety of moderately salt-sensitive crops, including, but not limited to, corn, pumpkins, melons, and cabbage. Equally important, the historical record documents the Tribe's attempts, often defeated by matters beyond its control (and unrelated to water quality), to cultivate and harvest such crops.

The Tribe and the government presented persuasive evidence that the salinity of the Gila River reaching the San Carlos Reservation today prevents the successful cultivation of such crops as alfalfa, pinto beans, squash, corn, melons, and garden vegetables. As the expert testimony at trial indicates, there are two important factors determining crop viability and yield: the quantity of the water and the quality of the water. Because the Tribe, like other parties to the Decree, is limited to an annual water duty of 6 AFA, it is critical that the water applied to the lands be of sufficient quality to permit the successful growth of the crops. Plaintiffs' experts, using well-accepted statistical modeling, demonstrated that commercial yields of salt-sensitive and moderately salt-sensitive crops are unlikely unless the quality of the water reaching the reservation improves. Witnesses from both sides agreed, however, that the Tribe can produce full yields of salt-tolerant crops, such as barley, oats, hay, and wheat.

The Court concludes, based on the evidence presented, that plaintiffs have documented the unlikelihood of successful commercial cultivation of salt-sensitive and moderately salt-sensitive crops using Gila River water at its current levels of quality.

F. Restoring Water Quality at the Reservation

As the above discussion indicates, the Court concludes that injunctive relief is required to restore to the Apache Tribe water of sufficient quality to sustain commercial production of the sorts of crops they grew prior to the entry of the Decree.

UVDs propose extending the Fort Thomas canal (joined with two other canals) to the reservation boundary. An extension of the canal, they argue, would supply the Tribe with water of the same quality as irrigators in the Fort Thomas region receive. The Tribe objects to this proposal for several reasons. First, extending the Fort Thomas canal will not deliver the water to the Tribe's irrigated lands, but will only get the canal water to the eastern boundary of the reservation. The Tribe is not in a financial position to complete the canal project. Also, UVDs apparently expect the Tribe to join the canal association and pay dues like other users. Second, water from the Fort Thomas canal may not be of the same quality as the Gila River would be, if some amount of the natural flow passed through the upper valleys without being diverted. The Tribe notes that the canal water, by the time it reaches the reservation, may have been applied more than once to cultivated lands and may be heavily supplemented with water pumped from the more saline groundwater. In other words, the canal water may not represent an improvement over the river water. Third, the Tribe will bear significant transportation and seepage losses from the reservation boundary to the fields. This may defeat the proposal entirely. Fourth, the Fort Thomas Canal has junior rights to some other canals and gets shut down earlier when users are limited to diverting on priority. The Tribe fears that it will forfeit its priority date by being placed on the canal. Fifth, the Tribe asserts its right under the Decree to the natural flow of the river. Even if the doctrine of prior appropriation permits a court to authorize a different point of diversion, an issue which the Court need not and does not reach, the circumstances presented here do not warrant the imposition of a costly and untested approach that may conflict with the Decree. Therefore, the Court will not, under the circumstances presented here, force the Tribe to accept an equivalent amount of water from a source designated by a junior appropriator.

The government and the Tribe offer a water quality management proposal drafted by Dr. Gerald T. Orlob. * * * One objective of his proposal is that the Gila River be maintained as a live stream as far as possible within the natural variability of its flows, and that the stream not be allowed to go dry "as a consequence of diversions." Finally, Dr. Orlob proposes sealing artesian "hot wells," discontinuing the use of certain wells of abnormally high salinity, minimizing drainage from irrigated fields to the stream, lining canals that have excessive losses to ground water, and beginning development of both monitoring and modeling of the river and ground water system.

UVDs object to Dr. Orlob's proposals as unrealistic and possibly devastating to farmers. UVDs argue, for example, that sealing particularly salty wells will ruin certain farmers who rely heavily on well water. The Court agrees with plaintiffs, however, that the river cannot tolerate inflows of extremely salty water. Indeed, the proposal to seal unusually saline wells is somewhat modest.

The Court considers it unnecessary to adopt Dr. Orlob's proposal in its entirety at this time. Certain aspects of the proposal would work sweeping changes in the management of the river, some of which may prove unnecessary or unwise. Rather, the Court directs representatives of the affected parties to convene, with the assistance of the Water Commissioner, to discuss alternative methods of altering the management of the river to improve the continuity and quality of flow of the Gila River reaching the San Carlos Reservation. The parties may conclude that they cannot agree on a proposed form of injunction, in which case they may submit proposed forms of injunction for the Court's review and possible adoption.

The Court realizes that the Tribe seeks immediate relief on the issue of water quality. The Court concludes, however, * * * that the parties are in a better position to consider alternative measures for the realistic improvement of water quality in light of the Court's findings and conclusions set forth above. Further, the Court is optimistic that a measured approach to improving water quality will reveal that the Tribe's water rights can be satisfied without drastically altering the farming practices in the upper valleys.

Until such time as the parties have met, conferred, and advised the Court on a proposed course of action, the Court reissues the preliminary injunction entered in September of 1992 [which prohibited the upstream non-Indian irrigators from diverting the entire flow of the river, leaving only irrigation return flows].

D. Determination of Water Rights

This section examines important issues in determining Indian reserved rights to water. The first two cases address the federal role in determinations of reserved water rights, including the federal trust responsibility and the government's competing roles in water development in the West.

The third case concerns the states' role in adjudicating Indian water rights. As seen in the *Big Horn*, *Gila River*, and other litigation discussed in previous sections, Indian reserved rights to water can be adjudicated in state court as part of a general stream adjudication. The *San Carlos* case (page 567) explains the legal foundation of that jurisdiction.

Notes

1. Pyramid Lake. In its natural state, Pyramid Lake was the second largest inland body of water in the western United States. Today, at some 70 feet below its natural level, it is about the size of Lake Tahoe. Pyramid Lake's only source of water is the Truckee River. The Pyramid Lake Reservation, set aside in 1859 for the Northern Paiute, includes both Pyramid Lake itself and the lower reaches of the Truckee River. Historically, the tribe was heavily dependent on the lake for Lahontan cutthroat trout and cui ui, a large sucker fish.

In 1902, Congress enacted the Reclamation Act, 32 Stat. 388, designed to alleviate the high cost of irrigation for arid western lands. The Reclamation Act empowered the Secretary of the Interior to withdraw arid lands from the public domain, initiate irrigation projects to develop the lands, and then restore the lands to entry under the homestead laws. Fifteen days after passage of the Reclamation Act, the Secretary of the Interior set aside 200,000 acres in Nevada for the Newlands Reclamation Project. In 1905, the government constructed Derby Dam on the Truckee River. The dam diverted water into the Truckee Canal, for storage in the Lahontan Reservoir and then into the Carson River for delivery to the Newlands Reclamation Project.

As a result of these diversions of water that otherwise would have reached Pyramid Lake, a small lake to the east, dependent upon the overflow from Pyramid Lake, dried up in 1939. The lowering of the water level in Pyramid Lake had such an adverse impact on the indigenous lake fish that both species were placed on the endangered species list. The lowered lake level also threatened to create a land bridge to a lake island, which had been declared a National Wildlife Refuge in 1913 for white pelicans and cormorants. In addition to the ecological damage, the lowered lake level had serious adverse effects on the Pyramid Lake Paiute themselves. Tribal members were dependent upon the lake for their livelihood: subsistence and commercial fishing, as well as income from tourism.

2. The *Orr Ditch* decree. While the Newlands Reclamation Project works were underway, private owners established water rights on the Truckee River and the Supreme Court decided the *Winters* case (see page 474). The federal government filed suit in federal district court in 1913 to adjudicate water rights on the Truckee in order to establish the quantity of water available for the project. In what became known as the *Orr Ditch* litigation, a special master issued a report in 1924 awarding the reservation more than 12,000 acre feet for irrigation of some 3000 acres with a priority date of 1859. The master also ruled that the Newlands project had 1500 cubic feet per second for irrigation of more than 230,000 acres, with a priority date of 1902.

In 1926, the Truckee-Carson Irrigation District signed a contract under which it would operate the Newlands Reclamation Project for the government. In 1934, following a prolonged period of drought, the parties entered into settlement negotiations. The federal government demanded and received a water right for the reservation to irrigate an additional 2745 acres. The parties signed the settlement agreement in 1935, and the district court entered a final decree adopting the agreement, known as the *Orr Ditch* decree, in 1944.

The *Orr Ditch* decree settled the then-existing water rights on the Truckee River. But there is (or at least was) water available in the river over and above that adjudicated in the decree. The decree did not dispose of all the available water of the river, but only the water dedicated to the reclamation lands, the reservation, and the then-existing private parties. It is this "extra" water—water not needed to fulfill the *Orr Ditch* decree or other contracts made by the Department of the Interior—that was at issue in the following *Pyramid Lake* case. Once that question was settled, the issue of the water rights determined by the *Orr Ditch* decree was taken up in the *Nevada* case that follows *Pyramid Lake* (page 551).

Pyramid Lake Paiute Tribe of Indians v. Morton
354 F. Supp. 252 (D.D.C 1972)

GESELL, District Judge.

This is an action by a recognized Indian tribe challenging a regulation issued by the Secretary of the Interior. The matter came before the Court for trial without a jury following an extended period of pretrial activity during which issues were narrowed and efforts to resolve the controversy by negotiation failed. Claiming that the regulation should be set aside as arbitrary, capricious, and an abuse of the Secretary's authority, the Tribe invokes applicable provisions of the Administrative Procedure Act. A declaration of rights and affirmative injunctive relief is also sought on the ground the Secretary has unlawfully withheld and unreasonably delayed required actions.

The regulation was signed by the Secretary on September 14, 1972, appears in the Federal Register, and became effective November 1, 1972. It is designed to implement pre-existing general regulations by establishing the basis on which water will be provided during the succeeding twelve months to the Truckee-Carson Irrigation District, which is located in Churchill County, Nevada, some 50 miles east of Reno. The Tribe contends that the regulation delivers more water to the District than required by applicable court decrees and statutes, and improperly diverts water that otherwise would flow into nearby Pyramid Lake located on the Tribe's reservation.

This Lake has been the Tribe's principal source of livelihood. Members of the Tribe have always lived on its shores and have fished its waters for food. Following directives of the Department of Interior in 1859, which were confirmed by Executive Order signed by President Grant in 1874, the Lake, together with land surrounding the Lake and the immediate valley of the Truckee River which feeds into the Lake, have been reserved for the Tribe and set aside from the public domain. The area has been consistently recognized as the Tribe's aboriginal home.

Recently, the United States, by original petition in the Supreme Court of the United States, filed September, 1972, claims the right to use of sufficient water of the Truckee River for the benefit of the Tribe to fulfill the purposes for which the Indian Reservation was created, "including the maintenance and preservation of Pyramid Lake and the maintenance of the lower reaches of the Truckee as a natural spawning ground for fish and other purposes beneficial to and satisfying the needs" of the Tribe.

Appended to this Memorandum Opinion is a map which shows the available sources of water supply in relationship to Pyramid Lake and the District. The area involved is a water shortage area characterized by seasonal and yearly variations in available supply. Beneficial irrigation for farming and other uses within the District are accommodated through some 600 miles of main water ditches and drains and the water is ultimately parcelled out through 1,500 delivery points. The water fed into this system comes from the Carson River following storage in Lahontan Reservoir and by diversion of water from the Truckee River at Derby Dam where it passes through the Truckee Canal to be stored in the Lahontan Reservoir for subsequent or simultaneous release. The Secretary entered into a contract with the District in 1926 and this contract is still in effect.

As the map so clearly shows, any water diverted from the Truckee at Derby Dam for the District is thereby prevented in substantial measure from flowing further north into Pyramid Lake. The Lake is a unique natural resource of almost incomparable beauty. It has no outflow, and as a desert lake depends largely on Truckee River inflow to make up for evaporation and other losses. It is approximately five miles wide and twenty-five miles long and now has a maximum depth of 335 feet. Although the Lake has risen a few feet in recent years, it has dropped more than 70 feet since 1906. A flow of 385,000 acre feet of water per year from the Truckee River into the Lake is required merely to maintain its present level. The decreased level and inflow have had the effect of making fish native to the Lake endangered protected species, and have unsettled the erosion and salinity balance of the Lake to a point where the continued utility of the Lake as a useful body of water is at hazard.[2]

The regulation under attack is the most recent of a series of regulations issued from year to year since 1967 pursuant to general policies established by the Secretary. The Tribe contends that the Secretary's action is an arbitrary abuse of discretion in that the Secretary has ignored his own guidelines and failed to fulfill his trust responsibilities to the Tribe by illegally and unnecessarily diverting water from Pyramid Lake.

The focus of the inquiry has been to determine whether the 378,000 acre feet of water which the regulation contemplates will be diverted from the Truckee River at Derby Dam may be justified on a rational basis. This determination must be made in the light of three major factors which necessarily control the Secretary's action: namely, the Secretary's contract with the District, certain applicable court decrees, and his trust responsibilities to the Tribe. The Secretary and the Tribe are in substantial agreement that these are the factors to be weighed. The issue, therefore, comes down to whether or not the Secretary's resolution of conflicting demands created by these factors was effectuated arbitrarily rather than in the sound exercise of discretion.

The Court has carefully reviewed the processes by which the Secretary arrived at the disputed regulation. The Secretary had before him various written recommendations from interested agencies and experts, including responsible expert studies presented by the Tribe. There was a wide variation in these recommendations suggesting diversion of water in varying amounts ranging from 287,000 acre feet to 396,000 acre feet. All purported to be made on the basis of guidelines and policies previously set by the Secretary. After reviewing these written submissions, the Secretary conferred with the Assistant Secretary for Water and Power Resources (with

---

2. Native fish which naturally spawn in the Truckee can no longer do this and the Lake must be stocked at least until 1974 when construction to permit the fish again to pass into the river for spawning is to be completed.

authority over the Bureau of Reclamation) and the Assistant Secretary for Public Land Management (with authority over Indian Affairs) and made what one of these Assistants characterized as a "judgment call." It is affirmatively stated that the Secretary did not accept the recommendation of any particular person or group. The record, therefore, is completely devoid of any explanation or indication of the factors or computations which he took into account in arriving at the diversion figure of 378,000 acre feet. The grounds of his action are therefore not disclosed and there is no way of knowing the basis on which his conclusions rested. Since the record is as complete on this score as it ever can be, the Government has failed to meet its burden of establishing that this decision was anything but arbitrary.

Furthermore, while the Secretary's good faith is not in question, his approach to the difficult problem confronting him misconceived the legal requirements that should have governed his action. A "judgment call" was simply not legally permissible. The Secretary's duty was not to determine a basis for allocating water between the District and the Tribe in a manner that hopefully everyone could live with for the year ahead. This suit was pending and the Tribe had asserted well-founded rights. The burden rested on the Secretary to justify any diversion of water from the Tribe with precision. It was not his function to attempt an accommodation.

In order to fulfill his fiduciary duty, the Secretary must insure, to the extent of his power, that all water not obligated by court decree or contract with the District goes to Pyramid Lake. The United States, acting through the Secretary of Interior, "has charged itself with moral obligations of the highest responsibility and trust. Its conduct, as disclosed in the acts of those who represent it in dealings with the Indians, should therefore be judged by the most exacting fiduciary standards."

The vast body of case law which recognizes this trustee obligation is amply complemented by the detailed statutory scheme for Indian affairs set forth in Title 25 of the United States Code. Undertakings with the Indians are to be liberally construed to the benefit of the Indians, and the duty of the Secretary to do so is particularly apparent. It is not enough to assert the water and fishing rights of the Tribe by filing a suit in the United States Supreme Court.

The Secretary was obliged to formulate a closely developed regulation that would preserve water for the Tribe. He was further obliged to assert his statutory and contractual authority to the fullest extent possible to accomplish this result. Difficult as this process would be, and troublesome as the repercussions of his actions might be, the Secretary was required to resolve the conflicting claims in a precise manner that would indicate the weight given each interest before him. Possible difficulties ahead could not simply be blunted by a "judgment call" calculated to placate temporarily conflicting claims to precious water. The Secretary's action is therefore doubly defective and irrational because it fails to demonstrate an adequate recognition of his fiduciary duty to the Tribe. This also is an abuse of discretion and not in accordance with law.

The record before the Court clearly establishes the underlying defects and arbitrary nature of the challenged regulation. The Secretary erred in two significant respects. First, he disregarded interrelated court decrees, and, second, he failed to exercise his authority to prevent unnecessary waste within the District. The effect of this is to deprive the Tribe of water without legal justification.

Two decrees of the United States District Court for the District of Nevada, known as the *Orr Water Ditch* and *Alpine* decrees, govern the amounts and conditions under which water shall be available for beneficial uses in the District. Maximums of roughly 4.5 acre feet and 2.92 acre feet measured at farm headgates are provided in the *Orr* and *Alpine* decrees, respectively. Approximately 60–75 percent of the water needed to serve the District's 60,000 acres of land is covered by the *Alpine* decree, and the remaining needed water is covered by the *Orr* decree. The parties and this Court of course recognize that neither the Secretary nor this Court can adopt or require a regulation that would infringe upon these decrees, and their interpretation and application is, in a number of respects, uncertain. Nonetheless, regardless of ambiguities and inconsistencies, as the Secretary himself recognized in his own guidelines and regulations, he was required to take both decrees into account. The evidence demonstrates conclusively that the Secretary formulated the regulation by totally ignoring the *Alpine* decree and must have reached his calculations by relying solely on larger quantities provided by the *Orr Water Ditch* decree.

In addition, the evidence conclusively showed that the regulation is wholly inadequate to prevent waste within the District, causing substantial and wholly unnecessary diversion of water from the Truckee River to the obvious detriment of the Tribe. It was amply demonstrated that water could be conserved for Pyramid Lake without offending existing decrees or contractual rights of the District through better management which would prevent unnecessary waste. The amount of exposed water can be reduced to limit evaporation. Better management will lessen seepage and overflow; users can be assessed for water taken; techniques exist for measuring water more efficiently at headgates; land not entitled to water under the decrees and contract with the District can be prevented from taking the water; and by the mere employment of a few individuals the system can be so policed that it will function on a basis consistent with modern water control practices. All of this can be accomplished in spite of the fact that the District has an antiquated system. Failure to take appropriate steps, under the circumstances, by the regulation constitutes agency action unlawfully withheld and unreasonably delayed when viewed in the light of the Secretary's trust responsibilities to the Tribe.

Under the contract between the Secretary and the District the Secretary has the right to require the District to conduct its affairs in a non-wasteful manner but no such action was taken or is contemplated in the regulation. The operations of the District are not tightly controlled and water is taken practically on demand without necessary safeguards to prevent improper and wasteful use. This failure to act must be given particular emphasis since the proof showed that the Secretary has not in the past enforced his prior yearly regulations affecting the District and has acquiesced in excessive water deliveries to the farms. Moreover, the absence of effective enforcement provisions in the challenged regulation must be considered in the light of a formal statement by the District that it will disregard the new regulation and will divert water as it chooses by giving instructions to its own water masters.

Accordingly, the Court directs that on or before January 1, 1973, the Secretary shall submit to this Court a proposed amended regulation which is in conformity with the findings of fact and conclusions of law set forth in this Memorandum Opinion. The amendment shall provide, among other things, an effective means to measure water use, to minimize unnecessary waste, to end delivery of water within the District to land not entitled under the decrees, and to assure compliance by the District. Proper weight shall be given to both the *Orr Water Ditch* and *Alpine* decrees and the amount of water diverted shall be wholly consistent with the Secretary's fiduciary duty to the Tribe.

In this connection, the Court has noted that the manner in which the Secretary chooses to manage and commit water stored in Stampede Reservoir will have an effect on the situation. Inasmuch as the contract between the Secretary and the Department of Agriculture relating to Stampede bears on this aspect of the problem, the Court notes that the contract is ambiguous in its terms and was made without consultation with the Tribe. This contract cannot be interposed as an obstacle to the Lake receiving the maximum benefit from the upper Truckee flow into Stampede which may be available under a reasonable and proper interpretation of the decrees. The Secretary's trust obligations to the Tribe are paramount in this respect.

In the event the amended regulation fails to assure at least the delivery of 385,000 acre feet of water to Pyramid Lake, the Secretary shall accompany the regulation with a full, detailed, factual statement of the reasons why this result has not been achieved, together with a specific itemized plan indicating what further action will be taken consistent with the *Orr Water Ditch* and *Alpine* decrees to accomplish this result in the immediate future.

The previous case concerned allocation of Truckee Basin waters in excess of those subject to the 1944 Orr Ditch Decree. The case below sought to reopen the decree itself.

Nevada v. United States

463 U.S. 110 (1983)

JUSTICE REHNQUIST delivered the opinion of the Court.

In 1913 the United States sued to adjudicate water rights to the Truckee River for the benefit of the Pyramid Lake Indian Reservation and the planned Newlands Reclamation Project. Thirty-one years later, in 1944, the United States District Court for the District of Nevada entered a final decree in the case pursuant to a settlement agreement. In 1973 the United States filed the present action in the same court on behalf of the Pyramid Lake Indian Reservation, seeking additional water rights to the Truckee River. The issue thus presented is whether the Government may partially undo the 1944 decree, or whether principles of res judicata prevent it, and the intervenor Pyramid Lake Paiute Tribe, from litigating this claim on the merits.

I

Nevada has, on the average, less precipitation than any other State in the Union. Except for drainage in the southeastern part of the State into the Colorado River, and drainage in the northern part of the State into the Columbia River, the rivers that flow in Nevada generally disappear into "sinks." The present litigation relates to water rights in the Truckee River, one of the three principal rivers flowing through west central Nevada. It rises in the High Sierra in Placer County, Cal., flows into and out of Lake Tahoe, and thence down the eastern slope of the Sierra Nevada mountains. It flows through Reno, Nev., and after a course of some 120 miles debouches into Pyramid Lake, which has no outlet.

It has been said that Pyramid Lake is "widely considered the most beautiful desert lake in North America [and that its] fishery [has] brought it worldwide fame. A species of cutthroat trout . . . grew to world record size in the desert lake and attracted anglers from throughout the world." The first recorded sighting of Pyramid Lake by non-Indians occurred in January 1844 when Captain John C. Fremont and his party camped nearby. In his journal Captain Fremont reported that the lake "broke upon our eyes like the ocean" and was "set like a gem in the mountains." * * * When first viewed by Captain Fremont in early 1844, Pyramid Lake was some 50 miles long and 12 miles wide. Since that time the surface area of the lake has been reduced by about 20,000 acres.

The origins of the cases before us are found in two historical events involving the Federal Government in this part of the country. First, in 1859 the Department of the Interior set aside nearly half a million acres in what is now western Nevada as a reservation for the area's Paiute Indians. In 1874 President Ulysses S. Grant by Executive Order confirmed the withdrawal as the Pyramid Lake Indian Reservation. The Reservation includes Pyramid Lake, the land surrounding it, the lower reaches of the Truckee River, and the bottom land alongside the lower Truckee.

Then, with the passage of the Reclamation Act of 1902, the Federal Government was designated to play a more prominent role in the development of the West. That Act directed the Secretary of the Interior to withdraw from public entry arid lands in specified Western States, reclaim the lands through irrigation projects, and then to restore the lands to entry pursuant to the homestead laws and certain conditions imposed by the Act itself. Accordingly, the Secretary withdrew from the public domain approximately 200,000 acres in western Nevada, which ultimately became the Newlands Reclamation Project. The Project was designed to irrigate a substantial area in the vicinity of Fallon, Nev., with waters from both the Truckee and the Carson Rivers.

The Carson River, like the Truckee, rises on the eastern slope of the High Sierra in Alpine County, Cal., and flows north and northeast over a course of about 170 miles, finally disappearing into Carson sink. The Newlands Project accomplished the diversion of water from the Truckee River to the Carson River by constructing the Derby Diversion Dam on the Truckee River, and constructing the Truckee Canal through which the diverted waters would be transported to the Carson River. Experience in the early days of the Project indicated the necessity of a storage reservoir on the Carson River, and accordingly Lahontan Dam was constructed and Lahontan Reservoir behind that dam was created. The combined waters of the Truckee and Carson Rivers impounded in Lahontan Reservoir are distributed for irrigation and related uses on downstream lands by means of lateral canals within the Newlands Reclamation Project.

Before the works contemplated by the Project went into operation, a number of private landowners had established rights to water in the Truckee River under Nevada law. The Government also asserted on behalf of the Indians of the Pyramid Lake Indian Reservation a reserved right under the so-called "implied-reservation-of-water" doctrine set forth in *Winters v. United States*, 207 U.S. 564 (1908). The United States therefore filed a complaint in the United States District Court for the District of Nevada in March 1913, commencing what became known as the *Orr Ditch* litigation. The Government, for the benefit of both the Project and the Pyramid Lake Reservation, asserted a claim to 10,000 cubic feet of water per second for the Project and a claim to 500 cubic feet per second for the Reservation. The complaint named as defendants all water users on the Truckee River in Nevada. The Government expressly sought a final decree quieting title to the rights of all parties.

Following several years of hearings, a Special Master issued a report and proposed decree in July 1924. The report awarded the Reservation an 1859 priority date in the Truckee River for 58.7 second-feet and 12,412 acre-feet annually of water to irrigate 3,130 acres of Reservation lands. The Project was awarded a 1902 priority date for 1,500 cubic feet per second to irrigate, to the extent the amount would allow, 232,800 acres of land within the Project. In February 1926 the District Court entered a temporary restraining order declaring the water rights as proposed by the Special Master. "One of the primary purposes" for entering a temporary order was to allow for an experimental period during which modifications of the declared rights could be made if necessary.

Not until almost 10 years later, in the midst of a prolonged drought, was interest stimulated in concluding the *Orr Ditch* litigation. Settlement negotiations were commenced in 1934 by the principal organizational defendants in the case, Washoe County Water Conservation District and the Sierra Pacific Power Co., and the representatives of the Project and the Reservation. The United States still acted on behalf of the Reservation's interests, but the Project was now under the management of the Truckee-Carson Irrigation District (TCID). The defendants and TCID proposed an agreement along the lines of the temporary restraining order. The United States objected, demanding an increase in the Reservation's water rights to allow for the irrigation of an additional 2,745 acres of Reservation land. After some resistance, the Government's demand was accepted and a settlement agreement was signed on July 1, 1935. The District Court entered a final decree adopting the agreement on

September 8, 1944. No appeal was taken. Thus, 31 years after its inception the *Orr Ditch* litigation came to a close.

On December 21, 1973, the Government instituted the action below seeking additional rights to the Truckee River for the Pyramid Lake Indian Reservation; the Pyramid Lake Paiute Tribe was permitted to intervene in support of the United States. The Government named as defendants all persons presently claiming water rights to the Truckee River and its tributaries in Nevada. The defendants include the defendants in the *Orr Ditch* litigation and their successors, approximately 3,800 individual farmers that own land in the Newlands Reclamation Project, and TCID. The District Court certified the Project farmers as a class and directed TCID to represent their interests.

In its complaint the Government purported not to dispute the rights decreed in the *Orr Ditch* case. Instead, it alleged that *Orr Ditch* determined only the Reservation's right to "water for irrigation," not the claim now being asserted for "sufficient waters of the Truckee River . . . [for] the maintenance and preservation of Pyramid Lake, [and for] the maintenance of the lower reaches of the Truckee River as a natural spawning ground for fish." The complaint further averred that in establishing the Reservation the United States had intended that the Pyramid Lake fishery be maintained. Since the additional water now being claimed is allegedly necessary for that purpose, the Government alleged that the Executive Order creating the Reservation must have impliedly reserved a right to this water.[7]

The defendants below asserted res judicata as an affirmative defense, saying that the United States and the Tribe were precluded by the *Orr Ditch* decree from litigating this claim. Following a separate trial on this issue, the District Court sustained the defense and dismissed the complaint in its entirety.

The Court of Appeals for the Ninth Circuit affirmed in part and reversed in part. * * * We granted certiorari in the cases challenging the Court of Appeals' decision, and we now affirm in part and reverse in part.

II

The Government opens the "Summary of Argument" portion of its brief by stating: "The court of appeals has simply permitted a reallocation of the water decreed

---

7. Between 1920 and 1940 the surface area of Pyramid Lake was reduced by about 20,000 acres. The decline resulted in a delta forming at the mouth of the Truckee that prevented the fish indigenous to the lake, the Lahontan cutthroat trout and the cui-ui, from reaching their spawning grounds in the Truckee River, resulting in the near extinction of both species. Efforts to restore the fishery have occurred since that time. Pyramid Lake has been stabilized for several years and, augmented by passage of the Washoe Project Act of 1956, the lake is being restocked with cutthroat trout and cui-ui. Fish hatcheries operated by both the State of Nevada and the United States have been one source for replenishing the lake. In 1976 the Marble Bluff Dam and Fishway was completed, enabling the fish to bypass the delta to their spawning grounds in the Truckee. Both the District Court and Court of Appeals observed that "these restoration efforts 'appear to justify optimism for eventual success.'"

in *Orr Ditch* to a single party—the United States—from reclamation uses to a Reservation use with an earlier priority. The doctrine of res judicata does not bar a single party from reallocating its water in this fashion...." We are bound to say that the Government's position, if accepted, would do away with half a century of decided case law relating to the Reclamation Act of 1902 and water rights in the public domain of the West.

It is undisputed that the primary purpose of the Government in bringing the *Orr Ditch* suit in 1913 was to secure water rights for the irrigation of land that would be contained in the Newlands Project, and that the Government was acting under the aegis of the Reclamation Act of 1902 in bringing that action.

* * * [W]e conclude that the Government is completely mistaken if it believes that the water rights confirmed to it by the *Orr Ditch* decree in 1944 for use in irrigating lands within the Newlands Reclamation Project were like so many bushels of wheat, to be bartered, sold, or shifted about as the Government might see fit. Once these lands were acquired by settlers in the Project, the Government's "ownership" of the water rights was at most nominal; the beneficial interest in the rights confirmed to the Government resided in the owners of the land within the Project to which these water rights became appurtenant upon the application of Project water to the land.

The Government's brief is replete with references to its fiduciary obligation to the Pyramid Lake Paiute Tribe of Indians, as it properly should be. But the Government seems wholly to ignore in the same brief the obligations that necessarily devolve upon it from having mere title to water rights for the Newlands Project, when the beneficial ownership of these water rights resides elsewhere.

Both the briefs of the parties and the opinion of the Court of Appeals focus their analysis of res judicata on provisions relating to the relationship between private trustees and fiduciaries, especially those governing a breach of duty by the fiduciary to the beneficiary. While these undoubtedly provide useful analogies in cases such as these, they cannot be regarded as finally dispositive of the issues. This Court has long recognized "the distinctive obligation of trust incumbent upon the Government" in its dealings with Indian tribes. These concerns have been traditionally focused on the Bureau of Indian Affairs within the Department of the Interior.

But Congress in its wisdom, when it enacted the Reclamation Act of 1902, required the Secretary of the Interior to assume substantial obligations with respect to the reclamation of arid lands in the western part of the United States. Additionally, in § 26 of the Act of Apr. 21, 1904, Congress provided for the inclusion of irrigable lands of the Pyramid Lake Indian Reservation within the Newlands Project, and further authorized the Secretary, after allotting five acres of such land to each Indian belonging to the Reservation, to reclaim and dispose of the remainder of the irrigable Reservation land to settlers under the Reclamation Act.*

---

* [In footnote 2 of the opinion, the Court noted that "Congress abandoned the plan, however, before it was ever implemented. Act of June 18, 1934 [Indian Reorganization Act]."—ed.]

Today, particularly from our vantage point nearly half a century after the enactment of the Indian Reorganization Act of 1934, it may well appear that Congress was requiring the Secretary of the Interior to carry water on at least two shoulders when it delegated to him both the responsibility for the supervision of the Indian tribes and the commencement of reclamation projects in areas adjacent to reservation lands. But Congress chose to do this, and it is simply unrealistic to suggest that the Government may not perform its obligation to represent Indian tribes in litigation when Congress has obliged it to represent other interests as well. In this regard, the Government cannot follow the fastidious standards of a private fiduciary, who would breach his duties to his single beneficiary solely by representing potentially conflicting interests without the beneficiary's consent. The Government does not "compromise" its obligation to one interest that Congress obliges it to represent by the mere fact that it simultaneously performs another task for another interest that Congress has obligated it by statute to do.

With these observations in mind, we turn to the principles of res judicata that we think are involved in this case.

III

Simply put, the doctrine of res judicata provides that when a final judgment has been entered on the merits of a case, "[it] is a finality as to the claim or demand in controversy, concluding parties and those in privity with them, not only as to every matter which was offered and received to sustain or defeat the claim or demand, but as to any other admissible matter which might have been offered for that purpose." The final "judgment puts an end to the cause of action, which cannot again be brought into litigation between the parties upon any ground whatever."

To determine the applicability of res judicata to the facts before us, we must decide first if the "cause of action" which the Government now seeks to assert is the "same cause of action" that was asserted in *Orr Ditch*; we must then decide whether the parties in the instant proceeding are identical to or in privity with the parties in *Orr Ditch*. We address these questions in turn.

A

* * * [T]he only conclusion allowed by the record in the *Orr Ditch* case is that the Government was given an opportunity to litigate the Reservation's entire water rights to the Truckee, and that the Government intended to take advantage of that opportunity.

In its amended complaint in *Orr Ditch*, the Government averred:

> "16. On or about or prior to the 29th day of November, 1859, the Government of the United States, having for a long time previous thereto recognized the fact that certain Pah Ute and other Indians were, and they and their ancestors had for many years been, residing upon and using certain lands in the northern part of the said Truckee River Valley and around said

Pyramid Lake . . . and the said Government being desirous of protecting said Indians and their descendants in their homes, fields, pastures, fishing, and their use of said lands and waters, and in affording to them an opportunity to acquire the art of husbandry and other arts of civilization, and to become civilized, did reserve said lands from any and all forms of entry or sale and for the sole use of said Indians, and for their benefit and civilization. On, to wit, the 23d day of March, 1874, the said lands, having been previously surveyed, were by order of the then President of the United States, for the purposes aforesaid, withdrawn from sale or other disposition, and set apart for the Pah Ute and other Indians aforesaid.

"The United States by setting aside said lands for said purposes and creating said reservation, and by virtue of the matters and things in this paragraph set forth, did on, to wit, the 29th day of November, 1859, reserve from further appropriation, appropriate and set aside for its own use in, on, and about said Indian reservation, and the land thereof, from and of the waters of the said Truckee River, five hundred (500) cubic feet of water per second of time."

This cannot be construed as anything less than a claim for the full "implied-reservation-of-water" rights that were due the Pyramid Lake Indian Reservation.

B

Having decided that the cause of action asserted below is the same cause of action asserted in the *Orr Ditch* litigation, we must next determine which of the parties before us are bound by the earlier decree. As stated earlier, the general rule is that a prior judgment will bar the "parties" to the earlier lawsuit, "and those in privity with them," from relitigating the cause of action.

There is no doubt but that the United States was a party to the *Orr Ditch* proceeding, acting as a representative for the Reservation's interests and the interests of the Newlands Project, and cannot relitigate the Reservation's "implied-reservation-of-water" rights with those who can use the *Orr Ditch* decree as a defense. We also hold that the Tribe, whose interests were represented in *Orr Ditch* by the United States, can be bound by the *Orr Ditch* decree.[14] This Court left little room for an argument to the contrary in *Heckman v. United States*, 224 U.S. 413 (1912), where it plainly said that "it could not, consistently with any principle, be tolerated that, after the United States on behalf of its wards had invoked the jurisdiction of its courts . . . these wards

---

14. We, of course, do not pass judgment on the quality of representation that the Tribe received. In 1951 the Tribe sued the Government before the Indian Claims Commission for damages, basing its claim of liability on the Tribe's receipt of less water for the fishery than it was entitled to. In a settlement the Tribe was given $8 million in return for its waiver of further liability on the part of the United States.

should themselves be permitted to relitigate the question." We reaffirm that principle now.[15]

---

15. This Court held in *Hansberry v. Lee*, 311 U.S. 32, 44 (1940), that persons vicariously represented in a class action could not be bound by a judgment in the case where the representative parties had interests that impermissibly conflicted with those of persons represented. The Tribe seeks to take advantage of this ruling, arguing that the Government's primary interest in *Orr Ditch* was to obtain water rights for the Newlands Reclamation Project and that by definition any water rights given to the Tribe would conflict with that interest. We reject this contention.

We have already said that the Government stands in a different position than a private fiduciary where Congress has decreed that the Government must represent more than one interest. When the Government performs such duties it does not by that reason alone compromise its obligation to any of the interests involved.

The Justice Department's involvement in *Orr Ditch* began with a letter from the Secretary of the Interior to the Attorney General requesting that a single suit be brought by the Government for a determination "of all water rights in Lake Tahoe and Truckee River above the intake of the Truckee-Carson Reclamation project." A Special Assistant United States Attorney assigned to the matter was apparently the first to recognize that the Government should in the same suit seek to establish the water rights to the Pyramid Lake Indian Reservation. In a memorandum where the Special Assistant explained the reserved-water-rights holding of Winters, he advanced the view that "[these] Indian reservation water rights are important and should be established to the fullest extent because they are senior and superior to most if not all the other rights on the river."

Contemporaneously with this report, the Acting Director of the Reclamation Service notified the Commissioner of Indian Affairs that an assertion of the Reservation's rights should be included in *Orr Ditch*. The claim was advanced accordingly and thereafter the Bureau of Indian Affairs was kept aware of the *Orr Ditch* proceedings; during the settlement negotiations the BIA directly participated. The BIA is the agency of the Federal Government "charged with fulfilling the trust obligations of the United States" to Indians, and there is nothing in the record of this case to indicate that any official outside of the BIA attempted to influence the BIA's decisions in a manner inconsistent with these obligations.

The record suggests that the BIA alone may have made the decision not to press claims for a fishery water right, for reasons which hindsight may render questionable, but which did not involve other interests represented by the Government. For instance, in a 1926 letter to a federal official on the Pyramid Lake Reservation, the Commissioner of Indian Affairs explained:

> "We feel that the Indians would be wise to assume that Truckee River water will be used practically as far as it can be for irrigation, and that the thing for the Indians to do is, if possible, instead of trying to stop such development to direct it so that it will inure to their benefit.
>
> . . . .
>
> ". . . [If] their ultimate welfare depends in part on their being able to hold their own in a civilized world . . . they should look forward to a different means of livelihood, in part at least, from their ancestral one, of fishing and hunting. They should expect not only to farm their allotments but also to do other sorts of work and have other ways of making a living."

Furthermore, the District Court found that during the pendency of the *Orr Ditch* proceedings "a serious and reasonable doubt existed as to whether any *Winters* reserved water right could be claimed at all for an executive order Indian reservation."

In pressing for a different conclusion, the Tribe relies primarily on a finding by the District Court that it was the intention of the Government in *Orr Ditch* "to assert as large a water right as possible for the Indian reservation, and to do everything possible to protect the fish for the benefit of the Indians and the white population insofar as it was 'consistent with the larger interests involved in the propositions having to do with the reclamation of thousands of acres of arid and

We then turn to the issue of which defendants in the present litigation can use the *Orr Ditch* decree against the Government and the Tribe. There is no dispute but that the *Orr Ditch* defendants were parties to the earlier decree and that they and their successors can rely on the decree. The Court of Appeals so held, and we affirm.

The Court of Appeals reached a different conclusion concerning TCID and the Project farmers that it now represents.

In these cases, as we have noted, the Government as a single entity brought the action seeking a determination both of the Tribe's reserved rights and of the water rights necessary for the irrigation of land within the Newlands Project. But it separately pleaded the interests of both the Project and the Reservation. During the settlement negotiations the interests of the Project, and presumably of the landowners to whom the water rights actually accrued, were represented by the newly formed TCID and the interests of the Reservation were represented by the Bureau of Indian Affairs. The settlement agreement was signed by the Government and by TCID. It would seem that at this stage of the litigation the interests of the Tribe and TCID were sufficiently adverse for the latter to oppose the Bureau's claim for additional water rights for the Reservation during the settlement negotiations.

* * * The United States undoubtedly owes a strong fiduciary duty to its Indian wards. It may be that where only a relationship between the Government and the tribe is involved, the law respecting obligations between a trustee and a beneficiary in private litigation will in many, if not all, respects adequately describe the duty of the United States. But where Congress has imposed upon the United States, in addition to its duty to represent Indian tribes, a duty to obtain water rights for reclamation projects, and has even authorized the inclusion of reservation lands within a

---

now useless land for the benefit of the country as a whole.'" The Tribe's focus on this ambiguous finding, however, has not blinded us to the District Court's specific finding on the alleged conflict.

> "[There] was a foreseeable conflict of purposes created by the Congress within the Interior Department and as between the Bureau of Reclamation on the one hand in asserting large water rights for its reclamation projects and the Bureau of Indian Affairs on the other in the performance of its obligations to protect the rights and interests of the Indians on the Pyramid Lake Paiute Indian Reservation. [This] conflict of purposes was apparent prior to and during the *Orr Ditch* proceedings and was resolved within the executive department of government by top-level executive officers acting within the scope of their Congressionally-delegated duties and authority and were political and policy decisions of those officials charged with that responsibility, which decisions resulted in the extinguishment of the alleged fishery purposes water right. . . . The government lawyers in *Orr Ditch*, both departmental, agency and bureaus, as well as those charged with the responsibility for the actual conduct of the litigation, are not chargeable with an impermissible conflict of purpose or interest in carrying out the decisions and directions of their superiors in the executive department of government. . . ."

The District Court's finding reflects the nature of a democratic government that is charged with more than one responsibility; it does not describe conduct that would deprive the United States of the authority to conduct litigation on behalf of diverse interests.

project, the analogy of a faithless private fiduciary cannot be controlling for purposes of evaluating the authority of the United States to represent different interests.

At least by 1926, when TCID came into being, and very likely long before, when conveyances of the public domain to settlers within the Reclamation Project necessarily carried with them the beneficial right to appropriate water reserved to the Government for this purpose, third parties entered into the picture. The legal relationships were no longer simply those between the United States and the Paiute Tribe, but also those between the United States, TCID, and the several thousand settlers within the Project who put the Project water to beneficial use. We find it unnecessary to decide whether there would be adversity of interests between the Tribe, on the one hand, and the settlers and TCID, on the other, if the issue were to be governed by private law respecting trusts. We hold that under the circumstances described above, the interests of the Tribe and the Project landowners were sufficiently adverse so that both are now bound by the final decree entered in the *Orr Ditch* suit.

We turn finally to those defendants below who appropriated water from the Truckee subsequent to the *Orr Ditch* decree. These defendants, we believe, give rise to a difficult question, but in the final analysis we agree with the Court of Appeals that they too can use the *Orr Ditch* decree against the plaintiffs below. While mutuality has been for the most part abandoned in cases involving collateral estoppel, it has remained a part of the doctrine of res judicata. Nevertheless, exceptions to the res judicata mutuality requirement have been found necessary, and we believe that such an exception is required in these cases.

Orr Ditch was an equitable action to quiet title, an in personam action. But as the Court of Appeals determined, it "was no garden variety quiet title action." As we have already explained, everyone involved in *Orr Ditch* contemplated a comprehensive adjudication of water rights intended to settle once and for all the question of how much of the Truckee River each of the litigants was entitled to. Thus, even though quiet title actions are in personam actions, water adjudications are more in the nature of in rem proceedings. Nonparties such as the subsequent appropriators in these cases have relied just as much on the *Orr Ditch* decree in participating in the development of western Nevada as have the parties of that case. We agree with the Court of Appeals that under "these circumstances it would be manifestly unjust . . . not to permit subsequent appropriators" to hold the Reservation to the claims it made in *Orr Ditch*; "[any] other conclusion would make it impossible ever finally to quantify a reserved water right."[16]

---

16. The Tribe makes the argument that even if res judicata would otherwise apply, it cannot be used in these cases because to do so would deny the Tribe procedural due process. The Tribe argues that in *Orr Ditch* they were given neither [notice nor a] full and fair opportunity to be heard. * * * In these cases, the Tribe, through the Government as their representative, was given adequate notice and a full and fair opportunity to be heard. If in carrying out its role as representative, the Government violated its obligations to the Tribe, then the Tribe's remedy is against the Government, not against third parties. As we have noted earlier, the Tribe has already taken advantage of that remedy.

IV

In conclusion we affirm the Court of Appeals' finding that the cause of action asserted below and the cause of action asserted in *Orr Ditch* are one and the same. We also affirm the Court of Appeals' finding that the *Orr Ditch* decree concluded the controversy on this cause of action between, on the one hand, the *Orr Ditch* defendants, their successors in interest, and subsequent appropriators of the Truckee River, and, on the other hand, the United States and the Tribe. We reverse the Court of Appeals, however, with respect to its finding concerning TCID, and the Project farmers it represents, and hold instead that the *Orr Ditch* decree also ended the dispute raised between these parties and the plaintiffs below.

Notes

1. The trust doctrine and water rights. Professor Ralph Johnson critiqued Justice Rehnquist's interpretation of the trust responsibility in the *Nevada* case:

> To fully appreciate the implications of the trust duty in the *Nevada* case, one must keep in mind that tribes today are much more competent at looking out for their own interests than they were in 1944. Most tribes have better access to lawyers, who are in turn more knowledgeable in the field of federal Indian law. In the 1940s, tribes had virtually no access to attorneys, except through the Department of the Interior and the United States Attorney General's office. Before 1944, tribes were ordinarily represented by the Solicitor General's office, whose representation was often compromised by its conflicting duty to defend the interests of federal agencies such as the Bureau of Reclamation and Department of Agriculture. Since 1966, tribes have been able to sue in their own names through private attorneys, and have often done so when the Solicitor General and Attorney General have declined to bring suit on their behalf. Although the trust policy might be less important today, in 1944 it was essential.
>
> Nevertheless, Justice Rehnquist treats the events of 1944 as if they occurred today. He seems unaware of the special reasons that a trust relationship exists with Indian tribes and not with other racial minorities, and of the fact that departments of government have not labored under the financial, cultural, and racial handicaps that have affected Indian tribes. In short, he ignores the rationale for upholding the trust relationship that was both necessary and appropriate in 1944.

Ralph W. Johnson, *Chief Justice Rehnquist and the Indian Cases*, 16 Public Land L. Rev. 1, 10–11 (1995).

Problems with application of trust responsibility principles to water rights continue. In *Hopi Tribe v. United States*, 113 Fed. Cl. 43, 45 (2013), the federal government conceded that it held the tribe's water rights in trust, but argued that this general trust relationship did "not suffice to establish a specific trust duty to maintain water quality." In the case, summarized above at page 393, the Court of Federal Claims agreed with the federal government and dismissed (for lack of subject matter jurisdiction) the tribe's claim that the United States had an enforceable duty to ensure safe levels of arsenic in reservation drinking water supplies.

Nonetheless, the trust doctrine continues to be important for Indian water rights. For more recent commentary, see Robert T. Anderson, *Indian Water Rights and the Federal Trust Responsibility*, 46 Natural Res. J. 399 (2006); Judith V. Royster, *Indian Water and the Federal Trust: Some Proposals for Federal Action*, 46 Natural Res. J. 375 (2006).

2. Finality, preclusion, and water decrees. In 1963, the Court decided *Arizona v. California I*, 373 U.S. 546 (1963) (page 481). Under the decree entered in 1964, *Arizona v. California*, 376 U.S. 340 (1964), the Court retained jurisdiction to modify the decree. In the late 1970s, the five Indian tribes awarded water rights in *Arizona I*, supported by the United States, sought to modify the decree to increase their PIA rights by 15 to 22 percent on the ground that those acres had been omitted prior to the 1964 decree. (The government contended that the omission was due to the complexity of the case; the tribes claimed that the omission was due to the government's conflict of interest in *Arizona I*, when it represented both the tribes and competing federal interests). In *Arizona v. California III*, 460 U.S. 605 (1983), the Court, per Justice White, ruled against the tribes and the government, primarily based on the need for finality:

> Recalculating the amount of practicably irrigable acreage runs directly counter to the strong interest in finality in this case. A major purpose of this litigation, from its inception to the present day, has been to provide the necessary assurance to States of the Southwest and to various private interests, of the amount of water they can anticipate to receive from the Colorado River system.

Subsequently, two of the *Arizona I* tribes claimed damages for breach of trust based on the government's inadequate representation in *Arizona I*. In *Fort Mojave Indian Tribe v. United States*, 32 Fed. Cl. 29 (1994), *aff'd without opinion*, 64 F.3d 677 (Fed. Cir. 1995), the claims court dismissed the tribes' action, noting that more than thirty years had elapsed since the alleged breach. Because of the time delay, witnesses and documents were lost. The tribe, the court held, "simply failed to demonstrate" that the government "acted other than in a good faith effort to promote the Tribes' interests." The court concluded:

> Plaintiffs' rationale for pursuing this litigation is perfectly understandable. Water rights in the Colorado River Basin are extremely valuable and plaintiffs believe that they were allocated less water rights than they were entitled. The Tribes' reservations appear economically depressed and an increase in water rights could be a key to future industrialization. Moreover, plaintiffs apparently did not choose to have the United States represent them in *Arizona I* and were unable to select their own counsel. Perhaps most frustrating from plaintiffs' perspective is that looking back, an argument can be

made that the United States could have presented the Tribes' PIA claims in a more aggressive manner than it did. * * * But this is the seducing aspect of hindsight. * * * Any such errors that may have occurred appear to be errors of judgment which counsel, acting in a reasonably prudent manner, potentially can make in the course of complex litigation.

Similarly, the Arizona Supreme Court held that the 1935 Globe Equity Decree, entered by the federal district court in Arizona, precluded the San Carlos Apache Tribe from litigating its claims to water from the mainstream of the Gila River in the state-court Gila River general stream adjudication. But the court decided that the decree did not address, and therefore did not preclude, the tribe's claims to water from tributaries of the Gila River. *In re the General Adjudication of All Rights to Use Water in the Gila River System and Source*, 127 P.3d 882 (Ariz. 2006).

By contrast, the Washington Supreme Court held that federal proceedings in *United States v. Ahtanum Irrigation District*, 330 F.2d 897 (9th Cir. 1964), adjudicated the non-tribal rights in Ahtanum Creek (a tributary of the Yakima River that forms the northern boundary of the Yakama Reservation), but did not quantify the practicably irrigable acreage on the Yakama Reservation. *In re Yakima River Drainage Basin*, 177 Wash. 2d 299 (2013). The state trial court determined the PIA based on a 1957 pretrial order in the federal lawsuit, but the state supreme court ruled that the pretrial order only referred to the PIA claimed by the United States. At no time did the federal court make a finding of fact as to PIA, and consequently, the state supreme court remanded to the trial court for a determination. (In the federal litigation, the United States claimed 5,100 acres of PIA; the state trial court determined PIA to be 4,107 acres; the United States and the Yakama Nation argue in the current litigation that the correct figure is 6,381 acres.)

3. Subsequent developments concerning Pyramid Lake. The Pyramid Lake saga has continued, with both negotiation and litigation playing a part.

a. Pyramid Lake water settlements. In 1990, Congress enacted the Fallon Paiute Shoshone Indian Tribes Water Rights Settlement Act, Pub. L. No. 101–618, 104 Stat. 3289, which, among other provisions, incorporated a preliminary agreement between the Pyramid Lake Paiute Tribe and certain private water users. The Act required the Secretary of the Interior to negotiate an operating agreement for the Truckee River and the Newlands Reclamation Project. Any agreement had to provide for the enhancement of flows for the Pyramid Lake fishery in order to meet the requirements of the Endangered Species Act. *See generally* A. Dan Tarlock, *The Creation of New Risk Sharing Water Entitlement Regimes: The Case of the Truckee-Carson Settlement*, 25 Ecol. L.Q. 674 (1999).

In 1993, the Pyramid Lake Paiute Tribe and the Nevada Department of Conservation and Natural Resources entered into a memorandum of understanding concerning the tribe's claim to waters of the Truckee River that are not subject to vested or perfected rights. The tribe agreed to pursue its claims to water under Nevada water law, and the state agreed that the tribe's proposed instream flow was a beneficial use under Nevada law. In 1998, the Nevada state engineer granted the tribe's ensuing application under Nevada state law for the remaining unappropriated water in the Truckee River. These rights are junior to all existing rights and are subject to state law. The Nevada state legislature amended state water law in 1999 to protect the tribe's instream water right from forfeiture due to non-use. Nev. Rev. Stat. § 533.060(2). *See* Michael C. Blumm, David H. Becker & Joshua D. Smith, *The Mirage of Indian Reserved Water Rights and Western Streamflow Restoration in the McCarran Amendment Era: A Promise Unfulfilled*, 36 Envt'l L. 1157, 1188–1193 (2006).

As part of the 1996 Truckee River Water Quality Agreement, the tribe dropped Clean Water Act suits brought in 1988 against the cities of Reno and Sparks in exchange for the two cities and the Department of the Interior agreeing to spend $24 million to purchase existing water rights on the Truckee river and dedicate the water to instream flow approved by the state engineer. By 2006, the federal government and the two cities had acquired approximately 4,500 acre-feet of water rights for the tribe, at a cost of some $8 million.

Churchill County and the City of Fallon attempted to block restoration plans by challenging the validity of the Fallon Paiute Shoshone Indian Tribes Water Rights Settlement Act, arguing that the National Environmental Policy Act had been violated. The court held that the agency's action was not arbitrary or capricious. *Churchill Cnty. v. Norton*, 276 F.3d 1060 (9th Cir. 2001). *See* William H. Rodgers, Jr., Environmental Law in Indian Country 628–631 (Thomson/West 2005) (discussing the case).

In September 2008, the Pyramid Lake Paiute Tribe, the United States, the states of California and Nevada, and several water agencies concluded the Truckee River Operating Agreement (TROA). The TROA, authorized by the 1990 Settlement Act, took eighteen years of negotiations. *See Truckee River Operating Agreement Settles Decades of Water Rights Dispute*, 13 Western Water Law 3 (Nov. 2008). One of the purposes of the TROA is to provide for enhanced spawning flows for the Pyramid Lake fisheries. To that end, the TROA allows signatory parties, and non-signatories who agree to be bound by the terms of the TROA, to receive credit for storing in Truckee River reservoirs water that they would otherwise be entitled to divert. One category of credit water is Fish Credit Water, which the U.S. and the Pyramid Lake Paiute Tribe will establish to benefit the tribal fisheries. The U.S. Bureau of Reclamation adopted the TROA by rule. 73 Fed. Reg. 74031 (2008).

b. The Tribe's effort to change use from irrigation to instream. In the ongoing Pyramid Lake litigation, the tribe and the United States as trustee filed applications with the Nevada State Engineer for temporary one-year transfers of water from irrigation uses to in-stream flows to protect the tribal fishery. The Nevada State Engineer ruled that fishing was a primary purpose of the reservation, Ruling No. 5185, Nevada State Engineer (Dec. 6, 2002), and the federal district court agreed that fisheries was a purpose to which the tribe could apply its reserved water right. *United States v. Orr Water Ditch Co.*, 309 F. Supp. 2d 1245 (D. Nev. 2004). The Ninth Circuit did not reach that issue on appeal, merely noting that the Orr Ditch decree permits parties to the decree to change the "purpose of use" of their water rights "in the manner provided by law." *United States v. Truckee-Carson Irrigation Dist.*, 429 F.3d 902, 904 (9th Cir. 2005). The appeals court then affirmed the decisions of the district court and the engineer that, under the Orr Ditch decree, the tribe could transfer to instream flow use water decreed for actual use in irrigation, but could not transfer the transportation loss.

c. State groundwater allocations affecting tribal rights. The Pyramid Laiute Tribe challenged an allocation of groundwater by the State Engineer, alleging that the withdrawals would adversely affect the tribe's water rights under the Orr Ditch decree. In *United States v. Orr Water Ditch Co.*, 600 F.3d 1152 (9th Cir. 2010), the court held that the tribe's decreed water rights could not be diminished by state groundwater allocations. In addition, the court ruled that the federal district court had jurisdiction to review the State Engineer's decision as part of its equitable power to enforce and administer the Orr Ditch decree. The opinion also addressed a 1998 State Engineer's ruling that the tribe was entitled to all water in the Truckee River remaining after all decreed and other rights had been satisfied. The Ninth Circuit held that the federal court had no jurisdiction over the tribe's challenge that groundwater allocations would affect those rights, because they were state-law rights rather than rights awarded by the federal decree.

4. FOIA requests for tribal water rights litigation information. As *Nevada* makes clear, the federal government may represent tribes in water rights cases, and the tribes are bound by judgments against the United States as trustee. This federal involvement, however, may implicate the Freedom of Information Act (FOIA), 5 U.S.C. § 552, which requires the federal government to make certain documents available to the public upon request.

In 2001, the U.S. Supreme Court held that memoranda between the Bureau of Indian Affairs and the Klamath Tribes with respect to the appropriate scope of the tribes' water claims in the Klamath Basin were not protected from disclosure under FOIA. *Dept. of the Interior v. Klamath Water Users Protective Ass'n*, 532 U.S. 1 (2001). The bureau and the tribes claimed that the documents were protected from disclosure under FOIA by the statute's attorney work-product and deliberative process privileges. The district court agreed, but the Ninth Circuit reversed, and a unanimous Supreme Court affirmed, ruling that the communications did not qualify under the FOIA exemption because they were not inter-agency memoranda. Even though some circuit courts have ruled that documents prepared by government consultants may be exempt from disclosure, Justice Souter distinguished the case of Indian tribes. Although they are owed a trust duty from the federal government, tribes cannot keep sensitive BIA-tribal communications relevant to a water adjudication from their opponents because they "are self-advocates at the expense of others seeking benefits inadequate to satisfy everyone."

In *Flathead Joint Board of Control v. U.S. Dept. of the Interior*, 309 F. Supp. 2d 1217 (D. Mont. 2004), however, the court distinguished the Supreme Court decision in a case where the plaintiff sought information in connection with the Flathead Tribes' claims to water in a general stream adjudication. The district court ruled that the exemption for inter-agency memoranda, which the Supreme Court held inapplicable to the documents requested in *Klamath Water Users*, did apply in this case because the information sought was generated by the federal agencies, not the tribes. Only those documents that the government generated for its own use and then disseminated to the tribes were subject to disclosure under FOIA. In addition, the court held in favor of the government on most of its claims of non-disclosure under the FOIA exemption for privileged or confidential commercial or financial information. The court noted that the information requested by the Joint Board generally fell into this category because water rights are a valuable property right.

5. The Endangered Species Act and tribal water rights. In 1997, the Secretary of the Interior established the Working Group on the Endangered Species Act and Indian Water Rights to investigate concerns raised by tribes that the Endangered Species Act (ESA) was being applied so as interfere with *Winters* rights. In 2000, the working group issued its report, which made recommendations for the U.S. Fish and Wildlife Service (FWS) when making environmental baseline determinations under the ESA. Although one objective of the Working Group's report was that FWS consultations "should address the future possible exercise of Indian water rights," the report in fact recommended only that tribal rights decreed in litigation, confirmed by a settlement act, or otherwise quantified by Congress should be included in FWS consultations. A number of tribes argued that all tribal rights, quantified or not, should be considered. See Judith V. Royster, *Indian Water and the Federal Trust: Some Proposals for Federal Action*, 46 Natural Res. J. 375, 384–389 (2006); Sarah Britton, *Vollmann Report* in Tribal Water Rights 121–22 (John E. Thorson, Sarah Britton & Bonnie G. Colby eds., U. Ariz. Press 2006).

Note on the McCarran Amendment and State Water Adjudications

In 1952, Congress enacted the McCarran Amendment, 43 U.S.C. § 666, as a rider to the Justice Department appropriations bill, authorizing the joinder of the federal government as a party in state court general stream adjudications. The Supreme Court subsequently held that the McCarran Amendment permitted state courts to determine federally reserved water rights. *United States v. District Court in and for Eagle County*, 401 U.S. 520 (1971) (federal reserved water rights for a national forest). Five years later, the Court extended that holding to state court adjudication of tribal reserved rights to water. *Colorado River Water Conservation Dist. v. United States*, 424 U.S. 800 (1976). For a comprehensive history of the McCarran Amendment, see John E. Thorson et al., *Dividing Western Waters: A Century of Adjudicating Rivers and Streams*, 8 U. Denv. Water L. Rev. 355 (2005) & Part II, 9 U. Denv. Water L. Rev. 299 (2006).

The *Colorado River* case established three primary principles of state court adjudication of Indian water rights. First, the Court held that once the federal government is joined in a state general stream adjudication, it must litigate Indian reserved rights to water as well as other federal water rights. Second, the Court held that the McCarran Amendment did not by itself divest federal courts of their concurrent jurisdiction to determine Indian water rights. And third, the Court created what has come to be known as the *Colorado River* abstention doctrine.

The Supreme Court again took up the *Colorado River* abstention doctrine in the following case.

Arizona v. San Carlos Apache Tribe of Arizona
463 U.S. 545 (1983)

JUSTICE BRENNAN delivered the opinion of the Court.

These consolidated cases form a sequel to our decision in *Colorado River Water Conservation District v. United States*, 424 U.S. 800 (1976). That case held that (1) the McCarran Amendment, 43 U.S.C. § 666, which waived the sovereign immunity of the United States as to comprehensive state water rights adjudications,[1] provides state courts with jurisdiction to adjudicate Indian water rights held in trust by the United States, and (2), in light of the clear federal policies underlying the McCarran Amendment, a water rights suit brought by the United States in federal court was properly dismissed in favor of a concurrent comprehensive adjudication reaching the same issues in Colorado state court. The questions in these cases are parallel: (1) What is the effect of the McCarran Amendment in those States which, unlike Colorado, were admitted to the Union subject to federal legislation that reserved "absolute jurisdiction and control" over Indian lands in the Congress of the United States? (2) If the courts of such States do have jurisdiction to adjudicate Indian water rights, should concurrent federal suits brought by Indian tribes, rather than by the United States, and raising only Indian claims, also be subject to dismissal under the doctrine of *Colorado River*?

I

Colorado River arose out of a suit brought by the Federal Government in the United States District Court for the District of Colorado seeking a declaration of its rights, and the rights of a number of Indian Tribes, to waters in certain rivers and their

---

1. The McCarran Amendment provides in relevant part:
"(a) Consent is hereby given to join the United States as a defendant in any suit (1) for the adjudication of rights to the use of water of a river system or other source, or (2) for the administration of such rights, where it appears that the United States is the owner of or is in the process of acquiring water rights by appropriation under State law, by purchase, by exchange, or otherwise, and the United States is a necessary party to such suit. The United States, when a party to any such suit, shall (1) be deemed to have waived any right to plead that the State laws are inapplicable or that the United States is not amenable thereto by reason of its sovereignty, and (2) shall be subject to the judgments, orders and decrees of the court having jurisdiction, and may obtain review thereof, in the same manner and to the same extent as a private individual under like circumstances. . . ."

tributaries located in one of the drainage basins of the State of Colorado. In the suit, the Government asserted reserved rights, governed by federal law, as well as rights based on state law. Shortly after the federal suit was commenced, the United States was joined, pursuant to the McCarran Amendment, as a party in the ongoing state-court comprehensive water adjudication being conducted for the same drainage basin. The Federal District Court, on motion of certain of the defendants and intervenors, dismissed the federal suit, stating that the doctrine of abstention required deference to the state proceedings. The Court of Appeals reversed the District Court, and we in turn reversed the Court of Appeals.

We began our analysis in *Colorado River* by conceding that the District Court had jurisdiction over the federal suit under 28 U.S.C. § 1345, the general provision conferring district court jurisdiction over most civil actions brought by the Federal Government. We then examined whether the federal suit was nevertheless properly dismissed in view of the concurrent state-court proceedings. This part of the analysis began by considering "whether the McCarran Amendment provided consent to determine federal reserved rights held on behalf of Indians in state court," since "given the claims for Indian water rights in [the federal suit], dismissal clearly would have been inappropriate if the state court had no jurisdiction to decide those claims." We concluded:

> "Not only the Amendment's language, but also its underlying policy, dictates a construction including Indian rights in its provisions. [*United States v. District Court for Eagle County*, 401 U.S. 520 (1971),] rejected the conclusion that federal reserved rights in general were not reached by the Amendment for the reason that the Amendment '[deals] with an all-inclusive statute concerning "the adjudication of rights to the use of water of a river system."' This consideration applies as well to federal water rights reserved for Indian reservations."

In sum, considering the important federal interest in allowing all water rights on a river system to be adjudicated in a single comprehensive state proceeding, and "bearing in mind the ubiquitous nature of Indian water rights in the Southwest," it was clear to us "that a construction of the Amendment excluding those rights from its coverage would enervate the Amendment's objective."

We buttressed this conclusion with an examination of the legislative history of the McCarran Amendment. We also noted:

> "Mere subjection of Indian rights to legal challenge in state court . . . would no more imperil those rights than would a suit brought by the Government in district court for their declaration. . . . The Government has not abdicated any responsibility fully to defend Indian rights in state court, and Indian interests may be satisfactorily protected under regimes of state law. The Amendment in no way abridges any substantive claim on behalf of Indians under the doctrine of reserved rights. Moreover, as *Eagle County* said, 'questions [arising from the collision of private rights and reserved rights of the

United States], including the volume and scope of particular reserved rights, are federal questions which, if preserved, can be reviewed [by the Supreme Court] after final judgment by the Colorado court.'"

We then considered the dismissal itself. We found that the dismissal could not be supported under the doctrine of abstention in any of its forms, but that it was justified as an application of traditional principles of "'[wise] judicial administration, giving regard to conservation of judicial resources and comprehensive disposition of litigation.'" We stated that, although the federal courts had a "virtually unflagging obligation . . . to exercise the jurisdiction given them," there were certain very limited circumstances outside the abstention context in which dismissal was warranted in deference to a concurrent state-court suit. In the case at hand, we noted the comprehensive nature of the state proceedings and the considerable expertise and technical resources available in those proceedings. We concluded:

"[A] number of factors clearly counsel against concurrent federal proceedings. The most important of these is the McCarran Amendment itself. The clear federal policy evinced by that legislation is the avoidance of piecemeal adjudication of water rights in a river system. This policy is akin to that underlying the rule requiring that jurisdiction be yielded to the court first acquiring control of property, for the concern in such instances is with avoiding the generation of additional litigation through permitting inconsistent dispositions of property. This concern is heightened with respect to water rights, the relationships among which are highly interdependent. Indeed, we have recognized that actions seeking the allocation of water essentially involve the disposition of property and are best conducted in unified proceedings. The consent to jurisdiction given by the McCarran Amendment bespeaks a policy that recognizes the availability of comprehensive state systems for adjudication of water rights as the means for achieving these goals."

For these reasons, and others,[3] we affirmed the judgment of the District Court dismissing the federal complaint.

II

The two petitions considered here arise out of three separate consolidated appeals that were decided within three days of each other by the same panel of the Court of Appeals for the Ninth Circuit. In each of the underlying cases, either the United States as trustee or certain Indian Tribes on their own behalf, or both, asserted the right to have certain Indian water rights in Arizona or Montana adjudicated in federal court.

The Montana Cases (No. 81-2188)

---

3. The other factors were the apparent absence at the time of dismissal of any proceedings in the District Court other than the filing of the complaint, the extensive involvement of state water rights in the suit, the 300-mile distance between the Federal District Court in Denver and the state tribunal, and the Government's apparent willingness to participate in other comprehensive water proceedings in the state courts.

In January 1975, the Northern Cheyenne Tribe brought an action in the United States District Court for the District of Montana seeking an adjudication of its rights in certain streams in that State. Shortly thereafter, the United States brought two suits in the same court, seeking a determination of water rights both on its own behalf and on behalf of a number of Indian Tribes, including the Northern Cheyenne, in the same streams. Each of the federal actions was a general adjudication which sought to determine the rights inter sese of all users of the stream, and not merely the rights of the plaintiffs. On motion of the Northern Cheyenne, its action was consolidated with one of the Government actions. The other concerned Tribes intervened as appropriate.

At about the time that all this activity was taking place in federal court, the State of Montana was preparing to begin a process of comprehensive water adjudication under a recently passed state statute. In July 1975, the Montana Department of Natural Resources and Conservation filed petitions in state court commencing comprehensive proceedings to adjudicate water rights in the same streams at issue in the federal cases.

Both sets of contestants having positioned themselves, nothing much happened for a number of years. The federal proceedings were stayed for a time pending our decision in *Colorado River*. When that decision came down, the State of Montana, one of the defendants in the federal suits, brought a motion to dismiss, which was argued in 1976, but not decided until 1979. Meanwhile, process was completed in the various suits, answers were submitted, and discovery commenced. Over in the state courts, events moved even more slowly, and no appreciable progress seems to have been made by 1979.

In April 1979, the United States brought four more suits in federal court, seeking to adjudicate its rights and the rights of various Indian Tribes in other Montana streams. One month later, the Montana Legislature amended its water adjudication procedures "to expedite and facilitate the adjudication of existing water rights." The legislation provided for the initiation of comprehensive proceedings by order of the Montana Supreme Court, the appointment of water judges throughout the State, and the consolidation of all existing actions within each water division. It also provided, among other things, that the Montana Supreme Court should issue an order requiring all claimants not already involved in the state proceedings, including the United States on its own behalf or as trustee for the Indians, to file a statement of claim with the Department of Natural Resources and Conservation by a date set by the court or be deemed to have abandoned any water rights claim. The Montana court issued the required order, and the United States was served with formal notice thereof.

In November 1979, the two judges for the District of Montana jointly considered the motions to dismiss in each of the federal actions, and granted each of them. * * * On appeal, a divided Court of Appeals reversed.

The Arizona Cases (No. 81-2147)

In the mid-1970s, various water rights claimants in Arizona filed petitions in state court to initiate general adjudications to determine conflicting rights in a number of river systems. In early 1979, process was served in one of the proceedings on approximately 12,000 known potential water claimants, including the United States. In July 1981, process was served in another proceeding on approximately 58,000 known water claimants, again including the United States. In each case, the United States was joined both in its independent capacity and as trustee for various Indian Tribes.

In March and April 1979, a number of Indian Tribes whose rights were implicated by the state water proceedings filed a series of suits in the United States District Court for the District of Arizona, asking variously for removal of the state adjudications to federal court, declaratory and injunctive relief preventing any further adjudication of their rights in state court, and independent federal determinations of their water rights. A number of defendants in the federal proceedings filed motions seeking remand or dismissal. The District Court, relying on *Colorado River*, remanded the removed actions, and dismissed most of the independent federal actions without prejudice. It stayed one of the remaining actions pending the completion of state proceedings.

The Tribes appealed from these decisions, with the exception of the remand orders. The Court of Appeals reversed, holding that the Enabling Act under which Arizona was admitted to statehood, and the Arizona Constitution, both of which contain wording substantially identical to the Montana Enabling Act and Constitution, disabled Arizona from adjudicating Indian water claims.

We granted certiorari, in order to resolve a conflict among the Circuits regarding the role of federal and state courts in adjudicating Indian water rights. We now reverse.

III A

At the outset of our analysis, a number of propositions are clear. First, the federal courts had jurisdiction here to hear the suits brought both by the United States and the Indian Tribes. Second, it is also clear in these cases, as it was in *Colorado River*, that a dismissal or stay of the federal suits would have been improper if there was no jurisdiction in the concurrent state actions to adjudicate the claims at issue in the federal suits.

Finally, it should be obvious that, to the extent that a claimed bar to state jurisdiction in these cases is premised on the respective State Constitutions, that is a question of state law over which the state courts have binding authority. Because, in each of these cases, the state courts have taken jurisdiction over the Indian water rights at issue here, we must assume, until informed otherwise, that—at least insofar as state law is concerned—such jurisdiction exists. We must therefore look, for our purposes, to the federal Enabling Acts and other federal legislation, in order to determine whether there is a federal bar to the assertion of state jurisdiction in these cases.

B

That we were not required in *Colorado River* to interpret the McCarran Amendment in light of any statehood Enabling Act was largely a matter of fortuity, for Colorado is one of the few Western States that were not admitted to the Union pursuant to an Enabling Act containing substantially the same language as is found in the Arizona and Montana Enabling Acts. Indeed, a substantial majority of Indian land—including most of the largest Indian reservations—lies in States subject to such Enabling Acts.

* * * [T]he parties in these cases have engaged in a vigorous debate as to the exact meaning and significance of the Arizona and Montana Enabling Acts. We need not resolve that debate, however, nor need we resort to the more general doctrines that have developed to chart the limits of state authority over Indians, because we are convinced that, whatever limitation the Enabling Acts or federal policy may have originally placed on state-court jurisdiction over Indian water rights, those limitations were removed by the McCarran Amendment. Congress clearly would have had the right to distinguish between disclaimer and nondisclaimer States in passing the McCarran Amendment. But the Amendment was designed to deal with a general problem arising out of the limitations that federal sovereign immunity placed on the ability of the States to adjudicate water rights, and nowhere in its text or legislative history do we find any indication that Congress intended the efficacy of the remedy to differ from one State to another. Moreover, we stated in *Colorado River* that "bearing in mind the ubiquitous nature of Indian water rights in the Southwest, it is clear that a construction of the Amendment excluding those rights from its coverage would enervate the Amendment's objective." The "ubiquitous nature of Indian water rights" is most apparent in the very States to which Congress attached jurisdictional reservations. To declare now that our holding in *Colorado River* applies only to that minority of Indian water claims located in States without jurisdictional reservations would constitute a curious and unwarranted retreat from the rationale behind our previous holding, and would work the very mischief that our decision in *Colorado River* sought to avoid.

IV

The second crucial issue in these cases is whether our analysis in *Colorado River* applies with full force to federal suits brought by Indian tribes, rather than by the United States, and seeking adjudication only of Indian water rights. This question is not directly answered by *Colorado River*, because we specifically reserved in that case "[whether] similar considerations would permit dismissal of a water suit brought by a private party in federal district court." On reflection, however, we must agree with JUSTICE STEVENS, who, in dissenting from our decision, wrote: "[The] Federal Government surely has no lesser right of access to the federal forum than does a private [party], such as an Indian asserting his own claim. If this be so, today's holding will necessarily restrict the access to federal court of private plaintiffs asserting water rights claims in Colorado."

The United States and the various Indian respondents raise a series of arguments why dismissal or stay of the federal suit is not appropriate when it is brought by an Indian tribe and only seeks to adjudicate Indian rights. (1) Indian rights have traditionally been left free of interference from the States. (2) State courts may be inhospitable to Indian rights. (3) The McCarran Amendment, although it waived United States sovereign immunity in state comprehensive water adjudications, did not waive Indian sovereign immunity. It is therefore unfair to force Indian claimants to choose between waiving their sovereign immunity by intervening in the state proceedings and relying on the United States to represent their interests in state court, particularly in light of the frequent conflict of interest between Indian claims and other federal interests and the right of the Indians under 28 U.S.C. § 1362 to bring suit on their own behalf in federal court.[17] (4) Indian water rights claims are generally based on federal rather than state law. (5) Because Indian water claims are based on the doctrine of "reserved rights," and take priority over most water rights created by state law, they need not as a practical matter be adjudicated inter sese with other water rights, and could simply be incorporated into the comprehensive state decree at the conclusion of the state proceedings.

Each of these arguments has a good deal of force. We note, though, that very similar arguments were raised and rejected in *United States v. District Court for Eagle County*, 401 U.S. 520 (1971), and *Colorado River*. More important, all of these arguments founder on one crucial fact: If the state proceedings have jurisdiction over the Indian water rights at issue here, as appears to be the case, then concurrent federal proceedings are likely to be duplicative and wasteful, generating "additional litigation through permitting inconsistent dispositions of property." Moreover, since a judgment by either court would ordinarily be res judicata in the other, the existence of such concurrent proceedings creates the serious potential for spawning an unseemly and destructive race to see which forum can resolve the same issues first—a race contrary to the entire spirit of the McCarran Amendment and prejudicial, to say the least, to the possibility of reasoned decisionmaking by either forum. The United States and many of the Indian Tribes recognize these concerns, but in responding to them they cast aside the sort of sound argument generally apparent in the rest of their submissions and rely instead on vague statements of faith and hope. The United States, for example, states that adjudicating Indian water rights in federal court, despite the existence of a comprehensive state proceeding, would not

---

17. This argument, of course, suffers from the flaw that, although the McCarran Amendment did not waive the sovereign immunity of Indians as parties to state comprehensive water adjudications, it did (as we made quite clear in *Colorado River*) waive sovereign immunity with regard to the Indian rights at issue in those proceedings. Moreover, contrary to the submissions by certain of the parties, any judgment against the United States, as trustee for the Indians, would ordinarily be binding on the Indians. In addition, there is no indication in these cases that the state courts would deny the Indian parties leave to intervene to protect their interests. Thus, although the Indians have the right to refuse to intervene even if they believe that the United States is not adequately representing their interests, the practical value of that right in this context is dubious at best.

"entail any duplication or potential for inconsistent judgments. The federal court will quantify the Indian rights only if it is asked to do so before the State court has embarked on the task. And, of course, once the United States district court has indicated its determination to perform that limited role, *we assume* the State tribunal will turn its attention to the typically more complex business of adjudicating all other claims on the stream. *In the usual case,* the federal court will have completed its function earlier and its quantification of Indian water rights will simply be incorporated in the comprehensive State court decree." (emphasis added).

Similarly, the Navajo Nation states:

"There is no reasonably foreseeable danger that [the] federal action [brought by the Navajo] will duplicate or delay state proceedings or waste judicial resources. While the Navajo claim proceeds in federal court, the state court *can* move forward to assess, quantify, and rank the 58,000 state claims. The Navajo federal action will be concluded long before the state court has finished its task." (emphasis added).

The problem with these scenarios, however, is that they assume a cooperative attitude on the part of state courts, state legislatures, and state parties which is neither legally required nor realistically always to be expected. The state courts need not "turn their attention" to other matters if they are prompted by state parties to adjudicate the Indian claims first. Moreover, considering the specialized resources and experience of the state courts, it is not at all obvious that the federal actions "will be concluded long before" the state courts have issued at least preliminary judgments on the question of Indian water rights.

The McCarran Amendment, as interpreted in *Colorado River,* allows and encourages state courts to undertake the task of quantifying Indian water rights in the course of comprehensive water adjudications. Although adjudication of those rights in federal court instead might in the abstract be practical, and even wise, it will be neither practical nor wise as long as it creates the possibility of duplicative litigation, tension and controversy between the federal and state forums, hurried and pressured decisionmaking, and confusion over the disposition of property rights.

Colorado River, of course, does not require that a federal water suit must always be dismissed or stayed in deference to a concurrent and adequate comprehensive state adjudication. Certainly, the federal courts need not defer to the state proceedings if the state courts expressly agree to stay their own consideration of the issues raised in the federal action pending disposition of that action. Moreover, it may be in a particular case that, at the time a motion to dismiss is filed, the federal suit at issue is well enough along that its dismissal would itself constitute a waste of judicial resources and an invitation to duplicative effort. Finally, we do not deny that, in a case in which the arguments for and against deference to the state adjudication were otherwise closely matched, the fact that a federal suit was brought by Indians on their own behalf and sought only to adjudicate Indian rights should be figured into the balance. But the most important consideration in *Colorado River*, and the most important consideration in any federal water suit concurrent to a comprehensive state proceeding, must be the "policy underlying the McCarran Amendment," and, despite the strong arguments raised by the respondents, we cannot conclude that water rights suits brought by Indians and seeking adjudication only of Indian rights should be excepted from the application of that policy or from the general principles set out in *Colorado River*. In the cases before us, assuming that the state adjudications are adequate to quantify the rights at issue in the federal suits, and taking into account the McCarran Amendment policies we have just discussed, the expertise and administrative machinery available to the state courts, the infancy of the federal suits, the general judicial bias against piecemeal litigation, and the convenience to the parties, we must conclude that the District Courts were correct in deferring to the state proceedings.

V

Nothing we say today should be understood to represent even the slightest retreat from the general proposition we expressed so recently in *New Mexico v. Mescalero Apache Tribe*, 462 U.S., at 332: "Because of their sovereign status, [Indian] tribes and their reservation lands are insulated in some respects by a 'historic immunity from state and local control,' and tribes retain any aspect of their historical sovereignty not 'inconsistent with the overriding interests of the National Government.'" Nor should we be understood to retreat from the general proposition, expressed in *Colorado River*, that federal courts have a "virtually unflagging obligation . . . to exercise the jurisdiction given them." But water rights adjudication is a virtually unique type of proceeding, and the McCarran Amendment is a virtually unique federal statute, and we cannot in this context be guided by general propositions.

We also emphasize, as we did in *Colorado River*, that our decision in no way changes the substantive law by which Indian rights in state water adjudications must be judged. State courts, as much as federal courts, have a solemn obligation to follow federal law. Moreover, any state-court decision alleged to abridge Indian water rights protected by federal law can expect to receive, if brought for review before this Court, a particularized and exacting scrutiny commensurate with the powerful federal interest in safeguarding those rights from state encroachment.

The judgment of the Court of Appeals in each of these cases is reversed, and the cases are remanded for further proceedings consistent with this opinion.

JUSTICE MARSHALL, dissenting.

In *Colorado River Water Conservation District v. United States*, this Court recognized a narrow rule of abstention governing controversies involving federal water rights. We stated that in light of "the virtually unflagging obligation of the federal courts to exercise the jurisdiction given them," "[only] the clearest of justifications," will warrant abstention in favor of a concurrent state proceeding. Substantially for the reasons set forth in Justice Stevens' dissenting opinion, I believe that abstention is not appropriate in these cases. Unlike the federal suit in *Colorado River*, the suits here are brought by Indian Tribes on their own behalf. These cases thus implicate the strong congressional policy, embodied in 28 U.S.C. § 1362, of affording Indian tribes a federal forum. Since § 1362 reflects a congressional recognition of the "great hesitancy on the part of tribes to use State courts," tribes which have sued under that provision should not lightly be remitted to asserting their rights in a state forum. Moreover, these cases also differ from *Colorado River* in that the exercise of federal jurisdiction here will not result in duplicative federal and state proceedings, since the District Court need only determine the water rights of the Tribes. I therefore cannot agree that this is one of those "exceptional" situations justifying abstention.

JUSTICE STEVENS, with whom JUSTICE BLACKMUN joins, dissenting.

"Nothing in the McCarran Amendment or in its legislative history can be read as limiting the jurisdiction of the federal courts." *Colorado River Water Conservation District v. United States*, 424 U.S. 800, 821, n. 2 (1976) (Stewart, J., dissenting). That Amendment is a waiver, not a command. It permits the United States to be joined as a defendant in state water rights adjudications; it does not purport to diminish the United States' right to litigate in a federal forum and it is totally silent on the subject of Indian tribes' rights to litigate anywhere. Yet today the majority somehow concludes that it commands the federal courts to defer to state-court water rights proceedings, even when Indian water rights are involved. Although it is customary for the Court to begin its analysis of questions of statutory construction by examining the text of the relevant statute, one may search in vain for any textual support for the Court's holding today.

Notes

1. Extending the *Colorado River* doctrine. In *United States v. Oregon*, 44 F.3d 758 (9th Cir. 1994), the Ninth Circuit held that the McCarran Amendment's waiver of federal sovereign immunity in state lawsuits for general stream adjudications extends to comprehensive determinations that begin in an administrative agency and are later reviewed by the state court. The court determined that Oregon's proceedings were sufficiently comprehensive to qualify under the McCarran Amendment, even though post-1909 water rights were not subject to reopening and groundwater claims were not included in the proceedings. The Oregon statute has been a model for similar statutes in California, Arizona, Nevada, and Texas.

The *Oregon* court also denied the intervenor Klamath Tribe's due process claim. The tribe alleged that state decisionmaking would be biased against the tribe's water rights, citing the state Justice Department's position in prior litigation that no tribal water rights existed. The court held that even if the state Justice Department was biased, it would not have any significant role to play in the actual adjudication by the state water agency or in judicial review of that decision. Moreover, the court noted that the federal courts had already determined the legal issues. All that was left for the state was the factual issue of quantification. The court found that the tribe had failed to establish how the state's prior hostility to tribal water rights could affect that determination.

2. Limiting the *Colorado River* doctrine. Despite its preference for abstention, the *Colorado River* Court ruled that the McCarran Amendment does not divest federal courts of their jurisdiction to determine federally reserved water rights. Subsequent federal decisions refusing to abstain, however, have been rare. In one case, the Ninth Circuit affirmed the district court's refusal to abstain in favor of state court, citing a number of differences from the facts in *Colorado River*. *United States v. Adair*, 723 F.2d 1394, 1404–07 (9th Cir. 1983). The *Adair* court noted that at the time the federal lawsuit was filed, no state proceedings were underway. In fact, seven years later, the state proceedings had not progressed beyond the fact-gathering stage. Consequently, the court ruled that to dismiss a completed federal court determination of federal rights would result in duplicative efforts and a waste of judicial resources. Moreover, the court noted that the federal lawsuit sought to determine only the federal-law issue of priority of reserved rights, and therefore would not intrude on the role of the state court in any general stream adjudication. Similarly, the Ninth Circuit also declined to order abstention where the federal court was asked to interpret the rights of the Yakama Nation to fisheries water pursuant to a federal consent decree awarding non-Indian irrigation rights. *Kittitas Reclamation Dist. v. Sunnyside Valley Irrigation Dist.*, 763 F.2d 1032, 1034–35 (9th Cir. 1985) ("The parties intended no general adjudication of water rights and no party moved to dismiss the federal suit."). With these rare exceptions, however, federal courts have abstained under *Colorado River*.

3. Administration of state court decrees. The McCarran Amendment provides that state courts may litigate claims "for the administration of" water rights that have been adjudicated as part of a general stream adjudication. 43 U.S.C. § 666(a). See, e.g., *Wyoming v. United States*, 933 F.Supp. 1030, 1035–35 (D. Wyo. 1996). State courts thus retain jurisdiction to execute, interpret, and enforce their decrees. The Ninth Circuit determined that such state court jurisdiction is exclusive of federal courts, relying on the doctrine of prior exclusive jurisdiction. *State Engineer v. South Fork Band of the Te-Moak Tribe*, 339 F.3d 804, 809–14 (9th Cir. 2003).

Note on Water Settlements

Negotiated consent decrees in Indian water rights litigation have been employed since early in the twentieth century, but water rights settlement acts became an important tool beginning in the 1970s. The increased use of settlements was in reaction to the drawbacks of general stream adjudications as a means of determining Indian reserved rights to water.

1. Advantages and disadvantages of settlements.

The use of state general stream adjudications to determine Indian reserved rights to water has proved to have a number of well-documented drawbacks.

One significant drawback arises from the nature of general stream adjudications. Because they are comprehensive proceedings, often involving thousands of water rights, general stream adjudications may run for literally decades. The costs of such prolonged litigation are extensive, running into the tens of millions of dollars. During the course of the litigation, tribal and federal resources are devoted to the proceedings rather than to other uses and priorities. A state may permit new state-law uses to begin during the adjudication, further complicating the process.

Moreover, state court may be an unfriendly forum for tribes. State judges are, in most states, ultimately answerable to the voters. To the extent that tribal water rights are in conflict with, or perceived to be in conflict with, the water rights of state users, state courts may favor state users. In addition, in a majority of western states, the state water agency is more than simply a party to the water rights litigation. In most of the states, the water agency makes at least preliminary findings and determinations. Where the state water agency is both a representative of state interests and a preliminary fact-finder, tribes may well distrust the process to fairly consider tribal interests.

In addition to the historic conflict between states and tribes, state court rulings in general stream adjudications have varied significantly. Although the U.S. Supreme Court cautioned states to follow federal law in determining tribal water rights, state court interpretations of federal law are not uniform. For example, one state finds that the only purpose for which a reservation was created was agriculture, while another finds a broad purpose of creating a viable homeland. One state restricts the uses that tribes may make of their water rights, while others do not. One state determines that Indian water rights do not extend to groundwater, while others find that groundwater may, at least under certain circumstances, be used to fulfill the tribal right. These variances in the application of federal reserved water rights principles are not necessarily tailored to the needs of the parties, but rather to the various state courts' interpretation of federal precedent.

A final and crucial drawback to litigation of Indian water rights is the end result. The ultimate purpose of litigating Indian water rights is not only a declaration of those rights, but the ability to put the water to uses that best serve the needs of the Indian community. In general stream adjudications, Indian tribes receive determinations of water rights, but those rights are paper rights only. At the end of a long, costly litigation process, the tribe has a recognized water right, but not "wet" water or the means of putting the decreed water to actual use. Moreover, given that the tribe itself may spend upwards of a million dollars to obtain the paper right, few if any tribal resources remain available to fund water projects and delivery systems. Similarly, the federal government may spend considerable resources helping to litigate Indian water rights, without being able to offer financial assistance for water projects after the water rights are determined.

In light of these substantial drawbacks of state general stream adjudications, negotiated settlements of Indian rights to water have significant advantages.

First, the settlement acts resolve tribal claims to water with respect to both the states and the federal government. At the heart of every settlement act is a quantification of the tribal right to water. Tribes waive their reserved rights to water under the *Winters* doctrine and their water claims against the United States. They agree, in general, to a lesser quantity of water than they could receive under the *Winters* approach of securing sufficient water to fulfill the purposes for which the land was set aside. In exchange, the tribes receive guarantees of financial assistance in developing their water resources.

Thus, the second and crucially important advantage of negotiated settlements is the promise of "wet" water. Every settlement act authorizes appropriations for water development or management projects, or more generally for economic development purposes. A few more recent settlements include mandatory appropriations. Costs are shared among the various interested parties, including the tribes, the states, and the federal government. The importance of this feature cannot be overstated. Tribes with litigated paper rights to water face enormous obstacles in getting that water into use; tribes with negotiated rights have some guarantee that financial assistance is forthcoming.

Third, water rights settlements are faster and less expensive than litigation through a general stream adjudication. Negotiated settlements are by no means quick or cheap. But compared to adjudications, negotiated settlements take less time and use fewer tribal, state, and federal resources to conclude. As settlements become more common, parties have greater expertise in the process, and prior settlements may serve as models for future negotiations.

Fourth, water settlements are flexible and tailored to the needs and circumstances of the parties. Unlike variances in adjudication decrees that result from inconsistent state court interpretation of federal law, variances in negotiated settlements serve the interests of all parties. Settlement acts often clarify issues that are not entirely resolved under federal precedent. For example, a significant number of settlement acts protect tribal uses of water for other than agricultural irrigation. Some settlements specify that the water rights may be used for any purpose, while others protect the tribe's ability to use part of its water rights for an instream flow to ensure that sufficient water remains in the river itself. Similarly, settlement acts may specifically address groundwater rights. Settlements in the Southwest tend to do so, while settlements in the Northern Plains tend not to, indicating the relative importance of the groundwater issue in those regions.

As part of their flexibility, settlement acts often address issues that are outside the scope of a general stream adjudication. Often these involve issues of water use and administration for which there is currently no general statutory or regulatory authority. For example, the Secretary of the Interior placed a moratorium on the approval of tribal water codes back in 1975, pending the adoption of federal regulations. No regulations were ever issued, and thus tribes that require federal approval of their laws face a serious roadblock in regulating water rights. Several of the settlement acts address this issue directly, providing for the creation of a tribal water code to administer water rights, often with the Secretary of the Interior administering tribal water rights until the adoption of a tribal code.

As another example, tribes' ability to engage in water marketing is open to question under current law. Water marketing, generally defined as the lease or sale of water rights to another user, is gaining wide acceptance in western states as a means of ensuring that water is put to the most economic and beneficial use, without requiring the water rights holder to forego the value of the right. Water marketing can be enormously beneficial to tribes, ensuring that tribes receive the economic value of their water rights, particularly during times when the tribe itself is not able to put the water right to actual use. States and state-law water users may also benefit from tribal water marketing by having a reliable source of additional water at a reasonable cost.

Under current federal law, the sale or encumbrance of Indian property requires federal consent. Because tribal water rights are property rights, it is likely that the lease of these rights requires congressional authorization. While no statute generally permits tribal water marketing, most of the settlement acts do. The tribes' ability to market their water rights is generally subject to certain limitations. Virtually all of the acts prohibit the permanent sale of tribal water rights, but rather authorize leasing. A significant number restrict the lease term to no more than 99–100 years. Tribes are often limited to marketing water from certain sources or, more often, to certain users such as nearby municipalities, benefitting local governments as well as the tribes. In most cases, the marketed water is expressly subject to state law during the period it is used off-reservation by the non-tribal users.

On occasion, water rights settlements address other water-related issues outside the scope of litigation. For example, one settlement included a hiring preference for tribal members in connection with a water project. Another addressed tribal-state relations in connection with water quality standards under the Clean Water Act.

The final advantage of water rights settlements over litigation is harder to quantify. Parties in litigation are in conflict with one another. It is the nature of litigation to have winners and losers. Even in a general stream adjudication, the proceedings can be adversarial. Negotiated settlements, at their best, are less so. The aim of a negotiated settlement is to reach a result that is beneficial to and acceptable to all parties. States, tribes, and the federal government must necessarily work together to reach a settlement before it is presented to Congress. The parties may not emerge from the process as friends, but a good process fosters respect and understanding. If negotiated water settlements lead to greater cooperation in state-tribal relations, that alone is an advantage worth pursuing.

Negotiated water settlements are not without their disadvantages. As noted above, faster and cheaper does not mean fast and cheap. Moreover, implementation of water settlements has been slow. Further proceedings are often necessary, funding must be appropriated, water projects designed and constructed, and so forth.

Oversight Hearing on Indian Water Rights: Promoting the Negotiation and Implementation of Water Settlements in Indian Country U.S. Senate Committee on Indian Affairs (March 15, 2012) (statement of Judith V. Royster).

2. Settlement act provisions. Between 1982 and 2016, Congress enacted 30 water rights settlement acts into law, including the first settlement in a dual-system appropriation/riparian state. Choctaw Nation of Oklahoma and the Chickasaw Nation Water Settlement, Pub. L. No. 114-322, § 3608, 130 Stat. 1628 (2016). All of these settlement acts contain provisions to address the unique needs and circumstances of the parties. Some of these provisions from the more recent settlement acts are summarized below:

- **Aamodt Litigation Settlement Act,** Pub. L. 111-291, 124 Stat. 3064 (2010): The Aamodt Litigation, one of the longest running federal cases, resolved issues between several Pueblos and neighboring communities who use the same water sources. Non-Pueblo users must eventually obtain water from a non-Pueblo water utility system and in return the Pueblos agree to not make priority calls against such groundwater users. The agreement also authorized importing water to relieve pressure on the aquifer. The Act does not authorize water marketing, but provides that the Pueblos retain all rights to use and protect the water rights granted through the Act in a manner consistent with federal law.

- **Taos Pueblo Indian Water Rights Settlement Act,** Pub. L. 111-291, 124 Stat. 3064 (2010): The Taos Pueblo settlement permits a diversion of over 2,200 acre-feet to protect the water rights of the Pueblo and authorizes the use of $124 million in federal funds to acquire additional water rights, improve water production, and restore a natural wetland — the Buffalo Pasture The pueblo may market its water rights, provided such marketing is consistent with the Act.

- **White Mountain Apache Tribe Water Rights Quantification Act of 2010,** Pub. L. 111-291, 124 Stat. 3064 (2010): The agreement required safe drinking water and the construction of reservoirs on the reservation. This settlement confirms the tribe's right to divert 74,000 acre-feet from Salt River. The Act does not authorize the tribe to market its water rights.

- **Northwestern New Mexico Rural Water Projects Act (Navajo-Gallup Water Supply Project/Navajo Nation Water Rights),** Pub. L. No. 111-11; 123 Stat 1367 (2009): This settlement established the Reclamation Water Settlements Fund to fund Indian water rights settlements in Arizona, Montana, and New Mexico. The Act also authorized diverting water and developing additional groundwater on Navajo lands for agricultural, carriage, industrial, commercial, municipal and domestic purposes. The settlement obligated the federal government to provide 606,000 acre-feet to the Navajo Nation and pay costs related to the construction and operation of the Navajo-Gallup Water Supply Project. In total, the Act authorizes approximately $1 billion to fund the settlements and build the Navajo project. Although the Act mentions that acquired water will be subject to state law, it does not authorize water marketing.

- **Shoshone-Paiute Tribes of Duck Valley Water Rights Settlement Act,** Pub. L. No. 111-11; 123 Stat 1405 (2009): The Shoshone-Paiute settlement entitled the tribes to over 111,000 acre feet per year from the East Fork Owyhee River Basin and 2,606 acre-feet of groundwater. The agreement also stipulated that any water rights forfeited or abandoned by upstream users will become part of the tribes' rights. Although the Act mentions that the tribes may use and store surface water not used by upstream water rights users, the Act does not authorize water marketing.

- **Soboba of Luiseño Indians Settlement Act,** Pub. L. No. 110-297; 122 Stat. 2975 (2008): This agreement resolved a dispute over the Tribe's water rights by creating a fifty-year plan to protect the San Jacinto River Basin. The settlement grants the tribe priority access to 9,000 acre-feet per year. The settlement also authorized construction of new water projects to implement the tribe's water rights and permits the tribe to lease water to other users within the specified water management plan area.

- **Crow Tribe Water Rights Settlement Act of 2010,** Pub. L. No. 111-291, 124 Stat. 3064 (2010). In one of the largest water rights settlements ever with the federal government, the principal goal was to rehabilitate and improve the Crow Irrigation Project to provide municipal, rural, and industrial water on the reservation. Although the Act called for compliance with NEPA and the Endangered Species Act, it exempted federal implementation from EIS requirements. It also preserved federal statutes affecting water quality, such as the Clean Water Act, the Safe Drinking Water Act, and CERCLA, and established a Crow Settlement Fund to carry out its provisions. The Act provides that allotment water rights "shall be satisfied from the tribal water rights," and allottees are entitled to "a just and equitable allocation of water for irrigation purposes."

Any land transfers from the tribe necessary to implement the compact will not affect tribal civil and criminal jurisdiction. Lands acquired by the federal government to implement the agreement, however, will become reservation lands held in trust.

The Act required the Tribe to approve a tribal water code to manage, regulate, and govern all tribal water rights consistent with the compact. The code must include a "due process system for the consideration and determination by the Tribe" of allotment water rights. The tribe may lease water consistent with the water code and the compact.

The Act called for a federal management plan to govern streamflows below and lake levels at Yellowtail Dam on the Bighorn River. Any instream flow requirements below the dam are "an obligation on the part of the Tribe to withhold from development or otherwise refrain from diverting or removing [water] from the Bighorn River." The tribe has "the exclusive right to develop and market power generation" from the Yellowtail Afterbay Dam, so long as it constructs power generation facilities within fifteen years.

For descriptions and analysis of the water settlement acts, see Cohen's Handbook of Federal Indian Law § 19.05[2] (Nell Jessup Newton et al., eds. 2012); 2 Waters and Water Rights § 37.04(c)(1) (Amy K. Kelley. ed., 3d ed. LexisNexis/Matthew Bender 2016); Indian Water Rights: An Analysis of Current and Pending Indian Water Rights Settlements (Bureau of Indian Affairs and Confederated Tribes of the Chehalis Reservation 2004). For additional information on tribal water rights settlements, see the Native American Water Rights Database available through the Native American Rights Fund's website: www.narf.org.

If you were representing a tribal client interested in a water rights settlement with the applicable state, what provisions would be important to your client? Does that analysis change if you are representing a state or non-tribal entity in such negotiations? What is the role of water marketing in this analysis? Of federal funding?

3. Non-congressionally-approved settlements. Negotiated settlements may also be concluded without being enacted into law by Congress. For example, see the Klamath Hydroelectric Settlement Agreement (Feb. 18, 2010). Forty-five entities and organizations agreed to 1) support fish production for harvesting in the Klamath Basin; 2) develop reliable water supplies and hydroelectric power sources for use by communities, agriculture, and nearby national wildlife refuges; and 3) increase sustainability in the basin by providing an adequate and consistent amount of water for all agreed-to purposes with the agreement area. This agreement called for removing four hydroelectric dams by 2020 to increase water flow and enhance fish habitat, and restore salmon populations. The Karuk Tribe, Klamath Tribes and Yurok Tribe are parties to this agreement. *See* David N. Allen, *The Klamath Hydroelectric Settlement*

Agreement: Federal Law, Local Compromise, and the Largest Dam Removal Project in History, 16 Hastings W-NW J. Envt'l L. & Pol'y 427 (2010).

Chapter 8

Usufructuary Rights: Hunting, Fishing, and Gathering

Usufructuary rights are use rights, or non-possessory interests in land. That is, they are interests in lands owned by others. Because they are non-possessory does not mean that they are not real property interests, however. The common law has long recognized such interests as real property, labeling them as easements or profits *a prendre*. Easements are rights to cross another's land; profits *a prendre* are rights to go on another's land and take and remove a resource. Off-reservation hunting, fishing, and gathering rights, the subject of this chapter, are therefore profits *a prendre*.

Indian hunting, gathering, and fishing rights are peculiar kinds of profits *a prendre*, however. They were affirmed or recognized by one sovereign for the benefit of another sovereign. Often, their recognition was an essential element of agreements in which Indian peoples ceded vast amounts of lands to the United States, clearing the way for settlement. In the Stevens Treaties of the Pacific Northwest, for example, the tribes explicitly bargained for retention of their hunting, fishing, and gathering rights, because those rights were essential to the native way of life, and because the tribes knew that the relatively small reservations with which the treaties left them did not include many of their hunting, fishing, and gathering places. Therefore, in a very real sense the usufructuary rights the tribes reserved in their treaties were *the* essential consideration for non-Indian settlement.

Recognition and protection of usufructuary rights is a central concern of many tribes today, particularly in the Pacific Northwest and western Great Lakes regions. These reserved rights to hunt, fish, and gather are the means by which tribes maintain traditional cultural practices and often are of great commercial importance as well. Indeed, the world-view of many tribes, even prior to white contact, was premised on a usufructuary view of the universe. Although many tribes had elaborate systems of private rights in land, tribes had generally not conceived of the Anglo-American notion of fee simple absolute land ownership. Instead, the native world was premised on a more complex system of (sometimes conflicting) use rights.

This chapter considers the modern survival of tribal usufructuary rights, their scope and extent, whether they include a right to protect habitat, their regulation, and their loss and diminishment.

A. Off-Reservation Rights

1. Modern Survival of the Rights

Minnesota v. Mille Lacs Band of Chippewa Indians
526 U.S. 172 (1999)

JUSTICE O'CONNOR delivered the opinion of the Court.

In 1837, the United States entered into a Treaty with several Bands of Chippewa Indians. Under the terms of this Treaty, the Indians ceded land in present-day Wisconsin and Minnesota to the United States, and the United States guaranteed to the Indians certain hunting, fishing, and gathering rights on the ceded land. We must decide whether the Chippewa Indians retain these usufructuary rights today. The State of Minnesota argues that the Indians lost these rights through an Executive Order in 1850, an 1855 Treaty, and the admission of Minnesota into the Union in 1858. After an examination of the historical record, we conclude that the Chippewa retain the usufructuary rights guaranteed to them under the 1837 Treaty.

I. A.

In 1837, several Chippewa Bands, including the respondent Bands here, were summoned to Fort Snelling (near present-day St. Paul, Minnesota) for the negotiation of a treaty with the United States. The United States representative at the negotiations, Wisconsin Territorial Governor Henry Dodge, told the assembled Indians that the United States wanted to purchase certain Chippewa lands east of the Mississippi River, lands located in present-day Wisconsin and Minnesota. The Chippewa agreed to sell the land to the United States, but they insisted on preserving their right to hunt, fish, and gather in the ceded territory. In response to this request, Governor Dodge stated that he would "make known to your Great Father, your request to be permitted to make sugar, on the lands; and you will be allowed, during his pleasure, to hunt and fish on them." To these ends, the parties signed a treaty on July 29, 1837. In the first two articles of the 1837 Treaty, the Chippewa ceded land to the United States in return for 20 annual payments of money and goods. The United States also, in the fifth article of the Treaty, guaranteed to the Chippewa the right to hunt, fish, and gather on the ceded lands:

> "The privilege of hunting, fishing, and gathering the wild rice, upon the lands, the rivers and the lakes included in the territory ceded, is guaranteed [sic] to the Indians, during the pleasure of the President of the United States."
> 1837 Treaty with the Chippewa.

In 1842, many of the same Chippewa Bands entered into another Treaty with the United States, again ceding additional lands to the Federal Government in return for annuity payments of goods and money, while reserving usufructuary rights on the ceded lands. 1842 Treaty with the Chippewa. This Treaty, however, also contained a provision providing that the Indians would be ""subject to removal therefrom at the pleasure of the President of the United States." Art. 6.

In the late 1840s, pressure mounted to remove the Chippewa to their unceded lands in the Minnesota Territory.

Whatever the impetus behind the removal effort, President Taylor responded to this pressure by issuing an Executive Order on February 6, 1850. The order provided:

> "The privileges granted temporarily to the Chippewa Indians of the Mississippi, by the Fifth Article of the Treaty made with them on the 29th of July 1837, 'of hunting, fishing and gathering the wild rice, upon the lands, the rivers and the lakes included in the territory ceded' by that treaty to the United States; and the right granted to the Chippewa Indians of the Mississippi and Lake Superior, by the Second Article of the treaty with them of October 4th 1842, of hunting on the territory which they ceded by that treaty, 'with the other usual privileges of occupancy until required to remove by the President of the United States,' are hereby revoked; and all of the said Indians remaining on the lands ceded as aforesaid, are required to remove to their unceded lands."

The officials charged with implementing this order understood it primarily as a removal order, and they proceeded to implement it accordingly.

The Government hoped to entice the Chippewa to remove to Minnesota by changing the location where the annuity payments—the payments for the land cessions—would be made. The Chippewa were to be told that their annuity payments would no longer be made at La Pointe, Wisconsin (within the Chippewa's ceded lands), but, rather, would be made at Sandy Lake, on unceded lands, in the Minnesota Territory. The Government's first annuity payment under this plan, however, ended in disaster. The Chippewa were told they had to be at Sandy Lake by October 25 to receive their 1850 annuity payment. By November 10, almost 4,000 Chippewa had assembled at Sandy Lake to receive the payment, but the annuity goods were not completely distributed until December 2. In the meantime, around 150 Chippewa died in an outbreak of measles and dysentery; another 230 Chippewas died on the winter trip home to Wisconsin.

The Sandy Lake annuity experience intensified opposition to the removal order among the Chippewa as well as among non-Indian residents of the area. In the face of this opposition, Commissioner of Indian Affairs Luke Lea wrote to the Secretary of the Interior recommending that the President's 1850 order be modified to allow the Chippewa "to remain for the present in the country they now occupy." * * * [On August 25, 1851,] the Secretary of the Interior issued the requested authorization, instructing the Commissioner "to suspend the removal of the Chippeway [sic] Indians until the final determination of the President." Commissioner Lea immediately telegraphed the local officials with instructions to "[s]uspend action with reference to the removal of Lake Superior Chippewas for further orders." As the State's own expert historian testified, "[f]ederal efforts to remove the Lake Superior Chippewa to the Mississippi River effectively ended in the summer of 1851."

Although Governor Ramsey still hoped to entice the Chippewa to remove by limiting annuity payments to only those Indians who removed to unceded lands, this plan, too, was quickly abandoned. In 1853, Franklin Pierce became President, and he appointed George Manypenny as Commissioner of Indian Affairs. The new administration reversed Governor Ramsey's policy, and in 1853, annuity payments were once again made within the ceded territory. As Indian Agent Henry Gilbert explained, the earlier "change from La Pointe to [Sandy Lake] was only an incident of the order for removal," thus suggesting that the resumption of the payments at La Pointe was appropriate because the 1850 removal order had been abandoned.

In 1849, white lumbermen built a dam on the Rum River (within the Minnesota portion of the 1837 ceded Territory), and the Mille Lacs Band of Chippewa protested that the dam interfered with its wild rice harvest. This dispute erupted in 1855 when violence broke out between the Chippewa and the lumbermen, necessitating a call for federal troops. In February 1855, the Governor of the Minnesota Territory, Willis Gorman, who also served as the ex officio superintendent of Indian affairs for the Territory, wrote to Commissioner Manypenny about this dispute. In his letter, he noted that "[t]he lands occupied by the timbermen have been surveyed and sold by the United States and the Indians have no other treaty interests *except hunting and fishing.*" (emphasis added). There is no indication that Commissioner Manypenny disagreed with Governor Gorman's characterization of Chippewa treaty rights. In June of the same year, Governor Gorman wrote to Mille Lacs Chief Little Hill that even if the dam was located within the Mille Lacs Reservation under the 1855 Treaty, the dam "was put there long before you had any rights there except to hunt and fish." Thus, as of 1855, the federal official responsible for Indian affairs in the Minnesota Territory acknowledged and recognized Chippewa rights to hunt and fish in the 1837 ceded Territory.

On the other hand, there are statements by federal officials in the late 19th century and the first half of the 20th century that suggest that the Federal Government no longer recognized Chippewa usufructuary rights under the 1837 Treaty.

Although the United States abandoned its removal policy, it did not abandon its attempts to acquire more Chippewa land. * * * [Indian Agent Henry] Gilbert negotiated such a Treaty with several Chippewa Bands, 1854 Treaty with the Chippewa, 10 Stat. 1109, although for reasons now lost to history, the Mille Lacs Band of Chippewa was not a party to this Treaty. The signatory Chippewa Bands ceded additional land to the United States, and certain lands were set aside as reservations for the Bands. In addition, the 1854 Treaty established new hunting and fishing rights in the territory ceded by the Treaty.

When the Senate finally passed the authorizing legislation in December 1854, Minnesota's territorial delegate to Congress recommended to Commissioner Manypenny that he negotiate a treaty with the Mississippi, Pillager, and Lake Winnibigoshish Bands of Chippewa Indians. Commissioner Manypenny summoned representatives of those Bands to Washington, D.C., for the treaty negotiations, which were held in February 1855. The purpose and result of these negotiations was the sale of

Chippewa lands to the United States. To this end, the first article of the 1855 Treaty contains two sentences:

> "The Mississippi, Pillager, and Lake Winnibigoshish bands of Chippewa Indians hereby cede, sell, and convey to the United States all their right, title, and interest in, and to, the lands now owned and claimed by them, in the Territory of Minnesota, and included within the following boundaries, viz: [describing territorial boundaries]. And the said Indians do further fully and entirely relinquish and convey to the United States, any and all right, title, and interest, of whatsoever nature the same may be, which they may now have in, and to any other lands in the Territory of Minnesota or elsewhere."

Article 2 set aside lands in the area as reservations for the signatory tribes. The Treaty, however, makes no mention of hunting and fishing rights, whether to reserve new usufructuary rights or to abolish rights guaranteed by previous treaties. The Treaty Journal also reveals no discussion of hunting and fishing rights.

A little over three years after the 1855 Treaty was signed, Minnesota was admitted to the Union. The admission Act is silent with respect to Indian treaty rights.

B.

In 1990, the Mille Lacs Band of Chippewa Indians and several of its members filed suit in the Federal District Court for the District of Minnesota against the State of Minnesota, the Minnesota Department of Natural Resources, and various state officers (collectively State) seeking, among other things, a declaratory judgment that they retained their usufructuary rights under the 1837 Treaty and an injunction to prevent the State's interference with those rights. The United States intervened as a plaintiff in the suit; nine counties and six private landowners intervened as defendants. * * * [Subsequently,] the District Court permitted several Wisconsin Bands of Chippewa to intervene as plaintiffs.

Simultaneously with this litigation, the Fond du Lac Band of Chippewa Indians and several of its members filed a separate suit against Minnesota state officials, seeking a declaration that they retained their rights to hunt, fish, and gather pursuant to the 1837 and 1854 Treaties. Two Minnesota landowners intervened as defendants.

In both cases, the district court found that the tribes retained their treaty rights to hunt, fish, and gather. The Eighth Circuit affirmed, consistent with a ruling of the Seventh Circuit that the Wisconsin Chippewa bands retained the same rights on ceded land located in Wisconsin. *See Lac Courte Oreilles Band of Lake Superior Chippewa Indians v. Voigt*, 700 F.2d 341 (7th Cir. 1983), *appeal dismissed and cert. denied sub nom. Besadny v. Lac Courte Oreilles Band of Lake Superior Chippewa Indians*, 464 U.S. 805 (1983).

II.

We are first asked to decide whether President Taylor's Executive Order of February 6, 1850, terminated Chippewa hunting, fishing, and gathering rights under the 1837 Treaty. The Court of Appeals began its analysis of this question with a statement of black letter law: "'The President's power, if any, to issue the order must stem either from an act of Congress or from the Constitution itself.'" 124 F.3d, at 915 (quoting *Youngstown Sheet & Tube Co. v. Sawyer*, 343 U.S. 579, 585 (1952)). The court considered whether the President had authority to issue the removal order under the 1830 Removal Act (hereinafter Removal Act). The Removal Act authorized the President to convey land west of the Mississippi to Indian tribes that chose to "exchange the lands where they now reside, and remove there." According to the Court of Appeals, the Removal Act only allowed the removal of Indians who had consented to removal. Because the Chippewa had not consented to removal, according to the court, the Removal Act could not provide authority for the President's 1850 removal order.

In this Court, no party challenges the Court of Appeals' conclusion that the Removal Act did not authorize the President's removal order. The landowners argue that the Removal Act was irrelevant because it applied only to land exchanges, and that even if it required consent for such land exchanges, it did not prohibit other means of removing Indians. We agree that the Removal Act did not forbid the President's removal order, but as noted by the Court of Appeals, it also did not authorize that order.

Because the Removal Act did not authorize the 1850 removal order, we must look elsewhere for a constitutional or statutory authorization for the order. In this Court, only the landowners argue for an alternative source of authority; they argue that the President's removal order was authorized by the 1837 Treaty itself. There is no support for this proposition, however. The Treaty makes no mention of removal, and there was no discussion of removal during the Treaty negotiations. Although the United States could have negotiated a treaty in 1837 providing for removal of the Chippewa—and it negotiated several such removal treaties with Indian tribes in 1837—the 1837 Treaty with the Chippewa did not contain any provisions authorizing a removal order. The silence in the Treaty, in fact, is consistent with the United States' objectives in negotiating it. Commissioner of Indian Affairs Harris explained the United States' goals for the 1837 Treaty in a letter to Governor Dodge on May 13, 1837. In this letter, Harris explained that through this Treaty, the United States wanted to purchase Chippewa land for the pine woods located on it; the letter contains no reference to removal of the Chippewa. Based on the record before us, the proposition that the 1837 Treaty authorized the President's 1850 removal order is unfounded. Because the parties have pointed to no colorable source of authority for the President's removal order, we agree with the Court of Appeals' conclusion that the 1850 removal order was unauthorized.

The State argues that even if the removal portion of the order was invalid, the 1837 Treaty privileges were nevertheless revoked because the invalid removal order was severable from the portion of the order revoking Chippewa usufructuary rights. Although this Court has often considered the severability of statutes, we have never addressed whether Executive Orders can be severed into valid and invalid parts, and if so, what standard should govern the inquiry. In this case, the Court of Appeals assumed that Executive Orders are severable, and that the standards applicable in statutory cases apply without modification in the context of Executive Orders. Because no party before this Court challenges the applicability of these standards, for purposes of this case we shall assume, arguendo, that the severability standard for statutes also applies to Executive Orders.

The inquiry into whether a statute is severable is essentially an inquiry into legislative intent. We stated the traditional test for severability over 65 years ago: "Unless it is evident that the legislature would not have enacted those provisions which are within its power, independently of that which is not, the invalid part may be dropped if what is left is fully operative as a law." *Champlin Refining Co. v. Corporation Comm'n of Okla.*, 286 U.S. 210, 234 (1932). Translated to the present context, we must determine whether the President would not have revoked the 1837 Treaty privileges if he could not issue the removal order.

We think it is clear that President Taylor intended the 1850 order to stand or fall as a whole. The 1850 order embodied a single, coherent policy, the predominant purpose of which was removal of the Chippewa from the lands that they had ceded to the United States. The federal officials charged with implementing the order certainly understood it as such.

When the 1850 order is understood as announcing a removal policy, the portion of the order revoking Chippewa usufructuary rights is seen to perform an integral function in this policy. The order tells the Indians to "go," and also tells them not to return to the ceded lands to hunt and fish. The State suggests that President Taylor might also have revoked Chippewa usufructuary rights as a kind of "incentive program"" to encourage the Indians to remove had he known that he could not order their removal directly. The State points to no evidence, however, that the President or his aides ever considered the abrogation of hunting and fishing rights as an "incentive program." Moreover, the State does not explain how this incentive was to operate. As the State characterizes Chippewa Treaty rights, the revocation of those rights would not have prevented the Chippewa from hunting, fishing, and gathering on the ceded territory; the revocation of Treaty rights would merely have subjected Chippewa hunters, fishers, and gatherers to territorial, and, later, state regulation. The State does not explain how, if the Chippewa were still permitted to hunt, fish, and gather on the ceded territory, the revocation of the Treaty rights would have encouraged the Chippewa to remove to their unceded lands.

There is also no evidence that the Treaty privileges themselves—as opposed to the presence of the Indians—caused any problems necessitating the revocation of those privileges. In other words, there is little historical evidence that the Treaty privileges would have been revoked for some other purpose. The only evidence in this regard is Governor Ramsey's statement to the Minnesota Territorial Legislature that settlers in the Sauk Rapids and Swan River area were complaining about the Chippewa Treaty privileges. But the historical record suggests that the settlers were complaining about the Winnebago Indians, and not the Chippewa, in that area.

We conclude that President Taylor's 1850 Executive Order was ineffective to terminate Chippewa usufructuary rights under the 1837 Treaty. The State has pointed to no statutory or constitutional authority for the President's removal order, and the Executive Order, embodying as it did one coherent policy, is inseverable. We do not mean to suggest that a President, now or in the future, cannot revoke the Chippewa usufructuary rights in accordance with the terms of the 1837 Treaty. All we conclude today is that the President's 1850 Executive Order was insufficient to accomplish this revocation because it was not severable from the invalid removal order.

III.

The State argues that the Mille Lacs Band of Chippewa Indians relinquished its usufructuary rights under the 1855 Treaty with the Chippewa. Specifically, the State argues that the Band unambiguously relinquished its usufructuary rights by agreeing to the second sentence of Article 1 in that Treaty:

> "And the said Indians do further fully and entirely relinquish and convey to the United States, any and all right, title, and interest, of whatsoever nature the same may be, which they may now have in, and to any other lands in the Territory of Minnesota or elsewhere."

This sentence, however, does not mention the 1837 Treaty, and it does not mention hunting, fishing, and gathering rights. The entire 1855 Treaty, in fact, is devoid of any language expressly mentioning—much less abrogating—usufructuary rights. Similarly, the Treaty contains no language providing money for the abrogation of previously held rights. These omissions are telling because the United States treaty drafters had the sophistication and experience to use express language for the abrogation of treaty rights. In fact, just a few months after Commissioner Manypenny completed the 1855 Treaty, he negotiated a Treaty with the Chippewa of Sault Ste. Marie that expressly revoked fishing rights that had been reserved in an earlier Treaty. See Treaty with the Chippewa of Sault Ste. Marie, Art. 1, 11 Stat. 631.

The State argues that despite any explicit reference to the 1837 Treaty rights, or to usufructuary rights more generally, the second sentence of Article 1 nevertheless abrogates those rights. But to determine whether this language abrogates Chippewa Treaty rights, we look beyond the written words to the larger context that frames the Treaty, including "the history of the treaty, the negotiations, and the practical construction adopted by the parties." *Choctaw Nation v. United States*, 318 U.S. 423, 432 (1943). In this case, an examination of the historical record provides insight into how the parties to the Treaty understood the terms of the agreement. This insight is especially helpful to the extent that it sheds light on how the Chippewa signatories to the Treaty understood the agreement because we interpret Indian treaties to give effect to the terms as the Indians themselves would have understood them. *See Washington v. Washington State Commercial Passenger Fishing Vessel Assn.*, 443 U.S. 658, 675–676 (1979); *United States v. Winans*, 198 U.S. 371, 380–381 (1905).

The 1855 Treaty was designed primarily to transfer Chippewa land to the United States, not to terminate Chippewa usufructuary rights. It was negotiated under the authority of the Act of December 19, 1854. This Act authorized treaty negotiations with the Chippewa "for the extinguishment of their title to all the lands owned and claimed by them in the Territory of Minnesota and State of Wisconsin." The Act is silent with respect to authorizing agreements to terminate Indian usufructuary privileges, and this silence was likely not accidental. During Senate debate on the Act, Senator Sebastian, the chairman of the Committee on Indian Affairs, stated that the treaties to be negotiated under the Act would "reserv[e] to them [i.e., the Chippewa] those rights which are secured by former treaties."

In the winter of 1854–1855, Commissioner Manypenny summoned several Chippewa chiefs to Washington, D.C., to begin negotiations over the sale of Chippewa land in Minnesota to the United States. The negotiations ran from February 12 through February 22. Commissioner Manypenny opened the negotiations by telling the Chippewa chiefs that his goal for the negotiations was to buy a portion of their land, and he stayed firm to this proposed course throughout the talks, focusing the discussions on the purchase of Chippewa land. Indeed all of the participants in the negotiations, including the Indians, understood that the purpose of the negotiations was to transfer Indian land to the United States.

Like the authorizing legislation, the Treaty Journal, recording the course of the negotiations themselves, is silent with respect to usufructuary rights. The journal records no discussion of the 1837 Treaty, of hunting, fishing, and gathering rights, or of the abrogation of those rights. This silence suggests that the Chippewa did not understand the proposed Treaty to abrogate their usufructuary rights as guaranteed by other treaties. It is difficult to believe that in 1855, the Chippewa would have agreed to relinquish the usufructuary rights they had fought to preserve in 1837 without at least a passing word about the relinquishment.

After the Treaty was signed, President Pierce submitted it to the Senate for ratification, along with an accompanying memorandum from Commissioner Manypenny describing the Treaty he had just negotiated. Like the Treaty and the Treaty journal, this report is silent about hunting, fishing, and gathering rights.

To summarize, the historical record provides no support for the theory that the second sentence of Article 1 was designed to abrogate the usufructuary privileges guaranteed under the 1837 Treaty, but it does support the theory that the Treaty, and Article 1 in particular, was designed to transfer Chippewa land to the United States. At the very least, the historical record refutes the State's assertion that the 1855 Treaty "unambiguously" abrogated the 1837 hunting, fishing, and gathering privileges. Given this plausible ambiguity, we cannot agree with the State that the 1855 Treaty abrogated Chippewa usufructuary rights. We have held that Indian treaties are to be interpreted liberally in favor of the Indians, and that any ambiguities are to be resolved in their favor.

To attack the conclusion that the 1855 Treaty does not abrogate the usufructuary rights guaranteed under the 1837 Treaty, the State relies primarily on our decision in *Oregon Dept. of Fish and Wildlife v. Klamath Tribe*, 473 U.S. 753 (1985). [The

Klamath decision is excerpted at page 528.] * * * *Klamath* does not control this case. * * * [T]he State's argument that similar language in two Treaties involving different parties has precisely the same meaning reveals a fundamental misunderstanding of basic principles of treaty construction. Our holding in *Klamath* was not based solely on the bare language of the 1901 agreement [that the Tribe agreed to "cede, surrender, grant, and convey to the United States all their claim, right, title and interest in and to" a tract of land that had been erroneously excluded from the reservation]. Rather, to reach our conclusion about the meaning of that language, we examined the historical record and considered the context of the treaty negotiations to discern what the parties intended by their choice of words. This review of the history and the negotiations of the agreements is central to the interpretation of treaties. As we described above, an analysis of the history, purpose, and negotiations of this Treaty leads us to conclude that the Mille Lacs Band did not relinquish their 1837 treaty rights in the 1855 Treaty.

IV.

Finally, the State argues that the Chippewa's usufructuary rights under the 1837 Treaty were extinguished when Minnesota was admitted to the Union in 1858. In making this argument, the State faces an uphill battle. Congress may abrogate Indian treaty rights, but it must clearly express its intent to do so. *United States v. Dion*, 476 U.S. 734, 738–740 (1986); *see also Washington v. Washington State Commercial Passenger Fishing Vessel Assn.*, *supra*, at 690; *Menominee Tribe v. United States*, 391 U.S. 404, 413 (1968). There must be "clear evidence that Congress actually considered the conflict between its intended action on the one hand and Indian treaty rights on the other, and chose to resolve that conflict by abrogating the treaty." *United States v. Dion, supra*, at 740. There is no such "clear evidence" of congressional intent to abrogate the Chippewa Treaty rights here. The relevant statute—Minnesota's enabling Act—provides in relevant part:

> "[T]he State of Minnesota shall be one, and is hereby declared to be one, of the United States of America, and admitted into the Union on an equal footing with the original States in all respects whatever."

This language, like the rest of the Act, makes no mention of Indian treaty rights; it provides no clue that Congress considered the reserved rights of the Chippewa and decided to abrogate those rights when it passed the Act. The State concedes that the Act is silent in this regard, and the State does not point to any legislative history describing the effect of the Act on Indian treaty rights.

With no direct support for its argument, the State relies principally on this Court's decision in *Ward v. Race Horse*, 163 U.S. 504 (1896). In *Race Horse*, we held that a Treaty reserving to a Tribe "'the right to hunt on the unoccupied lands of the United States, so long as game may be found thereon, and so long as peace subsists among the whites and Indians on the borders of the hunting districts'" terminated when Wyoming became a State in 1890. This case does not bear the weight the State places on it, however, because it has been qualified by later decisions of this Court.

The first part of the holding in *Race Horse* was based on the "equal footing doctrine," the constitutional principle that all States are admitted to the Union with the same attributes of sovereignty (i.e., on equal footing) as the original 13 States. As relevant here, it prevents the Federal Government from impairing fundamental attributes of state sovereignty when it admits new States into the Union. According to the *Race Horse* Court, because the Treaty rights conflicted irreconcilably with state regulation of natural resources—"an essential attribute of its governmental existence,"—the Treaty rights were held an invalid impairment of Wyoming's sovereignty. Thus, those rights could not survive Wyoming's admission to the Union on "equal footing" with the original States.

But *Race Horse* rested on a false premise. As this Court's subsequent cases have made clear, an Indian tribe's treaty rights to hunt, fish, and gather on state land are not irreconcilable with a State's sovereignty over the natural resources in the State. *See, e.g., Washington v. Washington State Commercial Passenger Fishing Vessel Assn.*, 443 U.S. 658 (1979). Rather, Indian treaty rights can coexist with state management of natural resources. Although States have important interests in regulating wildlife and natural resources within their borders, this authority is shared with the Federal Government when the Federal Government exercises one of its enumerated constitutional powers, such as treaty making. U.S. Const., Art. VI, cl. 2. *See, e.g., United States v. Winans*, 198 U.S., at 382–384. Here, the 1837 Treaty gave the Chippewa the right to hunt, fish, and gather in the ceded territory free of territorial, and later state, regulation, a privilege that others did not enjoy. Today, this freedom from state regulation curtails the State's ability to regulate hunting, fishing, and gathering by the Chippewa in the ceded lands. But this Court's cases have also recognized that Indian treaty-based usufructuary rights do not guarantee the Indians "absolute freedom" from state regulation. *Oregon Dept. of Fish and Wildlife v. Klamath Tribe*, 473 U.S., at 765, n.16. We have repeatedly reaffirmed state authority to impose reasonable and necessary nondiscriminatory regulations on Indian hunting, fishing, and gathering rights in the interest of conservation. *See Puyallup Tribe v. Department of Game of Wash.*, 391 U.S. 392, 398 (1968); *Washington v. Washington State Commercial Passenger Fishing Vessel Assn., supra*, at 682. This "conservation necessity" standard accommodates both the State's interest in management of its natural resources and the Chippewa's federally guaranteed treaty rights. Thus, because treaty rights are reconcilable with state sovereignty over natural resources, statehood by itself is insufficient to extinguish Indian treaty rights to hunt, fish, and gather on land within state boundaries.

We do not understand Justice Thomas to disagree with this fundamental conclusion. *Race Horse* rested on the premise that treaty rights are irreconcilable with state sovereignty. It is this conclusion—the conclusion undergirding the *Race Horse* Court's equal footing holding—that we have consistently rejected over the years. Justice Thomas's only disagreement is as to the scope of State regulatory authority. His disagreement is premised on a purported distinction between "rights" and "privileges." This Court has never used a distinction between rights and privileges to justify any differences in State regulatory authority. Moreover, as Justice Thomas acknowledges, the starting point for any analysis of these questions is the Treaty language itself. The Treaty must be interpreted in light of the parties' intentions, with any ambiguities resolved in favor of the Indians. There is no evidence that the Chippewa understood any fine legal distinctions between rights and privileges. Moreover, under Justice Thomas's view of the 1837 Treaty, the guarantee of hunting, fishing, and gathering privileges was essentially an empty promise because it gave the Chippewa nothing that they did not already have.

The equal footing doctrine was only part of the holding in *Race Horse*, however. We also announced an alternative holding: The Treaty rights at issue were not intended to survive Wyoming's statehood. We acknowledged that Congress, in the exercise of its authority over territorial lands, has the power to secure off-reservation usufructuary rights to Indian Tribes through a treaty, and that "it would be also within the power of Congress to continue them in the State, on its admission into the Union." We also acknowledged that if Congress intended the rights to survive statehood, there was no need for Congress to preserve those rights explicitly in the statehood Act. We concluded, however, that the particular rights in the treaty at issue there — "the right to hunt on the unoccupied lands of the United States" — were not intended to survive statehood.

The Chief Justice reads *Race Horse* to establish a rule that "temporary and precarious" treaty rights, as opposed to treaty rights "which were 'of such a nature as to imply their perpetuity,'" are not intended to survive statehood. But the "temporary and precarious" language in *Race Horse* is too broad to be useful in distinguishing rights that survive statehood from those that do not. In *Race Horse*, the Court concluded that the right to hunt on federal lands was temporary because Congress could terminate the right at any time by selling the lands. Under this line of reasoning, any right created by operation of federal law could be described as "temporary and precarious," because Congress could eliminate the right whenever it wished. In other words, the line suggested by *Race Horse* is simply too broad to be useful as a guide to whether treaty rights were intended to survive statehood.

The focus of the *Race Horse* inquiry is whether Congress (more precisely, because this is a treaty, the Senate) intended the rights secured by the 1837 Treaty to survive statehood. The 1837 Treaty itself defines the circumstances under which the rights would terminate: when the exercise of those rights was no longer the "pleasure of the President." There is no suggestion in the Treaty that the President would have to conclude that the privileges should end when a State was established in the area. Moreover, unlike the rights at issue in *Race Horse*, there is no fixed termination point to the 1837 Treaty rights. The Treaty in *Race Horse* contemplated that the rights would continue only so long as the hunting grounds remained unoccupied and owned by the United States; the happening of these conditions was "clearly contemplated" when the Treaty was ratified. By contrast, the 1837 Treaty does not tie the duration of the rights to the occurrence of some clearly contemplated event. Finally, we note that there is nothing inherent in the nature of reserved treaty rights to suggest that they can be extinguished by implication at statehood. Treaty rights are not impliedly terminated upon statehood. The *Race Horse* Court's decision to the contrary—that Indian treaty rights were impliedly repealed by Wyoming's statehood Act—was informed by that Court's conclusion that the Indian treaty rights were inconsistent with state sovereignty over natural resources and thus that Congress (the Senate) could not have intended the rights to survive statehood. But as we described above, Indian treaty-based usufructuary rights are not inconsistent with state sovereignty over natural resources. Thus, contrary to the State's contentions, *Race Horse* does not compel the conclusion that Minnesota's admission to the Union extinguished Chippewa usufructuary rights guaranteed by the 1837 Treaty.

Accordingly, the judgment of the United States Court of Appeals for the Eighth Circuit is affirmed.

CHIEF JUSTICE REHNQUIST, with whom JUSTICE SCALIA, JUSTICE KENNEDY and JUSTICE THOMAS join, dissenting.

The Court holds that the various Bands of Chippewa Indians retain a usufructuary right granted to them in an 1837 Treaty. To reach this result, the Court must successively conclude that: (1) an 1850 Executive Order explicitly revoking the privilege as authorized by the 1837 Treaty was unlawful; (2) an 1855 Treaty under which certain Chippewa Bands ceded "all" interests to the land does not include the treaty right to come onto the land and hunt; and (3) the admission of Minnesota into the Union in 1858 did not terminate the discretionary hunting privilege, despite established precedent of this Court to the contrary. Because I believe that each one of these three conclusions is demonstrably wrong, I dissent.

I.

I begin with the text of the Treaty negotiated in 1837. In that Treaty, the Chippewa ceded land to the United States in exchange for specified consideration. Article 1 of the Treaty describes the land ceded by the Chippewa to the United States. Article 2 of the 1837 Treaty provides * * * [that] in exchange for the land cessions, the Chippewa agreed to receive an annuity payment of money, goods, and the implements necessary for creating blacksmith's shops and farms, for a limited duration of 20 years. * * * [Article 5, quoted in the Court's opinion, guarantees the "privilege of hunting, fishing, and gathering the wild rice" on the ceded lands "during the pleasure of the President of the United States."]

Thus, the Treaty by its own plain terms provided for a quid pro quo: Land was ceded in exchange for a 20-year annuity of money and goods. Additionally, the United States granted the Chippewa a quite limited "privilege" to hunt and fish, "guarantied . . . during the pleasure of the President."

II.

In 1850, President Taylor expressly terminated the 1837 Treaty privilege by Executive Order. * * * In deciding that this seemingly ironclad revocation was not effective as a matter of law, the Court rests its analysis on four findings. * * * I shall address each of these dubious findings in turn.

The Court's first proposition is the seemingly innocuous statement that a President's Executive Order must be authorized by law in order to have any legal effect. In so doing, the Court quotes our decision in *Youngstown Sheet & Tube Co. v. Sawyer*, 343 U.S. 579, 585 (1952), which held that President Truman's seizure of the steel mills by Executive Order during the Korean War was unlawful. However, the Court neglects to note that treaties, every bit as much as statutes, are sources of law and may also authorize Executive actions. *See Dames & Moore v. Regan*, 453 U.S. 654, 680 (1981). In *Dames & Moore*, we noted that where the President acts with the implied consent of Congress in his Executive actions, "he exercises not only his own powers but also those delegated by Congress," and that such an action was entitled to high deference as to its legality. This case involves an even stronger case for deference to Executive power than *Dames & Moore*, in which Presidential power under an Executive agreement was impliedly authorized by Congress, because the Executive Order in this case was issued pursuant to a Treaty ratified by the advice and consent of the Senate, and thus became the supreme law of the land. The Court's contrary conclusion is simply wrong.

The Court's second assumption is that the Executive Order was a "removal order"—that its primary purpose was the removal of the Chippewa. This assumption rests upon scattered historical evidence that, in the Court's view, "[t]he officials charged with implementing this order understood it primarily as a removal order, and they moved to implement it accordingly." Regardless of what the President's remote frontier agents may have thought, the plain meaning of the text of President Taylor's order can only support the opposite conclusion. The structure of the Executive Order is not that of a removal order, with the revocation of the hunting privileges added merely as an afterthought. Instead, the first part of the order (not to mention the bulk of its text) deals with the extinguishment of the Indians' privilege to enter onto the lands ceded to the United States and hunt. Only then (and then only in its final five words) does the Executive Order require the Indians to "remove to their unceded lands."

If the structure and apparent plain meaning of the Executive Order reveal that the order was primarily a revocation of the privilege to hunt during the President's pleasure, what then should we make of the fact that the officials charged with "implementing" the order viewed their task as primarily effecting removal? The answer is simple. First, the bulk of the Executive Order that terminates the hunting privilege was self-executing. Second, while the President could terminate the legal right (i.e., the privilege to enter onto the ceded lands and hunt) without taking enforcement action, a removal order would require actual implementation. The historical evidence cited by the Court is best understood thus as an implementation of President Taylor's unequivocal (and legally effective) termination of the usufructuary privileges. But while the removal portion may have required implementation to be effective, this cannot turn the Executive Order into a "removal order." And even if the President's agents viewed the order as a removal order (a proposition for which the historical evidence is far more ambiguous than the Court admits), their interpretation is not binding on this Court; nor should it be, since the agents had nothing to do with the bulk of the order which terminated the Treaty privileges.

The Court's third finding is that the removal portion of the order is invalid because President Taylor had no authority to order removal. Although the Court sensibly concludes that the Removal Act of 1830 is inapplicable to this case, it then curiously rejects the notion that the 1837 Treaty authorizes removal, largely on the grounds that "[t]he Treaty makes no mention of removal." The Court is correct that the Treaty does not mention removal, but this is because the Treaty was essentially a deed of conveyance— it transferred land to the United States in exchange for goods and money. After the Treaty was executed and ratified, the ceded lands belonged to the United States, and the only real property interest in the land remaining to the Indians was the privilege to come onto it and hunt during the pleasure of the President. When the President terminated that privilege (a legal act that the Court appears to concede he had a right to make), he terminated the Indians' right to come onto the ceded lands and hunt. The Indians had no legal right to remain on the ceded lands for that purpose, and the removal portion of the order should be viewed in this context. Indeed, the Indians then had no legal rights at all with respect to the ceded lands, in which all title was vested in the United States. And this Court has long held that the President has the implied power to administer the public lands. Dealing with persons whose legal right to come onto the lands and hunt had been extinguished would appear to fall squarely under this power. Whether the President chose to enforce his revocation through an order to leave the land or the ambiguous lesser "measures to ensure that the Chippewa were not hunting, fishing, or gathering" proposed by the Court, is not ours to second-guess a century and a half later. Indeed, although the Court appears to concede that the President had the power to enforce the revocation order, it is difficult to imagine what steps he could have taken to prevent hunting other than ordering the Chippewa not to come onto the land for that purpose. The ceded lands were not a national park, nor did the President have an army of park rangers available to guard Minnesota's wildlife from Chippewa poachers. Removal was the only viable option in enforcing his power under the Treaty to terminate the hunting privilege. Thus, in my view, the final part of the Executive Order discussing removal was lawful.

The fourth element essential to today's holding is the conclusion that if the final part of the Executive Order requiring removal were not authorized, the bulk of the order would fail as not severable.

* * *Even if I were to assume that the President were without authority to order removal, I would conclude that the removal provision is severable from that terminating the Treaty privileges.

Rather than engage in the flawed analysis put forward by the Court, I would instead hold that the Executive Order constituted a valid revocation of the Chippewa's hunting and fishing privileges. Pursuant to a Treaty, the President terminated the Indians' hunting and fishing privileges in an Executive Order which stated, in effect, that the privilege to come onto federal lands and hunt was terminated, and that the Indians move themselves from those lands.

III.

Although I believe that the clear meaning of the Executive Order is sufficient to resolve this case, and that it is unnecessary to address the Court's treatment of the 1855 Treaty and the 1858 admission of Minnesota to the Union, I shall briefly express my strong disagreement with the Court's analysis on these issues also.

As the Court notes, in 1855, several of the Chippewa Bands agreed, in exchange for further annuity payments of money and goods, to "fully and entirely relinquish and convey to the United States, any and all right, title, and interest, of whatsoever nature the same may be, which they now have in, and to any other lands in the Territory of Minnesota or elsewhere." The plain meaning of this provision is a relinquishment of the Indians of "all" rights to the land. The Court, however, interprets this provision in a manner contrary to its plain meaning by first noting that the provision does not mention "usufructuary" rights. It argues, citing examples, that since the United States "had the sophistication and experience to use express language for the abrogation of treaty rights," but did not mention the 1837 Treaty rights in drafting this language, it perhaps did not intend to extinguish those rights, thus creating an interpretation at odds with the Treaty's language. Then, using our canons of construction that ambiguities in treaties are often resolved in favor of the Indians, it concludes that the Treaty did not apply to the hunting rights.

I think this conclusion strained, indeed. First, the language of the Treaty is so broad as to encompass "all" interests in land possessed or claimed by the Indians. Second, while it is important to the Court that the Treaty "is devoid of any language expressly mentioning—much less abrogating—usufructuary rights," the definition of "usufructuary rights" explains further why this is so. Usufructuary rights are "a real right of limited duration on the property of another." *See* Black's Law Dictionary 1544 (6th ed. 1990). It seems to me that such a right would fall clearly under the sweeping language of the Treaty under any reasonable interpretation, and that this is not a case where "even 'learned lawyers' of the day would probably have offered differing interpretations of the [treaty language]." *Cf. Washington v. Washington State Commercial Passenger Fishing Vessel Assn.*, 443 U.S. 658, 677 (1979). And third, although the Court notes that in other treaties the United States sometimes expressly mentioned cessions of usufructuary rights, there was no need to do so in this case, because the settled expectation of the United States was that the 1850 Executive Order had terminated the hunting rights of the Chippewa. Thus, rather than applying the plain and unequivocal language of the 1855 Treaty, the Court holds that "all" does not in fact mean "all."

IV.

Finally, I note my disagreement with the Court's treatment of the equal footing doctrine, and its apparent overruling sub silentio of a precedent of 103 years' vintage. In *Ward v. Race Horse*, 163 U.S. 504 (1896), we held that a Treaty granting the Indians "the right to hunt on the unoccupied lands of the United States, so long as game may be found thereon, and so long as peace subsists among the whites and the

Indians on the borders of the hunting districts" did not survive the admission of Wyoming to the Union since the Treaty right was "temporary and precarious."

But the Court, in a feat of jurisprudential legerdemain, effectively overrules *Ward* sub silentio. First, the Court notes that Congress may only abrogate Indian treaty rights if it clearly expresses its intent to do so. Next, it asserts that Indian hunting rights are not irreconcilable with state sovereignty, and determines that "because treaty rights are reconcilable with state sovereignty over natural resources, statehood by itself is insufficient to extinguish Indian treaty rights to hunt, fish, and gather on land within state boundaries." And finally, the Court hints that *Ward* rested on an incorrect premise—that Indian rights were inconsistent with state sovereignty.

Without saying so, this jurisprudential bait-and-switch effectively overrules *Ward*, a case which we reaffirmed as recently as 1985 in *Oregon Dept. of Fish and Wildlife v. Klamath Tribe*, 473 U.S. 753 (1985). *Ward* held merely that treaty rights which were only "temporary and precarious," as opposed to those which were "of such a nature as to imply their perpetuity," do not survive statehood. Here, the hunting privileges were clearly, like those invalidated in *Ward*, temporary and precarious: The privilege was only guaranteed "during the pleasure of the President"; the legally enforceable annuity payments themselves were to terminate after 20 years; and the Indians were on actual notice that the President might end the rights in the future.

Perhaps the strongest indication of the temporary nature of the Treaty rights is presented unwittingly by the Court in its repeated (and correct) characterizations of the rights as "usufructuary." As noted *supra*, usufructuary rights are by definition "of limited duration." Thus, even if the Executive Order is invalid; and even if the 1855 Treaty did not cover the usufructuary rights: Under *Ward*, the temporary and precarious Treaty privileges were eliminated by the admission of Minnesota to the Union on an equal footing in 1858. Today the Court appears to invalidate (or at least substantially limit) *Ward*, without offering any principled reason to do so.

V.

The Court today invalidates for no principled reason a 149-year-old Executive Order, ignores the plain meaning of a 144-year-old treaty provision, and overrules sub silentio a 103-year-old precedent of this Court. I dissent.

JUSTICE THOMAS, dissenting.

I join The Chief Justice's dissent, but also write separately because contrary to the majority's assertion, in dicta, our prior cases do not dictate the conclusion that the 1837 Treaty curtails Minnesota's regulatory authority. [Justice Thomas based this conclusion on the language in the 1837 Treaty, which reserved only "privileges," not "rights."]

Notes

1. Treaty rights and the equal footing doctrine. In *Ward v. Race Horse*, 163 U.S. 504 (1896), the Court held that the admission of Wyoming into the Union terminated the Crow Tribe's off-reservation hunting rights because of the equal footing doctrine, which guarantees new states sovereignty equal to the original states. The *Race Horse* Court thought that survival of the tribe's off-reservation hunting right after statehood would conflict with Wyoming's sovereignty. Justice O'Connor's opinion in *Mille Lacs*, however, made clear that *Race Horse*'s assumption of this conflict was based on false premises because off-reservation treaty rights and state regulation can and do in fact co-exist. Thus, the Mille Lacs' off-reservation rights survived Minnesota statehood. But did the Court in *Mille Lacs* overrule *Race Horse*?

2. **The canons of treaty construction.** Both the majority and Chief Justice Rehnquist's four-member dissent emphasize the canons of treaty construction. Thus, all nine members of the Supreme Court seemed to agree that courts should employ the canons to interpret treaties. How then did the dissent conclude that the Mille Lacs' usufructuary rights were terminated?

3. **The relationship between land cessions and usufructuary rights.** The *Mille Lacs* Court ruled that the band's usufructuary rights survived the 1855 Treaty with the Chippewa, in which the tribe agreed to "fully and entirely relinquish and convey to the United States, any and all right, title, and interest, of whatsoever nature . . . to other lands in the Territory of Minnesota and elsewhere." Despite this apparently categorical relinquishment, the Court held that the band's usufructuary rights were not extinguished because they were not mentioned in the treaty language or negotiations, and the band would not have understood that the treaty meant to terminate its hunting and fishing rights. The Court also reiterated that "Indian treaties are to be interpreted liberally in favor of the Indians, and . . . any ambiguities are to be resolved in their favor." Thus, the canons of treaty construction counsel that generic land cessions do not extinguish unmentioned tribal usufructuary rights. This result appears to be consistent with *United States ex rel. Hualpai Indians v. Santa Fe Pacific Railroad Co.*, excerpted at page 170, which held that unrecognized aboriginal title may survive land conveyances from the United States to non-Indians. In light of that result, it seems logical that usufructuary rights recognized in treaties and other instruments must survive statutes that diminish treaty boundaries unless Congress specifically terminated those rights. Notice, however, that the rule for extinguishing sovereign authority may be different than the rule for extinguishing property rights. See *South Dakota v. Yankton Sioux Tribe*, 522 U.S. 329 (1998), excerpted at page 138. Why should this be so?

In 2009, the Sixth Circuit held that removal terminated a tribe's fishing rights. *Ottawa Tribe of Oklahoma v. Logan,* 577 F.3d 634 (6th Cir. 2009). The Ottawa Tribe of Oklahoma argued that it retained treaty rights to fish in Lake Erie, its ancestral waters. The district court rejected the tribe's argument based on its interpretation of an 1831 removal treaty, which terminated "the privileges of every description" held under a series of earlier treaties. The Sixth Circuit affirmed, but based on a 1795 treaty and an interpretation of that treaty by the U.S. Supreme Court in *Williams v. City of Chicago*, 242 U.S. 434 (1917), which involved a tribal claim to the filled lakebed of Lake Michigan. The appeals court interpreted *Williams* to hold that the treaty gave the tribes only a "right of continued occupancy" which ended when the tribe "abandoned" its territory under congressional removal statutes. A concurrence suggested that the result could have been different had the tribe been able to show, based on the historical record, that it understood its fishing rights to be "a separate bundle of rights from its right to occupy land associated with those rights," noting that under the Supreme Court's *Mille Lacs* decision, usufructuary rights may exist apart from occupancy rights

4. Usufructs as real property interests. The Chief Justice's dissent in *Mille Lacs*, like the majority opinion, acknowledged the band's usufructuary rights to be real property interests. ("After the Treaty was executed and ratified, the only real property interest in the land remaining to the Indians was the privilege to come onto it and hunt during the pleasure of the President.") But the Chief Justice, relying on Black's Law Dictionary, mischaracterized usufructuary rights as "right[s] of limited duration in the land of another." In truth, usufructuary rights may be of limited duration, or they may be perpetual, depending on the intent of the parties to the agreement. *See* Tiffany on Real Property § 839, at 429 (3rd ed. 1939); *see also* Restatement of Property: Servitudes §§ 4.1, 4.3 (2000). The only express temporal condition on the usufructuary rights in the Chippewa treaty of 1837 was "at the pleasure of the President."

5. "At the pleasure of the President." The majority opinion did not consider the meaning of this term because the issues before the Court were (1) whether the 1850 removal order was lawful, (2) whether the 1855 treaty terminated the usufructs, and (3) whether statehood terminated them. However, the Seventh Circuit, in another case interpreting the 1837 Chippewa treaty, construed this language "not [to] confer the unlimited discretion it appears to; rather, it required the Indians be denied their usufructuary privileges only if the Indians were instrumental in causing disturbances with the white settlers," because that is how the Indians understood the treaty language. *Lac Courte Oreilles Band of Lake Superior Chippewa Indians v. Voigt*, 700 F.2d 341, 357 (7th Cir. 1983). Other defeasible usufructuary rights are considered *infra* at section 2, page 482.

Note on the Non-Indian Backlash

The federal courts' recognition of tribal treaty rights, in particular treaty fishing rights, has been an emotional issue in both the Pacific Northwest and the western Great Lakes, leading in both areas to a non-Indian backlash. In Wisconsin, much of the non-Indian animosity focused on the practice of spear fishing. Spear fishing is a traditional practice of the Chippewa, and takes place on inland lakes in the spring, as soon as the ice melts, during the short spawning season. Spear fishing takes place at night; spearers stand in small boats or canoes, use a light to attract the fish near the surface, and then use a long five-tine spear to take the fish. Today, spearers usually wear a miner's hat with a light attached. Historically, flaming torches provided light. The Chippewa band most involved in spear fishing today, the Lac du Flambeau Band, was probably so named by French explorers because of its spear fishing practice.

Following the 1988 spear fishing season, a northern Wisconsin resident named Dean Crist formed Stop Treaty Abuse (STA). The stated purpose of the organization was to stop Chippewa members from exercising their off-reservation treaty rights to take fish by net and spear. To that end, STA organized protests at the landings from which spear fishing boats are launched. During 1989 and 1990, some of these protests attracted as many as 1000 to 3000 protestors.

The following excerpt is the federal district court's findings of fact concerning incidents at landings and on lakes, not including incidents involving Crist:

> On the lakes where plaintiffs and other tribal members speared in 1989, 1990 and 1991, protesters used high-powered motorboats to create wakes and rock the boats in which spearers were standing, threw stones at the spearers who were trying to launch their boats from the landings, crowded the landings to try to prevent spearers from getting their boats to the water, encircled the launch areas with their motor boats to interfere with the spearers' efforts to launch their boats and move them away from the landings, taunted and threatened spearers and their supporters, yelled racial and sexual insults, shined lights in the eyes of spearers as they were spearing, and mocked the religious and cultural significance of spearing. Often, protesters threw rocks that struck spearers and caused injury. At one lake, protesters used slingshots to hurl rocks at spearers. At another lake, a protester struck a spearer with a fishing lure he cast at the spearer. This interference and harassment took place despite the presence at the lakes of numerous law enforcement officers recruited from the entire state and mobilized into an emergency force for the spearing season and despite the establishment of fenced-off areas intended to separate protesters and supporters from the boat launching areas.
>
> At landings where plaintiffs speared in 1989 and 1990, protesters yelled such comments as, "All you Indians that are on welfare" or "All you Indians that are filling up our jails" and asked Indian women at the landings, "What do you use that spawn for, to douche?" Indians with long hair were called "Tonto" or "redskin." Protesters asked spearers where they got their boats and trailers and made statements to the effect that taxpayers had paid for the boats. At Arbor Vitae Lake, protesters sang a variation of the song, "Tom Dooley," to plaintiff Tom Maulson as he tried to spear: "Hang down your head, Tom Maulson, hang down your head and die." At many landings, STA board member Al Soik and his wife Elaine Soik beat on drums to the chant of "Hey, how are ya? Hey, how are ya?" in mockery of an Indian chant. On several occasions, Elaine Soik wrapped a bandanna around her head, stuck a twig in her hair as a feather, and caricatured an Indian ceremonial dance. On Minocqua Lake, STA leader Jack Lanta stated, "Niggers are better than Indians." At Big Arbor Vita, Jack Lanta said, "Those Indians are all on welfare that are out there spearing." At one landing, protesters commented in reference to some young Indian men who had brought drums to the landing, "The hardest work they've ever done in their life is pounding on that drum."

On one occasion on Trout Lake, STA leader Howie Caputo yelled, "Go home, timber niggers" to plaintiff Maulson while circling Maulson's spearing boat in his own motorboat. Other STA members made comments to the effect that Indians couldn't find their food stamps because they kept them under their work boots. Members of STA, including board member Tommy Handrick, frequently called spearers "welfare warriors," "wagon burners" and "timber niggers." At Squirrel, Willow Springs and Namekagon lakes, protesters yelled, "Timber nigger" and "You're a defeated people; you are a conquered people." At Sand and Dam Lake, protesters chanted, "Spear an Indian, save a walleye. Drown 'em, drown 'em." Especially during the 1990 spearing season, it was customary to reserve the derogatory chants until after 10:30 p.m., by which time most of the press and camera crews had left the landings.

Protesters yelled, "Dead Indian, dead Indian" and sang, "A half breed here; a half breed there," to the tune of "Old McDonald had a farm." At Eau Pleine Reservoir, they referred to Indian women as squaws and bitches and said, "The only good Indian is a dead Indian." In 1989, they said that "Custer had the right idea" and "Tom Maulson is nothing but a fucking Jew. We need another Hitler to take care of him."

At numerous landings, protesters came up to spearing supporter Anita Koser and talked about stabbing her in the back. Protesters made such statements as "Wait until the lights go out. Then we're going to have some fun"; "If those law enforcement officers weren't there, we'd really have some fun" and "You're not going to go home tonight except in a body bag." Protesters told plaintiff Hockings "You're not going to get home tonight. You're not going to get off the boat landing. You're not going to get off the water. I'll shoot you in the back of the head."

Lac du Flambeau Band of Lake Superior Chippewa Indians v. Stop Treaty Abuse-Wisconsin, Inc., 843 F.Supp. 1284, 1288–89 (W.D. Wis. 1994).

Based on these incidents and others involving Crist, the court held that the defendants had violated the plaintiffs' civil rights under 42 U.S.C. § 1982. The court decided that 1) the defendants had interfered with plaintiffs' property right (the treaty right to fish), 2) the interference was motivated by racial prejudice, and 3) the interference would not have occurred but for the prejudice. The Seventh Circuit affirmed both the district court's award of a permanent injunction and its award to the plaintiffs of more than $240,000 in attorneys' fees. *Lac du Flambeau Band of Lake Superior Chippewa Indians v. Stop Treaty Abuse-Wisconsin, Inc.*, 41 F.3d 1190 (7th Cir. 1994).

The following case is an unusual one in that the survival of native usufructuary rights is due not to the language and interpretation of a treaty, but to state constitutional language. Hawaiian native rights are complex and deeply entwined with Hawaiian history See Cohen's Handbook of Federal Indian Law § 4.07[4] (Nell

Jessup Newton, et al. eds. 2012). Here we concentrate only on the following case, which interprets the meaning of the state constitutional promise to "protect all rights, customarily and traditionally exercised for subsistence, cultural, and religious purposes."

Public Access Shoreline Hawaii (PASH) v. Hawai'i County Planning Commission
903 P.2d 1246 (Haw. 1995)

KLEIN, Justice.

[T]his case . . . concerns a challenge by Public Access Shoreline Hawaii (PASH) and Angel Pilago to the Hawai'i County Planning Commission's (HPC) decision denying them standing to participate in a contested case hearing on an application by Nansay Hawai'i, Inc. (Nansay) for a Special Management Area (SMA) use permit.

In order to pursue development of a resort complex on land within a SMA on the island of Hawai'i (Big Island), Nansay applied to the HPC for a SMA use permit. PASH, an unincorporated public interest membership organization based in Kailua-Kona, and Pilago opposed the issuance of the permit and requested contested case hearings before the HPC. The HPC denied the requests on the ground that, under its rules, neither PASH nor Pilago had standing to participate in a contested case. The HPC subsequently issued a SMA use permit to Nansay.

The HPC received a SMA use permit application from Nansay for a resort development on the Big Island. Nansay sought approval of its plans to develop a community complex including: two resort hotels with over 1,000 rooms; 330 multiple family residential units; 380 single family homes; a golf course; a health club; restaurants; retail shops; an artisan village; a child care center; and other infrastructure and improvements over a 450 acre shoreline area in the ahupua'a of Kohanaiki on the Big Island. On September 28, 1990, the HPC held a public hearing on Nansay's permit application, as required by the agency's rules.

* * * Although the HPC Rules allow formal intervention through specified procedures, PASH was denied standing to participate in a contested case hearing because the agency found that its asserted interests were "substantially similar" to those of the general public. The HPC's restrictive interpretation of standing requirements is not entitled to deference. * * * Accordingly, we review *de novo* whether PASH has demonstrated its interests were injured.

* * * Through unrefuted testimony, PASH sufficiently demonstrated that its members, as "native Hawaiian[s] who [have] exercised such rights as were customarily and traditionally exercised for subsistence, cultural, and religious purposes on undeveloped lands[,] [have] an interest in a proceeding for the approval of [a SMA permit] for the development of lands within the ahupua'a which are [sic] clearly distinguishable from that of the general public."

IV. THE OBLIGATION TO PRESERVE AND PROTECT CULTURAL AND HISTORIC RESOURCES

* * * [T]he HPC is obligated to protect customary and traditional rights to the extent feasible under the Hawai'i Constitution and relevant statutes. Article XII, section 7 of the Hawai'i Constitution (1978) provides:

"The State reaffirms and *shall protect all rights, customarily and traditionally exercised for subsistence, cultural and religious purposes* and possessed by ahupua'a tenants who are descendants of native Hawaiians who inhabited the Hawaiian Islands prior to 1778, *subject to the right of the State to regulate such rights.*"

(Emphasis added.) HRS § 1-1 (Supp. 1992) provides:

"The common law of England, as ascertained by English and American decisions, is declared to be the common law of the State of Hawai'i in all cases, except as otherwise expressly provided by the Constitution or laws of the United States, or by the laws of the State, or fixed by Hawaiian judicial precedent, *or established by Hawaiian usage*; provided that no person shall be subject to criminal proceedings except as provided by the written laws of the United States or of the State."

(Emphasis added.)

The aforementioned provisions were discussed by this court, in the context of an individual's asserted gathering rights, in *Kalipi v. Hawaiian Trust Co.*, 656 P.2d 745 (Hawaii 1982). Ten years later, in *Pele Defense Fund v. Paty*, we recognized that ancient Hawaii gathering rights may have extended beyond the boundaries of individual ahupua'a in certain cases. 837 P.2d at 1272 (Hawaii 1992). Nevertheless, neither *Kalipi* nor *Pele* precluded further inquiry concerning the extent that traditional practices have endured under the laws of this State.

[The court discussed *Kalipi*, in which it ruled that the state did not extinguish traditional native gathering rights protected by Article XII, section 7 of the Hawaiian Constitution by conveying or recognizing private fee simple ownership of land. So long as the land was "undeveloped" and the gathering produced "no actual harm," residents of an ahupua'a* could enter private property to gather traditional items for subsistence, cultural, or religious purposes. In *Pele*, the court extended traditional access and gathering rights beyond the *ahupua'a* in which the gatherer resides.]

* * * Traditional and customary rights are properly examined against the law of property as it has developed in this state. Thus, the regulatory power provided in article XII, section 7 does not justify summary extinguishment of such rights by the State merely because they are deemed inconsistent with generally understood elements of the western doctrine of "property."

---

* [An *ahupua'a* is a land division extending from the mountains to the sea along natural features and accounting for traditional cultural uses. — Eds.]

4. *The development of private property rights in Hawai'i*

Some of the generally understood western concepts of property rights were discussed in *Reppun v. Board of Water Supply*, 656 P.2d 57, 68 (Hawaii 1982).

> The western doctrine of "property" has traditionally implied certain rights. Among these are the right to the use of the property, the right to exclude others[,] and the right to transfer the property with the consent of the "owner". In conformance with creation of private interests in land, each of these rights were embodied in the delineation of post-[Mahele] judicial water rights. Ostensibly, this judge-made system of rights was an outgrowth of Hawaiian custom in dealing with water. However, the creation of private and exclusive interests in water, within a context of western concepts of property, compelled the drawing of fixed lines of authority and interests which were not consonant with Hawaiian custom."

Although the court in *Reppun* focused on interests in water, its discussion of the development of Hawaiian property rights is enlightening.

Our examination of the relevant legal developments in Hawaiian history leads us to the conclusion that the western concept of exclusivity is not universally applicable in Hawai'i. In other words, the issuance of a Hawaiian land patent confirmed a limited property interest as compared with typical land patents governed by western concepts of property. Cf. *United States v. Winans*, 198 U.S. 371 (1905) (observing that the United States Congress was competent "to secure to the Indians such a remnant of the great rights they possessed").

Although this premise clearly conflicts with common "understandings of property" and could theoretically lead to disruption, the non-confrontational aspects of traditional Hawaiian culture should minimize potential disturbances. In any event, we reiterate that the State retains the ability to reconcile competing interests under article XII, section 7. We stress that unreasonable or non-traditional uses are not permitted under today's ruling. *See, e.g., Winans* (noting that the trial court found "that it would not be justified in issuing process to compel the defendants to permit the Indians to *make a camping ground of their property while engaged in fishing*") (emphasis added).

There should be little difficulty accommodating the customary and traditional Hawaiian rights asserted in the instant case with Nansay's avowed purposes. A community development proposing to integrate cultural education and recreation with tourism and community living represents a promising opportunity to demonstrate the continued viability of Hawaiian land tenure ideals in the modern world.

5. *Customary Rights under Hawai'i law*

The *Kalipi* court properly recognized that "all the requisite elements of the doctrine of custom were [not] necessarily incorporated in § 1-1." Accordingly, HRS § 1-1 represents the codification of the doctrine of custom *as it applies in our State*. One of the most dramatic differences in the application of custom in Hawai'i is that passage of HRS § 1-1's predecessor fixed November 25, 1892 as the date Hawaiian usage must have been established in practice.

Other differences in the doctrine's applicability are readily discernible. For example, under English common law, "a custom for every inhabitant of an ancient messuage [meaning "[d]welling-house with the adjacent buildings and curtilage[,]" see *Black's Legal Dictionary* 990 (6th ed.1990) within a parish to take a profit a prendre in the land of an individual is bad." Blackstone's Commentaries, at 78 n.18. Strict application of the English common law, therefore, would apparently have precluded the exercise of traditional Hawaiian gathering rights. As such, this element of the doctrine of custom could not apply in Hawai'i.

In light of the confusion surrounding the nature and scope of customary Hawaiian rights under HRS § 1-1, the following subsections of this opinion discuss applicable requirements for establishing such rights in the instant case.

a.

Nansay argues that the recognition of rights exercised by persons who do not actually reside in the subject ahupua'a "represents such a departure from existing law . . . [that *Pele*] should be overruled or strictly limited to its specific facts." Nansay contends further that *Pele* is inconsistent with the fundamental nature of Hawaiian land tenure, which allegedly recognizes only three classes: government, landlord, and tenant.

We decline Nansay's invitation to overrule *Pele*; on the contrary, we reaffirm it and expressly deem the rules of law posited therein to be applicable here. In *Pele*, we held that article XII, section 7, which, inter alia, obligates the State to protect customary and traditional rights normally associated with tenancy in an ahupua'a, may also apply to the exercise of rights beyond the physical boundaries of that particular ahupua'a. *Pele*, 837 P.2d at 1272. * * * [W]e hold that common law rights ordinarily associated with tenancy do not limit customary rights existing under the laws of this state."

D.

We have stated previously that rights of access and collection will not necessarily prevent landowners from developing their lands. Our analysis in the instant case is consistent with these cases.

The *Kalipi* court justified the imposition of a non-statutory "undeveloped land" requirement by suggesting that the exercise of traditional gathering rights on fully developed property "would conflict with our understanding of the traditional Hawaiian way of life in which cooperation and non-interference with the well-being of other residents were integral parts of the culture." The court also stated that, without the undeveloped land limitation, "there would be nothing to prevent residents from going anywhere within the ahupua'a, including fully developed property, to gather the enumerated items." However, the court did not expressly hold that the exercise of customary gathering practices would be absurd or unjust when performed on land that is less than fully developed."

For the purposes of this opinion, we choose not to scrutinize the various gradations in property use that fall between the terms "undeveloped" and "fully developed." Nevertheless, we refuse the temptation to place undue emphasis on non-Hawaiian principles of land ownership in the context of evaluating deliberations on development permit applications. Such an approach would reflect an unjustifiable lack of respect for gathering activities as an acceptable cultural usage in pre-modern Hawai'i, see HRS § 5-7.5 (Supp. 1992), which can also be successfully incorporated in the context of our current culture. Contrary to the suggestion in *Kalipi* that there would be nothing to prevent the unreasonable exercise of these rights, article XII, section 7 accords an ample legal basis for regulatory efforts by the State. In other words, the State is authorized to impose appropriate regulations to govern the exercise of native Hawaiian rights in conjunction with permits issued for the development of land previously undeveloped or not yet fully developed."

Depending on the circumstances of each case, once land has reached the point of "full development" it may be inconsistent to allow or enforce the practice of traditional Hawaiian gathering rights on such property. However, legitimate customary and traditional practices must be protected to the extent feasible in accordance with article XII, section 7. Although access is only guaranteed in connection with undeveloped lands, and article XII, section 7 does not require the preservation of such lands, the State does not have the unfettered discretion to regulate the rights of ahupua'a tenants out of existence.

Thus, to the extent feasible, we hold that the HPC must protect the reasonable exercise of customary or traditional rights that are established by PASH on remand.

Notes

1. Hawaiian versus Chippewa usufructuary rights. How do the usufructuary rights recognized by the Hawai'i Supreme Court compare to the rights the U.S. Supreme Court upheld in *Mille Lacs*? How, for example, may they be established? Extinguished? Where may they be exercised?

In *State v. Hanapi*, 970 P.2d 485 (Haw. 1998), the Hawaiian Supreme Court ruled that native customary rights were a defense to trespass so long as the following three elements were proved: 1) the defendant is a native Hawaiian; 2) the asserted right is constitutionally protected as a customary and traditional native Hawaiian practice; and 3) the right is being exercised on undeveloped or less-than-fully-developed land.

2. No "taking." In another part of the principal opinion, the Hawai'i Supreme Court rejected as premature the developer's claim that recognition of traditional Hawaiian gathering rights fundamentally altered its property rights so as to work a "taking" of its private property for public use, warranting payment of constitutional "just compensation." The court suggested that if such rights were established at the development site, the planning commission would be obligated to protect them "to the extent feasible." Then, the court said, the developer could make the taking allegation, although the court also observed that "the government 'assuredly [can] . . . assert a permanent easement that [reflects] a pre-existing limitation upon the landowner's title.'" 903 P.2d at 1273, citing *Lucas v. South Carolina Coastal Council*, 505 U.S. 1003, 1028–29 (1992). Wouldn't Native Hawaiian gathering rights constitute a "pre-existing limitation" upon title sufficient to defeat a takings claim?

3. Protect "to the extent feasible." The Hawaiian court imposed on state agencies the duty to protect native usufructuary rights "to the extent feasible." Compare the trust obligation which the court in *Pyramid Lake Paiute Tribe v. Morton*, excerpted at page 547, ruled imposed a duty on the exercise of the Secretary of the Interior's discretionary authority in water project operations.

In *Ka Pa'Akai O Ka'Aina v. Land Use Comm'n*, 7 P.3d 1068 (Haw. 2000), the Hawai'i Supreme Court reversed a lower court's affirmance of the state Land Use Commission's approval of a reclassification of approximately 1,000 acres of land from a conservation district to an urban district because the commission's findings were insufficient to determine whether it had fulfilled its obligation to protect native usufructuary rights "to the extent feasible." The commission conditioned the reclassification on the developer's promise to protect and preserve native usufructuary rights. But the court held that was an impermissible delegation of the commission's affirmative duty. In order to fulfill its duty to protect and preserve native rights to the extent feasible, the court ruled the commission had to identify 1) the scope of valued cultural, historical, or natural resources in the area at issue, 2) the effect of the proposed action on the native rights, and 3) any feasible action to be taken by the commission to reasonably protect those rights.

4. Hawaiian water rights. In *Reppun v. Board of Water Supply*, 656 P.2d 57 (Haw. 1982), cited in the principal case, the Hawai'i Supreme Court ruled that although the state followed the riparian system of water rights, the state possessed greater authority to allocate water rights than other riparian states because it was obligated to assure a fair distribution of water among all those who could put it to productive use. The court concluded that "[r]iparian rights in Hawaii are thus analogous to the federally reserved water rights accruing to Indian reservation pursuant to *Winters v. United States*." Thus, Hawaiian water rights "are limited by the purposes for their establishment," and they do not include "an independent source of profit." They therefore "were not intended to be, and cannot be severed from the land in any fashion. Their sole purpose is to provide water to make tenants' lands productive—no other incident of ownership is attached." Compare Hawaiian water rights with the reserved rights recognized in the *Adair I* and *Big Horn I* decisions (pages 487 and 499).

In *In the Matter of Water Use Permit Applications*, 9 P.3d 409 (Haw. 2000), in what amounted to a veritable restatement of Hawaiian water law, the Hawai'i Supreme Court confirmed that the public trust doctrine is an integral part of Hawaiian water law, embedded in the Hawai'i Constitution. Partially reversing a water resources commission allocation of an interbasin water transfer from the windward to the leeward side of Oahu in the Waiahold Ditch, the court ruled that the state water code does not supplant the public trust doctrine, which burdens all water resources, including groundwater. According to the court, the doctrine includes resource protection as one of its purposes; therefore, retention of waters in their natural state cannot be waste. The court observed that while the public trust doctrine requires a balancing process, the doctrine includes a presumption in favor of public uses and requires a high level of scrutiny for commercial uses. The doctrine also requires a consideration of the cumulative impacts of existing and proposed uses on trust uses and implementation of mitigating measures, including the use of alternative water sources. The state may, according to the court, "compromise public rights" only with the "openness, diligence, and foresight commensurate with the high priority these rights command" under state law. Implementing the public trust doctrine may help to protect Native Hawaiian usufructuary rights, but where it conflicts with native rights, the court seemed to indicate that the Hawaiian constitution placed a higher priority on satisfying native rights.

2. Defeasible Usufructuary Rights

In both *Mille Lacs* and *PASH*, the usufructuary rights were defeasible, terminable upon the happening of an event. The Chippewa usufructs persist at "the pleasure of the President," while the Hawaiian rights do not apparently survive "full development." The Seventh Circuit has interpreted the Chippewa treaty usufructs to not burden privately owned land because the Chippewa understood that their rights could be limited by settlement, which the court considered analogous to privately owned lands. *Lac Courte Oreilles Band of Chippewa Indians v. Voigt*, 700 F.2d 341, 365 & n. 14 (7th Cir. 1983). On the other hand, the Supreme Court construed Stevens Treaty fishing rights in the *Winans* case (page 471), to burden private land titles. Perhaps the distinction has to do with the fact that the Stevens Treaty fishing rights are spatially limited to "usual and accustomed" fishing places, while the Chippewa usufructs apply throughout ceded lands.

Many native usufructuary rights were conditioned on being exercised on "unoccupied" or on "open and unclaimed" lands. Consider the following case, involving a Stevens Treaty hunting right which was limited to "open and unclaimed lands."

State of Washington v. Buchanan
978 P.2d 1070 (Wash. 1999)

GUY, C.J.

This is a criminal prosecution for illegal hunting of elk in the State-owned Oak Creek Wildlife Area. The defendant, a member of the Nooksack Indian Tribe, claims he has a treaty right to hunt elk in the Oak Creek Area, and that this right may not be restricted by state hunting regulations. The issues presented are (1) whether the geographic scope of the tribe's treaty right to hunt on open and unclaimed lands includes the Oak Creek Wildlife Area, (2) whether the Oak Creek Wildlife Area is open and unclaimed land, and (3) whether the tribe's treaty right to hunt outside the reservation was abrogated by Washington's admission to the Union "on equal footing" with the original states.

We reverse the dismissal of the criminal action and remand for trial. We hold that, on remand, the defendant may raise a treaty right to hunt as a defense to the criminal charges and may offer evidence in support of his position that the Oak Creek Wildlife Area is within the aboriginal hunting grounds of the Nooksack Tribe. We also hold that under the facts presented in this case, the Oak Creek Wildlife Area is "open and unclaimed" land within the meaning of the Nooksack's treaty. We decline, in this case, to reconsider prior case law on whether the equal footing doctrine applies to impliedly abrogate Indian treaty rights in Washington.

FACTS

On January 6, 1995, defendant Donald Buchanan was stopped by Department of Fish and Wildlife enforcement officers while Buchanan was hunting in the Oak Creek Wildlife Area, land which is owned and managed by the State of Washington. The defendant was in possession of two recently killed five-point, branch-antlered bull elks. At the time he was stopped, the defendant's Washington state hunting license had been revoked, and the Washington elk hunting season was closed.

The Oak Creek Wildlife Area, which is near Yakima, is open to the public at specified times each year for hunting, fishing and recreational purposes. During the fall and winter of 1994–95, state regulations permitted elk hunting in the Oak Creek Wildlife Area only from November 5 through 13, 1994. The number of branch-antlered elk that could be killed also was regulated during the hunting season, and only young "spike bulls" could be killed without a special permit. The purposes of the restrictions on elk hunting in the Oak Creek Wildlife Area are to maintain and manage the existing elk population. However, there is not an immediate threat to elk, as a species, in the Oak Creek Wildlife Area.

Defendant Buchanan is a resident of Kent, Washington, and a member of the Nooksack Indian Tribe. The Nooksack Tribe's reservation is located in Whatcom County, near Deming. The lands ceded to the United States by the Nooksack Tribe under the provisions of the Treaty of Point Elliott, which is the treaty involved here, are bordered on the east by the summit of the Cascade range. The Oak Creek Wildlife Area is east of the territory ceded to the United States by the Nooksacks.

Defendant Buchanan was charged with two felony counts of possessing big game during a closed season, and with one misdemeanor count of hunting while license is revoked. Defendant Buchanan moved to dismiss the charges on the ground that State hunting regulations do not apply to hunters, like Buchanan, who are members of Indian tribes that have a treaty right to hunt on open and unclaimed lands. He claims the only regulations that govern his hunting on open and unclaimed lands are those of the Nooksack Indian Tribe.

The trial court granted the motion to dismiss the charges, ruling: (1) the language of the Treaty of Point Elliot does not restrict hunting to open and unclaimed lands within the area ceded by the Indians to the United States, but instead gives tribal members a right to hunt anywhere in the "Territory of Washington"; (2) the term "open and unclaimed lands" includes public lands, such as the Oak Creek Wildlife

Area, which are put to uses compatible with an Indian hunting privilege; and (3) although Indian hunting privileges may be limited if necessary for conservation, the State, in this case, failed to demonstrate that application of State hunting regulations to treaty tribe hunters is necessary for conservation.

On appeal, the State challenged the trial court's conclusions and, additionally, argued that the Treaty of Point Elliot was abrogated by Congress when Washington was admitted to the Union on equal footing with the original states. The court of Appeals affirmed and declined to consider the equal footing argument, as that issue was not presented to the trial court and was not asserted to be of constitutional magnitude.

ISSUES

1. What is the geographic scope of the Nooksack Indian Tribe's treaty hunting right?

2. Is the State-owned Oak Creek Wildlife Area "open and unclaimed lands" within the meaning of the Treaty of Point Elliott?

3. Were those provisions of the Treaty of Point Elliott which conflict with the State's right to regulate off-reservation hunting abrogated by Congress when Washington was admitted to the Union upon "equal footing" with the original states?

DISCUSSION

The Treaty of Point Elliott was made in January 1855 and ratified March 8, 1859. As noted above, the Nooksack Indian Tribe was judicially determined to be a party to the treaty * * *. The first article of the treaty includes a description of lands ceded to the United States by the Indians. The treaty provides, in article 1, that the

> "said tribes and bands of Indians hereby cede, relinquish, and convey to the United States all their right, title, and interest in and to the lands and country occupied by them, bounded and described as follows: Commencing at [the inlets and bays of western Washington Territory] to the summit of the Cascade range of mountains."

Article 5 if the treaty provides:

> "The right of taking fish at usual and accustomed grounds and stations is further secured to said Indians in common with all citizens of the Territory, and of erecting temporary houses for the purpose of curing, together with the privilege of hunting and gathering roots and berries on open and unclaimed lands. Provided, however, that they shall not take shell-fish from any beds staked or cultivated by citizens."

This paragraph was substantially the same in all of the Stevens Treaties, and its language has been the subject of extensive litigation in both state and federal court during much of the last century.

Like any treaty between the United States and another sovereign nation, a treaty with Indians is the supreme law of the land and is binding on the State until Congress limits or abrogates the treaty. A treaty, including one between the United States and an Indian tribe, is essentially a contract between two sovereigns. When the signatory nations are not at war and neither is the vanquished, it is reasonable to assume the parties bargained at arm's length. In discussing the negotiations involved in another Stevens Treaty, that with the Nez Perce, Professor Wilkinson has observed:

> [T]he stereotype of Indian leaders at treaty talks as being passive and overmatched intellectually is wrong. The negotiators for the Nez Perce, and for the other tribes as well, had a complete understanding of the situation. The white people wanted their land, and had the population and technology to take it. The tribes, on the other hand, had considerable leverage: in time they would lose a military campaign, but they could exact great costs in terms of human life and monetary expenditure to fight a war on the fragile, far edge of American territory. The calculus was about power, and the tribes could make the calculations as well as the white people. The tribal negotiators were sophisticated and they used every technique and device available to them. . . . They made their arguments precisely and ably.

Charles F. Wilkinson, *Indian Tribal Rights and the National Forests: The Case of the Aboriginal Lands of the Nez Perce Tribe,* 34 Idaho L. Rev 435, 438 (1998).

The goal of treaty interpretation is the same as the goal of contract interpretation to determine the intent of the parties. The analysis of the parties' intention begins with the language of the treaty and the context in which the written words are used. In interpreting a treaty between the United States and an Indian tribe, the treaty must "be construed, not according to the technical meaning of its words to learned lawyers, but in the sense in which they would naturally be understood by the Indians."

Where there is ambiguity in the language of a treaty, it must not be construed to the prejudice of the Indians. However, courts may not ignore treaty language that, viewed in its historical context and given a fair appraisal, clearly runs counter to the tribe's claims. Additionally, treaties must be construed liberally in favor of Indians.

A key principle of treaty interpretation is known as the "reservation of rights doctrine." First announced in *United States v. Winans,* 198 U.S. 371, a case involving interpretation of a Stevens Treaty made with the Yakama Indians, the reservation of rights doctrine holds that a treaty between the federal government and an Indian tribe is not a grant of rights to the Indians but, rather, a grant from them. In other words, the Indians ceded certain rights possessed by them at the time of making the treaty but reserved whatever rights were not expressly granted to the United States.

Under the reservation of rights doctrine, tribal members have possessed certain rights, such as hunting and fishing rights, from time immemorial. A treaty between a tribe and the United States documents a grant of some rights from the tribe to the federal government. However, those rights not expressly ceded in the treaty, as well as those expressly reserved, remain with the tribe.

The reservation of rights doctrine has consistently been applied to the fishing and hunting provisions of the Stevens Treaties. The treaty language at issue here is the following:

> The right of taking fish at usual and accustomed grounds and stations is further secured to said Indians . . . together with the privilege of hunting . . . on open and unclaimed lands.

This court has interpreted the words "privilege" and "right" as used in the treaty, to be synonymous. The United States Supreme Court has interpreted the treaty language "securing" or "secured" rights to be synonymous with "reserving" rights previously exercised. *Fishing Vessel*, 443 U.S. at 678.

The State argues that the hunting right reserved by the treaty was limited to the right previously exercised, that is, to the ceded lands or to lands upon which the Nooksack Tribe traditionally hunted. We agree.

The scope of a tribe's off-reservation hunting rights is generally found in an Indian tribe's aboriginal use of or title to land and its reservation of the right in a treaty, or by agreement, executive order or statute.

> The reservation system, in addition to minimizing confrontations between encroaching settlers and the resident Indians, was also intended to transform Indians into "a pastoral and civilized people." As a result, game populations were not one of the primary factors considered in the federal government's choice of reservation lands, and many tribes were removed to reservations located far from their traditional hunting grounds. In response to a strong desire on the part of tribes to retain access to these areas, treaties with Northwest Indians provided for . . . "the privilege of hunting . . . on open and unclaimed lands[.]" In essence, these treaty provisions preserved a portion of the aboriginal rights exercised by the signatory tribes.

[Bradley I. Nye, *Where Do the Buffalo Roam? Determining the Scope of American Indian Off-Reservation Hunting Rights in the Pacific Northwest*, 67 Wash. L. Rev. 175, 177–78 (1992) (footnotes omitted).]

> To determine the existence of original Indian title to land, and the right to hunt and fish following from that title, courts have generally required a showing of actual use and occupancy over an extended period of time. In *Mitchel v. United States* [34 U.S. (9 Pet.) 711 (1835)], the United States Supreme Court said:
>
>> Indian possession or occupation was considered with reference to their habits and modes of life; their hunting grounds were as much in their actual possession as the cleared fields of the whites; and their rights to its exclusive enjoyment in their own way and for their own purposes were as much respected, until they abandoned them, made a cession to the government, or an authorized sale to individuals.

In claims against the United States based upon original title, a requirement of exclusive use and occupancy has been satisfied by a showing that two or more tribes jointly or amicably hunted in the same area to the exclusion of others . . .

The existence of aboriginal hunting and fishing rights, however, does not necessarily turn upon the existence of original title to lands and is not dependent upon recognition in a treaty or act of Congress. Aboriginal rights remain in the Indians unless granted to the United States by treaty, abandoned, or extinguished by statute. When a treaty has been signed, aboriginal use may still be important to determine the extent of the rights reserved under the treaty.

[Felix S. Cohen's Handbook of Federal Indian Law 442–43 (Rennard Strickland & Charles Wilkinson, eds. 1982)] (footnotes omitted).

There is no evidence in the record on appeal to support a finding that the Nooksack Tribe actually occupied or used, over an extended period of time, the Oak Creek Wildlife Area for hunting. The only area which the record shows the Tribe clearly used for hunting lies within the lands ceded to the United States in the treaty.

The geographic scope of the hunting right cannot be resolved from the language of the treaty alone. We hold that application of the reservation of rights doctrine is the more legally sound approach to interpreting the hunting rights provision of the Treaty of Point Elliott. Under such an analysis, open and unclaimed lands within the aboriginal hunting grounds of the Nooksack Tribe are reserved under the treaty for hunting by tribal members, so long as the lands remain open and unclaimed. The geographic area available for hunting would certainly include the territory ceded to the United States and described in article I of the Treaty of Point Elliott, and may include other areas if those areas are proven to have been actually used for hunting and occupied by the Nooksack Tribe over an extended period of time. Because the trial court did not so limit the geographic scope of the Nooksack's treaty, we reverse the dismissal of the charges against the defendant Buchanan. However, we hold that, on remand, the defendant should have the opportunity to prove that the Nooksack Tribe's aboriginal hunting grounds include the land within the Oak Creek Wildlife Area.

We next consider whether the Oak Creek Wildlife Area is "open and unclaimed land" under the meaning of the Treaty of Point Elliot.

* * * This court has previously interpreted the meaning of "open and unclaimed lands" as that term is used in Stevens Treaties in two decisions. Under both decisions, publicly-owned lands are considered "open and unclaimed." In [*State v.*] *Miller*, 102 Wn. 2d [678], 680 n.2 [1984], the court held that national forest land is "open and unclaimed" land within the meaning of the treaty. In [*State v.*] *Chambers*, 81 Wn. 2d [929]. 936 [(1973], this court approved a jury instruction defining "open and unclaimed lands" as "lands which are not in private ownership." These decisions are consistent with those of other jurisdictions interpreting Stevens Treaties.

The State, relying on [*United States v.*] *Hicks*, [587 F. Supp. 1162 (W.D. Wash. 1984)] argues that once the hunting regulations with respect to elk went into effect, the use of the Oak Creek Wildlife Area for hunting was not a compatible use and, therefore, the lands were not open and unclaimed. Our acceptance of this argument would permit the State to avoid its burden of proving that regulations imposed on Indian treaty hunters are necessary for conservation purposes. The State has designated the Oak Creek Wildlife Area for use for hunting, fishing, and recreation. Limits on these activities in the Oak Creek Wildlife Area are by State regulation. The regulations must comply with standards developed by this court and the United States Supreme Court, and be necessary for conservation if the regulations are restrictive of treaty rights. The trial court's unchallenged finding in this case is that the State has not met its burden in this regard.

The State also relies on *State v. Cutler*, 708 P.2d 853 (Idaho 1985), to support its argument that lands which are located in a State-owned wildlife area which is operated as a wintering range for elk and deer are not "open and unclaimed lands" under the terms of the Stevens Treaties. Treaty hunters have a right to hunt on such lands, unrestricted by State regulation, unless the regulations are necessary for conservation purposes. In this case, the Oak Creek Wildlife Area is publicly owned, is obviously unoccupied, and its purposes are compatible with and, in fact, include hunting. The trial court and Court of Appeals correctly determined that the Oak Creek Wildlife Area is open and unclaimed land. Finally, the State urges this court to hold that the federal statute creating the State of Washington and admitting the state "into the Union on an equal footing with the original States," impliedly abrogated the treaty hunting rights of Indians living in Washington.

In support of its argument the State primarily relies on *Ward v. Race Horse*, 163 U.S. 504 (1896), a case in which the Supreme Court held that Congress, in admitting Wyoming to the Union on equal footing with the original states, effectively abrogated the Indian treaty hunting rights of certain treaty Indians in Wyoming.

After oral argument in this case, the United States Supreme Court effectively overruled *Race Horse* in *Minnesota v. Mille Lacs*, 526 U.S. 172, 220 (1999) (Rehnquist, C.J., dissenting) (noting the majority's "apparently overruling sub silentio" of *Race Horse*). The Supreme Court rejected use of the equal footing language to find an abrogation of Indian treaty rights, holding "treaty rights are not impliedly terminated upon statehood."

This decision is consistent with the decisions over the past 100 years, since *Race Horse* was decided, in which the Supreme Court has clarified and refined the law governing interpretation and abrogation of Indian treaty hunting and fishing rights. In contrast to the language in *Race Horse*, where the Court discussed the treaty's "grant" of rights to the Indians, the Supreme Court now views the grant as one from the Indians, with a reservation of rights not granted. *Winans*, 198 U.S. at 381. The Court has further stated that although Congress has the sole power to eliminate a treaty right, its intention to abrogate Indian treaty rights must be clear and plain. *United States v.*

Dion, 476 U.S. 734, 738 (1986). Absent explicit statutory language, the Court is "extremely reluctant" to find congressional abrogation of treaty rights. *Fishing Vessel*, 443 U.S. at 690. It therefore will not construe statutes as abrogating a treaty right in a backhanded way but will require "clear evidence that Congress actually considered the conflict between its intended action on the one hand and Indian treaty rights on the other, and chose to resolve that conflict by abrogating the treaty." *Dion*, 476 U.S. at 739–40.

Furthermore, the Supreme Court has undermined the premise upon which *Race Horse* was decided by holding that "treaty rights to hunt, fish . . . are not irreconcilable with a State's sovereignty over the natural resources in the State." *Mille Lacs*, 526 U.S. at 204. Washington's enabling act differs from the statute admitting Wyoming to the Union, in that the statute admitting Washington reserves from Washington the right to control lands owned or held by any Indian or Indian tribe. This clause makes it clear that Congress had the Indians' treaty rights in mind when it created the State of Washington, but did not go on to expressly abrogate the treaty hunting rights. Under *Dion* and *Mille Lacs*, we are unable to hold that, in the enabling act, Congress impliedly abrogated Indian treaty rights.

Reversed.

Notes

1. "Open and unclaimed lands." Why did the Washington Supreme Court conclude that the state wildlife area is "open and unclaimed"? Could the state do anything to change the status of the area? Under what conditions may the state regulate Buchanan's hunting, if it is treaty-protected? Could the state ban all hunting in the Oak Creek Area for conservation? In this regard, see the *Puyallup* cases, excerpted at pages 620 and 625.

2. The geographic scope of the hunting right. Why was the geographic scope of Buchanan's hunting right not bounded by the lands ceded in his tribe's treaty? What must he do on remand to show that his hunting right may be exercised in the Oak Creek Wildlife Area? Note that the Washington Supreme Court's unwillingness to restrict the scope of the usufructuary right to ceded lands is consistent with the U.S. Supreme Court's decision in *Seufert Bros. v. United States*, 249 U.S. 194 (1919) (refusing to restrict treaty fishing rights to lands expressly ceded by the treaty), discussed at page 630.

3. Treaty hunting versus fishing rights. The *Buchanan* court contrasted the hunting versus the fishing rights reserved in the Stevens Treaties. According to the court, the fishing right is "a permanent one, unless abrogated by Congress." But the hunting right, "by its terms, is of a temporary and self-limiting nature. The right was intended to diminish as lands became settled, without the need for congressional action." In other words, unlike the treaty fishing right, the treaty hunting right is a defeasible usufruct.

4. Hunting in national parks and forests. In *United States v. Hicks*, 587 F.Supp. 1162 (W.D. Wash. 1984), the court considered another Stevens Treaty hunting claim and concluded that "[l]ands cease to be 'open and unclaimed' when they are put to uses incompatible with hunting." Therefore, the court determined that Olympic National Park was not open and unclaimed land because one of the purposes of the park was to preserve the elk there and because Congress had prohibited hunting. The court distinguished national parks from national forests, since only the parks prohibited hunting.

The Tenth Circuit disagreed with the court in *Hicks* and held that the lands in the Big Horn National Forest were occupied since the establishment of the forest in 1887, because those lands were no longer available for settlement. *Crow Tribe of Indians v. Repsis*, 73 F.3d 982 (10th Cir. 1995). The *Repsis* court also held that the treaty hunting right did not survive Wyoming statehood, a result which the Supreme Court subsequently rejected in *Mille Lacs*, excerpted at page 586.

5. Other public lands. The Seventh Circuit noted that some public lands, such as schools, highways, and hospitals, would probably be considered "settled," and thus not subject to treaty usufructuary rights, because of public health and safety concerns. *Lac Courte Oreilles Band of Lake Superior Chippewa Indians v. Wisconsin (LCO II)*, 760 F.2d 177, 182–83 (7th Cir. 1986). But the court cautioned that lands could not be "laundered" by passing them through private ownership and then back into public ownership for the purpose of extinguishing treaty rights.

3. Regulation of Treaty Rights

As a general proposition, Indians and Indian tribes are usually subject to state authority for off-reservation activities. *See Mescalero Apache Tribe v. Jones*, 411 U.S. 145 (1973). Does that general proposition hold true for off-reservation activities conducted pursuant to treaty-reserved rights? That is, does the state have the right to regulate Indians engaged in the exercise of their off-reservation reserved rights to hunt, fish, and gather?

Puyallup Tribe v. Department of Game of Washington [*Puyallup I*]
391 U.S. 392 (1968)

MR. JUSTICE DOUGLAS delivered the opinion of the Court.

These cases present a question of public importance which involves in the first place a construction of the Treaty of Medicine Creek made with the Puyallup and Nisqually Indians in 1854 and secondly the constitutionality of certain conservation measures adopted by the State of Washington allegedly impinging on those treaty rights.

These suits were brought by respondents in the state court against the Indians for declaratory relief and for an injunction. The trial court held for respondents and with exceptions not relevant to our problem the Supreme Court affirmed in part and remanded for further findings on the conservation aspect of the problem. We granted the petitions for certiorari and consolidated the cases for oral argument.

While the Treaty of Medicine Creek created a reservation for these Indians, no question as to the extent of those reservation rights, if any, is involved here.[1] Our question concerns the fishing rights protected by Article III, which so far as relevant reads as follows:

> "The right of taking fish, at all usual and accustomed grounds and stations, is further secured to said Indians, in common with all citizens of the Territory, and of erecting temporary houses for the purpose of curing, together with the privilege of hunting, gathering roots and berries, and pasturing their horses on open and unclaimed lands. . . ."

The fish to which the Treaty rights pertain in these cases are salmon and steelhead, anadromous fish that hatch in the fresh water of the Puyallup River and the Nisqually River. The steelhead is a trout; the salmon are of four species—chinook, silver, chum, and pink. They come in from the ocean, pass through the salt water of Puget Sound, enter the fresh waters at the mouths of rivers, and go up these rivers to spawn. The adult salmon die after spawning, but not necessarily the steelhead. In time the fry return to the ocean and start the cycle anew.

People fish for these species far offshore. As respects fishing within its territorial waters, Washington specifies the time when fishing may take place, the areas open to fishing, and the gear that may be used.

Fishing licenses are prescribed. Steelhead may be taken only by hook and not commercially. Salmon may be taken commercially with nets of a certain type in certain areas. Set nets or fixed appliances are barred in "any waters" of the State for the taking of salmon or steelhead. So is "monofilament gill net webbing."

---

1. It should be noted that while a reservation was created by Article II of the Treaty, Article VI provided that the President might remove the Indians from the reservation "on remunerating them for their improvements and the expenses of their removal, or may consolidate them with other friendly tribes or bands." Article VI also gave the President authority alternatively to divide the reservation into lots and assign them to those individuals or families who were willing to make these places their permanent home. In 1887 Congress passed the General Allotment Act authorizing the division of the reservation land among the individual Indians. In 1893 Congress passed the Puyallup Allotment Act, which established a commission to make the allotments. And by the Act of April 28, 1904, Congress gave "the consent of the United States" to the removal of prior restrictions on alienation by these Indians. The trial court in No. 247 found that all lands within the boundaries of the reservation created by the Treaty have been transferred to private ownership pursuant to these Acts of Congress, with the exception of two small tracts used as a cemetery for members of the tribe; and much of it is now in the City of Tacoma. Whether in light of this history the reservation has been extinguished is a question we do not reach. The Washington Supreme Court seems to hold that the right to fish in streams once within the old reservation is protected by the Article III guarantee. There are indeed no other fishing rights specifically reserved in the Treaty of Medicine Creek except those covered by Article III.

Nearly every river in the State has a salmon preserve at its mouth; and Commencement Bay at the mouth of the Puyallup River is one of those preserves.

The Puyallup Indians use set nets to fish in Commencement Bay and at the mouth of the Puyallup River and in areas upstream. The Nisqually Indians use set nets in the fresh waters of the Nisqually River. These Indians fish not only for their own needs but commercially as well, supplying the markets with a large volume of salmon. The nets used are concededly illegal if the laws and regulations of the State of Washington are valid; and it is to that question that we now turn.

The "right of taking fish at all usual and accustomed places, in common with" citizens of the Territory under a treaty with the Yakimas was involved in *United States v. Winans*, 198 U.S. 371 [1905]. The lands bordering the Columbia River at those places were acquired by private owners who under license from the State acquired the right to fish there and sought to exclude the Indians by reason of their ownership. The Court held that the right to fish at these places was a "continuing" one that could not be destroyed by a change in ownership of the land bordering the river. To construe the treaty as giving the Indians "no rights but such as they would have without the treaty" would be "an impotent outcome to negotiations and a convention, which seemed to promise more and give the word of the Nation for more." In *Seufert Bros. Co. v. United States*, 249 U.S. 194 [1919], the Court construed the same provision liberally so as to include all "accustomed places" even though the Indians shared those places with other Indians and with white men, rejecting a strict, technical construction not in keeping with the justice of the case.

It is in that spirit that we approach these cases in determining the scope of the treaty rights which the Puyallups and Nisqually obtained.

The treaty right is in terms the right to fish "at all usual and accustomed places." We assume that fishing by nets was customary at the time of the Treaty; and we also assume that there were commercial aspects to that fishing as there are at present. But the manner in which the fishing may be done and its purpose, whether or not commercial, are not mentioned in the Treaty. We would have quite a different case if the Treaty had preserved the right to fish at the "usual and accustomed places" in the "usual and accustomed" manner. But the Treaty is silent as to the mode or modes of fishing that are guaranteed. Moreover, the right to fish at those respective places is not an exclusive one. Rather, it is one "in common with all citizens of the Territory." Certainly the right of the latter may be regulated. And we see no reason why the right of the Indians may not also be regulated by an appropriate exercise of the police power of the State. The right to fish "at all usual and accustomed" places may, of course, not be qualified by the State, even though all Indians born in the United States are now citizens of the United States. But the manner of fishing, the size of the take, the restriction of commercial fishing, and the like may be regulated by the State in the interest of conservation, provided the regulation meets appropriate standards and does not discriminate against the Indians.

In *Tulee v. Washington*, 315 U.S. 681 [1942], we had before us for construction a like treaty with the Yakima Indians which guaranteed the right to fish "at all usual and accustomed places, in common with the citizens" of Washington Territory. Tulee, a member of the tribe, was fishing without a license off the Yakima Indian Reservation; the State convicted him for failure to obtain a license. We reversed, saying:

> "While the treaty leaves the state with power to impose on Indians, equally with others, such restrictions of a purely regulatory nature concerning the time and manner of fishing outside the reservation as are necessary for the conservation of fish, it forecloses the state from charging the Indians a fee of the kind in question here."

In other words, the "right" to fish outside the reservation was a treaty "right" that could not be qualified or conditioned by the State. But "the time and manner of fishing . . . necessary for the conservation of fish," not being defined or established by the treaty, were within the reach of state power.

The overriding police power of the State, expressed in nondiscriminatory measures for conserving fish resources, is preserved. In *United States v. Winans, supra*, a forerunner of the *Tulee* case, the Court said:

> "Surely it was within the competency of the Nation to secure to the Indians such a remnant of the great rights they possessed as 'taking fish at all usual and accustomed places.' Nor does it restrain the State unreasonably, if at all, in the regulation of the right."

The use of purse seines and other nets[12] in the salt waters is permitted for commercial purposes under terms and conditions prescribed by the State; and their use in these areas is open to all, Indians as well as others. The use of set nets[13] in fresh water streams or at their mouths is barred not only to Indians but to all others. An expert for the State testified that the reason for that prohibition was conservation:

---

12. A purse seine is a type of gear that encircles a school of fish, lead weights taking the net down, and a boat operating at each end of the net. A line runs through rings on the bottom of the net, making it possible to close the bottom of the net.

A gill net has a mesh which fish cannot back out of once their heads get through. Gill net fishing is drift fishing, the net being up to 1,800 feet in length.

Purse seines and drift gill nets are used in salt water.

13. Set gill nets are often anchored at one end, stretched on a cork line, and held down by weights, while drifting at the other end. They are often located one above another at a short distance. Fish are taken by hand out of the nets as a boat travels its length. The mesh in the gill net varies, depending on the size of the species of salmon that are running—chinook, 8 to 8H inches; silver, chum, and sockeye, 5H inches. Set gill nets run from 40 to 150 feet depending on the width of the river at the point they are used.

"The salmon are milling and delaying, and especially in times of low water or early arrival of the run or for any number of reasons, the delay may be considerable.

"Once again the fish are available to the net again and again. This is the main reason for the preserve, so that the milling stock will not be completely taken.

"Then further, this is a point in the bay at the river mouth where you very definitely have a funneling effect. The entire run is funneled into a smaller area and it is very vulnerable."

Fishing by hook and line is allowed in these areas because when salmon are "milling near the river mouth," they are not "feeding and they don't strike very well, so the hook and line fishery will take but a small percentage of the available stock no matter how hard they fish."

Whether the prohibition of the use of set nets in these fresh waters was a "reasonable and necessary" conservation measure was left for determination by the trial court when the state Supreme Court, deeming the injunction too broad, remanded the case for further findings. When the case was argued here, much was said about the pros and the cons of that issue. Since the state court has given us no authoritative answer to the question, we leave it unanswered and only add that any ultimate findings on the conservation issue must also cover the issue of equal protection implicit in the phrase "in common with."

Affirmed.

Notes

1. Salmon preserves. Justice Douglas noted that "really every river in the State has a Salmon preserve at its mouth." These preserves imposed the burden of conservation on the tribes, while allowing non-Indian commercial harvests in the ocean and Puget Sound and non-Indian recreational harvests upriver. The real question in the case, which Justice Douglas neither identified nor attempted to answer, was: who was the beneficiary of the "preserves"?

2. State regulation of the manner and size of harvests. Justice Douglas opined that "[t]he right to fish at 'all usual and accustomed' places may, of course, not be qualified by the State." Wouldn't a ban on commercial harvests amount to "qualifying" the treaty right?

3. Justice Douglas as a conservationist. Justice Douglas was the foremost environmentalist ever to sit on the Supreme Court. *See* Richard J. Lazarus, *Restoring What's Environmental About Environmental Law in the Supreme Court*, 47 U.C.L.A. L. Rev. 703, 724–25 (2000) (reporting that Justice Douglas sided with the environmental result 15 times in 15 cases). Dean Getches considered Douglas' environmental sensitivities to outweigh his sympathies to the tribes in *Puyallup I*. David H. Getches, *Conquering the Cultural Frontier: The New Subjectivism of the U.S. Supreme Court in Indian Law*, 84 Cal. L. Rev. 1573, 1632, n.284 (1996).

Department of Game of the State of Washington v. Puyallup Tribe [*Puyallup II*]
414 U.S. 44 (1973)

MR. JUSTICE DOUGLAS delivered the opinion of the Court.

[In *Puyallup I*, we] found the state court decision had not clearly resolved the question whether barring the "use of set nets in fresh water streams or at their mouths" by all, including Indians, and allowing fishing only by hook and line in these areas was a reasonable and necessary conservation measure. The case was remanded for determination of that question and also "the issue of equal protection implicit in the phrase 'in common with'" as used in the Treaty.

In Washington the Department of Fisheries deals with salmon fishing, while steelhead trout are under the jurisdiction of the Department of Game. On our remand the Department of Fisheries changed its regulation to allow Indian net fishing for salmon in the Puyallup River (but not in the bay or in the spawning areas of the river). The Department of Game, however, continued its total prohibition of net fishing for steelhead trout. The Supreme Court of Washington upheld the regulations imposed by the Department of Fisheries which, as noted, were applicable to salmon; and no party has brought that ruling back here for review. The sole question tendered in the present cases concerns the regulations of the Department of Game concerning steelhead trout. We granted the petitions for certiorari.

The Supreme Court of Washington, while upholding the regulations of the Department of Game prohibiting fishing by net for steelhead in 1970, held (1) that new fishing regulations for the Tribe must be made each year, supported by "facts and data that show the regulation is necessary for the conservation" of the steelhead; (2) that the prohibition of net fishing for steelhead was proper because "the catch of the steelhead sports fishery alone in the Puyallup River leaves no more than a sufficient number of steelhead for escapement necessary for the conservation of the steelhead fishery in that river."

The ban on all net fishing in the Puyallup River for steelhead grants, in effect, the entire run to the sports fishermen. Whether that amounts to discrimination under the Treaty is the central question in these cases.

At issue presently is the problem of accommodating net fishing by the Puyallups with conservation needs of the river. Our prior decision recognized that net fishing by these Indians for commercial purposes was covered by the Treaty. We said that "the manner of fishing, the size of the take, the restriction of commercial fishing, and the like may be regulated by the State in the interest of conservation, provided the regulation . . . does not discriminate against the Indians." There is discrimination here because all Indian net fishing is barred and only hook-and-line fishing entirely pre-empted by non-Indians, is allowed.

Only an expert could fairly estimate what degree of net fishing plus fishing by hook and line would allow the escapement of fish necessary for perpetuation of the species. If hook-and-line fishermen now catch all the steelhead which can be caught within the limits needed for escapement, then that number must in some manner be fairly apportioned between Indian net fishing and non-Indian sports fishing so far as that particular species is concerned. What formula should be employed is not for us to propose. There are many variables—the number of nets, the number of steelhead that can be caught with nets, the places where nets can be located, the length of the net season, the frequency during the season when nets may be used. On the other side are the number of hook-and-line licenses that are issuable, the limits of the catch of each sports fisherman, the duration of the season for sports fishing, and the like.

The aim is to accommodate the rights of Indians under the Treaty and the rights of other people.

We do not imply that these fishing rights persist down to the very last steelhead in the river. Rights can be controlled by the need to conserve a species; and the time may come when the life of a steelhead is so precarious in a particular stream that all fishing should be banned until the species regains assurance of survival. The police power of the State is adequate to prevent the steelhead from following the fate of the passenger pigeon; and the Treaty does not give the Indians a federal right to pursue the last living steelhead until it enters their nets.

We reverse the judgment below insofar as it treats the steelhead problem and remand the cases for proceedings not inconsistent with this opinion.

Note on Limiting Treaty Rights on Public Safety Grounds

In *Washington v. Washington State Commercial Passenger Fishing Vessel Ass'n* (page 633), the Court stated that: "Although nontreaty fishermen might be subjected to any reasonable state fishing regulation serving any legitimate purpose, treaty fishermen are immune from all regulation save that required for conservation." Nonetheless, at least two district courts have allowed states to regulate the exercise of off-reservation treaty hunting rights on grounds of public safety.

In *Lac Courte Oreilles Band of Lake Superior Chippewa Indians v. Wisconsin (LCO IV)*, 668 F. Supp. 1233 (W.D. Wis. 1987), the court rejected the state's argument that it could regulate for any legitimate purpose. However, the court ruled that treaty rights were subject to state health and safety regulations, noting that "it appears logical that if the state may intrude upon treaty reserved rights to preserve a species or resource, it may intrude as well to preserve its citizens from certain public health or safety hazards." Limiting state health and safety regulations in the same manner as conservation regulations, the court announced that they must be "reasonable and necessary to prevent or ameliorate a substantial risk" to the public health and safety and not discriminate against the tribes or in favor of non-Indian harvesters.

Limitations based on public safety concerns may change over time. For example, the Seventh Circuit, per Judge Posner, suggested that public safety no longer warranted a ban on off-reservation night deer hunting and reversed a state ban on night hunting ("shining" or "spotlighting") of deer. *Lac Courte Oreilles Band of Superior Chippewa Indians of Wisconsin v. Wisconsin,* 769 F.3d 543 (7th Cir. 2014) (emphasizing changed conditions and the fact that the Minnesota ban was out of step with other midwestern states like Michigan and Minnesota). An ensuing district court decision also emphasized changed conditions:

> [The tribe's] right to hunt deer at night throughout the ceded territory was prohibited in the final judgment entered in 1991 only because [of public safety concerns] . . . . Now, with the benefit of 24 years of state experience with night hunting, the tribes have been able to show that the prohibition on off-reservation night deer hunting is no longer necessary for public safety purposes, when properly regulated. It remains [the tribe's] right, as well as its responsibility, to promulgate and enforce the regulations; not [the state's]. [The state's] role is limited to showing that plaintiffs' regulations are inadequate.

Lac Courte Oreilles Band of Lake Superior Chippewa Indians v. Wisconsin, 2015 WL 5944238 at *2 (W.D. Wis. Oct. 13, 2015).

In *Confederated Tribes of the Colville Reservation v. Anderson,* 761 F. Supp. 2d 1101 (E.D. Wash. 2011), the court ruled that the state of Washington could enforce its hunting regulations against tribal members hunting on off-reservation at "in common with" hunting grounds. As in its *LCO IV* decision, the court limited state hunting regulations to those reasonable and necessary to prevent a public safety threat, and which were not discriminatory.

Note on Tribal Hunting and Fishing Regulations

As mentioned in Chapter 4 in relation to tribal environmental laws (pages 319–320), tribes may enact laws separate from state and federal law. Some tribes have consequently enacted hunting and fishing regulations. For example, the Confederated Tribes of the Colville Reservation adopted the Colville Tribal Hunting and Fishing Chapter at Chapter 4-1 of the Tribes' Code, available at https://www.cct-fnw.com/new-page/. The purpose of the Colville Hunting and Fishing Code is "to restore, preserve, protect and perpetuate the fish and game resources (wildlife) on the Colville Indian Reservation, the North Half, and off the Colville Reservation to the extent that wildlife passes through or would pass through the usual and accustomed fishing grounds and stations, hunting areas, or aboriginal lands of the Tribes." Colville Tribal Code 4-1-2. In *Colville Confederated Tribes v. Everybodytalksabout,* Nos. FW-2002-01087 and FW-2002-01124 (Aug. 6, 2003), the Colville tribal court interpreted the meaning of the Code concerning hunting in violation of the tribal code. Because the alleged hunter refused to cooperate with an investigating tribal officer, the officer issued him citations for possession of large game during a closed season and for obstruction of the officer's investigation. But the tribes dismissed the citation for possession of large game outside of the designated season, and the court dismissed the obstruction of justice citation, deciding that failure to cooperate with an investigation did not amount to obstruction of justice.

Federal courts in both the Pacific Northwest and the Great Lakes regions have held that tribes have the authority to regulate their members who are exercising off-reservation treaty usufructuary rights. States may generally regulate tribal members exercising off-reservation rights only if the tribes do not impose effective regulations of their own. *See, e.g., Lac Courte Oreilles Band of Lake Superior Chippewa Indians v. Wisconsin [LCO IV]*, 668 F. Supp. 1233 (W.D. Wis. 1987); *United States v. Washington*, 520 F.2d 676 (9th Cir. 1975); *Settler v. Lameer*, 507 F.2d 231 (9th Cir. 1974). The district court in *LCO IV* offered an outline of what might constitute effective tribal regulation:

> for the purpose of preclusion of state regulation, tribal regulations must adequately address legitimate state concerns in the areas of conservation of resources and public health and safety. There must be effective enforcement mechanisms, including competent and adequately trained enforcement personnel. There must be a form of official tribal identification for tribe members exercising off-reservation rights. And there must be a full exchange of relevant information between the plaintiff tribes and the state, including the exchange of scientific and management information as well as data on the harvest of any given resource in any given geographic area. Cooperation among the Department of Natural Resources, the tribes, and perhaps the Great Lakes Indian Fish and Wildlife Commission will help to ensure the full exchange of information necessary to the common state and tribal goals of preserving the resource and ensuring public health and safety. If necessary, however, I will consider an order directing the establishment of a joint tribal-state natural resources commission.

Note on On-Reservation versus Off-Reservation Rights

Within Indian country, tribal rights to hunt, fish, and gather are impliedly reserved as incidents of sovereignty that the tribes have never relinquished. Tribal authority to regulate hunting and fishing on trust lands within Indian country is generally paramount. *See Montana v. United States*, 450 U.S. 544 (1981), and *New Mexico v. Mescalero Apache Tribe*, 462 U.S. 324 (1983) (pages 249 and 257, respectively). Tribes do not, however, retain the right to regulate hunting and fishing by nonmembers on fee lands unless the tribe can show substantial direct effects on tribal interests. *See Montana* and *South Dakota v. Bourland*, 508 U.S. 679 (1993) (page 273). In the absence of tribal regulation of nonmembers on fee lands, state regulation appears to apply, if only by default.

In *Puyallup III*, the Court extended the state's regulatory power to on-reservation fishing by Indians. *Puyallup Tribe v. Dep't of Game of State of Washington*, 433 U.S. 165, 173–77 (1977). Under two congressional acts, the Puyallup Tribe ceded all but 22 acres of its original 18,000-acre reservation. None of the remaining acres was riparian to the Puyallup River. Nonetheless, because the Court had denied certiorari in a case holding that the Puyallup Reservation had not been disestablished, *United States v. Washington*, 496 F.2d 620 (9th Cir 1974), *cert. denied*, 419 U.S. 1032 (1974), the Court had to accept the fact that the fishing rights at issue took place within the reservation. The Court noted, however, that fishing on the Puyallup River was not exclusive to the tribe, but rather in common with non-Indians. It also observed that unregulated on-reservation fishing had the potential to "completely destroy" the fish runs.

> Though it would be decidedly unwise, if Puyallup treaty fishermen were allowed untrammeled on-reservation fishing rights, they could interdict completely the migrating fish run and "pursue the last living [Puyallup River] steelhead until it enters their nets." In this manner the treaty fishermen could totally frustrate both the jurisdiction of the Washington courts and the rights of the non-Indian citizens of Washington recognized in the Treaty of Medicine Creek. In practical effect, therefore, the petitioner is reasserting the right to exclusive control of the steelhead run that was unequivocally rejected in both *Puyallup I* and *Puyallup II*. At this stage of this protracted litigation, we are unwilling to re-examine those unanimous decisions or to render their holdings virtually meaningless. We therefore reject petitioner's claim to an exclusive right to take steelhead while passing through the reservation.

Subsequently, however, the Court refused to extend *Puyallup III* to allow general state regulation of hunting and fishing on reservations. *New Mexico v. Mescalero Apache Tribe*, 462 U.S. 324, 331–32 (1983) (page 257). In *Mescalero*, the Court ruled that states may regulate Indians in Indian country only in "exceptional circumstances," and those were present in *Puyallup III*. The Court then distinguished that case:

> *Puyallup [III]* upheld the State of Washington's authority to regulate on-reservation fishing by tribal members. Like *Montana v. United States*, the decision in *Puyallup* rested in part on the fact that the dispute centered on lands which, although located within reservation boundaries, no longer belonged to the Tribe; all but 22 of the 18,000 acres had been alienated in fee simple. The Court also relied on a provision of the Indian treaty which qualified the Indians' fishing rights by requiring that they be exercised "in common with all citizens of the Territory," and on the State's interest in conserving a scarce, common resource.

The Court then held that the State of New Mexico had no authority to concurrently regulate non-Indian hunting and fishing on the Mescalero Apache Reservation.

4. Scope and Extent of "the Right of Taking Fish"

United States v. Winans

198 U.S. 371 (1905)

[The *Winans* case is excerpted at page 471. Recall the holding:]

The right to resort to the fishing places in controversy was a part of larger rights possessed by the Indians, upon the exercise of which there was not a shadow of impediment, and which were not much less necessary to the existence of the Indians than the atmosphere they breathed. New conditions came into existence, to which those rights had to be accommodated. Only a limitation of them, however, was necessary and intended, not a taking away. In other words, the treaty was not a grant of rights to the Indians, but a grant of rights from them—a reservation of those not granted. And the form of the instrument and its language was adapted to that purpose. Reservations were not of particular parcels of land, and could not be expressed in deeds as dealings between private individuals. The reservations were in large areas of territory and the negotiations were with the tribe. They reserved rights, however, to every individual Indian, as though named therein. They imposed a servitude upon every piece of land as though described therein. There was an exclusive right of fishing reserved within certain boundaries. There was a right outside of those boundaries reserved "in common with citizens of the Territory." As a mere right, it was not exclusive in the Indians. Citizens might share it, but the Indians were secured in its enjoyment by a special provision of means for its exercise. They were given "the right of taking fish at all usual and accustomed places," and the right "of erecting temporary buildings for curing them." The contingency of the future ownership of the lands, therefore, was foreseen and provided for—in other words, the Indians were given a right in the land—the right of crossing it to the river—the right to occupy it to the extent and for the purpose mentioned. No other conclusion would give effect to the treaty. And the right was intended to be continuing against the United States and its grantees as well as against the State and its grantees.

Notes

1. Application to private lands. The *Winans* decision affirmed the continuing treaty right of the Yakama Nation to fish at its "usual and accustomed places, in common with citizens of the Territory," even though the land had been acquired by non-Indians. The treaty rights, the Court held, "imposed a servitude upon every piece of land as though described therein." That servitude is in the nature of both an easement, a right to cross private land to reach the fishing places, and a piscary profit *a prendre*, the right to go onto another's land and remove a resource, in this case, fish. *See generally* Michael C. Blumm & Brett M. Swift, *The Indian Treaty Piscary Profit: A Property Rights Approach,* 69 U. Colo. L. Rev. 407, 440–57 (1998).

In *Seufert Bros. v. United States*, 249 U.S. 194 (1919), the Court extended the *Winans* reasoning to lands on the south side of Celilo Falls, on the Columbia River, which the Yakama Nation had not ceded in its treaty (the treaty language spoke of the midpoint of the Columbia River). The Court determined that the tribes would not have understood the effect of the treaty language as limiting the exercise of their traditional fishing practices. Moreover, the Court pointed out that there was sufficient notice of the existence of the usufruct from the treaty language and from the "habitual and customary use of the [south side of the river], which must have been so open and notorious . . . that any person, not negligently or wilfully blind to the conditions of the property he was purchasing, must have known of them."

2. Regulatory cases. As we saw in the previous section, the Supreme Court addressed state regulation of treaty fishing before it addressed allocation of the harvest. The following is a brief overview of the regulatory decisions.

In *Tulee v. Washington*, 315 U.S. 681 (1942), the Court reversed a state criminal conviction of Sampson Tulee for salmon fishing without a state dip net license. No licenses were required for hook-and-line fisherman, effectively exempting non-Indian recreational fishers from the license fee of $5.00. The Court determined that the license fee served both to raise money for state government and to regulate harvests for conservation purposes. Because the tribe would not have understood at treaty time that its members would have to pay to exercise their treaty rights, and because the state could not show that the license fee was "indispensable" for effective conservation, the Court struck the licensing fee, even though it was facially nondiscriminatory.

In *Puyallup I* (page 620), the Court limited *Tulee's* indispensability requirement to license fees and suggested that the state could regulate tribal harvests in the interest of conservation if the measure did not discriminate against tribal harvests and was "reasonable and necessary" for conservation. *Puyallup Tribe v. Dept. of Game*, 391 U.S. 392 (1968). Professor Ralph Johnson wrote a sharp critique of the Court's *Puyallup I* decision, predicting that the state would soon use it as a means of "conserving" salmon for the non-Indian harvesters whose license fees were an important source of state revenue. Ralph W. Johnson, *The States Versus Indian Off-Reservation Fishing: A United States Supreme Court Error*, 47 Wash. L. Rev. 207 (1972).

Puyallup II (page 625) followed quickly on the heels of *Puyallup I* and involved a state conservation measure which confirmed Professor Johnson's fears. *Dept. of Game v. Puyallup Tribe*, 414 U.S. 44 (1973). The state banned net fishing on the Puyallup River, which in effect banned tribal harvests, while permitting non-Indian hook-and-line harvests. The Court struck down the measure as discriminatory, even though it was facially neutral.

3. Apportionment of the "in common with" harvest. In *Puyallup III* (pages 628–629), the Court addressed apportionment of the harvest for the first time. *Puyallup Tribe v. Dept. of Game*, 433 U.S. 165 (1977). Apparently fearful that an exclusive salmon fishery on the lower seven miles of the Puyallup River would allow the tribe to take all the harvestable fish, the Court upheld a state court allocation of 45% of the harvest to the tribe, suggesting that the place where the fish were harvested was less important in the case of a migrating fish like salmon than that the harvests were fairly apportioned overall.

Efforts to fairly apportion salmon harvests had already been the subject of two district court decisions. In the first, the tribes and the federal government challenged longstanding state regulations in Oregon which limited Columbia River harvests above The Dalles Dam to hook-and-line fisheries, closing the upper river to net fishing traditionally employed by the tribes. The state interpreted the treaty fishing right to give the tribes only the same rights as other citizens. District Judge Robert

Belloni, in memorable words, replied that "[s]uch a ruling would not seem unreasonable if all history, anthropology, biology, prior case law, and the intention of the parties to the treaty were to be ignored." *Sohappy v. Smith*, 302 F. Supp. 899, 905 (D. Or. 1969). Judge Belloni determined that the state's "conservation" regulations were actually designed to conserve fish for non-Indian harvests, not conserve the species. He therefore ruled that tribal fishers were entitled to a "fair share" of the harvests. Based on that standard, he established detailed substantive and procedural standards aimed at elevating tribal fishing to a "coequal" status, including "meaningful" tribal participation in developing harvest regulations, and limited the state to "the least restrictive regulations which can be imposed [on tribal harvests] consistent with assuring [sufficient numbers of spawning fish]." See Ed Goodman, *Protecting Habitat for Off-Reservation Tribal Hunting and Fishing Rights: Tribal Co-management as a Reserved Right*, 30 Envtl. L. 279, 349–52 (2000) (discussing implementation of the Columbia River Fisheries Management Plan, an outgrowth of Judge Belloni's decision).

Because the *Sohappy* decision applied only in Oregon, tribal members continued to be prosecuted in Washington for violating state harvest regulations. Consequently, the tribes and the federal government filed suit in federal court in Washington, claiming that Judge Belloni's "fair share" principle meant that the tribes were entitled to one-half the harvest of salmon destined to pass through their historic fishing grounds. Judge George Boldt agreed, invalidating the state's regulatory scheme as discriminatory. Judge Boldt noted that state regulatory practices had reduced tribal harvests to two percent of the total harvest, and observed that despite three years of trial preparation, the state failed to produce "any credible evidence showing any instance, remote or recent, when definitely identified members of any plaintiff tribe exercised his off reservation rights by any conduct or means detrimental to the perpetuation of any species of anadromous fish." *United States v. Washington*, 384 F. Supp. 312, 338 n.26 (W.D. Wash. 1974). Judge Boldt then interpreted the treaty language recognizing the tribes' "right of taking fish in common with" white settlers to mean "sharing equally the opportunity to take fish," or 50 percent of the harvest.

Judge Boldt's decision was quickly affirmed by the Ninth Circuit, *United States v. Washington*, 520 F.2d 676 (9th Cir. 1975), but the state and its citizens vigorously resisted its implementation. Widespread noncompliance included shooting threats. Then, in 1977, the state supreme court ruled that the state lacked the statutory and constitutional authority to implement Judge Boldt's decree. *Purse Seine Vessel Owners Ass'n v. Tollefson*, 571 P.2d 1373 (Wash. 1977); *Puget Sound Gillnetters Ass'n v. Moos*, 565 P.2d 1151 (Wash. 1977). Consequently, Judge Boldt was forced to enter numerous orders that effectively made him the regulator of the fishery, "the fishmaster" as his critics alleged. His authority to do so was upheld by the Ninth Circuit, which noted that the state's "extraordinary machinations" to resist the federal court decree resembled the South's efforts to resist desegregation. *Puget Sound Gillnetters v. U.S. District Court*, 573 F.2d 1123, 1126 (9th Cir. 1978).

This conflict between the state and federal courts led to the following case:

Washington v. Washington State Commercial Passenger Fishing Vessel Association

443 U.S. 658 (1979)

MR. JUSTICE STEVENS delivered the opinion of the Court.

To extinguish the last group of conflicting claims to lands lying west of the Cascade Mountains and north of the Columbia River in what is now the State of Washington, the United States entered into a series of treaties with Indian tribes in 1854 and 1855. The Indians relinquished their interest in most of the Territory in exchange for monetary payments. In addition, certain relatively small parcels of land were reserved for their exclusive use, and they were afforded other guarantees, including protection of their "right of taking fish, at all usual and accustomed grounds and stations . . . in common with all citizens of the Territory."

The principal question presented by this litigation concerns the character of that treaty right to take fish. Various other issues are presented, but their disposition depends on the answer to the principal question. Before answering any of these questions, or even stating the issues with more precision, we shall briefly describe the anadromous fisheries of the Pacific Northwest, the treaty negotiations, and the principal components of the litigation complex that led us to grant these three related petitions for certiorari.

I

Anadromous fish hatch in fresh water, migrate to the ocean where they are reared and reach mature size, and eventually complete their life cycle by returning to the fresh-water place of their origin to spawn. Different species have different life cycles, some spending several years and traveling great distances in the ocean before returning to spawn and some even returning to spawn on more than one occasion before dying. The regular habits of these fish make their "runs" predictable; this predictability in turn makes it possible for both fishermen and regulators to forecast and to control the number of fish that will be caught or "harvested." Indeed, as the terminology associated with it suggests, the management of anadromous fisheries is in many ways more akin to the cultivation of "crops"—with its relatively high degree of predictability and productive stability, subject mainly to sudden changes in climatic patterns—than is the management of most other commercial and sport fisheries.

Regulation of the anadromous fisheries of the Northwest is nonetheless complicated by the different habits of the various species of salmon and trout involved, by the variety of methods of taking the fish, and by the fact that a run of fish may pass through a series of different jurisdictions. Another complexity arises from the fact that the State of Washington has attempted to reserve one species, steelhead trout, for sport fishing and therefore conferred regulatory jurisdiction over that species upon its Department of Game, whereas the various species of salmon are primarily harvested by commercial fishermen and are managed by the State's Department of Fisheries. Moreover, adequate regulation not only must take into account the potentially conflicting interests of sport and commercial fishermen, as well as those of Indian and non-treaty fishermen, but also must recognize that the fish runs may be harmed by harvesting either too many or too few of the fish returning to spawn.

The anadromous fish constitute a natural resource of great economic value to the State of Washington. Millions of salmon, with an average weight of from 4 or 5 to about 20 pounds, depending on the species, are harvested each year. Over 6,600 non-treaty fishermen and about 800 Indians make their livelihood by commercial fishing; moreover, some 280,000 individuals are licensed to engage in sport fishing in the State.

II

One hundred and twenty-five years ago when the relevant treaties were signed, anadromous fish were even more important to most of the population of western Washington than they are today. At that time, about three-fourths of the approximately 10,000 inhabitants of the area were Indians. Although in some respects the cultures of the different tribes varied—some bands of Indians, for example, had little or no tribal organization while others, such as the Makah and the Yakima, were highly organized—all of them shared a vital and unifying dependence on anadromous fish.

Religious rites were intended to insure the continual return of the salmon and the trout; the seasonal and geographic variations in the runs of the different species determined the movements of the largely nomadic tribes. Fish constituted a major part of the Indian diet, was used for commercial purposes, and indeed was traded in substantial volume. The Indians developed food-preservation techniques that enabled them to store fish throughout the year and to transport it over great distances. They used a wide variety of methods to catch fish, including the precursors of all modern netting techniques. Their usual and accustomed fishing places were numerous and were scattered throughout the area, and included marine as well as fresh-water areas.

All of the treaties were negotiated by Isaac Stevens, the first Governor and first Superintendent of Indian Affairs of the Washington Territory, and a small group of advisers. Contemporaneous documents make it clear that these people recognized the vital importance of the fisheries to the Indians and wanted to protect them from the risk that non-Indian settlers might seek to monopolize their fisheries. There is no evidence of the precise understanding the Indians had of any of the specific English terms and phrases in the treaty. It is perfectly clear, however, that the Indians were vitally interested in protecting their right to take fish at usual and accustomed places, whether on or off the reservations, and that they were invited by the white negotiators to rely and in fact did rely heavily on the good faith of the United States to protect that right.

Referring to the negotiations with the Yakima Nation, by far the largest of the Indian tribes, the District Court found:

> "At the treaty council the United States negotiators promised, and the Indians understood, that the Yakimas would forever be able to continue the same

off-reservation food gathering and fishing practices as to time, place, method, species and extent as they had or were exercising. The Yakimas relied on these promises and they formed a material and basic part of the treaty and of the Indians' understanding of the meaning of the treaty."

The Indians understood that non-Indians would also have the right to fish at their off-reservation fishing sites. But this was not understood as a significant limitation on their right to take fish. Because of the great abundance of fish and the limited population of the area, it simply was not contemplated that either party would interfere with the other's fishing rights. The parties accordingly did not see the need and did not intend to regulate the taking of fish by either Indians or non-Indians, nor was future regulation foreseen.

Indeed, for several decades after the treaties were signed, Indians continued to harvest most of the fish taken from the waters of Washington, and they moved freely about the Territory and later the State in search of that resource. The size of the fishery resource continued to obviate the need during the period to regulate the taking of fish by either Indians or non-Indians. Not until major economic developments in canning and processing occurred in the last few years of the 19th century did a significant non-Indian fishery develop. It was as a consequence of these developments, rather than of the treaty, that non-Indians began to dominate the fisheries and eventually to exclude most Indians from participating in it—a trend that was encouraged by the onset of often discriminatory state regulation in the early decades of the 20th century.

In sum, it is fair to conclude that when the treaties were negotiated, neither party realized or intended that their agreement would determine whether, and if so how, a resource that had always been thought inexhaustible would be allocated between the native Indians and the incoming settlers when it later became scarce.

III

Unfortunately, that resource has now become scarce, and the meaning of the Indians' treaty right to take fish has accordingly become critical. The United States Court of Appeals for the Ninth Circuit and the Supreme Court of the State of Washington have issued conflicting decisions on its meaning. In addition, their holdings raise important ancillary questions that will appear from a brief review of this extensive litigation.

The federal litigation was commenced in the United States District Court for the Western District of Washington in 1970. The United States, on its own behalf and as trustee for seven Indian tribes, brought suit against the State of Washington seeking an interpretation of the treaties and an injunction requiring the State to protect the Indians' share of the anadromous fish runs. Additional Indian tribes, the State's Fisheries and Game Departments, and one commercial fishing group, were joined as parties at various stages of the proceedings, while various other agencies and groups, including all of the commercial fishing associations that are parties here, participated as amici curiae.

The District Court * * * held that the Indians were then entitled to a 45% to 50% share of the harvestable fish that will at some point pass through recognized tribal fishing grounds in the case area. The share was to be calculated on a river-by-river, run-by-run basis, subject to certain adjustments. Fish caught by Indians for ceremonial and subsistence purposes as well as fish caught within a reservation were excluded from the calculation of the tribes' share. In addition, in order to compensate for fish caught outside of the case area, i.e., beyond the State's jurisdiction, the court made an "equitable adjustment" to increase the allocation to the Indians. The court left it to the individual tribes involved to agree among themselves on how best to divide the Indian share of runs that pass through the usual and accustomed grounds of more than one tribe, and it postponed until a later date the proper accounting for hatchery-bred fish. With a slight modification, the Court of Appeals for the Ninth Circuit affirmed, and we denied certiorari.

The injunction entered by the District Court required the Department of Fisheries (Fisheries) to adopt regulations protecting the Indians' treaty rights. After the new regulations were promulgated, however, they were immediately challenged by private citizens in suits commenced in the Washington state courts. The State Supreme Court, in two cases that are here in consolidated form in No. 77-983, ultimately held that Fisheries could not comply with the federal injunction.

As a matter of federal law, the state court * * * held that [the treaties] did not give the Indians a right to a share of the fish runs, and second concluded that recognizing special rights for the Indians would violate the Equal Protection Clause of the Fourteenth Amendment. The opinions might also be read to hold, as a matter of state law, that Fisheries had no authority to issue the regulations because they had a purpose other than conservation of the resource. In this Court, however, the Attorney General of the State disclaims the adequacy and independence of the state-law ground and argues that the state-law authority of Fisheries is dependent on the answers to the two federal-law questions discussed above. We defer to that interpretation, subject, of course, to later clarification by the State Supreme Court. Because we are also satisfied that the constitutional holding is without merit, our review of the state court's judgment will be limited to the treaty issue.

When Fisheries was ordered by the state courts to abandon its attempt to promulgate and enforce regulations in compliance with the federal court's decree—and when the Game Department simply refused to comply—the District Court entered a series of orders enabling it, with the aid of the United States Attorney for the Western District of Washington and various federal law enforcement agencies, directly to supervise those aspects of the State's fisheries necessary to the preservation of treaty fishing rights. The District Court's power to take such direct action and, in doing so, to enjoin persons who were not parties to the proceeding was affirmed by the United States Court of Appeals for the Ninth Circuit. * * * Subsequently, the District Court entered an enforcement order regarding the salmon fisheries for the 1978 and subsequent seasons, which, prior to our issuance of a writ of certiorari to review the case, was pending on appeal in the Court of Appeals.

Because of the widespread defiance of the District Court's orders, this litigation has assumed unusual significance. We granted certiorari in the state and federal cases to interpret this important treaty provision and thereby to resolve the conflict between the state and federal courts regarding what, if any, right the Indians have to a share of the fish, to address the implications of international regulation of the fisheries in the area, and to remove any doubts about the federal court's power to enforce its orders.

IV

The treaties secure a "right of taking fish." The pertinent articles provide:

> "The right of taking fish, at all usual and accustomed grounds and stations, is further secured to said Indians, in common with all citizens of the Territory, and of erecting temporary houses for the purpose of curing, together with the privilege of hunting, gathering roots and berries, and pasturing their horses on open and unclaimed lands: Provided, however, That they shall not take shell fish from any beds staked or cultivated by citizens."

A treaty, including one between the United States and an Indian tribe, is essentially a contract between two sovereign nations. When the signatory nations have not been at war and neither is the vanquished, it is reasonable to assume that they negotiated as equals at arm's length. There is no reason to doubt that this assumption applies to the treaties at issue here.

Accordingly, it is the intention of the parties, and not solely that of the superior side, that must control any attempt to interpret the treaties. When Indians are involved, this Court has long given special meaning to this rule. It has held that the United States, as the party with the presumptively superior negotiating skills and superior knowledge of the language in which the treaty is recorded, has a responsibility to avoid taking advantage of the other side. "[The] treaty must therefore be construed, not according to the technical meaning of its words to learned lawyers, but in the sense in which they would naturally be understood by the Indians." This rule, in fact, has thrice been explicitly relied on by the Court in broadly interpreting these very treaties in the Indians' favor.

Governor Stevens and his associates were well aware of the "sense" in which the Indians were likely to view assurances regarding their fishing rights. During the negotiations, the vital importance of the fish to the Indians was repeatedly emphasized by both sides, and the Governor's promises that the treaties would protect that source of food and commerce were crucial in obtaining the Indians' assent. It is absolutely clear, as Governor Stevens himself said, that neither he nor the Indians intended that the latter "should be excluded from their ancient fisheries," and it is accordingly inconceivable that either party deliberately agreed to authorize future settlers to crowd the Indians out of any meaningful use of their accustomed places to fish. That each individual Indian would share an "equal opportunity" with thousands of newly arrived individual settlers is totally foreign to the spirit of the negotiations. Such a "right," along with the $207,500 paid the Indians, would hardly have been sufficient to compensate them for the millions of acres they ceded to the Territory.

It is true that the words "in common with" may be read either as nothing more than a guarantee that individual Indians would have the same right as individual non-Indians or as securing an interest in the fish runs themselves. If we were to construe these words by reference to 19th-century property concepts, we might accept the former interpretation, although even "learned lawyers" of the day would probably have offered differing interpretations of the three words. But we think greater importance should be given to the Indians' likely understanding of the other words in the treaties and especially the reference to the "right of taking fish"—a right that had no special meaning at common law but that must have had obvious significance to the tribes relinquishing a portion of their pre-existing rights to the United States in return for this promise. This language is particularly meaningful in the context of anadromous fisheries—which were not the focus of the common law—because of the relative predictability of the "harvest." In this context, it makes sense to say that a party has a right to "take"—rather than merely the "opportunity" to try to catch—some of the large quantities of fish that will almost certainly be available at a given place at a given time.

This interpretation is confirmed by additional language in the treaties. The fishing clause speaks of "securing" certain fishing rights, a term the Court has previously interpreted as synonymous with "reserving" rights previously exercised. *Winans*, 198 U.S., at 381. Because the Indians had always exercised the right to meet their subsistence and commercial needs by taking fish from treaty area waters, they would be unlikely to perceive a "reservation" of that right as merely the chance, shared with millions of other citizens, occasionally to dip their nets into the territorial waters. Moreover, the phrasing of the clause quite clearly avoids placing each individual Indian on an equal footing with each individual citizen of the State. The referent of the "said Indians" who are to share the right of taking fish with "all citizens of the Territory" is not the individual Indians but the various signatory "tribes and bands of Indians" listed in the opening article of each treaty. Because it was the tribes that were given a right in common with non-Indian citizens, it is especially likely that a class right to a share of fish, rather than a personal right to attempt to land fish, was intended.

In our view, the purpose and language of the treaties are unambiguous; they secure the Indians' right to take a share of each run of fish that passes through tribal fishing areas. But our prior decisions provide an even more persuasive reason why this interpretation is not open to question. For notwithstanding the bitterness that this litigation has engendered, the principal issue involved is virtually a "matter decided" by our previous holdings.

The Court has interpreted the fishing clause in these treaties on six prior occasions. In all of these cases the Court placed a relatively broad gloss on the Indians' fishing rights and—more or less explicitly—rejected the State's "equal opportunity" approach; in the earliest and the three most recent cases, moreover, we adopted essentially the interpretation that the United States is reiterating here.

Not only all six of our cases interpreting the relevant treaty language but all federal courts that have interpreted the treaties in recent times have reached the foregoing conclusions, as did the Washington Supreme Court itself prior to the present litigation. *State v. Satiacum*, 314 P.2d 400, 406 (Wash. 1957). A like interpretation, moreover, has been followed by the Court with respect to hunting rights explicitly secured by treaty to Indians "'in common with all other persons,'" *Antoine v. Washington*, 420 U.S. 194, 205–206, and to water rights that were merely implicitly secured to the Indians by treaties reserving land—treaties that the Court enforced by ordering an apportionment to the Indians of enough water to meet their subsistence and cultivation needs. *Arizona v. California*, 373 U.S. 546, 598–601; *Winters v. United States*, 207 U.S. 564, 576.

The purport of our cases is clear. Nontreaty fishermen may not rely on property law concepts, devices such as the fish wheel, license fees, or general regulations to deprive the Indians of a fair share of the relevant runs of anadromous fish in the case area. Nor may treaty fishermen rely on their exclusive right of access to the reservations to destroy the rights of other "citizens of the Territory." Both sides have a right, secured by treaty, to take a fair share of the available fish. That, we think, is what the parties to the treaty intended when they secured to the Indians the right of taking fish in common with other citizens.

V

We also agree with the Government that an equitable measure of the common right should initially divide the harvestable portion of each run that passes through a "usual and accustomed" place into approximately equal treaty and nontreaty shares, and should then reduce the treaty share if tribal needs may be satisfied by a lesser amount. Although this method of dividing the resource, unlike the right to some division, is not mandated by our prior cases, it is consistent with the 45%–55% division arrived at by the Washington state courts, and affirmed by this Court, in *Puyallup III* with respect to the steelhead run on the Puyallup River. The trial court in the *Puyallup* litigation reached those figures essentially by starting with a 50% allocation based on the Indians' reliance on the fish for their livelihoods and then adjusting slightly downward due to other relevant factors. The District Court took a similar tack in this case, i.e., by starting with a 50–50 division and adjusting slightly downward on the Indians' side when it became clear that they did not need a full 50%.

The division arrived at by the District Court is also consistent with our earlier decisions concerning Indian treaty rights to scarce natural resources. In those cases, after determining that at the time of the treaties the resource involved was necessary to the Indians' welfare, the Court typically ordered a trial judge or special master, in his discretion, to devise some apportionment that assured that the Indians' reasonable livelihood needs would be met. *Arizona v. California, supra,* at 600; *Winters, supra*. This is precisely what the District Court did here, except that it realized that some ceiling should be placed on the Indians' apportionment to prevent their needs from exhausting the entire resource and thereby frustrating the treaty right of "all [other] citizens of the Territory."

Thus, it first concluded that at the time the treaties were signed, the Indians, who comprised three-fourths of the territorial population, depended heavily on anadromous fish as a source of food, commerce, and cultural cohesion. Indeed, it found that the non-Indian population depended on Indians to catch the fish that the former consumed. Only then did it determine that the Indians' present-day subsistence and commercial needs should be met, subject, of course, to the 50% ceiling.

It bears repeating, however, that the 50% figure imposes a maximum but not a minimum allocation. As in *Arizona v. California* and its predecessor cases, the central principle here must be that Indian treaty rights to a natural resource that once was thoroughly and exclusively exploited by the Indians secures so much as, but no more than, is necessary to provide the Indians with a livelihood—that is to say, a moderate living. Accordingly, while the maximum possible allocation to the Indians is fixed at 50%, the minimum is not; the latter will, upon proper submissions to the District Court, be modified in response to changing circumstances. If, for example, a tribe should dwindle to just a few members, or if it should find other sources of support that lead it to abandon its fisheries, a 45% or 50% allocation of an entire run that passes through its customary fishing grounds would be manifestly inappropriate because the livelihood of the tribe under those circumstances could not reasonably require an allotment of a large number of fish.

[The Court modified the lower courts' allocation of fish as follows:] Accordingly, any fish (1) taken in Washington waters or in United States waters off the coast of Washington, (2) taken from runs of fish that pass through the Indians' usual and accustomed fishing grounds, and (3) taken by either members of the Indian tribes that are parties to this litigation, on the one hand, or by non-Indian citizens of Washington, on the other hand, shall count against that party's respective share of the fish.

VII

In addition to their challenges to the District Court's basic construction of the treaties, and to the scope of its allocation of fish to treaty fishermen, the State and the commercial fishing associations have advanced two objections to various remedial orders entered by the District Court.[1] It is claimed that the District Court has ordered

---

1. The associations advance a third objection as well—that the District Court had no power to enjoin individual nontreaty fishermen, who were not parties to its decisions, from violating the allocations that it has ordered. The reason this issue has arisen is that state officials were either unwilling or unable to enforce the District Court's orders against nontreaty fishermen by way of state regulations and state law enforcement efforts. Accordingly, nontreaty fishermen were openly violating Indian fishing rights, and, in order to give federal law enforcement officials the power via contempt to end those violations, the District Court was forced to enjoin them. The commercial fishing organizations, on behalf of their individual members, argue that they should not be bound by these orders because they were not parties to (although the associations all did participate as amici curiae in) the proceedings that led to their issuance.

If all state officials stand by the Attorney General's representations that the State will implement the decision of this Court, this issue will be rendered moot because the District Court no longer will be forced to enforce its own decisions. Nonetheless, the issue is still live since state

a state agency to take action that it has no authority to take as a matter of state law and that its own assumption of the authority to manage the fisheries in the State after the state agencies refused or were unable to do so was unlawful.

These objections are difficult to evaluate in view of the representations to this Court by the Attorney General of the State that definitive resolution of the basic federal question of construction of the treaties will both remove any state-law impediment to enforcement of the State's obligations under the treaties, and enable the State and Fisheries to carry out those obligations. Once the state agencies comply, of course, there would be no issue relating to federal authority to order them to do so or any need for the District Court to continue its own direct supervision of enforcement efforts.

The representations of the Attorney General are not binding on the courts and legislature of the State, although we assume they are authoritative within its executive branch. Moreover, the State continues to argue that the District Court exceeded its authority when it assumed control of the fisheries in the State, and the commercial fishing groups continue to argue that the District Court may not order the state agencies to comply with its orders when they have no state-law authority to do so. Accordingly, although adherence to the Attorney General's representations by the executive, legislative, and judicial officials in the State would moot these two issues, a brief discussion should foreclose the possibility that they will not be respected. State-law prohibition against compliance with the District Court's decree cannot survive the command of the Supremacy Clause of the United States Constitution. It is also clear that Game and Fisheries, as parties to this litigation, may be ordered to prepare a set of rules that will implement the Court's interpretation of the rights of the parties even if state law withholds from them the power to do so. Once again the answer to a question raised by this litigation is largely dictated by our *Puyallup* trilogy. There, this Court mandated that state officers make precisely the same type of allocation of fish as the District Court ordered in this case.

Whether Game and Fisheries may be ordered actually to promulgate regulations having effect as a matter of state law may well be doubtful. But the District Court may prescind that problem by assuming direct supervision of the fisheries if state recalcitrance or state-law barriers should be continued. It is therefore absurd to argue, as do the fishing associations, both that the state agencies may not be ordered to implement the decree and also that the District Court may not itself issue detailed

---

implementation efforts are now at a standstill and the orders are still in effect. Accordingly, we must decide it.

In our view, the commercial fishing associations and their members are probably subject to injunction under either the rule that nonparties who interfere with the implementation of court orders establishing public rights may be enjoined, or the rule that a court possessed of the res in a proceeding in rem, such as one to apportion a fishery, may enjoin those who would interfere with that custody. But in any case, these individuals and groups are citizens of the State of Washington, which was a party to the relevant proceedings, and "they, in their common public rights as citizens of the State, were represented by the State in those proceedings, and, like it, were bound by the judgment." Moreover, a court clearly may order them to obey that judgment.

remedial orders as a substitute for state supervision. The federal court unquestionably has the power to enter the various orders that state official and private parties have chosen to ignore, and even to displace local enforcement of those orders if necessary to remedy the violations of federal law found by the court. Even if those orders may have been erroneous in some respects, all parties have an unequivocal obligation to obey them while they remain in effect.

In short, we trust that the spirit of cooperation motivating the Attorney General's representation will be confirmed by the conduct of state officials. But if it is not, the District Court has the power to undertake the necessary remedial steps and to enlist the aid of the appropriate federal law enforcement agents in carrying out those steps. Moreover, the comments by the Court of Appeals strongly imply that it is prepared to uphold the use of stern measures to require respect for federal-court orders.[36]

The judgments of the Court of Appeals for the Ninth Circuit and the Supreme Court of the State of Washington are vacated and the respective causes are remanded to those courts for further proceedings not inconsistent with this opinion.

[The dissenting opinion of Justice POWELL, with whom Justice STEWART and Justice REHNQUIST joined, is omitted.]

Notes

1. **Expanding the piscary profit.** Prior to the *Passenger Fishing Vessel* case, the Court had interpreted the Stevens Treaty fishing right to include an affirmative access right (*Winans*), which burdened both lands ceded by treaty and those not (*Seufort Bros.*), as well as negative rights to be insulated from state license fees (*Tulee*, discussed in *Puyallup I*) and discriminatory regulations, even if they were facially neutral (*Puyallup II*). In *Passenger Fishing Vessel*, the Court went a significant step further: finding in the treaty's "in common with" language an affirmative right to harvest up to half of the available fish. A subsequent Ninth Circuit decision affirmed a district court ruling that the tribal harvest allocation included both hatchery and spawning salmon. *United States v. Washington*, 694 F.2d 1374, 1379–85 (9th Cir. 1982). The question of whether the treaty fishing right includes a right to protect the habitat on which the fish depend remains unresolved. *See* section 5 below (pages 649–665).

2. **Fish harvests as "crops."** The Supreme Court seemed impressed with the relative stability of salmon runs:

> The regular habits of these fish make their "runs" predictable; this predictability in turn makes it possible for both fishermen and regulators to

---

36. "The state's extraordinary machinations in resisting the [1974] decree have forced the district court to take over a large share of the management of the state's fishery in order to enforce its decrees. Except for some desegregation cases . . . , the district court has faced the most concerted official and private efforts to frustrate a decree of a federal court witnessed in this century. The challenged orders in this appeal must be reviewed by this court in the context of events forced by litigants who offered the court no reasonable choice."

forecast and to control the number of fish that will be caught or 'harvested.' Indeed, as the terminology suggests, the management of anadromous fisheries is in many ways more akin to the cultivation of "crops"—with its relatively high degree of predictability and productive stability, subject mainly to sudden changes in climatic patterns—than is the management of other commercial and sport fisheries.

The analogy to crop harvests, however inaccurate, led the Court to conclude that the treaty "right of taking fish" amounts to "a right to 'take'—rather than merely the 'opportunity' to try to catch—some of the large quantities of fish that will almost certainly be available at a given place at a given time." Thus, the Court rejected the state's argument that the treaty right meant mere equality of treatment with other fishers subject to state regulation, a proposition the Court first dismissed three-quarters of a century before in the *Winans* decision (page 471).

3. No "crowding out." The Court observed that "neither [Governor Stevens] nor the Indians intended that the latter 'should be excluded from their ancient fisheries,' and it is accordingly inconceivable that either party deliberately agreed to authorize future settlers to crowd the Indians out of any meaningful use of their accustomed places to fish." The Court also noted that "[b]ecause the Indians had always exercised the right to meet their subsistence and commercial needs by taking fish from treaty area waters, they would be unlikely to perceive a 'reservation' of that right as merely the chance, shared with millions of other citizens, occasionally to dip their nets into the territorial waters." These statements helped the district court in a subsequent decision, discussed at pages 650–651, to rule that the Court had all but concluded that implied within the treaty right of taking fish was the right to protect the habitat on which the fish depended. *United States v. Washington*, 506 F.Supp. 207 (W.D. Wash. 1980), *vacated*, 759 F.2d 1353 (9th Cir. 1985).

4. The "moderate living" standard. Perhaps the most notable paragraph of the *Passenger Fishing Vessel* opinion was where the Court, after explaining that the 50% figure was a maximum, not a minimum allocation, stated that "the central principle here must be that Indian treaty rights to a natural resource that once was thoroughly and exclusively exploited by the Indians secures so much as, but not more than, is necessary to provide the Indians with a livelihood—that is to say, a moderate living." The Court then suggested that the share allocated to the tribes could be reduced in response to changing circumstances, such as a tribe "dwind[ling] to just a few members, or if it should find other sources of support that lead it to abandon its fisheries," because the tribe's livelihood would not require a 50% allocation. Does that statement mean a tribe's gaming revenues could lead to a reduction in its treaty fishing rights?

Justice Thurgood Marshall's papers revealed that the "moderate living" standard resulted from a successful eleventh hour attempt to avoid a rehearing, with the possible outcome of overruling *Puyallup II*, which had broadened the scope of the treaty fishing right beyond a mere access right. Justice Stevens created the "moderate living" standard as a ceiling on the right, a ceiling argued by no party to the case, in an effort to assure his colleagues that the tribes would not reap an economic windfall as a result of the opinion. He estimated that the tribes would actually harvest only around 20 percent of the harvestable fish because he assumed (erroneously, as it turned out) that the tribes' effort to have their harvest share apply to hatchery fish would fail. *See* David H. Getches, *Conquering the Cultural Frontier: The New Subjectivism of the Supreme Court in Indian Law,* 84 Cal. L. Rev. 1573, 1637–39 (1996). In fact, the Ninth Circuit later affirmed a district court's determination that the tribes had a right to a harvest share of both hatchery and wild fish. *United States v. Washington,* 759 F.2d 1353, 1360 (9th Cir. 1985).

5. In-Lieu Fishing Sites. In 1945, to compensate tribes for the devastation of many tribal "usual and accustomed fishing grounds" caused by federal dams, Congress authorized the creation of several "in-lieu" fishing sites and added to them in 1988 "for the permanent use and enjoyment of Indian tribes." One such site was Maryhill, where Lester Ray Jim, a Yakama tribal member, was cited by the state of Washington for unlawfully harvesting an undersized sturgeon. However, in *State v. Jim,* 273 P.3d 434 (Wash. 2012), the Washington Supreme Court affirmed an appeals court dismissal of the charge and held that the state lacked criminal jurisdiction over the in-lieu fishing site because federal regulations made clear that the fishing right at such sites was reserved exclusively for the tribes.

6. The moderate living standard in the Chippewa litigation. The Court in *Passenger Fishing Vessel* allocated the fish resource between the treaty and the non-treaty fisheries. In the *LCO* litigation in Wisconsin, the court initially refused to allocate the resources in the ceded territory, on two grounds: (1) that neither party had presented evidence that any species was endangered or scarce, and (2) that the Chippewa treaties differed significantly in language from the Pacific Northwest treaties. The court did, however, adopt the *Passenger Fishing Vessel* standard that the treaties reserved the right to resources sufficient to provide the tribes with a moderate living. *Lac Courte Oreilles Band of Lake Superior Chippewa Indians v. Wisconsin (LCO III),* 653 F. Supp. 1420 (W.D. Wis. 1987). The following year, the court held that the tribes

> have established the monetary measurement of a "modest standard of living" and have proven that they could not achieve this standard even if they were permitted to harvest every available resource in the ceded territory and even if they were capable of doing so. In other words, the modest living standard imposes no practical limit on the amount of the natural resources that can be harvested by tribal members.

LCO V, 686 F. Supp. 226, 227 (W.D. Wis. 1988). The court finally allocated the resources in 1990:

> I conclude that the parties [to the treaties] did not intend that plaintiffs' reserved rights would entitle them to the full amount of the harvestable resources in the ceded territory, even if their modest living needs would otherwise require it. The non-Indians gained harvesting rights under those same treaties that must be recognized. The bargain between the parties included competition for the harvest.

How to quantify the bargained-for competition is a difficult question. The only reasonable and logical resolution is that the contending parties share the harvest equally. Plaintiffs' moderate living needs drive the division. In the unlikely event that those needs decline to the point at which they can be met with less than half the harvest, the division will have to be adjusted to reflect the reduced needs.

LCO VII, 740 F. Supp. 1400, 1416–18 (W.D. Wis. 1990).

7. Hatchery fish as part of the treaty harvest share. In 1970, the tribes and the federal government originally asked the district court in *United States v. Washington* for three types of declaratory relief: 1) a harvest share; 2) inclusion of hatchery fish in that harvest share; and 3) recognition that the treaty protected the habitat upon which the fish depend for survival. Judge Boldt's decision dealt only with the first. After the Supreme Court largely affirmed Judge Boldt in 1979, the tribes and the federal government revived their second and third claims in what became known as Phase II of *United States v. Washington*. (The habitat protection claim is considered in section 5 below, pages 649–655.)

Although three members of the Supreme Court, in the *Puyallup II* decision (p. 492), had suggested that the treaty right would not extend to hatchery fish subsidized by non-Indian fishers, the hatchery fish claim was upheld by Judge Orrick (Judge Boldt having retired) in 1980. He ruled that the Supreme Court's emphasis on supplying the tribes with a "moderate living" virtually decided the issue because, given the preponderance of hatchery fish among certain salmon species, the exclusion of hatchery fish would tend to "crowd out" the tribes from their historic fisheries. *United States v. Washington*, 506 F. Supp. 187, 198–99 (W.D. Wash. 1980). The court also noted that hatchery fish and wild fish are hard to differentiate prior to harvest; hatchery fish serve as substitutes for wild fish lost due to state-authorized habitat destruction; the state lacks any ownership interest in hatchery fish released into its waters; and federal and tribal hatcheries also contribute hatchery fish. A panel of the Ninth Circuit affirmed on the basis of the lack of state ownership of the released fish, the competition between hatchery and natural fish for the same resources in a given stream, and the mitigation function of the hatcheries (attempting to compensate for habitat loses due to developments like dams), 694 F.2d 1374, 1379 (9th Cir. 1982), as did an en banc panel. 759 F.2d 1353, 1360 (9th Cir. 1985).

8. New Zealand's quota system. Although legislatively established, New Zealand's quota system is similar to the allocation established in the Boldt decision. New Zealand uses a "quota management system" to allocate harvest rights among commercial fishers. The Treaty of Waitangi Settlement Act of 1992 waived all future Maori commercial fishing claims in exchange for government payment of $150 million to the Maori so that they could purchase Sealord Products Ltd., the largest fishing company in the country. Sealord owned about 25 percent of all commercial fishing rights in the country. The Act also gave the Maori a right to 20 percent of the quota for any new species brought under the quota management system. As in the United

States, quotas are assessed with reference to the "total allowable catch," meaning that as resources decline, so too do Maori harvest rights. For a comparison of treaty fishing rights in New Zealand and Washington see Kristi Stanton, *A Call for Co-Management: Treaty Fishing Allocation in New Zealand and Western Washington*, 11 Pac. Rim. L. & Pol'y J. 745 (2002) (advocating more cooperative co-management of resources between governments and indigenous populations).

9. **What are "usual and accustomed" places?** There is a fair amount of case law, much of it involving intertribal disputes, concerning which tribe may claim a particular site or the scope of a tribe's fishing places. *See, e.g., Upper Skagit Indian Tribe v. Washington*, 590 F.3d 1020 (9th Cir. 2010) (holding that the Suquamish Tribe's usual and accustomed fishing grounds did not include Skagit Bay and Saratoga Passage on the east side of Whidbey Island in Puget Sound, agreeing with the Upper Skagit Tribe that the Suquamish never had the right to fish in these areas); *United States v. Confederated Tribes of the Colville Indian Reservation*, 606 F.3d 698 (9th Cir. 2010) (deciding that both the Yakama Indian Nation and the Wenatchi Constituent Tribe (one of the Confederated Tribes on the Colville reservation) possessed nonexclusive fishing rights "that they share in 'in common with' non-treaty and non-agreement fishermen" to the Whatshapum fishery in north central Washington); *Muckleshoot Indian Tribe v. Lummi Indian Nation*, 234 F.3d 1099 (9th Cir. 2000) (finding that the Lummi Tribe's usual and accustomed fishing grounds extended only to the northern suburbs of Seattle, as they existed in 1974); *United States v. Lummi Tribe*, 235 F.3d 443 (9th Cir. 2000) (determining that the Lummi Tribe's usual and accustomed grounds include Admiralty Inlet, but not the Strait of Juan de Fuca or the mouth of Hood Canal); *United States v. Lummi Tribe,* 876 F.3d 1004 (9th Cir. 2017) (declaring that the Lummi Tribe's fishing rights extend to waters west of Whidbey Island); *United States v. Muckleshoot Tribe,* 235 F.3d 429 (9th Cir. 2000) (finding that the Muckleshoot Tribe's usual and accustomed grounds include only Elliot Bay); *United States v. Washington*, 235 F.3d 438 (9th Cir. 2000) (deciding that the Chehalis Tribe was not party to the treaty of Olympia, and therefore Chehalis harvests should be counted against the state's 50 percent share).

On a related issue, the Ninth Circuit upheld a district court decision that refused to reopen the Boldt decision to include fishing rights for the Samish Tribe. *United States v. Washington*, 593 F.3d 790 (9th Cir. 2010). The court denied the claim on the grounds that the Samish Tribe had obtained federal recognition in 1996, nearly two decades after district court had rejected the tribe's claim; it did not live as a continuous, separate, and distinct Indian community; and it was not a political successor of any the tribes that were signatories to the 1855 Treaty of Point Elliot. The court, in an opinion by Judge Canby, thought that reopening the earlier decree due to the Samish Tribe's subsequent federal recognition would be inconsistent with considerations of finality which fishing rights cases share with water adjudications.

In 2014, a divided Ninth Circuit reversed a district court and ruled that the eastern boundary of the Lummi Nation's usual and accustomed fishing ground had not been established by "law of the case." The court therefore decided that the boundary dispute between the Lummi and the Klallam Tribes would have to be resolved at trial before the district court. *United States v. Lummi Nation*, 763 F.3d 1180 (9th Cir. 2014).

10. Commercial use of reserved resources. In *Passenger Fishing Vessel*, the Supreme Court noted that:

> Fish constituted a major part of the Indian diet, was used for commercial purposes, and indeed was traded in substantial volume. The Indians developed food-preservation techniques that enabled them to store fish throughout the year and to transport it over great distances. They used a wide variety of methods to catch fish, including the precursors of all modern netting techniques.

As a result of this treaty-time commercial activity, tribes today are generally able to exploit treaty-reserved resources on a commercial basis. For example:

> [The Chippewa tribes] assert, and defendants dispute, that the Chippewa commercially disposed of a substantial part of the fish and game they obtained by fishing and hunting during the treaty era. Plaintiffs assert they are free now to commercially to dispose of fish and game they obtain by off-reservation fishing and hunting performed under the treaties. Specifically, they assert they may now trade and sell to non-Indians, in the modern manner, from their current harvests.
>
> Their assertion is valid. The Chippewa were clearly engaged in commerce throughout the treaty era. Commercial activity was a major factor in Chippewa subsistence.

Lac Courte Oreille Band of Lake Superior Chippewa Indians v. Wisconsin (LCO III), 653 F. Supp. 1420, 1430 (W.D. Wis. 1987).

In addition, tribes are not confined to the methods of fishing or otherwise gathering resources that they used at treaty time. Courts in the Great Lakes and Pacific Northwest have specifically recognized the right to take advantage of improvements in hunting and fishing techniques. See *LCO III*, 653 F. Supp. at 1430; *United States v. Washington (Boldt I)*, 384 F. Supp. 312, 402 (W.D. Wash. 1974), aff'd, 520 F.2d 676 (9th Cir. 1975).

In light of these standards, consider the following case. Do the Chippewa off-reservation usufructuary rights include the right to harvest timber commercially? If not, why is timber different than all other resources reserved in the ceded territory?

Lac Courte Oreilles Band of Lake Superior Chippewa Indians v. Wisconsin [*LCO-Timber*]

758 F. Supp. 1262 (W.D. Wis. 1991)

CRABB, Chief Judge.

The initial question is the most basic: whether the usufructuary rights plaintiffs reserved under the treaties of 1837 and 1842 include the right to harvest the commercial timber resource in the ceded territory.

For the reasons that follow, I find and conclude that the usufructuary rights reserved to plaintiffs under the treaties of 1837 and 1842 do not include the right to harvest the commercial timber resource. When the Chippewa entered into those treaties they ceded to the United States their rights to the pine timber forever. It is a closer question whether plaintiffs understood that they were selling their rights to all the other timber as well. Whether they did understand this or not, they never contemplated retaining a usufructuary right to harvest timber commercially within the ceded territory because harvesting and selling timber were not among plaintiffs' usual and customary activities at the time the treaties were signed.

Ascertaining what the Chippewa were actually doing at the time of the treaties is a prerequisite to determining what they would have understood they were reserving.

The evidence before Judge Doyle [in a prior proceeding in the case] showed that at the time of the treaties, the Chippewa used particular species of trees for a myriad of purposes. The evidence did not show that the Chippewa exploited a timber resource, either for their own use or for commercial purposes. That distinction is a critical one.

[C]ommercial timber is a unique and specific object of harvesting. Harvesters of commercial timber look for a collection of trees of a size, quality and density that make them valuable to harvest. This is not what the Chippewa harvesters were interested in exploiting at treaty time. They were seeking particular trees for their unique characteristics, for example, the gum of the balsam or the roots of the jack pine. They did not harvest trees for use as logs or for saw boards.

The record before Judge Doyle contained no evidence that in 1837 or 1842 the Chippewa were harvesting and using timber. There is no evidence to suggest that at that time the Chippewa would have had the equipment, knowledge and skills necessary to take timber from the forest, or that they would have even contemplated doing so.

Logging large areas of trees would have had no purpose for the Chippewa: their mobile hunting and gathering lifestyle gave them no reason to build log homes or barns or to clear the land. To the contrary, they depended heavily on retaining many different species of trees and other forms of plant life from which they derived many specialized products and which served as habitat for the animals they hunted.

Plaintiffs argue that the lack of evidence of logging activity in 1837 and 1842 is not determinative of their right to engage in this form of harvest. They argue that it is necessary only to prove that they were exploiting trees for some commercial purpose at treaty time because the law of the case is that plaintiffs may use any harvesting methods employed in 1837 and 1842 and developed since, and logging is simply an advanced form of harvesting. Therefore, they maintain, they may apply logging techniques to the forest resources they were exploiting in other ways at treaty time.

* * * [T]he harvesting of this resource cannot be characterized as merely a modern adaptation of a traditional harvesting method. Logging is not a "modern" technique, but rather one that has been in use for centuries, and it is an activity that is wholly different in purpose and effect from utilizing parts of trees for specialized purposes.

The uses the Chippewa made of trees in 1837 and 1842 were essentially uses that preserved the living trees. They did not take the trunk of the tree that loggers concentrate on; they used the sap, bark, branches, leaves, needles and roots. Even when they used wood in large quantities as fuel for their extensive maple sugar and syrup-making it is reasonable to assume that they used fallen, dry logs for this purpose rather than green living trees. This use of forest products contrasts sharply with commercial logging, which destroys the forest resource unless it is managed carefully as an element of an overall silviculture plan.

In short, I find that at treaty time, the Chippewa were not exploiting timber for their own use or for commercial purposes, although they were exploiting the various species of trees in the forest for a multitude of purposes other than for timber. I find and conclude also that commercial logging is not simply a modern means of harvesting but an entirely different activity from any the Chippewa engaged in at treaty time.

Because plaintiffs did not reserve a usufructuary right to harvest the commercial timber resource under their treaties with the United States, defendants may regulate plaintiffs' harvesting of this resource in the same manner they regulate the non-Indian harvest.

5. Habitat Protection for the Treaty Fishing Right

The habitat protection issue was outlined some years ago by Professor Blumm and Brett Swift:

> Unfortunately, today the salmon runs included in the treaty right to take fish have dwindled to a fraction of their former size, as a century of dam building, timber harvesting, and other habitat-damaging activities have taken a severe toll. Despite expensive programs aimed at restoring salmon populations, several salmon runs have been listed under the Endangered Species Act. As a result, a central promise of the treaties—that tribal members could earn livelihoods from fishing—has gone unfulfilled.
>
> Not surprisingly, Indian tribes in recent years have invoked the treaty right of taking fish in order to protect salmon habitats that are so critical to preserving the salmon populations necessary to sustain a livelihood from fishing. Nearly twenty years ago, the Supreme Court inferred that the treaties included protection for salmon habitat. The Court, in affirming that the treaties reserved to the tribes one-half of the harvest, observed that the treaties forbade the crowding out of tribal fisherman by property rules, fish wheels, license fees, or general regulations. The Court also declared that the tribes were entitled to more than the mere chance to dip their nets into empty waters. The use of the treaty fishing right to prevent habitat-damaging activity or development, however, is controversial. A district court ruling that

Indians exercising the treaty fishing right could enjoin habitat-damaging activities was vacated by an en banc panel of the Ninth Circuit, which refused to decide the habitat issue by summary judgment in the absence of concrete facts.

For more than a dozen years, the habitat issue has lain dormant as the tribes devoted their attention to developing and implementing salmon restoration plans under the Northwest Power Act and the Endangered Species Act. That era appears about to end, however, as some tribal leaders are exhibiting increasing impatience with the lack of restoration progress. Thus, the courts may soon be forced to revisit the question of whether the treaty right to fish includes the right to protect fish habitat where necessary to ensure sufficient fish in the river to fulfill the treaty promise.

Michael C. Blumm & Brett M. Swift, *The Indian Treaty Piscary Profit and Habitat Protection in the Pacific Northwest: A Property Rights Approach*, 69 U. Colo. L. Rev. 407, 409–411 (1998).*

Notes

1. The first habitat protection opinion. In 1970, when the Stevens Treaty tribes petitioned the district court for a harvest allocation, they also asked for a declaration that the treaty fishing right included a right to protect the habitat on which the fish depended for survival. Their theory was that an allocated share—even 50%—of salmon runs that were near extinction was inconsistent with the treaty promise. The district court deferred the habitat issue until the allocation issue was resolved. When the Supreme Court, in *Passenger Fishing Vessel* in 1979, interpreted the purpose of the treaty fishing right to supply the tribes with a livelihood, the tribes reiterated their request for a declaration that the treaty right included a right to protect habitat, in what became known as "Phase II" of *United States v. Washington*. In 1980, the district court agreed with the tribes, determining that "[t]he fundamental prerequisite to exercising the right to take fish is the existence of fish to be taken." The court concluded that:

> Were this trend [loss of salmon habitat] to continue, the right to take fish would eventually be reduced to the right to dip one's net into the water ... and bring it out empty. Such a result would render nugatory the nine-year effort in Phase I, sanctioned by this Court, the Ninth Circuit, and the Supreme Court, to enforce the treaties' reservation to the tribes of a sufficient quantity of fish to meet their fair needs.

United States v. Washington, 506 F. Supp. 187 (W.D. Wash. 1980), *vacated*, 759 F.2d 1353 (9th Cir. 1985). The district court tied the state's (and federal government's)

---

* Michael C. Blumm & Brett Swift, *The Indian Treaty Piscary Profit and Habitat Protection in the Pacific Northwest: A Property Rights Approach*, 69 U. Colo. L. Rev. 407 (1998). Reprinted with permission of the *University of Colorado Law Review*.

obligations to protect habitat to the tribes' "moderate living" needs, a phrase drawn from the Supreme Court's *Passenger Fishing Vessel* decision (Phase I). Thus, the state and federal governments were to refrain from authorizing activities that degraded fish habitat unless they could prove that habitat-damaging development would not interfere with the tribes' moderate living needs. When the harvest share allocation from Phase I was set at 50% of the harvest, the court presumed that the tribes' moderate living needs were unmet.

A panel of the Ninth Circuit modified the district court's opinion by banning discriminatory developments and articulating the scope of the state's authority in terms of "reasonable steps commensurate with the resources and abilities [of both the state and the tribes] to preserve and enhance the fishery." The court also ruled without explanation that the habitat protection duty applied only to the state, not private parties. *United States v. Washington*, 694 F.2d 1374, 1387–89 (9th Cir. 1982). The tribes successfully sought rehearing *en banc*, but a majority of the *en banc* panel ruled that articulating the scope of the habitat protection right in a case without concrete facts (the tribes had merely asked for a declaratory judgment) was judicially imprudent, possibly producing legal rules that would be "imprecise in definition and uncertain in dimension." The court observed that the legal standards governing the state's obligations should "depend for their definition and articulation upon concrete facts which underlie a dispute in a concrete case." *United States v. Washington*, 759 F.2d 1353, 1357 (9th Cir. 1985).

2. Water flows for habitat protection. As we saw in Chapter VII, Section C, tribes in the Pacific Northwest in particular are generally entitled to a reserved water right for their fisheries. There is a strong connection between water rights and habitat protection. In one notable decision involving a water right for fisheries, the district court quantified the Spokane Tribe's water rights in terms of water temperature, in order to promote salmon spawning. *United States v. Anderson*, 6 Indian L. Rep. F-129 (E.D. Wash. July 23, 1979) (determining that the amount of water reserved was that necessary to preserve trout fishing, which the court determined required temperatures of 68 degrees or less, and in no case less than 20 cubic feet per second), *aff'd*, 591 F.Supp. 1 (E.D. Wash. 1982), *aff'd in part and rev'd in part on other grounds*, 736 F.2d 1358 (9th Cir. 1984). *See also Colville Confederated Tribes v. Walton*, 647 F.2d 42, 46, 48 (9th Cir. 1981) (finding reserved water rights to establish replacement fishing grounds); *United States v. Adair*, 723 F.2d 1394, 1411, 1414–15 (9th Cir. 1983) (declaring reserved water to support fishing for a "moderate living").

Habitat protection can also depend on water allocation decisions that are made by the state and federal governments. In 1980, the federal Bureau of Reclamation reduced river flows from the Cle Elum Dam in the Yakima Basin at the end of the irrigation season in order to store water for the next season. The reduced flows threatened salmon redds (nests) with dewatering, because the salmon had spawned unusually high in the Yakima River that fall due to unusually high irrigation releases from the dam. The Yakama Nation, which had been unable to exercise its fishing rights in the river for several years due to depleted numbers of returning salmon, requested the basin watermaster to order the Bureau to maintain the flows to protect the redds. The watermaster in turn asked the district court if he had the authority to do so. The district court answered in the affirmative, ordering the watermaster to take a number of steps to preserve the redds, including maintaining streamflows. *Kittatas Reclamation Dist. v. Sunnyside Valley Irrig. Dist.*, 763 F.2d 1032 (9th Cir. 1985). This case had the kind of concrete facts the *en banc* panel of the Ninth Circuit sought in Phase II of *United States v. Washington*.

The irrigation districts appealed the district court decision, and the Ninth Circuit three times affirmed the lower court decision, growing progressively vaguer about the nature of the treaty obligations each time (in response to the district court, panel, and *en banc* decisions in Phase II of *United States v. Washington*), but nevertheless upholding the lower court. The first unpublished decision in 1982 stated that: "[t]he parties to a treaty bear a duty to refrain from actions interfering with either the Indians' access to fishing grounds or the amount of fish there." (No. 80-3505, slip op. Sept. 10. 1982). The second opinion, in February 1985, again affirmed the decision to require flow releases, but stated: "we need not decide the exact scope of the treaty fishing right. It is enough to note that the Indian fishing rights are protected and under those circumstance the release of water is justified in order to avoid damage to the redds." 752 F.2d 1456 (9th Cir. 1985). The second opinion was revoked after the *en banc* decision in the Phase II case and replaced with an opinion that merely observed that there was "no abuse of discretion in the [district] court's decision," and that under the circumstances the court's flow directives constituted "reasonable emergency measures." *Kittitas Reclamation Dist.*, 763 F.2d at 1035.

3. Other habitat protection decisions. In several other decisions, lower courts reached results consistent with implying habitat protection in the treaty fishing right. *See, e.g., No Oilport! v. Carter*, 520 F. Supp. 334, 372–73 (W.D. Wash. 1980) (concerning a pipeline which would have been buried under rivers with treaty fishing); *Muckleshoot v. Hall*, 698 F.Supp. 1504 (W.D. Wash. 1988) (concerning a proposed marina); *Northwest Sea Farms v. U.S. Army Corps of Engineers*, 931 F. Supp. 1515 (W.D. Wash. 1996) (concerning a proposed net pen "fish farm").

4. The tribal salmon restoration plan. In 1995, the Columbia River Inter-Tribal Fish Commission, comprised of the four Columbia Basin tribes with Stevens Treaty fishing rights, released *Wy-Kan-Ush-Mi Wa-Kish-Wit*, or *The Spirit of the Salmon*, which, unlike competing federal and state salmon restoration plans, aimed to restore Columbia Basin salmon runs to their historic populations in their historic habitats. The plan emphasized natural production and healthy ecosystems through "gravel-to-gravel" management that would focus on improved stream flows, reservoir drawdowns, and improved riparian habitat through changed land use practices. The tribal plan also embraced "supplementation," a controversial hatchery technique that seeks to produce spawning fish from native broodstock and rear them in habitat that closely resembles natural rearing habitat. Anti-hatchery critics claim that supplementation is simply another hatchery technique that risks genetic damage to native fish populations. Although parts of the tribal plan have been incorporated into the federal and state Columbia Basin salmon restoration plans, the plan as a whole has gone unimplemented. *See generally* Melissa Powers, *The Spirit of the Salmon: How the Tribal Restoration Plan Could Restore Columbia Basin Salmon*, 30 Envtl. L. 867 (2000).

5. The Northwest Power Act. Habitat protection for Columbia Basin salmon was promised by the 1980 Northwest Power Act, 16 U.S.C. §§ 839 *et seq.*, which also incorporated the tribes as coequal fishery managers with the Northwest states. *See* Michael C. Blumm, Michael A. Schoessler & Christopher Beckwith, *Beyond the Parity Promise: Struggling to Save Salmon in the Mid-1990s*, 27 Envtl. L. 21 (1997). Unfortunately, the Act's promise of restoring salmon runs damaged by the operation of the federal Columbia River dams has never been fulfilled. *See generally* Michael C. Blumm, Sacrificing the Salmon: A Legal and Policy History of the Decline of Columbia Basin Salmon 129–60 (BookWorld Pub. 2002). One reason for the disappointing track record is captured in the decision of the Ninth Circuit, which made the statutory directive requiring the Bonneville Power Administration and other federal power managers to give "equitable treatment" to fish and wildlife when making hydroelectric power production decisions essentially unenforceable. *Confederated Tribes v. Bonneville Power Administration*, 342 F.3d 924 (9th Cir. 2003) (rejecting arguments by the tribes, environmental groups, and the state of Oregon that Bonneville unreasonably delayed implementing the equitable treatment directive). For a pessimistic perspective that describes the failure of the Endangered Species Act, which has largely supplanted the Northwest Power Act, at least in terms of regulating mainstem Columbia Basin fish flows and dam passage, *see* Michael C. Blumm, Erica J. Thorson & Joshua A. Smith, *Practiced at the Art of Deception: The Failure of Columbia Basin Salmon Recovery Under the Endangered Species Act*, 36 Envtl. L. 709 (2006).

In 2016, the federal district court in Oregon issued a lengthy opinion that struck down the National Marine Fisheries Service's biological opinion (BiOp) on Columbia Basin hydroelectric operations for the sixth time during the past two decades. The court determined that the BiOp's conclusion that some 73 "reasonable and prudent alternatives" (RPAs) would avoid jeopardy to listed salmon species was arbitrary because it employed an improper "jeopardy" standard ("trending toward recovery"), failed to consider the climate change-induced effects on the RPAs, and relied on measures that were reasonably certain to occur. The court also concluded that the federal agencies responsible for implementing the RPAs (the Corps of Engineers, the Bureau of Reclamation, and the Bonneville Power Administration) violated NEPA by not preparing a comprehensive environmental impact statement (EIS) the measures implementing the BiOp that would consider the alternative of breaching the four federal Lower Snake River dams, although the court did not enjoin ongoing hydroelectric operations. *Nat'l Wildlife Fed'n v. Nat'l Marine Fisheries Serv.*, 184 F. Supp. 2d 861 (D. Or. 2016). However, an ensuing 2017 decision called for increased spring and summer spills at federal dams to facilitate juvenile salmon passage while the EIS is being prepared. *Id.*, 2017 WL 1829588 (D. Or.). *See* Michael C. Blumm, Julianne L. Fry & Olivier Jamin, *Still "Crying Out for a Major Overhaul" After All These Years: Salmon and Another Failed Biological Opinion on Columbia Basin*

Hydroelectric Operations, 47 Envtl. L. 287 (2017). The Ninth Circuit affirmed within just two weeks of oral argument in *Nat'l. Wildlife Fed'n. v. Nat'l Marine Fisheries Serv.,* 886 F.3d 803 (9th Cir. 2018). Some members of Congress have drafted a bill that would reverse Judge Simon's decision, keep the existing biological opinion in force until 2022, and foreclose the dam breaching alternative. *See* Associated Press, *Bill in Congress Seeks to Preserve the Snake River Dams,* U.S. News (July 2, 2017), https://www.usnews.com/news/best-states/washington/articles/2017-07-02/bill-in-congress-seeks-to-preserve-the-snake-river-dams.

United States v. Washington
No. CV 9213RSM, 2007 WL 2437166 (W.D. Wash., Aug. 22, 2007)

MARTINEZ, District Judge.

This is a designated subproceeding of *United States, et al., v. State of Washington, et al.,* C70-9213. The United States, in conjunction with the Tribes, initiated this subproceeding in early 2001, seeking to compel the State of Washington to repair or replace any culverts that are impeding salmon migration to or from the spawning grounds.

This subproceeding arises from the language in Article III of the 1855 Treaty of Point Elliot ("Stevens Treaties") in which the Tribes were promised that "[t]he right of taking fish, at all usual and accustomed grounds and stations, is further secured to said Indians, in common with all citizens of the Territory. . . ." The Tribes state that they brought this action

> to enforce a duty upon the State of Washington to refrain from constructing and maintaining culverts under State roads that degrade fish habitat so that adult fish production is reduced, which in turn reduces the number of fish available for harvest by the Tribes. In part due to the reduction of harvestable fish caused by those actions of the State, the ability of the Tribes to achieve a moderate living from their Treaty fisheries has been impaired.

The Tribes requested mandatory relief "requiring Washington to identify and then to open culverts under state roads and highways that obstruct fish passage, for fish runs returning to or passing through the usual and accustomed grounds and stations of the plaintiff tribes." Specifically, they request a declaratory judgment, establishing that (1) the right of taking fish secured by the Treaties imposes a duty upon the State of Washington to refrain from diminishing the number of fish passing through, or to or from the Tribes' usual and accustomed fishing grounds by improperly constructing or maintaining culverts under State-owned roads and highways; and that (2) the State has violated, and continues to violate, the duty owed the Tribes under the Stevens Treaties. Further, the Tribes request a prohibitory injunction, prohibiting the State of Washington and its agencies from constructing or maintaining any culverts that reduce the number of fish that would otherwise return to or pass through the usual and accustomed fishing grounds of the Tribes. Finally, they request a mandatory injunction, requiring the State to (1) identify, within eighteen months, the location of all culverts constructed or maintained by State agencies, that diminish the number of fish in the manner set forth above, and (2) fix, within five years after judgment, and thereafter maintain all culverts built or maintained by any State agency, so that they do not diminish the number of fish as set forth above.

The Tribes, in their Request, assert that between 1974, the year that this case was originally decided, and 1986, Tribal harvests of anadromous fish (salmon and steelhead) rose dramatically, eventually reaching some 5 million fish. Then harvests declined, so that by 1999 harvests were back down to the 1974 levels. The Tribes contend that "[a] significant reason for the decline of harvestable fish has been the destruction and modification of habitat needed for their survival."

The Request addresses one specific type of habitat modification: the placement of culverts rather than bridges where roadways cross rivers and streams. The Tribes allege that when such culverts are improperly built or maintained, they block fish passage up or down the stream, "thereby preventing out-migration of juvenile fish to rearing areas or the salt water, or the return of adult fish to spawning beds, or both." According to the Tribes, culverts under State-owned or maintained roads block fish access to at least 249 linear miles of stream, thus closing off more than 400,000 square meters of productive spawning habitat, and more than 1.5 million square meters of productive rearing habitat for juvenile fish. The Tribes state that, by the State's own estimates, removal of the obstacles presented by blocked culverts would result in an annual increase in production of 200,000 fish, many of which would be available for Tribal harvest.

The State does not dispute the fact that a certain number of culverts under State-owned roads present barriers to fish migration. The State notes that 18% of the culverts on land managed by the Department of Natural Resources were identified as barriers in a 2000 inventory. Washington State Parks have identified 120 culverts as fish passage barriers. And of the thousands of culverts passing under roads maintained by the Washington State Department of Transportation, the State asserts that "most," but not all, allow free passage of migrating fish—meaning that many do not.

The State argues that the Tribes have produced no evidence that the blocked culverts "affirmatively diminish[] the number of fish available for harvest." The Tribes have, however, produced evidence of greatly diminished fish runs. While there may be other contributing causes for this, the conclusion is inescapable that if culverts block fish passage so that they cannot swim upstream to spawn, or downstream to reach the ocean, those blocked culverts are responsible for some portion of the diminishment. It is not necessary for the Tribes to exactly quantify the numbers of "missing" fish to proceed in this matter.

The issue then becomes a purely legal one: whether the Tribes' treaty-based right of taking fish imposes upon the State a duty to refrain from diminishing fish runs by construction or maintaining culverts that block fish passage.

* * * The Tribes' showing that fish harvests have been substantially diminished, together with the logical inference that a significant portion of this diminishment is due to the blocked culverts which cut off access to spawning grounds and rearing areas, is sufficient to support a declaration regarding the culverts' impairment of treaty rights.

In finding a duty on the part of the State to refrain from blocking fish access to spawning grounds and rearing habitat, the Court has been guided by well-established principles of treaty construction. [The court discussed the relevant case law.]

It was thus the right to *take* fish, not just the right to fish, that was secured by the treaties. The significance of this right to the Tribes, its function as an incentive for the Indians to sign the treaties, and the Tribes' reliance on the unchanging nature of that right, have been set forth in expert declarations provided by the Tribes.

It was thus the government's intent, and the Tribes' understanding, that they would be able to meet their own subsistence needs forever, and not become a burden on the treasury.

Thus, the Tribes were persuaded to cede huge tracts of land—described by the Supreme Court as "millions of acres"—by the promise that they would forever have access to this resource, which was thought to be inexhaustible. It was not deemed necessary to write any protection for the resource into the treaty because nothing in any of the parties' experience gave them the reason to believe that would be necessary.

As [an expert historian] stated, the representatives of the Tribes were personally assured during the negotiations that they could safely give up vast quantities of land and yet be certain that their right to take fish was secure. These assurances would only be meaningful if they carried the implied promise that neither the negotiators nor their successors would take actions that would significantly degrade the resource. Such resource-degrading activities as the building of stream-blocking culverts could not have been anticipated by the Tribes, who themselves had cultural practices that migrated negative impacts of their fishing on the salmon stocks.

In light of these affirmative assurances given the Tribes as an inducement to sign the Treaties, together with the Tribes' understanding of the reach of those assurances, as set forth by the Supreme Court in the language quoted above, this Court finds that the Treaties do impose a duty upon the State to refrain from building or maintaining culverts in such a manner as to block the passage of fish upstream or down, to or from the Tribes' usual and accustomed fishing places. This is not a broad "environmental servitude" or the imposition of an affirmative duty to take all possible steps to protect fish runs as the State protests, but rather a narrow directive to refrain from impeding fish runs in one specific manner. The Tribes have presented sufficient facts regarding the number of blocked culverts to justify a declaratory judgment regarding the State's duty to refrain from such activity. This duty arises directly from the right of taking fish that was assured to the Tribes in the Treaties, and is necessary to fulfill the promises made to the Tribes regarding the extent of that right.

Notes

1. **The role of the federal government.** The federal government joined with the tribes in bringing this case. Yet the federal government itself has built and maintains

numerous culverts on federal lands throughout western Washington. Might not the declaratory relief granted by the district court be extended to the federal government's culverts? If so, is this a case where the federal trustee in effect sued itself? See Michael C. Blumm & Jane G. Steadman, *Indian Treaty Fishing Rights and Habitat Protection: The* Martinez *Decision Supplies a Resounding Judicial Reaffirmation*, 49 Nat. Res. J. 653 (2009) (noting, among other issues, that the decision did not decide an appropriate remedy for the treaty habitat violation).

2. The nature of the relief. The court's order was limited to declaratory relief. In 2010, after lengthy settlement negotiations on the appropriate remedy failed (basically over the issues of the scope and timing of culvert repair), Judge Martinez heard motions for summary judgment in 2013 and proceeded to issue an injunction requiring the state to begin repairing more than 600 state-owned road culverts blocking salmon migration, giving the state 17 years to complete the task. The court ruled that an injunction was necessary because the state had reduced repair efforts in recent years, resulting in a net increase of fish blocking culverts, meaning that at the current rate, repairs would never be completed. The decision found that the state's duty to fix the culverts did not arise from a "broad environmental servitude" but instead from a "narrow and specific treaty-based duty that attaches when the state elects to block rather than bridge a salmon-bearing stream. . . ." *United States v. Washington*, No. C70-9213, 2013 WL 1334391 (W.D. Wash.) (determining that the tribes had been irreparably harmed "economically, socially, educationally, and culturally by the generally reduced salmon harvest."). The Ninth Circuit affirmed in 2016 in the following decision.

United States v. Washington
827 F.3d 836 (9th Cir 2016), superseded by 853 F.3d 946 (9th Cir. 2017)

[Some 46 years after the tribes filed suit, a unanimous Ninth Circuit panel affirmed Judge Martinez's injunction requiring the state to correct road culverts blocking salmon migration because they violated treaty fishing rights. In doing so, the court rejected the state's claim that the federal government had waived the treaty right by actions and inaction over the years, stating that the federal government had no authority to waive tribal rights, and it also rejected the state's argument that the federal government should be required to fix its culverts first on sovereign immunity grounds. If the federal government violated the treaties with its culverts, according to the court, that was a case that the tribes could pursue, but they had chosen not to do so. After discussing the centrality of salmon to the tribes negotiating the Stevens Treaties and long and tortuous litigation leading up to the decision, the court invoked the canons of treaty interpretation (most citations omitted)]:

We have long construed treaties between the United States and Indian tribes in favor of the Indians. Chief Justice Marshall wrote in the third case of the Marshall Trilogy, "The language used in treaties with the Indians should never be construed to their prejudice." "If words be made use of which are susceptible of a more extended meaning than their plain import, as connected with the tenor of the treaty, they should be considered as used only in the latter sense."

Negotiations for the Stevens Treaties were conducted in the Chinook language, a trading jargon of only about 300 words. The Treaties were written in English, a language the Indians could neither read nor write. Because treaty negotiations with Indians were conducted by "representatives skilled in diplomacy," because negotiators representing the United States were "assisted by . . . interpreter[s] employed by themselves," because the treaties were "drawn up by [the negotiators] and in their own language," and because the "only knowledge of the terms in which the treaty is framed is that imparted to [the Indians] by the interpreter employed by the United States," a "treaty must . . . be construed, not according to the technical meaning of its words to learned lawyers, but in the sense in which they would naturally be understood by the Indians." "[W]e will construe a treaty with the Indians as [they] understood it, and as justice and reason demand, in all cases where power is exerted by the strong over those to whom they owe care and protection, and counterpoise the inequality by the superior justice which looks only to the substance of the right, without regard to technical rules." "[W]e look beyond the written words to the larger context that frames the Treaty, including the history of the treaty, the negotiations, and the practical construction adopted by the parties."

The Supreme Court has interpreted the Stevens Treaties on several occasions. In affirming Judge Boldt's decision, the Court wrote:

> [I]t is the intention of the parties, and not solely that of the superior side, that must control any attempt to interpret the treaties. When Indians are involved, this Court has long given special meaning to this rule. It has held that the United States, as the party with the presumptively superior negotiating skills and superior knowledge of the language in which the treaty is recorded, has a responsibility to avoid taking advantage of the other side. "[T]he treaty must therefore be construed, not according to the technical meaning of its words to learned lawyers, but in the sense in which they would naturally be understood by the Indians." This rule, in fact, has thrice been explicitly relied on by the Court in broadly interpreting these very treaties in the Indians' favor.

Washington has a remarkably one-sided view of the Treaties. In its brief, Washington characterizes the "treaties' principal purpose" as "opening up the region to settlement." Opening up the Northwest for white settlement was indeed the principal purpose of the United States. But it was most certainly not the principal purpose of the Indians. Their principal purpose was to secure a means of supporting themselves once the Treaties took effect.

The Indians did not understand the treaties to promise that they would have access to their usual and accustomed fishing places, but with a qualification that would allow the government to diminish or destroy the fish runs. Governor Stevens did not make, and the Indians did not understand him to make, such a cynical and disingenuous promise. The Indians reasonably understood Governor Stevens to promise not only that they would have access to their usual and accustomed fishing places, but also that there would be fish sufficient to sustain them. They reasonably understood that they would have, in Stevens' words, "food and drink . . . forever." As the Supreme Court wrote in *Fishing Vessel*:

> Governor Stevens and his associates were well aware of the "sense" in which the Indians were likely to view assurances regarding their fishing rights. During the negotiations, the vital importance of the fish to the Indians was repeatedly emphasized by both sides, and the Governor's promises that the treaties would *protect that source of food and commerce* were crucial in obtaining the Indians' assent. It is absolutely clear, as Governor Stevens himself said, that neither he nor the Indians intended that the latter should be excluded from their ancient fisheries, and it is accordingly inconceivable that either party deliberately agreed to authorize future settlers to crowd the Indians out of any *meaningful use* of their accustomed places to fish. (emphasis added).

Even if Governor Stevens had not explicitly promised that "this paper secures your fish," and that there would be food "forever," we would infer such a promise. In *Winters v. United States*, the treaty creating the Fort Belknap Reservation in Montana did not include an explicit reservation of water for use on the reserved lands, but the Supreme Court inferred a reservation of water sufficient to support the tribe. The purpose of the treaty was to reserve land on which the Indians could become farmers. Without a reservation of water, the "lands were arid, and . . . practically valueless." "[B]etween two inferences, one of which would support the purpose of the agreement and the other impair or defeat it," the Court chose the former.

Similarly, in *United States v. Adair*, the Klamath Tribe in Oregon had entered into an 1854 treaty under which it relinquished 12 million acres, reserving for itself approximately 800,000 acres. The treaty promised that the tribe would have the right to "hunt, fish, and gather on their reservation," but contained no explicit reservation of water rights. A prime hunting and fishing area on the reservation was the Klamath Marsh, whose suitability for hunting and fishing depended on a flow of water from the Williamson River. A primary purpose of the treaty was to "secure to the Tribe a continuation of its traditional hunting and fishing" way of living. Because game and fish at the Klamath Marsh depended on a continual flow of water, the treaty's purpose would have been defeated without that flow. In order to "support the purpose of the agreement," we inferred a promise of water sufficient to ensure an adequate supply of game and fish.

Thus, even if Governor Stevens had made no explicit promise, we would infer, as in *Winters* and *Adair*, a promise to "support the purpose" of the Treaties. That is, even in the absence of an explicit promise, we would infer a promise that the number of fish would always be sufficient to provide a "moderate living" to the Tribes. Just as the land on the Belknap Reservation would have been worthless without water to irrigate the arid land, and just as the right to hunt and fish on the Klamath Marsh would have been worthless without water to provide habitat for game and fish, the Tribes' right of access to their usual and accustomed fishing places would be worthless without harvestable fish.

In *Washington III*, we vacated the district court's declaration of a broad and undifferentiated obligation to prevent environmental degradation. We did not dispute that the State had environmental obligations, but, in the exercise of discretion under the Declaratory Judgment Act, we declined to sustain the sweeping declaratory judgment issued by the district court. We wrote, "The legal standards that will govern the State's precise obligations and duties under the treaty with respect to the myriad State actions that may affect the environment of the treaty area will depend for their definition and articulation upon concrete facts which underlie a dispute in a particular case."

We concluded [that] "[t]he State of Washington is bound by the treaty. If the State acts for the primary purpose or object of affecting or regulating the fish supply or catch in noncompliance with the treaty as interpreted by past decisions, it will be subject to immediate correction and remedial action by the courts. In other instances, the measure of the State's obligation will depend for its precise legal formulation on all of the facts presented by a particular dispute."

There is no allegation in this case that in building and maintaining its barrier culverts the State has acted "for the primary purpose or object of affecting or regulating the fish supply or catch in noncompliance with the treaty." The consequence of building and maintaining the barrier culverts has been to diminish the supply of fish, but this consequence was not the State's "primary purpose or object." The "measure of the State's obligation" therefore depends "on all the facts presented" in the "particular dispute" now before us.

The facts presented in the district court establish that Washington has acted affirmatively to build and maintain barrier culverts under its roads. The State's barrier culverts within the Case Area block approximately 1,000 linear miles of streams suitable for salmon habitat, comprising almost 5 million square meters. If these culverts were replaced or modified to allow free passage of fish, several hundred thousand additional mature salmon would be produced every year. Many of these mature salmon would be available to the Tribes for harvest.

Salmon now available for harvest are not sufficient to provide a "moderate living" to the Tribes. The district court found that "[t]he reduced abundance of salmon and the consequent reduction in tribal harvests has damaged tribal economies, has left individual tribal members unable to earn a living by fishing, and has caused cultural and social harm to the Tribes in addition to the economic harm." The court found, further, that "[m]any members of the Tribes would engage in more commercial and subsistence salmon fisheries if more fish were available."

We therefore conclude that in building and maintaining barrier culverts within the Case Area, Washington has violated, and is continuing to violate, its obligation to the Tribes under the Treaties.

B. Waiver by the United States

[Rejecting the state's waiver claim, the court concluded:] "The United States may abrogate treaties with Indian tribes, just as it may abrogate treaties with fully sovereign nations. However, it may abrogate a treaty with an Indian tribe only by an Act of Congress that "clearly express[es an] intent to do so." Congress has not abrogated the Stevens Treaties. So long as this is so, the Tribes' rights under the fishing clause remain valid and enforceable. The United States, as trustee for the Tribes, may bring suit on their behalf to enforce the Tribes' rights, but the rights belong to the Tribes.

The United States cannot, based on laches or estoppel, diminish or render unenforceable otherwise valid Indian treaty rights. The same is true for waiver. Because the treaty rights belong to the Tribes rather than the United States, it is not the prerogative of the United States to waive them.

[The court proceeded to uphold the district court's injunction, finding that it was based on "extensive" record evidence, including from the state itself, that barrier culverts have substantial adverse effects on salmon, and that the district court did not ignore the state's expertise, citing a state expert's conclusion that removing barrier culverts would produce "the biggest bang for the buck." The court also thought the state's cost estimates for fixing the culverts were exaggerated, and that the injunction violated no federalism principles.]

Conclusion

In sum, we conclude that in building and maintaining barrier culverts Washington has violated, and continues to violate, its obligation to the Tribes under the fishing clause of the Treaties. The United States has not waived the rights of the Tribes under the Treaties, and has not waived its own sovereign immunity by bringing suit on behalf of the Tribes. The district court did not abuse its discretion in enjoining Washington to correct most of its high-priority barrier culverts within seventeen years, and to correct the remainder at the end of their natural life or in the course of a road construction project undertaken for independent reasons.

Affirmed.

Notes

1. Commentary on the culverts case. For an assessment of the case, see Michael C. Blumm, *Indian Treaty Fishing Rights and the Environment: Affirming the Right of Habitat Protection and Restoration*, 92 Wash. L. Rev. 1 (2017) (suggesting that the decision could have effects beyond the state of Washington and beyond road culverts), an article published before the Ninth Circuit amended its decision in ways which did not affect the analysis.

2. Affirmed by an equally divided Court. The state sought a rehearing en banc, but the full Ninth Circuit denied rehearing in May 2017, although nine judges dissented from the denial. *United States v. Washington*, No. 13-35474 (May 19, 2017). The dissents may have persuaded the Court to accept certiorari, which it did on January 12, 2018, 138 S. Ct. 735. In June, however, the Supreme Court affirmed the Ninth Circuit by an equally divided Court, with Justice Kennedy taking no part in the decision. 584 U.S. __, 2018 WL 2767653 (June 11, 2018).

3. No environmental servitude. Why is it that the culverts case does not establish an environmental servitude, the possibility that worried the Ninth Circuit panel in the 1982 decision, discussed at page 651? Could not the principles of this case be extended, for example, to state-authorized timber harvests that damaged salmon habitat? Could they be extended to federally-authorized timber harvests? Consider the case of *Klamath Tribes v. U.S. Forest Service*, No. 969-381-HA (D. Or., Oct. 2, 1996), which addressed the effects of federal timber harvests on the Klamath Tribes' treaty hunting rights.

As a result of a 1954 termination act, the Klamath reservation no longer exists, and the tribes' usufructuary rights now exist on federal lands, mostly national forest lands. Under a 1995 appropriations rider, the Forest Service planned eight expedited timber sales, exempt from environmental statutes, on the tribe's ceded territory. The tribes filed suit, alleging that the sales amounted to a breach of the federal government's fiduciary duties because the sales would destroy prime old-growth habitat for mule deer which were necessary for the tribes' subsistence. The district court determined that the 1995 timber rider did not abrogate the tribes' treaty rights, because it did not mention them. The court further ruled that the federal fiduciary obligation required more than mere consultation with the tribes; the government also had "a substantive duty to protect 'to the fullest extent possible' the tribes' treaty rights, and the resources on which those rights depend." The court therefore enjoined the sales until the federal government "assure[d], in consultation with the Klamath Tribes on a government-to-government basis, that the resources on which the tribes depend will be protected." *See* Ed Goodman, *Protecting Habitat for Off-Reservation Tribal Hunting and Fishing Rights: Tribal Co-management as a Reserved Right*, 30 Envtl. L. 279, 297–98 (2000); *see also* U.S. Interior Solicitor, Fishing Rights of the Yurok and Hoopa Valley Tribes (Op. No. M-36979, Oct. 4, 1993) (recognizing, in the context of fishing rights reserved by executive order, that protection of on-reservation tribal rights to resources may require the regulation of off-reservation activities that affect the tribes' ability to enjoy meaningful use of their reserved rights).

The result in the *Klamath Tribes* case—that the trust doctrine imposes on the government a substantive duty to protect treaty rights and resources "to the fullest extent practicable"—seems similar to the results in *Pyramid Lake Paiute Tribe v. Morton*, excerpted at page 547 (trust doctrine requires the Secretary of Interior to use statutory and contractual authority "to the fullest extent possible" to preserve water for the tribe), and *PASH v. Hawaii County Planning Comm'n*, excerpted at page 606 (Hawaiian constitution requires state agencies to protect native usufructuary rights "to the fullest extent feasible"). But compare those results to *Nevada v. United States*, excerpted at page 551 (trust doctrine does not allow the federal government to reallocate water from reclamation uses to tribal uses). What might account for the different results?

4. Rejecting a Damage Claim Due to Dam Construction and Operations. In *Nez Perce Tribe v. Idaho Power Company*, 847 F. Supp. 791 (D. Idaho 1994), the tribe unsuccessfully sought money damages due to the negative effects of the operation of Idaho Power Company's federally licensed dams in Hells Canyon on the Snake River. The tribe claimed the construction and operation of the dams violated its 1855 treaty as well as a Federal Power Act provision which made licensees liable for all property damage due to the construction, maintenance, and operation of their projects. The court rejected both claims, concluding that the tribe had no vested right to the fish damaged by the project and rephrasing its claim as "[t]he ultimate issue presented is whether the treaty provides the Tribe with an absolute right to preservation of the fish runs in the condition existing in 1855, free from environmental damage caused by a changing and developing society. Only if such a right exists is the Tribe entitled to an award of monetary damages." The court proceeded to declare that "Indian tribes do not have an absolute right to the preservation of the fish runs in their original 1855 condition, free from all environmental damage caused by the migration of increasing numbers of settlers and the resulting development of the land." The *Nez Perce* court repeatedly characterized the tribe's claim as seeking an "absolute right to preservation of the fish runs in the condition they existed in 1855." However, the scope of protection afforded to an owner of a profit a prendre, like "the right of taking fish," is only to restrain "unreasonable interferences" with the exercise of the profit. *See* Restatement (Third) of Property: Servitudes § 4.9 (2000).

There were actually two separate grounds for the Nez Perce's claim for damages: 1) diminished salmon runs due to the construction and operation of Idaho Power's dams; and 2) inundation of several tribal "usual and accustomed" fishing grounds. A magistrate judge mistakenly thought that the tribe had not originally raised the second issue until oral argument, and therefore dismissed the claim. When it became evident that the claim was indeed in the record, a separate decision was required. The magistrate concluded that Idaho Power could be held liable in conversion for inundating the fishing grounds, but the district court refused that recommendation and held that the tribe's fishing right amounted to nothing more than the right to cross land to reach the river. The district court opined that the tribe's claim amounted to an unwarranted attempt to prohibit all development of the river banks. Order on Second Report and Recommendation and Dismissing the Action, No. 91-0517-S-HLR (D. Idaho, Sept. 28, 1994).

Is this result consistent with *Winans* (page 471), where the Supreme Court described the treaty fishing right as impressing a "servitude ... a right in land" over all ceded lands?

Although the tribe appealed the district court's decision to the Ninth Circuit, it settled the case with the power company before the appeal was heard. Under the settlement, Idaho Power paid the tribe $11.5 million, plus an additional $5 million for the tribe's "full support" in the company's efforts to relicense the three dams in Hell's Canyon. See *Nez Perce Tribe v. Idaho Power Company*, CV-91-0517-S-HLR (D. Idaho Mar. 21, 1997) (district court's acceptance of the settlement). See generally *Nez Perce Water Rights Settlement Articles*, 42 Idaho L. Rev. 545–793 (2007).

5. The shellfish case. The result in *Nez Perce* was based on the court's unwillingness to view the tribe's treaty right as a property right, for damage to which section 10(c) of the Federal Power Act afforded a remedy. A subsequent Ninth Circuit decision makes it appear that the district court's conclusion was unlikely to withstand appeal. In *United States v. Washington*, 135 F.3d 618 (9th Cir. 1998), *amended by* 157 F.3d 630 (9th Cir. 1998), the court interpreted the "shellfish provision" in certain Stevens Treaties—which provides that the tribes "shall not take shellfish from any beds staked or cultivated by citizens"—to not exclude privately-owned shellfish beds from tribal harvests. According to the court, the only beds that were excluded were beds that were artificially enhanced by shellfish growers, who bore the burden of proving the efficacy of their efforts. The decision specifically recognized that unenhanced, privately-owned shellfish beds were burdened by the treaty, meaning that private ownership and the continuation of treaty harvests were not inconsistent with each other because the land ownership was burdened with the treaty usufruct, a prior property right. See Mariel J. Combs, United States v. Washington: *The Boldt Decision Reincarnated*, 29 Envtl. L. 683 (1999).

6. **The Cushman Dam Case.** The Skokomish Tribe sought damages against the city of Tacoma, Tacoma Public Utilities, and the United States for the operation of the Cushman hydroelectric project, which had damaged the tribe's fishery. The Ninth Circuit, affirming the district court, held that under the plain language of section 10(c) of the Federal Power Act, the United States was exempt from liability. *Skokomish Indian Tribe v. United States*, 410 F.3d 506, 512 (9th Cir. 2005). It further ruled that section 10(c) did not create a federal private right of action against the city and its utility, but only preserved existing state-law claims against licensees. All the tribe's state-law claims, the court held, were time-barred. For withering criticism of the decision, see William H. Rodgers, Jr., *Judicial Regrets and the Case of the Cushman Dam*, 36 Envtl. L. 397 (2006).

7. **Treaty rights versus property rights?** The Supreme Court in *Menominee Tribe of Indians v. United States*, 391 U.S. 404 (1968) (page 665), assumed that treaty fishing rights were property rights. The Court stated: "We find it difficult to believe that Congress, without explicit statement, would subject the United States to a claim for compensation by destroying property rights conferred by treaty." When is a treaty right to fish a property right, and when is it not?

8. **Treaty fishing rights and environmental regulation.** There is some evidence that environmental regulators are beginning to take treaty fishing rights seriously in their decisionmaking. For example, in 2014, the state of Oregon rejected a permit from Ambre Energy, an Australian company seeking a permit to construct a terminal on the Columbia River to export coal to Asia. The state denied the permit largely on the ground that would it would harm tribal fisheries. Then Governor John Kitzhaber declared that "Columbia River tribes have fundamental rights to these fisheries," and "any project that threatens those rights should be held to high standards." Timothy Carma, *Oregon Blocks Major Coal Export Terminal,* The Hill (Aug. 19, 2014), http://thehill.com/policy/energy-environment/215463-oregon-blocks-major-coal-export-terminal.

In 2016, the U.S. Army Corps of Engineers rejected a permit for the largest coal port ever proposed in North America, at Cherry Point, Washington, north of the Lummi Tribe's coastal reservation. The Corps determined that the project would interfere with the tribe's treaty rights to fish for herring and crabs as well as have adverse effects on tribal village and burial site. *See* Lynda V. Mapes, *Tribes Prevail, Kill Proposed Coal Terminal at Cherry Point,* Seattle Times (May 9, 2016), https://www.seattletimes.com/seattle-news/environment/tribes-prevail-kill-proposed-coal-terminal-at-cherry-point/. The Corps' reasoning in rejecting the permit makes for surprisingly good reading. Memorandum from Michelle Walker, Chief, Regulatory Branch, U.S. Army Corps of Engineers (May 9, 2016), https://perma.cc/6XB3-HGXL.

Also in 2016, a county government in Oregon denied Union Pacific Railroad Company's application for a permit to construct a second mainline track in the Columbia River Gorge in and near the city of Mosier. In doing so, the county reversed a planning commission approval of the project because the county board of commissioners determined the project would adversely affect treaty fishing rights. Union Pacific appealed that decision to the Columbia River Gorge Commission, an interstate compact agency that hears appeals of county National Scenic Area decisions. The Gorge Commission affirmed Wasco County's denial. *Union Pacific Railroad Co. v. Wasco County,* CRGC Nos. 16-01, 16-02 (Sept. 8, 2017), http://www.gorgecommission.org/images/uploads/appeals/20170908_Final_Opinion_and_Order_%2816-01%2C_16-02_%28Consolidated%29%29.pdf. Appeal of this decision is pending in the Oregon Court of Appeals. Union Pacific concurrently sought an injunction in federal district court claiming that the county decision and Gorge Commission's appeal were preempted by the Interstate Commerce Commission Termination Act and unconstitutionally burdened interstate commerce. Three tribes with treaty rights in the Columbia River Gorge moved to dismiss the federal court action under FRCP Rule 19 because the railroad failed to join the tribes as necessary parties to the suit; the tribes have sovereign immunity from suit. The court decided that it could not proceed without the tribes as defendants and dismissed the case. *Union Pacific Railroad Co. v. Runyon,* 2017 WL 923915 (D. Or. Mar. 8, 2017).

B. Loss and Diminishment of the Rights

Menominee Tribe of Indians v. United States
391 U.S. 404 (1968)

MR. JUSTICE DOUGLAS delivered the opinion of the Court.

The Menominee Tribe of Indians was granted a reservation in Wisconsin by the Treaty of Wolf River in 1854. By this treaty the Menominees retroceded certain lands they had acquired under an earlier treaty and the United States confirmed to them the Wolf River Reservation "for a home, to be held as Indian lands are held." Nothing was said in the 1854 treaty about hunting and fishing rights. Yet we agree with the Court of Claims that the language "to be held as Indian lands are held" includes the right to fish and to hunt. The record shows that the lands covered by the Wolf River Treaty of 1854 were selected precisely because they had an abundance of game. The essence of the Treaty of Wolf River was that the Indians were authorized to maintain on the new lands ceded to them as a reservation their way of life which included hunting and fishing.[2]

What the precise nature and extent of those hunting and fishing rights were we need not at this time determine. For the issue tendered by the present decision of the Court of Claims is whether those rights, whatever their precise extent, have been extinguished.

That issue arose because, beginning in 1962, Wisconsin took the position that the Menominees were subject to her hunting and fishing regulations. Wisconsin prosecuted three Menominees for violating those regulations and the Wisconsin Supreme Court held that the state regulations were valid, as the hunting and fishing rights of the Menominees had been abrogated by Congress in the Menominee Indian Termination Act of 1954.

Thereupon the tribe brought suit in the Court of Claims against the United States to recover just compensation for the loss of those hunting and fishing rights. The Court of Claims by a divided vote held that the tribe possessed hunting and fishing rights under the Wolf River Treaty; but it held, contrary to the Wisconsin Supreme Court, that those rights were not abrogated by the Termination Act of 1954. We granted the petition for a writ of certiorari in order to resolve that conflict between the two courts. On oral argument both petitioner and respondent urged that the judgment of the Court of Claims be affirmed. The State of Wisconsin appeared as amicus curiae and argued that that judgment be reversed.

In 1953 Congress by concurrent resolution instructed the Secretary of the Interior to recommend legislation for the withdrawal of federal supervision over certain American Indian tribes, including the Menominees. Several bills were offered, one for the Menominee Tribe that expressly preserved hunting and fishing rights. But the one that became the Termination Act of 1954, viz., H.R. 2828, did not mention hunting and fishing rights. Moreover, counsel for the Menominees spoke against the

---

2. As stated by the Supreme Court of Wisconsin:
"It would seem unlikely that the Menominees would have knowingly relinquished their special fishing and hunting rights which they enjoyed on their own lands, and have accepted in exchange other lands with respect to which such rights did not extend. They undoubtedly believed that these rights were guaranteed to them when these other lands were ceded to them 'to be held as Indian lands are held.' Construing this ambiguous provision of the 1854 treaty favorably to the Menominees, we determine that they enjoyed the same exclusive hunting rights free from the restrictions of the state's game laws over the ceded lands, which comprised the Menominee Indian Reservation, as they had enjoyed over the lands ceded to the United States by the 1848 treaty." *State v. Sanapaw*, 21 Wis. 2d 377, 383, 124 N.W.2d 41, 44 (1963).

bill, arguing that its silence would by implication abolish those hunting and fishing rights. It is therefore argued that they were abolished by the Termination Act.

The purpose of the 1954 Act was by its terms "to provide for orderly termination of Federal supervision over the property and members" of the tribe. Under its provisions, the tribe was to formulate a plan for future control of tribal property and service functions theretofore conducted by the United States. On or before April 30, 1961, the Secretary was to transfer to a tribal corporation or to a trustee chosen by him all property real and personal held in trust for the tribe by the United States.

The Menominees submitted a plan, looking toward the creation of a county in Wisconsin out of the former reservation and the creation by the Indians of a Wisconsin corporation to hold other property of the tribe and its members. The Secretary of the Interior approved the plan with modifications; the Menominee Enterprises, Inc., was incorporated; and numerous ancillary laws were passed by Wisconsin integrating the former reservation into its county system of government. The Termination Act provided that after the transfer by the Secretary of title to the property of the tribe, all federal supervision was to end and "the laws of the several States shall apply to the tribe and its members in the same manner as they apply to other citizens or persons within their jurisdiction."

It is therefore argued with force that the Termination Act of 1954, which became fully effective in 1961, submitted the hunting and fishing rights of the Indians to state regulation and control. We reach, however, the opposite conclusion. The same Congress that passed the Termination Act also passed Public Law 280, as amended, 18 U.S.C. § 1162. The latter came out of the same committees of the Senate and the House as did the Termination Act; and it was amended[11] in a way that is critical here only two months after the Termination Act became law. As amended, Public Law 280 granted designated States, including Wisconsin, jurisdiction "over offenses committed by or against Indians in the areas of Indian country" named in the Act, which in the case of Wisconsin was described as "All Indian country within the State." But Public Law 280 went on to say that "Nothing in this section . . . shall deprive any Indian or any Indian tribe, band, or community of any right, privilege, or immunity afforded under Federal treaty, agreement, or statute *with respect to hunting, trapping, or fishing* or the control, licensing, or regulation thereof." (Emphasis added.) That provision on its face contains no limitation; it protects any hunting, trapping, or fishing right granted by a federal treaty. Public Law 280, as amended, became the

---

11. As originally enacted Public Law 280 exempted the Menominees from its provisions. The House Reports on Pub. L. 280 and on Pub. L. 661 indicate that the Menominees had specifically asked for exemption from the provisions of the bill that eventually became Pub. L. 280, on the ground that their tribal law and order program was functioning satisfactorily. Subsequently, the tribe reconsidered its position and sponsored H.R. 9821, amending Pub. L. 280 to extend its provisions to the Menominee Reservation. The Department of the Interior recommended favorable action on the proposed amendment, and the amendment was enacted into law on August 24, 1954, two months after the passage of the Menominee Termination Act.

law in 1954, nearly seven years before the Termination Act became fully effective in 1961. In 1954, when Public Law 280 became effective, the Menominee Reservation was still "Indian country" within the meaning of Public Law 280.

Public Law 280 must therefore be considered in pari materia with the Termination Act. The two Acts read together mean to us that, although federal supervision of the tribe was to cease and all tribal property was to be transferred to new hands, the hunting and fishing rights granted or preserved by the Wolf River Treaty of 1854[12] survived the Termination Act of 1954.

This construction is in accord with the overall legislative plan. The Termination Act by its terms provided for the "orderly termination of Federal *supervision* over the property and members" of the tribe. (Emphasis added.) The Federal Government ceded to the State of Wisconsin its power of supervision over the tribe and the reservation lands, as evident from the provision of the Termination Act that the laws of Wisconsin "shall apply to the tribe and its members in the same manner as they apply to other citizens or persons within [its] jurisdiction."

The provision of the Termination Act that "all statutes of the United States which affect Indians because of their status as Indians shall no longer be applicable to the members of the tribe" plainly refers to the termination of federal supervision. The use of the word "statutes" is potent evidence that no *treaty* was in mind.

We decline to construe the Termination Act as a backhanded way of abrogating the hunting and fishing rights of these Indians. While the power to abrogate those

---

12. The Act creating the Wisconsin Territory contained an express reservation of Indian rights, though both the Enabling Act of 1846 and the Act admitting Wisconsin to the Union in 1848 were silent on the subject. It was only a few months after Wisconsin achieved statehood that the Menominees ceded all of their Wisconsin lands to the United States in anticipation of the tribe's removal to other lands west of the Mississippi. Treaty of October 18, 1848, 9 Stat. 952. But as already noted, this removal never fully succeeded, and the Menominee Reservation created by the Treaty of Wolf River was carved out of the lands the Indians had previously ceded to the United States.

The State argues that since it was admitted into the Union on an equal footing with the original States, its sovereignty over the lands designated in 1854 as the Menominee Reservation attached in some degree between the time the Indians ceded all of their Wisconsin lands to the United States in 1848 and the time when the United States ceded back a certain portion of those lands for the reservation in 1854. Wisconsin contends that any hunting or fishing privileges guaranteed the Menominees free from state regulation did not survive the dissolution of the reservation and the termination of the trusteeship of the United States over the Menominees. At that time, it is said, Wisconsin's long dormant power to exercise jurisdiction over those reservation lands was awakened by the termination of the reservation.

If any hiatus in title to the reservation lands in question occurred between 1848 and 1854, any jurisdiction that the State may have acquired over those would not have survived the Treaty of 1854. The Treaty of Wolf River was, under Article VI of the Constitution, the "supreme law of the land," and the exercise of rights on reservation lands guaranteed to the tribe by the Federal Government would not be subject to state regulation, at least in absence of a cession by Congress. In this connection it should be noted that in 1853 the Wisconsin Legislature consented to the establishment of the Menominee Reservation subsequently confirmed by the 1854 Treaty, an action which can be fairly construed as a disclaimer of any jurisdiction the State may have possessed.

rights exists (see *Lone Wolf v. Hitchcock*, 187 U.S. 553, 564–567) "the intention to abrogate or modify a treaty is not to be lightly imputed to the Congress."

Our conclusion is buttressed by the remarks of the legislator chiefly responsible for guiding the Termination Act to enactment, Senator Watkins, who stated upon the occasion of the signing of the bill that it "in no way violates any treaty obligation with this tribe."

We find it difficult to believe that Congress, without explicit statement, would subject the United States to a claim for compensation by destroying property rights conferred by treaty, particularly when Congress was purporting by the Termination Act to settle the Government's financial obligations toward the Indians.

Accordingly the judgment of the Court of Claims is Affirmed.

MR. JUSTICE MARSHALL took no part in the consideration or decision of this case.

MR. JUSTICE STEWART, with whom MR. JUSTICE BLACK joins, dissenting.

The [Menominee Termination Act] is plain on its face: after termination the Menominees are fully subject to state laws just as other citizens are, and no exception is made for hunting and fishing laws. Nor does the legislative history contain any indication that Congress intended to say anything other than what the unqualified words of the statute express. In fact two bills which would have explicitly preserved hunting and fishing rights were rejected in favor of the bill ultimately adopted—a bill which was opposed by counsel for the Menominees because it failed to preserve their treaty rights.

The Court today holds that the Termination Act does not mean what it says. The Court's reason for reaching this remarkable result is that it finds "in pari materia" another statute which, I submit, has nothing whatever to do with this case.

That statute, Public Law 280, granted to certain States, including Wisconsin, general jurisdiction over "Indian country" within their boundaries. Several exceptions to the general grant were enumerated, including an exception from the grant of criminal jurisdiction for treaty-based hunting and fishing rights. But this case does not deal with state jurisdiction over Indian country; it deals with state jurisdiction over Indians after Indian country has been terminated. Whereas Public Law 280 provides for the continuation of the special hunting and fishing rights while a reservation exists, the Termination Act provides for the applicability of all state laws without exception after the reservation has disappeared.

The Termination Act by its very terms provides:

> "All statutes of the United States which affect Indians because of their status as Indians shall no longer be applicable to the members of the tribe. . . ."

Public Law 280 is such a statute. It has no application to the Menominees now that their reservation is gone.

The 1854 Treaty granted the Menominees special hunting and fishing rights. The 1954 Termination Act, by subjecting the Menominees without exception to state law, took away those rights. The Menominees are entitled to compensation.

I would reverse the judgment of the Court of Claims.

Oregon Dept. of Fish and Wildlife v. Klamath Indian Tribe
473 U.S. 753 (1985)

JUSTICE STEVENS delivered the opinion of the Court.

In 1901 the Klamath Indian Tribe ceded 621,824 acres of reservation land to the United States. The question presented in this case is whether the Tribe thereafter retained a special right to hunt and fish on the ceded lands free of state regulation. In answering that question we consider not only the terms of the 1901 Cession Agreement but also the predecessor 1864 Treaty that established the Tribe's original reservation and certain other events in the history of the Tribe.

I

In the early 19th century, the Klamath and Modoc Tribes and the Yahooskin Band of Snake Indians claimed aboriginal title to approximately 22 million acres of land extending east from the Cascade Mountains in southern Oregon. In 1864 these Tribes (now collectively known as the Klamath Indian Tribe) entered into a Treaty with the United States, ceding "all their right, title and claim to all the country claimed by them" and providing that a described tract of approximately 1.9 million acres "within the country ceded" would be set apart for them, to be "held and regarded as an Indian reservation." The 1864 Treaty also provided that the Tribes would have "secured" to them "the exclusive right of taking fish in the streams and lakes, included in said reservation, and of gathering edible roots, seeds, and berries within its limits."[2] No right to hunt or fish outside the reservation was preserved.

The boundaries of the reservation were first surveyed by the United States in 1871. Members of the Tribe immediately complained that the surveyor had erroneously excluded large areas of land from the reservation as described in the 1864 Treaty. These complaints continued after the Government resurveyed the boundaries, and slightly enlarged them, in 1888. In response to these complaints, in 1896 Congress authorized a Boundary Commission to determine the amount and value of the land that had been incorrectly excluded from the reservation.

In October 1896, the three-member Boundary Commission visited the reservation, traveled its disputed boundaries with a Klamath Indian guide, and interviewed a number of Klamath Indians who had participated in the negotiation of the 1864

---

2. Relying on our decision in *Menominee Tribe v. United States*, 391 U.S. 404 (1968), the Court of Appeals for the Ninth Circuit has held that the language of the 1864 Treaty also served to reserve for the Tribe a right to hunt and trap game within the reservation, as well as the rights to fish and gather.

Treaty. These Indians specifically recalled that the parties to the 1864 Treaty had intended to include the Sycan and Sprague River Valleys within the eastern portion of the reservation because those valleys had been an important source of fish and game for members of the Tribe. Based on its review of the 1864 negotiations and the geographical description provided in the Treaty itself, the Boundary Commission concluded that over 617,000 acres of land had been erroneously excluded from the reservation in previous Government surveys.

The Boundary Commission determined that the excluded land had an average value of 83.36 cents per acre. This figure took into account "the good timber land and the meadows of the Sycan and Sprague River valleys" as well as the "rocky and sterile mountain ranges, producing very ordinary timber and little grass." The Commission's valuation was based on the use of the land for stock grazing and as a source of timber. Its report did not discuss hunting or fishing on the excluded lands, nor did it advert to any valuation for the right to conduct such activities on the land.

Upon receiving the Boundary Commission's report, Congress appropriated funds in 1898 for a precise "resurvey of the exterior boundaries of the Klamath Reservation," and authorized the Secretary of the Interior "to negotiate through an Indian inspector with said Klamath Indians for the relinquishment of all their right and interest in and to" the excluded lands.

The course of negotiations with the Tribe extended over the next two years. The Tribe was assisted by counsel and actively asserted its interests when those interests diverged from the proposals of the United States. Yet the historical record provided by a number of congressional documents contains no reference to continuation of any special hunting or fishing rights for members of the Tribe after payment for the excluded lands. No objection by the Tribe to resolving the problem by selling the excluded lands to the Government appears anywhere in the record. Although one Government inspector felt that the price recommended by the Boundary Commission was too high, the Commission's recommendation ultimately was accepted. The final Cession Agreement was signed by 191 adult male members of the Tribe on June 17, 1901.

In the 1901 Agreement, the United States agreed to pay the Tribe $537,007.20 for 621,824 acres of reservation land. In return, the Tribe agreed in Article I to "cede, surrender, grant, and convey to the United States all their claim, right, title and interest in and to" that land. The reservation was thereby diminished to approximately two-thirds of its original size as described in the 1864 Treaty. The 1901 Agreement also provided in Article IV that "nothing in this agreement shall be construed to deprive [the Tribe] of any benefits to which they are entitled under existing treaties not inconsistent with the provisions of this agreement."

The 1901 Agreement was ratified by Congress in 1906. Between 1901 and 1906, virtually all of the ceded land was closed to settlement entry and placed in national forests or parks, a status much of the land retains to this day. The parties have stipulated that members of the Tribe continued to hunt and fish on the ceded lands, from the time of the cession to the commencement of this litigation in 1982. During that period, there is no record of any assertion by the State of Oregon, or any denial by the Tribe, of state regulatory jurisdiction over Indian hunting or fishing on the ceded lands. It is also stipulated that hunting, fishing, trapping, and gathering were "crucial to the survival" of the Klamath Indians in 1864, 1901, and 1906, and that these activities continue to "play a highly significant role" in the lives of Klamath Indians.

II

In 1954, Congress terminated federal supervision over the Klamath Tribe and its property, including the Klamath Reservation. The Termination Act required members of the Tribe to elect either to withdraw from the Tribe and receive the monetary value of their interest in tribal property, or to remain in the Tribe and participate in a non-governmental tribal management plan. The Termination Act also authorized the sale of that portion of the reservation necessary to provide funds for the compensation of withdrawing members, and the transfer of the unsold portion to a private trustee.[12] The Termination Act further specified that its provisions would not "abrogate any fishing rights or privileges of the tribe or the members thereof enjoyed under Federal treaty."

In 1969, the Indian Claims Commission awarded the Tribe $4,162,992.80 as additional compensation for the lands ceded by the 1901 Agreement. As had been the case in 1896 and in 1901, the amount of the Commission's award was based on the estimated value of the land for stock grazing and timber harvesting, which the parties had agreed constituted the "highest and best uses" for the land. The Claims Commission's opinion did not specify a value for, or mention, hunting or fishing rights.

III

In 1982 the Tribe filed this action against the Oregon Department of Fish and Wildlife and various state officials, seeking an injunction against interference with tribal members' hunting and fishing activities on the lands ceded in 1901. The State conceded that it had no authority to interfere with tribal hunting or fishing on lands sold or transferred pursuant to the 1954 Termination Act, but it asserted the right to enforce state regulations against the Tribe on the lands that had been ceded in 1901.

[The District Court entered summary judgment in favor of the Tribe, on the ground that the 1901 Agreement did not abrogate the usufructuary rights guaranteed by the 1864 Treaty. The Court of Appeals affirmed.] We now reverse.

IV

At issue in this case is an asserted right of tribal members to hunt and fish outside the reservation boundaries established in 1901, free of state regulation. The Tribe

---

12. Of the 2,133 persons listed on the final tribal roll of 1954, 1,660 elected to withdraw from the Tribe and receive monetary compensation. The remaining 473 tribe members retained a participatory interest in the management of the remainder of the reservation. At least as of 1979, the Klamath Tribe continued to maintain a tribal constitution, a tribal government, and a tribal Game Commission.

argues that this special right continued on the lands that were ceded in the 1901 Agreement, even though the reservation boundaries were diminished and the exclusivity of the 1864 Treaty rights necessarily expired on the ceded lands. The Tribe agrees that ceded lands now privately owned may be closed to tribal hunting and fishing, and that the Federal Government validly may regulate Indian activity on the ceded lands now held as national parks or forests. It is also clear that non-Indians may hunt and fish on at least some of the ceded lands and that members of the Tribe are entitled to the same hunting and fishing privileges as all other residents of Oregon. Our inquiry, therefore, is whether a special right, nonexclusive but free of state regulation, was intended to survive in the face of the language of the 1901 Agreement ceding "all . . . right . . . in and to" the ceded lands.[16]

The Court of Appeals' holding was predicated on its understanding that the hunting and fishing rights reserved to the Tribe by the 1864 Treaty were not appurtenant to the land within the reservation boundaries. We agree with the Court of Appeals that Indians may enjoy special hunting and fishing rights that are independent of any ownership of land, and that, as demonstrated in 25 U.S.C. §564m(b), the 1954 Termination Act for the Klamath Tribe, such rights may survive the termination of an Indian reservation. Moreover, the Court of Appeals was entirely correct in its view that doubts concerning the meaning of a treaty with an Indian tribe should be resolved in favor of the tribe. Nevertheless, we cannot agree with the court's interpretation of the 1901 Cession Agreement or with its reading of the 1864 Treaty.

V

Before the 1864 Treaty was executed, the Tribe claimed aboriginal title to about 22 million acres of land. The Treaty language that ceded that entire tract—except for the 1.9 million acres set apart for the Klamath Reservation—stated only that the Tribe ceded "all their right, title, and claim" to the described area. Yet that general conveyance unquestionably carried with it whatever special hunting and fishing rights the Indians had previously possessed in over 20 million acres outside the reservation. Presumptively, the similar language used in the 1901 Cession Agreement should have the same effect.

More importantly, the language of the 1864 Treaty plainly describes rights intended to be exercised within the limits of the reservation. This point can be best

---

16. We have not previously found such absolute freedom from state regulation on nonreservation lands, even in the face of Indian cession agreements that expressly reserved a right to hunt or fish on ceded nonreservation lands. *See, e.g., Puyallup Tribe v. Department of Game of Washington*, 391 U.S. at 398 (State may regulate "manner" of Indian fishing although treaty reserved right to take fish "at all usual and accustomed places" including places outside the reservation); *United States v. Winans*, 198 U.S. at 384 (although reserved right to take fish at "all usual and accustomed places" outside the reservation implies an easement over private lands, it does not otherwise "restrain the state unreasonably . . . in the regulation of the right"); *see also Washington v. Washington Commercial Passenger Fishing Vessel Assn.*, 443 U.S. 658, 682–684 (1979) (reserved Indian right to "take fish" off the reservation is not an "untrammeled right" and is subject to "nondiscriminatory" conservation regulation by the State).

understood by consideration of the entire portion of the Treaty in which the right of taking fish is described. The relevant language of the 1864 Treaty is found in Article I:

> "That the following described tract, within the country ceded by this treaty, shall, until otherwise directed by the President of the United States, be set apart as a residence for said Indians, [and] held and regarded as an Indian reservation. . . . And the tribes aforesaid agree and bind themselves that, immediately after the ratification of this treaty, they will remove to said reservation and remain thereon, unless temporary leave of absence be granted to them by the superintendent or agent having charge of the tribes.

> "It is further stipulated and agreed that no white person shall be permitted to locate or remain upon the reservation, except the Indian superintendent and agent, employees of the Indian department, and officers of the army of the United States . . . [and] that in case persons other than those specified are found upon the reservation, they shall be immediately expelled therefrom; and the exclusive right of taking fish in the streams and lakes, included in said reservation, and of gathering edible roots, seeds, and berries within its limits, is hereby secured to the Indians aforesaid. . . ."

The fishing right thus reserved is described as a right to take from the streams and lakes "included in said reservation," and the gathering right is for edible roots, seeds, and berries "within its limits." This limiting language surely indicates that the fishing and gathering rights pertained to the area that was reserved for the Indians and from which non-Indians were excluded. Although hunting is not expressly mentioned in the Treaty, it is clear that any exclusive right to hunt was also confined to the reservation. The fact that the rights were characterized as "exclusive" forecloses the possibility that they were intended to have existence outside of the reservation; no exclusivity would be possible on lands open to non-Indians. Moreover, in view of the fact that Article I restricted members of the Tribe to the reservation, to "remain thereon, unless temporary leave of absence be granted," it is manifest that the rights secured to the Indians by that same Article did not exist independently of the reservation itself.

The language of the 1901 Agreement must be read with these terms of the 1864 Treaty in mind. In 1954 when Congress terminated the Klamath Reservation, it enacted an express provision continuing the Indians' right to fish on the former reservation land. The 1901 Agreement contained no such express provision concerning the right to hunt and fish on the lands ceded by the Tribe. Instead, the 1901 Agreement contained a broad and unequivocal conveyance of the Tribe's title to the land and a surrender of "all their claim, right, title, and interest in and to" that portion of the reservation. The 1901 Agreement thus was both a divestiture of the Tribe's ownership of the ceded lands and a diminution of the boundaries of the reservation within which the Tribe exercised its sovereignty. In the absence of any language reserving any specific rights in the ceded lands, the normal construction of the words used in the 1901 Agreement unquestionably would encompass any special right to use the ceded lands for hunting and fishing.

This conclusion is unequivocally confirmed by the fact that the rights secured by the 1864 Treaty were "exclusive." Since the 1901 Cession Agreement concededly diminished the reservation boundaries, any tribal right to hunt and fish on the ceded, off-reservation lands can no longer be "exclusive" as specified in the 1864 Treaty. Indeed, even if the Tribe had expressly reserved a "privilege of fishing and hunting" on the ceded lands, our precedents demonstrate that such an express reservation would not suffice to defeat the State's power to reasonably and evenhandedly regulate such activity. In light of these precedents, the absence of any express reservation of rights, as found in other 19th-century agreements, only serves to strengthen the conclusion that no special off-reservation rights were comprehended by the parties to the 1901 Agreement.

As both the District Court and the Court of Appeals noted, Article IV of the 1901 Agreement preserved all of the Klamath Indians' "benefits to which they are entitled under existing treaties, not inconsistent with the provisions of this agreement." Article IV thus made it clear that none of the benefits that the Tribe had preserved within its reservation in the 1864 Treaty would be lost. But because the right to hunt and fish reserved in the 1864 Treaty was an exclusive right to be exercised within the reservation, that right could not consistently survive off the reservation under the clear provisions of cession and diminution contained in Article I. Moreover, a glaring inconsistency in the overall Treaty structure would have been present if the Tribe simultaneously could have exercised an independent right to hunt and fish on the ceded lands outside the boundaries of the diminished reservation while remaining bound to honor its 1864 Treaty commitment to stay within the reservation absent permission. Article IV cannot fairly be construed as an implicit preservation of benefits previously linked to the reservation when those benefits could be enjoyed thereafter only outside the reservation boundaries.

In sum, the language of the 1864 Treaty indicates that the Tribe's rights to hunt and fish were restricted to the reservation. The broad language used in the 1901 Agreement, virtually identical to that used to extinguish off-reservation rights in the 1864 Treaty, accomplished a diminution of the reservation boundaries, and no language in the 1901 Agreement evidences any intent to preserve special off-reservation hunting or fishing rights for the Tribe. Indeed, in light of the 1901 diminution, a silent preservation of off-reservation rights would have been inconsistent with the broad language of cession as well as with the Tribe's 1864 Treaty agreement to remain within the reservation.

VI

The Tribe acknowledges that the 1901 Agreement is silent with regard to hunting and fishing rights, but argues that that silence itself, viewed in historical context, demonstrates an intent to preserve tribal hunting and fishing rights in the ceded land. The Tribe asserts that Congress' "singular" purpose in negotiating and ratifying the 1901 Agreement was "to benefit the Indians by honoring the United States' Treaty obligations," and that an intent to extinguish hunting and fishing rights would be inconsistent with this purpose. We disagree for two reasons.

First, an end to the Tribe's special hunting and fishing rights on lands ceded to the Government, if accomplished with the understanding and assent of the Tribe in return for compensation, is not at all inconsistent with an intent to honor the 1864 Treaty. Having acknowledged an intent to remedy its breach of the 1864 Treaty, the United States might have opted to restore the correct boundaries of the reservation and compensate the Indians for any loss occasioned by the erroneous surveys, or, instead, to acquire the erroneously excluded land for a price intended to represent fair compensation. Both options are consistent with an intent to honor the Treaty obligations. Choice of the purchase and compensation option is also consistent with an intent, on both sides, to end any special privileges attaching to the excluded land. Moreover, since the boundary restoration option would have unquestionably preserved such rights for the Tribe, the rejection of that option is also consistent with an intent not to preserve those rights.

Second, Congress in 1901 was motivated by additional goals. By 1896, non-Indian settlers had moved onto the disputed reservation lands, the State of Oregon had completed a military road across the reservation, and conflicts between members of the Tribe and non-Indians perceived as interlopers were sufficient to require congressional attention. Negotiations with the Tribe were authorized in order to settle these conflicts as well as to honor fairly the terms of the 1864 Treaty. These goals again suggest two equally consistent options: restoration of the correct reservation boundaries and exclusion of non-Indians as the 1864 Treaty required, or purchase of the excluded, entered-upon lands. Rather than restore the excluded lands to the Tribe— an option that would have left intact the Tribe's exclusive right to hunt and fish on those lands—Congress chose to remove the excluded lands from the reservation, leaving them open for non-Indian use, and to compensate the Indians for the taking.

The historical record of the lengthy negotiations between the Tribe and the United States provides no reason to reject the presumption that the 1901 Agreement fairly describes the entire understanding between the parties. The Tribe was represented by counsel, the tribal negotiating committee members spoke and understood English, and the Tribe secured a number of alterations to the United States' original proposals. Although members of the Tribe had stressed the importance of hunting and fishing on the excluded lands in order to establish their claim to title with the Boundary Commission in 1896, there is no record of even a reference to a right to continue those activities on those lands in the course of negotiating for the cession of the land and all rights "in and to" it. The failure to mention these rights in the face of this language, as well as the specific terms of the 1864 Treaty that would appear to render their continued exercise inconsistent with diminution, strongly supports the conclusion that there existed no contemporary intention specially to preserve those rights.

The Tribe finally contends that the absence of any payment expressly in compensation for hunting and fishing rights on the ceded lands demonstrates that the parties did not intend to extinguish such rights in 1901. This contention again rests entirely on the assumption that the 1864 Treaty created hunting and fishing rights that were separate from and not appurtenant to the reservation. As explained above, that assumption is incorrect. Moreover, the fact that there was no separate valuation of the right to hunt and fish on the ceded lands is consistent with the view that the parties did not understand any such separate right to exist, and that the value of fish, game, and vegetation on the ceded lands was subsumed within the estimated value of the land in general. Indeed, had the parties actually intended to preserve independent hunting and fishing rights for the Tribe on the ceded lands, the Boundary Commission presumably would have computed the value of such rights and explicitly subtracted that amount from the price to be paid for land so encumbered.

Moreover, the Tribe has since been afforded an opportunity to recover additional compensation for the ceded lands, in light of the "unconscionable" amount paid in 1906. Yet in that proceeding [before the Indian Claims Commission], which resulted in an award to the Tribe of over $4 million, the Tribe apparently agreed that the "highest and best uses" for the ceded lands were commercial lumbering and livestock grazing, again without mention of any hunting or fishing rights. The absence of specific compensation for the rights at issue is entirely consistent with our interpretation of the 1901 Agreement.

VII

Thus, even though "legal ambiguities are resolved to the benefit of the Indians," courts cannot ignore plain language that, viewed in historical context and given a "fair appraisal," clearly runs counter to a tribe's later claims. Careful examination of the entire record in this case leaves us with the firm conviction that the exclusive right to hunt, fish, and gather roots, berries, and seeds on the lands reserved to the Klamath Tribe by the 1864 Treaty was not intended to survive as a special right to be free of state regulation in the ceded lands that were outside the reservation after the 1901 Agreement. The judgment of the Court of Appeals is therefore reversed.

Note on the Restoration of Menominee and Klamath Tribes

Both the Menominee and the Klamath Tribes have since been "restored" to federal recognition and supervision. The Menominee Tribe was the first terminated tribe to be restored. Menominee Restoration Act of 1973, 25 U.S.C. §903 *et seq.* During termination, the Menominee land base had been retained virtually intact by Menominee Enterprises, Inc. Upon restoration, the land base was again placed in trust status as the Menominee Reservation. Initially, the State of Wisconsin took civil and criminal jurisdiction over the Menominee Nation under Public Law 280, but in 1976 the state retroceded all its civil and criminal jurisdiction to the federal government. The Menominee Nation today is the only tribe in Wisconsin not subject to Public Law 280.

The Klamath Tribes were among the last of the terminated tribes that have been restored to federal recognition. Klamath Restoration Act of 1986, 25 U.S.C. §566 *et seq.* Like most restoration acts, the Klamath Act restored "all rights and privileges" which the tribes enjoyed prior to termination. In addition, it expressly provided that nothing in the Restoration Act shall affect "any hunting, fishing, trapping, gathering, or water right of the tribe and its members." Because the Klamath land base had been lost during termination—much of it to national forests purchased by the United States—the Act provided a mechanism for the Secretary to take lands into trust for the Klamath Tribes. The Restoration Act also subjected the Klamath people to state civil and criminal jurisdiction equivalent to that exercised by Public Law 280 states.

United States v. Dion
476 U.S. 734 (1986)

JUSTICE MARSHALL delivered the opinion of the Court.

Respondent Dwight Dion, Sr., a member of the Yankton Sioux Tribe, was convicted of shooting four bald eagles on the Yankton Sioux Reservation in South Dakota in violation of the Endangered Species Act, 16 U.S.C. § 1531 *et seq.* (1982 ed. and Supp. II). The District Court dismissed before trial a charge of shooting a golden eagle in violation of the Bald Eagle Protection Act, 16 U.S.C. § 668 *et seq.* (Eagle Protection Act). Dion was also convicted of selling carcasses and parts of eagles and other birds in violation of the Eagle Protection Act and the Migratory Bird Treaty Act, 16 U.S.C. § 703 *et seq.* The Court of Appeals for the Eighth Circuit affirmed all of Dion's convictions except those for shooting bald eagles in violation of the Endangered Species Act. As to those, it stated that Dion could be convicted only upon a jury determination that the birds were killed for commercial purposes. It also affirmed the District Court's dismissal of the charge of shooting a golden eagle in violation of the Eagle Protection Act. We granted certiorari, and we now reverse the judgment of the Court of Appeals insofar as it reversed Dion's convictions under the Endangered Species Act and affirmed the dismissal of the charge against him under the Eagle Protection Act.

I

The Eagle Protection Act by its terms prohibits the hunting of the bald or golden eagle anywhere within the United States, except pursuant to a permit issued by the Secretary of the Interior. The Endangered Species Act imposes an equally stringent ban on the hunting of the bald eagle. The Court of Appeals for the Eighth Circuit, however, sitting en banc, held that members of the Yankton Sioux Tribe have a treaty right to hunt bald and golden eagles within the Yankton Reservation for noncommercial purposes.[2] It further held that the Eagle Protection Act and Endangered Species Act did not abrogate this treaty right. It therefore directed that Dion's convictions for shooting bald eagles be vacated, since neither the District Court nor the jury made any explicit finding whether the killings were for commercial or noncommercial purposes.[3]

---

2. The court held that tribal members have no treaty right to sell eagles, or to hunt eagles for commercial purposes. Dion does not challenge that holding here, and its validity is not before us.
3. On remand from the en banc court, an Eighth Circuit panel rejected a religious freedom claim raised by Dion. Dion does not pursue that claim here, and accordingly we do not consider it.

The Court of Appeals relied on an 1858 treaty signed by the United States and by representatives of the Yankton Tribe. Under that treaty, the Yankton ceded to the United States all but 400,000 acres of the land then held by the Tribe. The treaty bound the Yanktons to remove to, and settle on, their reserved land within one year. The United States in turn agreed to guarantee the Yanktons quiet and undisturbed possession of their reserved land, and to pay to the Yanktons, or expend for their benefit, various moneys in the years to come. The area thus reserved for the Tribe was a legally constituted Indian reservation. The treaty did not place any restriction on the Yanktons' hunting rights on their reserved land.

All parties to this litigation agree that the treaty rights reserved by the Yankton included the exclusive right to hunt and fish on their land. As a general rule, Indians enjoy exclusive treaty rights to hunt and fish on lands reserved to them, unless such rights were clearly relinquished by treaty or have been modified by Congress. These rights need not be expressly mentioned in the treaty. Those treaty rights, however, little avail Dion if, as the Solicitor General argues, they were subsequently abrogated by Congress. We find that they were.

II

It is long settled that "the provisions of an act of Congress, passed in the exercise of its constitutional authority, . . . if clear and explicit, must be upheld by the courts, even in contravention of express stipulations in an earlier treaty" with a foreign power. This Court applied that rule to congressional abrogation of Indian treaties in *Lone Wolf v. Hitchcock*, 187 U.S. 553, 566 (1903). Congress, the Court concluded, has the power "to abrogate the provisions of an Indian treaty, though presumably such power will be exercised only when circumstances arise which will not only justify the government in disregarding the stipulations of the treaty, but may demand, in the interest of the country and the Indians themselves, that it should do so."

We have required that Congress' intention to abrogate Indian treaty rights be clear and plain. "Absent explicit statutory language, we have been extremely reluctant to find congressional abrogation of treaty rights. . . ." We do not construe statutes as abrogating treaty rights in "a backhanded way;" in the absence of explicit statement, "'the intention to abrogate or modify a treaty is not to be lightly imputed to the Congress.'" Indian treaty rights are too fundamental to be easily cast aside.

We have enunciated, however, different standards over the years for determining how such a clear and plain intent must be demonstrated. In some cases, we have required that Congress make "express declaration" of its intent to abrogate treaty rights. In other cases, we have looked to the statute's "'legislative history'" and "'surrounding circumstances'" as well as to "'the face of the Act.'" Explicit statement by Congress is preferable for the purpose of ensuring legislative accountability for the abrogation of treaty rights. We have not rigidly interpreted that preference, however, as a per se rule; where the evidence of congressional intent to abrogate is sufficiently compelling, "the weight of authority indicates that such an intent can also be found by a reviewing court from clear and reliable evidence in the legislative history of a statute." What is essential is clear evidence that Congress actually considered the conflict between its intended action on the one hand and Indian treaty rights on the other, and chose to resolve that conflict by abrogating the treaty.

A.

The Eagle Protection Act renders it a federal crime to "take, possess, sell, purchase, barter, offer to sell, purchase or barter, transport, export or import, at any time or in any manner any bald eagle commonly known as the American eagle or any golden eagle, alive or dead, or any part, nest, or egg thereof." The prohibition is "sweepingly framed"; the enumeration of forbidden acts is "exhaustive and careful." The Act, however, authorizes the Secretary of the Interior to permit the taking, possession, and transportation of eagles "for the religious purposes of Indian tribes," and for certain other narrow purposes, upon a determination that such taking, possession, or transportation is compatible with the preservation of the bald eagle or the golden eagle.

Congressional intent to abrogate Indian treaty rights to hunt bald and golden eagles is certainly strongly suggested on the face of the Eagle Protection Act. The provision allowing taking of eagles under permit for the religious purposes of Indian tribes is difficult to explain except as a reflection of an understanding that the statute otherwise bans the taking of eagles by Indians, a recognition that such a prohibition would cause hardship for the Indians, and a decision that that problem should be solved not by exempting Indians from the coverage of the statute, but by authorizing the Secretary to issue permits to Indians where appropriate.

The legislative history of the statute supports that view. The Eagle Protection Act was originally passed in 1940, and did not contain any explicit reference to Indians. Its prohibitions related only to bald eagles; it cast no shadow on hunting of the more plentiful golden eagle. In 1962, however, Congress considered amendments to the Eagle Protection Act extending its ban to the golden eagle as well. As originally drafted by the staff of the Subcommittee on Fisheries and Wildlife Conservation of the House Committee on Merchant Marine and Fisheries, the amendments simply would have added the words "or any golden eagle" at two places in the Act where prohibitions relating to the bald eagle were described.

Before the start of hearings on the bill, however, the Subcommittee received a letter from Assistant Secretary of the Interior Frank Briggs on behalf of the Interior Department. The Interior Department supported the proposed bill. It noted, however, the following concern:

> "The golden eagle is important in enabling many Indian tribes, particularly those in the Southwest, to continue ancient customs and ceremonies that are of deep religious or emotional significance to them. We note that the Handbook of American Indians (Smithsonian Institution, 1912) volume I, page 409, states in part, as follows:
>
>> "Among the many birds held in superstitious and appreciative regard by the aborigines of North America, the eagle, by reason of its majestic, solitary, and mysterious nature, became an especial object of worship.

This is expressed in the employment of the eagle by the Indian for religious and esthetic purposes only.

. . . .

"There are frequent reports of the continued veneration of eagles and of the use of eagle feathers in religious ceremonies of tribal rites. The Hopi, Zuni, and several of the Pueblo groups of Indians in the Southwest have great interest in and strong feelings concerning eagles. In the circumstances, it is evident that the Indians are deeply interested in the preservation of both the golden and the bald eagle. If enacted, the bill should therefore permit the Secretary of the Interior, by regulation, to allow the use of eagles for religious purposes by Indian tribes."

The House Committee reported out the bill. In setting out the need for the legislation, it explained in part:

"Certain feathers of the golden eagle are important in religious ceremonies of some Indian tribes and a large number of the birds are killed to obtain these feathers, as well as to provide souvenirs for tourists in the Indian country. In addition, they are actively hunted by bounty hunters in Texas and some other States. As a result of these activities if steps are not taken as contemplated in this legislation, there is grave danger that the golden eagle will completely disappear."

The Committee also reprinted Assistant Secretary Briggs' letter in its Report, and adopted an exception for Indian religious use drafted by the Interior Department. The bill as reported out of the House Committee thus made three major changes in the law, along with other more technical ones. It extended the law's ban to golden eagles. It provided that the Secretary may exempt, by permit, takings of bald or golden eagles "for the religious purposes of Indian tribes." And it added a final proviso: "Provided, That bald eagles may not be taken for any purpose unless, prior to such taking, a permit to do so is procured from the Secretary of the Interior." The bill, as amended, passed the House and was reported to the Senate Committee on Commerce.

At the Senate hearings, representatives of the Interior Department reiterated their position that, because "the golden eagle is an important part of the ceremonies and religion of many Indian tribes," the Secretary should be authorized to allow the use of eagles for religious purposes by Indian tribes. The Senate Committee agreed, and passed the House bill with an additional amendment allowing the Secretary to authorize permits for the taking of golden eagles that were preying on livestock. That Committee again reprinted Assistant Secretary Briggs' letter, and summarized the bill as follows: "The resolution as hereby reported would bring the golden eagle under the 1940 act, allow their taking under permit for the religious use of the various Indian tribes (their feathers are an important part of Indian religious rituals) and upon request of a Governor of any State, be taken for the protection of livestock and game." The bill passed the Senate, and was concurred in by the House, with little further discussion.

It seems plain to us, upon reading the legislative history as a whole, that Congress in 1962 believed that it was abrogating the rights of Indians to take eagles. Indeed, the House Report cited the demand for eagle feathers for Indian religious ceremonies as one of the threats to the continued survival of the golden eagle that necessitated passage of the bill. Congress expressly chose to set in place a regime in which the Secretary of the Interior had control over Indian hunting, rather than one in which Indian on-reservation hunting was unrestricted. Congress thus considered the special cultural and religious interests of Indians, balanced those needs against the conservation purposes of the statute, and provided a specific, narrow exception that delineated the extent to which Indians would be permitted to hunt the bald and golden eagle.

Respondent argues that the 1962 Congress did not in fact view the Eagle Protection Act as restricting Indian on-reservation hunting. He points to an internal Interior Department memorandum circulated in 1962 stating, with little analysis, that the Eagle Protection Act did not apply within Indian reservations. We have no reason to believe that Congress was aware of the contents of the Vaughn memorandum. More importantly, however, we find respondent's contention that the 1962 Congress did not understand the Act to ban all Indian hunting of eagles simply irreconcilable with the statute on its face.

Respondent argues, and the Eighth Circuit agreed, that the provision of the statute granting permit authority is not necessarily inconsistent with an intention that Indians would have unrestricted ability to hunt eagles while on reservations. Respondent construes that provision to allow the Secretary to issue permits to non-Indians to hunt eagles "for Indian religious purposes," and supports this interpretation by pointing out testimony during the hearings to the effect that large-scale eagle bounty hunters sometimes sold eagle feathers to Indian tribes. We do not find respondent's argument credible. Congress could have felt such a provision necessary only if it believed that Indians, if left free to hunt eagles on reservations, would nonetheless be unable to satisfy their own needs and would be forced to call on non-Indians to hunt on their behalf. Yet there is nothing in the legislative history that even remotely supports that patronizing and strained view. Indeed, the Interior Department immediately after the passage of the 1962 amendments adopted regulations authorizing permits only to "individual Indians who are authentic, bona fide practitioners of such religion."

Congress' 1962 action, we conclude, reflected an unmistakable and explicit legislative policy choice that Indian hunting of the bald or golden eagle, except pursuant to permit, is inconsistent with the need to preserve those species. We therefore read the statute as having abrogated that treaty right.

B

Dion also asserts a treaty right to take bald eagles as a defense to his Endangered Species Act prosecution. He argues that the evidence that Congress intended to abrogate treaty rights when it passed the Endangered Species Act is considerably more slim than that relating to the Eagle Protection Act. The Endangered Species Act and its legislative history, he points out, are to a great extent silent regarding Indian hunting rights. In this case, however, we need not resolve the question of whether the Congress in the Endangered Species Act abrogated Indian treaty rights. We conclude that Dion's asserted treaty defense is barred in any event.

Dion asserts that he is immune from Endangered Species Act prosecution because he possesses a treaty right to hunt and kill bald eagles. We have held, however, that Congress in passing and amending the Eagle Protection Act divested Dion of his treaty right to hunt bald eagles. He therefore has no treaty right to hunt bald eagles that he can assert as a defense to an Endangered Species Act charge.

We do not hold that when Congress passed and amended the Eagle Protection Act, it stripped away Indian treaty protection for conduct not expressly prohibited by that statute. But the Eagle Protection Act and the Endangered Species Act, in relevant part, prohibit exactly the same conduct, and for the same reasons. Dion here asserts a treaty right to engage in precisely the conduct that Congress, overriding Indian treaty rights, made criminal in the Eagle Protection Act. Dion's treaty shield for that conduct, we hold, was removed by that statute, and Congress' failure to discuss that shield in the context of the Endangered Species Act did not revive that treaty right.

It would not promote sensible law to hold that while Dion possesses no rights derived from the 1858 treaty that bar his prosecution under the Eagle Protection Act for killing bald eagles, he nonetheless possesses a right to hunt bald eagles, derived from that same treaty that bars his Endangered Species Act prosecution for the same conduct. Even if Congress did not address Indian treaty rights in the Endangered Species Act sufficiently expressly to effect a valid abrogation, therefore, respondent can assert no treaty defense to a prosecution under that Act for a taking already explicitly prohibited under the Eagle Protection Act.

III

We hold that the Court of Appeals erred in recognizing Dion's treaty defense to his Eagle Protection Act and Endangered Species Act prosecutions. * * * The judgment of the Court of Appeals is reversed in part, and the case is remanded for further proceedings consistent with this opinion.

Notes

1. **Endangered Species Act.** The Court in *Dion* declined to decide whether the Endangered Species Act also abrogated the Sioux treaty right to hunt. The following year, however, a federal district court reached the issue in a case involving the Florida panther, a species so endangered that only about 30 animals remained. *United States v. Billie*, 667 F. Supp. 1485 (S.D. Fla. 1987). James Billie, chairman of the Florida Seminole Tribe, killed a panther and was prosecuted under the ESA.

The court applied the test articulated in *Dion*: "What is essential is clear evidence that Congress actually considered the conflict between its intended action on the one hand and Indian treaty rights on the other, and chose to resolve that conflict by abrogating the treaty." As to the language of the statute, the court concluded that the

ESA's "general comprehensiveness, its non-exclusion of Indians, and the limited exceptions for certain Alaskan natives" meant that Congress had considered the conflict and chose to abrogate the Seminole treaty right to hunt. The court bolstered its conclusion by reference to the legislative history, relying on two bills introduced the year before the ESA was adopted, neither of which was enacted, but both of which contained broader exemptions for Indian hunting for religious purposes.

Nonetheless, Billie was not convicted under the ESA. His federal jury deadlocked 7–5 in favor of acquittal. The judge declared a mistrial, and the Justice Department declined to re-prosecute. For an argument that the ESA does not abrogate treaty rights, see Robert J. Miller, *Speaking with Forked Tongues: Indian Treaties, Salmon, and the Endangered Species Act*, 70 Or. L. Rev. 543 (1991).

2. Migratory Bird Treaty Act. Another federal district court reached a very different conclusion with regard to the Migratory Bird Treaty Act (MBTA), 16 U.S.C. §§ 703–712. *United States v. Bresette*, 761 F. Supp. 658 (D. Minn. 1991). The MBTA makes it unlawful to "possess, offer for sale, [or] sell" any part of any migratory bird. 16 U.S.C. § 703. The defendants agreed that their conduct was proscribed by the Act.

Walter Bresette, a member of the Red Cliff Band of Chippewa, sold items called "dream catchers" at two stores, one located on the Red Cliff Chippewa Reservation and one located in a mall in Duluth, Minnesota. The dream catchers, which are suspended over beds to protect the sleeper from bad dreams, are "traditional Chippewa objects of artistic and spiritual value made of materials which include bird feathers." Several of the dream catchers sold at Bresette's Duluth store included feathers from migratory birds such as the Canada goose and red-tailed hawk. The feathers were supplied by members of the Chippewa tribes of Wisconsin and Minnesota and were taken either within reservations or within the off-reservation area where the Chippewa retained treaty rights to hunt, fish, and gather. *See Minnesota v. Mille Lacs Band of Chippewa Indians*, 526 U.S. 172 (1999) (p. 460).

The court held first that the Chippewa treaty-reserved usufructuary rights, "which undeniably include the taking of migratory birds and their feathers, encompassed the sale of their catch." Then, the court applied the *Dion* consideration-and-choice test to determine whether the MBTA abrogated the Chippewa treaty right. Like the ESA, the MBTA was silent as to Indian treaty rights. The court held:

> In the instant case the statute contains no indication that Congress considered Indian treaty rights and chose to abrogate them. The statute allows "indigenous inhabitants of the State of Alaska to take and collect migratory birds for food and clothing," but this is irrelevant for purposes of treaty rights analysis because Native Alaskans do not have treaty rights. * * * To treat the consideration of indigenous Alaskans' rights as the consideration of Native American treaty rights nationwide, for the simple reason that both groups are regarded as Indian, is disingenuous.

As to the legislative history, the court found "insufficient evidence that treaty rights were specifically considered and eliminated in the creation of the Migratory Bird

Treaty Act." The court concluded that the MBTA did not abrogate the Chippewa treaty rights, and dismissed the case against Bresette.

3. The Lacey Act. The Lacey Act makes violation of tribal (and state) wildlife laws a federal offense. 16 U.S.C. § 3372(a)(1). In *United States v. Brown*, 777 F.3d 1025 (8th Cir. 2015), the Eighth Circuit affirmed the dismissal of federal criminal charges against members of the Minnesota Chippewa Tribe under the Lacey Act for violating the Leech Lake Conservation Code by fishing on-reservation with gillnets for commercial purposes and subsequently selling the fish to non-Indians. The tribal code prohibited commercial fishing without a permit and banned gillnetting for other than personal use.

The appeals court agreed with the lower court that the Chippewa Tribe reserved exclusive on-reservation fishing rights under its 1837 treaty and an 1855 Executive Order, and that these rights included commercial fishing with no specifications as to how to fish. The Eighth Circuit decided that although the tribe might be able to enforce its code against the defendants, "[t]ribal fishing laws enforceable in tribal court do not change the scope of treaty protections which tribal members may assert as a defense to prosecution by the United States." The court also found no treaty abrogation under the standards set by the Supreme Court's *Dion* decision because Congress never abrogated the treaty rights by actually considering and choosing to abrogate them in clear and plain legislation. The *Brown* decision seems consistent with the purpose of the Lacey Act, which was to make state and tribal laws enforceable in federal court as federal offenses in order to deter interjurisdictional travel to defeat application of local wildlife laws, not to have the federal government interfere with tribal prosecutorial discretion of their wildlife codes.

4. Secretarial Order on Tribal Rights, Federal Trust Responsibilities, and the Endangered Species Act. In 1997, the Secretaries of Commerce and Interior issued an order requiring that restrictions on treaty harvests: 1) must be "reasonable and necessary" for the conservation of the species; 2) are permitted only if the conservation purpose cannot be achieved by reasonable regulation of non-Indian activities alone; 3) must be the least restrictive alternative to achieve the benefits sought; 4) cannot discriminate against treaty harvests; and 5) are permitted only if voluntary tribal conservation measures are inadequate to achieve the conservation purpose. U.S. Departments of Commerce and Interior, *American Indian Tribal Rights, Federal-Tribal Trust Responsibilities, and the Endangered Species Act* (Order No. 3206, June 5, 1997) (available at http://elips.doi.gov/). *See* Charles F. Wilkinson, *The Role of Bilateralism in Fulfilling the Tribal Rights—Endangered Species Secretarial Order*, 72 Wash. L. Rev. 1063 (1997).

5. Eagles not endangered species. In June 2007, bald eagles were removed from the endangered and threatened species list. The Secretary of the Interior's announcement noted that: "In 1963, the lower 48 states were home to barely 400 nesting pairs of bald eagles. Today, after decades of conservation effort, they are home to some 10,000 nesting pairs, a 25-fold increase in the last 40 years." *See* https://www.fws.gov/endangered/. Bald eagles, however, like golden eagles, remain subject to the protections of the Eagle Protection Act and the Migratory Bird Treaty Act. For an argument that Congress should amend the Eagle Protection Act to allow the U.S. Fish and Wildlife Service to issue take permits to tribes, rather than individuals, and turn over much of the administration of the permit program to tribes collectively, *see* Kathryn E. Kovacs, *Eagles, Indian Tribes, and the Exercise of Freedom of Religion*, 47 Loyola LA L. Rev. 53 (2013).

6. Religious Freedom Restoration Act, 42 U.S.C. § 2000bb *et seq.* Although the Supreme Court held that the Religious Freedom Restoration Act (RFRA) was unconstitutional as applied to state and local government action, *City of Boerne v. Flores*, 521 U.S. 507 (1997), federal courts have since assumed that it continues to be valid as applied to federal action. *See, e.g., Navajo Nation v. U.S. Forest Service*, 535 F.3d 1058 (9th Cir. 2008) (page 22). Under this approach to RFRA, the statute continues to apply to federal laws such as the Bald and Golden Eagle Protection Act, the Endangered Species Act, and the Migratory Bird Treaty Act.

a. RFRA and the taking of eagles. Federal courts have routinely rejected claims that federal statutes protecting eagles violate RFRA. Although the courts have disagreed as to whether the statutory permit requirements place a "substantial" burden on the practitioner's exercise of native religion, as required under RFRA, they have agreed that the government has a compelling interest in protecting both bald and golden eagles and that, in general, the statutes represent the least restrictive means of furthering that interest. *See, e.g., United States v. Friday*, 535 F.3d 938 (10th Cir. 2008) (Eagle Protection Act does not impose a substantial burden, and statute is least restrictive means to achieve compelling government interest); *United States v. Oliver*, 255 F.3d 588 (8th Cir. 2001) (Eagle Protection Act is least restrictive means to achieve compelling interest); *United States v. Hugs*, 109 F.3d 1375 (9th Cir. 1997) (Eagle Protection Act imposes substantial burden but is least restrictive means to achieve compelling interest). *See also United States v. Tawahongva*, 456 F. Supp. 2d 1120 (D. Ariz. 2006) (Migratory Bird Treaty Act does not impose substantial burden, but even if it did, is the least restrictive means to achieve compelling interest).

b. RFRA, eagles, and non-Indian practitioners. An *en banc* Tenth Circuit ruled that the possession of eagle feathers by persons not members of federally recognized tribes was subject to strict scrutiny under RFRA. *United States v. Hardman*, 297 F.3d 1116 (10th Cir. 2002). But the court determined that protecting eagle populations was a compelling interest, as was the federal obligation to preserve Native American culture and religion. Consequently, in one of the cases on appeal, the Tenth Circuit concluded that the federal government had not met its burden of showing that limiting permits for eagle feathers to members of federally recognized tribes was the least restrictive alternative means of preserving eagle populations and tribal culture. In two other cases, the court remanded for further factual determinations.

On remand, the district court concluded that the application of the Eagle Protection Act to a follower of a Native American faith who was not a member of a recognized tribe violated RFRA, but the Tenth Circuit reversed. *United States v. Wilgus*, 638 F.3d 1274 (10th Cir. 2011). The court concluded that the competing compelling state interests were 1) protecting the bald eagle as a national symbol, and 2) protecting and fostering Native American culture and religion, which the court interpreted to mean protecting the culture of federally recognized tribes. Consequently, it determined that the Eagle Protection Act's restriction of eagle feather permits to members of federal recognized tribes met the test of being the least restrictive means of forwarding the government's "dual competing interests," which the court described as navigating between "Scylla and Charybdis."

The Ninth Circuit considered and rejected the Tenth Circuit's *Hardman* rule in *United States v. Antoine,* 318 F.3d 919 (9th Cir. 2003), where the court upheld the conviction of a member of a Canadian tribe for possessing eagle parts without a permit in violation of the Eagle Protection Act. Unlike the Tenth Circuit, the Ninth Circuit concluded that the permit requirement established by the Eagle Protection Act did not violate RFRA. *See also United States v. Vasquez-Ramos,* 531 F.3d 987 (9th Cir. 2008) (reaffirming *Antoine* and rejecting defendants' argument that because eagles were removed from the Endangered Species List, the government no longer had a compelling interest).

7. **International travel with eagle items.** The prohibitions in the Bald and Golden Eagle Protection Act include a ban on travel with eagle parts into or out of the United States, including travel by Native Americans who use eagle items in the practice of their religion. In September 1999, the U.S. Fish and Wildlife Service introduced eagle transport permits that allow enrolled members of federally recognized tribes to travel overseas with eagle parts and feathers. These permits will enable tribal members to obtain permits required by the Convention on International Trade in Endangered Species, which regulates the global movement of hundreds of plant and animal species, including bald and golden eagles. *See* U.S. Fish and Wildlife Service Fact Sheet, *International Travel with Eagle Items: Guidelines for Native Americans* (2000).

Anderson v. Evans

371 F.3d 475 (9th Cir. 2004)

Opinion by Judge BERZON for sections I and II; Opinion by Judge GOULD for sections III and IV.

BERZON, Circuit Judge.

"[W]hile in life the great whale's body may have been a real terror to his foes, in his death his ghost [became] a powerless panic to [the] world." Herman Melville, Moby Dick 262 (W.W. Norton & Co. 1967) (1851). This modern day struggle over whale hunting began when the United States granted support and approval to the Makah Tribe's ("the Tribe's") plan to resume whaling.

The Tribe, a traditional Northwest Indian whale hunting tribe, had given up the hunt in the 1920s. In recent years, the Tribe's leaders came to regret the cultural impact on the Tribe of the lapse of its whale hunting tradition. As part of a general effort at cultural revival, the Tribe developed plans to resume pursuing gray whales off the coast of Washington State and in the Strait of Juan de Fuca. The worldwide hunt for whales in the years the real-life Captain Ahabs roamed the high seas, however, seriously depleted the worldwide stock of the cetaceans. As a result of the near extinction of some species of whales, what had been a free realm for ancient and not-so-ancient mariners became an activity closely regulated under both federal and international law. This case is the second in which we have considered whether the federal government's approval of the Tribe's plans to pursue once again the Leviathan of the deep runs afoul of that regulation. *See Metcalf v. Daley,* 214 F.3d 1135 (9th Cir. 2000) [excerpted at page 266].

The plaintiffs, citizens and animal conservation groups * * * contend that the Tribe's whaling plan cannot be implemented because the Tribe has not complied with the Marine Mammal Protection Act of 1972 ("MMPA"), 16 U.S.C. § 1361 et seq. * * * We also conclude that the MMPA applies to the Tribe's proposed whale hunt.

I. Background A. *The Whales*

The record discloses that there are two genetically distinct North Pacific gray whale populations—an eastern stock, also known as the California gray whale, and a western stock, confined to East Asian waters. The California gray whales migrate annually between the North Pacific and the West Coast of Mexico. These whales were at one time nearing extinction and were therefore listed on the Endangered Species Act list. Protected by the endangered species designation and by other conservation measures, the California gray whale stock revived, so that by 1994 the whale was removed from the endangered species list. The NMFS has determined that the eastern North Pacific gray whale stock has now recovered to between 17,000 and 26,000 whales, a number near its carrying capacity. Most of the migrating whales pass through the Olympic Coast National Marine Sanctuary ["Marine Sanctuary"], adjacent to the Makah Tribe's home territory on the coast of Washington State, on their way to the Bering and Chukchi Seas, and again when heading south for the winter.

B. *The Makah Tribe and Its Efforts to Resume Whaling*

The Tribe is composed of Native Americans whose traditional territory is in Washington State, on the northwestern Olympic Peninsula. In 1855, the United States entered into a treaty with the Tribe, the Treaty of Neah Bay, providing that the Tribe would give up most of its land on the Olympic Peninsula. *See* 12 Stat. 939, 940 (1855). In exchange, the Tribe was given, *inter alia,* the "right of taking fish and of whaling or sealing at usual and accustomed grounds and stations. . . ." That the Treaty of Neah Bay is the only treaty between the United States and a Native American tribe that specifically protects the right to hunt whales suggests the historic importance of whaling to the Makah Tribe.

Despite the central place of whaling in their lives, the Tribe ended their whaling expeditions in the late 1920s. Explanations regarding the reasons for the abandonment of this custom include: the federal government's discouragement and lack of assistance; a decline in demand for whale oil; social and economic dislocation within the Tribe; and the drastic decline of the gray whale population.

Then came, in the early 1990s, both a renewed interest within the Tribe in reviving its traditional whaling customs and the removal of the California gray whale from the Endangered Species Act list. The Tribe therefore determined to resume its traditional whale hunting. In the seventy years since the last hunt, however, whaling had become an activity tightly regulated internationally, through the International Whaling Commission, and domestically, through the Whaling Convention Act, and the MMPA, as well as through more general federal environmental legislation.

* * * [T]he NOAA and the NMFS issued a Federal Register notice on December 13, 2001 announcing a quota for the "land[ing]" of five gray whales in 2001 and 2002 and approving the latest Makah Management Plan.

GOULD, Circuit Judge, with whom HILL and BERZON, Circuit Judges, concur:

III. MMPA Analysis

In addition to arguing their NEPA claim, plaintiffs maintain that the federal defendants issued a gray whale quota to the Tribe in violation of the Marine Mammal Protection Act (MMPA), 16 U.S.C. § 1361 et. seq., which prohibits the taking of marine mammals absent a permit or waiver. The Tribe has not applied for a permit or waiver under the MMPA. Defendants maintain that the MMPA does not apply because * * * the Tribe has an Indian treaty whaling right that is not affected by the MMPA.

B. *Conservation Necessity*

We consider whether the MMPA must apply to the Tribe to effectuate the conservation purpose of the statute.[21] In *Fryberg,* we set out a three-part test for determining when reasonable conservation statutes affect Indian treaty rights: (1) the sovereign has jurisdiction in the area where the activity occurs; (2) the statute is non-discriminatory; and (3) the application of the statute to treaty rights is necessary to achieve its conservation purpose.[22] Applying this rule, the MMPA may regulate any

---

21. The conservation necessity principle finds its roots in the state context, allowing state regulation of Indian treaty rights even though states do not otherwise possess Congress's authority to qualify treaty rights. *Minnesota v. Mille Lacs Band of Chippewa Indians,* 526 U.S. 172, 205 (1999). *See also Antoine v. Washington,* 420 U.S. 194 (1975) (tribal hunting and fishing rights may be restricted by a regulation that is a "reasonable and necessary conservation measure") (citations omitted); *Puyallup Tribe v. Dept. of Game (Puyallup I),* 391 U.S. 392, 398 (1968) (states may regulate tribal hunting and fishing rights if the regulation meets "appropriate standards" and is non-discriminatory). The invocation of the conservation necessity principle, however, is not limited to state regulation. *See United States v. Fryberg,* 622 F.2d 1010, 1014–1015 (9th Cir.1980). Indeed, because the states do not have the power held by Congress to regulate affairs with Indian nations, state regulation of treaty hunting or fishing rights may be more limited in scope than federal regulation. We express no opinion as to whether and, if so, the extent to which our decision has relevance to assessment of state conservation regulation that touches on treaty rights.

22. *Fryberg* addressed whether the Eagle Protection Act, 16 U.S.C. § 668 et seq., abrogated treaty hunting rights by prohibiting the taking and killing of bald eagles. Though the ultimate issue in *Fryberg* was abrogation, *Fryberg* also articulated a test for identifying conservation statutes that affect treaty rights. That test was based on Supreme Court authority that allows conservation statutes to affect treaty rights to the extent necessary to achieve their conservation purpose. The

pre-existing Makah Tribe whaling rights under treaty if (1) the United States has jurisdiction where the whaling occurs; (2) the MMPA applies in a non-discriminatory manner to treaty and non-treaty persons alike; and (3) the application of the statute to regulate treaty rights is necessary to achieve its conservation purpose.

As to the first prong of the test, the MMPA extends to "any person subject to the jurisdiction of the United States," and reaches 200 nautical miles outward from the seaward boundary of each coastal state. Thus, the MMPA would clearly apply to the Tribe's whaling off the coast of Washington State in the Strait of Juan de Fuca. As to the second prong, the MMPA places a general moratorium on all persons except certain Native Alaskans with subsistence needs. The MMPA cannot be said to discriminate between treaty and non-treaty persons because members of the Tribe are not being singled out any more than non-treaty people in the lower forty-eight states.

The third prong of the *Fryberg* test requires that the application of the MMPA to the Tribe be necessary to achieve its conservation purpose. This prong frames for us the critical issue under this test: whether restraint on the Tribe's whaling pursuant to treaty rights is necessary to effectuate the conservation purpose of the MMPA. In assessing this issue, we are mindful that the major objective of the MMPA is to ensure that marine mammals continue to be "significant functioning element[s] in the ecosystem." In fact, "[marine mammals] should not be permitted to diminish below their optimum sustainable population." To carry out these conservation objectives, the MMPA implements a sweeping moratorium in combination with a permitting process to ensure that the taking of marine mammals is specifically authorized and systematically reviewed. For example, the MMPA requires that the administering agency consider "distribution, abundance, breeding habits, and times and lines of migratory movements of such marine mammals" when deciding the appropriateness of waiving requirements under the MMPA. And, when certain permits are issued, the permit may be suspended if the taking results in "more than a negligible impact on the species or stock concerned." One need only review Congress's carefully selected language to realize that Congress's concern was not merely with survival of marine mammals, though that is of inestimable importance, but more broadly with ensuring that these mammals maintain an "optimum sustainable population" and remain "significant functioning elements in the ecosystem." The MMPA's requirements for

---

Supreme Court authority relied on by *Fryberg* remains good law. *See Antoine v. Washington,* 420 U.S. 194 (1974); *Wash. Dep't of Game v. Puyallup Tribe,* 414 U.S. 44 (1973) (*Puyallup II*); *Puyallup Tribe v. Wash. Dep't of Game,* 391 U.S. 392 (1968) (*Puyallup I*); *Kennedy v. Becker,* 241 U.S. 556 (1916). Moreover, *Fryberg* did not purport to substitute the conservation necessity test for an abrogation analysis. Rather, *Fryberg* used the conservation purpose of the statute to bolster its conclusion that Congress clearly intended to abrogate treaty rights by enacting the Eagle Protection Act. Later, the same conclusion was reached by the Supreme Court in *United States v. Dion,* 476 U.S. 734 (1986), though the Supreme Court did not discuss the conservation necessity principle. Still, regardless of *Fryberg's* posture as an abrogation case, we conclude that the conservation necessity test articulated by *Fryberg* has not been undermined by later cases and is supported by the Supreme Court authorities above cited.

taking are specifically designed to promote such objectives. Without subjecting the Tribe's whaling to review under the MMPA, there is no assurance that the takes by the Tribe of gray whales, including both those killed and those harassed without success, will not threaten the role of the gray whales as functioning elements of the marine ecosystem, and thus no assurance that the purpose of the MMPA will be effectuated.[23]

If the Tribe's plans for whaling could proceed without regulation, we cannot be certain that future whaling by the Tribe will not jeopardize the gray whale population either through its current plan or through future expanded quotas. While the Tribe's current Gray Whale Management Plan allows the Tribe to hunt whales with rifles and motorized boats, the Tribe is not limited to a particular method of hunting by the terms of the Treaty of Neah Bay. The Tribe, therefore, could use evolving technology to facilitate more efficient hunting of the gray whales. The tribal council of the Makah Tribe has shown admirable restraint in limiting its aim to a small number of whales, and seeking the umbrella approval of the United States for a share of a quota approved by the IWC [International Whaling Commission]. But it is not clear the extent to which the Tribe's treaty right is limited to the approvals of the IWC or the Tribe's Gray Whale Management Plan. The intent of Congress cannot be hostage to the goodwill or good judgment or good sense of the particular leaders empowered by the Tribe at present; it must be assumed that Congress intended to effectuate policies for the United States and its residents, including the Makah Tribe, that transcend the decisions of any subordinate group.

If the MMPA's conservation purpose were forced to yield to the Makah Tribe's treaty rights, other tribes could also claim the right to hunt marine mammals without complying with the MMPA. While defendants argue that the Makah Tribe is the only tribe in the United States with a treaty right expressly guaranteeing the right to whale, that argument ignores the fact that whale hunting could be protected under less specific treaty language. The EA prepared by the federal defendants notes that other Pacific Coast tribes that once hunted whales have reserved traditional "hunting and fishing" rights in their treaties. These less specific "hunting and fishing" rights might be urged to cover a hunt for marine mammals. Although such mammals might not be the subject of "fishing," there is little doubt they are "hunted."

Defendants argue that the conservation necessity test under *Fryberg* is not triggered until species preservation emerges as an issue. We have rejected the idea that species preservation must be an issue for the conservation necessity principle to apply.

---

23. While we conclude here that the Tribe must undergo the MMPA permitting process to ensure the conservation goals of the Act are effectuated, we do not purport to address what limitations on the scope of a permit, if any is issued, would be appropriate to achieve the conservation purpose of the Act. Any disputes arising under the MMPA's terms regarding whether, and the means by which, any whaling may be carried out will emerge clearly and concretely in the permitting process, and can be resolved at that juncture by the responsible agencies or on judicial review thereafter.

Satisfaction of the *Fryberg* test depends on the conservation purpose of the statute. Here the purpose of the MMPA is not limited to species preservation. Whether the Tribe's whaling will damage the delicate balance of the gray whales in the marine ecosystem is a question that must be asked long before we reach the desperate point where we face a reactive scramble for species preservation. To effectuate the purpose of the MMPA, which is to make informed, proactive decisions regarding the effect of marine mammal takes, we conclude that the MMPA must apply to the Tribe, even if its treaty rights must be considered and given weight by NMFS in implementing the MMPA, an issue we do not decide.

The application of the MMPA to the Tribe to uphold the conservation purpose of the MMPA goes hand in hand with the principles embedded in the Treaty of Neah Bay itself. The treaty language, when considered on its face, supports our conclusion that the conservation purpose of the MMPA requires it be applied to the Tribe. The Treaty of Neah Bay provides the Tribe with a right to fish and hunt whales "in common with all citizens of the United States." We have recognized that the "in common with" language creates a relationship between Indians and non-Indians similar to a cotenancy, in which neither party may "permit the subject matter of [the treaty] to be destroyed." *United States v. Washington*, 520 F.2d 676, 685 (9th Cir. 1975). While this "in common with" clause does not strip Indians of the substance of their treaty rights, *see Washington v. Washington Commercial Passenger Fishing Vessel Ass'n*, 443 U.S. 658, 677 n. 22 (1979), it does prevent Indians from relying on treaty rights to deprive other citizens of a fair apportionment of a resource. In *Washington Commercial Passenger Fishing Vessel Ass'n*, the Supreme Court concluded that: "Nontreaty fishermen may not rely on property law concepts, devices such as the fish wheel, license fees, or general regulations to deprive the Indians of a fair share of the relevant runs of anadromous fish in the case area. Nor may the treaty fishermen rely on their exclusive right of access to the reservations to destroy the rights of other 'citizens of the Territory.' Both sides have a right, secured by the treaty, to take a fair share of the available fish. That, we think, is what the parties to the treaty intended when they secured to the Indians a right of taking fish in common with other citizens." This holding might be read to suggest that the Tribe's treaty right gives the Tribe a right to a "fair share" of whales that are to be taken. The "fair share" formula, however, does not provide a ready answer in this case, which involves now-protected marine mammals rather than salmon and other fish available, within limits, for fishing. The question presented to us is not how whaling rights can be fairly apportioned between Indians and non-Indians. Rather, the Tribe asserts a treaty right that would give the Tribe the exclusive ability to hunt whales free from the regulatory scheme of the MMPA. Just as treaty fisherman are not permitted to "totally frustrate . . . the rights of the non-Indian citizens of Washington" to fish, *Puyallup Tribe v. Dept. of Game of Wash.*, 433 U.S. 165, 175, (1977) (*Puyallup III*), the Makah cannot, consistent with the plain terms of the treaty, hunt whales without regard to processes in place and designed to advance conservation values by preserving marine mammals or to engage in whale watching, scientific study, and other non-consumptive uses. The Supreme Court has recognized that regulation for the purpose of conservation is permissible despite the existence of treaty rights. *Washington Commercial Passenger Fishing Vessel Ass'n,* 443 U.S. at 682 ("Although nontreaty fishermen might be subjected to any reasonable state fishing regulation serving any legitimate purpose, treaty fishermen are immune from all regulation *save that required for conservation.*") (emphasis added). Mindful of that recognition, we conclude that to the extent there is a "fair share" of marine mammal takes by the Tribe, the proper scope of such a share must be considered in light of the MMPA through its permit or waiver process. The MMPA will properly allow the taking of marine mammals only when it will not diminish the sustainability and optimum level of the resource for all citizens. The procedural safeguards and conservation principles of the MMPA ensure that marine mammals like the gray whale can be sustained as a resource for the benefit of the Tribe and others.

Having concluded that the MMPA is applicable to regulate any whaling proposed by the Tribe because the MMPA's application is necessary to effectuate the conservation purpose of the statute, and because such application is consistent with the language of the Neah Bay Treaty, we conclude that the issuance by NOAA of a gray whale quota to the Tribe, absent compliance with the MMPA, violates federal law. Whether or not the Tribe may have sufficient justification to gain a permit or waiver allowing whaling under the MMPA, we must now set aside NOAA's approval of the Tribe's whaling quota absent MMPA compliance as "arbitrary, capricious, an abuse of discretion, or otherwise not in accordance with law."

Of course, in holding that the MMPA applies to the Tribe, we need not and do not decide whether the Tribe's whaling rights have been abrogated by the MMPA.[26] We simply hold that the Tribe, to pursue any treaty rights for whaling, must comply with the process prescribed in the MMPA for authorizing a "take" because it is the procedure that ensures the Tribe's whaling will not frustrate the conservation goals of the MMPA.

Note on Abrogation versus Regulation

In footnote 22, the Ninth Circuit stated that the conservation necessity test, as applied to federal regulation, "has not been undermined" by *United States v. Dion.* Do you agree? If the Ninth Circuit is correct, when should courts apply the consideration-and-choice approach of *Dion* and when should they apply the conservation necessity test? Is the Ninth Circuit saying that the *Dion* test is only

---

26. Having determined that the procedures of the MMPA apply to the Tribe, in light of the conservation principle and the "in common with" language of the treaty, we need not resolve the abrogation issue presented by the plaintiffs: The NMFS might authorize prescribed whaling to proceed under the MMPA, albeit with conditions designed to ensure the perpetuation of the resident whale population. Unlike other persons applying for a permit or waiver under the MMPA, the Tribe may urge a treaty right to be considered in the NMFS's review of an application submitted by the Tribe under the MMPA.

appropriate when the question is whether Congress has abrogated a tribal treaty right, not merely regulated it? In *Dion*, the Supreme Court did conclude that the Eagle Protection Act "abrogated" the treaty right, but so held on the basis that Congress determined that hunting was inconsistent with species preservation, "except pursuant to permit." What is the difference between a treaty right that is "regulated" and a treaty right that is "abrogated" but may nonetheless be exercised pursuant to a permit? If the Ninth Circuit's approach is adopted, courts will be able to subject tribal treaty rights to federal regulation without ever considering whether that was Congress's intent. *See* Zachary Tomlinson, Note, *Abrogation or Regulation? How* Anderson v. Evans *Discards the Makah's Treaty Whaling Right in the Name of Conservation Necessity*, 78 Wash. L. Rev. 1101, 1111–29 (2003). See also *Metcalf v. Daley,* excerpted at page 335.

Chapter 9

International Approaches to Indigenous Lands and Resources

A. International Instruments for the Protection of Indigenous Rights

Three types of international law bind nation states according to Article 38 of the Statute of the International Court of Justice: 1) "international conventions, whether general or particular, establishing rules expressly recognized by the contesting states"; 2) "international custom, as evidence of a general practice accepted as law"; and 3) "the general principles of law recognized by civilized nations". Statute of the International Court of Justice, available at: http://www.icj-cij.org/en; *see also* Ian Brownlie, Principles of Public International Law (Oxford U. Press 2003).

There are three primary international instruments concerning protection of indigenous rights to lands and resources: the U.N. Declaration on the Rights of Indigenous Peoples, the Convention Concerning Indigenous and Tribal Peoples in Independent Countries (ILO Convention No. 169), and the American Declaration on the Rights of Indigenous Peoples. Each is excerpted below. Look at each document separately. What rights does it establish for indigenous peoples? How would those rights differ from current United States law? In the case of the ILO Convention, below, should the United States become a signatory? Would tribes be better off under United States law, the U.N. Declaration, the ILO convention, or the American Declaration?

Note: U.N. Declaration on the Rights of Indigenous Peoples

On September 13, 2007, the United Nations General Assembly adopted the U.N. Declaration on the Rights of Indigenous Peoples. The vote on the Declaration was 143 Member States in favor, 11 abstentions, and four opposed. The four countries that voted against approval—Australia, Canada, New Zealand, and the United States—all subsequently announced their support. In 2009, Australia endorsed the Declaration. In April 2010, New Zealand endorsed the Declaration. In November 2010, Canada endorsed the Declaration, but maintains that the document is merely aspirational. And, in December 2010, President Obama announced that the United States supported the Declaration.

The language of the Declaration was debated for more than two decades before it was adopted. A Draft Declaration was agreed upon by the members of the Working

Group on Indigenous Populations in 1993 and again in 1994. On August 26, 1994, the U.N. Sub-Commission on Prevention of Discrimination and Protection of Minorities unanimously adopted the draft Declaration and submitted it to the U.N. Commission on Human Rights. At its March 1995 session, the Commission created an open-ended Intersessional Working Group to consider the draft Declaration and bring its conclusions back to the full Commission. In addition, in 2000, the Economic and Social Council established the Permanent Forum on Indigenous Issues as an advisory body to the Council.

In 2006, the United Nations General Assembly abolished the U.N. Commission on Human Rights and replaced it with the Human Rights Council. The Council is a subsidiary of the General Assembly, which elected the initial 47 member countries. The United States is not a member. The Council held its first session in June 2006, at which it received the report of the open-ended Intersessional Working Group and adopted the Declaration of the Rights of Indigenous Peoples.

The exact legal status of General Assembly declarations of rights is fuzzy. They have no binding legal effect, but at the same time they are considered authoritative internationally. To the extent that they represent the understanding of the U.N., they are at least a source to be considered.

For information on the United States' position on the Declaration, see Announcement of U.S. Support for the United Nations Declaration on the Rights of Indigenous Peoples, available at: https://2009-2017.state.gov/s/srgia/154553.htm. For information on the intersection of the Declaration and Federal Indian Law, see Rebecca Tsosie, *Reconceptualizing Tribal Rights: The Interface of Federal Indian Law and International Human Rights Law*, 2017 NO. 4 RMMLF-INST 10, Rocky Mountain Mineral Law Foundation Special Institute, Indian Law and Natural Resources: The Basics and Beyond (2017).

U.N. Declaration on the Rights of Indigenous Peoples
As Adopted by the U.N. General Assembly 13 September 2007

Article 3

Indigenous peoples have the right to self-determination. By virtue of that right they freely determine their political status and freely pursue their economic, social and cultural development.

Article 8

1. Indigenous peoples and individuals have the right not to be subjected to forced assimilation or destruction of their culture.

2. States shall provide effective mechanisms for prevention of, and redress for:

(a) Any action which has the aim or effect of depriving them of their integrity as distinct peoples, or of their cultural values or ethnic identities;

(b) Any action which has the aim or effect of dispossessing them of their lands, territories or resources;

(c) Any form of forced population transfer which has the aim or effect of violating or undermining any of their rights;

(d) Any form of forced assimilation or integration;

(e) Any form of propaganda designed to promote or incite racial or ethnic discrimination directed against them.

Article 10

Indigenous peoples shall not be forcibly removed from their lands or territories. No relocation shall take place without the free, prior and informed consent of the indigenous peoples concerned and after agreement on just and fair compensation and, where possible, with the option of return.

Article 11

1. Indigenous peoples have the right to practise and revitalize their cultural traditions and customs. This includes the right to maintain, protect and develop the past, present and future manifestations of their cultures, such as archaeological and historical sites, artefacts, designs, ceremonies, technologies and visual and performing arts and literature.

2. States shall provide redress through effective mechanisms, which may include restitution, developed in conjunction with indigenous peoples, with respect to their cultural, intellectual, religious and spiritual property taken without their free, prior and informed consent or in violation of their laws, traditions and customs.

Article 12

1. Indigenous peoples have the right to manifest, practice, develop and teach their spiritual and religious traditions, customs and ceremonies; the right to maintain, protect, and have access in privacy to their religious and cultural sites; the right to the use and control of their ceremonial objects; and the right to the repatriation of their human remains.

2. States shall seek to enable the access and/or repatriation of ceremonial objects and human remains in their possession through fair, transparent and effective mechanisms developed in conjunction with indigenous peoples concerned.

Article 20

1. Indigenous peoples have the right to maintain and develop their political, economic and social systems or institutions, to be secure in the enjoyment of their own means of subsistence and development, and to engage freely in all their traditional and other economic activities.

2. Indigenous peoples deprived of their means of subsistence and development are entitled to just and fair redress.

Article 25

Indigenous peoples have the right to maintain and strengthen their distinctive spiritual relationship with their traditionally owned or otherwise occupied and used lands, territories, waters and coastal seas and other resources and to uphold their responsibilities to future generations in this regard.

Article 26

1. Indigenous peoples have the right to the lands, territories and resources which they have traditionally owned, occupied or otherwise used or acquired.

2. Indigenous peoples have the right to own, use, develop and control the lands, territories and resources that they possess by reason of traditional ownership or other traditional occupation or use, as well as those which they have otherwise acquired.

3. States shall give legal recognition and protection to these lands, territories and resources. Such recognition shall be conducted with due respect to the customs, traditions and land tenure systems of the indigenous peoples concerned.

Article 27

States shall establish and implement, in conjunction with indigenous peoples concerned, a fair, independent, impartial, open and transparent process, giving due recognition to indigenous peoples' laws, traditions, customs and land tenure systems, to recognize and adjudicate the rights of indigenous peoples pertaining to their lands, territories and resources, including those which were traditionally owned or otherwise occupied or used. Indigenous peoples shall have the right to participate in this process.

Article 28

1. Indigenous peoples have the right to redress, by means that can include restitution or, when this is not possible, just, fair and equitable compensation, for the lands, territories and resources which they have traditionally owned or otherwise occupied or used, and which have been confiscated, taken, occupied, used or damaged without their free, prior and informed consent.

2. Unless otherwise freely agreed upon by the peoples concerned, compensation shall take the form of lands, territories and resources equal in quality, size and legal status or of monetary compensation or other appropriate redress.

Article 29

1. Indigenous peoples have the right to the conservation and protection of the environment and the productive capacity of their lands or territories and resources. States shall establish and implement assistance programmes for indigenous peoples for such conservation and protection, without discrimination.

2. States shall take effective measures to ensure that no storage or disposal of hazardous materials shall take place in the lands or territories of indigenous peoples without their free, prior and informed consent.

3. States shall also take effective measures to ensure, as needed, that programmes for monitoring, maintaining and restoring the health of indigenous peoples, as developed and implemented by the peoples affected by such materials, are duly implemented.

Article 31

1. Indigenous peoples have the right to maintain, control, protect and develop their cultural heritage, traditional knowledge and traditional cultural expressions, as well as the manifestations of their sciences, technologies and cultures, including human and genetic resources, seeds, medicines, knowledge of the properties of fauna and flora, oral traditions, literatures, designs, sports and traditional games and visual and performing arts. They also have the right to maintain, control, protect and develop their intellectual property over such cultural heritage, traditional knowledge, and traditional cultural expressions.

2. In conjunction with indigenous peoples, States shall take effective measures to recognize and protect the exercise of these rights.

Article 32

1. Indigenous peoples have the right to determine and develop priorities and strategies for the development or use of their lands or territories and other resources.

2. States shall consult and cooperate in good faith with the indigenous peoples concerned through their own representative institutions in order to obtain their free and informed consent prior to the approval of any project affecting their lands or territories and other resources, particularly in connection with the development, utilization or exploitation of mineral, water or other resources.

3. States shall provide effective mechanisms for just and fair redress for any such activities, and appropriate measures shall be taken to mitigate adverse environmental, economic, social, cultural or spiritual impact.

Article 37

1. Indigenous peoples have the right to the recognition, observance and enforcement of treaties, agreements and other constructive arrangements concluded with States or their successors and to have States honour and respect such treaties, agreements and other constructive arrangements.

2. Nothing in this Declaration may be interpreted as diminishing or eliminating the rights of indigenous peoples contained in treaties, agreements and other constructive arrangements.

Article 38

States in consultation and cooperation with indigenous peoples, shall take the appropriate measures, including legislative measures, to achieve the ends of this Declaration.

Article 43

The rights recognized herein constitute the minimum standards for the survival, dignity and well-being of the indigenous peoples of the world.

Article 45

Nothing in this Declaration may be construed as diminishing or extinguishing the rights indigenous peoples have now or may acquire in the future.

Note: ILO Convention No. 169

The Convention Concerning Indigenous and Tribal Peoples in Independent Countries, known as Convention No. 169, was proposed by the International Labour Organisation on June 7, 1989. A convention is a source of international law, but it is legally binding only on its signatories. Nonetheless, even though a convention is not binding on a non-signatory nation, conventions are suggestive of world opinion.

As of 2018, twenty-three countries had ratified ILO Convention 169; most of those nations are located in Central and South America. The United States is not a signatory to Convention No. 169.

The Convention Concerning Indigenous and Tribal Peoples in Independent Countries, 1989

[ILO Convention No. 169]

PART I. GENERAL POLICY

Article 4

1. Special measures shall be adopted as appropriate for safeguarding the persons, institutions, property, labour, cultures and environment of the peoples concerned.

2. Such special measures shall not be contrary to the freely-expressed wishes of the peoples concerned.

3. Enjoyment of the general rights of citizenship, without discrimination, shall not be prejudiced in any way by such special measures.

Article 7

1. The peoples concerned shall have the right to decide their own priorities for the process of development as it affects their lives, beliefs, institutions and spiritual well-being and the lands they occupy or otherwise use, and to exercise control, to the extent possible, over their own economic, social and cultural development. In addition, they shall participate in the formulations, implementation and evaluation of plans and programmes for national and regional development which may affect them directly.

2. The improvement of the conditions of life and work and levels of health and education of the peoples concerned, with their participation and co-operation, shall be a matter of priority in plans for the overall economic development of areas they inhabit. Special projects for development of the areas in question shall also be so designed as to promote such improvements.

3. Governments shall insure that, whenever appropriate, studies are carried out, in co-operation with the peoples concerned to assess the social, spiritual, cultural and environmental impact on them of planned development activities. The results of these studies shall be considered as fundamental criteria for the implementation of these activities.

4. Governments shall take measures, in co-operation with the peoples concerned, to protect and preserve the environment of the territories they inhabit.

PART II. LAND

Article 13

1. In applying the provisions of this Part of the Convention governments shall respect the special importance for the cultures and spiritual values of the peoples concerned of their relationship with the lands or territories, or both as applicable, which they occupy or otherwise use, and in particular the collective aspects of this relationship.

2. The use of the term "lands" in Articles 15 and 16 shall include the concept of territories, which covers the total environment of the areas which the peoples concerned occupy or otherwise use.

Article 14

1. The rights of ownership and possession of the peoples concerned over the lands which they traditionally occupy shall be recognized. In addition, measures shall be taken in appropriate cases to safeguard the right of the peoples concerned to use lands not exclusively occupied by them, but to which they have traditionally had access for their subsistence and traditional activities. Particular attention shall be paid to the situation of nomadic peoples and shifting cultivators in this respect.

2. Governments shall take steps as necessary to identify the lands which the peoples concerned traditionally occupy, and to guarantee effective protection of their rights of ownership and possession.

3. Adequate procedures shall be established within the national legal system to resolve land claims by the peoples concerned.

Article 15

1. The rights of the peoples concerned to the natural resources pertaining to their lands shall be specially safeguarded. These rights include the right of these peoples to participate in the use, management and conservation of these resources.

2. In cases in which the State retains the ownership of mineral or sub-surface resources or rights to other resources pertaining to lands, governments shall establish or maintain procedures through which they shall consult these peoples, with a view to ascertaining whether and to what degree their interests would be prejudiced, before undertaking or permitting any programmes for the exploration or exploitation of such resources pertaining to their lands. The peoples concerned shall wherever possible participate in the benefits of such activities, and shall receive fair compensation for any damages which they may sustain as a result of such activities.

Article 16

1. Subject to the following paragraphs of this Article, the peoples concerned shall not be removed from the lands which they occupy.

2. Where the relocation of these peoples is considered necessary as an exceptional measure, such relocation shall take place only with their free and informed consent. Where their consent cannot be obtained, such relocation shall take place only following appropriate procedures established by national laws and regulations, including public inquiries where appropriate, which provide the opportunity for effective representation of the peoples concerned.

3. Whenever possible, these peoples shall have the right to return to their traditional lands, as soon as the grounds for relocation cease to exist.

4. When such return is not possible, as determined by agreement or, in the absence of such agreement, through appropriate procedures, these peoples shall be provided in all possible cases with lands of quality and legal status at least equal to that of the lands previously occupied by them, suitable to provide for their present needs and future development. Where the peoples concerned express a preference for compensation in money or in kind, they shall be so compensated under appropriate guarantees.

5. Persons thus relocated shall be fully compensated for any resulting loss or injury.

Article 17

1. Procedures established by the peoples concerned for the transmission of land rights among members of these peoples shall be respected.

2. The peoples concerned shall be consulted whenever consideration is being given to their capacity to alienate their lands or otherwise transmit their rights outside their own community.

3. Persons not belonging to these peoples shall be prevented from taking advantage of their customs or of lack of understanding of the laws on the part of their members to secure the ownership, possession or use of land belonging to them.

Article 18

Adequate penalties shall be established by law for unauthorized intrusion upon, or use of, the lands of the peoples concerned, and governments shall take measures to prevent such offences.

Article 19

National agrarian programmes shall secure to the peoples concerned treatment equivalent to that accorded to other sectors of the population with regard to:

(a) the provision of more land for these peoples when they have not the area necessary for providing the essentials of a normal existence, or for any possible increase in their numbers;

(b) the provision of the means required to promote the development of the lands which these peoples already possess.

Note: American Declaration on the Rights of Indigenous Peoples

On June 15, 2016, after nearly 30 years of advocacy and negotiation, the Organization of American States (OAS) adopted the American Declaration on the Rights of Indigenous Peoples. For a copy of the Declaration, see http://www.narf.org/wordpress/wp-content/uploads/2015/09/2016oas-declaration-indigenous-people.pdf. A draft of the Proposed Declaration was approved by the Inter-American Commission on Human Rights in 1995. The Organization of American States (OAS) General Assembly received the draft Declaration in 1997 and instructed the Permanent Council to study it. In June 1999, the Working Group to Prepare the Draft American Declaration on the Rights of Indigenous Peoples, part of the Committee on Juridical and Political Affairs of the Permanent Council, was established. Documents pertaining to the Working Group's on-going efforts are available at www.oas.org/consejo/CAJP/Indigenous%20documents.asp.

The OAS Charter was signed in 1948 and entered into force in December 1951. Today, the OAS has 35 member states, including all the sovereign states of the Americas. The legal status of an OAS Declaration is much like that of a U.N. General Assembly Declaration: it is not a source of binding law, but is considered authoritative and may become a source of customary international law. According to Professor James Anaya, "[a] norm of customary international law emerges—or *crystallizes*—when a preponderance of states (and other actors with international legal personality) converge on a common understanding of the norm's content and expect future behavior to conform to the norm." S. James Anaya, International Human Rights and Indigenous Peoples 80 (Wolters Kluwer 2009).

The American Declaration offers specific protection for indigenous peoples in North America, Mexico, Central and South America, and the Caribbean. It affirms the right of self-determination, rights to education, health, self-government, culture, lands, territories and natural resources, and it includes provisions that address the particular situation of indigenous peoples in the Americas, including protections for those living in voluntary isolation and those affected by a state's internal armed conflict.

American Declaration on the Rights of Indigenous Peoples

PREAMBLE

The member states of the Organization of American States (hereinafter the states),

RECOGNIZING: That the rights of indigenous peoples are both essential and of historic significance to the present and future of the Americas; The important presence in the Americas of indigenous peoples and their immense contribution to development, plurality, and cultural diversity and reiterating our commitment to their economic and social well-being, as well as the obligation to respect their rights and cultural identity; and That the existence of indigenous cultures and peoples of the Americas is important to humanity; and REAFFIRMING that indigenous peoples are original, diverse societies with their own identities that form an integral part of the Americas;

CONCERNED that indigenous peoples have suffered from historic injustices as a result of, inter alia, their colonization and dispossession of their lands, territories and resources, thus preventing them from exercising, in particular, their right to development in accordance with their own needs and interests;

RECOGNIZING the urgent need to respect and promote the inherent rights of indigenous peoples which derive from their political, economic and social structures and from their cultures, spiritual traditions, histories and philosophies, especially their rights to their lands, territories and resources;

RECOGNIZING FURTHER that respect for indigenous knowledge, cultures and traditional practices contributes to sustainable and equitable development and proper management of the environment;

BEARING IN MIND the progress achieved at the international level in recognizing the rights of indigenous peoples, especially the 169 ILO Convention and the United Nations Declaration on the Rights of Indigenous Peoples;

BEARING IN MIND ALSO the progress made in nations of the Americas, at the constitutional, legislative, and jurisprudential levels to safeguard, promote, and protect the rights of indigenous peoples, as well as the political will of states to continue their progress toward recognition of the rights of indigenous peoples in the Americas;

RECALLING the commitments undertaken by the Member States to guarantee, promote, and protect the rights and institutions of indigenous peoples, including those undertaken at the Third and Fourth Summits of the Americas;

RECALLING AS WELL the universality, inseparability, and interdependence of human rights recognized under international law;

CONVINCED that recognition of the rights of indigenous peoples in this Declaration will foster among states and indigenous peoples harmonious and cooperative relations based on the principles of justice, democracy, respect for human rights, nondiscrimination, and good faith;

CONSIDERING the importance of eliminating all forms of discrimination that may affect indigenous peoples, and taking into account the responsibility of states to combat them;

ENCOURAGING States to respect and comply with and effectively implement all their obligations as they apply to indigenous peoples under international instruments, in particular those related to human rights, in consultation and cooperation with the peoples concerned;

DECLARE:

SECTION ONE: Indigenous Peoples. Scope of Application

Article I. 1. The American Declaration on the Rights of Indigenous Peoples applies to the indigenous peoples of the Americas.

2. Self-identification as indigenous peoples will be a fundamental criteria for determining to whom this Declaration applies. The states shall respect the right to such self-identification as indigenous, individually or collectively, in keeping with the practices and institutions of each indigenous people.

Article II. The states recognize and respect the multicultural and multilingual character of the indigenous peoples, who are an integral part of their societies.

Article III. Indigenous peoples have the right to self-determination. By virtue of that right they freely determine their political status and freely pursue their economic, social and cultural development.

Article IV. Nothing in this Declaration may be interpreted as implying for any State, people, group or person any right to engage in any activity or to perform any act contrary to the Charter of the Organization of American States and the Charter of the United Nations or construed as authorizing or encouraging any action which would dismember or impair, totally or in part, the territorial integrity or political unity of sovereign and independent States.

SECTION TWO: Human Rights and Collective Rights

Article V. Full effect and observance of human rights. Indigenous peoples and persons have the right to the full enjoyment of all human rights and fundamental freedoms, as recognized in the Charter of the United Nations, the Charter of the Organization of American States and international human rights law.

Article VI. Collective rights. Indigenous peoples have collective rights that are indispensable for their existence, wellbeing, and integral development as peoples. In this regard, the states recognize and respect, the right of the indigenous peoples to their collective action; to their juridical, social, political, and economic systems or institutions; to their own cultures; to profess and practice their spiritual beliefs; to use their own tongues and languages; and to their lands, territories and resources. States shall promote with the full and effective participation of the indigenous peoples the harmonious coexistence of rights and systems of the different population, groups, and cultures.

Article X. Rejection of assimilation.

1. Indigenous peoples have the right to maintain, express, and freely develop their cultural identity in all respects, free from any external attempt at assimilation.

2. The States shall not carry out, adopt, support, or favor any policy to assimilate the indigenous peoples or to destroy their cultures.

Article XI. Protection against genocide. Indigenous peoples have the right to not be subjected to any form of genocide or attempts to exterminate them.

Article XII. Guarantees against racism, racial discrimination, xenophobia, and other related forms of intolerance. Indigenous peoples have the right not to be subject to racism, racial discrimination, xenophobia, and other related forms of intolerance. The states shall adopt the preventive and corrective measures necessary for the full and effective protection of this right.

SECTION THREE: Cultural identity

Article XIII. Right to cultural identity and integrity.

1. Indigenous peoples have the right to their own cultural identity and integrity and to their cultural heritage, both tangible and intangible, including historic and

ancestral heritage; and to the protection, preservation, maintenance, and development of that cultural heritage for their collective continuity and that of their members and so as to transmit that heritage to future generations.

2. States shall provide redress through effective mechanisms, which may include restitution, developed in conjunction with indigenous peoples, with respect to their cultural, intellectual, religious and spiritual property taken without their free, prior and informed consent or in violation of their laws, traditions and customs.

3. Indigenous people have the right to the recognition and respect for all their ways of life, world views, spirituality, uses and customs, norms and traditions, forms of social, economic and political organization, forms of transmission of knowledge, institutions, practices, beliefs, values, dress and languages, recognizing their interrelationship as elaborated in this Declaration.

Article XIV. Systems of Knowledge, Language and Communication.

1. Indigenous peoples have the right to preserve, use, develop, revitalize, and transmit to future generations their own histories, languages, oral traditions, philosophies, systems of knowledge, writing, and literature; and to designate and maintain their own names for their communities, individuals, and places.

2. The states shall adopt adequate and effective measures to protect the exercise of this right with the full and effective participation of indigenous peoples.

3. Indigenous peoples have the right to promote and develop all their systems and media of communication, including their own radio and television programs, and to have equal access to all other means of communication and information. The states shall take measures to promote the broadcast of radio and television programs in indigenous languages, particularly in areas with an indigenous presence. The states shall support and facilitate the creation of indigenous radio and television stations, as well as other means of information and communication.

4. The states, in conjunction with indigenous peoples, shall make efforts to ensure that those peoples can understand and be understood in their languages in administrative, political, and judicial proceedings, where necessary through the provision of interpretation or by other effective means.

Article XVI. Indigenous spirituality.

1. Indigenous peoples have the right to freely exercise their own spirituality and beliefs and, by virtue of that right, to practice, develop, transmit, and teach their traditions, customs, and ceremonies, and to carry them out in public and in private, individually and collectively.

2. No indigenous people or person shall be subject to pressures or impositions, or any other type of coercive measures that impair or limit their right to freely exercise their indigenous spirituality and beliefs.

3. Indigenous Peoples have the right to preserve, protect, and access their sacred sites, including their burial grounds; to use and control their sacred objects relics, and to recover their human remains.

4. States, in conjunction with indigenous peoples, shall adopt effective measures, to promote respect for indigenous spirituality and beliefs, and to protect the integrity of the symbols, practices, ceremonies, expressions, and spiritual protocols of indigenous peoples, in accordance with international law.

Article XIX. Right to protection of a healthy environment.

1. Indigenous peoples have the right to live in harmony with nature and to a healthy, safe, and sustainable environment, essential conditions for the full enjoyment of the right to life, to their spirituality, worldview and to collective well-being.

2. Indigenous peoples have the right to conserve, restore, and protect the environment and to manage their lands, territories and resources in a sustainable way.

3. Indigenous peoples are entitled to be protected against the introduction of, abandonment, dispersion, transit, indiscriminate use or deposit of any harmful substance that could negatively affect indigenous communities, lands, territories and resources.

4. Indigenous peoples have the right to the conservation and protection of the environment and the productive capacity of their lands or territories and resources. States shall establish and implement assistance programmes for indigenous peoples for such conservation and protection, without discrimination.

SECTION FOUR: Organizational and Political Rights

Article XX. Rights of association, assembly, and freedom of expression and thought.

1. Indigenous peoples have the rights of association, assembly, organization and expression, and to exercise them without interference and in accordance with their worldview, inter alia, values, usages, customs, ancestral traditions, beliefs, spirituality, and other cultural practices.

2. Indigenous peoples have the right to assemble on their sacred and ceremonial sites and areas. For this purpose they shall have free access and use to these sites and areas.

3. Indigenous peoples, in particular those who are divided by international borders, shall have the right to travel and to maintain and develop contacts, relations, and direct cooperation, including activities for spiritual, cultural, political, economic, and social purposes, with their members and other peoples.

4. These states shall adopt, in consultation and cooperation with the indigenous peoples, effective measures to ensure the exercise and application of these rights.

Article XXI. Right to autonomy or self-government.

1. Indigenous peoples, in exercising their right to self-determination, have the right to autonomy or self-government in matters relating to their internal and local affairs, as well as ways and means for financing their autonomous functions.

2. Indigenous peoples have the right to maintain and develop their own decision-making institutions. They also have the right to participate in the decision making in matters which would affect their rights. They may do so directly or through their representatives, and accordance with their own norms, procedures, and traditions.

They also have the right to equal opportunities to access and to participate fully and effectively as peoples in all national institutions and fora, including deliberative bodies.

Article XXII. Indigenous law and jurisdiction.

1. Indigenous peoples have the right to promote, develop and maintain their institutional structures and their distinctive customs, spirituality, traditions, procedures, practices and, in the cases where they exist, juridical systems or customs, in accordance with international human rights standards.

2. The indigenous law and legal systems shall be recognized and respected by the national, regional and international legal systems.

3. The matters referring to indigenous persons or to their rights or interests in the jurisdiction of each state shall be conducted so as to provide for the right of the indigenous people to full representation with dignity and equality before the law. Consequently, they are entitled, without discrimination, to equal protection and benefit of the law, including the use of linguistic and cultural interpreters.

4. The States shall take effective measures in conjunction with indigenous peoples to ensure the implementation of this article.

Article XXIV. Treaties, agreements, and other constructive arrangements.

1. Indigenous peoples have the right to the recognition, observance, and enforcement of the treaties, agreements and other constructive arrangements concluded with states and their successors, in accordance with their true spirit and intent in good faith and to have the same be respected and honored by the States. States shall give due consideration to the understanding of the indigenous peoples as regards to treaties, agreements and other constructive arrangements.

2. When disputes cannot be resolved between the parties in relation to such treaties, agreements and other constructive arrangements, these shall be submitted to competent bodies, including regional and international bodies, by the States or indigenous peoples concerned.

3. Nothing in this Declaration may be interpreted as diminishing or eliminating the rights of indigenous peoples contained in treaties, agreements and other constructive arrangements.

SECTION FIVE: Social, Economic, and Property Rights

Article XXV. Traditional forms of property and cultural survival. Right to land, territory, and resources.

1. Indigenous peoples have the right to maintain and strengthen their distinctive spiritual, cultural, and material relationship to their lands, territories, and resources and to assume their responsibilities to preserve them for themselves and for future generations.

2. Indigenous peoples have the right to the lands, territories and resources which they have traditionally owned, occupied or otherwise used or acquired.

3. Indigenous peoples have the right to own, use, develop and control the lands, territories and resources that they possess by reason of traditional ownership or other traditional occupation or use, as well as those which they have otherwise acquired.

4. States shall give legal recognition and protection to these lands, territories and resources. Such recognition shall be conducted with due respect to the customs, traditions and land tenure systems of the indigenous peoples concerned.

5. Indigenous peoples have the right to legal recognition of the various and particular modalities and forms of property, possession and ownership of their lands, territories, and resources in accordance with the legal system of each State and the relevant international instruments. The states shall establish the special regimes appropriate for such recognition, and for their effective demarcation or titling.

Article XXVIII. Protection of Cultural Heritage and Intellectual Property.

1. Indigenous peoples have the right to the full recognition and respect for their property, ownership, possession, control, development, and protection of their tangible and intangible cultural heritage and intellectual property, including its collective nature, transmitted through millennia, from generation to generation.

2. The collective intellectual property of indigenous peoples includes, inter alia, traditional knowledge and traditional cultural expressions including traditional knowledge associated with genetic resources, ancestral designs and procedures, cultural, artistic, spiritual, technological, and scientific, expressions, tangible and intangible cultural heritage, as well as the knowledge and developments of their own related to biodiversity and the utility and qualities of seeds and medicinal plants, flora and fauna.

3. States, with the full and effective participation of indigenous peoples, shall adopt measures necessary to ensure that national and international agreements and regimes provide recognition and adequate protection for the cultural heritage of indigenous peoples and intellectual property associated with that heritage. In adopting these measures, consultations shall be effective intended to obtain the free, prior, and informed consent of indigenous peoples.

Article XXIX. Right to development.

1. Indigenous peoples have the right to maintain and determine their own priorities with respect to their political, economic, social, and cultural development in conformity with their own world view. They also have the right to be guaranteed the enjoyment of their own means of subsistence and development, and to engage freely in all their economic activities

2. This right includes the development of policies, plans, programs, and strategies in the exercise of their right to development and to implement them in accordance with their political and social organization, norms and procedures, their own world views and institutions.

3. Indigenous peoples have the right to be actively involved in developing and determining development programmes affecting them and, as far as possible, to administer such programmes through their own institutions.

4. States shall consult and cooperate in good faith with the indigenous peoples concerned through their own representative institutions in order to obtain their free and informed consent prior to the approval of any project affecting their lands or territories and other resources, particularly in connection with the development, utilization or exploitation of mineral, water or other resources.

5. Indigenous peoples have the right to effective measures to mitigate adverse ecological, economic, social, cultural, or spiritual impacts for the implementation of development projects that affect their rights. Indigenous peoples who have been deprived of their own means of subsistence and development have the right to restitution and, where this is not possible, to fair and equitable compensation. This includes the right to compensation for any damage caused to them by the implementation of state, international financial institutions or private business plans, programs, or projects.

Article XXX. Right to peace, security, and protection.

1. Indigenous peoples have the right to peace and security.

2. Indigenous peoples have the right to recognition and respect for their institutions for the maintenance of their organization and control of its communities and peoples.

3. Indigenous peoples have the right to protection and security in situations or periods of internal or international armed conflict pursuant to international humanitarian law.

4. States, in compliance with international agreements to which they are party, in particular international humanitarian law and international human rights law, including the Fourth Geneva Convention of 1949 relative to the protection of civilian persons in time of war, and Protocol II of 1977 relating to the protection of victims of non-international armed conflicts, in the event of armed conflicts shall take adequate measures to protect the human rights, institutions, lands, territories, and resources of the indigenous peoples and their communities. Likewise, States:

a. Shall not recruit indigenous children and adolescents into the armed forces under any circumstances;

b. Shall take measures of effective reparation and provide adequate resources for the same, in jointly with the indigenous peoples affected, for the damages incurred caused by an armed conflict.

c. Shall take special and effective measures in collaboration with indigenous peoples to guarantee that indigenous women, children live free from all forms of violence, especially sexual violence, and shall guarantee the right to access to justice, protection, and effective reparation for damages incurred to the victims.

6. Military activities shall not take place in the lands or territories of indigenous peoples, unless justified by a relevant public interest or otherwise freely agreed with or requested by the indigenous peoples concerned . . . .

B. Indian Claims before International Forums

How useful are international forums for American Indian tribes seeking to challenge United States government action? As a case study, consider the saga of the Dann sisters.

The Western Shoshone Tribe entered into the Treaty of Ruby Valley with the United States in 1863. The treaty affirmed the boundaries of the Western Shoshone lands while granting the United States access to those lands for specified purposes, including "mining and agricultural settlements . . . and ranches." Treaty with the Western Shoshone, Oct. 1, 1863, 18 Stat. 689. In 1977, the Indian Claims Commission awarded the tribe $26 million for the taking of more than 24 million acres of the land described in the treaty. The Commission was unable to discover any formal extinguishment of legal title; instead, it concluded that the gradual encroachment by settlers extinguished the title. The award, however, went unclaimed; the Shoshone refused to accept it. *Temoak Band of Western Shoshone Indians v. United States,* 40 Ind. Cl. Comm'n 318 (1977); *aff'd* 593 F.2d 994 (Ct. Cl. 1979).

In 1973, the Bureau of Land Management (BLM) sued Western Shoshone elders Mary and Carrie Dann—who grazed cattle and horses on land surrounding their Crescent Valley, Nevada ranch—for trespass and for exceeding their federal grazing permit. The Danns claimed that the pastures were Shoshone land, and challenged the United States to prove federal ownership. In 1985 the U.S. Supreme Court ruled that "payment" for the land in question occurred when the federal government placed the $26 million into a trust account for the loss of the tribe's aboriginal title. The fact that the money had never been collected was irrelevant. *United States v. Dann,* 470 U.S. 39, 50 (1985). For discussion and analysis, see Rebecca Tsosie, *Property, Power, and American "Justice": The Story of* United States v. Dann, *in* Indian Law Stories (Carole Goldberg, Kevin K. Washburn & Philip P. Frickey, eds, Found. Press 2011); Allison Dussias, *Squaw Drudges, Farm Wives, and the Dann Sisters' Last Stand: American Indian Women's Resistance to Domestication and the Denial of their Property Rights,* 77 N.C.L. Rev. 637, 707–26 (1999).

Controversy over the land continued. The BLM intensified its efforts to impound livestock and fine the Shoshones for overgrazing; the United States expanded resource development on historical Shoshone land, including gold mining and geothermal energy production, raising concerns about sacred sites and water resources. Moreover, new waste dumping plans threatened to add to the thousands of metric tons of radioactive material already deposited in the area by weapons testing.

The Dann sisters raised these and other issues in two international forums: the Inter-American Commission on Human Rights and the United Nations Committee on the Elimination of Racial Discrimination. The decisions of those bodies are excerpted below:

Inter-American Commission on Human Rights, Report No. 75/02, Case 11.140, Mary and Carrie Dann
United States December 27, 2002

35. In their initial petition and subsequent observations, the Petitioners have contended that the State is responsible for violations of the rights of Mary and Carrie Dann under Articles II (right to equality before the law), III (right to religious freedom and worship), VI (right to a family and to protection thereof), XIV (right to work and to fair remuneration), XVIII (right to a fair trial) and XXIII (right to property) of the American Declaration [of the Rights and Duties of Man] in respect of their use and occupancy of the Western Shoshone ancestral lands.

76. With respect to the merits of the Petitioners' claims, the State denies that it has violated the Danns' rights under the American Declaration. Indeed, the State argues that the matters raised by the Petitioners do not involve human rights violations, but rather involve lengthy litigation of land title and land use questions that have been and are still subject to careful consideration by all three branches of the United States government. In this connection, the State contends that the Danns' title to the lands at issue has been extinguished by lengthy litigation in the United States' courts, including the U.S. Supreme Court, and that compensation for the loss of title has been placed in a trust fund for the Danns and other members of the Western Shoshone people, pending development of a plan for the distribution of the funds.

95. The Petitioners claim that the State has violated the rights of the Danns under Articles I, XVIII, and XXVI of the American Declaration of the Rights and Duties of Man. As the Commission concluded in its admissibility report in this matter, the Commission is competent to determine these allegations as against the United States. The State is a Member of the Organization of American States that is not a party to the American Convention on Human Rights, as provided for in Article 20 of the Commission's Statute and Article 23 of the Commission's Rules of Procedure, and deposited its instrument of ratification of the OAS Charter on June 19, 1951. The events raised in the Petitioners' claim occurred subsequent to the State's ratification of the OAS Charter. The Danns are natural persons, and the Petitioners are authorized under Article 23 of the Commission's Rules of Procedure to lodge the petition on behalf of the Danns.

124. As indicated above, in addressing complaints of violations of the American Declaration it is necessary for the Commission to consider those complaints in the context of the evolving rules and principles of human rights law in the Americas and in the international community more broadly, as reflected in treaties, custom and other sources of international law. Consistent with this approach, in determining the claims currently before it, the Commission considers that this broader corpus of international law includes the developing norms and principles governing the human rights of indigenous peoples. As the following analysis indicates, these norms and principles encompass distinct human rights considerations relating to the ownership, use and occupation by indigenous communities of their traditional lands.

Considerations of this nature in turn controvert the State's contention that the Danns' complaint concerns only land title and land use disputes and does not implicate issues of human rights.

125. In particular, a review of pertinent treaties, legislation and jurisprudence reveals the development over more than 80 years of particular human rights norms and principles applicable to the circumstances and treatment of indigenous peoples. Central to these norms and principles is a recognition that ensuring the full and effective enjoyment of human rights by indigenous peoples requires consideration of their particular historical, cultural, social and economic situation and experience. In most instances, this has included identification of the need for special measures by states to compensate for the exploitation and discrimination to which these societies have been subjected at the hands of the non-indigenous.

128. Perhaps most fundamentally, the Commission and other international authorities have recognized the collective aspect of indigenous rights, in the sense of rights that are realized in part or in whole through their guarantee to groups or organizations of people. And this recognition has extended to acknowledgement of a particular connection between communities of indigenous peoples and the lands and resources that they have traditionally occupied and used, the preservation of which is fundamental to the effective realization of the human rights of indigenous peoples more generally and therefore warrants special measures of protection. The Commission has observed, for example, that continued utilization of traditional collective systems for the control and use of territory are in many instances essential to the individual and collective well-being, and indeed the survival of, indigenous peoples and that control over the land refers both its capacity for providing the resources which sustain life, and to the geographic space necessary for the cultural and social reproduction of the group. The Inter-American Court of Human Rights has similarly recognized that for indigenous communities the relation with the land is not merely a question of possession and production but has a material and spiritual element that must be fully enjoyed to preserve their cultural legacy and pass it on to future generations.

129. The development of these principles in the inter-American system has culminated in the drafting of Article XVIII of the Draft American Declaration on the Rights of Indigenous Peoples, which provides for the protection of traditional forms of ownership and cultural survival and rights to land, territories and resources. While this provision, like the remainder of the Draft Declaration, has not yet been approved by the OAS General Assembly and therefore does not in itself have the effect of a final Declaration, the Commission considers that the basic principles reflected in many of the provisions of the Declaration, including aspects of Article XVIII, reflect general international legal principles developing out of and applicable inside and outside of the inter-American system and to this extent are properly considered in interpreting and applying the provisions of the American Declaration in the context of indigenous peoples.

138. In evaluating the Petitioners' claims in light of [the Commission's] evidentiary findings, the Commission first wishes to expressly recognize and acknowledge

that the State, through the development and implementation of the Indian Claims Commission process, has taken significant measures to recognize and account for the historic deprivations suffered by indigenous communities living within the United States and commends the State for this initiative. As both the Petitioners and the State have recognized, this process provided a more efficient solution to the sovereign immunity bar to Indian land claims under U.S. law and extended to indigenous communities certain benefits relating to claims to their ancestral lands that were not available to other citizens, such as extended limitation periods for claims.

139. Upon evaluating these processes in the facts as disclosed by the record in this case, however, the Commission concludes that these processes were not sufficient to comply with contemporary international human rights norms, principles and standards that govern the determination of indigenous property interests.

140. The Commission first considers that Articles XVIII and XXIII of the American Declaration specially oblige a member state to ensure that any determination of the extent to which indigenous claimants maintain interests in the lands to which they have traditionally held title and have occupied and used is based upon a process of fully informed and mutual consent on the part of the indigenous community as a whole. This requires at a minimum that all of the members of the community are fully and accurately informed of the nature and consequences of the process and provided with an effective opportunity to participate individually or as collectives. In the case of the Danns, however, the record indicates that the land claim issue was pursued by one band of the Western Shoshone people which no apparent mandate from the other Western Shoshone bands or members. There is also no evidence on the record that appropriate consultations were held within the Western Shoshone at the time that certain significant determinations were made. This includes in particular the ICC's finding that the entirety of the Western Shoshone interest in their ancestral lands, which interests affect the Danns, was extinguished at some point in the past.

141. To the contrary, despite the fact that it became clear at the time of the Danns' request to intervene that the collective interest in the Western Shoshone territory may not have been properly served through the proceedings pursued by the Temoak Band, the courts ultimately did not take measures to address the substance of these objections but rather dismissed them based upon the expediency of the ICC processes. In the Commission's opinion and in the context of the present case, this was not sufficient in order for the State to fulfill its particular obligation to ensure that the status of the Western Shoshone traditional lands was determined through a process of informed and mutual consent on the part of the Western Shoshone people as a whole.

142. The insufficiency of this process was augmented by the fact that, on the evidence, the issue of extinguishment was not litigated before or determined by the ICC, in that the ICC did not conduct an independent review of historical and other evidence to determine as a matter of fact whether the Western Shoshone properly claimed title to all or some of their traditional lands. Rather, the ICC determination was based upon an agreement between the State and the purported Western Shoshone

representatives as to the extent and timing of the extinguishment. In light of the contentions by the Danns that they have continued to occupy and use at least portions of the Western Shoshone ancestral lands, and in light of the findings by the Ninth Circuit Court of Appeals as to the merits of the ICC's extinguishment finding, it cannot be said that the Danns' claims to property rights in the Western Shoshone ancestral lands were determined through an effective and fair process in compliance with the norms and principles under Articles XVIII and XXIII of the American Declaration.

143. Further, the Commission concludes that to the extent the State has asserted as against the Danns title in the property in issue based upon the ICC proceedings, the Danns have not been afforded their right to equal protection of the law under Article II of the American Declaration. The notion of equality before the law set forth in the Declaration relates to the application of substantive rights and to the protection to be given to them in the case of acts by the State or others. Further, Article II, while not prohibiting all distinctions in treatment in the enjoyment of protected rights and freedoms, requires at base that any permissible distinctions be based upon objective and reasonable justification, that they further a legitimate objective, regard being had to the principles which normally prevail in democratic societies, and that the means are reasonable and proportionate to the end sought.

144. The record before the Commission indicates that under prevailing common law in the United States, including the Fifth Amendment to the U.S. Constitution, the taking of property by the government ordinarily requires a valid public purpose and the entitlement of owners to notice, just compensation, and judicial review. In the present case, however, the Commission cannot find that the same prerequisites have been extended to the Danns in regard to the determination of their property claims to the Western Shoshone ancestral lands, and no proper justification for the distinction in their treatment has been established by the State. In particular, as concluded above, any property rights that the Danns may have asserted to the Western Shoshone ancestral lands were held by the ICC to have been "extinguished" through proceedings in which the Danns were not effectively represented and where the circumstances of this alleged extinguishment were never actually litigated nor the merits of the finding finally reviewed by the courts. And while compensation for this extinguishment was awarded by the ICC, the value of compensation was calculated based upon an average extinguishment date that does not on the record appear to bear any relevant connection to the issue of whether and to what extent all or part of Western Shoshone title in their traditional lands, including that of the Danns, may no longer subsist. Further, the Commission understands that the amount of compensation awarded for the alleged encroachment upon Western Shoshone ancestral lands did not include an award of interest from the date of the alleged extinguishment to the date of the ICC decision, thus leaving the Western Shoshone uncompensated for the cost of the alleged taking of their property during this period.

145. All of these circumstances suggest that the Danns have not been afforded equal treatment under the law respecting the determination of their property

interests in the Western Shoshone ancestral lands, contrary to Article II of the Declaration. While the State has suggested that the extinguishment of Western Shoshone title was justified by the need to encourage settlement and agricultural developments in the western United States, the Commission does not consider that this can justify the broad manner in which the State has purported to extinguish indigenous claims, including those of the Danns, in the entirety of the Western Shoshone territory. In the Commission's view, this is particularly apparent in light of evidence that the Danns and other Western Shoshone have at least until recently continued to occupy and use regions of the territory that the State now claims as its own.

170. The Commission, based upon the foregoing considerations of fact and law, and in light of the response of the State to Report 113/01, hereby ratifies the following conclusions.

171. The Commission wishes to emphasize that it is not for this body in the circumstances of the present case to determine whether and to what extent the Danns may properly claim a subsisting right to property in the Western Shoshone ancestral lands. This issue involves complex issues of law and fact that are more appropriately left to the State for determination through those legal processes it may consider suitable for that purpose. These processes must, however, conform with the norms and principles under the American Declaration applicable to the determination of indigenous property rights as elucidated in this report. This requires in particular that the Danns be afforded resort to the courts for the protection of their property rights, in conditions of equality and in a manner that considers both the collective and individual nature of the property rights that the Danns may claim in the Western Shoshone ancestral lands. The process must also allow for the Danns' full and informed participation in the determination of their claims to property rights in the Western Shoshone ancestral lands.

172. Based upon the foregoing analysis, the Commission hereby concludes that the State has failed to ensure the Danns' right to property under conditions of equality contrary to Articles II, XVIII and XXIII of the American Declaration in connection with their claims to property rights in the Western Shoshone ancestral lands.

173. In accordance with the analysis and conclusions in the present report, THE INTER-AMERICAN COMMISSION ON HUMAN RIGHTS REITERATES THE FOLLOWING RECOMMENDATIONS TO THE UNITED STATES:

> 1. Provide Mary and Carrie Dann with an effective remedy, which includes adopting the legislative or other measures necessary to ensure respect for the Danns' right to property in accordance with Articles II, XVIII and XXIII of the American Declaration in connection with their claims to property rights in the Western Shoshone ancestral lands.
>
> 2. Review its laws, procedures and practices to ensure that the property rights of indigenous persons are determined in accordance with the rights established in the American Declaration, including Articles II, XVIII and XXIII of the Declaration.

Note: The Inter-American Human Rights System

The Inter-American Commission on Human Rights and the Inter-American Court of Human Rights have been active in investigating and protecting indigenous claims, including claims to ancestral lands and resources. *See* Jo M. Pasqualucci, *The Evolution of International Indigenous Rights in the Inter-American Human Rights System*, 6 Human Rts L. Rev. 281, 295–306 (2006); S. James Anaya and Robert A. Williams, Jr., *The Protection of Indigenous Peoples' Rights over Lands and Natural Resources Under the Inter-American Human Rights System*, 14 Harv. Hum. Rts. J. 33 (2001). Professor Pasqualucci analyzed the Inter-American Court of Human Rights' approach to indigenous land rights in light of the U.N. Declaration on the Rights of Indigenous Peoples. She concluded that the court's decisions "generally conform" to the UN Declaration, "except in the area of state expropriation of natural resources on indigenous ancestral lands," where the court permits some government development rights "to the detriment of the indigenous peoples." Jo M. Pasqualucci, *International Indigenous Land Rights: A Critique of the Jurisprudence of the Inter-American Court of Human Rights in Light of the United Nations Declaration on the Rights of Indigenous Peoples*, 27 Wis. Int'l L.J. 51, 54 (2009).

In 2001, the Inter-American Court of Human Rights (IACHR) issued "the first legally binding decision by an international tribunal to uphold the collective land and resource rights of indigenous peoples in the face of a state's failure to do so." S. James Anaya and Claudio Grossman, *The Case of* Awas Tingni v. Nicaragua: *A New Step in the International Law of Indigenous Peoples*, 19 Ariz. J. Int'l & Comp. L. 1, 2 (2002). In that case, the IACHR held that Nicaragua had violated the property rights of the Awas Tingni indigenous community, and ordered the country to title and protect the Awas Tigni in their traditional lands.

Tribes and Native communities have petitioned the Inter-American Commission on Human Rights (IACHR) to address environmental wrongs. For example, in 2005, the Inuit Circumpolar Conference requested assistance from the IACHR to address the human rights abuses arising from the United States' greenhouse gas emissions, which were leading to climate change in the Inuit Arctic environment. *See* Elizabeth Ann Kronk Warner, *Working to Protect the Seventh Generation: Indigenous Peoples as Agents of Change*, 13 Santa Clara J. of Int'l L. 273 (2015). On March 2, 2015, the Navajo Nation filed a petition in the IACHR seeking redress for human rights violations arising from the authorization of a commercial ski facility to use treated sewage effluent, or "reclaimed wastewater," to produce artificial snow on the San Francisco Peaks in North Arizona. The San Francisco Peaks are of great religious and cultural significant to the Navajo people, and at least thirteen other indigenous peoples in the United States. Navajo Nation, Petition to the Inter-American Commission on Human Rights (March 2, 2015), available at: http://www.nnhrc.navajo-nsn.gov/docs/sacredsites/Navajo%20Nation%20Petition%20to%20IACHR%20March%202%202015.pdf. The Navajo Nation and other tribes' efforts to protect the San Francisco Peaks under the U.S. Constitution failed in 2008. *Navajo Nation v. U.S. Forest Service*, 535 F.3d 1058 (9th Cir. 2008), excerpted at pages 22–34.

Committee on the Elimination of Racial Discrimination: Early Warning and Urgent Action Procedure, Decision 1 (68): United States of America

Sixty-eighth session Geneva, 20 February–10 March 2006

A. Introduction

4. The Committee has received credible information alleging that the Western Shoshone indigenous peoples are being denied their traditional rights to land, and that measures taken and even accelerated lately by the State party in relation to the status, use and occupation of these lands may cumulatively lead to irreparable harm to these communities. In light of such information, and in the absence of any response from the State party, the Committee decided at its 68th session to adopt the present decision under its early warning and urgent action procedure. This procedure is clearly distinct from the communication procedure under article 14 of the Convention. Furthermore, the nature and urgency of the issue examined in this decision go well beyond the limits of the communication procedure.

B. Concerns

6. The Committee is concerned by the State party's position that Western Shoshone peoples' legal rights to ancestral lands have been extinguished through gradual encroachment, notwithstanding the fact that the Western Shoshone peoples have reportedly continued to use and occupy the lands and their natural resources in accordance with their traditional land tenure patterns. The Committee further notes with concern that the State party's position is made on the basis of processes before the Indian Claims Commission, "which did not comply with contemporary international human rights norms, principles and standards that govern determination of indigenous property interests", as stressed by the Inter-American Commission on Human Rights in the case Mary and Carrie Dann versus United States (Case 11.140, 27 December 2002).

7. The Committee is of the view that past and new actions taken by the State party on Western Shoshone ancestral lands lead to a situation where, today, the obligations of the State party under the Convention are not respected, in particular the obligation to guarantee the right of everyone to equality before the law in the enjoyment of civil, political, economic, social and cultural rights, without discrimination based on race, colour, or national or ethnic origin. The Committee recalls its General recommendation 23 (1997) on the rights of indigenous peoples, in particular their right to own, develop, control and use their communal lands, territories and resources, and expresses particular concern about:

a) Reported legislative efforts to privatize Western Shoshone ancestral lands for transfer to multinational extractive industries and energy developers.

b) Information according to which destructive activities are conducted and/or planned on areas of spiritual and cultural significance to the Western Shoshone peoples, who are denied access to, and use of, such areas. It notes in particular the reinvigorated federal efforts to open a nuclear waste repository at the Yucca Mountain; the alleged use of explosives and open pit gold mining activities on Mont Tenabo and Horse Canyon; and the alleged issuance of geothermal energy leases at, or near, hot springs, and the processing of further applications to that end.

c) The reported resumption of underground nuclear testing on Western Shoshone ancestral lands;

d) The conduct and/or planning of all such activities without consultation with and despite protests of the Western Shoshone peoples;

e) The reported intimidation and harassment of Western Shoshone people by the State party's authorities, through the imposition of grazing fees, trespass and collection notices, impounding of horse and livestock, restrictions on hunting, fishing and gathering, as well as arrests, which gravely disturb the enjoyment of their ancestral lands.

f) The difficulties encountered by Western Shoshone peoples in appropriately challenging all such actions before national courts and in obtaining adjudication on the merits of their claims, due in particular to domestic technicalities.

C. Recommendations

10. The Committee urges the State party to adopt the following measures until a final decision or settlement is reached on the status, use and occupation of Western Shoshone ancestral lands in accordance with due process of law and the State party's obligations under the Convention:

a) Freeze any plan to privatize Western Shoshone ancestral lands for transfer to multinational extractive industries and energy developers;

b) Desist from all activities planned and/or conducted on the ancestral lands of Western Shoshone or in relation to their natural resources, which are being carried out without consultation with and despite protests of the Western Shoshone peoples;

c) Stop imposing grazing fees, trespass and collection notices, horse and livestock impoundments, restrictions on hunting, fishing and gathering, as well as arrests, and rescind all notices already made to that end, inflicted on Western Shoshone people while using their ancestral lands.

Notes

1. **Committee on the Elimination of Racial Discrimination (CERD).** Article 8 of the International Convention on the Elimination of All Forms of Racial Discrimination (ICERD) established the United Nations CERD for the purpose of monitoring states' implementation of ICERD. It was the first body created by the United Nations with the purpose of reviewing state actions under a specific human rights agreement. This model has been followed by several subsequent conventions: the

Human Rights Committee; the Committee on the Elimination of Discrimination against Women; the Committee against Torture; the Committee on Economic, Social and Cultural Rights; and the Committee on the Rights of the Child. For more information about CERD and ICERD see Committee on the Elimination of Racial Discrimination, *Monitoring Racial Equality and Non-discrimination*, http://www2.ohchr.org/english/bodies/cerd/.

2. **Indigenous peoples.** In 1997 CERD acknowledged the "International Decade of the World's Indigenous Peoples," by reaffirming its position that discrimination against indigenous peoples was within the scope of ICERD. CERD requires states with indigenous populations in their territories to include full information on the situation of such peoples in their periodic reports. At the time of the March 10, 2006 decision, the United States had not yet submitted its fourth and fifth periodic reports which were due November 30, 2003. In June 2013, the United States issued its Period Report to CERD, which discusses indigenous peoples at pages 167-184. The full report is available at: https://www.state.gov/j/drl/rls/cerd_report/210605.htm.

3. **Early warning and urgent action procedure.** In its decision in the *Dann* case, CERD stressed that the early warning and urgent action procedure was "clearly distinct" from its communication procedure under article 14 of ICERD. In 1993, CERD adopted a working paper to guide it in its efforts to prevent and respond to violations of the Convention. The working paper noted that serious violations of the Convention could potentially be prevented though "early warning measures" and "urgent procedures." Early warning measures aim to prevent escalation of existing problems into conflicts, and urgent procedures attempt to respond to problems that require immediate attention in order to prevent or limit serious violations of the Convention. For more information about these procedures and for examples of recent decisions, see Committee on the Elimination of Racial Discrimination, *Early-Warning Measures and Urgent Procedures*, http://www.ohchr.org/EN/HRBodies/CERD/Pages/EarlyWarningProcedure.aspx.

4. **United States' response.** In addition to not providing a timetable for when it would submit its late periodic reports, the United States also did not submit a timely response to CERD's list of issues regarding the *Dann* case, and it did not appear before CERD to discuss the matter prior to the issuance of the decision.

Index

A

Aboriginal Title
  Generally, 155–185, 711
  Alaska, 114, 117, 179–185
  Australia, 178–179
  Canada, 176–178
  Extinguishment, 170–175, 711–720
  New Zealand, 179
  Takings, 180–185
Administrative Law, 291–293, 396–398
Agricultural Resources, 358–359
Alaska Native Claims Settlement Act, 108–115, 117, 185
Alaska Natives, 108, 109, 114, 115
  Aboriginal title, 114–117, 179, 185
  Indian country, 108–113
  Subsistence rights, 115–117
Alaskan National Interest Lands Conservation Act, 116–117
Allotments
  Generally, 74–77, 117–120, 229–245, 399–401
  Descent and devise, 235–243
  Diminishment (of reservations), see Indian Country
  Fractionation, 75, 235–245
  History, 74–77, 229–231
  Indian country, 104, 117–120, 363
  Land Buy-Back Program, 244–245
  Mineral rights, 231–235
  Rights-of-way, 367–370
  Takings, 95–99
  Taxation, federal, 419–422
  Taxation, state, 435
  Taxation, tribal, 117–120
  Tribal jurisdiction, 117–120
  Water rights, 530–536
American Declaration on the Rights of Indigenous Peoples, 702–710
American Indian Agricultural Resources Management Act, 358–359
American Indian Probate Reform Act, 235, 242–244, 360
  see also Indian Land Consolidation Act
American Indian Religious Freedom Act, 17, 78
Archaeological Resources Protection Act, 45–46
Australian Aborigines, 178–179

B

Bald and Golden Eagle Protection Act, see Eagle Protection Act
Bedlands, see Submerged Lands
Breach of Trust, see Claims Against United States
Bureau of Indian Affairs, see Department of the Interior
Bureau of Land Management, see Department of the Interior

C

Canadian First Nations, 176–178
Canons of Construction, 138, 219, 253–254, 448–449, 452, 602
Chevron Doctrine, 291–293

Citizen Suits, *see* Environmental Protection and Regulation
Claims Against United States
  Breach of trust actions, 228, 372–401
  Claims court, *see* Claims Against the United States: Court of Federal Claims
  Claims process, 186–188
  Compensation for takings
    Aboriginal title, 180–185
    Allotments, 231–242
    Executive Order reservations, 209–214
    Indian Claims Commission, 186–187,
    Leases and contractual rights, 407–412
    Recognized title, 188–205
    Submerged lands, 223–226
  Court of Claims, *see* Claims Against the United States: Court of Federal Claims
  Court of Federal Claims, 187–188, 398–399
  Minerals, 188–191, 231–235, 374–386, 407–412,
  Submerged lands, 223–229
  Timber, 180–184, 188–191
  Trust funds, 399–401
Claims Court Jurisdiction, 186–188
Clean Air Act, 152, 291, 302–312, 326
Clean Water Act, 283, 293–302, 307–308, 315, 326, 528, 538
Cobell litigation, *see* Claims Against United States: Trust funds
Compensation For Takings, *see* Claims Against the United States: Compensation for takings
Comprehensive Environmental Response, Compensation, and Liability Act, 317–318, 325–327
Conflict of Interest, *see* Federal Authority in Indian Affairs

Constitutional Issues
  Equal footing doctrine, *see* Equal footing doctrine
  Establishment clause, *see* Religion
  Free exercise of religion clause, *see* Religion
  Takings, *see* Claims Against United States
Convention Concerning Indigenous and Tribal Peoples in Independent Countries, 700–702
Court of Federal Claims, *see* Claims Against United States: Court of Federal Claims
Cultural Resources
  Federal protection, 43–69
  Indian attitudes and values, 3–11

D

Dakota Access Pipeline, 346–348
Dawes Act, *see* Allotments
Department of the Interior
  Bureau of Indian Affairs, 73, 93276 322–325, 331399–400
  Bureau of Land Management, 48, 227–229, 332, 354–356, 711
  Land leases, *see* Leases and Other Agreements
  Mineral leases and agreements, *see* Indian Mineral Development Act; Indian Mineral Leasing Act; Mineral Resources
  Mismanagement of resources, *see* Claims Against United States: Breach of trust actions
  Secretarial approval
    Federal recognition of tribes, 93–94, 128
    Lands taken into trust, 124–129, 168, 537
    Leases and other agreements, 350–354, 356–362
    Tribal constitutions and laws, 425–435

Trust responsibility, *see* Trust Relationship
Descent and devise, *see* Allotments
Diminishment (of reservations), *see* Indian Country
Disclaimer States, 572
Disestablishment (of reservations), *see* Indian Country
Doctrine of Discovery, 88, 155–161

E

Eagle Protection Act, 678–683, 685–687, 694
    see also Usufructuary Rights: Hunting rights
Eastern Land Claims, *see* Nonintercourse Act
Eminent Domain, *see* Federal Authority in Indian Affairs
Endangered Species Act, 496, 563, 566, 582, 649–650, 653, 678–686
Energy Resources, 349, 360–361, 362–363, 366
    see also Mineral Resources; Rights-of-Way
Environmental Justice, 344–348
Environmental Protection and Regulation
    Generally, 282–348
    Air quality, *see* Clean Air Act
    Citizen suits, 313–316, 322–326
    Endangered species, *see* Endangered Species Act
    Environmental impact statements, *see* National Environmental Policy Act
    EPA Policy on Environmental Programs on Indian Reservations, 283–285
    Fee lands regulation, 301–302
    Habitat protection, 497, 649–665
    Hazardous waste, *see* Comprehensive Environmental Response, Compensation, and Liability Act
    Historic preservation, 46–54
    Landfills, *see* Indian Lands Open Dump Clean-up Act
    Mining, *see* Surface Mining Control and Reclamation Act
    Natural Resources Damages, 317–318
    Oil contamination, *see* Oil Pollution Act
    State regulation, 286–291
    Tribal environmental law, 8, 319–320, 414
    Tribes as regulated parties, 320–327
    Tribes as states, 293–316, 528
    Water quality, *see* Clean Water Act
Environmental Protection Agency
    Generally, 282–317
    Indian policy, 283–285
Equal Footing Doctrine, 215–219, 222–223, 471–477, 586–602, 612–619
Executive Order 13007-Indian Sacred Sites, 41–43
Executive Order on Consultation and Coordination with Tribal Governments, 353–356
Executive Order Reservations, 209–214
Exhaustion Doctrine, *see* Federal Court Jurisdiction

F

Federal Authority in Indian Affairs, *see also* Department of the Interior
    Generally, 99–103
    Navigation servitude, *see* Submerged Lands
    Plenary power, 99–101
    Preemption of state authority, *see* Preemption
    Statutes of general applicability, 282–283
    Taxation, *see* Taxation
    Treaty abrogation, 95–99, 665–694
Federal Court Jurisdiction

Claims court, *see* Claims Against United States
Political question, 95–99, 100, 102, 163
Relation to tribal court jurisdiction, 321
Water rights, *see* Water Rights: McCarran Amendment
Federal Indian Policy, History of, 71–78
Federal Power Act, 663–664
Federal Recognition of Tribes, 93–94, 128
Fishing Rights, *see* Usufructuary Rights
Forest Resources, 349, 350, 358–359, 453–458
See also Usufructuary Rights: Timber rights
Fractionation, *see* Allotments
Freedom of Information Act, 42–43, 565–566

G

Gathering Rights, *see* Usufructuary Rights
General Allotment Act, *see* Allotments
Grazing, 349, 358–359, 711–719

H

Hawaiian Natives, *see* Native Hawaiians
Hazardous Materials Transportation Act, 327
HEARTH Act, 361–362
Helping Expedite and Advance Responsible Tribal Ownership Act, *see* HEARTH Act
History of Federal Indian Policy, *see* Federal Indian Policy, History of
Hunting Rights, *see* Usufructuary Rights: Hunting rights

I

Indian Claims Commission, 186–187
see also Claims Against United States

Indian Country
Generally, 103–153
Alaska, 108–115
Allotments, 117–120
Dependent Indian communities, 108–114, 121–122
Diminishment, 75, 129–153
Land into trust, 124–129
Oklahoma, 104–108, 117–120, 121–124, 151
Reservations, 104–108
See also Lands into trust; Diminishment
Statutory text, 104, 363
Surplus lands, *see* Diminishment
Tribal inability to create unilaterally, 122–124
Indian Health Service, 322–326
Indian Land Consolidation Act, 235–244
see also American Indian Probate Reform Act
Indian Lands Open Dump Clean-up Act, 326
Indian Long-Term Leasing Act, 357
See also HEARTH Act
Indian Mineral Development Act, 358, 395, 414–418, 464
Indian Mineral Leasing Act, 357–386, 394–395, 434, 449–452
Indian Policy, *see* Federal Indian Policy, History of
Indian Reorganization Act
Generally, 76, 231
Lands taken into trust under, 124–128
Leasing, 356–357
Secretarial approval of tribal action, 425–435
Indian Title, *see* Aboriginal Title
Indian Tribal Energy Development and Self-Determination Act, 360–361, 366, 395
Indian Tucker Act, *see* Tucker Act

Indigenous Peoples, 695–710
Inter-American Commission on Human Rights, 711–717
Inter-American Court of Human Rights, 717
International Indigenous Rights, *see* Indigenous Peoples
International Labour Organisation, 700
   See also Convention Concerning Indigenous and Tribal Peoples in Independent Countries

L

Lacey Act, 685
Laches, 163–168, 226, 401–406
Land Buy-Back Program, *see* Allotments
Land Use, *see* Regulatory Authority
Leases and Other Agreements, *see also* Nonintercourse Act
   Agricultural, 358–359
   Cancellation and rescission, 401–418
   Grazing, 358–359
   Historical overview, 356–362
   Minerals, *see* Mineral Resources
   National Environmental Policy Act, applicability of, 327–334
   Secretarial approval, 350–353
   Surface leases, 357, 361–362
   Timber, 358–359
   Water, 529–530

M

McCarran Amendment, *see* Water Rights: McCarran Amendment
Migratory Bird Treaty Act, 68–685
Mineral Resources
   see also Energy Resources
   Generally, 75–76, 349, 356–361
   Allotted lands, 75, 117–120, 231–235
   Environmental regulation, *see* Surface Mining Control and Reclamation Act
   Federal mismanagement, 374–386, 394–395, 396–397
   Mineral agreements, *see* Indian Mineral Development Act
   Mineral leases, *see* Indian Mineral Leasing Act
   Taxation
      State, 449–452, 458–464
      Tribal, 117–120, 425–435
   Tribal ownership, 188–192, 349
   Tribal role in management, 401–418
Moderate Living, *see* Usufructuary Rights: Moderate living standard

N

National Environmental Policy Act, 327–343, 401–406
National Historic Preservation Act, 46–54
National Indian Forest Resources Management Act, 358–359
Native American Graves Protection and Repatriation Act, 55–69
Native Hawaiians
   Hawaiian customary rights, 606–611
   Hawaiian water rights, 611–612
Navigation Servitude, *see* Submerged Lands
Nonintercourse Act, 72, 161–163, 168–169, 350, 359, 529–530

O

Oil Pollution Act, 317–318
Organization of American States, 702–710

P

Plenary Power, *see* Federal Authority in Indian Affairs: Plenary power
Practicably Irrigable Acreage, *see* Water Rights: Practicably irrigable acreage
Preemption

Regulatory authority, 257–263
Taxation, 440–441, 449–469
Profits a Prendre, *see* Usufructuary Rights

R

Railroads, 170–176
Recognized Title, 188–209
Regulatory Authority,
    Generally, 247–281
    Environmental, *see* Environmental Protection and Regulation
    Federal preemption, *see* Preemption
    Hunting, fishing, and gathering, 249–263
        See also Usufructuary Rights
    Land use, 249–275
    Water rights, *see* Water Rights: Administration and regulation
    Zoning, 264–272
Religion, *see also* American Indian Religious Freedom Act; Religious Freedom Restoration Act; Sacred Sites
    Establishment, 35–41, 54–55
    Free exercise of religion, 11–34
    Relationship to culture, 48–55
Religious Freedom Restoration Act, 22–34, 686–687
Religious Land Use and Institutionalized Persons Act, 34
Removal Era, 73
Renewable Energy Resources, 349, 362–363
    see also Energy Resources
Reorganization Era, *see* Indian Reorganization Act
Reservations
    Diminishment, *see* Indian Country: Diminishment
    History, 73–77
    Indian country status of, 104–108
Resource Conservation and Recovery Act, 286–291, 312–316, 322–326
Right of Occupancy, *see* Aboriginal Title
Rights-of-way
    Grant of, 363–370
    Regulation, 275–276, 370–372
    Taxation, 438–439
Riverbeds, *see* Submerged Lands

S

Sacred Sites
    Generally, 11–55, 205–206, 208, 706–707
    Cultural protection, 43–55
    Disclosure of location, 42–43
    Establishment of religion, 35–55
    Executive Order 13007-Indian Sacred Sites, 41–42
    Free exercise of religion, 11–34
    Restoration to tribes (Taos Blue Lake), 208
    Takings, 192–208
Safe Drinking Water Act, 282–283, 294
Salmon (anadromous fish), *see* Usufructuary Rights: Fishing rights
Secretarial Approval, *see* Department of the Interior: Secretarial approval
Secretarial Order on Tribal Rights, Federal Trust Responsibilities, and the Endangered Species Act, 685
Self-determination Era, 77–78
Sovereign Immunity
    Federal, *see* Claims Against United States; Tucker Act; Water Rights: McCarran amendment
    State, 220–222
    Tribal, 103, 168–170, 321–327, 369–370, 665
State Authority,
    Generally, 79–89
    Equal footing doctrine, *see* Equal Footing Doctrine
    Federal preemption of, *see* Preemption
    Regulatory authority

Environmental, 285–291
Land use / zoning, 264–273
Nonmembers, 247–276, 280–281
Usufructuary rights, *see* Usufructuary rights
Taxation, *see* Taxation: State taxation
Water administration, *see* Water Rights: Administration and regulation
Water rights adjudication, *see* Water Rights: McCarran Amendment
Stevens Treaty Rights, *see* Usufructuary Rights: Fishing rights
Submerged Lands
    Generally, 215–229
    Environmental authority, 301–302, 538
    Navigation servitude, 222–226
    Nonnavigable waters, 222
    Ownership, 215–222
    Takings, 223–226
    Trust responsibility, 227–229
Superfund Act, *see* Comprehensive Environmental Response, Compensation and Liability Act
Surface Mining Control and Reclamation Act, 406–407
Surplus Lands, *see* Indian Country: Diminishment

T

Takings, *see* Claims Against United States: Compensation for takings
Taxation
    Federal, 419–424
    State
        Of Indians, 104–108, 440–452, 468
        Of non-Indians, 453–469
    Tribal, 377, 424, 439, 463
        On fee lands, 435–438
        On trust lands, 117–120, 424-435, 438–440

Terminated Tribes
    Termination and restoration, 77, 677–678
    Usufructuary rights, 665–677
    Water rights, 487–493
Timber Rights, *see* Usufructuary Rights: Timber rights. *See also* Forest Resources
Trade and Intercourse Acts, *see* Nonintercourse Act
Treaties
    Abrogation, 95–99, 253–254, 693–694
        See also Indian Country: Diminishment
        Canons of construction, *see* Canons of Construction
    Usufructuary rights recognized by, *see* Usufructuary Rights
    Water rights implied by, *see* Water Rights
Tribal Court Jurisdiction, 120–121, 275–281, 321–325
Tribal Energy Resource Agreements, *see* Indian Tribal Energy Development and Self-Determination Act
Tribal Governmental Authority
    Generally, 78–92
    Regulatory jurisdiction
        Environmental, 283–285, 293–320
        Land use / zoning, 248–275
        Usufructuary rights, *see* Usufructuary rights
    Sovereign immunity, *see* Sovereign Immunity: Tribal
    Taxation, *see* Taxation: Tribal taxation
    Tribal court jurisdiction, *see* Tribal Court Jurisdiction
    Water administration, *see* Water Rights
Trust Funds, *see* Claims Against United States: Trust funds
Trust Relationship

Generally, 80–83, 94–103, 350–353, 372–373
Breach of trust actions, *see* Claims Against United States
Federal agencies
Bureau of Indian Affairs, *see* Department of Interior: Bureau of Indian Affairs
Bureau of Land Management, *see* Department of Interior: Bureau of Land Management
Environmental Protection Agency, 283–285
Indian Health Service, *see* Indian Health Service
Funds, *see* Claims Against United States: Trust funds
Natural resources, 372–397
Submerged lands, *see* Submerged Lands: Trust responsibility
Water, *see* Water Rights: Trust responsibility
Tucker Act, 187–188, 372–374
See also Claims Against United States: Court of Claims; Claims Against United States: Court of Federal Claims

U

United Nations, 43, 695–699
United Nations Committee on the Elimination of Racial Discrimination, 711, 719–720
United Nations Declaration on the Rights of Indigenous Peoples, 695–699
United Nations General Assembly Resolution: Protection of Religious Sites, 43
Usufructuary Rights
Generally, 471–474, 585–694
Allocation of, 629–645
As profits a prendre, 585, 630, 663
Commercial rights in, 647–649
Defeasibility, 612–620
Fishing rights
Hatchery fish, 642, 645, 652–653
Shellfish, 664
Usual and accustomed places, 646–647
Habitat protection, 649–665
Hunting Rights
Open and unclaimed lands, 612–620
Religious freedom, 686–687
Termination, 665–694
Implied water rights for, 494–498, 651–652
Loss or diminishment 665–694
"Moderate living" standard, 494–496, 643–645
New Zealand Maori, 645–646
Non-Indian backlash, 603–605
On executive order reservations, 213–214
On-reservation versus off-reservation, 628–629
State regulation, 620–627
Taxation, 423
Timber rights, 647–649
see also Forest Resources
Tribal regulation 627–628
Whaling rights, *see* Whaling

W

Water Rights
Generally, 471–584
Administration and regulation, 521–528, 537–538, 577
Allotments, 530–536
Fishing rights, support of, *see* Instream flow rights
Groundwater, 513–521
Hawaiian water rights, 611–612
Instream flow rights, *see* Quantification

Marketing, 529–530
McCarran Amendment, 566–577
Moderate living standard, 494–496
Non-Indians, 530–537
Off-reservation, 487–493, 497–498
Practicably irrigable acreage, *see* Quantification 4
Prior appropriation, 479–480
Priority date, 478–480, 485, 493–494
Purposes of reservations, 485–486, 494
Quantification
   Generally, 481–484, 486–487
   Instream flow rights, 486–487, 494–498, 521–529
   Practicably irrigable acreage, 481–484, 486, 562
Riparianism, 480
Sale and lease, *see* Marketing
Settlements, 480, 498, 520, 530, 537, 563–564, 577–584
Sources, 471–478
Trust responsibility, 545–563
Uses of, 521–530
Water quality, 538–545
   See also Clean Water Act
Whaling, 335–343, 687–69
Wheeler-Howard Act, *see* Indian Reorganization Act
Winters Doctrine, *see* Water Rights

Z

Zoning, 264–272